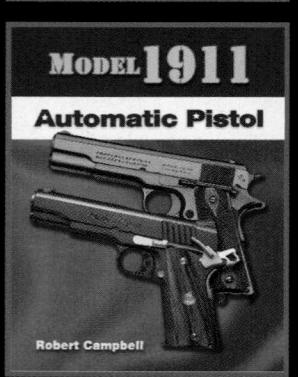

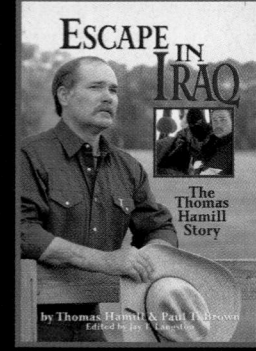

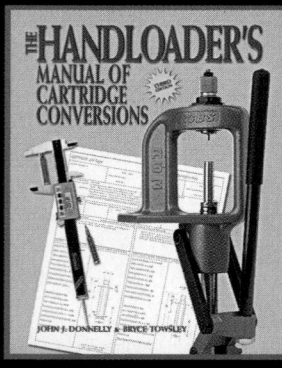

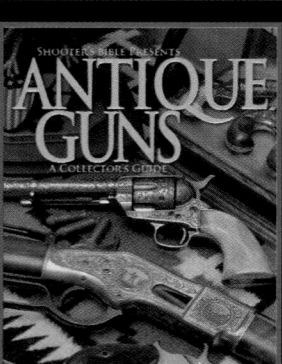

Shooter's Bible

97th Edition

Stoeger Publishing Company, Accokeek, Maryland

STOEGER PUBLISHING COMPANY
is a division of Benelli U.S.A.

Benelli U.S.A.
Vice President and General Manager: Stephen Otway
Vice President of Marketing and Communications: Stephen McKelvain

Stoeger Publishing Company
President: Jeffrey K. Reh
Managing Editor: Harris J. Andrews
Creative Director: Cynthia T. Richardson
Marketing & Communications Manager: Alex Bowers
Imaging Specialist: Williams Graves
National Sales Manager: Jennifer Thomas
Sales Manager Assistant: Julie Brownlee
Publishing Assistant: Amy Jones
Proofreader: Celia Beattie

Specifications Editor: Wayne van Zwoll

Published by:
Stoeger Publishing Company
17603 Indian Head Highway, Suite 200
Accokeek, Maryland 20607-2501

ISBN:0-88317-320-4 BK0501

Library of Congress Control Number: 2005924232

Manufactured in the United States of America
Distributed to the book trade and the sporting goods trade by:
Stoeger Industries, Stoeger Publishing Company
17603 Indian Head Highway, Suite 200
Accokeek, Maryland 20607-2501
301 283-6300 *Fax:* 301 283-6986

Note: Every effort has been made to record specifications and descriptions of guns, ammunition and accessories accurately, but the Publisher can take no responsibility for errors or omissions. The prices shown for guns, ammunition and accessories are manufacturers' suggested retail prices (unless otherwise noted) and are furnished for information only. These were in effect at press time and are subject to change without notice. Purchasers of the book have complete freedom of choice in pricing for resale.

Front Cover: The new Model 77 Mark II Frontier rifle with 16½-inch sporter barrel and Burris Scout 2.75x scope and the .22 caliber Mark III Hunter pistol are two new offerings from Ruger for 2006.

CONTENTS

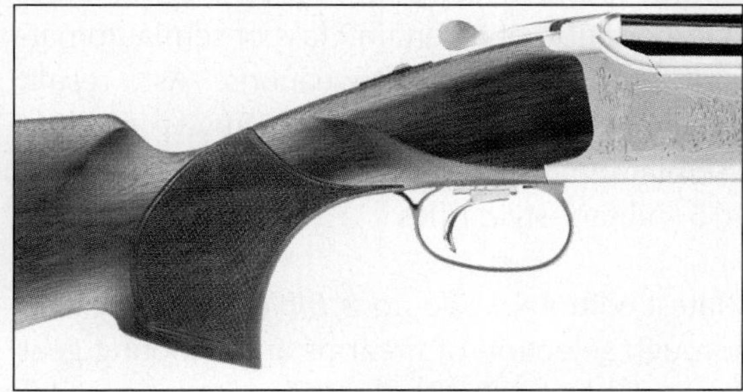

INTRODUCTION

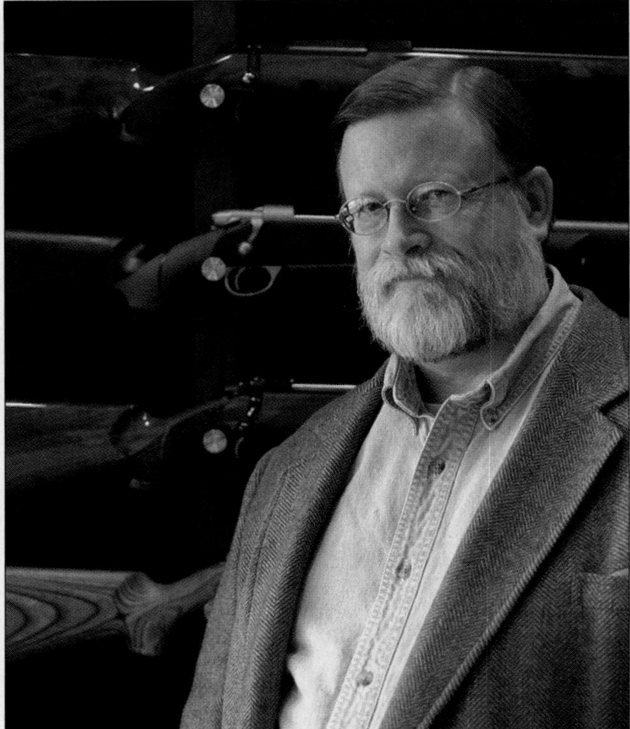

Once again the editorial and creative staff at Stoeger Publishing are pleased to offer a new edition of our classic annual—the *Shooter's Bible*. As usual, wherever possible, the extensive listings of firearms and related shooting products have been upgraded and new pricing information has been added. As always, we are indebted to our specifications editor, Wayne van Zwoll, for his extensive knowledge of firearms technology and the firearms trade.

In taking a look at new offerings, the hot little .17 caliber cartridges—the venerable .17 HMR and its younger rimfire cousins the .17 Remington, and .17 Mach2—have become American standbys with manufacturers continuing to offer new rifles chambered for the small but potent loads. Several major manufacturers, including Anschutz, Dakota, Sako, Winchester and Marlin, have issued new rifles chambered for the .17s. Thompson Center has introduced the R55, a handsome synthetic-stocked autoloader in .17 Mach 2. Other gun makers, Les Baer, and of course Ruger, have put their faith in the newer .204 Ruger cartridge.

A recent event effecting the firearms market is the expiration late last year of Title XI of the 1994 Federal Violent Crime Control Act that banned the manufacture and importation of a certain class of semiautomatic rifles—the so-called "assault weapons." As a result, several manufacturers are planning to revive production of semiautomatic versions of the popular M-16 and AR-15 military-style rifles.

In this latest edition of *Shooter's Bible*, we're presenting a thorough selection of firearms and shooting gear currently available on the market. Our feature articles this year span the shooting spectrum from histories of Spain's Llama handguns and Knight high-tech muzzleloaders, to a hunter's musings on his favorite rifle. We've got a feature on plinking—arguably some of the most fun you can have with a firearm—and another celebrating small game hunting with dogs, an American tradition that has become all too rare with the decline of small farms and the rural way of life.

The Stoeger publishing team here in Accokeek, Maryland, hopes you enjoy this latest edition of our eighty-one-year-old standard.

Good shooting!

Harris J. Andrews, Managing Editor

Special thanks to the National Rifle Association, for access to their image archives.

FEATURE ARTICLES

A Special Clean-Sweep Rifle

by Sam Fadala

The first day of September marks a full month of bowhunting in my state. Everything is open to the string-gun. And so I grab my all-glass limb Pronghorn Ferret IV recurve to try my fortunes in the field. But I don't have to tag anything because Wyoming is not either/or. Soon the same tags will be legal for rifles. Then I'll carry a muzzleloader, 30-30, or 38-55. But I don't have to bag anything with these rifles either if I don't want to. But when the final grains of sand drift lazily into the lower bell, it's time to break out the "real artillery" before the season ends. My Frank Wells custom 7mm Magnum usually gets the nod. That deadly rifle having passed its 30th birthday, however, I decided to give it a rest. Needed: a new clean-sweep rifle to fill those big game tags in the 11th hour of the season. I didn't know that the rifle would turn out to be ideal for any big game hunter anywhere.

I had tested a number of commercial, all-weather rifles for an arti-

Hunters in the mountainous terrain of northern Mexico will face shots at ranges that vary from quite close to very far. The clean-sweep rifle in standard .30-06 is fully capable of handling them all.

The theme of the clean-sweep rifle was all-weather ruggedness—take it anywhere with confidence that it will stand up to both weather and terrain.

cle. Their reliable ruggedness was impressive, and I decided to have one of my own. To make things more exciting, the new rifle would be a semi-custom model, chambered for a strong cartridge capable of harvesting game from moose at rock-throwing range to antelope, flyspeck-on-a-window distance. The new clean-sweep rifle must bear up under the rigors of tough terrain and harsh elements.

Shopping for a new rifle is exciting, but having one built kicks the experience up a notch. Individual elements come together like pieces of a jigsaw puzzle: action, barrel, stock, scope, scope mounts; even carry strap and sling swivels are important. Henry Ford said a customer could order any color Model T he wanted—as long as it was black. My new rifle would be as black as the bottom of

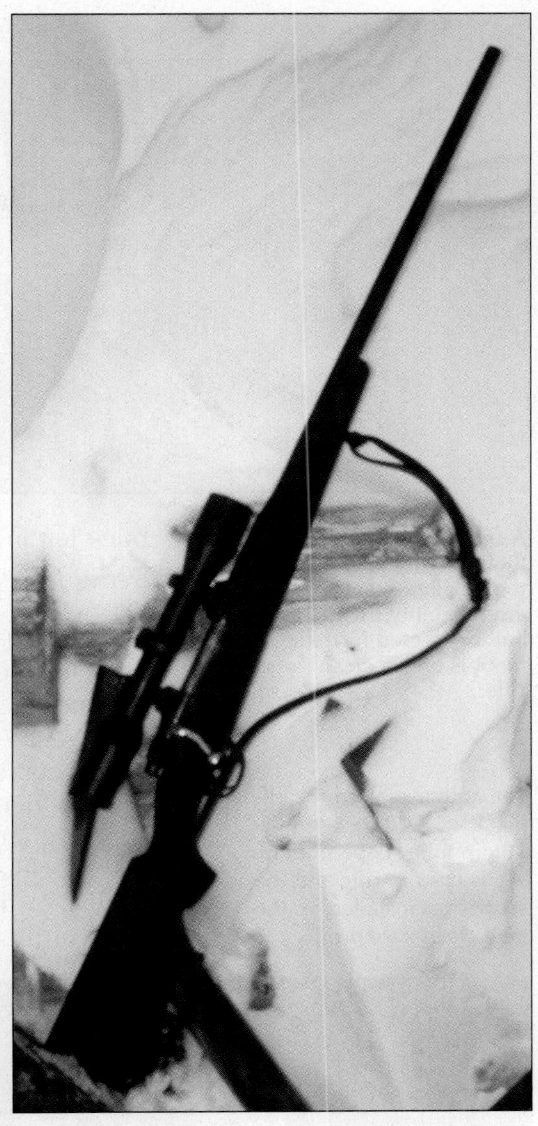

The author's clean-sweep rifle was not intended to be pretty; but it's hard to deny the sweeping lines of the McMillan stock and handsome fluted barrel—all in basic black.

an unlighted mineshaft at midnight.

I chose the Mauser 98 action for my clean-sweep rifle. Peter Paul Mauser, along with brother Wilhelm and American Samuel Norris, earned a patent for Paul's action in 1868 when the German inventor was only 30 years old. The refined 1898 version still resides with us with today's design outdistancing the original by a league. The soul of my new rifle would be the Global Trading 98 action from Legacy Sports International—Italian-made double square bridge with three-position wing safety, hinged floor plate and excellent trigger. Strong, smooth, dependable

The cut-rifled Morrison Precision barrel of my 25-284, with its consistent cloverleaf groups, brought me to the doorstep of the Hereford, Arizona shop once again for a No. 3 contour custom barrel. Bernard Morrison, metallurgical engineer by trade and barrel-making wizard by vocation, greeted the project with enthusiasm. Since a round trip from my home to the Morrison shop in Arizona eats up 36 hours of road time, our initial planning review was conducted on the singing wire.

I informed Morrison that I wanted a 24-inch medium weight barrel resulting in a nine-pound rifle. Lightweights are wonderful to carry. But when the season dwindles to a few hours, I want a rifle that steadies down in the field, not a flyweight. Barrel and action decided on, Bernie agreed to assemble the package. "Since you want a synthetic," Morrison advised, "I recommend McMillan. I've had nothing but great success with McMillan stocks." Go for it, says I. The black action with black barrel would rest in a black McMillan Super Grade fiberglass masterpiece. As Sherlock would say, the game was afoot! But would a new rifle be exciting for a fellow with a quarter century as a full-time gun writer? Teddy Roosevelt retained nine-year-old enthusiasm all his life. Me, too. So as the parts came together I grew increasingly anxious to see and shoot the finished project.

Barrel, action, stock—time for a glass sight. My Wells rifle wore a Swarovski 2.5X-10X 30mm tube scope. I'd pirate it away for the new rifle. There are many fine scopes on the market. I'm lucky to own examples such as Leupold's LPS and Bushnell's Elite 4200. These and other scopes perform flawlessly under all conditions, especially early and late in the day when game is on the move. But this time around I elected the big black Swarovski because it fit the overall nature of the new rifle. The scope with high optical resolution and adjustable ocular would promote specific bullet placement at all reasonable ranges. Combine target definition with Morrison barrel accuracy and delivering a bullet spot-on escalates geometrically.

A scope is no more accurate than the mounts that attach it to the rifle. In keeping with the reliability theme, the author elected for Talley mounts on his clean-sweep rifle.

The author pirated the all-black 2.5X-10X Swarovski 30mm tube scope from his Wells custom rifle and the scope was installed on the new clean-sweep rifle.

A little story about high-resolution magnification: I arrived on a northern Wyoming ranch on the last day of the season to fill my final big game tag. This was important. My clan, with two elk in the freezer, did not need the meat. But another family, newly arrived from out of state and just beginning to draw wages, could use the protein. The ranch foreman greeted me at the bunkhouse. "Hey Sam," he said, "you're in for tough sledding. We're overloaded with deer, but we had more hunters than planned on and there's not a buck left in the valley." He was right. It was hike up into the timber or go home empty-handed. I climbed. In early afternoon the magnified view of my B&L glass picked up a buck. No, that's not right. Actually, it was a big pine tree hiding all but the head and neck of a buck. Filled with the confidence of a high-resolution scope (happened to be a Bushnell 2.5X-10X with 50mm objective) mounted on an accurate rifle (my Wells 7Mag), I lined up and—Pow! Neck shot and meat in the pot.

"Accuracy is overrated," a gun authority wrote. In a sense, he was right. A friend has taken several elk in a row with one shot per customer shooting a rifle that is incapable of better than five shots inside a two-inch circle at a hundred yards. On the other hand, consider a situation similar to the one above—another family, also new in town, also in need of meat. Once again my freezer was friendly with fatless boned game. The only tag I had left was for a doe antelope. I've learned to prepare this meat to please the palate, especially my favorite recipe—leg o' lope. Tagging a doe would be no big deal where I live.

But this time it was a big deal. I couldn't figure out why the antelope were wilder than eagle-chased turkeys. Hunters? There were none in the immediate area. I failed to get a good opportunity two afternoons in a row. On the third try I located a lone doe. I stalked to one hill away and pulled out the little Nikon rangefinder. Distance was a fur piece—322 yards. I had an ideal rest, took aim, fired. Done. Accuracy paid off again. On the way out of the country I saw the cause of herd panic. A big timber wolf looked down at me from the crest of a hill. No wonder the antelope were jumpy.

A good scope is no more reliable than the mounts attaching it to the rifle. In keeping with the black cat theme, a set of midnight Talley mounts was selected for security. Add an Uncle Mike's carry strap from Michaels of Oregon,

A larger view of the Mauser-type action of the author's clean-sweep rifle.

along with the same company's latest (excellent) QD Premier swivels, and the deed was done. But wait a minute. We have the makings of a rifle, but what caliber? In my experience the 7mm Remington Magnum is North America's number one all-around cartridge. My chronograph shows bullets in the 160-162-grain realm ripping the atmosphere at 3,200 feet-per-second muzzle velocity with a stout charge of IMR-7828 powder. Not every 7Mag will do that due to chamber and bore variations. But mine have. However, I did not go with the Big 7 this time.

I elected the centurion .30-06 Springfield cartridge, born in 1903 as the .30-03 Springfield and only slightly neck-shortened to become the .30-06. Twenty-first-century factory ammunition and handloads push the hundred-year-old round to the original ballistics of the .300 H&H Magnum, a cartridge praised in poetry and sermon by lovers of high velocity and magnum energy. Holland & Holland built the .300 in 1925 by modifying a .375 H&H case. English factories proudly loaded "Holland's Super 30," as Britishers called the .300, with cordite powder

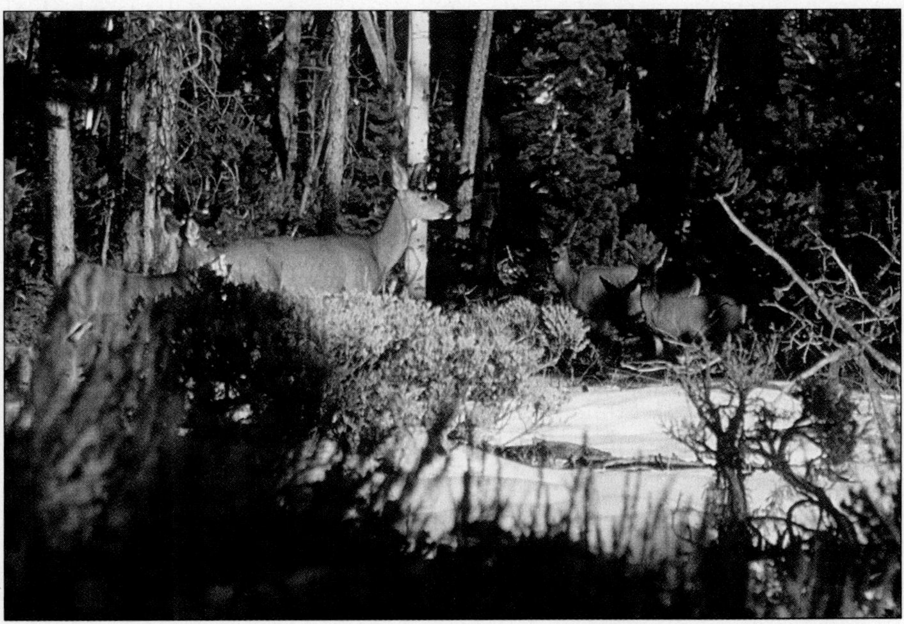

A herd of mule deer stalked for a close shot—with camera. Older does are an ideal harvest. That's why game departments issue tags for them.

The author considers the .30-06 Springfield cartridge to be 100 years old. Since it was created, the .30-03 Springfield with only .070-inch neck shortening and no other modification.

for 3,000 feet per second with a 150-grain bullet, a 180-grain missile at 2,700, and a 220-grain pill at 2,350. Less conservative American ammo crafters perked the .300 H&H to 3,200 feet per second with the 150-grain bullet, 2,900 for the 180-grain pill, 2,610 with the 220-grain. Previous tests with a 24-inch barrel Sauer '06 showed a 180-grain bullet departing the muzzle at a chronographed 2,938 feet per second, the case loaded with a full cargo of H-4831SC (Short Cut), fast enough for flat trajectory with high retained downrange energy. Later tests revealed almost 3,000 feet per second with IMR-4831 powder. Factory-wise, the latest Federal Vital*Shok failed to meet the advertised 2,880 feet-per-second muzzle velocity claim with its 180-grain Bear Claw bullet. Rather, it surpassed that mark with a chronographed velocity over 2,900 in my test rifle. Handload or factory, the "new" hundred-year-old .30-06 generated the same vaulted velocity and energy attributed to the original potency of the giant-killing .300 H&H.

Finally, I made it down south to pick up my new rifle. Bernie Morrison tackled the scope mounting detail with usual proficiency and the new clean-sweep rifle was finished. The fluted barrel, however, looked longer than a trip across Texas. Bernie's cheerful Cherokee Indian face lighted up. "Of course it looks longer than 24 inches," he pronounced. "That's because it's 26 inches, which is where the rifle balanced perfectly." He was right. The rifle challenged the scales of justice, "hanging" in the offhand stance perfectly. I was able to shoot from "hind legs" beyond my usual capability with Mr. Clean Sweep, as I named the rifle. Scale weight was nine pounds with scope. Just what I wanted. From the sitting posture, Moses stick (staff) locked in place, delivering a bullet on the money every shot was no big trick. I was happier than a kid with his first .22 rifle for Christmas.

Although the author chose the 180-grain bullet as an all-around game-taker, the .30-06 handles a multitude of good projectiles including, from the left, the 200-grain Northern Precision, 170-grain Hornady (loaded to 30-30 velocity), and the 165-grain Swift.

Now it was break-in time. Breaking in a cut rifled barrel is almost as much fun as painting a picket fence, and as just about as interesting as watching wet socks dry. But it had to be done, so I dutifully obeyed the rules. Shoot once. Clean. Shoot once. Clean. And so forth. I used JB Compound from Brownells followed by Hoppe's new Elite Gun Cleaner and Bore Gel. But would the .30-06 cartridge realize the accuracy potential of the Morrison barrel? I'm not opposed to the idea of inherent accuracy by virtue of cartridge design. All in all, short fat powder columns seem the way to go for best bullet grouping. Consider the 6PPC, .308, and the accurate new short magnums. However, I was not surprised when the Mauser action/Morrison

Accuracy paid off with a shot that took this northern Wyoming antelope at 322 yards. An accurate rifle, combined with a good scope is key to making a successful long-range shot.

barrel/McMillan stock combination, carefully wedded as a unit, proved capable of clustering five shots into a half-inch at 100 meters at my shooting site. The new rifle "liked" a wide range of bullets. There were favorites, of course, but every projectile proved accurate, some grouping a little tighter than others. In keeping with the current trend, factory ammunition continued to amaze with accuracy similar to carefully built handloads.

I enjoy a big rack or fine set of horns as much as anyone. Not long ago in Mexico I took my 15th B&C worthy Coues buck. I don't enter them, but each has been witnessed, measured, and verified at the time. Trophies are great, but I really like the meat. It was the wise use of that wild gift that prompted me to write my game care/cookery book. The new rifle with 180-grain bullet at around 2,900 to almost 3,000 feet per second will "make meat" without fanfare. I'll rely on faster-opening 180-grain bullets for deer-sized game with bonded projectiles for elk and (depending upon the luck of the draw) moose. One bullet weight, one sight-in, one trajectory for all hunting.

Confidence in Mr. Clean Sweep swelled like the ocean in storm. Here was an all-weather rifle that could be counted on under all conditions in any terrain from dense thicket to open mountain with the new ballistics of the old find-it-anywhere .30-06 cartridge packing the mail. And though I never intended the rifle to be pretty, the sweep of the McMillan stock, contour of the fluted barrel, plus black on black color scheme make it beautiful after all. At least to my eye. During the rifle's first season, loaded with a horizon-to-horizon variety of bullets and powders, Mr. Clean Sweep took nine edibles and one coyote, all at rangefinder measured yards, and with only 10 shots.

Big Rifles, Little Deer

by Wayne van Zwoll

The author approaches the buck he shot at just over 200 yards the last day of the hunt.

They had the big eye fixed on a clump of ocotillo. Mirage shimmered across the canyon floor and made the ocotillo swim. But, squinting, I saw the curve of an antler.

"Venado. Grande." Alejandro spread his hands to show many points and a wide basket.

Patrick had his binocular braced against a palo verde. Tom had his rifle on the bipod.

Alejandro had spotted this buck early. He and the other vaqueros carried good binoculars and saw detail that escaped me and Tom and Patrick. We had better binoculars, and the spotting scope. Top-quality glass helps you find deer, just like an expensive saddle helps you rope steers. But to get the most from it, you must put the saddle on a capable horse.

"Let's shoot that buck," whispered Patrick. He slipped over to help Tom adjust the tripod. A laser rangefinder had registered 370 yards; every detail had to be right.

Midmorning sun had warmed the patch of ocotillo, and the buck would want more shade soon. It is a habit of Coues deer to chase the shade.

Tom took a long time aiming. An experienced rifleman knows it is better to refine a hold than to miss. Sometimes you wait too long and lose a shot. But more often you make a better shot. This deer would not lie much longer, and if it got up, it could vanish, even without trying to.

We'd come into central Sonora only the night before, after a bit of a hang-up at the border. John Mullins, Patrick's right-hand man, did not have the necessary papers for driving beyond the "tourist belt." He would have to return to Tucson and come later. We loaded the essential gear in the remaining trucks and got back on the road late. The pavement got progressively worse as a red sun set on our motorcade. Long after dark, David Miller and Curt Crum turned onto a dirt track. Two hours and very few miles later, the left rear tire of their heavily loaded pickup slipped between bars in a cattle-guard. The truck crashed down on its axle.

Patrick Holehan's Remington 600 doesn't look like one. The author used this 6mm to take a Coues buck.

Perhaps to conserve steel, Mexican ranchers install cattle-guards with the bars running the same direction as the road. And they omit bars in the middle. A couple of tire-widths is all you should need, the reasoning goes. We pow-wowed, then cabled Patrick's Suburban to David's trailer. A downhill pull, it was our sole option, as there was no getting in front of the pickup on the narrow road, here cut into a steep hill.

The axle hung below ground level, the wheel dangling over a pit deep enough to swallow a small silo. We were very far from any place comfortable, and farther from any place with an F-250 rear axle. It was a joyous moment indeed when the tire climbed out of the well. No oil stains anywhere.

At midnight, we rumbled down the last grade to camp. In the dusty, moonlit yard of a stucco cabin a half-barrel burbled mesquite smoke from a fire not yet dead. Diamond-chip stars glittered when we killed the pickup lights, then dimmed again in lantern's glare as the three cowboys emerged from the night to help us fish bedrolls from the Suburban and unload coolers.

"We don't have to get up early," said Patrick.

The night gave us new energy, though, and we got out just after dawn, coffeed up and keen to find the trophy-class Coues bucks Patrick and

David had found here. We split, then rendezvoused at Alejandro's whistle. The next move was up to Tom.

But as he pressured the trigger, the buck rose and stepped into thicker ocotillos. Tom moved the rifle's muzzle slightly to follow. When the buck stepped clear, there would be no more waiting.

"Boom!" The .300 Weatherby rocked the hills with its report. In the binocular, I'd seen the buck appear, a sifting of gray. There was no antler in the big eye now, and no movement.

We marked the spot, then circled to a cow trail and angled down into the ocotillos. Water flowed over a table of smooth rock at the base of the canyon wall. Tall yellow willows shaded it. Past the water, the trail climbed onto a bench with a grade that surprised me. All had looked flat from above.

Alejandro and his companions found the deer easily. It was a fine buck, shot perfectly through the lungs. Tom had used David Miller's rifle, built by the gunmaker on a Model 70 action. It had a long, fluted barrel and a laminated stock, also a Leupold 6.5-20x scope with a special reti-

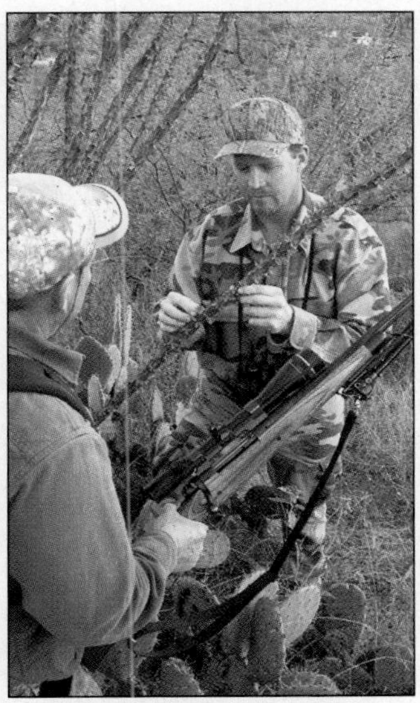

John Mullins, a Coues deer guide, examines an ocotillo in leaf. "Deer hide in thickets of this."

Tom Riley shot this beautiful Coues deer in central Sonora with a David Miller rifle.

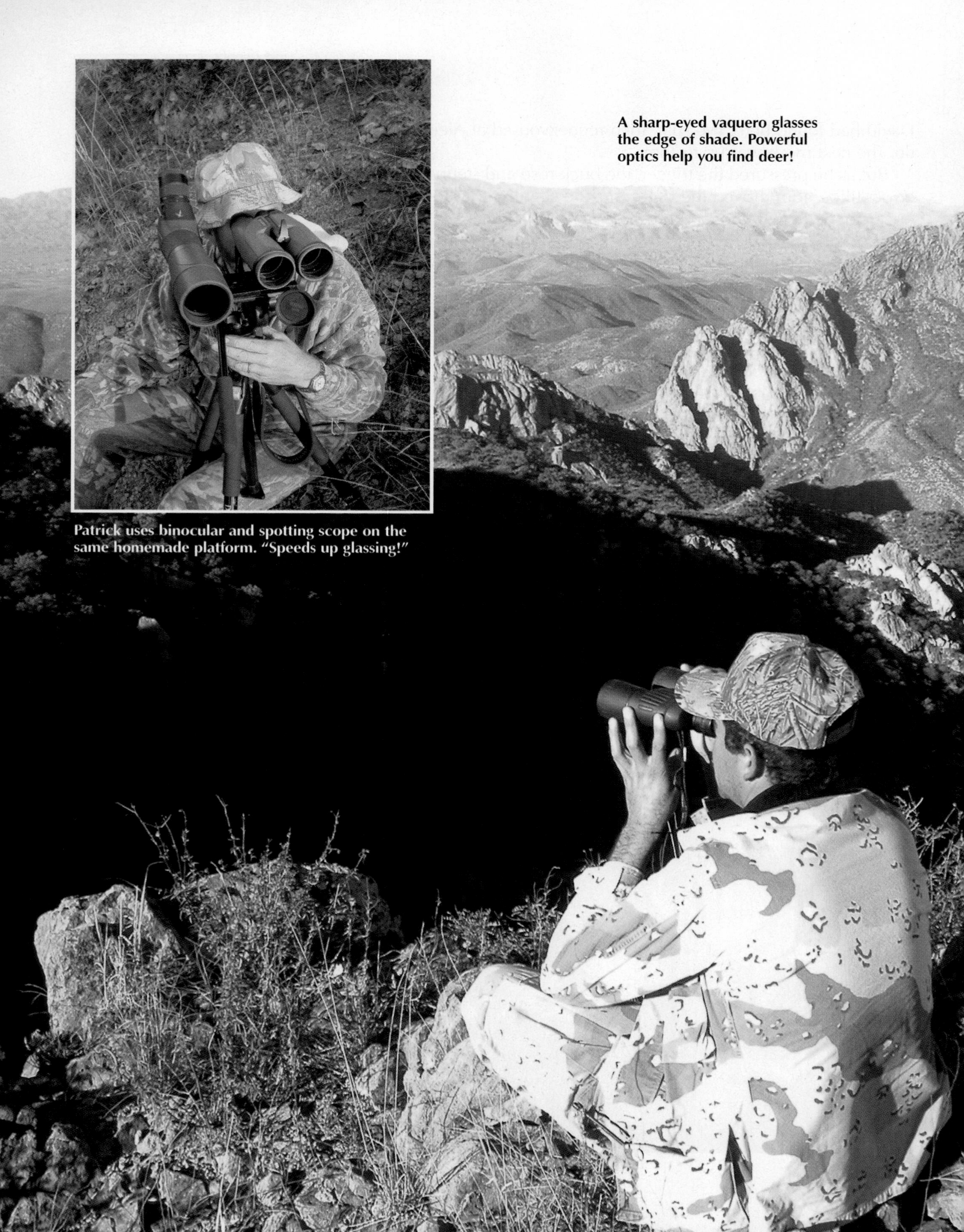

Patrick uses binocular and spotting scope on the same homemade platform. "Speeds up glassing!"

A sharp-eyed vaquero glasses the edge of shade. Powerful optics help you find deer!

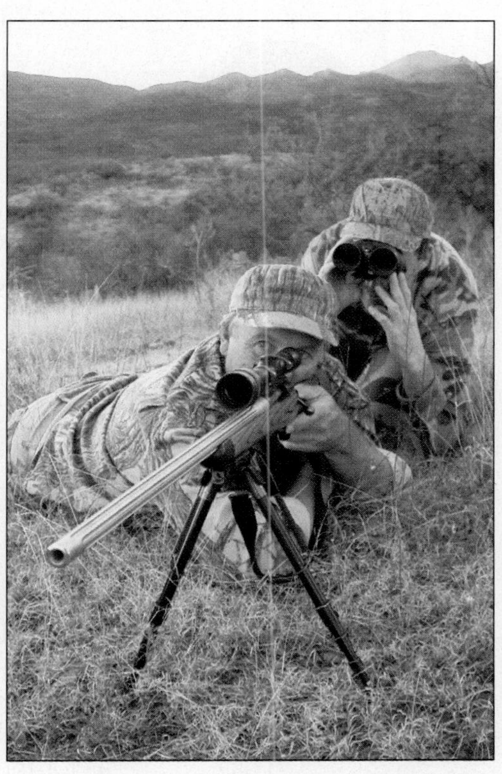

Curt Crum takes aim with a David Miller Marksman. Coues deer are often shot at long range.

cle David had fashioned to make long shots easier. Years earlier, I'd killed a Coues buck with a rifle like this. At 410 yards, it too had been perfectly shot. To ascribe all to luck had seemed unreasonable, so I'd taken the .300 onto a barren flat and fired at paper, prone, using the 168-grain Sierra MatchKings David and Curt had meticulously loaded by hand. One three-shot group measured just over an inch at 400 yards.

This time, I again carried a borrowed rifle: Patrick's. He is also a riflemaker. The P.L. Holehan's Gone Huntin' oufitting service gets him into the field "to test what I build." But he no longer even tries to keep a straight face when he says that. Patrick loves to hunt. And he works hard to see that other hunters have as much fun as he does. Coues deer are a passion, as they've been for David Miller. David's quest for really big Coues bucks keeps him prowling the hills in Mexico and Arizona for weeks each winter. They'd all been gracious enough to invite me on a hunting/scouting trip with Safari Club International's new chief executive, Tom Riley. And Tom had kicked it off well.

But for the next couple of days, we saw only small bucks. Warm, dry days put the lid on deer movement, though the rut was about to commence. David and Curt hunted together, taking four-wheelers up the rough roads much faster than would have been possible with a pickup. They were a seasoned team, used to the long hours of glassing that brings old bucks to bag. They sometimes took lunch, sometimes came back to the adobe cabin. They always had deer to report, but the 100-inch buck we all were looking for eluded them.

One day, as the others napped, I laced up jogging shoes and headed up the dirt road. The grades and mile-high elevation soon had me gasping. Struggling to top a hill a couple of miles from camp, I cut cat tracks. Cougars take goodly numbers of Coues deer, especially, it seems, the bucks. As with mule deer, the bucks are most often alone; groups of females and young have many eyes and ears to warn of approaching predators. Also, hunting pressure in Coues country can drive bucks to the most rugged places, where lions lurk. I doubted that hunting in this part of Sonora had much effect on deer movements. The road we'd taken to the remote cabin was just 20 miles long, but driving it—not counting time at the cattle-guard—had taken longer than running my first marathon. Cowboys sometimes poach deer. Still, the area was vast, with few roads and plenty of cover.

I crested the last ridge heaving. The sweep of country to the south and east brought me up short. Hills and hogbacks and shadowed canyons rolled away to mountains, mostly nameless, that stretched, rank upon blue rank, to a horizon hazy with distance. Beyond the road at my feet, none were visible. No sign of people. No reflections from rooftops or power lines. No noise save peeps from a cactus wren.

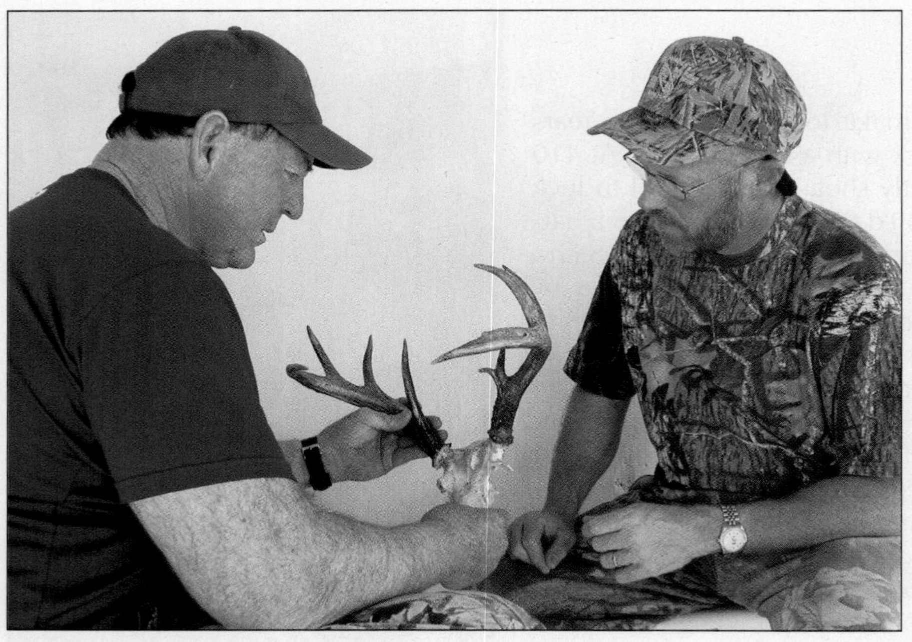

Tom Riley and Patrick Holehan examine the antlers of Tom's fine first-day deer.

Alaska is a wild place, but nowhere is wilderness more plainly revealed than in this part of Sonora.

I turned around and jogged back.

The next morning, just after dawn, Jacinto and José spied an impressive buck slipping along the shadowed side of a spire. I was just a few yards away, glassing opposite slopes with Patrick. But this time the deer won. The vaqueros' signals to us alerted it, and it hurried over a saddle. We never saw it again.

To tell you the truth, I like Coues deer hunting as much for the nights as for the days. You cannot shoot deer at night, but you can stand off by yourself as vaqueros tend the mesquite fire. Your back to the blaze, you see constellations not visible north of the Mason-Dixon line. And because there's no artificial light when Sonora sleeps, each pinprick of brilliance in the heavens is unalloyed. It is as if your eyes are suddenly sharper. The moon moves in a dignified sweep to knife-edge horizons black against a gun-barrel sky. And after you've tired of counting into the Milky Way, and the vaqueros have left the half-barrel for their cots, you fetch more mesquite and pile it on the coals to thicken the swarms of sparks climbing into the night. You warm your back, then your belly and hands, and you breathe deeply of the desert. Then you slide your cot away from the cabin porch, away from the snoring inside, away from the light of the dying fire, out to a quiet place in the yard, where night winds ride like a river over dams of prickly pear and the stars are once again bright. You zip your sleeping bag shut and open yourself to feeling small. Because you are. Because the nearest of the diamond chips is light-years away. That one—over there—may have flamed out when you were young. And that one above it is bigger than any wilderness you can imagine, its girth broader than the orbit of yon white-china moon.

Then it is morning, and you must hunt.

We did hunt hard, though I'm not a competent Coues deer hunter. I lack patience and would rather walk than glass. But Coues bucks are always switched on, and sneaking up on one in oak brush or ocotillo is very difficult. These animals have good ears, good eyes and a sense of smell that should be illegal. They do not know how to relax. While I'd rather kill a Coues buck—or any game—up close, I appreciate the David Miller mantra: If you can't shoot long, you aren't really serious about taking trophy-class Coues deer.

Vaqueros cross a stream with Tom Riley's buck, shot at 375 yards the first morning.

My chance came late in the hunt. We had glassed up several deer just after dawn in a canyon we'd left alone all week. None of the bucks was big, though we were heartened to see two tussling, head to head, a mile and a half to the south. Rut was at last evident.

I'd run out of time, however, and when the sun got warm enough to push deer to deeper shade, we collected all the expensive glass, the vaqueros and the guides and packed them again into the Suburban. David and Curt trailed us this morning, glassing where we'd already glassed because Coues deer can lie all but invisible, then move after you leave. Or the sun can move; shadows that obscured a buck then expose him to your binocular. Or you can just plain miss a buck. Even vaqueros do that.

We motored around a hill that looked very promising, and Patrick wanted to climb it. I was all for that, but our activity might affect the opposite slope, where David and Curt would glass next. We lurched down the two-track, angling east, then around the hill north. And suddenly we saw him, high on a ridge to our front.

Patrick reached for his binocular and I for my rifle at the same time. Even at a distance, there was no question. The antlers had mass and length, and plenty of height. I was on the ground now, and resting the rifle. The crosswire quivered above his shoulder. "He's a fine deer," hissed Patrick. "Shoot him."

I'm deliberate, and had been hunting Coues deer enough to know

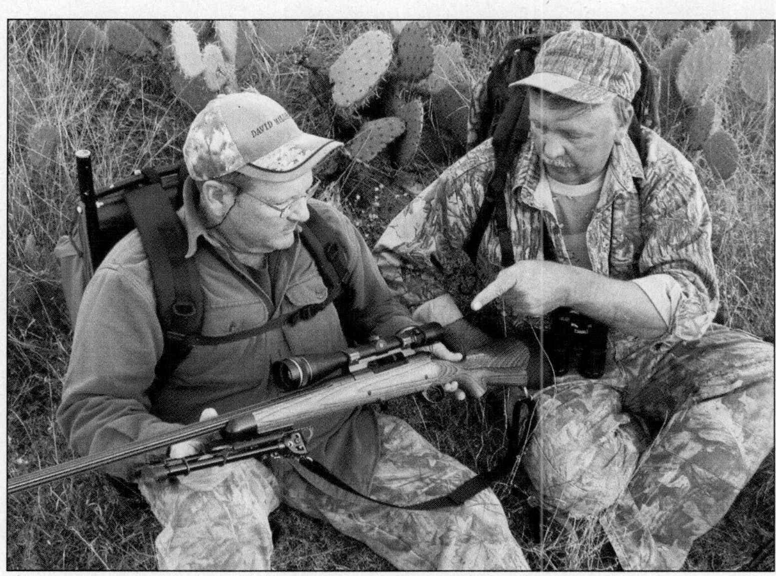

David Miller and Curt Crum conduct a "field test" of a Marksman rifle from their Tucson shop.

that ranging them can be tricky. They're not much bigger than collies, and they almost always look farther than they are. I guessed this one at 275, and said so. "He's closer to 200," Patrick shot back. I could almost hear him bite his lip. He wanted to say what I felt: that there wouldn't be much time. The buck was looking directly at us, tail half-masted. A pair of does behind him skittered up the slope.

Water is life in the desert, but few streams are more picturesque than this one, deep in Sonora.

Forcing myself to hold pressure on the trigger, I brought the reticle down to where I wanted the bullet to land, briefly congratulating myself for having taken an hour with the little 6mm at noon the first day, to check zero from various positions. It was Patrick's wife's gun, a lightweight Model 600 Remington to which Patrick had fitted a straight bolt handle. He'd reshaped the stock and installed a 4-12x Swarovski. Svelte, if unfinished, this rifle lacked the reach of David Miller artillery. But what I needed now was only precision.

When the butt jabbed me and shook the images in the scope, I cycled the action right away. But in the melee on the hill, I saw that the buck was running low, looking tired. Near the crest he stumbled, then spun in a tight circle and fell. He struggled to rise but couldn't, and rolled down the slope toward us. I fired once again, standard procedure when a moving animal is about to vanish in cover. But the shot was both poorly aimed and unnecessary.

We took photographs then, as we had with Tom's buck. The vaqueros field-dressed the deer. "I'd like to see the end of this road," Patrick said. The vaqueros

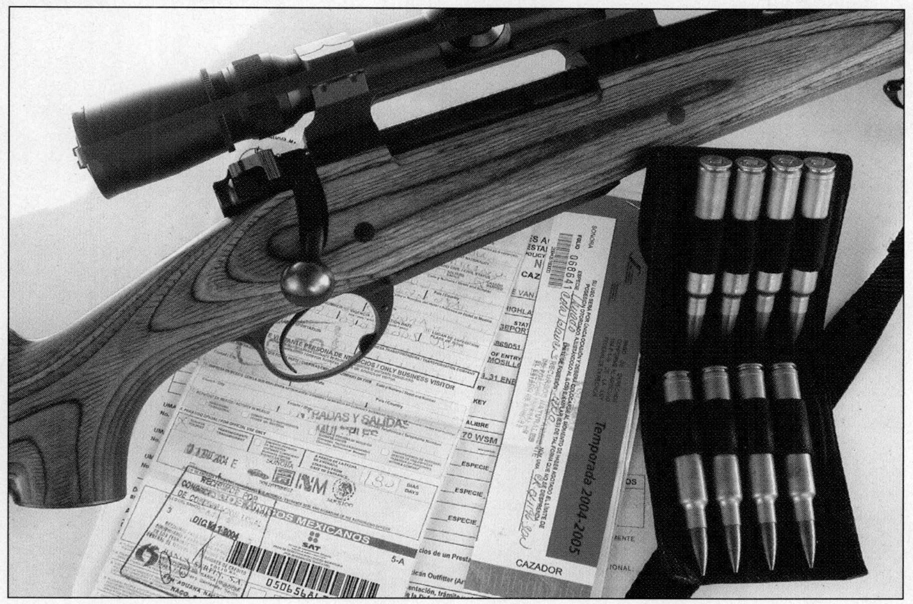

Gun permits and other paperwork are a necessary hurdle if you want to hunt in Mexico.

carried the buck down to the Suburban.

The two-track ended less than a mile from where I'd shot the deer. A small firepit marked the spot as a popular camp. Building fence or rounding up cattle, vaqueros would rest where there was water, shade and protection from wind. Exploring on foot to the south, we found the stream cascading over huge round boulders. A cold green pool lay at their base. Prickly pear and cholla competed with cheat grass on the dry slopes. Beyond those, jagged brown peaks sawed into the blue morning sky.

I urged the guides, vaqueros and hunters to leave me a while. I watched the vehicles lurch back up the two-track, then I started back on foot. No need now to scrutinize every shaded crevice or clump of oaks. A swinging step became a dog-trot. Eyes on the rocks in front of my feet, I felt the grade in my legs. At the canyon's head, I switchbacked to a saddle, then stopped to catch my breath and look north to hills already hazy with noon heat.

Come nightfall, I'd stand again by the mesquite fire in the half-barrel and listen to vaqueros joke softly in fast Spanish. I'd step away to watch the shooting stars, later return to tend the blaze alone and fuel a parade of sparks. I'd move the cot to the edge of the prickly pears and listen to the night.

Sonora is a seductive mistress, even when the hunt ends.

This Coues buck beats the 100-inch score minimum many hunters set as a goal.

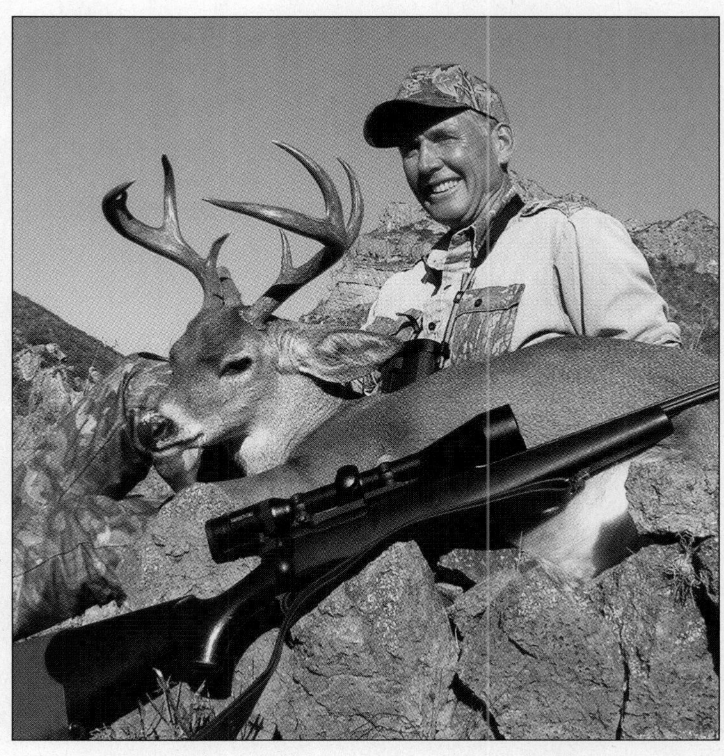

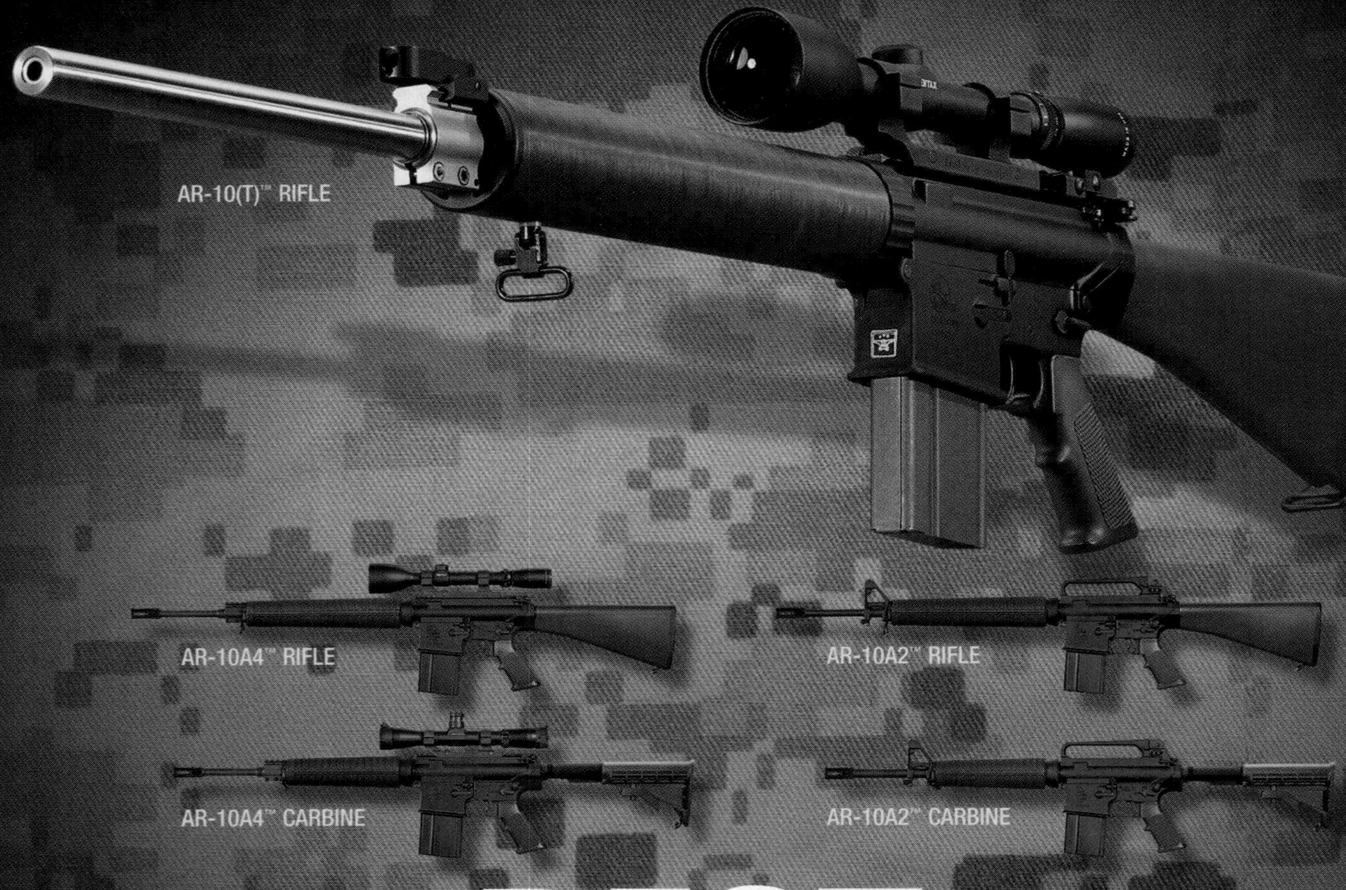
AR-10(T)™ RIFLE
AR-10A4™ RIFLE
AR-10A2™ RIFLE
AR-10A4™ CARBINE
AR-10A2™ CARBINE

Remington's AccuTip Ammunition

by C. Rodney James

Remington's AccuTip ammunition features a pointed polycarbonate tip on a copper-jacketed boat-tailed bullet to ensure maximum expansion upon impact.

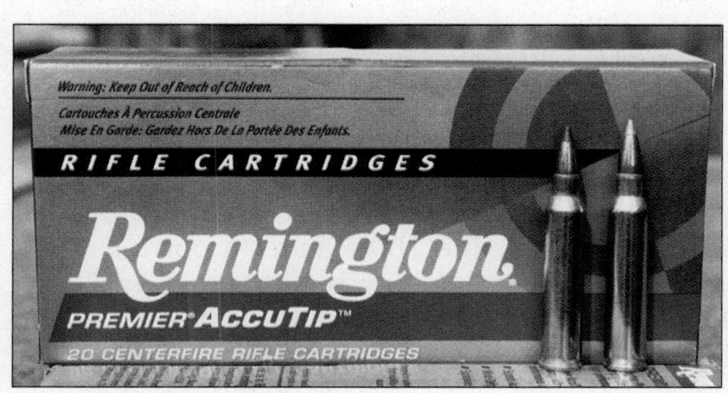

It was mid October 2003 that Remington announced release of a new premium varmint round in a boat-tail configuration with a polymer-point, the AccuTip. The promise was sub minute-of-angle accuracy and rapid expansion. Polymer point ammunition has always delivered the goods in terms of expansion, but accuracy has at times been lacking. The AccuTip is offered in weights ranging from 20 to 75 grains in 17 Remington, 221 Remington Fireball, 222 Remington, 223 Remington, 22/250 Remington and 243 Winchester. I opted to test the 223 since this was the one cartridge offered in two bullet weights—50 grain and 55 grain.

Sales of this ammunition have been brisk (and supplies for writers short), a good indication that word-of-mouth reaction was favorable. The acid test for accuracy was with a vintage 40-X Remington Rangemaster built in 1974. I had always had a hankering for a half-minute rifle and originally thought of using it for varmint work. I ordered up one with a stainless barrel and a magazine. The 27-inch heavy barrel is bored with a 1/14-inch twist. With a scope, the rifle weighs in at over 14 pounds. After a limited number of forays on foot into the field it became a bench rifle though it had accounted for a number of "HO"chucks, once at well over 200 yards in the hands of a shooting partner, Lew Gray, sitting at my bench. We had been sighting-in the rifle when a chuck, that had the habit of crossing the back field at close to 4:00 p.m., appeared on schedule.

I mentioned to Lew that instead of punching another hole in the paper he might wish to try the four-o'clock chuck. Before sliding through the fence row the chuck stopped for a backward look across the empty bean field. This was a mistake. A 55-grain soft-point took him under the

The Remington 40-X Rangemaster has a well-deserved reputation for tack-driving accuracy. The rifles are built and tested to deliver sub minute-of-angle accuracy with target loadings, and they do! Armalite AR-180 auto-loader is a military-style sporter with accuracy on a par with its military counterpart, the AR-18. This is to say about 3 inches at a 100 yards.

REMINGTON 40-X RANGEMASTER

ARMALITE AR-180

chin and flipped him backwards about 10 feet. The range was close to 250 yards. My 40-X was built and tested by a bench-rest shooter named Gary Southard in what is now known as the Remington "custom shop" though at that time the 40-X was simply listed as a standard item at $300. The trigger breaks crisply at an ounce over 2 pounds. The rifle came with two test targets one measuring .3 inch the other .28 inch. I assumed (correctly) this was done indoors from a rest. This rifle is currently equipped with a Weaver T Series 10x40 target scope. Outside, I have accounted for chucks with it out to nearly 400 yards. Both Lew Gray and Gary Southard have gone to their reward, but my 40-X has no visible barrel wear and is still a tack driver.

For giggles I thought I'd see how these varmint rounds might work in an original Armalite AR-180 (from 1966) which has seen exceedingly limited use as a plinker and a (as yet untried) home-defense item. The 180 has an excellent barrel and delivers 55-grain military rounds into 3 inches at 100 yards. Handloads have yielded occasional 1-inch groups at this distance from a rest. The 180 features a polymer stock and weighs 9 pounds. The 18-inch barrel is bored with a 1-12-inch twist. I purchased the (only available) scope for this rifle, a 2.75X20mm compact model made for Armalite. It features a crosshair with a heavy inverted post (for use in low-light situations). Shooting this rifle with precision is difficult owing to its heavy, rather creepy, trigger that breaks around the 8-pound mark.

Testing was done over two sunny September afternoons with temperatures in the high 70s and conditions ranging from calm to faint breeze running to about 3 mph. Mirage was boiling which made the 200-yard targets flicker in midafternoon heat. The original plan was to shoot each loading at both 100 and 200 yards. Making reliable hits on woodchuck-size targets with the 180 much beyond 100 yards proved problematic in view of the trigger situation and the heavy scope post that blocked much of the target area. In view of these handicaps targeting was limited to 100-yard shooting with this rifle.

After foulers and sight adjusters work began. Shooting was done from a newly built mobile shooting bench with two-point sandbag rests. As could be expected, the 40-X delivered the goods much as I hoped, although there were the usual surprises, both real and imaginary. The results are shown in the table on page 30 . While it may appear that the 55-grain bullet has the advantage over the 50-grain load (and while this difference appears real, with four observations at the 100-yard mark), by 200 yards the group differences are so slight that apparent advantage has evaporated. A group-size difference of .05 inch is not statistically significant and of no import whatsoever to a chuck on the receiving end of either bullet. Every shot in both groups would easily nail a chuck at 200 yards.

Genuine surprises were experienced with the 180, although the overall results were much as expected. Since the Armalite was designed as a military rifle for use with the 55-grain bullet, I expected this loading to be the best performer. It was not. Not only did the 55

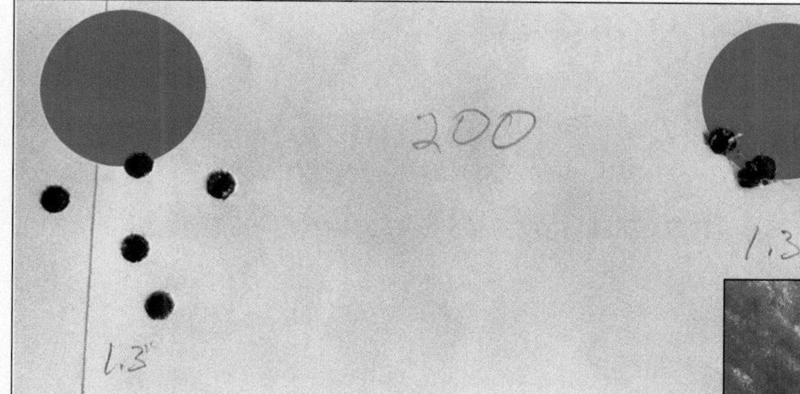

The two best groups with the 50-grain AccuTip both measured 1.3 inches at 200 yards.

produce a measurably larger group, at least seven stoppages (using two different magazines) were experienced with this ammunition. The 50-grain loading, however, ran through this rifle without a hiccup and shaved over an inch from the heavier bullet's group average. (See the table on page 30 for results.)

Why did this happen? The best answer is probably that the military loading is with a faster-burning powder (and more of it) intended for maximum velocity and reliability of function. The Remington varmint load is balanced for accuracy and as such is intended for bolt-action and single-shot rifles where a slightly slower-burning powder provides better accuracy. This comes at the expense of the necessary quick pressure spike to provide reliable functioning. Interestingly enough, the problem did not appear to be a feature of the 50-grain loading with its advertised velocity of 3,300 fps as opposed to the 55's 3,240 fps. The "why?" here was likely a faster-burning powder generating enough reward bolt speed for reliable functioning for this autoloader. Chronographed velocities are shown in the table on page 30.

As a varmint rifle, the 180 and its ilk must be considered about a hundred-yard gun. With a trigger job and a more powerful scope this might be extended half that distance. Owners of high-end target autoloaders might give these 55-grain cartridges a try, although the function problem would still likely be there in those designed for military-style ammunition. A slightly flatter pressure curve is thus the most likely cause for the bolt not getting back quite far enough for reliable feeding. The old caveat still holds true: Autoloaders are more ammunition sensitive than manually operated rifles.

In conclusion, the AccuTip gets my tip of the hat for living up to its promise of a commercial varmint round with accuracy close to target ammunition. The only way a shooter is going to beat this one is by fabricating handloads tailored to his particular rifle. Even with the best of these, I doubt the advantage for a varmint shooter will be all that great except at ranges over the 300-yard mark.

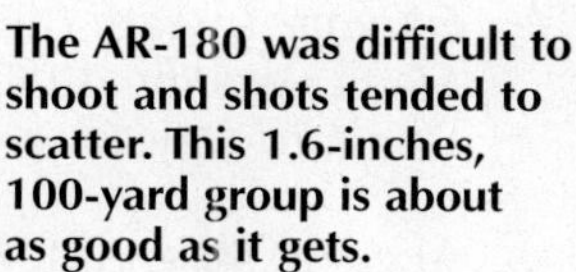

The AR-180 was difficult to shoot and shots tended to scatter. This 1.6-inches, 100-yard group is about as good as it gets.

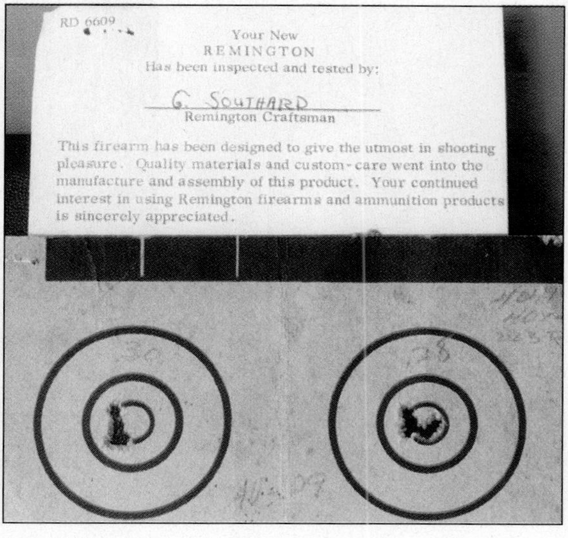

This 100-yard test target, signed by Gary Southard came with the rifle. It was fired with 52-grain Remington HP target bullets backed by 26 grains of IMR 4895 with the Remington 7½ primer.

ACCURACY RESULTS

REMINGTON 40-X RANGEMASTER (27" barrel)

AccuTip 55 gr. b.t. Polytip — 5-shot groups
100 Yards: 0.6", 0.7", 0.5", 0.9" AV 0.68"
200 Yards: 1.5", 1.7", 1.4", 2.0"
Average: 1.65"

AccuTip 50 gr. b.t. Polytip — 5-shot groups
100 Yards: 0.9", 1.0", 1.5", 1.15" AV 1.14"
200 Yards: 1.3", 1.3", 1.8", 2.0"
Average: 1.60"

CHRONOGRAPHED VELOCITIES
AccuTip 55 gr. b.t. Polytip
3216, 3250, 3218, 3219, 3250
Highest Velocity: 3250
Lowest Velocity: 3216
Extreme Spread: 0034
Mean Velocity: 3230
Standard Deviation: 0017

AccuTip 50 gr. b.t. Polytip
3271, 3281, 3296, 3314, 3179
Highest Velocity: 3314
Lowest Velocity: 3179
Extreme Spread: 0135
Mean Velocity: 3268
Standard Deviation: 00

ARMALITE AR-180 (18" barrel)

AccuTip 55 gr. b.t. Polytip — 5-shot groups
100 Yards: 2.5", 4.3", 3.8" 1.9"
Average: 3.13"

AccuTip 50 gr. b.t. Polytip — 5-shot groups
100 Yards: 1.2", 1.6", 2.3" 3.0"
Average: 2.03"

CHRONOGRAPHED VELOCITIES
AccuTip 55 gr. b.t. Polytip
2915, 2937, 2961, 3009, 3013
Highest Velocity: 3013
Lowest Velocity: 2915
Extreme Spread: 0098
Mean Velocity: 2967
Standard Deviation: 43

AccuTip 50 gr. b.t. Polytip
3089, 2984, 3001, 3084, 3001
Highest Velocity: 3089
Lowest Velocity: 2984
Extreme Spread: 0105
Mean Velocity: 3031
Standard Deviation: 0050

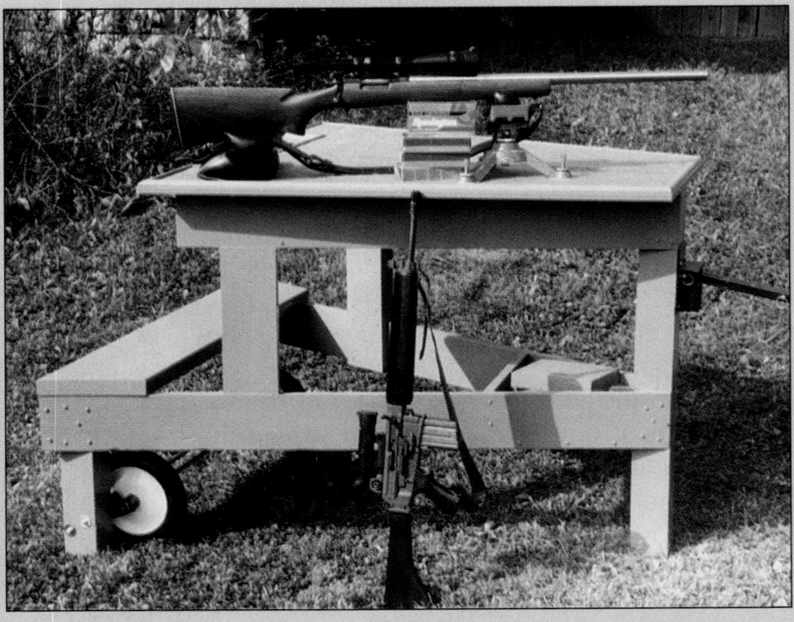

Shots were chronographed at approximately 10 feet from the muzzle with an Oehler 35P Chronograph. Temperatures were 68°-70° F. Shooting was done from a two-point rest and heavy, movable bench.

BURRIS
HUNT. LIKE YOU MEAN IT™
Short
Magnum
Eye Relief
Low
SHORT MAG
Ballistic Plex™
SHORT MAG™
The new line of Short Mag™ riflescopes designed and crafted to provide:
• Outstanding brightness, clarity, and resolution using index-matched HiLume® lens multicoatings and a state-of-the-art lens formulation for edge-to-edge clarity.
• 3.5"- 5" of lightweight magnum eye relief.
• Low mounting for better balance and cheek weld.
• Performance and balance on lightweight, compact, hard kicking, short action rifles.
• Trajectory compensation for long range shots utilizing the simple and proven Ballistic Plex™.
Optimize your rifle and time in the field with a Burris Short Mag™ and Ballistic Plex.
4X
2X-7X
3X-9X
4.5X-14X PA
Standard Trajectories
100
200
300
400
500
ExampleCartridges that calibrate for 100 to 500 yards.
.243 100grain
.270 150grain
7mm-08 140grain
7 Mags 175grain
30-06 165grain
Magnum Trajectories
200
300
400
500
600
ExampleCartridges that calibrate for 200 to 600 yards.
.25WSSM 120grain
.270WSM 150grain
7mmWSM 160grain
300WSM 150grain
325WSM 180grain
All riflescopes are warranted forever. Burris Company, 331 E. 8th Street, Greeley, CO 80631 (970) 356-1670
www.burriscompany.com

Plinking—Our Most Popular Shooting Sport

by Ken Horowitz

Just as the bull elephant turned to charge, I raised the original John Rigby double rifle to firing position and dropped the trophy on the spot. Much to my amazement, this was accomplished in the final daylight hours of my other four triumphs, thus managing to bag all of Africa's big five in the very same day. This feat, right on the heels of having won that giant gold medal for putting 10 rounds into the same hole at 1,000 yards made me the all-time shooting champion of the universe. If this sounds like a wild dream, you're right on track, for it is nothing but sheer nonsense, far outside the borders of ordinary fantasy.

But for that matter, even more traditional tales of shooting have more wishful thinking associated with them than reality. Those mountain sojourns with the 400- to 500-yard shots that we read about every month in mainstream magazines are experienced by so few shooters that their hype is totally out of proportion to the actual number of events. Most of those professionally photographed snazzy defense pieces we see every month are more likely to stay in a drawer than to be carried, let alone fired in anger, and even the traditional deer rifle sees relatively minor use over the couple of days a year that the typical hunter sits in a tree stand trying to stay awake.

To be sure, lots of us engage in some sort of organized or semi-structured shooting sport, including hunting, competition, training and practice, all with rifle, pistol and shotgun, but when all the smoke clears, our number one shooting passion is no more sophisticated than mak-

Youngster plinking off the bench with his 22LR under the watchful eyes and careful guidance of his grandfather. Informal sessions such as these are a great way to introduce people to the shooting sports and will engender a lifetime of memories.

ing tin cans dance, popping a balloon, busting a dirt clod, watching a homemade pendulum swing. Yes, good ol' plinking is our secret pastime and where many of us would rather be than on a more regulated course of fire. With its virtual universal platform, just about every firearm imaginable can be used in this most enjoyable recreational pursuit; while most of it is done with run-of-the-mill rimfire rifles and pistols, plinking's informal nature allows the use of center-fire pistols and rifles, even shotguns and front-stuffers.

Typical 22LR plinking rifles include ubiquitous Marlin Model 60 *(top)*, author's first rifle, a Marlin Glenfield Model 101 *(center)* and a 1960's vintage Mossberg Model 352 KB *(bottom)*.

Plinking is also a great way to get new shooters started. For people who have never fired a gun before, punching paper can get tiresome and frustrating, partly because skills need to be developed and partly because of misguided expectations. For most new shooters I've mentored, group size means nothing in the beginning. They have a tendency to think in terms of bull's-eyes only and see those shots outside the center as evidence of failures. When knocking down plastic bottles on the other hand, misses are magically erased from their minds whenever a target is struck, even if it's only the accidental result of a ground splatter. This is exactly the kind of excitement that attracts people to the shooting sports. Skills can be honed later, but if we let that interest wane after a handful of holes in a paper bull's-eye target, there will be no opportunity to develop into a better shooter.

What exactly is plinking? A quick click on the web inundated me with close to 10,000 hits! Without giving credit to any one specific "official" definition of this highly unofficial pastime, there seems to be general agreement that it is informal shooting of reactive targets. Perhaps the "plinking" name itself is based on the sound of hits on tin or steel cans, maybe even the clinking of breaking glass. While this connection is apocryphal at best, it is at least credible.

When I was growing up as a city kid, shooting was pretty much limited to an occasional treat at a seaside arcade where tube fed 22 Shorts were the order of the day. The diminutive rifles were chained to the table in such a way that it wasn't possible to swing them in an unsafe direction. The sights were poor and none of us kids really knew how to use them, but after a few hits at toppling ducks that reset themselves, I was hooked. Of course, my dad was always standing there behind me and he ponied up the coins for a few plays. With my city pedigree, I didn't realize at the time that these

Pistols chambered for the 22LR can provide hours of fun in any of several action types, including the Ruger Mark I single-action semiautomatic *(top)*, the Smith & Wesson Model 73 double-action revolver *(center)* and the Taurus DA semiautomatic *(bottom)*.

kinds of rifles could be used anywhere other than at the arcade.

My best friend Tommy always had a lot of things and in our day that meant that we all had a lot of things. When he proudly showed the air gun he had found under the Christmas tree, I didn't get it at first. It was one of those sanitized versions with an oversized barrel through which a pin had been riveted. A lever action cocked the spring-loaded piston, the net result of which was a whoosh of air out of the barrel and a sound that wasn't quite as appealing as any of our standard cap guns.

Then one day my older brother, applying the engineering logic that only kids know, figured that a wad of wet toilet tissue, wrung out and stuffed into the barrel ahead of the cross rivet, would fly a considerable way upon firing the air rifle. Now we were in business. Tommy, the possessor of all those goodies, soon came down from his apartment with a collection of toy soldiers. Even kids know the headaches of wartime supply logistics, so we strategically selected our position, the bathroom window, where we had a ready supply of ammunition and a sink to get it wet. Since I lived in a second-floor apartment overlooking an adjacent flat-roofed building, we simply crawled out the dining room window onto the roof, set up the enemy soldiers and fired away from the bathroom. We were in plinking heaven, although at the time, I had never heard the word. Things went pretty well until my little brother decided he needed the bathroom for other purposes. Lots of sibling yelling later, we let him take a few shots and nature's calling somehow got delayed until the adults came home.

As I got older, other youthful pursuits upstaged shooting toy soldiers with wads of compacted toilet tissue and real shooting opportunities weren't to be had in the confines of the city. However, once I got to be in the age group with wheels it wasn't long before Tommy and I discovered an indoor shooting range on a highway about 15 miles outside the city. It was part of a sports shop and they rented 22 caliber rifles for anyone who purchased range time who needed one. While the rifles were high quality with good peep sights, the re-sighting of a rental coupled with the economics of rental versus buying and it wasn't long before I got my first rifle, a Marlin Glenfield Model 101 that set me back about eighteen very big dollars at the time. In retrospect, that rifle shot much better than it should have, but I didn't know any better, so I got really good, really fast (that was when the peepers could hold a sight picture).

It didn't take long before the standard paper bull's-eye targets became routine, even a bit tiresome and a deck of discarded playing cards provided a lot more fun. To make things even more challenging, if the range officer wasn't too savvy, Tommy and I would "accidentally" shoot each other's target holders to get them to swing.

Odd lots of leftover ammunition, including centerfire such as these 9mm "orphans" make ideal plinking fodder. None of the leftovers below, ranging from 2 to 6 rounds is worthwhile zeroing and determining point of aim for competition or other organized purpose, but they are all more than suitable to knock around a couple of tin cans or plastic bottles.

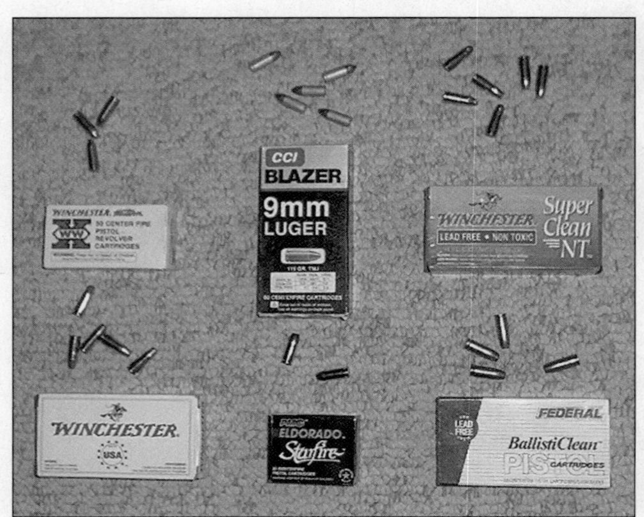

Some of the author's favorite plinking materials include spent shotshell hulls, clay targets and heavy plastic bottles. Plinking treasures are everywhere.

Then we discovered another place to shoot, this one a public outdoor range. It was prone only, but it provided us a new kind of target. Even though paper targets were normally used at this facility, the range officer didn't mind if we put some twigs and other non-ricocheting natural materials in front of the berm. Leaves, twigs, pine cones and acorns were a lot more fun than paper punching and while my lifelong affair with plinking may have been born earlier, for certain, it was sealed.

Working my way through school, I was lucky enough to hook up with a friend whose family had some rural land where we could set up cans, balloons, cards, twigs, plastic bottles and anything else we wanted as long as it was safe and we cleaned up after we were done.

Years later, when I looked around to join a shooting club, one of my elimination criteria were those clubs that didn't have a plinking range. While I enjoy all sorts of target sports, with pistol, rifle and shotgun, plinking still rules. While it may not carry the panache of a formal competition, each shot still carries the instant exhilaration of success or miss. There's no waiting to peek downrange through the spotting scope. Either that plastic bottle goes dancing, the balloon pops, the clay breaks, or nothing happens.

For new shooters, the instant confirmation of success is a timely reinforcement that can often mean the difference between a ho-hum experience and one that will spark a lifelong interest in the shooting sports. For anyone not fully understanding sight alignment, group size and the like, even a good target may be disappointing to the newer shooter, but a bad hit on a reactive target is a rewarded success.

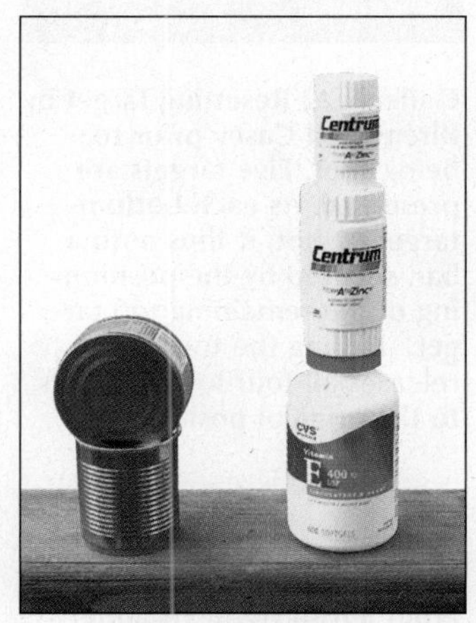

How about a stackable challenge? Using just a bit of imagination can make plinking even more fun. A couple of cat-food cans on the left or plastic vitamin bottles on the right make very challenging plinking targets. The object is to hit the top target off the stack without sending the lower target flying. It's not easy!

Anyone who has done a fair amount of plinking has favorite targets. For me, the two best that I like are rigid white plastic bottles like the ones you get with over the counter vitamins and clay birds. The bottles are hard enough and have enough resistance so that they really fly when hit. With metal cans, without enough resistance, the bullet will often pass through the target with no apparent reaction. Using clay birds, you can keep breaking the parts into smaller pieces, especially with a 22 rimfire and each successive target presents an increased challenge. If I'm having a really good accuracy day, smaller targets such as empty shotshell hulls and bottle caps really fly when hit.

Plinking isn't limited to 22 rimfires, although that's undoubtedly how most of it is done. I've gone plinking with center-fire handguns up to 44 Magnum, and with rifles up to 30 caliber, even with .410 shotgun slugs, but by and large, 22 rimfires, including the ubiquitous 22LR, is where the action is. According to reliable industry sources,

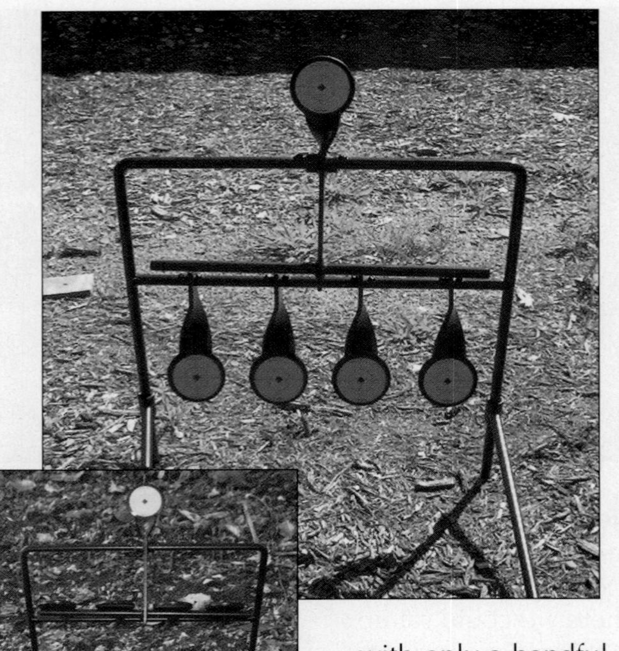

Gallery .22 Resetting Target by Birchwood Casey prior to being shot. Five targets are presented. As each bottom target is shot, it flips onto a bar, secured by the positioning of the remaining top target. Hitting the top target releases all four lower targets to the original position.

annual worldwide sales of 22LR ammunition are about 5 billion rounds, or somewhere in the neighborhood of 80 percent of all rounds produced. By and large, most of these are of the common high velocity non-competition type.

It's not unusual for a new shooter to go through a brick or more of 22LRs the first time at the range. Even though this is entirely too much ammunition to go through and do much in the way of technique, you'd be surprised at how much is developed by the end of the day. After a shooter becomes confident that targets can be hit, I've found more attentive listening than I'd otherwise get by giving a big lecture and a few rounds at a bull's-eye. My approach is to show them how to shoot safely, whether hit or miss, with only a handful of comments on aiming and trigger control. Then, after they have the first exhilaration out of their systems (usually about 200 rounds later), I'll show them improvement techniques. By that time, they're hooked and the techniques for improvement mean something.

Hundreds of rounds fired at a bull's-eye target by a new shooter can be very boring for the neophyte. Coupled with a lecture on the finer aspects of trigger letoff, the best-meaning instructor can do more to discourage participation in our sport than even the most virulent anti-gunner. To get a shooter's interest, make it fun. The first time out on the range, even with a lot of shooting, likely won't instill any bad marksmanship habits that can't be corrected at a later session. As long as they're shooting safely, let them get comfortable with the process.

To satisfy curiosity, new plinkers like to fire at least a handful of cartridges in other calibers, but I've found that other than this curiosity, few of them prefer much recoil, a burden that we needn't give them. With exceptions, of course, I've found that most new shooters I've encountered shy away from anything more potent than a standard 38 Special. Interestingly, on the lower end, rimfires lighter than a common 22LR don't seem to hold much interest either.

From left to right: Qualifier Spinner Target by Birchwood Casey, .22 Rimfire Indicator Spinner Target by Hoppes and Sight and Sound .22 Rimfire Spinner Target by Champion.

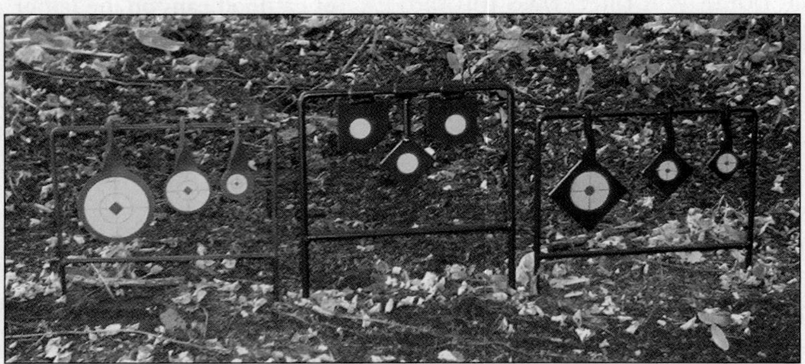

Several years ago, I quickly supplemented my regular stock of 22LRs with all kinds of 22 Shorts, CB Caps and other light fodder for use by my mother-in-law in a small revolver on her first shooting venture. I had been concerned about her potential reaction to recoil, both mentally and as a result of her arthritis. Very quickly, she made it clear that she didn't like anything less than the kick of plain vanilla High Velocity 22LRs. Moreover, the revolver was soon set aside in favor of a full-sized 22 autoloader and a piggy bank's worth of CCI Stingers.

These competition posts have targets that swing from one side to the other upon being hit. Both use a simple but effective camming action that holds the target in place but is easily overcome by the strike of a 22LR bullet. While practice by a single shooter is fun, these targets really come into their own when two shooters compete to get all targets onto the opponent's side. Of course, the opponent is doing the same. On the left is the Champion .22 Target Tree, which free stands on a base, while the Hoppes Dualing Post on the right is tapped into the ground.

Besides makeshift targets, there is a wide choice of commercially made rigs that run the gamut from hanging spinners and swingers to targets that shift left and right upon being hit. There are even targets that automatically reset; automatically, that is, upon being hit by the shooter. Following the ammunition market, most of the commercially made setups are designed for 22LR (as well as lighter ones for air-gun pellets), but there are some heavier duty models for center-fire pistols. These commercial models come with instructions and warnings from the manufacturers as to type of ammunition and minimum distances at which the targets should be set. Beyond these warnings, no matter the target, the shooter should always follow safe shooting practices, including knowing the target and what is behind it.

Also available are commercial quick setup frames that provide an easy way for a shooter to hang reactive and paper targets. Having both on the same frame allows the shooter to sight-in on the paper and then plink away at reactive items of choice without leaving a shooting position. I've found this is great for those sessions where I'm using up those odd lots of ammunition that may shoot to different points of aim.

Even some of the more organized competition target games share the same reactive target benefit that draws so many to plinking. I've frequently heard metallic silhouetting, whether handgun or rifle, jestingly referred to as "plinking for grownups." Many of the "stage" events, both combat and dress-up, such as cowboy action shooting, are not much more than organized plinking. For those shooters who keep their interest in our most popular of shooting sports a deep dark secret, the formality of competition somehow legitimizes it. For the rest of us, I have no qualms whatsoever in proudly boasting my fondness for this real sport of sports, even while batting the breeze with other shooters at a more organized competition.

Whether out of the closet or in secret, plinking is by far our number one target sport. All you need is a gun, a safe place to shoot and an imagination.

The quickly set-up Field Target Holder by Champion allows the use of paper targets or plinkables with the use of different clips to hold them to the crossbars. A favorite setup is this dual-purpose setup with dangling cans, plastic bottles and spent shotshells plus a paper sighting-in target on the left. Getting the plinking targets off the ground assures that they react only from direct hits, not ground splatter.

Optics Worth the Money

by Wayne van Zwoll

You can buy cheap and cheat yourself, and spend big to buy only fluff. Here are developments and products worthy of your hard-earned cash!

Dots in the Darkness: Aimpoint

Kenneth Mardklint smiled. "Some hunters don't trust sights that use batteries. But our sights give you 20,000 hours of aiming from a 3-volt lithium cell. That's a long time to hold a rifle."

Five years ago, I'd spoken with Kenneth on a visit to Aimpoint, the Swedish company that built the first red dot sight. In 1975 Gunnar Sandberg invented what he called the single-point sight. You saw the target with one eye and the sight's dot reticle with the other, so you couldn't look through the sight at all! Next came the Aimpoint Electronic, with windage and elevation adjustments and five brightness settings for the illuminated dot. An improved version came out in 1977. A decade later, after further improvements, the company introduced its Model 1000 with an integral Weaver-type base. It was soon supplanted by the Aimpoint 3000, featuring 2x magnification. In 1991 the 5000 appeared, with a 30mm tube and 20 percent bigger field. An XD (extreme duty) diode later made the 5000 three times as bright as the old diode, while battery life leaped from 100 to 500 hours!

Hunting moose in Sweden, I found Aimpoint's 7000 an ideal sight for the thick forest. In a damp dawn I waited as fog swirled through tall black conifers and the distant shouts of drivers grew louder. The first moose appeared silently, its long legs swinging easily. It passed wide to the east, but the Aimpoint's dot, throttled to low intensity, stayed easily visible as I kept the .30-06 muzzle moving ahead of the moose. At 90 yards, I didn't need magnification. When the bull crossed a clearing, I triggered the Blaser,

SmartScope affords little latitude in ring spacing but mounts as low as many ordinary scopes.

The author mounted this Simmons Master Series 3-9x40 on a Remington AWR in 6.8 SPC.

keeping the dot on the shoulder's leading edge.

That bull dropped immediately when my Norma bullet threaded his lungs. A cow moose that tried to slip past me on the last drive of the day also died. In the gathering dusk, under a dark, leaking canopy, I might have lost a black reticle. But the Aimpoint's dot grabbed my eye, and the shot followed right away.

The sight's unlimited eye relief is not just a boon for stock-crawlers; it enables you to shoot your rifle as fast as you might a shotgun. Your eye can be 3 inches back, or 9. There's a generous "eyebox" too, so you needn't worry if your eye is off axis a little; the dot will probably still be visible, and even if it's off-center, your bullet will hit where you see it.

Long shooting? Because you see all the target around the dot, it's easy to make lethal hits to 200 yards. A Blaser rifle delivered 1½-minute groups for me at 100. One reason: Aimpoint's compound front lens. An ordinary single lens up front will still reflect the dot produced by the diode in the rear bottom of the tube. Aimpoint's "doublet" brings the dot to your eye in a line parallel with the optical axis of the sight. The reflective path of a single-lens sight varies with your eye position. If the dot isn't centered in the sight, you'll have parallax error at distances other than the one for which the sight was corrected. With Aimpoint, you hit where you see the dot.

"Aimpoint sights are not nitrogen-filled," notes Mike Kingston, the company's North American representative. "It's unnecessary. Aimpoints don't fog, and they don't leak, even with adjustment caps off." After hunting in rain with that 7000, I believe him. Durability and reliability have endeared Aimpoint sights to soldiers. In fact, military sales account for 75 percent of total revenues, with the biggest commitments to U.S. and French armies. The firm's hunting sights are marketed in 40 countries. One of every 10 Swedish hunters using optical sights carries an Aimpoint.

This year, there's another reason to install an Aimpoint on your woods rifle or shotgun. Advanced Circuit Efficiency Technology (ACET) reduces power demand,

This Simmons Master Series 3-9x looks at home on a Hill Country Rifles' Model 70 in .70 WSM.

This Wyoming elk fell to the author's Howa in 6.5x55 and a Nikon Monarch 4x scope.

boosting battery life on the new Aimpoint 9000 to 50,000 hours! That's with brightness set on 7, on a dial numbered to 10. The 9000 series comprises three models, and you get a choice of reticles: 2-minute or 4-minute dot. "Our sights aren't cheap," says Mike. "They're simply the best red dot sights you can get. Now they're more rugged than ever, and with battery life at 50,000 hours, you can stay in the woods for nearly six years before replacing the cell!"

A Smarter SmartScope at ADK

In 2004 Adirondack Optics, a small company in upstate New York, announced a rifle scope that also works like a camera—and can be set to photograph what you see through the scope when you pull the trigger. SmartScope was designed by Terry Gordon, a young entrepreneur who knew from the start that producing the instrument would "be a costly effort." But his team included some talented and persistent engineers. Bankrolling the project called for more help. Local investors ponied up. They even convinced the state of New York to pitch in.

Adirondack Optics built the scope first, with high quality a requisite. Terry reasoned that no hunter would compromise a hunt for the sake of a photo. The first SmartScope became three: a 1.5-6x40, 3-10x44 and 6-16x44. All have 30mm tubes with quarter-minute adjustments and 3 inches of eye relief. There's a parallax adjustment on the 3-10x and 6-

16x. The mil dot reticle lies in the front focal plane, so apparent reticle dimensions change with magnification but not in relation to your target. "Point of impact can't shift during power change," says Terry, "because lens movement is behind it. Also, you can use the reticle to judge range without considering power." European hunters have long favored first-plane reticles, a design already used on other scopes in the Czech factory that builds SmartScope for ADK. The intent is to move all production Stateside, to consolidate assembly and shed a 15-percent import tariff.

An internal digital camera is what makes this ADK product different. A small screen saddling the ocular bell has the on-off switch and a button that lets you take photos through the scope. The camera uses standard digital cards. "They're Smart Media now," Terry tells me. "But a CD card is coming." The camera is powered by a pair of 1.5-volt AA batteries housed at midsection in a turret compartment.

Most hunters will want to use SmartScope to photograph an animal at hunting's moment of truth. That, too, is easy. You set the camera for automatic function before the hunt. Then, when you fire at game, SmartScope takes a digital picture automatically as your rifle recoils. It's not a blurry image, because the camera is designed to record what it saw 7 milliseconds before recoil—an average lock time.

According to the author, 4x is the most versatile magnification. A Kahles sight helped take this buck.

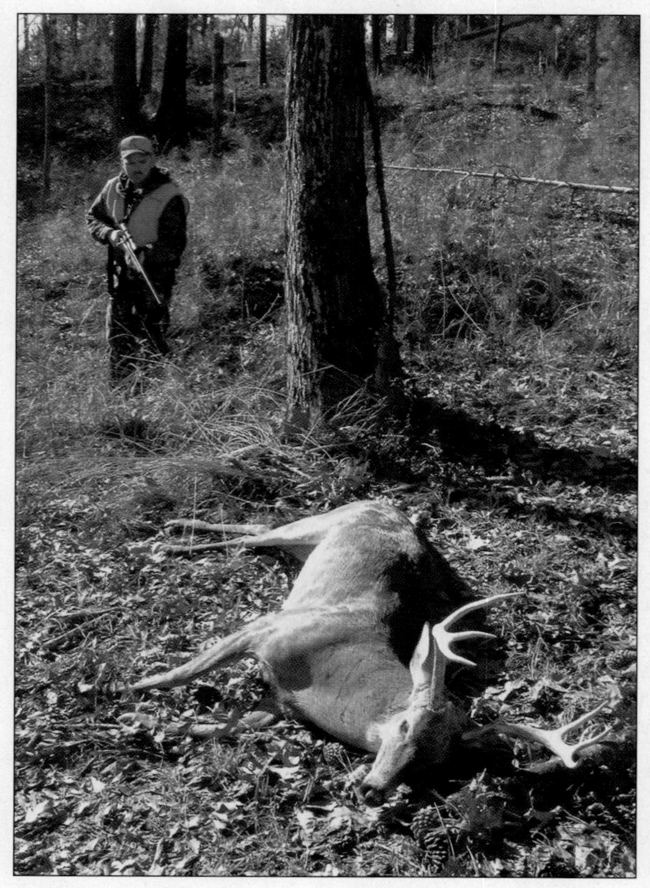

My field test of SmartScope should have netted me a trophy. I'm embarrassed to admit botching a very easy shot by horsing a heavy trigger and pulling the borrowed rifle off target. Fortunately, the forest shadows were too black for a photo. At the range, I vented my frustrations on paper, first with a 14-caliber wildcat that fired a 12-grain bullet from a modified .221 Fireball case. The negligible recoil triggered the camera without fail. A tight five-shot group from prone confirmed what photos of the reticle told me. Next I put my sling on the rifle with the tough trigger, a .300 Ultra Mag. My group this time was abominable. Reviewing the five photos, I saw the crosswire off-center in three. Images from successful hunters showed the reticle right where it should be on the target deer.

SmartScope's fully multi-coated lenses deliver the resolution and brightness of the most expensive scopes. But the camera does extract a price. At 22 to 26 ounces, SmartScope weighs half again as much as many 30mm scopes, and a mid-ship battery case leaves little free tube for scope rings. Finally, SmartScope is costly: $1,500 and up. But there's no other way to hunt with camera and rifle at once, and the crew from upstate New York has done an outstanding job of building an instrument that not long ago would have been considered a pipe dream. Now, it is more likely to emerge the pioneering effort in an industry trend. Phone Adirondack Optics at 800-815-6814.

With lots of tube for easy mounting, and a slim, traditional profile, the Simmons Master Series is an impressive sight inside as well. And it retails for just $150.

FX-II and FX-III: Best New Old Sights

Leupold has overhauled its variable-power hunting scopes. It has replaced the Multicoat 4 lens treatment in Vari-X IIIs with an "index-matched" system in the new VX-III. Idexed lens coatings, say people at the Beaverton, Oregon, facility, promise more light to your eye and a sharper, color-true image. Multicoat 4 is now standard on VX-II scopes, successor to the Vari-X IIs that wore lesser coatings but were extremely popular with hunters. My hunter surveys for the Rocky Mountain Elk Foundation in the 1990s showed that Leupold Vari-X II 3-9x scopes outnumbered the second- and third-most-used sights combined! Leupold's fine catalogs helped; they dress up scopes the way that pinup calendars fill out swimsuits.

Also without blemish is Leupold's warranty. The firm will make good on any scope that malfunctions; it has replaced and reconditioned scopes that merely fell into the wrong hands. One day on a steep, snowy slope the horse I was leading lost its footing and toppled over backwards, crushing the eyepiece of my Leupold scope against the bolt handle of my rifle. The Leupold folks could have told me to take my .338 out of the scabbard next time. Instead, they repaired the scope. No charge. No chiding.

Lest this tale trigger an avalanche of abused scopes, I'll add that no firm can afford to underwrite the misbehavior of its customers. Most hunters understand this and don't abuse the warranty. But as with blue-chip stocks in a dowry, they like knowing it's there.

Leupold knows how to court loyalty. When you buy the scope with a Golden Ring, you buy into a brotherhood. The image of the Leupold hunter is Marlboroesque. But what keeps me loyal to Leupold is its attention to fixed-power scopes—the M8s I lusted after in my youth, when a nickel would keep me in air-gun BBs for a weekend. Then a new 4x cost $59.50. Leupold continued to catalog fixed-power scopes after other makers dropped them and still has a broad selection. This year Leupold replaced the M8 series with new FX-II and FX-III scopes.

The FX-II 4x33 weighs 9.3 ounces, same as before. But the lenses feature Multicoat 4 coatings, a step up from the treatment given M8s. Coin-slotted quarter-minute click adjustments replace the traditional friction-fit dials. Available in matte finish or gloss, with wide Duplex or

Terry Gordon, who came up with SmartScope, here shoots with it on a Heym straight-pull rifle.

standard Duplex reticle, this scope has a whopping 4 inches of eye relief. Naturally, the new FX-II 6x36 offers the same improvements. You can also order this 10-ounce sight with Dot or Post & Duplex reticle.

Another new 6x is the 11-ounce FX-III 6x42. The "III" means that like VX-III variables, its lenses feature index-matched coatings. Windage and elevation dials are finger-friendly. A competition model has target knobs and adjustable objective. It weighs 15 ounces—a couple of ounces more than the FX-III 12x40 AO target scope with adjustable objective. I've found 12x sights ideal for lightweight rifles usually shot at long range. Pronghorn guns and "walking varmint rifles" qualify.

For hunters who prowl the oak thickets and lodgepole jungles, Leupold has the FX-II Ultralight 2.5x20. At 6½ ounces, it's lighter than some iron sights. The FX-II Scout scope has more eye relief, but of course it can't match the standard model's 40-foot field of view at 100 yards. Neither will FXII 2x20 and 4x28 pistol scopes. An 18-inch eye relief extracts a big price in field; theirs span 21 and 9 feet at 100 yards.

I was using a fixed-power scope in Oregon 30 years ago when on a rocky ridge I surprised a very fine mule deer and laid him low with an early Model 70 in .30-06. With the same rifle and scope, I made what is still my longest shot at big game. Another mule deer. The biggest buck I've killed dropped to a .35 Whelen wearing a fixed-power. So did my first Canadian moose and the animals that gave themselves to my first safari. All these scopes were 4x. I like 2½ x and 3x models as well, and mourned under sackcloth for days when Leupold discontinued its M8 3x. My first bull elk collapsed in the field of a 2½ x scope, my first mature six-pointer to a .30-06 Improved with a 3x. I've rarely needed more power; the longest shot I've attempted at an elk gave me a one-shot kill with a 3-9x variable set at 3x, where it's stayed on every hunt. The few times I've appreciated higher magnification, I've been satisfied with 6x. Higher power offers more detail, but only in well-lit places and only when you're holding the rifle still. Wobbles magnified blur both the target and reticle.

Though modern variables are reliable and show minimal shift in point of impact between power settings, they're necessarily heavier and more complex than fixed-power scopes. They cost more and have more lenses, which means less light gets to your eye. Variables saddle you with one more concern if you use a second-plane reticle for range-finding, because the reticle/target relationship changes with power.

Practice with a 4x scope, and it's unlikely you'll want more choices. Especially if it's a Leupold.

Simmons and Redfield Rally Under Meade

When a few years ago ATK bought a collection of companies then held by Blount, it had no plan for the optics brands, Weaver, Simmons and Redfield. A huge enterprise with commitments in aerospace and military munitions, ATK sold the optics firms to Meade Optical Company of Irvine, California. Meade had built a solid business designing, building and selling astronomical telescopes. But CEO Steve Murdock was eager to take on the rifle scopes. "We want to improve these products. We have the technology here, plus coated lenses that show us stars light-years away."

Meade zeroed in on the Simmons line. Consulting engineers Mark Thomas and Forrest Babcock no doubt foresaw the application of new ideas to other scope ventures at Meade. Performance was the goal. Keep it simple. No lighted reticles or bullet-drop-compensating gizmos. Not even an AO dial. Refinements could come later. "Our aim was to design a 3-9x scope that hunters would consider a best buy," Mark said.

The team succeeded. Simmons Master Series scopes are lighter and stronger than their forebears. There's up to 17 percent greater windage and elevation range, longer eye relief and a bigger "eyebox" so you get on target as soon as your cheek hits the comb. Inside, a revolutionary erector suspension improves the reliability of windage and elevation adjustments.

This custom-built rifle in .256 Newton wears a 3x Lyman scope. A useful but discontinued sight.

The 3-9x40 prototype of the Simmons Master that I tested recently weighed a wispy 10½ ounces. Mounting the scope on a Winchester 70 .270 WSM built by Hill Country Rifles, I "shot around the square" to check repeatability of adjustment. Moving 20 clicks at a time, I fired five groups. The last struck an inch to 4 o'clock of the first. Point-of-impact shift, high to low power, came to about ¾ inch.

"We didn't think you'd shoot under it!" Mark and

The author fired this three-shot group at 200 yards with a Heym rifle and SmartScope.

Forrest groaned. "It's not finished!" Truly, they did make an extra effort to deliver the prototype in time for an at-deadline photo shoot. And the first scopes released for testing often need refining. "Windage and elevation dials are already different," said Simmons Product Manager Everett Jones at the time. "Adjustment knobs have more surface for easier grip. And the contacts inside have been reshaped to eliminate unwanted vertical or horizontal shift."

Though the company lists eye relief as 3¾ inches, I found the actual "sweet spot" about 4 inches from the lens. There is a bigger eyebox. You can move your eye forward and back, even slightly off-axis, without blackout. That means faster aim, quicker second shots. "It's one of those features you appreciate when you use a scope," Steve told me, "not a cheap cosmetic trick." The eyepiece is of fast-focus design.

The most noteworthy development on this scope is one you won't see. It's a slotted beryllium and copper ring fitted to the rear of the erector assembly. It replaces front-end biasing springs commonly used to hold the tube against the windage and elevation pegs. "With this arrangement, you get smoother, more predictable impact shift as you turn the dials, and no drag from a forward spring," said Forrest. The design delivers a sturdier gimbal joint (the fitting that allows the erector tube 360-degree movement up front).

Sticker price has long been a concern at Simmons. "And despite the improvements, we're keeping it low," confirms Sherry Kerr, whose public relations firm has long represented the brand. The 3-9x40 lists for just $150. Sherry tells me its features will be shared with other sights in Simmons' line, including the Aetec. The new biasing arrangement will appear in a revitalized Redfield line of optics as well.

You're well advised to buy the best sight you can afford. Still, you can easily spend more money than you have to. Simple is good. And what a scope does matters more than where its heritage or place of manufacture.

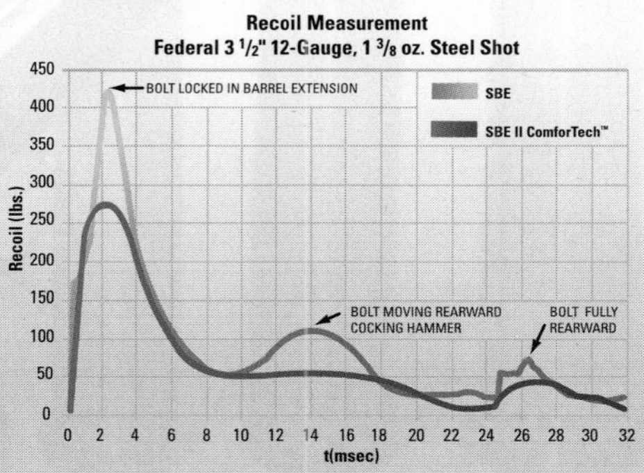

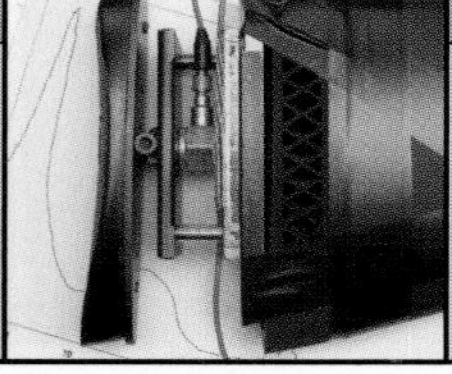

The .250 Savage CP1 Competitor *(above)* features a Weaver 2.5 x 8 scope and its interchangeable barrel, fitted-with a Bushnell 2-6 scope, is in .270 Winchester. The barrel's recoil reducing device has been removed and replaced by a thread protector.

Inset: Besides the sliding safety on the rotary breech that blocks the transfer bar, another safety is placed "Glock style" in the center of the trigger.

can be fired safely (from .22 LR to .458 Winchester Magnum—a list of more than 400 calibers). I asked Al about the most popular calibers with his customers and he said that these included the .223, 7mm-08 Remington, .243 and .308 Winchester. He also said the .44 Magnum was very popular since some states do not allow rifle cartridges for handgun hunting.

The Competitor's grip design is completely ambidextrous with the grip centered under the action, and its exceptional balance makes shooting offhand easy. What is also a plus is that barrels can easily be changed, retaining the same rotary cannon breech mechanism and ambidextrous stock. The stock is available in synthetic and laminated or natural wood.

The standard barrel is 14 inches long with muzzle breaks and nonstandard barrels are available from 10½ to 23 inches. When you purchase extra barrels for your Competitor, you'll find that additional paperwork is not necessary since the serial number is on the action, not the barrel. A unique feature of the Competitor is that it has two safeties, a sliding one that blocks the transfer bar and a Glock-type trigger safety that is inactivated when the trigger is depressed.

In late 2004, Competitor introduced a new pistol, the CP2, with a new action designed to accept really high-pressure rounds such as the Winchester Short Magnums. Also in 2004, Competitor resumed manufacture of their own stocks that are ½ inch higher in the grip and 4 inches longer than their earlier offerings. With a longer stock, it is now easier to attach a bipod.

An extraordinary range of options are available from the factory. Dealing with a small company is a big plus since it is like ordering from a custom shop, one where you can expect quality and many options. The two calibers I own—ones that can put 3 shots into an inch at 100 yards—are the .250 Savage and .270 Winchester. These are two excellent varmint and whitetail calibers.

Examples of high-pressure cartridges are, from left to right, .22-250 Remington, .270 Winchester, .7mm-08 Remington, .308 Winchester, .358 Winchester and .450 Marlin.

RPM-XL: In 1978 Jim Rock, a silhouette shooter of national stature, purchased the manufacturing rights for this pistol from California gun designer Rex

Merrill. Rock moved the operation to its present facility in Tucson, Arizona, in 1989. Originally two frame sizes were available, the regular size and a beefed-up wide-frame variant that was 7/8 of an inch wider. The under-lug on the larger frame is 5/16 inch and only 1/4 inch on the discontinued regular model. The newer 5/16 under-lug greatly increases the lock-up strength. Although the regular model has been discontinued, extra barrels and repairs are still offered for the older frame size.

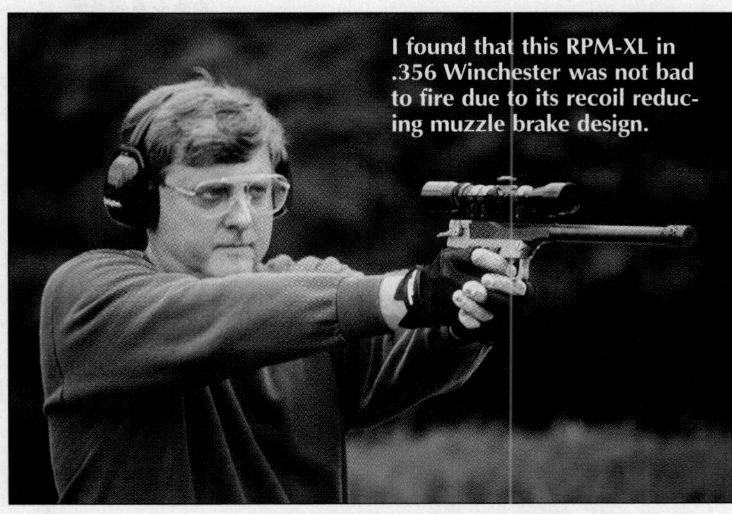

I found that this RPM-XL in .356 Winchester was not bad to fire due to its recoil reducing muzzle brake design.

There are more than 50 calibers available ranging from .22 LR to the big .454 Casull and 45-70 Government. A favorite of mine is the 7-30 Waters. The .308 Winchester is also quite popular according to Jim Rock. The RPM-XL is also offered in a number of wildcat calibers including 7mm Merrill, .270 Rocket and .375 Rocket.

The RPM-XL has no external hammer; the mechanism cocks the pistol when the action is opened to load. The safety can be released by applying pressure with the right thumb to the safety lever which is located in the center of the thumb rest on the wooden grip. Without depressing the safety lever, the gun will "click" on squeezing the trigger but the firing pin will be blocked from striking the primer. When cocked, an indicator protrudes from the back of the frame. The RPM-XL has a smooth trigger and the pull can be easily externally adjusted from 1 to 4 pounds by using an Allen wrench. Without a doubt, these handguns have the best triggers of any that I have been able to test.

Clerke Arms Xtender Conversion: The concept of owning one semi-auto pistol for both personal defense and hunting usually does not work, but at times, with the right parts, a semi auto in 45 ACP designed primarily for close-range defense can be converted to a long-range single shot using .223 Remington. To make this transformation with your Model 1911, all it takes is a conversion unit available from Tom Gregory at Northern Rockies Armory and about 5 minutes of time. The only tool needed is a screwdriver to perform a series of temporary alterations.

The man who designed this system, Bo Clerke of Belgrade,

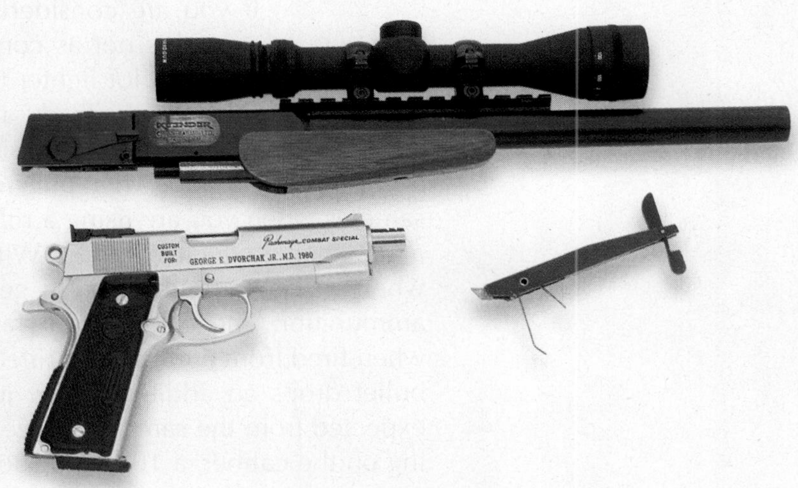

A Clerke Arms Xtender Conversion system is available for the 1911. It comes with a barrel, clamp, breech, extractor mechanism, two replacement grip screws and universal wooden forearm. The scope is a Burris 3 x 12 which makes long shots with the .223 easy.

Optics: To Scope or Not...

Optics, which I highly recommend on any handgun used for hunting, will not help you to shoot a firearm any better, rather they make it easier to see the target along with most obstructions that lie along the bullet's path. This helps you to better place that bullet for a humane kill. Today's handgun hunter is fortunate since most all manufacturers offer handgun scopes. Of all the different types and powers available, I prefer variables. When hunting, I leave the power set to the lowest—usually two or three—and, if I have time and the game is spotted farther off, I get a good rest, crank up the power and take my best shot.

Over the years I have used optics from Bushnell, Burris, Leupold, Redfield, Simmons and Weaver, all of which held up to use on big caliber handguns. Certainly, there are other good scopes but these are what I have used over the years, and I know firsthand that they hold up. Electronic scopes or dot scopes can be useful but do not offer any magnification. Although I have used the Bushnell HoloGraphic when I headed to the backcountry, I prefer a sighting device that does not rely on batteries and electronics. Yet, many hunters with failing eyesight have switched to these with considerable success.

Montana, told me that his design dates back to 1982 when he first applied it to a shotgun. His first handguns were built with silhouette shooting in mind and later the handgun conversion became popular with varmint hunters and with some police officers who carried the 1911-A1. An officer told me that he liked the quick change concept that converted his handgun into a long-range arm suitable for special extended range situations. When it comes to accuracy, the unit I tested in .223 is extremely accurate and reliable.

Savage Striker: Currently, the Striker is the only bolt-action handgun commercially available. When it was introduced, the Striker, a bolt-action repeater, offered a level of high performance that hunters associated with long-barreled rifles. These powerful handguns, designed to handle just about any cartridge including the Winchester Short Magnums, are accurate at both short and long ranges. Earlier bolt-action designs, while they may have performed well, suffered from the bolt handle being placed on the right side of the firearm. To chamber a round, the right-handed shooter had to change his grip to work the bolt. Savage mounted the bolt on the left, allowing a right-handed shooter to maintain his grip while working the bolt left-handed.

The Striker is strong, accurate, innovative and reasonably priced. On the downside, the trigger was not the best Savage has offered, but in recent production it has been replaced by the revolutionary AccuTrigger which will become standard.

Getting Started At Handgun Hunting

If you are considering hunting with a handgun, getting started is not as complicated as you may think. For one thing, a handgun is a lot lighter to lug through the woods although it can be a little harder to steady a firearm that is held with two hands rather than steadied against the shoulder.

As I stated before, when pursuing game, the tactics are basically the same as when you are using a rifle but consideration must be given to a handgun's effective range. With a handgun's shorter barrel, even when chambered with what is generally considered to be rifle-caliber ammunition, the velocity generated is less than would be expected when fired from a full-length rifle barrel. Due to the lower velocity, the bullet drops an additional few inches or more than what would be expected from the same cartridge when fired from a rifle. Yet, depending on the caliber, a 100-yard shot is practical with most handguns.

At extended ranges such as 200 to even 300 yards, success is both possible and consistent given the right caliber, optics and shooter. As any marksman knows, the most important aspect of this equation is that the person squeezing the trigger, one who takes the challenge of handgun hunting seriously, practices at short as well as long ranges.

The Steadyhold Grip locks into the forend stud post on any firearm, as this Savage Striker which, for many, makes it more comfortable to steady offhand.

As anyone who has hunted with bow, black powder, slug or handgun knows, with practice, any and all of these can be effectively used to humanely harvest all types and sizes of game. When you achieve success with a handgun, it takes on a different perspective and means a bit more. Remember, after good equipment selection, success depends entirely on you. To get started, or to expand from target shooting to hunting, here are some thoughts drawn on my experience as to what one can expect in selecting the caliber, ballistics and equipment options available if you make that switch to the "little gun."

The .22 LR—Practice Makes Perfect

When you begin hunting with a handgun, it is always a good idea to start small and work up to more potent calibers. This is why most handgun hunters have at least one .22 caliber rimfire for practice. It is a simple fact that to get good with anything, you need familiarity with it, and to do that with firearms you need to shoot a lot. With .22 rimfire ammunition still reasonably priced, this is the best way to get that necessary practice. I recommend getting a handgun in .22 LR that is similar in mechanics to what you will be hunting with in a larger caliber. If you like the Smith & Wesson Model 29 in .44 Magnum, for instance, then get a Smith & Wesson .22 LR in the same length barrel and if the big gun is scoped, put the same scope on the rimfire. Once you master the small caliber, switching to the larger one becomes easy.

While single-shot pistols remain the most popular with modern handgun hunters, there is something available—from revolvers to bolt action—for everyone. Handgun hunting is not difficult, when getting started try to fire the pistol that you are initially interested in before you purchase it to find out if it is really what you expected. I recommend that you take a hard look at the .308 Winchester in the single shots and then take it from there. I think you will find the challenge of hunting with a handgun truly rewarding.

Rimfire ammo, especially the .22 LR on the left is the best choice for practice. Next in line is the .17 Mach 2, then the .22 Magnum and, at far right, the round created by necking down the .22 Magnum, the .17 HMR.

Popular Hunting Handguns

Handgun	Caliber	Barrel	Ammunition	Muzzle Velocity	3-Shot Group
Competitor Single-Shot Pistol	.250 Savage	14"	Remington 100 Gr.	2545 (fps)	1.00"
	.270 Winchester	15"	Winchester 150 Gr. Partition Gold	2636 (fps)	1.25"
Thompson/Center Contender	.17 HRF	14"	Hornady 17 Gr.	2466 (fps)	2.10"
	.22 Magnum	10"	PMC Predator JHP	1618 (fps)	2.50"
	.223 Remington	16"	Black Hills 52 Gr.	3099 (fps)	0.55"
	.223 Remington	16"	Black Hills 55 Gr. SP	3050 (fps)	0.95"
	.300 Savage	14"	Winchester 150 Gr. ST	2330 (fps)	1.10"
	7-30 Waters (Fox Ridge barrel)	15"	Federal 120 Gr.	2502 (fps)	1.25"
	30-30 Winchester	16"	Winchester 150 Gr. Silvertip	2132 (fps)	1.25"
	.300 Savage (SSK Ind. barrel)	14"	Winchester 150 Gr. Silvertip	2333 (fps)	1.20"
	.375 Winchester (Fox Ridge barrel)	15"	Winchester 200 Gr. PP	1889 (fps)	1.75"
	.375 JDJ (SSK Ind. barrel)	14"	Hornady 220 Gr. Flat Point	2000 (fps)	1.00"
	45/70 Government (SSK Ind. barrel)	14"	Winchester 300 Gr. JHP	1488 (fps)	1.70"
Thompson/Center Encore	.22-250 Remington	15"	Hornady 55 Gr.	3153 (fps)	0.60"
			Varmint Express	2320 (fps)	1.20"
	.260 Remington	15"	Remington 140 Gr.		
	7mm-08 Remington	15"	Federal 140 Gr. Nosler Partition	2440 (fps)	1.10"
	.308 Winchester	15"	Winchester 150 Gr. Ballistic Silvertip	2582 (fps)	1.10"
	.358 Winchester (SSK Ind. barrel)	15"	Winchester 200 Gr. Silvertip	2233 (fps)	1.20"
Savage Bolt-Action Striker	.300 WSM	14"	Winchester Fail Safe 180 Gr.	2500 (fps)	0.95"
	.270 WSM	14"	Winchester Ballistic Silvertip 130 Gr.	2628 (fps)	1.10"
RPM-XL	.223 Remington	12"	Black Hills 50 Gr. V-Max	2958 (fps)	0.60"
	.356 Winchester	12"	Winchester 200 Gr. PP	2155 (fps)	1.55"
	6.5 JDJ (SSK Ind. barrel)	14"	Sierra 120 Gr., 34.0 Gr. IMR 4064, CCI 200	2531 (fps)	1.10"

Chronograph: Oehler 35-P; Temperature: 77 degrees F.; Humidity 80 percent; Range: 100 yards

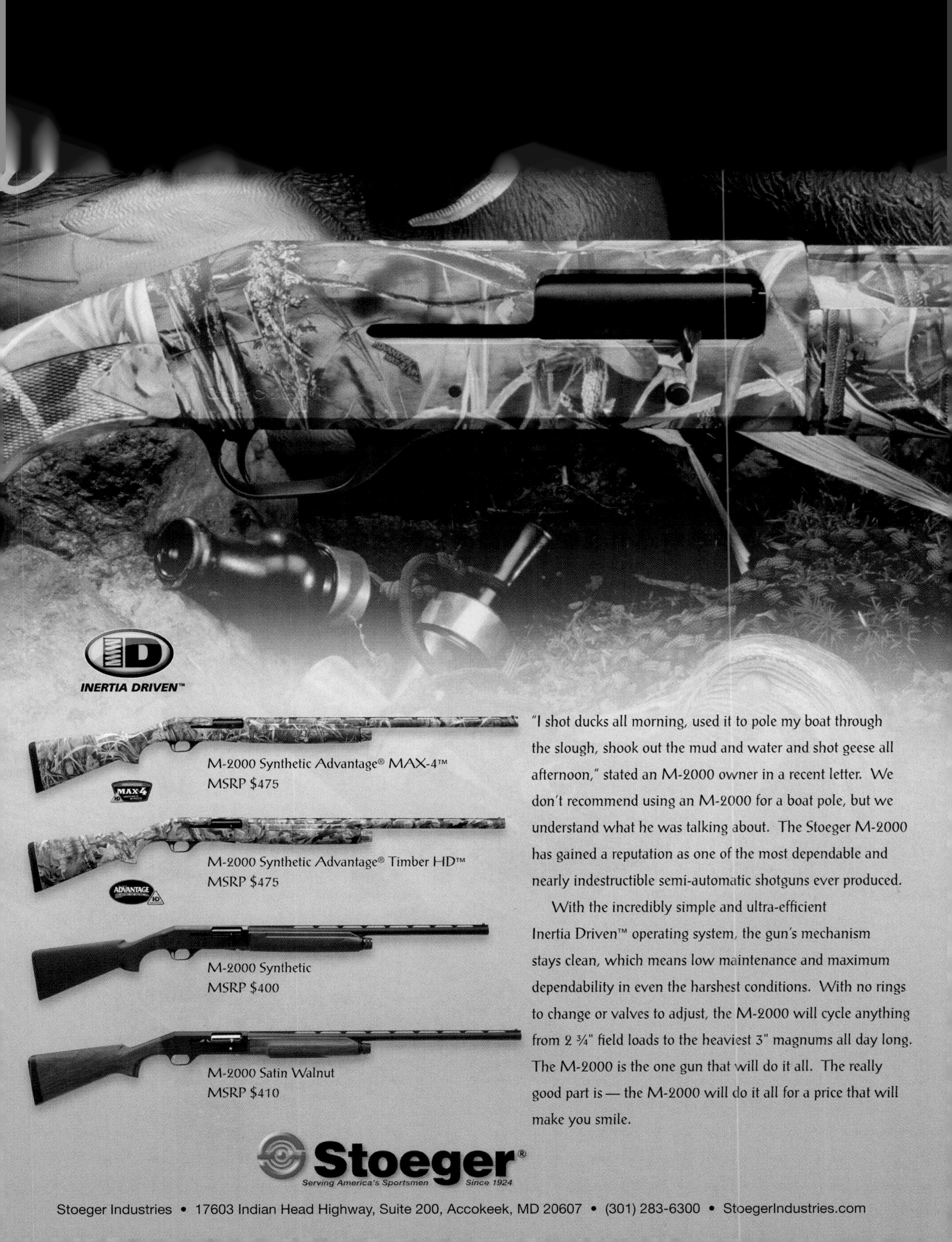

INERTIA DRIVEN™
M-2000 Synthetic Advantage® MAX-4™
MSRP $475
MAX-4
M-2000 Synthetic Advantage® Timber HD™
MSRP $475
ADVANTAGE
M-2000 Synthetic
MSRP $400
M-2000 Satin Walnut
MSRP $410
"I shot ducks all morning, used it to pole my boat through the slough, shook out the mud and water and shot geese all afternoon," stated an M-2000 owner in a recent letter. We don't recommend using an M-2000 for a boat pole, but we understand what he was talking about. The Stoeger M-2000 has gained a reputation as one of the most dependable and nearly indestructible semi-automatic shotguns ever produced.
With the incredibly simple and ultra-efficient Inertia Driven™ operating system, the gun's mechanism stays clean, which means low maintenance and maximum dependability in even the harshest conditions. With no rings to change or valves to adjust, the M-2000 will cycle anything from 2 ¾" field loads to the heaviest 3" magnums all day long. The M-2000 is the one gun that will do it all. The really good part is — the M-2000 will do it all for a price that will make you smile.
Stoeger®
Serving America's Sportsmen Since 1924
Stoeger Industries • 17603 Indian Head Highway, Suite 200, Accokeek, MD 20607 • (301) 283-6300 • StoegerIndustries.com

Test-Firing the 504 Remington

by C. Rodney James

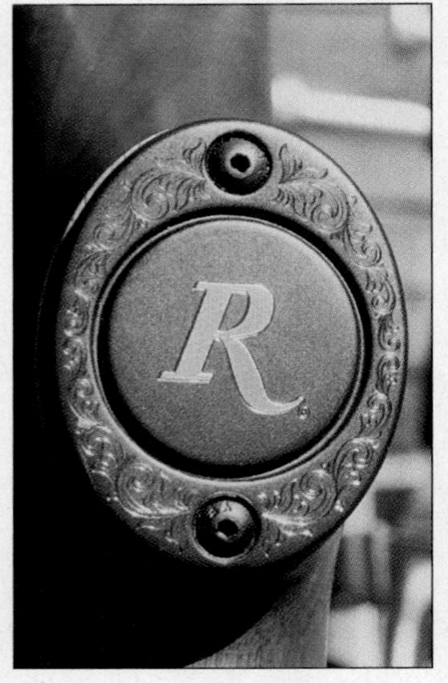

Fancied-up grip caps like white-line spacers in butt plates do nothing for accuracy or (in this writer's opinion) for esthetics either.

Introduced in 2004, Remington's new, long rifle, bolt-action repeater brings this company back into the marketplace with a premium-grade sporting rifle. The 504 is reminiscent of their discontinued 513S, 541äS, and 40X magazine-fed sporters. The 504 is competing in the class of the Sako Finnfire, Kimber sporters and the briefly reintroduced (now gone) Winchester 52 Sporter. Suggested list is $710.

The initial offering for the 504 is .22 LR though other calibers may follow. The rifle features an attractive, American walnut stock with clean, precision-cut checkering. The wood has a dull finish with the grain well filled. The butt plate is a black high-adhesion rubber that sticks where you put it without the slippage common with smooth metal and polymer. The 504 features a steel grip cap with a dark finish, stamped engraving and a bright golden "R" in the center. This will undoubtedly make it stand out on a vertical rifle rack, but was a bit gaudy for my taste. The rifle is fitted fore and aft with quick-detach, steel swivel studs.

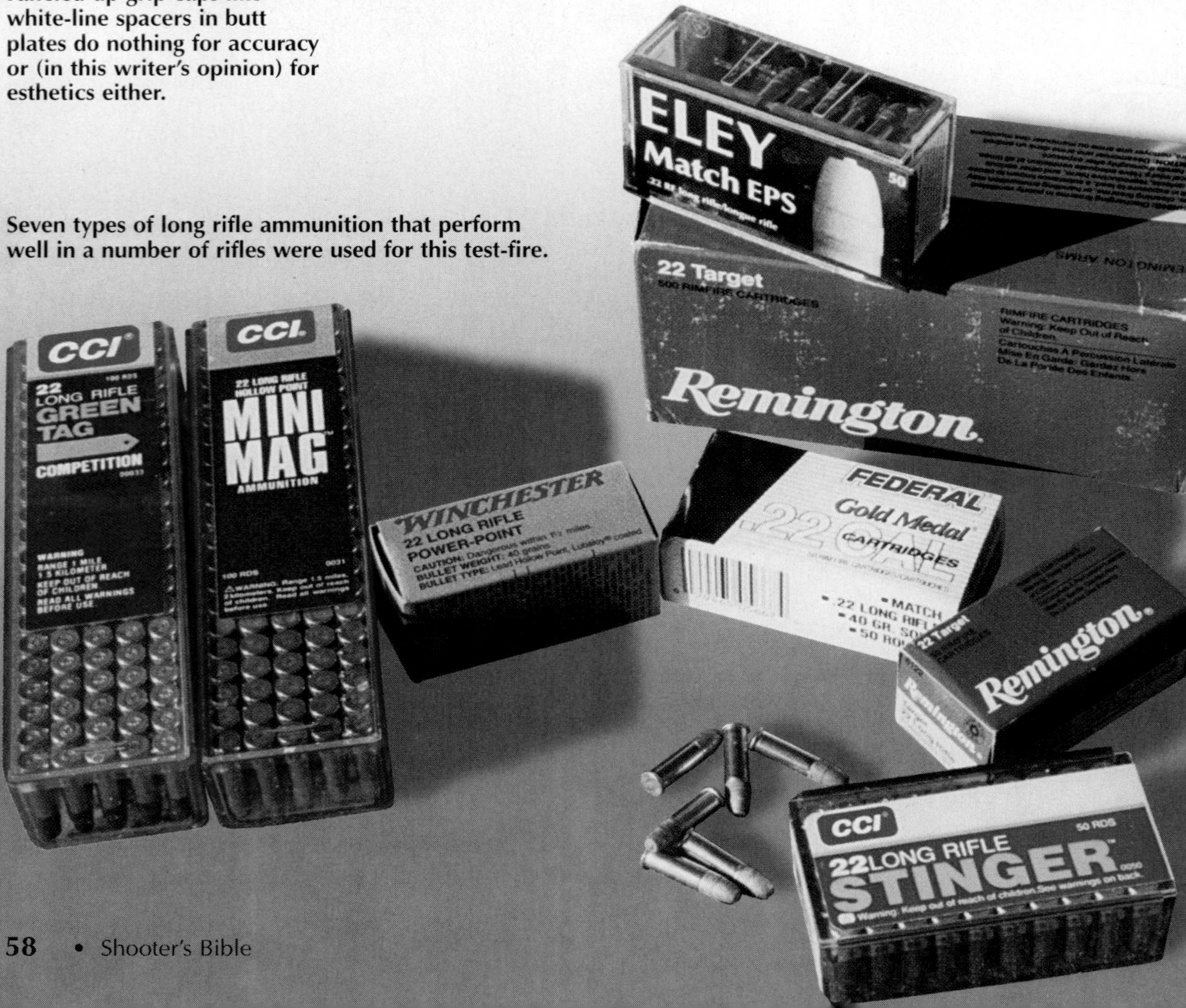

Seven types of long rifle ammunition that perform well in a number of rifles were used for this test-fire.

The barrel and action are carbon steel with what is listed as a "satin blued finish." To my eye the finish is black with a very low luster and appears to be glass-bead blasted. It seems to be quite hard as opposed to the traditional blue finish. In this regard it is practical though slightly jarring to we traditionalists who were imprinted in the fifties with the notion of how gun finishes should look.

Remington sees this rifle as the rimfire answer to the Model 700. The barrel channel is machined with Model 700-style pressure-pad bedding. To wit: the stock is milled so that there are two points of contact—at the front of the receiver and under the barrel, about an inch-and-a-half inside the fore-end tip. The rifling is five-groove right, based on the system used in the Model 40-X rimfire target rifle. The 20-inch barrel is step-crowned and of a light sporter style. There are no sights mounted but a set of Weaver-style bases is included with the rifle. The barrel is set into a steel receiver milled from a single piece of carbon steel bar. Fitting of the barrel is via dual clamp screws and a setscrew at the bottom to allow for retrofitting of custom and alternate caliber barrels. Overall length is 39½ inches and weight is 6 pounds.

The bolt is nickel-plated for smooth operation and features a cocking indicator and dual extractors. The bolt cocks on closing and can be field stripped without tools.

The manual states that the trigger is factory set at 4 pounds. My test rifle's trigger broke at 3¾ pounds. in each of five tests with my Chatillon trigger gauge. The trigger is factory adjustable for pull, over-travel and sear engagement. The trigger on the test rifle had some creep in it. The adjustments are sealed with lacquer and not identified and an uninformed individual would be ill advised to tinker with them. The 504 is fitted with a rocker safety on the right side.

Replacing the traditional-stamped steel magazine is one made of magnesium alloy. It is a compact, staggered design—light, very solid and, owing to the precision of the forming process, it feeds flawlessly. Capacity is six rounds. The fit is flush. Magnesium does have a tendency to corrode and is attacked by many elements in the environment. Sweat, acids, salts and ammonia are especially bad.

In cleaning, do not wipe the magazine

The new 504 *(right)* was tested against the vintage 513 target gun. In terms of accuracy, they were equal!

down with bore cleaners containing ammonia or its chemical relatives. The magazine should be wiped down with a good silicone cloth or a rust-resisting oil, but be sure there is no component in this oil that may attack the magnesium alloy. The magazine release is on the bottom in front of the magazine. A push on the catch pops the magazine out every time.

Magazine fit is flush and the release always pops it out.

The word from Remington is that the 504 is comparable in accuracy to their earlier production target guns. In the spirit of inquiry, and since the opportunity presented itself, I took advantage of a friend's offer to shoot his (fine condition) 513 Remington target rifle, built in the fifties or early sixties.

The 513 "Matchmaster" is a second-tier target rifle that sold in 1965 for $88.95. It was purchased a few years ago at a gun show for $230. It features a 27-inch heavy barrel, traditional blued finish, checkered steel butt plate, walnut stock (varnished) with a beaver-tail fore end. Steel, 1¾-inch sling swivels and sling were included. The barrel is tapped for scope blocks. The rifle features the same rocker safety as the 504. The magazine is steel holding six rounds. Overall length is 45 inches and weight is 10 pounds. The trigger pull measured a crisp 4 pounds. The specimen I tested was in fine shape with no visible chamber erosion or anything else that might indicate wear or abuse affecting the rifle's accuracy. For the test-fire, the 504 was fitted with a Burris 4X-12X variable. The 513 came equipped with a vintage 8X Lyman Targetspot.

Testing was done outdoors over three, humid July afternoons and one morning with the breeze occasionally running at about 5 mph in the same direction as the shots. In all, conditions were relatively calm with less than 3 mph cross winds. Temperatures ranged from the high 70s to the mid 80s. The rifles were fired from a sandbag rest. The range was 50 yards.

The new 504 magazine *(left)* is compact and reliable with a one-piece dent-resistant body—an improvement over the traditional stamped-steel variety.

Seven types of long rifle ammunition including competition-target, practice and hunting-style loadings were selected on the basis that these had performed well in a number of the author's other rifles. Before each type of ammunition was tested, an initial, fouling-shot (or two) of that ammunition was fired before record groups were fired. In one instance (Remington /Eley Match EPS) the bores required half a dozen fouling shots owing to the fouling incompatibility between the Eley (featuring a heavy wax lubricant) and Winchester Power Point causing the latter to shoot erratically until the Eley fouling was shot out. Here was a good reminder that

Stock finish on the 504 *(right)* is durable and tough—an improvement over earlier varnish finishes that must be kept touched up or stripped and refinished.

even with current makes of L.R. ammunition, fouling incomparability can be a major factor affecting short-run accuracy. If you change ammunition, it is a good idea to swab the bore or fire enough foulers of the current ammunition to be sure the previous type's fouling is gone and not adversely affecting your results. Each type of ammunition was fired in three 5-shot groups. As a control, a single 5-shot group of that ammunition was fired through a Winchester Mä52C, Bull-barrel match rifle to monitor any unusual events such as fouling, wind, or any other unexpected behavior in a particular lot of ammunition that might be skewing the results. The performance figures for the tests are shown in table on page 62.

When it comes to the shooting qualities of these two Remington rifles, it is a matter of personal preference. I like the holding qualities of a longer barreled, heavier rifle—8 to 9 pounds is about right. The 513 is a steady-holding rifle, but its length and weight make it something of a burden to haul through the woods. The spring magazine release did not work particularly well with the after-market magazine in the 513. I far prefer the 513's polished blue finish to the 504's matt blue and see no advantage to the shiny grip cap. The 504's hard, dull stock finish (an epoxy varnish) is head and shoulders above the old varnish finishes in both looks and practicality. If I were adding design features to the 504 it would be a heavier barrel and one about 24 inches in length with a genuine match chamber in it. I still like polished blue metal finishes and no grip caps (please). The rubber butt plate is very practical, but I still like that checkered steel on the old 513.

Trigger pulls on both rifles are about equal, but if I owned a 504 I would send it off to have the pull adjusted to about 3¼ pounds. The 513

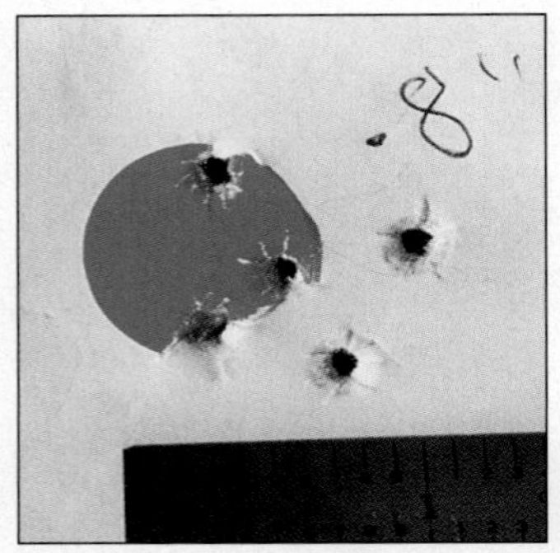

Groups like this can be achieved by finding the right ammunition. Test everything and keep records!

and 504 both feature dual extractors, but the 513 always ejected the empty cases over the side, whereas the 504 required a smart snap of the bolt to do this—a habit every 504 owner should develop.

The Remington engineers have certainly built a sporting rifle with target-rifle accuracy. As can be seen by the (admittedly) limited results produced by the massive 52C (13 ½ pounds with scope) with its match chamber, the 504 is not likely to threaten anything used in the Olympics. Nevertheless, as a nifty little squirrel rifle that can be carried with ease and comfort, it will knock squirrels out of treetops all day!

Three 5-Shot Groups: Average and Control Groups at 50 Yards

	Remington 504	Remington 513	Winchester 52C
Remington Target Standard Velocity	1.6", 1.5", 1.1", 1.40" AV	1.5", 1.1", 1.2" 1.27" AV	0.7"
CCI Mini Mag HP	0.8", 1.4", 1.1", 1.10" AV	1.5", 0.9", 0.8", 1.07" AV	0.5"
CCI Green Tag	1.6", 1.6", 1.0", 1.40" AV	1.1", 1.3", 0.8",1.07 " AV	0.6"
Eley/Rem Match EPS	1.0", 1.7", 1.0", 1.23" AV	0.9", 0.9", 0.8", 0.87" AV	0.9"
Winchester Power Point	1.0", 1.2", 1.3", 1.17" AV	1.3", 1.1" 0.85", 1.08" AV	0.9"
CCI Stinger HP	1.5", 0.9", 1.1", 1.17" AV	0.9", 1.7", 1.7", 1.43" AV	0.8"
Federal Gold Medal Match	1.0", 1.6", 1.8", 1.47" AV	1.3", 1.1", 0.6", 1.0" AV	0.6"

Aggregate average all groups:
Rem 504 1.28"
Rem 513 1.11"

By subtracting the best group from the worst with each rifle—1.8" –0.8" = 1.0" for the 504 and 1.7"-0.6" =1.1" for the 513—it can be seen that the group-size range with both rifles with all the tested ammunition is (effectively) one inch. That .17-inch difference is not significant and could be a result of wind, shooter error or the expected variation within any lot of ammunition.

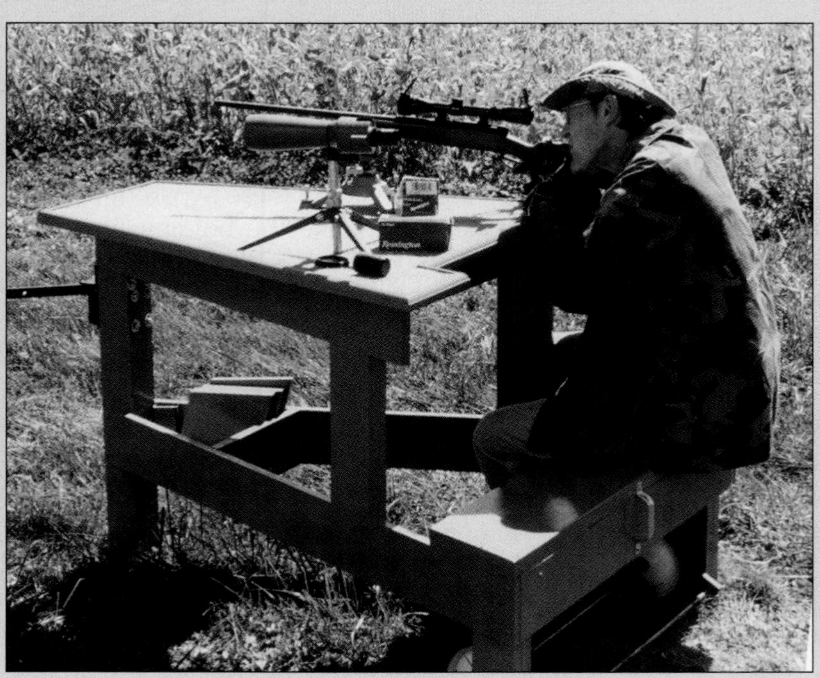

Testing was at 50 yards.

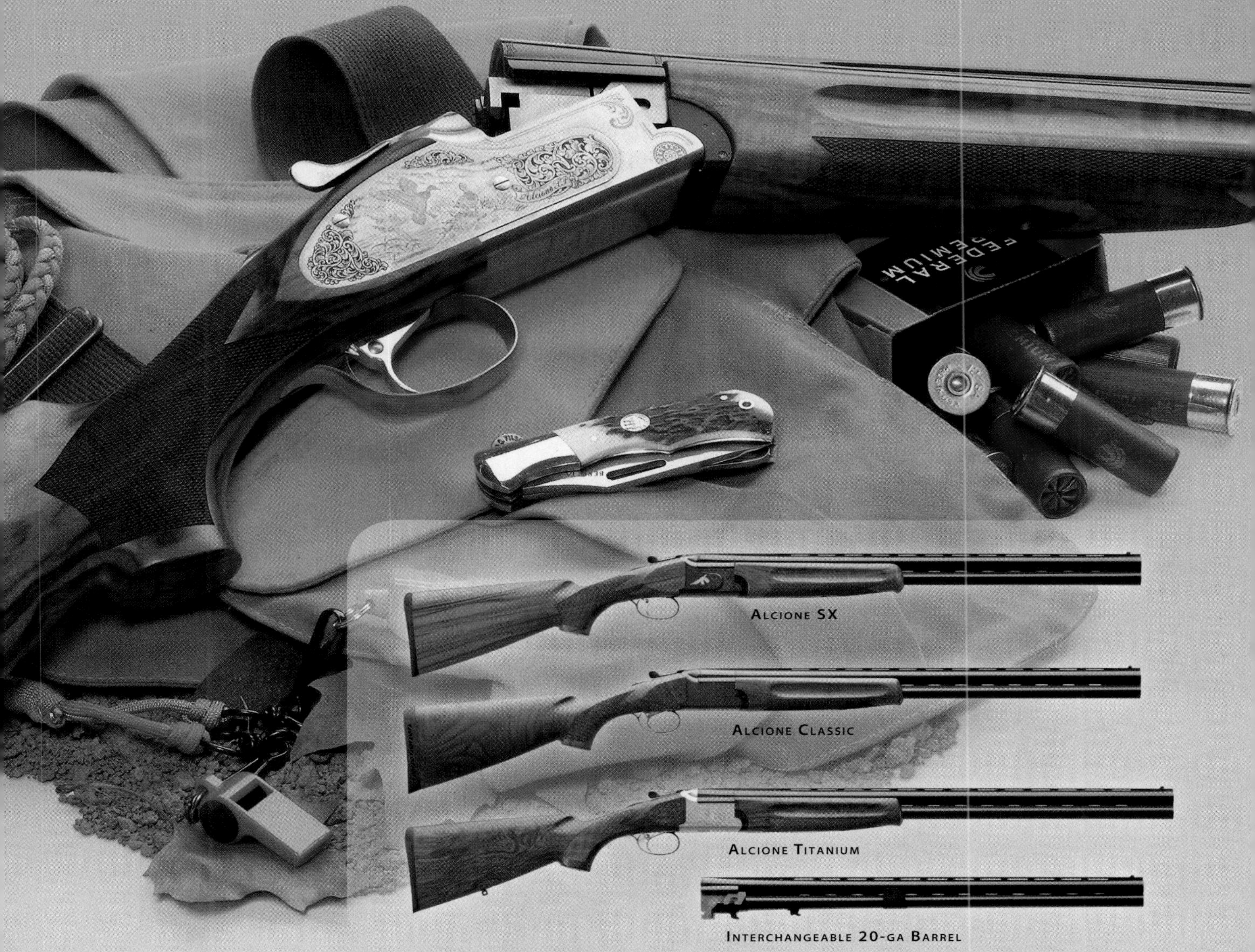

Twenty Years of Knight Rifles
by Toby Bridges

The scoped .50 caliber stainless steel LK-93 "Wolverine" used by the author to take this high-racked pronghorn would have been illegal to use during the majority of the special "muzzleloader-only" seasons of the late 1980s. Thanks much to the efforts of Tony Knight and Knight Rifles, regulations that blocked the modernization of muzzleloading rifles and loads have been greatly relaxed.

Since the mid-1950s, roughly a half-dozen individuals can be credited with establishing and setting the course for the muzzleloading market as we know it today. First, there was Turner Kirkland, who founded Dixie Gun Works and brought us the first truly modern-made reproduction muzzle-loaded rifle. Then, there was Val Forgett, another pioneer who introduced modern-day shooters to near exact copies of original Colt percussion revolvers, while earning the reputation of being the "father" of the Italian reproduction firearms industry. And, let's not forget Warren Center, who designed and manufactured the best-selling muzzle-loaded sporting rifle of all times, the Thompson/Center Arms "Hawken" rifle.

Even the very first MK-85 rifles displayed the lines, features and quality of workmanship one would have expected from a company with years of gunmaking experience. Truth is, the rifle shown here was built in Tony Knight's garage.

Another valuable contributor to muzzleloading shooting sports was Dan Pawlak who developed the first successful black powder substitute—Pyrodex. Likewise, the efforts of Del Ramsey, a quiet and gentle-mannered muzzleloading shooter, changed the way hunters looked at the game-taking effectiveness of hunting projectiles with his introduction of the plastic sabot system to the muzzleloading world.

No one can argue that the contributions of these five individuals did not have a profound impact on today's muzzleloader shooting and hunting. Without their efforts, muzzleloading as we now know it would very likely be an entirely different sport. Even so, there is one more individual who has probably made an even greater impact on this 700-year-old pursuit, and that is none other than William "Tony" Knight, who brought us the refined in-line percussion ignition system that set the stage for more than 80 percent of all muzzle-loaded rifles now built and sold annually.

The Knight MK-85

During the late 1970s and early 1980s, after working a number of years on the railroad, Tony Knight opened a custom gunsmithing operation in rural north-central Missouri. At about the same time, several of his friends had taken up muzzleloading in order to cash in on the special muzzleloader-only elk seasons in Colorado. And the traditionally styled side-hammer rifles they turned to often proved to be less than what they had bargained for. Frequently, these hunters would return from their hunts with horror stories about how the rifles failed to fire in bad weather, and how cumbersome the 10-pound-plus muzzleloaders seemed when carried all day at high altitudes.

And that's when the wheels began to turn in this ingenious gunsmith's head. Tony Knight's full attention shifted from the custom rework of Remington Model 600 carbine center-fire rifles for which he was known to designing a brand-new type of muzzle-loaded big game rifle—a lighter, faster handling muzzleloader with the lines and balance of a fine center-fire rifle, and one with far more reliable ignition and capable of producing 1½-inch groups at 100 yards.

In the fall and winter of 1983, Knight began whittling on the stock and machining the metal parts for just such a rifle. The walnut stock even came from a tree cut on the family farm, and the barrel for his first

Tony Knight took this south Texas buck with one of his now famous MK-85 in-line percussion rifles, shooting a saboted bullet system that was just as advanced as the modern muzzleloader.

prototype was a Numrich Arms barrel with a slow, one turn-in-66 inches rate of twist. The very first Knight rifle fired a patched round-ball!

However, what this and two subsequent prototypes featured was a very unique in-line percussion ignition system, meaning that the nipple was positioned directly in the rear center of the breech plug. When the plunger-style hammer traveled forward in the receiver to hit the capped nipple, fire from the exploding percussion cap had to travel only a fraction of an inch into the powder charge—and in a straight unobstructed path. Not only was ignition more spontaneous than with muzzleloaders of traditional side-hammer design, but, thanks to the much shorter flash channel, ignition with the Knight system proved far more certain.

Other features of the Knight in-line ignition system included a "center-fire rifle type" receiver that allowed quick and easy installation of a telescopic sight. Still another appealing feature was the fully removable breech plug for easier and more thorough cleaning. The simplicity of the Knight design allowed the rifle to be totally broken down in just a minute or two, permitting this muzzleloader barrel to be cleaned from the breech end, just like a modern center-fire rifle.

When Tony Knight built his final prototype in late 1984, he added a second safety. This particular prototype was built with a trigger taken from a sporting Mauser rifle, and featured a sliding, side-mounted safety. The rifle also featured a secondary safety in the form of a knurled nut fitted onto a threaded extension at the rear of the plunger hammer. To cock the rifle, the shooter simply grabbed this portion of the hammer and pulled straight back. To engage the secondary safety, the nut was turned forward, and even if the hammer fell, the secondary safety would contact the rear of the receiver well before the nose of the hammer traveled far enough to strike the capped nipple. Tony Knight was awarded a patent for this double safety system.

I first spoke with Tony on the phone in late November 1985, and remember how he excitedly described his new muzzle-loaded big game rifle. I immediately became intrigued and in January 1986, I became the proud owner of Knight MK-85 serial number 37. When I slipped the new .50 caliber in-line rifle from the shipping box, I was amazed at the quality of the workmanship, and the design of the ignition system. I was also pleased at how well the rifle shouldered and handled, not to mention all of the neat new muzzleloading rifle features I was looking at for the first time. I can remember thinking to myself, "Imagine, a muzzleloading deer rifle that can be carried always cocked and ready. Just slip off the safety, and the rifle is ready to shoot!"

Even the very first 25 production rifles produced in 1985 featured a nicely tapered 24-inch round barrel, a set of quality Williams sights, a handsomely contoured walnut stock, a comfortable rubber recoil pad, and an excellent quality Timney featherweight trigger. Plus, the rifles came superbly finished. The more closely I examined my early MK-85 rifle, the harder it was for me to accept that these very modern in-line muzzleloaders were being built one at a time in Knight's garage-turned-production facility.

A Faster Rate of Rifling Twist

The first 150 or so Knight MK-85 rifles were built with a turn-in-48 inches rate of rifling twist, primarily for shooting the popular "Maxi-style" heavy lead conical bullets of the time. In late 1986, the newly established Modern Muzzleloading, Inc. began building the in-line rifle with a snappier turn-in-32 inches rate of rifling twist for shooting the modern plastic saboted bullets. Tony Knight and Del Ramsey, owner of Muzzleload Magnum Products, had become good friends, and both realized that a rifle as modern as the MK-85 deserved a muzzleloading projectile system just as advanced. And through the following years, the two companies have worked closely hand in hand to take muzzle-loading into the 21st century.

In the fall of 1986, I harvested my first in-line taken whitetail—shooting a saboted bullet. And to make the moment even more special,

The first production Knight MK-85 rifles featured very refined lines and excellent workmanship. Here the rear "secondary" safety is in the forward "on" position and prevents the hammer from going far enough forward to hit the nipple.

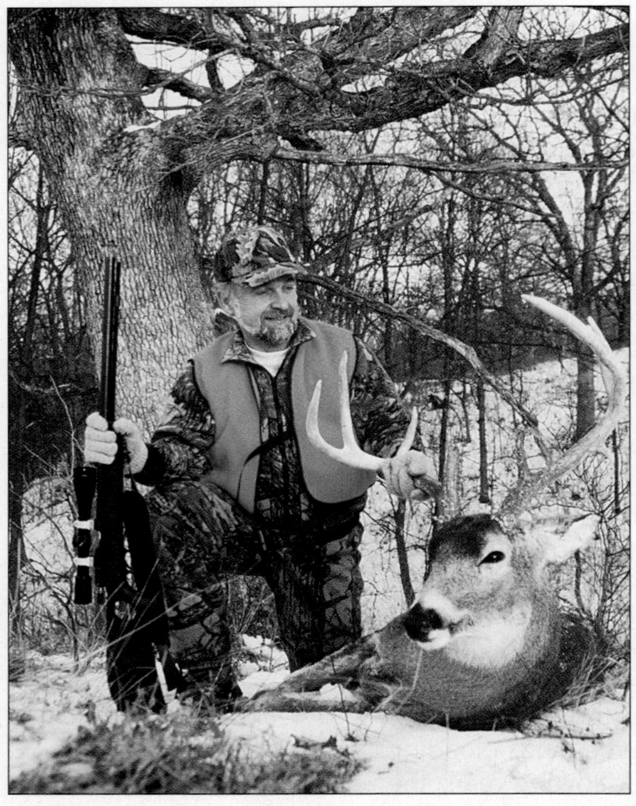

The author's smile is nearly as wide as the rack of this late muzzleloader season buck that was taken with a .50 caliber Knight LK-93 "Wolverine".

I did it while hunting with Tony Knight on his family farm in northern Missouri. Like just about everyone who picked up and shot a Knight in-line rifle for the first time, I quickly became hooked on the improved performance and reliability. And from that time forward, the sport of muzzleloading had changed forever.

During the spring of 1987, Modern Muzzleloading, Inc. adopted a faster turn-in-28 inches rate of rifling twist for improved accuracy with saboted bullets. And by that time they were offering the MK-85 in .45, .50 and .54 caliber. In 1992, the company introduced a more economically priced model known the BK-92 "Black Knight," and the following year brought out a still lower priced model they dubbed the LK-93 Legend, which the following year became the Wolverine. All of these newer models were based on the original Knight plunger-hammer design, but in 1995 the company dared to try a new modified bolt design known as the MK-95 Magnum Elite.

Knight's First "Bolt-Action" Muzzleloader

This rifle featured a shorter hammer that powered a firing pin that traveled through a separate short bolt of simple design. The front of this bolt featured a C-shaped groove (similar to the groove of a shell holder used on a cartridge reloading press), into which the shooter could slip a primed plastic .38 Special case. Instead of a nipple, the breech plug of the Magnum Elite featured a chamber. And when the bolt was closed, the rifle was primed and ready to be fired. The system allowed ignition conscious shooters to rely on much hotter large rifle primers for ignition rather than the standard old No. 11 percussion cap.

The MK-95 Magnum Elite was only somewhat successful for one main reason. It was the most expensive production muzzle-loaded rifle of its day, with a black composite stocked stainless steel rifle retailing for $929.95. But those hunters who bought one of the rifles realized the superiority of the hotter and the fully enclosed weatherproof primer ignition system. Many of those same hunters still head out every fall with their Knight Magnum Elite slung over a shoulder, preferring the rifle over the many bolt-action in-line muzzleloading designs that have been introduced since.

Knight Rifles (a.k.a. Modern Muzzleloading, Inc.) went to a redesigned bolt-action in-line model the following year, with the introduction of the original DISC Rifle. This model relies on still hotter No. 209 shotshell primers for ignition, using a flat plastic disc to hold the primer compressed between the front of the bolt and the rear of the breech plug. The system is easy to prime and de-prime, making it extremely popular with hunters who hate fumbling with trying to get a tiny No. 11 percussion cap onto a nipple.

I was fortunate enough to have the opportunity to hunt with one of the first three prototypes of the DISC Rifle, taking the very first elk ever harvested with one. Prior to the hunt, I had sighted the rifle "dead on" at 100 yards, and found the .50 caliber DISC Rifle loaded with a 100-grain charge of Pyrodex Pellets and a saboted 300-grain Barnes all-copper Expander MZ fully capable of printing honest 1½-inch groups at that distance. However, on that first elk hunt, I actually dropped my 6x6 bull at just 15 yards. The bull was coming to the seductive cow calls being made by my guide, and if I hadn't pulled the trigger, I would have most likely gotten stepped on.

One of the complaints some hunters had with the DISC Rifle was that enough fire escaped from the compressed juncture of the plastic disc and rear of the stainless steel breech plug that the finish on the bottom of a quality scope was often damaged. To remedy this problem, just a couple of years ago Knight Rifles went to an improved version of the model—known as the DISC Extreme.

Latest Knight Rifle Models

The redesigned bolt of this rifle permits the use of a cylindrical primer carrier the company refers to as a "Full Plastic Jacket". And when the bolt is pushed forward, the front of this primer carrier sits inside the front recess of the receiver. Also, instead of compressing the flat frontal

Knight's "Magnum Elite" featured a simple bolt and separate hammer arrangement. This was the first of today's modern "bolt-action" in-line muzzle-loaded big game rifles.

William "Tony" Knight with a great Iowa gobbler taken with a hefty charge of No. 6 shot out of an MK-86 muzzleloading shotgun.

surface of the carrier against a flat rear surface of the breech plug, as with the original DISC Rifle, the breech plug of the DISC Extreme features a nipple-like extension, around which the front of the "Full Plastic Jacket" fits. The system does a much better job of preventing blowback. Knight offers this model in .45, .50 and an all-new .52 caliber.

At the 2004 SHOT Show, Knight Rifles introduced its latest model, the all-new Revolution. Here again is a radical departure from the previous successful Knight in-line rifle designs, showing that this company is not afraid to bring something new and exciting to today's muzzleloading shooter. This rifle doesn't rely on either a plunger-style hammer or a bolt-action design. At first glance, Knight's new Revolution looks more like a circa 1880 single-shot cartridge rifle, with a receiver that looks like something of a cross between a Winchester "High Wall" and a Sharps -Borchardt Model 1878. But in reality, it is a very modern .50 caliber in-line muzzleloading big game rifle.

Internally, this rifle is a unique design. The action is of the type generally referred to as "hammerless", which actually means that it does not feature an external hammer. To cock this action, the shooter must first depress a release at the top of the pistol grip. Then the action is opened by pushing down, then forward on a lever extending from the trigger guard. At this point, a primed "Full Plastic Jacket" is inserted into the opening at the top rear of the receiver. Then the lever is pulled back up, closing the action and locking it into place.

The Revolution features a cross-bolt type safety just to the rear of the trigger. And the safety can be slipped into the "on" position before opening, cocking and priming the rifle. When it's time to do the required cleanup after an afternoon at the range or a successful day in the deer woods, the entire internal mechanism can be quickly and easily pulled from the rifle by simply lifting a release just forward of the trigger guard. The only other part that has to be removed is the breech plug, which can be threaded out through the rear receiver opening.

Modern Muzzleloading, Inc., better know today as simply Knight Rifles, has offered several other models through the years as well. During the early 1990s, the company introduced an in-line muzzleloading shotgun known as the MK-86, designed specifically for the turkey hunter. This was actually a dual-purpose muzzleloader, with

Knight's big 375-grain .475" diameter all-copper "Red Hot" Bullet for the .52 caliber DISC Extreme leaves the muzzle of the 26-inch barrel at 1,992 f.p.s. when loaded ahead of a 150-grain charge of FFg Triple Seven. The load generates 3,300 f.p.e. at the muzzle.

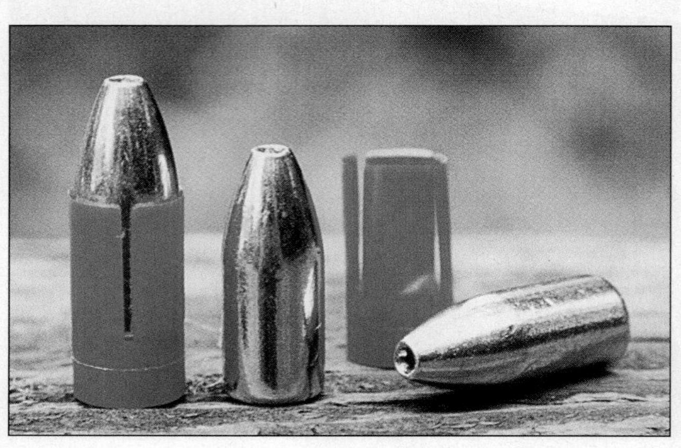

When the action of the "Revolution" is opened, the majority of the internal mechanism drops out the bottom of the receiver. All of this is removed for cleaning by lifting one simple catch release.

optional interchangeable .50 or .54 caliber rifle barrels available. But, it was the tight-patterning barrel with a screw-in extra-full choke that interested muzzleloading hunters most. The gun has been replaced by the current easier-loading TK-2000 in-line shotgun. Interestingly, this front-loaded turkey-hunting shotgun features a modern version of the "jug" choke of the late 1800s rather than a modern constriction choke.

Another model offered during the early 1990s was the big "Hawkeye" in-line .50 caliber handgun. This 14-inch barreled behemoth weighed right at 4½ pounds, but could be loaded with enough fine grain "P" grade Pyrodex and a saboted bullet to produce more than adequate energy levels for taking deer-sized game out to about 75 yards. However, during the early 1990s Knight discovered that there just wasn't enough interest in hunting with a muzzle-loaded pistol.

Of all the Knight rifle models available today, this writer finds the bolt-action DISC Extreme to be a high performance muzzle-loaded big game rifle that's hard to match, let alone beat. I've particularly enjoyed shooting the new .52 caliber version, which comes with a unique stemmed breech plug that carries fire from a No. 209 primer to the forward part of the powder charge. Knight claims that it results in a more efficient burn of the powder. All I know is that when this big-bore front-loader is stuffed with a 150-grain charge of FFg Triple Seven and one of Knight's huge 375-grain saboted all-copper .475" diameter "Red Hot" Bullets, this rifle is one unbelievable powerhouse!

This load is good for 1,992 f.p.s. at the muzzle, which translates into 3,300 f.p.e. at the muzzle. The big 1.2-inch-long all-copper spire-point hollow-point bullet has a ballistic coefficient of around .400, and at 200 yards the load will retain a little more than 2,200 f.p.e. Talk about

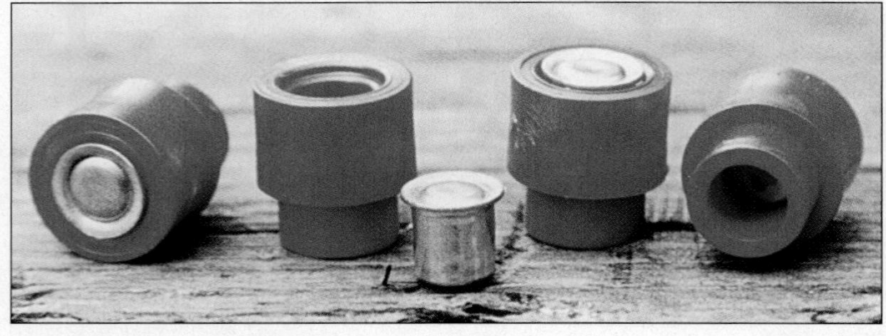

The "Full Plastic Jacket" primer carrier is shown here sitting at the face of the Knight DISC Extreme bolt.

an elk load! For whitetails, I shoot a more modest 130-grain charge of FFFg Triple Seven (using the standard non-stemmed breech plug) behind a 275-grain all-copper .475" diameter "Red Hot" hollow-point. This load gets the bullet out of the 26-inch barrel at 2,120 f.p.s., and with 2,745 f.p.e. At 200 yards the big blunt-nosed hollow-point plows into a whitetail with around 1,200 foot-pounds of remaining energy.

It hasn't been all that long ago that such muzzleloader performance was considered only a dream. A lot of water has certainly passed beneath the bridge since Tony Knight sat down to take his ideas for a modern muzzle-loaded rifle and turn them into reality. Today, we have just about every major muzzleloading gunmaker offering one or more in-line rifle models. And over the past 20 years, a few other companies have introduced models of somewhat original design or with innovative new features. But all can still trace their modern roots to that small garage gunsmithing operation in northern Missouri during the early 1980s.

I, for one, just want to say, "Thanks Tony, I've enjoyed the ride!"

The "stemmed" breech plug at right comes standard in the .52 caliber DISC Extreme. The design ignites magnum 150-grain charges of granular Triple Seven near the front rather than at the rear. Shown with the standard "non-stemmed" DISC Extreme breech plug for comparison.

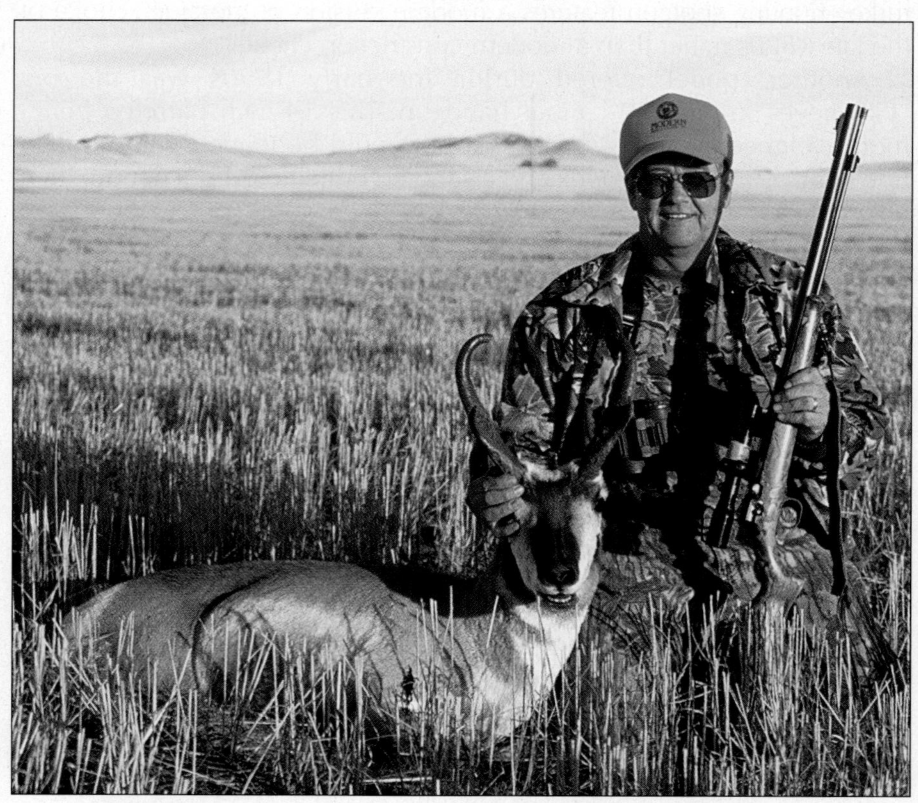

William "Tony" Knight revolutionized the sport of muzzleloading with the introduction of the first modern in-line ignition percussion rifle with all the features the modern-day hunter wanted.

The Story of Llama

by Gene Gangarosa Jr.

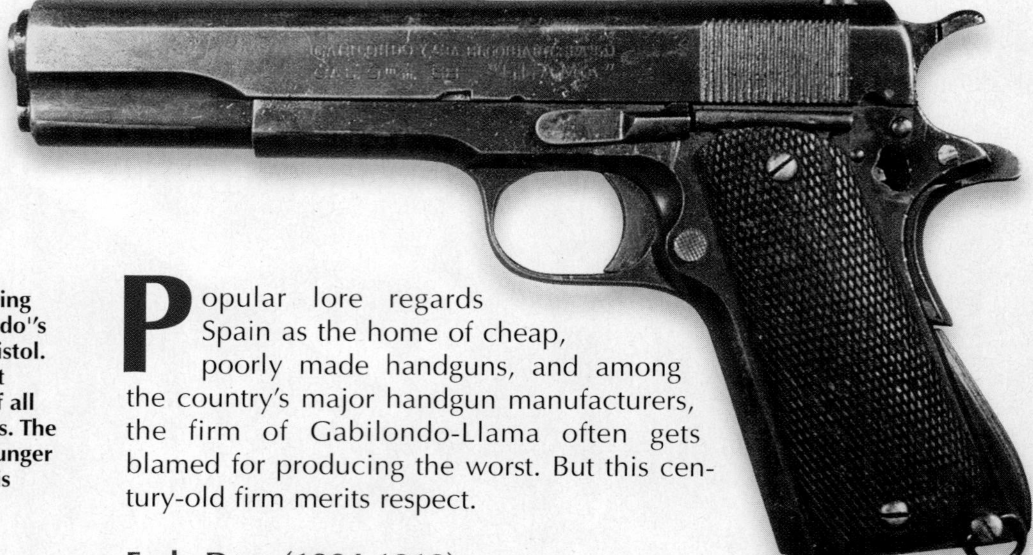

The Llama "EXTRA," dating from 1934, was Gabilondo's first Model 1911-style pistol. It was closest to the Colt Model 1911A1 design of all early Llama-brand pistols. The manual safety and its plunger spring are missing on this well-used example.

Popular lore regards Spain as the home of cheap, poorly made handguns, and among the country's major handgun manufacturers, the firm of Gabilondo-Llama often gets blamed for producing the worst. But this century-old firm merits respect.

Early Days (1904-1918)

Established in 1904 in Eibar Spain as Gabilondo y Urresti, the partnership was named for two cousins, one of whom left the company in 1909. Production began with small, cheap "Velo-Dog" (Velo—velocipede + Dog) revolvers, small caliber pistols marketed to bicyclists for protection against marauding canines. But times were changing, and great interest already existed among Spanish firearm manufacturers for the newly introduced automatic pistols. Gabilondo's Radium, introduced around 1910, was a .25 ACP pistol that resembled FN's pocket model, but with some novel design features. Rather than remove the six-round magazine to reload in the usual manner, the shooter slid the Radium's right grip panel down to lower the magazine follower. After introducing rounds directly into the magazine, raising the grip tensioned the magazine spring.

In 1914 Gabilondo introduced a 9-shot, .32 ACP caliber automatic pistol called the Ruby. It succeeded beyond Gabilondo's wildest dreams when the French Army, desperate for small arms due to the demands of the First World War, adopted it in 1915 as a sidearm for soldiers issued the Chauchat automatic rifle. Gabilondo received a contract for 10,000 pistols per month, later raised to 30,000 a month. Italy and Romania placed additional orders as well. Gabilondo, with a small workshop and only half a dozen employees, were unable to meet the demand, so they subcontracted with other manufacturers. In time dozens of firms joined in, each distinctively marking its own version of the Ruby-type pistol. By 1918 France alone had bought over 700,000 Ruby clones, of which Gabilondo made about 200,000. Regrettably, serious quality-control issues arose due to poor parts interchangeability between multiple manufacturers. These production problems helped saddle Spanish handguns with a reputation for poor quality.

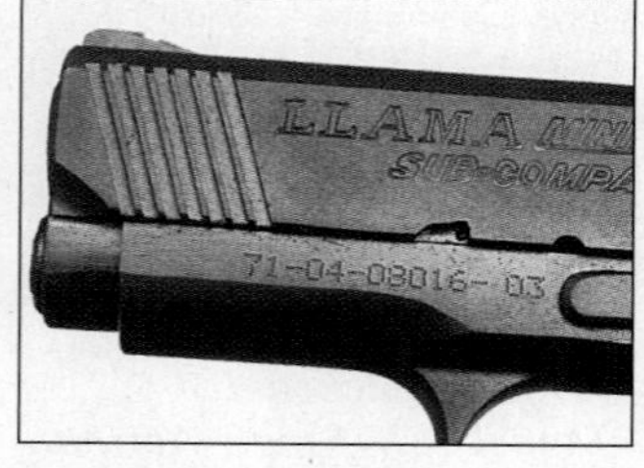

In Spain's current gun identification system, effective January 1995, the first two digits refer to the manufacturer (in this case Fabrinor). The next two digits identify the product, 04 standing for automatic pistol. Then comes a five-digit serial number, which resets to 00001 each year. The last two digits give the year of production.

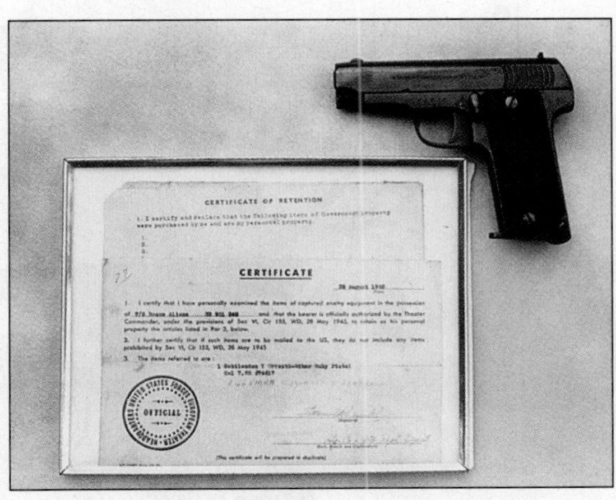

Gabilondo's .32 ACP caliber "Ruby" pistol brought Spain's arms industry to worldwide attention during World War One. Many remained in use long afterward; a G.I. liberated this one from a German soldier during World War Two.

Postwar Changes (1919-1927)

With the end of World War I, Allied pistol orders dried up, and Gabilondo was compelled to revamp its product line. In 1919 the firm moved its plant to Elgoibar, a small town in the Basque country of northern Spain, and reorganized as Gabilondo y Compañia. While other manufacturers continued making Ruby-type pistols for a shrunken market, Gabilondo introduced new lines to supplement it, beginning with the Búfalo in 1919. Chambered for .32 ACP or .380 ACP, the first variant resembled FN's Model 1910 by positioning the recoil spring around the barrel. A smaller .25 ACP Búfalo resembling a shrunken Ruby appeared in 1920. Both Búfalo types featured a grip safety designed by an inventor/dealer named Beristain, who marketed them with his "BC" logo on the grips. The coarse, curved slide serrations on the Búfalo were typical of Gabilondo's wartime Ruby pistol, being easier to manufacture than the straight slide serrations usually seen on other automatic pistols.

In 1925 Gabilondo y Compañia introduced the Danton, a modified Búfalo design made in .25, .32 and .380 calibers. Magazine capacities varied from six rounds in the .25 vest-pocket model, to as many as 12 rounds in the full-sized "War Model." From 1929 until production ended in 1933 the smallest Danton variants included a grip safety.

The Plus Ultra, produced from 1927 to 1933, enlarged the Ruby design by extending the barrel and stretching the frame to house a 22-round magazine. Some included a selector switch permitting fully automatic fire, and saw use in war-torn China and in Spain's civil war.

Enter the Llama (1927-1945)

Around 1925 Gabilondo decided to produce a clone of Colt's Model 1911 pistol. Initial efforts centered around a .45 ACP caliber pistol again called the Ruby. It had a crude, angular appearance, but by 1927 Gabilondo had reworked it into a more graceful design inspired by Colt's new Model 1911A1, naming it Llama Model IV. Pronounced "YAW-mah," Llama means flame. In 1932 Spain's patent office granted protection the Llama brand name, explaining the addition of the torch logo found on many subsequent Gabilondo pistols.

The Llama Model IV was a large locked-breech pistol,

The Búfalo appeared in two variants, the smaller 6.35mm (.25 ACP) type shown here being based on the Ruby. The proofmarks on this example indicate production before 1925. Note the grip safety, a feature the Ruby lacked.

The Llama Model 82 *(bottom)* derived some features from the failed Omni pistol but mechanically owed more to Beretta's Model 92 shown above it. Both Models 82 and 92, like other contemporary military pistols, feature ambidextrous controls.

8½ inches long, chambered for the 9mm Largo (9x23mm) Spanish service cartridge. Unlike the American Colt M1911A1, the Model IV had a more vertical grip and lacked a grip safety. Grips were checkered walnut with a diamond pattern around the screws. The mechanically identical Model V was produced with English markings for export. The similar Model VII, introduced in 1932, chambered 9mm Largo for sales in Spain or .38 Super for the overseas market.

Though automatic pistols comprised the bulk of Gabilondo's business, the company never forgot its roots in revolver production. In 1931 the firm introduced a new "Ruby" revolver line based on Smith & Wesson's Military & Police model.

Gabilondo began producing the small (6 inches overall) .32 ACP Model I and .380 ACP Model II in 1933. Though outwardly resembling the Model IV, Gabilondo's small pistols used a simple blowback breech mechanism, common in small-caliber automatic pistols.

Gabilondo's competitors Unceta and Echeverria sold large numbers of pistols to Spain's military and police. Between 1931 and 1935, in an attempt to enter this market, Gabilondo contracted with an agent named Tauler to prepare a line of service pistols. With Tauler, Gabilondo made variants of its Llama Models I, II, III, IV, and VII, a product line combining full-sized models for open carry on a belt holster with concealable models. Gabilondo stamped a "GC" monogram onto the right side of Tauler-contract pistol frames for identification. Tauler's Model P, marked "MODEL MILITARY AND POLICE," was a 9mm Largo full-sized locked-breech pistol with an added grip safety. It saw modest use in official circles, inspiring Gabilondo to create the 9mm Largo or .45 ACP "Llama Extra" in 1934. This looked very similar to the Colt Model 1911A1. The grip safety later became standard on Llama models. In 1939 Gabilondo formalized these changes into the Llama Model VIII, one of the company's longest-lived designs.

To bolster foreign sales, Gabilondo contracted with José Cruz Mugica, an Eibar-based shotgun manufacturer and exporter. From 1931 to 1954 Mugica-marked Llama Models III, VII, VIII, X and XI pistols were exported, notably to Siam (Thailand) and China. Mugica also marketed a Gabilondo-made .25 caliber Ruby variant as the "Perfect."

The Model X appeared in 1935. A miniaturized Model 1911A1 look-alike (6½ inches long; 21 ounces unloaded) using a blowback breech and lacking a grip safety, this chambered the popular .32 ACP cartridge. The following year Gabilondo discontinued Models I and II, and the blowback-operated Model III in .380 caliber replaced the Model II.

Gabilondo's .380 caliber Model VI also lacked a grip safety but had a miniature version of the locked breech used in the company's full-sized pistols. Heavier and more expensive to manufacture than the Model III, the Model VI remained in production only briefly. In 1936 Gabilondo also introduced a full-sized Model IX to chamber 7.65mm (.30 Luger), 9mm Parabellum or .45 ACP cartridges. Another 1936 introduction, the Model XI or "Llama Especial," chambered 9mm Parabellum ammunition only. Because the 9mm Parabellum is 4mm shorter than the 9mm Largo cartridge, the Model XI had a sleek, compact appearance, making it one of the most visually appealing handguns ever made. None of these models included a grip safety, a solid backstrap being easier to manufacture as part of the frame.

The post-World War Two Llama Model IX-A added an extended manual safety, a grip safety, a toe extension to the frame and, on later examples, a ventilated sight rib. Gabilondo typically included a lanyard loop on any of its pistols offering potential for official use.

Gabilondo's role in the Spanish Civil War of 1936-1939 remains uncertain. The Basque region saw fierce fighting between the leftist Republican government (supported by the USSR and various international volunteers) and the Nationalists under fascist general Francisco Franco, who won with help from Hitler and Mussolini. A factory letter stated Gabilondo's records were lost in the fighting. In their absence, and with the passing of eyewitnesses, history can shed no light on the company's role in the war, which ended with establishment of Francisco Franco's long-lived fascist dictatorship. Gabilondo, along with Star, Bonifacio Echeverria, and Astra-Unceta y Cia, was one of only three Spanish manufacturers allowed to continue producing handguns after the civil war.

Though Spain officially stayed neutral in World War II, Astra-Unceta produced 104,450 pistols for Nazi Germany (Astra Models 200, 300, 400, 600 and 900). Echeverria sent 27,750 pistols to Germany (Star Models B, S, and D) and another 15,000 Model Bs to Bulgaria. During the war Gabilondo produced about 50,000 Llama Models III, IV, VIII, IX and XIs. Many served as substitute-standard pistols in various armed forces, or, in Germany, as models cleared by government inspectors for private purchase by approved personnel. Some wartime Llama models sent to Germany show the Gustave Genschow company's "Geco" import mark. Gabilondo sometimes re-chambered its 9mm Largo/.38 Llama Model VIII to 9mm Parabellum to make it more attractive. Similarly some .380 Model IIIs were re-barreled to .32 ACP for sales to Germany. Gabilondo stressed the Model IV's "tolerant chamber," which they claimed handled 9mm Parabellum cartridges safely and reliably.

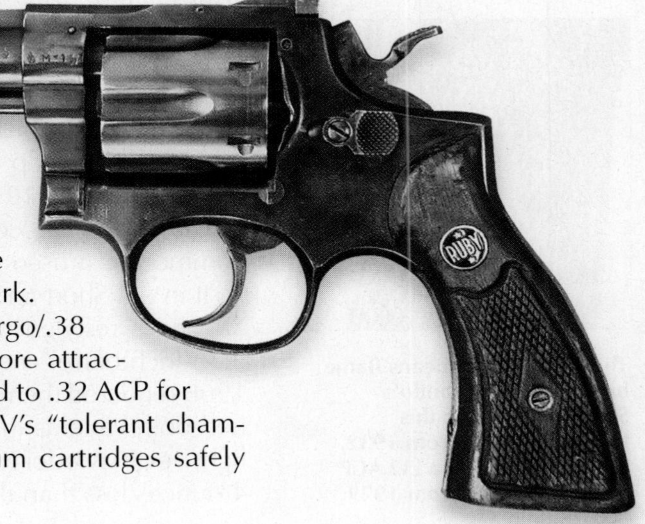

Ruby Extra revolvers, produced from 1955 to 1970, served Gabilondo well. This particular specimen was made in 1967, and a Central American police force used it for 20 years before its importation into the USA.

The .32 ACP Llama X-A replaced the Model X in 1955, adding a grip safety to the basic design. By the time Gabilondo made this example in 1979, a ventilated sight rib had been added.

New Directions (1945-present)

Echeverria introduced the 9mm Largo "Star Model Super A" in 1946 for Spanish army service. Gabilondo competed, but Spain's government rejected their Model VIII entry for excessive weight. In 1954 Echeverria introduced the similar "Star Super B" chambering 9mm Parabellum. As Spain sought NATO membership, 9mm Parabellum pistols grew in importance among Spanish manufacturers.

Gabilondo set up Spain's first investment casting facility in 1954 and revamped its line in 1955, eliminating Models III, IV, V, VII, IX, X and XI. Similar pistols incorporating grip safeties and, later, a raised sighting rib atop the slide, replaced them, the model designations receiving an -A suffix. The .380 Llama Model III-A supplanted the III, the .32 ACP X-A replaced the X, the IX-A chambered the .45 ACP, etc. The new pistols included a slight extension to the frame's bottom front portion or toe. This extension gave additional support to the shooter's hand and simplified manufacture since the frames no longer had to be notched in front for the magazine floor plate.

Prewar Llama pistols featured only a tiny knob at the manual safety's forward end, like Colt M1911 and early 1911A1 pistols, for the shooting-hand thumb to push the safety lever. Experience showed this knob to be too small, so post-1955 Llama pistols used an enlarged safety with a ledge running its full length.

In 1955 the Model VIII appeared in a long-barreled (8.6-inch) .38 Super caliber version. This sold well in Central and South America, where shooters favor the .38 Super as an automatic pistol round, but less so in the USA, where shooters preferred the Colt Government Model so chambered. More important for U.S. sales, the .45 ACP caliber Llama Model IX-A formed the backbone of the Llama line for three decades and served as the chief design influence for the current Llama line.

Gabilondo also boosted revolver sales in 1955 by introducing the "Ruby Extra." This included the .38 Long Colt Model XII, .38 Special Model XIII and .22LR or .32 S&W caliber Model XIV. These inexpensive, well-made revolvers saw extensive police use in Latin America. In the Philippines the Ruby Extra sold second only to Smith & Wesson before Gabilondo discontinued the series in 1970.

The word Llama means flame in Spanish. Gabilondo's Spanish patent on this trademark dates from 1932, as shown here on a .32 ACP caliber Model X from 1979.

Gabilondo's top 1955 introduction, the .22 Long Rifle Model XV, was a miniaturized M1911A1 lookalike with unlocked breech and grip safety. It was one of the company's best-selling types for decades and remains common as a used gun. In 1963 Gabilondo introduced the rare Models XVII in .22 Short and XVIII in .25 ACP. Mechanically similar to the Model XV, these restyled "Executive Models" were only 4.7 inches long with 2.36-inch barrel and weighed only 12⅓ ounces. The Gun Control Act of 1968 rendered them unimportable into the USA, so Gabilondo discontinued both variants in 1969. Gabilondo then introduced the Model XIX, a lightweight Model XV with aluminum alloy frame. It weighed 17 ounces, 4 ounces less than the all-steel Model XV.

In 1966 Gabilondo relocated pistol production to Vitoria to expand its investment-casting plant, while continuing revolver manufacture in Elgoibar. The enlarged installation increased Gabilondo's business in contract work for other firearms manufacturers and in non-firearms manufacturing. The added business gave Gabilondo valuable financial stability in the years ahead which Unceta and Echeverria lacked.

The ensuing years were good for Gabilondo. In 1969 Gabilondo introduced the improved Martial series of revolvers, replaced in 1976 by the even better Comanche line. These included variants chambered for .22 Long Rifle, .38 Special, .357 Magnum and .44 Magnum. Imported to the USA until 1995, the Comanche was even more popular in Europe. In 1972 Llama-Gabilondo passed the half-million mark in handgun production, and in 1983 they reached one million. Yet there was no time to rest on their laurels. Gabilondo made serious efforts to diversify and update its handgun offerings. Spain's military and police still used aging single-action models, many chambered for the obsolete 9mm Largo cartridge. In the late 1970s Spain's Army called on Unceta, Echeverria and Gabilondo to submit double-action 9mm Parabellum pistols with a large magazine capacity and ambidextrous controls for future adoption.

Gabilondo's first entry was the innovative "Llama Omni." Though it used a variation of the Browning breech lock introduced in the Model 1911, in all other respects the Omni represented a radical shift in design. But it fell short in Spanish testing. Introduced commercially in 1982, the Omni also flopped with civilian enthusiasts, even after being offered in a 7-shot .45 ACP variant. They found it too exotic, and its high price discouraged cost-conscious customers who typically chose Llama handguns. Gabilondo discontinued the Omni in 1986 but had a replacement, the Model 82, in the wings. Inspired by the Beretta Model 92, the impressive Model 82 won the Spanish armed forces contract in 1987, beating Unceta's Astra Models 80 and 90 and Echeverria's Star Models 30 and 31. Stoeger Industries imported the Model 82 into the United States from 1988 to 1993. In 1989 Gabilondo introduced a higher-performance version as the Model 87 with an integral compensator and extended operating controls to attract competitive shooters. Both types sold poorly in the United States despite experiencing modest success elsewhere.

As Gabilondo introduced double-action models, they took the opportunity in 1985 to revamp its tradi-

In 1987 the Spanish armed forces selected Gabilondo's Llama Model 82 (top) to replace the Star Super B *(center),* which in 1946 had supplanted the Astra Model 400, *(bottom),* adopted in 1921. The Model 82's victory represented Gabilondo's first ever against formidable Unceta and Echeverria competitors for official service in their native country.

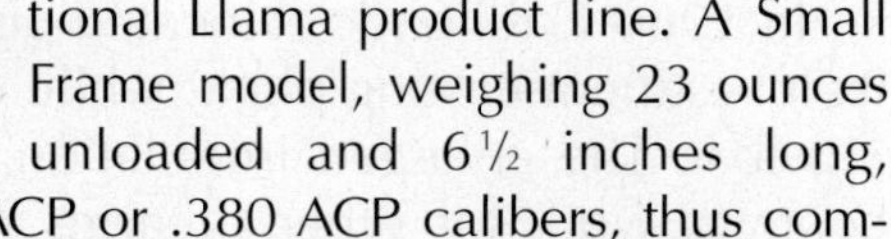

The Llama Micromax, introduced in 1995, is the latest variant of the company's small Model 1 1911-A1 copy.

tional Llama product line. A Small Frame model, weighing 23 ounces unloaded and 6 1/2 inches long, chambered .22LR, .32 ACP or .380 ACP calibers, thus combining the earlier Models XV, X-A and III-A lines. A Compact Frame or Model XI-B chambered 9mm Parabellum (9-round magazine) or .45 ACP (7-round magazine). The Compact Frame pistol had a 4 5/16-inch barrel and unloaded weight of 34-36 ounces, making it slightly smaller than the 9mm Parabellum/.45 ACP Llama Large Frame pistol, at 8 1/2 inches long with a 5-inch barrel and 40-ounce unloaded weight about the size of Colt's Government Model/Model 1911A1. In 1988 a .38 Super variant replaced the 9mm Large Frame.

In 1991 Gabilondo announced a new line of personal-defense revolvers. The 23-ounce Piccolo had an aluminum alloy frame, a 2-inch barrel and a 6-shot cylinder. The similar Scorpio revolver had a steel frame and an unloaded weight of 29 ounces. Both resembled the snub-nosed variant of Smith & Wesson's Model 10 revolver. Though neither was offered in the USA they sold well overseas.

For many years Stoeger Industries handled the U.S. and Canadian distribution of the Llama handgun line. In 1993 Import Sports Inc. of Wanamassa, New Jersey, took over. Import Sports reduced the Gabilondo product line to M1911-type pistols which were reworked to appeal to U.S. shooters. In 1994 Import Sports announced the new .45 ACP caliber Llama Model IX-C with 12-round magazine, an ambitious and dramatic attempt to update the Llama series. The large IX-C, 8 1/2 inches long with a 5 1/8-inch barrel and an unloaded weight of 44 ounces, outweighed the Government Model pistol by 5 ounces. Its double-column magazine, inspired by Para-Ordnance, and thick, checkered neoprene grips, gave the IX-C a very wide grip. Worse, the U.S. Congress' passage of a 10-round magazine restriction took effect in January 1995. Small changes accompanied the switch to a 10-round magazine; a skeleton hammer replaced the earlier spur and a widened beavertail grip safety protected the shooter's hand. The Model IX-D, designed around the IX-C's magazine, was slightly smaller. Neither gun lasted long, but three features they pioneered still impact the Llama line. The elimination of the sighting rib atop the slide lowered manufacturing costs. A semi-arched mainspring housing split the difference between the Model 1911's flat housing and the M1911A1's arched housing, and pleases a wide variety of shooters. The third feature, the Swartz safety, had been developed and used briefly in the 1930s by Colt. The Swartz safety prevents the firing pin from moving until the shooter properly squeezes the grip safety. It makes the pistol safe from accidental firing if dropped, but unlike more modern firing-pin locks it has no effect on the trigger pull.

The 9mm Parabellum Llama Model XI "ESPECIAL" was typical of pre-World War Two Llama pistols in lacking a grip safety and having a more vertical grip than the Colt Model 1911. The Model XI was the first Gabilondo pistol to include a "toe" extension on the front of the gripstrap and a rounded hammer.

In 1995 Gabilondo unveiled the Max-I in 9-round 9mm Parabellum and 7-round .45 ACP variants, in Government (5 1/8-inch barrel, 36 ounces) and Compact (4 1/4-inch barrel, 34 ounces) sizes. A .45 ACP caliber Max-I Compensator variant appeared next year with a barrel extension which vented gases downward to control muzzle rise.

Gabilondo eliminated the Small Frame's .32 caliber option (Model X-A) in 1993 and the .22 caliber Model XV the following year. In 1997 the surviving .380 caliber variant received a matte finish, an extended slide latch and grip safety, elimination of the sighting rib, and enlarged high-visibility sights to become the "Llama Micromax .380."

In 1995 Gabilondo revamped the Compact Frame Model IX-D to create the .45 ACP caliber "Llama Max-II Compact Frame" with a 4¼-inch barrel, 3-dot sights, black rubber grips and double-column magazine holding 10 rounds for U.S. and Canadian private sales or 13 rounds elsewhere.

Last of the 1995 additions was the Llama Minimax, whose name derived from the phrase "Minumum size/maximum firepower." This compact pistol (3½-inch barrel, 7⅓-inch overall length, 35 ounces unloaded, 6-round magazine) comes in 9mm, .40 S&W or .45 ACP. The Minimax shares the Max-I's skeletonized hammer, combat-style sights and extended operating controls. It adds a considerably modified locking system built around a barrel flared at the muzzle. Gabilondo followed it up in 1997 with the 10-shot Minimax-II in .45 ACP. It resembled Para-Ordnance's P12•45 but cost dramatically less. Regrettably, the Minimax-II lasted just one year.

In late 1998 Llama-Gabilondo began producing the Llama Minimax Sub-Compact, with a 3.14-inch barrel, to replace the 10-shot Minimax-II. Gabilondo offered the Minimax Sub-Compact chambered for 9mm, .40 S&W or .45 ACP, all variants having a 10-round magazine. With its dramatically small dimensions—only 6.33 inches long, with a 3.14-inch barrel and a height of 4¾ inches—this pistol really lives up to the "Minimax" slogan. Import Sports introduced the Minimax Sub-Compact to the important U.S. market with a dramatic flourish, unveiling it at the 1999 SHOT show.

The late 1990s were hard times for handgun manufacture in Spain. Echeverria went out of business in 1997 and Unceta collapsed in 1998. Thanks to strong representation in the United States with its Llama line, Gabilondo just managed to survive. In November 1999 it underwent yet another reorganization, being bought out by a firm called Fabrinor S.A.L. comprised of former Gabilondo employees. In the early 21st century, Fabrinor's M1911-type pistols occupy a lucrative niche. At this writing Fabrinor produces the .45 ACP caliber Max-I in "Government Frame" and "Compact Frame" iterations, the Minimax, the Minimax Sub-Compact and the Micromax in .32 ACP and .380 ACP chambering.

In a century of operation, Gabilondo has never gotten the measure of respect it deserves. However, the company has offered good value for money throughout its existence, and continues to do so as Spain's last surviving manufacturer to "carry the flame," by continuing the country's long tradition of handgun manufacture.

A current version of the Llama trademark, on a Minimax Sub-Compact dated 2003, resembles a cigarette lighter.

Rabbits and Beagles: Tips from an Expert

By Keith Sutton

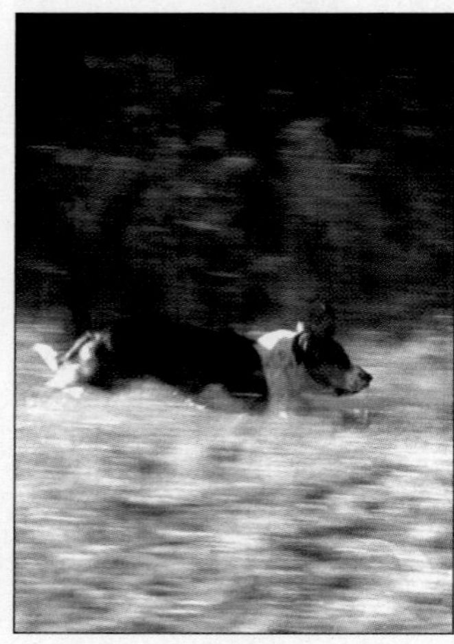

A good beagle loves running rabbits almost as much as eating.

The beagle is believed to be one of the oldest hunting breeds.

Some things fit together so perfectly that when one of the components is missing, the whole thing seems out of kilter. Rabbits and beagles are one such pairing. Compared to this combination, setters and quail or catfish and hushpuppies are mere also-rans. It's certainly possible to hunt rabbits without dogs. Many hunters do. But it's difficult to hunt them as well, and it's usually not half as much fun.

There are two main reasons why beagling for rabbits is so appealing. First is the rabbit's instinctive habit of circling. Rabbits have a small home range, and they won't leave it even when hounded by beagles. So, when flushed from cover, a rabbit will likely bound away, leaving the dogs behind, then slow down until it feels menaced again, when it once again easily outdistances the beagles. But somewhere out yonder, usually not more than a couple hundred yards, Br'er Rabbit begins circling back to the spot where he initially hopped out.

The hunters follow the chase by listening to the baying of the dogs. That's the second big thrill of this fast-paced sport. The hurly-burly of a pack of beagles running a rabbit is heavenly music to the hunter's ears.

Before long, the chase turns back the hunter's way, and he climbs up on a stump to watch and wait. With luck, he'll catch a glimpse of the rabbit running, maybe hopping, depending on how far it's leading the dogs. Then, when the time is right, the shotgun is shouldered, the hunter takes aim, and another rabbit is added to the bag.

Beagle History

Despite a limited recorded history, it is generally believed that the beagle is one of the oldest breeds and is one of the breeds closest in appearance to the original hounds.

Records of its ancestry point to ancient Greece and France. There is also some evidence that beagle-type dogs were used during the Crusades as an established hunting dog. Talbot hounds were brought to Great Britain from France in 1066 and are considered to be ancestors to the beagle and the foxhound.

The beagle came into prominence in the 1500s during the reign of King Henry VII of England (1485-1509). The breed's popularity further increased during the reign of his daughter, Elizabeth I (1558-1603). It was the custom in those days for the hunting parties to take the dogs to the fields in baskets attached to the saddles of their horses.

By the 1700s, two types of hounds existed for hunting rabbits: the Southern Hound and the much quicker North Country Beagle. Since fox hunting was becoming increasingly popular, beagles were being kept less and less in favor of foxhounds. Fortunately for the continuing existence of the beagle, farmers in England, Ireland and Wales continued to keep packs of beagles to hunt with.

In the mid-1800s, Reverend Phillip Honeywood established his pack in Essex, England, which is thought to be the progenitor of the modern beagle. He was breeding for hunting skills though, not looks. A fellow Englishman, Thomas Johnson, was responsible for breeding lines of beagles that could hunt and also look attractive.

Beagles were imported to America in 1876, and in 1888, wealthy sportsmen promoted the beagle by forming the National Beagle Club. The club was established to hold pack field trials and bench shows. American breeders began developing beagles that would fit American needs. The English variety of hound had been trained to track foxes and was bred to an average height of 15 to 17 inches at the shoulder. The smaller American beagle was bred for rabbit hunting.

Usually. Sometimes the chase is so enthralling, the hunter doesn't want it to end. During these times, the gun remains cradled in the bend of an arm, while the hunter just enjoys the magical sights and sounds.

Lewis Peeler, a 48-year-old insurance salesman from Wynne, Arkansas, has been hunting rabbits in eastern Arkansas since he was a boy. He's packed away more than 35 years experience beagling for cottontails and swamp rabbits, and you'd be hard pressed to find a more cordial and knowledgeable dog handler. I've tagged along with him on many hunts and have learned a great deal about the specialized tactics he uses when hunting rabbits with beagles. He knows the blueprint for success and depends on science, not luck, to find his quarry.

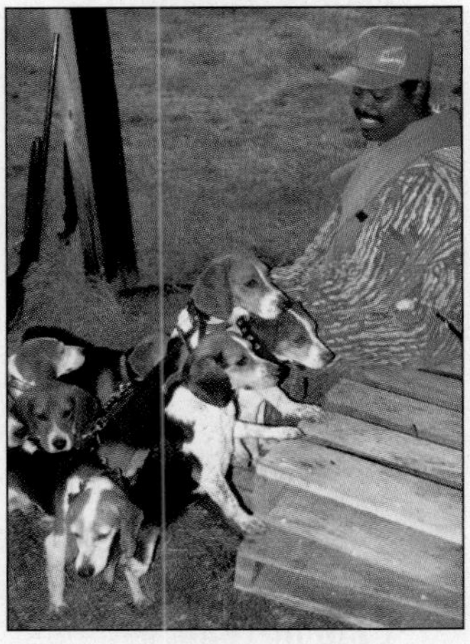

Putting together a good pack of beagles takes time and effort.

Listen to some of the advice he offers. Veteran beagle men and novices alike will discover something of value.

"One of the most important things to learn about hunting rabbits with dogs," Peeler says, "is not to rush your dogs. If you have a good dog, he'll get in there and work out all the good places where rabbits will hide. But if you stay too close to him, he'll tend to go through the cover too fast and move on.

"Dogs will often gauge their pace by your actions, and if you tend to want to go on, they will, too. It's best to stay back and give them time to work the cover out and get their noses into everything."

Peeler says it's just as important to sit tight once the chase is on.

"After the dogs jump a rabbit, many people follow them and try to head the rabbit off," he says. "The best thing to do, though, is to move to

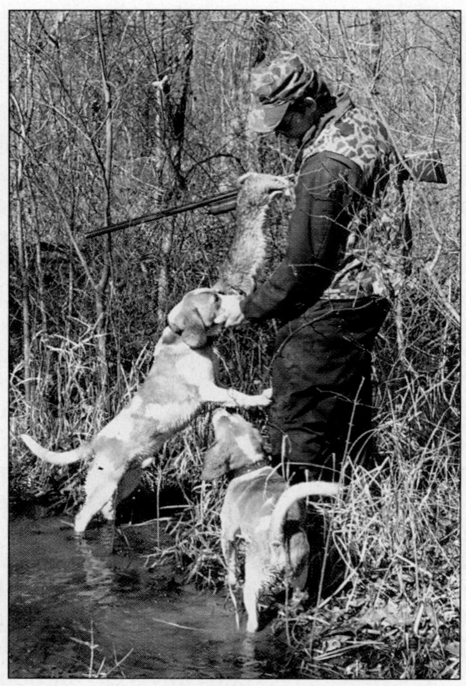

Lewis Peeler with two of his beagles. According to Peeler, hunters must learn to work in concert with their dogs in order to enjoy consistently successful rabbit hunting.

Beagle Trivia

- The origin of the word "beagle" is uncertain, although it has been suggested that the word derives from the French *begueule* (meaning "open throat") or from an Old English, French or Welsh term meaning "small."
- In the 14th century, beagles became popular among the British monarchy. Pocket Beagles, only nine inches tall at the withers, were kept by Elizabeth I, and there are references to Glove Beagles, dogs small enough to fit on a gloved hand, being kept in packs by Edward II and Henry VII.
- Beagles were imported into the United States in 1876 and recognized by the American Kennel Club in 1884.
- The National Beagle Club held its first field trial in 1888.
- Lyndon B. Johnson owned three beagles named Him, Her and Edgar.
- There has never been a time since the American

the area where they jumped the rabbit, and then pick a good place where you can see well. Then just wait for the rabbit to circle back. To me, that's the most enjoyable part of rabbit hunting, waiting there and listening to the chase. Why chase the rabbit down? That's why you have the dogs in the first place, so let the dogs do that."

Patience is a virtue too few rabbit hunters are blessed with, Peeler notes.

"Patience is especially important when the cover you're hunting is real thick," he says, "because the rabbit may just play around with the dogs. Sometimes he won't budge until they push him real hard. You have to be even more patient when hunting swamp rabbits because they'll run a much bigger circle than just regular cottontails."

This last fact was borne out on a hunt I made with Peeler in the L'Anguille River bottoms in east Arkansas. The cover we hunted was thick enough to hide a blaze-orange elephant. Saplings of sweetgum, sassafras, persimmon and elm shot up 8 to 12 feet tall and stood 50,000 stems to the acre, and though Lewis was only a few feet away, he was totally invisible, despite the fact that he was dressed in a hunter-orange vest and hat that should have made him as conspicuous as a bear in a belly boat.

Like I said: thick enough to hide a blaze-orange elephant.

Rabbits were plentiful. Lew's two lemon-and-white beagles, Bear and Rebel, hadn't stopped running since we'd released them. And as luck would have it, we bagged two plump cottontails in our first half-hour of hunting. After a short chase, each rabbit had circled back to within a few feet of the point where it was flushed.

The third rabbit, though, had distinctly different plans. More than 30 minutes passed before the dogs came back into earshot. They had followed the rabbit on a long circuitous route that took them half a mile away. We listened as they grew closer, then we finally headed in opposite directions through the thickets, hoping one of us would manage to be in the right place at the right time when the little brown ghost came passing through.

The hullabaloo grew louder and louder as I strained my eyes to see through the dense cover. Any second now, and ...

Boooom! The report from Lew's shotgun off to my left startled me. I looked in that direction and saw him fight his way through a brier patch, from the midst of which he retrieved a rabbit nearly as big as one of the beagles running the race. Not surprisingly, when the pack of dogs came into sight, they snuffled and bawled their way right past the spot where I had been standing, proving once again that a rabbit had gotten the best of me.

Lewis placed the big swamp rabbit on the ground, then pulled a cottontail from his game bag. When he hoisted the two up for me to see, it was obvious there were some major differences. Both were similar in appearance—peppered brown coloration, fluffy white tails, long ears, big feet. But the swamp rabbit was nearly twice the size of the cottontail Lew had shot earlier. It was like comparing a beagle to a St. Bernard.

"I'd be the last to complain about shooting a mess of these nice cottontails," Lew said. "But when you can throw in a few of the big swampers, too, it really makes things exciting."

Though we hunted with two dogs that day, Peeler prefers to hunt with no fewer than three beagles, and considers four the optimum number.

"Beagles have different characteristics," he says. "Some are good jump dogs. They'll get in there and really work the tracks and get the rabbits moving. Other beagles are better chase dogs. They'll get on the trail once the rabbit's moving and keep after him. You want both kinds in your dog pack, and you have a better chance of that if you hunt with several dogs."

Peeler is also quick to point out that finding a good swamp rabbit dog is a rare treat. On a good day, a beagle chasing swampers and cottontails will work five times as hard as a dog chasing cottontails alone. For a dog to work productively in bottomland rabbit areas, it should have a Labrador retriever's affinity for cold water and must be persistent, well trained, keen-nosed and in topnotch physical condition. Swampers run straight, hard and long. They're crafty, running or swimming through water, holing up in hollow trees and scurrying through every available bit of cover to throw the hounds off the track. Only the best rabbit dogs can keep up at a steady pace throughout the day.

Hunting under the proper weather conditions can tip the odds in the hunter's favor, says Peeler.

"Moist, cool weather is best because the ground holds the scent better," he explains. "Extremely cold days or dry days aren't good, and dogs usually won't do as well when there's snow on the ground, either. Cool fall days when the ground's a bit moist are really the best."

Of course, not every rabbit hunter can afford the luxury of a pack of beagles. Training dogs and giving them proper care can be expensive and time-consuming. The investment of time and money is too prohibitive for many sportsmen busy with other day-to-day affairs.

Nevertheless, many hunters are smitten with a passion for beagles and bunnies, and any work required to savor this exciting combo is a labor of love.

For those fortunate few, there will be a time this season when they're wishing the beagle music would never end. Lewis Peeler will be one of them.

Kennel Club's inception in 1884 that the beagle was not one of the most popular breeds in this country. From 1953 through 1959 the little hound with the big ears was America's most popular dog.

- **It ranked number four on the AKC's Top Dog Breeds of 2004.**
- **In a pilot program launched in the mid-1980s, the U.S. Department of Agriculture recruited beagles to sniff out contraband food being brought into the United States through airports. These dogs, part of the "Beagle Brigade," sniff baggage for prohibited food articles to battle pests that endanger the nation's farm products. The USDA chose beagles because they wanted dogs that could do the job without being intimidating to travelers.**
- **Beagles are used by law enforcement personnel to detect arson accelerants at suspicious fires. And beagles also are popular with pest control companies due to their ability to smell termites.**
- **Who was the most famous beagle of all time? Undoubtedly, it was Charlie Brown's dog.**

NEW Products: **Anschutz Rifles**

1702 D HB

1416 D HB

ANSCHUTZ 1702 D HB

Action: bolt
Stock: walnut
Barrel: 23 in.
Sights: none
Weight: 8 lbs.
Caliber: .17 Mach 2
Magazine: 5-round detachable box
Features:
Price: $1512

ANSCHUTZ 1416 D HB, 1502 D HB, 1517 D HB

Action: bolt
Stock: walnut
Barrel: 23 in.
Sights: none
Weight: 6.2 lbs.
Caliber: .22 LR, .17 Mach 2 and .17 HMR, respectively
Magazine: 5-round detachable box
Features:
Price:................. $813-$878

NEW Products: **Browning Rifles**

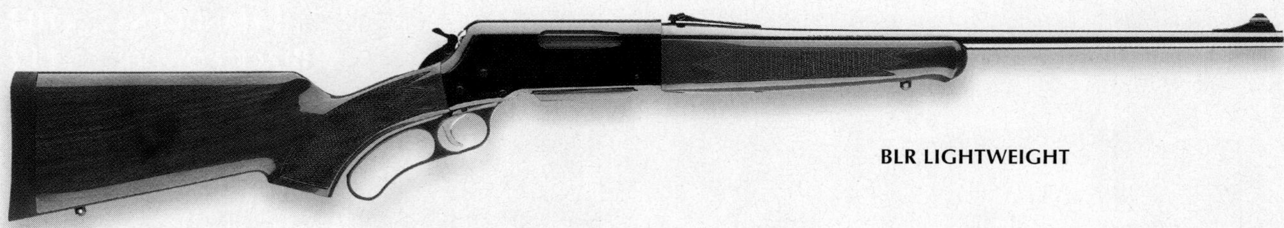
BLR LIGHTWEIGHT

BLR LIGHTWEIGHT RIFLES

Action: lever
Stock: checkered walnut
Barrel: 18 or 20 in.
Sights: open
Weight: 6.5 to 7.75 lbs.
Caliber: .22-250, .243, 7mm-08, .308, .358, .450, .270 WSM, 7mm WSM, .300 WSM, .325 WSM, .270, .30-06, 7mm Rem. Mag., .300 Win. Mag.
Magazine: 3- to 5-round detachable box
Features: Long- and short-actions; rotating bolt heads; sporter barrel; stock with pistol grip and schnabel forend
Price: .... $765 to $836

NEW Products: **Dakota Rifles**

PREDATOR

Action: bolt
Stock: checkered walnut
Barrel: match-grade stainless
Sights: none
Weight: 9.0 lbs.
Caliber: .17 VarTarg, .17 Rem., .17 Tactical, .20 VarTarg, .20 Tactical, .20 PPC, .204 Ruger, .221 Fireball, .222 Rem., .222 Rem. Mag., .223 Rem., .22 BR, 6 PPC, 6 BR
Magazine: none
Features: many options, including fancy walnut
Price: $1995

NEW Products: **Lazzeroni Rifles**

MODEL 2005 GLOBAL HUNTER

MODEL 2005 GLOBAL HUNTER

Action: bolt
Stock: synthetic
Barrel: 22 or 26 in.
Sights: none
Weight: 6.1 (short action) or 74. (long action)
Caliber: nine Lazzeroni chamberings, from 6.53 Scramjet to 10.57 Meteor
Magazine: 3-round internal box
Features: Fluted stainless sporter barrel; long- or short-action; lightweight graphite composite stock and alloy bottom metal.
Price: $5900

Bench technique is critical to accurate shooting. Sandbags won't guarantee a tight group if your body isn't in exactly the same position each shot and pressure on the rifle identical, shot to shot.

NEW Products: **Legacy Rifles**

HOWA M-1500 JRS CLASSIC SUPREME

PUMA M-92 CARBINE

HOWA M-1500 JRS CLASSIC SUPREME

Action: bolt
Stock: laminated
Barrel: 22 or 24 in.
Sights: none
Weight: 7.25 to 7.75 lbs.
Caliber: .223, .22-250, .243, 6.5x55, .25-06, .270, .308, .30-06, 7mm Rem. Mag., .300 Win. Mag., .338 Win. Mag., .270 WSM, 7mm WSM, .300 WSM.
Magazine: 3- to 5-round internal box
Features: Improved 3-position thumb safety; Boyds stock available in black walnut or laminate; optional thumbhole stock
Blue: . . . . $646 to $675
Stainless: . . . . $755 to $784

PUMA M-92 RIFLES AND CARBINE

Action: lever
Stock: walnut
Barrel: 16, 18, and 20 in.
Sights: open
Weight: 6 to 7.5 lbs.
Caliber: .38/.357, .44 Mag., .45 Colt, .454 Casull, .480 Ruger
Magazine: full-length tube; capacity varies with barrel length.
Features: 18-inch barrel ported; available with 24-inch octagon barrel; HiViz sights; .45 carbine with large-loop lever; stainless and blued finishes available
Price: . . . . from $457

NEW Products: **Les Baer Rifles**

SVR

Action: autoloader
Stock: synthetic
Barrel: 18 and 24 in.
Sights: none
Weight: 13 lbs.
Caliber: .204 Ruger
Magazine: 5-round detachable box
Features: Les Baer 416-R stainless barrel; chromed National Match carrier and extractor; titanium firing pin; aluminum gas block with Picatinny top; match-grade stainless; two-stage, 24-inch Jewell trigger; Picatinny rail; optional Leupold Long Range 8.5-25x50mm Vari-X III package; Versa Pod bipod; all-weather Baer Coat finish; camo finish and special rifling twist available as options
Price: $3075

NEW Products: **Marlin Rifles**

MODEL 717M2

MODEL 917VSF

MODEL 1894CL

Action: lever
Stock: walnut
Barrel: 22 in.
Sights: open
Weight: 6 lbs.
Caliber: 32-20 Win.
Magazine: 6 round under-barrel tube
Features: Micro-Groove finish barrel; solid top receiver; hammer block safety; half-length tube magazine; Marble adjustable semi-buckhorn rear and carbine front sights; straight-grip stock with cut checkering and hard rubber butt pad; 39.5-inch overall length
Price: $836

MODEL 717M2

Action: autoloading
Stock: hardwood
Barrel: 18 in.
Sights: open
Weight: 5 lbs.
Caliber: .17 Mach 2
Magazine: 7-round detachable box
Features: Sportster barrel; last-shot bolt hold-open; manual bolt hold-open; cross-bolt safety;adjustable ramp front sight; receiver grooved for scope mount; Monte Carlo walnut-finshed laminated hardwood stock with pistol grip; 37-inch overall length.
Price: $264

MODEL 917VSF

Action: bolt
Stock: laminated
Barrel: 22 in.
Sights: none
Weight: 6.75 lbs.
Caliber: .17 HMR
Magazine: 7-round detachable box
Features: Heavy fluted stainless barrel; thumb safety; receiver grooved for scope mount; Monte Carlo laminated gray/black hardwood stock with pistol grip and rubber rifle butt pad; 41-inch overall length.
Price: $450

NEW Products: **Nosler Rifles**

BOLT-ACTION

NOSLER BOLT-ACTION RIFLE

Action: bolt
Stock: Turkish walnut
Barrel: 24 in.
Sights: optical
Weight: 7.75 lbs.
Caliber: .300 WSM
Magazine: 3-round internal box
Features: Hand-lapped, match-grade Wiseman barrel; three-position safety; Timney trigger; Leupold VX-III 2.5-8x36 scope serial-numbered to the rifle; production limited to 500 units
Price: $4000

NEW Products: **Remington Rifles**

NEW PRODUCTS

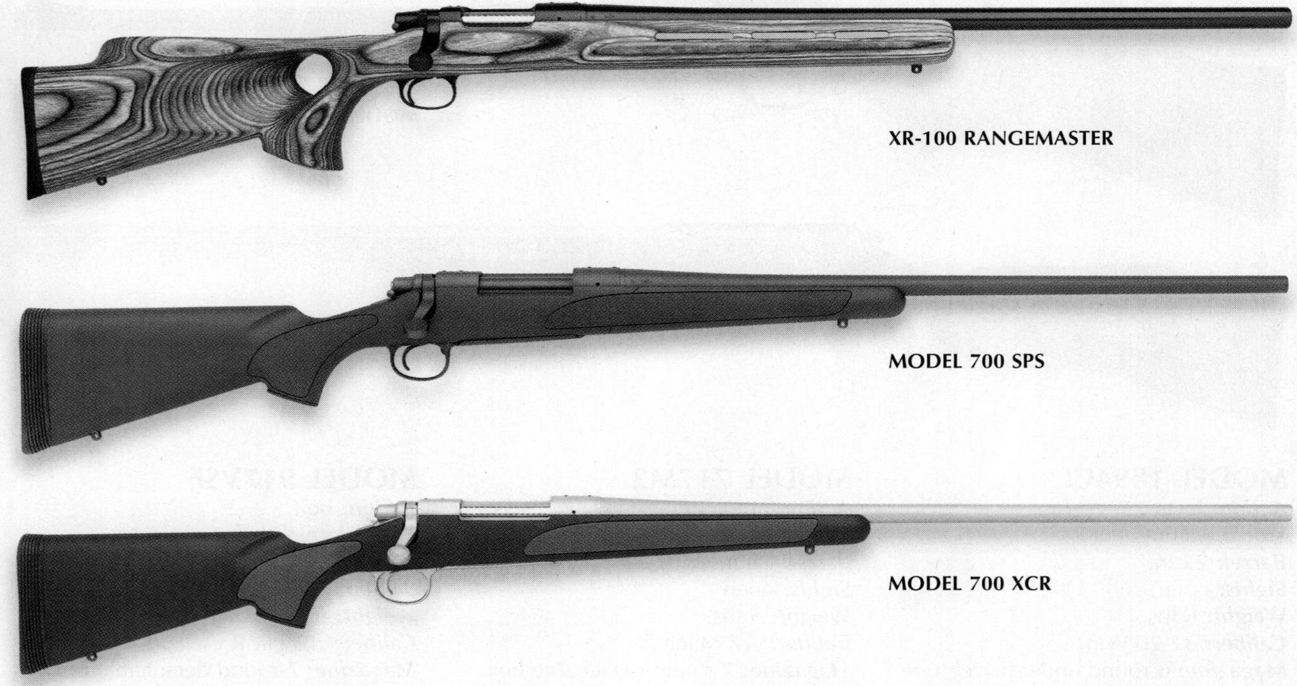

XR-100 RANGEMASTER

MODEL 700 SPS

MODEL 700 XCR

XR-100 RANGEMASTER

Action: bolt
Stock: laminated thumb-hole
Barrel: 26 in.
Sights: none
Weight: 9.2 lbs.
Caliber: .204, .223, .22-250
Magazine: none
Features: Varmint-contour heavy chrome-moly barrel; 40-XB target trigger; gray laminate thumbhole stock
Price: $879

MODEL 700 SPS

Action: bolt
Stock: synthetic
Barrel: 24 or 26 in.
Sights: none
Weight: 7.25 to 7.5 lbs.
Caliber: .204 Ruger to .300 Ultra Mag
Magazine: 3- to 5-round detachable box
Features: also available in youth models with 20- and 22-inch barrels; chrome-moly or stainless, sporter
Price: .... from $520

MODEL 700 XCR

Action: bolt
Stock: synthetic
Barrel: 24 or 26 in.
Sights: none
Weight: 7.5 lbs.
Caliber: 11 chamberings, from .270 to .375 Ultra Mag
Magazine: 3- to 5-round internal box
Features: Stainless barreled action; TriNyte corrosion control coating; Hogue grip panels; stock finish is Realtree Hardwoods Gray HD; R3 recoil pad.
Price: $993

Practice not only your shooting techniques, but fast reloading during the off-season. Smooth bolt operation comes with repetition; so does loading the magazine quickly from your pouch.

NEW Products: **Sako Rifles**

75 GREY WOLF

QUAD

75 GREY WOLF

Action: bolt
Stock: laminated
Barrel: 22½ or 24½ in.
Sights: none
Weight: 7¼ to 7¾ lbs.
Caliber: .223, .22-250, .243, 7mm08, .260, .308, .25-06, .270, .30-06, .270 WSM, 7mm WSM, .300 WSM.
Magazine: 4- to 6-round detachable box
Features: Satin-finished stainless cold hammer-forged barrel; four action sizes; gray laminated stock
Price: $1549

QUAD

Action: bolt
Stock: synthetic
Barrel: 22 in.
Sights: none
Weight: 5.75 lbs.
Caliber: .22 LR, .22 WMR, .17 Mach 2, .17 WMR
Magazine: 5-round detachable box
Features: Switch-barrel combo set of four sporter-weight barrels (.22 LR, .22 WMR, .17 Mach 2, .17 HMR); color-coded barrels feature quick change system with single retaining screw; double locking lug action, bolt lift 50 degrees, adjustable single-stage trigger; two-position sliding safety; 40 inches overall; foam-padded metal case.
4 barrel set:.............. $1739
Single Barrel: $948

NEW Products: **Tikka Rifles**

T3 BIG BOAR CARBINE

T3 SUPER VARMINT

T3 BIG BOAR CARBINE

Action: bolt
Stock: synthetic
Barrel: 19-in.
Sights: none
Weight: 6.1 lbs.
Caliber: .308, .30-06, .300 WSM
Magazine: 3-round detachable box
Features: Chrome-moly sporter barrel
Price: $719

T3 SUPER VARMINT

Action: bolt
Stock: synthetic
Barrel: 23½-in. heavy
Sights: none
Weight: 9.3 lbs
Caliber: .223, .22-250, .308
Magazine: 3- or 4-round detachable box
Features: stainless action and barrel, top rail and adjustable comb.
Price: $1668

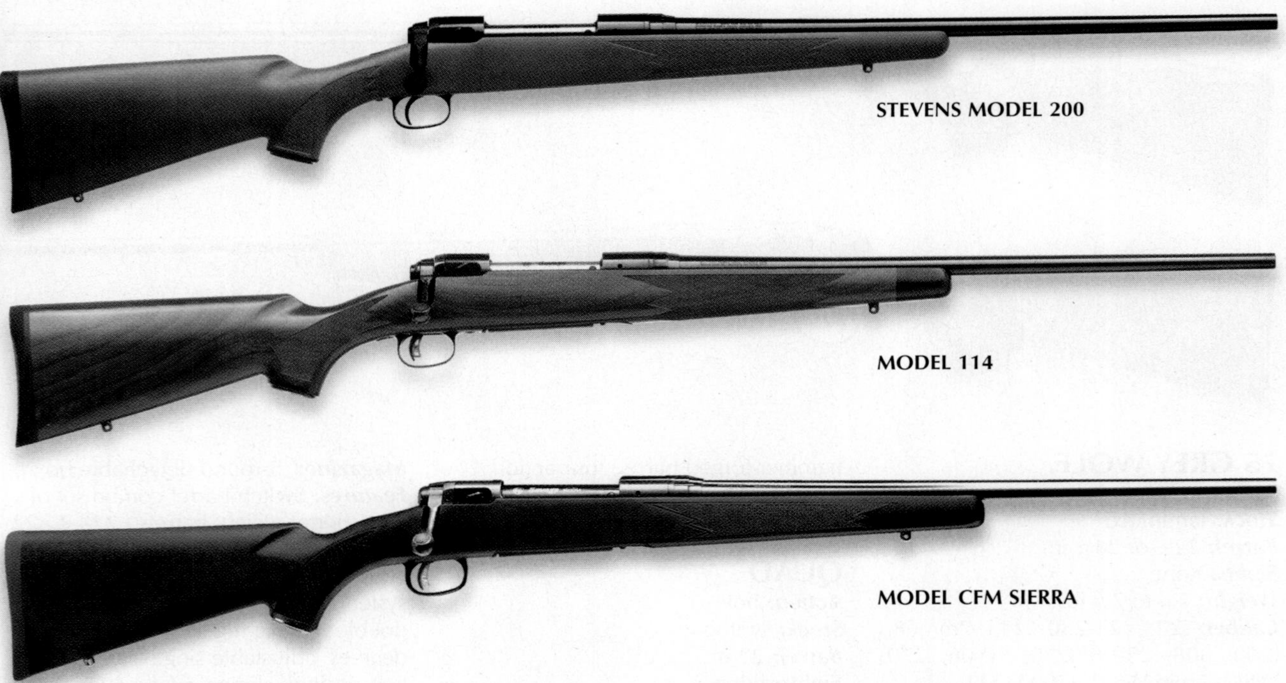

STEVENS MODEL 200

MODEL 114

MODEL CFM SIERRA

MODEL 200

Action: bolt
Stock: synthetic
Barrel: 22- and 24-in. sporter
Sights: none
Weight: 7½ lbs.
Caliber: 10 chamberings, from .223 to .300 Win. Mag.
Magazine: blind box
Features: pillar-bedded
Price: **$316**

MODEL 14/114

Action: bolt
Stock: checkered walnut
Barrel: 22 and 24 in.
Sights: none
Weight: 7¼ lbs.
Caliber: .223 to .300 Win. Mag.
Magazine: 3 to 5 round detachable box
Features: AccuTrigger
Price: **$616**

MODEL CFM SIERRA

Action: bolt
Stock: synthetic
Barrel: 20-in. sporter
Sights: none
Weight: 6 lbs.
Caliber: .243, 7mm-08, .308, .270 WSM, .300 WSM.
Magazine: 3 to 5 round detachable box
Features: AccuTrigger
Price: **$552**

After you shoot at game, reload and keep your eye to the scope. Your best chance for a follow-up shot is almost always from where you are. Move, and you can miss it.

NEW Products: **Ruger Rifles**

MODEL 77 MARK II FRONTIER

MODEL 77 MARK II FRONTIER

Action: bolt
Stock: laminated
Barrel: 16½-in sporter
Sights: none
Weight: 6.75 lbs.
Caliber: .243, 7mm-08, .308, .300 WSM
Magazine: 3- or 5-round internal box
Features: rib for barrel-mounted scope
Price: $799

MODEL 77 MARK II ALL-WEATHER

Action: bolt
Stock: synthetic
Barrel: 22 in.
Sights: none
Weight: varies with caliber
Caliber: .204 Ruger, 7mm-08 Rem., .305 Rem. Mag.
Magazine: box, 4 rounds
Features: Stainless steel components; one-piece bolt with non-rotating, Mauser-type controlled-feed extractor; three-position safety; integral scope rings.
Price: . . . . $ 716.00

NEW Products: **Thompson/Center Rifles**

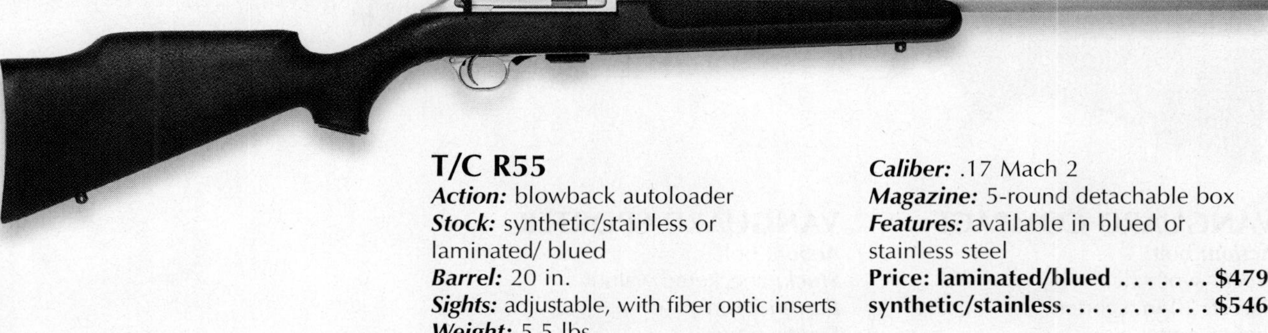

T/C R55

Action: blowback autoloader
Stock: synthetic/stainless or laminated/ blued
Barrel: 20 in.
Sights: adjustable, with fiber optic inserts
Weight: 5,5 lbs.
Caliber: .17 Mach 2
Magazine: 5-round detachable box
Features: available in blued or stainless steel
Price: laminated/blued $479
synthetic/stainless. $546

Bench technique is critical to accurate shooting. Sandbags won't guarantee a tight group if your body isn't in exactly the same position each shot and pressure on the rifle identical, shot to shot.

NEW PRODUCTS

NEW Products: **Walther Rifles**

G22 CARBINE

Action: blowback autoloading
Stock: synthetic
Barrel: 20 in.
Sights: adjustable on handle and front strut
Weight: 6 lbs.
Caliber: .22 LR
Magazine: detachable box
Features: Weaver-style accessory rail; black or green synthetic stock.
Price: $420

NEW Products: **Weatherby Rifles**

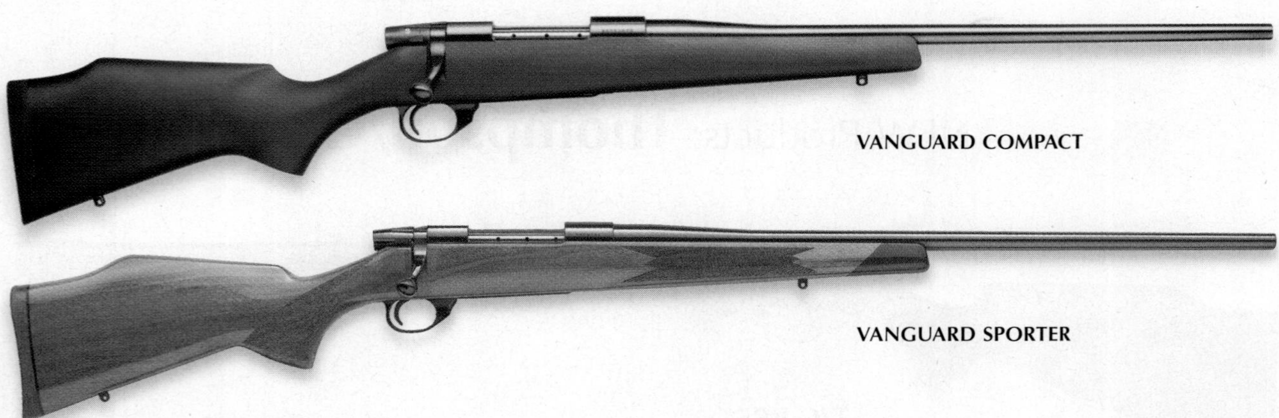
VANGUARD COMPACT

VANGUARD SPORTER

VANGUARD COMPACT

Action: bolt
Stock: synthetic
Barrel: 20-in. sporter
Sights: none
Weight: 6.75 lbs.
Caliber: .22-250, .243, .308
Magazine: 5-round internal box
Features: Chrome-moly or stainless steel barrel.
Price: $549

VANGUARD SPORTER

Action: bolt
Stock: checkered walnut
Barrel: 24-in.
Sights: none
Weight: 7.75 lbs.
Caliber: 13 chamberings, from .223 to .338 Win. Mag.
Magazine: 3- to 5-round internal box
Features: Chrome-moly or stainless steel barrel; pillar-bedded composite stock with Aramid, fiberglass and graphite components.
Price: blue................. $582
stainless $701

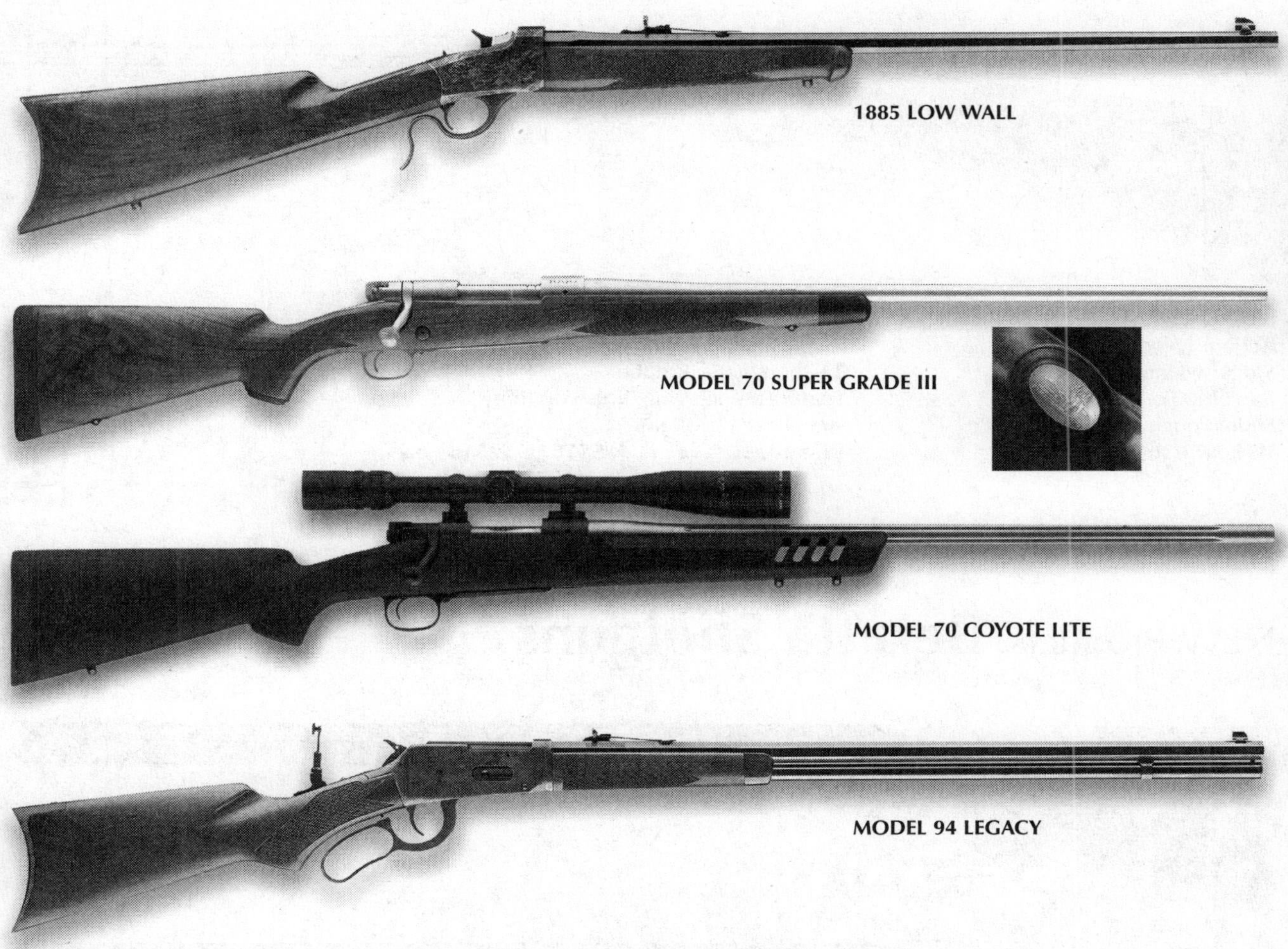

1885 LOW WALL

MODEL 70 SUPER GRADE III

MODEL 70 COYOTE LITE

MODEL 94 LEGACY

1885 LOW WALL AND HIGH WALL

Action: dropping block
Stock: checkered walnut
Barrel: 24 in. (Low Wall) 28 in. (High Wall)
Sights: open (Low Wall) and none
Weight: 8 lbs. (Low Wall), 8.5 lbs. (High Wall)
Caliber: .17 Mach 2 (Low Wall), and .270, 7mm and .300 WSM
Magazine: none
Features: Case-colored breech; straight-grip walnut stock with crescent butt.
1885 High Wall. $1085
1885 Low Wall $1014

MODEL 70 SUPER GRADE III

Action: bolt
Stock: checkered walnut
Barrel: 24- and 26-in. sporter
Sights: none
Weight: 7.75 to 8 lbs.
Caliber: nine chamberings, from .25-06 to .325 WSM
Magazine: 3- to 5-round internal box
Features: new, slimmer stock, inletted swivel studs
Price: standard $1036
magnum. $1067

MODEL 70 COYOTE LITE

Action: bolt
Stock: synthetic
Barrel: 24 in.
Sights: none
Weight: 7.5 lbs.
Caliber: eight chamberings, from .223 to .325 WSM (all WSSM and WSM rounds)
Magazine: 3- to 5-round internal box
Features: Chrome-moly or stainless barrel; lightweight carbon Bell & Carlson synthetic stock with double swivel studs and ventilated forend.
Price:. . . . . from $839 to $930

MODEL 94 LEGACY

Action: lever
Stock: walnut
Barrel: 26 in. round or octagon
Sights: open, with rear Marble's tang peep
Weight: 7 to 7.5 lbs.
Caliber: .30-30 and .38-55
Magazine: 7-round full-length tube
Features: Case-colored or blued receiver; Marble adjustable tang sight; steel crescent butt and forend cap,
Price: round blued $783
round case-colored $839
octagon blued. $882
octagon case-colored $939

NEW Products: **Winchester Rifles**

MODEL 9422 TRIBUTE

MODEL 9422 TRIBUTE

Action: lever
Stock: walnut
Barrel: 20½ and 22½ in.
Sights: open
Weight: 6 lbs.
Caliber: .22 LR and .22 WMR
Magazine: 15-round (LR) and 11-round (WMR) tube
Features: engraving, finish options, straight or pistol grip
Price:. . . . . $516 to $2313

NEW Products: **Beretta Shotguns**

UGB25XCEL

XTREMA2

UGB25XCEL

Action: hinged breech autoloading
Stock: checkered walnut
Barrel: 30 or 32 in.
Chokes: screw-in tubes
Weight: 7.75 to 9 lbs.
Bore/Gauge: 12
Magazine: 3
Features: Three-alloy steel Optima-Bore barrel with fully chromed bore and chamber; Beretta Optimachoke and Extended Optimachoke choke tubes; light alloy streamlined receiver with modified Greener-style cross-locking bolt; rising locking block; short recoil operating principle allows the use of all 12 gauge 2½-inch competition cartridges; button-operated safety on trigger guard; high-resistance fiberglass-reinforced technopolymer trigger plate; side feed, bottom ejection, recoil reduction system, ventilated interchangeable rib; fore-end stock with adjustable drop.
Price: $3195

XTREMA2

Action: autoloader
Stock: synthetic, with rubber grip inserts
Barrel: backbored, 24, 26 and 28 in.
Chokes: choke tubes
Weight: 7¾ lbs.
Bore/Gauge: 12
Magazine Capacity: 3
Features: Spring-mass recoil reducer in stock (optional); rubber grip inserts; buttplate spacers to lengthen pull, camo finish available; accepts all 12-gauge ammunition, including 3½-inch.
Price: $1295
Camo $1395
Slug. $1495
"Kick-Off" recoil reduction . . . . $100 additional

NEW Products: **Beretta Shotguns**

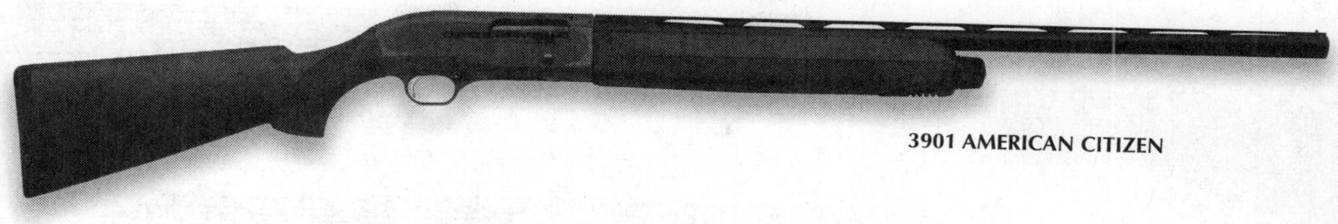

3901 AMERICAN CITIZEN

3901 AMERICAN

Action: autoloading
Stock: walnut or synthetic
Barrel: 26 or 28 in.
Chokes: screw-in tubes
Weight: 7.75 lbs. (12 ga.), 7 lbs. (20 ga.)
Bore/Gauge: 12 and 20
Magazine: 3
Features: High-strength steel alloy hammer forged barrel; 3-inch chamers; Beretta Mobilchoke system; removable trigger group.
Price: Citizen, synthetic $750
Statesman, walnut............ $850
Ambassador, select walnut $950

NEW Products: **Browning Shotguns**

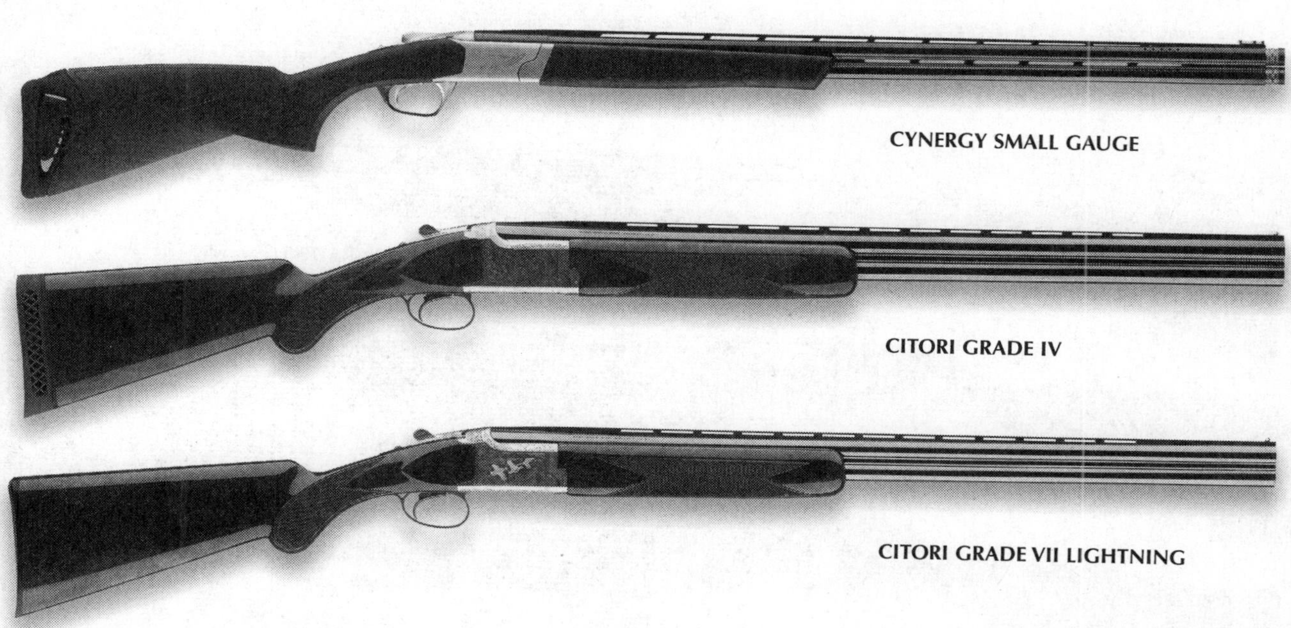

CYNERGY SMALL GAUGE

CITORI GRADE IV

CITORI GRADE VII LIGHTNING

CYNERGY SMALL GAUGE

Action: over/under
Stock: walnut
Barrel: 26 or 28 in. (Field), 30 or 32 in. (Sporting)
Chokes: screw-in tubes
Weight: 6.25 to 6.5 lbs
Bore/Gauge: 20 and 28
Magazine: none
Features: Boxlock action; 20 gauge comes with ported barrels; mechanical single trigger
Price: Field $2062
Sporting $3080

CITORI GRADE IV AND VII LIGHTNING

Action: over/under
Stock: select walnut
Barrel: 26 and 28 inches, backbored, 3-in. chambers in 12, 20 and .410
Chokes: screw-in tubes
Weight: 6½ to 8 pounds
Bore/Gauge: 12, 20, 28 and .410
Magazine: none
Features: Boxlock action with automatic ejectors; engraved receivers
Price: 12, 20 Grade IV $2608
28, .410 Grade IV.......... $2929
12, 20 Grade VII........... $4146
28, .410 Grade VII $4466

NEW Products: **CZ Shotguns**

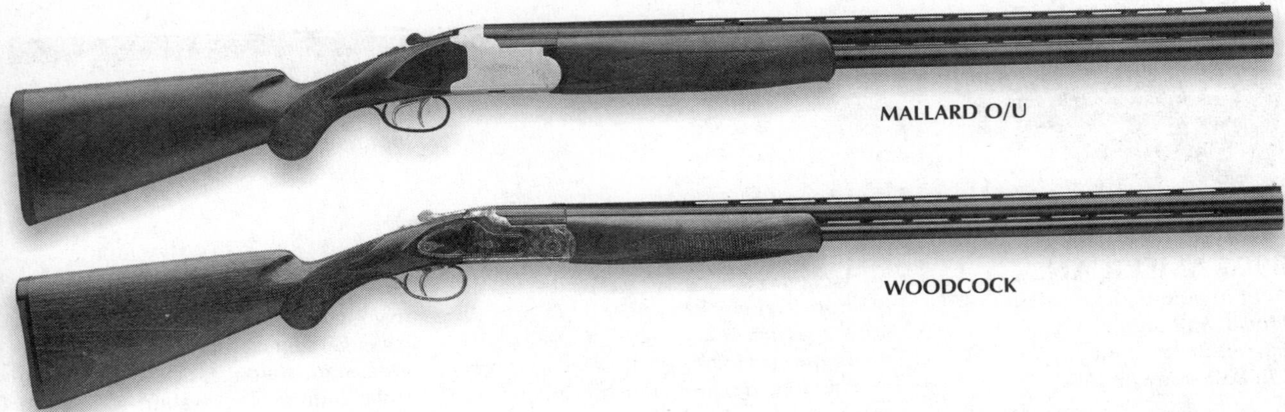

MALLARD O/U

WOODCOCK

CZ SHOTGUNS

Action: boxlock
Stock: checkered Turkish or American walnut
Barrel: 26 and 28 in.
Chokes: choke tubes in 12 and 20 gauge, fixed chokes in 28
Weight: 5 .75 to 7.75 lbs.
Bore/Gauge: 12, 20, 28, .410
Magazine Capacity: no magazine
Features: silvered or case-colored receivers; Woodcock and Redhead Deluxe have auto ejectors.Ringneck with hand engraving.
Price: side-by-sides . . . $795 to $1045
Mallard O/U. $495
single-trigger O/Us . . . $695 to $1129

NEW Products: **Franchi Shotguns**

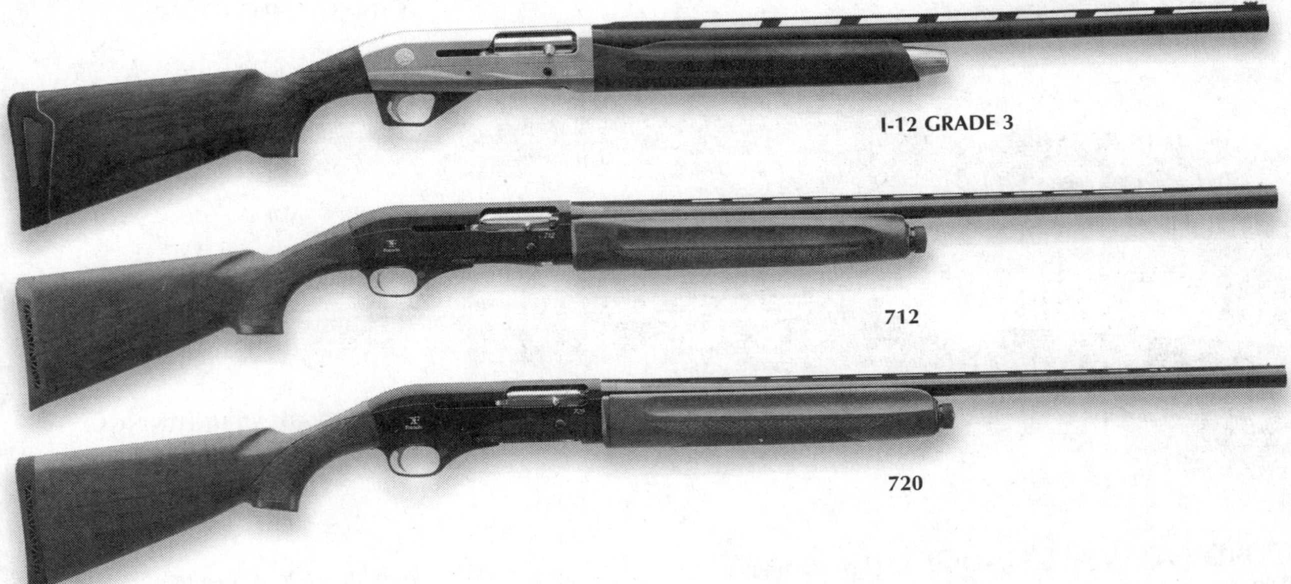

I-12 GRADE 3

712

720

I-12

Action: autoloader
Stock: synthetic or walnut
Barrel: 26 or 28 in.
Chokes: screw-in tubes
Weight: 7.5 lbs.
Bore/Gauge: 12
Magazine: 3 rounds
Features: Benelli inertia-driven system; 3-inch chambers; recoil pad with gel insert, vent rib
Price:. . . . . $660 (black)
. . . . $730 (camo)
. . . . $760 (walnut)

712, 720

Action: autoloader
Stock: walnut with WeatherCoat protection
Barrel: 30 in. (12 gauge), 28 in. (20 gauge)
Chokes: screw-in tubes
Weight: 7 lbs (712), 6.25 lbs (720)
Bore/Gauge: 12 and 20
Magazine: 5 (712) and 4 (720)
Features: Satin nickel receiver finish; 3-inch chambers
Price: $850

NEW Products: **Kimber Shotguns**

VALIER

VALIER

Action: side-by-side, sidelock
Stock: Turkish walnut
Barrel: 26 or 28-in.
Chokes: IC & Mod.
Bore/Gauge: 20

Features: Chrome lined barrels; chambered for 3-inch shells; hand engraved, case colored receivers and furniture; hinged forward trigger; gold line cocking indicators; straight grip, Turkish walnut stock—14.75 inch length-of-pull; finished in niter and rust blue.

Valier Grade I with extractors, Grade II features tuned ejectors.
Grade I (20 gauge). $3,879
Grade II (20 gauge) $4,480

NEW Products: **Marlin Shotguns**

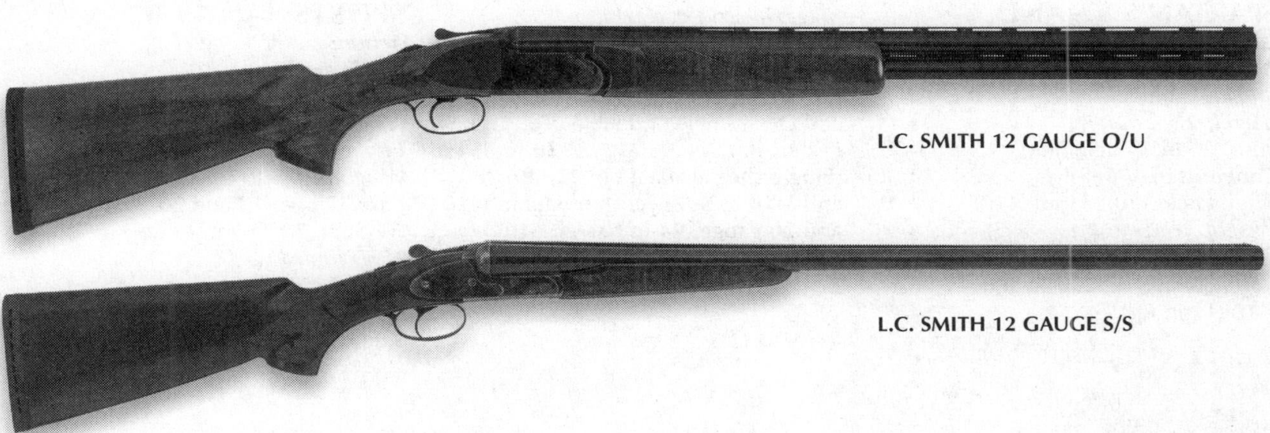

L.C. SMITH 12 GAUGE O/U

L.C. SMITH 12 GAUGE S/S

L.C. SMITH

Action: side-by-side and over/under
Stock: checkered walnut
Barrel: 26 and 28 in.
Chokes: screw-in tubes
Weight: 6 lbs. (20 gauge side-by-side) to 7.75 lbs (12 gauge O/U)

Bore/Gauge: 12 and 20
Magazine: no magazine
Features: automatic ejectors; 3-inch chamber
Price:. . . . from approximately $1900

Good shooting starts with your feet. If your torso is twisted uncomfortably, it will unwind as you release muscle tension at the shot. Practice pointing your feet quickly where the shot will come.

NEW PRODUCTS

NEW Products: **Remington Shotguns**

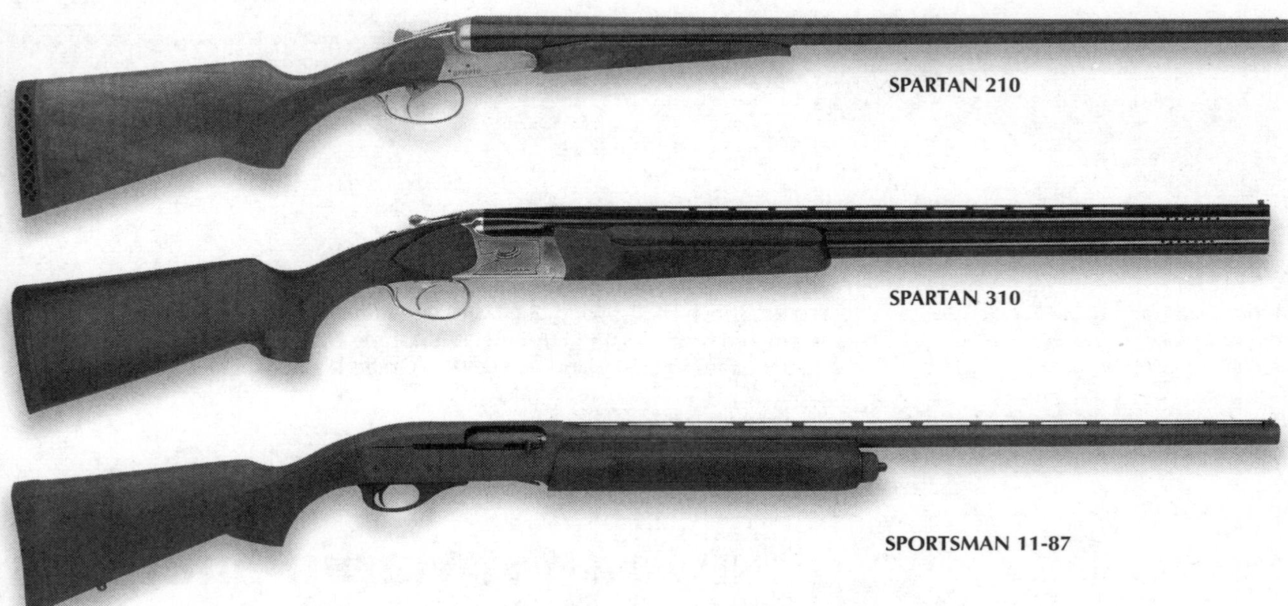

SPARTAN S X S AND O/U SHOTGUNS

Action: hinged breech
Stock: walnut
Barrel: 26- or 28-in. (also, 20-in. Coach Gun)
Chokes: screw-in tubes (fixed chokes in 28 and .410)
Weight: 6.25 to 7 lbs. (SxS) and 7.5 lbs. (O/U)
Bore/Gauge: 12, 20, 28 and .410 (16 in O/U)
Magazine: no magazine
Features: Chrome-lined barrels; all-steel breech; single selective trigger and selective ejectors; automatic safety. (SXS and O/U), single or double triggers (SxS)
Price: . . . . $320 to $519
(Single-shot available in 12, 20, 28 and .410 at $97; youth model in .410 and 20 gauge, 24-in barrel, $104)

SPORTSMAN 11-87

Action: autoloading
Stock: synthetic
Barrel: 26 and 28 in. (21-in. on Slug and Youth guns)
Chokes: RemChoke tubes
Weight: 7.75 to 8.5 lbs (6.5 lbs. Youth)
Bore/Gauge: 12 and 20 (12 Slug, 20 Youth)
Magazine: 4
Features:
Price: Field and Youth $624
Slug. $705

NEW Products: **Weatherby Shotguns**

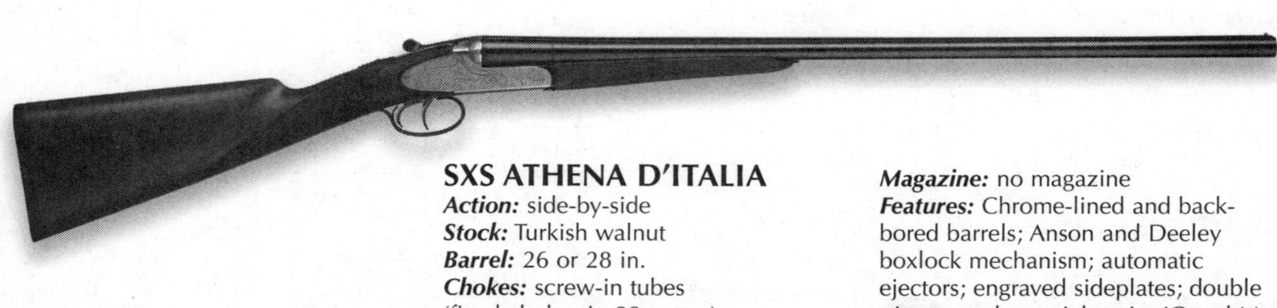

SXS ATHENA D'ITALIA

Action: side-by-side
Stock: Turkish walnut
Barrel: 26 or 28 in.
Chokes: screw-in tubes (fixed chokes in 28-gauge)
Weight: 6.75 to 7.25 lbs.
Bore/Gauge: 12, 20, 28
Magazine: no magazine
Features: Chrome-lined and back-bored barrels; Anson and Deeley boxlock mechanism; automatic ejectors; engraved sideplates; double triggers and a straight grip, IC and M chokes in 28 gauge.
Price: . . . . from $2800

NEW Products: **Beretta Handguns**

PX4 STORM

Action: autoloader
Grips: polymer, with interchangeable backstraps
Barrel: 4 in.
Sights: fixed 3-dot
Weight: 27.5 oz.
Caliber: 9mm, .40 S&W
Capacity: 17 (9mm), 14 (.40 S&W)
Features: SA/DA operation and de-cocker mechanism; grip inserts adapt grip size; accessory rail for lights and lasers
Price: $630

NEW Products: **Browning Handguns**

BUCK MARK HUNTER .22 PISTOL

Action: autoloader
Grips: composite or wood
Barrel: 5¼ in. to 7¼ in.
Sights: adjustable open
Weight: 34 to 38 ounces
Caliber: .22 LR
Capacity: 10
Features: Heavy chrome-moly or stainless barrel; integrated scope base; Truglo front sight.
Price: Hunter $360
Camper Stainless. $310
Standard Stainless $345
5.5 Target, 5.5 Field $511

Sight alignment is crucial on a pistol, with its short barrel. Misalignment of the front sight with the target is a misdemeanor; misalignment of the front sight with the rear sight is a felony.

NEW Products: **CZ Handguns**

NEW PRODUCTS

75 COMPACT .40 S&W

Action: autoloader
Grips: checkered synthetic
Barrel: 3.9 in.
Sights: fixed open
Weight: 37.8 oz.
Caliber: .40 S&W
Capacity: 10
Features: First shot single- or double-action; ambidextrous safety; M3 rail for tactical lights and lasers.
Price: $539

NEW Products: **Charles Daly Handguns**

ZDA PISTOL

Action: autoloader
Grips: polymer
Barrel: 3½ in.
Sights: fixed
Weight: 26 oz.
Caliber: 9mm, .40 S&W
Capacity: 15, 12
Features: Double-action and de-cocker; ambidextrous slide lock; low shot indicator for magazine
Price: $589

Back-up for bear country? Few handgun rounds will stop a grizzly, and you'll need a very heavy pistol to shoot them. Besides, hitting a charging bear is very difficult. Better to tote pepper spray.

NEW Products: **Charles Daly Handguns**

NEW PRODUCTS

1873 REVOLVER

Action: single-action revolver
Grips: walnut or simulated ivory
Barrel: 4¾, 5½, 7½ in.
Sights: fixed
Weight: 40 to 44 oz.
Caliber: .357 Mag., .45 Colt
Capacity: 6

Features: Available in civilian, artillery and cavalry models; brass or steel backstop and trigger guard.
Steel Frame $479
Stainless Frame $659

NEW Products: **FN Handguns**

FIVE-SEVEN IOM

Action: autoloader
Grips: textured synthetic
Barrel: 4¾-in, chrome-lined
Sights: adjustable rear, blade front
Weight: 18 oz.
Caliber: 5.7x28
Capacity: 20
Features: Single-action with an internal hammer; polymer frame and traditional trigger
Price: $1074

NEW Products: **Heckler & Koch Handguns**

P2000 AND P2000 SK

Action: DA autoloading
Grips: polymer
Barrel: 3.6 in. (2000) and 2.5 in. (2000 SK)
Sights: 3-dot
Weight: 24 oz. (2000) and 22 oz. (2000 SK)
Caliber: 9mm, .357 SIG, .40 S&W
Capacity: 9 to 13
Features: Pre-cock hammer; ambidextrous magazine releases and interchangeable grip straps; mounting rail for lights and lasers.
P2000 . . . . $887
P2000 SK $929

HK LP2000

NEW Products: **Para Ordnance Handguns**

"LT. COLONEL" COMPACT

STEALTH HI-CAP .45

HAWG 9

"LT. COLONEL" COMPACT

Action: autoloader
Grips: checkered wood
Barrel: 4¼-in.
Sights: 3-dot
Weight: 34 oz.
Caliber: .45 ACP
Capacity: 7
Features: Single action; stainless slide and frame, Power Extractor
Price: $988

PXT HIGH CAPACITY SA 9MM

Action: autoloader
Grips: polymer
Barrel: 3-in.
Sights: 3-dot
Weight: 24 oz.
Caliber: 9mm
Capacity: 12
Features: Single-action; alloy receiver
Price: $840

STEALTH HI-CAP .45

Action: autoloader
Grips: polymer
Barrel: 5 in.
Sights: 3-dot
Weight: 38 oz.
Caliber: .45 ACP
Capacity: 14
Features: Double-action; available in stainless
Blue $943
Stainless $1016

HAWG 9

Action: autoloader
Grips: polymer
Barrel: 3-in.
Sights: 3-dot
Weight: 24 oz.
Caliber: 9mm
Capacity: 12 + 1
Features: Single action; ramped barrel; alloy receiver; spurred hammer
Price: $840

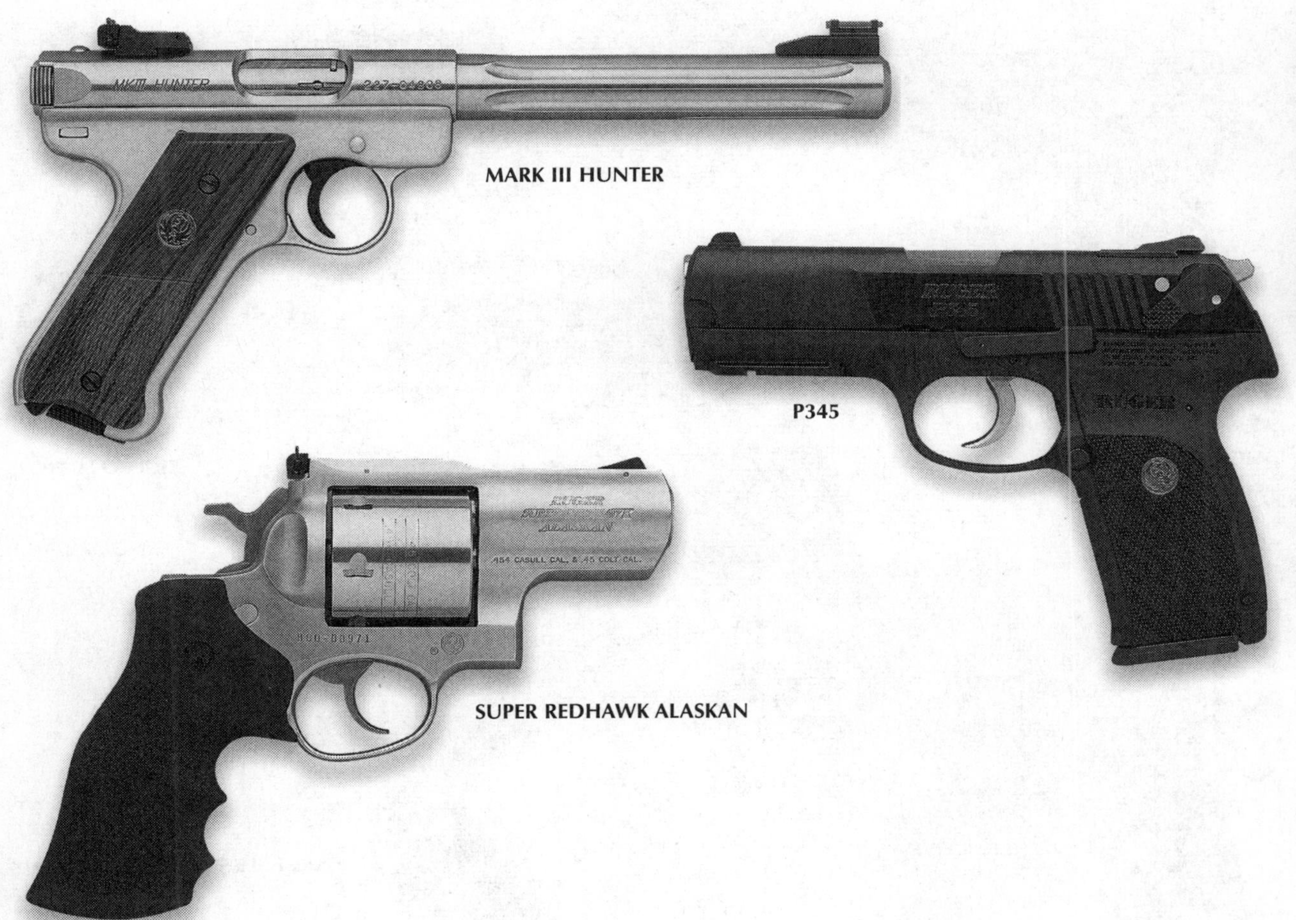

MARK III HUNTER

P345

SUPER REDHAWK ALASKAN

MARK III

Action: autoloader
Grips: synthetic
Barrel: 5½ in.
Sights: open, adjustable
Weight:
Caliber: .22 LR
Capacity: 10
Features: Bull barrel; contoured ejection port and tapered bolt ears; manual safety; loaded chamber indicator; magazine disconnect; adjustable rear sight; stainless finish; come drilled and tapped for a Weaver-type scope base adapter
Price:.................... $ 483

22/45 MARK III

Action: autoloader
Grips: synthetic
Barrel: 4 in.
Sights: open, fixed
Weight:
Caliber: .22 LR
Capacity: 10
Features: Slab bull barrel; manual safety; loaded chamber indicator; magazine disconnect; adjustable rear sight; blued finish.
Price:.................... $ 305

SUPER REDHAWK ALASKAN

Action: double-action revolver
Grips: Hogue Monogrip
Barrel: 2½ in.
Sights: adjustable open
Weight: 42 oz.
Caliber: .454 Casull, .480 Ruger
Capacity: 6
Features:
Price: $819

P345

Action: DA autoloading
Grips: polymer, integral with frame
Barrel: 4¼ in.
Sights: fixed
Weight: 29 oz.
Caliber: .45 ACP
Capacity: 8
Features: Double-action; polymer frame, fieldstrips without tools into five subassemblies.
Price: $548

NEW Products: **Sigarms Handguns**

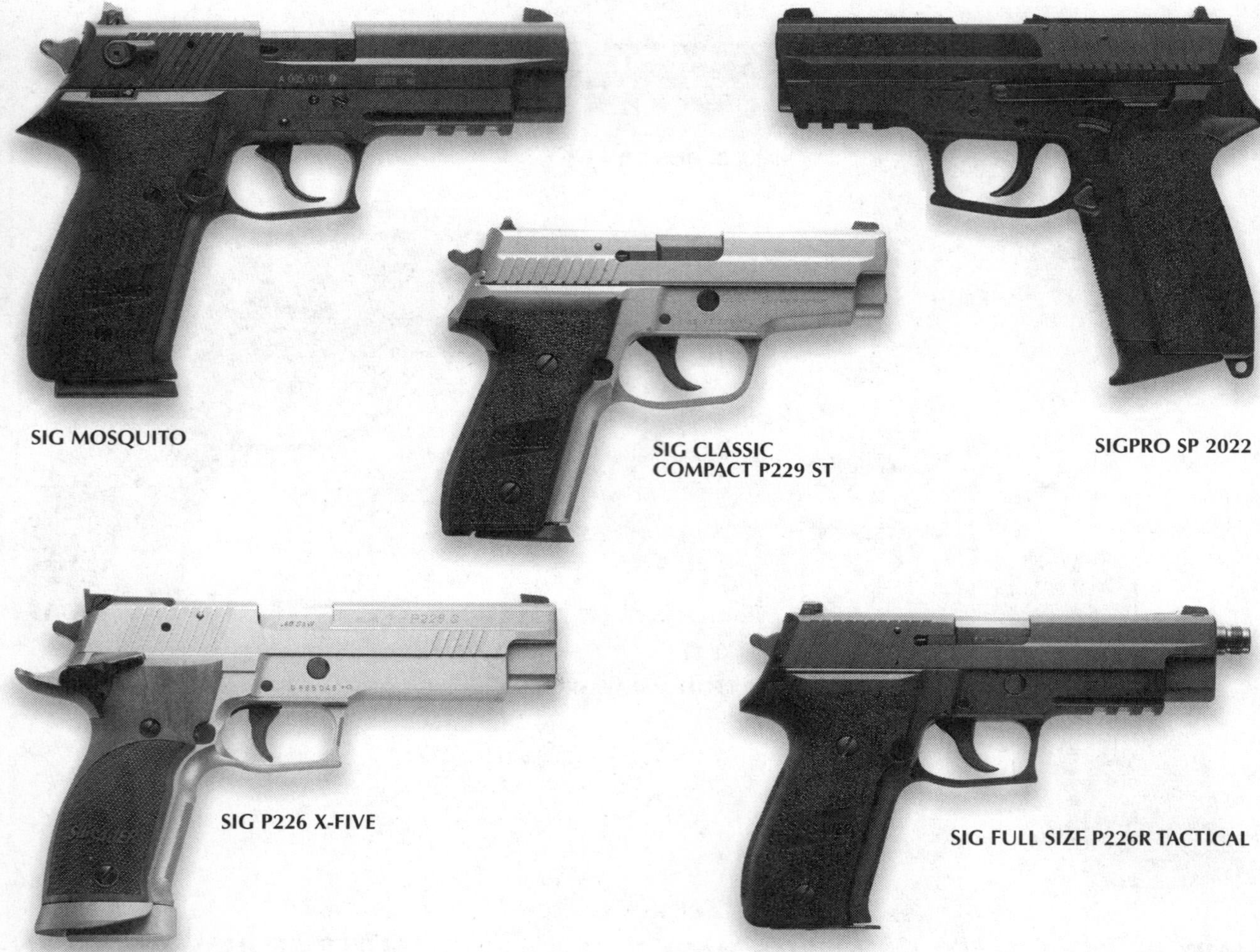

SIG MOSQUITO

SIG CLASSIC COMPACT P229 ST

SIGPRO SP 2022

SIG P226 X-FIVE

SIG FULL SIZE P226R TACTICAL

MOSQUITO

Action: autoloader
Grips: polymer
Barrel: 4 in.
Sights: adjustable
Weight: 25 oz.
Caliber: .22 LR
Capacity: 10
Features: Double action; polymer frame; ambidextrous grip; Picatinny rail
Price: $349

PRO SP 2022

Action: DA autoloader
Grips: interchangeable polymer
Barrel: 4 in.
Sights: fixed (available with night sights)
Weight: 30 oz.
Caliber: 9mm, .357 SIG, .40 S&W
Capacity: 15, 12, 10
Features: Double-action; stainless slide; polymer frame
Price: . $640 ($715 with night sights)

P226 X-FIVE

Action: autoloader
Grips: wood
Barrel: 5 in.
Sights: adjustable
Weight: 47 oz.
Caliber: 9mm, .40 S&W
Capacity: 19, 14
Features: Single-action; factory-tuned trigger
Price: $2499

CLASSIC COMPACT P229 ST

Action: autoloader
Grips: polymer
Barrel: 4 in.
Sights: fixed
Weight: 41 oz.
Caliber: .40 S&W
Capacity: 12
Features: Double action; stainless slide and frame

FULL SIZE P226R TACTICAL

Action: autoloader
Grips: polymer
Barrel: 5 in.
Sights: SIGlite night sights
Weight: 32 oz.
Caliber: 9mm
Capacity: 15
Features: Double-acion; alloy frame, stainless slide

1911

460XVR

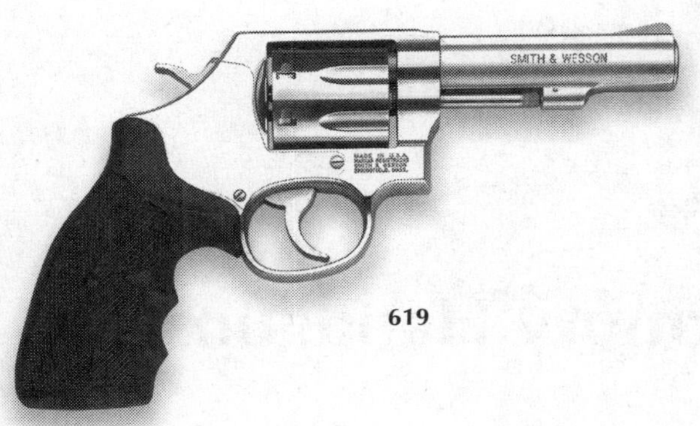

619

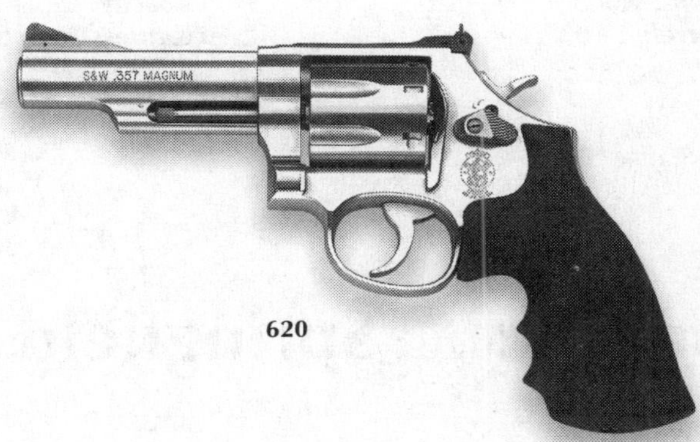

620

1911

Action: SA autoloading
Grips: checkered composite, checkered wood
Barrel: 5 in. (4 in. for Model 945)
Sights: adjustable open
Weight: 28 to 41 oz., depending on model
Caliber: .45 ACP (.38 Super in SW1911DK)
Capacity: 8 (10 in SW1911DK)
Features: Single-action
Price: . . . . from $960 to $2112

460XVR

Action: double-action revolver
Grips: stippled rubber
Barrel: $8\frac{3}{8}$ in., stainless
Sights: adjustable open
Weight: 72 oz.
Caliber: .460 S&W
Capacity: 5
Features: Ported barrel also fires .454 Casull and .45 Colt.
Price: $1253

619 AND 620 MEDIUM-FRAME REVOLVERS

Action: double-action revolver
Grips: checkered rubber
Barrel: 4 in.
Sights: adjustable open (M620) and fixed (M619)
Weight: 38 oz.
Caliber: .357 Magnum
Capacity: 7
Features:
Price: (M620) $669
(M619) $615

MODEL 60 SMALL-FRAME REVOLVER

Action: double-action revolver
Grips: wood
Barrel: 5 in.
Sights: adjustable open
Weight: 30.5 oz.
Caliber: .357
Capacity: 5
Features:
Price: $671

NEW Products: **Smith & Wesson Handguns**

MODEL 60

MODEL 625 JERRY MICULEK

MODEL 625 JERRY MICULEK PROFESSIONAL SERIES REVOLVER

Action: double-action revolver
Grips: wood
Barrel: 4 in.
Sights: adjustable open, removable front bead
Weight: 43 oz.
Caliber: .45 ACP
Capacity: 6
Features: Wide trigger; smooth wood grip; gold bead front sight on a removable blade; comes with five full-moon clips for fast loading.
Price: $845

NEW Products: **Springfield Armory Handguns**

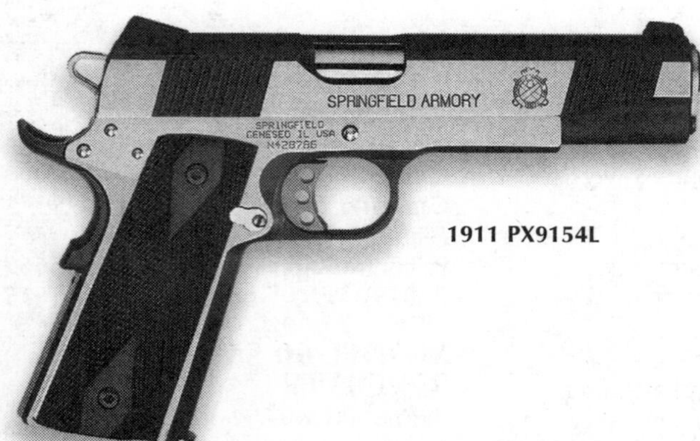

1911 PX9154L

GI 45 1911A1

1911

Action: autoloading
Grips: polymer and wood, depending on model
Barrel: 3, 4 and 5 in.
Sights: fixed and target
Weight: 23 and 24 oz. (Defender and Micro), 28 oz. (Champion), 30 oz. (full-size Lightweight) and 38 oz.
Caliber: .40 S&W, .45 ACP
Capacity: depends on model, magazine
Features: Single-action
Price: .... from $502

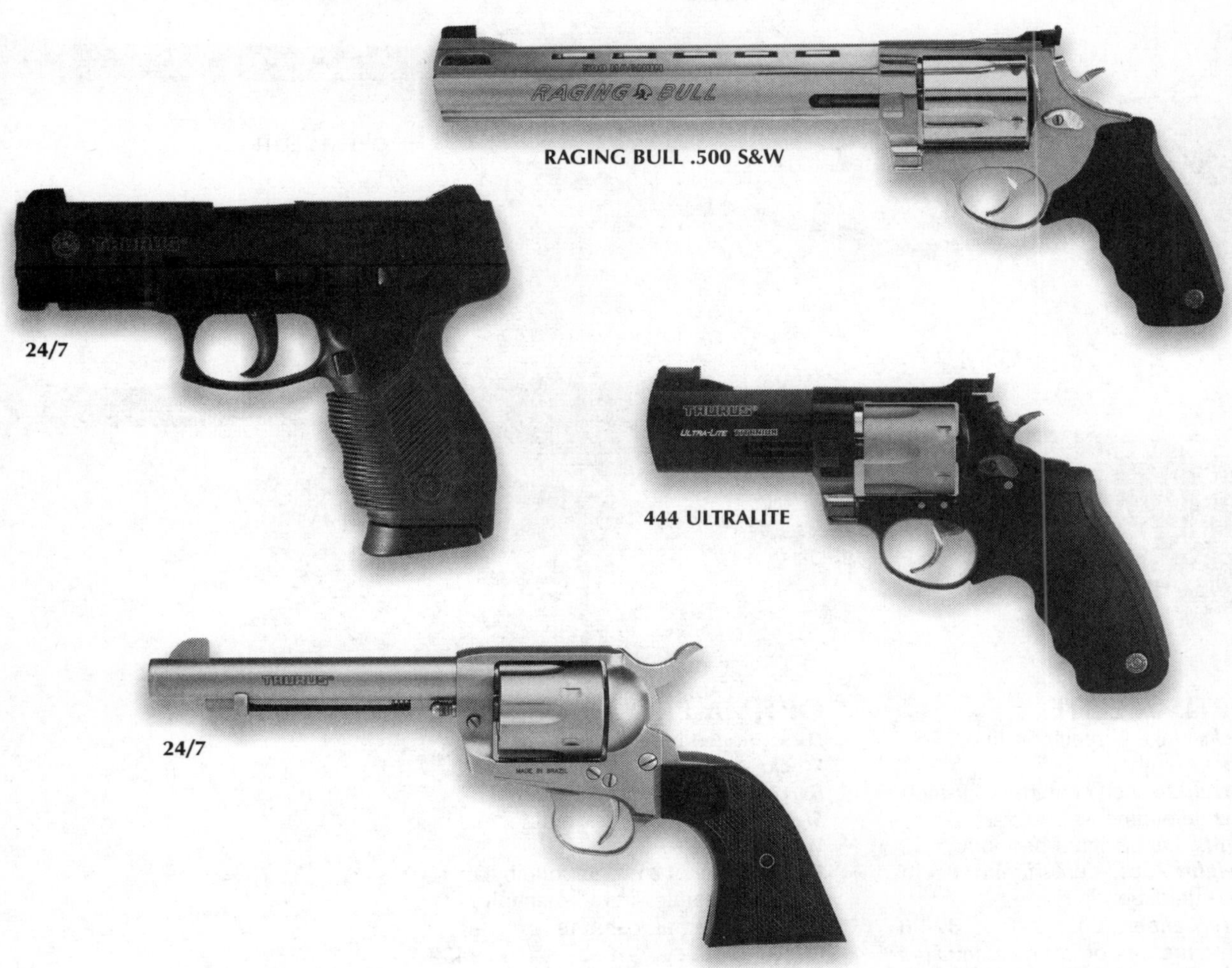

RAGING BULL .500 S&W

24/7

444 ULTRALITE

24/7

MODEL 24/7

Action: autoloader
Grips: polymer with rubber overlay
Barrel: 6 in.
Sights: 3-dot
Weight: 32 oz.
Caliber: .40 S&W
Capacity: 15
Features: Double-action; reversible magazine release; Picatinny rail
Price: blued. $576
stainless $594

NINE BY SEVENTEEN

Action: autoloader
Grips: hard rubber
Barrel: 4 in.
Sights: 3-dot
Weight: 26 oz.
Caliber: 9mm
Capacity: 17
Features: Double-action with de-cocker
Price: blued. $523
stainless $539

GAUCHO

Action: single-action revolver
Grips: hard rubber
Barrel: 5½ in.
Sights: fixed
Weight: 37 oz.
Caliber: .45 Colt
Capacity: 6
Features:
Price: blued. $484
stainless or blued with case-colored frame $500

444 ULTRALITE

Action: double-action revolver
Grips: rubber
Barrel: 4 in.
Sights: adjustable with fiber optic insert
Weight: 28 oz.
Caliber: .44 Magnum
Capacity: 6
Features: alloy frame, titanium cylinder
Price: blued. $650
stainless $699

RAGING BULL .500 S&W

Action: double-action revolver
Grips: rubber
Barrel: 10 in., vent rib
Sights: adjustable
Weight: 72 oz.
Caliber: .500 S&W
Capacity: 5
Features: ported muzzle, stainless barrel and action.
Price: $899

OPTIMA ELITE

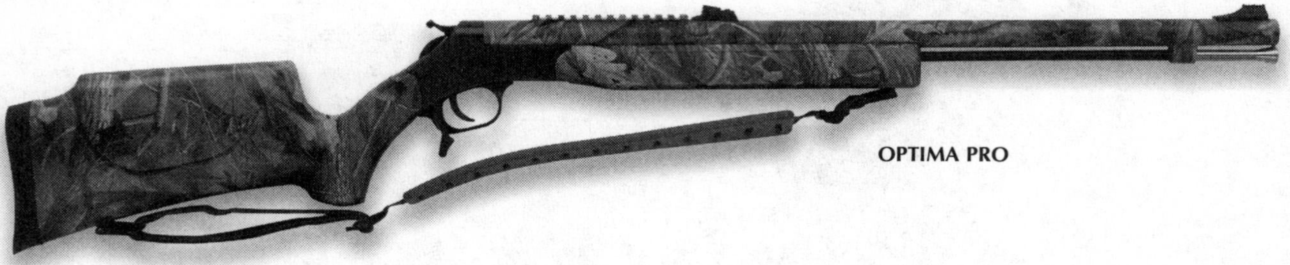

OPTIMA PRO

OPTIMA ELITE

Lock: hinged breech, in-line
Stock: synthetic
Barrel: 24-inch centerfire, 29-inch muzzleloading
Sights: DuraBright fiber optic
Weight: 7 lbs. (centerfire) or 8¾ lbs. (muzzleloader)
Bore/Caliber: .243, .270 or .30-06 centerfire; .45 or .50 muzzleloader
Features: Hinged breech; interchangeable barrels; stainless 209 breechplug
Price: black chrome-moly $355
camo chrome-moly or black stainless. $415
camo stainless. $475

OPTIMA PRO

Lock: hinged breech, in-line
Stock: synthetic
Barrel: 26 in.
Sights: DuraBright fiber optic
Weight: 7½ lbs.
Bore/Caliber: 12 gauge, full choke
Features: Stainless 209 breechplug; Weaver-style rail; camo finish
Price: $450

Before loading a caplock rifle, hold the muzzle close to a patch of grass and fire a primer only. If the grass shudders, the nipple is clear and the gun ready for loading.

NEW Products: **Ultra Light Arms Black Powder**

BOLT-ACTION MUZZLELOADER

Lock: bolt
Stock: Kevlar/Graphite
Barrel: 24 in.
Sights: none; drilled for scope mounts
Weight: 5 lbs.
Bore/Caliber: .45 and .50
Features: 209 primer; recoil pad; sling swivels
Price: $1000

NEW Products: **Traditions Black Powder**

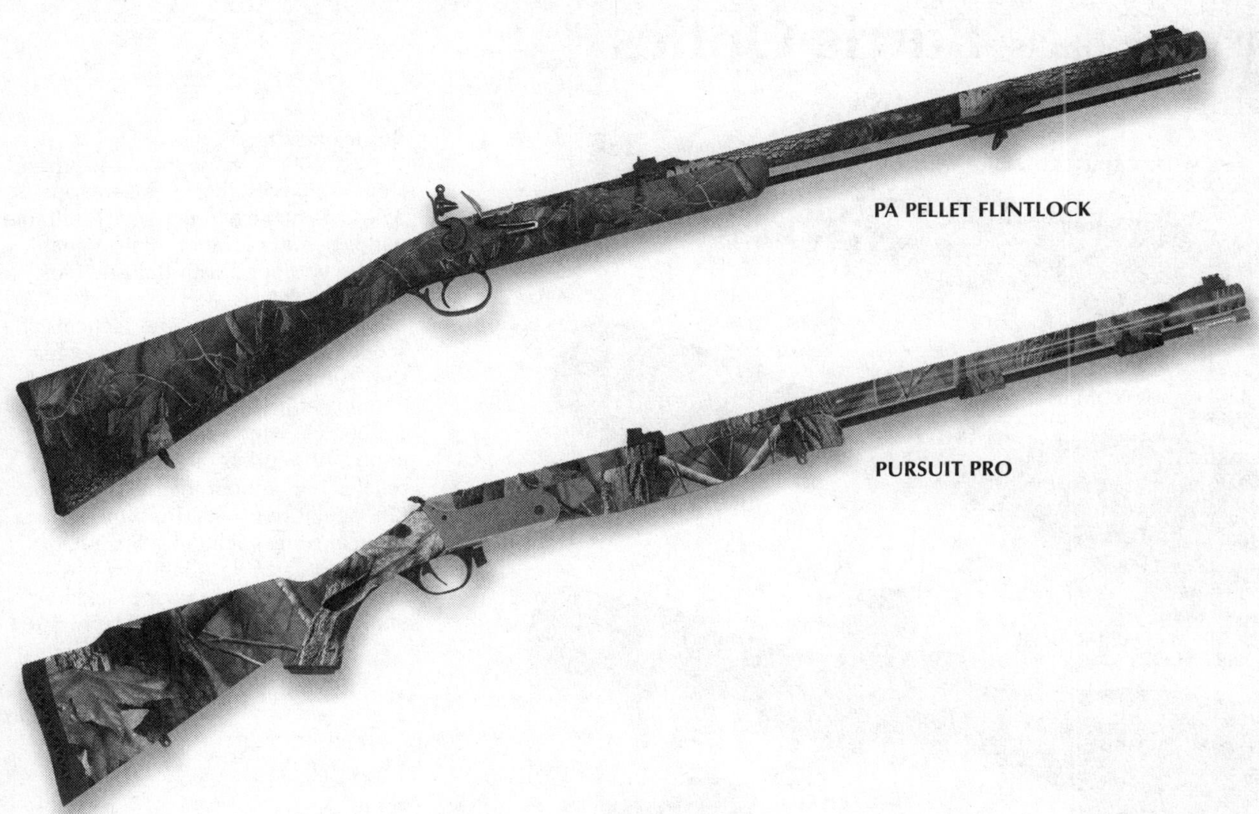

PA PELLET FLINTLOCK

PURSUIT PRO

PA PELLET FLINTLOCK

Lock: flint
Stock: synthetic
Barrel: 24 in.
Sights: TruGlo fiber optic
Weight: 7½ lbs.
Bore/Caliber: .50
Features: Camo finish
Price: $319

PURSUIT PRO

Lock: hinged breech
Stock: synthetic
Barrel: 28 in.
Sights: TruGlo fiber optic
Weight: 8½ lbs.
Bore/Caliber: .50
Features: Fluted barrel; camo finish
Price:. . . . . $345 to $389

NEW Products: **Aimpoint Optics**

Aimpoint's new Model 9000 offers twice as much dot time. Advanced Circuit Efficiency Technology reduces power demand, so batteries in the new Aimpoint 9000 lasts 50,000 hours. That's with brightness set on 7 on a dial numbered to 10. The 9000 series comprises three models, and you can choose a 2-minute or 4-minute dot.

NEW Products: **Burris Optics**

3-9X SHORT MAG SCOPE

4.5-14X SHORT MAG SCOPE

3-12X XTREME TACTICAL RIFLE SCOPE

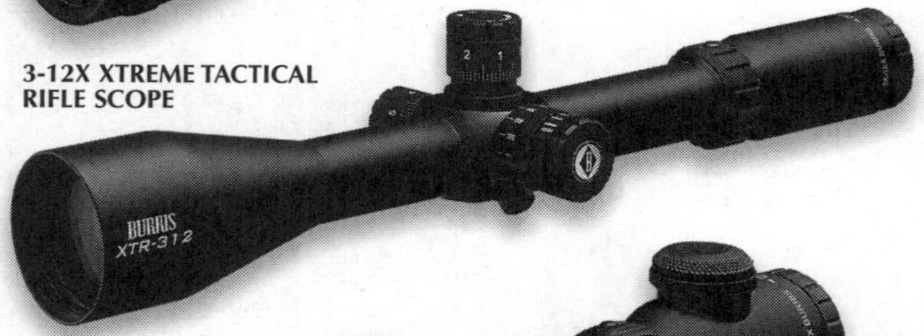

1.5-6X SIG LRS

3X10 SIG LRS

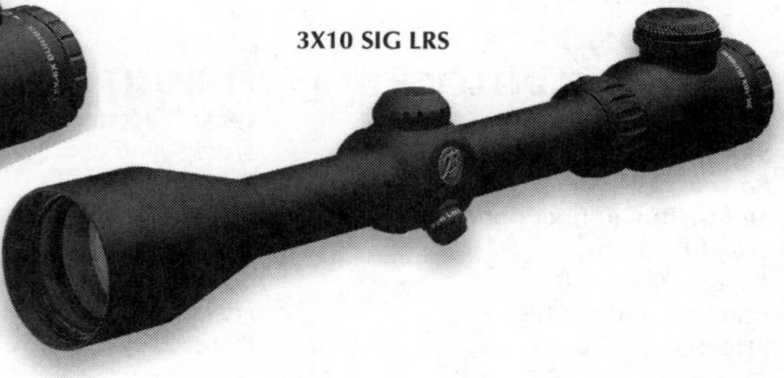

Burris offers new "Short Mag" scopes: 1x, 4x, 2-7x, 3-9x and 4.5-14x. These short-coupled sights have generous 3½- to 5-inch eye relief and re-settable windage and elevation dials. Variables can be equipped with Ballistic Plex reticles.

The new Burris Xtreme Tactical Rifle scopes in 1.5-6x, 10x and 3-12x feature 30mm tubes with side-mounted parallax adjustments and steel-on-steel target-style windage and elevation knobs. All models offer illuminated reticles but without the bubble of the LRS ocular housings. The Burris Tactical series includes a SpeedDot sight and Laser flashlight you can mount on the rail of your black gun.

Short Mag Scopes . . . . $316 to $581

NEW Products: **Bushnell Optics**

ELITE 3200 4-12

HOLOSIGHT XLP

Bushnell offers two new Elite 4200 scopes—a 1.5-6x36 and a 2.5-10x50. Elite scopes come with RainGuard lens coating that breaks up water droplets so you can see clearly through a wet lens. Bushnell's 3200 line now boasts a 7-21x40 Varmint scope with front AO sleeve, fast-focus eyepiece and 3.7 inches of eye relief. Another 3200, the 3-10x40, is a versatile sight for hunters. In the Legend line, you'll find a 4-12x40 with front AO. The Banner Super 17 AO scope includes a bullet drop compensator for 17-caliber bullets. Bushnell's new 1x28 Red/Green Dot Trophy scopes offer a red or green dot, 3 MOA or 10 MOA, a crosswire or a circle-dot. An alternative for hunters who kick the thickets for whitetails is the new HOLOsight. It's lighter in weight, lower in profile and now uses AAA batteries.

Bushnell's rangefinder series includes the new Elite 1500. It has a 7x eyepiece, 26mm objective with RainGuard lens coating. Powered by a 9-volt battery, it can determine distance to 1500 yards.

3200 SCOPES

7-21x40. . . . . $298
7-21x $550

ELITE 4200

1.5-6x36 . . . . $604
2.5-10x50 . . . . $748
HOLOsight $300
Legend 4-12x40 . . . . $266
Banner Super 17 AO $134
Elite 1500 Rangefinder $574

NEW Products: **Kahles Optics**

CL HELIA 3-9X42

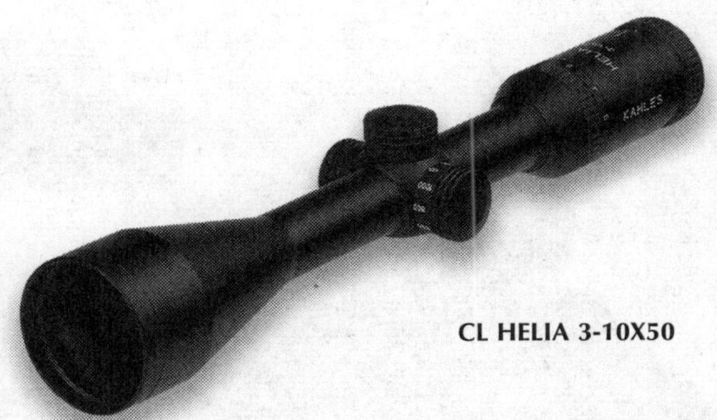

CL HELIA 3-10X50

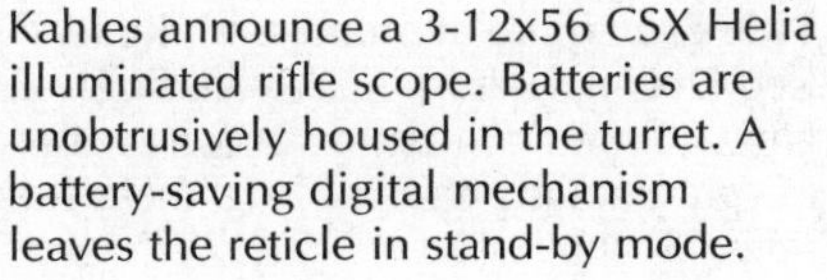

Kahles announce a 3-12x56 CSX Helia illuminated rifle scope. Batteries are unobtrusively housed in the turret. A battery-saving digital mechanism leaves the reticle in stand-by mode. Touch the dial and the reticle instantly brightens to the level you set before. The 56mm objective on this scope brings total weight to just under 19 ounces.

NEW Products: Kahles Optics

NEW PRODUCTS

CL HELIA 4-12X52

CSX HELIA 1.5-6X42

The latest Kahles scope series is called CL, for Compact Light. The turret-mounted "AO" dial refines focus and eliminates parallax error. Kahles CL scopes are available in three configurations: 3-9x42, 3-10x50 and 4-12x52. Manufactured in Austria, these sights are assembled at the company's U.S. headquarters in Cranston, Rhode Island. They will retail for a little more than the AV scopes.

3-12x56 CSX Helia illuminated rifle scope: $1954

NEW Products: Legacy Sports International Optics

NIKKO-STERLING GOLD CROWN 4X32

NIKKO-STERLING GOLD CROWN 3-9X42

NIKKO-STERLING REFLEX RED DOT SIGHTS 40MM

Legacy introduces three Gold Crown riflescopes from Nikko-Sterling optics this year: 4x32, 4x32 AO and 3-9x42. All three 1-inch scopes feature multi-coated lenses, plex reticles, and fast-focus eyepieces. They come with flip-up scope covers and list for under $70! Even more affordable are Reflex Red Dot sights from Nikko-Sterling. New 30mm and 40mm versions with integral mounts have 11 brightness settings, 5 MOA dots.

FX-II 2.5X28
FX-II 6X36
FX-III 6X42
MARK 4 1.5-5X20
MARK 4 3.5-10X40 LRT M1
VX-1 2-7X28 RIMFIRE

After many years of success with M8s, Leupold is improving the series. The new 4x is called the FX-II 4x33 and weighs 9.3 ounces. The lenses have Multicoat 4 coatings. Coin-slotted quarter-minute click adjustments replace traditional friction-fit dials. The FX-II is available in matte finish or gloss, with wide Duplex or standard Duplex reticle and 4 inches of eye relief! The new 10-ounce FX-II 6x36 offers the same improvements but comes with Leupold Dot and Post & Duplex reticles. Leupold's other new 6x is the 11-ounce FX-III 6x42 with a matched-lens system. A 15-ounce competition model features target knobs and adjustable objective. For longer shots, there's an FX-III 12x40 target scope with adjustable objective. Trim and lightweight at just 13 inches and 13 ounces, this is an ideal sight for "walking varmint rifles." The 6.5-ounce FX-II Ultralight 2.5x20 is lighter than some iron sights and delivers a 40-foot field of view at 100 yards. There's also an FX-II Scout scope, designed for forward mounting on the likes of Ruger's 77 Frontier. Leupold has added FXII 2x20 and 4x28 pistol scopes to its line as well.

Leupold's 2005 catalog lists a new VX-1 2-7x28 Rimfire scope with fine Duplex reticle and short-range parallax setting, friction dials and the multicoating once used on Vari-X II lenses. There's a VX-II 9x33 EFR for rimfires too. Handgunners can now buy a 2.5-8x32 Leupold VX-III. At 6 ounces, it has 18 inches of eye relief, finger-click adjustments and the index-matched optical coatings.

The company's Mark 4 scopes, designed for tactical use and law enforcement, include a couple of new 1.5-5x20 variables. The 1-inch "Precision" scope weighs less than 10 ounces. The 30mm Mid Range/Tactical scales 15. It offers a new reticle designed to permit fine aim at long range but with the speed of a Circle Dot. Another new Mark 4 listing is the 3.5-10x40 Long Range/Tactical. All Mark 4 scopes have Leupold's best lens coatings.

NEW Products: **Meade Optics**

The Simmons Master Series scopes are lighter, simpler and stronger than their predecessors. At 10.5 ounces, the 3-9x40 is lighter than most competitive models. There's up to 17 percent greater windage and elevation range, longer eye relief and a bigger "eye box" so you find targets quicker. Innovation on Master Series sights, however, is mostly where you can't see it. A slotted beryllium and copper ring fitted to the rear of the erector assembly holds the scope's internal lenses. The new biasing ring pre-loads the tube so it bears hard against the windage and elevation pegs, eliminating the need for biasing springs and solving several technical problems. Result: smoother, more predictable point of impact shift as you turn the dials, and no drag from the customary forward springs. The 3-9x40 Simmons Master lists $150.

At the January SHOT show, the company revealed a new Redfield scope, a notch up in price from the Simmons but with the same biasing ring. It will be available later in 2005.

NEW Products: **Nikon Optics**

BUCKMASTER 3-9X50

1200 LASER RANGEFINDER

Buckmasters scopes have a new look, with rounded objective housings and a quick-focus eyepiece. AO models have been stripped of the up-front sleeve and given a more convenient turret-mounted dial. In a fit of altruism, Nikon left the prices essentially the same as last year.

Nicon's top-ranked LX roof prism binoculars have been renamed LXLs. They're lighter in weight and feature lead-free, arsenic-free glass. A stickier rubber jacket makes them easier to grip. Nikon's has also added a 1200 laser rangefinder that sells for about $430. MAP for the Realtree version is $20 higher.

To perfectly align scope rings use a ring alignment tool. Just mount each half as you would a scope and line them up.

NEW Products: **Redfield Optics**

This year heralds the start of a new line of Redfields. Five new models include 3-15x52 and 5-25x52 scopes, both with 1-inch tubes. The 1.5-7x42, 4-20x56 and 6-30x56 feature 30mm tubes. All feature "five times" magnification ranges. The three Redfields with the highest magnifications wear adjustable objectives and ⅛-minute clicks. The other two models have ¼-minute detents. All the new Redfields have fully multi-coated optics and ED (extra-low dispersion) objective lenses. The fast-focus eyepiece gives you 4 inches of eye relief. External lens surfaces wear a HydroShield coat. Scopes come with a standard plex reticle and external black matte finish.

One of the most intriguing features of the new Redfield is its erector tube suspension. As in the Simmons Master Series scopes designed by Mark Thomas and Forrest Babcock, a slotted beryllium and copper ring is fitted to the rear of the erector assembly (the part that holds the scope's internal lenses). The ring is designed to compress, preloading the tube so it bears against the windage and elevation pegs. This design eliminates the need for biasing springs yields smoother, more predictable point of impact shift as you adjust windage and elevation.

Price: . . . . $550 to $800

3-15X52

NEW Products: **Sightron Optics**

S II 3.5-10X44 **S II 4.5-14X44** **S II 6.5-20X50**

Sightron is announcing three "SS" scopes with side-mounted parallax dials. The 3.5-10x44, 4.5-14x44 and 6.5-20x50. Plex, Dot and Mil Dot reticles are cataloged for the high-power models and the 3.5-10x comes with Plex or Mil Dot. SS scopes are fully multi-coated, waterproof and shipped with sunshades and dust covers.

A new 30mm S III-series 6-24x50 features greater adjustment latitude than do most 1-inch scopes of similar power. Select Plex, Dot or Mil Dot reticle. For whitetail and turkey hunters, Sightron has a new 2.5x32SG scope with more than 4 inches of eye relief. Sightron is also cataloging a hunting-size spotting scope. It comes with 25x and 20-60x eyepieces, plus a Cordura soft case zippered to allow quick access to the ends. The S II WP2060x63 scope is waterproof, camera-adaptable and fully multi-coated.

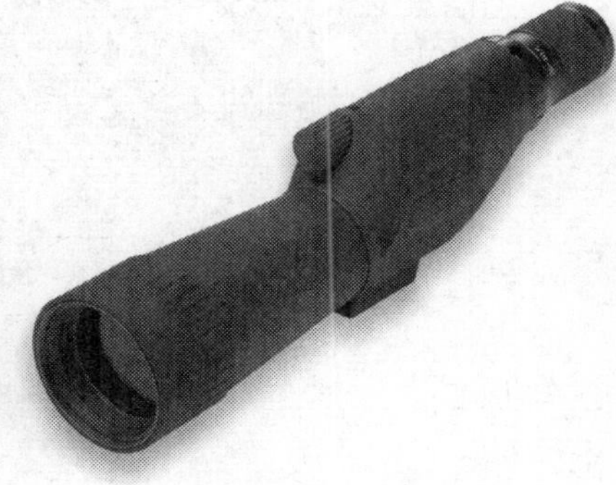

NEW Products: **Trijicon Optics**

Trijicon has announced several new items for 2005. TR22 2.5-10x56 AccuPoint is a battery-free illuminated scope with a 30mm tube and a delta-shaped, tritium-lit reticle. Fiber optic assist is adjustable. Trijicon will also bring to civilian shooters its ACOG (Advanced Combat Optical Gunsight). Developed for military use, the compact, rail-mounted ACOG has been adopted by the USMC.

NEW Products: **Weaver Optics**

Weaver has added the ETX spotting scopes, 48x90 and 73x125. They are relatively short, and are camera-adaptable. Magnification is right for long-range target shooting.

NEW Products: **Barnes Ammunition**

BANDED SOLIDS

EXPANDER MZ COMBO

Barnes X-Bullets have spawned the blue-jacketed XLC, coated to improve ballistic performance. For 2005, Barnes has essentially doubled the Triple-Shock line with 16 new bullets, from .224 to .458 in diameter.

Barnes has carried the driving-band design into its six new bluff-nosed solid bullets—two each in .375, .416 and .458. There's a 750-grain XLC bullet for the .577 Nitro, and two new Expander MZ bullets for muzzleloaders. Both the 245-grain and the 285-grain MZs are .50 caliber.

EXPANDER MZ BOX

NEW Products: **Brenneke Ammunition**

This year Brenneke brings back a traditional 1⅛-ounce, 12-gauge design with felt wad called the Classic. There's also the lead-free SuperSabot that's housed in a conventional plastic sleeve with integral wad. Another new slug, the Gold Magnum, comes in 3-inch 12-gauge ammunition. The 1⅜-ounce projectile has a yellow coating to reduce fouling.

NEW Products: **Hornady Ammunition**

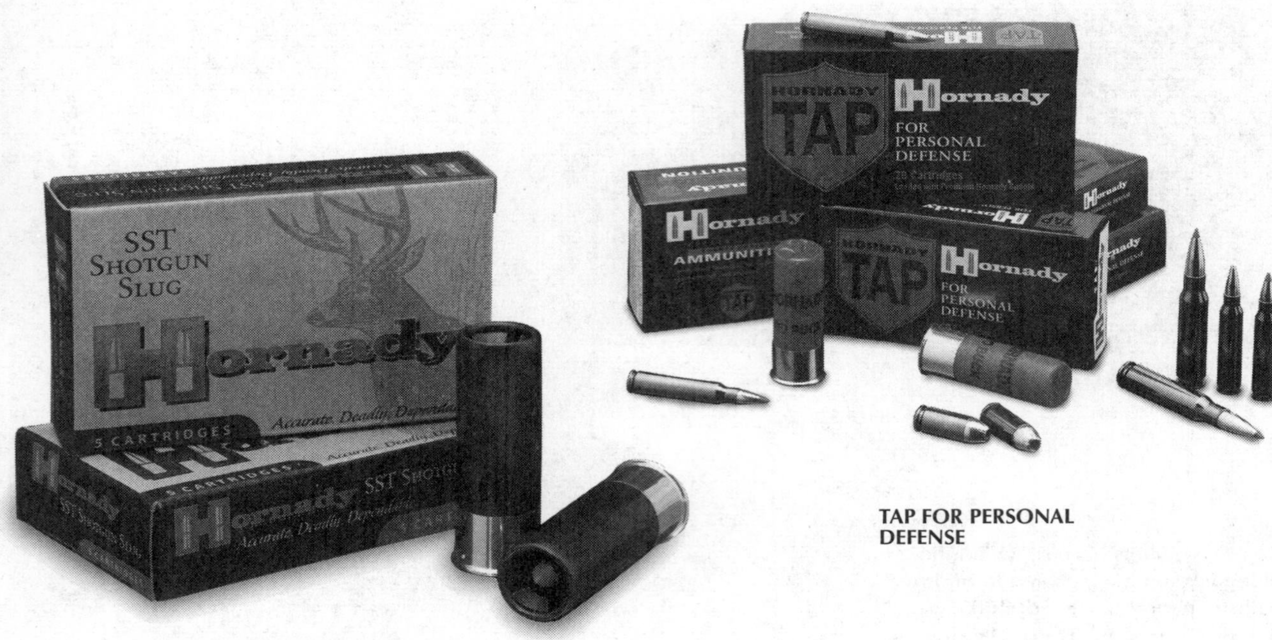

TAP FOR PERSONAL DEFENSE

SST SHOTGUN SLUG

Hornady's InterBond stable now includes three round-nose bullets: 300-grain .375, 400-grain .416 and 500-grain .458. The newest in the line of Polymer-tipped InterBond bullets is a 225-grain .338 spitzer. Hornady has added to its selection of hunting ammunition with SST bullets in 154-grain 7mm Remington Magnum and 180-grain .300 Weatherby Magnum loads. There's also a 195-grain SP load for the 8x57 JS. Handgunners get new options in .500 S&W ammo: 350- and 500-grain XTPs, with starting velocities of 1900 and 1425 fps. Hornady has also launched a new line of ammunition for personal defense. The TAP series includes 9mm, .40 S&W and .45 ACP ammo, .223 and .308 rifle loads and 12-gauge 00 buckshot rounds.

Borrowing from its successful Speed Sabot system for muzzleloaders, Hornady has used the big SST bullets in a loaded shotshell. The SST slug clocks 2,000 fps and delivers 2,664 ft-lbs. of energy.

NEW Products: **Kenny Jarrett Ammunition**

Shooters who know of Kenny Jarrett's legendary long range rifles will be itching for a look at Jarrett ammunition. The Baron of the Beanfield announced the high-performance cartridges last year but is just now rolling out the 10-round boxes. The cases are from Norma with Jarrett's headstamp. Calibers include .243, .270, 7mm Remington Magnum, .30-06, .300 Winchester Magnum, .300 Jarrett, .375 H&H and .416 Remington Magnum. Bullet options for each include Nosler Ballistic Tip and Swift A-Frame.

NEW Products: **Magtech Ammunition**

Solid copper hollowpoint bullets highlight new hunting ammunition from MagTech. Available in .44 Magnum, .454 Casull and .500 S&W, the new hunting cartridges deliver top-rung velocities with deep penetration and high weight retention. Choose a 200-grain .44 Magnum bullet at 1,296 fps, or 225- and 240-grain .454 loads at 1,640 or 1,771 fps. The .500 kicks a 325-grain bullet downrange at 1,801 fps. For more pleasant shooting, try a 275-grain bullet at 1,667. The MagTech line includes several new loads in 9mm, .38 Special, .357 Magnum, .380 Auto, .40 S&W and .45 Auto. Bullet types in the company stable range from semi-wadcutter lead to FMJ and jacketed hollowpoint.

SOLID COPPER HOLLOWPOINT

NEW Products: **Nosler Ammunition**

Now the Solid Base is back along with its stable mates in Federal ammunition. The firm has designed CT (Combined Technology) Partition Gold and now CT AccuBond bullets. Nosler's latest pioneering effort is not into different bullet designs but into ammunition. Beginning in 2005, the company started loading cartridges, in brass produced by a contractor with Nosler's headstamp and to Nosler's specifications.

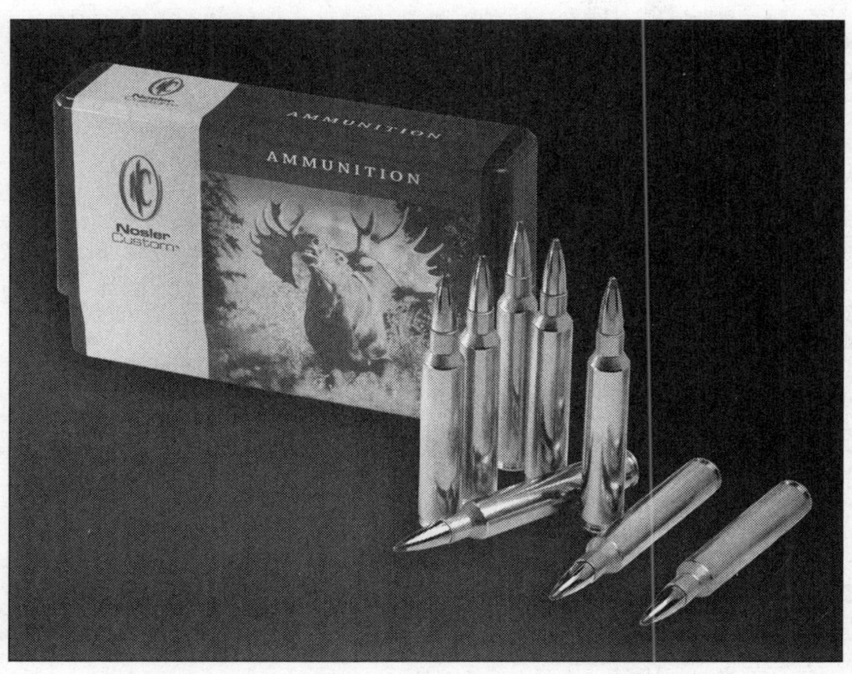

NEW Products: **Remington Ammunition**

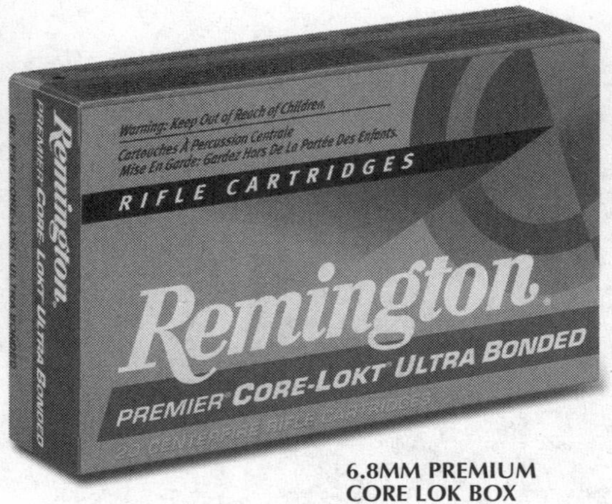

6.8MM PREMIUM
CORE LOK BOX

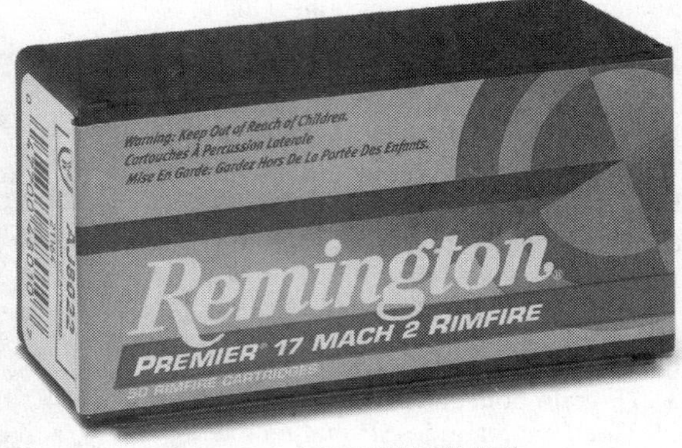

.17 MACH 2 AMMO

MANAGED-RECOIL BUCKHAMMER

6.8MM CARTRIDGE— AND ACCUTIP UPDATE

When the U.S. 5th Special Forces Group needed a round with more punch and reach than the .223 (5.56mm NATO), Remington engineers worked with Special Forces officers and the U.S. Army Marksmanship Unit to neck the .30 Remington case to 6.8mm (.277). The new cartridge is shorter than the .308 at 2.26 inches but adds 17 percent more capacity than the .223, exiting at 2800 fps to deliver an even ton of muzzle energy. The 6.8mm Remington SPC is also loaded with a 115-grain Sierra MatchKing or bonded Remington Core-Lokt bullets.

New Remington Premier Match offerings include the .223 (62-grain HP Match), .308 (168-grain MatchKing), .300 Winchester Magnum and .300 Remington Short Ultra Mag (both with 190-grain MatchKings). Remington has also replaced all its polymer-tipped bullets except the Swift Scirocco with its own AccuTip bullets, available in cartridges from the .17 Remington to the .300 Win. Mag. Remington is also offering 32- and 40-grain AccuTip bullets in the .204 Ruger cartridge. Competitive shooters will welcome the wind-resistant 69-grain Sierra MatchKing BTHP in .223 loads and rimfire shooters will now find .17 Mach 2 ammo in gold-and-green boxes.

NITRO PHEASANT

SHURSHOT PHEASANT

PHEASANT LOADS

SHOTGUN LOADS

For 2005, Remington has announced Nitro Pheasant loads with extra-hard Copper-Lokt plated shot (#4,5 and 6 shot at velocities as high as 1400 fps). The Power-Piston wad reduces flattening by setback and ensures uniform patterns with payloads ranging from 1-ounce 20-gauge to 1⅜-ounce 12. Remington BuckHammers are now available in a 3-inch, 20-gauge load that clocks 1,550 fps and delivers 2,470 ft-lbs of energy at the muzzle. Both 20-gauge loads feature 1-ounce BuckHammers.

Try shooting lighter loads in your turkey gun. Many times a high-velocity one-and-three-quarter ounce load will put more pellets where they count than heavier two-ounce loads.

NEW Products: **Sierra Ammunition**

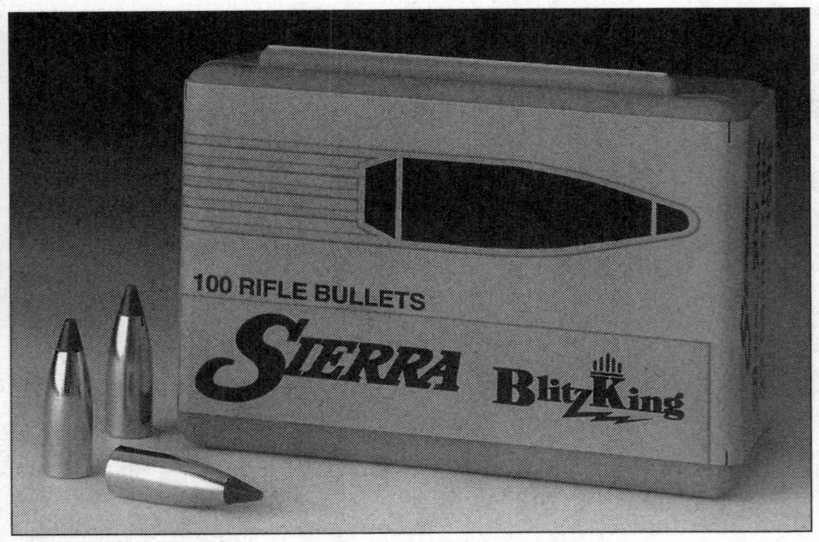

The success of Ruger's .204 cartridge may have been unexpected, but it's no longer being ignored. Ammunition and components are popping up far from the Hornady lab where the round was developed. Two of the latest bullets come in green boxes. Sierra now offers 32-grain and 39-grain BlitzKings for the .204. Given the reputation of MatchKing and GameKing bullets, no one will be surprised if these bullets show themselves to be extremely accurate. Or if they turn up in loaded ammunition under other labels.

NEW Products: **Winchester Ammunition**

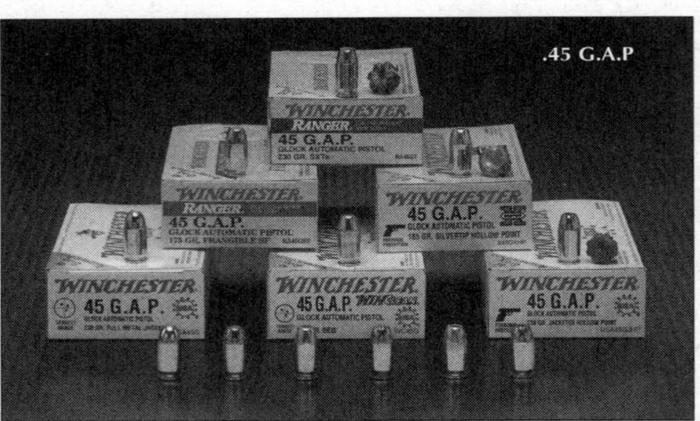

.45 G.A.P and .325 WSM ammunition. The .45 G.A.P. can fit in actions and magazine wells designed for the 9mm Luger, so pistols can be shorter and grips more compact to fit smaller hands. Winchester is offering four loads. Three of these feature bullets of 230 grains, traditional weight for military "hardball" ammo. In the economical USA line, an FMJ bullet at 850 fps will be joined by a JHP bullet at 880 fps and a non-toxic, completely jacketed bullet at 875. This latter "Winclean" cartridge includes a lead-free primer and is intended for target shooting in confined areas. Winchester's light-bullet load for the .45 G.A.P is a Super-X 185-grain Silvertip Hollow Point at 1000 fps.

RIFLES

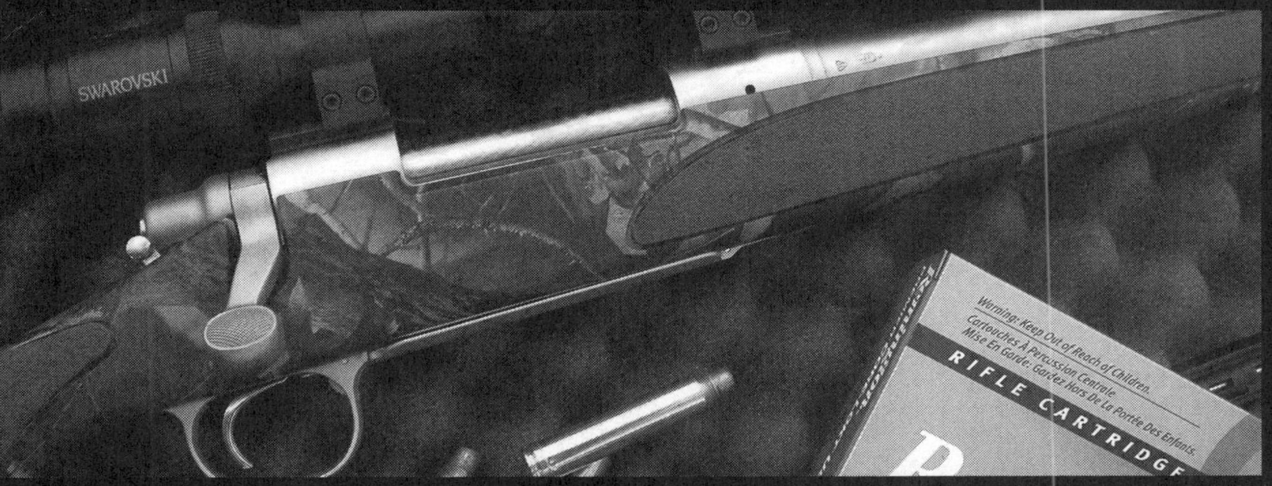
SWAROVSKI
Warning: Keep Out of Reach of Children.
Cartouches À Percussion Centrale.
Mise En Garde: Gardez Hors De La Portée Des Enfants.
RIFLE CARTRIDGE

Accu-Tek Rifles

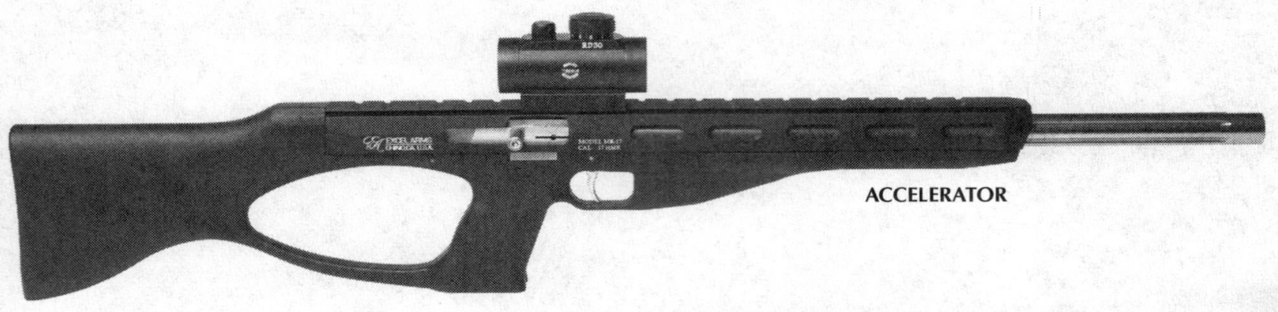
ACCELERATOR

ACCELERATOR RIFLE

Action: autoloading
Stock: synthetic
Barrel: 18 in.
Sights: none
Weight: 8
Caliber: 17 HMR, 22 WMR
Magazine: detachable box, 9 rounds
Features: Fluted stainless steel bull barrel; pistol grip stock; aluminum shroud with integral Weaver scope and sight rail; manual safety and firing pin block; last round bolt hold-open feature
MSRP: . . . . **$ 465**

RIFLES

Anschutz Rifles

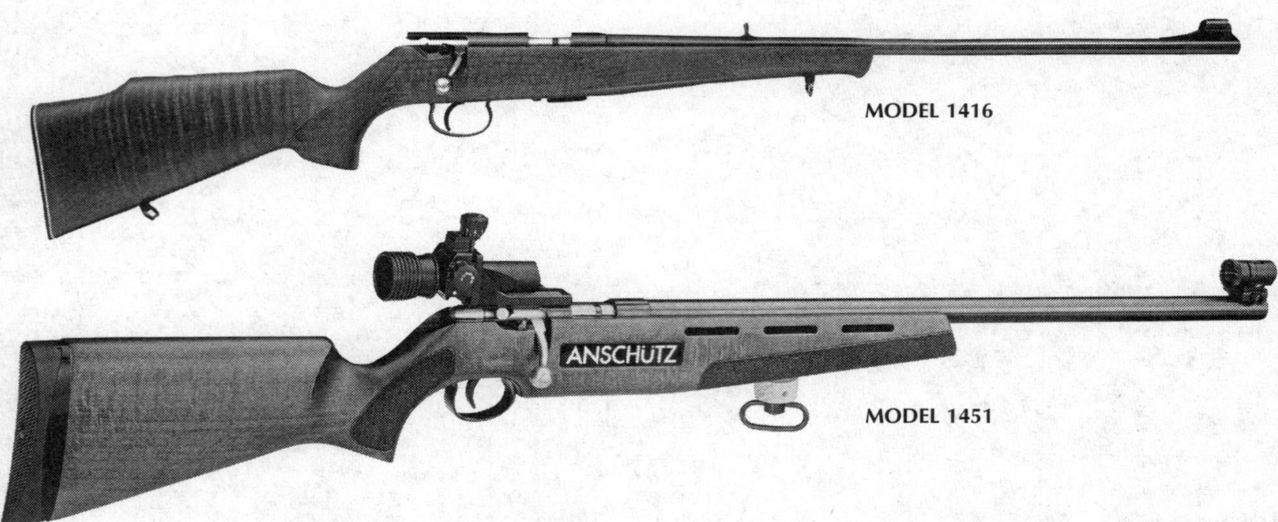

MODEL 1416

MODEL 1451

MODEL 1416

Action: bolt
Stock: checkered walnut
Barrel: 22 in.
Sights: open
Weight: 5.5 lbs.
Caliber: .22LR, .22 WMR
Magazine: detachable box, 5-round .22 LR, 4-round .22 WMR
Features: M64 action; 2-stage match trigger; stock available in classic or Monte Carlo
Classic: **$796**
Monte Carlo:. **$819**

MODEL 1451

Action: bolt
Stock: Sporter Target, hardwood
Barrel: heavy 22 in.
Sights: open
Weight: 6.3 lbs.
Caliber: .22 LR
Magazine: detachable box, 10-round
Features: M64 action
1451: **$515**

Anschutz Rifles

MODEL 1517

MODEL 1827 FORTNER

MODEL 1903

MODEL 1517

Action: bolt
Stock: walnut
Barrel: target-grade sporter, 22 in.
Sights: none
Weight: 6.0 lbs.
Caliber: .17 HMR
Magazine: 4
Features: M64 action, heavy and sporter barrels, Monte Carlo and Classic stocks available; target-grade barrel, adjustable trigger (2.5 lbs.)
Classic. $834
Monte Carlo $855

MODEL 1730 AND 1740 CLASSIC SPORTER

Action: bolt
Stock: sporter, walnut
Barrel: 23 in.
Sights: none
Weight: 7.3 lbs.
Caliber: .22 Hornet and .222
Magazine: detachable box, 5-round
Features: M54 action; Meister grade about $250 additional
1730 .22 Hornet, Monte Carlo $1729
1730 .22 Hornet with heavy barrel $1621
1740 .222 with heavy barrel. . $1621
1740 .222, Monte Carlo $1729

MODEL 1710

Action: bolt
Stock: walnut
Barrel: target-grade sporter, 22 in.
Sights: none
Weight: 6.7 lbs.
Caliber: .22 LR
Magazine: 5
Features: M54 action; two-stage trigger, Monte Carlo stock; silhouette stock available
Model 1710 . . . . $1469
with fancy wood $1743
Silhouette Model 1712 . . . . . . $1554

MODEL 1827 FORTNER

Action: bolt
Stock: Biathlon, walnut
Barrel: medium 22 in.
Sights: none
Weight: 8.8 lbs.
Caliber: .22 LR
Magazine: detachable box, 5 rounds
Features: M54 action
1827:. $1850
with thumbhole stock: $1940

MODEL 1903

Action: bolt
Stock: Standard Rifle, hardwood
Barrel: heavy 26 in.
Sights: none
Weight: 10.5 lbs.
Caliber: .22 LR
Magazine: none
Features: M64 action, adjustable cheekpiece, forend rail
1903: $690
left-hand: $730

Anschutz Rifles

MODEL 1907

MODEL 1912 SPORT

MODEL 2013 BENCHREST

MODEL 54.18 MS R "SILHOUETTE"

RIFLES

MODEL 1907

Action: bolt
Stock: Standard Rifle, walnut
Barrel: heavy 26 in.
Sights: none
Weight: 10.5 lbs.
Caliber: .22 LR
Magazine: none
Features: M54 action, adjustable cheekpiece and butt, forend rail
1907:. $1375
left-hand: $1475

MODEL 1912 SPORT

Action: bolt
Stock: International, laminated
Barrel: heavy 26 in.
Sights: none
Weight: 11.4 lbs.
Caliber: .22 LR
Magazine: none
Features: M54 action, adjustable cheekpiece and butt, forend rail
1912:. $1690
left-hand: $1785

MODEL 2013 BENCHREST

Action: bolt
Stock: Benchrest (BR-50) walnut
Barrel: heavy 20 in.
Sights: none
Weight: 10.3 lbs.
Caliber: .22 LR
Magazine: none
Features: M54 action
2013:. $1575

MODEL 54.18 MS

Action: bolt
Stock: Silhouette, walnut
Barrel: heavy 22 in.
Sights: none
Weight: 8.1 lbs.
Caliber: .22 LR
Magazine: none
Features: M54 action
54.18:. $1225

Armalite Rifles

AR-10A2 CARBINE

Action: autoloading
Stock: synthetic
Barrel: 16 in.
Sights: open
Weight: 9
Caliber: .308
Magazine: detachable box, 10 rounds
Features: forged A2 receiver; NM two stage trigger; chrome lined barrel; recoil check muzzle device; green or black synthetic stock
MSRP: **$1,383**

AR-10B

Action: autoloading
Stock: synthetic
Barrel: 20 in.
Sights: open
Weight: 9.5
Caliber: .308
Magazine: detachable box, 20 rounds
Features: multi-slot recoil-check muzzle device; M-16 style front sight base, single stage trigger (two stage NM optional); chrome lined barrel; forged aluminum upper receiver; M-16 style tapered handguards; AR-10 SOF with M4 type fixed stock
MSRP: **$1,635**

AR-10T AND AR-10A4 CARBINE

Action: autoloading
Stock: synthetic
Barrel: 24 in.; (Carbine: 16 in.)
Sights: open; (Carbine: none)
Weight: 10.4; (Carbine: 9)
Caliber: .308
Magazine: detachable box, 10 rounds
Features: forged flattop receiver; stainless T heavy barrel; carbine with chrome lined barrel and recoil check muzzle device; two stage NM trigger;
AR-10T: **$2,080**
AR-10A4 Carbine: **$1,383**

AR-10A4 SPR (SPECIAL PURPOSE RIFLE)

Action: autoloading
Stock: synthetic
Barrel: 20 in.
Sights: none
Weight: 9.6
Caliber: .308, 243 WIN
Magazine: detachable box, 10 rounds
Features: forged flattop receiver; chrome lined heavy barrel; optional recoil-check muzzle device; green or black synthetic stock; Picatinny rail sight base
MSRP: **$1,383**

Armalite Rifles

RIFLES

AR-30M RIFLE

Action: bolt
Stock: synthetic
Barrel: 26 in.
Sights: none
Weight: 12
Caliber: .300 WIN MAG, .308 WIN, .338 LAPUA
Magazine: detachable box
Features: Triple lapped match grade barrel; manganese phosphated steel and hard anodized aluminum finish; forged and machined removable buttstock; available with bipod adapter, scope rail and muzzle brake; receiver drilled and slotted for scope rail
MSRP:
.308 Win & .300 Win Mag: . . $1,372
.338 Lapua: $1,585

AR-50

Action: bolt
Stock: synthetic
Barrel: 31 in.
Sights: none
Weight: 35
Caliber: .50BMG
Magazine: none
Features: receiver drilled and slotted for scope rail; Schillen standard single stage trigger; vertically adjustable butt plate; vertical pistol grip; manganese phosphated steel and hard anodized aluminum finish; available in right or left handed version
MSRP: **. $2,745**

M-15A2, M-15A2 CARBINE AND M-15 NATIONAL MATCH RIFLE

Action: autoloading
Stock: synthetic
Barrel: 16 in., (M-15A2), 20 in., (M-15 A4) (T) 24 in.
Sights: open
Weight: 7 (Carbine); 8.27
Caliber: .223 REM
Magazine: detachable box, 10 rounds; 7 rounds (Carbine)
Features: forged A2 receiver; heavy, stainless, chrome lined floating match barrel; barrel; recoil check muzzle device; green or black synthetic stock; Carbine with M-16 style front sight base; National Match Rifle with NM two stage trigger and NM sleeved floating barrel; M-15 A4 (T) with flattop receiver, and tubular handguard
M-15A2: $1,023
M-15 A4 (T) 24 in. barrel: . . . $1,383
Carbine: $1,023
National Match Rifle: $1,435

M-15 A4 SPR II (SPECIAL PURPOSE RIFLE)

Action: autoloading
Stock: synthetic
Barrel: 20 in.
Sights: none
Weight: 9
Caliber: .308, 243 WIN
Magazine: detachable box, 10 rounds
Features: forged flattop receiver; NM sleeved floating stainless barrel; Picatinny rail; two stage trigger; green or black synthetic stock; Picatinny gas block front sight base
MSRP: **. $1,383**

Auto-Ordnance Rifles

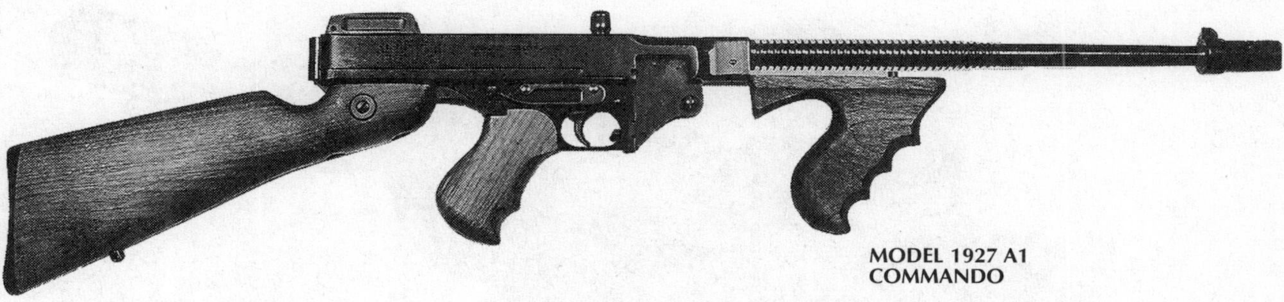

MODEL 1927 A1
COMMANDO

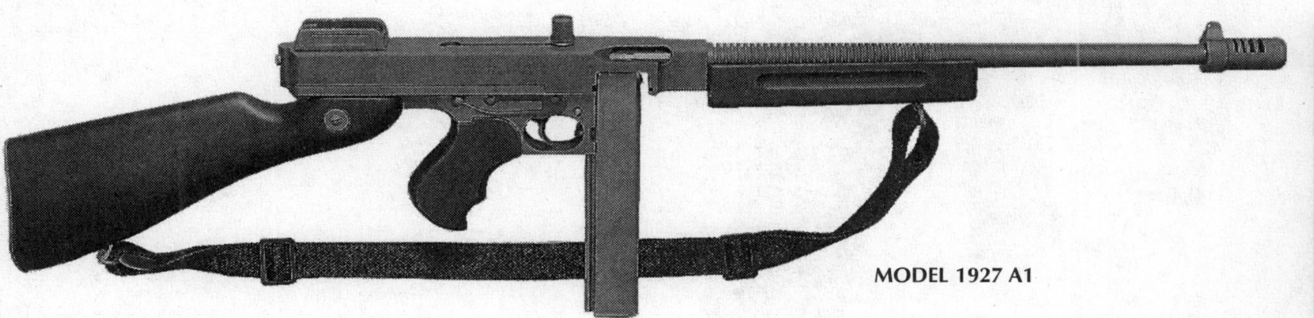

MODEL 1927 A1

RIFLES

AUTO-ORDNANCE RIFLES

This veteran design, the Thompson Submachine Gun, became famous during the "Roaring Twenties" and World War II. These replicas are legal autoloaders, not machine guns.

MODEL 1927 A1 COMMANDO

Action: autoloading
Stock: walnut, horizontal fore-grip
Barrel: 16 in.
Sights: open
Weight: 13.0 lbs.
Caliber: .45 ACP
Magazine: detachable box 20-round
Features: Top-cocking, autoloading blowback; carbine version with side-cocking lever, 11.5 lbs.
1927:. $1088
carbine:. $1041

MODEL 1927A1

Action: autoloading
Stock: walnut, vertical foregrip
Barrel: 16 in.
Sights: open
Weight: 13.0 lbs.
Caliber: .45 ACP
Magazine: detachable box, 20-round
Features: top-cocking, autoloading blowback; lightweight version 9.5 lbs.
standard:. $1109
lightweight:. $958

If you drop .22 cartridges on the ground or even on a shooting mat or the floor, wipe them off thoroughly before loading. Outside bullet lubricant picks up grit that can scour your bore.

Barrett Rifles

RIFLES

MODEL 468

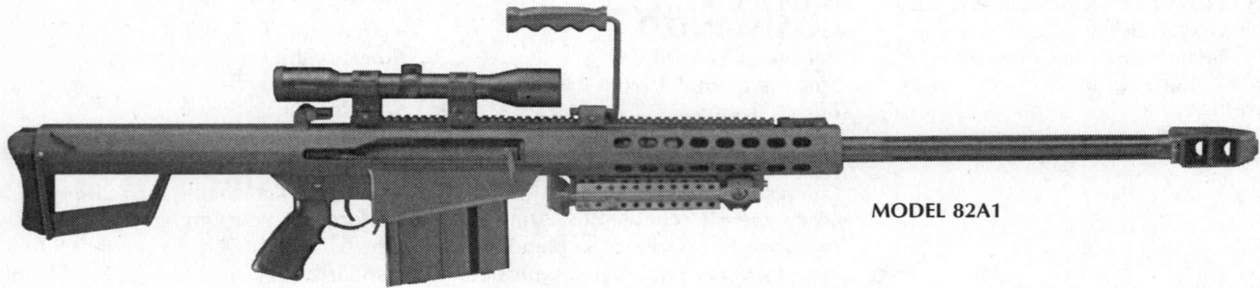

MODEL 82A1

MODEL 468

Action: semi-automatic
Stock: synthetic
Barrel: 16 in.
Sights: target
Weight: 7.3 lbs.
Caliber: 6.8 Rem SPC
Magazine: 5, 10, 30 round available
Features: two-stage trigger, muzzle brake
M468: . . . . price on request

MODEL 82A1

Action: autoloading
Stock: synthetic
Barrel: 29 in.
Sights: target
Weight: 28.5 lbs.
Caliber: .50 BMG
Magazine: 10
Features: Picatinny rail and scope mount, fluted barrel, detachable bipod and carrying case
82A1: . . . . price on request

Barrett Rifles

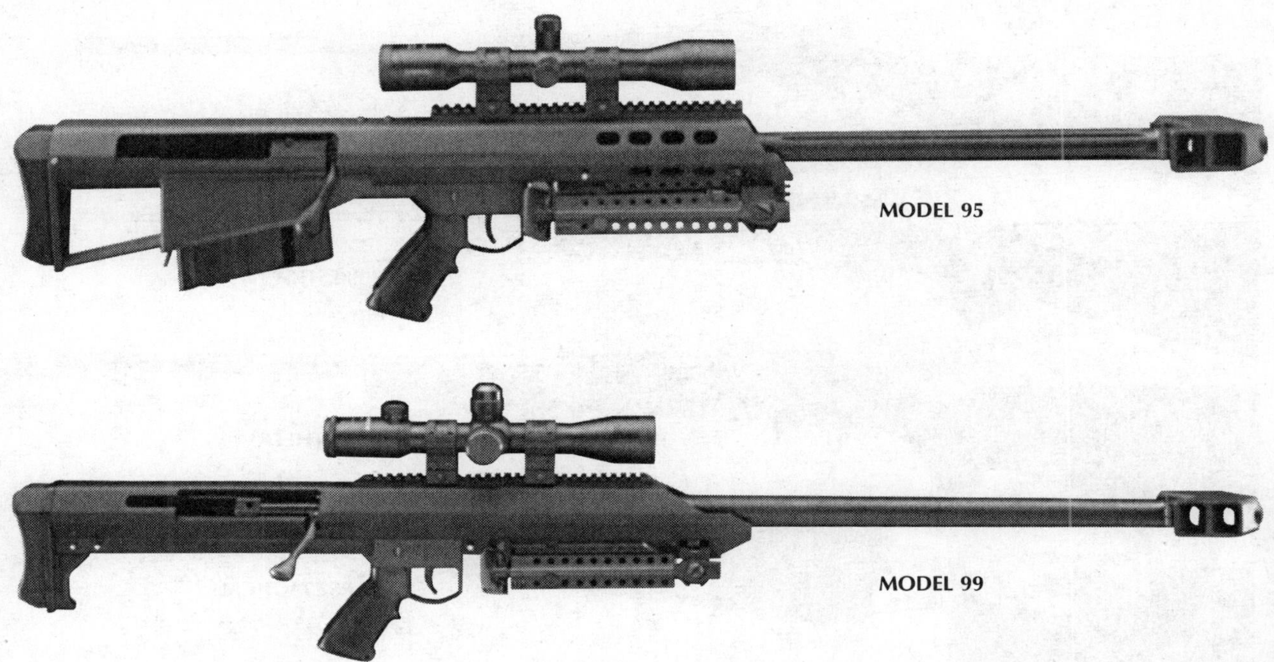

MODEL 95

MODEL 99

RIFLES

MODEL 95, MODEL 99

Action: bolt
Stock: synthetic
Barrel: 29 in. or 33 in. (M99)
Sights: none
Weight: 25.0 lbs.
Caliber: .50 BMG
Magazine: 5 (M95) or none (M99)
Features: Picatinny rail, detachable bipod, M95 has fluted barrel and weighs 22 lbs.
M95, M99 . . . . price on request

Benelli Rifles

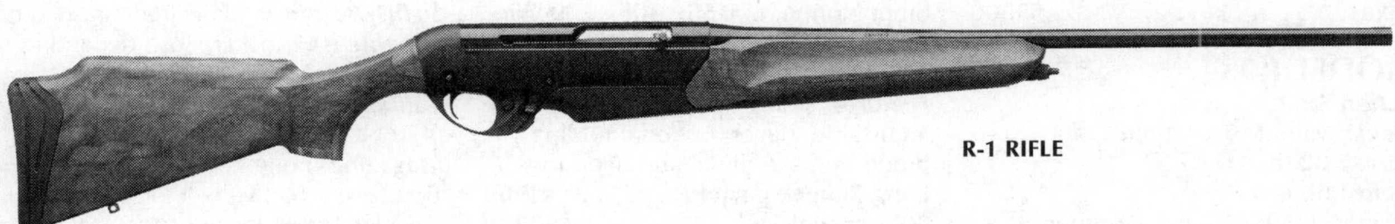

R-1 RIFLE

R-1 RIFLE

Action: autoloading
Stock: walnut
Barrel: 22 in. (Standard Rifle); 20 in. (Standard Carbine); 24 in. (Magnum Rifle), 20 in. (Magnum Carbine)
Sights: none
Weight: 7.1 lbs. (Standard Rifle); 7.0 lbs. (Standard Carbine); 7.2 lbs. (Magnum Rifle), 7.0 lbs. (Magnum Carbine)
Caliber: Standard 30-06; Magnum .300 Win. Mag.
Magazine: 3-4 shot detachable box
Features: auto-regulating gas-operated system; three lugged rotary bolt; select satin walnut stock; receiver drilled and tapped for scope mount; base included
Standard Rifle & Carbine $1065
Magnum Rifle & Carbine. $1080

Blaser Rifles

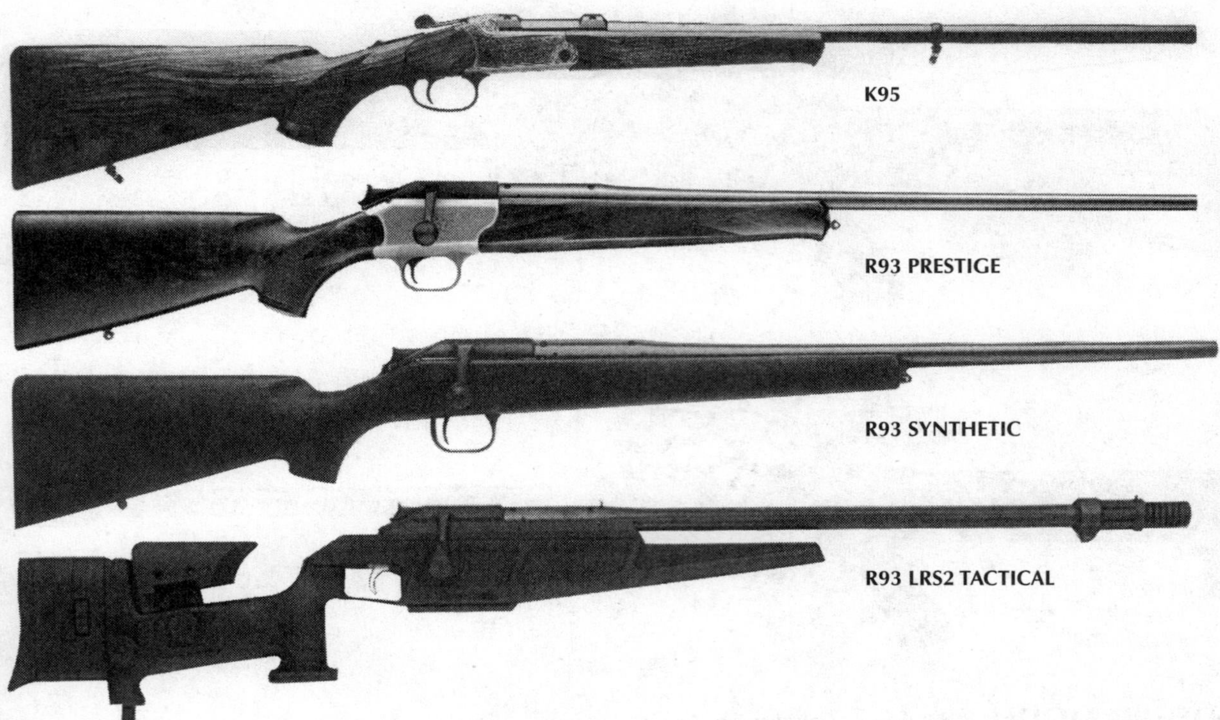

RIFLES

MODEL K95

Action: hinged breech
Stock: walnut
Barrel: 24 in. and 26 in. (magnum)
Sights: none
Weight: 5.5 lbs.
Caliber: .222, .22 Hornet, .25-06, .243, .270, .308, .30-06; magnum: 7mm Rem., .300 Win., .300 Wby.
Magazine: none
Features: easy takedown with no loss of zero; magnum calibers weigh 5.8 lbs.; Luxus has hand engraving on receiver
Prestige: $3300
Luxus: $3800

MODEL R93

Action: bolt
Stock: walnut or synthetic
Barrel: 22 in.
Sights: none
Weight: 6.5 lbs., 7 lbs. (Magnum)
Caliber: .22-250, .243, .25-06, 6.5x55, .270, 7x57, 7mm/08, .308, .30-06; Magnums: .257 Wby. Mag., 7mm Rem. Mag., .300 Win. Mag., .300 Wby. Mag., .300 Rem UM, .338 Win. Mag., .375 H&H, .416 Rem. Mag.
Magazine: in-line box, 5 rounds
Features: straight-pull bolt with expanding collar lockup; left-hand versions available, add $141
Prestige: $2600
Synthetic: $2000
Luxus: $3400
Attache $4800

MODEL R93 LONG RANGE SPORTER 2

Action: bolt
Stock: tactical composite
Barrel: heavy, fluted 26 in.
Sights: none
Weight: 8.0 lbs.
Caliber: .223 Rem., .243, .22-250, 6mm Norma, 6.5x55, .308, .300 Win. Mag., .338 Lapua Mag.
Magazine: in-line box, 5 rounds
Features: straight-pull bolt; fully adjustable trigger; optional folding bipod, muzzle brake and hand rest
Long Range Sporter: $2900
.338 Lapua: $3300

MODEL R93 LRS2 TACTICAL RIFLE PACKAGE

Action: bolt
Stock: synthetic tactical with adjustments
Barrel: heavy, fluted 26 in.
Sights: none
Weight: 10 lbs.
Caliber: .308, .300 Win. Mag., .338 Lapua
Magazine: in-line box, 5 rounds
Features: package includes bipod, sling, Leupold Tactical scope, mirage band, muzzle brake
Long Range Tactical: $4200
.338 Lapua: $5000

S2 SAFARI

Action: tilting block, double-barrel
Stock: select Turkish walnut, checkered
Barrels: 24 inches, gas-nitrated, sand-blasted, independent
Sights: open rear, blade front on solid rib
Weight: 10.1 to 11.2 lbs., depending on caliber.
Caliber: .375 H&H, .500/.416 NE, .470 NE, .500 NE
Magazine: none
Features: selective ejectors, Pachmayr Decelerator pad, snap caps, leather sling, Americase wheeled travel case, scope mount of choice
Price: (standard grade) $8500
(extra barrel set): $5300
Also available: S2 double rifle in standard chamberings, from .222 to 9.3x74R, 7.7 pounds.

Brown Precision Rifles

CUSTOM TEAM CHALLENGER

HIGH COUNTRY

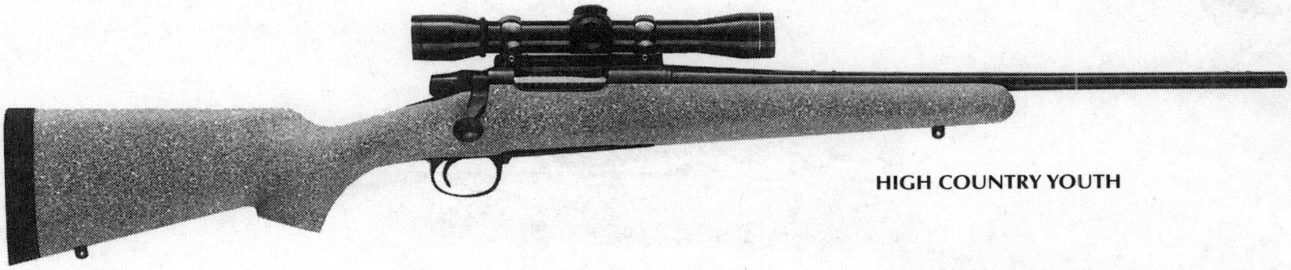

HIGH COUNTRY YOUTH

RIFLES

CUSTOM TEAM CHALLENGER

Action: autoloading
Stock: composite
Barrel: heavy Shilen match grade 18 in.
Sights: open
Weight: 7.0 lbs.
Caliber: .22 LR
Magazine: rotary, 10 rounds
Features: also available with stainless barrel
Team Challenger: $1595
stainless: $1695

HIGH COUNTRY

Action: bolt
Stock: composite classic stock
Barrel: choice of contours, lengths
Sights: none
Weight: 6.0 lbs.
Caliber: any popular standard caliber
Magazine: box, 5 rounds
Features: Remington 700 barreled action; tuned trigger; choice of stock colors and dimensions
High Country: $3495

HIGH COUNTRY YOUTH

Action: bolt
Stock: composite sporter, scaled for youth
Barrel: length and contour to order
Sights: none
Weight: 5.0 lbs.
Caliber: any popular standard short action
Magazine: box, 5 rounds
Features: Remington Model 700 or Model 7 barreled action; optional muzzle brake, scopes, stock colors and dimensions; included: package of shooting, reloading, and hunting accessories
Youth: $1895

"Swamping" was done by old-time gunmakers to give muzzle-loader barrels slightly greater diameter at the front end than in the middle, for a pendulum effect that steadied the rifle quickly.

Brown Precision Rifles

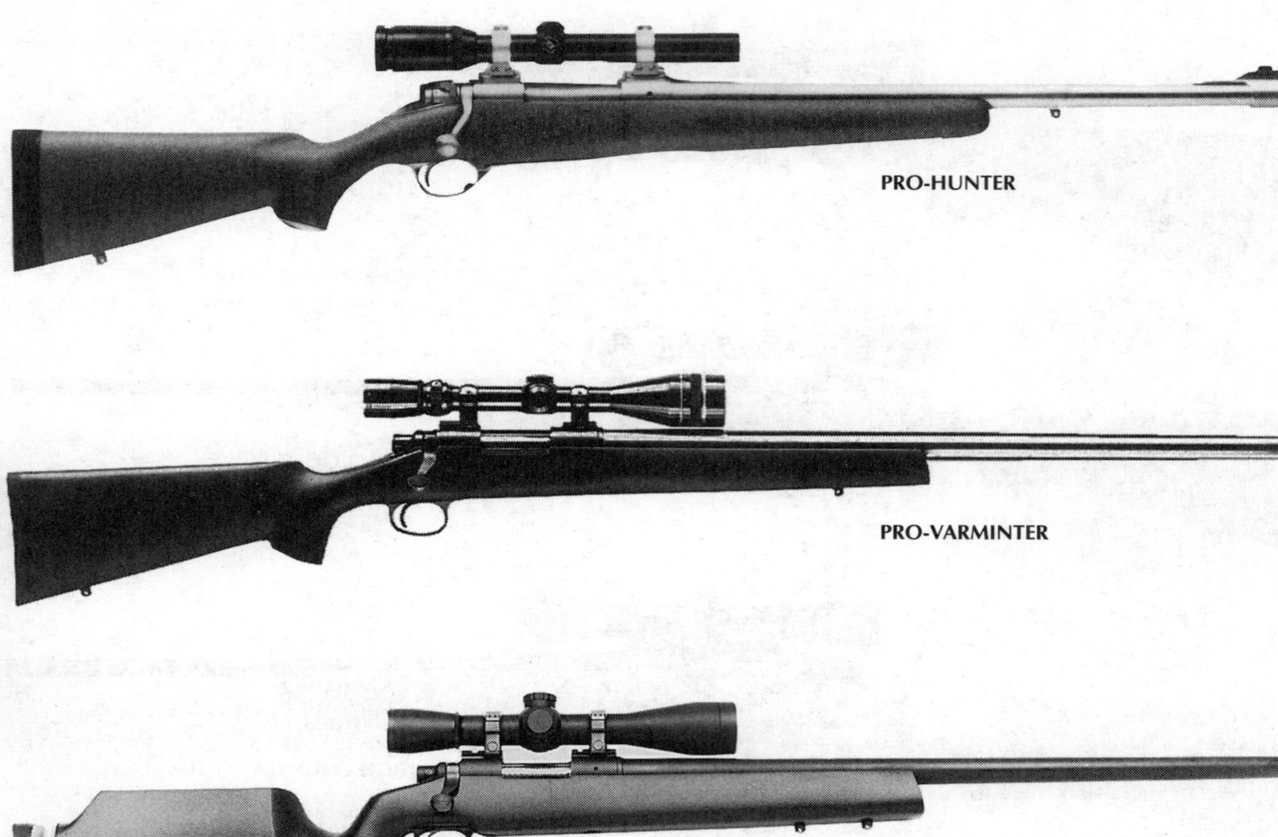

PRO-HUNTER

PRO-VARMINTER

TACTICAL ELITE

PRO HUNTER

Action: bolt
Stock: composite sporter
Barrel: Shilen match grade stainless
Sights: none
Weight: 8.0 lbs.
Caliber: any standard and belted magnum caliber up to .375 H&H
Magazine: box, 3 to 5 rounds
Features: Model 70 action with Mauser extractor; tuned trigger; optional Talley peep sight and banded ramp front sight or Talley mounts with 8-40 screws; optional muzzle brake, Mag-Na-Porting, Americase aluminum hard case
Pro Hunter:. $4295
in left-hand: $4395

PRO VARMINTER

Action: bolt
Stock: composite, varmint or bench rest
Barrel: heavy stainless match grade 26 in.
Sights: none
Weight: 9.0 lbs.
Caliber: all popular calibers
Magazine: box (or single shot)
Features: Remington 40X or 700 action (right or left-hand); bright or bead-blasted finish; optional muzzle brake; after-market trigger; scope and mounts optional
Model 700, right-hand:. $3295
Model 700, left-hand: $3595
Rem. 40X (with target trigger): $3895

TACTICAL ELITE

Action: bolt
Stock: composite tactical
Barrel: Shilen match-grade, heavy stainless
Sights: none
Weight: 9.0 lbs.
Caliber: .223, .308, .300 Win. Mag., (others on special order)
Magazine: box, 3 or 5 rounds
Features: Remington 700 action, Teflon metal finish; adjustable butt plate; tuned trigger; optional muzzle brakes, scopes
Elite: $3995

Browning Rifles

.22 SEMI-AUTOMATIC

A-BOLT HUNTER

A-BOLT ECLIPSE

A-BOLT HUNTER MEDALLION BOSS

A-BOLT WSSM MEDALLION

RIFLES

.22 SEMI-AUTOMATIC

Action: autoloading
Stock: walnut
Barrel: 19 in.
Sights: open
Weight: 5.2 lbs.
Caliber: .22 LR
Magazine: tube in stock, 11 rounds
Features: Grade VI has high grade walnut, finer checkering, engraved receiver
Grade I:. $535
Grade VI: $1145

A-BOLT HUNTER

Action: bolt
Stock: walnut
Barrel: 20 to 26 in.
Sights: none
Weight: 7.0 lbs.
Caliber: all popular cartridges from .22 Hornet to .30-06, including WSM's and WSSM's.
Magazine: detachable box, 4 to 6 rounds
Features: BOSS (ballistic optimizing shooting system) available; Micro Hunters weigh 6.3 lbs. with 20 in. barrel and shorter stock. Left-hand Medallion available. Eclipse thumbhole stock available with light or heavy barrel (9.8 lbs.) and BOSS.
Hunter: $705
Medallion:. $805
Medallion BOSS:. $936
Medallion, white gold:. . $1155-1183
Medallion, white gold BOSS: $1235-1263
Micro Hunter: . . . . $684 - 714
Eclipse Hunter: $1134

A-BOLT HUNTER MAGNUM

Action: bolt
Stock: walnut
Barrel: 23 and 26 in.
Sights: none
Weight: 7.5 lbs.
Caliber: popular magnums from 7mm Rem. to .375 H&H, including .270, 7mm and .300 WSM plus .25, .223 and .243 WSSMs.
Magazine: detachable box, 3 rounds
Features: rifles in WSM calibers have 23 in. barrels and weigh 6.5 lbs. WSSM have 22 in. barrels; BOSS (Ballistic Optimizing Shooting System) available; left-hand available.
Magnum:. $734
Medallion Magnum: $835
Medallion Magnum BOSS: $915
Eclipse Magnum:. $1086

Browning Rifles

A-BOLT STALKER

BAR

BAR SAFARI, BOSS, WALNUT

BLR LIGHTWEIGHT 81

RIFLES

A-BOLT STALKER

Action: bolt
Stock: synthetic
Barrel: 22, 23 and 26 in.
Sights: none
Weight: 7.5 lbs.
Caliber: most popular calibers and magnums, including .270, 7mm and .300 WSMs; and .25, .223 and .243 WSSMs.
Magazine: detachable box, 3 to 6 rounds
Features: BOSS (Ballistic Optimizing Shooting System) available; stainless option. Rifles in WSM calibers have 23 in. barrels and weigh 6.5 lbs.

Stalker:. $705-734
BOSS:. $785-835
Stainless :. $897-947
Stainless, BOSS:. $977-1027
Stainless, left-hand: $925-954
Stainless, left-hand, Boss:$1005-1034
Varmint Stalker:. $860-913

BAR

Action: autoloading
Stock: walnut or synthetic
Barrel: 20, 23, and 24 in.
Sights: open ***Weight:*** 7.5 lbs.
Caliber: .243, .25-06, .270, .308, .30-06, 7mm Rem. Mag., .300 Win. Mag., .270 WSM, 7mm WSM, .300 WSM, .338 Win. Mag.
Magazine: detachable box, 3 to 5 rounds
Features: gas operated; lightweight model with alloy receiver and 20 in. barrel weighs 7.2 lbs.; magnum with 24 in. barrel weighs 8.6 lbs. \BOSS (Ballistic Optimizing Shooting System) available; higher grades also available.

Lightweight Stalker: $883
WSM's: $964
Magnums:. $964
Safari (no sights): $889
Magnums:. $972
Safari, BOSS:. $988
WSM & Mag.:. $1071

MODEL BLR LIGHTWEIGHT 81

Action: lever
Stock: straight-grip walnut
Barrel: 20, 22 or 24 in.
Sights: open
Weight: 6.5 or 7.3 lbs.
Caliber: .22-250, .243, 7mm-08, .308, .358, .450 Marlin, .270, .30-06 (22 in.), 7mm Rem. Mag., .300 Win. Mag. (24 in.)
Magazine: 5 and 4 (magnums)
Features: short action, alloy receiver, front-locking bolt, rack-and-pinion action

BLR Lightweight $731
BLR Long Action $775
WSMs $802

BL 22

BUCK MARK

BL 22

Action: lever
Stock: walnut
Barrel: 20 or 24 in.
Sights: open
Weight: 5.0 lbs.
Caliber: .22 LR or .17 MACH2
Magazine: under-barrel tube, 15 rounds
Features: short stroke, exposed hammer, lever action; straight grip; also available in Grade II with fine checkered walnut.

Grade I:. $462
.17 MACH2. . . . . $484
Grade II:. $524
.17 MACH2 . . . . $546
With 24″ octagon bbl.: $726
.17 MACH2. . . . . $748
FLD Series (nickel receiver)
. . . . $494 - $577

BUCK MARK

Action: autoloading
Stock: laminate
Sights: open
Weight: 5.2 lb.s
Caliber: .22 LR
Magazine: detachable box, 10 rounds
Features: also in target model with heavy barrel

Sporter:. $572
Target, heavy barrel: $589
Classic Carbon (3.6 lbs.): $652

Moly-coating bullets decreases bore friction and may reduce copper fouling. It is no sure cure for poor accuracy and does not affect the terminal performance of the bullet.

Bushmaster Rifles

A2 CARBINE

AK A3 CARBINE

A3 20 INCH RIFLE

RIFLES

A2 CARBINE

Action: auto loader
Stock: polymer
Barrel: 16 in.
Sights: open, adjustable
Weight: 7.22
Caliber: 223 Rem. (5.56mm)
Magazine: detachable box, 10 rounds
Features: Lightweight forged aluminum receiver with M16A2 design improvements; heavy profile barrel with chrome-lined bore and chamber; M16A2 sight system; overall length 34.74 inches; manganese phosphate finish
MSRP: $985

A3 CARBINE, AK A3 CARBINE AND AK A2 RIFLE

Action: autoloader
Stock: polymer
Barrel: 16 in., 14.5 in, (AK A3 Carbine and Rifle)
Sights: open adjustable
Weight: 6.7, 7.33 (AK A3 Carbine and Rifle)
Caliber: .223 Rem. (5.56mm)
Magazine: detachable box, 10 rounds
Features: Forged upper and lower receivers with M16A2 design improvements; heavy-profile barrel with chrome lined bore and chamber; M16A2 sight system; overall length 34.75 inches; manganese phosphate finish; AK muzzle brake permanently-attached
A3 Carbine:. $1085
AK A3 Carbine: $1105
AK A2 Rifle: $1005

A2 AND A3 20-INCH RIFLES

Action: autoloader
Stock: polymer
Barrel: 20 in.
Sights: open, adjustable
Weight: 8.27
Caliber: 223 Rem. (5.56mm)
Magazine: detachable box, 10 rounds
Features: Forged aluminum receivers; A3 upper receiver with slotted rail; optional removable carry handle; military spec. heavy barrel with chrome lined bore and chamber; ribbed front handguard; M16A2 rear sight system; overall length 38.25 in. manganese phosphate finish;
A2 20 inch Rifle: $995
A3 20 inch Rifle: $1095
RealTree Grey Camo Rifle: . . . $1055

Bushmaster Rifles

A2 AND A3 .308 CALIBER CARBINES W/ SKELETON STOCK & IZZY BRAKE

Action: autoloader
Stock: polymer
Barrel: 16 in.
Sights: none
Weight:
Caliber: .308 Winchester
Magazine: detachable box, 20 rounds (accepts all FN-FAL types)
Features: Flat top forged aluminum upper receiver with Picatinny rail and ambidextrous controls for bolt and magazine release; heavy alloy steel barrel with Izzy muzzle brake; manganese phosphate finish
A2 Carbine: . . . . $ 1800
A3 Carbine: . . . . $ 1825

A2 .308 20INCH RIFLE

Action: autoloader
Stock: polymer
Barrel: 20 in.
Sights: open
Weight: 9.57
Caliber: 308 Winchester
Magazine: detachable box. 20 round (accepts all FN-FAL types)
Features: Heavy alloy steel barrel with Bushmaster's Izzy muzzle brake; forged aluminum receiver; integral solid carrying handle with M16A2 rear sight; overall length 42.75 in.
A2 .308 20-inch Rifle: . . . . . . $ 1810
A2 .308 w/ AK Brake: . . . . . . $ 1750

CARBON 15 TYPE 21 RIFLE

Action: autoloader
Stock: synthetic
Barrel: 16 in.
Sights: none
Weight: 4.0
Caliber: .223 Rem. (5.56mm)
Magazine: detachable box, 10 rounds (accepts all m16 types)
Features: Carbon fiber upper and lower receivers; anodized aluminum Picatinny rail; stainless match grade barrel; quick-detach compensator; overall length 35 inches.
MSRP: **. $ 916**

CARBON 15 TYPE 97 RIFLE

Action: autoloader
Stock: synthetic
Barrel: 16 in.
Sights: none
Weight: 3.9
Caliber: 5.56mm., 223 Rem.
Magazine: detachable box, 10 rounds (accepts all M16 types)
Features: Fluted, stainless steel match grade barrel with Quick-Detach compensator; upper receiver mounted with anodized aluminum Picatinny rail; overall length 35 in.
MSRP: **. . . . . $ 1039**

Bushmaster Rifles

M4 A2 CARBINE

VARMINTER

VARMINTER SPECIAL

V MATCH RIFLE

M4 TYPE CARBINE

Action: autoloader
Stock: polymer
Barrel: 16 in.
Sights: open adjustable
Weight: 6.59
Caliber: .223 Rem. (5.56 mm)
Magazine: detachable box, 10 rounds
Features: Forged aluminum receivers with M16A2 design improvements; M4 profile chrome lined barrel with permanently attached Mini Y Comp muzzle brake; M16A2 rear sight system; BATF approved, fixed position tele-style buttstock; manganese phosphate finish
MSRP: **$1065**

VARMINTER RIFLE

Action: autoloader
Stock: synthetic
Barrel: 24 in.
Sights: none
Weight: 8.75
Caliber: .223 Remington (5.56 mm)
Magazine: detachable box, 5 rounds; (accepts all M16 types)
Features: Free-floating fluted heavy DCM competition barrel; V Match tubular forend with special cooling vents and bipod stud; Bushmaster competition trigger; overall length 42.25 in.
MSRP: **$1245**

VARMINT SPECIAL RIFLE

Action: autoloader
Stock: synthetic
Barrel: 24 in.
Sights: none
Weight:
Caliber: .223 Rem. (5.56 mm)
Magazine: detachable box, 5 rounds
Features: Flat-top upper receiver with B.M.A.S. scope risers; lower receiver includes two stage competition trigger and tactical pistol grip; polished stainless steel barrel;
MSRP: **$1245**

V MATCH RIFLE AND CARBINE

Action: autoloader
Stock: synthetic
Barrel: 16 in. (Carbine), 20 or 24 in. (Rifle)
Sights: none
Weight: 6.9 (Carbine), 8.05 (Rifle)
Caliber: .223 Rem. (5.56mm)
Magazine: detachable box, 10 rounds
Features: Forged aluminum V Match flat-top upper receiver with M16A2 design improvements and Picatinny rail; heavy, chrome lined free floating barrel; front sight bases available in full sight or no sight versions; overall length 34.75 in
Carbine: **$1045**
Rifle: **$1055**

Bushmaster Rifles

XM15 E2S A2 20 INCH STAINLESS STEEL

A2 DISSIPATOR CARBINE WITH TELESTOCK

A3 DISSIPATOR CARBINE WITH TELESTOCK

16 INCH MODULAR CARBINE

RIFLES

XM15 E2S A2 20-INCH STAINLESS STEEL RIFLE

Action: autoloader
Stock: synthetic
Barrel: 20 in.
Sights: open
Weight:
Caliber: .223 Rem. (5.56 mm)
Magazine: detachable box, 5 rounds; (accepts all M16 types)
Features: Heavy configuration, match grade stainless barrel; available in either A2 or A3 (with removable carry handle) configurations
MSRP: **$1055**

A2 AND A3 DISSIPATOR CARBINES

Action: autoloader
Stock: polymer
Barrel: 16 in.
Sights: adjustable
Weight: 7.68
Caliber: .223 Rem. (5.56mm)
Magazine: detachable box, 10 rounds
Features: Lightweight forged aluminum receivers; manganese phosphate finished heavy profile barrel with chrome lined bore and chamber; ribbed full length Dissipator handguards; M16A2 sight system; removable carry handle; overall length 34.74 inches
A2 Dissipator $1040
with Telestock $1065
A3 Dissipator $1150
with Telestock $1175

16-INCH MODULAR CARBINE

Action: autoloader
Stock: synthetic
Barrel: 16 in.
Sights: open adjustable
Weight: 7.3
Caliber: .223 Rem. (5.56mm)
Magazine: detachable box, 10 rounds (accepts all M16 types)
Features: Forged aluminum A3 type flattop upper receiver; chrome-lined moly steel fluted barrel with milled gas block; A. B.M.A.S. four rail free-floater tubular forend with Picatinny rails; skeleton stock; ambidextrous pistol grip; overall length 34.5 in.
MSRP: **$1650**

Charles Daly Rifles

FIELD GRADE MAUSER

Action: bolt, Zastava Mauser
Stock: molded black polymer, classic style with cheekpiece, reverse checkering
Barrel: hammer-forged, chrome vanadium (also stainless), 22 inches (standard) and 24 inches (magnum).
Sights: none (drilled and tapped for scope mounts)
Weight: 7.5 and 7.8 lbs.
Caliber: .22-250, .243, .25-06, .270, .308, .30-06, 7mm Rem. Mag, .300 Win. Mag.
Magazine: box, capacity 5+1 (standard), 3+1 (magnum)
Features: fully adjustable trigger, long Mauser claw extractor

Price: (blue, standard). $459
(blue, magnum). $489
(stainless, standard). $549
(stainless, magnum). $579
Superior grade and
Superior mini $599
Superior magnum $629
Superior safari. $789

Chey Tac Rifles

7.62 SNIPER SYSTEM

.330 LAPUA

M-200

M310

RIFLES

7.62 SEMI-AUTOMATIC SNIPER SYSTEM

Action: autoloader
Stock: synthetic
Barrel: 20-26 in.
Sights: variable power optics/ electro-optics
Weight: 16
Caliber: 7.62x51mm
Magazine: detachable box, 5 – 20 rounds
Features: Flash/sound suppressor; picatinny type rail; adjustable trigger pull; maximum length 48 inches; accessories include, detachable bipod, hard transport/storage case, soft carrying case, cleaning/maintenance equipment and spotting scope; available in tan, gray-green, gray or taupe

.338 LAPUA MAGNUM RIFLE

Action: autoloader
Stock: synthetic
Barrel: 20-26 in.
Sights: none
Weight: 11.5 (carbon fiber barrel), 16 (steel barrel)
Caliber: .338 Lapua
Magazine: detachable box
Features: CNC machine matched upper & lower receivers; integral Picatinny rail; left sided, non-reciprocating changing handle; titanium firing pin; 3.5-lb. trigger pull; integrated buffer system; fully adjustable stock

.223/5.56 NATO RIFLE

Action: autoloader
Stock: synthetic
Barrel: 18-26 inches
Sights: none
Weight: 5.5 Lbs. (Carbon Fiber Barrel) 9.5 Lbs. (Steel Barrel)
Caliber: .223 / 5.56 mm
Magazine: detachable box
Features: CNC machine-matched upper & lower receivers; integral Picatinny rail; steel or carbon fiber barrel; titanium firing pin; 3.5-lb. trigger pull; frame: 20 inches

.300 WINCHESTER SHORT MAGNUM RIFLE

Action: autoloader
Stock: synthetic
Barrel: 20-26 inches
Sights: none
Weight: 7, 11.5 (carbon fiber barrel)
Caliber: .300 WSM
Magazine: detachable box
Features: CNC machine-matched upper & lower receivers; integral Picatinny rail; left-sided, non-reciprocating changing handle; 3.5-lb. trigger pull; integrated buffer system; adjustable, stock; frame: 21 inches

Christensen Arms Rifles

CARBON CHALLENGER THUMBHOLE

CARBON ONE CUSTOM

CARBON ONE HUNTER

CARBON RANGER

CARBON TACTICAL

RIFLES

CARBON CHALLENGER THUMBHOLE

Action: autoloading
Stock: synthetic or wood thumbhole
Barrel: graphite sleeved 20 in.
Sights: none
Weight: 4.0 lbs.
Caliber: .22 LR
Magazine: rotary, 10 rounds
Features: 10/22 Ruger action; custom trigger and bedding
Challenger: $1500
.22 Mag. $1850

CARBON ONE CUSTOM

Action: bolt
Stock: synthetic or wood sporter
Barrel: graphite sleeved 26 in.
Sights: none
Weight: 6.0 lbs.
Caliber: all popular magnums
Magazine: box, 3 rounds
Features: Remington 700 action; optional custom trigger
Custom:. $3650

CARBON ONE HUNTER

Action: bolt
Stock: synthetic
Barrel: graphite sleeved 26 in.
Sights: none
Weight: 7.0
Caliber: any popular
Magazine: box, 3 or 5 rounds
Features: Remington 700 action
Hunter: . . . . $1599 - $1999

CARBON RANGER

Action: bolt
Stock: retractable tactical skeleton
Barrel: graphite sleeved, up to 36 in.
Sights: none
Weight: 18.0 lbs.
Caliber: .50 BMG
Magazine: box, 5 rounds
Features: Omni Wind Runner action; custom trigger; guaranteed 5 shots in 8 in. at 1000 yds.
Ranger: $5500

CARBON TACTICAL

Action: bolt
Stock: synthetic
Barrel: graphite sleeved, 26 in.
Sights: none
Weight: 7.0 lbs.
Caliber: most popular calibers
Magazine: box, 3 or 5 rounds
Features: guaranteed accuracy ½ in. at 100 yards; optional custom trigger, muzzle brake
Tactical: $2750

Cimarron Rifles

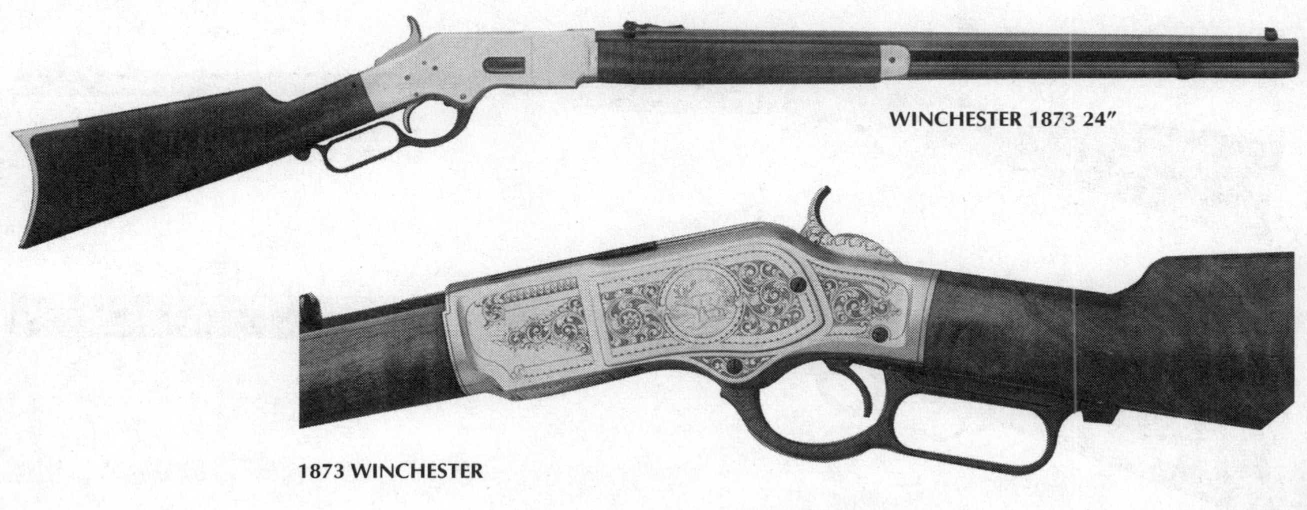

WINCHESTER 1873 24"

1873 WINCHESTER

1873 "DELUXE" SPORTING RIFLE

1885 HIGH WALL

1873 WINCHESTER

Action: lever
Stock: walnut, straight grip
Barrel: 24 in.
Sights: open
Weight: 7.5 lbs.
Caliber: .45 Colt, .44 WCF, .357, .32 WCF, .38 WCF, .44 Special
Magazine: under-barrel tube, 11 rounds
Features: Available: "Sporting" model, "Deluxe" model, "Long Range" model (30 in. barrel), and carbine (19 in. barrel); Deluxe model has pistol grip

Sporting: **$1149**
Deluxe: **$1214**
Long Range: **$1079**
Long Range Deluxe: **$1144**
Carbine: **$1025**

1885 HIGH WALL

Action: dropping block
Stock: walnut, straight grip
Barrel: octagon 30 in.
Sights: open
Weight: 9.5 lbs.
Caliber: .45-70, .45-90, .45/120, . 40-65, .38-55, .348 Win., .30-40 Krag
Magazine: none
Features: reproduction of the Winchester single shot hunting rifle popular in the 1880s

1885 Sporting: **$995**
1885 Deluxe: **$1175**

Synthetic stocks are sturdier than walnut, but not always lighter in weight. Choose one of carbon fiber and Kevlar, not injection-molded material. You'll pay more, carry less.

Cimarron Rifles

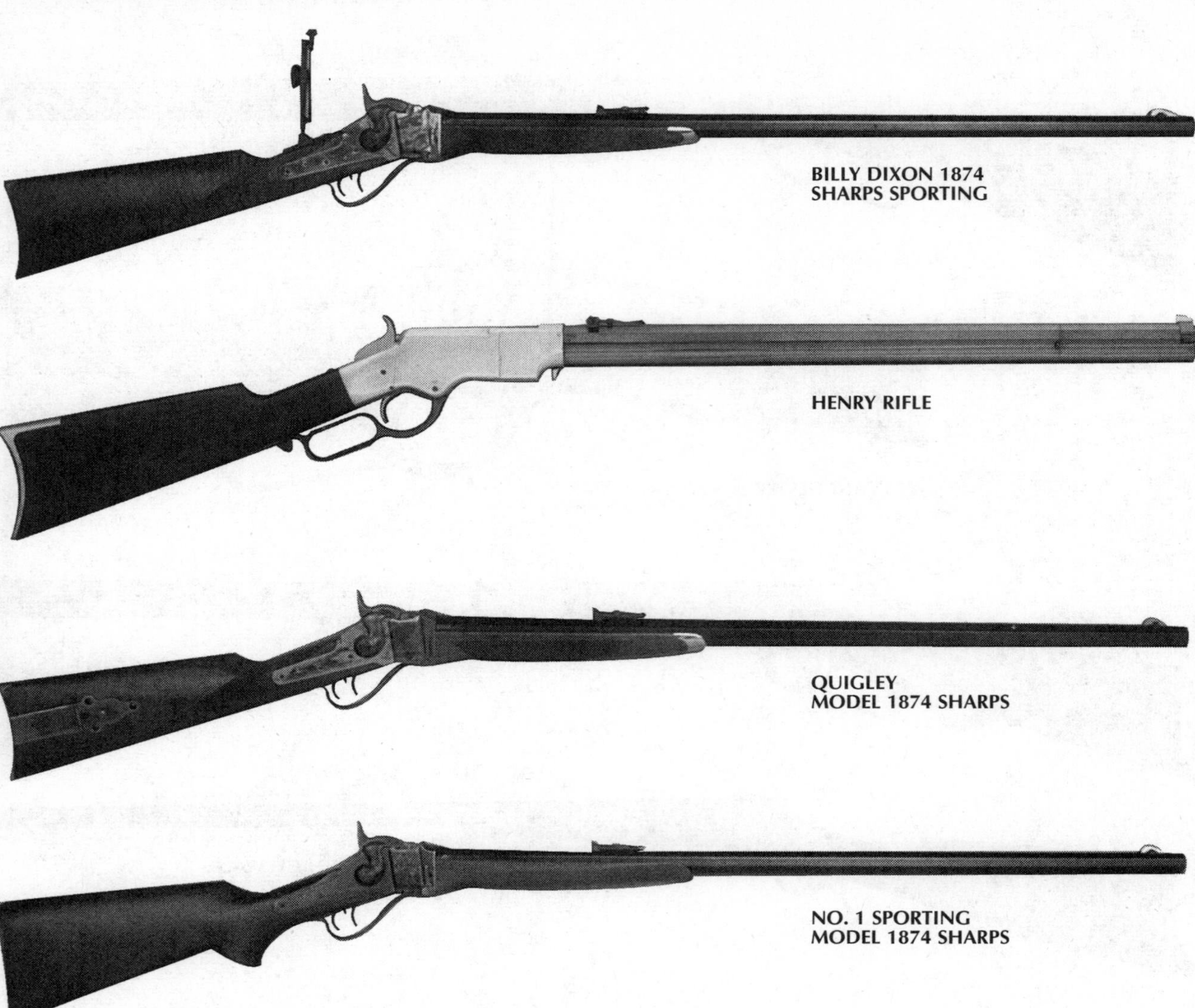

BILLY DIXON 1874 SHARPS SPORTING

Action: dropping block
Stock: walnut, straight grip
Barrel: octagon 32 in.
Sights: open
Weight: 10.5 lbs.
Caliber: .45-70, .45-90, .45-110, .50-90
Magazine: none
Features: Single-shot reproduction
Billy Dixon:. $1349

HENRY RIFLE

Action: lever
Stock: walnut, straight grip
Barrel: 24 in.
Sights: open
Weight: 7.5 lbs.
Caliber: .44 WCF, .45 LC
Magazine: under-barrel tube, 11 rounds
Features: replica of the most famous American rifle of the Old West
Henry:. $1149

QUIGLEY MODEL 1874 SHARPS

Action: dropping block
Stock: walnut, straight grip
Barrel: octagon 34 in.
Sights: open
Weight: 10.5 lbs.
Caliber: .45-70, .45-90, .45-120
Magazine: none
Features: single-shot reproduction
Quigley: $1430

NO. 1 SPORTING MODEL 1874 SHARPS

Action: dropping block
Stock: walnut, pistol grip
Barrel: 32 in. octagon
Sights: open
Weight: 10.5 lbs.
Caliber: .45-70, .50-70
Magazine: none
Features: single-shot reproduction; shotgun style buttplate; barrel features cut rifling, lapped and polished
No. 1 Sporting: $1350

Colt Rifles

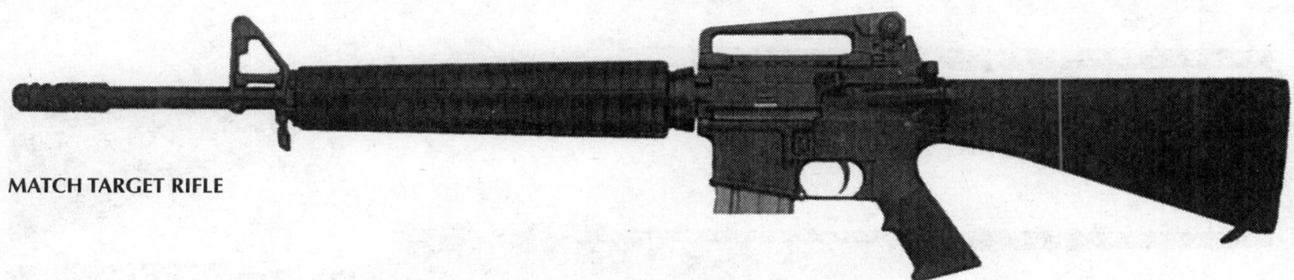

MATCH TARGET RIFLE

MATCH TARGET RIFLE

Action: autoloading
Stock: combat-style, synthetic
Barrel: 16 or 20 in.
Sights: open
Weight: 8.0 lbs.
Caliber: .223
Magazine: detachable box, 9 rounds
Features: suppressed recoil; accepts optics; 2-position safety; available with heavy barrel, compensator
Target:.................. $1300

Cooper Arms Rifles

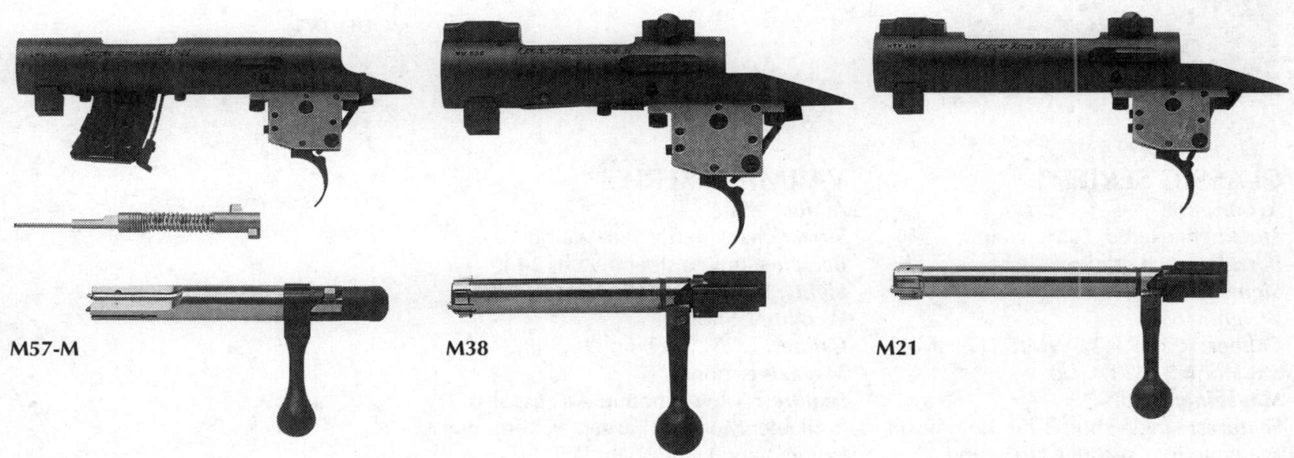

M57-M M38 M21

M57-M CALIBERS:

22LR, 22WMR, 17HMR

M38 CALIBERS:

.17 Ackley Hornet, .22 Hornet, .22 K-Hornet, .218 Bee, .218 Mashburn Bee

M21 CALIBERS:

.17 Rem, .17 Mach IV, Tactical 29, .221 Fireball, .222 Rem Mag, .223, .223 AI, .22 PPC, 6 PPC, .204 Ruger

M22 CALIBERS:

.22-250 Rem, .22-250 AI, .25-06 AI, .243 Win, .243 Win, .243 AI, 220 Swift, .257 Roberts, .257 AI, 7-08, 6mm Rem, 6x284, .22 BR, 6 BR, .308 Win, .20 Rem

M15 CALIBERS:

.223 WSSM, .243 WSSM

Cooper Arms Rifles

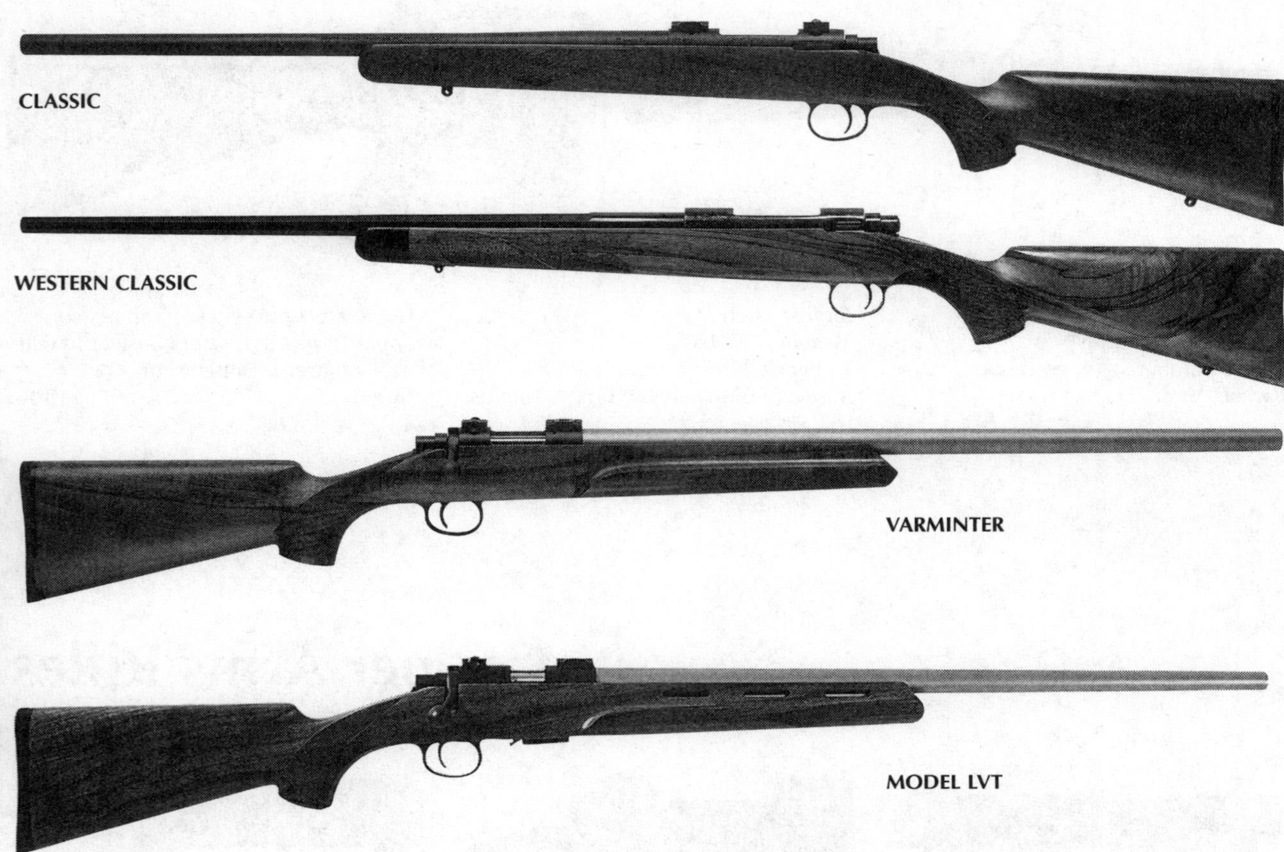

CLASSIC SERIES

Action: bolt
Stock: checkered, Claro walnut
Barrel: match grade 22 in.
Sights: none
Weight: 6.5
Caliber: .22 LR, .22 WMR, .17 HMR, .38 Hornet, .223, .308
Magazine: none
Features: single shot; 3-lug bolt; also available in: Custom Classic and Western Classic with upgraded wood
Classic: . . . . $1295 -1395
Custom Classic: $1995-2350
Western Classic:. $2595-2995

VARMINT SERIES

Action: bolt
Stock: checkered, Claro walnut
Barrel: stainless steel match, 24 in.
Sights: none
Weight: 7.5 lbs.
Caliber: .223, .38 Hornet, .308
Magazine: none
Features: 3-lug action in 4 sizes; also available: Montana Varminter, Varminter Extreme and Lightweight LVT
Varminter: $1095-1395
Montana Varminter:. . . . $1395-1595
Varminter Extreme: $1795-1995
LVT (.22 LR): $1395

CZ (Ceska Zbrojovka Uhersky Brod) Rifles

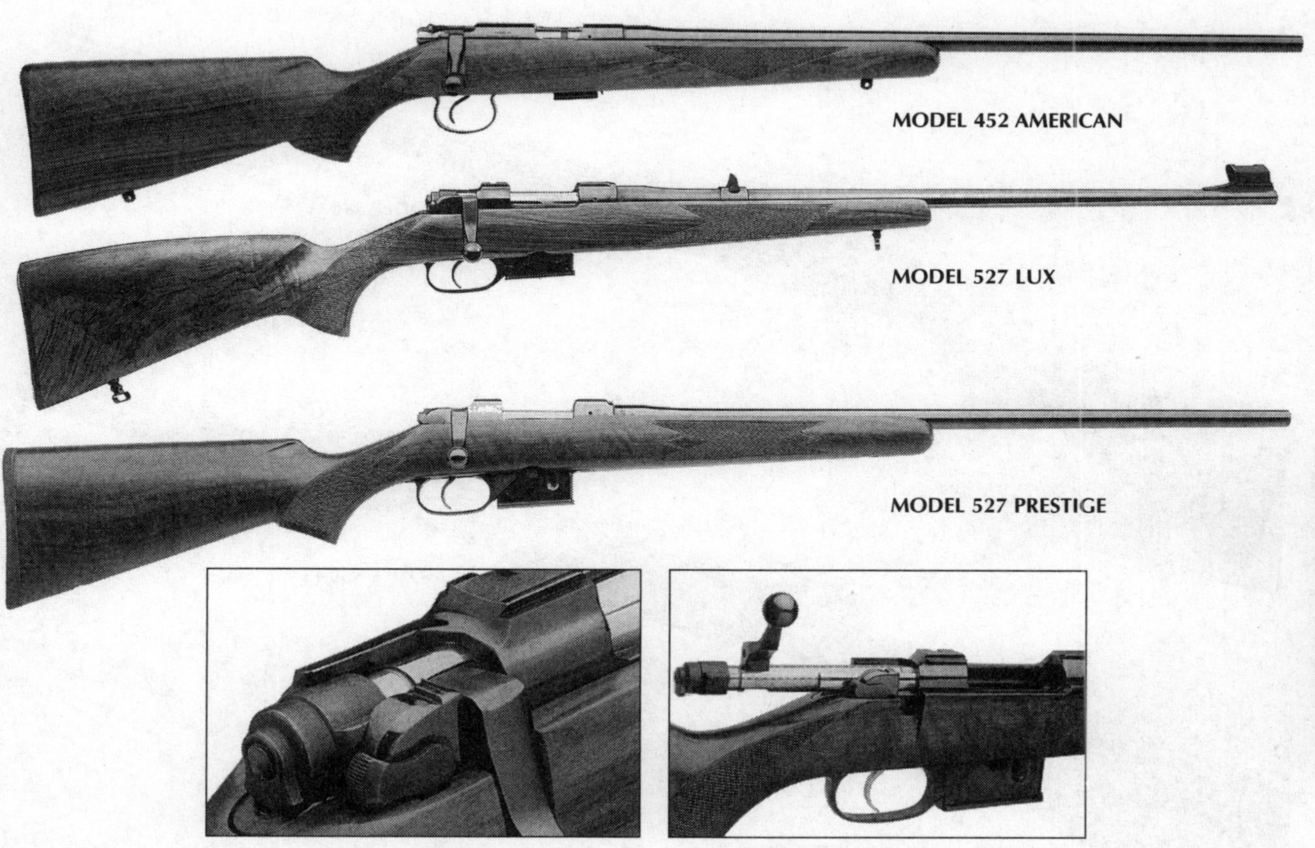

MODEL 452 AMERICAN

MODEL 527 LUX

MODEL 527 PRESTIGE

FINE MACHINING AND POLISHING ARE CZ TRADEMARKS

A SHORT-STROKE, LOW-LIFT BOLT AND DETACHABLE BOX MAGAZINE ARE DESIGNED FOR SMOOTH FEEDING.

RIFLES

MODEL 452 AMERICAN

Action: bolt
Stock: checkered walnut sporter
Barrel: 22 in.
Sights: none
Weight: 7.0 lbs.
Caliber: .22 LR, .17 HMR, .17 MACH2, .22 WMR
Magazine: detachable box, 5 rounds
Features: adjustable trigger; European-style stock and open sights; Varmint version has heavy 22 in. barrel. Youth Scout rifle has shortened stock, 16 in. barrel.

American and Lux, .22 LR: $389
.22 WMR. $419
.17 HMR $458
.17 MACH2. . . . . $433

MODEL 527

Action: bolt
Stock: checkered, walnut sporter
Barrel: 24 in.
Sights: open
Weight: 6.2 lbs.
Caliber: .22 Hornet, .222, .223
Magazine: detachable box, 5 rounds
Features: CZ 527 Carbine in .223, 7.62x39, CZ 527 full stock (FS) in .22 Hornet, .222 and .223 with 20 in. barrel and 527 Prestige in .22 Hornet and .223 with 22 in. barrel

American $599
Varmint. $597
Varmint Kevlar $799
Lux $599
Carbine: $606
FS:. $690
Prestige: $880

CZ (Ceska Zbrojovka Uhersky Brod) Rifles

MODEL 550

MODEL 550 FS

MODEL 550

Action: bolt
Stock: checkered walnut sporter
Barrel: 24 in.
Sights: open
Weight: 7.3 lbs.
Caliber: .243, 6.5x55, .270, 7x57, 7x64, .308, .30-06, 9.3x62
Magazine: box, 5 rounds
Features: adjustable single set trigger; detachable magazine optional; full-stocked model (FS) available; CZ 550 Safari Magnum has magnum length action, express sights in calibers: .375 H&H, .416 Rigby, .458 Win.

FS: **$705**
Safari magnum: **$875**
American **$623**
Prestige: **$854**
Medium Magnum **$690**

MODEL 550 VARMINT

Action: bolt
Stock: walnut
Barrel: heavy varmint 24 in.
Sights: open
Weight: 8.5 lbs.
Caliber: .308 Win., 22-250
Magazine: box, 5 rounds
Features: adjustable single set trigger, laminated stock optional; detachable magazine optional; also available: CZ 550 medium magnum in .7mm Rem. Mag. and .300 Win. Mag.

Varmint: **$652**
Varmint Laminate: **$749**
Medium Magnum: **$823**

Dakota Arms Rifles

MODEL 10 SINGLE SHOT

Action: dropping block
Stock: select walnut
Barrel: 23 in.
Sights: none
Weight: 5.5 lbs.
Caliber: from .22 LR to .375 H&H: magnum: .338 Win. to .416 Dakota
Magazine: none
Features: receiver and rear of breech block are solid steel; removable trigger plate
standard or magnum: $3995
barreled actions: $2150
action only: $1675

MODEL 76

Action: bolt
Stock: select walnut
Barrel: 23 to 24 in.
Sights: none
Weight: 6.5 lbs.
Caliber: Safari: from .257 Roberts to .458 Win. Mag. Classic: from .22-250 through .458 Win. Mag.(inc. WSM). African: .404 Jeffery, .416 Dakota, .416 Rigby, .450 Dakota
Magazine: box, 3 to 5 rounds
Features: three-position striker-blocking safety allows bolt operation with safety on; stock in oil-finished English, Bastogne or Claro walnut; African model weighs 9.5 lbs. and the Safari is 8.5 lbs.
Classic: $3995
Safari: $4995
African: $5795

MODEL 97 HUNTER

Action: bolt
Stock: walnut or composite
Barrel: 24 in.
Sights: open
Weight: 7.0 lbs.
Caliber: Hunter; .25-06 through .375 Dakota; Lightweight Hunter: .22-250 through .330; Varmint hunter: .17 Rem. through .22-250
Magazine: blind box, 3 to 5 rounds
Features: 1 in. black recoil pad, 2 sling swivel studs; Varmint model has #4 chrome-moly barrel, adjustable trigger, ½ in. black pad and weighs 8 lbs.
Hunter: $1995
97 with semi-fancy wood stock: $2495
action only: $1000
barreled action: $1300

Bonding a bullet's core to its jacket helps reduce core/jacket separation during upset, increasing penetration. Bonded bullets make sense for tough game, but generally aren't needed for deer.

Dakota Arms Rifles

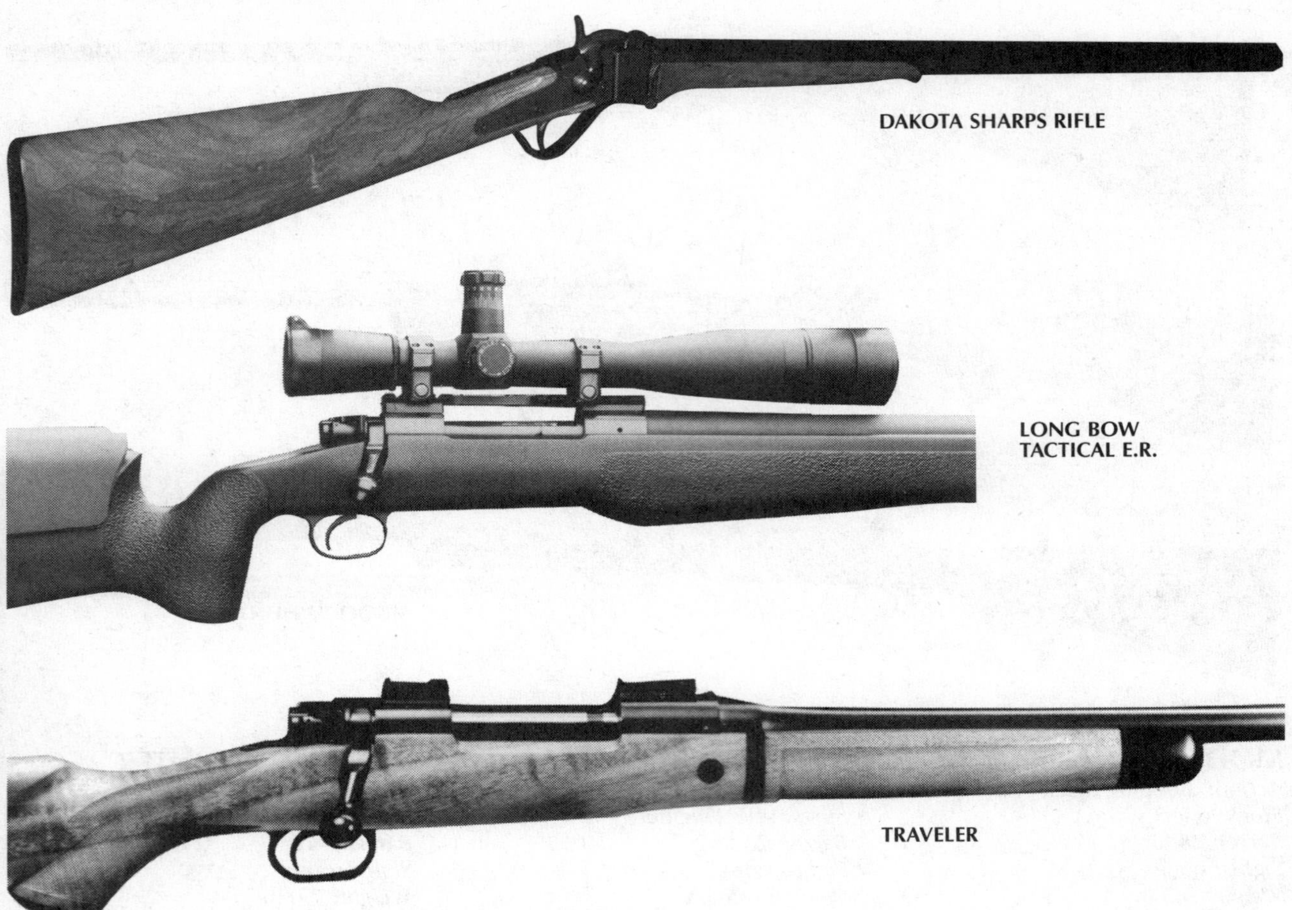

DAKOTA SHARPS RIFLE

LONG BOW TACTICAL E.R.

TRAVELER

RIFLES

DOUBLE RIFLE

Action: hinged breech
Stock: exhibition walnut, pistol grip
Barrel: 25 in.
Sights: open
Weight: 9.5 lbs.
Caliber: most common calibers
Magazine: none
Features: round action, elective ejectors, recoil pad, Americase
Double Rifle: $27,500

DAKOTA SHARPS RIFLE

Action: dropping block
Stock: walnut, straight grip
Barrel: octagon 26 in.
Sights: open
Weight: 8.0 lbs.
Caliber: .17 HRM to .30-40 Krag
Magazine: none
Features: small frame version of 1874 Sharps
Dakota Sharps: $3100

LONG BOW TACTICAL E.R.

Action: bolt
Stock: McMillan fiberglass, matte finish
Barrel: stainless, 28 in.
Sights: open
Weight: 13.7 lbs.
Caliber: .338 Lapua, .300 Dakota and .330 Dakota
Magazine: blind, 3 rounds
Features: Adjustable cheekpiece; 3 sling swivel studs; bipod spike in forend; controlled round feeding; one-piece optical rail; 3-position firing pin block safety; deployment kit; muzzle brake
Tactical E.R.: $4500
Action only: $2400

TRAVELER

Action: bolt
Stock: take-down, checkered walnut
Barrel: choice of contours, lengths
Sights: none
Weight: 8.5 lbs.
Caliber: all popular cartridges
Magazine: box, 3 to 5 rounds
Features: The Dakota Traveler is based on the Dakota 76 design. It features threadless disassembly. Weight and barrel length depend on caliber and version.
Classic: $4995
Safari: $5995
African: $6795

Dixie Rifles

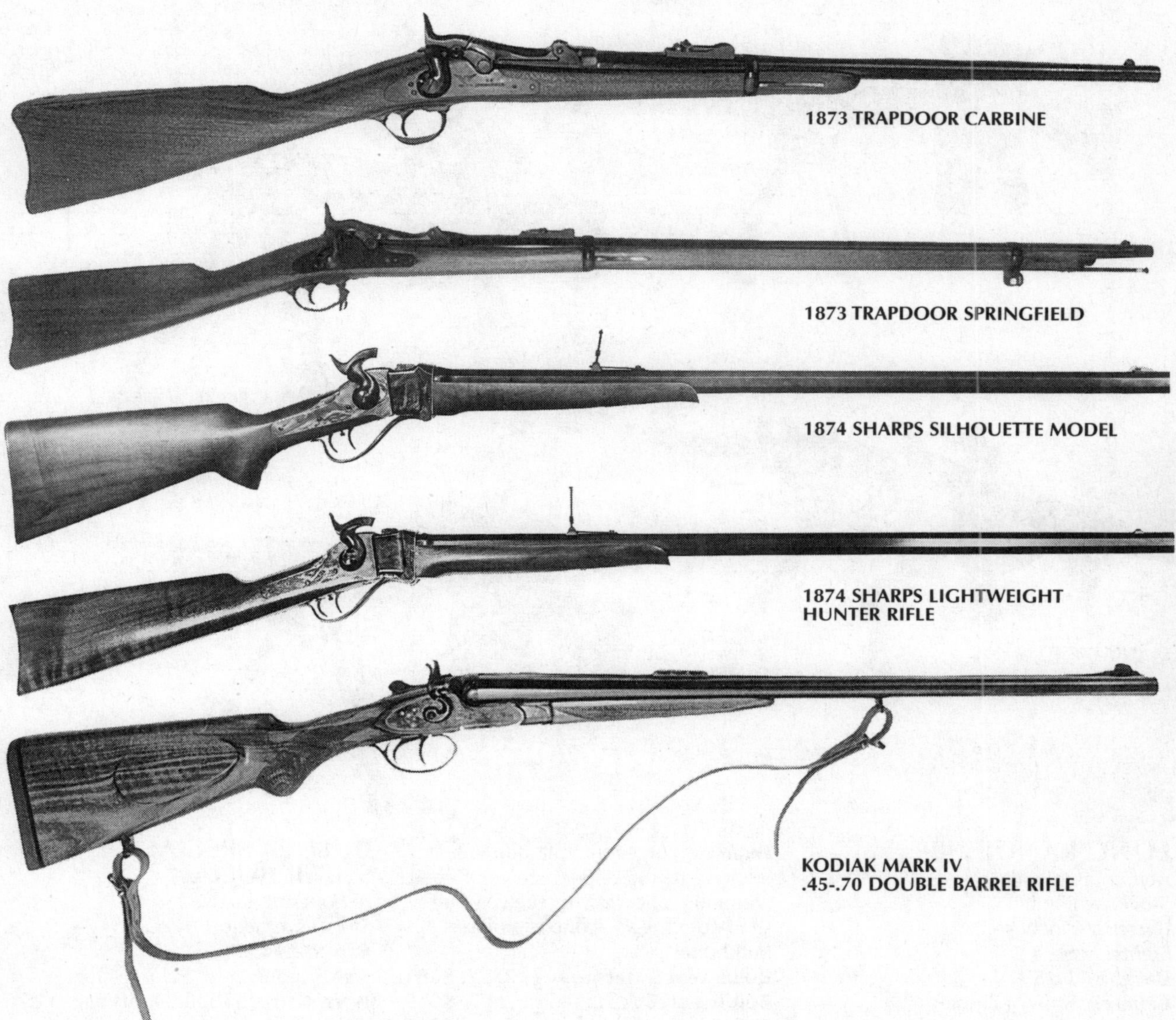

1873 TRAPDOOR CARBINE

1873 TRAPDOOR SPRINGFIELD

1874 SHARPS SILHOUETTE MODEL

1874 SHARPS LIGHTWEIGHT HUNTER RIFLE

KODIAK MARK IV .45-.70 DOUBLE BARREL RIFLE

RIFLES

1873 SPRINGFIELD "TRAPDOOR"

Action: hinged breech
Stock: walnut
Barrel: 26 or 32 in. (22 in carbine)
Sights: adjustable
Weight: 8.0 lbs.
Caliber: .45-70
Magazine: none
Features: single shot rifle, first cartridge rifle of U.S. Army; Officer's Model (26 in.) has checkered stock; weight with 32 in. Barrel: 8.5 lbs. and 7.5 lbs. for carbine

1873 Springfield "Trapdoor" . . . $940
Officer's Model $1125
Carbine $835

1874 SHARPS LIGHTWEIGHT HUNTER

Action: dropping block
Stock: walnut
Barrel: 30 in.
Sights: ajustable
Weight: 10.0 lbs.
Caliber: .45-70
Magazine: none
Features: case-colored receiver, drilled for tang sights; also 1874 Sharps Silhouette Hunter in .40-65 or .45-70

Hunter $1025
Silhouette $1075

KODIAK DOUBLE RIFLE BY PEDERSOLI

Action: hinged breech
Stock: walnut
Barrel: 24 in.
Sights: open, folding leaf
Weight: 10.0 lbs.
Caliber: .45-70
Magazine: none
Features: double-barrel rifle with exposed hammers

Kodiak Double Rifle $2600

DPMS Panther Rifles

RIFLES

LONG RANGE .308

Action: autoloader
Stock: synthetic
Barrel: 24 inches
Sights: none
Weight: 11.28
Caliber: .308 Winchester
Magazine: detachable box, 9 rounds
Features: Extruded aluminum upper receiver; milled aluminum lower receiver; Picatinny rail; stainless steel bull barrel; A-15 trigger group; length 43.6 inches
MSRP: **$1149**

BULL SWEET SIXTEEN, TWENTY AND TWENTY-FOUR

Action: autoloader
Stock: synthetic
Barrel: 16, 20, or 24 in.
Sights: none
Weight: 7.75 (16 in.), 9.5 (20 in.), 9.8 (24 in.)
Caliber: .223 Rem.
Magazine: detachable box, 30 rounds
Features: Forged aircraft aluminum alloy A3 flattop upper receiver; forged aluminum alloy lower receiver with semi-auto trigger group; stainless steel bull barrel
Bull Sweet Sixteen: $885
Bull Twenty $915
Bull Twenty-Four: $945

16-INCH AP4 POST BAN W/Miculek Comp.

Action: autoloader
Stock: syntheic
Barrel: 16 in.
Sights: open
Weight: 7.25
Caliber: 5.56 x 45mm
Magazine: detachable box, 30 rounds
Features: Forged aluminum alloy A3 flattop upper receiver with detachable carry handle; forged aluminum alloy lower receiver with semi-auto trigger group; AP4 contour chrome-moly steel barrel with fixed Miculek compensator; length: 34 inches
MSRP: $899

BULL 24 SPECIAL & SUPER BULL 24

Action: autoloader
Stock: synthetic
Barrel: 24 in.
Sights: none
Weight: 10.25 (Bull 24 Special), 11.75 (Super Bull)
Caliber: .223 Rem.
Magazine: detachable box, 30 rounds
Features: Forged aircraft aluminum alloy A3 flattop upper receiver; flattop hi-rider upper receiver on Super Bull; forged aluminum alloy lower receiver with semi-auto trigger group; stainless steel fluted bull barrel; Super Bull with extra heavy stainless steel bull barrel (1.150-in. diameter); length, 43 inches (Bull 24 Special), 42.5 inches (Super Bull)
Bull 24 Special: $1189
Super Bull 24: $1199

DPMS Panther Rifles

CLASSIC

LITE 16

A2 TACTICAL 16 INCH

BULL CLASSIC

CLASSIC
Action: autoloader
Stock: synthetic
Barrel: 16, 20 (Classic) in.
Sights: open
Weight: 9 (Classic), 7.06 (Classic Sixteen)
Caliber: 5.56 x 45mm
Magazine: detachable box, 30 rounds
Features: Forged aircraft aluminum alloy upper receiver with A2 fixed carry handle; forged aluminum alloy lower receiver with semi-auto trigger group; heavy chrome-moly steel barrel with A2 flash hider; chrome plated steel bolt carrier with phosphated steel bolt;
Classic: $809
Classic Sixteen: $799

LITE 16
Action: autoloader
Stock: synthetic
Barrel: 16 in.
Sights: open
Weight: 5.7
Caliber: 5.56 x 45mm
Magazine: detachable box, 30 rounds
Features: Forged aluminum alloy upper receiver with A1 fixed carry handle; forged aluminum alloy lower receiver with semi-auto trigger group; chrome-moly steel lite-contour barrel with A2 flash hider; chrome plated steel bolt carrier with phosphated steel bolt; A1 rear and front sights
MSRP: **. $720**

A2 TACTICAL 16-INCH
Action: autoloader
Stock: synthetic
Barrel: 16 in.
Sights: open
Weight: 9.75
Caliber: 5.56 x 45mm
Magazine: detachable box, 30 rounds
Features: Forged aluminum alloy upper receiver with A2 fixed carry handle; forged aluminum alloy lower receiver with semi-auto trigger group; heavy chrome-moly steel barrel with A2 flash hider; length: 34.75 inches
MSRP: **. $809**

BULL CLASSIC
Action: autoloader
Stock: synthetic
Barrel: 20 in.
Sights: open
Weight: 9.75
Caliber: .223 Rem.
Magazine: detachable box, 30 rounds
Features: Forged aluminum alloy upper receiver with A2 fixed carry handle; forged aluminum alloy lower receiver with semi-auto trigger group; stainless steel bull barrel;; length: 38.5 inches
MSRP: **. $905**

DPMS Panther Rifles

LO-PRO CLASSIC

DCM

AP4 CARBINE

CARBINE 16 INCH

LO-PRO CLASSIC

Action: autoloader
Stock: synthetic
Barrel: 16 in.
Sights: none
Weight: 7.75
Caliber: .223 Rem.
Magazine: detachable box, 30 rounds
Features: Extruded aluminum alloy flattop Lo-Pro upper receiver; forged aluminum alloy lower receiver with semi-auto trigger group; chrome-moly steel bull barrel; length, 34.75 inches
MSRP: **$710**

DCM

Action: autoloader
Stock: synthetic
Barrel: 20 in.
Sights: none
Weight: 9
Caliber: .223 Rem.
Magazine: detachable box, 30 rounds
Features: Forged aluminum alloy upper receiver with A2 fixed carry handle and adjustable NM rear sight; forged aluminum alloy lower receiver with two stage semi-auto trigger group; stainless steel heavy barrel; length: 38.5 inches
MSRP: **$1099**

AP4 CARBINE

Action: autoloader
Stock: synthetic
Barrel: 16 in.
Sights: none
Weight: 6.7
Caliber: 5.56 x 45mm
Magazine: detachable box, 30 rounds
Features: Forged aluminum alloy A3 flattop upper receiver with detachable carry handle and adjustable rear sight; forged aluminum alloy lower receiver with semi-auto trigger group; chrome-moly steel barrel; telescoping stock: 36.24 in. extended, 32.5 collapsed
MSRP: **$899.00**

CARBINE

Action: autoloader
Stock: synthetic
Barrel: 11.5 and 16 in.
Sights: none
Weight: 6.9 (11.5 in.), 7.06 (16 in.)
Caliber: 5.56 x 45mm
Magazine: detachable box, 30 rounds
Features: Forged aluminum alloy upper receiver with A2 fixed carry handle and adjustable rear sight; forged aluminum alloy lower receiver with semi-auto trigger group; chrome-moly steel barrel flash hider; telescoping AP4 (6 position) stock: 35.5 in. extended, 31.75 collapsed (11.5 in.), 36.26 in. extended, 32.75 collapsed (16 in.)
11.5-inch Carbine: $799
16-Inch Carbine: $799

DPMS Panther Rifles

.22 LR

RACE GUN

ARTIC

TUBER

.22LR & DCM .22LR

Action: autoloader
Stock: synthetic
Barrel: 16 in., 20 in. (DCM)
Sights: open
Weight: 7.8, 8.7 (DCM)
Caliber: .22 LR
Magazine: detachable box, 10 rounds
Features: Extruded aluminum alloy Lo-Pro flattop upper receiver; cast aluminum alloy lower receiver with semi-auto trigger group; DCM has A2 fixed carry handle; forged aluminum alloy lower receiver with semi-auto trigger group; chrome-moly steel bull barrel; heavy stainless barrel (DCM); length: 34.5 inches, 38.25 inches (DCM)
.22LR: $670
DCM .22LR: $770

RACE GUN

Action: autoloader
Stock: synthetic
Barrel: 24 in.
Sights: open
Weight: 16
Caliber: .223 Rem.
Magazine: detachable box, 30 rounds
Features: Extruded aluminum alloy flattop lo-pro upper receiver; forged aluminum alloy lower receiver with JP adjustable trigger group; high polish stainless steel fluted bull barrel; chrome plated steel bolt carrier with phosphated steel bolt; Hot Rod free float handguard with bipod stud installed; Badger Ordnance Tac Latch included on charge handle; JP micro adjustable rear and front sights; length: 40 inches
MSRP: **. $1719**

ARCTIC

Action: autoloader
Stock: synthetic
Barrel: 20 in.
Sights: none
Weight: 9
Caliber: .223 Rem.
Magazine: detachable box, 30 rounds
Features: Forged aluminum alloy A3 flattop upper receiver; forged aluminum alloy lower receiver with semi-auto trigger group; stainless steel fluted bull barrel; white coated, vented aluminum free float handguards
MSRP: **. $1099**

TUBER

Action: autoloader
Stock: synthetic
Barrel: 16 in.
Sights: none
Weight: 7.64
Caliber: .223 Rem.
Magazine: detachable box, 30 rounds
Features: Forged aluminum alloy A3 flattop upper receiver; forged aircraft aluminum alloy lower receiver with semi-auto trigger group; chrome-moly steel heavy barrel; aluminum free-float 2-inch tube handguard with M-203 handgrip; length: 34.75 inches
MSRP: **. $746**

SINGLE-SHOT AR RIFLE

Action: autoloader
Stock: synthetic
Barrel: 20 in.
Sights: open
Weight: 9
Caliber: 5.56 x 45mm
Magazine: detachable box, 30 rounds
Features: Forged aluminum alloy upper receiver with A2 fixed carry handle and adjustable rear sight; single-shot forged aluminum alloy lower receiver with standard trigger group; chrome-moly steel barrel; length: 38.25 inches
MSRP: **. $814**

Ed Brown Rifles

BUSHVELD

Action: bolt
Stock: McMillan composite
Barrel: 24 in., match-grade Shilen
Sights: open
Weight: 8.5 lbs.
Caliber: .375 H&H, .416 Rem. Mag., .458 Win. Mag., .458 Lott
Magazine: deep box, 4 rounds
Features: lapped barrel, 3 position safety, steel bottom metal, Talley scope mounts with 8-40 screws; optional QD scope rights, barrel-mounted swivel
Bushveld: . . . . $2995 - 3195

DENALI

Action: bolt
Stock: McMillan composite
Barrel: 22 or 23 in.
Sights: none
Weight: 6.8 lbs.
Caliber: .270 WSM, 7mm WSM, .300 WSM
Magazine: box, 3 or 4 rounds
Features: Short action; lapped barrel, 3 position safety, steel bottom metal, Talley scope mounts with 8-40 screws. Also available: Long-action version in .25-06, .270, .280, .30-06, 7mm Rem. Mag., 7mm Wby., .300 Win. Mag.
Denali: $2895

MODEL 40A2 MARINE SNIPER

Action: bolt
Stock: McMillan composite tactical
Barrel: heavy match 24 in.
Sights: none
Weight: 9.3 lbs.
Caliber: .308
Magazine: box, 5 rounds
Features: lapped barrel, 3 position safety, steel bottom metal; available in left-hand
Marine Sniper: $2995

DAMARA

Action: bolt
Stock: McMillan composite
Barrel: #1.5, 22 in.
Sights: none
Weight: 6.1 lbs.
Caliber: .22-250, .243, 6mm, .260, 7mm/08, .308, 270 WSM, 7mm WSM, .300 WSM
Magazine: box, 5 rounds (WSM: 3)
Features: lapped barrel, 3 position safety, steel bottom metal; Talley scope mounts with 8-40 screws; also available in long-action: .25/06, .270, .280, 7mm Rem. Mag., 7mm Wby., .300 Win. Mag., .300 Wby. Mag.
Damara: $3100

Ed Brown Rifles

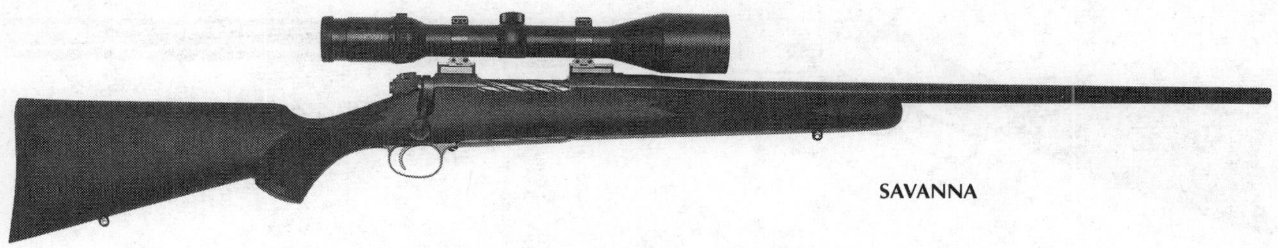

SAVANNA

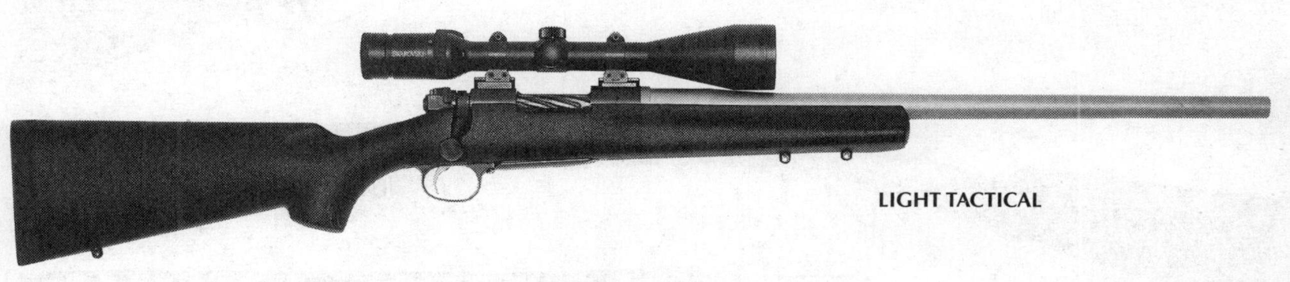

LIGHT TACTICAL

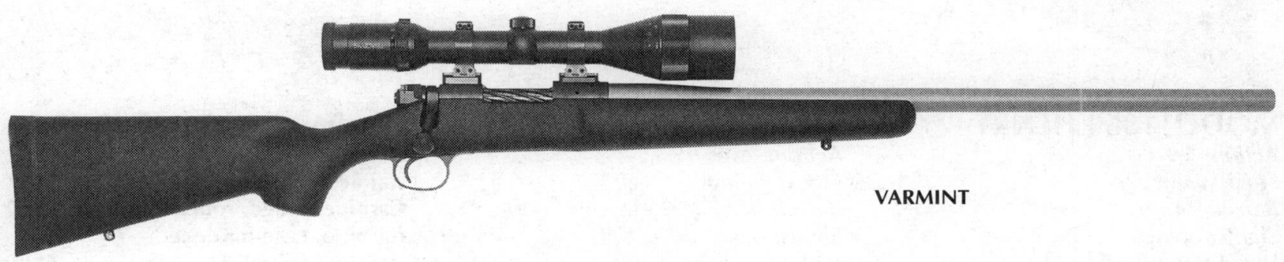

VARMINT

RIFLES

SAVANNAH

Action: bolt
Stock: McMillan composite
Barrel: #3 lightweight 24 in.
Sights: open
Weight: 7.5 lbs.
Caliber: .270 WSM, 7mm WSM, .308, .300 WSM
Magazine: box, 3 or 5 rounds
Features: short action; lapped barrel, 3 position safety, steel bottom metal; long-action model in .270, .280, 7mm Rem. Mag., .30-06, 7mm Wby. Mag., .340 Wby., .300 Win. Mag., .300 Wby. Mag., .338 Win. Mag. with 26 in. #4 barrel in magnums, 8.0 lbs.
Savannah: $2895

TACTICAL

Action: bolt
Stock: McMillan composite tactical
Barrel: heavy 26 in.
Sights: none
Weight: 11.3 lbs.
Caliber: .308, .300 Win. Mag., .338 Lapua
Magazine: box, 3 or 5 rounds
Features: Jewell trigger; Talley scope mounts with 8-40 screws. Also available: Lightweight Tactical with sporter stock, 21 in. medium barrel, 8.8 lbs., in .204 Ruger, .223 and .308
Tactical: $2995
Light Tactical: $2895

VARMINT

Action: bolt
Stock: McMillan composite varmint
Barrel: medium 24 in. or heavy 24 in.
Sights: none
Weight: 9.0 lbs.
Caliber: .204 Ruger, .223, .22-250, .220 Swift, .308
Magazine: none
Features: lapped barrel, 3 position safety, steel bottom metal; optional 2 oz. trigger
Varmint: $2895

EMF Replica Rifles

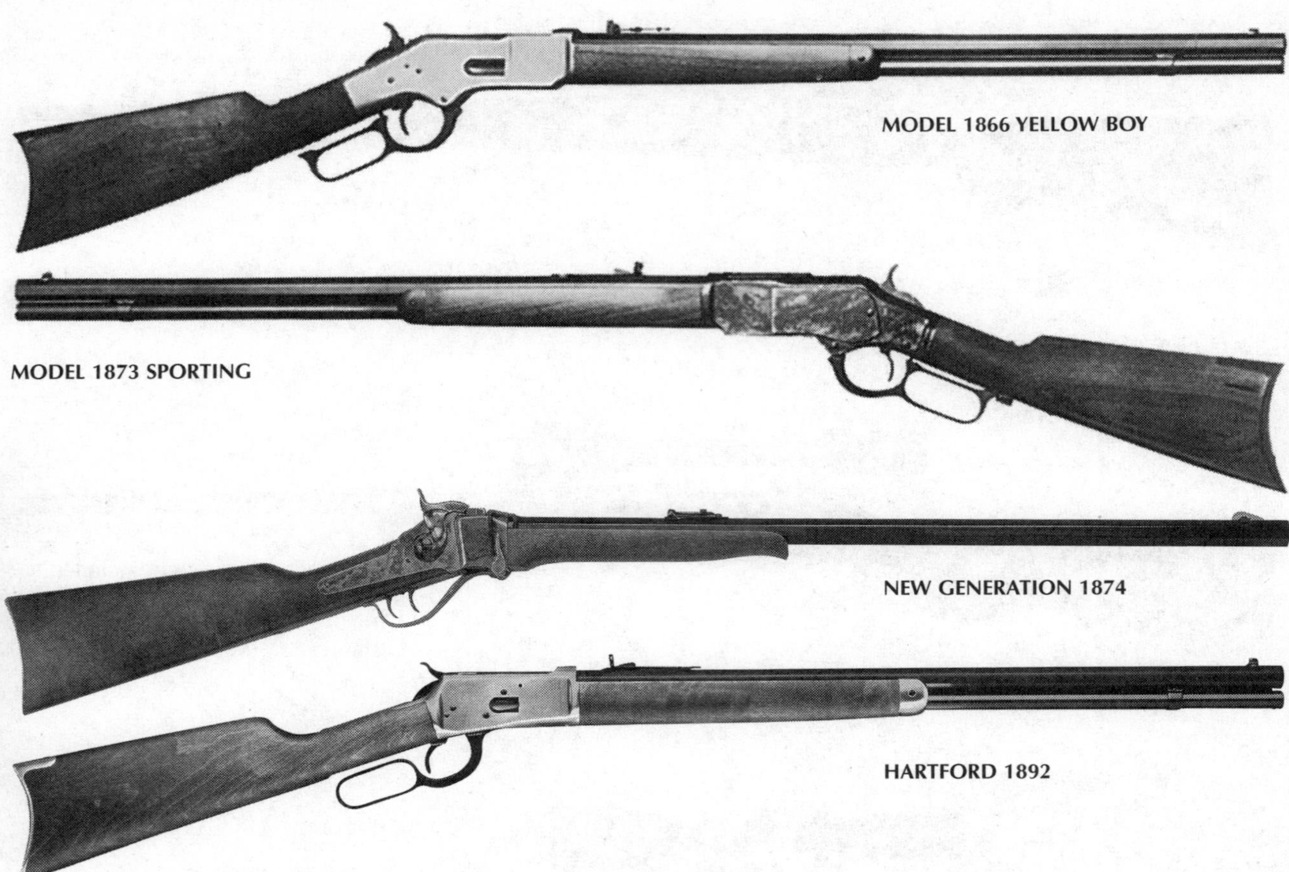

MODEL 1860 HENRY

Action: lever
Stock: walnut
Barrel: 24 in.
Sights: open
Weight: 9.3 lbs.
Caliber: .44-40 and .45 LC
Magazine: under-barrel tube, 11 rounds
Features: blued barrel, brass frame
1860 Henry: $1045
white barrel $1150

MODEL 1866 YELLOW BOY

Action: lever
Stock: walnut
Barrel: 24 in.
Sights: open
Weight: 8.0 lbs.
Caliber: .45 LC, .38 Special and .44-40
Magazine: under-barrel tube, 11 rounds
Features: blued barrel, brass frame
Yellow Boy: $850
carbine:. $875
white barrel: $875

MODEL 1873 SPORTING

Action: lever
Stock: walnut
Barrel: octagon 24 in.
Sights: open
Weight: 8.1 lbs.
Caliber: .32-20, .357, .38-40, .44-40, .45 LC; carbine: .32-30, .357, .45LC
Magazine: under-barrel tube, 11 rounds
Features: Magazine tube in blued steel; frame is casehardened; carbine has 20 in. barrel
standard:. $985
carbine:. $985
short "Border" model:. $1179

HARTFORD 1892

Action: lever
Stock: walnut
Barrel: octagon or round 24 in.
Sights: open
Weight: 7.5 lbs.
Caliber: .357 and .45 LC
Magazine: under-barrel tube, 11 rounds
Features: blued, casehardened or stainless steel; carine has 20 in. barrel
blued: $462
case-hardened: $462
stainless: $487
Carbine, blued, round barrel: . . $399
Carbine, case-hardened, round barrel:. $399
Carbine, stainless, round barrel:. $437

NEW GENERATION 1874 SHARPS

Action: dropping block
Stock: walnut
Barrel: octagon 28 in.
Sights: open
Weight: 9.0 lbs.
Caliber: .45-70
Magazine: none
Features: Created by Christian Sharps, this rifle played a major role in the Civil War. Single shot, double-set triggers, Schnabel forearm, barrel in blue, white or brown patina.
1874 Sharps:. $900
with brown patina: $900
with white patina:. $960

Harrington & Richardson Rifles

RIFLES

BUFFALO CLASSIC

Action: hinged breech
Stock: checkered walnut
Barrel: 32 in.
Sights: target
Weight: 8.0 lbs.
Caliber: .45-70
Magazine: none
Features: single-shot, break-open action; steel buttplate; Williams receiver sight; Lyman target front sight; antique color case-hardened frame
standard or target: $438

ULTRA

Action: hinged breech
Stock: hand-checkered, laminate
Barrel: 22, 24, and 26 in.
Sights: none
Weight: 7.0 lbs.
Caliber: .22 WMR, .223 Rem. and .243 (Varmint), .25-06, .30-06, .270, .308 Win
Magazine: none
Features: Single-shot with break-open action and side lever release. Monte Carlo stock with sling swivels on stock and forend; scope mount included. Weight varies to 8 lbs. with bull barrel.
Ultra: $349
Ultra in .22 WMR: $203

Heckler & Koch Rifles

SR9 (T) & PSG1 MARKSMAN'S RIFLE

Action: autoloading
Stock: synthetic
Barrel: 19.7 in.
Sights: open
Weight: 10.9
Caliber: 7.62x51mm.
Magazine: detachable box, 5 or 20 rounds
Features: Delayed roller-locked bolt system; polygonal rifling; low-recoil buffer system; Kevlar reinforced fiberglass thumbhole stock; adjustable buttstock (SR9 target version); overall length 42.5 inches
SR9 (T):................. $5000
PSG1 Marksman's Rifle:.... $10,000

Heckler & Koch Rifles

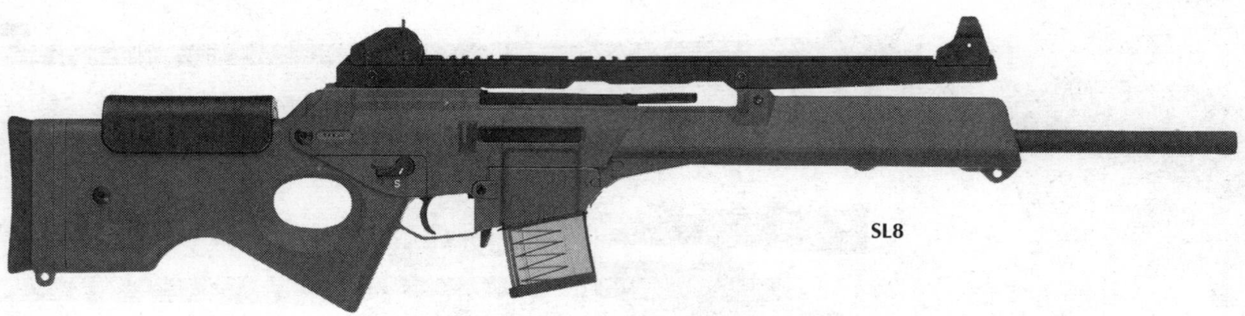

SL8

SL8

Action: autoloading
Stock: synthetic
Barrel: 20.80 in.
Sights: open
Weight: 8.60
Caliber: 5.56x45mm.
Magazine: detachable box, 10 rounds
Features: Delayed roller-locked bolt system; match grade barrel with external fluting; available with Weaver type scope/sight rail or 13-inch Picitinny rail
MSRP: . . . .

HK 94

Action: autoloading
Stock: synthetic
Barrel: 16.54 in.
Sights: none
Weight: 6.43 (A2 fixed stock), 7.18 (A3 collapsible stock)
Caliber: 9x19mm Parabellum
Magazine: detachable box, 15 or 30 rounds
Features: Delayed roller-locked bolt system; Stoner-style rotating bolt; A2 fixed tock or A3 collapsible stock; HK claw-lock sight mounts; sold with tool kit
MSRP: . . . .

SP89

Action: autoloading
Stock/grip: synthetic
Barrel: 4.5 in.
Sights: open
Weight: 4.4
Caliber: 9mm.
Magazine: detachable box, 15 or 30 rounds.
Features: Delayed roller-locked bolt system; overall length 13 inches; 10.25-inch sight radius
MSRP: . . . .

Henry Repeating Arms Rifles

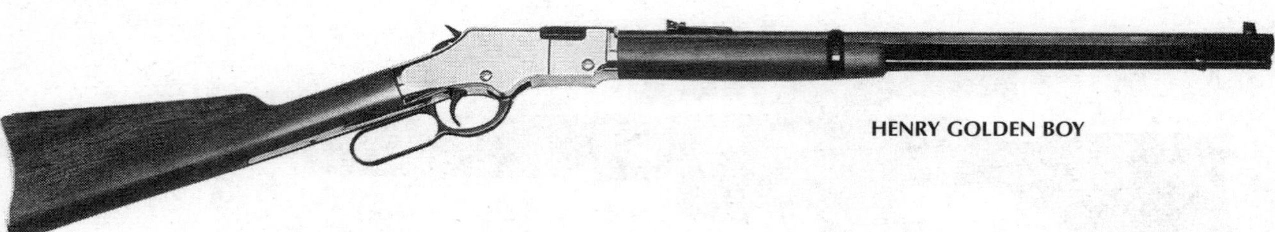

HENRY GOLDEN BOY

HENRY GOLDEN BOY

Action: lever
Stock: walnut, straight-grip
Barrel: octagon 20 in.
Sights: open
Weight: 6.8 lbs.
Caliber: .22 LR, .22 WMR, .17 HMR
Magazine: under-barrel tube, 16 to 22 rounds
Features: brass receiver and buttplate per Winchester 66
Golden Boy (.22 LR): $410
.22 Mag. $485
.17 HMR $490
Golden Boy Deluxe (engraved receiver, .22 LR) . . . $1000 - 1200

Henry Repeating Arms Rifles

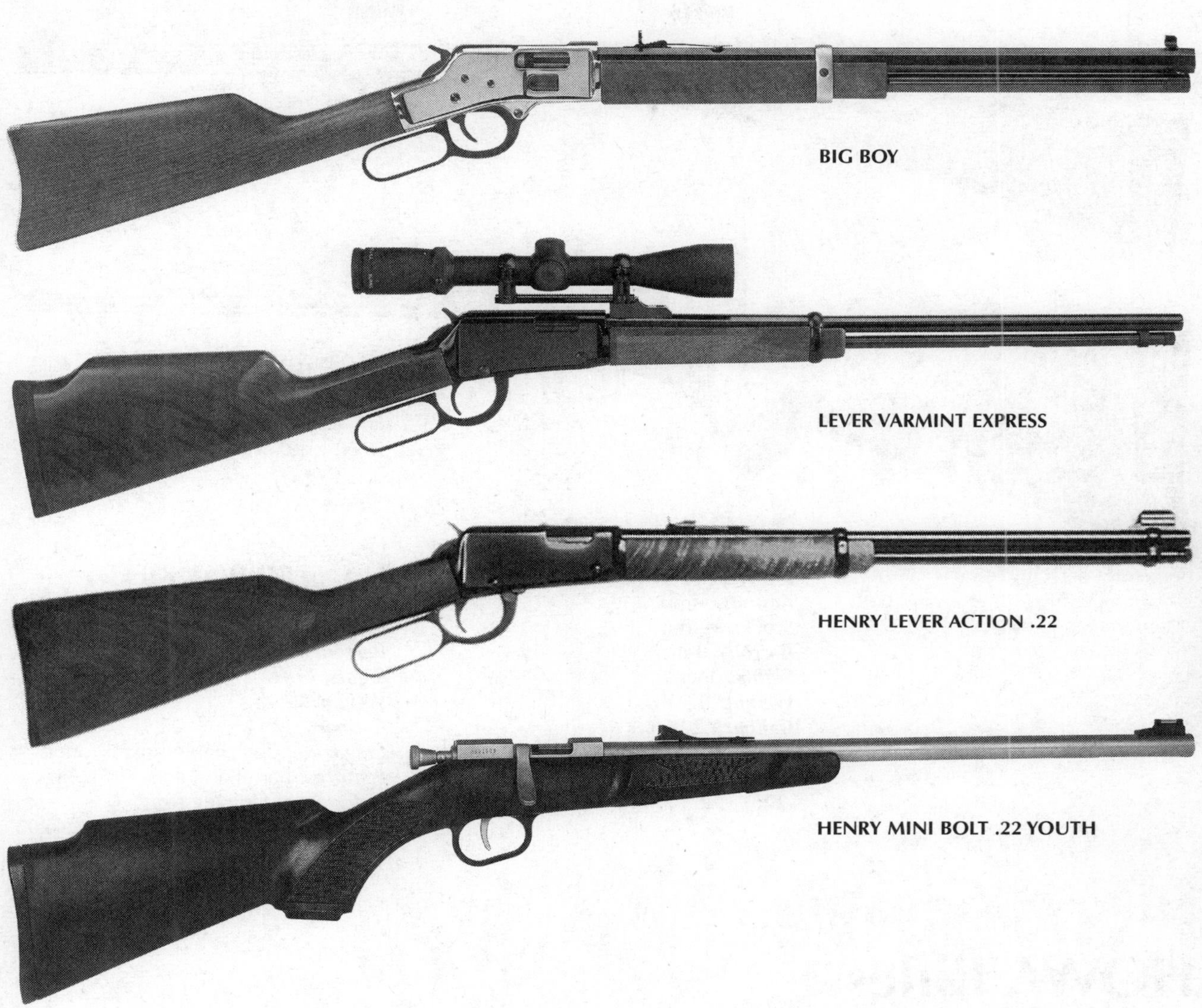

BIG BOY

LEVER VARMINT EXPRESS

HENRY LEVER ACTION .22

HENRY MINI BOLT .22 YOUTH

RIFLES

MODEL BIG BOY

Action: lever
Stock: walnut
Barrel: 20 in. octagon
Sights: open
Weight: 8.7lbs.
Caliber: .44 Mag., .45 LC
Magazine: 10 lbs.
Features: brass receiver, barrel band, buttplate
Big Boy $775

MODEL LEVER VARMINT EXPRESS

Action: lever
Stock: walnut
Barrel: 20 in.
Sights: none
Weight: 5.8 lbs.
Caliber: .17 HMR
Magazine: 11
Features: Monte Carlo stock; scope mount included
Varmint Express $475

HENRY LEVER ACTION .22

Action: lever
Stock: American walnut
Barrel: 18 in.
Sights: open
Weight: 5.5 lbs.
Caliber: .22 S, .22 L, .22 LR
Magazine: under-barrel tube, 15 to 21 rounds
Features: also available: carbine and youth model, .22 WMR with checkered stock, 19 in. barrel
rifle, carbine or youth: $280
magnum: $410

MINI BOLT .22 YOUTH

Action: bolt
Stock: synthetic
Barrel: stainless 16 in.
Sights: illuminated
Weight: 3.3 lbs.
Caliber: .22 S, .22 L, .22 LR
Magazine: none
Features: single-shot; designed for beginners
Mini Bolt: $205
Acu-Bolt (20 in. bbl. & 4x scope included). $335

Henry Repeating Arms Rifles

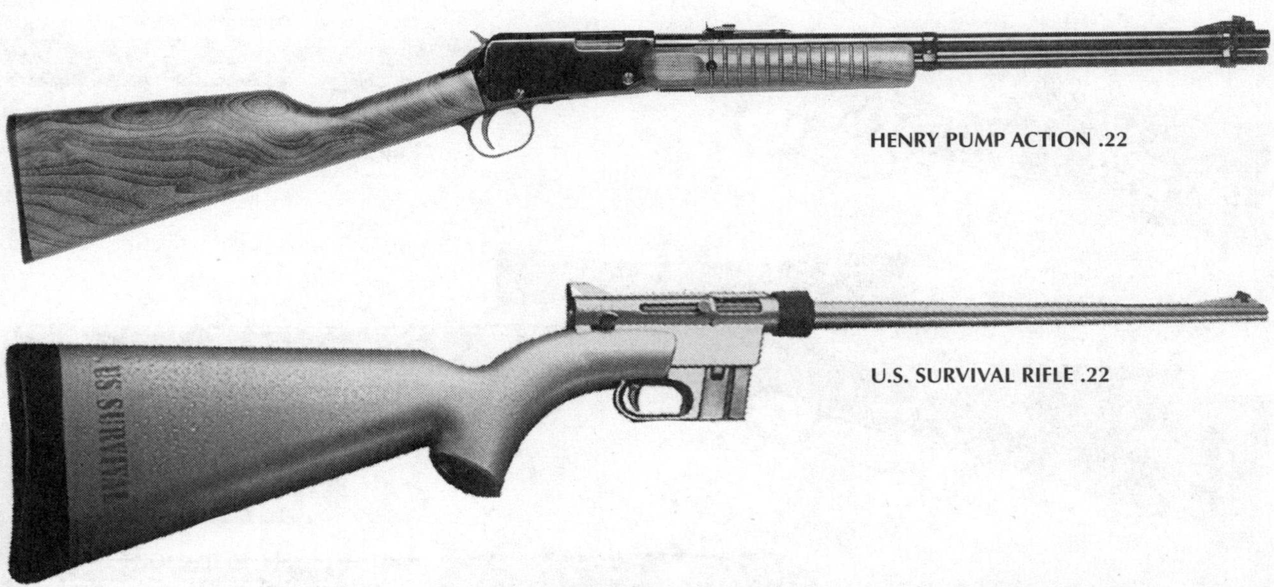

HENRY PUMP ACTION .22

U.S. SURVIVAL RIFLE .22

RIFLES

PUMP-ACTION .22

Action: pump
Stock: walnut
Barrel: 18 in.
Sights: open
Weight: 5.5 lbs.
Caliber: .22 LR
Magazine: under-barrel tube, 15 rounds
Features: alloy receiver
.22: $310

U.S. SURVIVAL RIFLE

Action: Autoloading
Stock: synthetic butt stock
Barrel: 16 in.
Sights: open
Weight: 4.5 lbs.
Caliber: .22 LR
Magazine: detachable box, 8 rounds
Features: barrel and action stow in water-proof, floating stock
Survival Rifle (black or silver): . $205
camo. $260

HOWA Rifles

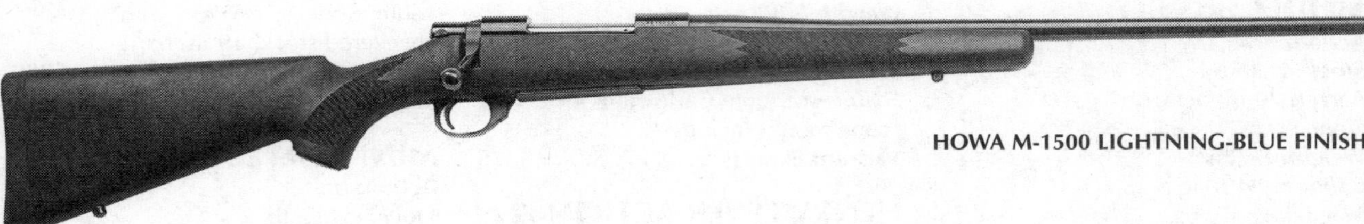

HOWA M-1500 LIGHTNING-BLUE FINISH

MODEL 1500 LIGHTNING

Action: bolt
Stock: Black Polymer with cheekpiece or camo
Barrel: 22 in.
Sights: none
Weight: 7.6 lbs.
Caliber: Popular standard and magnum calibers from .223 Rem. to.300 WSM
Magazine: box, 5 rounds
Features: choice of blue or stainless; 22 in. (standard) or 24 in. (magnum) barrels; new, modern checkered grips, palm swell and foreend; barreled actions are available; 3-position safety
Black, blue finish standard: . . . $508
magnum:. $531
black, stainless standard:. $620
magnum:. $649
camo, blue finish standard:. . . . $545
magnum:. $568
camo, stainless, standard $661
magnum:. $690

HOWA Rifles

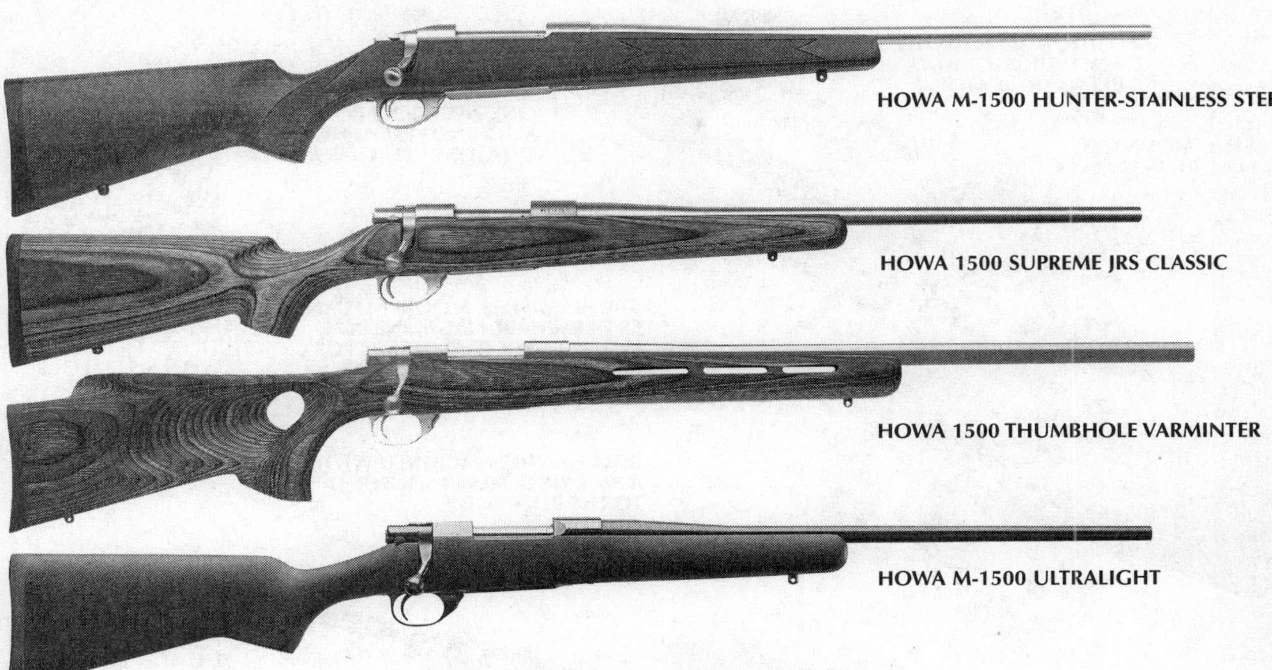

HOWA M-1500 HUNTER-STAINLESS STEEL

HOWA 1500 SUPREME JRS CLASSIC

HOWA 1500 THUMBHOLE VARMINTER

HOWA M-1500 ULTRALIGHT

RIFLES

HOWA M-1500 SUPREME SERIES

Action: bolt
Stock: laminated or black matte
Barrel: 22 or 24 in.
Sights: none
Weight: 7.6 lbs.
Caliber: .223, .25-06, .22-250, .243, 6.5x55, .270, .308, .30-06, 7mm Rem. Mag., .300 Win. Mag., .338 Win. Mag., .270 WSM, 7mm WSM, .300 WSM
Magazine: 5 or 3
Features: stainless or blue, nutmeg or pepper stock; also: Hunter rifles with walnut stock

Blue, JRS stoc:. $646
Stainless, JRS stock $755
Magnum, blue, JRS stock $675
Magnum, stainless, JRS stock . . $784
Also available in thumbhole stock: . . . . add $58

HOWA 1500 THUMBHOLE VARMINTER

Action: bolt
Stock: laminated
Barrel: heavy 22 in.
Sights: none
Weight: 9.9 lbs.
Caliber: .223, .22-250, .243 Win., .308
Magazine: 5
Features: nutmeg, pepper or black stock color, blued or stainless; also: Sporter thumbhole version (7.6 lbs.) in 19 calibers including WSMs

blue. $733
stainless $805
blued sporter $704
magnum $738
stainless Sporter $813
magnum $842

MODEL 1500 HUNTER

Action: bolt
Stock: American black walnut with cheekpiece
Barrel: 22 in.
Sights: none
Weight: 7.6 lbs.
Caliber: popular standard and magnum calibers from .223 Rem. to.300 WSM
Magazine: box, 5 rounds
Features: choice of blue or stainless; 22 in. (standard) or 24 in. (magnum) barrels; varmint model in .223, .22-50 and .308; checkered grips and foreend

blue finish standard $574
magnum $595
stainless standard $682
magnum $704

MODEL 1500 VARMINT

Action: bolt
Stock: Black Polymer or American walnut
Barrel: 22 in.
Sights: none
Weight: 9.3 lbs.
Caliber: .223, .22-50 and .308
Magazine: box, 5 rounds
Features: choice of blue or stainless; 24 in. barrels; wood stocks with weather-resistant finish and laser-stippled grip and forearm panels

blue finish black polymer:. $546
walnut. $610
camo. $582
stainless black polymer $664
walnut. $719
camo. $704

MODEL 1500 ULTRALIGHT

Action: bolt
Stock: Black texture wood
Barrel: 20 inches
Sights: none
Weight: 6.4 lbs.
Caliber: .243 Win., .308, 7mm-08
Magazine: box, 5 rounds
Features: mill-cut lightweight receiver; wood stock with textured flat black finish, blue finish; Youth model available

Ultralight "Mountain Rifle". . . . $539
stainless (.308 only) $658
Ultralight "Youth Model" $539
stainless $658

All Howa Rifles imported by Legacy Sports International, Alexandria VA

H-S Precision Rifles

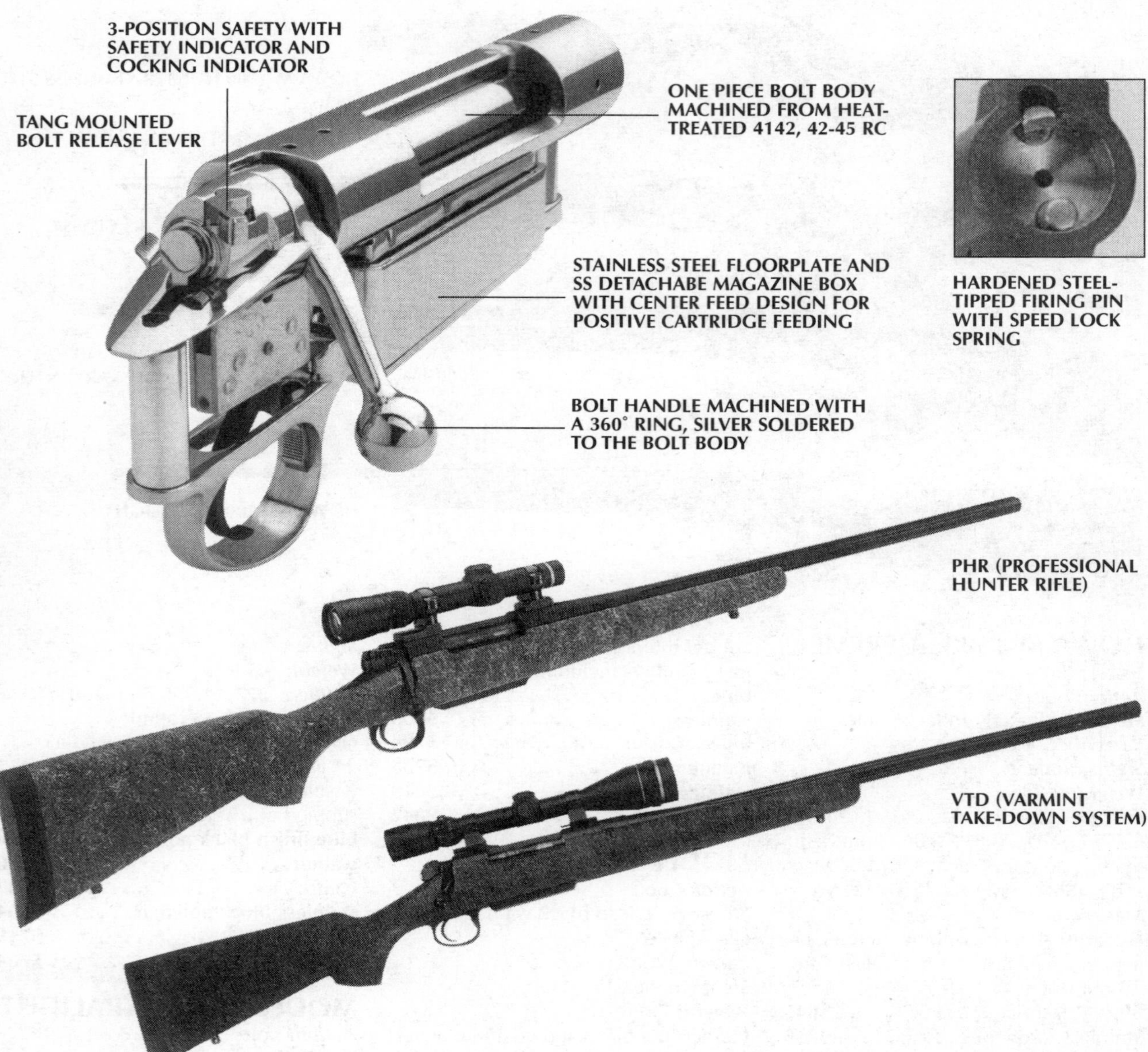

RIFLES

PHR (PROFESSIONAL HUNTER RIFLE)

Action: bolt
Stock: composite
Barrel: 24 to 26 in.
Sights: none
Weight: 8.0 lbs.
Caliber: all popular magnum calibers up to .375 H&H and .338 Lapua
Magazine: detachable box, 3 rounds
Features: Pro series 2000 action: full-length bedding block, optional 10x Model with match-grade stainless, fluted barrel, muzzle brake, built-in recoil reducer; Lightweight SPR rifle is chambered in standard calibers

PHR: $2375
SPR: $2175

TAKE-DOWN RIFLES

Action: bolt
Stock: 2-piece composite
Barrel: any contour and weight 22 to 26 in.
Sights: none
Weight: 8.0 lbs.
Caliber: any popular standard or magnum chambering
Magazine: detachable box, 3 or 4 rounds
Features: rifle disassembles in front of action and reassembles to deliver identical point of impact; price includes carrying case, TD versions with sporter or tactical stocks; customer's choice of barrels and chambering; left-hand model: add $200

Take-Down:. $3600

H-S Precision Rifles

VAR (VARMINT RIFLE)

RIFLES

VAR (VARMINT)

Action: bolt
Stock: composite
Barrel: heavy 24 in.
Sights: none
Weight: 11.0 lbs.
Caliber: all popular varmint calibers
Magazine: detachable box, 4 rounds
Features: Pro-series 2000 action; full-length bedding block; also 10x version with fluted, stainless barrel, optional muzzle
VAR: $2275

Jarrett Custom Rifles

SQUIRREL KING HUNTING RIFLE

SQUIRREL KING

Action: autoloading
Stock: Brown Precision composite
Barrel: match grade 18 in.
Sights: none
Weight: 6.0 lbs.
Caliber: .22 LR
Magazine: rotary, 10 rounds
Features: built on Ruger 10/22 action; target and hunting configurations available; Talley rings and bases included; guaranteed ½″ groups at 50 yards
Hunting model: $2150
Target model: $2400

Jarrett Custom Rifles

ORIGNIAL BEANFIELD

WIND WALKER

RIFLES

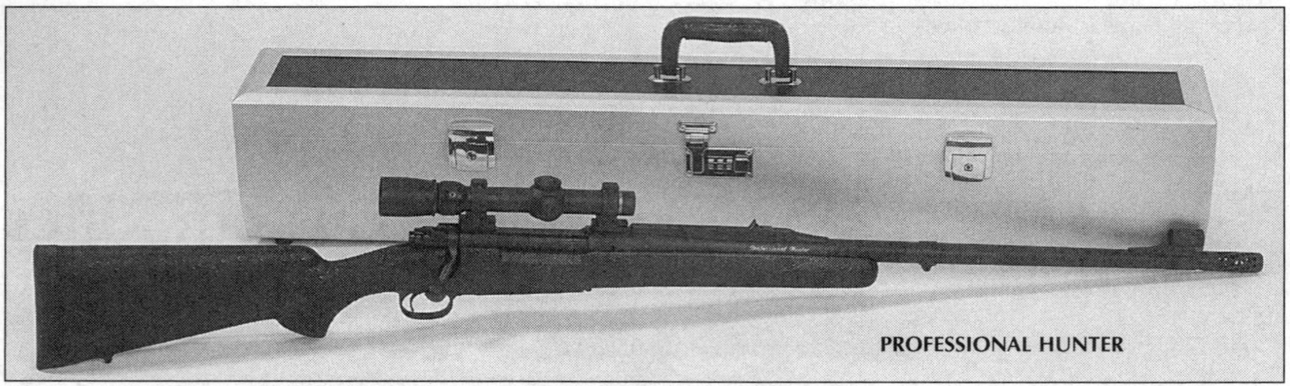

PROFESSIONAL HUNTER

ORIGNIAL BEANFIELD RIFLE

Action: bolt
Stock: McMillan synthetic
Barrel: #4 match grade, 24 in.
Sights: none
Weight: 8.5 lbs.
Caliber: any popular standard or magnum
Magazine: box, 3 or 5 rounds
Features: Shilen trigger; Remington 700 or Winchester 70 action; Talley scope mounts, case, sling, load data and 20 rounds of ammunition; Wind Walker has skeletonized 700 action (7.3 lbs.), muzzle brake.
Original Beanfield.......... $4850

WIND WALKER

Action: bolt
Stock: synthetic
Barrel: 20 in.
Sights: none
Weight: 7.5 lbs.
Caliber: any popular short-action
Magazine: box, 3 or 5 rounds
Features: Remington Model 700 short action; includes Talley scope mounts, choice of scope plus case, sling, load data and 20 rounds of ammunition
Wind Walker: $6650

PROFESSIONAL HUNTER

Action: bolt
Stock: synthetic
Barrel: 24 in.
Sights: open
Weight: 9.0 lbs.
Caliber: any popular standard or wildcat chambering
Magazine: 5 or 3
Features: muzzle brake, also, two Leupold 1.5-5x scopes zeroed in Talley QD rings
Professional Hunter:........ $9390

Kimber Rifles

MODEL 84M CLASSIC

MODEL 8400 CLASSIC

MODEL 84M MONTANA

MODEL 84M SUPER AMERICA

MODEL 84M CLASSIC

Action: bolt
Stock: checkered, Claro walnut
Barrel: light sporter, 22 in.
Sights: none
Weight: 5.6
Caliber: .243, .22-250, .260, 7mm-08, .308
Magazine: box, 5 rounds
Features: also Varmint model (7.4 lbs.) in .22-250 & .204 Ruger with 26 in. stainless, fluted barrel; Long Master Classic (7.4 lbs) in .223, .243 and .308 with 24 in. stainless, fluted barrel and Long Master VT (10 lbs.) in .22-250 with stainless, bull barrel, laminated target stock; Pro Varmint with 22 in. barrel in .204 Ruger and .223 Rem., 24 in. barrel in .22-250; Short Varmint/Target (SVT) with 18.25 in. barrel in .223 Rem.

Classic: $945
Varmint : $1038
Long Master Classic: $1038
Long Master VT: $1162
ProVarmint:. $1115
SVT:. $1162

MODEL 8400 CLASSIC

Action: bolt
Stock: walnut
Barrel: 24 in.
Sights: none
Weight: 6.6 lbs.
Caliber: .270, 7mm, .325 WSM and .300 WSM
Magazine: 3
Features: 3-position safety

8400 Classic $1080
8400 Montana, WSMs. $1222
8400 Super America $2023

MODEL 84M MONTANA

Action: bolt
Stock: synthetic
Barrel: 22 in.
Sights: none
Weight: 5.3 lbs..
Caliber: .308, .243, .260, 7mm-08
Magazine: 5
Features: stainless steel

84M Montana, standard calibers $1124

MODEL 84M SUPER AMERICA

Action: bolt
Stock: AAA walnut
Barrel: 22 in.
Sights: none
Weight: 5.3 lbs.
Caliber: .308, .243, .260, 7mm-08, .223 Rem.
Magazine: 5
Features: 24 LPI wrap checkering on select wood

84M Super America $1828

Kimber Rifles

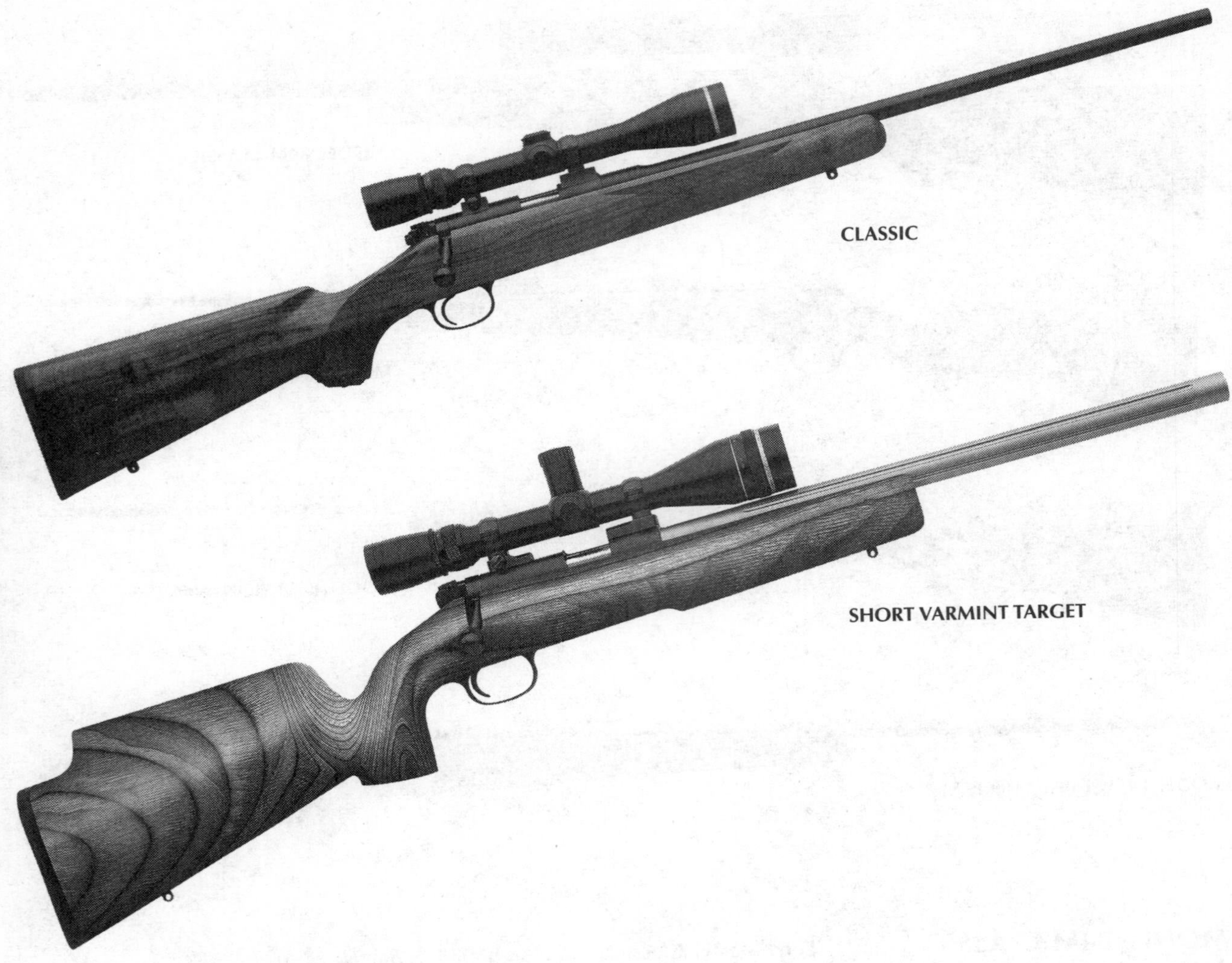

CLASSIC

Action: bolt
Stock: checkered, AA walnut
Barrel: 22 in. match grade
Sights: none
Weight: 6.5
Caliber: .22 LR
Magazine: detachable box, 5 rounds
Features: Model 70-type, 3-position safety; bead blasted finish; deluxe checkering, hand-rubbed finish; 50-yard groups less than .4 in.; also available: no-frills Hunter model; Super America with fancy AA walnut stock with wrap-around checkering; Classic varmint with walnut stock & 20 in. fluted barrel; Pro varmint with laminated stock; custom classic with AAA walnut, matte finish and ebony forend.

Classic: **$1147**
Hunter: **$809**
Super America: **$1865**
Classic Varmint: **$1055**
Pro Varmint: **$1108**
Custom Classic: **$1507**

HS (HUNTER SILHOUETTE)

Action: bolt
Stock: high-comb walnut
Barrel: medium-heavy, half-fluted 24 in.
Sights: none
Weight: 7.0 lbs.
Caliber: .22 LR
Magazine: detachable box, 5 rounds
Features: designed for NRA rimfire silhouette competition
HS: **$915**

SVT (SHORT VARMINT TARGET)

Action: bolt
Stock: heavy, competition style Laminate
Barrel: extra heavy, fluted, stainless 18.25 in.
Sights: none
Weight: 7.5 lbs.
Caliber: .22 LR
Magazine: detachable box, 5 rounds
Features: bead-blasted blue; gray laminated stock
SVT: **$949**

Krieghoff Rifles

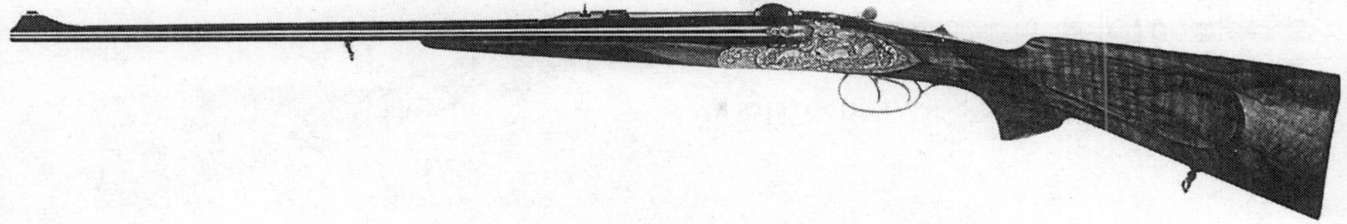

CLASSIC SIDE-BY-SIDE DOUBLE RIFLE

CLASSIC SIDE-BY-SIDE

Action: hinged breech
Stock: select walnut
Barrel: 23.5 in.
Sights: open
Weight: 8.0 lbs.
Caliber: 7x65R, .308, .30-06, .30R Blaser, 8x57, 9.3x74, .375 H&H, .416 Rigby, .458 Win., .470 N.E., .500 N.E.
Magazine: none
Features: thumb-cocking, break-action; double triggers; optional 21.5 in. barrel; engraved side plates; weight depends on chambering and barrel contour

standard calibers: $7850
magnum calibers: $9450
extra barrels with forearm (fitted): $4500
magnum barrels:........... $5500

L.A.R. Rifles

GRIZZLY BIG BOAR

GRIZZLY BIG BOAR

Action: bolt
Stock: all steel sleeve with rubber butt pad
Barrel: 36 in.
Sights: none
Weight: 30.4 lbs.
Caliber: .50 BMG
Magazine: none
Features: Bull Pup single-shot; descending pistol grip; bi-pod; finish options

Grizzly:.................. $2295
Parkerized: $2395
nickel-frame:............. $2545
full nickel:................ $2645
stainless.................. $2545

Lone Star Rifles

ROLLING BLOCK

ROLLING BLOCK

Action: single shot
Stock: walnut
Barrel: 28 – 34 in.
Sights: many options
Weight: 6.0 to 16 lbs.
Caliber: .25, .20 WCF, .25-35, .30-30, .30-40, .32-20, .32-40, .38-50, .38-55, .40-50SS, .40-50SBN, .40-70SMB, .40-70SS, .40-82, .40-90SS, .45-70, .45-90, .45-100, .45-110, .45-120, .44-60, .44-77SBN, .44-90SBN, .44-100 Rem. Sp., .50-70, .50-90, .50-140
Magazine: none
Features: true-to-form replicas of post-Civil War Remington rolling blocks; single set or double set triggers, case-colored actions on Silhouette, Creedmoor, Sporting, Deluxe Sporting, Buffalo, Custer Commemorative, #5, #7
Standard:. $1595
Sporting: $1995
#7: $3500
Buffalo Rifle: $2900
Take Down: $4000

RIFLES

Magnum Research Rifles

BARRACUDA STOCK MAGNUM LITE

MOUNTAIN EAGLE SPORT BARREL

TACTICAL RIFLE

MAGNUM LITE RIMFIRE

Action: autoloading
Stock: composite or laminated
Barrel: graphite sleeved, 16.75 in.
Sights: none
Weight: 5.2 lbs.
Caliber: .22LR, .22 WMR, .17 HMR and .17M2
Magazine: rotary, 9 rounds
Features: Ruger 10/22 action; carbon-fiber barrel with steel liner
with composite stock: $599
with laminated stock: $759
magnum with composite: $799
magnum with laminated: $959
.17 HMR: . . . . $$709 – 999
.17 M2: . . . . $599 – 759

MAGNUM LITE CENTERFIRE

Action: bolt
Stock: composite
Barrel: graphite, sleeved 24 or 26 in.
Sights: none
Weight: 7.8 lbs.
Caliber: .280, .30-06, 7mm Rem. Mag., .300 Win. Mag., 7 WSM, .300 WSM
Magazine: box, 3 or 4 rounds
Features: adjustable trigger, free-floating match-grade barrel; platform bedding; left-hand available
Magnum Lite: $2295
Varmint model: $2295

TACTICAL RIFLE

Action: bolt
Stock: H-S Precision, synthetic tactical
Barrel: graphite sleeved 26 in.
Sights: none
Weight: 8.3 lbs.
Caliber: .223, .22-250, .300 WSM, .308, .300 Win. Mag.
Magazine: box, 3 or 5 rounds
Features: accurized Rem. 700 action; adjustable comb; adjustable trigger and length of pull
Tactical: $2400

Marlin Rifles

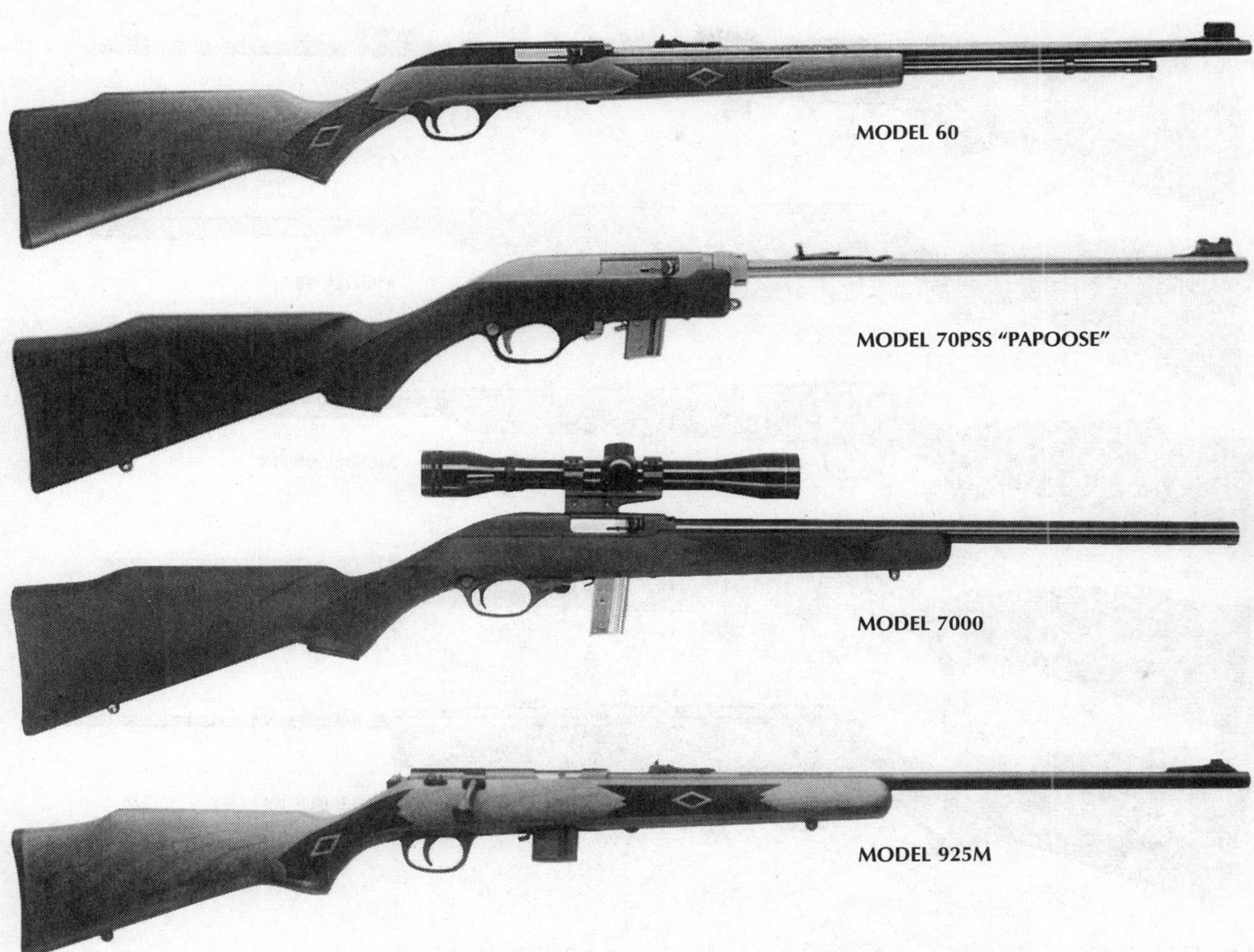

MODEL 60

MODEL 70PSS "PAPOOSE"

MODEL 7000

MODEL 925M

MODEL 60

Action: autoloading
Stock: hardwood
Barrel: 19 in.
Sights: open
Weight: 5.5 lbs.
Caliber: .22 LR
Magazine: under-barrel tube, 14 rounds
Features: last shot hold-open device; stainless, synthetic and laminated stocked versions available; also available with camo-finished stock

standard $195
camo. $231
stainless $247
stainless, synthetic $269
stainless, laminated two-tone . . $312

MODEL 70 PSS PAPOOSE

Action: autoloading
Stock: synthetic
Barrel: 16 in.
Sights: open
Weight: 3.3 lbs.
Caliber: .22 LR
Magazine: detachable box, 7 rounds
Features: take-down rifle; nickel-plated swivel studs; floatable, padded carrying case included

Papoose. $318

MODEL 7000

Action: autoloading
Stock: synthetic
Barrel: target weight, 28 in.
Sights: none
Weight: 5.3 lbs.
Caliber: .22 LR
Magazine: detachable box, 10 rounds
Features: also available as Model 795 and 795 SS, with sights and lighter barrel (weight: 4.5 lbs.)

7000 . . . . $263
795 . . . . $168
795 SS. $247

MODEL 925M

Action: bolt
Stock: hardwood
Barrel: 22 in.
Sights: open
Weight: 6.0 lbs.
Caliber: .22 WMR
Magazine: detachable box, 7 rounds
Features: T-900 Fire Control System, Micro-Groove barrel; also available with Mossy Oak camo-finish stock

925M $255
925MC (camo) $294

Marlin Rifles

MODEL 925

Action: bolt
Stock: hardwood
Barrel: 22 in.
Sights: open
Weight: 5.5 lbs.
Caliber: .22 LR
Magazine: detachable box, 7 rounds
Features: T-900 Fire Control System, Micro-Groove rifling; can be ordered with scope; also available with Mossy Oak camo stock finish

925 . . . . $223
925 with scope $232
925C (camo). $263

MODEL 981T

Action: bolt
Stock: synthetic
Barrel: 22 in.
Sights: open
Weight: 6.0 lbs.
Caliber: .22 L, S, or LR
Magazine: under-barrel tube, 17 rounds
Features: Micro-Groove rifling, T-900 Fire Control System

918T $225

MODEL 983T

Action: bolt
Stock: synthetic
Barrel: 22 in.
Sights: open
Weight: 6.0 lbs.
Caliber: .22 WMR
Magazine: under-barrel tube, 12 rounds
Features: T-900 Fire Control System, Micro-Groove rifling; available as Model 983 with walnut stock or laminated stock and stainless barrel

983T $273
Model 983 . . . . $365
Model 983S. $377

MODEL 917V

Action: bolt
Stock: hardwood
Barrel: heavy 22 in.
Sights: none
Weight: 6.0 lbs.
Caliber: .17 HMR
Magazine: detachable box, 7 rounds
Features: T-900 Fire Control System, 1-in. scope mounts provided; also available: 917VS stainless steel with laminated hardwood stock (7 lbs.)

917V $284
917VS $425
917 VSF (fluted barrel):. $450

LITTLE BUCKAROO

Action: bolt
Stock: hardwood
Barrel: 16 in.
Sights: open
Weight: 4.3 lbs.
Caliber: .22 S, L or LR
Magazine: none
Features: T-900 Fire Control System; stainless version available

Little Buckaroo (Model 915Y) . . $221
Stainless (Model 915YS) $247

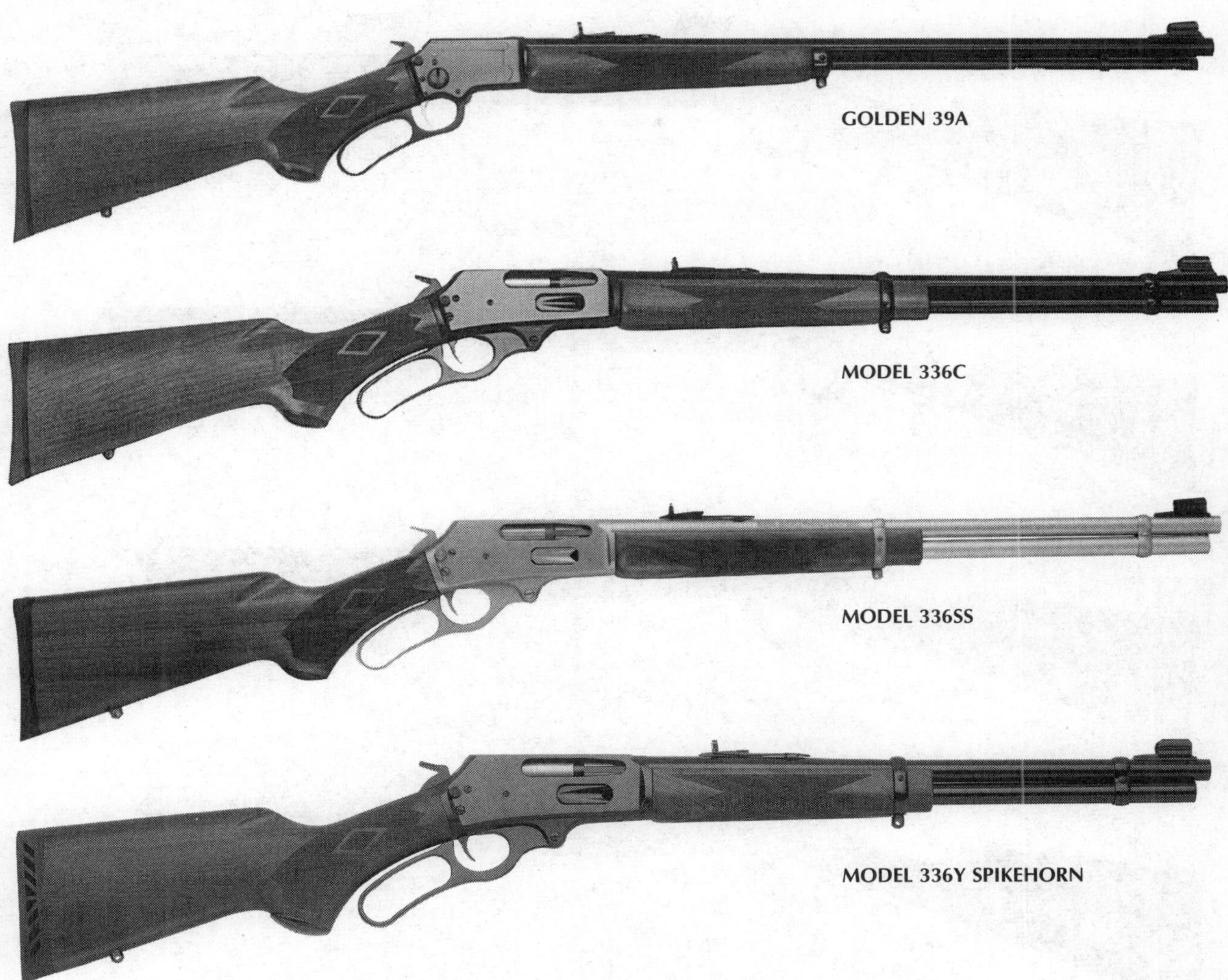
GOLDEN 39A
MODEL 336C
MODEL 336SS
MODEL 336Y SPIKEHORN

GOLDEN 39A

Action: lever
Stock: checkered walnut, pistol grip
Barrel: 24 in.
Sights: open
Weight: 6.5 lbs.
Caliber: .22 LR
Magazine: under-barrel tube, 19 rounds
Features: Micro-Groove rifling, single-screw take-down; swivel studs
Golden 39A $596

MODEL 336C

Action: lever
Stock: checkered walnut, pistol grip
Barrel: 20 in.
Sights: open
Weight: 7.0 lbs.
Caliber: .30-30 Win., and .35 Rem.
Magazine: tube, 6 rounds
Features: blued, hammer-block safety, offset hammer spur for scope use
Model 336C $558
Model 336A, .30-30 only, birch stock $477
Model 336W, .30-30 only, gold-plated $482

MODEL 336SS

Action: lever
Stock: checkered walnut, pistol grip
Barrel: 20 in.
Sights: open
Weight: 7.0 lbs.
Caliber: .30-30
Magazine: under-barrel tube, 6 rounds
Features: offset hammer spur for scope use; Micro-Groove rifling
336SS $692

MODEL 336Y SPIKEHORN

Action: lever
Stock: walnut
Barrel: 16.5 in.
Sights: open
Weight: 6.5 lbs.
Caliber: .30-30
Magazine: 5
Features: pistol grip stock; 12.5-inch pull for small shooters
336Y Spikehorn. $566

Marlin Rifles

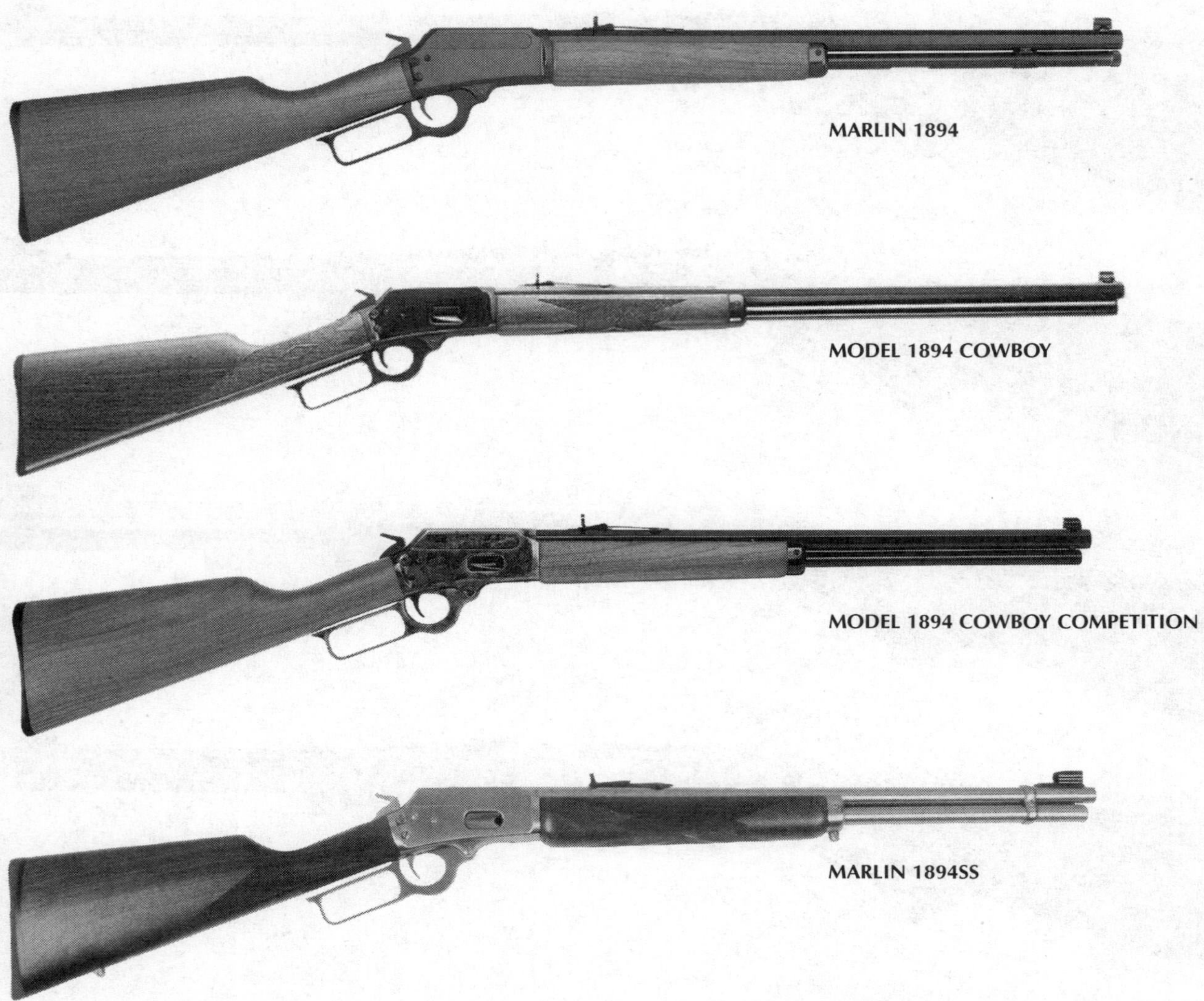

MARLIN 1894

MODEL 1894 COWBOY

MODEL 1894 COWBOY COMPETITION

MARLIN 1894SS

MODEL 1894

Action: lever
Stock: checkered American walnut
Barrel: 20 in.
Sights: open
Weight: 6.0 lbs.
Caliber: .44 Rem. Mag./.44 Special
Magazine: tube, 10 rounds
Features: straight grip stock with Mar-Shield finish
Price: $591

MODEL 1894 COWBOY

Action: lever
Stock: walnut, straight grip, checkered
Barrel: tapered octagon 24 in.
Sights: open
Weight: 6.5 lbs.
Caliber: .357 Mag./38 Special, .44 mag./.44 Special and .45 Colt
Magazine: tube, 10 rounds
Features: blued finish, hammer-block safety, hard rubber buttplate; Competition model available in .38 Special or .45 Colt with 20 in. barrel
1894 Cowboy $872
Cowboy in .32 H&R Mag $849

MODEL 1894 COWBOY COMPETITION

Action: lever
Stock: walnut
Barrel: 20 in.
Sights: open
Weight: 7.0 lbs.
Caliber: .38 Spl., .45 Long Colt
Magazine: 10
Features: case-colored receiver
1894 Cowboy Competition.... $986

MODEL 1894 SS

Action: lever
Stock: checkered walnut, straight grip
Barrel: 20 in.
Sights: open
Weight: 6.0 lbs.
Caliber: .44 Rem. Mag.
Magazine: under-barrel tube, 10 rounds
Features: Micro-groove rifling
1894 SS.................. $716
1894C (blued).............. $591
1894 CL (in .32/30 with 22 in. bbl., 6-shot) $836

Marlin Rifles

MODEL 1895

Action: lever
Stock: checkered walnut, pistol grip
Barrel: 22 in.
Sights: open
Weight: 7.5 lbs.
Caliber: .45-70 Govt.
Magazine: tube, 4 rounds
Features: blued, hammer-block safety, offset hammer spur for scope use; Model 1895G has 18.5 in. barrel and straight grip.

1895 . . . . $654
1895G. $668
1895GS in stainless steel. $805
1895 Cowboy (26″ octagon barrel). $849

MODEL 1895M

Action: lever
Stock: checkered walnut, straight grip
Barrel: Ballard rifled, 18.5 in.
Sights: open
Weight: 7.0 lbs.
Caliber: .450
Magazine: tube, 4 rounds
Features: blued finish, hammer-block safety, offset hammer spur for scope use.

1895M $719

MODEL 444

Action: lever
Stock: walnut, pistol grip, fluted comb, checkering
Barrel: 22 in.
Sights: open
Weight: 7.5 lbs.
Caliber: .444 Marlin
Magazine: tube, 5 rounds
Features: blued, hammer-block safety, offset hammer spur for scope use.

Model 444: $654

Remove blood from your rifle as soon as you spot it. Blood is salty and causes rust in short order. Wash bloodied rifles with cold water, dry immediately with a rag, then apply light gun oil.

Merkel Rifles

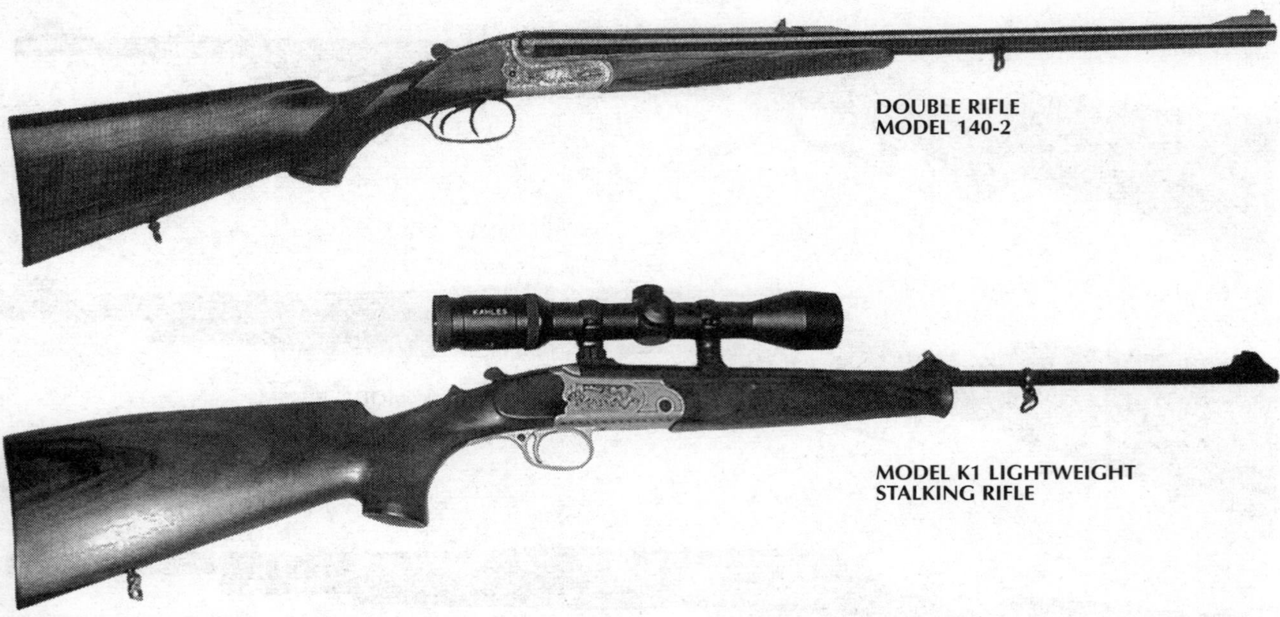

DOUBLE RIFLE MODEL 140-2

MODEL K1 LIGHTWEIGHT STALKING RIFLE

RIFLES

MODEL K1 LIGHTWEIGHT STALKING RIFLE

Action: hinged breech
Stock: select walnut
Barrel: 24 in.
Sights: open
Weight: 5.6 lbs.
Caliber: .243, .270, 7x57R, 7mm Rem. Mag., .308, .30-06, .300 Win. Mag., 9.3x74R
Magazine: none
Features: single-shot; Franz Jager action; also available: Premium and Jagd grades

Stalking Rifle: $3395
Premium: $4395
Jagd: $4695

DOUBLE RIFLE MODEL 140-2

Action: hinged breech
Stock: select walnut
Barrel: length and contour to order
Sights: open
Weight: 9.0 lbs.
Caliber: .375 H&H, .416 Rigby, .470 N.E.
Magazine: none
Features: Anson & Deely box-lock; double triggers; includes oak and leather luggage case; higher grade available; also Model 141.1, lightweight double in .308, .30-06, 9.3x74R

Safari Double:. $10195
higher grade:. $11395
Model 141.1: $7195

After mounting a scope, check eye relief from the prone position, muzzle slightly high. Shooting at game, you're likely to thrust your head forward and get clobbered. Mount scopes well forward.

Navy Arms Rifles

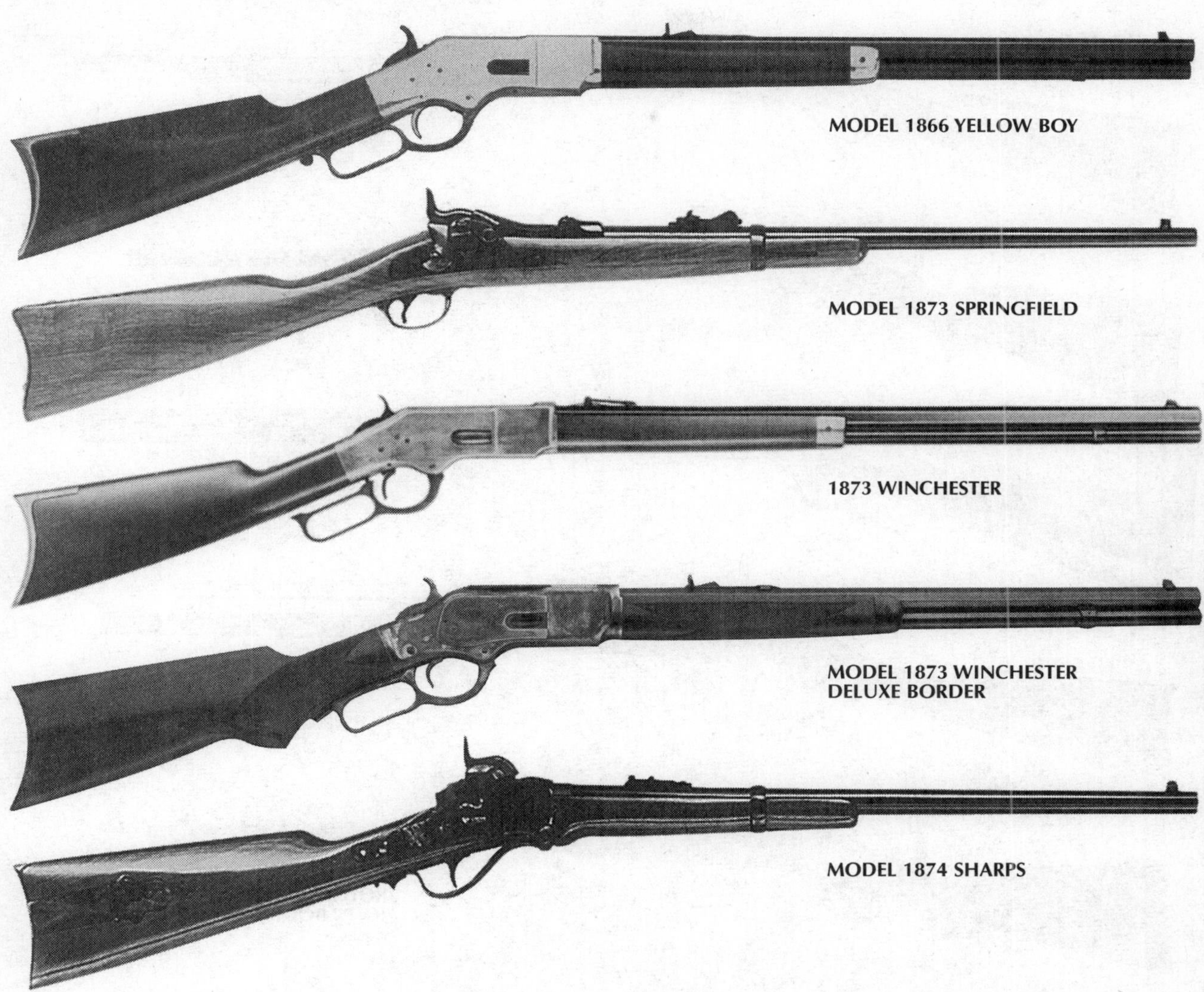

MODEL 1866 YELLOW BOY

MODEL 1873 SPRINGFIELD

1873 WINCHESTER

MODEL 1873 WINCHESTER DELUXE BORDER

MODEL 1874 SHARPS

MODEL 1866 YELLOW BOY

Action: lever
Stock: walnut, straight grip
Barrel: octagon 20 in.
Sights: open
Weight: 7.5 lbs.
Caliber: .38 Special, .44-40, .45 Colt
Magazine: under-barrel tube, 10 rounds
Features: also available: Yellow Boy with 24 in. barrel (8.3 lbs.)
1866 Yellow Boy: $915

MODEL 1873 SPRINGFIELD

Action: dropping block
Stock: walnut
Barrel: 22 in.
Sights: open
Weight: 7.0 lbs.
Caliber: .45-70
Magazine: none
Features: "Trapdoor" replica, saddle bar with ring
1873 Springfield:. $1475

MODEL 1873 WINCHESTER

Action: lever
Stock: walnut, straight grip
Barrel: 24 in.
Sights: open
Weight: 8.3 lbs.
Caliber: .357 Mag., .44-40, .45 Colt
Magazine: under-barrel tube, 13 rounds
Features: case-colored receiver; also: Carbine, Border, Deluxe (checkered) Border and Sporting models
1873 Winchester: $1047
Carbine: $1025
Border Model:. $1047
Deluxe Border Model:. $1183
Sporting Rifle:. $1183

MODEL 1874 SHARPS

Action: dropping block
Stock: walnut
Barrel: 22 in.
Sights: open
Weight: 7.8 lbs.
Caliber: .45-70
Magazine: none
Features: also: No. 3 Long Range Sharps with double set triggers, 34 in. barrel (10.9 lbs.) and Buffalo Rifle with double set triggers, 28 in. octagon barrel (10.6 lbs.)
Carbine: $1186
No. 3: $2205

Navy Arms Rifles

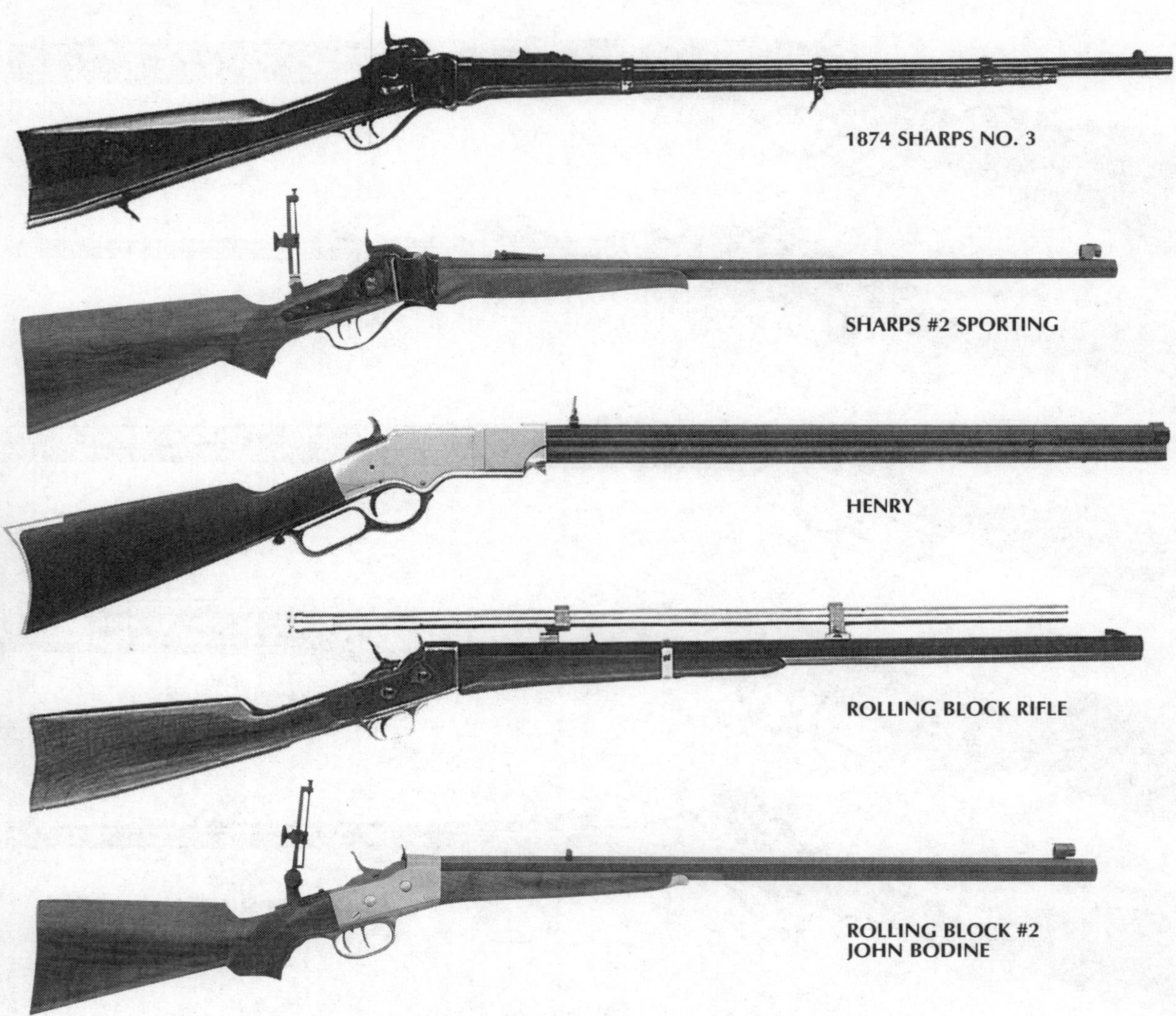

1874 SHARPS NO. 3

SHARPS #2 SPORTING

HENRY

ROLLING BLOCK RIFLE

ROLLING BLOCK #2
JOHN BODINE

RIFLES

MODEL SHARPS #2 SPORTING

Action: dropping block
Stock: walnut
Barrel: 30 in.
Sights: target
Weight: 10.0 lbs.
Caliber: .45-70
Magazine: none
Features: also #2 Silhouette Creedmoor and Quigley (with 34 in. barrel)
Sporting and Creedmoor..... $1603
Silhouette................ $1639
Quigley.................. $1703

HENRY

Action: lever
Stock: walnut, straight grip
Barrel: 24 in.
Sights: open
Weight: 9.0 lbs.
Caliber: .44-40, .45 Colt
Magazine: under-barrel tube, 13 rounds
Features: blued or case-colored receiver
Henry:.................... $1222
Military Henry $1164

ROLLING BLOCK RIFLE

Action: dropping block
Stock: walnut
Barrel: 26 or 30 in.
Sights: open
Weight: 9.0 lbs.
Caliber: .45-70
Magazine: none
Features: case-colored receiver; optional brass telescopic sight; drilled for Creedmoor sight; also; checkered #2 model with tang and globe sights
John Bodine $1640

MODEL ROLLING BLOCK #2 JOHN BODINE

Action: dropping block
Stock: walnut
Barrel: 30 in.
Sights: adjustable tang
Weight: 12.0 lbs.
Caliber: .45-70
Magazine: none
Features: double set triggers, nickel-finish breech
John Bodine $1640

New England Firearms Rifles

SPORTSTER 17 HMR

SURVIVOR

SYNTHETIC HANDI-RIFLE

HARDWOOD HANDI-RIFLE

SPORTSTER 17 HMR & 17 MACH2

Action: hinged breech
Stock: synthetic
Barrel: heavy varmint 22 in.
Sights: none
Weight: 6.0 lbs.
Caliber: .17 Hornady Magnum Rimfire, .17 MACH2
Magazine: none
Features: Monte Carlo stock; sling swivel studs, recoil pad; Sportster Youth available with 20 in. barrel (5.5 lbs.), in .22 LR or .22 WMR.
Sportster:............. $183 - 188
Youth:..................... $157

SURVIVOR

Action: hinged breech
Stock: synthetic
Barrel: 22 in. bull
Sights: open
Weight: 6.0 lbs.
Caliber: .223 & .308
Magazine: none
Features: single-shot; recoil pad; hollow synthetic stock with storage compartment, thumbscrew take down
Survivor: $296

HANDI-RIFLE

Action: hinged breech
Stock: Monte Carlo synthetic or hardwood
Barrel: 22 or 26 in.
Sights: none
Weight: 7.0 lbs.
Caliber: .223, .22-250, .243, .270, .30-06
Magazine: none
Features: offset hammer; open-sight version of Handi-Rifle in .22 Hornet, .30-30, .357 Mag., .44 Mag., .45-70 Govt. Youth models in .223, .243 and 7mm-08.
Handi-Rifle:................ $296
with hardwwod stock:........ $284
Synthetic stainless: $354
Youth:..................... $284

New Ultra Light Arms

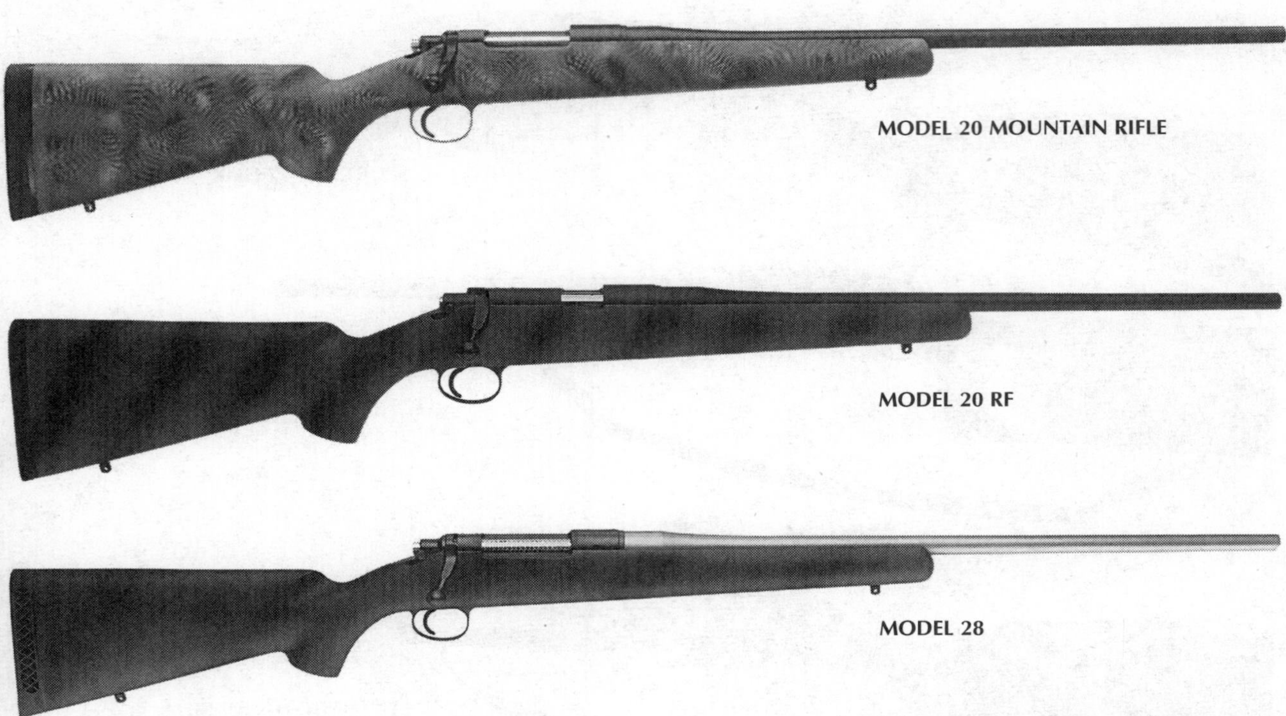

MODEL 20 MOUNTAIN RIFLE

MODEL 20 RF

MODEL 28

RIFLES

MODEL 20 MOUNTAIN RIFLE

Action: bolt
Stock: Kevlar/graphite composite
Barrel: 22 in.
Sights: none
Weight: 4.75 lbs.
Caliber: short action: 6mm, .17, .22 Hornet, .222, .222 Rem. Mag., .22-250, .223, .243, .250-3000 Savage, .257, .257 Ackley, 7x57, 7x57 Ackley, 7mm-08, .284, .300 Savage, .308, .358
Magazine: box, 4, 5 or 6 rounds
Features: two-position safety; choice of 7 or more stock colors; available in left-hand

Mountain Rifle: $2800
left-hand: $2900

MODEL 20 RF

Action: bolt
Stock: composite
Barrel: Douglas Premium #1 Contour 22 in.
Sights: none
Weight: 5.25 lbs.
Caliber: .22 LR
Magazine: none (or detachable box, 5 rounds)
Features: single shot or repeater; drilled and tapped for scope; recoil pad, sling swivels; fully adjustable Timney trigger; 3-position safety; color options

single-shot: $1100
repeater: $1150

MODEL 24

Action: bolt
Stock: Kevlar composite
Barrel: 22 in.
Sights: none
Weight: 5.25 lbs.
Caliber: long action: .270, .30-06, .25-06, .280, .280 Ackley, .338-06, .35 Whelen; Magnum (Model 28): .264, 7mm, .300, .338, .300 WSM, .270 WSM, 7mm WSM; Model 40: (magnum) .300 Wby. and .416 Rigby
Magazine: box, 4 rounds
Features: Model 28 has 24 in. bbl. and weighs 5.5 lbs.; Model 40 has 24 in. bbl. (6.5 lbs.) All available in left-hand versions.

Model 24: $2900
Model 24, left-hand: $3000
Model 28 or Model 40: $3200
Model 28 or Model 40, left-hand: $3300

Hunt with a "dry" rifle. Wipe excess lubricant from the bore, as it can make a first shot go wild. Oil on exposed action parts collects grit.

Pedersoli Replica Rifles

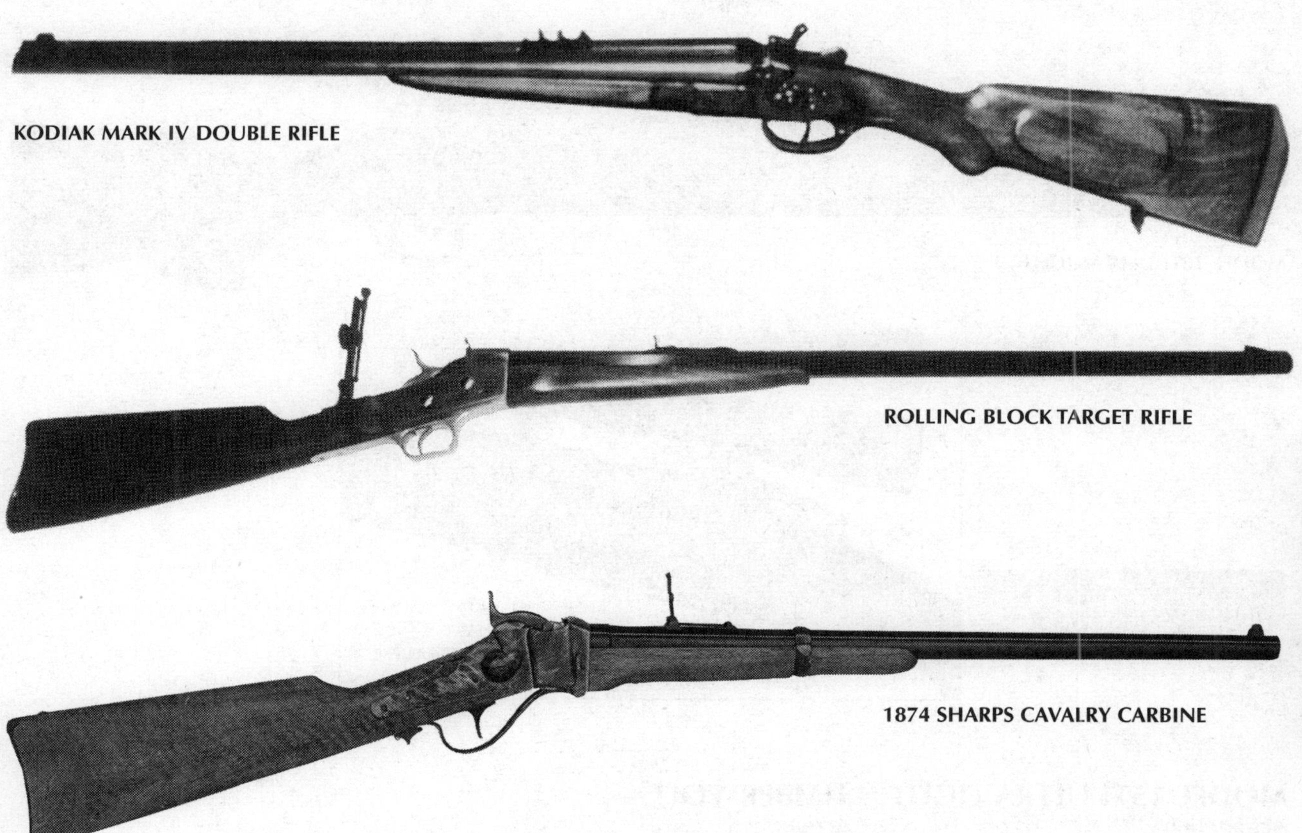

KODIAK MARK IV DOUBLE RIFLE

ROLLING BLOCK TARGET RIFLE

1874 SHARPS CAVALRY CARBINE

KODIAK MARK IV DOUBLE

Action: hinged breech
Stock: walnut
Barrel: 22 and 24 in.
Sights: open
Weight: 8.2 lbs.
Caliber: .45-70, 9.3x74R, 8x57JSR
Magazine: none
Features: .45-70 weighs 8.2 lbs.; also available: Kodiak Mark IV with interchangeable 20-gauge barrel

45-70:. $3250
8x57, 9.3x74: $3250
Kodiak Mark IV: $4925

ROLLING BLOCK TARGET

Action: dropping block
Stock: walnut
Barrel: octagon 30 in.
Sights: target
Weight: 9.5 lbs.
Caliber: .45-70 and .357 (10 lbs.)
Magazine: none
Features: Creedmoor sights; Also available: Buffalo, Big Game, Sporting, Baby Carbine, Custer, Long Range Creedmoor

Rolling Block Target, steel:. . . . $995

SHARPS 1874 CAVALRY MODEL

Action: dropping block
Stock: walnut
Barrel: 22 in.
Sights: open
Weight: 8.4 lbs.
Caliber: .45-70
Magazine: none
Features: also available: 1874 Infantry (set trigger, 30 in. bbl.), 1874 Sporting (.40-65 or .45-70, set trigger, 32 in. oct. bbl.), 1874 Long Range (.45-70 and .45-90, .45-120, 34 in. half oct. bbl., target sights)

Cavalry:. $1200
Infantry (one trigger): $1300
Infantry (two triggers): $1375
Sporting: $1220
Long Range: $1695
Long Range Big Bore: $1750

PGW Defense Technology

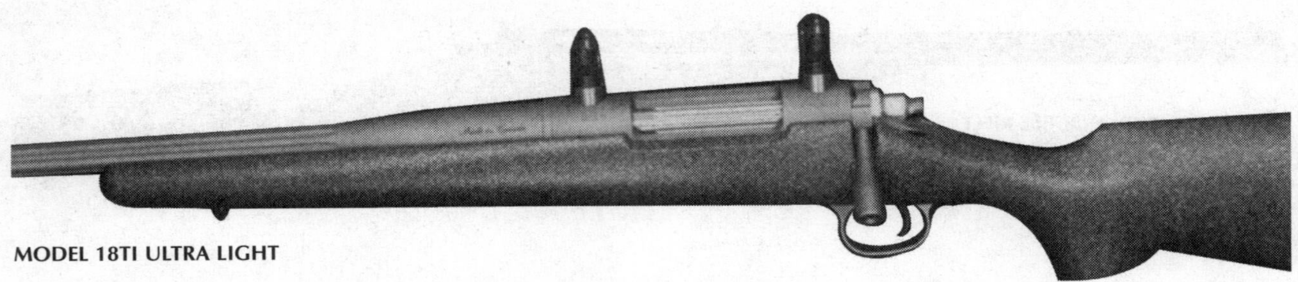

MODEL 18TI ULTRA LIGHT

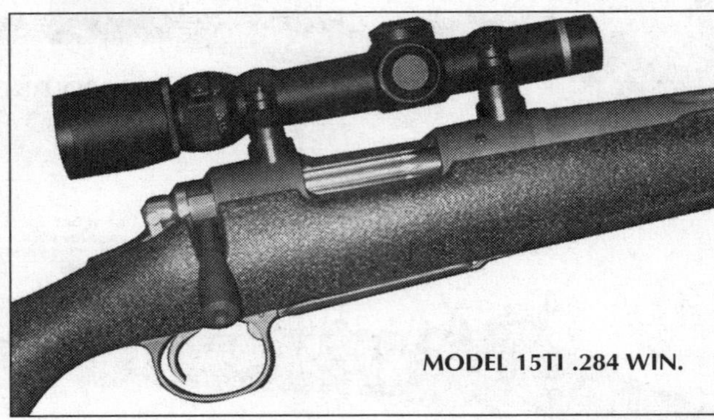

MODEL 15TI .284 WIN.

RIFLES

MODEL 15TI ULTRA LIGHT

Action: bolt
Stock: composite
Barrel: 22 in.
Sights: none
Weight: 5.0 lbs.
Caliber: most short-action calibers
Magazine: box, 5 rounds
Features: Rem. 700 short action, custom alloy scope mounts, new firing pin and bolt shroud tuned; also: Model 18Ti with long 700 action
Model 15Ti:. $2800
Model 18Ti:. $2800

TIMBERWOLF

Action: bolt
Stock: McMillan fiberglass
Barrel: fluted, match grade
Caliber: .338 Lapua
Magazine: 5-shot
Features: stainless receiver; adjustable trigger; 3-position safety, titanium rail with guide rib
Price: $5500
Also available:
in .408 . . . . $6300
Coyote in 7.62 (5 or 10-shot magazine) $3700
LRT .50 caliber Take-Down . . . $4500
LRT-2 in .338 or .408 . . . $2975 - 3700

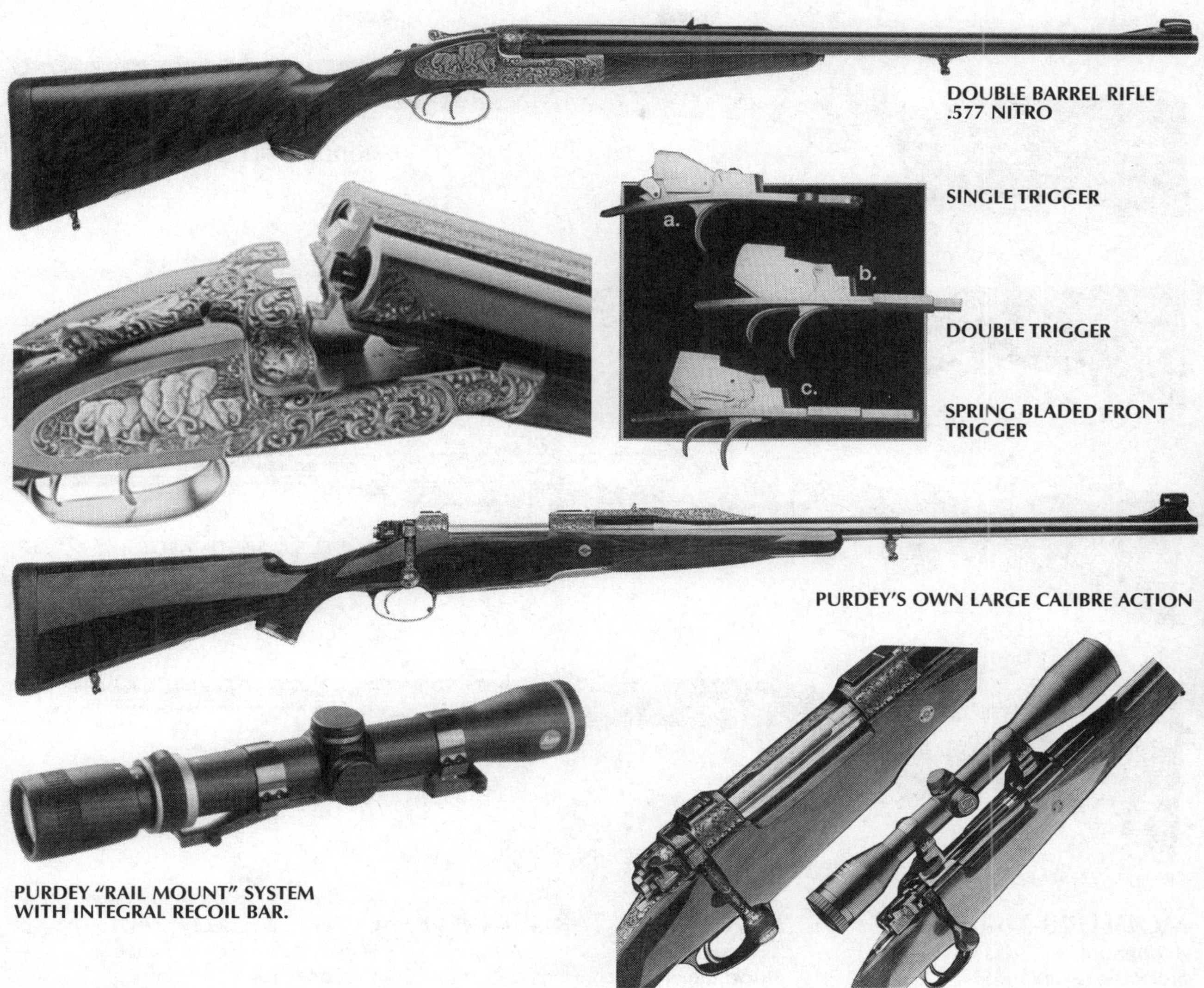

DOUBLE BARREL RIFLE
.577 NITRO

SINGLE TRIGGER

DOUBLE TRIGGER

SPRING BLADED FRONT TRIGGER

PURDEY'S OWN LARGE CALIBRE ACTION

PURDEY "RAIL MOUNT" SYSTEM WITH INTEGRAL RECOIL BAR.

DOUBLE BARREL RIFLE .577 NITRO

Purdey's double-barrel Express rifles are built to customer specifications on actions sized to each particular cartridge. Standard chamberings include .375 H&H Magnum and .470, .577 and .600 Nitro Express. The Purdey side-by-side action patented in 1880 is still made now with only very minor changes. The action mechanism, designed by Frederick Beesley, retains a portion of the energy in the mainsprings to facilitate the opening of the gun.

The over-under is derived from the Woodward, patented in 1913. The action blocks for all guns are cut from certified forgings, for consistency of grain throughout, and are so fitted to the barrels as to give an absolute joint. The actioner then fits the fore-part, the locks, the strikers and the safety work before finally detonating the action.

A – SINGLE TRIGGER

The Purdey single trigger works both by inertia and mechanically. It is simple, effective and fast. The firing sequence is fixed, therefore no barrel selection is possible.

B & C – DOUBLE TRIGGERS

The standard double triggers (B) can be augmented with an articulated front trigger (C). This device alleviates damage to the back of the trigger finger on discharge.

Purdey makes its own dedicated actions for bolt rifles in the following calibers: .375 H&H, .416/450 Rigby or other, .500 and .505 Gibbs.

The action length is suited to cartridge length in each caliber. Mauser Square Bridge and Mauser '98 actions are available.

RAIL MOUNT SYSTEM

This is Purdey's own system for big bolt rifles. It is very secure and facilitates fast on/off. Rings and mounts are all made with an integral recoil bar from a single piece of steel. This system is recommended for Purdey actions and Mauser Square Bridge actions.

Remington Arms Rifles

MODEL 40-XB TACTICAL

MODEL 40-XB

MODEL 552 SPEEDMASTER

MODEL 572 FIELDMASTER

RIFLES

MODEL 40-XBBR KS

Action: bolt
Stock: fiberglass
Barrel: 24 in.
Sights: none
Weight: 9.75 lbs.
Caliber: .22 LR
Magazine: single shot
Features: benchrest with stainless barrel, Aramid-fiber reinforced Remington green stock
Price: $1894

MODEL 40-XB TACTICAL

Action: bolt
Stock: black with green fiberglass
Barrel: 27.25 in.
Sights: none
Weight: 10.25 lbs.
Caliber: .308 Win.
Magazine: 5 shot, hinged floorplate; features built to order
.308 XB Tactical $2108

MODEL 40-X TARGET RIFLE

Action: bolt
Stock: target, benchrest or tactical
Barrel: 24 or 27 in.
Sights: none
Weight: 10.25 –11.25 lbs.
Caliber: 18 popular standard and magnum calibers
Magazine: box, 3 or 5 rounds
Features: rimfire and single-shot versions available; walnut, laminated and composite stocks; forend rail, match trigger
40-X: . . . . $1636 - 2108
Left-hand . . . . $1709 - 2044

MODEL 552 BDL DELUXE SPEEDMASTER

Action: autoloading
Stock: walnut
Barrel: 21 in.
Sights: Big Game
Weight: 5.75 lbs.
Caliber: .22 S, .22 L, .22 LR
Magazine: under-barrel tube, 15 rounds (LR), 17 (L) and 20 (S)
Features: classic autoloader made 1966 to date
552: $413

MODEL 572 BDL DELUXE FIELDMASTER

Action: pump
Stock: walnut
Barrel: 21 in.
Sights: Big Game
Weight: 5.5 lbs.
Caliber: .22 S, .22 L, .22 LR
Magazine: under-barrel tube, 15-20 rounds
Features: grooved receiver for scope mounts
Fieldmaster: $427

Remington Arms Rifles

MODEL 597

MODEL 673

REMINGTON 700 CDL

MODEL 700 CUSTOM C GRADE

MODEL 597

Action: autoloading
Stock: synthetic or laminated
Barrel: 20 in.
Sights: Big Game
Weight: 5.5 to 6.5 lbs.
Caliber: .22 LR, .22 WMR, .17 HMR
Magazine: detachable box, 10 rounds (8 in magnums)
Features: magnum version in .22 WMR and .17 HMR (both 6 lbs.); also: heavy-barrel model
Model 597: $156
stainless: $240
stainless laminated: $295
22 WMR $351
magnum (.17 HMR): $377
heavy-barrel: $288
heavy-barrel magnum: . . . $428 - 455

MODEL 673

Action: bolt
Stock: laminated
Barrel: 22 in.
Sights: open
Weight: 7.5 lbs.
Caliber: .350 Rem. Mag., .308 Win., 6.5 Rem. Mag., 300 SAUM
Magazine: 3 + 1
Features: vent rib, Model Seven action
Model 673 . . . . $859

REMINGTON 700 CDL

Action: bolt
Stock: walnut
Barrel: 24 inches (standard) and 26 inches (magnum, Ultra Mag)
Sights: none (drilled and tapped for scope mounts)
Weight: 7.5 lbs.
Caliber: .243, .25-06 Rem., .35 Whelen, .270, 7mm-08, 7mm Rem. Mag., 7mm Ultra Mag, .30-06, .300 Win. Mag. .300 Ultra Mag
Magazine: 4-round box (3 in magnums, Ultra Mags)
Features: fully adjustable trigger
Price: (standard) $743
(Ultra Mag) $769
Mag & Ultra Mag, lefthand (6 calibers) . . . . $769 - 796

MODEL 700 CUSTOM C GRADE

Action: bolt
Stock: fancy American walnut
Barrel: 24 in. (Ultra Mag 26 in.)
Sights: none
Weight: 7.5 lbs.
Caliber: any popular standard or magnum chambering
Magazine: 3 to 5
Features: some custom-shop options available
Model 700 Custom C Grade . . $1733

Remington Arms Rifles

MODEL 700 AFRICAN BIG GAME

MODEL 700 AFRICAN PLAINS RIFLE (APR)

MODEL 700 CLASSIC

MODEL 700 BDL DM

MODEL 700 AFRICAN BIG GAME

Action: bolt
Stock: laminated
Barrel: 26 in.
Sights: open
Weight: 9.5 lbs.
Caliber: .375 H&H, .375 RUM, .458 Win, .416 Rem.
Magazine: box, 3 rounds
Features: barrel-mounted front swivel
African Big Game:. $1726

MODEL 700 AFRICAN PLAINS RIFLE

Action: bolt
Stock: laminated
Barrel: 26 in.
Sights: none
Weight: 7.75 lbs.
Caliber: 10 offerings from 7mm Rem. Mag. to .375 RUM
Magazine: box, 3 rounds in magazine
Features: epoxy bedded action, machined steel trigger and floor plate.
African Plains Rifle:. $1716

MODEL 700 CLASSIC

Action: bolt
Stock: walnut
Barrel: 24 in.
Sights: none
Weight: 7.25 lbs.
Caliber: .308 Win.
Magazine: box, 5 rounds
Features: one-year run per caliber
700 Classic:. $716

MODEL 700 BDL CUSTOM DELUXE

Action: bolt
Stock: walnut
Barrel: 22 – 26 in.
Sights: open
Weight: 7.25 – 7.5 lbs.
Caliber: popular standard calibers from .17 Rem. to .300 RUM
Magazine: box, 3 or 5 rounds
Features: hinged floorplate, sling swivel studs, hooded ramp front & adjustable rear sights
BDL: $716
BDL Magnum:. $743
BDL Ultra-Mags:. $743

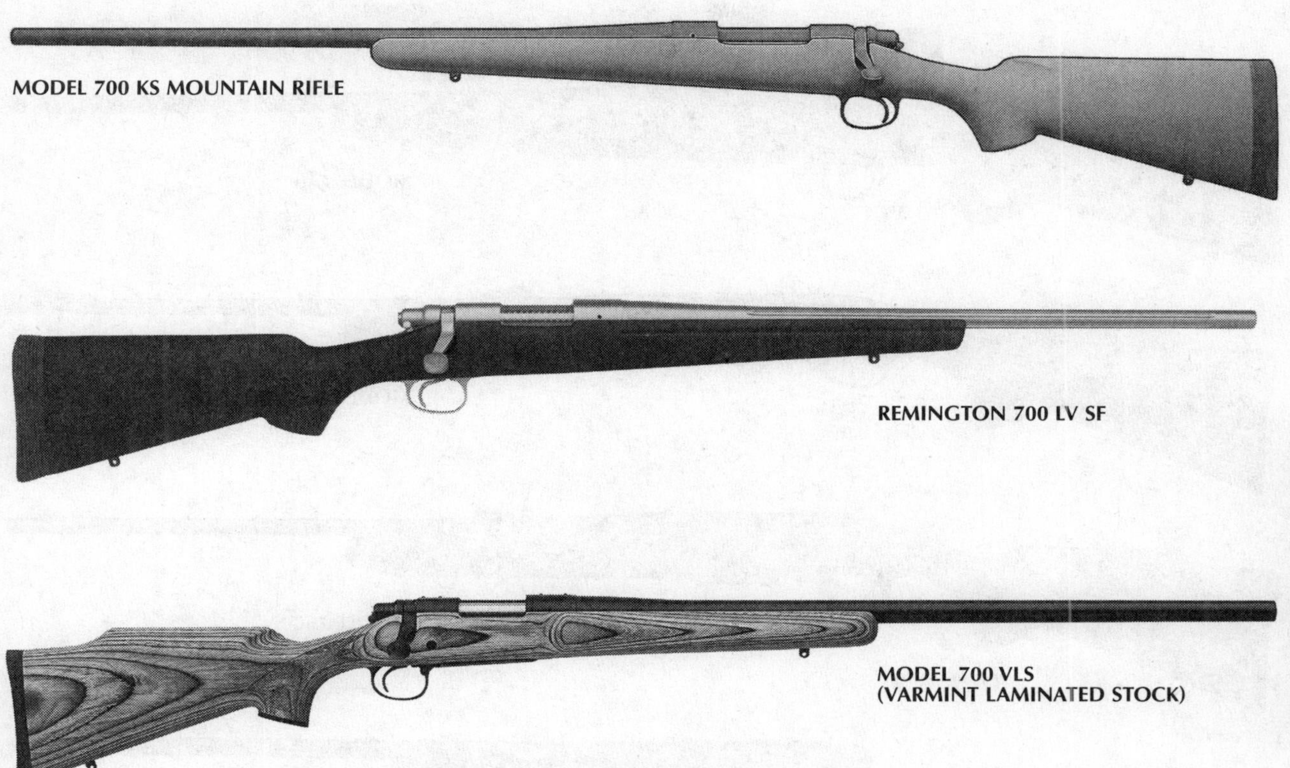

MODEL 700 CUSTOM KS MOUNTAIN RIFLE

Action: bolt
Stock: lightweight composite black matte
Barrel: 24 or 26 in., blued or stainless
Sights: none
Weight: 6.5 – 7.0 lbs. (magnums)
Caliber: 13 choices from .270 to .375 RUM
Magazine: box, 3 or 4 rounds
standard: $1314
stainless: $1500
Left-hand: . . . . $1393 - 1580

MODEL 700 MOUNTAIN RIFLE DM

Action: bolt
Stock: walnut or laminate
Barrel: 22 in.
Sights: none
Weight: 6.5 lbs.
Caliber: .260, .270, 7mm-08, .280, .30-06
Magazine: detachable box, 4 rounds
Features: also; LSS with laminated stock, stainless steel
Mountain DM: $783
LSS: $833

REMINGTON 700 LIGHT VARMINT (LV SF)

Action: bolt
Stock: synthetic
Barrel: 22 inches, stainless, fluted
Sights: none (drilled and tapped for scope mounts)
Weight: 6.7 lbs.
Caliber: .17 Rem., .204 Ruger, .221 Fireball, .22-250, .223
Magazine: 4 or 5round box
Features: fully adjustable trigger
Price: $952

MODEL 700 TITANIUM

Action: bolt
Stock: synthetic
Barrel: stainless 22 in. (24 in. SAUM)
Sights: none
Weight: 5.25 – 6.25 lbs.
Caliber: .260, .270, 7mm-08, .308, .30-06, 7mm SAUM, .300 SAUM
Magazine: box, 2 -4 rounds
Features: Titanium receiver; fluted bolt, skeleton handle, RC recoil pad
Titanium: $1272
Magnums: $1312

MODEL 700 VSF TARGET

Action: bolt
Stock: composite
Barrel: heavy 26 in.
Sights: none
Weight: 9.5 lbs.
Caliber: .223, .22-250,.243, .308
Magazine: box, 5 rounds
Features: fluted barrel, stock with beavertail fore-end, tactical style dual front swivel studs for bi-pod; VSSF II also available in .204 Ruger and .220 Swift
VSF (desert tan): $932
VSSF II: $1025
VLS (laminate): $759
Left hand: $959

Remington Arms Rifles

MODEL 710

MODEL 7400

MODEL 7600

REMINGTON 504

MODEL 710

Action: bolt
Stock: synthetic
Barrel: 22 or 24 in.
Sights: none
Weight: 7.3 lbs.
Caliber: .270, .30-06, 7mm Rem. Mag., .300 Win. Mag.
Magazine: detachable box, 3 or 4 rounds
Features: steel receiver; 60° bolt throw; includes mounted 3-9x40 Bushnell scope
710 with scope: $426

MODEL 7400

Action: autoloading
Stock: walnut or synthetic
Barrel: 22 in.
Sights: open
Weight: 7.5 lbs.
Caliber: .243, .270, .308, .30-06
Magazine: detachable box, 4 rounds
Features: also; 7400 carbine with 18 in. barrel (7.25 lbs.)
walnut: $651
synthetic: $547

MODEL 7600

Action: pump
Stock: walnut or synthetic
Barrel: 22 in.
Sights: open
Weight: 7.5 lbs.
Caliber: .243, .270, .308, .30-06
Magazine: detachable box, 4 rounds
Features: also: 7600 carbine with 18 in. barrel (7.25 lbs.)
walnut: $615
synthetic: $511

REMINGTON 504

Action: bolt
Stock: checkered walnut
Barrel: 20 inches, button-rifled 1:14 ½
Sights: none (drilled and tapped for scope mounts)
Weight: 6.0 lbs.
Caliber: .22 Long Rifle, .17 MACH2
Magazine: 6-round detachable box
Features: fully adjustable trigger, nickel-plated bolt, removable barrel with "match" chamber,
Price: $710
Also available:
504-T LSHB .22 LR/.17 HMR . . . . $799 – 825
504 Custom "C" Grade .22 LR . . $1665

Remington Arms Rifles

ROLLING BLOCK MID-RANGE SPORTER RIFLE

Action: dropping block
Stock: walnut
Barrel: heavy 30 in. Round barrel
Sights: Buckhorn rear, blade front
Weight: 8.75 lbs.
Caliber: .45-70
Magazine: none
Features: single set trigger
Mid-Range Sporter: $1450
Rolling Block Silhouette: $1560

MODEL SEVEN AWR (CUSTOM SHOP)

Action: bolt
Stock: lightweight composite
Barrel: stainless 22 in.
Sights: none
Weight: 6.0 lbs.
Caliber: 6.8 Rem. SPC, 7mm SAUM, .300 SAUM
Magazine: box, 3 rounds
Features: Alaska Wilderness Rifle has lightweight composite stock; also: MS wood, full-length stock (6.5 lbs.); Model Seven KS in standard short-action calibers has 20 in. barrel
Model Seven AWR: $1546
MS (12 calbiers): $1332
KS (6 calibers): $1314

MODEL SEVEN LS

Action: bolt
Stock: synthetic
Barrel: 20 in.
Sights: open
Weight: 6.5 lbs.
Caliber: .223, .243, .260, 7mm-08, .308
Magazine: box, 4 or 5 rounds
Features: synthetic stock with stainless barrel, laminate with satin finished carbon steel; youth model with short hardwood stock;
LS: $735
LS Magnum (.300 & 7mm SAUM) $775
Youth (.260 Rem. only): $580
Stainless synthetic: . . . . . . $763 - 803
Also available:
Model Seven Youth (synthetic in .223, .243, 7mm-08) $580

MODEL SEVEN MAGNUM

Action: bolt
Stock: synthetic or laminate
Barrel: stainless or blued 22 in.
Sights: open
Weight: 7.25 lbs.
Caliber: 7mm SAUM, .300 SAUM
Magazine: box, 3 rounds
Features: also: laminated stock versions with chrome-moly steel
LS laminated: $775
SS synthetic: $803

Rifles, Inc.

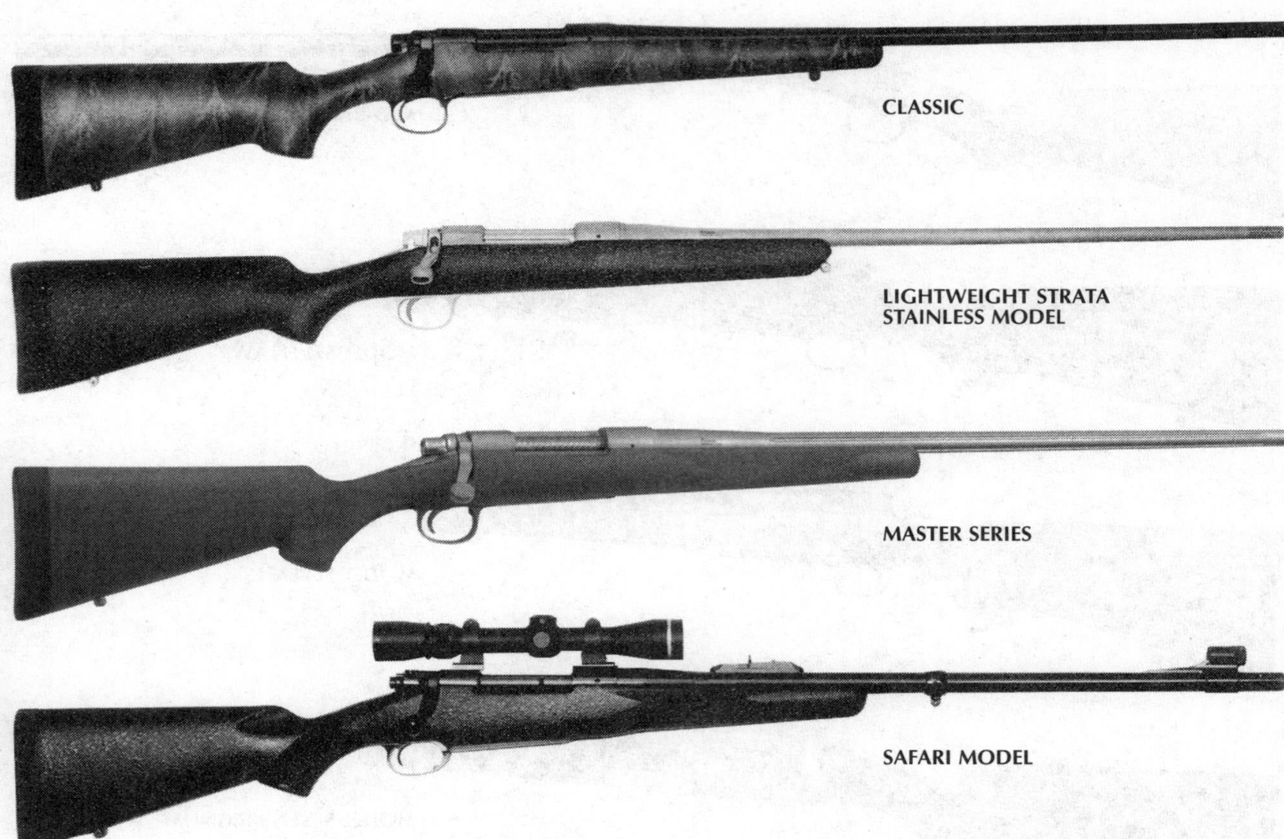

CLASSIC

LIGHTWEIGHT STRATA STAINLESS MODEL

MASTER SERIES

SAFARI MODEL

RIFLES

CLASSIC

Action: bolt
Stock: laminated fiberglass
Barrel: stainless steel, match grade 24 to 26 in.
Sights: none
Weight: 6.5 lbs.
Caliber: all popular chamberings up to .375 H&H
Magazine: box, 3 or 5 rounds
Features: Winchester 70 or Rem. 700 action; lapped bolt; pillar glass bedded stock; adjustable trigger; hinged floorplate; also: 27 in. fluted barrel, synthetic stock in .300 Rem. UM
Classic: $2000

LIGHTWEIGHT STRATA STAINLESS

Action: bolt
Stock: laminated with textured epoxy
Barrel: stainless match grade 22 to 25 in.
Sights: none
Weight: 5.0 lbs.
Caliber: all popular chamberings up to .375 H&H
Magazine: box, 3 or 5 rounds
Features: Stainless Rem. action, fluted bolt and hollowed-handle; pillar glass bedded stock; stainless metal finish; blind or hinged floorplate; custom Protektor pad; also: Lightweight 70 (5.75 lbs.); Lightweight Titanium Strata
Lightweight Strata: $2350
Lightweight 70: $2250
Titanium Strata:. $2900

MASTER SERIES

Action: bolt
Stock: laminated fiberglass
Barrel: match grade 24 to 27 in.
Sights: none
Weight: 7.75 lbs.
Caliber: all popular chamberings up to .300 Rem. Ultra Mag.
Magazine: box, 3 rounds
Features: Remington 700 action
Master Series: $2500

SAFARI MODEL

Action: bolt
Stock: laminated fiberglass
Barrel: stainless match grade 23 to25 in.
Sights: optional Express
Weight: 8.5 lbs.
Caliber: all popular chamberings
Magazine: box, 3 or 5 rounds, optional drop box
Features: Win. Model 70 action; drilled and tapped for 8-40 screws; Stainless Quiet Slimbrake; stainless or black Teflon finish; adjustable trigger; hinged floor-plate; barrel band optional
Safari: $2700

All Rifles, Inc. prices include customer-supplied action.

Rogue Rifle Company

STD-DELUXE WALNUT

CHIPMUNK

Action: bolt
Stock: walnut, laminated black, brown or camo
Barrel: 16 in.
Sights: target
Weight: 2.5 lbs.
Caliber: Sporting rifle in .17 HMR and .17 MACH2; Target model in .22, .22 LR, .22 WMR
Magazine: none
Features: single-shot; manual-cocking action; receiver-mounted rear sights; Target model weighs 5 lbs. and comes with competition-style receiver sight and globe front and adjustable trigger, extendable buttplate and front rail.

standard: . . . . $140 - 200
Target with options: $350
stainless:. . . . . $160 –220
bull barrel: . . . . $175 – 220
bullbarrel/stainless: . . . . . $195 - 240

Rossi Rifles

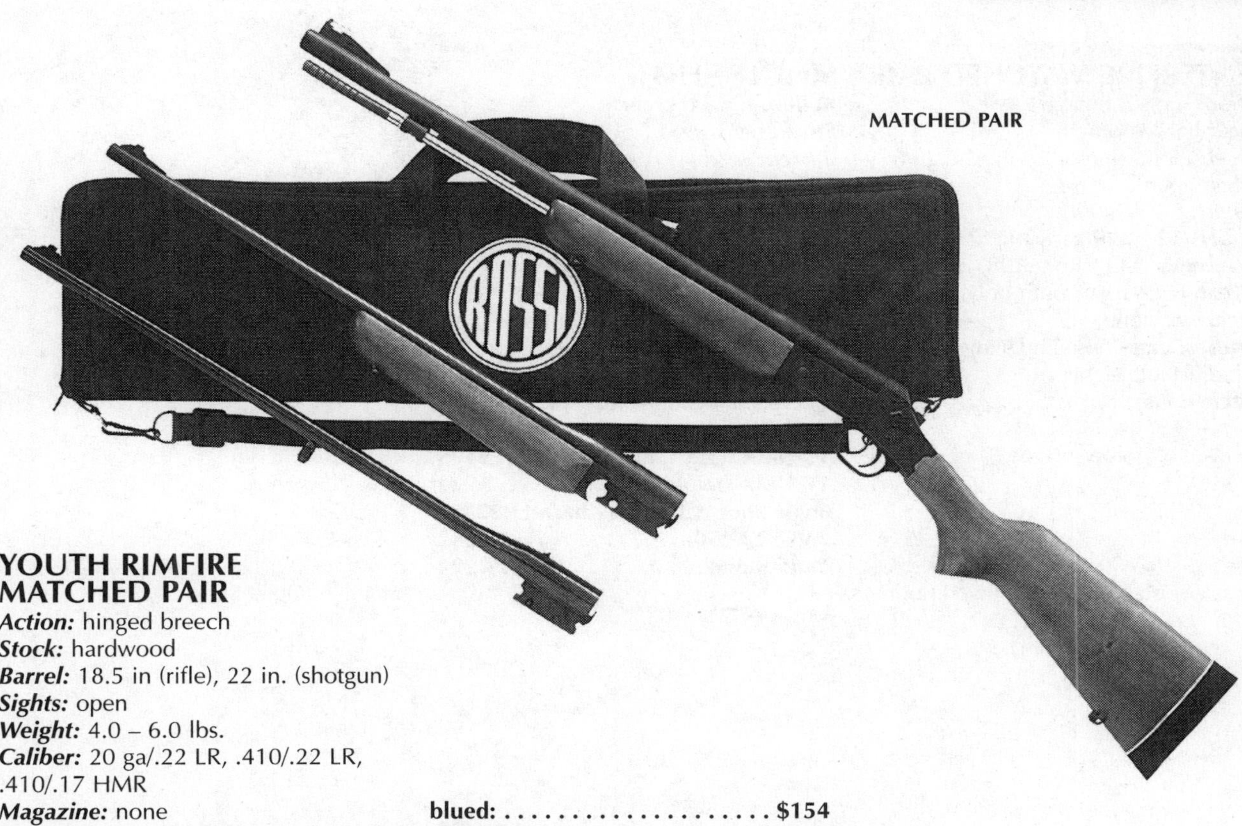

MATCHED PAIR

YOUTH RIMFIRE MATCHED PAIR

Action: hinged breech
Stock: hardwood
Barrel: 18.5 in (rifle), 22 in. (shotgun)
Sights: open
Weight: 4.0 – 6.0 lbs.
Caliber: 20 ga/.22 LR, .410/.22 LR, .410/.17 HMR
Magazine: none
Features: single shot; blue or stainless steel; single-stage trigger, adjustable sights; full size 12 or 20 gauge with .22 LR, .22 Mag or .17 HMR

blued: $154
stainless: $195
.410 and .17 HMR, blue:. $196
stainless: $243
full-size:. . . . . $160 - 200

Rossi Rifles

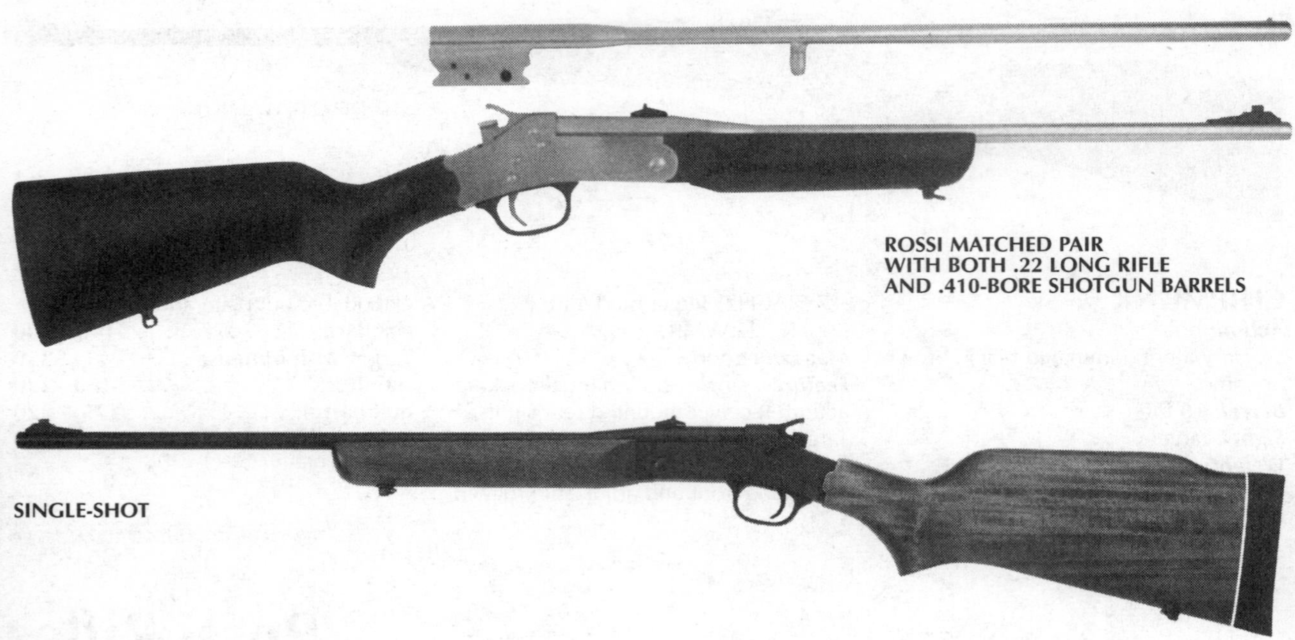

ROSSI MATCHED PAIR
WITH BOTH .22 LONG RIFLE
AND .410-BORE SHOTGUN BARRELS

SINGLE-SHOT

RIFLES

CENTERFIRE MATCHED PAIR

Action: hinged breech
Stock: hardwood
Barrel: 23 in. rifle or 28 in. shotgun
Sights: open
Weight: 5.0 – 6.0 lbs.
Caliber: 12 or 20 ga with .223 Rem., .243 Rem., .243 Win., .308, .30-06, .270 and .22-250 (Youth only)
Magazine: none
Features: carry case and sling included; adjustable sights
Matched Pair. $272

SINGLE SHOT

Action: hinged breech
Stock: hardwood
Barrel: 23 in.
Sights: open
Weight: 6.25 lbs.
Caliber: .17 HMR, .223, 243, .308, .30-06, .270, .22-250 , 7.62x39
Magazine: none
Features: single shot; recoil pad; sling swivels; extra-wide positive-action extractor; good rifle for first time shooters; all calibers except .17 HMR have Monte Carlo stock
.17 HMR blue: $175
.17 HMR stainless: $222
Single Shot with heavy barrel (.223, .243, .22-250): $232
Youth model: . . . . $164 - 224

Zero a big game rifle so the bullet strikes between 3 inches above point of aim at mid-range. That way, you'll achieve greatest "point-blank" range. For the .30-06 and kin, try a zero of 200 yards.

MODEL 10/22 RBM

M-77 MARK II ALL-WEATHER

M77RSM MKII

MODEL 77VT MARK II HEAVY BARREL TARGET

MODEL 10/22

Action: autoloading
Stock: walnut, birch, synthetic or laminated
Barrel: 18 in.
Sights: open
Weight: 5.0 lbs.
Caliber: .22 LR
Magazine: rotary, 10 rounds
Features: blowback action; also: International with full-stock, heavy-barreled Target and stainless steel versions; Magnum with 9-shot magazine
Model 10/22: $258
walnut: $324
stainless: $304
Target: $445
Target stainless, laminated: $495
magnum: $536
.17 HMR $536

MODEL 77 RFP MARK II

Action: bolt
Stock: synthetic
Barrel: 22 in.
Sights: none
Weight: 7.0 – 8.0 lbs.
Caliber: most popular standard and magnum calibers
Magazine: box, 3 - 5 rounds
Features: stainless steel barrel and action, (magnums with 24 in. barrel); scope rings included
RFP: $716

MODEL 77 RSM MAGNUM

Action: bolt
Stock: Circassian walnut
Barrel: 23 in. with quarter rib
Sights: open
Weight: 9.5 – 10.0 lbs.
Caliber: .375 H&H, .416 Rigby (10.3 lbs.), .458 Lott
Magazine: box, 3 or 4 rounds
Features: barrel-mounted front swivel; also: Express rifle in popular standard and magnum long-action calibers
Price: $1975

MODEL 77 VT MARK II

Action: bolt
Stock: brown laminate
Barrel: heavy stainless 26 in., target grey finish
Sights: none
Weight: 9.8 lbs.
Caliber: .223, .204, .22-250, .220 Swift, .243, .25-06, .308
Magazine: box, 4 or 5 rounds
Model 77 VT: $870

Ruger Rifles

MODEL 77/17 BOLT ACTION RIFLE

MODEL 96/17

MODEL 77/22VBZ VARMINT

MODEL M-77R MKII

RIFLES

MODEL 77/17

Action: bolt
Stock: walnut, synthetic or laminated
Barrel: 22 in.
Sights: none
Weight: 6.5 lbs.
Caliber: .17 HMR
Magazine: 9 rounds
Features: also: stainless (P) and stainless varmint with laminated stock (VMBBZ), 24 in. barrel (6.9 lbs.)
77/17 RM:. $613
77/17 RMP:. $613
K77/17 VMBBZ: $685
Also available:
.17 MACH2 (20 in, blue or stainless bbl.): . . . . . $674 - 746

MODEL 96 LEVER ACTION RIFLE

Action: Lever
Stock: Hardwood
Barrel: 18½ inches blued
Sights: Adjustable rear sight
Weight: 5.25 lbs.
Caliber: .17 HMR, .22 WMR, .44 Mag.
Magazine: 9 round rotary magazine
Features: Enclosed short-throw lever action; cross bolt safety; standard tip-off scope-mount base.
Price:. $ 390
.44 Mag. (4-round):. $546

MODEL 77/22 RIMFIRE RIFLE

Action: bolt
Stock: walnut
Barrel: 20 in.
Sights: none
Weight: 6.0 lbs.
Caliber: .22 LR, .22 Mag., .22 Hornet
Magazine: rotary, 6 -10 rounds
Features: also: Magnum (M) and stainless synthetic (P) versions; scope rings included for all; sights on S versions. VBZ has 24 in. medium stainless barrel (6.9 lbs.)
77/22R:. $613
77/22RM: $613
K77/22RP:. $613
K77/22 RMP:. $613
K77/22VBZ: $685
K77/22VMBZ:. $685
77/22RH (.22 Hornet): $649
K77/22VHZ (.22 Hornet):. $685

MODEL 77R MARK II

Action: bolt
Stock: walnut
Barrel: 22 in.
Sights: none
Weight: 7.25 – 8.25 lbs.
Caliber: most popular standard and magnum calibers
Magazine: box, 3 - 5 rounds
Features: scope rings included; RBZ has stainless steel, laminated stock; RSBZ with sights
77R: $716
RBZ: $773

Ruger Rifles

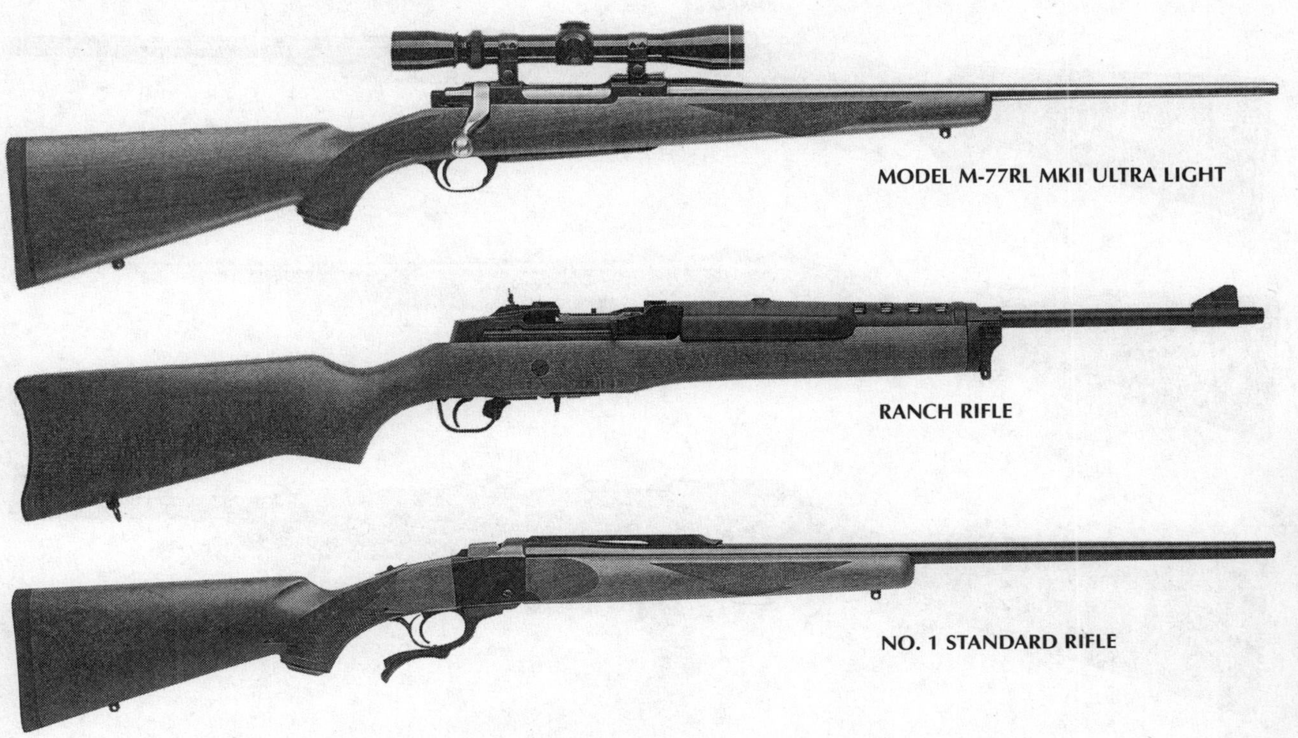

RIFLES

MODEL 77RL MARK II ULTRA LIGHT

Action: bolt
Stock: walnut
Barrel: 20 in.
Sights: none
Weight: 6.25 – 6.75 lbs.
Caliber: .223, .243, .257, .270, .308
Magazine: box, 4 or 5 rounds
77RL Ultra Light:. $773
International Model (18 in. bbl.): . . . $819

RANCH RIFLE

Action: autoloading
Stock: hardwood
Barrel: 18 in.
Sights: target
Weight: 6.5 – 7.0 lbs.
Caliber: .223
Magazine: detachable box, 5 rounds
Features: also: stainless, stainless synthetic versions of Mini-14/5; Ranch Rifle (with scope mounts) and Mini-thirty (in 7.62x39)
Ranch Rifle:. $750
Ranch rifle, stainless: $809
Ranch rifle, stainless synthetic:. $809
Mini-Thirty, stainless synthetic:. $809
Deerfield Carbine .44 Mag.. . . . $702

NO. 1 SINGLE-SHOT

Action: dropping block
Stock: select checkered walnut
Barrel: 22, 24, or 26 in. (RSI: 20 in.)
Sights: open
Weight: 7.25 – 8.25 lbs.
Caliber: all popular chamberings in Light Sporter, Medium Sporter, Standard Rifle
Magazine: none
Features: pistol grip; all rifles come with Ruger 1″ scope rings; 45-70 is available in stainless; No. 1 Stainless comes in .243, .25-06, 7mm Rem. Mag., .204, .30-06, .270, .300 Win. Mag., .308
No. 1: $966
Stainless steel:. $998

Adjust your trigger so it "breaks" at a comfortable weight. Heavy triggers require too much hand muscle in the squeeze. You'll move the rifle.

Ruger Rifles

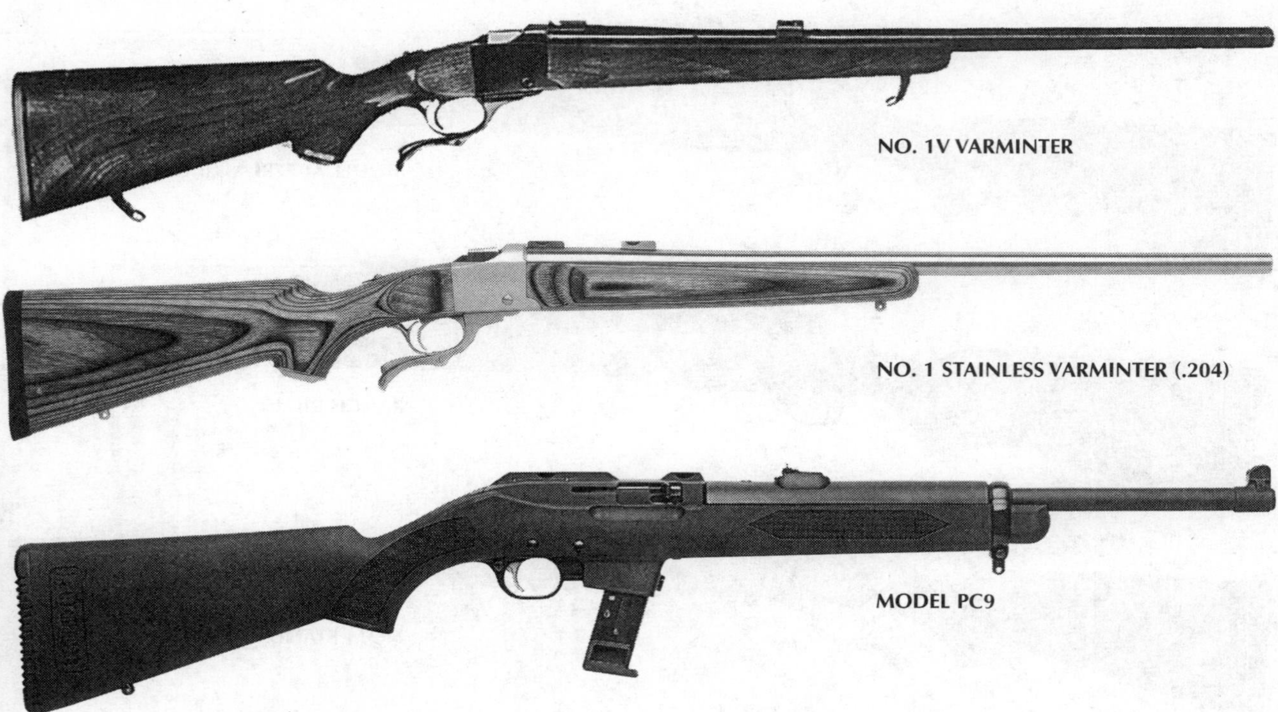
NO. 1V VARMINTER

NO. 1 STAINLESS VARMINTER (.204)

MODEL PC9

RIFLES

NO. 1V (VARMINTER)

Action: dropping block
Stock: select checkered walnut
Barrel: heavy 24 or 26 in. (.220 Swift)
Sights: open
Weight: 8.75 lbs.
Caliber: .22-250, .220 Swift, .223, .25-06
Magazine: box, 5 rounds
Features: Ruger target scope block, stainless available in .22-250; also: No. 1H Tropical (heavy 24 in. bbl.) in .375 H&H, .416 Rigby, .458 Lott, .458 Win. Mag., .405; No.1 RSI International (20 in. light bbl. and full-length stock) in .243, .270, .30-06, 7x57

Varmint: $966
Tropical: $966
International: $998
stainless Varminter (24 - 26 in. bbl. In .204 Ruger or .22-250): $998

MODEL PC4 CARBINE

Action: autoloading
Stock: synthetic
Barrel: 16.25 in.
Sights: open
Weight: 6.3 lbs.
Caliber: 9mm, .40 S&W
Magazine: detachable, 10 - 15 rounds
Features: delayed blowback action; optional ghost ring sight

Carbine: $623
with ghost ring sights: $647

Before taking a shot, inhale deeply, then let your lungs relax. A surge of oxygen improves your vision and sight picture; but if you hold your breath, you tense up and pulse becomes a problem.

Sako Rifles

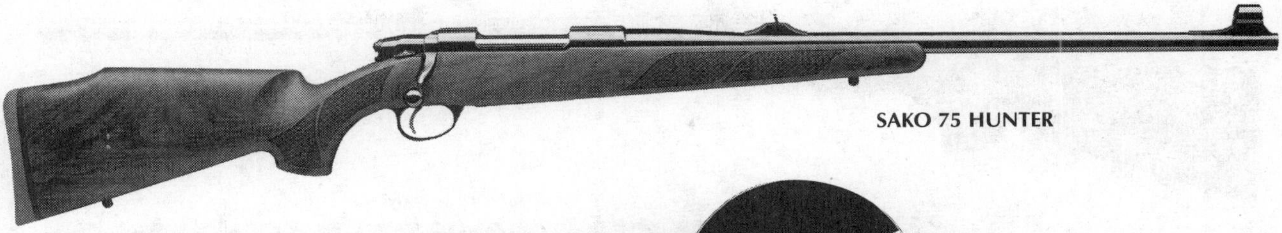

SAKO 75 HUNTER

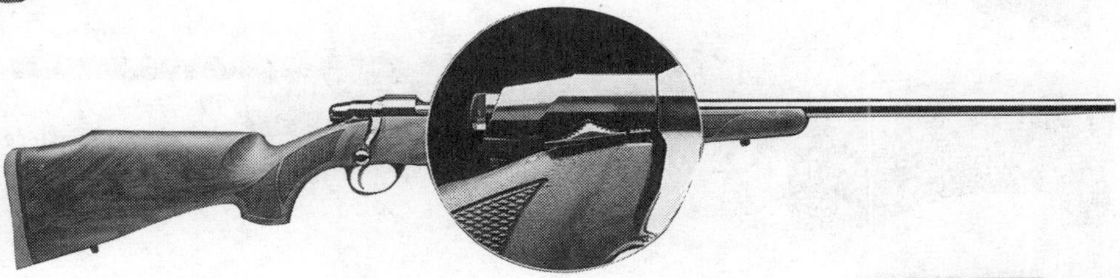

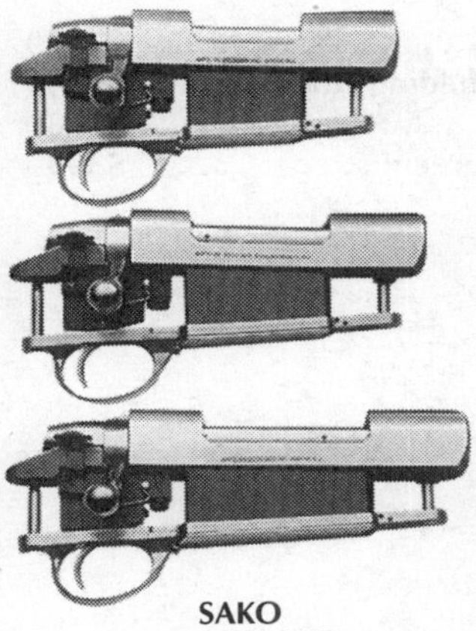

KEY

SAKO ACTIONS

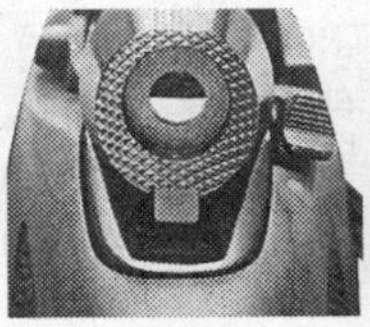

LOCKED

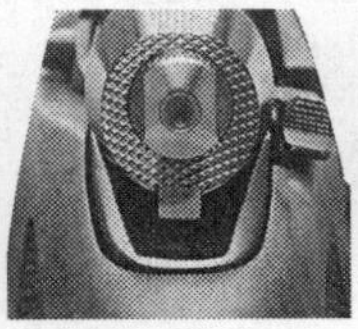

READY

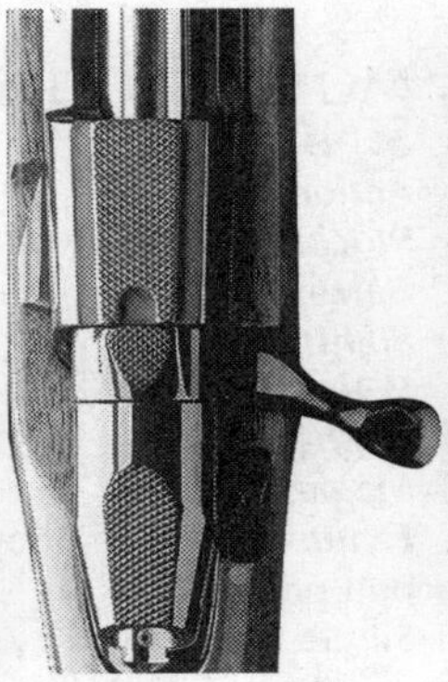

THUMB SAFETY, DOVETAILED RECEIVER

MODEL 75 VARMINT

MODEL 75 HUNTER

Action: bolt
Stock: walnut or synthetic
Barrel: hammer-forged 22, 24 or 26 in.
Sights: none
Weight: 7.0 lbs.
Caliber: most popular standard and magnum calibers from .222 Rem. to .375 H&H and .300, 7 and .270 WSM
Magazine: detachable box, 4 to 6 rounds
Features: barrel length depends on caliber; 4 action lengths; also: stainless synthetic and short-barreled Finnlight versions, Deluxe Grade with fancy walnut stock

Hunter: **$1419**
.375 H&H: **$1499**
Stainless synthetic: **$1499**
Left-hand (.25-06, .270, .30-06): **$1419**
Finnlight: **$1584**
Deluxe: **$2044**
.416 Rem: **$2418**

MODEL 75 VARMINT

Action: bolt
Stock: varmint-style walnut
Barrel: heavy 24 in.
Sights: none
Weight: 9.0 lbs.
Caliber: .223, .260 Rem., .22-250, .243, .308, .204 Ruger
Magazine: detachable box, 5 to 6 rounds
Features: also: single set trigger

Varmint: **$1684**
Varmint LS: **$1959**

Sako Rifles

MODEL 75 CUSTOM SINGLE SHOT

MODEL TRG-42

RIFLES

MODEL 75 CUSTOM SINGLE SHOT

Action: bolt
Stock: laminated
Barrel: 23 in.
Sights: none
Weight: 9.0 lbs.
Caliber: .308
Magazine: none
Features: stainless barrel, rubber butt pad
Single Shot:. $3448

MODEL TRG-22

Action: bolt
Stock: synthetic
Barrel: 26 in.
Sights: none
Weight: 10.3 lbs.
Caliber: .308
Magazine: detachable box, 10 rounds
Features: 3-lug bolt; fully adjustable trigger; optional bipod, brake; also: TRG 42 in .300 Win. Mag. and .338 Lapua (5-round magazine, 27 in. barrel, 11.3 lbs.)

TRG-22: $3589
TRG-22, folding stock: $5849
TRG-42: $3589
TRG-42, green: $3999

Sauer Rifles

202 STANDARD

202 VARMINT

MODEL 202

Action: bolt
Stock: Claro walnut
Barrel: 24 in.
Sights: none
Weight: 7.7 lbs.
Caliber: .243, .25-06, 6.5x55, .270, .308, .30-06
Magazine: detachable box, 5 rounds
Features: adjustable trigger; quick-change barrel; also: Supreme Magnum with 26 in. barrel in 7mm Rem., .300 Win., .300 Wby., .375 H&H; Varmint and Tactical versions too

Model 202: $2200
Magnum: . . . . $2400 - 2600
Synthetic:. . . . . $2200 - 2600
Lightweight: $3400
Varmint: $3400
Left-hand (.30-06, walnut): . . . $3700
SSG 3000 Tactical: . . . . $2900 - 5000

MODEL 12 VSS

MODEL 12FV

MODEL 12FVSS

MODEL 12BVSS

SAVAGE VARMINTER

MODEL 12, 112 10FP SERIES

Action: bolt
Stock: synthetic or laminated
Barrel: 20 or 26 in.
Sights: none
Weight: 8.3lbs.
Caliber: .223, .22-250, .243, .25-06, 7mm Rem. Mag., .308, .30-06, .300 WSM, .300 Win. Mag.
Magazine: 3 or 4
Features: single-shot or box magazine; new in these rifles for 2003 is the Savage AccuTrigger
12 VSS: $934

MODEL 12FV (SHORT ACTION)

Action: bolt
Stock: synthetic
Barrel: varmint , 26 in.
Sights: none
Weight: 9.0 lbs.
Caliber: .223, .22-250, .243, .308, .300 WSM, .204 Ruger
Magazine: box, 5 rounds
Features: also: 12VSS with fluted stainless barrel, Choate adjustable stock (11.3 lbs.) and V2BVSS with stainless fluted barrel, laminated or synthetic stock (9.5 lbs.)
FV $549
FVSS $667
BVSS laminated. $721

MODEL 112 BVSS (LONG-ACTION)

Action: bolt
Stock: lightweight composite
Barrel: fluted stainless 26 in.
Sights: none
Weight: 10.3 lbs.
Caliber: .25-06, 7mm Rem. Mag., .30-06, .300 Win. Mag.
Magazine: box, 4 rounds
Features: also: 112BVSS with laminated stock
BVSS $721

VARMINTER LOW PROFILE

Action: bolt
Stock: laminated
Barrel: heavy fluted stainless, button-rifled
Sights: none (drilled and tapped for scope mounts)
Weight: 9.0 lbs.
Caliber: .223 and .22-250, .204 Ruger
Magazine: 4-round box or single-shot
Features: fully adjustable AccuTrigger
Price: $778

Savage Rifles

MODEL 40 VARMINT HUNTER

MODEL 11G

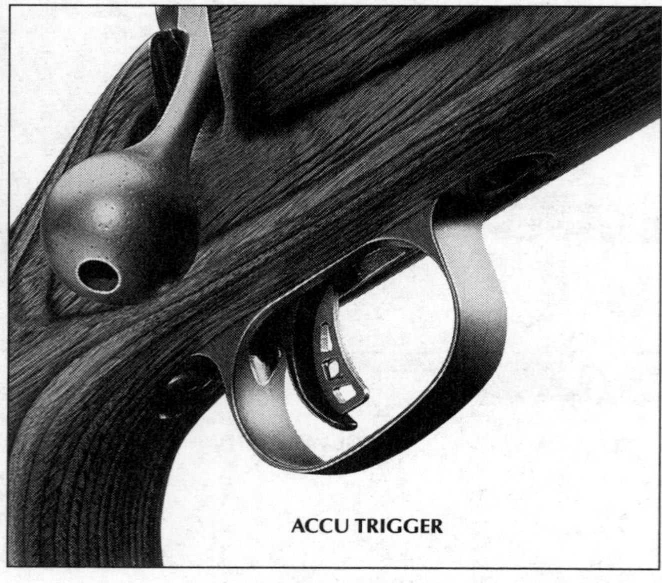

ACCU TRIGGER

MODEL 40 W/ACCUTRIGGER

Action: bolt
Stock: laminated, beavertail, with third swivel stud
Barrel: 24 inches, heavy, sleeved, free-floating
Sights: none (drilled and tapped for scope mounts)
Weight: 8.5 lbs.
Caliber: .22 Hornet
Magazine: none
Price: (Hornet) $436

MODEL 11F

Action: bolt
Stock: synthetic
Barrel: 22 in.
Sights: none
Weight: 6.8 lbs.
Caliber: .223, .22-250, .243, 7mm-08, .308, .270 WSM, 7mm WSM, .300 WSM,
Magazine: box, 5 rounds
Features: open sights available; also 11G with walnut stock, 10 GY Youth with short stock in .223, .243, and .308
11F $486
11G. $496

MODEL 11/111

Action: bolt
Stock: hardwood or synthetic
Barrel: 24 in.
Sights: none
Weight: 7.0 lbs.
Caliber: .270 WSM, 7mm WSM, .300 WSM, 7mm SUM, .300 SUM (all new for 2003 in various configurations)
Magazine: 3
Features: top tang safety; adjustable sights available
from $486

MODEL 116FSS (LONG ACTION)

Action: bolt
Stock: synthetic
Barrel: stainless 22, 24, or 26 in.
Sights: none
Weight: 6.5 lbs.
Caliber: .270, .30-06 (22 in.), 7mm Rem. Mag., .300 Win. Mag., .338 Win. Mag., .300 RUM (26 in.)
Magazine: box, 3 or 4 rounds
Features: also: 116BSS with checkered laminated stock
116FSS $552

MODEL 110 LONG RANGE

Action: bolt
Stock: lightweight composite
Barrel: heavy 24 in.
Sights: none
Weight: 8.5 lbs.
Caliber: .25-06, 7mm Rem. Mag., .30-06, .300 Win. Mag.
Magazine: box, 4 rounds
Features: also short-action Model 10 in .223, .308
Model 110FP: $601
Model 10: $601
Model 10GY (youth, 22 in. bbl.). . $496

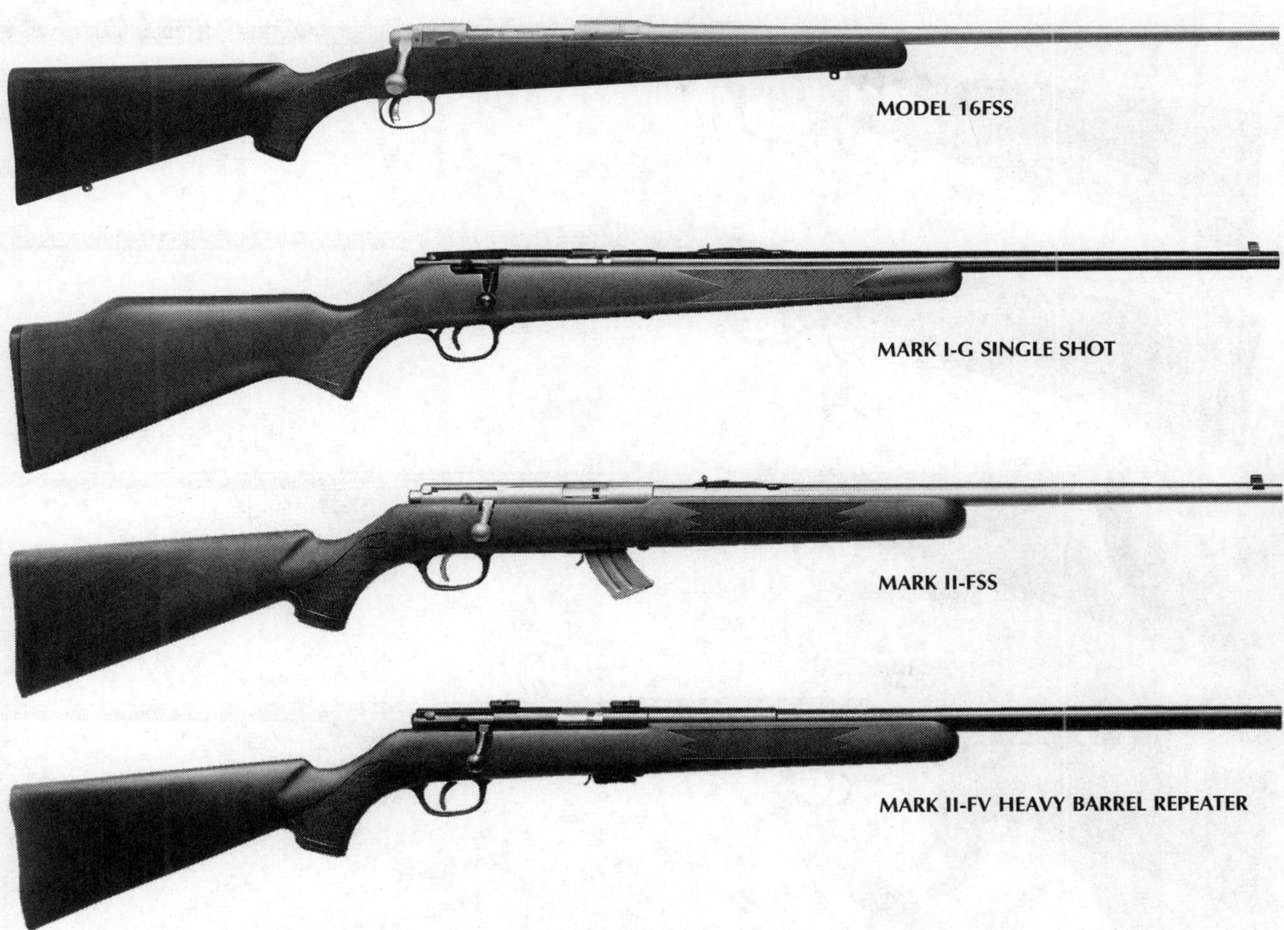

MODEL 16FSS (SHORT ACTION)

Action: bolt
Stock: synthetic
Barrel: stainless 22 or 24 in.
Sights: none
Weight: 6.0 lbs.
Caliber: .223, .243, .204 Ruger, 7mm WSM, .22-250 REM, 7-08, .308, .270 WSM, .300 WSM
Magazine: box, 3 or 4 rounds
Features: also: 16BSS with checkered laminated stock in .300 WSM only
16FSS $552

MARK I

Action: bolt
Stock: hardwood
Barrel: 19 or 21 in.
Sights: open
Weight: 5.5 lbs.
Caliber: .22 S, .22 L, .22 LR
Magazine: none
Features: also: MkIG Youth (19 in. barrel), MkILY Youth laminated stock, MIY Youth camo stock
Mark I FVT (with peep sights) . . $289
Mark I G $152
G Youth.................. $152
LY $187
Mark I GSB (.22 LR Short): $152

MARK II F

Action: bolt
Stock: synthetic
Barrel: 21 in.
Sights: open
Weight: 5.0 lbs.
Caliber: .22 LR
Magazine: detachable box, 5 rounds
Features: also: MkIIG with hardwood stock, MkIIFSS stainless, MkIIGY with short stock and 19 in. barrel
F $151
G........................ $169
FSS $213
GY $169
camo..................... $184

MARK II FV HEAVY-BARREL

Action: bolt
Stock: synthetic
Barrel: heavy 21 in.
Sights: none
Weight: 6.0 lbs.
Caliber: .22 LR
Magazine: detachable box, 5 or 10 rounds
Features: Weaver scope bases included; also: MkII LV with laminated stock (6.5 lbs.)
FV....................... $216
BV....................... $264

Savage Rifles

MODEL 30

Action: dropping block
Stock: walnut
Barrel: octagon 21 in.
Sights: open
Weight: 4.3 lbs.
Caliber: .22 LR, .22 WMR, .17 HMR
Magazine: none
Features: re-creation of Steven's Favorite

30G. $228
30GM $266
30R17 . . . . $292
Take-down .22. . . . . $249
Take-down .17. . . . . $314

MODEL 64F

Action: autoloading
Stock: synthetic
Barrel: 21 in.
Sights: open
Weight: 5.5 lbs.
Caliber: .22 LR
Magazine: detachable box, 10 rounds
Features: also; 64 FSS stainless, 64FV and FVSS heavy barrel, 64G hardwood stock

64F $135
64G. $162

MODEL 93

Action: bolt
Stock: synthetic, hardwood or laminated
Barrel: 21 in.
Sights: none
Weight: 5.0 lbs.
Caliber: .17 HMR
Magazine: 5
Features: scope bases included; eight versions with stainless or C-M steel, different stocks; varmint models weigh 6.0 lbs.

synthetic F $187
laminated stainless FVSS $267

MODEL 93G

Action: bolt
Stock: synthetic
Barrel: 21 in.
Sights: open
Weight: 5.8 lbs.
Caliber: .22 WMR, .17 HMR
Magazine: detachable box, 5 rounds
Features: 93G with hardwood stock; 93 FSS stainless, 93FVSS with heavy barrel, 93G with hardwood stock

Model 93G $195

Springfield Rifles

M1 GARAND

M1A STANDARD

M1A-A1 SCOUT RIFLE

MODEL M-6 SCOUT RIFLE/SHOTGUN COMBO FOLDING SURVIVAL GUN

RIFLES

M1 GARAND

Action: autoloading
Stock: walnut
Barrel: 24 in.
Sights: target
Weight: 9.5 lbs.
Caliber: .30-06, .308
Magazine: clip-fed, 8 rounds
Features: gas-operated; new stock, receiver, barrel; other parts mil-spec
M1 Garand .308:. $1378
M1 Garand .30-06:. $1348

M1A

Action: autoloading
Stock: walnut
Barrel: 22 in.
Sights: target
Weight: 9.2 lbs.
Caliber: .308
Magazine: detachable box, 5 or 10 rounds
Features: also with fiberglass stock and M1A/Scout with 18 in. barrel and scope mount (9.0 lbs.)
M1A:. $1586
M1A fiberglass:. $1498
M1A Camo:. $1507
M1A Scout Rifle:. $1727
M1A Scout Rifle, fiberglass: . . $1610
M1A Scout Rifle, camo: $1653

MODEL M-6 SCOUT

Action: hinged breech
Stock: synthetic
Barrel: 16 in.
Sights: open
Weight: 4.0
Caliber: .22LR and .410 or .22 Hornet and .410
Magazine: none
Features: over/under combination gun; lockable plastic case; also: stainless M-6
M-6: $215
M-6 stainless: $249

Steyr Rifles

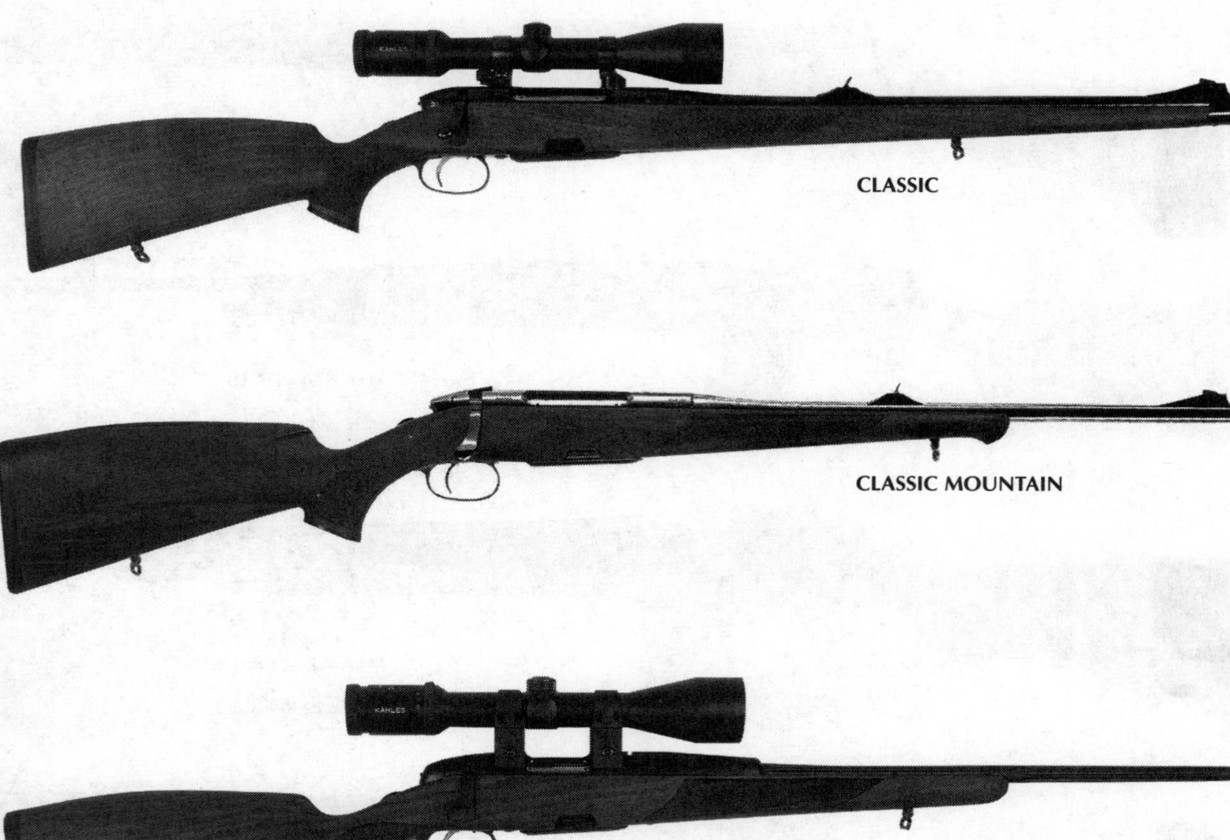

RIFLES

CLASSIC MANNLICHER

Action: bolt
Stock: European walnut
Barrel: 20 in., 23.6 in. and 25.6 in.
Sights: open
Weight: 7.4, 7.7 (magnum)
Caliber: .222, .223, .243, 6,5x55 SE, 6,5x57, 25-06, .270, 7x64, 7mm-08, 308, 30-06, 8x57 JS, 9,3x62, 7 mm Rem. Mag., .300 Win. Mag., 7 mm WSM, .270 WSM, .300 WSM
Magazine: box, 4 rounds,
Features: Three-position roller tang safety with front locking lugs and ice/residue groove; full stock or half stock models; total length 41.7 in.; set or direct trigger; sights as optional extras on half-stock models;
Half-stock: **$1566**
Mountain: **$1753**
Classic **$1893**

ULTRA LIGHT

Action: bolt
Stock: European walnut
Barrel: 19 in.
Sights: none
Weight: 5.9
Caliber: .222, .223, .243 Win., 7 mm-08 Rem., 308
Magazine: detachable box, 4 rounds
Features: High-strength aluminium receiver; bolt lugs lock into steel safety bushing; SBS (Safe Bolt System) safety system three position roller tang safety with front locking lugs and ice/residue groove; set trigger or direct trigger; integral Weaver-type scope mounting rail; total length 38.5 in.
MSRP: **$1505**

SCOUT

Action: bolt
Stock: synthetic
Barrel: 19 in.
Sights: open
Weight: 7
Caliber: .223, .243, 7 mm-08, .308, .376 Steyr
Magazine: detachable box, 5 rounds
Features: High-strength aluminium receiver; SBS (Safe Bolt System) safety system three position roller tang safety full; set or direct trigger; full Weaver-type rail; spare magazine in the butt stock; integral folding bipod; matte black finish; total length 38.5 in.
MSRP: **$2699**

SCOUT

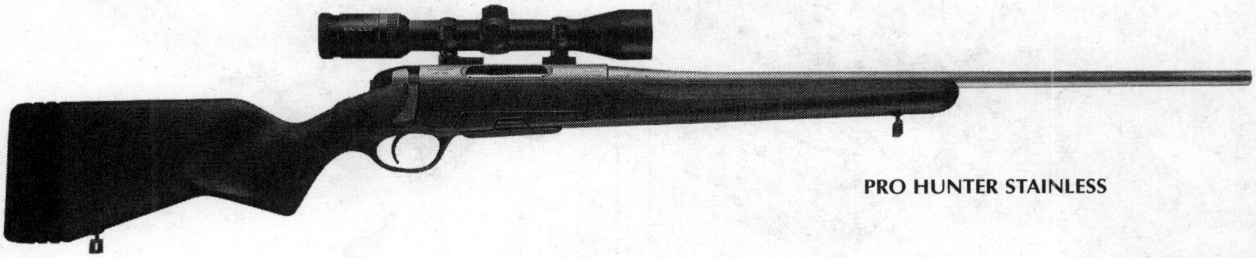

PRO HUNTER STAINLESS

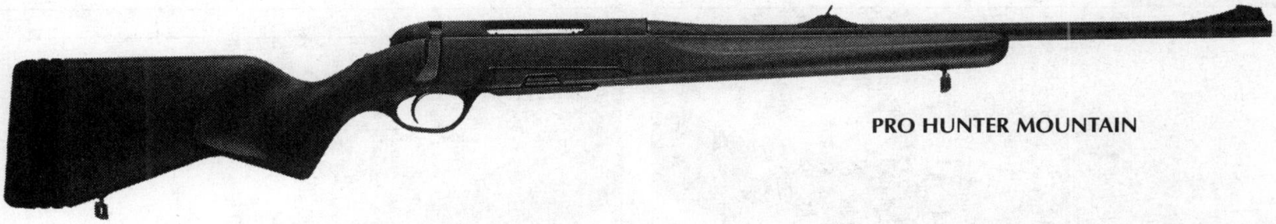

PRO HUNTER MOUNTAIN

STEYR PROHUNTER

Action: bolt
Stock: synthetic
Barrel: 20 in. (Mtn.), 23.6 in. and 25.6 in.
Sights: open
Weight: 7.8 (std.), 8.2 (mag.), 7.4 (Mtn.)
Caliber: .222, .223, .243, 6,5x55 SE, 6,5x57, 25-06, .270, 7x64, 7mm-08, 308, 30-06, 8x57 JS, 9,3x62, 7 mm Rem. Mag., .300 Win. Mag., 7 mm WSM, .270 WSM, .300 WSM
Magazine: detachable box, 5 rounds
Features: High-strength aluminium receiver; SBS safety system; three position roller tang safety; set or direct trigger; charcoal-gray, charcoal-black or Realtree Hardwoods HD stocks; heavy barrel available in .308 or .300 Win. Mag.;
MSRP: **ProHunter:. $776**
ProHunter Stainless: $861
ProHunter Mountain: $776
ProHunter Mountain Stainless: . . $861

Learn to use a sling for shooting as well as carrying. Brownell's Latigo sling is a fine example of one designed for shooting. It's leather, with an adjustable loop. Carrying straps don't qualify.

Szecsei & Fuchs Rifles

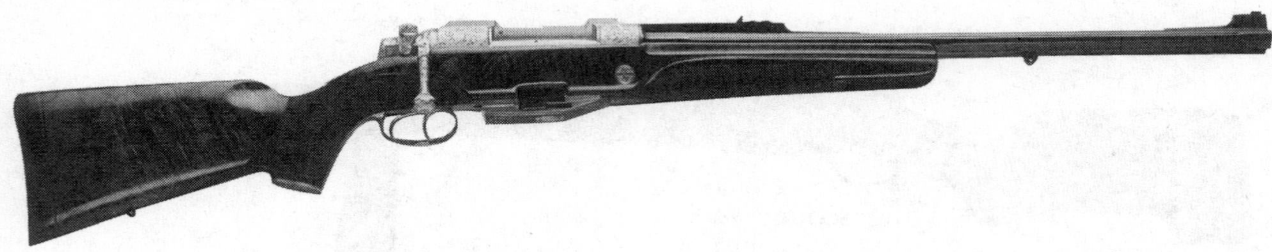

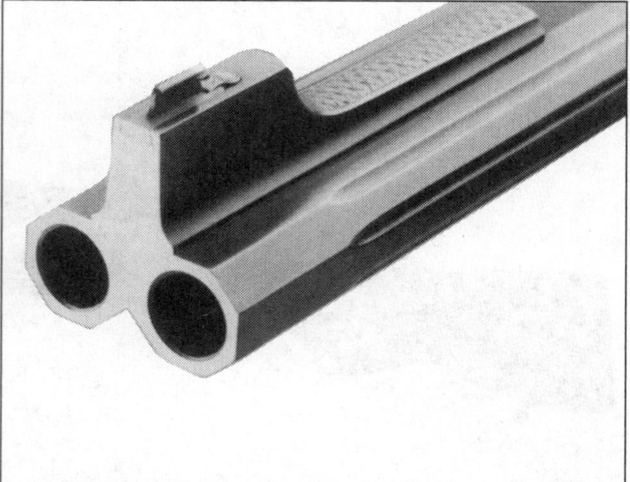

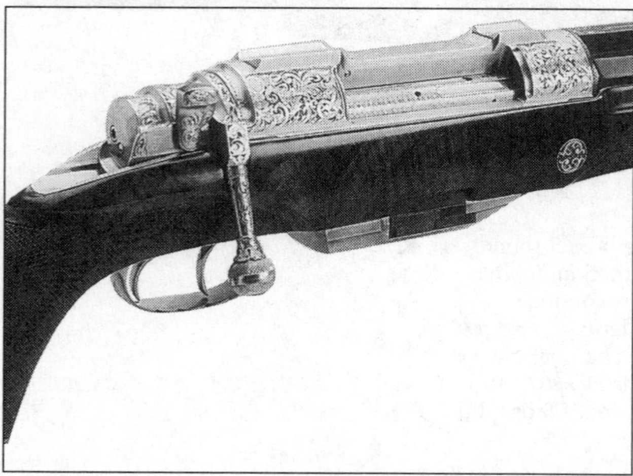

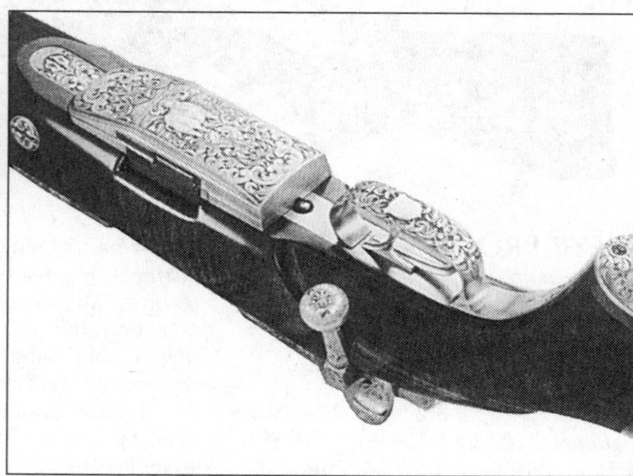

THE SZECSEI & FUCHS double-barrel bolt action rifle may be the only one of its kind. Built with great care and much handwork from the finest materials, it follows a design remarkable for its cleverness. And while the rifle is not light-weight, it can be aimed quickly and offers more large-caliber firepower than any competitor. The six-shot magazine feeds two rounds simultaneously, both of which can then be fired by two quick pulls of the trigger.

SPECIFICATIONS

Chamberings: .300 Win, 9.3 x 64, .358 Norma, .375 H&H, .404 Jeff, .416 Rem., .458 Win., .416 Rigby, .450 Rigby, .460 Short A-Square, .470 Capstick, .495 A-Square, .500 Jeffery

Weight: 14 lbs. with round barrels, 16 with octagon barrels.

Price: . . . . Available on request

Tactical Rifles

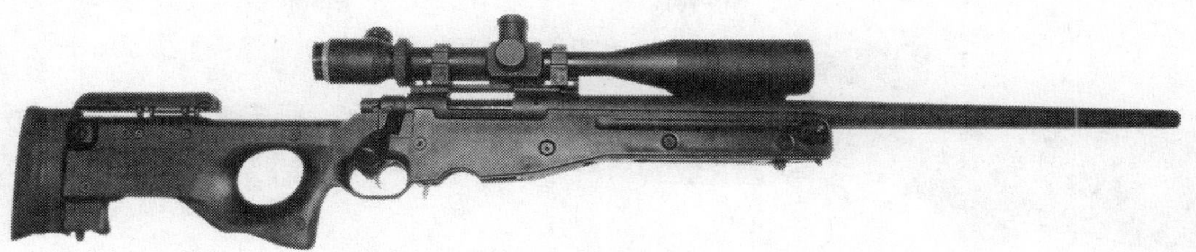

TACTICAL L.R.
Action: bolt, M700 Remington
Stock: thumbhole aluminum, with resin panels, optional adjustable cheekpiece
Barrel: heavy, match-grade, 26 inches
Sights: none (drilled and tapped for scope, supplied with Picatinny rail)
Weight: 13.4 lbs.
Caliber: 7.62 NATO (Magnum version available, in .300 WSM)
Magazine: 5-shot detachable box (10-round boxes available)
Features: adjustable trigger, soft rubber recoil pad, swivel studs; options include stainless fluted barrel.
Price: $2450

Taylor's Rifles

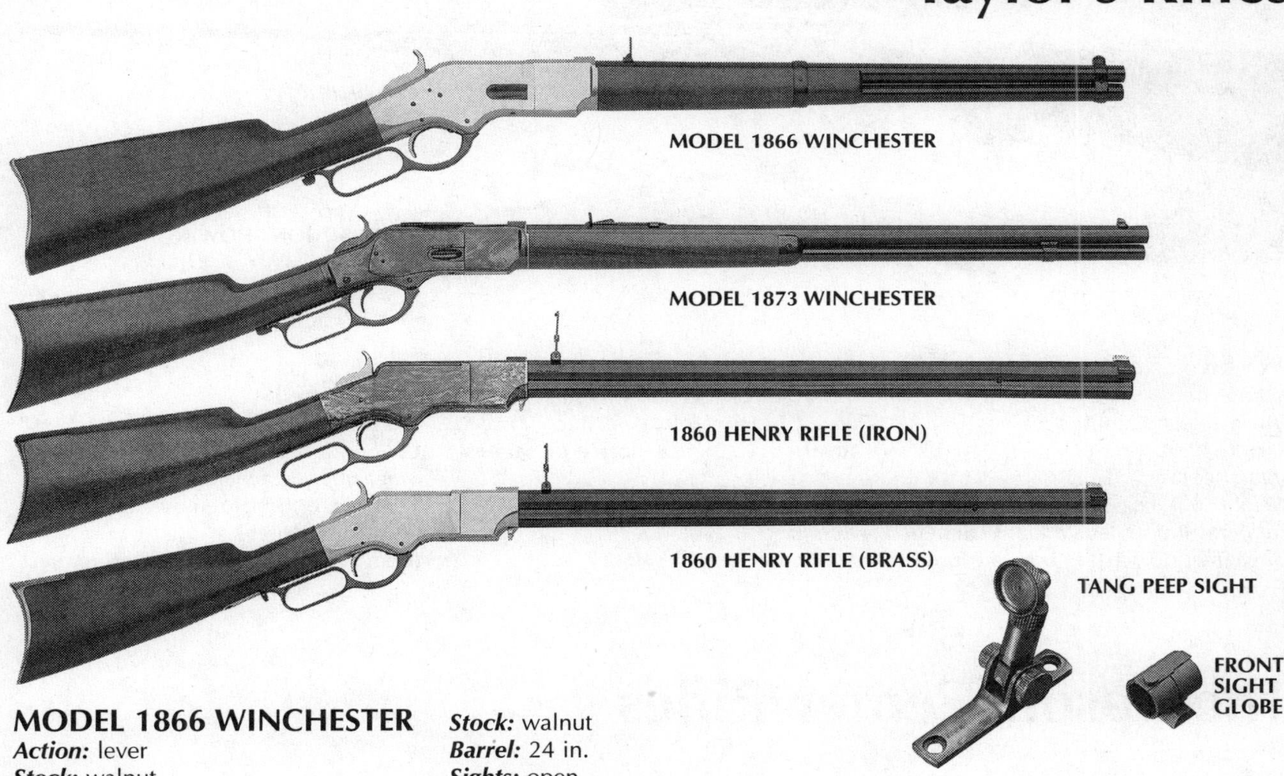

MODEL 1866 WINCHESTER
Action: lever
Stock: walnut
Barrel: 20 in.
Sights: open
Weight: 6.5 lbs.
Caliber: .38 Spl., .45 Long Colt
Magazine: under-barrel tube, 9 rounds
Features: brass frame, octagon barrel
1866: $915

MODEL 1873 WINCHESTER RIFLE
Action: lever
Stock: walnut
Barrel: 24 in.
Sights: open
Weight: 7.5 lbs.
Caliber: .44-40, .45 Long Colt
Magazine: under-barrel tube, 13 rounds
Features: optional: front globe and rear tang sights
1873 Winchester: $1045

1860 HENRY RIFLE
Action: lever
Stock: walnut
Barrel: 24 in.
Sights: open
Weight: 7.5 lbs.
Caliber: .44-40, .45 Long Colt
Magazine: under-barrel tube, 13 rounds
Features: brass frame; also: original-type steel-frame in .44-40 only
.44-40 Steel frame: $1220
brass frame:. $1160
charcoal blue:. $1220
white finish: $1185

Thompson & Campbell Rifles

INVER RIFLE

JURA RIFLE

CHROMIE RIFLE

PATENTED
INVER ACTION SHOWING
BEDDING PLATE.

RIFLES

INVER
Action: bolt
Stock: select walnut
Barrel: 22 in.
Sights: none
Weight: 8.0 lbs.
Caliber: all popular standard calibers
Magazine: detachable box, 4 rounds
Features: takedown barrels; optional removable sights and two-stage trigger; also: Chromie deluxe version
Inver:. . . . . price on request

JURA
Action: bolt
Stock: full length walnut
Barrel: 17 in.
Sights: none
Weight: 7.5 lbs.
Caliber: all popular standard calibers
Magazine: detachable box, 4 rounds
Features: optional removable sights, two-stage trigger
Jura:. . . . . price on request

Thompson/Center Rifles

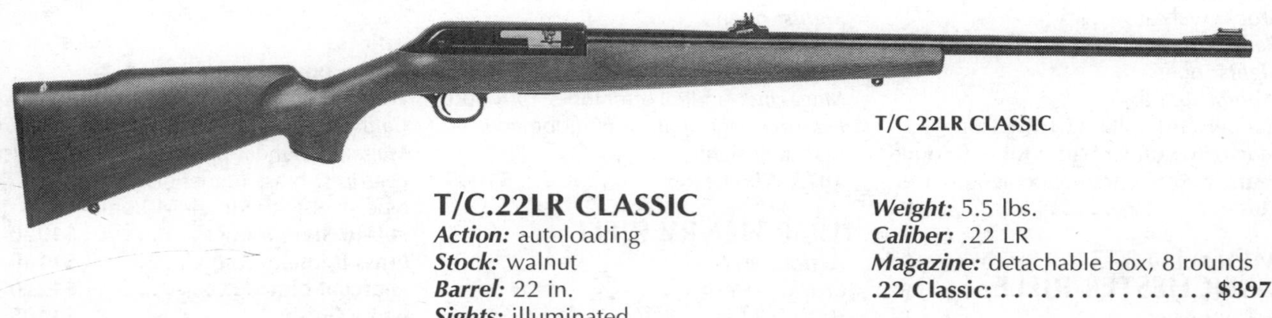

T/C 22LR CLASSIC

T/C.22LR CLASSIC
Action: autoloading
Stock: walnut
Barrel: 22 in.
Sights: illuminated
Weight: 5.5 lbs.
Caliber: .22 LR
Magazine: detachable box, 8 rounds
.22 Classic: $397

Thompson/Center Rifles

22 CLASSIC BENCHMARK

ENCORE RIFLE

ENCORE KATAHDIN

CONTENDER G2

RIFLES

MODEL 22 CLASSIC BENCHMARK

Action: autoloading
Stock: laminated
Barrel: 18 in., heavy
Sights: none
Weight: 6.8 lbs.
Caliber: .22 LR
Magazine: 10
Features: target rifle for bench shooting; drilled for scope
benchmark $506

ENCORE

Action: hinged breech
Stock: walnut
Barrel: 24 and 26 in.
Sights: open
Weight: 6.8 lbs.
Caliber: most popular calibers, from .22 Hornet to .300 Win. Mag. and .45-70
Magazine: none
Features: also: synthetic and stainless versions; Hunter package with .308 or .300 includes 3-9x40 T/C scope and hard case
walnut: $649
synthetic: $604
stainless: $680

KATAHDIN CARBINE

Action: hinged breech
Stock: synthetic
Barrel: 18 in.
Sights: illuminated
Weight: 6.6 lbs.
Caliber: .450, .45-70
Magazine: none
Features: integral muzzle brake
Carbine: $620

CONTENDER G2

Action: hinged breech
Stock: walnut
Barrel: 23 in.
Sights: none
Weight: 5.4 lbs.
Caliber: .17 HMR, .17 MACH2, .22 LR, .223, 6.8 Rem., .30-30, .204 Ruger, .45/70, .375 JDJ
Magazine: 1
Features: can recock without opening rifle
G2 Rifle $662
Also available:
.50 cal. muzzleloader $652

Tikka Rifles

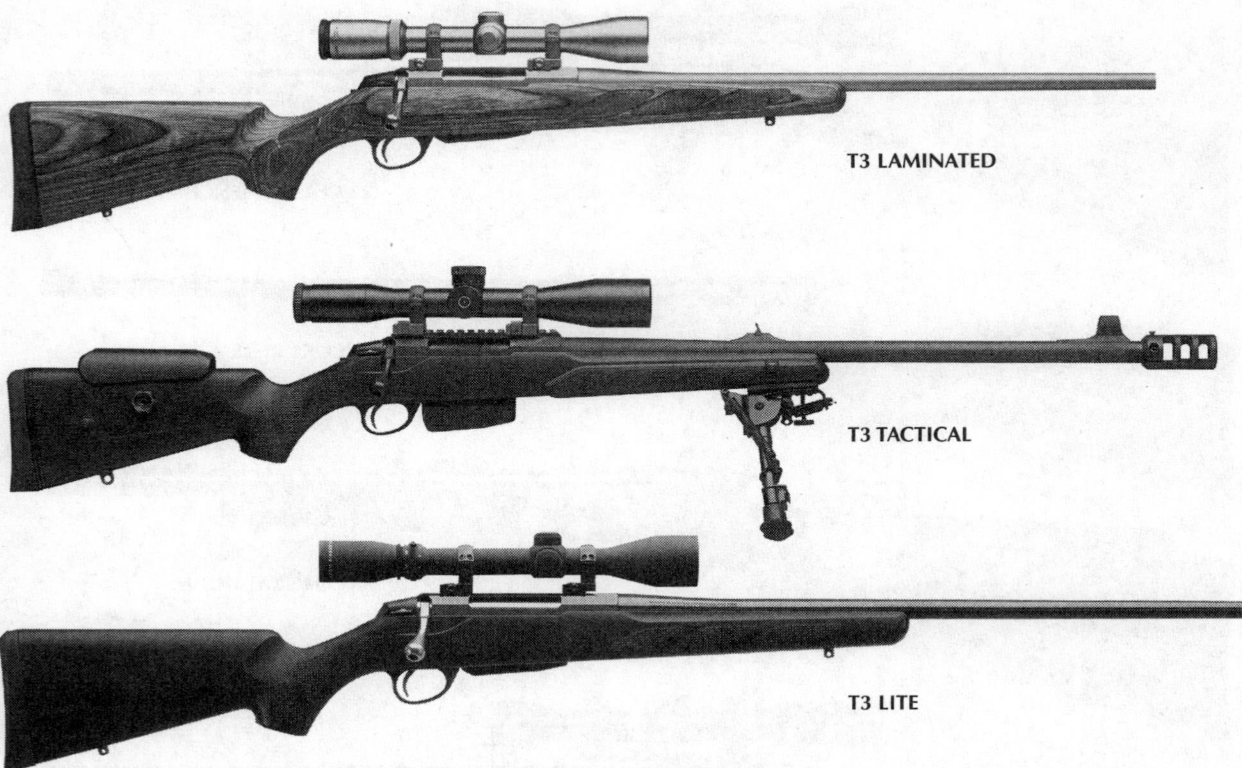

T3 LAMINATED

T3 TACTICAL

T3 LITE

T3 LAMINATED STAINLESS

Action: two-lug bolt
Stock: laminated
Barrel: free-floating, hammer-forged, 22 inches (standard) and 24 inches (magnum)
Sights: none (drilled and tapped for scope mounts)
Weight: 7.0 lbs.
Caliber: .243, .308, .25-06, .270, .30-06, .270 WSM, .300 WSM, 7mm Rem. Mag., .300 Win. Mag., .338 Win. Mag.
Magazine: 3-round detachable box
Features: fully adjustable trigger
Price: (standard) $908
(magnum) $944

T3 VARMINT AND TACTICAL

Action: two-lug bolt
Stock: synthetic
Barrel: heavy, 23 inches (Varmint) and 20 inches (Tactical), free-floating, hammer-forged
Sights: none (drilled and tapped for scope mounts)
Weight: 9.0 lbs. (Varmint), 8.5 lbs. (Tactical)
Caliber: .223, .22-250, .308 (Varmint), .223, .308 (Tactical)
Magazine: 5-round detachable box
Features: fully adjustable trigger
Price: $839
(Varmint, chrome-moly and stainless) $908
(Tactical) $1440

T3 LITE

Action: bolt
Stock: synthetic
Barrel: 23 to 24 in.
Sights: none
Weight: 6.0 lbs.
Caliber: from .223 Rem to .338 Win.
Magazine: 3 or 4 rounds
Features: blue or stainless, 3-shot 1 in. group at 100 yds. in factory testing
Price: $674
stainless $690
magnums. $709
stainless $725
Also available:
T3 Hunter (walnut/blue) . . $759 - 798

TIKKA T3 HUNTER

Action: bolt
Stock: walnut, (T3 Lite, synthetic)
Barrel: 22 7/16, 24 3/8 in.
Sights: none
Weight: 6 lb 10 oz to 6 lb 13 oz, (CK) (T3 Lite 6.2)
Caliber: 22-250 Rem, .223 Rem, .243 Win, .25-06 Rem, .270 Win, .270 WSM, 30-06, 308 Win, 6.5 x 55
Magazine: detachable box, 3 rounds
Features: Walnut stock with distinctive checkering pattern; blued action and cold hammer-forged barrel; laminated stock with stainless action and barrel, 2- to 4-pound adjustable trigger, integral scope rail, required rings are supplied with each gun;
MSRP: **. . . . . $ 690**
.270 WSM, 300 Win Mag, 300 WSM, 338 Win Mag 7mm Rem Mag: . . . . $ 725
T3 Laminated Stainless: . . . . . . $ 825
T3 Lite: . . . . $ 559-$587
T3 Lite Stainless: . . . $ 690 to 725.00

Tikka Rifles

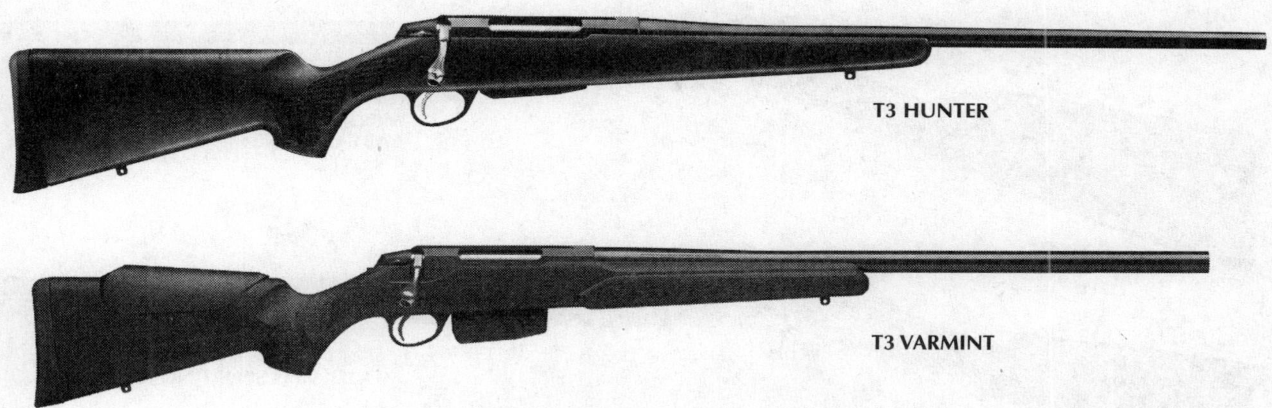

T3 HUNTER

T3 VARMINT

RIFLES

TIKKA T3 VARMINT

Action: bolt
Stock: synthetic
Barrel: 23 3/8 in.
Sights: none
Weight: 8
Caliber: 22-250 Rem, 223 Rem, 308 Win
Magazine: detachable box, 5 rounds
Features: modular synthetic stock with wide beavertail fore-end and non-reflective finish; raised-comb cheek piece; blued or stainless steel; heavy contour barrel
MSRP: $765
Stainless $825

Uberti Rifles

1860 HENRY RIFLE

MODEL 1866 YELLOWBOY CARBINE

1860 HENRY RIFLE

Action: lever
Stock: walnut, straight grip
Barrel: octagon 18, 22 and 24 in.
Sights: open
Weight: 7.9 lbs.
Caliber: .44-40, .45 Colt
Magazine: under-barrel tube, 13 rounds
Features: brass or steel frame
brass frame:. $1035
steel frame:. $1125

MODEL 1866 WINCHESTER CARBINE "YELLOWBOY"

Action: lever
Stock: walnut, straight grip
Barrel: 19 in.
Sights: open
Weight: 7.4 lbs.
Caliber: .38 Spl., .44-40, .45 Colt
Magazine: under-barrel tube
Features: brass frame
1866 Yellowboy Carbine: $755
1866 Rifle (24" BBL): $800

Uberti Rifles

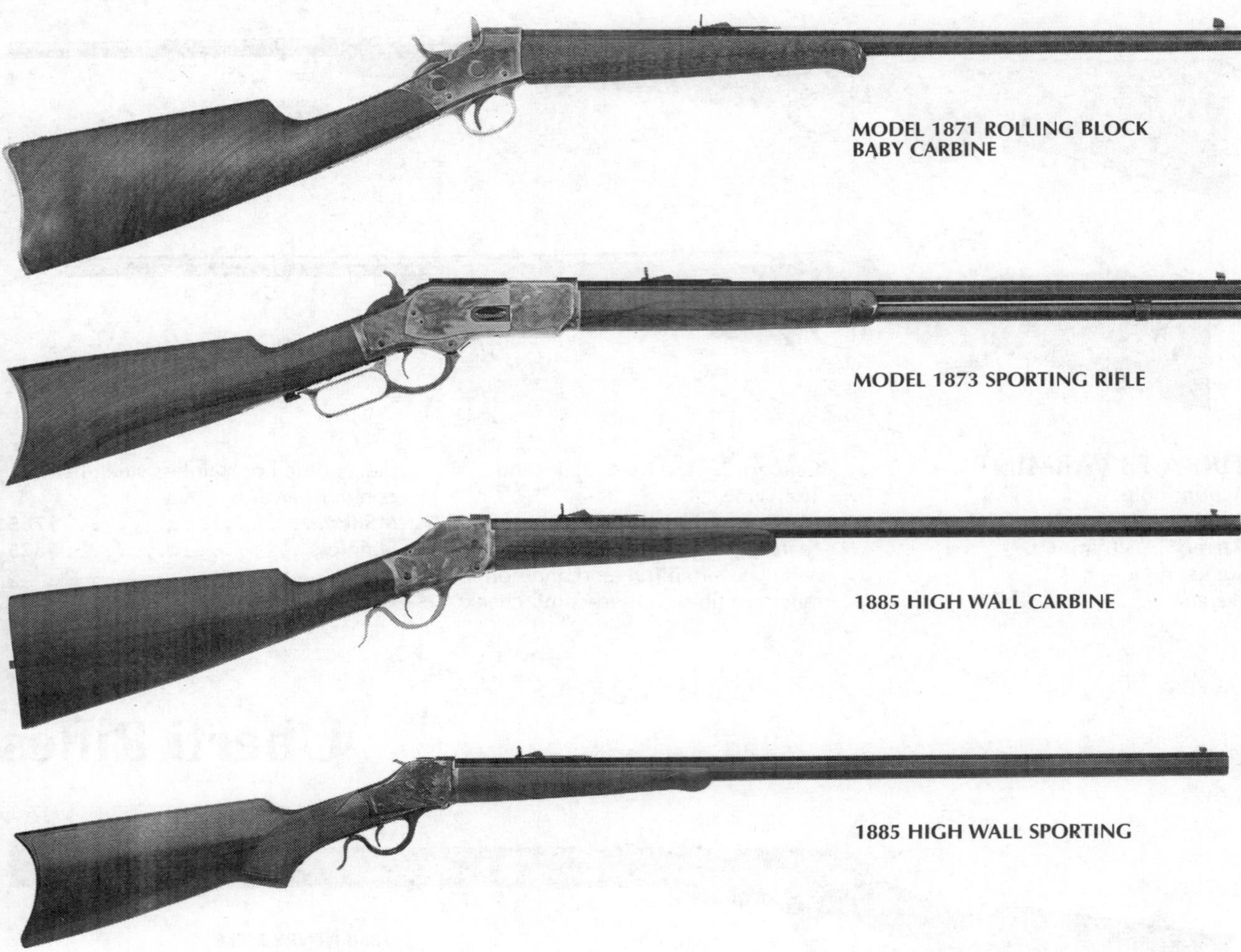

MODEL 1871 ROLLING BLOCK BABY CARBINE

MODEL 1873 SPORTING RIFLE

1885 HIGH WALL CARBINE

1885 HIGH WALL SPORTING

RIFLES

MODEL 1871 ROLLING BLOCK BABY CARBINE

Action: rolling block
Stock: walnut, straight grip
Barrel: 22 in.
Sights: open
Weight: 4.9 lbs.
Caliber: .22 LR, .22 WMR, .22 Hornet
Magazine: none
Features: case-colored receiver
Baby Carbine: $535
1871 Rifle (26″ BBL): $600

MODEL 1873 WINCHESTER SPORTING RIFLE

Action: lever
Stock: walnut, straight grip
Barrel: octagon 20, 24 in.
Sights: open
Weight: 7.5 lbs.
Caliber: .357 Mag., .44-40, .45 Colt
Magazine: under-barrel tube, 13 rounds
Features: optional pistol grip
straight grip (20″ BBL): $925
(24″ BBL): $965
pistol grip: . . . . $1055 - 1100

1885 HIGH-WALL CARBINE

Action: single shot dropping block
Stock: walnut
Barrel: 28 in.
Weight: 9.3 lbs.
Caliber: .45-70
Magazine: none
Features: Case-hardened frame with blued round barrel; total length 44.5 inches
Price: $850

1885 HIGH-WALL SPORTING RIFLE AND SPECIAL SPORTING RIFLE

Action: single shot dropping block
Stock: walnut
Barrel: 30 in., 32 in. (Octagon)
Sights: adjustable leaf
Weight: 9.9 lbs.
Caliber: 45-70, .45-90, .45-120
Magazine: none
Features: Case-hardened frame with blued barrel; optional sights: mid-range Vernier adjustable Creedmore or Lyman adjustable Creedmore; total length 47inches
Sporting Rifle: $850
Special Sporting Rifle: $1,035

Weatherby Rifles

MARK V TRR

ACCUMARK

MARK V DANGEROUS GAME RIFLE

MARK V DELUXE

RIFLES

MARK V THREAT RESPONSE RIFLE

Action: bolt
Stock: composite
Barrel: heavy 22 in.
Sights: none
Weight: 8.5 lbs.
Caliber: .223, .308
Magazine: box, 5 + 1 rounds
TRR: $1737

MARK V ACCUMARK

Action: bolt
Stock: composite
Barrel: 26 and 28 in. barrels
Sights: none
Weight: 7.0 lbs.
Caliber: Wby. Magnums: .257, .270, 7mm, .300, .340, .30-378, .338-378 and .300 Win. Mag., 7mm Rem. Mag.
Magazine: box, 3 or 5 rounds
Features: weight depends on caliber; hand-laminated, raised comb, Pachmayr recoil pad
magnums: $1726
with Accubrake: $1974

MARK V DANGEROUS GAME RIFLE

Action: bolt
Stock: composite
Barrel: 24 or 26 in.
Sights: open
Weight: 9.0 lbs.
Caliber: .300 Wby., .340 Wby., .375 H&H, .375 Wby., .416 Rem., .458 Win., .458 Lott; also: .378, .416, .460 Wby.
Magazine: box, 3 rounds
Features: express sights, barrel band swivel
Dangerous Game Rifle: $3095
.378, .416: $3266
.460: $3360

MARK V DELUXE

Action: bolt
Stock: Claro walnut
Barrel: 26 and 28 in.
Sights: none
Weight: 8.5 lbs.
Caliber: ..257 Wby. Mag to .460 Wby. Mag.
Magazine: box, 3 or 5 rounds
Features: 26 in. barrels for most magnum calibers; 28 in. barrel for .378, .416, .460 (with brake)
.378, .416 with Accubrake: . . . $2380
.460: $2797

Weatherby Rifles

MARK V FIBERMARK STAINLESS

MARK V LAZERMARK

MARK V SPORTER

MARK V SUPER VARMINT MASTER

RIFLES

MARK V FIBERMARK

Action: bolt
Stock: synthetic
Barrel: 24 and 26 in.
Sights: none
Weight: 8.0 lbs.
Caliber: popular magnum chamberings from .257 Wby. Mag. to .375 H&H Mag..
Magazine: box, 3 to 5 rounds
magnum: $1285
with Accubrake: $1542

MARK V LAZERMARK

Action: bolt
Stock: walnut
Barrel: 26 in.
Sights: none
Weight: 8.5 lbs.
Caliber: Wby. Magnums from .257 to .340
Magazine: box, 3 rounds
Features: laser-carved stock, button rifled Krieger barrel
Lazermark: $2202

MARK V SPORTER

Action: bolt
Stock: walnut
Barrel: 24 and 26 in.
Sights: none
Weight: 8.0 lbs.
Caliber: popular magnum chamberings from .257 Wby. Mag. to .340 Wby. Mag.
Magazine: box, 3 or 5 rounds
Features: checkered grip and forend
Mark V Sporter:. $1309

MARK V SUPER VARMINT MASTER

Action: bolt
Stock: composite
Barrel: 26 in.
Sights: none
Weight: 8.5 lbs.
Caliber: .223, .22-250, .220 Swift, .243
Magazine: box, 5 rounds
Features: Super VarmintMaster has heavy 26 in., fluted stainless barrel, flat-bottomed stock
SVM:. $1737

Weatherby Rifles

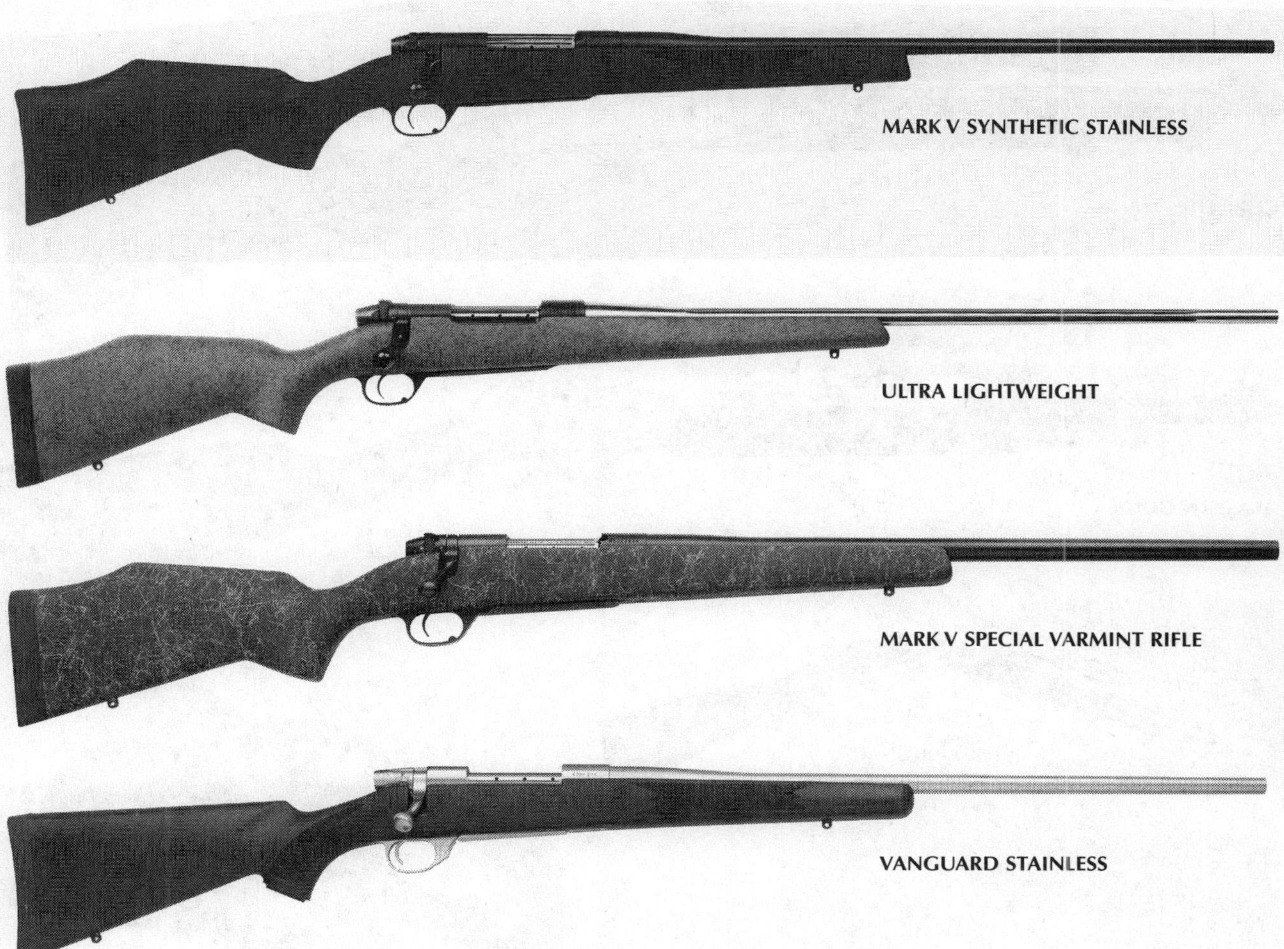

RIFLES

MARK V SYNTHETIC

Action: bolt
Stock: synthetic
Barrel: 24, 26 and 28 in.
Sights: none
Weight: 8.5 lbs.
Caliber: popular standard and magnum calibers from .22-250 to .257 Wby. Mag.
Magazine: box, 3 or 5 rounds
Features: also: stainless version.
Mark V Synthetic: $1057
magnum:................. $1116
with Accubrake: $1318

ULTRA LIGHTWEIGHT

Action: bolt
Stock: composite
Barrel: 24 and 26 in.
Sights: none
Weight: 6.0 lbs.
Caliber: .243, .240 Wby., .25-06, .270, 7-08, .280, 7mm Rem. Mag., .308, .30-06, .300 Win. Mag., Wby. Magnums: .257, .270, 7mm, .300
Magazine: box, 3 or 5 rounds
Features: lightweight action; 6-lug bolt
Ultra Lightweight:.......... $1670
magnums: $1752

MARK V SPECIAL VARMINT RIFLE

Action: bolt
Stock: composite
Barrel: 22 in.
Sights: none
Weight: 7.3 lbs.
Caliber: .223, .22-250
Magazine: 5 and 4
Features: 6-lug action;
barrel #3 contour, lapped, fluted
SVR.................... $1176

VANGUARD

Action: bolt
Stock: composite
Barrel: 24 in.
Sights: none
Weight: 7.8lbs.
Caliber: .223, .22-250, .243, .270, .308, .30-06, .257 Wby. Mag., 7mm Rem. Mag., .300 Win. Mag., .300 WSM, .270 WSM, .300 Wby. Mag., .338 Win. Mag.
Magazine: 5 to 3
Features: 2-lug action, made in Japan, 1½-inch factory guarantee for 3-shot group
synthetic $476
stainless $595

Wild West Guns

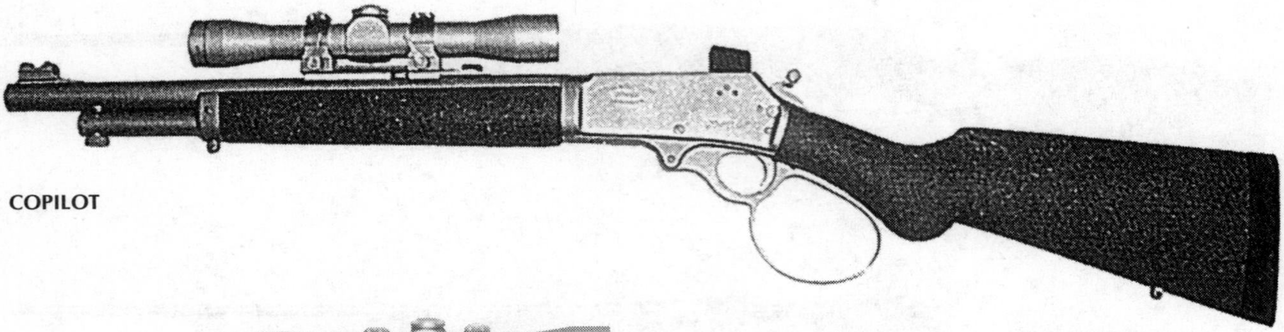

COPILOT

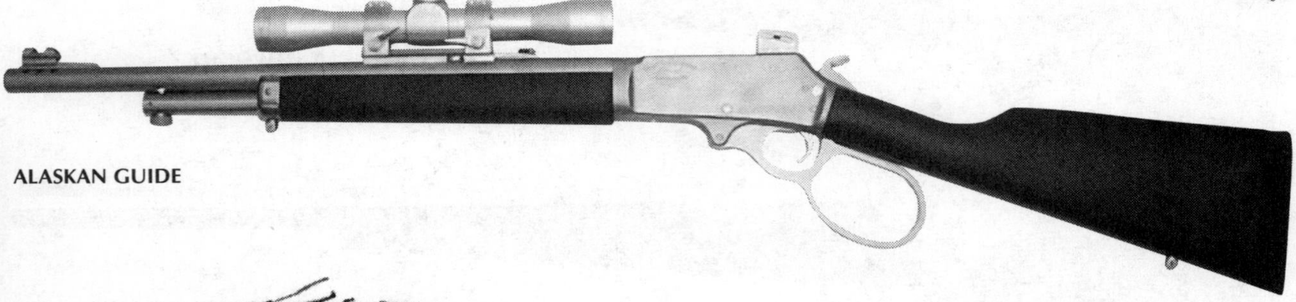

ALASKAN GUIDE

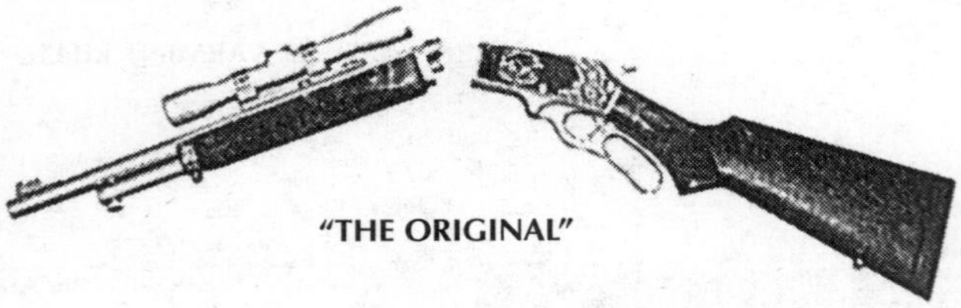

"THE ORIGINAL"

RIFLES

CO-PILOT

Action: lever
Stock: walnut
Barrel: 16, 18 or 20 inch
Sights: illuminated
Weight: 7.0 lbs.
Caliber: .45-70, .457 Magnum, .50 Alaskan
Magazine: under-barrel tube
Features: 1895 Marlin action; ported barrels; take-down feature; Alaskan Guide similar, not take-down

Co-Pilot: $1980
on supplied 1895 Marlin: $1595
.50 Alaskan conversion: $250
Alaskan Guide: $1320
Alaskan on supplied 1895 Marlin: $935
.50 Alaskan conversion: $250
Master Guide Take-Down:. . . . $1865
Take-Down on supplied 1895G: $1485

Store rifles in a cool, dry place – horizontal or muzzle down on brown wrapping paper so any excess oil drains out the muzzle instead of into the stock. Keep weight off recoil pads.

Winchester Rifles

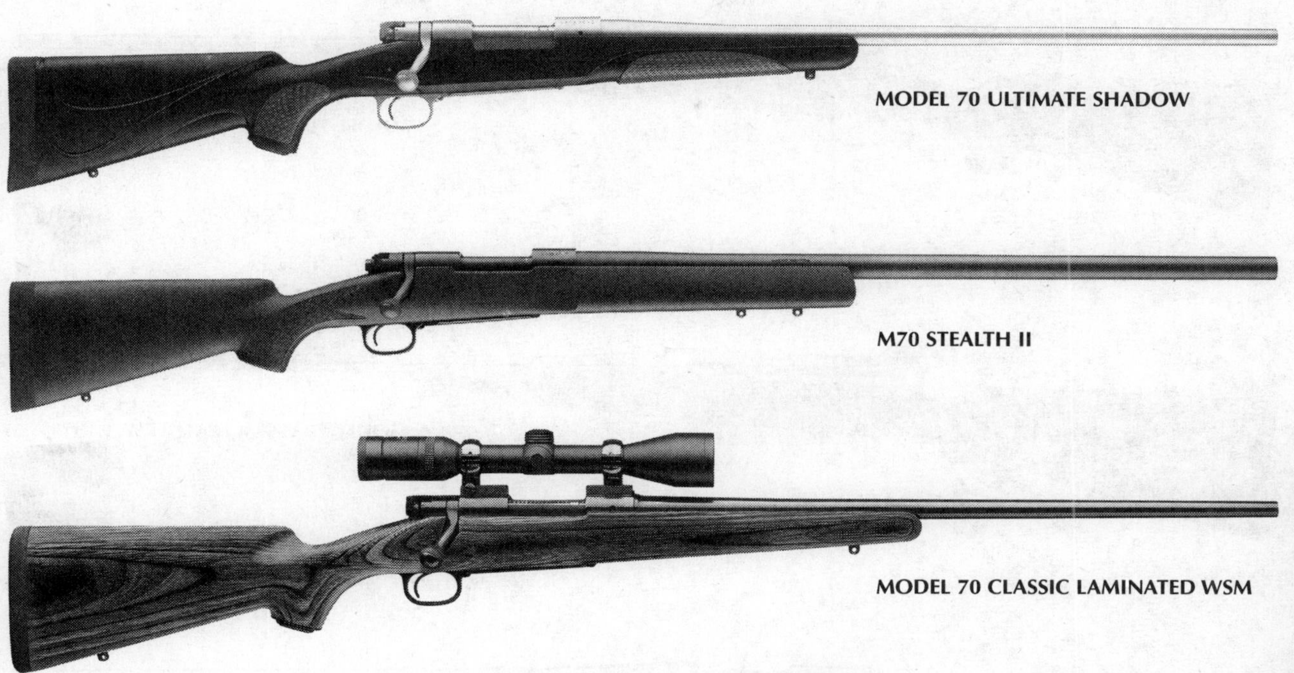

MODEL 70 ULTIMATE SHADOW

M70 STEALTH II

MODEL 70 CLASSIC LAMINATED WSM

RIFLES

MODEL 70 ULTIMATE SHADOW

Action: bolt
Stock: composite
Barrel: 22 and 24 in.
Sights: none
Weight: 6.5
Caliber: .223 WSSM, .243 WSSM, .25 WSSM, .270 WSM, 7mm WSM, .300 WSM
Magazine: box, 3 rounds
Features: push-feed; Ultimate Shadow has integrated, rubberized, oval gripping surfaces on the stock pistol grip and forend.
WSM's: $817
WSSM's: $838
Stainless: . . . . $861 - 883
Camo: . . . . $869 – 892
Camo, stainless: . . . . $914 - 937
Super Shadow: . . . . $554 – 576

MODEL 70 STEALTH II

Action: bolt
Stock: synthetic, beavertail forend with third stud, checkered pistol grip
Barrel: heavy, 26 inches
Sights: none (drilled and tapped for scope mounts)
Weight: 10 lbs.
Caliber: .22-250, .308, .223 WSSM, .243 WSSM, .25 WSSM
Magazine: 3-round box with hinged floorplate
Features: three-position safety, pillar bedding, matte black finish
Price: (.22-250 and .308) $832
WSSMs $886

MODEL 70 CLASSIC COMPACT

Action: bolt
Stock: walnut
Barrel: 20 in.
Sights: none
Weight: 6.0 lbs.
Caliber: .243, .308
Magazine: box, 4 rounds
Features: features 13-in. pull for small-frame people
Compact: $762

Heavy barrels are not intrinsically more accurate than lightweight barrels. But they are typically more consistent when shooting long strings because they don't "walk" as readily when they heat.

Winchester Rifles

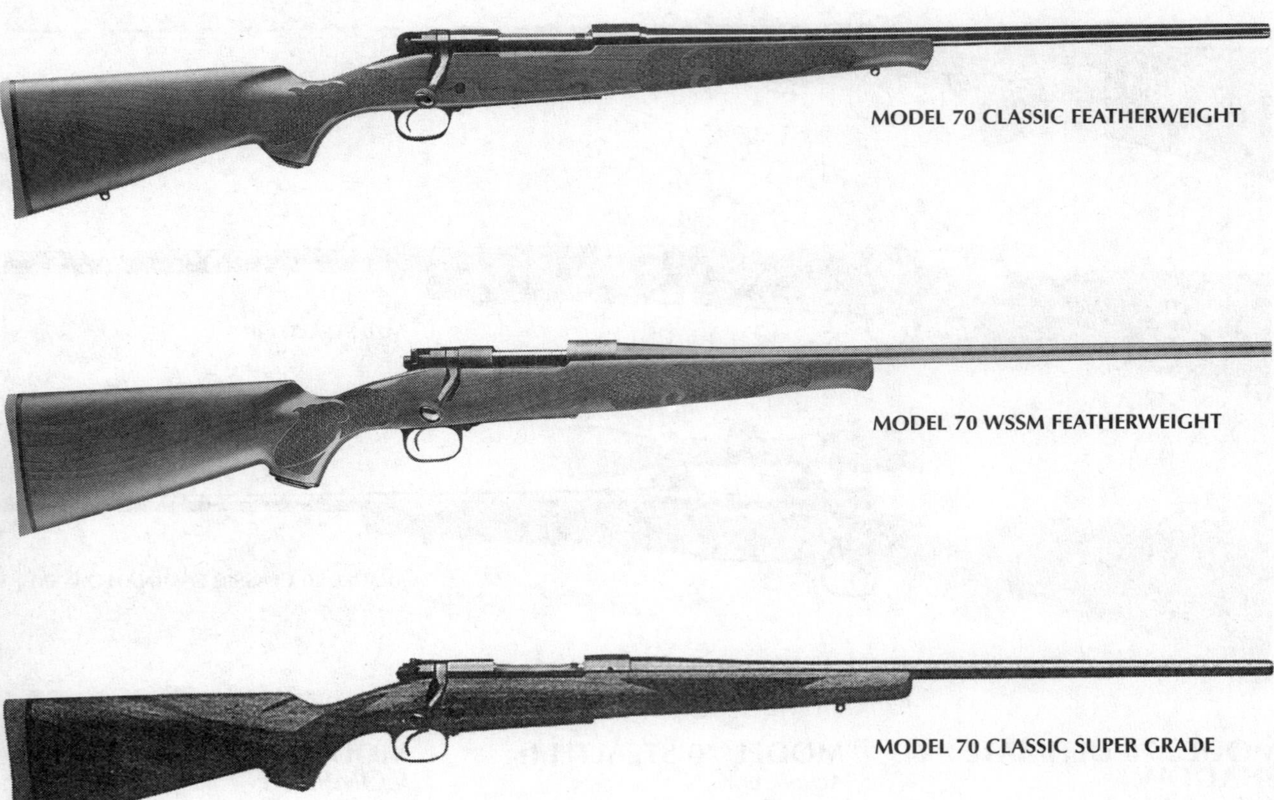

MODEL 70 CLASSIC FEATHERWEIGHT

MODEL 70 WSSM FEATHERWEIGHT

MODEL 70 CLASSIC SUPER GRADE

RIFLES

MODEL 70 CLASSIC FEATHERWEIGHT

Action: bolt
Stock: walnut
Barrel: 22 and 24 in.
Sights: none
Weight: 7.0 lbs.
Caliber: .22-250, .243, 6.5x55, .270, .270 WSM, 7-08, 7mm WSM, .308, .30-06, .300 WSM, .223 WSSM, .243 WSSM, .25 WSSM
Magazine: box, 3 or 5 rounds
Features: stainless available in .22-250, .243, .270, .308, .30-06
Classic Featherweight:........ $762
WSM's: $792
WSSM's: $814

MODEL 70 CLASSIC SPORTER III

Action: bolt
Stock: walnut
Barrel: 24 and 26 in.
Sights: none
Weight: 7.8 lbs.
Caliber: .25-06, .270, 7mm Rem. Mag., .30-06, .300 Win. Mag., .338 Win. Mag., .270 WSM, 7mm WSM, .300 WSM
Magazine: box, 3 or 5 rounds
Features: also in .270, 7mm and .300 WSM with laminated stock; left-hand models available.
Classic Sporter:............. $742
magnum:.................. $773
WSM:............... $773 - 810
Classic laminated WSM: $810

MODEL 70 CLASSIC STAINLESS

Action: bolt
Stock: synthetic
Barrel: 24 and 26 in.
Sights: none
Weight: 7.3 lbs.
Caliber: .270, .30-06, .300 Win. Mag., .338 Win. Mag., .375 H&H
Magazine: box, 3 or 5 rounds
Features: open sights on .375 H&H
Classic Stainless:............ $817
magnum:.................. $847
.375: $943

MODEL 70 CLASSIC SUPER GRADE

Action: bolt
Stock: walnut
Barrel: 24 and 26 in.
Sights: none
Weight: 7.8 lbs.
Caliber: .25-06, .30-06, .300 Win. Mag., .338 Win. Mag., .270 WSM, 7mm WSM, .300 WSM, .325 WSM
Magazine: box, 3 or 5 rounds
Features: also; Safari Express in .375 H&H (8.5 lbs.), .416 Rem. Mag. and .458 Win. with open sights
Classic Super Grade:........ $1036
magnum:................ $1067
Safari express:............ $1149

MODEL 70 COYOTE

MODEL 94 TRAILS END OCTAGON

MODEL 94 TRAPPER

MODEL 70 COYOTE

Action: bolt
Stock: laminated
Barrel: 24 in.
Sights: none
Weight: 9.0 lbs.
Caliber: .22-250, .308; also .270 WSM, 7mm WSM, .300 WSM, .223 WSSM, .243 WSSM, .25 WSSM
Magazine: box, 3 to 5 rounds
Features: push-feed action
Coyote, blue: . . . . $689 - 742
stainless: . . . . $734 – 787
Coyote Lite, blue . . . . $839 – 889
Coyote Lite, stainless: . . . $881 - 930

MODEL 70 WSSM

Action: bolt
Stock: walnut, synthetic or laminated
Barrel: 24 in.
Sights: none
Weight: 6.0 lbs.
Caliber: .223 WSSM, .243 WSSM, .25 WSSM
Magazine: 3
Features: shortened M70 action, new synthetic shadow stock with grip inserts; laminated Coyote weighs 9 lbs.
Super Shadow $576
Featherweight . . . . $814 - 859
Coyote. . . . . $742 – 930
Stealth: $886
Classic: . . . . $838 - 937

MODEL 94 TRAILS END

Action: lever
Stock: walnut, straight grip
Barrel: 20 in.
Sights: open
Weight: 6.5 lbs.
Caliber: .357 Mag., .44 Rem. Mag., .45 Colt
Magazine: 11 rounds
Features: Trails End Hunter round barrel in .25-35 Win., .30-30, .38-55 Win.; large-loop option
Ranger: $377
Trails End: $468
Trails End Hunter: $468
Octagon bbl., case color: $816

MODEL 94 TRAPPER

Action: lever
Stock: walnut
Barrel: 16 in.
Sights: open
Weight: 6.0 lbs.
Caliber: .30-30, .357 Mag., .44 Mag., .45 Long Colt
Magazine: under-barrel tube, 5 or 9 rounds
Features: saddle ring; 8 rounds only in .357, .44, .45
Trapper: $458

Winchester Rifles

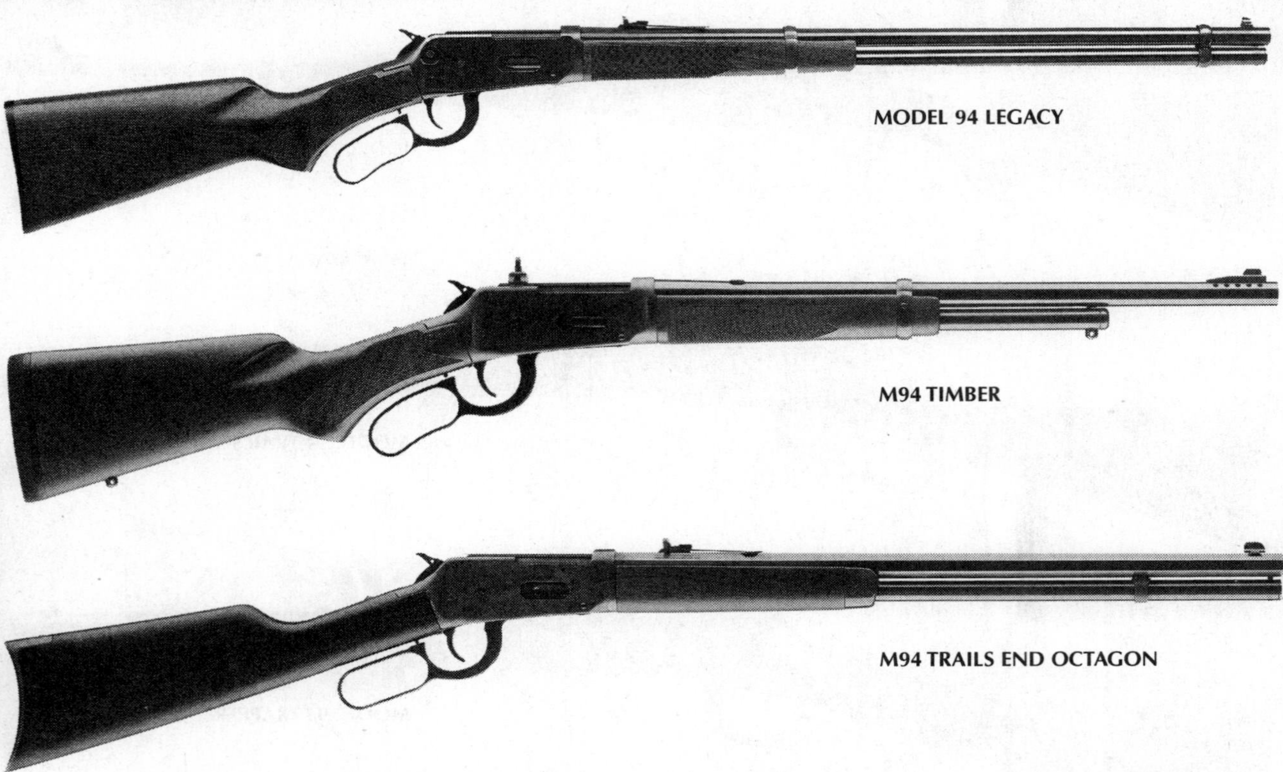

MODEL 94 LEGACY

M94 TIMBER

M94 TRAILS END OCTAGON

RIFLES

MODEL 94 LEGACY

Action: lever
Stock: checkered walnut, pistol grip
Barrel: 20 or 24 in.
Sights: open
Weight: 6.8 lbs.
Caliber: .30-30, .357 Mag., .44 Mag., .45 Long Colt
Magazine: under-barrel tube, 6 rounds
Features: deluxe version of 94; 11 rounds only in .357, .44, .45
Legacy: $485
octagon barrel: $882
octagon, case colored: $938

MODEL 94 TIMBER

Action: exposed-hammer lever
Stock: walnut with checkered forend and pistol grip
Barrel: 18-inch, ported
Sights: XS Ghost Ring rear and ramp front with bead
Weight: 6.0 lbs.
Caliber: .450 Marlin
Magazine: under-barrel ⅔-length tube, 4-shot
Features: Pachmayr recoil pad, crossbolt safety, receiver drilled and tapped for scope
Price: $597

MODEL 94 TRAILS END OCTAGON

Action: exposed-hammer lever
Stock: walnut, uncheckered, with straight grip, forend cap
Barrel: 20 inches, octagonal
Sights: step-adjustable semi-buckhorn rear, bead front
Weight: 6.8 lbs.
Caliber: .357 Magnum, .44 Magnum, .45 Colt
Magazine: full-length under-barrel tube, 11-shot
Features: Case colored receiver and furniture on TECC version
Price: (Octagon) $757
Case Colored. $816

Resist the urge to squeeze the trigger quickly as the sight bounces onto the target. Press when the sight picture looks good, hold pressure when it doesn't.

Armsco Shotguns

MODEL 103

Action: over/under
Stock: walnut pistol grip
Barrel: 26, 28 or 30 in.
Chokes: improved cylinder/modified, screw-in tubes
Weight: 7.0 lbs.
Bore/Gauge: 12, 16, 20, 28, 410
Magazine: none
Features: boxlock over/under, single trigger, silver, black or case-finished breech
Canvasback, black 12 & 20. . . . $695
Redhead Deluxe, silver, ejectors, 12 & 20 . . . . $795
28 & .410 . . . . $825
M103 Woodcock Deluxe, case-hardened, ejectors, 12 & 20. . $1056
28 & .410 . . . . $1129

MODEL 201

Action: side-by-side
Stock: walnut, straight or pistol grip
Barrel: 26 in.
Chokes: improved cylinder/modified, screw-in tubes
Weight: 6.3 lbs.
Bore/Gauge: 12, 16, 20, 28, 410
Magazine: none
Features: boxlock double, single trigger, silver, black or case-finished breech; IC/M in 16 ga. and .410
12 & 20. . . . . $869
28 & .410 . . . . $1045

MODEL 712

Action: autoloader
Stock: walnut or camo
Barrel: 24, 26 or 28 in.
Chokes: screw-in tubes
Weight: 7.0 lbs.
Bore/Gauge: 12
Magazine: 4
Features: matte or polished metal;
M712, 3-in., walnut $399
Camo $460
M712 Mag., 3.5-in., walnut. . . . $499
Camo $599
M720 20 ga. 3-in., walnut. $425
Camo $499

AYA Shotguns

MODEL 4/53

MODEL 4/53

Action: side-by-side
Stock: walnut, straight grip
Barrel: 26, 27 or 28 in.
Chokes: improved cylinder, modified, full
Weight: 7.0 lbs.
Bore/Gauge: 12, 16, 20, 28, .410
Magazine: none
Features: boxlock; chopper lump barrels, bushed firing pins, automatic safety and ejectors
Model 4/53 . . . . $2795 - 2935

Repeating shotguns give you more shots, but doubles are shorter overall for their barrel length, and, say many connoisseurs, much better balanced.

Benelli Shotguns

MODEL 1014

M4 PISTOL GRIP

M1 FIELD STEADY GRIP

NOVA H2O PUMP

M2 FIELD

SHOTGUNS

MODEL 1014 AND M4

Action: autoloader
Stock: synthetic
Barrel: 18.5 in.
Chokes: improved cylinder, modified, full
Weight: 8.0 lbs.
Bore/Gauge: 12
Magazine: 4 + 1
Features: M4 has pistol grip; gas operated, ghost-ring sight, modular buttstocks
M1014 . . . . $1575
M4 . . . . $1529

M1 FIELD STEADY GRIP, SUPER BLACK EAGLE STEADY GRIP

Action: autoloader
Stock: synthetic with vertical pistol grip
Barrel: 24 in.
Chokes: screw-in tubes
Weight: 7.3 lbs.
Bore/Gauge: 12
Magazine: 3
Features: Benelli inertia-system mechanism; Super Black Eagle also handles $3\frac{1}{2}$-inch shells
M1 Field $1195
Super Black Eagle $1485

NOVA H20 PUMP

Action: pump
Stock: synthetic
Barrel: 18.5 in.
Chokes: cylinder, fixed
Weight: 7.2 lbs.
Bore/Gauge: 12
Magazine: 4 + 1
Features: matte nickel finish, open rifle sights
synthetic $480

M2 FIELD

Action: autoloader
Stock: synthetic or satin walnut
Barrel: 21, 24, 26 or 28 in.
Chokes: screw-in tube
Weight: 6.9 to 7.1 lbs.
Bore/Gauge: 12
Magazine: 3
Features: Comfor tech recoil reduction system, Crio barrel, inertia-recoil system, 3-in. chamber, rotating bolt with dual lugs, Advantage Timber HD, Advantage: MAX-4 camo or black synthetic stock
Walnut $1035
Synthetic. $1065
Camo $1165
Slug . . . . $1135 - 1235

Benelli Shotguns

SPORT II

SUPER SPORT

SUPER BLACK EAGLE II

SUPER BLACK EAGLE II MAX-4

SHOTGUNS

SPORT II

Action: autoloader
Stock: satin walnut
Barrel: 28 or 30 in.
Chokes: screw-in tubes
Weight: 7.85 lbs.
Bore/Gauge: 12
Magazine: 4
Features: Comfor tech recoil reduction system, Crio barrel, inertia-recoil system, 3-in. chamber
Price **$1430**

SUPER SPORT

Action: autoloader
Stock: synthetic
Barrel: 24 or 26 in.
Chokes: screw-in tubes
Weight: 7.2 lbs.
Bore/Gauge: 12
Magazine: 3
Features: Comfor tech recoil reduction system, Crio barrel, inertia-recoil system, 3½-in. chamber, rotating bolt with dual lugs, Advantage HD camo or black synthetic stock
Price **$1600**

SUPER BLACK EAGLE II

Action: autoloader
Stock: synthetic
Barrel: 24 or 26 in.
Chokes: screw-in tubes
Weight: 7.2 lbs.
Bore/Gauge: 12
Magazine: 3
Features: Comfor tech recoil reduction system, Crio barrel, inertia-recoil system, 3½-in. chamber, rotating bolt with dual lugs, Advantage Timber HD, Advantage–MAX-4 camo or black synthetic stock, Super Black Eagle II Flyway comes with walnut stock and choice of three scroll engraved receivers.
Walnut **$1335**
Synthetic **$1365**
MAX-4 & HD Timber **$1465**
Flyway Editions **$2130**

Benelli Shotguns

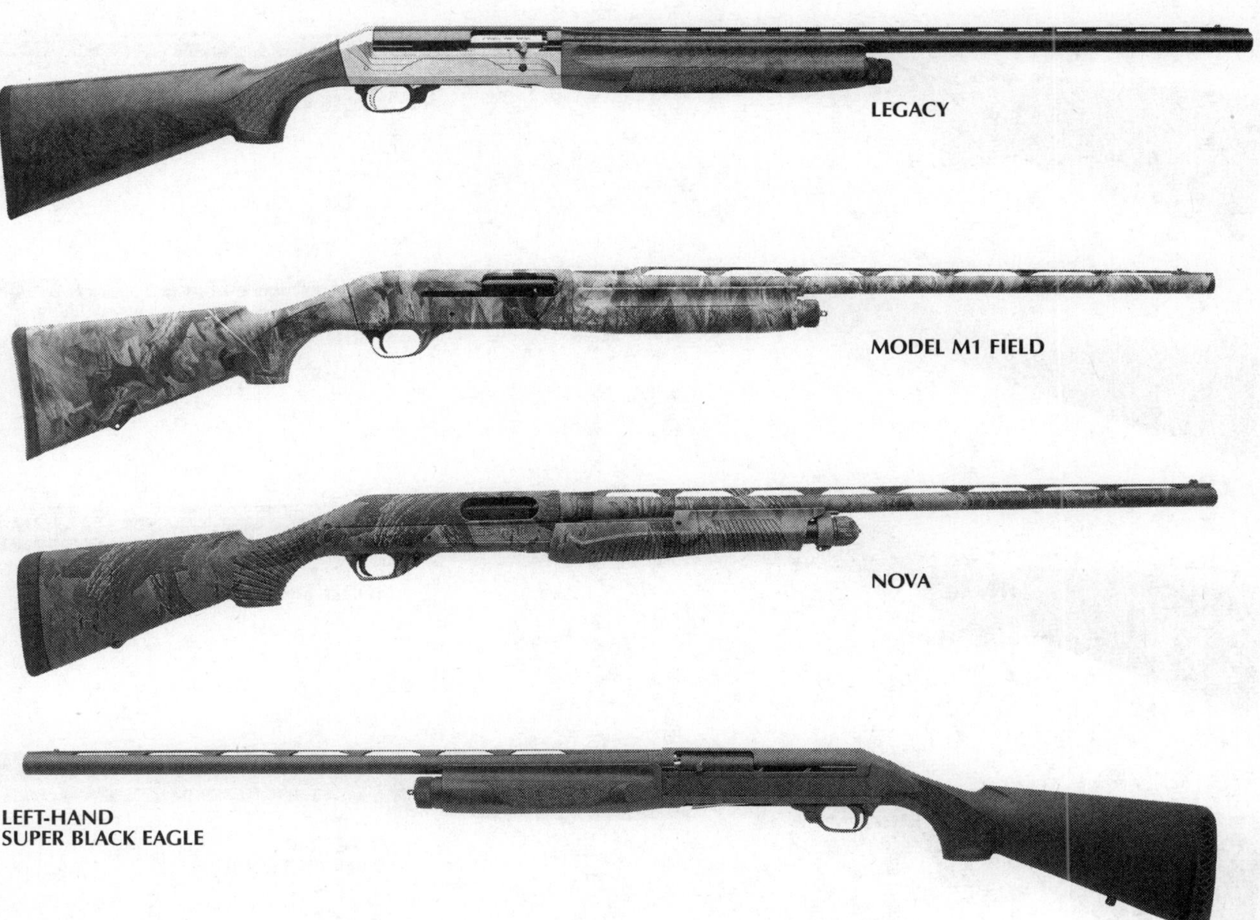

LEGACY

MODEL M1 FIELD

NOVA

LEFT-HAND
SUPER BLACK EAGLE

SHOTGUNS

LEGACY

Action: autoloader
Stock: walnut
Barrel: 24, 26 or 28 in.
Chokes: screw-in tubes
Weight: 7.5 lbs.
Bore/Gauge: 12, 20
Magazine: 3
Features: 3-inch chambers, inertia recoil system, rotating bolt with dual lugs; Executive series, Grades I, II and III at extra cost

Legacy **$1435**

MODEL M1 FIELD

Action: autoloader
Stock: walnut, synthetic or camo
Barrel: 21, 24, 26, 28 or 30 in.
Chokes: screw-in tubes
Weight: 7.3 lbs.
Bore/Gauge: 12, 20
Magazine: 3
Features: 3-inch chambers, inertial recoil system, rotating bolt with dual lugs, rifled slug (12-gauge) about $80 more; Sport: 8 pounds, walnut, 12 ga.; Montefeltro: walnut, 5.3 to 7.1 pounds.

synthetic **$1000**
wood **$1015**
camo **$1100**
tactical **$1040**
Montefeltro **$1035**
M1 Field Slug . . . . **$1055 - 1155**

NOVA

Action: pump
Stock: synthetic
Barrel: 24, 26 or 28 in.
Chokes: screw-in tubes
Weight: 8.1lbs.
Bore/Gauge: 12, 20
Magazine: 4
Features: molded polymer (steel reinforced) replaces traditional stock and receiver; bolt locks into barrel

Nova synthetic **$340**
camo **$405**
rifled slug **$505**
rifled slug, camo **$580**
youth . . . . **$340 - 405**

SUPER BLACK EAGLE

Action: autoloader
Stock: walnut or synthetic
Barrel: 24, 26 or 28 in.
Chokes: screw-in tubes
Weight: 7.3 lbs.
Bore/Gauge: 12
Magazine: 3
Features: 3½" chamber, inertial recoil system; rotating bolt with dual lugs; rifles slug and left-hand versions about $50 extra

synthetic **$1305**
walnut **$1315**
camo **$1400**
slug . . . . **$1380 - 1535**

Beretta Shotguns

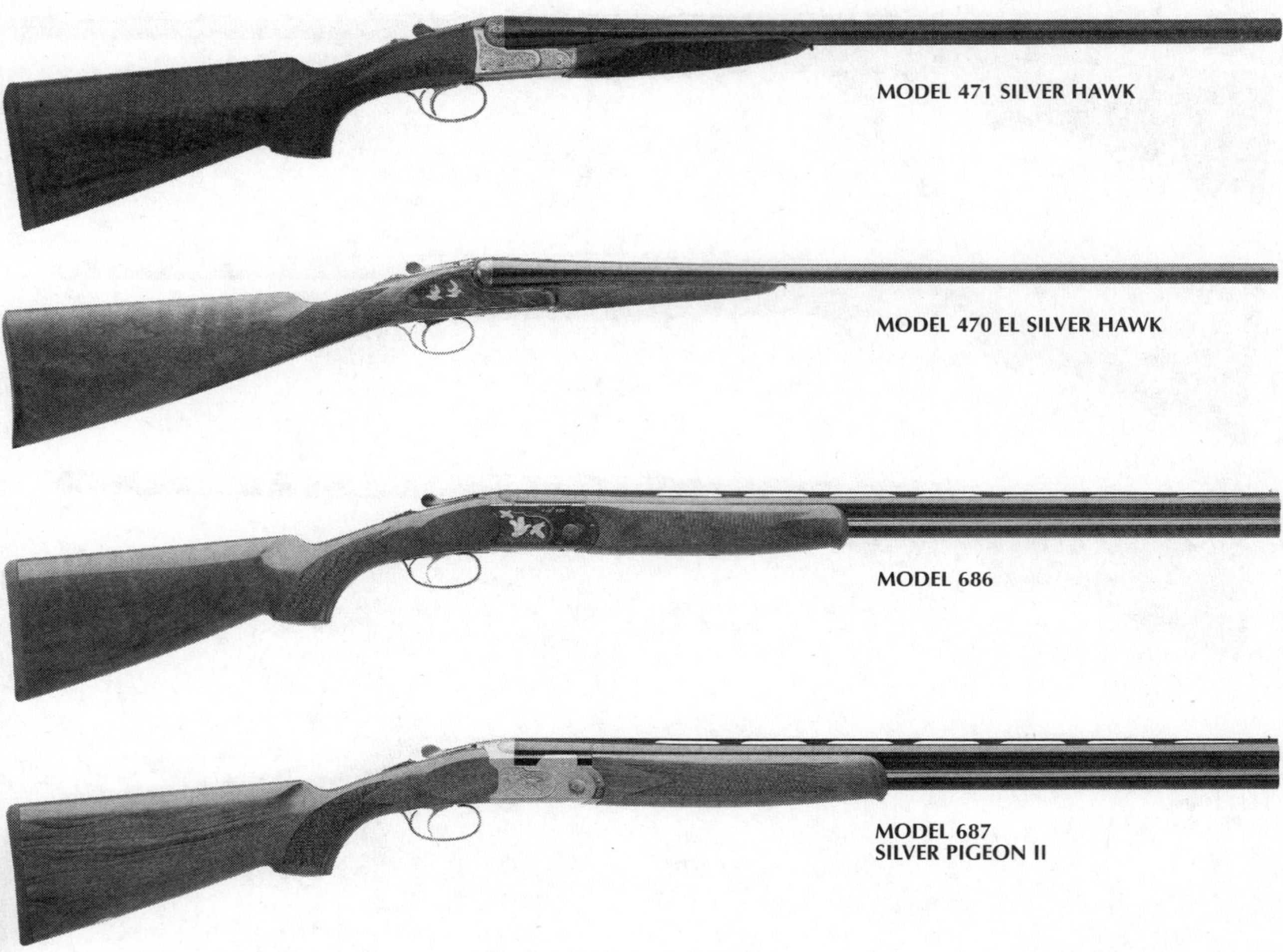

SILVER HAWK

Action: side-by-side
Stock: walnut
Barrel: 26 or 28 in.
Chokes: 12 Gauge Optima-Chokes, 20 Gauge Mobile Chokes
Weight: 6.5 lbs.
Bore/Gauge: 12, 20
Magazine: none
Features: boxlock; satin chromed receiver, single selective trigger, automatic ejectors; straight or pistol grips.
Model 471: $3295
with straight grip. $3495
Model 471 EL $6495

MODEL 686 ONYX

Action: over/under
Stock: walnut
Barrel: 26, 28, 30 or 32 in.
Chokes: screw-in tubes
Weight: 6.8-7.7 lbs.
Bore/Gauge: 12, 20, 28
Magazine: none
Features: boxlock; 3-inch chambers; single selective trigger; automatic ejectors; 3.5 has 3½-inch chambers
Onyx Pro: $1895
Onyx Pro 3.5. . . . . $1995

MODEL 687 PIGEON SERIES

Action: over/under
Stock: walnut
Barrel: 26 - 32 in.
Chokes: screw-in tubes
Weight: 6.8 lbs.
Bore/Gauge: 12, 20, 28/20 Combo
Magazine: none
Features: boxlock; 3-inch chambers; single selective trigger; automatic ejectors; Ultralight (12 ga. only);
Silver Pigeon S $1995
Silver Pigeon II $2395
Silver Pigeon III $2495
Silver Pigeon IV $2795
Silver Pigeon V $3295
EL Gold Pigeon II $4795
EELL Diamond Pigeon $5995

ULTRALIGHT SERIES

Action: O/U, improved box lock
Stock: select walnut
Barrel: 28 in.
Chokes: screw-in tubes (Mobilchoke)
Weight: 6.3 lbs., (Ultralight), 6.5 lbs. (Deluxe)
Bore/Gauge: 12
Magazine: none
Features: Aluminum, titanium-reinforced frame; Single selective trigger; automatic safety; 23/4-inch chamber; Schnabel fore-end; checkered stock; gold inlay
Ultralight: $1,995
Ultralight Delux: $2,495

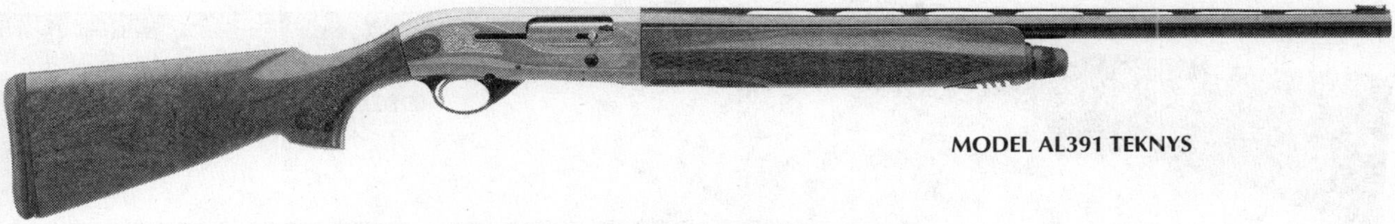

Beretta Shotguns

MODEL AL391 TEKNYS

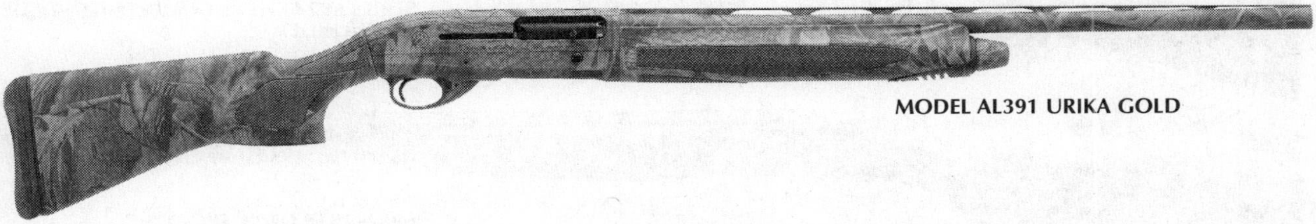

MODEL AL391 URIKA GOLD

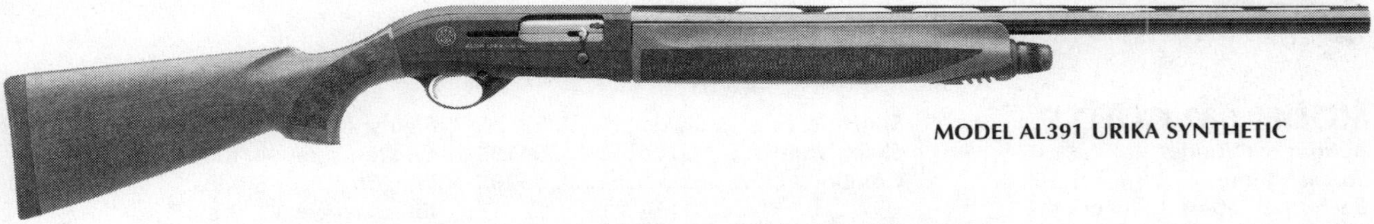

MODEL AL391 URIKA SYNTHETIC

MODEL DT 10 TRIDENT

AL391 TEKNYS

Action: autoloader
Stock: walnut
Barrel: 26, 28, 30 or 32 in.
Chokes: screw-in tubes
Weight: 7.3 lbs. (12 ga.), 5.9 lbs. (20 ga.)
Bore/Gauge: 12, 20
Magazine: 3
Features: Self-compensating gas system, Gel-Tek recoil pad, reversible cross-bolt, Optima-Bore overbored barrels (12-gauge), Optima-Choke

AL391 Teknys $1295
AL391 Teknys Gold $1595
AL391 Teknys Gold Sporting . $1795
AL391 Teknys Gold Trap $1895

MODEL AL391 URIKA

Action: autoloader
Stock: walnut or synthetic
Barrel: 24, 26, 28 or 30 in.
Chokes: screw-in tubes
Weight: 7.4 lbs.
Bore/Gauge: 12, 20
Magazine: 3
Features: gas-operated action; alloy receiver; stock adjust-ment shims;

wood or synthetic.......... $1095
camo.................... $1195
Youth $1095
Trap..................... $1195
Sporting $1195
Gold $1395

DT 10 TRIDENT

Action: over/under
Stock: walnut
Barrel: 28, 30, 32 or 34 in.
Chokes: screw-in tubes
Weight: 7.5 lbs.
Bore/Gauge: 12
Magazine: none
Features: boxlock; single selective trigger, automatic ejectors. Combo with top single or bottom single; Trap versions available

Sporting $6495
Trap..................... $6995
Trap, Bottom Single......... $7495
Trap, Combo Top Single $8995

Beretta Shotguns

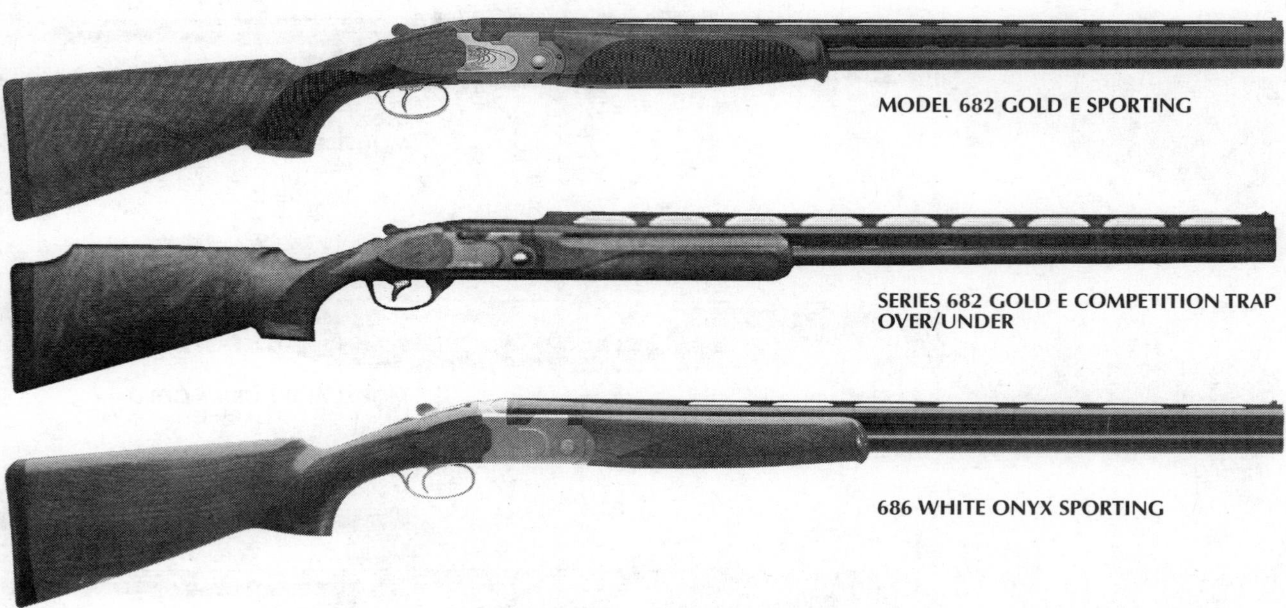

MODEL 682 GOLD E SPORTING

SERIES 682 GOLD E COMPETITION TRAP OVER/UNDER

686 WHITE ONYX SPORTING

MODEL 682 GOLD E

Action: over/under
Stock: walnut
Barrel: 28, 30 or 32 inches
Chokes: screw-in tubes
Weight: 8.8 lbs.
Bore/Gauge: 12
Magazine: none
Features: Skeet, Trap, Sporting, Combo and adjustable-stock models available

Sporting: $3595
Skeet, Trap: $4195
Combo: $5295

686 WHITE ONYX

Action: box-lock over/under
Stock: walnut, oil-finished and checkered, with black recoil pad
Barrels: 26 or 28 in., fitted with removable choke tubes
Sights: front bead
Chokes: screw-in tubes
Weight: 7.8 or 8.0 lbs.
Bore/Gauge: 12, 20, 28
Magazine: none
Features: single selective trigger, manual safety, selective ejectors

List price: $1795
686 White Onyx Sporting (12 ga., 30-32 in. bbl.) $1995

SHOTGUNS

Bernardelli Shotguns

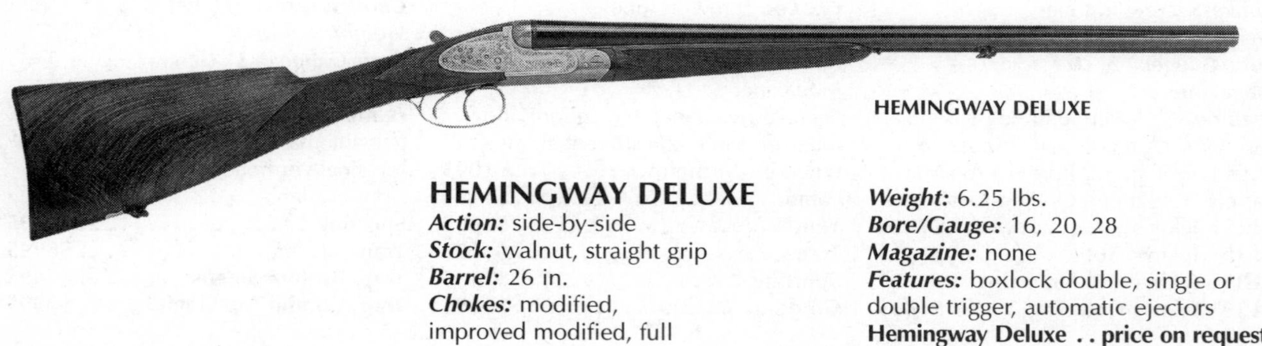

HEMINGWAY DELUXE

HEMINGWAY DELUXE

Action: side-by-side
Stock: walnut, straight grip
Barrel: 26 in.
Chokes: modified, improved modified, full
Weight: 6.25 lbs.
Bore/Gauge: 16, 20, 28
Magazine: none
Features: boxlock double, single or double trigger, automatic ejectors

Hemingway Deluxe . . price on request

Bernardelli Shotguns

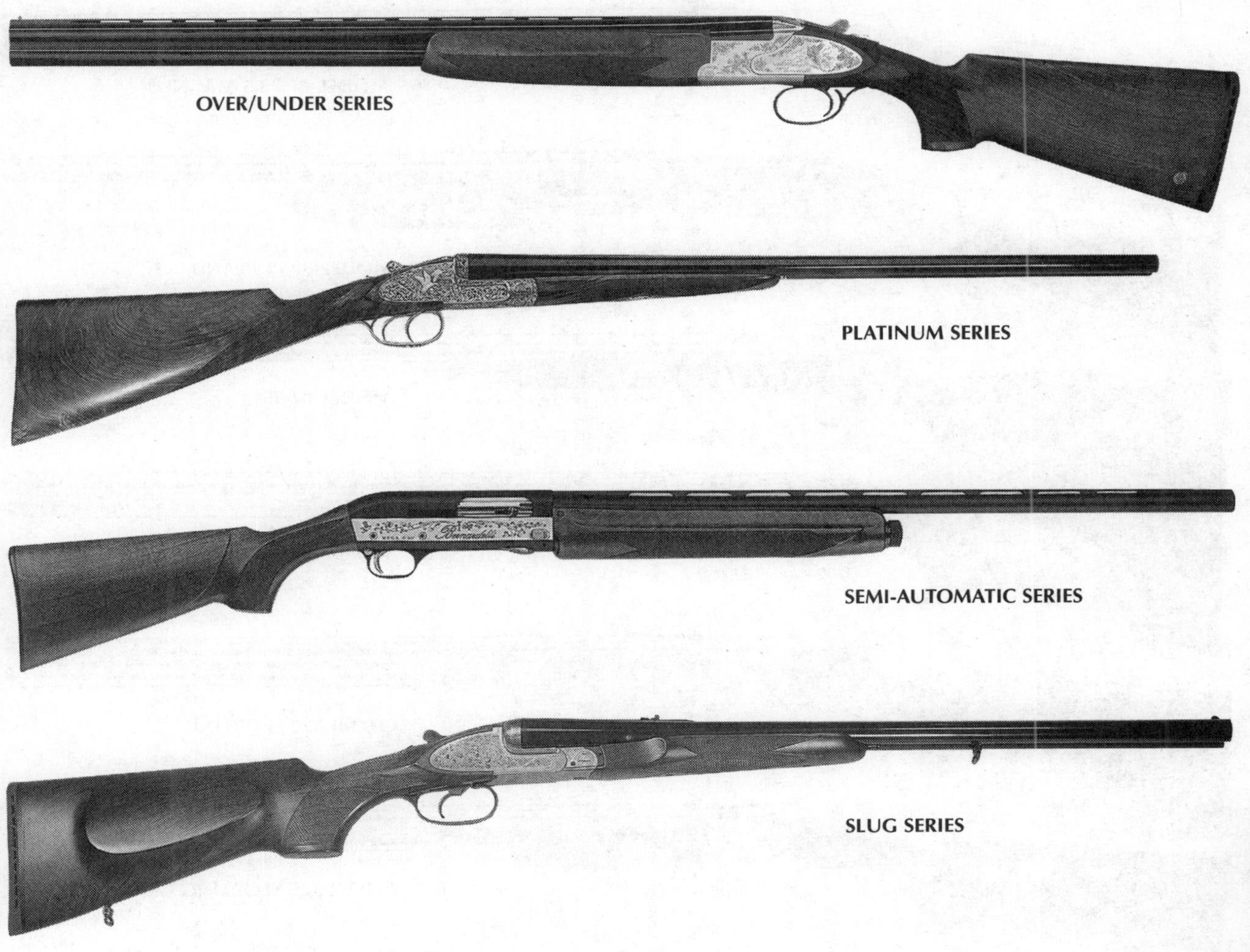

OVER/UNDER SERIES

PLATINUM SERIES

SEMI-AUTOMATIC SERIES

SLUG SERIES

OVER/UNDER SERIES

Action: over/under
Stock: walnut, pistol grip
Barrel: 26 or 28 in.
Chokes: modified, improved modified, full, screw-in tubes
Weight: 7.2 lbs.
Bore/Gauge: 12, 20
Magazine: none
Features: boxlock over/under, single or double triggers, vent rib, various grades
Over/Under. . . . . . . price on request

PLATINUM SERIES

Action: side-by-side
Stock: walnut, straight or pistol grip
Barrel: 26 or 28 in.
Chokes: modified, improved modified, full
Weight: 6.5 lbs.
Bore/Gauge: 12
Magazine: none
Features: sidelock double; articulated single selective or double trigger, triple-lug Purdey breeching automatic ejectors, various grades
Platinum Series . . . . price on request

SEMI-AUTOMATIC SERIES

Action: autoloader
Stock: walnut, synthetic or camo
Barrel: 24, 26 or 28 in.
Chokes: screw-in tubes
Weight: 6.7 lbs.
Bore/Gauge: 12
Magazine: 5
Features: gas-operated, concave top rib, ABS case included
Semi-Automatic. . . . price on request

SLUG SERIES

Action: side-by-side
Stock: walnut, pistol grip
Barrel: 24 in.
Chokes: modified, improved modified, full
Weight: 7.0 lbs.
Bore/Gauge: 12
Magazine: none
Features: boxlock double, single or double trigger, automatic ejectors, rifle sights
Slug Series. . . . . . . price on request

Browning Shotguns

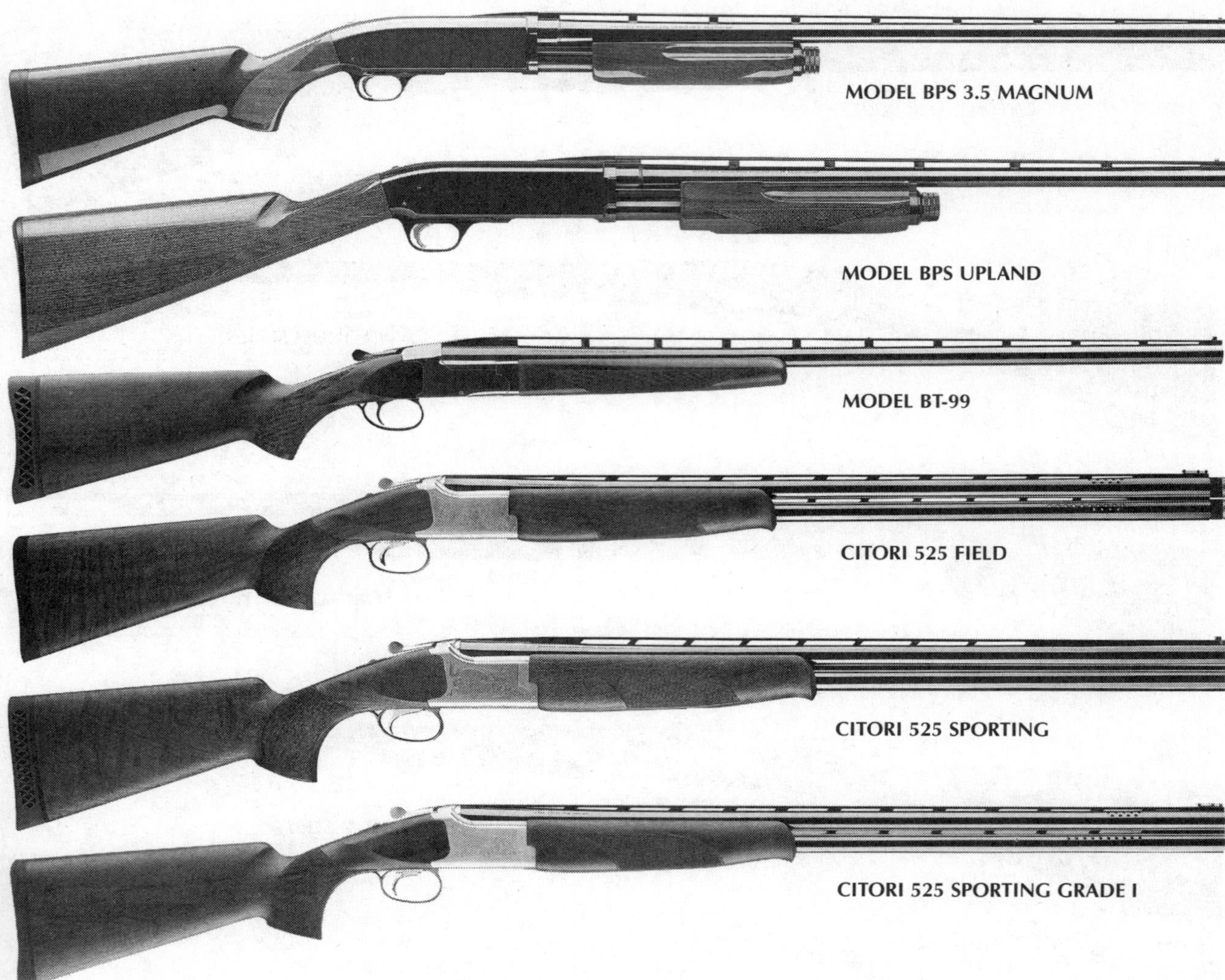

MODEL BPS 3.5 MAGNUM

MODEL BPS UPLAND

MODEL BT-99

CITORI 525 FIELD

CITORI 525 SPORTING

CITORI 525 SPORTING GRADE I

SHOTGUNS

MODEL BPS

Action: pump
Stock: walnut or synthetic
Barrel: 20, 22, 24, 26, 28 or 30 in.
Chokes: screw-in tubes
Weight: 8.0 lbs.
Bore/Gauge: 10, 12, 20, 28, .410
Magazine: 4
Features: Both 10 and 12 gauge available with 3.5-inch chambers; Upland Special has short barrel, straight grip; Deer Special has rifled barrel; Micro BPS has short barrel, stock

Hunter (walnut) $509
Stalker (synthetic) $492
Camo synthetic $605
28 or .410 . . . . $544
Magnum (3.5-inch) $579
Magnum Camo $688
Upland (12, 20) $509
Micro (20) $509
Rifled Deer (12) $624

MODEL BT-99

Action: hinged single-shot
Stock: walnut, trap-style
Barrel: 30, 32 or 34 in.
Chokes: screw-in tubes
Weight: 8.0 lbs.
Bore/Gauge: 12
Magazine: none
Features: boxlock single-shot competition gun with high-post rib

BT-99 . . . . $1329
with adjustable comb $1584
Micro $1329
Golden Clays $3509

CITORI 525

Action: over/under
Stock: walnut
Barrel: 26, 28, 30 or 32 in.
Chokes: screw-in tubes
Weight: 7.3 lbs.
Bore/Gauge: 12, 20, 28, .410
Magazine: none
Features: boxlock; European-style stock, pronounced pistol grip, floating top and side ribs; Golden Clays has gold inlays

Field $1981
Sporting $2778
Golden Clays $4450
Field (28 or .410) $2010
Sporting (28 or .410) $2787
Golden Clays (28 or .410) $4653
525 Sporting Grade I $2319
Golden Clays Ladies $1812

Browning Shotguns

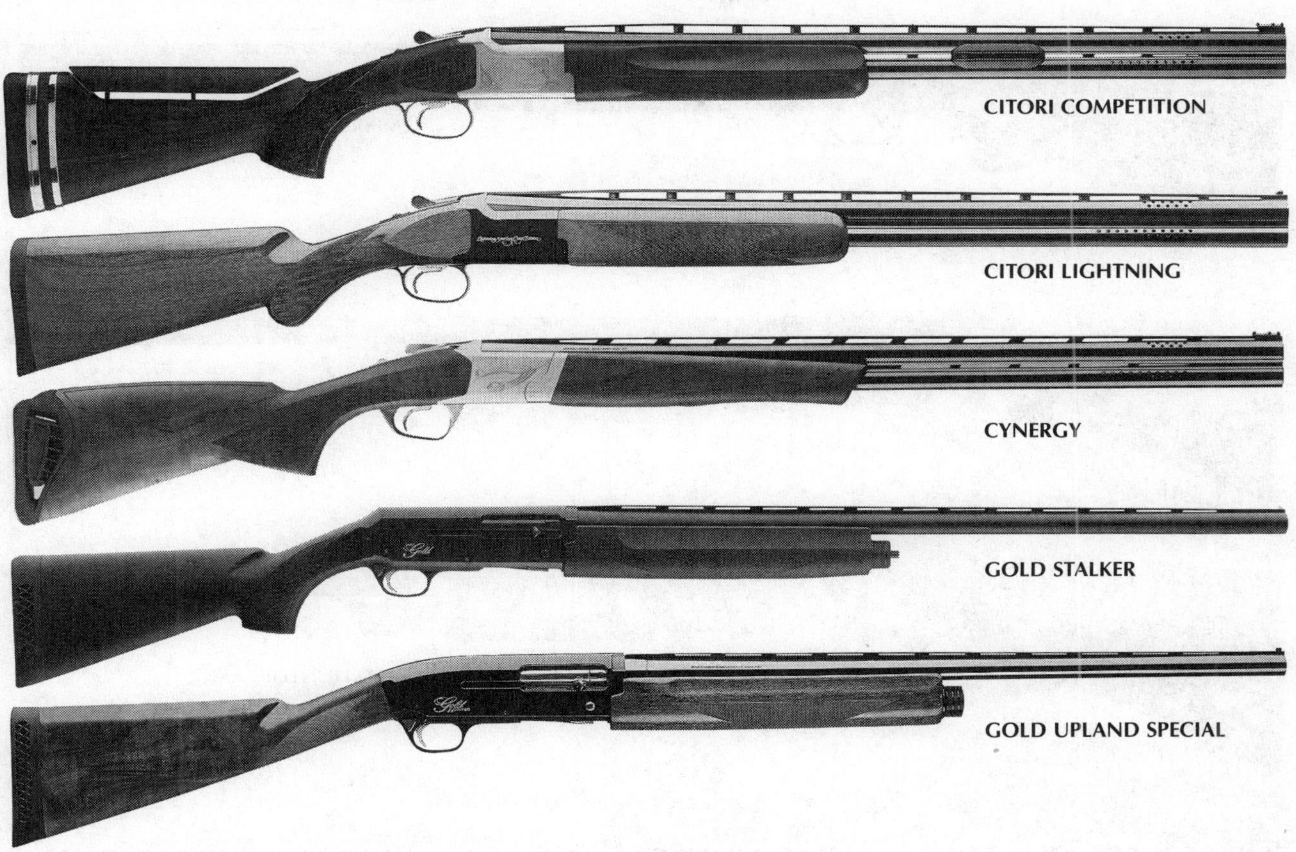

CITORI COMPETITION

Action: over/under
Stock: walnut
Barrel: 26, 28 or 30 in.
Chokes: screw-in tubes
Weight: 8.0 lbs.
Bore/Gauge: 12
Magazine: none
Features: boxlock; XS Pro-Comp has ported barrels, adjustable stock comb, GraCoil recoil reducer; Trap and Skeet Models are stocked and barreled accordingly

XT Trap $2275
XT Trap with adjustable comb . . $2549
XT Trap Gold w/adjustable comb. $4221
XS Skeet $2434
XS Skeet with adjustable comb . $2708

CITORI LIGHTNING

Action: over/under
Stock: walnut
Barrel: 26 or 28 in.
Chokes: screw-in tubes
Weight: 6.3 – 8.0 lbs.
Bore/Gauge: 12, 20, 28, .410
Magazine: none
Features: boxlock; single selective trigger, automatic ejectors; higher grades available; ported barrels optional

Citori Lightning. $1645
28 & .410 . . . . $1709
Citori White Lightning. $1714
28 & .410 . . . . $1790
Citori Lightning Feather $1869
Citori Superlight Feather. $1938

CYNERGY

Action: box-lock over/under, with reverse striker firing mechanism
Stock: walnut, oil-finished and checkered, or compostie, both with black recoil pad
Barrels: 26, 28, 30 or 32 inches, fitted with removable choke tubes
Sights: double beads on tapered rib
Chokes: screw-in tubes (three provided)
Weight: 7.7 lbs.
Bore/Gauge: 12
Magazine: none
Features: single selective trigger, manual safety, selective ejectors

List price: . . . . $1890 – 3046

Also available:
20 & 28 ga. . . . . $2062 – 3080

GOLD

Action: autoloader
Stock: walnut (Hunter) or synthetic (Stalker)
Barrel: 24, 26, 28 or 30 in.
Chokes: screw-in tubes
Weight: 8.0 lbs.
Bore/Gauge: 10, 12, 20
Magazine: 3
Features: gas-operated, 3½-inch chambers on 10 and one 12 gauge version; Youth and Ladies versions available

Stalker. $981
Hunter $1025
Sporting Clays. $1105
Upland Special $1025
Rifled Deer Stalker (22 in. bbl.) . $1086
Rifled Deer Hunter $1131
3½-inch Hunter. $1148
Gold Fusion $1129
Camo. . . . . $1127 - 1332
Gold Fusion HighGrade $2095
Micro $1025
Gold Light (10 ga.) $1336

Charles Daly Shotguns

EMPIRE II EDL HUNTER

FIELD HUNTER PUMP

FIELD HUNTER CAMO

SHOTGUNS

EMPIRE II EDL HUNTER

Action: over/under
Stock: walnut
Barrel: 26 or 28 in.
Chokes: screw-in tubes
Weight: 7.2 lbs.
Bore/Gauge: 12, 20, 28, .410
Magazine: none
Features: boxlock; single selective trigger, automatic safety, automatic ejectors

12 or 20 ga. $2029
28 ga. $2019
.410 . . . . $2019
Trap. $2099

FIELD HUNTER AUTOLOADER

Action: autoloader
Stock: synthetic
Barrel: 22, 24, 26, 28 or 30 in.
Chokes: screw-in tubes
Weight: 7.5 lbs.
Bore/Gauge: 12, 20, 28
Magazine: 4
Features: ventilated rib; Superior II Grade has walnut stock, ported barrel

12 or 20 ga. $389
28 ga. $459
camo. $459
3.5-in. magnum synthetic $469
3.5-in. magnum camo. $539
Superior Hunter $539
Superior Trap. $589

FIELD HUNTER PUMP

Action: pump
Stock: synthetic
Barrel: 26 or 28 in.
Chokes: screw-in tubes
Weight: 7.0 lbs.
Bore/Gauge: 12, 20
Magazine: 4
Features: ventilated rib

Field Hunter $219
camo. $289
3.5-in. magnum synthetic $259
3.5-in. magnum camo. $319

Choke tubes have made guns much more versatile. When you install them, be certain they're tight – and check them often. A loose tube can damage the barrel threads.

Charles Daly Shotguns

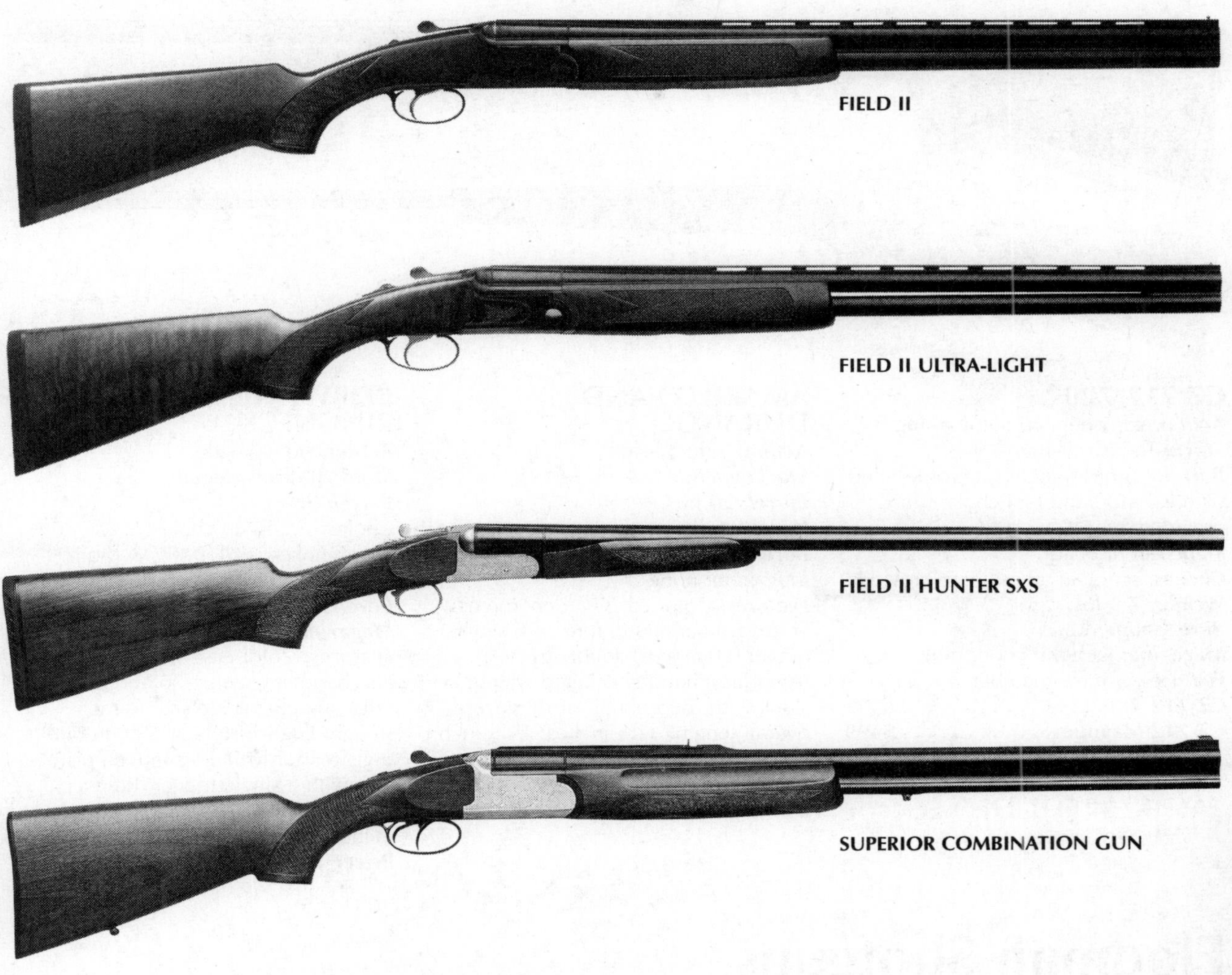

FIELD II

FIELD II ULTRA-LIGHT

FIELD II HUNTER SXS

SUPERIOR COMBINATION GUN

SHOTGUNS

FIELD II

Action: over/under
Stock: walnut
Barrel: 26 or 28 in.
Chokes: mod/full (28 in.), imp.cyl/mod (26 in.), full/full (.410)
Weight: 7.2 lbs.
Bore/Gauge: 12, 16, 20, 28, .410
Magazine: none
Features: boxlock; single selective trigger, automatic safety

Field II $1029
28-gauge $1129
.410 . . . . $1129
Ultra-Light (12, 20) $1199
Superior II. $1519
Superior II Trap $1699

FIELD II HUNTER SXS

Action: side-by-side
Stock: walnut
Barrel: 26, 28 or 30 in.
Chokes: imp.cyl/mod (26 in.), mod/full (28, 30 in.), full/full (.410)
Weight: 10.0 lbs.
Bore/Gauge: 12, 16, 20, 28, .410
Magazine: none
Features: boxlock; single selective trigger, automatic safety

12 or 20 ga. $1189
16, 28 ga. or .410 . . . . $1099
Superior Grade . . . . . . $1629 – 1659
Empire Grade $2119

SUPERIOR COMBINATION GUN

Action: over/under
Stock: walnut
Barrel: 24 in.
Chokes: improved cylinder
Weight: 7.5 lbs.
Bore/Gauge: 12
Magazine: none
Features: boxlock drilling; 12 gauge over .22 Hornet, .223 or .30-06 rifle; double triggers, sling swivels

Superior $1479
Empire Grade $2189
Superior Express (.30-06) $2259
Empire Express (.30-06, .375 H&H, .416 Rigby) . . . . $2949 – 3659

CZ Shotgun

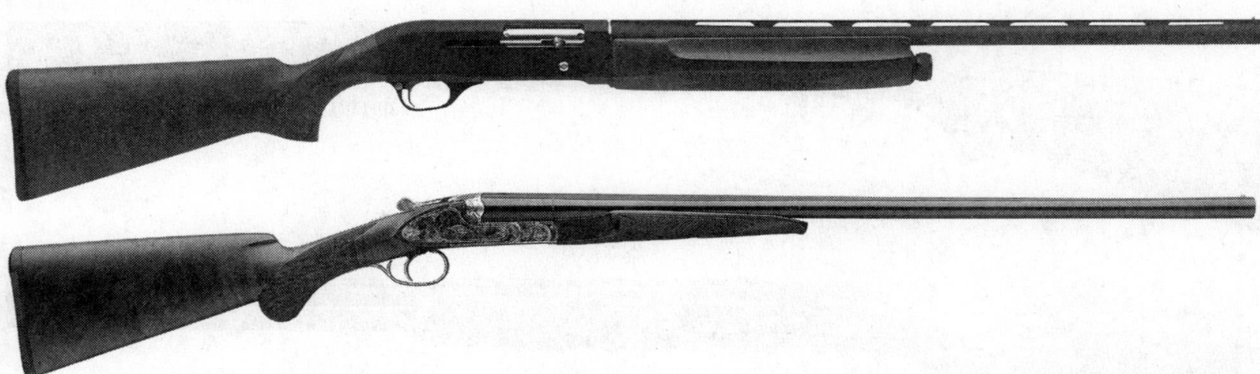

CZ 712/720

Action: gas-operated autoloading
Stock: Turkish walnut
Barrel: 26 or 28 inches, chrome-lined, with IC, Mod and Full choke tubes provided
Sights: front bead
Chokes: screw-in tubes (three provided)
Weight: 7.3 lbs.
Bore/Gauge: 12
Magazine: 4-shot without plug
Features: 3-inch chamber
CZ 712/720 . . . . $399
CZ 712 Magnum $499

AMARILLO AND DURANGO

Action: Side-by-side
Stock: walnut
Barrel: 20 in.
Weight: 6 lbs.
Bore/Gauge: 20, 12
Magazine: none
Features: Color case-hardened receiver, trigger guard and fore end, single trigger (Durango), double trigger (Amarillo); hand checkered walnut stock with round knob pistol grip; overall length: 37.5 inches; 14.5-inch LOP
Amarillo: $695
Durango: $695

BOBWHITE AND RINGNECK

Action: side-by-side
Stock: Turkish walnut
Barrel: 26 in.
Chokes: Screw-in chokes (12 & 20); fixed chokes in .410. (IC & Mod)
Weight: 5.2 lbs.
Bore/Gauge: 20, 28, 12, .410
Magazine: none
Features: Color case-hardened finish and hand engraving; 20 and 28 gauge built on appropriate size frame; straight English-style grip and double triggers (Bobwhite); American pistol grip with a single trigger (Ringneck); hand checkered; overall length 43 inches;14.5-inch LOP
Price: $869

SHOTGUNS

Flodman Shotguns

FLODMAN DOUBLE-RIFLE BARREL

FLODMAN COMBI BARREL

FLODMAN SHOTGUN BARREL

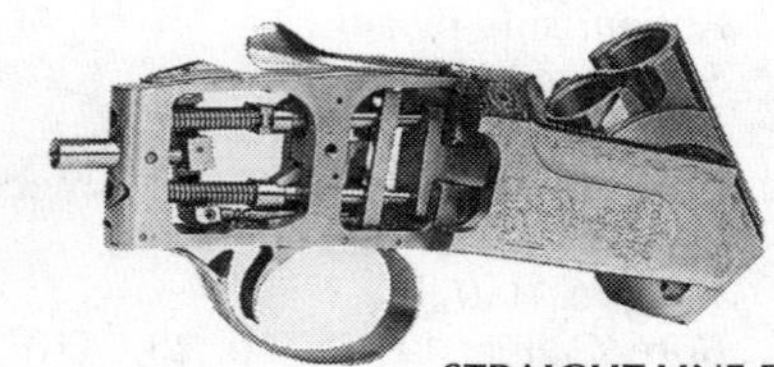

STRAIGHT-LINE RECOIL

FLODMAN SHOTGUN

Action: over/under
Stock: walnut, fitted to customer
Barrel: any standard length
Chokes: improved cylinder, modified, full
Weight: 7.0 lbs.
Bore/Gauge: 12, 20
Magazine: none
Features: boxlock offered in any standard gauge or rifle/shotgun combination; true hammerless firing mechanism, single selective trigger, automatic ejector
Flodman shotgun $15,500

Franchi Shotguns

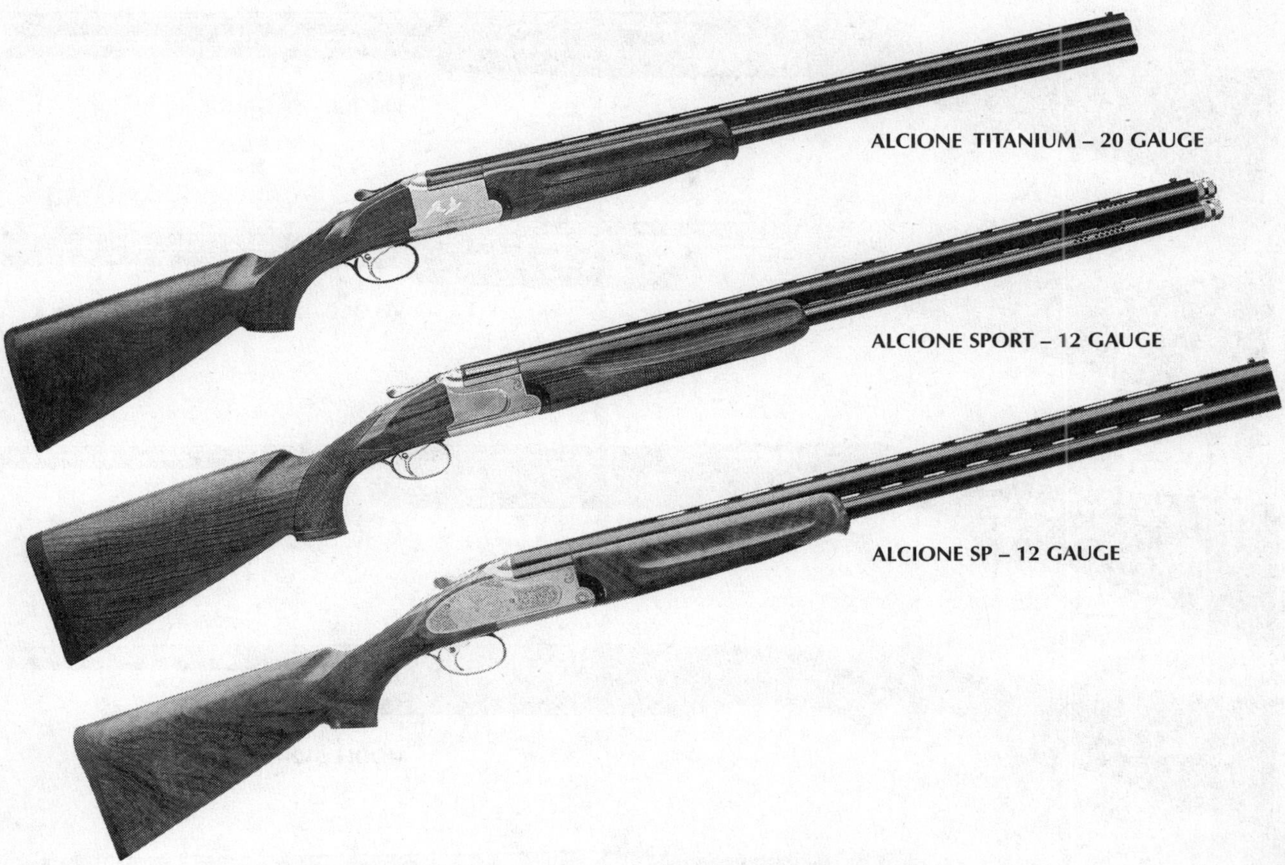

ALCIONE TITANIUM – 20 GAUGE

ALCIONE SPORT – 12 GAUGE

ALCIONE SP – 12 GAUGE

ALCIONE

Action: over/under
Stock: walnut
Barrel: 26 or 28 in.
Chokes: screw-in tubes
Weight: 5.4 lbs.
Bore/Gauge: 12, 20
Magazine: none
Features: boxlock; mechanical single selective trigger

Alcione Classic $1320
Alcione Field. $1310
Titanium $1470
SL Sport model $1700
SX $1980
Also available:
Alcione accessory barrels:
12 ga. Sport. . . . . $490 - 560
12 ga. Field . . . . $490 - 560
20 ga. Field $490

ALCIONE SP

Action: over/under
Stock: walnut
Barrel: 28 in.
Chokes: improved cylinder, modified, full
Weight: 7.5 lbs.
Bore/Gauge: 12
Magazine: none
Features: boxlock, engraved, coin-finish sideplates, fitted hard case

Alcione SP. $2780

SHOTGUNS

Shooting slugs but not enjoying it? Try Remington's new Managed Recoil ammunition. It takes the bite out of hard-kicking loads but leaves plenty of game-killing energy.

Franchi Shotguns

VELOCE – 20 GAUGE

VELOCE – 28 GAUGE ENGLISH STOCK

AL 48

MODEL 912 - 3.5" MAGNUM

MODEL 912 STEADY GRIP

SHOTGUNS

VELOCE

Action: over/under
Stock: walnut, straight English or pistol grip
Barrel: 26 or 28 in.
Chokes: screw-in tubes
Weight: 5.5 lbs.
Bore/Gauge: 20, 28
Magazine: none
Features: boxlock; alloy frame, steel breech insert, mechanical single selective trigger, engraved inside plate, 3-inch chambers (12 gauge), 2¾-inch chambers (28-gauge), aluminum alloy frame.

20 ga. $1470
28 ga. $1545
Veloce Squire Limited Edition (2 barrel set) $2470

MODEL AL 48

Action: autoloader
Stock: walnut pistol grip or English
Barrel: 24, 26 or 28 in.
Chokes: screw-in tubes
Weight: 5.6 lbs.
Bore/Gauge: 20, 28
Magazine: 4
Features: long recoil action

20 ga. $735
28 ga. $850
Deluxe 20 . . . . $970
Deluxe 28 . . . . $1020

MODEL 612, 620, 912

Action: autoloader
Stock: walnut, black synthetic or camo
Barrel: 24, 26, 28, or 30 in.
Chokes: screw-in tubes
Weight: 7.6 to 8.0 lbs.
Bore/Gauge: 12
Magazine: 5 + 1
Features: gas-operated, rotary bolt; Model 912 chambered for 2¾" to 3.5" shells; Model 912 Steady Grip has full grip.

walnut $850
synthetic $790
camo $900
Model 912 Steady Grip $850

Harrington & Richardson Shotguns

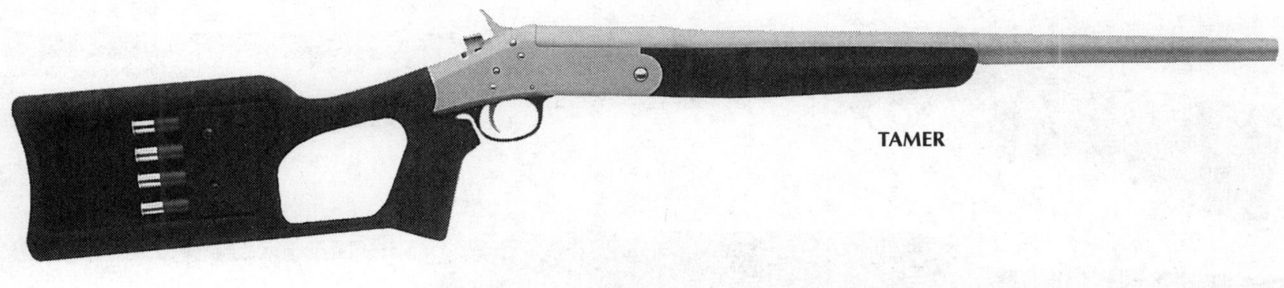
TAMER

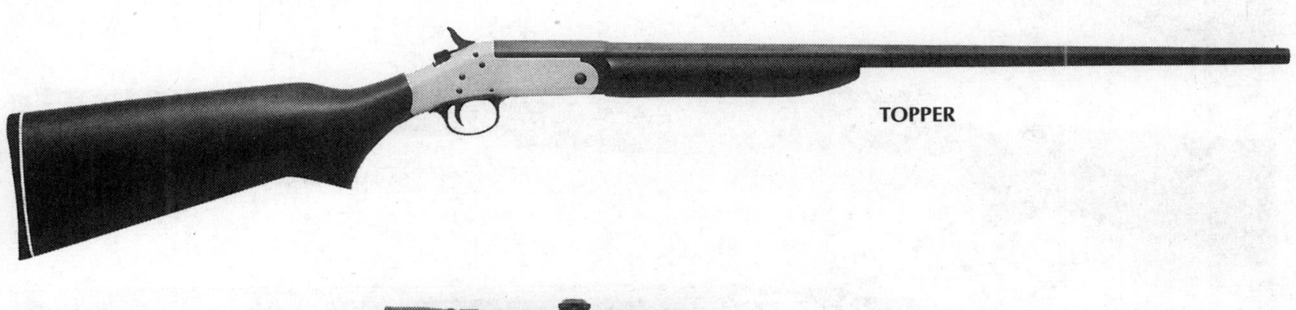
TOPPER

ULTRA SLUG HUNTER

SHOTGUNS

TAMER
Action: hinged single-shot
Stock: synthetic
Barrel: 19 in.
Chokes: full
Weight: 6 lbs.
Bore/Gauge: .410
Magazine: none
Features: thumbhole stock with recessed cavity for ammo storage
Tamer $169

TOPPER
Action: hinged single-shot
Stock: hardwood
Barrel: 26 or 28 in.
Chokes: screw-in tubes
Weight: 6.0 lbs.
Bore/Gauge: 12, 20, 28, .410
Magazine: none
Features: hinged-breech with side lever release, automatic ejection
Topper. $149
12 gauge 3.5-inch $175
Junior with walnut stock. $193
Deluxe Classic. $220

ULTRA SLUG HUNTER
Action: hinged single-shot
Stock: hardwood
Barrel: 24 in., rifled
Chokes: none
Weight: 7.5 lbs.
Bore/Gauge: 12, 20
Magazine: none
Features: factory-mounted Weaver scope base, swivels and sling
Ultra Slug Hunter $266
Youth $266
with camo laminated wood. . . . $328

Pattern your shotgun not only to determine pellet-strike percentages in 30-inch circles at 40 yards but to find the center of impact relative to your sightline. The gun must shoot where you look!

HK Fabarm Shotguns

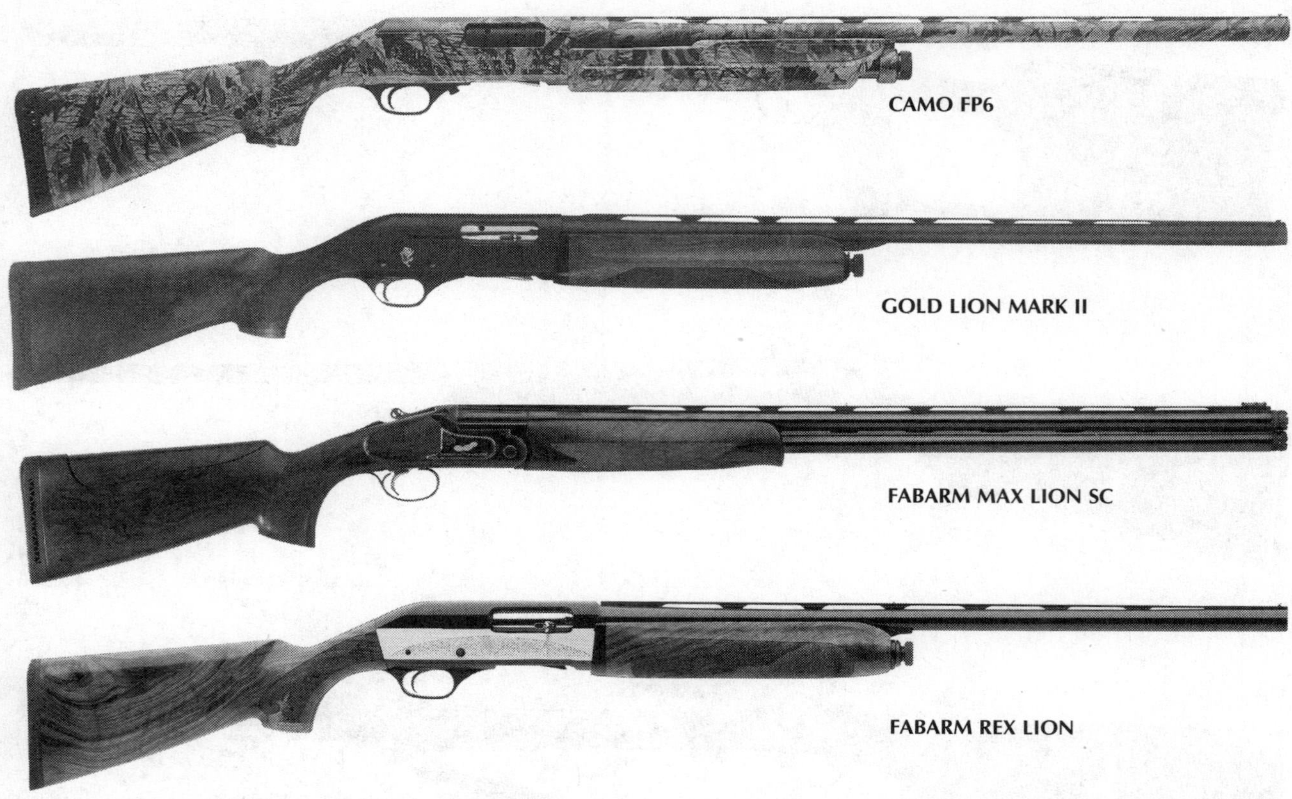

SHOTGUNS

MODEL FP6

Action: pump
Stock: walnut
Barrel: 26 or 28 in.
Chokes: screw-in tubes
Weight: 7.0 lbs.
Bore/Gauge: 12
Magazine: 4
Features: back-bored barrel
FP6 . . . . $549
camo $469

GOLDEN LION MARK II

Action: autoloader
Stock: walnut or synthetic
Barrel: 24, 26 or 28 in.
Chokes: screw-in tubes
Weight: 7.0 lbs.
Bore/Gauge: 12
Magazine: 4
Features: gas-operated actions, shim-adjustable buttstock
Golden Lion Mark II $939
Sporting Clays $1249

PARADOX LION

Action: over/under
Stock: walnut
Barrel: 24 in.
Chokes: screw-in tubes
Weight: 7.6 lbs.
Bore/Gauge: 12, 20
Magazine: none
Features: boxlock; choke tube on top barrel and rifled below; case-colored receiver; 6.6 lbs for 20 gauge; also, new Max Lion Sporting Clays with adjustable stock and 32 in. tube-choked barrels (7.9 lbs.)
Paradox Lion $1129
Max Lion SC $1799

REX LION AND GOLD LION

Action: autoloader
Stock: walnut
Barrel: 26 or 28 in.
Chokes: screw-in tubes
Weight: 7.7 lbs.
Bore/Gauge: 12
Magazine: 2
Features: gas operated, Turkish walnut stock, chrome-lined barrel
Rex Lion $1049
Gold Lion $939

Big shot leaves big holes in patterns far away, while little shot loses per-pellet energy faster. For turkey hunting, try #5 pellets. They deliver good penetration, head-tight patterns at long range.

HK Fabarm Shotguns

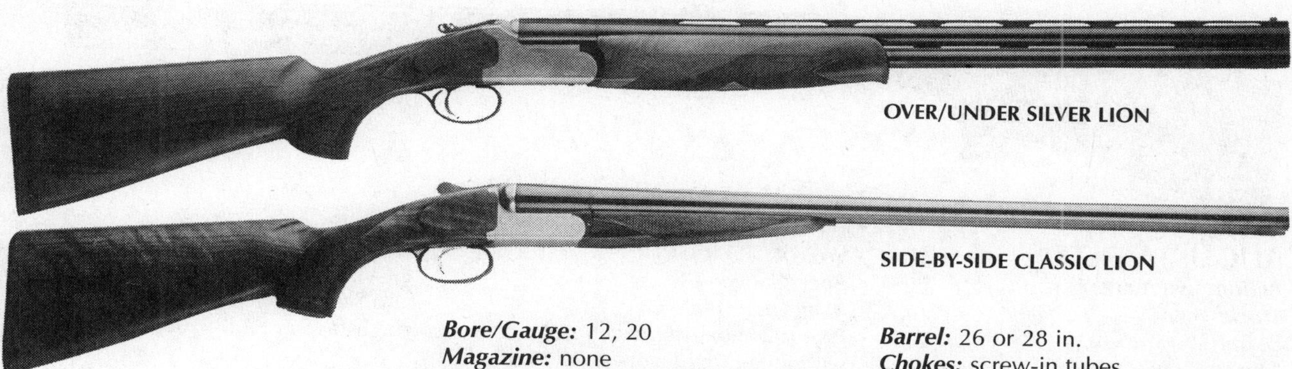

OVER/UNDER SILVER LION

SIDE-BY-SIDE CLASSIC LION

OVER/UNDER

Action: over/under
Stock: walnut
Barrel: 26 or 28 in.
Chokes: screw-in tubes
Weight: 7.0 lbs.
Bore/Gauge: 12, 20
Magazine: none
Features: boxlock; back-bored barrels, single selective trigger

Over/Under $1235
Silver Lion $1315
Sporting Clays $1871
UltraMag Camo $1315

SIDE-BY-SIDE

Action: side-by-side ***Stock:*** walnut
Barrel: 26 or 28 in.
Chokes: screw-in tubes
Weight: 7.0 lbs.
Bore/Gauge: 12
Magazine: none
Features: boxlock; back-bore barrels, single selective trigger

Grade I $1499
Classic Lion English $1604
Classic Lion Grade II $2246

Ithaca Shotguns

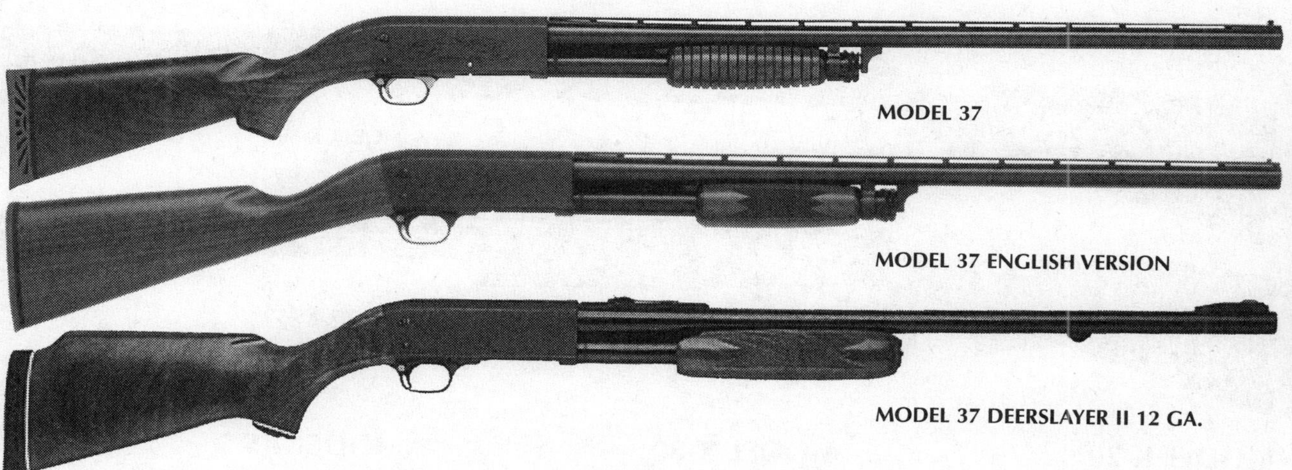

MODEL 37

MODEL 37 ENGLISH VERSION

MODEL 37 DEERSLAYER II 12 GA.

MODEL 37

Action: pump
Stock: walnut or synthetic
Barrel: 20, 22, 24, 26 or 28 in.
Chokes: screw-in tubes
Weight: 7.0 lbs.
Bore/Gauge: 12, 16, 20 ***Magazine:*** 4
Features: bottom ejection

Classic $812
Deluxe vent rib $627
M37 Guide Series slug gun,
12 or 20 . . . . $599
Turkey Slayer Guide 600
Ultralight 20 ga. $834
English straight-grip . . . .
Trap or Sporting Clays
with Briley tubes, starting . . $1495

MODEL 37 DEERSLAYER II

Action: pump ***Stock:*** walnut
Barrel: 20 or 25 in. rifled or smoothbore
Weight: 7.0 lbs.
Bore/Gauge: 12, 16, 20 ***Magazine:*** 4
Features: open sights; receiver fitted with Weaver-style scope base; also available: Deerslayer III with 26-in. heavy rifled barrel and Turkeyslayer (12 or 20) with 22 in. barrel, extra-full tube

Deerslayer $591
Deerslayer II $642

Kimber Shotguns

AUGUSTA FIELD

AUGUSTA FIELD

Action: over/under
Stock: walnut
Barrel: 26, 27.5 in.
Chokes: screw-in tubes
Weight: 7.5 lbs.
Bore/Gauge: 12
Magazine: none
Features: boxlock; backbored barrel with long forcing cones; adjustable single trigger, automatic ejectors, Hi-Viz sights (Sporting, Field, Trap and Skeet models available)
Augusta $5676

Krieghoff Shotguns

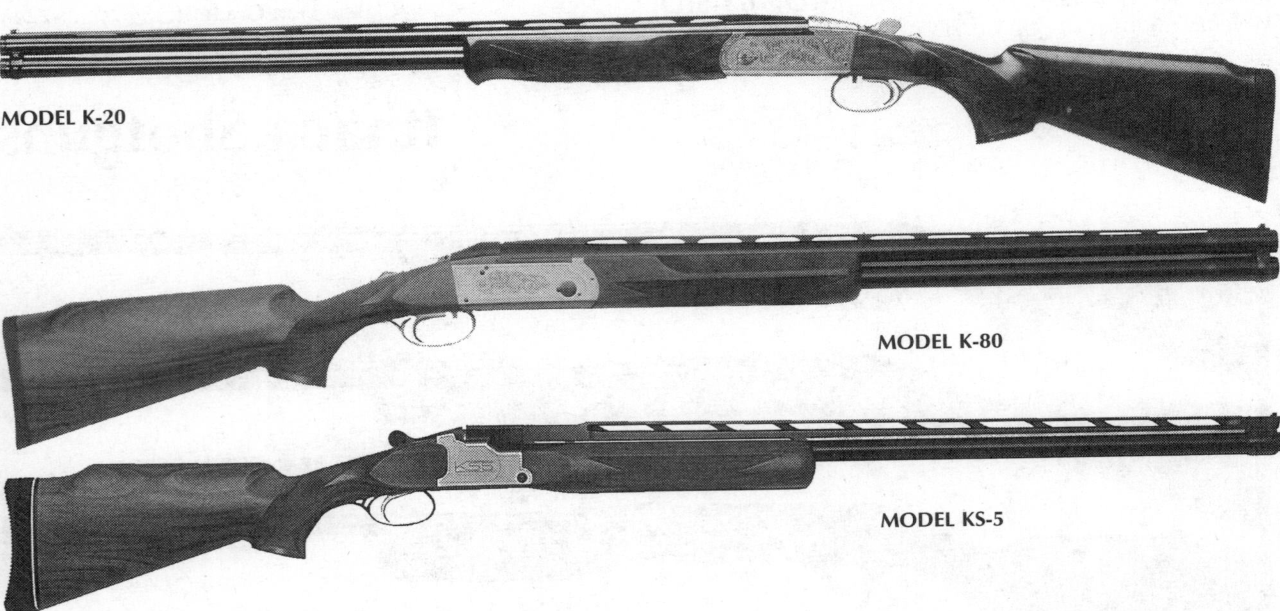

MODEL K-20

MODEL K-80

MODEL KS-5

MODEL K-20

Action: over/under
Stock: walnut
Barrel: 28 or 30 in.
Chokes: screw-in tubes
Weight: 7.2 lbs.
Bore/Gauge: 20, 28, .410
Magazine: none
Features: boxlock; single selective trigger, automatic ejectors, tapered rib, choice of receiver finish; fitted aluminum case
K-20 . . . . price on request

MODEL K-80

Action: over/under
Stock: walnut
Barrel: 28 or 30 in.
Chokes: screw-in tubes
Weight: 8.0 lbs.
Bore/Gauge: 12
Magazine: none
Features: boxlock; single selective trigger, automatic ejectors, tapered rib, choice of receiver finish; (Sporting Clays, Live Bird, Trap and Skeet models available)
K-80 . . . . price on request

MODEL KS-5

Action: hinged single-shot
Stock: walnut
Barrel: 30 in. or length to order
Chokes: screw-in tubes
Weight: 8.0 lbs.
Bore/Gauge: 12
Magazine: none
Features: boxlock; adjustable trigger (release trigger available), step rib, case-colored receiver, optional front hangers to adjust point of impact, optional adjustable comb
KS-5. . . . . price on request

Legacy Sports Shotguns

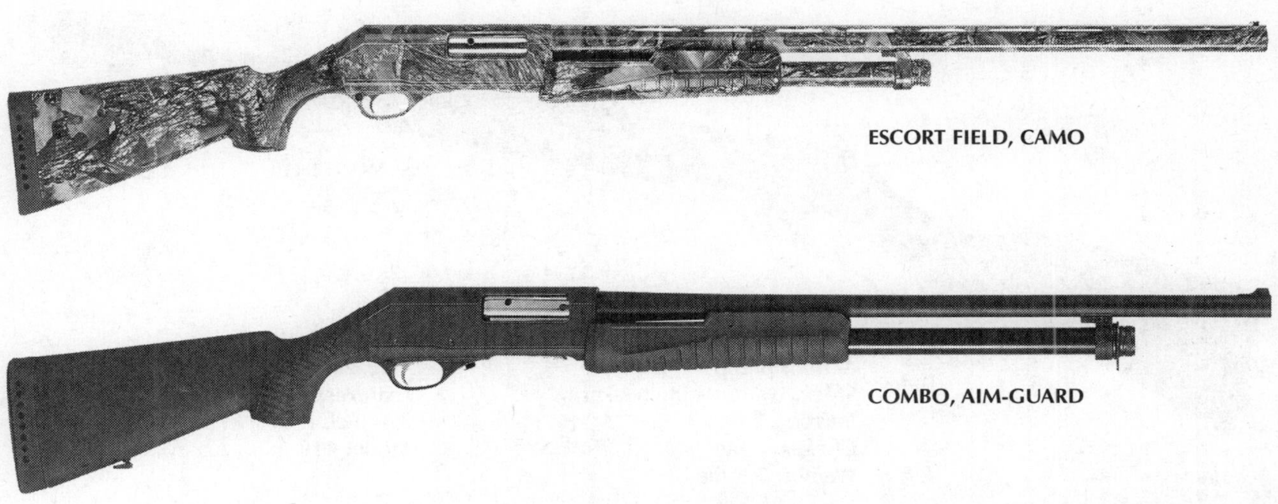

ESCORT FIELD, CAMO

COMBO, AIM-GUARD

ESCORT PUMP-ACTION SHOTGUN

Action: pump
Stock: Black or chrome polymer
Barrel: 18, 22, 26 or 28 in.
Sights: Hi Viz
Chokes: IC, M, F
Weight: 6.4 lbs. – 7.0 lbs.
Bore/Gauge: 12 & 20
Magazine: 5-shot with cut-off button
Features: Alloy receiver with $\frac{3}{8}$" milled dovetail for sight mounting. Black chrome or camp finish; black chrome bolt. Trigger guard safety. 5-shot magazine with cut-off button. Two stock adjustment shims. Three choke tubes; IC, M, F (except AimGuard). 24" Bbl comes with extra turkey choke tube and HI Viz TriViz sight combo.

Field Hunter, black $247
Aim Guard, 20" bbl. $211
Field Hunter Camo $312
Field Hunter, camo, TriViz sights. $363
Field Hunter slug, black . . . . . . $TBD
Combo, 20 to 28 in. barrel $270
Field Hunter slug combo . . . . . $TBD

ESCORT SEMI-AUTOMATIC SHOTGUN

Action: autoloader
Stock: polymer or walnut
Barrel: 18, 22, 26 & 28 in.
Sights: HiViz
Weight: 6.4 to 7.8 lbs.
Bore/Gauge: 12 & 20
Magazine: 5
Features: gas operated and chambered for 3" or $2\frac{3}{4}$-inch shells. Barrels are nickel-chromium-molybdenum steel with additional chrome plating internally and a ventilated anti-glare checkered rib. Bolts are chrome plated. Extras include three chokes, a migratory plug, and two spacers to adjust the slope of the stock. Camo waterfowl and turkey combo available with Hi Viz sights, 28" barrel, hard case.

AS walnut:. $421
AS Youth walnut $421
PS polymer:. $399
PS Aim Guard $392
PS Camo, Spark sights. $443
PS blue, 3.5 mag. $465
PS Waterfowl & Turkey $523
PS Slug, black. . . . . TBD
PS slug, camo. . . . . TBD
Combo, Waterfowler/Turkey (24 – 28 in. bbl., TriViz Sights, Turkey choke . . . . TBD

A quick fit test for length of pull: Rest the shotgun butt in the crook of your arm. If your finger rests comfortably on the trigger, the buttstock is about the right length.

Marlin Shotguns

MODEL 410

MODEL 410
Action: pump
Stock: walnut, cut checkering
Barrel: 22 in.
Chokes: none
Weight: 7.3 lbs.
Bore/Gauge: 410
Magazine: 4
Features: hammer block safety; 2½- inch only
Model 410 . . . . $614

Marocchi Shotguns

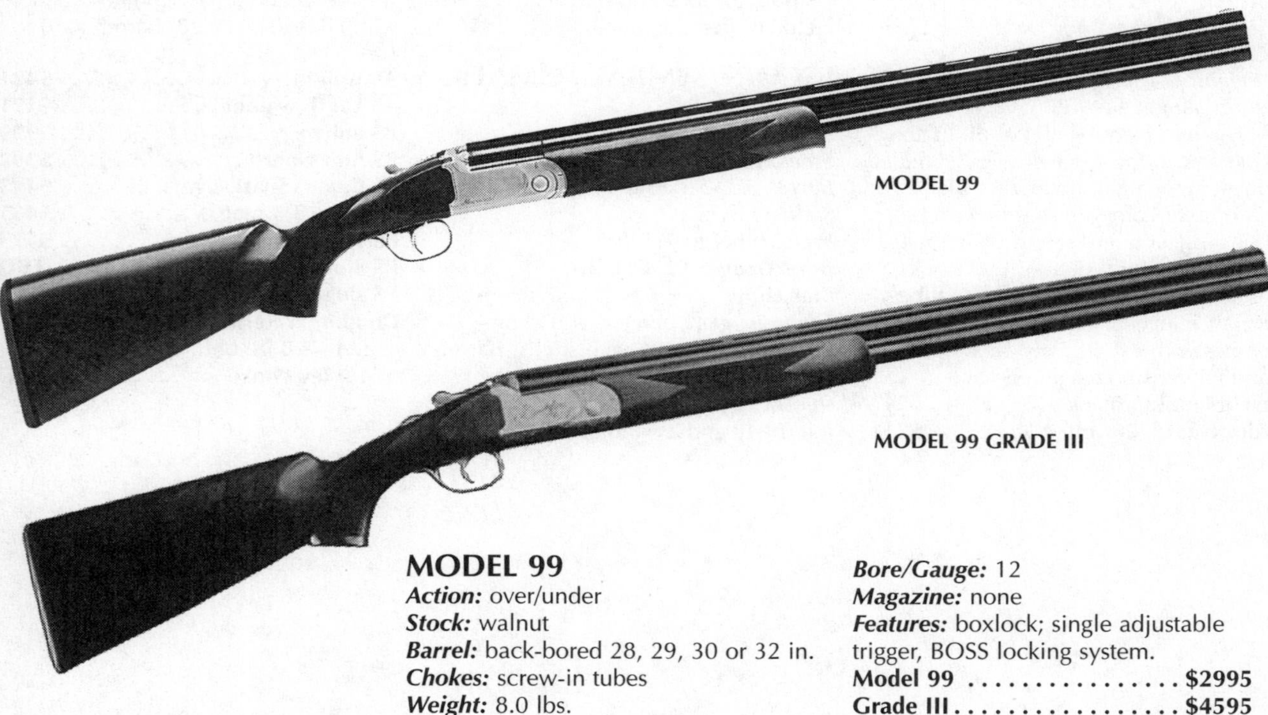

MODEL 99

MODEL 99 GRADE III

MODEL 99
Action: over/under
Stock: walnut
Barrel: back-bored 28, 29, 30 or 32 in.
Chokes: screw-in tubes
Weight: 8.0 lbs.
Bore/Gauge: 12
Magazine: none
Features: boxlock; single adjustable trigger, BOSS locking system.
Model 99 . . . . $2995
Grade III $4595

Merkel Shotguns

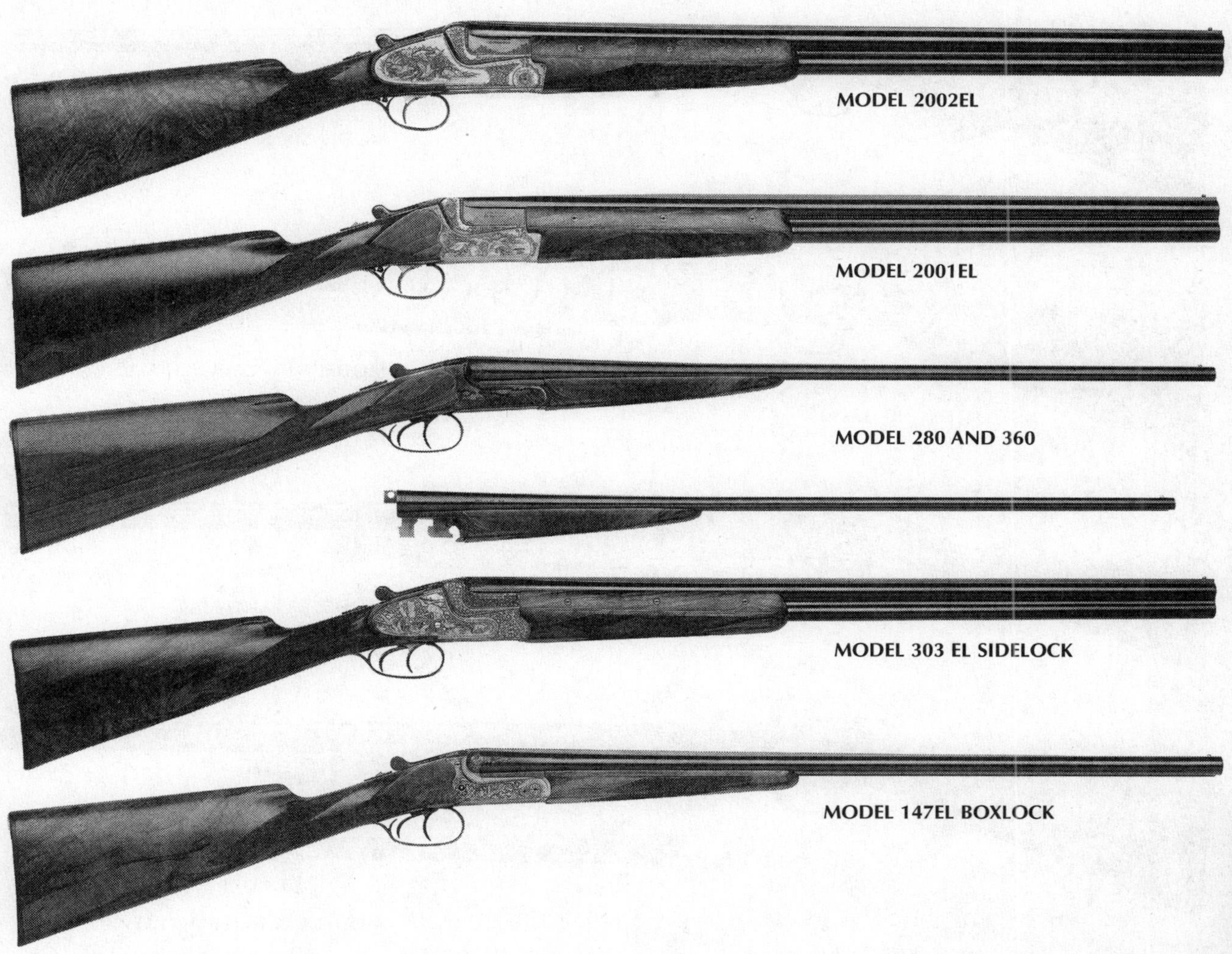

SHOTGUNS

MODEL 2000 EL

Action: over/under
Stock: walnut, straight or pistol grip
Barrel: 27 or 28 in.
Chokes: improved cylinder, modified, full
Weight: 7.3 lbs.
Bore/Gauge: 12, 20, 28
Magazine: none
Features: boxlock; single selective or double trigger; three-piece forend, automatic ejectors

2000 EL $6495
2001 EL (deluxe) $8295
2016 EL (16 ga.) $6496
2002 EL (with sideplates) . . . . P.O.R.

MODEL 280 AND 360

Action: side-by-side
Stock: walnut, straight grip
Barrel: 28 in.
Chokes: imp.cyl/mod (28 ga.), mod/full (.410)
Weight: 6.0 lbs.
Bore/Gauge: 28, .410
Magazine: none
Features: boxlock; double triggers, automatic ejectors; fitted luggage case (Model 280: 28 gauge and Model 360: .410)

Model 280 or Model 360 . . . . $4195
two-barrel sets $6495
S models with sidelocks $9395

MODEL 303 EL

Action: over/under
Stock: walnut, straight or pistol grip
Barrel: 27 or 28 in.
Chokes: improved cylinder, modified, full
Weight: 7.3 lbs.
Bore/Gauge: 16, 20, 28
Magazine: none
Features: sidelock; automatic ejectors, special-order features

303 EL $22,995

MODEL 147E

Action: side-by-side
Stock: walnut, straight or pistol grip
Barrel: 27 or 28 in.
Chokes: imp.cyl/mod or mod/full
Weight: 7.2 lbs.
Bore/Gauge: 12, 20
Magazine: none
Features: boxlock; single selective or double triggers; automatic ejectors; fitted luggage case

47E $3795
147E (deluxe) $4495
147EL (super deluxe). $5695

Mossberg Shotguns

MODEL 500 SPORTING

MODEL 835 PUMP ULTI-MAG CAMO

MODEL 835 ULTI-MAG

MODEL 835 ULTI-MAG COMBO

SHOTGUNS

MODEL 500

Action: pump
Stock: wood or synthetic
Barrel: 18, 22, 24, 26 or 28 in.
Chokes: screw-in tubes
Weight: 7.5 lbs.
Bore/Gauge: 12, 20, .410
Magazine: 5
Features: barrels mostly vent rib, some ported; top tang safety; camouflage stock finish options; 10-year warranty
Model 500 . . . . $316
camo. $364
Bantam Ported 24" bbl: $355
two-barrel combo set $404
Super Bantam Slugster. . . $316 - 364

MODEL 500 MARINER

Action: pump
Stock: synthetic
Barrel: 18 or 20 in.
Chokes: cylinder
Weight: 7.0 lbs.
Bore/Gauge: 12
Magazine: 5
Features: top tang safety; 12-gauge has "Marinecote" metal and 10-year warranty; 20 gauge and .410 variations available in blued finish
Mariner. $512

MODEL 835 ULTI-MAG

Action: pump
Stock: synthetic or camo
Barrel: 24 or 28 in.
Chokes: full
Weight: 7.0 lbs.
Bore/Gauge: 12
Magazine: 4
Features: barrel ported, back-bored with vent rib; 3.5-inch chamber; top tang safety; rifled slug barrel and combination sets available; 10-year warranty
Model 835 . . . . $394
Model 835, camo. . . . . . . $438 - 471
Combo: $502

NEF Shotgun

NEF PARDNER PUMP SHOTGUN

Action: hammerless pump
Stock: walnut , synthetic or camo
Barrel: 28 inches, with vent rib, screw-in choke tube; 22 in. Turkey model; combo comes with 22 in. rifled slug barrel
Sights: gold bead front, TruGlo front & rear on Turkey model
Chokes: screw-in Browning/Winchester/Mossberg tubes (one provided), turkey choke
Weight: 7.5 lbs.
Bore/Gauge: 12
Magazine: 5-shot tube, with 2-shot plug provided
Features: twin action bars, easy take-down
Price:. . . . . $208 - $305

New England Arms/FAIR Shotguns

MODEL 900

Action: over/under
Stock: walnut, straight or pistol grip
Barrel: all standard lengths
Chokes: screw-in tubes
Weight: 7.5 lbs.
Bore/Gauge: 12, 16, 20, 28, .410
Magazine: none
Features: boxlock; single selective trigger, automatic safety, automatic ejector; .410 has fixed choke
Model 900 . . . . $2700 - 3600

New England Firearms Shotguns

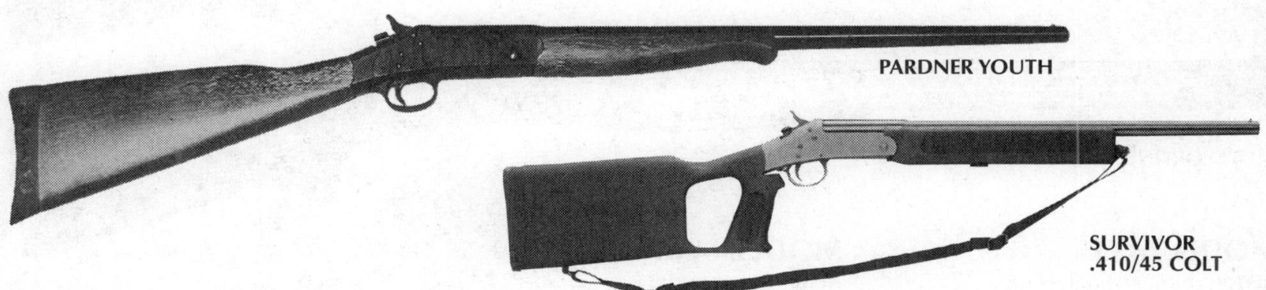

PARDNER YOUTH

SURVIVOR .410/45 COLT

SURVIVOR AND PARDNER

Action: hinged single-shot
Stock: synthetic
Barrel: 22, 26, 28 or 32 in.
Chokes: modified, full
Weight: 6.0 lbs.
Bore/Gauge: 12, 16, 20, 28, .410
Magazine: none
Features: Youth and camo-finish Turkey models available; Survivor has hollow pistol-grip buttstock for storage, chambers .410/.45 Colt

Survivor blue or silver . . . $213 - 232
Pardner $137
Pardner Turkey (3½", 10 and 12ga.) $187-286
Pardner Youth $145
Pardner Turkey Camo Youth . . . $195

New England Firearms Shotguns

TRACKER II RIFLED SLUG GUN

TURKEY & SPECIAL PURPOSE

TRACKER II RIFLED SLUG GUN

Action: hinged single-shot
Stock: hardwood
Barrel: rifled 24 in.
Chokes: none
Weight: 6.0 lbs.
Bore/Gauge: 12, 20
Magazine: none
Features: adjustable rifle sights, swivel studs standard

Tracker II $192

TURKEY & SPECIAL PURPOSE

Action: hinged single-shot
Stock: hardwood
Barrel: 24 in. (Turkey) or 28 in. (Waterfowl)
Chokes: full, screw-in tubes
Weight: 9.5 lbs.
Bore/Gauge: 10, 12
Magazine: none
Features: Turkey and Waterfowl models available with camo finish, swivel studs standard Turkey Gun

(camo, full choke) . . . . . $195 - $286
Turkey Gun (black, tubes) . $187 - $286
Special Purpose Waterfowl
10 ga. $280
with 28 in. barrel, walnut $221

SHOTGUNS

Perazzi Shotguns

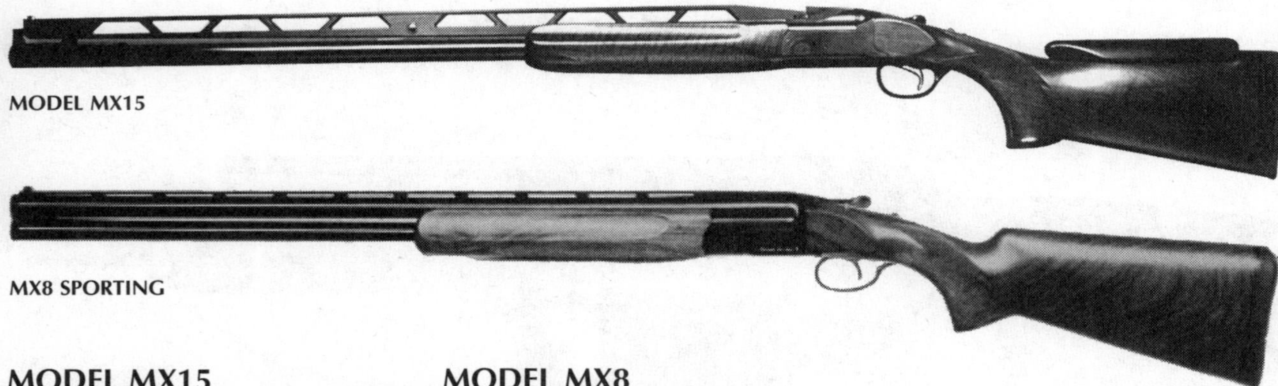

MODEL MX15

MX8 SPORTING

MODEL MX15

Action: hinged single-shot
Stock: walnut, adjustable comb
Barrel: 32 or 35 in.
Chokes: full
Weight: 8.4 lbs.
Bore/Gauge: 12
Magazine: none
Features: high trap rib

MX15 . . . . $9507

MODEL MX8

Action: over/under
Stock: walnut
Barrel: 28 - 34 in.
Chokes: screw-in tubes
Weight: 7.3lbs.
Bore/Gauge: 12 & 20
Magazine: none
Features: hinged-breech action; double triggers or single selective or non-selective trigger; Sporting, Skeet and Trap models and 28 ga. and .410 also available

MX8 . . . . $11,166

Purdey Shotguns

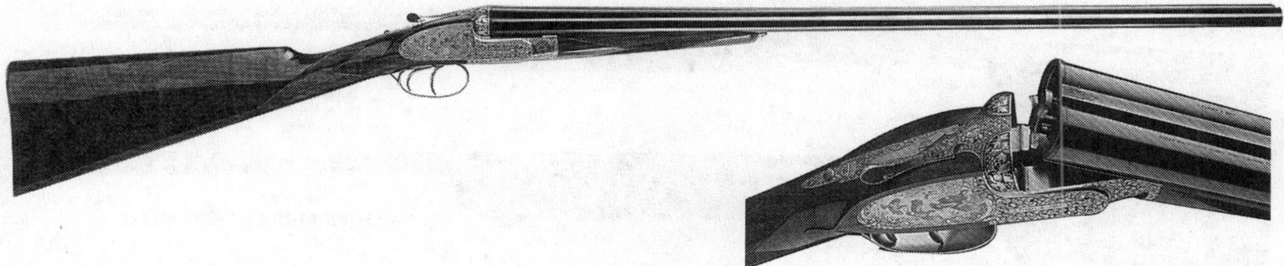

SIDE-BY-SIDE GAME GUN

Purdey easy opening action: All side-by-side guns are built on the easy opening system invented by Frederick Beesley. This system is incorporated in guns built from 1880 onwards.

Purdey offers dedicated action sizes for each of the bores 10, 12, 20, 28 & .410 cores. An extra pair of barrels can be ordered, even if you want a barrel set one gauge smaller. For example, you can have fitted 28 gauge barrels on a 20 gauge, and .410 on a 28 gauge. These guns are made with a single forend for both bores.

All Purdey barrels, both SxS and O/U, are of chopper lump construction. Each individual tube is hand filled and then "struck up" using striking files. This gives the tube the correct Purdey profile.

Once polished, the individual tubes are joined at the breech using silver solder. The loop iron is similarly fixed. Once together, the rough chokes can be cut and the internal bores finished using a traditional lead lapping technique.

Ribs are hand-filed to suit the barrel contour exactly, and then soft-soldered in place, using pine resin as the fluxing agent. Pine resin provides extra water resistance to the surfaces enclosed by the ribs.

OVER/UNDER GUN

The Over-Under gun is available in 12, 16, 20, 28 and .410, with each bore made on a dedicated action size. As with Side-by-Side, the shape of the action has an effect on the weight of the gun.

Conventionally, the Purdey over-under will shoot the lower barrel first, but can be made to shoot the top barrel first if required. All prices on request.

The standard for regulating and patterning the shooting of a gun is the percentage of the shot charge, which is evenly concentrated in a circle of 30" diameter at a range of 40 yards. (Purdey choke restrictions 1/1000 inch.)

12 Bore 2.75" 1.25 oz No.6	
Full Choke	.038 - .040
Choke	.035
.75 (mod)	.022
.5 Choke	.016-.017
.25 Choke	.010-.01
Imp Cyl	7-8
Cyl	3
Skeet	Open Bore

20 Bore 2.75"	
Full Choke	.038 - .040
Choke	.030
.75 (mod)	.018-.019
.5 Choke	.012-.013
.25 Choke	7-8
Imp Cyl	6
Cyl	3
Skeet	Open Bore

The Choke Section

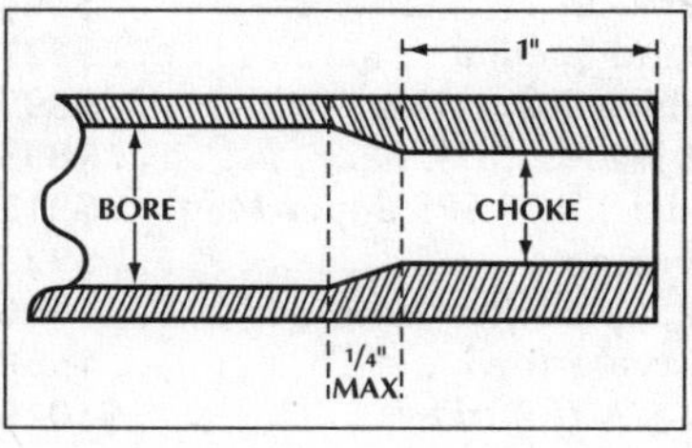

The Percentages Of Choke	
Cylinder	45%
Improved Cylinder	50%
1/4 Choke	55%
1/2 Choke	60%
3/4 or Modified Choke	65%
Choke	70%
Full Choke	75%
Skeet (2)	45%
Skeet (1)	40%

12 Bore 2.5" 1 oz. No. 6	
Full Choke	.038 - .040
Choke	.030
.75 (mod)	.018-.019
.5 Choke	.012-.013
.25 Choke	6-7
Imp Cyl	3
Cyl	2

28 Bore 2.75"	
Full Choke	.026
Choke	.020
.75 (mod)	.018
.5 Choke	.015
.25 Choke	.011
Imp Cyl	7
Cyl	3
Skeet	Open

Remington Shotguns

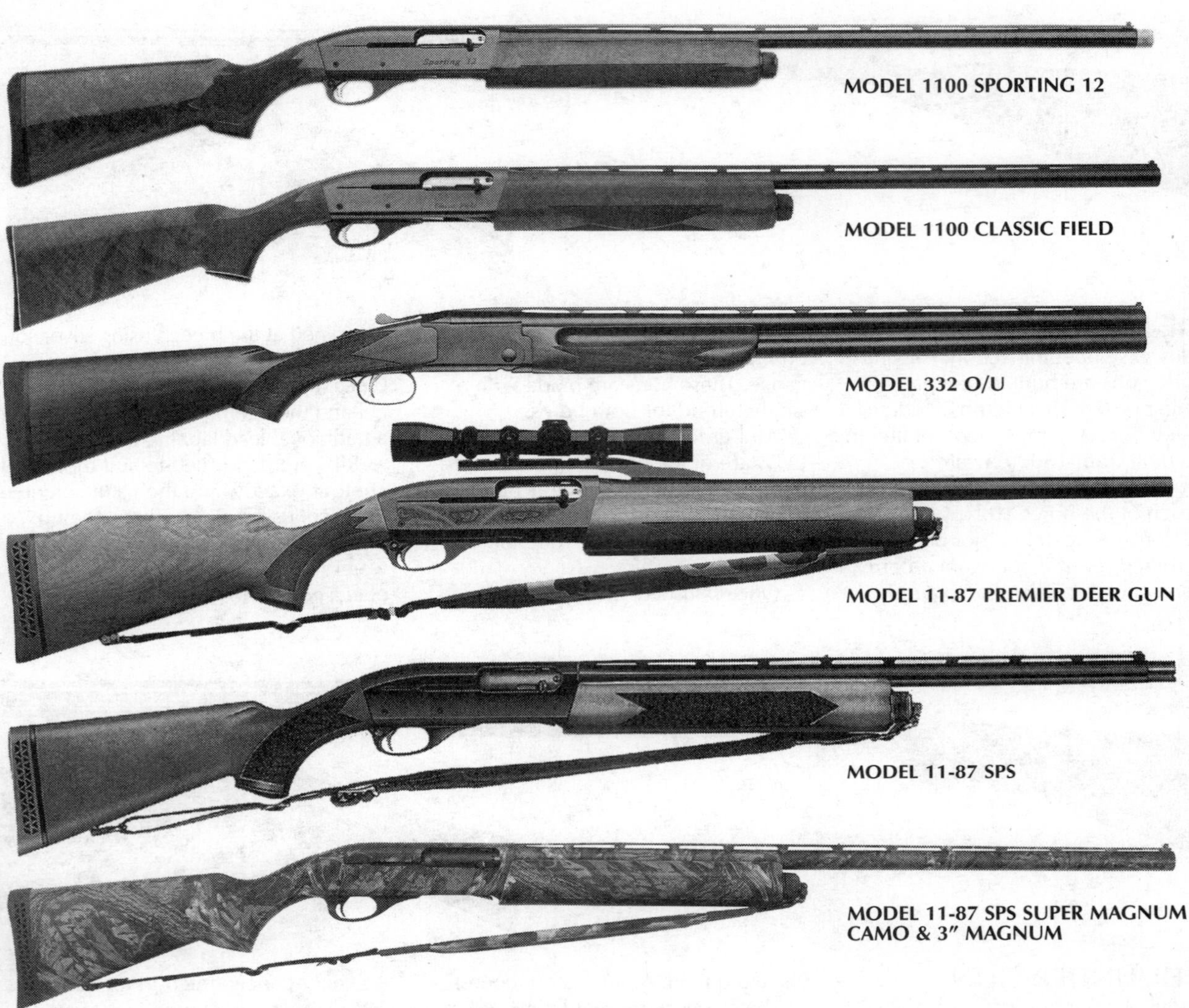
MODEL 1100 SPORTING 12

MODEL 1100 CLASSIC FIELD

MODEL 332 O/U

MODEL 11-87 PREMIER DEER GUN

MODEL 11-87 SPS

MODEL 11-87 SPS SUPER MAGNUM CAMO & 3″ MAGNUM

SHOTGUNS

MODEL 1100 CLASSIC FIELD

Action: autoloader
Stock: walnut
Barrel: 26 or 28 in.
Chokes: screw-in tubes
Weight: 6.75 – 7.25 lbs.
Bore/Gauge: 16 and 20 (26 in. only)
Magazine: 4
Features: gas-operated autoloading, vent rib
Classic Field $799
Also available:
M1100 Tournament Skeet (12 or 20 ga.) $901
M100 Classic Trap (12 ga.) $935
M100 Spporting (12, 20, 28 ga. & .410) . . . . $901 – 935

MODEL 332

Action: over/under
Stock: walnut, Hi-Gloss
Barrel: 26, 28 or 30 in.
Chokes: screw-in tubes
Weight: 7.5 to 8 lbs.
Bore/Gauge: 12
Magazine: none
Features: boxlock; ventilated rib; Model 332 patterned after classic Model 32
Model 332 . . . . $1691

MODEL 11-87 AUTOLOADERS

Action: autoloader
Stock: walnut or synthetic
Barrel: 21, 23, 26, 28 or 30 in.
Chokes: screw-in tubes
Weight: 6.25 – 8.25 lbs.
Bore/Gauge: 12 & 20
Magazine: 5
Features: gas-operated, handles 2¾ and 3-inch shells interchangeably; deer gun has cantilever scope mount, rifled bore; Upland Special has straight grip; Super Magnum chambers 3.5-inch shells
11-87 Premier. $827
Deer Gun $908
Upland Special $827
Premier Super Mag. $899
Left-Hand $893
Model 11-87 SPS Super Mag. . . $912
SPS camo $925
SPS Super Mag camo 996
SPS Waterfowl. $960
SPS NWTF Turkey $1016

Remington Shotguns

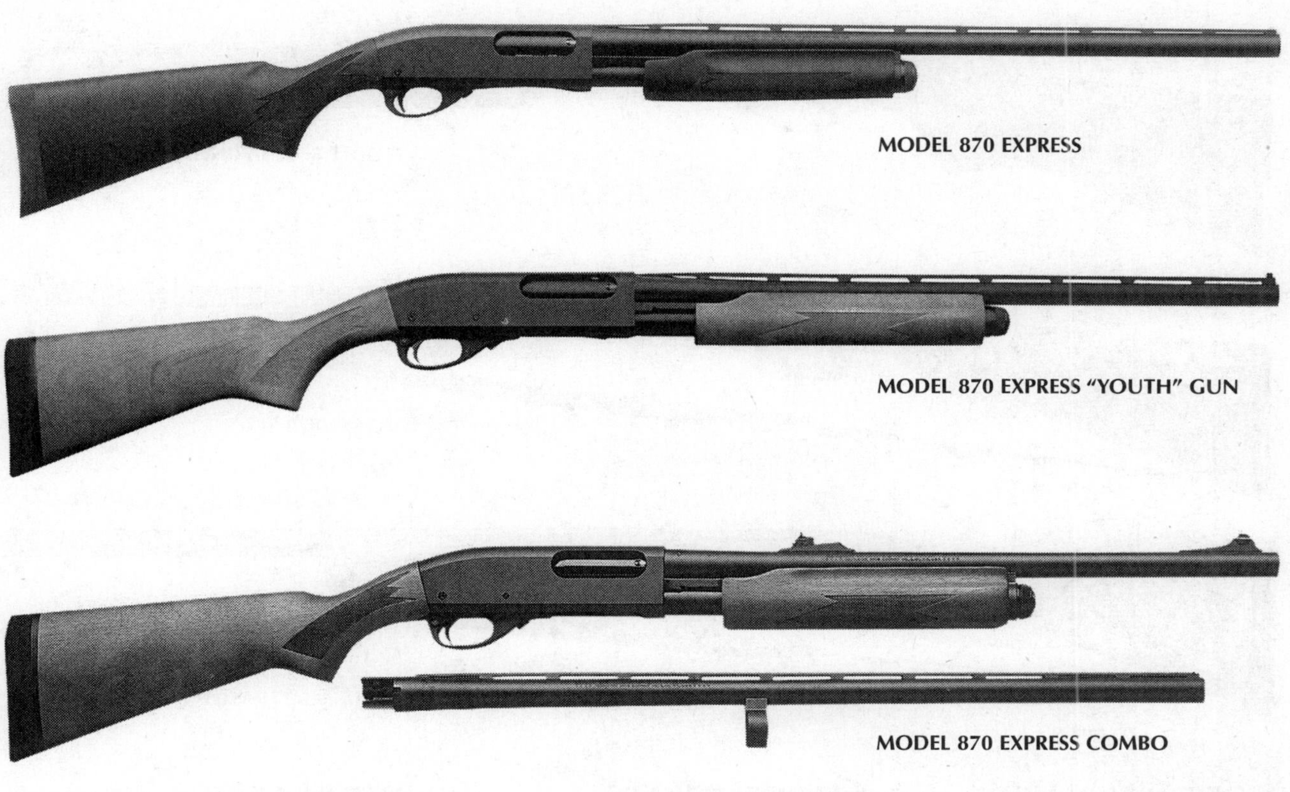

MODEL 870 EXPRESS

MODEL 870 EXPRESS "YOUTH" GUN

MODEL 870 EXPRESS COMBO

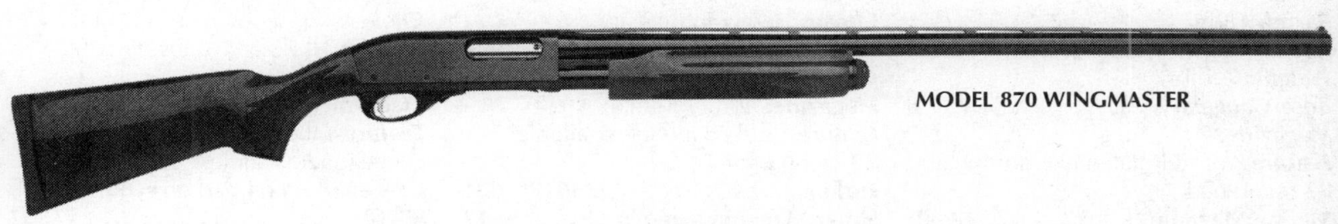

MODEL 870 WINGMASTER

MODEL 870 EXPRESS

Action: pump
Stock: Synthetic, hardwood or camo
Barrel: 18 to 28 in.
Chokes: screw-in tubes
Weight: 6 to 7.5 lbs.
Bore/Gauge: 12, 16, 20, 28, .410
Magazine: 5
Features: Super Magnum chambered for 3.5-inch shells; deer gun has rifled barrel, open sights

Express $332
Express LH $389
Express Super Magnum $376
Super Mag, camo $500
Express Youth 16 & 20 ga. $332
Youth Turkey $389
JR NWTF $419
Combo with Rem choke barrel and slug barrel . . $455 - 489
Express Super Mag. Turkey (31/2" Black synthetic) $389
Express Super Mag. Turkey, camo $500
Express Super Mag. Combo with deer barrel $523
Express Deer w/cantilever $439
Express Deer w/RS $332
Express Deer FR $372
Express Turkey $345
Turkey camo $399

MODEL 870 WINGMASTER

Action: pump
Stock: walnut
Barrel: 25 – 30 in.
Chokes: screw-in tubes
Weight: 6.5 – 7.5 lbs.
Bore/Gauge: 12, 16, 20, 28 & .410
Magazine: 3 – 4
Features: machine-cut checkering, blued receiver

Super Mag. $692
3-in. $625
Classic Trap $819
Wingmaster Jr. $625
Dale Earnhardt Special $820

Remington Shotguns

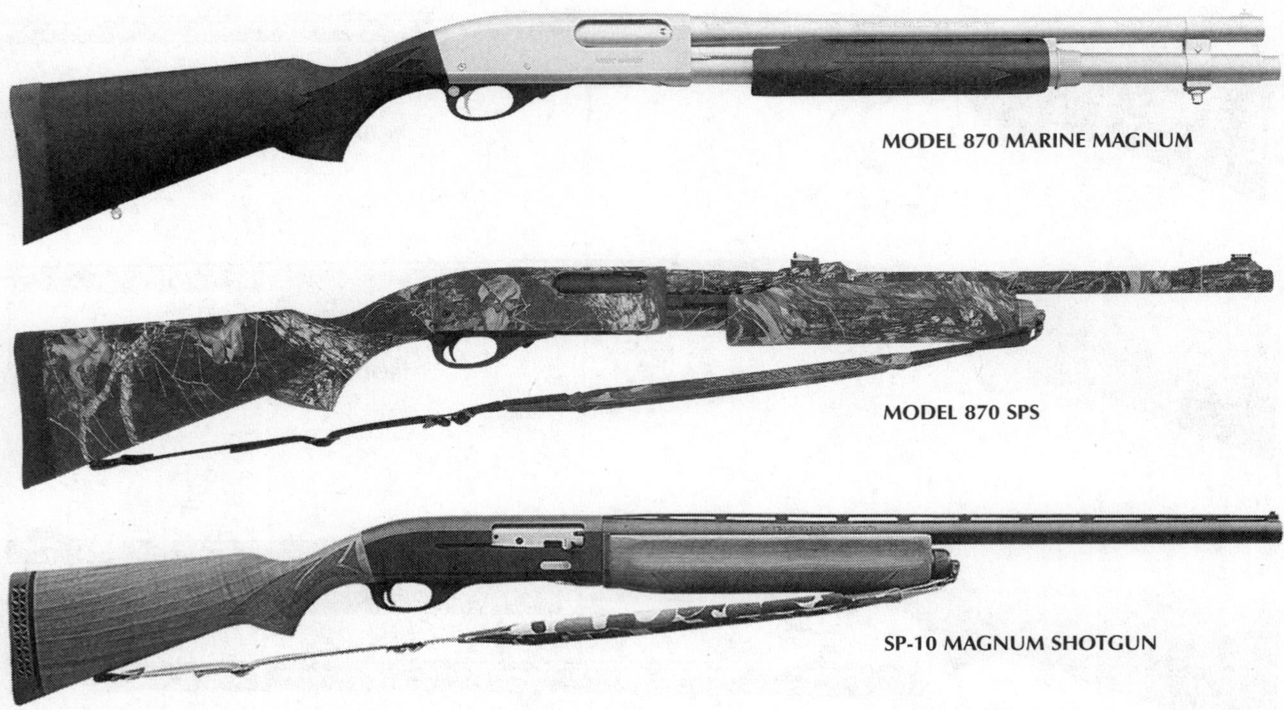

MODEL 870 MARINE MAGNUM

MODEL 870 SPS

SP-10 MAGNUM SHOTGUN

SHOTGUNS

MODEL 870 MARINE MAGNUM

Action: pump
Stock: synthetic
Barrel: 18 in.
Chokes: none, cylinder bore
Weight: 7.5 lbs.
Bore/Gauge: 12
Magazine: 7
Features: nickel-plated exterior metal; R3 recoil pad
Marine Magnum $600

MODEL 870 SPS

Action: pump
Stock: camo
Barrel: 20 to 28 in.
Chokes: screw-in tubes
Weight: 6.25 to 7.5 lbs.
Bore/Gauge: 12 & 20
Magazine: 4 (3: 3.5-inch)
Features: turkey models available; R3 recoil pad
Turkey . . . . $617 - 621
Super Magnum camo $617
with thumbhole stock
(12 ga., 3.5") $650

MODEL SP-10

Action: autoloader
Stock: walnut, synthetic or camo
Barrel: 26 or 30 in.
Chokes: screw-in tubes
Weight: 10.75 - 11.0 lbs.
Bore/Gauge: 10
Magazine: 2
Features: the only gas-operated 10 gauge made; stainless piston and sleeve; R3 recoil pad on synthetic
SP-10. . . . . $1387
camo. $1524

Clean gas-operated shotguns often by disassembling the forend unit and scrubbing working parts in mild solvent. Read instructions; some components must be dry, not oiled, to function properly.

Renato Gamba Shotguns

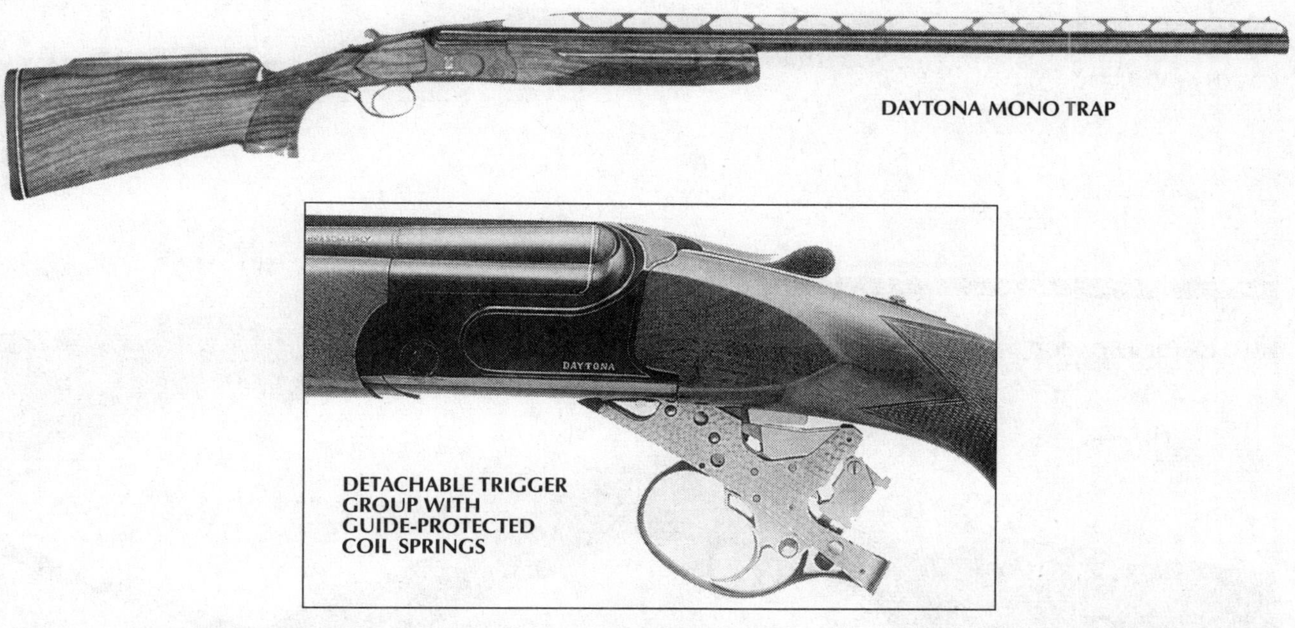

DAYTONA MONO TRAP

DETACHABLE TRIGGER GROUP WITH GUIDE-PROTECTED COIL SPRINGS

	TRAP	DOUBLE TRAP	SKEET	SPORTING CLAYS	HUNTING	MONO TRAP
GAUGE	12 - 20					
BARRELS		heat treated special chrome-nickel-molybdenum steel				
CHANBER		mm 70 (2"3/4) • mm 79 (3") on request				
BARRELS LENGTH	cm. 76 - cm.81 30" - 32"	cm. 76 30"	cm. 68-71 26"3/4 - 28"	cm. 71-74cm 76 - cm.81 28"- 29"- 30"- 32"	cm. 68- cm. 71 26"3/4 - 28"	cm. 81- cm. 86 32" - 34"
CHOKES	imp. mod/ full-mac/full	imp. cil./full	SK/SK	mod./full	imp. cit./imp.mod. mod./full	full
INTERCH. CHOKES	5 screw-in choke tubes set available on request					

SHOTGUNS

THE DAYTONA SHOTGUN

The Daytona shotgun is available in several styles oriented specifically to American Trap, International Trap, American Skeet, International Skeet, and Sporting Clays. The Daytona SL, (the side plate model), and the Daytona SLHH, (the side lock model), are the top of the Daytona line.

All employ the Boss locking system in a breech milled from one massive block of steel.

The trigger group: The trigger group is detachable and is removable without the use of tools. The frame that contains the hammers, sears and springs is milled from a single block of special steel and jeweled for oil retention. On special order, an adjustable trigger may be produced with one inch of movement that can accomodate shooters with exceptionally large or small hands. Internally, the hammer springs are constructed from coils that are contained in steel sleeves placed directly behind the hammers. With the fail safe capsule surrounding the springs, the shotgun will fire even if breakage occurs.

Hunter o/u . . . . from $1390
Le Maus o/u . . . . from 1580
Concorde o/u . . . . from 6100
Daytona 2K o/u . . . . from 7600

Old guns can still be used for hunting, but it's best to feed them light loads. Check any Damascus (wrapped-steel) barrel before using smokeless powder in it.

Rossi Shotguns

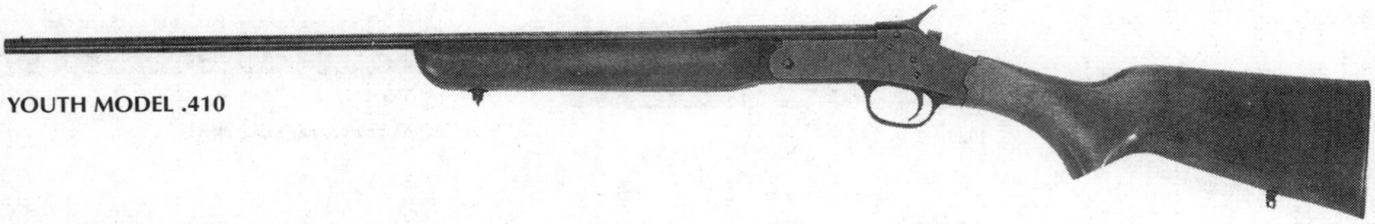

YOUTH MODEL .410

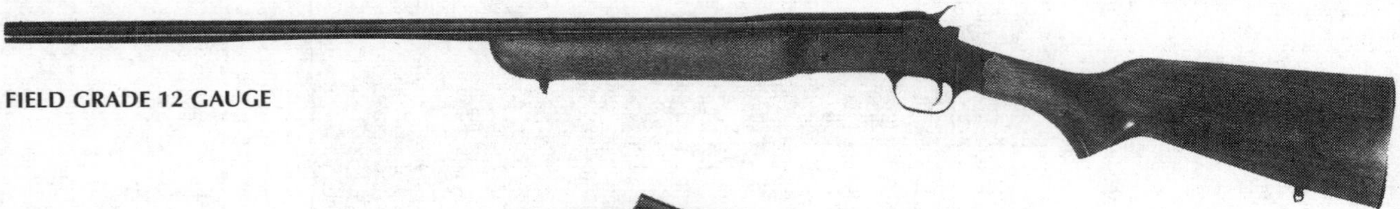

FIELD GRADE 12 GAUGE

MATCHED PAIR

SHOTGUNS

SINGLE BARREL SHOTGUNS

Action: hinged single-shot
Stock: hardwood
Barrel: 28 in.
Chokes: modified, full
Weight: 5.3 lbs.
Bore/Gauge: 12, 20, .410
Magazine: none
Features: exposed-hammer, transfer-bar action; Youth model available; rifle barrels have open sights

Single-Shot $115
Youth, 22" barrel. $115
Also available:
Rifled barrel slug gun (23 in. bbl., 12 or 20 ga.) . . . $190
Matched Pair (.50 cal/12 ga. rifled slug). $275

Lovely, lightweight double guns with thin barrel walls are best reserved for light lead-shot loads. Steel shot can damage delicate tubes and scour out fixed chokes.

Ruger Shotguns

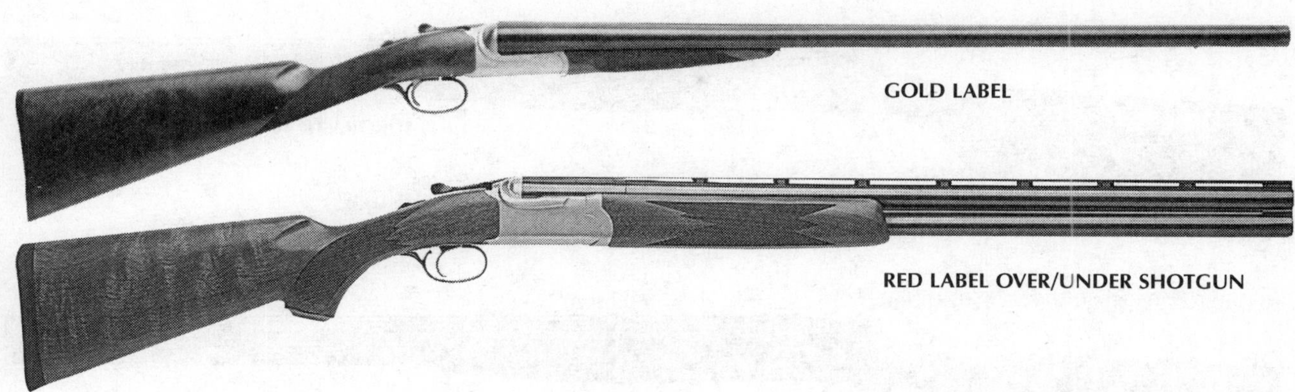

GOLD LABEL

RED LABEL OVER/UNDER SHOTGUN

GOLD LABEL

Action: over/under
Stock: walnut, straight or pistol grip
Barrel: 28 in.
Chokes: screw-in tubes
Weight: 6.5 lbs.
Bore/Gauge: 12
Magazine: none
Features: boxlock; round stainless frame
Gold Label $2000

RED LABEL SHOTGUNS

Action: over/under
Stock: walnut or synthetic, straight or pistol grip
Barrel: 26, 28, 30 in.
Chokes: screw-in tubes
Weight: 6 – 8 lbs.
Bore/Gauge: 12, 20, 28
Magazine: none
Features: boxlock; All-Weather version has stainless steel, synthetic stock; 28 ga. only available in 26" or 28" barrel
standard or All-Weather $1622
engraved $1811

Savage Shotguns

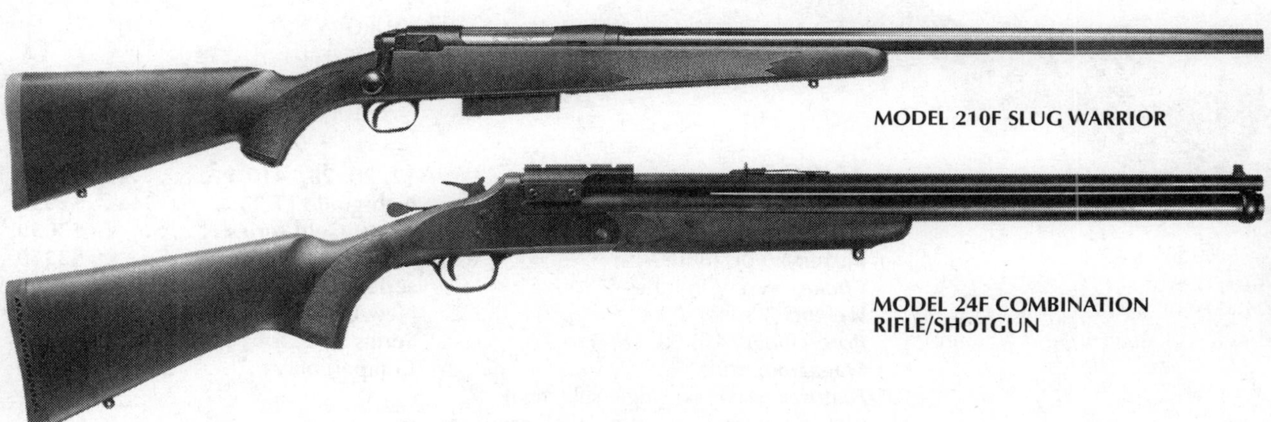

MODEL 210F SLUG WARRIOR

MODEL 24F COMBINATION RIFLE/SHOTGUN

MODEL 210F SLUG WARRIOR

Action: bolt
Stock: synthetic
Barrel: rifled, 24 in.
Chokes: none
Weight: 7.5 lbs.
Bore/Gauge: 12
Magazine: 2
Features: top tang safety, no sights, new camo version available
210F $475
Camo $513

MODEL 24F

Action: hinged single-shot
Stock: synthetic
Barrel: rifle over shotgun, 24 in.
Chokes: none
Weight: 8.0 lbs.
Bore/Gauge: 12, 20
Magazine: none
Features: open sights, hammer-mounted barrel selector; available in 20 ga./.22LR, 20/.22 Hornet, 20/.223, 12 ga./.22 Hornet, 12/.223, 12/.30-30
20 gauge $628
12 gauge $661

SIG Arms Shotguns

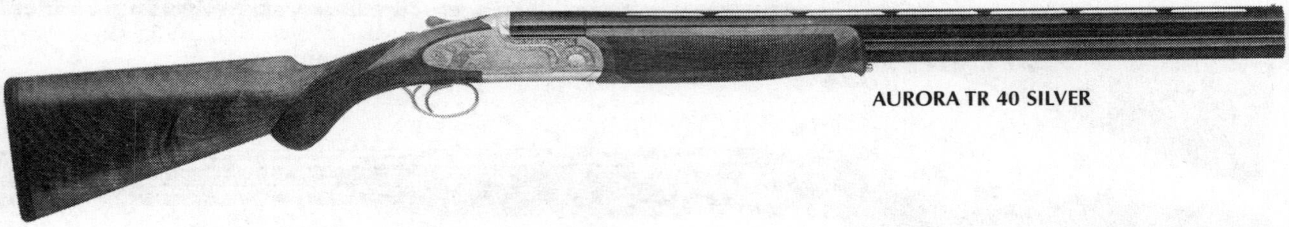

AURORA TR 40 SILVER

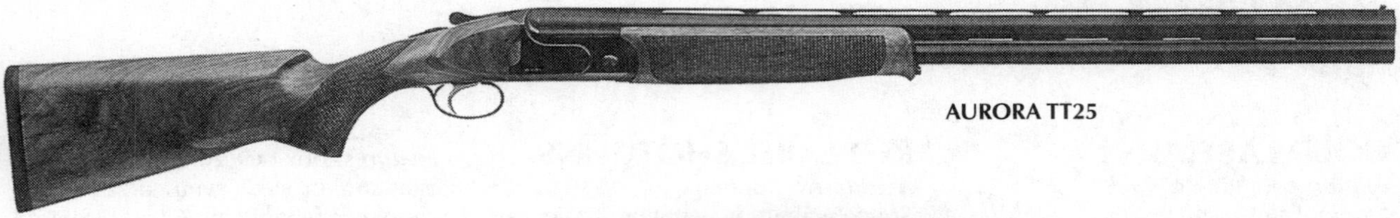

AURORA TT25

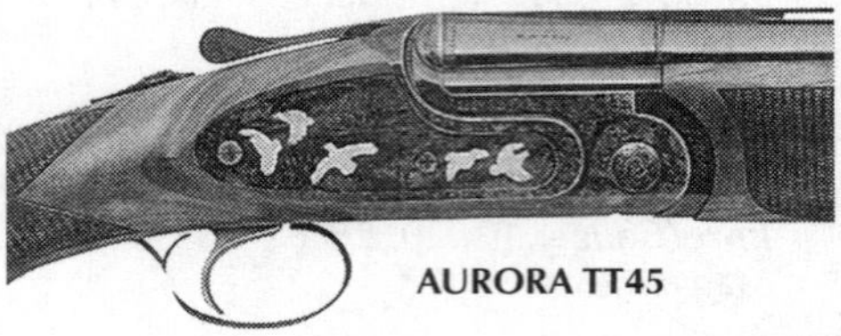

AURORA TT45

AURORA

SHOTGUNS

AURORA

Action: over/under
Stock: walnut
Barrel: 26 or 28 in.
Chokes: screw-in tubes
Weight: 7.3 lbs.
Bore/Gauge: 12, 20, 28, 410
Magazine: none
Features: boxlock, single selective trigger, automatic ejectors, replaceable hingepin; 20 gauge weighs 6.3 lbs., 28 ga. and .410 6.0 lbs.

12, 20, 28, .410 . . . . $2250
high-grade TT 25: $2950
TR 40 Gold series $3050
best-grade TT 45: $3350
series 20 . . . . $2250
New Englander $2161
Series 30 . . . . $2650
Compeition . . . . $2950 to 3350

Cock an exposed-hammer gun with the inside of your thumb's knuckle, your hand perpendicular to the hammer's travel. There's more leverage than with the thumb pad, less chance for slippage.

Silma Shotguns

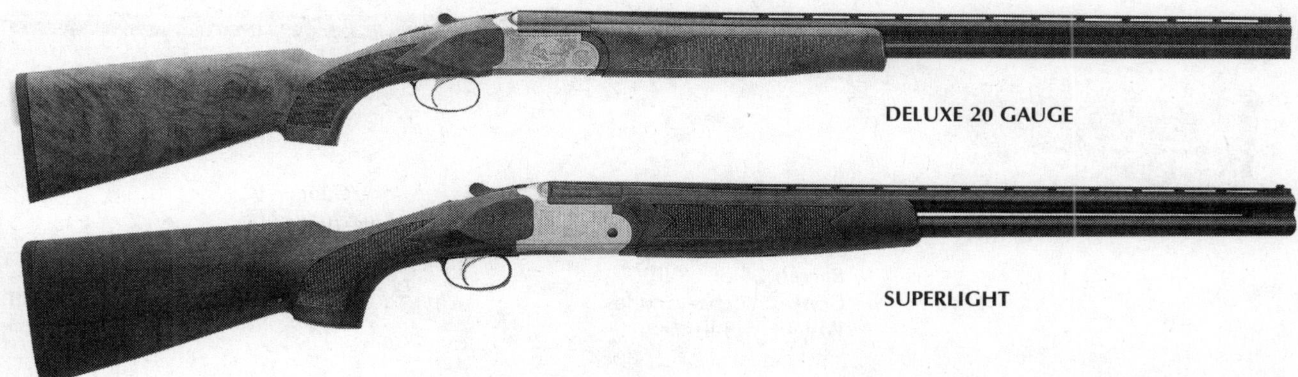

MODEL 70 EJ DELUXE

Action: box lock
Stock: walnut
Barrel: 28 in.
Bore/Gauge: 12 and 20 gauges (Standard); 12, 20, 28 gauges and .410 bore (Deluxe); 12 & 20 gauge (Superlight);12 gauge (Superlight deluxe); 12 and 20 (Clays)
Magazine: none
Features: all 12 gauge models, except Superlight, come with 3.5 inch chambers, high grade steel barrels and are proofed for steel shot. All models come with single selective trigger, automatic safety, automatic ejectors, ventilated rib, and recoil pad, gold plated.
Standard, 12 ga. $1016
Standard, 20 ga. $944
Deluxe, 12 ga.. . . . . $1089
Deluxe, 20 ga.. . . . . $1016
28 gauge & .410:. $1140
Superlight:. $1191
Clays: $1387

SKB Shotguns

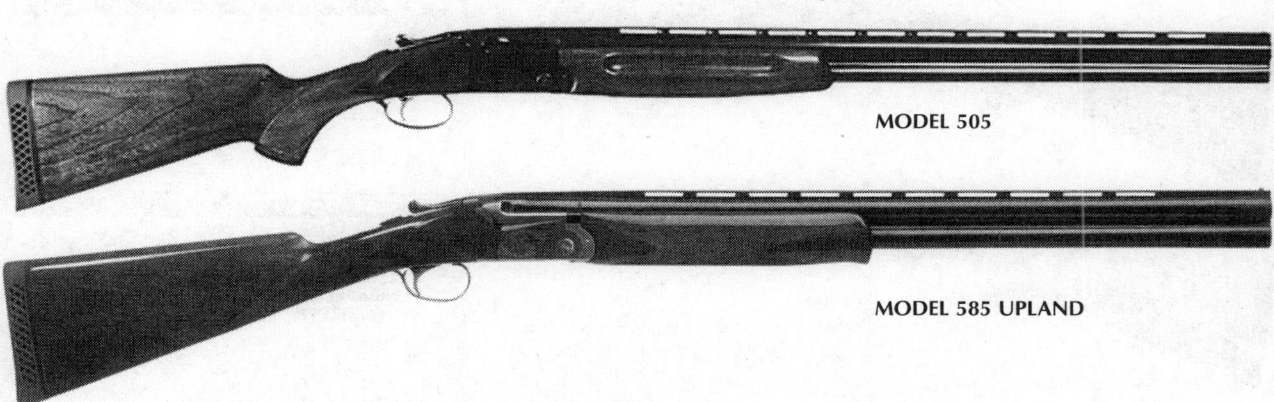

MODEL 505

Action: over/under
Stock: walnut
Barrel: 26 or 28 in.
Chokes: screw-in tubes
Weight: 8.4 lbs.
Bore/Gauge: 12, 20
Magazine: none
Features: boxlock; ventilated rib, automatic ejectors
Model 505 Field $1269

MODEL 585 FIELD

Action: over/under
Stock: walnut, straight or pistol grip
Barrel: 26 or 28 in.
Chokes: screw-in tubes
Weight: 9.0 lbs.
Bore/Gauge: 12, 20, 28, .410
Magazine: none
Features: boxlock; Field, Upland and Youth; silver and gold series available.
Field, Upland, Youth (12 and 20 ga.) $1549
28 ga. or .410 . . . . $1619
Field Set (12 and 20). $2479
Field Set (20 and 28). $2549
Field Set (28 and .410) $2549

Stevens Shotguns

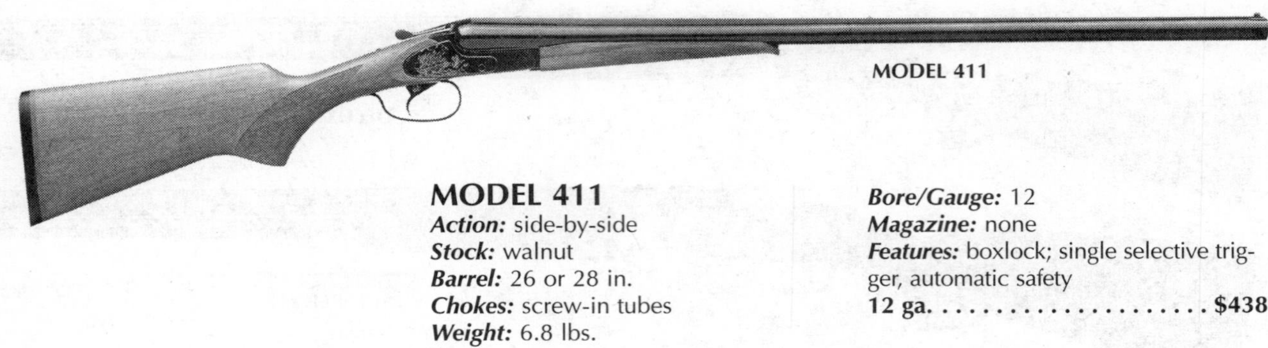
MODEL 411

MODEL 411
Action: side-by-side
Stock: walnut
Barrel: 26 or 28 in.
Chokes: screw-in tubes
Weight: 6.8 lbs.
Bore/Gauge: 12
Magazine: none
Features: boxlock; single selective trigger, automatic safety
12 ga. $438

Stoeger Shotguns

MODEL 2000

MODEL 2000 ADVANTAGE

MODEL 2000
SYNTHETIC ADVANTAGE MAX-4

SHOTGUNS

MODEL 2000
Action: autoloader
Stock: walnut or synthetic
Barrel: 24, 26, 28 or 30 in.
Chokes: screw-in tubes
Weight: 7.0 lbs.
Bore/Gauge: 12
Magazine: 4
Features: inertia-recoil system, ventilated rib.
walnut. $435
synthetic $420
camo. $495
slug (24" smooth bore) $430
synthetic/slug barrel combo . . . $495
camo shot/slug barrel combo . . $580

MODEL 2000 SYNTHETIC ADVANTAGE MAX-4
Action: autoloader
Stock: synthetic
Barrel: 26 or 28 in.
Chokes: screw-in tubes
Weight: 6.8 lbs.
Bore/Gauge: 12
Magazine: 4
Features: inertia-recoil system; ventilated rib; Advantage MAX-4 camo stock; fires 33/4- and 3-in. ammunition
Price $495

Stoeger Shotguns

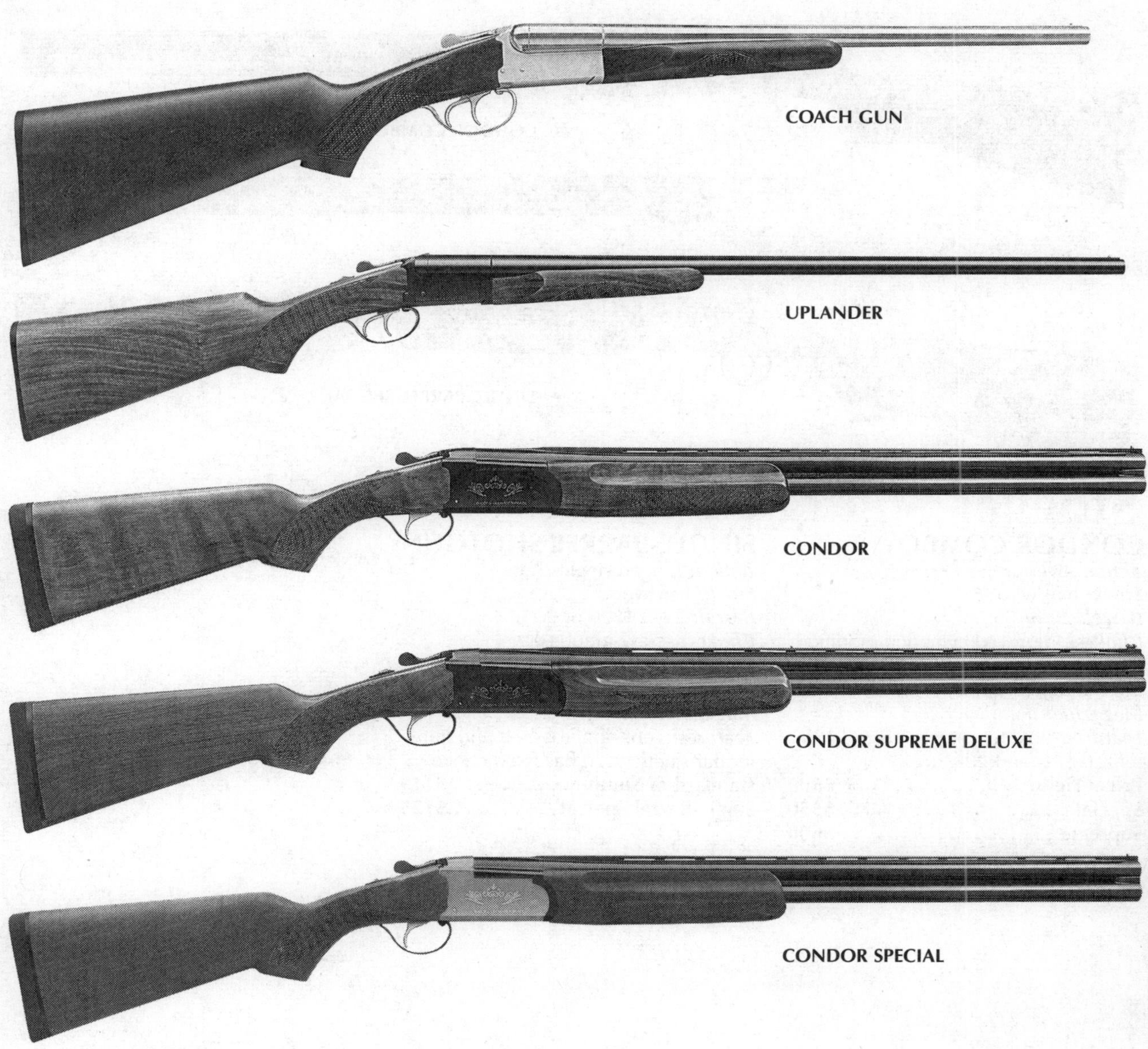

SHOTGUNS

COACH GUN AND UPLANDER

Action: side-by-side
Stock: Brazilian hardwood
Barrel: 20 in. (Uplander 26 or 28 in.)
Chokes: improved cylinder, modified
Weight: 6.4 lbs.
Bore/Gauge: 12, 16, 20, .410 and 28 ga. Uplander
Magazine: none
Features: boxlock; double triggers, automatic safety, nickel and matte nickel breech finish available; Uplander available with choke tubes, Youth stock; Uplander Supreme with ejectors, single trigger, American walnut stock

Coach Gun $320
nickel finish. $375
Coach Gun Supreme blue $380
stainless $390
nickel $410
Uplander. $335
Uplander Youth. $335
Uplander with choke tubes. . . . $350
Uplander Supreme $445

CONDOR

Action: over/under
Stock: Brazilian hardwood
Barrel: 26 or 28 in.
Chokes: improved cylinder, modified
Weight: 7.7 lbs.
Bore/Gauge: 12, 20
Magazine: none
Features: boxlock; single trigger

Condor $390
Special with stainless receiver . . $440
Supreme with American walnut stock, automatic ejectors . . . $500

Stoeger Shotguns

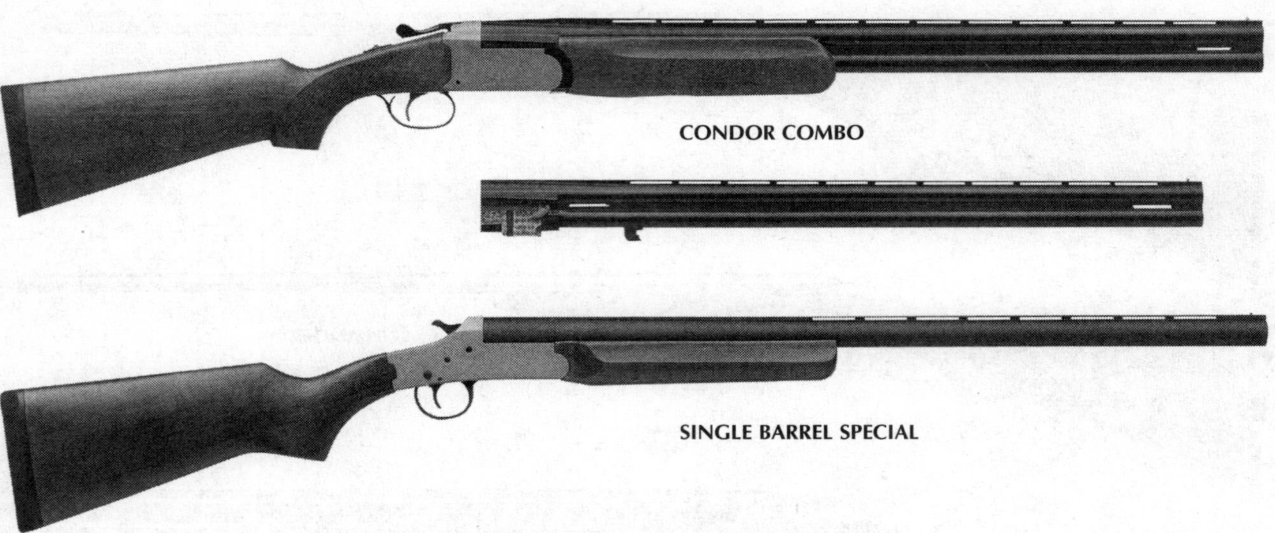

CONDOR COMBO

SINGLE BARREL SPECIAL

CONDOR COMBO

Action: over/under
Stock: hardwood
Barrel: 28 or 26 in.
Chokes: improved cylender, modified
Weight: 7.4 to 6.8 lbs.
Bore/Gauge: 12, 20
Magazine: none
Features: boxlock; single trigger, 2 barrel sets (12- and 20-gauge)
Price: Field $500
Special $550
Supreme $600

SINGLE-BARREL SHOTGUN

Action: hinged single-shot
Stock: hardwood
Barrel: 22, 24, 26 or 28 in.
Chokes: screw-in tubes
Weight: 5.4 lbs.
Bore/Gauge: 12, 20, .410
Magazine: none
Features: vent rib, crossbolt and transfer bar safety; .410 has fixed choke.
standard or Youth $119
Single-Barrel Special $125

When you shoulder a bird gun, remember that your eye serves the same purpose as a rifle's rear sight. Cheek the comb the same each time, so your eye is in the same place for the shot.

Tristar Sporting Arms Shotguns

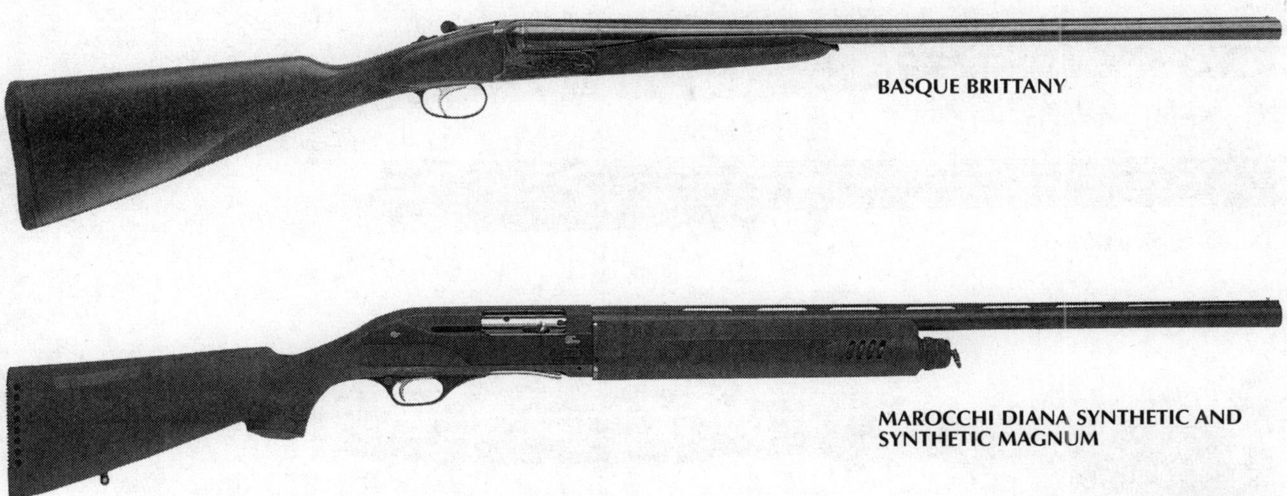

BASQUE BRITTANY

MAROCCHI DIANA SYNTHETIC AND SYNTHETIC MAGNUM

BASQUE SERIES

Action: side-by-side
Stock: walnut, straight or pistol grip
Barrel: 26 or 28 in.
Chokes: screw-in tubes
Weight: 6.8 lbs.
Bore/Gauge: 12, 16, 20, 28, 410
Magazine: none
Features: boxlock, single selective trigger, automatic ejectors, chromed bores, also: 20-inch Coach gun; chokes in 16 gauge: M/F and IC/M in 28 gauge and .410.

Gentry, 12 & 16 . . . . $824
20, 28 & .410 . . . . $839
Brittany, 12 & 20 . . . . $943
Brittany Sporting, 12 & 20 . . . $1049

MAROCCHI DIANA

Action: autoloader
Stock: walnut, synthetic or camo
Barrel: 24, 26, 28 or 30 in.
Chokes: screw-in tubes
Weight: 7.0 lbs.
Bore/Gauge: 12, 20, 28
Magazine: 4
Features: gas-operated, stock shims, slug model has sights, scope mount on rifled barrel

Synthetic, 3-in. $385
Walnut, 3-in.. . . . . $399
synthetic magnum, 3.5-in.. . . . . $479

SHOTGUNS

Recoil—or anticipation of it—can cause flinching and missing. A soft, thick recoil pad can pay big dividends, especially if you insist on shooting very lightweight guns with heavy loads.

Verona Shotguns

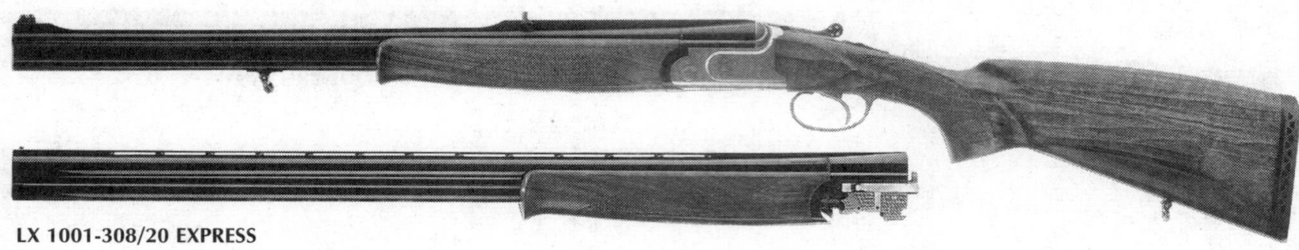

LX 1001-308/20 EXPRESS

LX 1001-20 GA OVER/UNDER BARREL SET

SX 801

SX 405

LX 680 COMPETITION

MODEL LX EXPRESS

Action: over/under
Stock: Turkish walnut
Barrel: 28 in.
Chokes: screw-in tubes
Weight: 8.0 lbs.
Bore/Gauge: .223, .243, .270, .308 or .30-06 over 20 gauge
Magazine: none
Features: single selective tirgger, automatic ejectors
Express Combo with Express and 20 gauge over/under set: . . . $2764

MODEL SX 801

Action: autoloader
Stock: walnut
Barrel: 28 or 30 in.
Chokes: screw-in tubes
Weight: 6.8 lbs.Bore/Gauge 12
Magazine: 3
Features: gas-operated, alloy receiver, sporting and competition models available; also model SX405: synthetic or camo, 22 in. slug or 26 in. field
Verona SX 801 . . . . $929 - 1139
Verona SX 405 . . . . $353
with Docter sight $611

MODEL LX 680 COMPETITION SERIES

Action: over/under
Stock: Turkish walnut
Barrel: 30 in. 932 on Trap Model)
Chokes: screw-in tubes
Weight: 7.5 lbs.
Bore/Gauge: 12
Magazine: none
Features: boxlock; removable competition trigger, ported barrels, deluxe case; also multiple-barrel sets
Verona LX 680 Sporting $1116
LX 680 Gold Trap or Skeet . . . $1616

Weatherby Shotguns

ATHENA GRADE III CLASSIC FIELD

SAS FIELD

SAS MOSSY OAK CAMO

SAS SLUG GUN

SHOTGUNS

ATHENA
Action: over/under
Stock: walnut
Barrel: 26 or 28 in.
Chokes: screw-in tubes
Weight: 8.0 lbs.
Bore/Gauge: 12, 20, 28
Magazine: none
Features: boxlock; single selective mechanical trigger, automatic ejectors
Grade III $2173
Grade V. $3037

ORION
Action: over/under
Stock: walnut, straight or pistol grip
Barrel: 26, 28, 30 or 32 in.
Chokes: screw-in tubes
Weight: 8.0 lbs.
Bore/Gauge: 12, 20 or 28
Magazine: none
Features: boxlock; single selective trigger, automatic ejectors
Upland $1299
Grade II $1622
Sporting Clays. $2059
Grade III $1955

SAS
Action: autoloader
Stock: walnut, synthetic or camo
Barrel: 24, 26, 28 or 30 in., vent rib
Chokes: screw-in tubes
Weight: 7.8 lbs.
Bore/Gauge: 12
Magazine: 4
Features: gas-operated, 3-inch chamber, magazine cutoff
walnut. $899
synthetic $849
camo. $949
Sporting Clays. $999

SAS SLUG GUN
Action: autoloader
Stock: walnut
Barrel: 22 in. rifled
Chokes: none
Weight: 7.3 lbs.
Bore/Gauge: 12
Magazine: 4
Features: self-compensating gas system; cantilever scope base included; "smart" follower, magazine cutoff, stock has shims to alter drop, pitch, cast-off
SAS Slug Gun $949

Winchester Shotguns

MODEL 1300 UNIVERSAL HUNTER

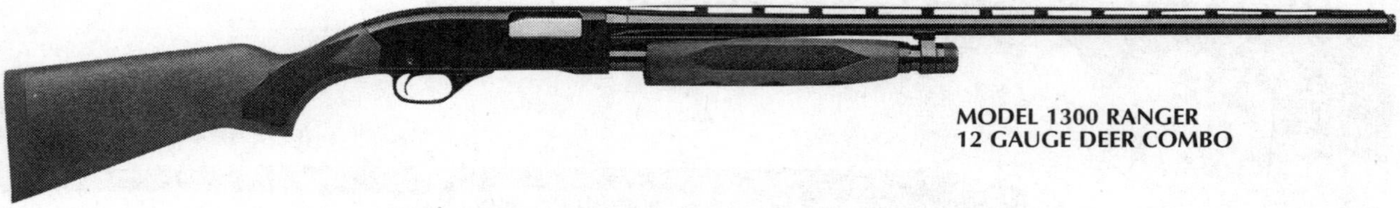

MODEL 1300 RANGER
12 GAUGE DEER COMBO

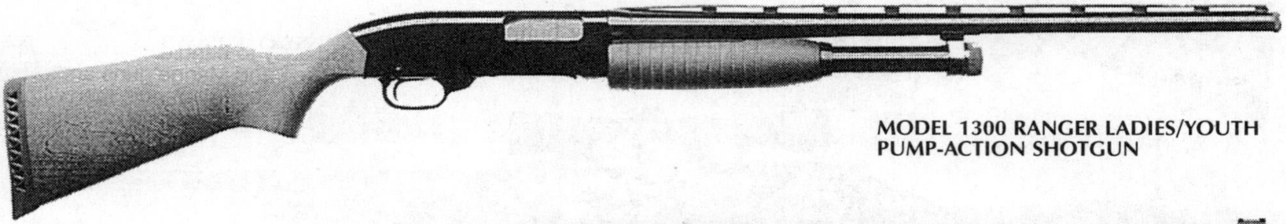

MODEL 1300 RANGER LADIES/YOUTH
PUMP-ACTION SHOTGUN

MODEL 9410 PACKER SHOTGUN

SHOTGUNS

MODEL 1300

Action: pump
Stock: walnut or synthetic
Barrel: 18, 22, 24, 26 or 28 in.
Chokes: screw-in tubes
Weight: 7.5 lbs.
Bore/Gauge: 12, 20
Magazine: 4
Features: Deer versions feature either smooth or rifled 22-inch barrels, rifle sights

synthetic $438
walnut $438
Ranger, hardwood $366
Turkey, camo $507
Deer, synthetic $376
Deer, synthetic with cantilever mount $420
Deer, combo $453
Universal Hunter $472

MODEL 9410

Action: lever
Stock: walnut
Barrel: 20 or 24 in.
Chokes: full
Weight: 7.0 lbs.
Bore/Gauge: 410
Magazine: 9
Features: 2.5-inch chamber; Truglo front sight, shallow V rear

9410 . . . . $626
Packer with 20-inch barrel $647
Packer w/TruGlo sights (no choke) $583
M9410 Ranger, hardwood $532

Some crack shotgun competitors lay their left center finger under the forend, pointing it at the target instead of wrapping it around the gun. The pointing and loose grip both help you hit.

Winchester Shotguns

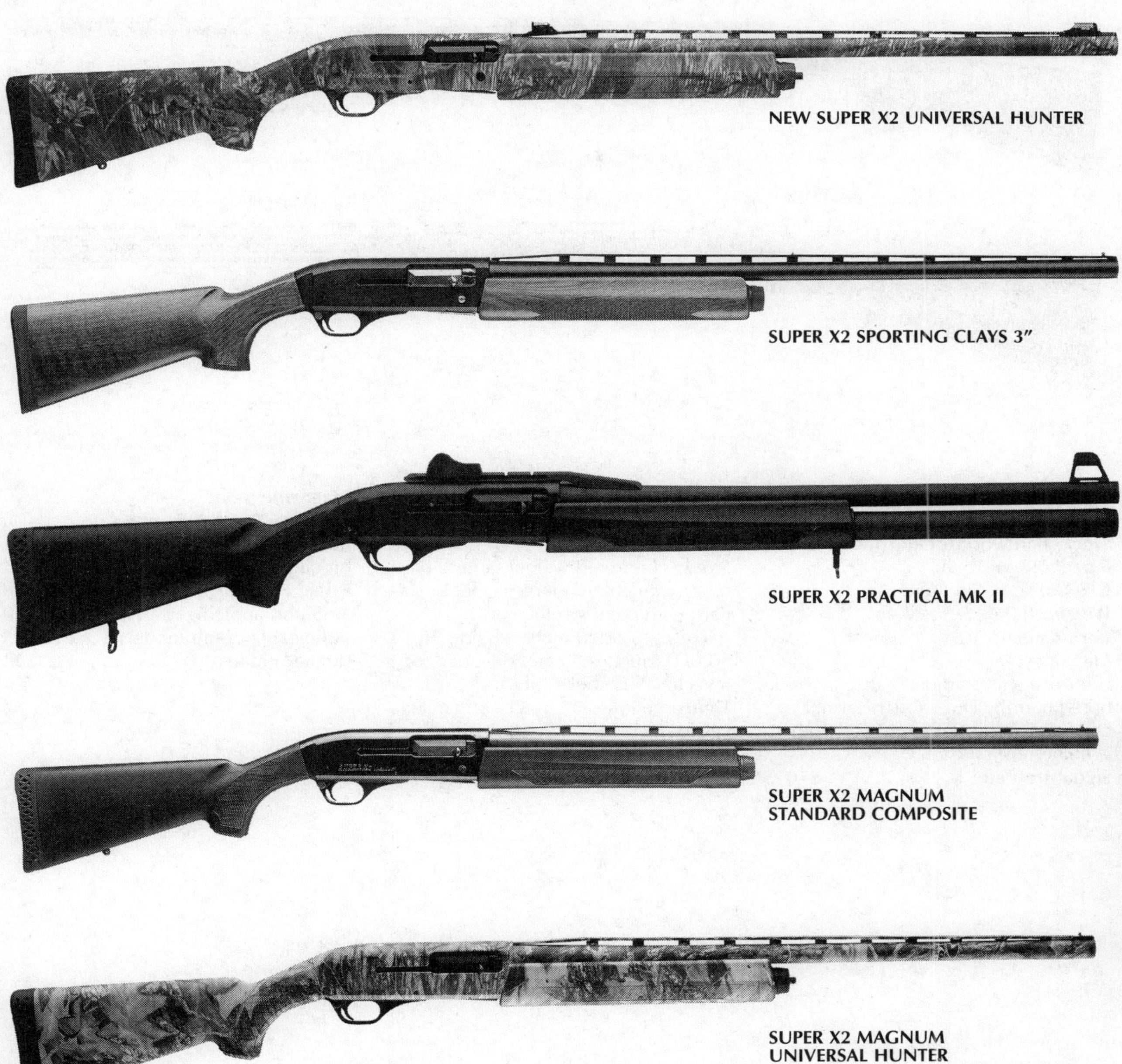

NEW SUPER X2 UNIVERSAL HUNTER

SUPER X2 SPORTING CLAYS 3"

SUPER X2 PRACTICAL MK II

SUPER X2 MAGNUM STANDARD COMPOSITE

SUPER X2 MAGNUM UNIVERSAL HUNTER

SHOTGUNS

SUPER X2

Action: autoloader
Stock: walnut or synthetic
Barrel: 22, 24, 26, 28 or 30 in.
Chokes: screw-in tubes
Weight: 8.0 lbs.
Bore/Gauge: 12
Magazine: 4
Features: gas-operated mechanism, back-bored barrels; all with "Dura-Touch" finish, some with Tru-Glo sights

Super X2 Light Field $945
Sporting Clays $998
Deer, rifled barrel, cantilever . . $957
Practical MK II, extended magazine. $1287
composite $908
Turkey. $1165
Universal Hunter Turkey $1179
Practical MKI w/TruGlo sights . . $1116

Winchester Shotguns

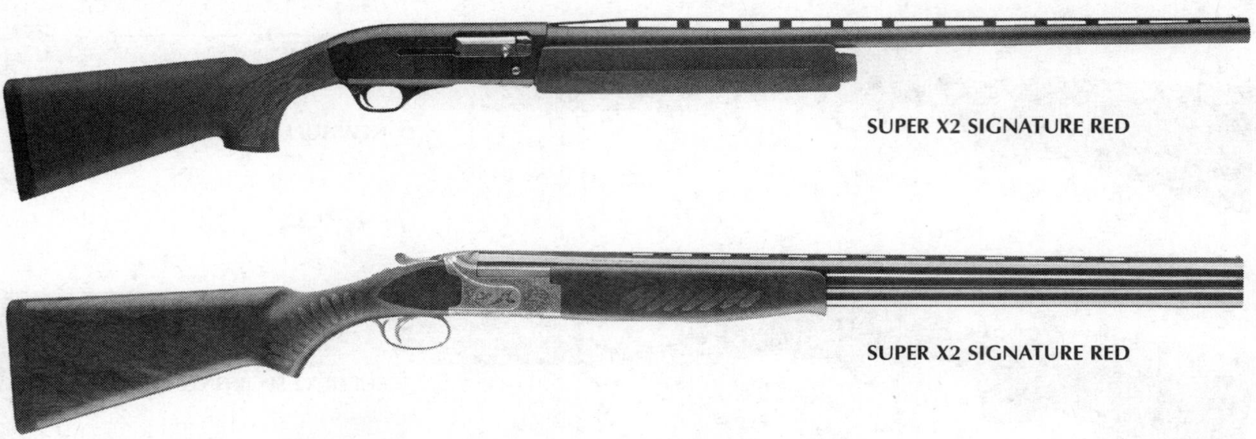

SUPER X2 SIGNATURE RED

SUPER X2 SIGNATURE RED

SUPER X2 SIGNATURE RED

Action: autoloader
Stock: hardwood, "Dura-Touch" finish
Barrel: 28 or 30 in.
Chokes: screw-in tubes
Weight: 8.0 lbs.
Bore/Gauge: 12
Magazine: 4
Features: shims adjust buttstock; backbored barrel; "Dura-Touch" armor coating now available on many other Winchesters
Signature Red $1015

WINCHESTER SELECT

Action: boxlock over-under with low-profile breech
Stock: checkered walnut (adjustable comb available on target models, standard with palm swell)
Barrels: 26 or 28 inches (field), 28, 30 or 32 inches (target) threaded for Invector Plus choke tubes.
Sights: bead front (TruGlo on target versions)
Weight: 7 to 7.3 lbs. (field), 7.5 to 7.8 lbs. (target) Bore/Gauge: 12
Magazine: none
Features: 3-inch chambers on field guns, ventilated middle rib on target guns
Price: Field $1498
Trap and Sporting $1950
(adjustable comb models) $2115
(higher grades) $2320

SHOTGUNS

Pull the shotgun firmly into your shoulder with your right hand; let the left gently and smoothly guide the muzzle.

HANDGUNS

Accu-Tek Handguns

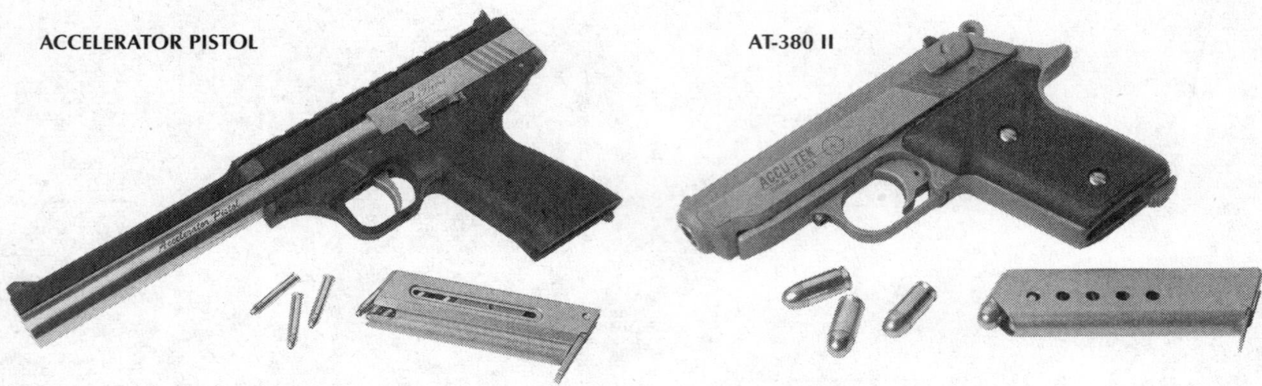
ACCELERATOR PISTOL AT-380 II

ACCELERATOR PISTOL

Action: autoloader
Grips: composite
Barrel: 8.5 in.
Sights: target
Weight: 54 oz.
Caliber: .22 WMR, .17 HMR
Capacity: 9 + 1
Features: Single action design; internal hammer; stainless steel bull barrel; aluminum rib incorporates fully adjustable target sights; integral Weaver scope base; firing pin block and last-round slide hold open features
MSRP: . . . . **$ 385**

AT-380 II

Action: autoloader
Grips: composite
Barrel: 2.8 in.
Sights: target
Weight: 23.5 oz
Caliber: 380.ACP
Capacity: 6 + 1
Features: Construction from high strength 17-4 stainless steel; one-hand manual safety; European type magazine release on bottom of grip; stainless steel magazine
MSRP: **$249**

American Derringer Handguns

MODEL 4

MODEL 4

Action: hinged breech
Grips: stag
Barrel: 4 in.
Sights: fixed open
Weight: 16.5 oz.
Caliber: .32 H&R, .357 Mag., .357 Max., .44 Mag., .45 Colt/.410, .45-70
Capacity: 2
Features: over/under Derringer also available with .45-70 over .45 Colt/.410
.357 Mag. $470
.357 Max. $475
.44 Mag. $540
.45 Colt/.410 . . . . $480

Auto-Ordnance Handguns

MODEL 1911A1

1911WGSE DELUXE

MODEL 1911A1

Action: autoloader
Grips: plastic
Barrel: 5 in.
Sights: fixed open
Weight: 39.0 oz.
Caliber: .45 ACP.
Capacity: 7 + 1
Features: single-action 1911 Colt design; Deluxe version has rubber wrap-around grips, 3-dot sights; Thompson 1911C stainless.

standard **$592**
WWII Parkerized **$581**
Deluxe **$597**
Thompson 1911C 45 cal. **$753**

Beretta Handguns

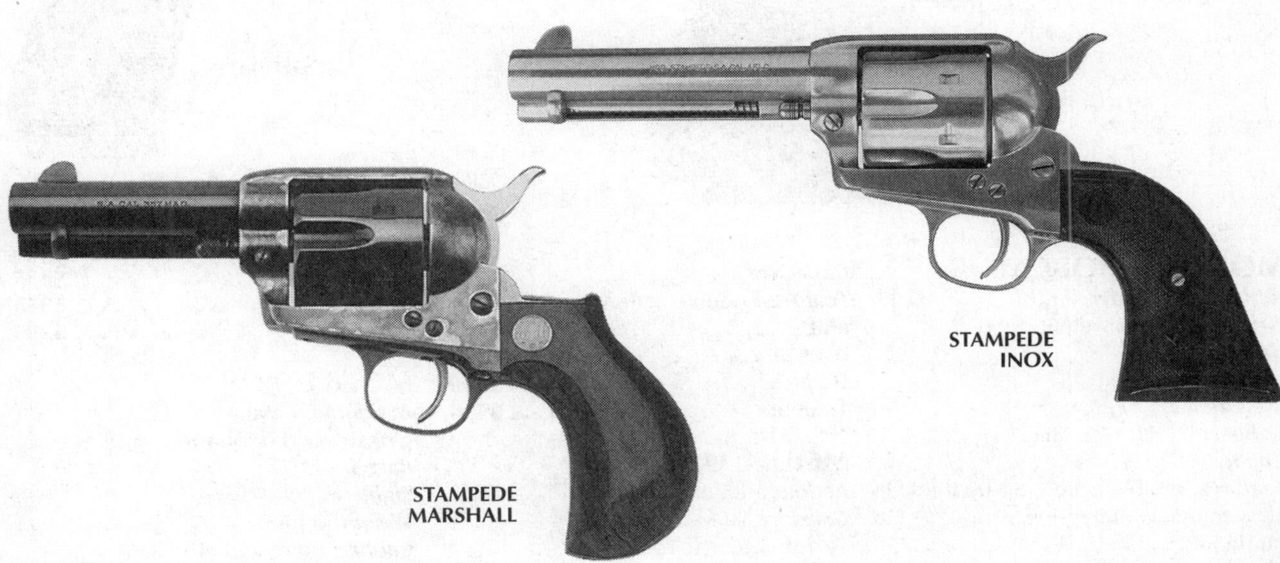

STAMPEDE INOX

STAMPEDE MARSHALL

BERETTA STAMPEDE INOX AND MARSHALL

Action: single-action revolver
Grips: black composite (Inox) and walnut (Marshall)
Barrel: $3\frac{1}{2}$ (Marshall), $4\frac{3}{4}$, $5\frac{1}{2}$ or $7\frac{1}{2}$ in. (Inox)
Sights: blade front, strap groove in rear
Weight: 37 oz. ($4\frac{3}{4}$-inch barrel)
Caliber: 357 Magnum, .45 Long Colt
Capacity: 6
Features: various finishes available on Stampede metal, including nickel, charcoal blue

Marshall **$575**
Stampede: **$540**
Stampede nickel **$575**
Stampede Inox **$710**

Beretta Handguns

MODEL 21 BOBCAT

MODEL U22 NEOS

MODEL 3032 TOMCAT

MODEL 92

MODEL 21 BOBCAT

Action: autoloader
Grips: plastic or walnut
Barrel: 2.4 in.
Sights: fixed open
Weight: 11.5 oz.
Caliber: .22 LR, .25 Auto
Capacity: 7 (.22) or 8 (.25)
Features: double action, tip-up barrel, alloy frame, walnut grips extra

matte **$275**
blued. **$315**
stainless **$340**

MODEL 3032 TOMCAT

Action: autoloader
Grips: plastic
Barrel: 2.5 in.
Sights: fixed open
Weight: 14.5 oz.
Caliber: .32 Auto
Capacity: 7 + 1
Features: double action; tip-up barrel

matte **$370**
blue. **$390**
stainless **$460**
Titanium **$450**

MODEL U22 NEOS

Action: autoloader
Grips: plastic
Barrel: 4.5 or 6 in.
Sights: target
Weight: 31.7 oz.
Caliber: .22 LR
Capacity: 10 + 1
Features: single action; removable colored grip inserts; model with 6 in. barrel weighs 36.2 oz.; Deluxe model features adjustable trigger, replaceable sights; optional 7.5-inch barrel

U22 Neos **$285**
Inox. **$335**
DLX. **$355**
Inox DLX. **$395**

MODEL 92

Action: autoloader
Grips: wood or plastic
Barrel: 4.3
Sights: 3-dot
Weight: 34.4 oz.
Caliber: 9mm and .40 S&W
Capacity: 10 + 1 (8 + 1 compact)
Features: chrome-lined bore; double action tritium sights available; reversible magazine catch

Model 92 . . . . **$715**
stainless **$795**
Brigadier **$795**
Brigadier stainless. **$845**
Inox Lasergrip **$975**

MODEL 92 VERTEC INOX

MODEL 84 CHEETAH

MODEL 92/96 VERTEC

MODEL 87 TARGET

MODEL 92/96 VERTEC
Action: autoloader
Grips: thin, vertical, dual-textured panels
Barrel: 4.7
Sights: fixed open
Weight: 32.2 oz.
Caliber: 9mm and .40 S&W
Capacity: 10 + 1
Features: double action, accessory rail for laser sight, flashlight
Vertec **$760**
Inox. **$825**
Inox Lasergrip (9mm) **$995**

MODEL 96
Action: autoloader
Grips: composite
Barrel: 5.9 in.
Sights: target
Weight: 40.0 oz.
Caliber: .40 S&W
Capacity: 10 + 1 (8 + 1 compact)
Features: double action, rubber magazine bumpers, competition-tuned trigger; tool set and ABS case
Model 96 . . . . **$715**
stainless **$795**

MODEL 84 CHEETAH
Action: autoloader
Grips: plastic or wood
Barrel: 3.8 or 4.4 in. (M86)
Sights: fixed open
Weight: 23.3 oz.
Caliber: .380 Auto
Capacity: 10 + 1 (8 in 85 Cheetah)
Features: double action, ambidextrous safety
Cheetah 84 . . . . **$625**
M84 nickel **$690**
Cheetah 85 . . . . **$590**
M85 nickel **$665**

MODEL 87 TARGET
Action: autoloader
Grips: plastic or wood
Barrel: 3.8 or 5.9 in. (Target)
Sights: fixed open
Weight: 20.1 oz.
Caliber: .22 LR
Capacity: 10 + 1
Features: blowback design; Target weighs 40.9 oz. with target sights
Model 87 . . . . **$625**
Target **$710**

Beretta Handguns

MODEL 9000 S

MODEL 9000 S

Action: autoloader
Grips: soft polymer
Barrel: 3.5 in.
Sights: fixed open
Weight: 27.0 oz.
Caliber: 9mm and .40 S&W
Capacity: 10 + 1
Features: double action, polymer frame, firing pin block
9000 S. $485

Bersa Handguns

THUNDER 380 LITE

MODEL 380 THUNDER

Action: autoloader
Grips: composite
Barrel: 3.5 in.
Sights: fixed open
Weight: 23.0 oz.
Caliber: .380 ACP
Capacity: 7 + 1
Features: double action; also Thunder .45
.380 . . . . $282
.380 concealed carry $292
.380 nickel $309
.380, 9-shot. $316
9mm, 10-shot matte $425
9mm, 10-shot stainless $467
.45 . . . . $425
.45 nickel $450
.45 stainless $467

Bond Arms Handguns

TEXAS DEFENDER

Action: hinged breech
Grips: composite
Barrel: 3 in.
Sights: fixed open
Weight: 20.0 oz.
Caliber: 25 cartridges from .22 LR to .45 Colt/.410 with interchangeable barrels
Capacity: 2
Features: double barrel, stainless steel; also available: Cowboy Defender at 19 oz., with no trigger guard

Texas Defender $379
Cowboy Defender $379
Century 2000 (3.5 in. barrel, 21 oz., .45 Colt or .410 Shot). . $394

TEXAS DEFENDER

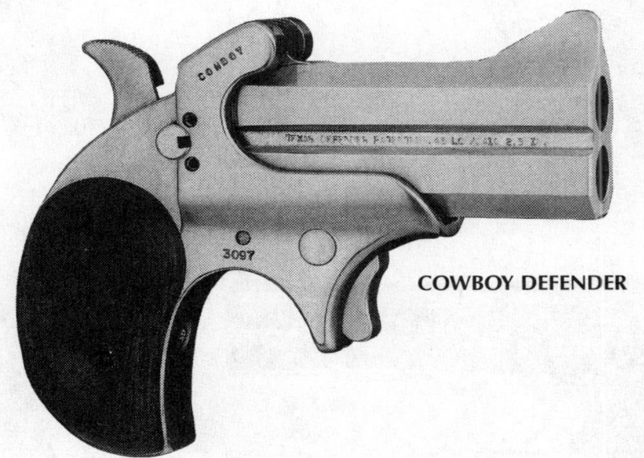

COWBOY DEFENDER

Before transporting handguns across state lines, be aware of laws that may require you to case or otherwise secure the gun in your car. Concealed-carry rules differ too.

Browning Handguns

BUCK MARK STANDARD (5.5″ BARREL)

BUCK MARK CLASSIC

BUCK MARK 5.5 TARGET

BUCK MARK BULLSEYE

HI-POWER

PRO-9

BUCK MARK

Action: autoloader
Grips: composite, laminated or wood
Barrel: 5.5 in.
Sights: target
Weight: 32.0 oz.
Caliber: .22 LR
Capacity: 10 + 1
Features: standard, camper, target, bullseye models available with various grips, barrel contours

Buck Mark. $319
Stainless $345
Nickel $377
Camper $287
Camper stainless $310
Camper nickel. $320
Bullseye (7.25 in. bbl.) $468
Bullseye Target $604
Micro (4 in. bbl.). $319
Micro nickel $377

PRO-9 AND HI-POWER

Action: autoloader
Grips: walnut, rubber or composite
Barrel: 4.75 in.
Sights: fixed
Weight: 30-35 oz.
Caliber: 9mm, .40 S& W
Features: Pro-9 (9mm only) has stainless steel slide and replaceable backstrap inserts. Hi-Power has optional adjustable sights.

Pro-9 . . . . $628
Hi-Power. . . . . $781 – 846
Hi-Power, adjustable sights $861

Charles Daly Handguns

MODEL 1911

MODEL 1911
TARGET STAINLESS

MODEL 1911
Action: autoloader
Grips: walnut
Barrel: 3.5, 4.0 or 5.0 in.
Sights: target
Weight: 33.0 oz.
Caliber: .45 ACP
Capacity: 7 + 1
Features: stainless and target models available (weights vary to 39 oz.)
Model 1911 . . . . $529
Stainless $629
Target $619
Target stainless $724

Cimarron Handguns

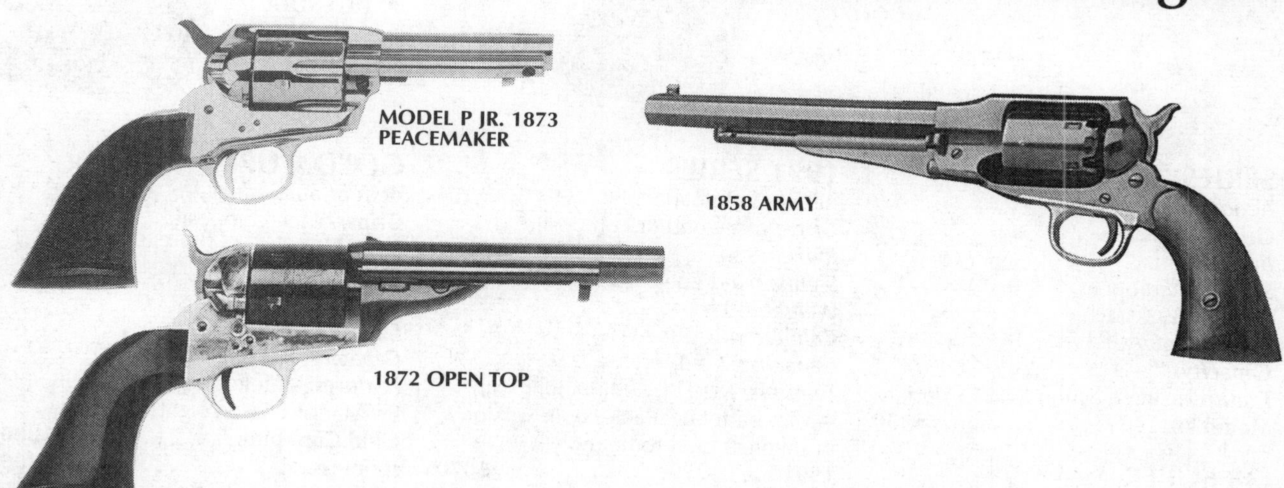
MODEL P JR. 1873
PEACEMAKER

1858 ARMY

1872 OPEN TOP

MODEL 1858 ARMY
Action: single-action revolver
Grips: walnut
Barrel: 7.5 in.
Sights: fixed open
Weight: 50.0 oz.
Caliber: .44
Capacity: 6
Features: black powder single action revolver also available in .36 Paterson
1858 Army $260

MODEL 1872 OPEN TOP
Action: single-action revolver
Grips: walnut
Barrel: 5.5 and 7.5 in.
Sights: fixed open
Weight: 40.0 oz.
Caliber: .38 Colt and S&W, .44 Colt and Russian, .45 Schofield
Capacity: 6
Features: modern steel, traditional design; weight varies up to 46 oz.
1872 . . . . $529

MODEL P JR. 1873 PEACEMAKER
Action: single-action revolver
Grips: composite
Barrel: 4.8, 5.5 and 7.5 in.
Sights: none
Weight: 44.0 oz.
Caliber: .32 WCP, .38 WCF, .357, .44 WCF, .45 LC
Capacity: 6
Features: fashioned after the 1873 Colt SAA but 20 percent smaller
Peacemaker. $499

Colt Handguns

SERIES 70

Action: autoloader
Grips: walnut
Barrel: 5 in.
Sights: fixed open
Weight: 39.0 oz.
Caliber: .45 ACP
Capacity: 7 + 1
Features: single-action M1911 design
Model 70 . . . . $990

.38 SUPER

Action: autoloader
Grips: rosewood or composite
Barrel: 5 in.
Sights: fixed open
Weight: 39.0 oz.
Caliber: .38 Super
Capacity: 9 + 1
Features: M1911 stainless models available, aluminum trigger
blue. $950
stainless $980
bright stainless $1200

1991 SERIES

Action: autoloader
Grips: rosewood or composite
Barrel: 5 in.
Sights: fixed open
Weight: 39.0 oz.
Caliber: .45 ACP
Capacity: 7 + 1
Features: M1911 Commander with 4.3 in. barrel available; both versions in stainless or chrome moly
1991 . . . . $870
stainless $920

MODEL XSE

Action: autoloader
Grips: rosewood
Barrel: 5 in.
Sights: 3-dot
Weight: 39.0 oz.
Caliber: .45 ACP
Capacity: 8 + 1
Features: stainless, M1911 with extended ambidextrous safety, upswept beavertail, slotted hammer and trigger; also available as 4.3-in. barreled Commander
XSE $1100

GOLD CUP

Action: autoloader
Grips: black composite
Barrel: 5 in.
Sights: target
Weight: 39.0 oz.
Caliber: .45 ACP
Capacity: 8 + 1
Features: stainless or chome-moly; Bo-Mar or Eliason sights
Gold Cup, blue $1300
stainless. $1400

DEFENDER

Action: autoloader
Grips: rubber finger-grooved
Barrel: 3 in.
Sights: 3-dot
Weight: 30.0 oz.
Caliber: .45 ACP
Capacity: 7 + 1
Features: stainless M1911, extended safety, upswept beavertail, beveled magazine well
Defender. $950

Colt Handguns

SINGLE ACTION ARMY

Action: single-action revolver
Grips: composite
Barrel: 4.3, 5.5 or 7.5 in.
Sights: fixed open
Weight: 46.0 oz.
Caliber: .32/20, .357 Mag., .38 Spl., .44-40, .45 Colt, .38/40
Capacity: 6
Features: case-colored frame, transfer bar, weight for .44-40, 48 oz. and 50 oz. for .45 Colt
Single Action Army $1380
Nickel. $1530

SINGLE ACTION ARMY

Comanche Handguns

MODEL II

Action: double-action revolver
Grips: rubber
Barrel: 3 or 6 in.
Sights: target
Weight: 22.0 oz.
Caliber: .38 Spl. (also in .22, .357)
Capacity: 6
Features: stainless or blue
Blue, 3 or 4 in. $225
Stainless, 3 or 4 in. $242
.22 blue, 6 in. $242
.22 stainless, 6 in. $267
.357 blue, 3, 4 or 6 in. $259
.357 stainless, 3, 4 or 6 in. $284

COMANCHE REVOLVER

SUPER SINGLE SHOT

Action: hinged breech
Grips: composite
Barrel: 10 in.
Sights: target
Weight: 48.0 oz.
Caliber: .45 LC/.410
Capacity: 1
Features: satin nickel finish (also in blue)
nickel $192
blue. $175

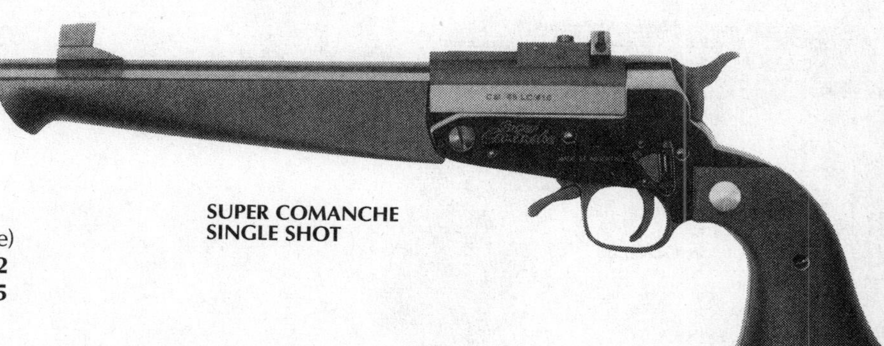

SUPER COMANCHE SINGLE SHOT

HANDGUNS

CZ Handguns

MODEL 75

MODEL 100

MODEL 75 CHAMPION

MODEL 75 IPSC

MODEL 83

MODEL 100

Action: autoloader
Grips: composite
Barrel: 3.9 in.
Sights: target
Weight: 24.0 oz.
Caliber: 9mm, .40 S&W
Capacity: 10 + 1
Features: single or double action, decocking lever
Model 100 . . . . $449

MODEL 75

Action: autoloader
Grips: composite
Barrel: 4.7 in.
Sights: 3-dot
Weight: 35.0 oz.
Caliber: 9mm or .40 S&W
Capacity: 10 + 1
Features: single or double action
9mm $509
.40 S&W $525

MODEL 75 CHAMPION

Action: autoloader
Grips: composite
Barrel: 4.5 in.
Sights: target
Weight: 35.0 oz.
Caliber: 9 mm or .40 S&W
Capacity: 10 + 1
Features: also available: IPSC version with 5.4-in. barrel
Champion $1646
IPSC $1152

MODEL 83

Action: autoloader
Grips: composite
Barrel: 3.8 in.
Sights: fixed open
Weight: 26.0 oz.
Caliber: 9mm
Capacity: 10 + 1
Features: single or double action
Model 83 . . . . $420

CZ Handguns

MODEL 85 COMBAT
Action: autoloader
Grips: composite
Barrel: 4.7 in.
Sights: target
Weight: 35.0 oz.
Caliber: 9 mm
Capacity: 10 + 1
Features: single or double action
Combat $599

2075 RAMI
Action: single- and double-action autoloading
Grips: lack composite
Barrel: 3 in.
Sights: blade front, shrouded rear
Weight: 25 oz.
Caliber: 9mm Luger, .40 S&W
Magazine Capacity: 10 (9mm), 8 (.40 S&W)
Features: firing pin block, manual safety, double-stack magazine
Price: $576

MODEL 85 COMBAT

2075 RAMI

MODEL 97
Action: autoloader
Grips: composite
Barrel: 4.8 in.
Sights: fixed open
Weight: 41.0 oz.
Caliber: .45 ACP
Capacity: 10 + 1
Features: single or double action
Model 97 . . . . $663

MODEL 75 COMPACT
Action: autoloader
Grips: composite
Barrel: 3.9 in.
Sights: fixed open
Weight: 32.0 oz.
Caliber: 9 mm
Capacity: 10 + 1
Features: single or double action
Compact $539

MODEL 97

MODEL 75 COMPACT

CZ Handguns

KADET MODEL 75

THE KADET ADAPTER IN ITS REAR (COCKED) POSITION

KADET MODEL 75

Action: autoloader
Grips: composite
Barrel: 4.9 in.
Sights: target
Weight: 38.0 oz.
Caliber: .22 LR
Capacity: 10 + 1
Features: single or double action
Kadet $510
.22 conversion kit for CZ 75/85 . . $299

Dan Wesson Handguns

ALASKAN GUIDE SUPER MAG

Action: revolver
Grips: rubber
Barrel: 4 in.
Sights: target
Weight:
Caliber: .445 Super Mag (.44 mag, .44 Special)
Capacity: 6
Features: Stainless steel frame; vented and compensated barrel; red ramp front sight, adjustable white outline rear sight; coated with Yukon Coat Teflon-based coating
MSRP: **. $1,059**

PATRIOT COMMANDER

Action: autoloader
Grips: cocobolo
Barrel: 4.74 in.
Sights: fixed open
Weight:
Caliber: .45 ACP
Capacity:
Features: Series 70 stainless steel frame; forged stainless steel slide; forged one-piece stainless steel match barrel; high ride beavertail grip safety; extended thumb safety; lowered and relieved ejection port;
MSRP: **. . . . . $929.**

PATRIOT CARRY CONCEALED

Action: autoloader
Grips: cocobolo
Barrel: 4.5 in.
Sights: fixed open
Weight:
Caliber: .45 ACP
Capacity:
Features: Series 70 stainless steel frame; forged stainless slide; forged one-piece stainless match barrel; tactical night dot front sight; XS 24/7 night post rear sight; high ride beavertail grip safety; extended thumb safety; lowered and relieved ejection port;
MSRP: **. $995**

PATRIOT-ED BROWN BOB-TAIL COMMANDER

Action: autoloader
Grips: cocobolo
Barrel: 4.75 in.
Sights: fixed open
Weight:
Caliber: 10mm, .45 ACP
Capacity:
Features: Series 70 stainless steel frame; forged stainless steel slide; forged one-piece stainless steel match barrel; high ride beavertail grip safety; extended thumb safety; lowered and relieved ejection port; checkered front-strap.
MSRP: **. $1,049**

PATRIOT EXPERT

Action: autoloader
Grips: cocobolo
Barrel: 5 in.,
Sights: target
Weight:
Caliber: 10 mm, .40 SW, .38 Super, .45 ACP
Capacity:
Features: Series 70 stainless steel frame; forged stainless steel slide; forged one-piece stainless steel match barrel; match grade trigger and sear; high ride beavertail grip safety; extended thumb safety; lowered and relieved ejection port;
MSRP: **. $1,019**

Dan Wesson Handguns

POINTMAN

Action: autoloader
Grips: exotic wood
Barrel: 5 in.
Sights: open fixed
Weight:
Caliber: .45 ACP
Capacity:
Features: Series 70 stainless frame; stainless slide; forged one-piece stainless match barrel; match grade trigger and sear; extended thumb safety; stainless high ride beavertail grip safety; Major with forged stainless steel target barrel, target sights, Ed Brown memory groove grip safety, STI extended thumb safety; Major Seven with hand-fit frame, slide, barrel, link and bushing, target sights and cocobolo grips
Pointman Aussie:. $859
Pointman Major $859
Pointman Major Seven $859
Pointman Major Stainless $809

RAZORBACK

Action: autoloader
Grips: black rubber
Barrel: 5 in.
Sights: target
Weight:
Caliber: 10 mm
Capacity:
Features: Series 70 stainless frame; forged stainless slide; forged one-piece stainless match barrel; solid match trigger; extended thumb safety; stainless high ride beavertail grip safety
MSRP: **. $959**

SUPER RAM SILHOUETTE

Action: revolver
Grips: rubber
Barrel: interchangeable
Sights: target
Weight: 64 oz. (8-in. barrel)
Caliber: .445 Super Mag
Capacity: 6
Features: Dan Wesson interchangeable barrel feature (2.5 to 10 in.); vented and slotted barrel; Bomar front hood and rear Sight; optional scope mounts
MSRP: **. $1,399**

MODEL 715 SMALL FRAME REVOLVER

Action: revolver
Grips: rubber
Barrel: interchangeable
Sights: target
Weight: 36 oz. (2.5-in. barrel)
Caliber: .22LR, .32H&R, .32-20, .357 magnum
Capacity: 6
Features: Dan Wesson interchangeable barrel feature (2.5 to 10 in.); yellow ramp front sight, fully adjustable white outline rear sight; optional scope mounts
MSRP: **. $709**

Downsizer Handguns

WSP

Action: hinged breech
Grips: composite
Barrel: 2.1 in.
Sights: none
Weight: 11.0 oz.
Caliber: .357 Mag., .45 ACP
Capacity: 1
Features: double action only, stainless steel
WSP $499

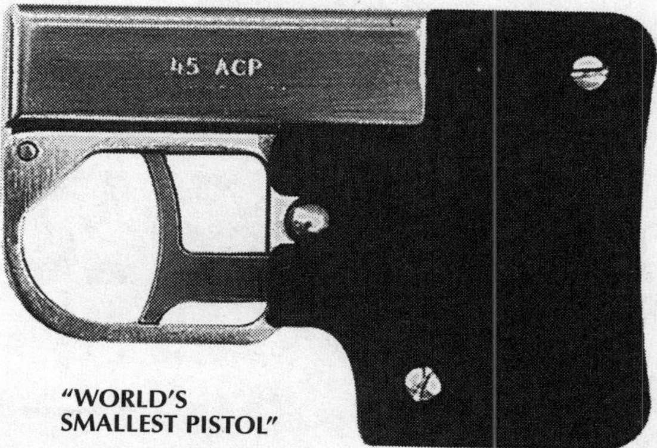

"WORLD'S SMALLEST PISTOL"

When shooting any pistol, position your trigger hand well up on the grip, your fore-arm in line with the barrel's horizontal axis and your wrist straight.

Ed Brown Handguns

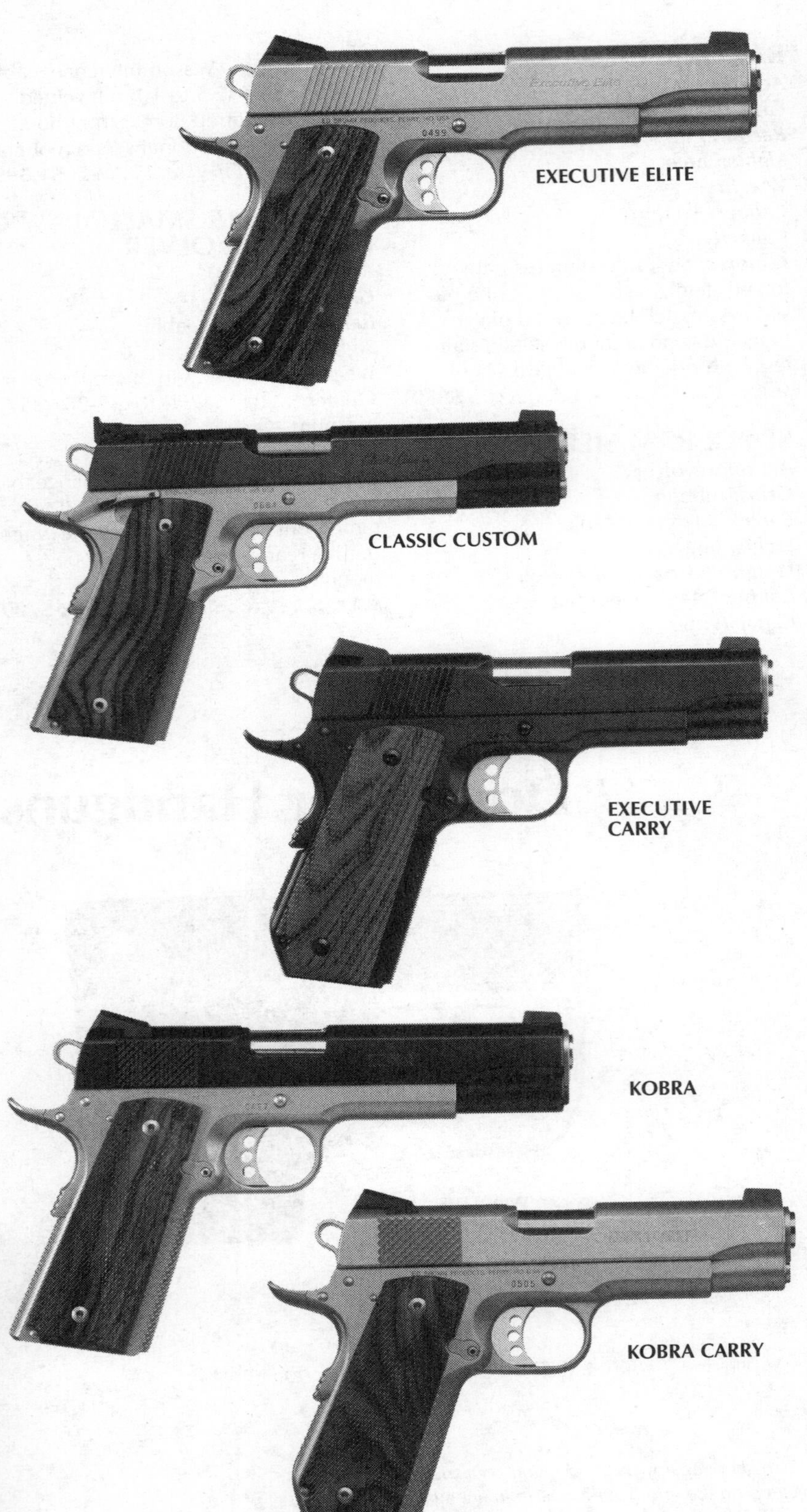

EXECUTIVE ELITE

Action: autoloader
Grips: checkered Cocobolo wood
Barrel: 5 in.
Sights: to order
Weight: 36.0 oz.
Caliber: .45 ACP
Capacity: 7 + 1 or more
Features: custom-grade M1911 Colt with many options to order
base model $2495

CLASSIC CUSTOM

Action: autoloader
Grips: Cocobolo wood
Barrel: 5 in.
Sights: target
Weight: 37.0 oz.
Caliber: .45 ACP
Capacity: 7 + 1
Features: single action, M1911 Colt design, Bo-Mar sights; checkered forestrap, ambidextrous safety, stainless available
Classic Custom $3095

EXECUTIVE CARRY

Action: autoloader
Grips: checkered Cocobolo wood
Barrel: 4.25 in.
Sights: low-profile combat
Weight: 33.0 oz.
Caliber: .45 ACP
Capacity: 7 + 1
Features: Bob-tail butt, checkered forestrap, stainless optional
Commander Bobtail $2495

KOBRA

Action: autoloader
Grips: Cocobolo wood
Barrel: 5 in.
Sights: low-profile combat
Weight: 36.0 oz.
Caliber: .45 ACP
Capacity: 7 + 1
Features: single-action M1911 Colt design, matte finish with Snakeskin treatment on forestrap, mainspring housing and rear of slide; stainless models available
Kobra. . . . . $1995 - 2195
Kobra Carry
with 4.3-in. barrel . . $2095 - 2295

HANDGUNS

EMF Handguns

MODEL 1873 DAKOTA

Action: single-action revolver
Grips: walnut
Barrel: 4.8, 5.5 and 7.5 in.
Sights: fixed open
Weight: 46.0 oz.
Caliber: .357 Mag., .44-40, .45 Colt
Capacity: 6
Features: case-colored frame; barrel length determines weight

1873 Dakota $400
combo cylinder $100

1873 DAKOTA SINGLE ACTION WITH 5.5" BARREL

MODEL 1875 REMINGTON

Action: single-action revolver
Grips: walnut
Barrel: 5.5 or 7.5 in.
Sights: fixed open
Weight: 48.0 oz.
Caliber: .357 Mag., .44, .45 Colt
Capacity: 6
Features: case-colored frame

Model 1875 . . . . $435
engraved $750
nickel $585

MODEL 1890 REMINGTON POLICE

Action: single-action revolver
Grips: walnut
Barrel: 5.8 in.
Sights: fixed open
Weight: 48.0 oz.
Caliber: .357 Mag., .44-40, .45 Colt
Capacity: 6
Features: lanyard loop, case-colored frame

Model 1890 . . . . $435
engraved $750
nickel $595

HARTFORD PINKERTON

Action: single-action revolver
Grips: walnut, birds-head
Barrel: 4 in.
Sights: fixed open
Weight: 44.0 oz.
Caliber: .357, .45 Colt
Capacity: 6
Features: case-colored frame

Hartford Pinkerton $570

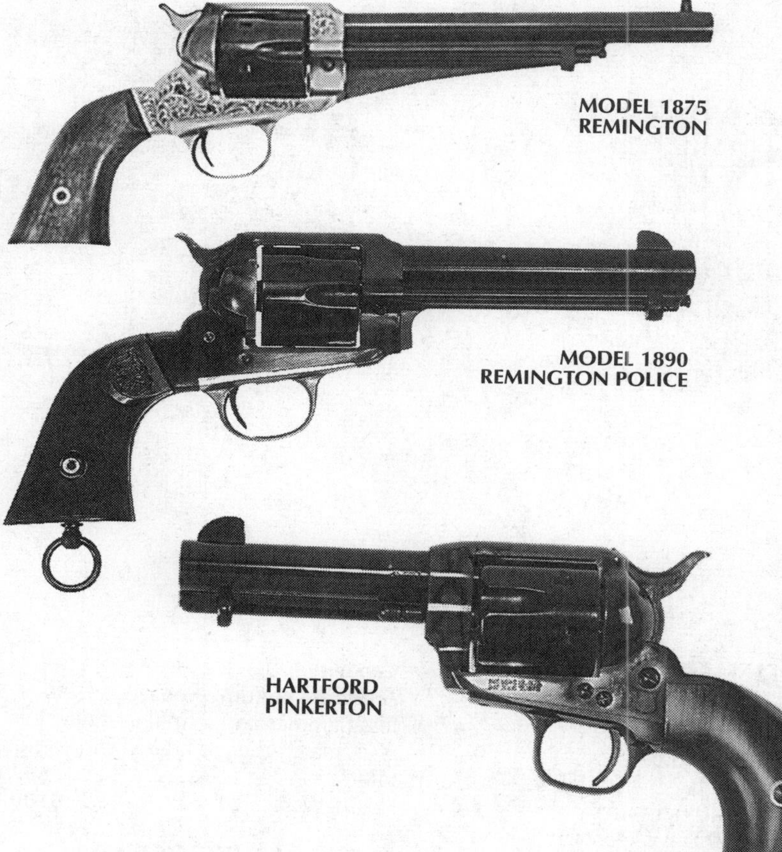

MODEL 1875 REMINGTON

MODEL 1890 REMINGTON POLICE

HARTFORD PINKERTON

1873 HARTFORD "BUNTLINE"

Enterprise Arms Handguns

BOXER P500

TACTICAL P325 PLUS

MODEL 500 BOXER

Action: autoloader
Grips: composite
Barrel: 5 in.
Sights: target
Weight: 44.0 oz.
Caliber: .40 S&W, .45 ACP
Capacity: 10 + 1
Features: match-grade components and fitting, stainless one-piece guide rod, lapped slide, flared ejection port
.45 ACP $1399
.40 S&W $1499

MEDALIST

Action: autoloader
Grips: composite
Barrel: 5 in.
Sights: target
Weight: 44.0 oz.
Caliber: .40 S&W, .45 ACP
Capacity: 10 + 1
Features: up-turned beavertail, stainless hammer and sear, flared ejection port, match trigger, lapped slide
.45 . . . . $979
.40 S&W $1099

TACTICAL P325 PLUS

Action: autoloader
Grips: composite
Barrel: 3.3 in.
Sights: low-profile combat
Weight: 37.0 oz.
Caliber: .45 ACP
Capacity: 10 + 1
Features: extended ambidextrous safety, lapped slide, up-turned beavertail, skeleton trigger and hammer; Tactical Ghost Ring or Novak sights; (also available with 4.3 and 5.0-inch barrels)
Tactical $979

TOURNAMENT

Action: autoloader
Grips: composite
Barrel: 5 in.
Sights: target
Weight: 44.0 oz.
Caliber: .38 Super, .40 S&W, .45 ACP
Capacity: 10 + 1
Features: up-turned beavertail, extended thumb safety, front cocking grooves, checkered front strap, all match components; 2-lb. trigger
TI with stainless bull barrel. . . $2300
TII with long slide. $2000
TIII ported, hard chromed, fashioned for scope use . . . $2700

HANDGUNS

European American Armory Handguns

WITNESS
BIG BORE BOUNTY HUNTER SINGLE ACTION
SMALL BORE BOUNTY HUNTER
WITNESS P COMPACT
WINDICATOR REVOLVER

BIG BORE BOUNTY HUNTER

Action: single-action revolver
Grips: walnut
Barrel: 4.5 or 7.5 in.
Sights: fixed open
Weight: 39 to 41 oz.
Caliber: .357 Mag., .44 Mag., .45 Colt
Capacity: 6
Features: case-colored or blued or nickel frame; version with 7.5 in. barrel weighs 42 oz.

Bounty Hunter. . . . . $369 - 379
nickel $399
case color . . . . $369 - 379
Also available:
Small Bore Bounty Hunter (.22 LR or .22 WMR). $269
nickel $299

WINDICATOR

Action: double-action revolver
Grips: rubber
Barrel: 2 or 4 in.
Sights: fixed open
Weight: 36.0 oz.
Caliber: .357 Mag., .38 Special
Capacity: 6
Features: transfer bar

.38, 2-inch $249
.38, 4-inch; .357, 2-inch $259
.357, 4-inch $279

WITNESS

Action: autoloader
Grips: rubber
Barrel: 4.5 in.
Sights: 3-dot
Weight: 33.0 oz.
Caliber: 9mm, .38 Super, .40 S&W, 10 mm, .45 ACP
Capacity: 10 + 1
Features: double action, polymer frame available

steel $459
polymer. $429
"Wonder" finish $459

WITNESS COMPACT

Action: autoloader
Grips: rubber
Barrel: 3.6 in.
Sights: 3-dot
Weight: 29.0 oz.
Caliber: 9mm, .40 S&W, 10 mm, .45 ACP
Capacity: 10 + 1
Features: double action, polymer frame and ported barrels available

steel $459
polymer. $449

Firestorm Handguns

MODEL 380

MODEL 45

MINI

MODEL 380

Action: autoloader
Grips: rubber
Barrel: 3.5 in.
Sights: 3-dot
Weight: 23.0 oz.
Caliber: .380
Capacity: 7 + 1
Features: double action, also available in .22 LR, 10-shot magazine
Model 380 . . . . $284
Duotone $292

MODEL 45

Action: autoloader
Grips: rubber
Barrel: 4.3 or 5.2 in.
Sights: 3-dot
Weight: 34.0 oz.
Caliber: .45 ACP
Capacity: 7 + 1
Features: single action, 1911 Colt design, from cocking grooves
Model 45 . . . . $309
Duotone $317

MINI

Action: autoloader
Grips: polymer
Barrel: 3.5 in.
Sights: target
Weight: 24.5 oz.
Caliber: 9mm, .40 S&W, .45 ACP
Capacity: 10 + 1 (7 + 1 in .45)
Features: double action
Mini $400
Duotone $409
Duotone .45 . . . . $417
nickel $425
.45 nickel $434

Freedom Arms Handguns

MODEL 83
PREMIER GRADE

MODEL 83 PREMIER GRADE

Action: single-action revolver with manual safety bar
Grips: hardwood or optional Micarta
Barrel: 4.75, 6, 7.5, 9 or 10 in.
Sights: fixed or adjustable
Weight: 52.5 oz.
Caliber: .357 Mag., .41 Mag., .44 Mag., .454 Casull, .475 Linebaugh
Capacity: 5
Features: sights, scope mounts and extra cylinders optional
Price:. . . . . $2035 to 2120

MODEL 83
454 CASULL FIELD GRADE

MODEL 83 RIMFIRE FIELD GRADE

Action: single-action revolver
Grips: Pachmyr or optional hardwood or Micarta
Barrel: 4.75, 6, 7.5, 9 or 10 in.
Sights: adjustable
Weight: 55.5 oz.
Caliber: .22 LR, .357 Mag., .41 mag., .44 Mag., 454 Casull, .475 Linebaugh
Capacity: 5
Features: sights, scope mounts and extra cylinders optional
Price:. . . . . $1573 to 1803

MODEL 97
PREMIER GRADE

MODEL 97 PREMIER GRADE

Action: single-action revolver with automatic transfer bar safety
Grips: hardwood or optional Micarta
Barrel: 4.5, 5.5, 7.5 or 10 in.
Sights: fixed or adjustable
Weight: 39.0 oz.
Caliber: .17 HMR, .22 LR, .32 H&R Mag., .357 Mag., .41 Mag., .44 Spl., .45 Colt
Capacity: 5 shot for .41 and bigger, 6 shot for smaller calibers
Features: sights, scope mounts and extra cylinders optional
Price:. . . . . $1718 to 1784

When using a two-handed grip, push with your right arm and pull with your left. The tension helps "lock" the pistol on target.

Glock Handguns

MODEL G19

9X19

MODEL G17

MODEL G27

MODEL G23

PORTED BARREL

.40

MODEL G22

MODEL G33

MODEL G26

.357

MODEL G31

9X19

MODEL G34

MODEL G29

10MM

MODEL G20

MODEL G30

9X19

MODEL G17

.40

MODEL G35

COMPACT PISTOLS

Action: autoloader
Grips: composite
Barrel: 3.8 in.
Sights: fixed open
Weight: 21.2 oz.
Caliber: 9mm, .40 S&W, .357 Mag., 10 mm, .45 ACP
Capacity: 9, 10, 13, 15 depending on cartridge, magazine
Features: trigger safety, double action, 10 mm and .45 ACP weigh 24.0 oz.
Compact Pistols. . . . price on request

FULL-SIZE PISTOLS

Action: autoloader
Grips: composite
Barrel: 4.5 in.
Sights: fixed open
Weight: 22.3 oz.
Caliber: 9 mm, .40 S&W, .357 Mag., 10 mm, .45 ACP
Capacity: 10, 13, 15, 17 depending on cartridge
Features: trigger safety, double action, 10 mm and .45 ACP weigh 26.3 oz.
Full-Size . . . . price on request

SUBCOMPACT PISTOLS

Action: autoloader
Grips: composite
Barrel: 3.5 in.
Sights: fixed open
Weight: 19.8 oz.
Caliber: 9mm, .40 S&W, .357, .45
Capacity: 9, 10, 6, depending on cartridge, magazine
Features: trigger safety, double action
Subcompact. . . . . . . price on request

Glock Handguns

G-36 SLIMLINE
Action: autoloader
Grips: synthetic
Barrel: 3.8 in.
Sights: fixed open
Weight: 21.0 oz.
Caliber: .45 ACP
Capacity: 6 + 1
Features: single-stack magazine for thinner grip
G36 . . . . price on request

G-37 SLIMLINE
Action: autoloader
Grips: synthetic
Barrel: 24-30 in.
Sights:fixed open
Weight:
Caliber: .45 Glock
Capacity: 10 + 1
Features: chambered for .45 Glock shortened 45 ACP cartridge
G-37:. . . . . price on request

G36 SLIMLINE
G37 SLIMLINE

Hammerli Handguns

HAMMERLI SP 20
X-ESSE .22 L.R. WITH LONG BARREL
X-ESSE .22 L.R. WITH SHORT BARREL

MODEL SP20
Action: autoloader
Grips: synthetic
Barrel: 4.6 in.
Sights: target
Weight: 40.0 oz.
Caliber: .22 LR, .32 S&W
Capacity: 5
Features: front-end magazine
.22 . . . . $1668
.32 . . . . $1743

MODEL X-ESSE SPORT
Action: autoloader
Grips: composite
Barrel: 4.5 or 5.5 in.
Sights: target
Weight: 36.0 oz.
Caliber: .22 LR
Capacity: 10
Features: single action
X-ESSE. $710

Heckler & Koch Handguns

MARK 23 SPECIAL OP

USP 45 TACTICAL PISTOL

MODEL P7M8

USP ELITE

USP 45 UNIVERSAL SELF-LOADING PISTOL

USP EXPERT

MARK 23 SPECIAL OP

Action: autoloader
Grips: polymer
Barrel: 5.9 in.
Sights: 3-dot
Weight: 42.0 oz.
Caliber: .45 ACP
Capacity: 10 + 1
Features: military version of USP
Mark 23 Special OP $2412

MODEL P7M8

Action: autoloader
Grips: polymer
Barrel: 4.1 in.
Sights: target
Weight: 28.0 oz.
Caliber: 9mm
Capacity: 8 + 1
Features: blue or nickel finish
Model P7M8 . . . . $1515

USP 45

Action: autoloader
Grips: polymer
Barrel: 4.4 in.
Sights: 3-dot
Weight: 30.0 oz.
Caliber: .45 ACP
Capacity: 12
Features: short-recoil action
USP 45 . . . . $839

USP 9 & 40

Action: autoloader
Grips: polymer
Barrel: 4.25 in.
Sights: 3-dot
Weight: 27.0 oz.
Caliber: 9mm, .40 S&W
Capacity: 13
Features: short-recoil action, also in kit form
USP. $769

MODEL USP ELITE

Action: autoloader
Grips: composite
Barrel: 6.0 in.
Sights: target
Weight: 36.0 oz.
Caliber: 9mm, .45 ACP
Capacity: 15
Features: short recoil action, fiber-reinforced polymer frame; universal scope mounting groves, ambidextrous magazine release
USP Elite. $1356
USP Expert (9mm, .45 ACP, .40 S&W with 5.2 in. bbl.) $1356

HANDGUNS

Heckler & Koch Handguns

USP 40 COMPACT LEM

USP 40 COMPACT LEM

Action: autoloader
Grips: composite
Barrel: 3.6 in.
Sights: fixed open
Weight: 24.0 oz.
Caliber: .40 S&W
Capacity: 12
Features: double-action only with improved trigger pull; also in 9mm
USP40 . . . . $799

Heritage Handguns

ROUGH RIDER 17

ROUGH RIDER SA

ROUGH RIDER

Action: single-action revolver
Grips: hardwood, regular or birds-head
Barrel: 3.5, 4.75, 6.5, 9 in.
Sights: fixed open
Weight: 31.0 oz.
Caliber: .22, .22 LR (.22 WMR cylinder available)
Capacity: 6
Features: action on Colt 1873 pattern, transfer bar, satin or blued finish, weight to 38 oz. dependent on barrel length
Rough Rider $145
with WMR cylinder. $160
satin, with WMR cylinder $200
satin, adjustable sights, WMR cylinder $240

ROUGH RIDER IN .17 HMR

Action: single-action revolver
Grips: laminated camo
Barrel: 6.5 or 9 in.
Sights: adjustable
Weight: 38.0 oz.
Caliber: .17 HMR
Capacity: 6
Features: Williams Fire Red ramp front sight and Millet rear
Rough Rider $240

High Standard Handguns

CAMP PERRY NATIONAL MATCH M1911A1

Action: autoloader
Grips: walnut
Barrel: 5 in.
Sights: target
Weight: 40 oz.
Caliber: .45 ACP
Capacity: 7 + 1
Features: Mil spec. slide; mil. spec. barrel and bushing; flared ejection port; beveled magazine well; match trigger with overtravel stop; 4-pound trigger pull; stippled front grip; available in stainless steel, blued or Parkerized finish
MSRP: **. $749**

CRUSADER COMBAT

Action: autoloader
Grips: cocobolo
Barrel: 4.5 in.
Sights: fixed open
Weight: 38 oz.
Caliber: .45 ACP
Capacity: 7+1
Features: Precision fitted frame and slide; flared ejection port; lightweight long trigger with over-travel stop; trigger pull tuned at 5 to 6 pounds; extended slide stop and safety; wide beavertail grip safety; available in stainless steel, blued or Parkerized finish
MSRP: **. $645**
TuTone: $675
Stainless: $695

High Standard Handguns

SUPERMATIC CITATION MS

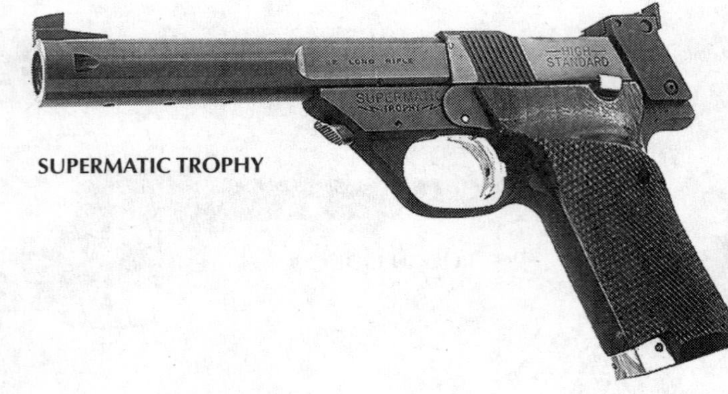

SUPERMATIC TROPHY

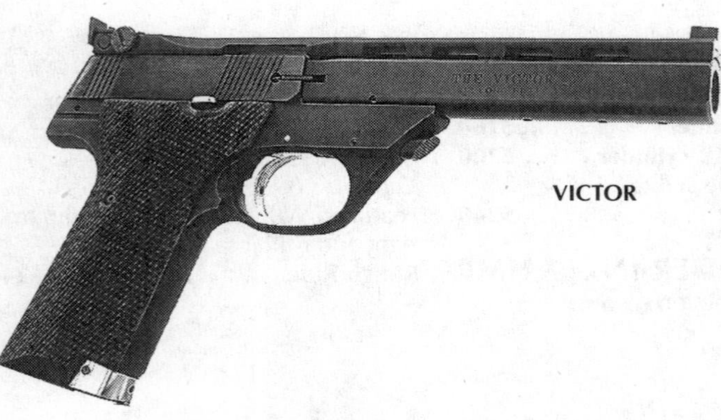

VICTOR

OLYMPIC

CRUSADER M1911

Action: autoloader
Grips: cocobolo; ***Barrel:*** 5 in.
Sights: fixed open
Weight: 40 oz.
Caliber: .38 Super, .45 ACP
Capacity: 7+1, (.38 Super) 9 + 1
Features: Precision fitted frame and slide; flared ejection port; lightweight long trigger with over-travel stop; trigger pull tuned at 5 to 6 pounds; extended slide stop and safety; wide beavertail grip safety; available in stainless steel, blued or Parkerized finish

MSRP: **$645**
Stainless: **$695**
.38 Super: **$695**

G-MAN MODEL

Action: autoloader
Grips: cocobolo; ***Barrel:*** 5 in.
Sights: fixed open
Weight: 39 oz.
Caliber: .45 ACP
Capacity: 8+1
Features: Custom-fit match grade stainless barrel and National Match bushing; polished feed ramp; throated barrel; lightweight trigger with over-travel stop; flared ejection port; wide, beavertail grip and ambidextrous thumb safties; black Teflon finish

MSRP: **$1,225**

SUPERMATIC CITATION MS

Action: autoloader
Grips: walnut
Barrel: 10 in.
Sights: target
Weight: 54.0 oz.
Caliber: .22 LR
Capacity: 10 + 1
Features: optional scope mount, slide conversion kit for .22 short

Citation **$775**
slide conversion kit **$317**

SUPERMATIC TROPHY

Action: autoloader
Grips: walnut
Barrel: 5.5 (bull) or 7.3 (fluted) in.
Sights: target
Weight: 44.0 oz.
Caliber: .22 LR
Capacity: 10 + 1
Features: left-hand grip optional

5.5 in. barrel **$795**
7.3 in barrel (46 oz.) **$845**

High Standard Handguns

OLYMPIC RAPID FIRE

VICTOR
Action: autoloader
Grips: walnut; *Barrel:* 4.5 or 5.5 in.
Sights: target; *Weight:* 45.0 oz.
Caliber: .22 LR
Capacity: 10 + 1
Features: optional slide conversion kit for .22 Short
4.5 in. barrel $745
5.5 in. barrel (46 oz.) $745
5.5 in. barrel with sights $795
7.25 in. barrel $625
7.25 in. barrel with sights $845
.22 Short conversion kit $317

OLYMPIC MILITARY
Action: autoloader
Grips: walnut; *Barrel:* 5.5 in.
Sights: target; *Weight:* 44.0 oz.
Caliber: .22 LR
Capacity: 10 + 1
Features: single action, blowback mechanism
Olympic Military. $795

OLYMPIC RAPID-FIRE
Action: autoloader
Grips: walnut; *Barrel:* 4 in.
Sights: target; *Weight:* 46.0 oz.
Caliber: .22 short
Capacity: 5
Features: push-button take-down, adjustable match trigger
Rapid-Fire $1027

Hi-Point Handguns

380 POLYMER COMP
380 POLYMER
9MM COMPACT POLYMER
9MM COMP GUN

380 POLYMER
Action: autoloader
Grips: polymer
Barrel: 3.5 in.
Sights: 3-dot
Weight: 30.0 oz.
Caliber: .380
Capacity: 8 + 1 (10-shot magazine available)
Features: last-round lock-open; comp model has 4 in. barrel
380 Polymer $120
comp. $135
with laser sight $190

9MM POLYMER
Action: autoloader
Grips: polymer
Barrel: 3.5 in.
Sights: 3-dot
Weight: 30.0 oz.
Caliber: 9mm
Capacity: 8 + 1 (10-shot magazine available)
Features: last-round lock-open, comp model has 4 in. barrel
9mm Polymer $140
comp. $169
with laser sight $219

BIG BORE PISTOL
Action: autoloader
Grips: polymer
Barrel: 4.5 in.
Sights: 3-dot
Weight: 32.0 oz.
Caliber: .45 ACP, .40 S&W
Capacity: 9 + 1, 10 + 1
Features: last-round lock-open
Big Bore $179

Kahr Handguns

MODEL P40

MODEL P9

MODEL P40

Action: autoloader
Grips: polymer
Barrel: 3.5 in.
Sights: fixed open
Weight: 18.7 oz.
Caliber: .40 S&W
Capacity: 6 + 1
Features: hammerless double action; target models available with 4 in. barrels, Hogue wood grips

P40 . . . . $676
stainless $719
Elite stainless. $783
P40 with 3 in. bbl. $707
Stainless $719
K40 Elite stainless $783
K40 Elite with night sights $892

MODEL P9

Action: autoloader
Grips: polymer
Barrel: 3.5 in.
Sights: fixed open
Weight: 17.7oz.
Caliber: 9mm
Capacity: 7 + 1
Features: hammerless double action

P9 . . . . $676
K9stainless $719
Elite stainless. $783
PM9 (3" bbl., black frame, stainless slide) $737
4 in. target bbl. $676
with night sights $814

Kel-Tec Handguns

P-11 CALIBER

P-32 CALIBER .32 AUTO

MODEL P-11

Action: autoloader
Grips: polymer
Barrel: 3.1 in.
Sights: fixed open
Weight: 14.4 oz.
Caliber: 9mm
Capacity: 10 + 1
Features: locked-breech mechanism

P-11 . . . . $320
parkerized $362
chrome $375

MODEL P-32

Action: autoloader
Grips: polymer
Barrel: 2.7 in.
Sights: fixed open
Weight: 6.6 oz.
Caliber: .32 Auto
Capacity: 7 + 1
Features: locked-breech mechanism

P-32 . . . . $306
parkerized $347
chrome $362

Kel-Tec Handguns

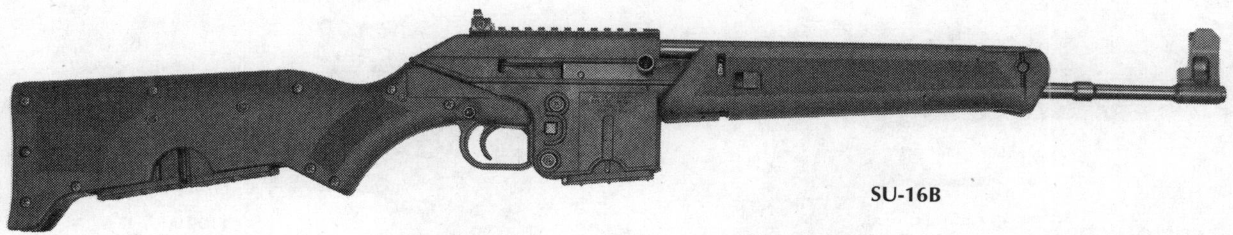

SU-16B

SUB RIFLE 2000 (READY TO FIRE)

P-3AT

SUB RIFLE 2000 CALIBERS 9MM & 40 S&W

MODEL P-3AT

Action: autoloader
Grips: polymer
Barrel: 2.8 in.
Sights: fixed open
Weight: 7.3 oz.
Caliber: .380
Capacity: 6 + 1
Features: locked-breech mechanism
P-3AT $311
parkerized $352
chrome $367

SUB RIFLE 2000

Action: autoloader
Grips: polymer
Barrel: 16 in.
Sights: target
Weight: 64.0 oz.
Caliber: 9mm and .40 S&W
Capacity: 10 + 1
Features: take-down, uses pistol magazines
Sub Rifle . . . . $391 - 428
SU-16 in .223 . . . . $640

HANDGUNS

Kimber Handguns

CUSTOM CDP II

COMPACT II & PRO CARRY II

CUSTOM II & CUSTOM TARGET II

ECLIPSE TARGET II

CDP11 SERIES

Action: autoloader
Grips: rosewood
Barrel: 3, 4, or 5 in.
Sights: low-profile night
Weight: 25 – 31 oz.
Caliber: .45 ACP
Capacity: 7 + 1
Features: alloy frame, stainless slide; also in 4 in. (Pro Carry and Compact) and 3 in. (Ultra) configurations
CDP $1165

COMPACT STAINLESS II

Action: autoloader
Grips: synthetic
Barrel: 4 in.
Sights: low-profile combat
Weight: 34.0 oz.
Caliber: .45 ACP, .40 S&W
Capacity: 7 + 1
Features: shortened single action 1911; also Pro Carry with alloy frame at 28 oz.; match-grade bushingless bull barrel
Compact II stainless $889
Pro Carry II. $789
Pro Carry II stainless. $862
Pro Carry HD II $897

CUSTOM II

Action: autoloader
Grips: synthetic or rosewood
Barrel: 5 in.
Sights: target or fixed
Weight: 38.0 oz.
Caliber: .38 Super, .40 S&W, .45 ACP, 10 mm, 9mm
Capacity: 7 + 1
Features: single action, 1911 Colt design, front cocking serrations, skeleton trigger and hammer
Custom II $760
Stainless II. $848
Target II $854
Stainless Target II $964

ECLIPSE II

Action: autoloader
Grips: laminated
Barrel: 5 in.
Sights: 3-dot night
Weight: 38.0 oz.
Caliber: .45 ACP, 10 mm
Capacity: 7 + 1
Features: matte-black oxide finish over stainless, polished bright on flats; also 3-inch Ultra and 4-inch Pro Carry versions; sights also available in low profile combat or target
Eclipse II $1074
Target II $1177
Ultra II $1074
Pro II. $1074
Pro Target II $1177

GOLD COMBAT II

Action: autoloader
Grips: rosewood
Barrel: 5 in.
Sights: low-profile night
Weight: 38.0 oz.
Caliber: .45 ACP
Capacity: 7 + 1
Features: M1911 Colt design with many refinements: checkered front strap, match bushing, ambidextrous safety, stainless match barrel
Gold Combat II. $1716
Gold Combat Stainless II $1657

Kimber Handguns

GOLD COMBAT II

STAINLESS GOLD MATCH II

STAINLESS ULTRA CARRY II

GOLD MATCH II

Action: autoloader
Grips: rosewood
Barrel: 5 in.
Sights: adjustable target
Weight: 38.0 oz.
Caliber: .45 ACP
Capacity: 7 + 1
Features: single action 1911 Colt design; match components, ambidextrous safety
Gold Match II **$1192**
Stainless **$1342**
Stainless in .40 S&W **$1373**
Team Match II **$1310**

TEN II HIGH CAPACITY

Action: autoloader
Grips: polymer
Barrel: 5 in.
Sights: low-profile combat
Weight: 34.0 oz.
Caliber: .45 ACP
Capacity: 10 + 1
Features: double-stack magazine, polymer frame; also in 4 in. (Pro Carry) configuration, from 32 oz.
Stainless Ten II **$771**
Pro Carry Ten II **$786**
Gold Match Ten II **$1061**

ULTRA CARRY II

Action: autoloader
Grips: synthetic
Barrel: 3 in.
Sights: low-profile combat
Weight: 25.0 oz.
Caliber: .40 S&W, .45 ACP
Capacity: 7 + 1
Features: smallest commercial 1911-style pistol
Ultra Carry II **$783**
Stainless II **$858**
Stainless II in .40 S&W **$903**

Unlike rifle or target pistol shooting, in which line of fire may be 30 degrees from a line across your feet or shoulders, defensive or combat pistol work is done at right angles to your stance.

Llama Handguns

MAX-I 45 GOVERNMENT DUOTONE FINISH

MICROMAX .380 MATTE FINISH

MINIMAX .45 SATIN CHROME FINISH

MAX-I GOVERNMENT

Action: autoloader
Grips: rubber
Barrel: 5 in.
Sights: 3-dot
Weight: 38.0 oz.
Caliber: .45 ACP
Capacity: 7 + 1
Features: single action M1911 Colt design; extended safety, beavertail, Duotone finish
Max-I $389

MICROMAX .380

Action: autoloader
Grips: polymer
Barrel: 4 in.
Sights: 3-dot
Weight: 29.0 oz.
Caliber: .380, .32 ACP
Capacity: 7 + 1, 8 + 1
Features: extended safety
matte $282
satin chrome $300

MINIMAX .45

Action: autoloader
Grips: rubber
Barrel: 3 in.
Sights: 3-dot
Weight: 28.0 oz.
Caliber: .40 S&W, .45 ACP
Capacity: 7 + 1 (.40), 6 + 1 (.45)
Features: single-action M1911 Colt design; extended beavertail grip
matte $309
Duo-Tone $316
satin chrome $334
Also available:
Minimax subcompact in .45 Auto, 10-shot matte: $316
satin chrome: $342
Duo-Tone: $325

Keep both eyes open when shooting any firearm, squinting slightly or using a patch or tape only if you must to avoid "doubling" the sight picture. A severe squint impairs vision in the open eye.

HANDGUNS

Magnum Research Handguns

BABY EAGLE
Action: autoloader
Grips: plastic composite
Barrel: 3.5, 4, 4.5 in.
Sights: 3-dot combat
Weight: 26.8 – 39.8 oz.
Caliber: 9mm, .40 S&W, .45 ACP
Capacity: 10 (15 for 9mm)
Features: squared, serrated trigger guard
Baby Eagle. $499

MARK XIX DESERT EAGLE
Action: autoloader
Grips: plastic composite
Barrel: 6 or 10 in.
Sights: fixed combat
Weight: 70.2 oz.
Caliber: .357 Mag., .44 Mag., .50 AE
Capacity: 9 + 1, 8 + 1, 7 + 1
Features: gas operated; all with polygonal rifling, integral scope bases
Desert Eagle, 6 in. barrel $1249
10 in. barrel (79 oz.). $1349
6 in. chrome or nickel. $1489
6 in. Titaniums/gold $1749

BFR (BIGGEST FINEST REVOLVER)
Action: single-action revolver
Grips: rubber
Barrel: 6.5, 7.5 or 10 in.
Sights: open adjustable
Weight: 50 – 67.3 oz.
Caliber: .45/70, .444, .450, .500 S&W, .30-30 Win. (long cylinder), .480 Ruger, .475 Linbaugh, .22 Hornet, .45 Colt/.410, .50 AE (short cylinder)
Capacity: 5
Features: both short and long-cylinder models entirely of stainless steel
BRF $899

BABY EAGLE

DESERT EAGLE PISTOL
MARK XIX .50 MAGNUM
TITANIUM FINISH

MARK XIX
COMPONENT SYSTEM

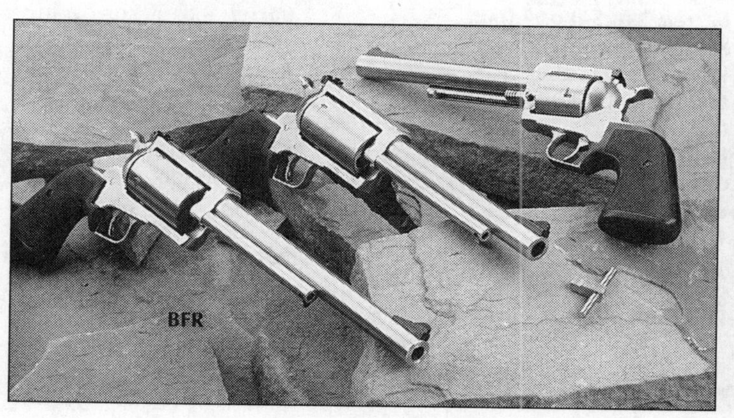
BFR

MOA Handguns

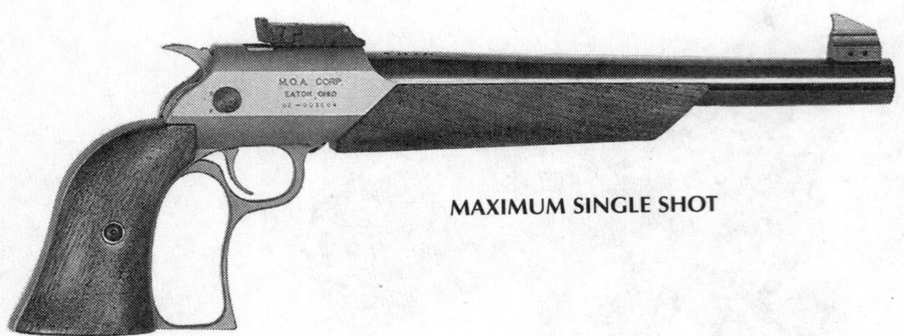

MAXIMUM SINGLE SHOT

MAXIMUM

Action: hinged breech
Grips: walnut
Barrel: 8.5, 10.5 or 14 in.
Sights: target
Weight: 56.0 oz.
Caliber: most rifle chamberings from .22 Hornet to .375 H&H
Capacity: 1
Features: stainless breech, Douglas barrel; extra barrels, muzzle brake available
Maximum $823
with stainless barrel $919
extra barrels $269

Navy Arms Handguns

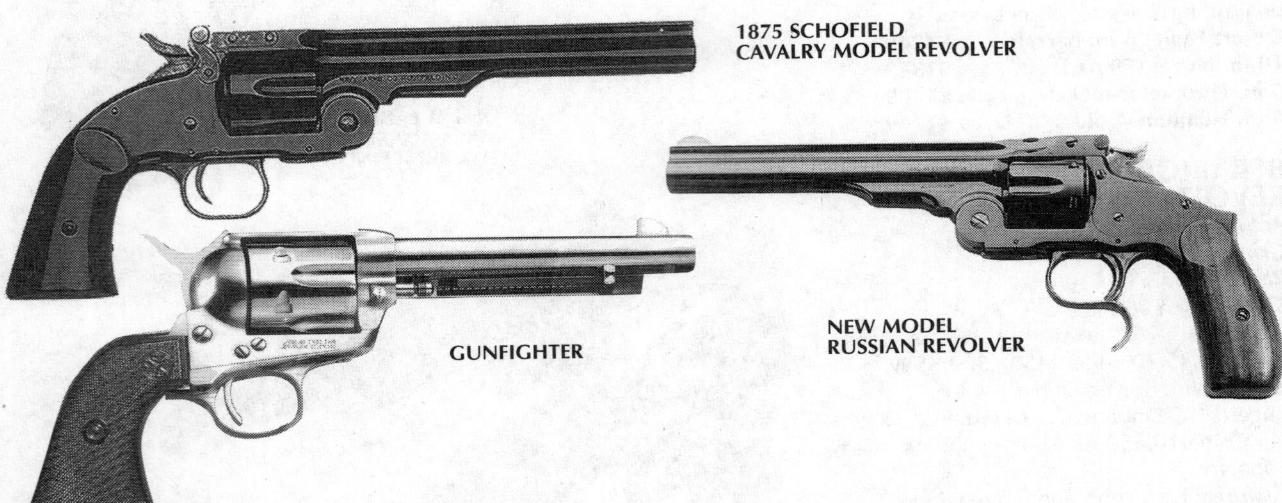
1875 SCHOFIELD CAVALRY MODEL REVOLVER

NEW MODEL RUSSIAN REVOLVER

GUNFIGHTER

MODEL 1875 SCHOFIELD

Action: double-action revolver
Grips: walnut
Barrel: 3.5, 5.0 or 7.0 in.
Sights: fixed open
Weight: 35.0 oz.
Caliber: .44-40, .45 Colt, .38 Spl.
Capacity: 6
Features: top-break action, automatic ejectors; 5 in barrel (37 oz.) and 7 in. barrel (39 oz.)
1875 Schofield $811
1873 U.S. Cavalry Model (7.5 in.). $550
Flat Top target (7.5 in.) $514

BISLEY

Action: single-action revolver
Grips: walnut
Barrel: 4.8, 5.5 or 7.5 in.
Sights: fixed open
Weight: 45.0 oz.
Caliber: .44-40, .45 Colt
Capacity: 6
Features: Bisley grip case-colored frame; weight to 48 oz.
Bisley $502

NEW MODEL RUSSIAN

Action: double-action revolver
Grips: walnut
Barrel: 6.5 in.
Sights: fixed open
Weight: 40.0 oz.
Caliber: .44 Russian
Capacity: 6
Features: top-break action
New Model Russian $893

GUNFIGHTER SERIES

Action: single-action revolver
Grips: walnut
Barrel: 4.8, 5.5, 7.5 in.
Sights: fixed open
Weight: 47.0 oz.
Caliber: .357, .44-40, .45 Colt
Capacity: 6
Features: case-colored frames, after 1873 Colt design
Gunfighter $479
stainless $569

North American Arms Handguns

GUARDIAN .32

Action: autoloader
Grips: polymer
Barrel: 2.5 in.
Sights: fixed open
Weight: 12.0 oz.
Caliber: .32 ACP or .25 NAA
Capacity: 6 + 1
Features: stainless, double action
Guardian. \$402

MINI REVOLVER

Action: single-action revolver
Grips: laminated rosewood
Barrel: 1.2 in.
Sights: fixed open
Weight: 5.0 oz.
Caliber: .22 Short, .22 LR, .22 WMR, .17 MACH2, .17 HMR
Capacity: 5
Features: holster grip
.22 Short, .22 LR, .17 MACH2 . \$193
with holster grip \$215
.22 Magnum, .17 HMR \$208
.22 Magnum with holster grip . . \$229

MINI MASTER SERIES REVOLVER

Action: single-action revolver
Grips: rubber
Barrel: 2 or 4 in.
Sights: fixed or adjustable
Weight: 8.8 oz (2 in.) or 10.7 oz (4 in.)
Caliber: .22LR or .22 Mag., .17 MACH2, .17 HMR
Capacity: 5
Features: conversion cylinder or adjustable sights available
.22 Mag, LR (2 in.), .17 MACH2 or .17 HMR. . . . \$258
.22 Mag w/conversion .22 LR (2 in.). \$287
.22 Mag or LR (4 in.). \$272
.22 Mag w/conversion .22 LR (4 in.) or .17 HMR with .17 MACH2 conversion . . \$301

GUARDIAN .380

Action: autoloader
Grips: composite
Barrel: 2.5 in.
Sights: fixed open
Weight: 18.8 oz.
Caliber: .380 ACP or .32 NAA
Capacity: 6
Features: stainless, double action
Guardian. \$449

GUARDIAN 32

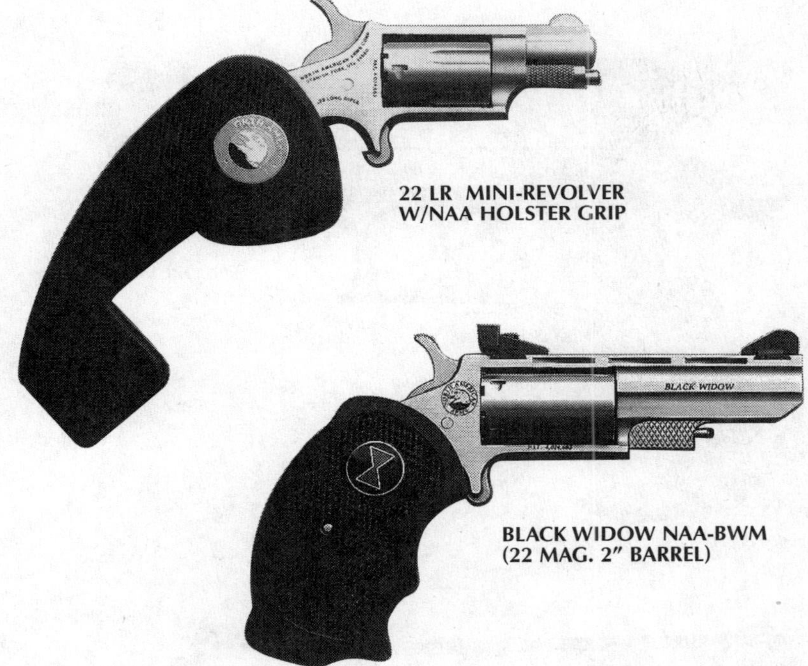

22 LR MINI-REVOLVER W/NAA HOLSTER GRIP

BLACK WIDOW NAA-BWM (22 MAG. 2" BARREL)

GUARDIAN.380

HANDGUNS

Olympic Arms Handguns

COHORT

COHORT

Action: autoloader
Grips: walnut
Barrel: 4 in. bull
Sights: target
Weight: 38.0 oz.
Caliber: .45 ACP
Capacity: 7 + 1
Features: single action on 1911 Colt design, extended beavertail, stainless or parkerized

Cohort $649

ENFORCER

ENFORCER

Action: autoloader
Grips: walnut
Barrel: 4 in. bull
Sights: low-profile combat
Weight: 36.0 oz.
Caliber: .45 ACP
Capacity: 6 + 1
Features: single action on 1911 Colt design; extended beavertail, stainless or parkerized

Enforcer $625

MATCHMASTER

Action: autoloader
Grips: walnut
Barrel: 5 or 6 in.
Sights: target
Weight: 40.0 – 44.0 oz.
Caliber: .45 ACP
Capacity: 7 + 1
Features: single action on 1911 Colt design; extended beavertail, stainless or parkerized

Matchmaster 5 in. $595
6 in. barrel (44 oz.). $645
Big Deuce (Two-Tone). $695

MATCHMASTER

Para Ordnance Handguns

PXT 1911

PARA CCW

PARA CARRY

PXT 1911 PISTOLS

Action: single-action autoloading
Grips: cocobolo with gold medallion and beavertail extension
Barrel: 3.5, 4.25 and 5 in.
Sights: blade front, white three-dot rear
Weight: 32 - 39 oz.
Caliber: .45 ACP
Magazine Capacity: 7+1
Features: match trigger, extended slide lock, Para Kote Regal finish, stainless competition hammer; ramped stainless barrel
List price: . . . . $840 - 988

CCW AND COMPANION CARRY

Action: Double-action autoloader
Grips: Cocobolo
Barrel: 2.5, 3.5 or 4.1 in.
Sights: low-profile combat
Weight: 32.0 – 34.0 oz.
Caliber: .45 ACP
Capacity: 7 + 1
Features: double action, stainless; Tritium night sights available
4.25 in. CCW $988
3.5 in. Companion Carry. $988

HANDGUNS

Para Ordnance Handguns

LDA

MODEL P12•45 ACP
(3.5″ BARREL, STAINLESS)

TAC-FOUR

LDA SERIES HIGH CAPACITY

Action: autoloader
Grips: composite
Barrel: 4.25 or 5.0 in. ramped
Sights: target
Weight: 37.0 – 40.0 oz.
Caliber: 9mm, .40 S&W or .45 ACP
Capacity: 14 + 1, 16 + 1, 18 + 1
Features: double action, double-stack magazine; stainless
LDA. . . . . $899 – 1135
Carry option, 3.5 in. barrel . . . $1075

LDA SINGLE STACK

Action: double-action autoloader
Grips: composite
Barrel: 3.5, 4.25 or 5 in.
Sights: target
Weight: 32.0 – 40.0 oz.
Caliber: .45 ACP
Capacity: 7 + 1
Features: ramped, stainless barrel
Price: . . . . $899 - 1135

P-SERIES

Action: single-action autoloader
Grips: composite
Barrel: 3.0, 3.5, 4.25, or 5.0 in.
Sights: fixed open
Weight: 24.0 – 40.0 oz.
Caliber: 9mm, .45 ACP
Capacity: 10 + 1 to 18 + 1
Features: customized 1911 Colt design, beveled magazine well, polymer magazine; also available with 3-dot or low-profile combat sights; stainless
P-Series . . . . $855 – 995

TAC-FOUR

Action: double-action autoloader
Grips: black polymer
Barrel: 4.25 in.
Sights: low-profile combat
Weight: 36.0 oz.
Caliber: .45 ACP
Capacity: 13 + 1
Features: double action, stainless; flush hammer, bobbed beavertail
Tac-Four $973

Rossi Handguns

MODEL R352

MODEL R461

MODEL R972 .357
MAGNUM 6-SHOT

MODEL R352

Action: double-action revolver
Grips: rubber
Barrel: 2 in.
Sights: fixed open
Weight: 24.0 oz.
Caliber: .38 Spl.
Capacity: 6
Features: stainless; R351 chrome-moly also available
R352 stainless $345
R351 blue $298
R851, 4 in. barrel blue $298

MODEL R462

Action: double-action revolver
Grips: rubber
Barrel: 2 in.
Sights: fixed open
Weight: 26.0 oz.
Caliber: .357 Mag.
Capacity: 6
Features: stainless; R461 chrome-moly also available
R462 stainless $345
R461 blue $298

MODEL R972

Action: double-action revolver
Grips: rubber
Barrel: 6
Sights: target
Weight: 34.0 oz.
Caliber: .357 Mag.
Capacity: 6
Features: stainless after S&W M19 pattern; also R971 chrome-moly with 4 in. barrel
R972 stainless $391
R971 blue $345

Zero ordinary pistol sights for a "6-o'clock" hold. The top of the blade front sight should appear at the top of the rear notch and tangent to the bottom of a bullseye.

Ruger Handguns

REDHAWK REVOLVER

STAINLESS REDHAWK

SUPER REDHAWK

SUPER REDHAWK GREY STAINLESS

NEW VAQUERO SINGLE ACTION

REDHAWK

Action: double-action revolver
Grips: Rosewood
Barrel: 5.5 or 7.5 in.
Sights: target
Weight: 49.0 oz.
Caliber: .44 Mag.
Capacity: 6
Features: stainless model available; 7.5 in. version weighs 54 oz.; scope rings available

Redhawk $633
stainless $695
stainless with rings $742

SUPER REDHAWK

Action: double-action revolver
Grips: rubber/black laminate
Barrel: 7.5 or 9.5 in.
Sights: target
Weight: 53.0 oz.
Caliber: .44 Mag., .454 Casull, .480 Ruger
Capacity: 6
Features: gray finish; 9.5 in. version weighs 58 oz.

.44 Magnum $742
.454, .480 Ruger $819

NEW VAQUERO

Action: single-action revolver
Grips: black, checkered
Barrel: 4.6, 5.5 or 7.5 in.
Sights: fixed open
Weight: 37.0 – 41.0 oz.
Caliber: .357, or .45 Colt
Capacity: 6
Features: gloss stainless or color case, reverse indexing pawl

Vaquero $583

NEW MODEL SUPER BLACKHAWK

Action: single-action revolver
Grips: walnut
Barrel: 4.6, 5.5, 7.5 or 10.5 in.
Sights: target
Weight: 45.0 – 55.0 oz.
Caliber: .44 Mag.
Capacity: 6
Features: weight to 51 oz. depending on barrel length; also available: Super Black-hawk Hunter, stainless with 7.5 in. barrel, black laminated grips, rib, scope rings

blue $562
stainless $577
Super Blackhawk Hunter $676

NEW MODEL SINGLE SIX

Action: single-action revolver
Grips: rosewood or Micarta
Barrel: 4.6, 5.5, 6.5 or 9.5 in.
Sights: fixed open
Weight: 33.0 – 45.0 oz.
Caliber: .22 LR, .22 WMR, .17 HMR, .17 MACH2
Capacity: 6
Features: adjustable sights available; weight to 38 oz. depending on barrel length

Single Six $411
stainless. . . . . $485 - 650
.32 H&R $675
.17 HMR/.17 MACH2 convertible $675

NEW MODEL SUPER BLACKHAWK

SUPER BLACKHAWK

NEW MODEL BLACKHAWK HUNTER

NEW MODEL SINGLE-SIX

NEW MODEL SINGLE-SIX WITH ROSEWOOD GRIPS

NEW MODEL SUPER SINGLE-SIX

HANDGUNS

Ruger Handguns

BISLEY SINGLE-ACTION TARGET

BISLEY

Action: single-action revolver
Grips: walnut
Barrel: 6.5 (.22 LR) or 7.5 in.
Sights: target
Weight: 43.0 to 50 oz.
Caliber: .22 LR, .357 Mag., .44 Mag., .45 Colt
Capacity: 6
Features: rimfire and centerfire (48 oz.); low-profile hammer
.22 . . . . $461
.357, .44, .45 . . . . $580

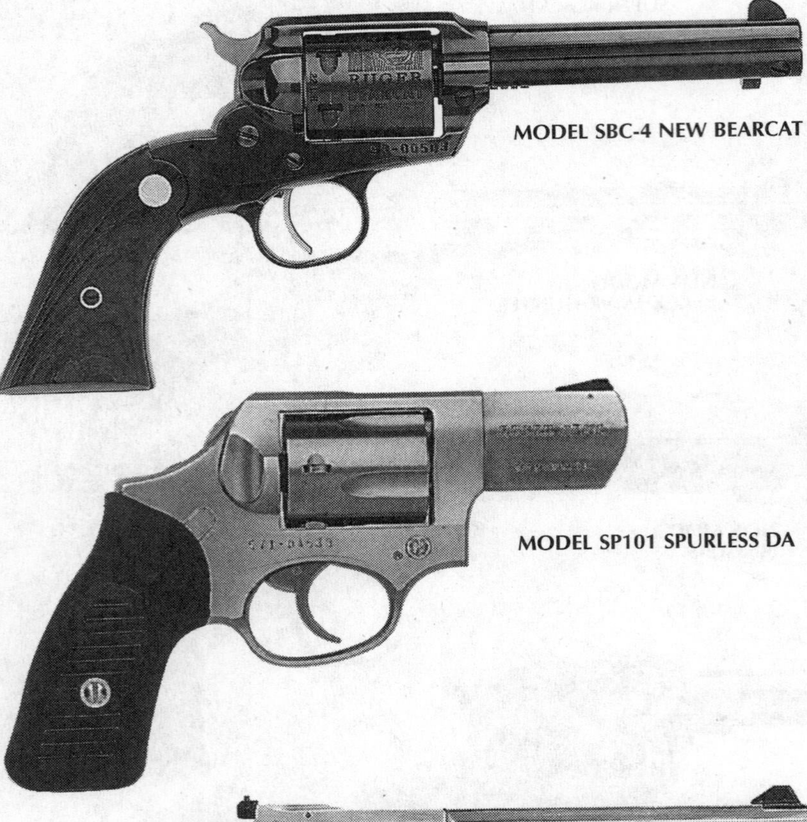

MODEL SBC-4 NEW BEARCAT

MODEL SP101 SPURLESS DA

MODEL SBC-4 NEW BEARCAT

Action: single-action revolver
Grips: rosewood
Barrel: 4 in.
Sights: fixed open
Weight: 24.0 oz.
Caliber: .22 LR
Capacity: 6
Features: transfer bar
New Bearcat $398
stainless $450

MODEL SP101

Action: double-action revolver
Grips: rubber with synthetic insert
Barrel: 2.3, 3.0, or 4.0
Sights: fixed open (adjustable on .32 H&R)
Weight: 25.0 – 30.0 oz.
Caliber: .32 H&R, .38 Spl., .357
Capacity: 5 or 6
Features: chrome-moly or stainless; weight to 30 oz. depending on barrel length
SP101 . . . . $515

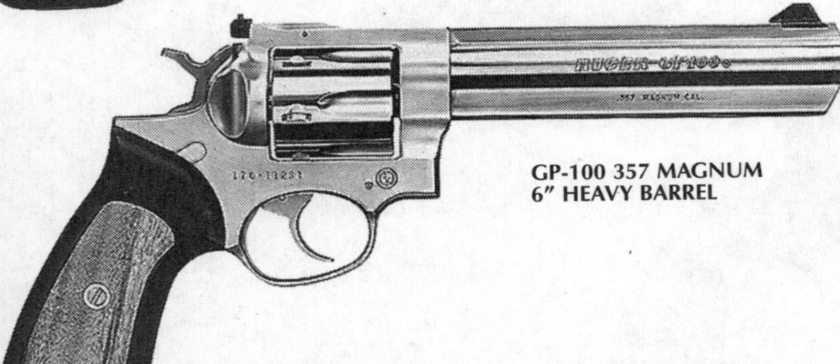

GP-100 357 MAGNUM
6" HEAVY BARREL

GP100

Action: single-action revolver
Grips: rubber with rosewood insert
Barrel: 3.4 or 6 in.
Weight: 38 – 46 oz.
Caliber: .38 Spl. or .357
Capacity: 6
Features: chrome-moly or stainless, weight to 46 oz. depending on barrel length
GP100. . . . . $541
GP100 stainless. $580

Ruger Handguns

MODEL P95D

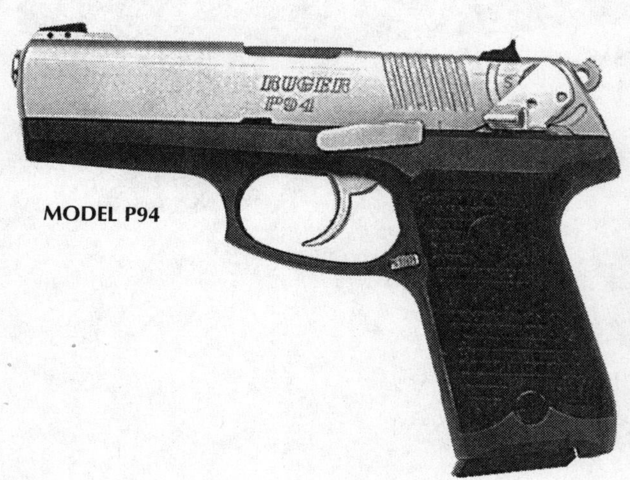

MODEL P94

MODEL P89D

P-SERIES

Action: autoloader
Grips: polymer
Barrel: 3.9 or 4.5 in.
Sights: fixed open
Weight: 30.0 oz.
Caliber: 9mm, .40 S&W, .45 Auto
Capacity: 10 + 1
(8 + 1 in .45, 15 + 1 in 9mm)
Features: double action, ambidextrous grip, safety; decocker on some models, manual safety on others.

P90 (.45 Auto, 4.5 in.). $525
KP90 stainless $565
P944 (.40 S&W, 4.2 in.) $495
stainless $575
P8915 (9mm, 4.5 in.) $475
Stainless $525
P9515 (9mm, 3.9 in.) $425
stainless $475

HANDGUNS

Savage Handguns

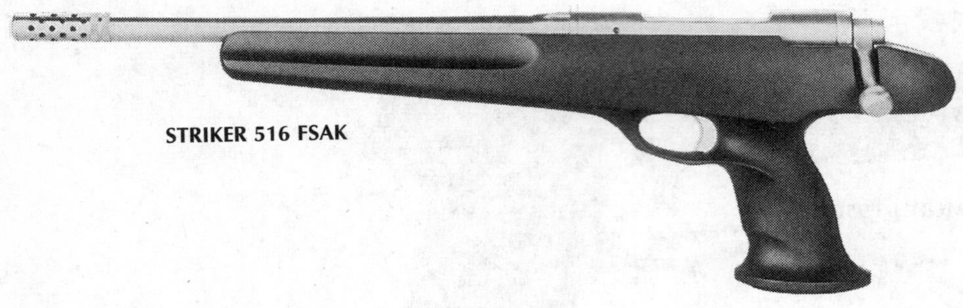

STRIKER 516 FSAK

STRIKER 516 FSAK
CAMO

STRIKER 501, 502, 503

Action: bolt
Grips: synthetic
Barrel: 10 in.
Sights: none
Weight: 64.0 oz.
Caliber: .22 LR, .22 WMR, .17 HMR
Capacity: 5 + 1
Features: left-hand bolt, right-hand ejection

.22 LR **$245**
.22 WMR **$269**
.17 HMR **$295**

STRIKER 516 FSAK

Action: bolt
Grips: synthetic
Barrel: 14 in.
Sights: none
Weight: 78.0 oz.
Caliber: .243, 7mm-08, .308, .270 WSM, 7mm WSM, .300 WSM
Capacity: 2 + 1
Features: stainless, with muzzle brake

FSAK **$621**

Red dot sights and the Bushnell Holo-Sight are particularly useful on handguns because they're lightweight and don't require your eye to be "on-axis" for an accurate shot.

Sigarms Handguns

P226
Action: autoloader
Grips: polymer
Barrel: 4.4 in.
Sights: fixed
Weight: 28.3 oz. - 30.6 oz
Caliber: 9mm; 357 SIG, 40 S&W with optional barrel
Capacity: 10 + 1
Features: Stainless steel slide; reversible magazine release; 6.3-inch sight radius; available in Nitron and two-tone finishes; overall length 7.7 inches
Nitron: $840
Two-tone: $896

MODEL P226

MODEL P229
Action: autoloader
Grips: polymer
Barrel: 3.9 in.
Sights: fixed open
Weight: 24.5 oz.
Caliber: 9mm, .357 Sig, .40 S&W
Capacity: 10 + 1
Features: "Nitron" stainless finish; tac rail,Siglite night sights available for about $100 extra; also P226 with 4.4 in. barrel
P229 . . . . $840
two-Tone. $896

MODEL P229

MODEL P232
Action: autoloader
Grips: polymer
Barrel: 3.6 in.
Sights: fixed open
Weight: 16.2 oz.
Caliber: .380
Capacity: 7 + 1
Features: double action, available with Siglite night sights
P232 . . . . $516
two-tone $535
stainless $559

MODEL P232

Optical sights on handguns should be of low power, for a big field and to keep barrel wobble from appearing so violent as to impair aim.

Sig Handguns

MODEL P239

MODEL P239

Action: autoloader
Grips: polymer
Barrel: 3.6 in.
Sights: target
Weight: 27.0 oz.
Caliber: 9mm, .357 Sig, .40 S&W
Capacity: 7 + 1
Features: stainless, double action

P239 . . . . $642
with Siglite night sights $745
two-tone $696
with night sights $800

MODEL PL 22
TRAILSIDE
COMPETITION

MODEL PL22 TRAILSIDE

Action: autoloader
Grips: rubber or walnut
Barrel: 4.5 or 6.0 in.
Sights: target
Weight: 26.0 oz.
Caliber: .22 LR
Capacity: 10 + 1
Features: all versions have a top rail for scope mounts

4.5 in. standard. $455
4.5 in. target. $534
6 in. standard $540
6 in. target $559
6 in. competition $710

PRO PISTOL
TWO TONE

PRO

Action: autoloader
Grips: polymer
Barrel: 3.9 in.
Sights: fixed open
Weight: 29.0 oz.
Caliber: .357 Sig, .40 S&W, 9mm
Capacity: 10 + 1
Features: polymer frame, stainless slide, double action; Siglite night sights available

Pro $640
Two-Tone. $671
Pro with night sights $700
Two-Tone with night sights $717

Smith & Wesson Handguns

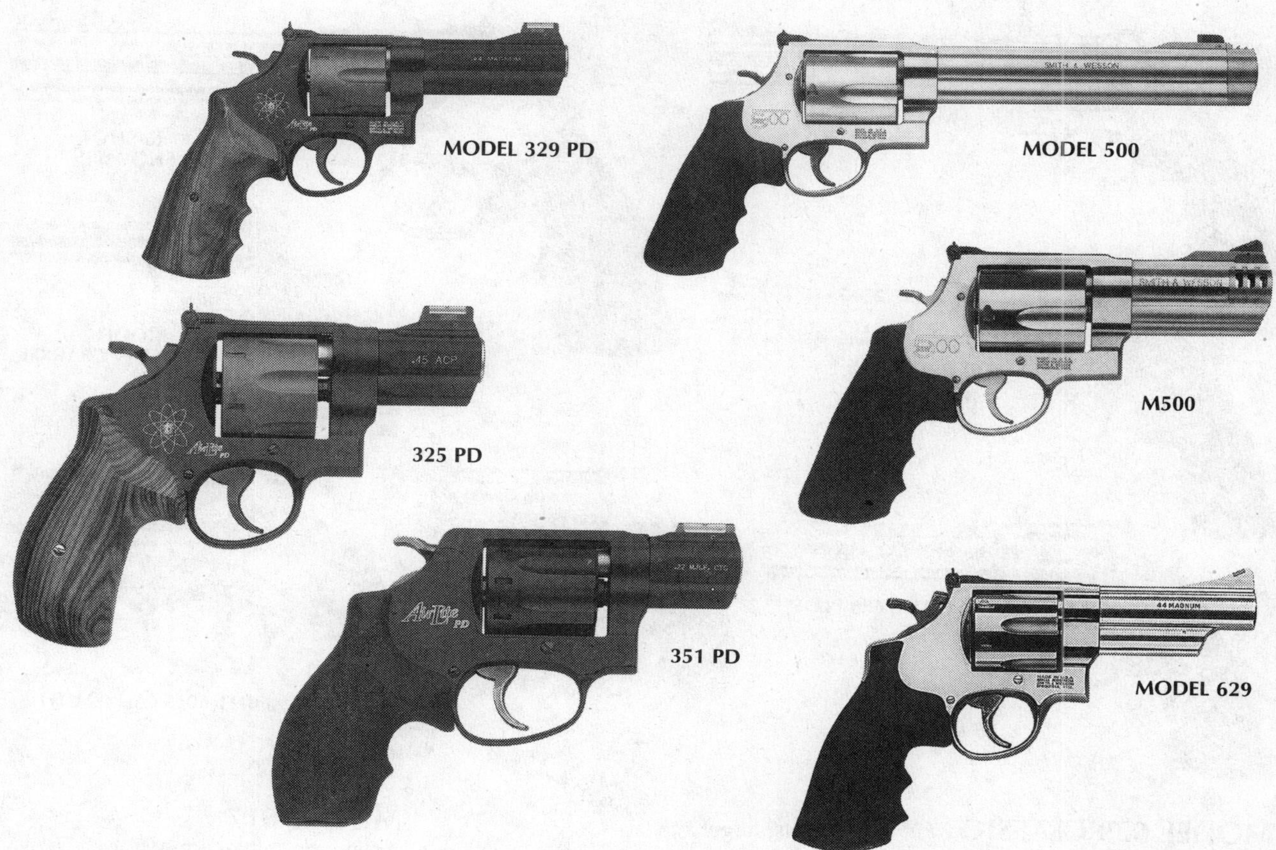
MODEL 329 PD
MODEL 500
325 PD
M500
351 PD
MODEL 629

S&W .500 "SHORT BARREL"

Action: double-action revolver
Grips: rubber
Barrel: 4 in., sleeved, with brake
Sights: adjustable rear, red ramp front
Weight: 56 oz.
Caliber: .500 S&W
Capacity: 5
Price: $1196

S&W MODELS 325 PD AND 351 PD REVOLVER

Action: double-action revolver
Grips: wood (.45), rubber (.22)
Barrel: 2¾ in. (.45), 1⅞ in. (.22)
Sights: adjustable rear, HiViz front (.45), fixed rear, red ramp front (.22)
Weight: 21.5 oz. (.45), 10.6 oz. (.22)
Caliber: .45 ACP (Model 325), .22 WMR (Model 351)
Capacity: 6 (.45), 7 (.22)
Price: (.45) $939
(.22) $647

MODEL 329 PD

Action: double-action revolver
Grips: wood
Barrel: 4 in.
Sights: adjustable fiber optic
Weight: 27.0 oz.
Caliber: .44 Mag.
Capacity: 6
Features: scandium frame, titanium cylinder
329 PD $960

MODEL 500

Action: double-action revolver
Grips: Hogue Sorbathane
Barrel: ported 8.4 in.
Sights: target
Weight: 72.5 oz.
Caliber: .500 S&W
Capacity: 5
Features: X-Frame, double-action stainless revolver
Model 500.......... $1130 – 1234
Model 460 (.460 S&W)...... $1253

MODEL 625

Action: double-action revolver
Grips: Hogue rubber, round butt
Barrel: 4 or 5 in.
Sights: target
Weight: 49.0 oz.
Caliber: .45 ACP
Capacity: 6
Features: N-frame, stainless; also in Model 610 10mm with 4 in. barrel; 5 in. Barrel: 51 oz.
Model 625 .... $817
625 jerry Miculek $845

MODEL 629

Action: double-action revolver
Grips: Hogue rubber
Barrel: 4 or 6 in.
Sights: target
Weight: 44.0 oz.
Caliber: .44 Mag.
Capacity: 6
Features: N-frame, stainless; 6 in. weighs 47 oz.
4 in. $787
6 in. $810

Smith & Wesson Handguns

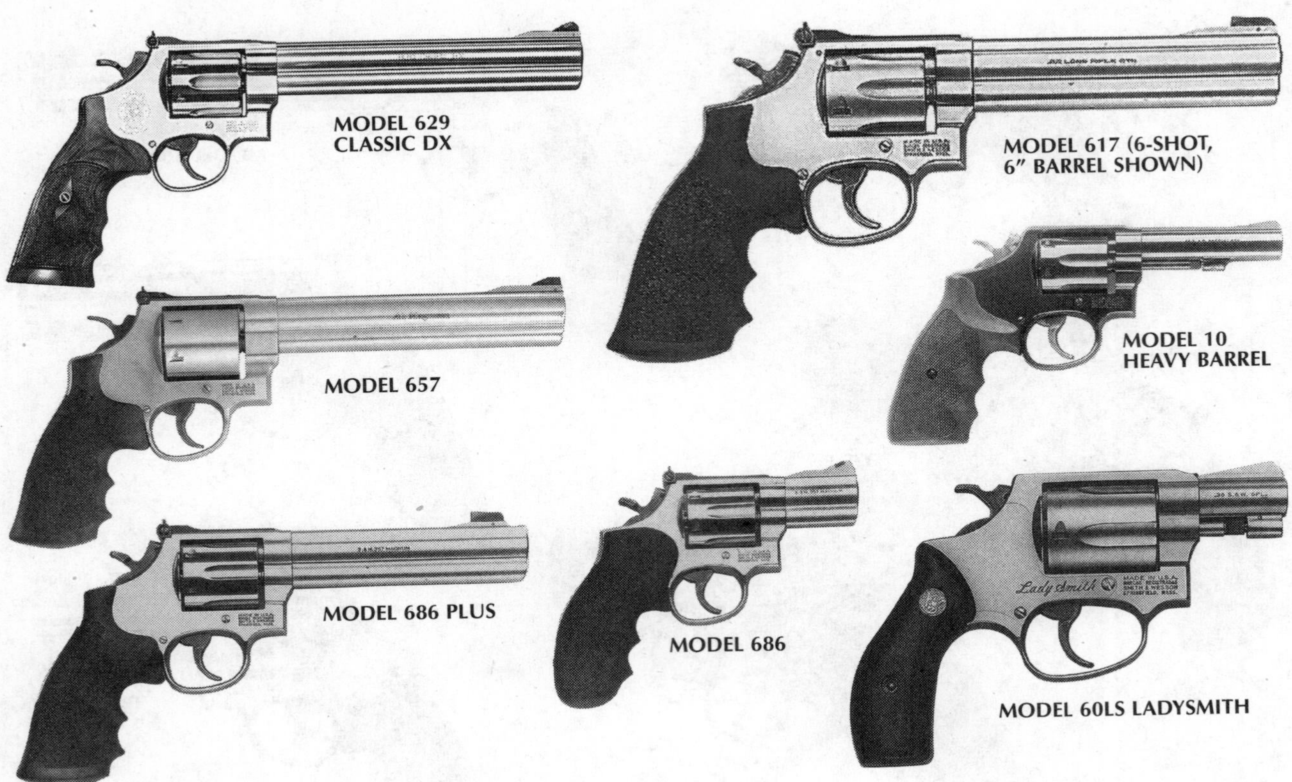
MODEL 629 CLASSIC DX

MODEL 617 (6-SHOT, 6" BARREL SHOWN)

MODEL 657

MODEL 10 HEAVY BARREL

MODEL 686 PLUS

MODEL 686

MODEL 60LS LADYSMITH

MODEL 629 CLASSIC

Action: double-action revolver
Grips: Hogue rubber
Barrel: 5.0, 6.5 or 8.4 in.
Sights: target
Weight: 51.0 oz.
Caliber: .44 Mag.
Capacity: 6
Features: N-frame, stainless, full lug; weight to 54 oz. depending on barrel length
5.0 or 6.5 in. . . . . $843 - 894
8.4 in. $871

MODEL 657

Action: double-action revolver
Grips: Hogue rubber
Barrel: 7.5 in.
Sights: target
Weight: 52.0 oz.
Caliber: .41 Mag.
Capacity: 6
Features: N-frame stainless
Model 657 . . . . $774

MODEL 686

Action: single-action revolver
Grips: combat or target
Barrel: 2.5, 4, 6, 8.4 in.
Sights: target
Weight: 34.5 oz.
Caliber: .357 Mag.
Capacity: 6
Features: stainless, K-frame 686 Plus holds 7 rounds; to 48 oz. depending on barrel length
2.5 in. $667
4 in. $694
6 in. $700
6 in. ported. $747
2.5 in. Plus $692
4 in. Plus. $716
6 in. Plus. $727

MODEL 10

Action: double-action revolve
Grips: Uncle Mike's Combat
Barrel: 4.0 in. heavy
Sights: fixed open
Weight: 33.5 oz.
Caliber: .38 Spl.
Capacity: 6
Features: "military and police" model; also in stainless, K-frame
Model 10 . . . . $554
stainless Model 64 . . . . $583
stainless with 2 in. barrel, round butt. $583

MODEL 617

Action: double-action revolver
Grips: Hogue rubber
Barrel: 4.0, 6.0, 8.4 in.
Sights: target
Weight: 42.0 oz.
Caliber: .22 LR
Capacity: 6
Features: stainless, target hammer and trigger, K-frame; weight to 54 oz. depending on barrel length
4 in. $707
6 in. $686
6 in., 10-shot. $734

MODEL 36-LS

Action: double-action revolver
Grips: laminated rosewood, round butt
Barrel: 1.8, 2.2, 3 in.
Sights: fixed open
Weight: 20.0 oz.
Caliber: .38 Spl.
Capacity: 5
Features: weight to 24 oz. depending on barrel length; stainless version in .357 Mag. available (60 LS)
Model 36 LS $568
60 LS. $621

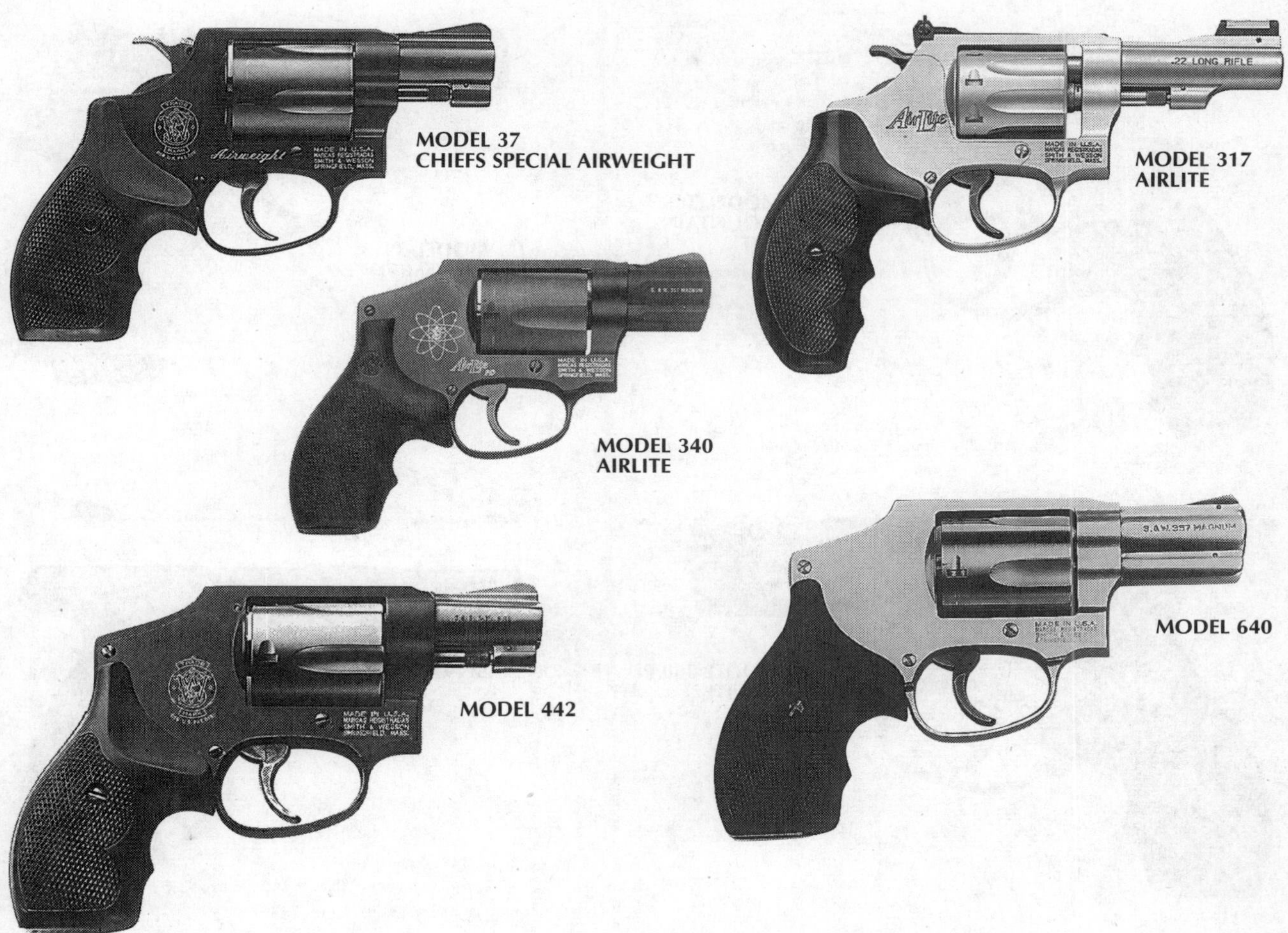

MODEL 37
CHIEFS SPECIAL AIRWEIGHT

MODEL 317
AIRLITE

MODEL 340
AIRLITE

MODEL 640

MODEL 442

MODEL 37 CHIEF'S SPECIAL AIRWEIGHT

Action: double-action revolver
Grips: uncle Mike's boot
Barrel: 1.8
Sights: fixed open
Weight: 11.9 oz.
Caliber: .38 Spl.
Capacity: 5
Features: alloy frame (also M37 in blue finish)
Model 637 . . . . $450
Model 37 . . . . $573

MODEL 317

Action: double-action revolver
Grips: rubber
Barrel: 1.8 or 3 in.
Sights: fixed open
Weight: 10.5 oz.
Caliber: .22 LR
Capacity: 8
Features: alloy frame
1.8 in. $603
3 in. $658

MODEL 340 AIRLITE

Action: double-action revolver
Grips: rubber
Barrel: 1.8 in.
Sights: fixed open
Weight: 12.0 oz.
Caliber: .357 Mag.
Capacity: 5
Features: Scandium alloy frame, titanium cylinder
Model 340 . . . . $838 - 862
with Hi-Viz sight $877

MODEL 442 AIRWEIGHT

Action: double-action revolver
Grips: rubber
Barrel: 1.8 in.
Sights: fixed open
Weight: 15.0 oz.
Caliber: .38 Spl.
Capacity: 5
Features: stainless Model 642 and 442 are concealed-hammer, double-action only
Model 442 . . . . $600

MODEL 640 CENTENNIAL

Action: double-action revolver
Grips: rubber
Barrel: 2.2
Sights: fixed open
Weight: 23.0 oz.
Caliber: .357
Capacity: 5
Features: stainless, concealed-hammer, double-action-only; also M649 Bodyguard single or double-action
M640 . . . . $658
M649 . . . . $651

Smith & Wesson Handguns

MODEL 386 MOUNTAIN LITE

MODEL 3913 LADYSMITH

MODEL 360 PD AIRLITE

SW9 VE

MODEL 386

Action: double-action revolver
Grips: rubber
Barrel: 3.2 in.
Sights: low-profile combat
Weight: 18.5 oz.
Caliber: .357 Mag.
Capacity: 7
Features: Scandium alloy frame, titanium cylinder
Model 386 . . . . $876
2.5 in. barrel $872

MODEL 360 AIRLITE

Action: double-action revolver
Grips: rubber
Barrel: 1.8 in.
Sights: fixed open
Weight: 12.0 oz.
Caliber: .357 Mag.
Capacity: 5
Features: Scandium alloy frame, titanium cylinder
Model 360 . . . . $818
with Hi-Viz sight $858
3.2 in. Kit Gun
with Hi-Viz sight $865

MODEL 3913 LADYSMITH

Action: autoloader
Grips: Hogue rubber
Barrel: 3.5 in.
Sights: low-profile combat
Weight: 24.8 oz.
Caliber: 9mm
Capacity: 8 + 1
Features: double action, stainless
Model 3913 . . . . $858

MODEL SW40G, P AND VE

Action: autoloader
Grips: polymer
Barrel: 4 in.
Sights: 3-dot
Weight: 24.4 oz.
Caliber: .40 S&W
Capacity: 10 + 1
Features: double action stainless slide, polymer frame, finish options
standard $379

MODEL SW 9 VE

Action: autoloader
Grips: polymer
Barrel: 4 in.
Sights: 3-dot
Weight: 24.7 oz.
Caliber: 9mm
Capacity: 10 + 1
Features: double action, stainless slide, polymer frame, finish options
SW9 VE $379

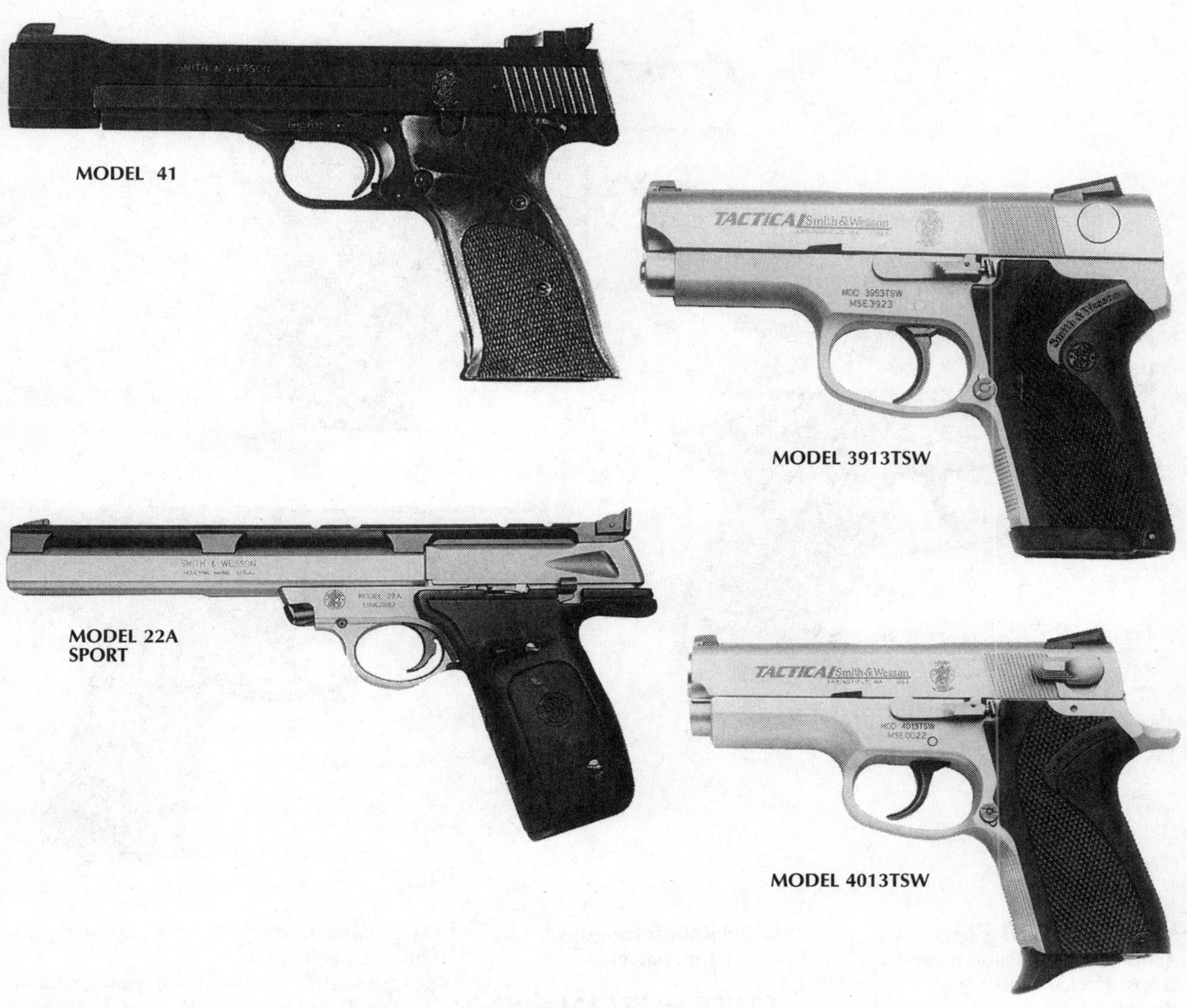

MODEL 41

MODEL 3913TSW

MODEL 22A SPORT

MODEL 4013TSW

MODEL 41

Action: autoloader
Grips: walnut
Barrel: 5.5 or 7 in.
Sights: target
Weight: 41.0 oz.
Caliber: .22 LR
Capacity: 12 + 1
Features: adjustable trigger; 7 in. Barrel: 44 oz.

Model 41 .... $1062

MODEL 22A SPORT

Action: autoloader
Grips: polymer
Barrel: 4, 5.5 or 7 in.
Sights: target
Weight: 28.0 oz.
Caliber: .22 LR
Capacity: 10 + 1
Features: scope mounting rib; 5.5 in. bull barrel available

4 in. $293
5.5 in. (31 oz.) $324
5.5 in. bull $407
5.5 in. bull, Hi-Viz sights $429
7 in. (33 oz.)............... $367
5.5 in. stainless $396

MODEL 3913 TSW (TACTICAL SERIES)

Action: autoloader
Grips: rubber
Barrel: 3.5 in.
Sights: 3-dot
Weight: 24.8 oz.
Caliber: 9mm
Capacity: 8 + 1
Features: alloy frame, stainless slide; also: 3953TSW double-action-only

Model 3913TSW $834

MODEL 4013TSW

Action: autoloader
Grips: rubber
Barrel: 3.5 in.
Sights: 3-dot
Weight: 26.8 oz.
Caliber: .40 S&W
Capacity: 9 + 1
Features: alloy frame, stainless slide, ambidextrous safety; also: 4053TSW double-action-only

Model 4013TSW $973

Smith & Wesson Handguns

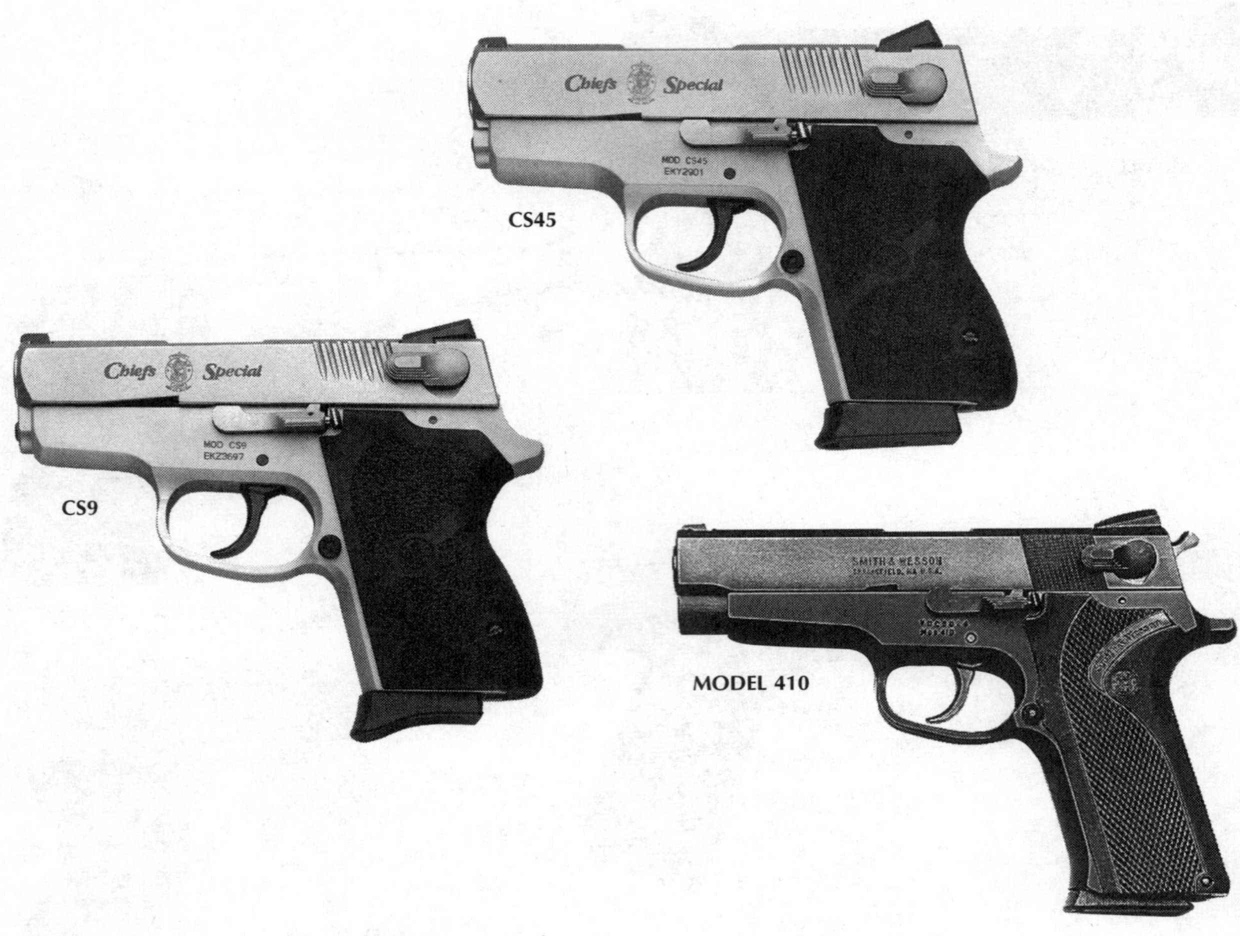

CS45

CS9

MODEL 410

MODEL 4040 PD

Action: double-action revolver
Grips: Hogue rubber
Barrel: 3.5 in.
Sights: 3-dot
Weight: 25.6 oz.
Caliber: .40 S&W
Capacity: 7 + 1
Features: first scandium-frame pistol
4040 PD $840

MODEL SW1911

Action: autoloader
Grips: rubber
Barrel: 5 in.
Sights: low-profile combat
Weight: 39.0 oz.
Caliber: .45 ACP
Capacity: 8 + 1
Features: stainless, extended beaver-tail, match trigger; single action
SW 1911. . . . . $960
w/Crimson Trace grips $1281
w/4.24 in. barrel. $1029

CHIEF'S SPECIAL

Action: autoloader
Grips: rubber
Barrel: 3 or 3.25 in.
Sights: 3-dot
Weight: 20.8 – 24.0 oz.
Caliber: 9mm, .45 ACP
Capacity: 7 + 1 (9mm) and 6 + 1 (.40 S&W)
Features: lightweight, compact
CS 9 . . . . $747
CS 45 . . . . $787

MODEL SW99OL

Action: autoloader
Grips: polymer
Barrel: 3.5, 4 or 5 in.
Sights: low-profile combat
Weight: 22.5 - 25 oz.
Caliber: .45 ACP, .40 S&W, 9mm
Capacity: 8 to 16
Features: double action pistol made in collaboration with Walther
Model 99 OL. $694
in .45 ACP. $736

MODEL 910, 410

Action: autoloader
Grips: rubber
Barrel: 4 in.
Sights: 3-dot
Weight: 28.5 oz.
Caliber: 9mm, .40 S&W
Capacity: 10 + 1
Features: alloy frame, chrome-moly slide, decocking lever; also M457 in .45 ACP, 7 + 1 capacity; Hi-Viz sights extra
Model 910 . . . . $587
Model 410 . . . . $649
Model 457 . . . . $649

Springfield Armory Handguns

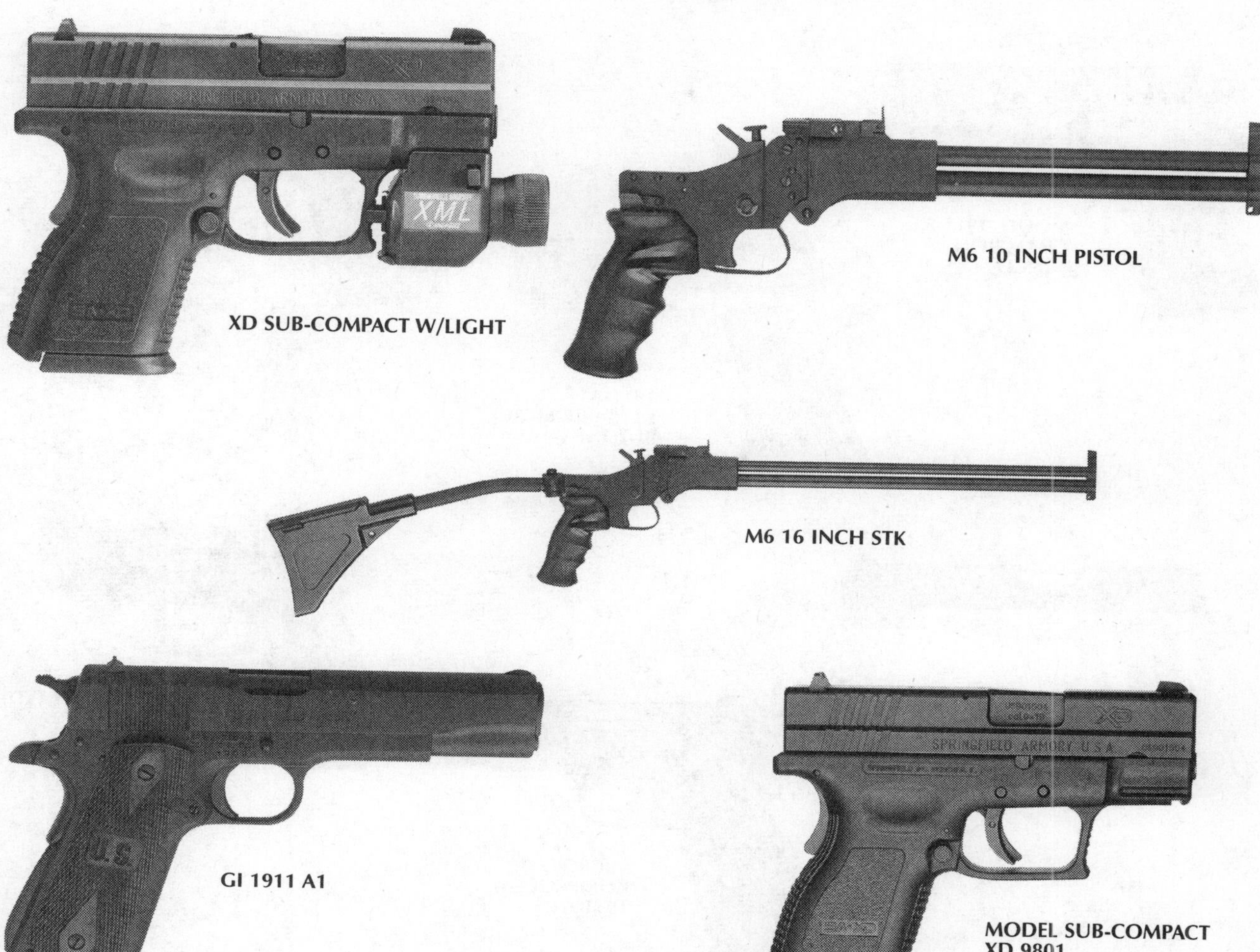

XD SUB-COMPACT W/LIGHT

M6 10 INCH PISTOL

M6 16 INCH STK

GI 1911 A1

MODEL SUB-COMPACT XD 9801

XD SUB-COMPACT W/XML LIGHT

Action: self-loading, short-recoil, locked-breech
Grips: black composite
Barrel: 3.1 in., cold hammer forged
Sights: 3-dot, fixed rear and front
Weight: 20.5 oz.
Caliber: 9x19mm and .40 S&W
Magazine Capacity: 10+1
Features: Polymer frame with heat-treated steel slide and rails, dual recoil springs, three safeties, cocking indicator, light rail (Mini Light optional)
Price: **$585**

GI 1911-A1

Action: autoloading, M1911 design
Grips: double-diamond walnut
Barrel: 5 in.
Sights: early service-style, fixed
Weight: 36 oz.
Caliber: .45 ACP
Capacity: 7+1
Features: forged frame, barrel, slide; titanium firing pin; standard ejection port; vertical slats; lanyard loop
Price: **$502**
Stainless: **$578**
GI Micro Compact (3 in. bbl.) . . **$578**

SPRINGFIELD M6 SCOUT

Action: hinged breech
Grips: synthetic
Barrel: 10 in.
Sights: open
Caliber: .22LR, .22 Hornet (upper barrel) and .45 LC or .410 (lower barrel)
Magazine Capacity: none
Features: over/under combination gun, stainless or parkerized finish.
Price: Parkerized **$199**
Stainless **$223**

MODEL SUB-COMPACT XD 9801

Action: autoloader
Grips: composite
Barrel: 3 in.
Sights: fixed open
Weight: 20.5 oz.
Caliber: 9mm, .40 S&W
Capacity: 10
Features: lightweight polymer frame, stainless magazines; black or OD green
XD **$514**
with Tritium sights **$599**
Bi-Tone **$542**

Springfield Armory Handguns

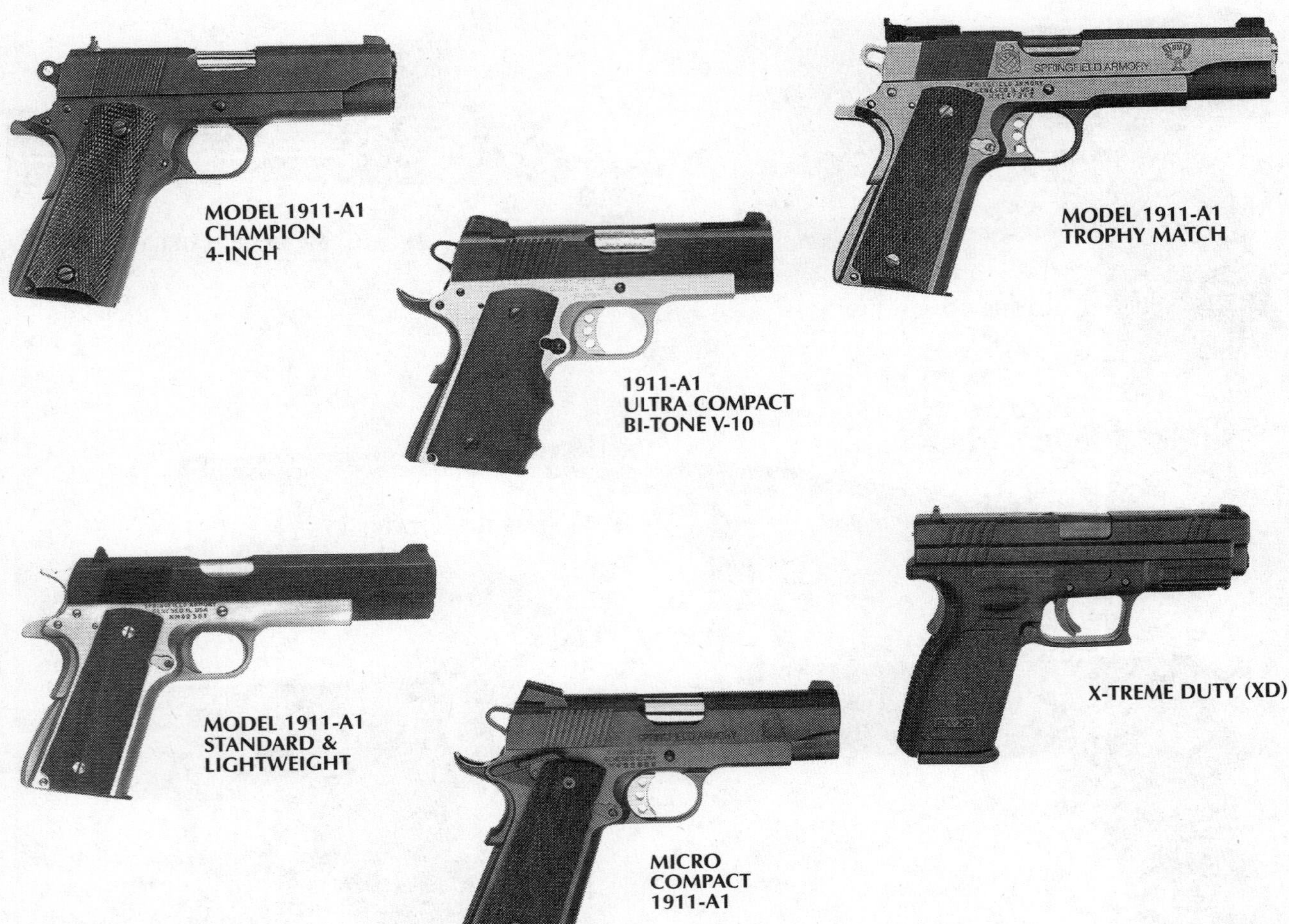

MODEL 1911-A1
CHAMPION
4-INCH

MODEL 1911-A1
TROPHY MATCH

1911-A1
ULTRA COMPACT
BI-TONE V-10

MODEL 1911-A1
STANDARD &
LIGHTWEIGHT

X-TREME DUTY (XD)

MICRO
COMPACT
1911-A1

MODEL 1911 CHAMPION

Action: autoloader
Grips: walnut
Barrel: 4 in.
Sights: fixed open
Weight: 34.0 oz.
Caliber: .45 ACP
Capacity: 7 + 1
Features: Ultra Compact with 3.5 in. barrel, Novak sights, stainless Bi-Tone finish option

Champion **$922**
Ultra Compact **$922**

MODEL 1911 TROPHY MATCH

Action: autoloader
Grips: Cocobolo
Barrel: match-grade, 5 in.
Sights: target
Weight: 38.0 oz.
Caliber: .45 ACP
Capacity: 7 + 1
Features: Videcki speed trigger, serrated front strap, stainless

Trophy Match **$1409**

MODEL 1911-A1

Action: autoloader
Grips: Cocobolo
Barrel: 5 in.
Sights: fixed open
Weight: 38.0 oz.
Caliber: .45 ACP, 9mm
Capacity: 7 + 1
Features: also Lightweight (31.5 oz.) and 3 in. Micro Compact (24 oz.) with alloy frames, stainless

M1911-A1 . . . . **$845 - 948**
Adjustable sights **$938**
Lightweight **$922**
Micro Compact **$1184**

XD SERVICE MODELS

Action: autoloader
Grips: walnut
Barrel: 4 in.
Sights: fixed open
Weight: 22.8oz.
Caliber: 9mm, .357 Sig, .40 S&W, .45 GAP
Capacity: 10 + 1
Features: short recoil, single action, black or OD green

XD **$514**
with Tritium sights **$599**
V-10 Ported **$542**
XD Tactical (5 in. bbl.) **$542**
Bi-Tone (.45 GAP only) **$571**

STI International Inc. Handguns

EDGE
EAGLE
LS AND BLS
EXECUTIVE
LSA LAWMAN

EAGLE

Action: autoloader
Grips: polymer
Barrel: 5 or 6 in.
Sights: target (5 in.), open fixed (6 in.)
Weight: 34.5oz. (5 in.), 40 oz. (6 in.)
Caliber: 9 mm, 9X21, .38Super, .40 S&W, .45ACP
Capacity:
Features: Modular steel frame; classic slide; long curved trigger; fully supported, ramped bull barrel; stainless STI grip and ambidextrous thumb safeties; blue finish
EAGLE (5 in.):. $1,794
EAGLE (6 in.):. $1,894

EDGE

Action: autoloader
Grips: polymer
Barrel:
Sights: target
Weight: 39 oz.
Caliber: 9 mm, .40 S&W, 10 mm, .45ACP
Capacity:
Features: Modular steel, long wide frame; overall length 8 5/8 in.; fully supported, ramped bull barrel; long curved trigger; stainless STI grip and ambidextrous thumb safeties; blue finish
MSRP: **. $1,874**

EXECUTIVE

Action: autoloader
Grips: polymer
Barrel: 5 in.
Sights: target
Weight: 39 oz.
Caliber: .40 S&W
Capacity:
Features: Modular steel, long wide frame; overall length 8⅝ in.; fully supported, ramped bull barrel; long curved trigger; stainless STI grip and ambidextrous thumb safeties
MSRP: **. $2,389**

LS AND BLS

Action: autoloader
Grips: rosewood
Barrel: 3.4 in.
Sights: fixed open
Weight: 30 oz. (LS), 28 oz (BLS)
Caliber: 9 mm, .40 S&W
Capacity: 7+1 (9mm), 6+1 (.40 S&W)
Features: Government size steel frame with full size grip (BLS with officer's size grip); fully supported, ramped bull barrel; undercut trigger guard and front strap; long curved trigger; STI grip and single sided thumb safeties; integral front sight with Heinie low-mount rear sight; flat blue finish; slide does not lock back after last round is fired
LS $889
BLS $789

LSA LAWMAN

Action: autoloader
Grips: rosewood
Barrel: 5 in.
Sights: fixed open
Weight: 40 oz.
Caliber: .45 ACP
Capacity:
Features: Forged steel government-length frame; overall length 8.5 inches; 1911 style slide; fully supported, ramped barrel with match bushing; STI aluminum trigger; STI grip and single sided thumb STI high rise beavertail safeties; two tone polymer finish (light brown over olive drab)
MSRP: **. $1,344**

STI International Inc. Handguns

RANGER II

Action: autoloader
Grips: rosewood
Barrel: 4.15 in.
Sights: fixed open
Weight: 30 oz.
Caliber: .45 ACP
Capacity: 7+1
Features: Commander size with full length 1911-style frame and fully supported barrel; hi-rise trigger guard; 1911-style flat topped slide; long curved trigger with stainless bow; hi-rise grip and single sided thumb safeties; blue finish
MSRP: **$1,029**

RANGEMASTER

Action: autoloader
Grips: rosewood
Barrel: 5 in.
Sights: target
Weight: 38 oz.
Caliber: .9mm, .45 ACP
Capacity:
Features: Single stack government length steel frame; flat top slide; full length dust cover; fully supported, ramped bull barrel; aluminum long curved trigger; polished stainless grip and ambidextrous thumb safeties; overall length 8.5 in.; polished blue finish
MSRP: **$1,440**

TARGETMASTER

Action: autoloader
Grips: rosewood
Barrel: 6 in.
Sights: tarrget
Weight: 40 oz.
Caliber: 9mm, .45 ACP
Capacity:
Features: Single stack government length frame; classic flat top slide; fully supported ramped match bull barrel; overall length 9.5 in.; tri-level adjustable sights; aluminum long curved trigger; STI stainless grip and ambidextrous thumb safeties; polished blue finish
MSRP: **$1,440**

TROJAN

Action: autoloader
Grips: rosewood
Barrel: 5 or 6 in.
Sights: target
Weight: 36 oz. (5 in.); 38 oz. (6 in.)
Caliber: 9 mm, .38Super, .40 S&W, .45 ACP
Capacity:
Features: Single stack government size frame; 5 in. or 6 in. classic flat top slide; fully supported match barrel; high rise grip safety, STI long curved polymer trigger and undercut trigger guard; flat blue finish
Trojan (5 in.): $1,024
Trojan (6 in.): $1,344

VIP

Action: Autoloader (SA)
Grips: polymer
Barrel: 3.9 in.
Sights: fixed open
Weight: 25 oz.
Caliber: 9mm, .38 Super, 9X21, .40 S&W,.45 ACP
Capacity: 10 + 1
Features: Modular aluminum frame; overall length 7.5 in.; classic flat top slide; fully supported, ramped bull barrel; STI long curved trigger; STI stainless grip and single sided thumb safeties
MSRP: **$1,653**

Swiss Arms Handguns

MODEL P210 SPORT

Action: autoloader
Grips: wood
Barrel: 4.8 in.
Sights: target
Weight: 24.0 oz.
Caliber: 9mm
Capacity: 8 + 1
Features: chrome-moly, single action
Swiss Army Service Model . . . $3031
Target grade $2695

P210-8-9

Taurus Handguns

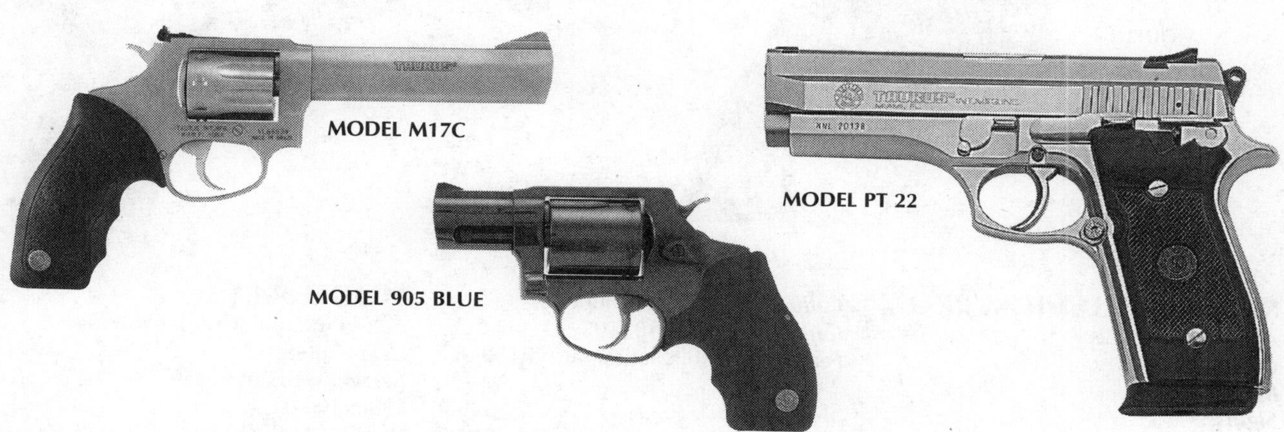
MODEL M17C
MODEL 905 BLUE
MODEL PT 22

MODEL 905

Action: double-action revolver
Grips: rubber
Barrel: 2 in.
Sights: fixed open
Weight: 21.0 oz.
Caliber: 9mm, .40 S&W, .45 ACP 9with 2, 4 or 6.5 inch barrel)
Capacity: 5
Features: stellar clips furnished; UltraLite weighs 17 oz.
blue. $383
stainless $430
.32 Mag. $438

MODEL M17C

Action: double-action revolver
Grips: rubber
Barrel: 2, 4, 5, 6.5 or 12 in.
Sights: target
Weight: 18.5 to 26.0 oz.
Caliber: .17 HMR
Capacity: 8
Features: 8 models available in blued and stainless steel; weight varies with barrel length
blue, 2, 4 or 5 in. barrel $359
Ultralite $391
stainless $406
Ultralite stainless $438
12 in. barrel $430

MODEL PT911 COMPACT

Action: autoloader
Grips: checkered rubber
Barrel: 4 in.
Sights: 3-dot
Weight: 28.2 oz.
Caliber: 9mm
Capacity: 10 + 1 or 15 + 1
Features: double action only; ambidextrous decocker
blue. $523
stainless $539

MODEL PT22

Action: autoloader
Grips: rosewood
Barrel: 2.8 in.
Sights: fixed open
Weight: 12.3 oz.
Caliber: .22 LR
Capacity: 8 + 1
Features: double action only, blue, nickel or DuoTone finish; also in .25 ACP (PT25)
PT22 . . . . $219
with gold trim. $234
with Mother of Pearl grips $250
with checkered wood $219

Taurus Handguns

MILLENIUM PRO

MODEL PT-945

MODEL 44

MODEL 82

MODEL PT-92

MODEL MILLENIUM PRO

Action: autoloader
Grips: polymer
Barrel: 3.25 in.
Sights: 3-dot
Weight: 18.7 oz.
Caliber: 9mm, .40 S&W, .45 ACP, .32 ACP, .380 ACP
Capacity: 10 + 1
Features: double action, polymer frame; also comes with night sights (BL or SS), add $78

.40 blue. $461
.40 stainless $476
.45 blue/composite $461
.45 stainless/composite $476
9mm, .32 or .380 BL. $422
9mm, .32 or .380 SS $438
9mm Titanium $508

MODEL PT945

Action: autoloader
Grips: checkered rubber, rosewood, or Mother of Pearl
Barrel: 4.3 in.
Sights: 3-dot
Weight: 29.5 oz.
Caliber: .45 ACP, .38 Super
Capacity: 8 + 1 (.38: 10 + 1)
Features: double action; also PT38 in .38 Super

blue. $563
stainless $578
stainless, gold, mother of Pearl . $641
stainless rosewood $625
Model 940 blue. $523
Model 940 stainless $539

MODEL 92

Action: autoloader
Grips: Rosewood or rubber
Barrel: 5 in.
Sights: fixed open
Weight: 34.0 oz.
Caliber: 9mm
Capacity: 10 + 1 or 17 + 1
Features: double action; also PT99 with adjustable sights

blue. $578
stainless $594
stainless gold, Mother of Pearl . $656

MODEL 44

Action: double-action revolver
Grips: rubber
Barrel: 4, 6.5 or 8.4 in.
Sights: target
Weight: 44.0 oz.
Caliber: .44 Mag. ***Capacity:*** 6
Features: vent rib, porting; weight to 57 oz. depending on barrel length

stainless, 4 in. $563
stainless, 6.5 in. $578
stainless, 8.4 in. $578

MODEL 82

Action: double-action revolver
Grips: rubber
Barrel: 4 in.
Sights: fixed open
Weight: 36.5 oz.
Caliber: .38 Spl. +P
Capacity: 6
Features: also, 21-ounce model 85 in .38 Spl, with 2 in. barrel, grip options

Model 82, blue $352
Model 82, stainless $398
Model 85, blue $375
Model 85, stainless $422

Taurus Handguns

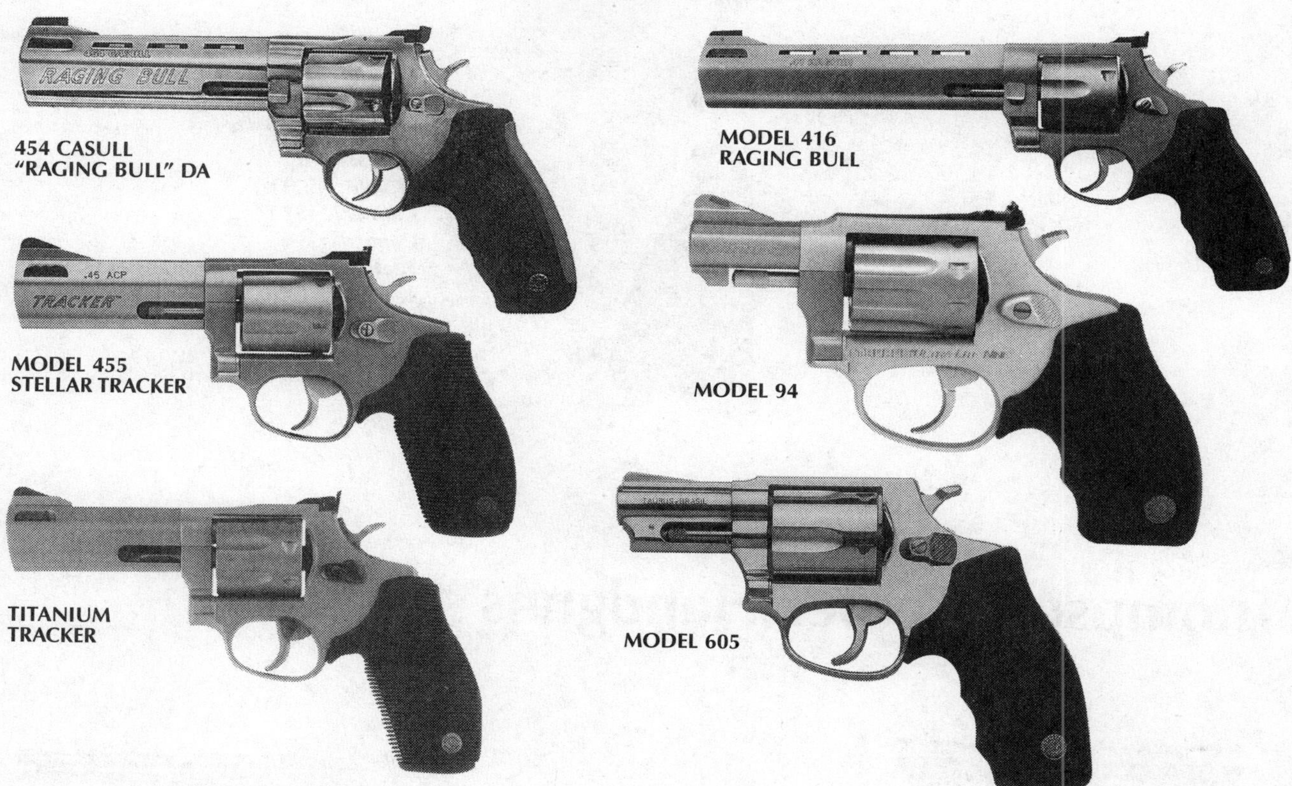

454 CASULL "RAGING BULL" DA

MODEL 416 RAGING BULL

MODEL 455 STELLAR TRACKER

MODEL 94

TITANIUM TRACKER

MODEL 605

PROTECTOR

Action: double-action revolver
Grips: rubber
Barrel: 2 in.
Sights: fixed open
Weight: 24.5 oz.
Caliber: .357 Mag. or .38 Spl.
Capacity: 5
Features: shrouded but accessible hammer; also Titanium and UltraLight versions to 17 oz.

blue $383
stainless $430
Shadow Gray Titanium $547

MODEL RAGING BULL

Action: double-action revolver
Grips: rubber
Barrel: 5, 6.5 or 8.3 in.
Sights: target
Weight: 53 - 63 oz.
Caliber: .41 Mag., .44 Mag., .480 Ruger, 454 Casull
Capacity: 6
Features: stainless vent rib, ported; also 72-ounce 5-shot Raging Bull in .500 Mag with 10 in. barrel

.41 . . . . $641
.44 Mag, blue $578
stainless .44 & .480 Ruger. $641
454 Casull, blue $797
454 Casull, stainless $859
.500 Mag. $899

MODEL TRACKER

Action: double-action revolver
Grips: rubber with ribs
Barrel: 4 or 6.5 in.
Sights: target
Weight: 24 – 45 oz.
Caliber: .22 LR, .41 Mag., .357 Mag., .44 Mag., .17 HMR
Capacity: 5 to 7 (full-moon clips)
Features: ported barrel on .44 Mag., .357 and .41 Mag.; available in Titanium

.22 LR $391
.41 Mag., stainless. $516
.41 Mag., Shadow Grey Titanium$688
.357 Mag. $508
.357 Mag. (Shadow Grey) $688
.44 Mag., blue. $500
.44 Mag., stainless. $547
.17 HMR $406

MODEL 94/941

Action: double-action revolver
Grips: hardwood
Barrel: 2, 4 or 5 in.
Sights: target
Weight: 18.5 – 27.5 oz..
Caliber: .22 LR, .22 Mag.
Capacity: 8 - 9
Features: small frame, solid rib

blue. $328
stainless $375
Magnum, blue. $344
Magnum, stainless. $391
.22 LR, Ultralite . . . . $359 – 406
.22 Mag., Ultralite. . . . . . $375 – 422

MODEL 605

Action: double-action revolver
Grips: rubber
Barrel: 2 in.
Sights: fixed open
Weight: 24.5 oz.
Caliber: .357 Mag.
Capacity: 5
Features: small frame, transfer bar; porting optional

Model 605 . . . . $375
stainless $422
Titanium (16 oz.) $375

Taurus Handguns

MODEL 608

MODEL 608

Action: double-action revolver
Grips: rubber
Barrel: 4, 6.5 or 8.4 in., ported
Sights: target
Weight: 49.0 oz.
Caliber: .357 Mag.
Capacity: 8
Features: large frame, transfer bar, weight to 53 oz. depending on barrel length
stainless, 4 in. $523
stainless, 6.5 or 8.4 in. $547

Thompson/Center Handguns

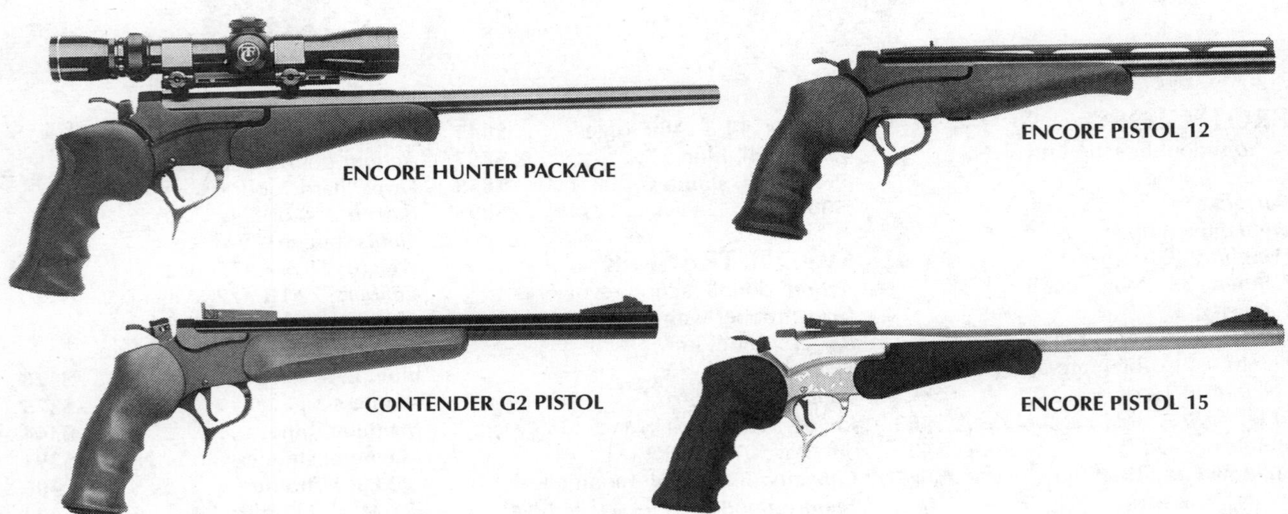
ENCORE HUNTER PACKAGE
ENCORE PISTOL 12
CONTENDER G2 PISTOL
ENCORE PISTOL 15

CONTENDER G2

Action: hinged breech
Grips: walnut
Barrel: 12 or 14 in.
Sights: target
Weight: 60.0 oz.
Caliber: .22 LR, .22 Hornet, .357 Mag., .17 MACH2, 6.8 Rem SPC, .44 Mag., .45/.410 (12 in.), .17 HMR, .22 LR, .22 Hornet, .223, 7-30, .30-30, .44 Mag., .45/.410, .45-70 (15 in.), .204 Ruger, .375 JDJ
Capacity: 1
Features: improved, stronger version of Contender
12 in. . . . . $562 – 591
14 in. (64 oz.). . . . . $569 – 605

ENCORE

Action: hinged breech
Grips: walnut or rubber
Barrel: 12 or 15 in.
Sights: target
Weight: 68.0 oz.
Caliber: many popular rifle and big-bore pistol rounds, from the .22 Hornet to the .30-06 and .45-70, the .454 Casull and .480 Ruger
Capacity: 1
Features: also in package with 2-7x scope, carry case; prices vary with caliber, options
12 in. $583
15 in. (72 oz.). $591
.45/.410 with rib. $620
stainless with rubber grips $673

Uberti Handguns

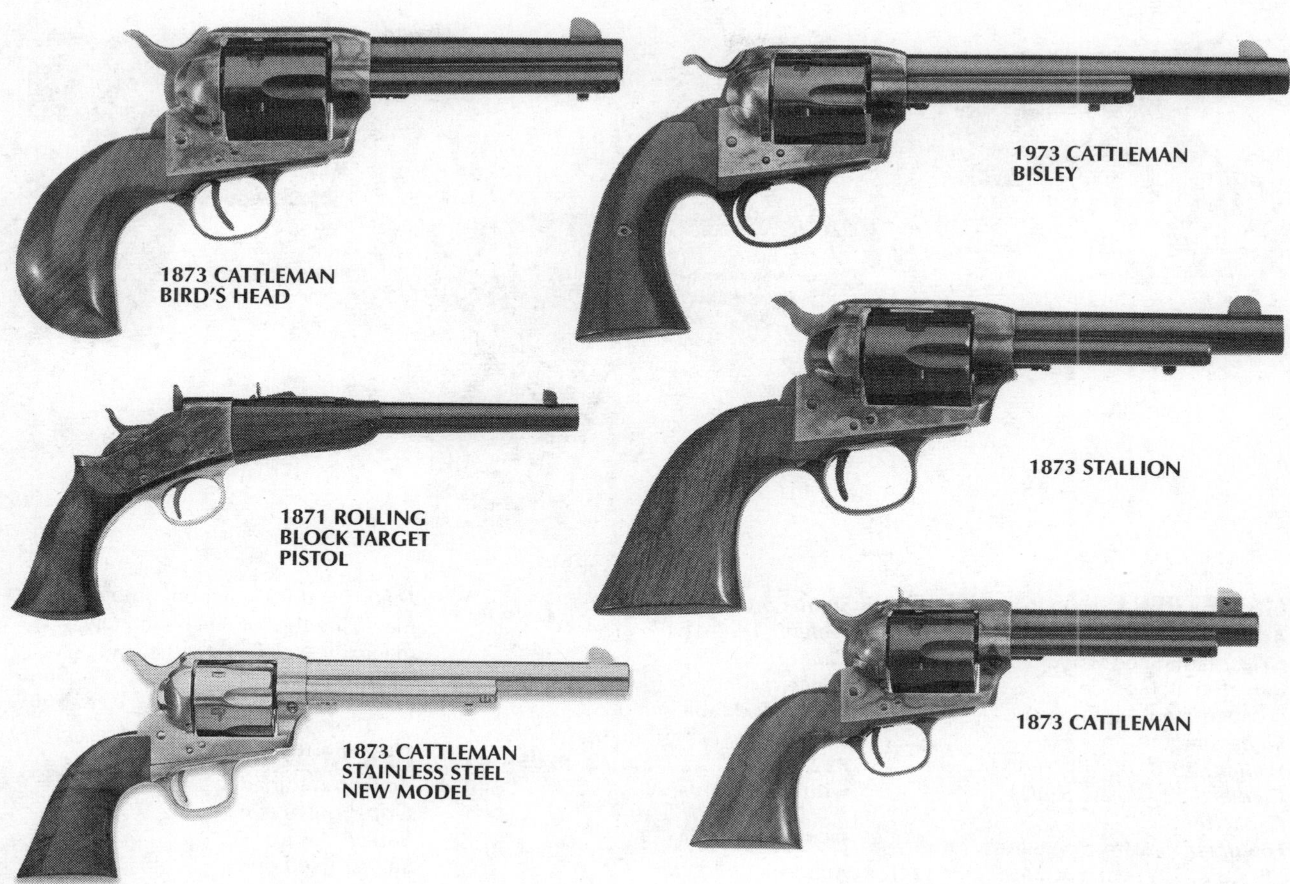

1873 CATTLEMAN BIRD'S HEAD

1973 CATTLEMAN BISLEY

1873 STALLION

1871 ROLLING BLOCK TARGET PISTOL

1873 CATTLEMAN

1873 CATTLEMAN STAINLESS STEEL NEW MODEL

1873 CATTLEMAN BIRD'S HEAD

Action: single-action revolver
Grips: walnut
Barrel: 3½, 4, 4½ or 5½ in.
Sights: fixed open
Weight: 2.31 lbs.
Caliber: .357 Mag., .44/40, .45 LC
Capacity: 6
Features: fluted cylinder, round tapered barrel, forged steel, color case-hardened frame, curved grip frame and grip, Flattop available with adjustable sights.
1873 Bird's Head $450

BISLEY

Action: single-action revolver
Grips: walnut
Barrel: 43/4, 51/2", 71/2 in.
Sights: adjustable
Weight: 2.51 lbs.
Caliber: .357 Mag., .44/40, .45 LC
Capacity: 6
Features: Bisley style grip, color case hardened frame, fluted cylender.
Bisley $450
Bisley Flattop $455

1873 STALLION

Action: single-action revolver
Grips: walnut
Barrel: 51/2 in.
Sights: open fixed
Weight: 1.98 lbs.
Caliber: .22 LR, .38 SP
Capacity: 6
Features: color case-hardened steel frame, fluted cylender
1873 Stallion. $390

1871 ROLLING BLOCK PISTOL

Action: rolling block
Grips: walnut
Barrel: 9.5 in.
Sights: target
Weight: 45.0 oz.
Caliber: .22 LR, .22 Mag.
Capacity: 1
Features: case-colored breech, brass guard
1871 Rolling Block $425

1873 SINGLE ACTION CATTLEMAN

Action: single-action revolver
Grips: walnut
Barrel: 4.8, 5.5, 7.5 or 18 in.
Sights: fixed open
Weight: 37.0 oz. (5.5 in.)
Caliber: .357 Mag., .44-40, .45 Colt
Capacity: 6
Features: case colored frame, Old Model/New Model available. Target sights available on some models; Birds Head or Bisley grips available
1873 . . . . $410
nickel finish. $490
Old West antique finish $490
Matte black millennium $270
charcoal blue $465
stainless New Model $495
Buntline $480

Walther Handguns

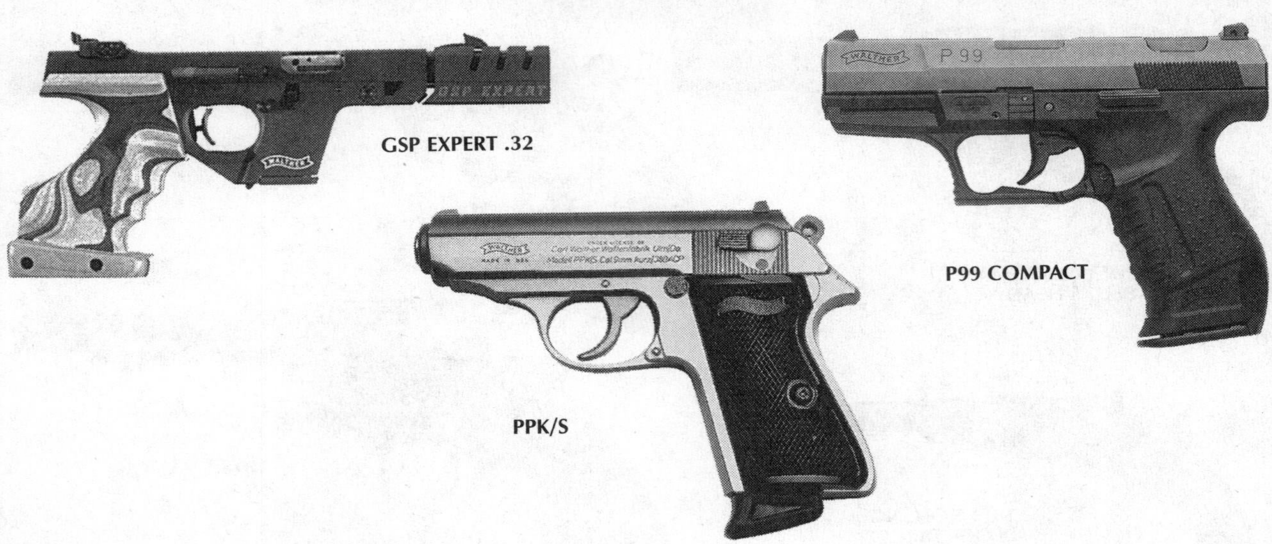

GSP EXPERT .32

PPK/S

P99 COMPACT

GSP EXPERT

Action: autoloader
Grips: laminated wood
Barrel: match-grade compensated 4.2 in.
Sights: target
Weight: 29.0 oz.
Caliber: .22 LR, .32 S&W
Capacity: 5
Features: forward magazine
.22 . . . . $1240
.32 . . . . $1420

P22

Action: autoloader
Grips: polymer
Barrel: 3.4 or 5 in.
Sights: 3-dot
Weight: 19.6 oz.
Caliber: .22 LR
Capacity: 10 + 1
Features: double action; 20.3 ounces with 5 in. barrel
P22 . . . . $295 – 415
with laser sights $405

P99 COMPACT

Action: autoloader
Grips: polymer
Barrel: 4 in.
Sights: low-profile combat
Weight: 25.0 oz.
Caliber: 9mm, .40 S&W
Capacity: 10 + 1
Features: double action, ambidextrous magazine release, high-capacity magazines available
P99 Compact $665
P99 Military $665

PPK AND PPK/S

Action: autoloader
Grips: polymer
Barrel: 3.4 in.
Sights: fixed open
Weight: 22.0 oz.
Caliber: .380 and .32 ACP
Capacity: 7 + 1
Features: double action, blue or stainless, decocker
PPK $543

Wildey Handguns

WILDEY AUTOMATIC PISTOL

Action: autoloader
Grips: composite
Barrel: 5, 6, 7, 8, 10, 12 or 14 in.
Sights: target
Weight: 64.0 oz.
Caliber: .45 Win. Mag., .44 Auto Mag, .45 and .475 Wildey
Capacity: 7 + 1
Features: gas operated, ribbed barrel
starting at $1525
Silhouette (18 in. barrel). $2696

BLACK POWDER

Austin & Halleck Black Powder

MODEL 320 REALTREE-HARDWOODS CAMO

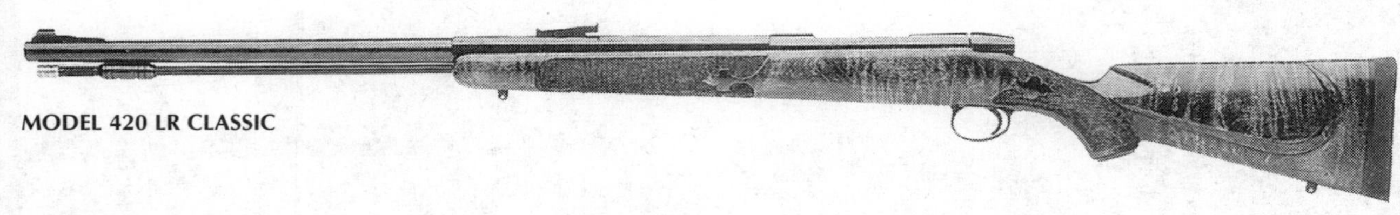

MODEL 420 LR CLASSIC

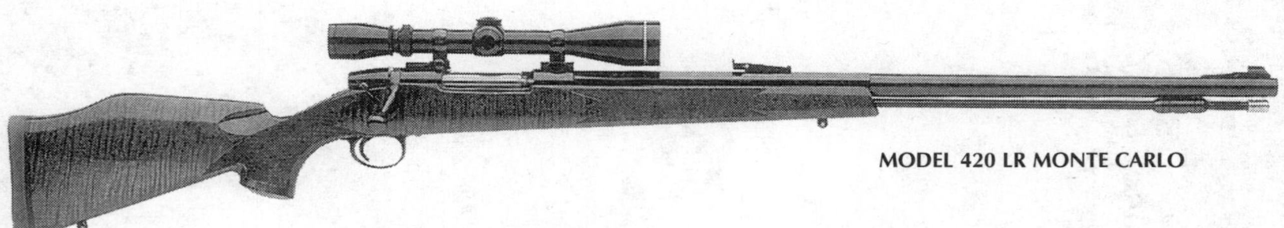

MODEL 420 LR MONTE CARLO

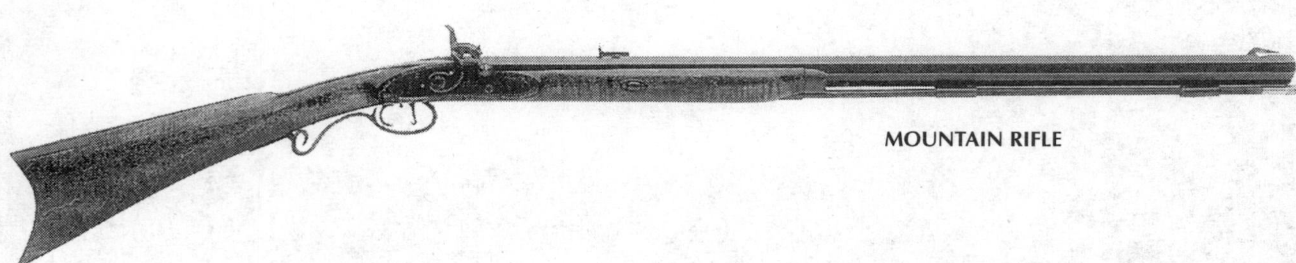

MOUNTAIN RIFLE

BOLT ACTION M320, 420

Lock: in-line
Stock: curly maple, synthetic, camo
Barrel: 26 in., 1:28 twist
Sights: adjustable open
Weight: 7.8 lbs.
Bore/Caliber: .50
Features: match trigger
synthetic $419
stainless synthetic $449
camo $459
stainless camo $489
curly maple $549
stainless maple $579

MOUNTAIN RIFLE

Lock: traditional cap or flint
Stock: curly maple
Barrel: 32 in., 1:66 or 1:28 twist
Sights: fixed
Weight: 7.5 lbs.
Bore/Caliber: .50
Features: double set triggers
percussion $539
select percussion $719
flint $589
select flint $769

Cabela's Black Powder

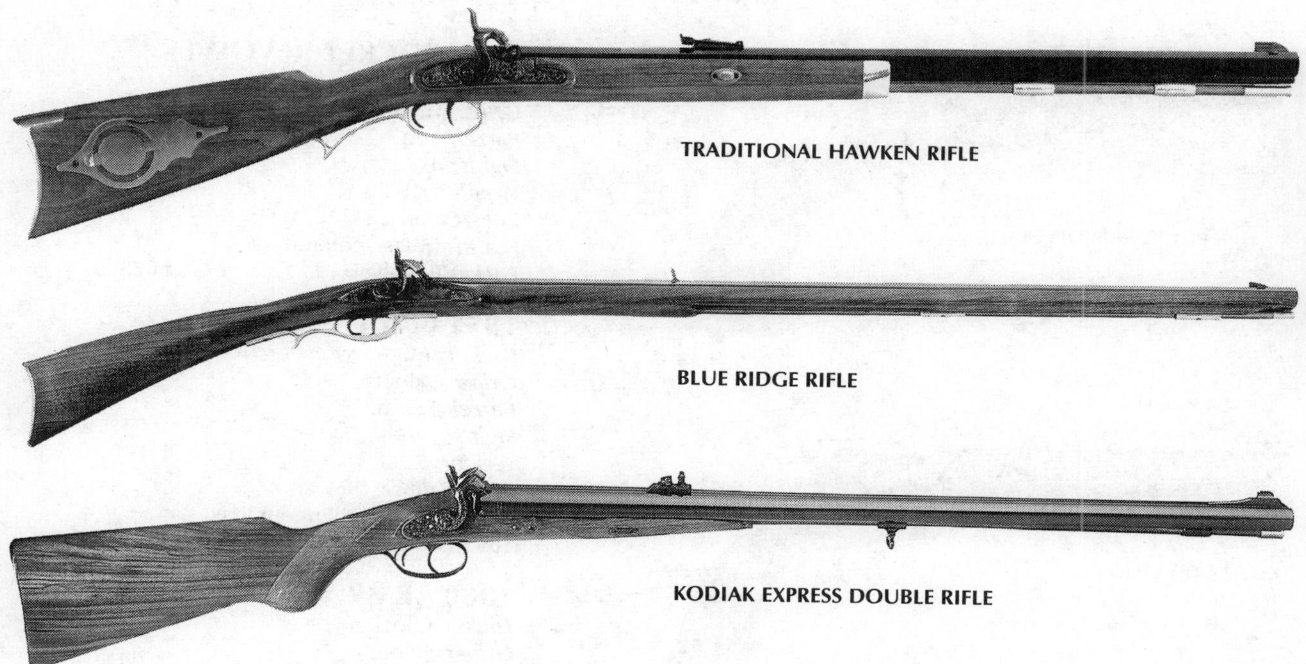

TRADITIONAL HAWKEN RIFLE

BLUE RIDGE RIFLE

KODIAK EXPRESS DOUBLE RIFLE

HAWKEN

Lock: traditional cap or flint
Stock: walnut
Barrel: 24 in., 1:28 twist
Sights: adjustable open
Weight: 9.0 lbs.
Bore/Caliber: .50 or .54
Features: brass furniture, double-set trigger
percussion (right or left-hand) . $270
flint $300

BLUE RIDGE

Lock: side-hammer caplock
Stock: walnut
Barrel: 39 in., 1:48 twist
Sights: none
Weight: 7.8 lbs.
Bore/Caliber: .32, .36, .45 and .50
Features: double set triggers, case-colored locks
caplock $430
flint $450

KODIAK EXPRESS DOUBLE RIFLE

Lock: traditional caplock
Stock: walnut, pistol grip
Barrel: 28 in., 1:48 twist
Sights: folding leaf
Weight: 9.3 lbs.
Bore/Caliber: .50, .54, .58 and .72
Features: double triggers
from $770

DOUBLE SHOTGUN

Lock: traditional caplock
Stock: walnut
Barrel: 27, 28 or 30 in.
Sights: none
Weight: 7.0 lbs.
Bore/Caliber: 20, 12 or 10 ga.
Features: screw-in choke tubes: X-Full, Mod, IC, double triggers; weight to 10 lbs. depending on gauge
from $550

Before loading a caplock rifle, hold the muzzle close to a patch of grass and fire a primer only. If the grass shudders, the nipple is clear and the gun ready for loading.

Colt Black Powder

1849
POCKET REVOLVER

1849 POCKET REVOLVER

Lock: caplock revolver
Grips: walnut
Barrel: 4 in.
Sights: fixed
Weight: 1.5 lbs.
Bore/Caliber: .31
Features: case-colored frame
Pocket Revolver $675

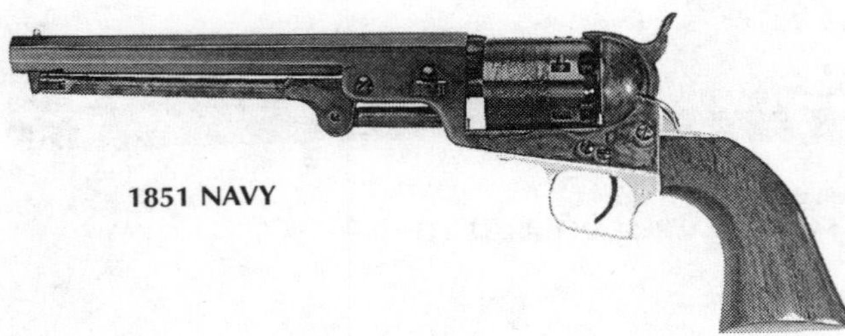

1851 NAVY

1851 NAVY

Lock: caplock revolver
Grips: walnut
Barrel: 7.5 in.
Sights: fixed
Weight: 2.5 lbs.
Bore/Caliber: .36
Features: case-colored frame
1851 Navy $695

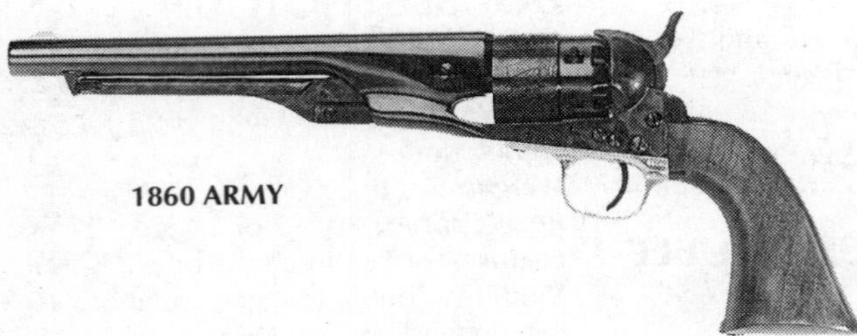

1860 ARMY

1860 ARMY

Lock: caplock revolver
Grips: walnut
Barrel: 8 in.
Sights: fixed
Weight: 2.6 lbs.
Bore/Caliber: ..44
Features: case-colored frame, hammer, plunger; also with fluted cylinder and adapted for shoulder stock
1860 Army $695

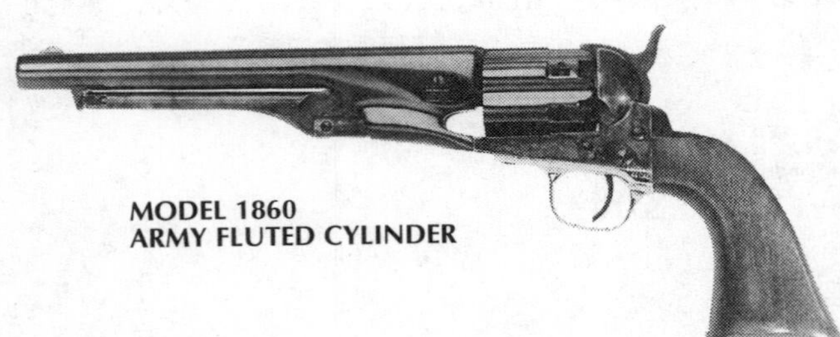

MODEL 1860
ARMY FLUTED CYLINDER

THIRD MODEL DRAGOON

Lock: caplock revolver
Grips: walnut
Barrel: 7.5 in.
Sights: fixed
Weight: 4.1 lbs.
Bore/Caliber: .44
Features: case-colored frame, hammer, lever, plunger
Dragoon $750

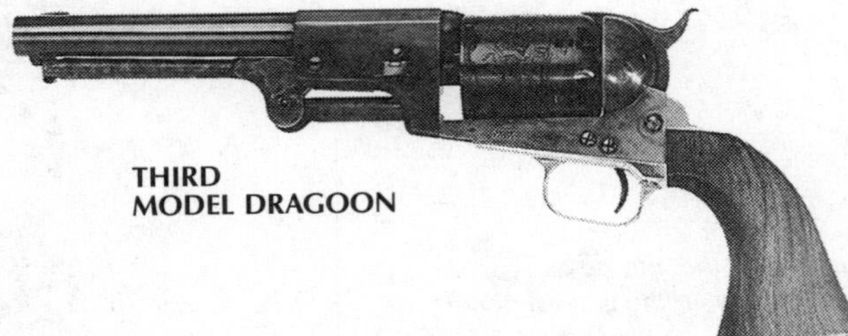

THIRD
MODEL DRAGOON

Colt Black Powder

WALKER

Lock: caplock revolver
Grips: walnut
Barrel: 9 in.
Sights: fixed
Weight: 4.6 lbs.
Bore/Caliber: .44
Features: case-colored frame, authentic remake of 1847 Walker
Walker $750

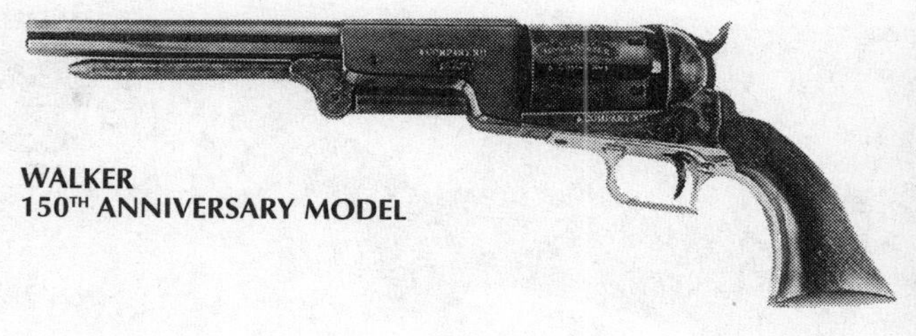

WALKER
150TH ANNIVERSARY MODEL

1861 NAVY

Lock: caplock revolver
Grips: walnut
Barrel: 7.5 in.
Sights: fixed
Weight: 2.6 lbs.
Bore/Caliber: .36
Features: revolver with case-colored frame, hammer, lever, plunger
1861 Navy $695

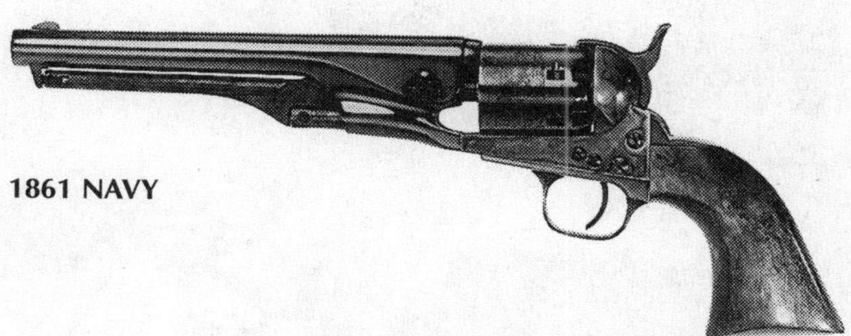

1861 NAVY

TRAPPER 1862 POCKET POLICE

Lock: caplock revolver
Grips: walnut
Barrel: 3.5 in.
Sights: fixed
Weight: 1.25 lbs.
Bore/Caliber: .36
Features: revolver with case-colored frame, separate brass ramrod
Pocket Police. $675

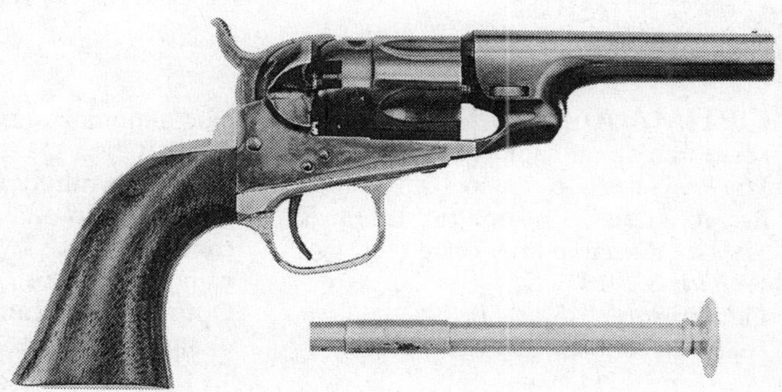

TRAPPER
1862 POCKET POLICE

COLT 1861 RIFLE

Lock: traditional caplock
Stock: walnut
Barrel: 40 in.
Sights: folding leaf
Weight: 9.2 lbs.
Bore/Caliber: .58
Features: authentic reproduction of 1861 Springfield
1861 Musket. $1000

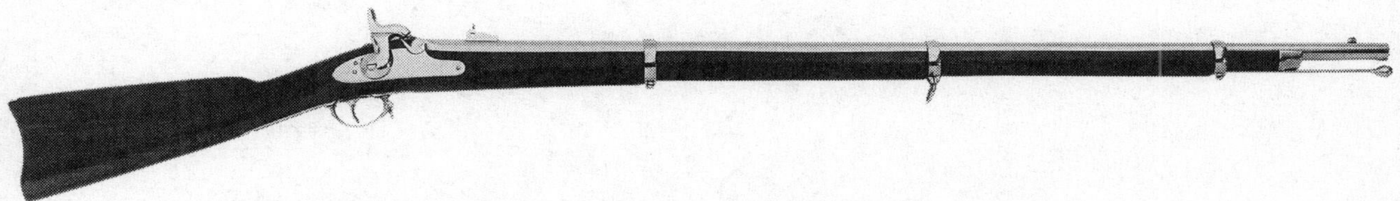

COLT 1861 RIFLE

CVA Black Powder

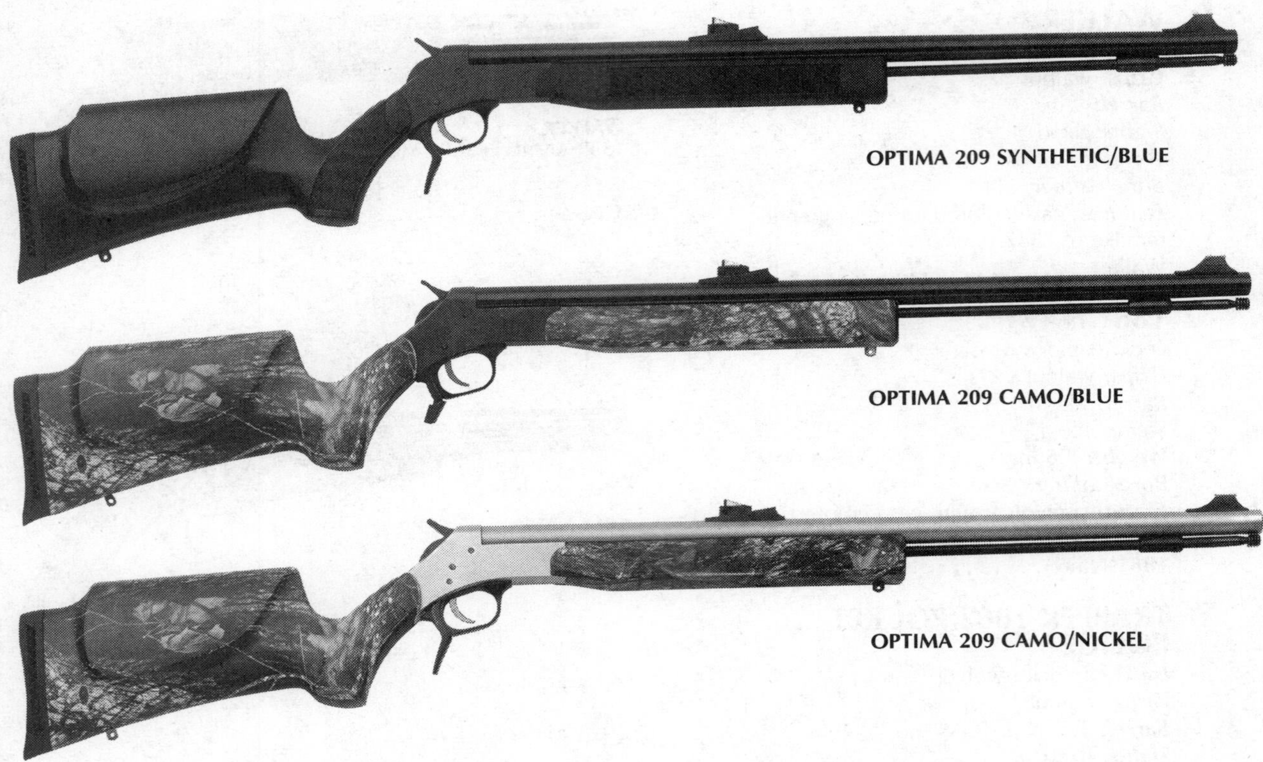

OPTIMA 209 SYNTHETIC/BLUE

OPTIMA 209 CAMO/BLUE

OPTIMA 209 CAMO/NICKEL

OPTIMA AND OPTIMA PRO

Lock: traditional caplock
Stock: synthetic or camo
Barrel: 26 in. (29 in. on Pro), 1:28 twist
Sights: adjustable fiber optic
Weight: 8.2 lbs.
Caliber/Bore: .45 or .50
Features: stainless steel 209 breech plug, ambidextrous stock; add $75 for Pro (8.8 lbs.)

Optima, synthetic/blue $225
synthetic/nickel. $255
camo/blue. $280
camo/nickel $300
Optima Pro w/camo
stock & bbl.. . . . . $400

Conical lead bullets need fast-twist barrels: 1 turn in 28 inches. Patched balls typically shoot best with slow twist: 1 in 66. The popular compromise in many muzzleloaders: 1-in-48 twist.

CVA Black Powder

KODIAK 209 MAGNUM

KODIAK 209 MAGNUM

Lock: in-line
Stock: synthetic
Barrel: 28 in.
Sights: fiber optic
Weight: 7.5 lbs.
Bore/Caliber: .45 or .50
Features: ambidextrous solid stock in black or Mossy Oak Camo, stainless steel 209 breech plug

Mossy Oak Camo/ Nickel Barrel:. $329.95
Mossy Oak Camo/ Blue Barrel: $309.95
Black FiberGrip/ Nickel Barrel:. $289.95
Black FiberGrip/ Blue Barrel: $259.95

Warning: Continuation of 1997 Recall
Do not use CVA In-Line rifles with 1995 or 1996 serial numbers
Serious injury may result

In 1997, Connecticut Valley Arms, Inc., voluntarily implemented a recall of in-line muzzleloading rifles manufactured in 1995 and 1996. If you currently own or possess a CVA in-line rifle with a 95 or 96 serial number, or you purchased one or gave it or sold it to another person, and the barrel has not been replaced, you should contact a Company Representative immediately by calling the customer service number below:
1-770-449-4687 (8:30 a.m. to 4:00 p.m. EST)
sample serial # 61-13-xxxxxx-95
sample serial # 61-13-xxxxxx-96

To identify the rifle, read the serial number on the barrel opposite the firing bolt. The only CVA rilfes subject to the voluntary recall are in-line models with serial numbers ending with the last two digits of 95 or 96. No other firearm models within the CVA product line are affected by the voluntary recall.

Blackpowder Products, Inc. purchased the assets of Connecticut Valley Arms, Inc. in May, 1999. Blackpowder products, Inc. assumed no liability for any product manufactured or sold prior to January 1, 1998. Blackpowder Products, Inc. is continuing the Connecticut Valley Arms, Inc. recall, and will cover all reasonable related shipping charges. Please do not return your in-line rifle before contacting a Company Representative at the above customer service number.

Be sure you check state game regulations before buying an in-line muzzleloader or scoping your smokepole. Some states insist that "primitive weapons" be primitive!

Dixie Black Powder

BLACK POWDER

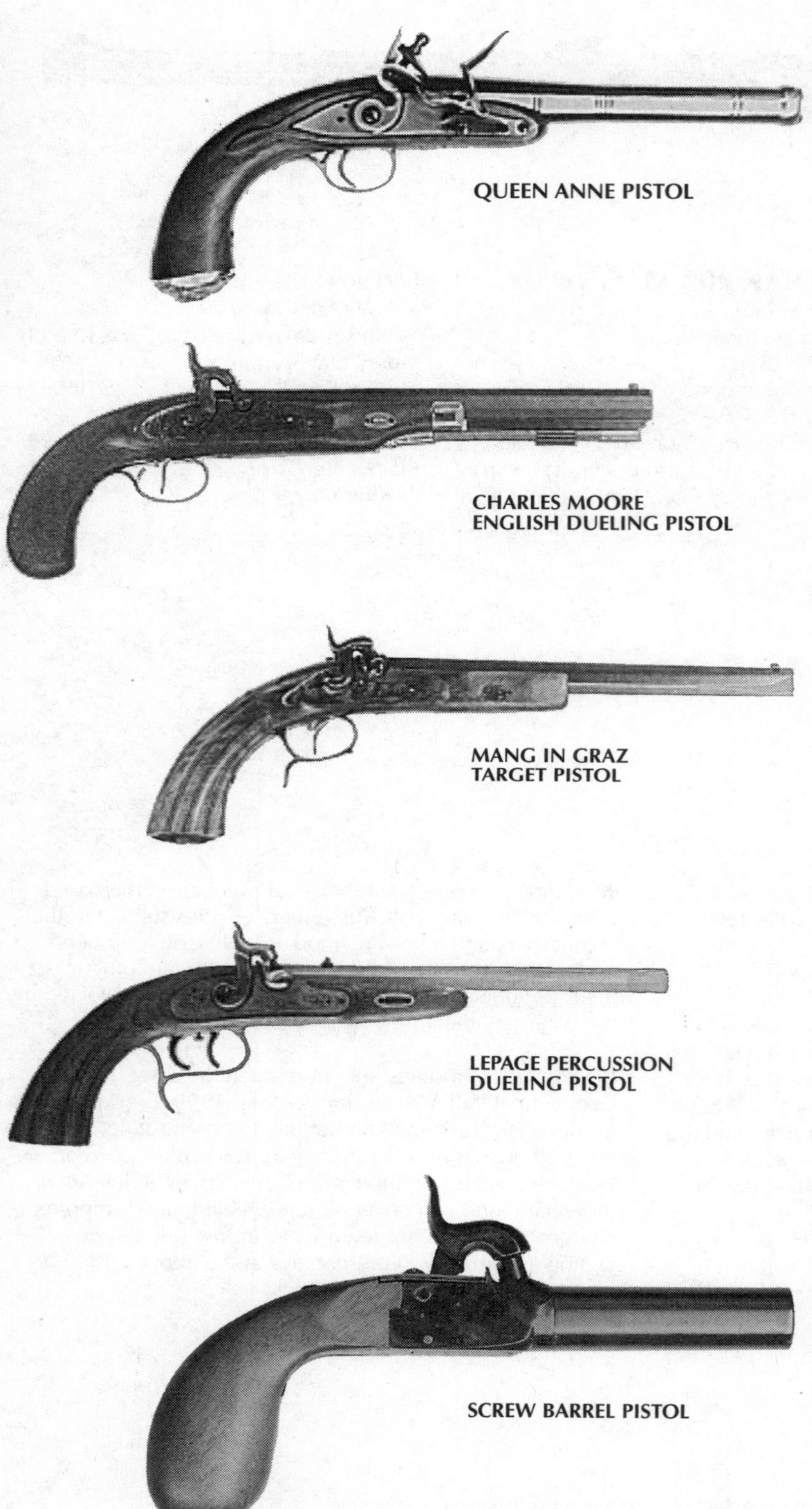

QUEEN ANNE PISTOL

CHARLES MOORE ENGLISH DUELING PISTOL

MANG IN GRAZ TARGET PISTOL

LEPAGE PERCUSSION DUELING PISTOL

SCREW BARREL PISTOL

PEDERSOLI QUEEN ANNE PISTOL

Lock: traditional flintlock
Grips: walnut
Barrel: 7.5 in.
Sights: none
Weight: 2.2 lbs.
Bore/Caliber: .45
Features: brass furniture
Queen Anne Pistol $290
unfinished kit $205

PEDERSOLI CHARLES MOORE ENGLISH DUELING PISTOL

Lock: traditional cap or flint
Grips: walnut
Barrel: 11 in.
Sights: fixed
Weight: 2.8 lbs.
Bore/Caliber: .45
Features: silver-plated furniture, case-colored
cap $395
flint. $445

PEDERSOLI MANG TARGET PISTOL

Lock: traditional caplock
Grips: hardwood
Barrel: 10.4 in., 1:15 twist
Sights: fixed
Weight: 2.5 lbs.
Bore/Caliber: .38
Features: half-stock, finger rest on guard
Mang Target Pistol. $960

LEPAGE DUELING PISTOL

Lock: traditional caplock
Grips: hardwood
Barrel: 9 in.
Sights: fixed
Weight: 2.5 lbs.
Bore/Caliber: .45
Features: double set trigger
LePage Dueling Pistol $470

SCREW BARREL PISTOL

Lock: traditional caplock
Grips: hardwood
Barrel: 3 in.
Sights: none
Weight: 0.75 lbs.
Bore/Caliber: .445
Features: barrel detaches for loading; folding trigger
Screw Barrel Pistol $168

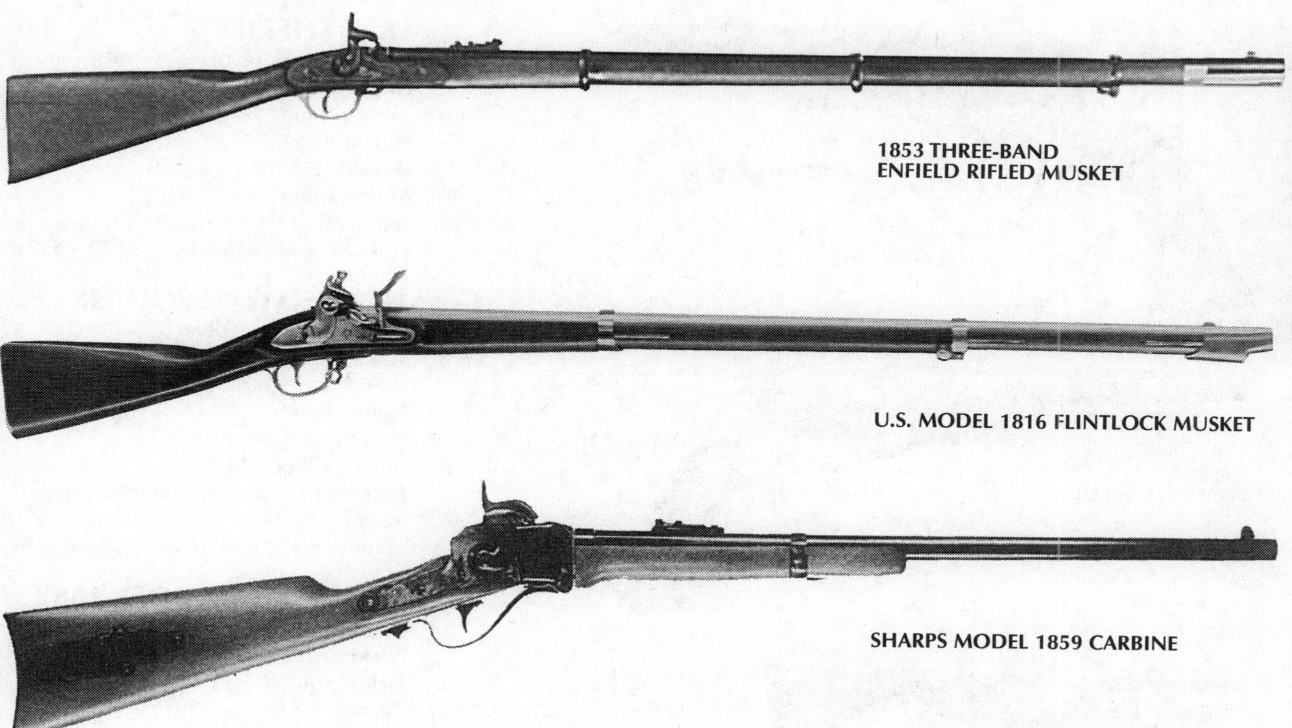

1853 THREE-BAND ENFIELD RIFLED MUSKET

U.S. MODEL 1816 FLINTLOCK MUSKET

SHARPS MODEL 1859 CARBINE

PENNSYLVANIA RIFLE

Lock: traditional cap or flint
Stock: walnut
Barrel: 41 in.
Sights: fixed
Weight: 8.0 lbs.
Bore/Caliber: .45 or .50
Features: brass furniture
Pennsylvania Rifle . . . . . $525 - $595
unfinished kit. . . . . $475 - $495

PEDERSOLI WAADTLANDER RIFLE

Lock: traditional caplock
Stock: walnut
Barrel: 30 in., 1;48 twist
Sights: aperture
Weight: 10.5 lbs.
Bore/Caliber: .45
Features: recreation of Swiss Target rifle, circa 1839 - 1860, case-colored hardware, double set trigger
Waadtlander $1900

1853 THREE-BAND ENFIELD

Lock: traditional caplock
Stock: walnut
Barrel: 39 in.
Sights: fixed
Weight: 10.5 lbs.
Bore/Caliber: .58
Features: case-colored lock, brass furniture; also 1858 two-band Enfield with 33 in. barrel
three-band $595
unfinished kit $595
two-band. $600

MODEL U.S. 1816 FLINTLOCK MUSKET

Lock: traditional flintlock
Stock: walnut
Barrel: 42 in. smoothbore
Sights: fixed
Weight: 9.8 lbs.
Bore/Caliber: .69
Features: most common military flintlock from U.S. armories, complete with bayonet lug and swivels
Musket by Pedersoil $1025

NEW MODEL 1859 MILITARY SHARPS CARBINE

Lock: dropping block
Stock: walnut
Barrel: 22 in.
Sights: adjustable open
Weight: 7.8 lbs.
Bore/Caliber: .54
Features: case-colored furniture, including saddle ring; also 1859 military rifle with 30-inch barrel (9 lbs.); both by Pedersoli
Sharps Carbine $875
with 30 in. barrel $995

EMF Hartford Black Powder

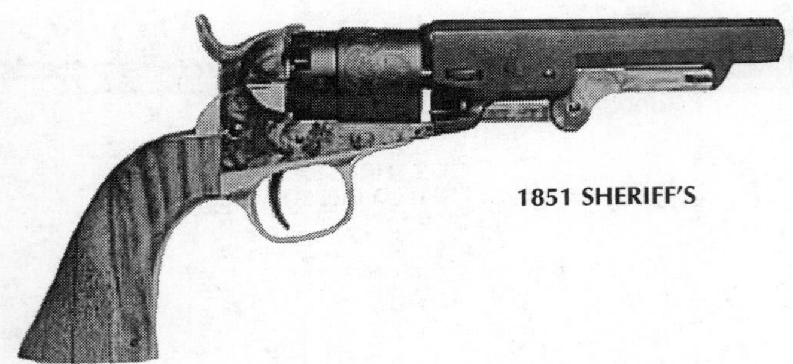

1851 SHERIFF'S

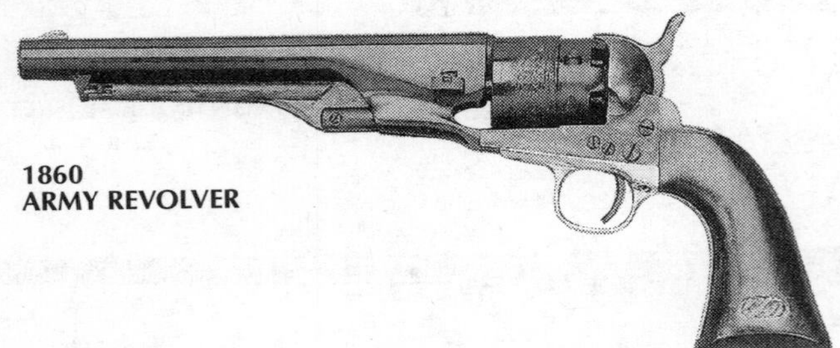

1860
ARMY REVOLVER

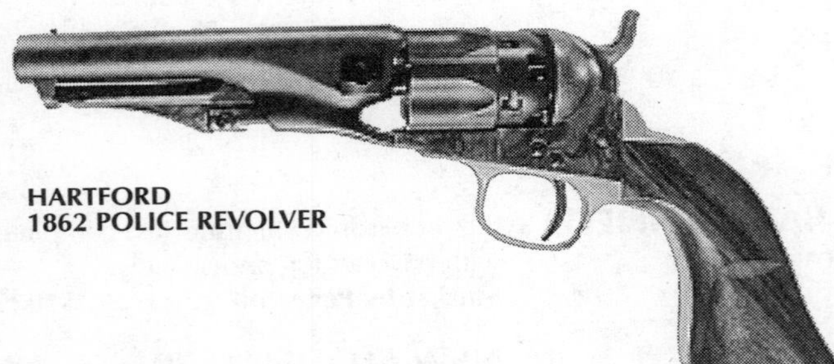

HARTFORD
1862 POLICE REVOLVER

1851 SHERIFF'S

Lock: caplock revolver
Grips: walnut
Barrel: 5 in.
Sights: none
Weight: 2.4 lbs.
Bore/Caliber: .44
Features: brass guard, strap
1851 Sheriff's Model . . . $140 - $170

1860 ARMY REVOLVER

Lock: caplock revolver
Stock: walnut
Barrel: 8 in.
Sights: fixed
Weight: 2.6 lbs.
Bore/Caliber: .44
Features: case-colored frame, brass guard, strap
1860 Army. . . . . $245 - $290

HARTFORD MODEL 1862 POLICE REVOLVER

Lock: caplock revolver
Grips: walnut
Barrel: 5.5 in.
Sights: fixed
Weight: 2.1 lbs.
Bore/Caliber: .36
Features: 5-shot cylinder
1862 Police Revolver $240

Pyrodex pellets make loading faster and easier than measuring black powder or granular Pyrodex (a black powder substitute).

EMF Hartford Black Powder

1858 REMINGTON

Lock: caplock revolver
Grips: walnut
Barrel: 8 in.
Sights: fixed
Weight: 2.5 lbs.
Bore/Caliber: .44
Features: brass or stainless steel frame
brass $180

1851 NAVY

Lock: caplock revolver
Grips: walnut
Barrel: 7.5 in.
Sights: fixed
Weight: 2.5 lbs.
Bore/Caliber: .36 or .44
Features: brass frame
1851 Navy . . . . $235 - $270

1847 WALKER

Lock: caplock revolver
Grips: walnut
Barrel: 9 in.
Sights: fixed
Weight: 4.6 lbs.
Bore/Caliber: .44
Features: largest commercial Colt single-action, named after Texas Ranger
1847 Walker $380

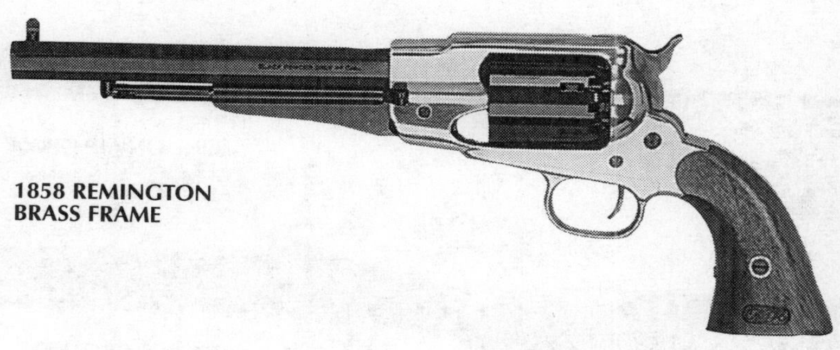

1858 REMINGTON BRASS FRAME

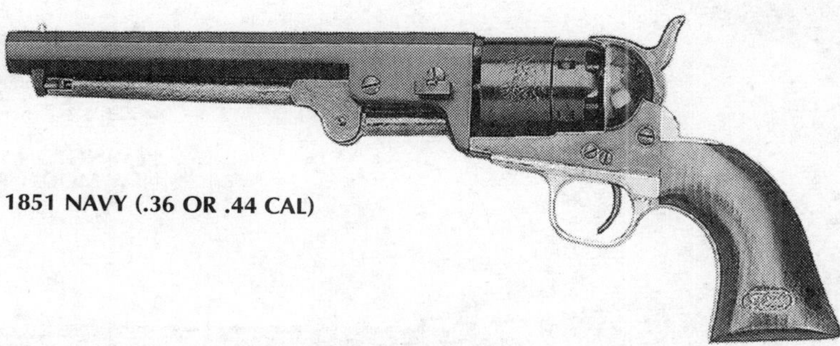

1851 NAVY (.36 OR .44 CAL)

1847 WALKER (.44 CAL)

Traditional #11 percussion caps are being replaced with musket caps and #209 shotshell primers because these options are "hotter" and provide surer ignition in guns that accept them.

Euroarms of America Black Powder

LONDON ARMORY P-1858 ENFIELD

COOK & BROTHER
CONFEDERATE CARBINE MODEL 2300

REMINGTON 1858
NEW MODEL ARMY

1803 HARPERS FERRY FLINTLOCK RIFLE

1841 MISSISSIPPI RIFLE

LONDON ARMORY P1858 ENFIELD

Lock: traditional caplock
Stock: walnut
Barrel: 33 in.
Sights: adjustable open
Weight: 8.8 lbs.
Bore/Caliber: .58
Features: steel ramrod, 2-band
P1858 Enfield $513
1853 rifled musket $528
1861 London Enfield. $475

COOK & BROTHER CONFEDERATE

Lock: traditional caplock
Stock: walnut
Barrel: 24 in.
Sights: fixed
Weight: 7.9 lbs.
Bore/Caliber: .577
Features: carbine; also rifle with 33 in. barrel
carbine $513
rifle $552

REMINGTON 1858 NEW MODEL ARMY

Lock: caplock revolver
Grips: walnut
Barrel: 8 in.
Sights: fixed
Weight: 2.5 lbs.
Bore/Caliber: .44
Features: brass guard; also engraved version
New Model Army $220
engraved $302

1803 HARPER'S FERRY FLINTLOCK

Lock: traditional flintlock
Stock: walnut
Barrel: 35 in.
Sights: fixed
Weight: 10.0 lbs.
Bore/Caliber: .54
Features: half-stock, browned steel
1803 Harper's Ferry $735

1841 MISSISSIPPI RIFLE

Lock: traditional caplock
Stock: walnut
Barrel: 33 in.
Sights: fixed
Weight: 9.5 lbs.
Bore/Caliber: .54 or .58
Features: brass furniture
1841 Mississippi. $575

Euroarms of America Black Powder

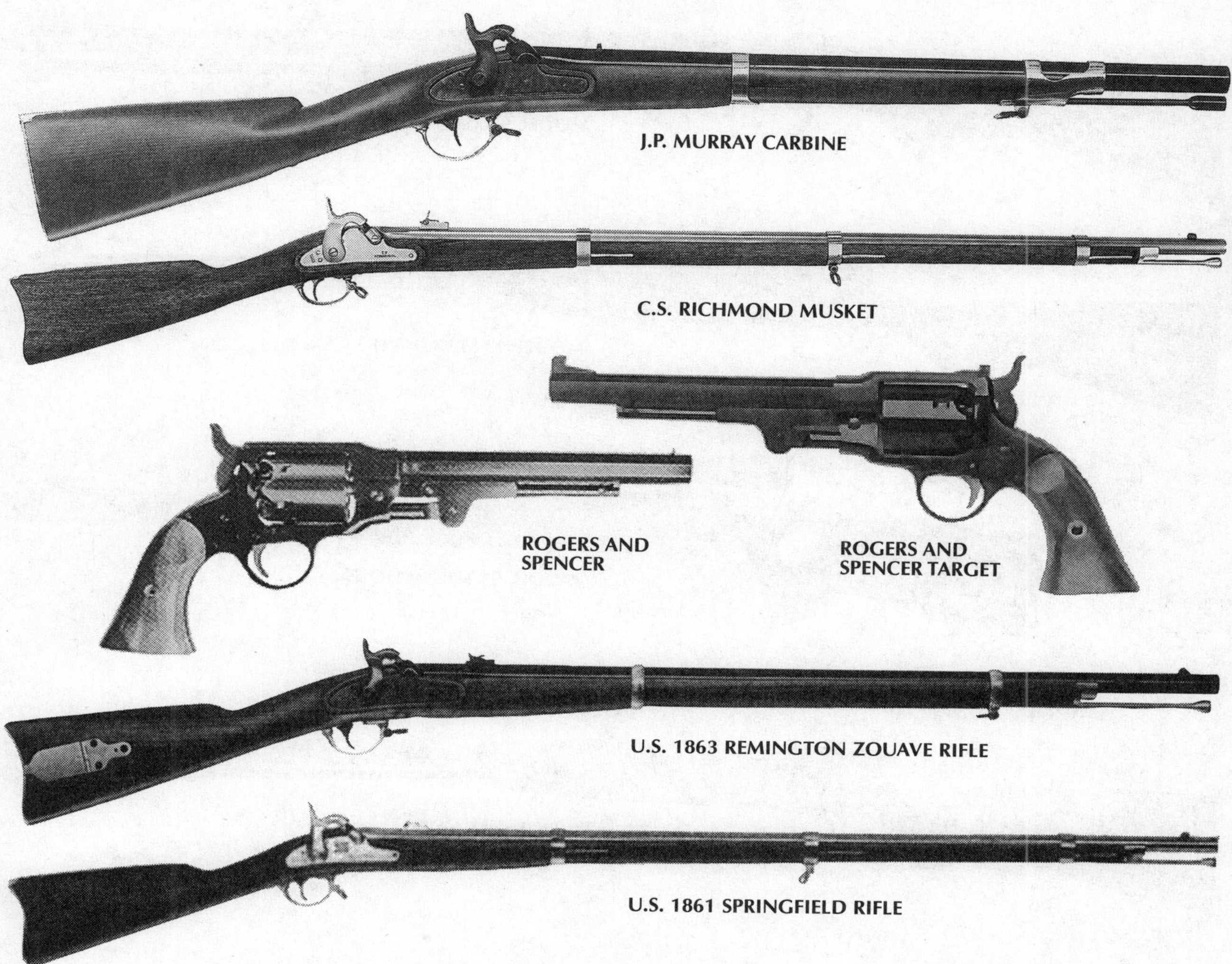

J.P. MURRAY CARBINE

C.S. RICHMOND MUSKET

ROGERS AND SPENCER

ROGERS AND SPENCER TARGET

U.S. 1863 REMINGTON ZOUAVE RIFLE

U.S. 1861 SPRINGFIELD RIFLE

J.P. MURRAY CARBINE

Lock: traditional caplock
Stock: walnut
Barrel: 23 in.
Sights: fixed
Weight: 7.5 lbs.
Bore/Caliber: .58
Features: brass furniture, replica of rare Confederate Cavalry Carbine
J.P. Murray Carbine. $521

C.S. RICHMOND MUSKET

Lock: traditional caplock
Stock: walnut
Barrel: 40 in.
Sights: fixed
Weight: 9.0 lbs.
Bore/Caliber: .58
Features: 3-band furniture, swivels
C.S. Richmond Musket $579

ROGERS AND SPENCER

Lock: caplock revolver
Grips: walnut
Barrel: 7.5 in.
Sights: fixed
Weight: 2.9 lbs.
Bore/Caliber: .44
Features: recommended ball diameter .451; also target model with adjustable sight
Rogers and Spencer $260
with London gray finish $283
Target $275

U.S. 1841 MISSISSIPPI RIFLE

Lock: traditional caplock
Stock: walnut
Barrel: 33 in.
Sights: fixed
Weight: 9.5 lbs.
Bore/Caliber: .54 or .58
Features: brass furniture; also 1863 Remington Zouave rifle
Mississippi. $575
Zouave $469

U.S. 1861 SPRINGFIELD

Lock: traditional caplock
Stock: walnut
Barrel: 40 in.
Sights: fixed
Weight: 10.0 lbs.
Bore/Caliber: .58
Features: sling swivels; also London P-1852 rifled musket, London Enfield P-1861 (7.5 lbs.)
Springfield. $579

Gonic Arms Black Powder

MODEL 93 MAG

MODEL 93 STANDARD

MODEL 93 THUMBHOLE

TK 2000 SHOTGUN

MODEL 93

Lock: in-line
Stock: laminated or synthetic, pillar bedded
Barrel: 26 in. stainless, 1:24 twist
Sights: adjustable open
Weight: 7.0 lbs.
Bore/Caliber: .50
Features: various stock configurations, including thumbhole; scope mounting provisions
Model 93 .... $999

MODEL TK 2000 SHOTGUN

Lock: in-line
Stock: synthetic or camo
Barrel: 26 in.
Sights: fiber optic
Weight: 7.6 lbs.
Bore/Caliber: 12 ga.
Features: adjustable trigger, screw-in choke tubes; uses 209 primers
synthetic $350
camo $400

Knight Black Powder

BLACK POWDER

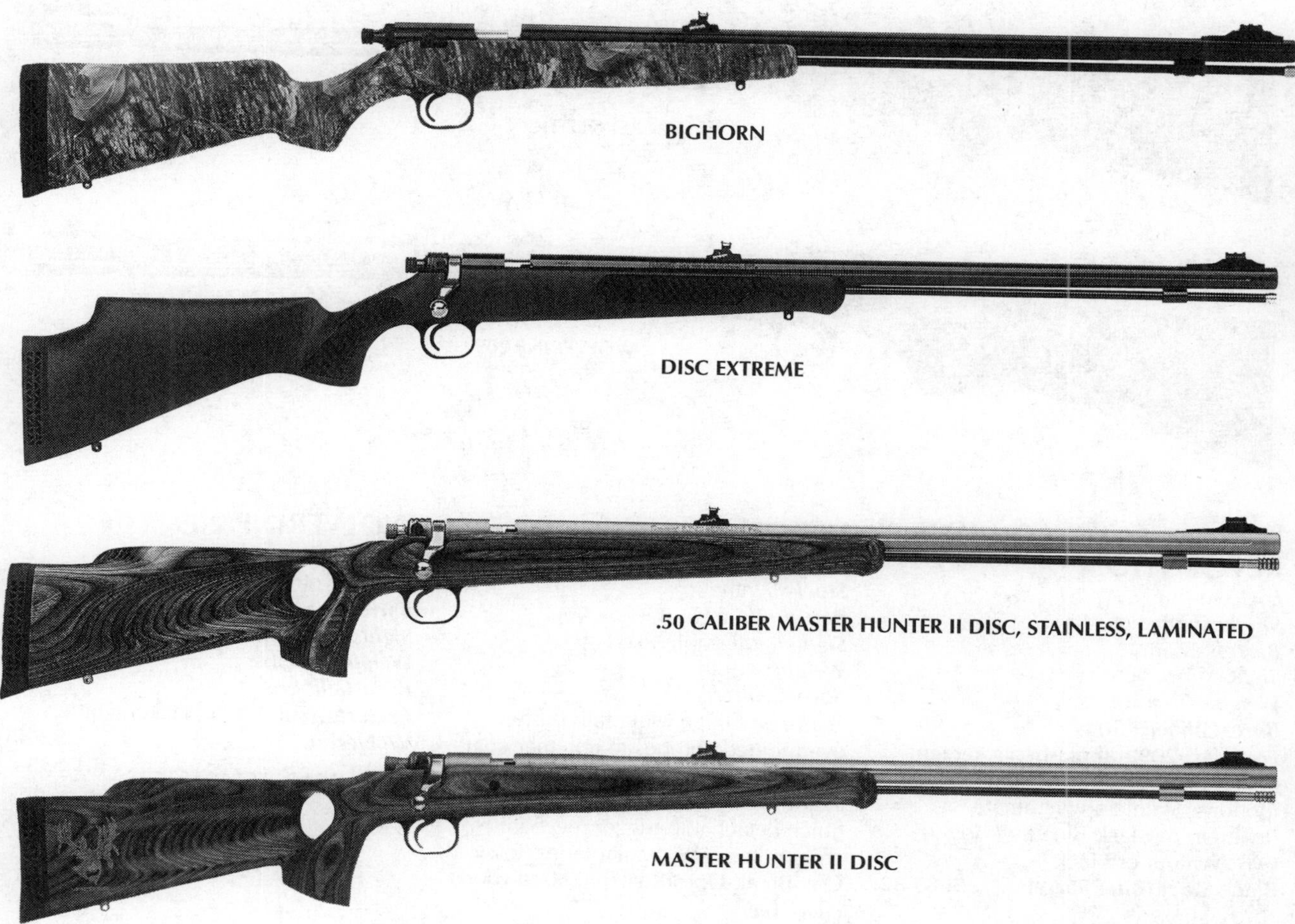

BIGHORN

DISC EXTREME

.50 CALIBER MASTER HUNTER II DISC, STAINLESS, LAMINATED

MASTER HUNTER II DISC

BIGHORN

Lock: In-Line
Stock: synthetic
Barrel: 26 in.
Sights: fiber optic or adjustable open
Weight: 7.6 lbs.
Bore/Caliber: .50
Features: 3 ignition systems: #11 nipple, musket nipple and the 209 Extreme shotgun primer system; full set of non-fiber optic sights

SS Black Thumbhole: $389.45
Realtree Hardwoods
Green HD: $399.95
MS Black: $315.95
MS MO Breakup: $357.95
SS Black: $357.95

DISC EXTREME

Lock: In-Line
Stock: synthetic or laminated
Barrel: 26 in.
Sights: fiber optic
Weight: 7.8 lbs.
Bore/Caliber: .45, .50, .52
Features: Green Mountain action and barrel; full plastic jacket ignition system; quick-release bolt system

SS Thumbhole: $698.87
SS Laminated: $698.87
MS Black: $516.08
(.45 cal.: . . . . $578.95)
SS Black: $591.34
(.50 cal.: . . . . $631.45)
Realtree Hardwood
Green HD: $631.45
(.52 cal.: . . . . $652.95)

MASTER HUNTER DISC EXREME

Lock: In-Line
Stock: Synthetic
Barrel: 26 in.
Sights: fiber optic
Weight: 7.8 lbs.
Bore/Caliber: .45, .50, .52 calibers.
Features: Green Mountain action and cryogenically accurized barrel; full plastic jacket ignition system; quick-release bolt system

SS Laminated: $698
SS Mossy Oak Breakup: $631.45
SS Thumbhole: 698
(.50 cal.: . . . . $610)
MS Black: $578
(.45 cal.: . . . . $578)
SS Black: $591
(.50 cal.: . . . . $631)
Realtree Hardwood
Green HD: $631
(.52 cal.: . . . . $652)

Knight Black Powder

REVOLUTION

WOLVERINE 209

KNIGHT BLACKPOWDER REVOLUTION

Lock: in-line
Stock: synthetic
Barrel: 27 in.
Sights: fiber optic
Weight: 7.14 lbs.
Bore/Caliber: .50
Features: 209 full plastic jacket ignition system,sling swivel studs. Options: Stainless w/laminate, Realtree, or Black Blued w/Mossy Oak, Walnut or black
Black Stock/Blue Barrel: . . . $605.32

VISION

Lock: In-Line
Stock: synthetic
Barrel: 26 in.
Sights: adjustable fixed
Weight: 7.9 lbs.
Bore/Caliber: .50
Features: Green Mountain barrel; overmolded composite polymer coated stainless steel receiver break-open action; full plastic primer jackets; quick detachable trigger mechanism; cross bolt safety; available in Mossy Oak Break-Up orRealTree Hardwoods HD-Green
Price: $421

WOLVERINE 209

Lock: in-line
Stock: synthetic or camo
Barrel: 22 in., 1:28 twist
Sights: fiber optic
Weight: 7.0 lbs.
Bore/Caliber: .50
Features: Full Plastic Jacket ignition
Wolverine $290
Camo $354

Lenartz Black Powder

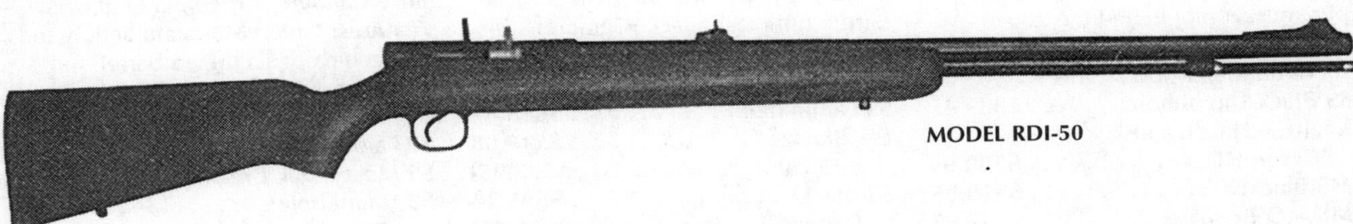

MODEL RDI-50

MODEL RDI-50

Lock: in-line
Stock: walnut
Barrel: 26 in., 1:28 twist
Sights: adjustable open
Weight: 7.5 lbs.
Bore/Caliber: .50
Features: adjustable trigger; uses 209 primers, converts to #11
RDI-5 . . . . price on request

Lyman Black Powder

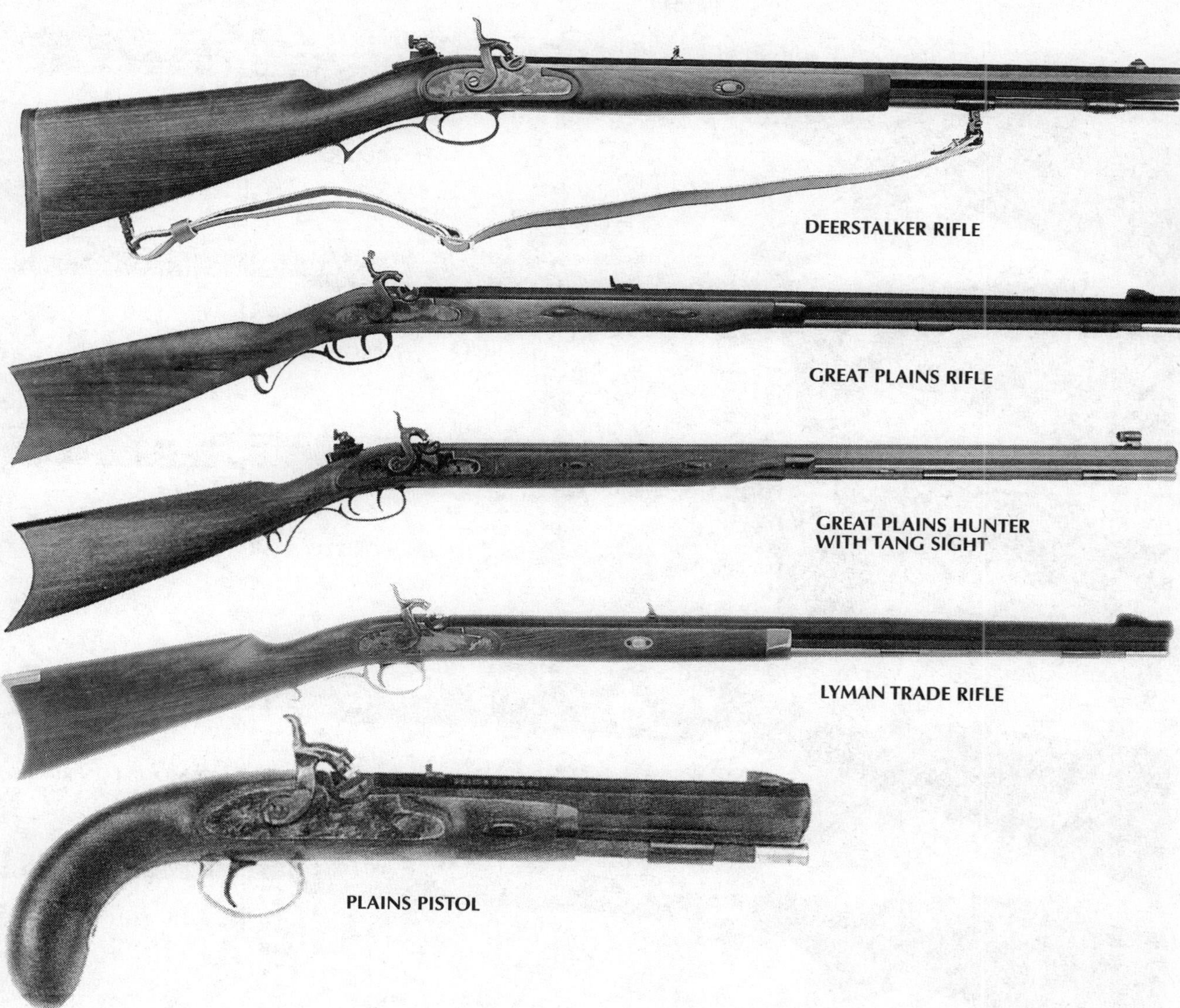

DEERSTALKER RIFLE

GREAT PLAINS RIFLE

GREAT PLAINS HUNTER WITH TANG SIGHT

LYMAN TRADE RIFLE

PLAINS PISTOL

DEERSTALKER

Lock: traditional cap or flint
Stock: walnut
Barrel: 24 in.
Sights: aperture
Weight: 7.5 lbs.
Bore/Caliber: .50 or .54
Features: left-hand models available

caplock **$347**
left-hand **$365**
stainless caplock **$450**
flintlock **$400**
left-hand **$416**

GREAT PLAINS RIFLE

Lock: traditional cap or flint
Stock: walnut
Barrel: 32 in., 1:66 twist
Sights: adjustable open
Weight: 8.0 lbs.
Bore/Caliber: .50 or .54
Features: double set triggers, left-hand models available; also Great Plains Hunter with 1:32 twist

caplock **$540**
unfinished kit **$413**
flintlock **$570**
unfinished kit **$445**

LYMAN TRADE RIFLE

Lock: traditional cap or flint
Stock: walnut
Barrel: 28 in., 1:48 twist
Sights: adjustable open
Weight: 8.0 lbs.
Bore/Caliber: .50 or .54
Features: brass furniture

caplock **$355**
flint **$390**

PLAINS PISTOL

Lock: traditional caplock
Stock: walnut
Barrel: 6 in.
Sights: fixed
Weight: 2.2 lbs.
Bore/Caliber: .50 or .54
Features: iron furniture

Plains Pistol **$280**
unfinished kit **$222**

Markesbery Black Powder

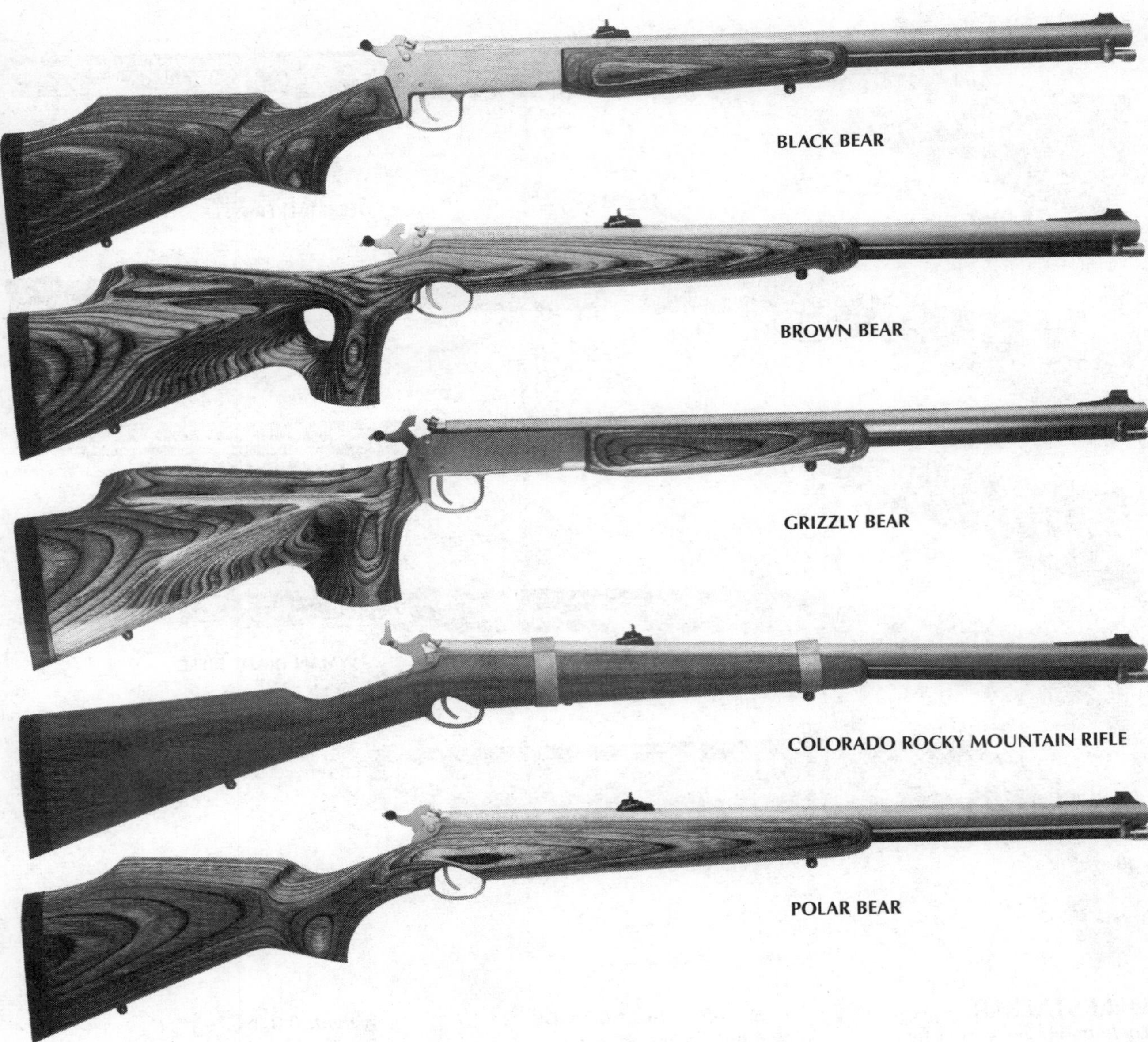

BLACK BEAR

Lock: in-line
Stock: two-piece laminated
Barrel: 24 in., 1:26 twist
Sights: adjustable open
Weight: 6.5 lbs.
Bore/Caliber: .36, .45, .50, .54
Features: also Grizzly Bear with thumbhole stock, Brown Bear with one-piece thumbhole stock, both checkered, aluminum ramrod
Black Bear, blue $549
Brown Bear $600
Grizzly Bear $600

COLORADO ROCKY MOUNTAIN RIFLE

Lock: in-line
Stock: walnut, laminated
Barrel: 24 in., 1:26 twist
Sights: adjustable open
Weight: 7.0 lbs.
Bore/Caliber: .36, .45, .50, .54
Features: #11 or magnum ignition
Rocky Mountain Rifle $549

POLAR BEAR

Lock: in-line
Stock: laminated
Barrel: 24 in., 1:26 twist
Sights: adjustable open
Weight: 7.8 lbs.
Bore/Caliber: .36, .45, .50, .54
Features: one-piece stock

Navy Arms Black Powder Handguns

1847 COLT WALKER
Lock: caplock revolver
Grips: walnut
Barrel: 9 in.
Sights: fixed
Weight: 4.5 lbs.
Bore/Caliber: .44
Features: case-colored frame, brass guard
1847 Colt Walker. $348

LE MAT CALVARY MODEL
Lock: caplock revolver
Grips: walnut
Barrel: 7.6 in.
Sights: fixed
Weight: 3.4 lbs.
Bore/Caliber: .44
Features: 9-shot cylinder; Navy, Cavalry, Army models available
Le Mat $748

COLT 1862 NEW MODEL POLICE
Lock: caplock revolver
Grips: walnut
Barrel: 5.5 in.
Sights: fixed
Weight: 2.7 lbs.
Bore/Caliber: .36
Features: last of the percussion Colts, has brass guard, case-colored frame
New Model Police $266

ROGERS AND SPENCER
Lock: caplock revolver
Grips: walnut
Barrel: 7.5 in.
Sights: fixed
Weight: 3.0 lbs.
Bore/Caliber: .44
Features: octagonal barrel, 6-shot cylinder
Rogers and Spencer $363

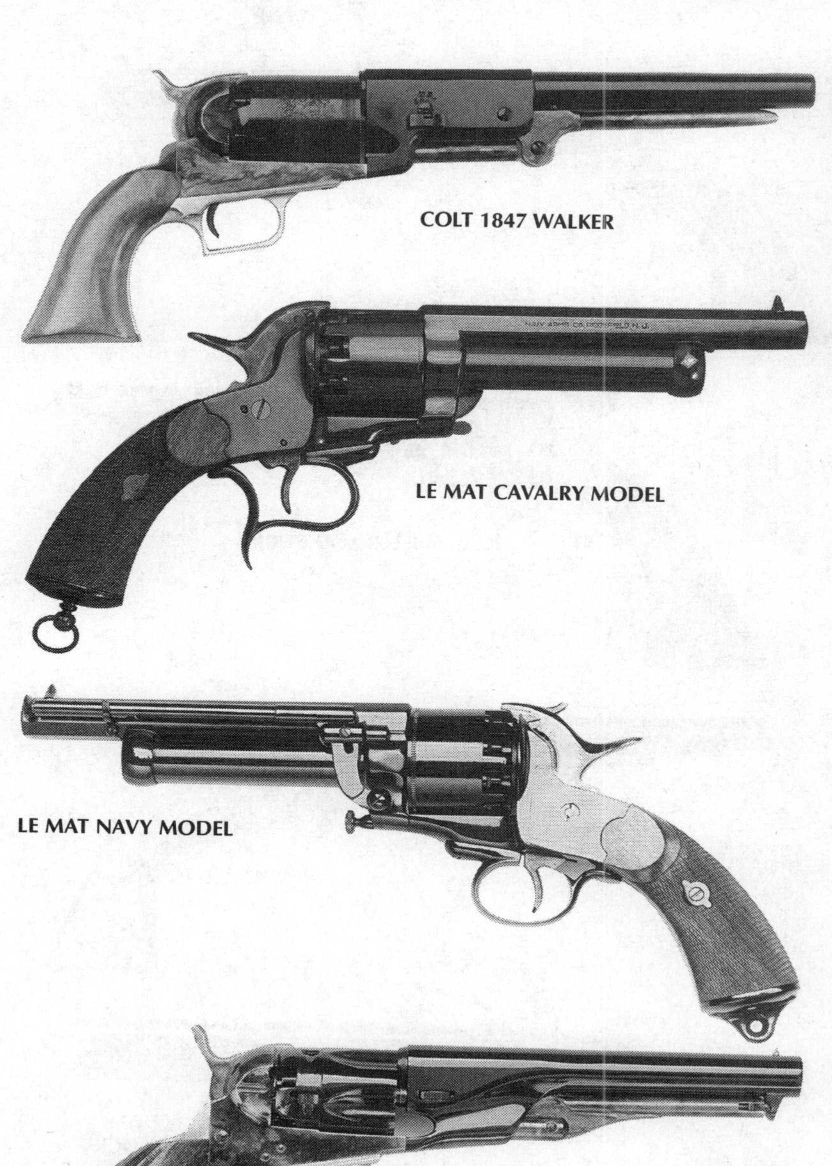

COLT 1847 WALKER

LE MAT CAVALRY MODEL

LE MAT NAVY MODEL

1862 NEW MODEL POLICE

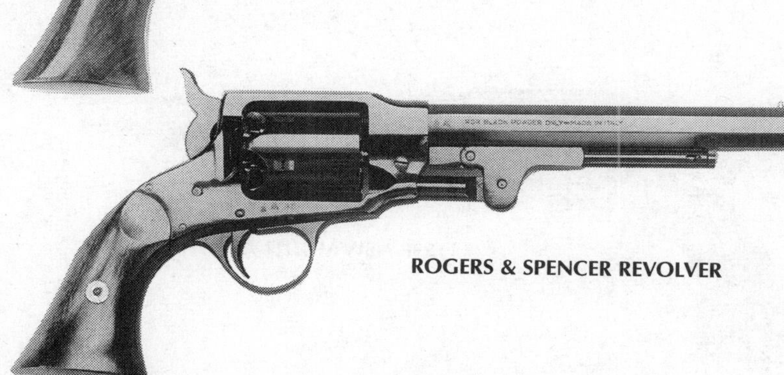

ROGERS & SPENCER REVOLVER

Navy Arms Black Powder Handguns

BLACK POWDER

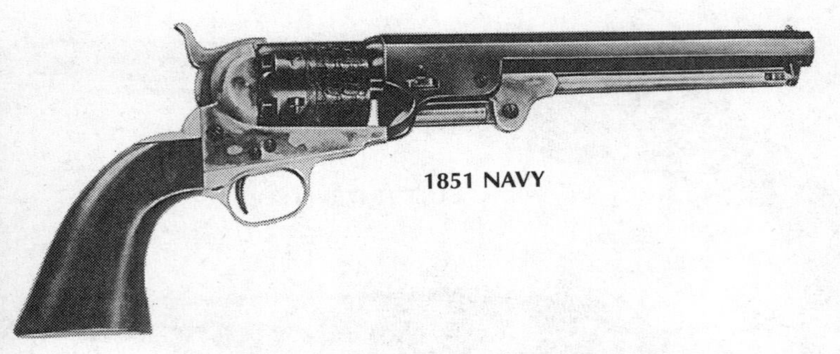
1851 NAVY

1851 NAVY

Lock: caplock revolver
Grips: walnut
Barrel: 7.5 in.
Sights: fixed
Weight: 2.7 lbs.
Bore/Caliber: .36 and .44
Features: brass guard and strap
1851 Navy $242
1851 Navy Frontiersman (.36 cal., 5 in. bbl.) $235

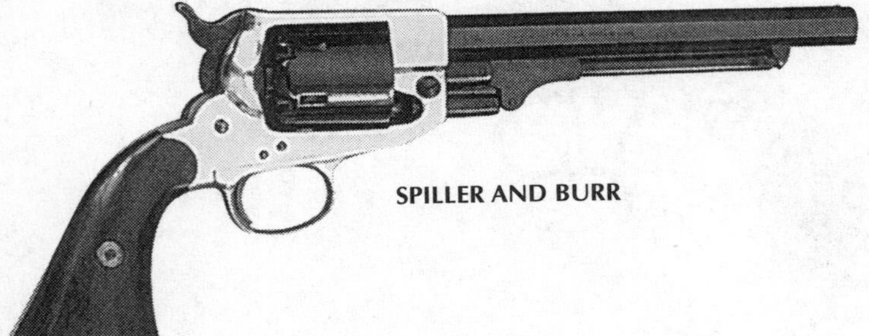
SPILLER AND BURR

SPILLER AND BURR

Lock: caplock revolver
Grips: walnut
Barrel: 7 in.
Sights: fixed
Weight: 2.6 lbs.
Bore/Caliber: .36
Features: brass frame
Spiller and Burr $197

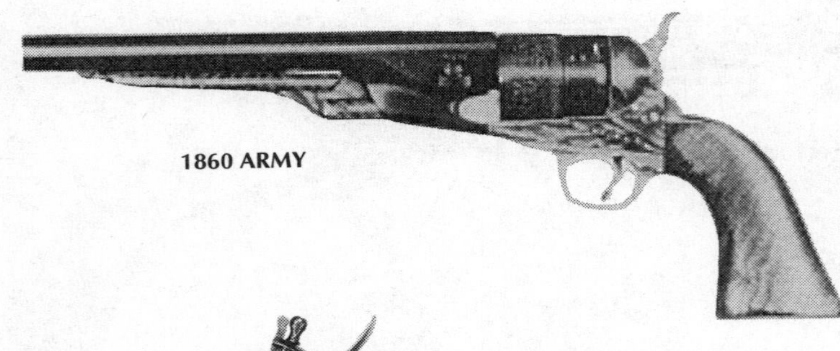
1860 ARMY

1860 ARMY

Lock: caplock revolver
Grips: walnut
Barrel: 8 in.
Sights: fixed
Weight: 2.6 lbs.
Bore/Caliber: .44
Features: brass guard, steel backstrap
1860 Army $221

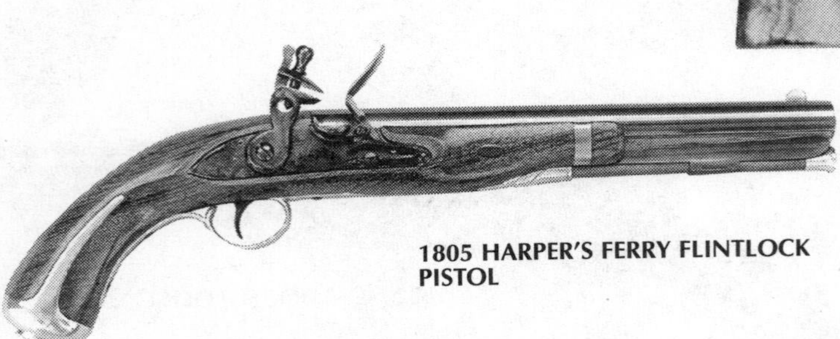
1805 HARPER'S FERRY FLINTLOCK PISTOL

HARPER'S FERRY FLINTLOCK PISTOL

Lock: traditional flintlock
Grips: walnut
Barrel: 10 in.
Sights: fixed
Weight: 2.6 lbs.
Bore/Caliber: .58
Features: case-colored lock, brass furniture, browned barrel
Harper's Ferry $412

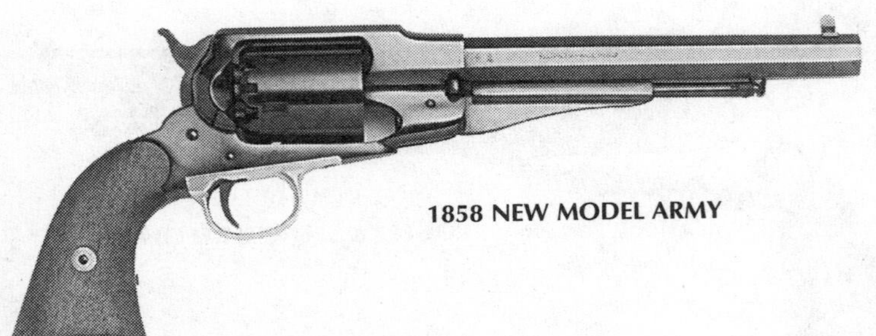
1858 NEW MODEL ARMY

1858 NEW MODEL ARMY REMINGTON

Lock: caplock revolver
Grips: walnut
Barrel: 8 in.
Sights: fixed
Weight: 2.5 lbs.
Bore/Caliber: .44
Features: brass guard, steel frame with top strap
1858 New Model Army Rem. . . $269
with brass frame $183
stainless $358
color, case-hardened......... $320

Navy Arms Black Powder Rifles

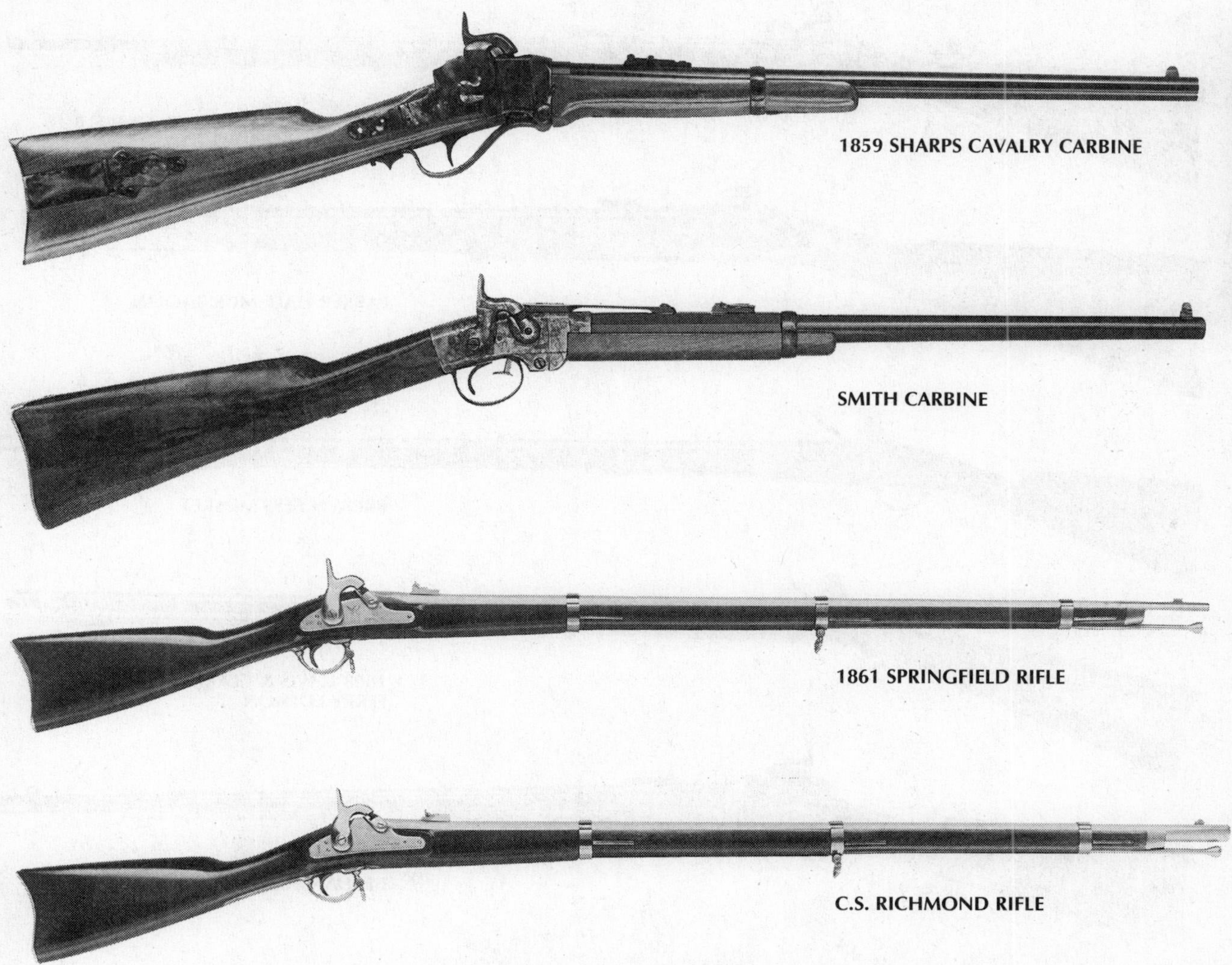

1859 SHARPS CAVALRY CARBINE

SMITH CARBINE

1861 SPRINGFIELD RIFLE

C.S. RICHMOND RIFLE

1859 SHARPS CAVALRY CARBINE

Lock: traditional caplock
Stock: walnut
Barrel: 22 in.
Sights: adjustable open
Weight: 7.8 lbs.
Bore/Caliber: .54
Features: infantry rifle also available
carbine $1187
rifle $1386

SMITH CARBINE

Lock: traditional caplock
Stock: walnut
Barrel: 22 in.
Sights: adjustable open
Weight: 7.8 lbs.
Bore/Caliber: .50
Features: cavalry and artillery models available
Smith Carbine $791

1861 SPRINGFIELD

Lock: traditional caplock
Stock: walnut
Barrel: 40 in.
Sights: fixed
Weight: 10.0 lbs.
Bore/Caliber: .58
Features: three-band furniture polished bright
1861 Springfield $926

C.S. RICHMOND RIFLE

Lock: traditional caplock
Stock: walnut
Barrel: 40 in.
Sights: fixed
Weight: 10.0 lbs.
Bore/Caliber: .58
Features: polished furniture
C.S. Richmond $862

Navy Arms Black Powder Rifles

BLACK POWDER

PARKER-HALE 1858 ENFIELD RIFLE

PARKER-HALE MUSKETOON

BROWN BESS MUSKET

1803 LEWIS & CLARK HARPERS FERRY EDITION

BERDAN 1859 SHARPS RIFLE

PARKER-HALE 1858 ENFIELD RIFLE

Lock: traditional caplock
Stock: walnut
Barrel: 33 in.
Sights: adjustable open
Weight: 9.6 lbs.
Bore/Caliber: .58
Features: brass furniture
Parker-Hale Enfield $762

PARKER-HALE MUSKETOON

Lock: traditional caplock
Stock: walnut
Barrel: 24 in.
Sights: adjustable open
Weight: 7.5 lbs.
Bore/Caliber: .58
Features: brass furniture
Parker-Hale Musketoon $684

BROWN BESS MUSKET

Lock: traditional flintlock
Stock: walnut
Barrel: 42 in.
Sights: fixed
Weight: 9.5 lbs.
Bore/Caliber: .75
Features: full stock without bands
Brown Bess Musket $1062

1803 LEWIS & CLARK HARPER'S FERRY EDITION

Lock: traditional flintlock
Stock: walnut
Barrel: 35 in.
Sights: fixed
Weight: 8.5 lbs.
Bore/Caliber: .54
Features: case-colored lock, brass patch box
1803 Harper's Ferry $882

BERDAN 1859 SHARPS RIFLE

Lock: traditional caplock
Stock: walnut
Barrel: 30 in.
Sights: adjustable open
Weight: 8.5 lbs.
Bore/Caliber: .54
Features: case-colored receiver, double set trigger
Berdan 1859 Sharps $1387

Pedersoli Black Powder

LE PAGE TARGET PISTOL

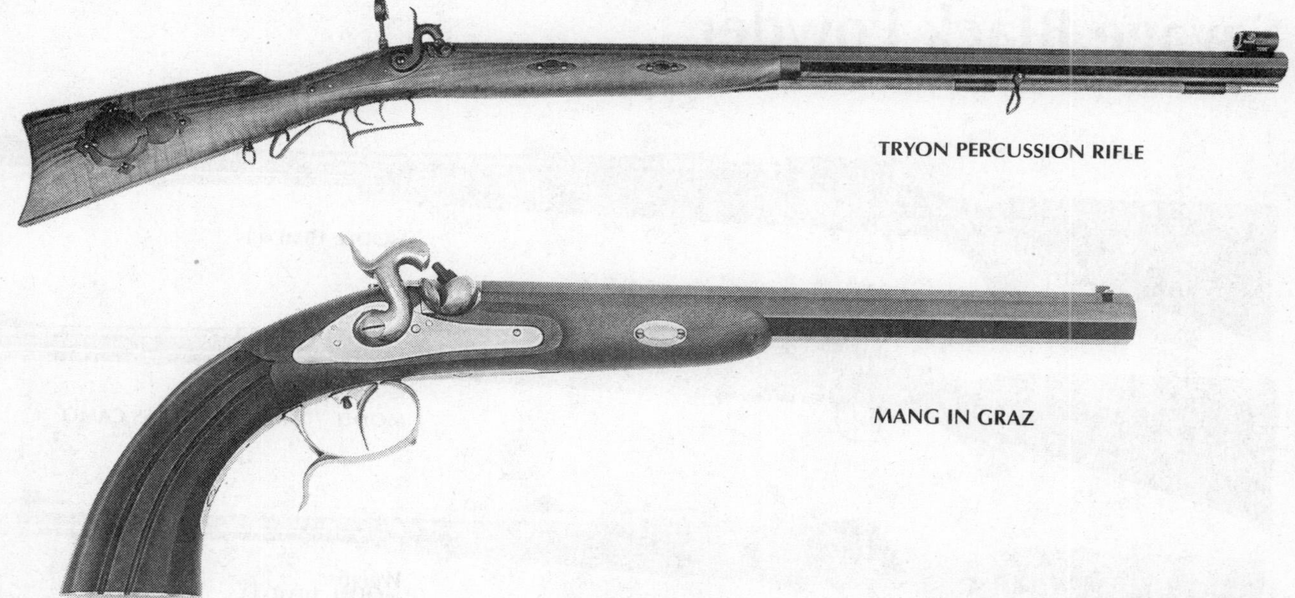

TRYON PERCUSSION RIFLE

MANG IN GRAZ

LEPAGE TARGET PISTOL

Lock: traditional flintlock
Grips: walnut
Barrel: 10.5 in., 1:18 twist
Sights: fixed
Weight: 2.5 lbs.
Bore/Caliber: .44 or .45
Features: smoothbore .45 available
LePage. $900
caplock in .36, .38, .44 . . . . $700

"MANG IN GRAZ"

Lock: traditional caplock
Grips: walnut
Barrel: 11 in., 1:15 or 1:18 (.44) twist
Sights: fixed
Weight: 2.5 lbs.
Bore/Caliber: .38 or .44
Features: grooved butt
Price: $1195

MORTIMER TARGET RIFLE

Lock: flintlock
Stock: English-style European walnut
Barrel: octagon to round 36 in.
Sights: target
Weight: 8.8 lbs.
Bore/Caliber: .54
Features: case-colored lock; stock has cheekpiece and hand checkering; 7-groove barrel
Mortimer Target $1225

TRYON-PERCUSSION RIFLE

Lock: traditional caplock
Stock: walnut
Barrel: 32 in., 1:48 or 1:66 (.54) twist
Sights: adjustable open
Weight: 9.5 lbs.
Bore/Caliber: .45, .50, .54
Features: Creedmoor version with aperture sight available
Tyron-Percussion $750
Creedmoor $960

Ruger Black Powder

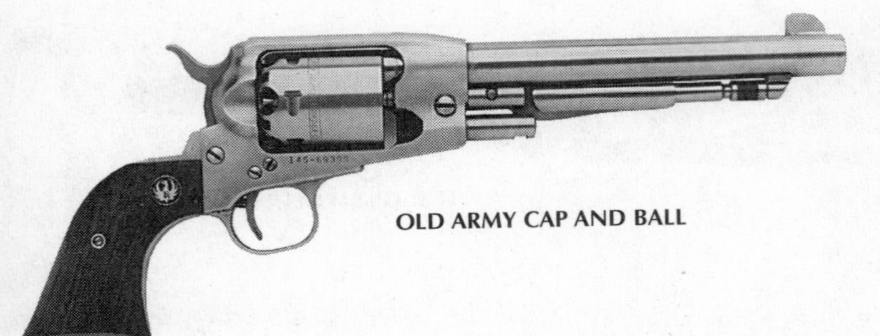
OLD ARMY CAP AND BALL

OLD ARMY CAP AND BALL

Lock: caplock revolver
Grips: walnut
Barrel: 5.5 or 7.5 in.
Sights: fixed
Weight: 3.0 lbs.
Bore/Caliber: .45
Features: Civil War-era reproduction in modern steel, music wire springs
blue. $541
stainless (adjustable sights) $577
gloss stainless with ivory grips . . $623

Savage Black Powder

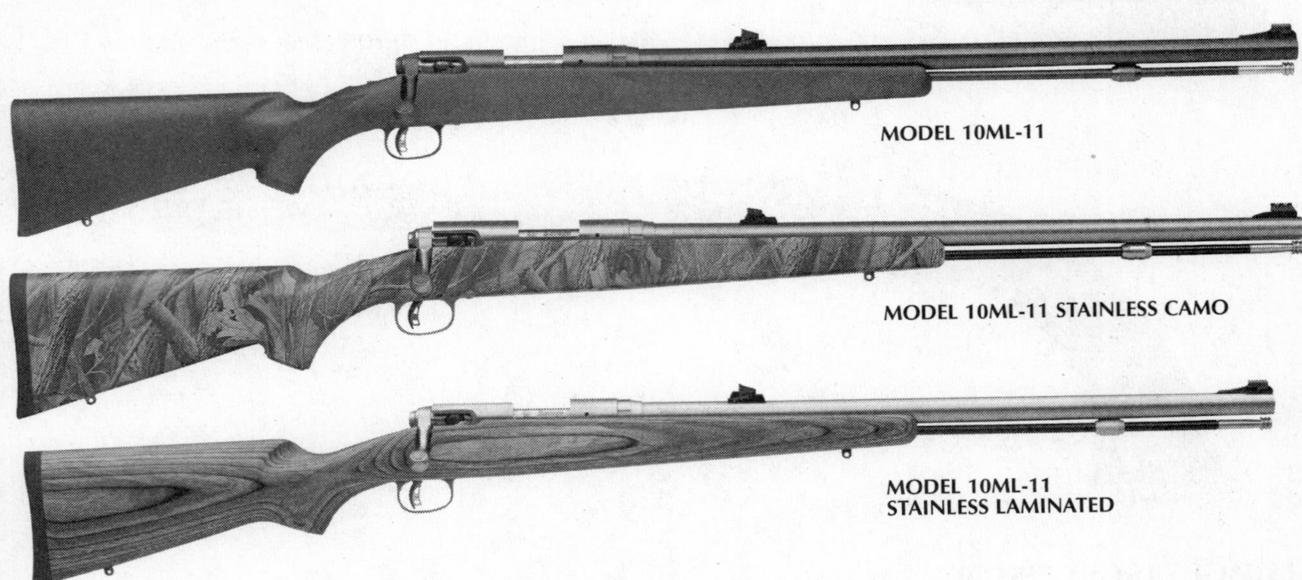
MODEL 10ML-11

MODEL 10ML-11 STAINLESS CAMO

MODEL 10ML-11 STAINLESS LAMINATED

MODEL M10ML-11 MUZZLELOADER

Lock: in-line
Stock: synthetic, camo or laminated
Barrel: 24 in.
Sights: adjustable fiber optic
Weight: 8.0 lbs.
Bore/Caliber: .50
Features: bolt action mechanism, 209 priming

blue synthetic $531
stainless $589
blue camo $569
stainless camo. $628
stainless laminated $667

Shiloh Black Powder

1863 SHARPS

1874 SPORTER

1874 CREEDMOOR TARGET RIFLE (WITHOUT SIGHTS)

MODEL 1863 SHARPS

Lock: traditional caplock
Stock: walnut
Barrel: 30 in.
Sights: adjustable open
Weight: 9.5 lbs.
Bore/Caliber: .50 or .54
Features: sporting model with half-stock, double set trigger military model with 3-band full stock; also carbine with 22 in. barrel (7.5 lbs.)
sporting rifle and carbine $1547
military rifle $1793

MODEL 1874 SPORTER

Lock: black powder cartridge
Stock: walnut
Barrel: 30 in. heavy or standard
Sights: adjustable open
Weight: 9.0 lbs.
Bore/Caliber: .38-55 to .50-90
Features: shotgun or military-style buttstock; double set triggers; Buckhorn rear sight, blade front.
Sporter #1 (cheek rest & pistol grip) $1638
Sporter #3 (staight grip) $1547

MODEL 1874 CREEDMOOR TARGET

Lock: black powder cartridge
Stock: walnut
Barrel: 32 in. half octagon
Sights: none
Weight: 9.0 lbs.
Bore/Caliber: all popular black powder cartridges from .38-55 to .50-90
Features: shotgun buttstock, pistol grip; single trigger; fancy walnut, pewter tip
Price: $2485
#2 Creedmoor Silhouette (30" round, tapered barrel) . . . $2485

When you seat a ball or bullet, make sure it's in contact with the powder. Let the ramrod drop a few inches onto the charge. If it bounces, the ball or bullet is probably seated properly.

Thompson/Center Black Powder

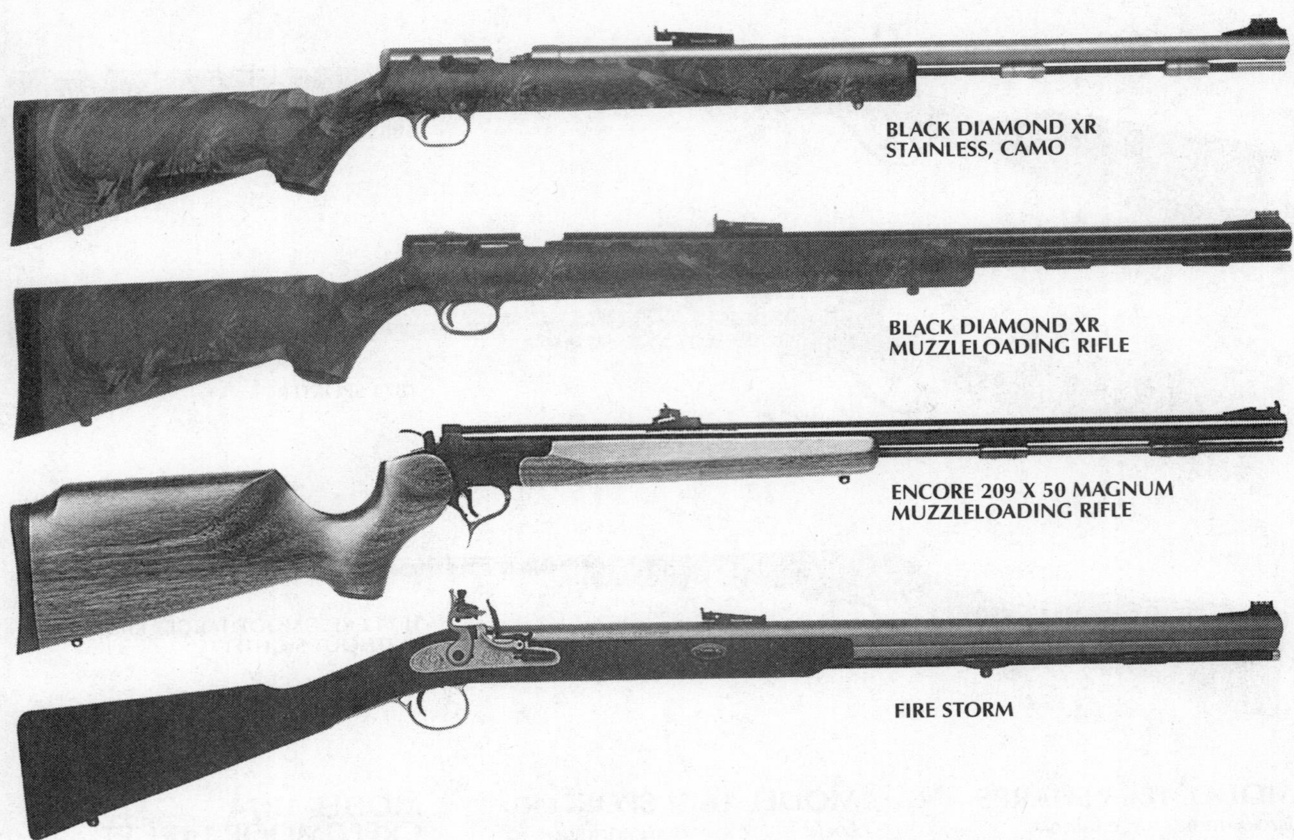

BLACK DIAMOND XR
STAINLESS, CAMO

BLACK DIAMOND XR
MUZZLELOADING RIFLE

ENCORE 209 X 50 MAGNUM
MUZZLELOADING RIFLE

FIRE STORM

BLACK DIAMOND RIFLE XR

Lock: in-line
Stock: walnut or synthetic
Barrel: 26 in., 1:28 twist
Sights: adjustable fiber optic
Weight: 6.6 lbs.
Bore/Caliber: .50
Features: musket, cap or no. 11 nipple
blue synthetic $337
stainless camo $440

ENCORE 209X50 RIFLE

Lock: in-line
Stock: walnut or synthetic
Barrel: 26 in., 1:28 twist
Sights: adjustable fiber optic
Weight: 7.0 lbs.
Bore/Caliber: .50
Features: automatic safety, interchangeable barrel with Encore centerfire barrels; also available 209x45 9.45)
blue synthetic $637
stainless synthetic $713
blue walnut $678
blue camo $696
stainless camo $772
blue walnut .45 . . . . $683
stainless synthetic .45 . . . . $727

FIRE STORM

Lock: traditional cap or flint
Stock: synthetic
Barrel: 26 in., 1:48 twist
Sights: adjustable fiber optic
Weight: 7.0 lbs.
Bore/Caliber: .50
Features: aluminum ramrod
blue $436
stainless $488

Traditions Black Powder

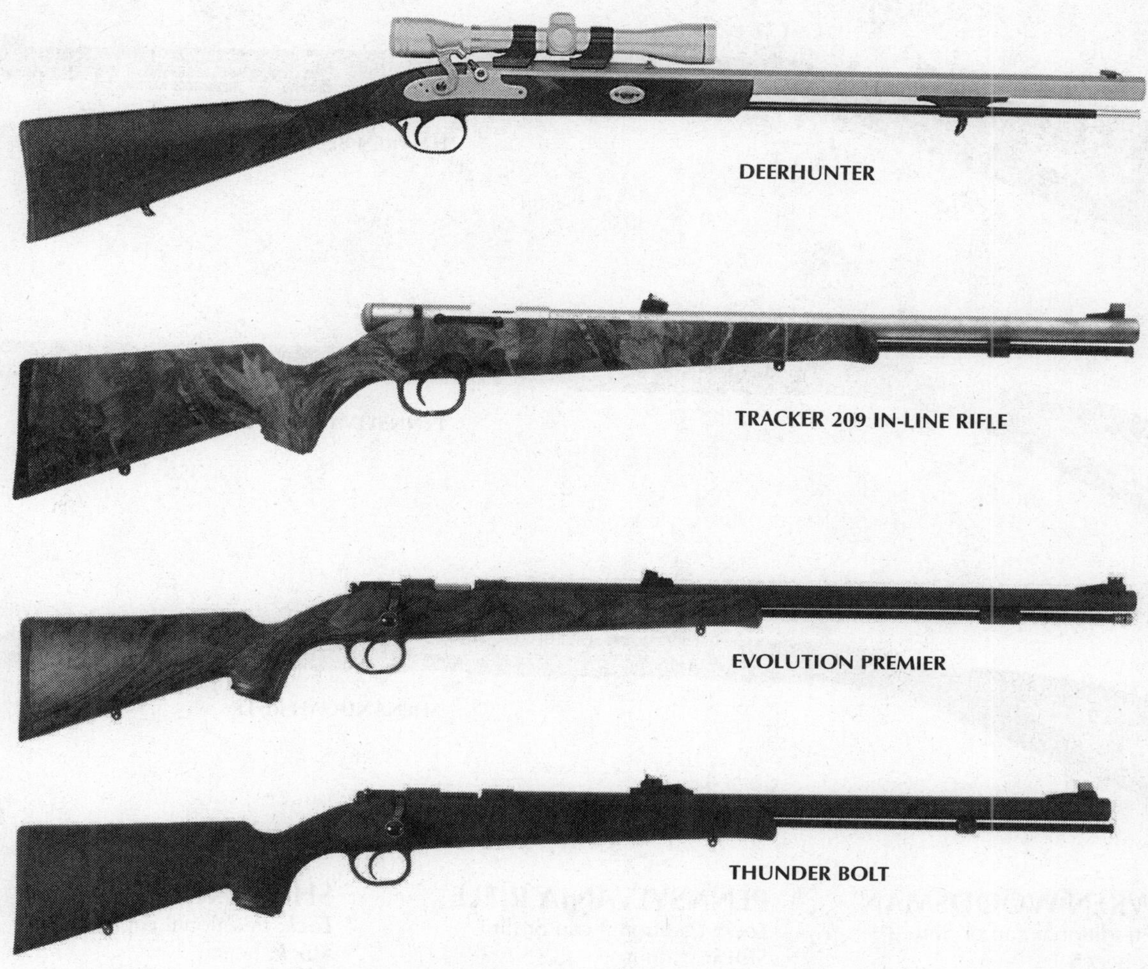

DEERHUNTER

TRACKER 209 IN-LINE RIFLE

EVOLUTION PREMIER

THUNDER BOLT

DEERHUNTER RIFLE

Lock: traditional cap or flint
Stock: hardwood, synthetic or camo
Barrel: 24 in., 1:48 twist
Sights: fixed
Weight: 6.0 lbs.
Bore/Caliber: .32, .50, .54
Features: blackened furniture; also economy-model Panther, 24 in .50 or .54

cap, blue, hardwood . . . $199 - $205
flint, blue, hardwood $219
cap, nickel, synthetic $179
flint, blue, synthetic $189
flint, nickel, cynthetic $199
flint, nickel, camo $249

TRACKER 209

Lock: in-line
Stock: synthetic or camo
Barrel: 22 in., 1:28 twist (1:24 .45)
Sights: fiber optic
Weight: 6.5 lbs.
Bore/Caliber: .45 or .50
Features: 209 primer ignition

blue synthetic $139
nickel synthetic $159
nickel camo. $199

EVOLUTION

Lock: bolt
Stock: synthetic, laminated, or camo
Barrel: 26 in.
Sights: fiber optics
Weight: 7.0 lbs.
Bore/Caliber: .50
Features: fluted, tapered barrel, drilled & tapped for scope. 209 ignition, swivel studs, rubber butt pad; LD model in .45 or .50 has tru-Glo sights.

Premier, blue. $349
stainless $469
stainless, camo $369
LD blue synthetic. . . . . . $249 - $259
blue camo $279
nickel synthetic. $279
nickel camo. $309

THUNDER BOLT

Lock: bolt
Stock: synthetic
Barrel: 24 in. (21 in. youth)
Sights: adjustable
Weight: 7.0 lbs.
Bore/Caliber: .45 or.50
Features: 209-ignition, checkered stock, sling swivels, rubber butt pad, drilled & tapped for scope.

blue synthetic $179
nickel synthetic. $189
blue camo $199
nickel camo. $219
youth. $179

Traditions Black Powder

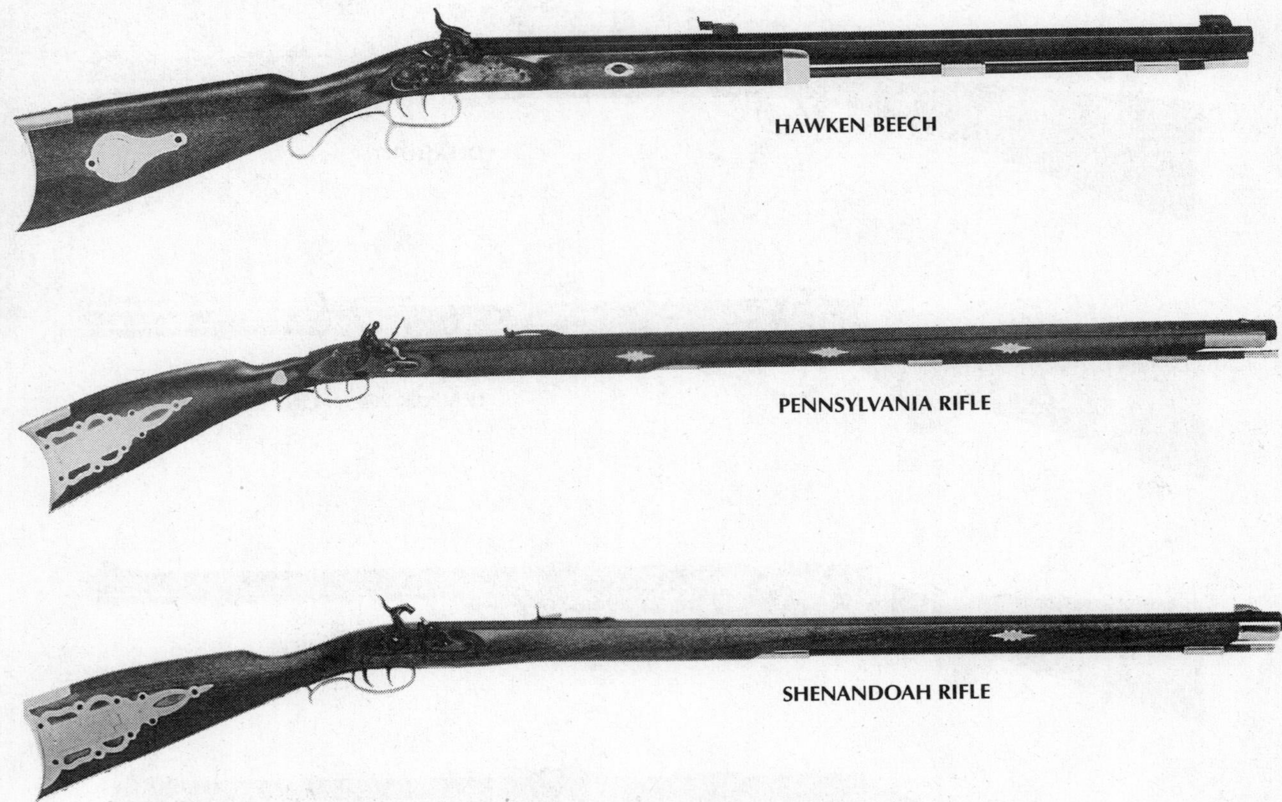

HAWKEN WOODSMAN

Lock: traditional cap or flint
Stock: beech
Barrel: 28 in., 1:48 twist
Sights: adjustable open
Weight: 7.7 lbs.
Bore/Caliber: .50 or .54
Features: brass furniture
caplock $295
lefthand caplock $309
flintlock. $309
also available: Crockett (.32 caplock). $325

PENNSYLVANIA RIFLE

Lock: traditional cap or flint
Stock: walnut
Barrel: 20 in., 1:66 twist
Sights: adjustable open
Weight: 8.5 lbs.
Bore/Caliber: .50
Features: brass furniture
caplock $529
flintlock. $545

SHENANDOAH RIFLE

Lock: traditional cap or flint
Stock: beech
Barrel: 33 in., 1:66 twist
Sights: fixed
Weight: 7.2 lbs.
Bore/Caliber: .50
Features: brass furniture; squirrel rifle in .36
caplock $425
flintlock. $439
caplock .36 . . . . $435
flintlock .36. . . . . $469
also available: Kentucky, flint or caplock . . . . . $269 - $295

Traditions Black Powder

KENTUCKY PISTOL

Lock: traditional caplock
Grips: beech
Barrel: 10 in.
Sights: fixed
Weight: 2.5 lbs.
Bore/Caliber: .50
Features: brass furniture
Kentucky Pistol $169

IN-LINE PISTOLS (BUCKHUNTER)

Lock: in-line
Grips: walnut or synthetic
Barrel: 9.5 or 12.5 in.
Sights: adjustable open
Weight: 2.1 lbs.
Bore/Caliber: .50
Features: blue or nickel furniture; also with extra-long barrel and brake
9.5 in. $279
12.5 in. $279
14.8 in. with brake (also in .45) . . $309

PIONEER PISTOL

Lock: traditional caplock
Grips: walnut
Barrel: 9.6 in.
Sights: fixed
Weight: 1.9 lbs.
Bore/Caliber: .45
Features: German silver furniture
Pioneer $174

WILLIAM PARKER PISTOL

Lock: traditional caplock
Grips: walnut
Barrel: 10.4 in.
Sights: fixed
Weight: 2.3 lbs.
Bore/Caliber: .50
Features: checkered with brass furniture
William Parker $295

TRAPPER PISTOL

Lock: traditional cap or flint
Grips: beech
Barrel: 9.8 in.
Sights: adjustable open
Weight: 2.9 lbs.
Bore/Caliber: .50
Features: brass furniture
Trapper $219
flintlock. $235

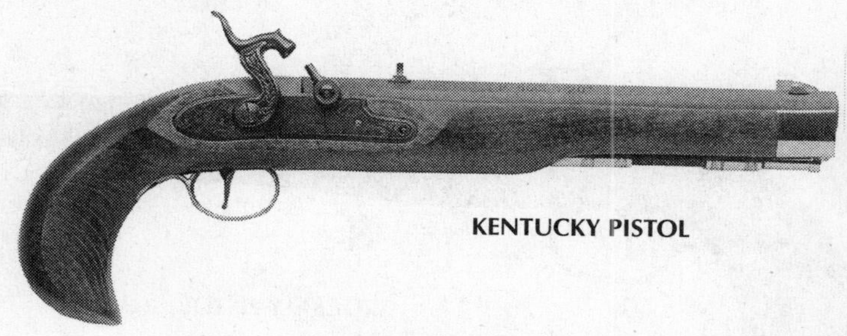
KENTUCKY PISTOL

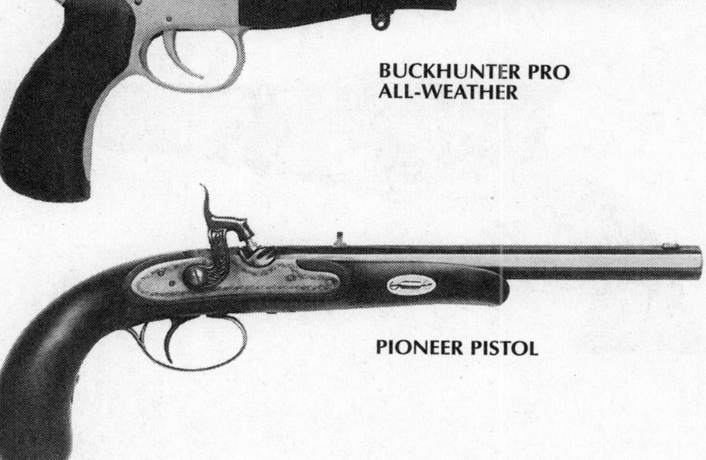
BUCKHUNTER PRO ALL-WEATHER

PIONEER PISTOL

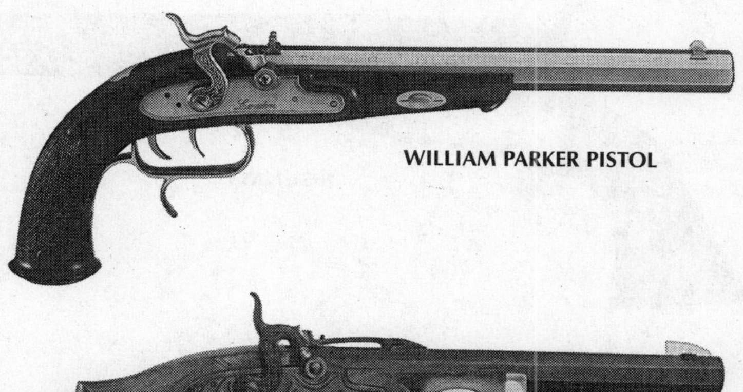
WILLIAM PARKER PISTOL

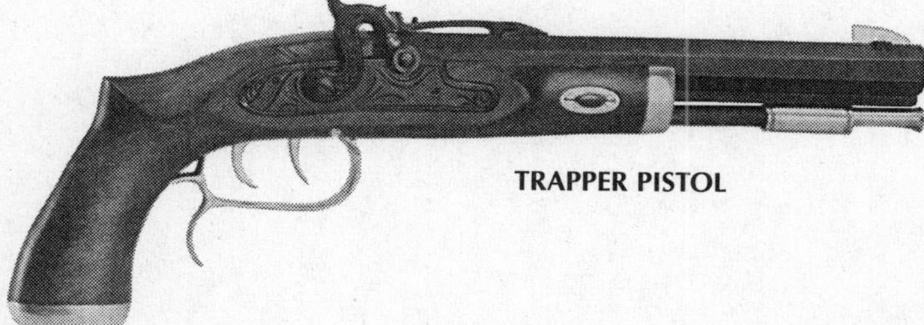
TRAPPER PISTOL

Traditions Black Powder

BLACK POWDER

CROCKETT PISTOL

1858 ARMY

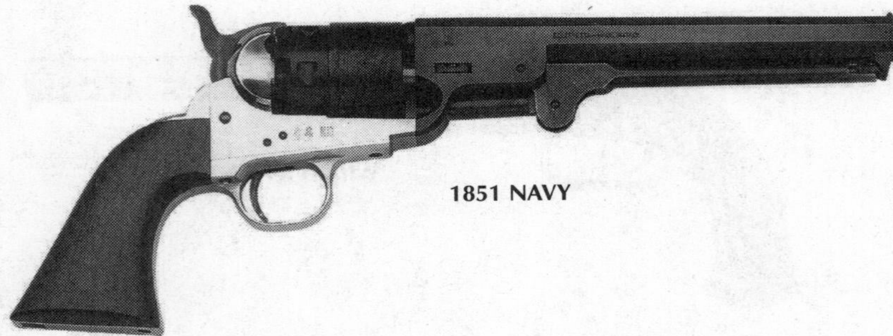
1851 NAVY

CROCKETT PISTOL

Lock: traditional caplock
Grips: hardwood
Barrel: 10 in.
Sights: fixed
Weight: 2.0 lbs.
Bore/Caliber: .32 caplock
Features: blued, octagon barrel
Price: $159

1858 ARMY REVOLVER

Lock: caplock
Grips: walnut
Barrel: 8 in.
Sights: fixed
Weight: 2.6 lbs.
Bore/Caliber: .44
Features: octagon barrel, steel frame
Price: $235
Stainless with target sights $385
1858 New Army (brass) $185
1858 Bison $215

1851 NAVY REVOLVER

Lock: caplock
Grips: walnut
Barrel: 7.5 in.
Sights: fixed
Weight: 2.8 lbs.
Bore/Caliber: .36 and .44
Features: blued, octagon barrel, brass frame
Price: $169
Steel frame (.44 only) $199
1851 Navy U.S. Marshall
(old silver, 5 in. bbl.). $309
1851 Navy Old Silver
(7.5 in. bbl.) $269
also available:
1860 Army (nickel, brass or steel,
8 in. round bbl.) . . . . $185 - $295
1873 Single Action
(steel, 4.75 or 7.5 in. bbl.) . . $365
1863 Pocket Model
(.31, 3.5 in. bbl) $215

Uberti Black Powder

1847 WALKER

Lock: caplock revolver
Grips: walnut grips
Barrel: 9 in.
Sights: fixed
Weight: 4.45 lbs.
Caliber: .44
Features: color, case-hardened frame, brass trigger guard
1847 Walker $320

1848 DRAGOON

Lock: caplock revolver
Grips: walnut
Barrel: 7.5 in.
Sights: fixed
Weight: 4.06 lbs.
Caliber: .44
Features: comes in 1st, 2nd and 3rd models, color, case-hardened frame, brass trigger guard
1848 Dragoon. $295
1848 Whiteneyville Dragoon . . $355

1858 REMINGTON NEW ARMY

Lock: caplock revolver
Grips: walnut
Barrel: 8 in.
Sights: fixed
Weight: 2.8 lbs.
Bore/Caliber: .44
Features: octagonal barrel, brass guard
New Army. $270
stainless $325

1860 ARMY REVOLVER

Lock: caplock revolver
Grips: walnut
Barrel: 8 in.
Sights: fixed
Weight: 2.6 lbs.
Bore/Caliber: .44
Features: case-colored frame
1860 Army $260
with fluted cylinder. $260

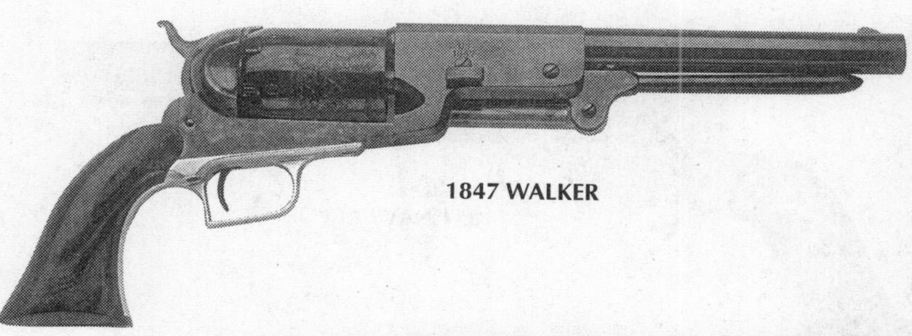

1847 WALKER

1848 3RD MODEL DRAGOON

1848 WHITENEYVILLE DRAGOON

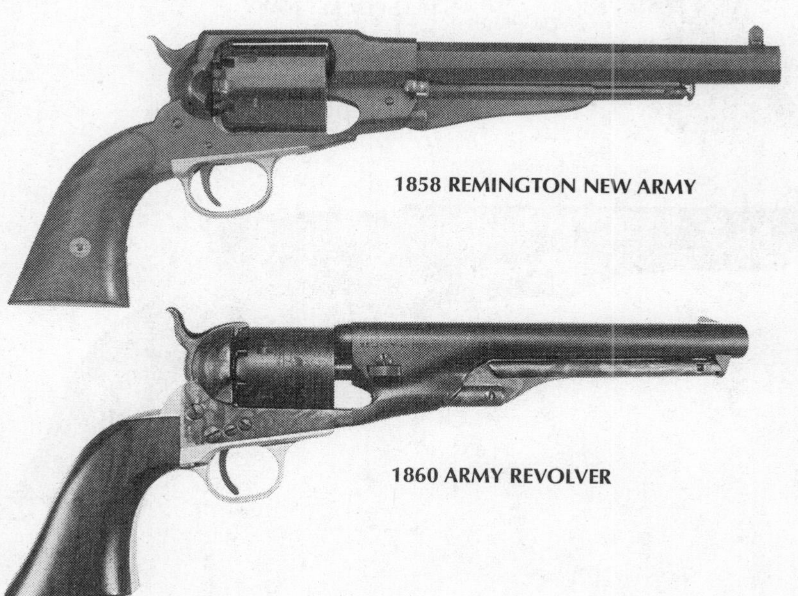

1858 REMINGTON NEW ARMY

1860 ARMY REVOLVER

Uberti Black Powder

1851 NAVY REVOLVER

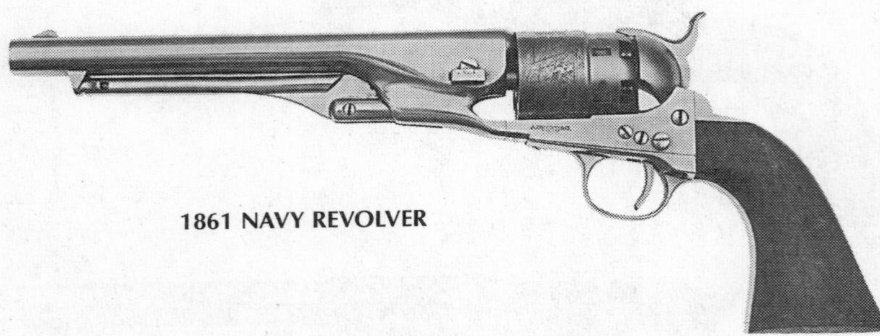
1861 NAVY REVOLVER

1862 POCKET NAVY

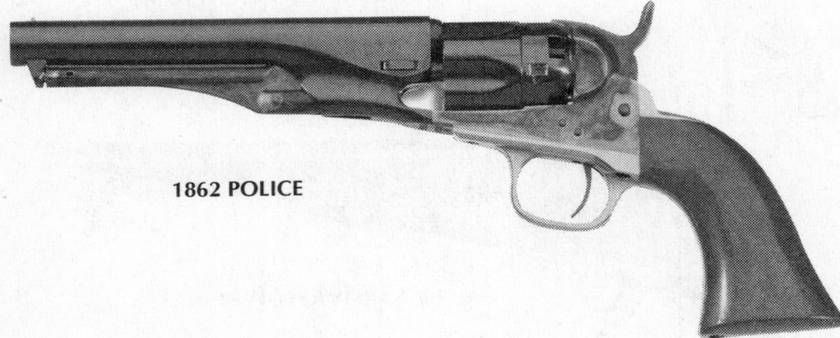
1862 POLICE

1851 NAVY REVOLVER

Lock: caplock revolver
Grips: walnut
Barrel: 7.5 in.
Sights: fixed
Weight: 2.8 lbs.
Bore/Caliber: .36
Features: case-colored frame; brass round or square trigger-guard
1851 Navy $250

1861 NAVY REVOLVER

Lock: caplock revolver
Grips: walnut
Barrel: 7.5 in.
Sights: fixed
Weight: 2.8 lbs.
Bore/Caliber: .36
Features: case-colored frame; brass or steel trigger-guard
1861 Navy $270

1862 POCKET NAVY

Lock: caplock revolver
Grips: walnut
Barrel: 5.5,.
Sights: fixed
Weight: 1.68 lbs.
Bore/Caliber: .36
Features: color case-colored frame, 6-shot cylinder, forged steel barrel,
Pocket Navy. $270

1862 POLICE

Lock: caplock revolver
Grips: walnut
Barrel: 6.5 in
Sights: fixed
Weight: 1.59 lbs.
Bore/Caliber: .36
Features: color case-colored frame, 6-shot cylender, forged steel barel,
1862 Pocket Police $270

Uberti Black Powder

PATERSON REVOLVER

Lock: caplock revolver
Grips: walnut
Barrel: 7.5 in.
Sights: none
Weight: 2.6 lbs.
Bore/Caliber: .36
Features: 5-shot cylinder
Paterson $375
with Load Lever $400

POCKET REVOLVERS

Lock: caplock revolver
Grips: walnut
Barrel: 4 in.
Sights: fixed
Weight: 1.46 to 1.56 lbs.
Bore/Caliber: .31
Features: color case-colored frame, 5-shot cylinders, forged steel barrel
1848 Baby Dragoon $270
1849 Wells Fargo 4" $270
1849 Pocket 4" $270

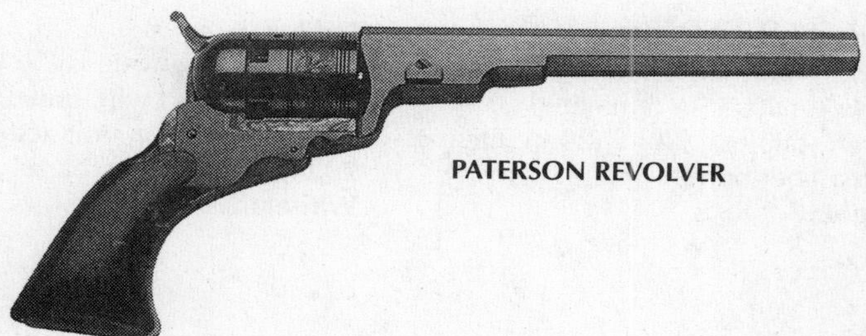

PATERSON REVOLVER

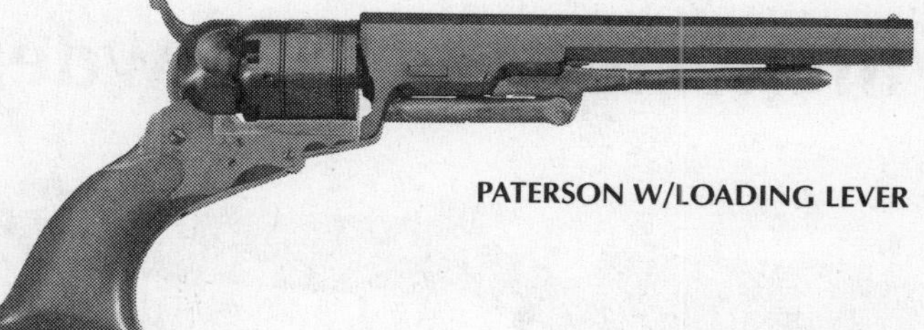

PATERSON W/LOADING LEVER

1849 POCKET

1849 WELLS FARGO

1848 BABY DRAGOON

White Rifles Black Powder

HUNTER SERIES

Lock: in-line
Stock: synthetic or laminated
Barrel: stainless, 22 in. (24 in. Elite)
Sights: fiber-optic
Weight: 7.7 lbs.
Caliber/Bore: .45 or .50
Features: Elite weighs 8.6 lbs., aluminum ramrod with bullet extractor, also: Thunderbolt bolt action with 209-ignition, 26 in. barrel

Whitetail. $430
Blacktail and Elite $500
Thunderbolt $600
Also available:
Odyssey (ss/laminated thumbhole stock) $1300

Winchester Black Powder

APEX STAINLESS SYNTHETIC

WINCHESTER MODEL X-150

APEX MUZZLELOADER

Lock: in-line
Stock: synthetic or camo
Barrel: 28 in., 1:28 twist
Sights: fiber optic
Weight: 7.2 lbs.
Caliber/Bore: .45 or .50
Features: "swing-action" breech

blue synthetic $311
full camo. $416
stainless synthetic. $370
stainless camo. $415

MODEL X-150 MUZZLELOADING RIFLE

Lock: in-line
Stock: synthetic or camo
Barrel: 26 in. fluted, 1:28 twist
Sights: fiber optic
Weight: 7.9 lbs.
Bore/Caliber: .45 or .50
Features: 209 primer ignition, stainless bolt action

blue synthetic $230
blue camo $280
stainless camo. $350

CUSTOM GUNMAKERS

Axtell Rifle Company
Sheridan, Montana

In 1973, Riflesmith, Inc. began manufacturing replicas of the late 19th-century sights traditionally installed on Sharps and other long-range rifles. In 1989 the Axtell Rifle Company began manufacture of a New Model 1877 Sharps.

Casual gun enthusiasts are more familiar with the 1874 Sharps "buffalo guns" of book and film. The Model 1877 is nonetheless better. It evolved from calls for a more accurate long-range target rifle following a match at the Creedmoor Rifle Range on Long Island between American and Irish shooters. The 1874 Sharps had proven itself there but even the winners wanted faster lock time and a heavier barrel.

Of the new 1877 Sharps, explains Carmen Axtell, "It's not a cheap rifle to build. Our prices reflect cost more than profit. And you'll never be disappointed." The rifles are remarkably true to the line, balance and mechanism of the originals. Also noticeable is the meticulous fitting and finishing of parts. The case coloring is exquisite and the wood and metal finish are even better than on the original!

Axtell Rifle Company makes several variations of the 1877 Sharps: Custom Express, No. 1 Creedmoor, No. 2 Long Range, Lower Sporter, Lower Business, and Overbaugh Scheutzen. All 10 chamberings are original Sharps rounds, from the .45-70, .45-90 and .45-100 Express to the various 40- and 45-caliber cartridges popular during the late 1800s.

Les Baer Custom
Hillsdale, Illinois

Well known among pistol shooters seeking superior M1911 .45 target guns, Les Baer is equally talented in turning out street-worthy hardware. His Hillsdale, Illinois shop has served law enforcement officers and consumers wanting best-quality pistols for home protection. Les offers compact Comanche and Stinger 1911s, as well as standard-size pistols. You can buy frames in steel, stainless steel and alloy to build your own .45. Slides and barrels are available too. Other components include safeties, triggers, bushings, sights and magazines. Les has earned the loyalty of many national pistol champions as well as people like Clint Smith, who runs a training facility for police and civilian shooters

The shop also deals in autoloading "AR" series rifles (like the M-16) for tactical shooters and service rifle competitors. Components too: from hand-stops and stocks to barrels, bolts and upper and lower receivers. His NRA Match rifle has a 30-inch, hand-lapped fast-twist barrel, floating handguard, titanium striker and two-stage Jewell trigger, plus many other refinements. The Picatinny rail, available on other Baer .223s, accommodates scope rings and a receiver sight.

Les, incidentally, established quite a reputation racing automobiles. His guns show the fine machine work and close tolerances of track-worthy V-8 engines; and Les goes about gun-building with the same intensity he brought to racing.

Mark Bansner

Adamstown, Pennsylvania

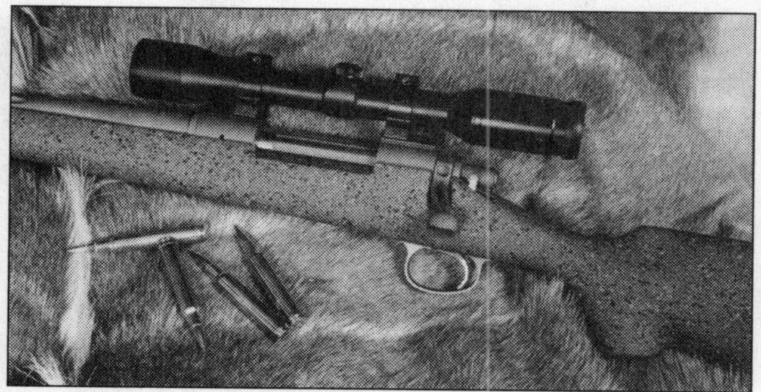

More than 25 years ago Mark Bansner started a gunshop with an idea to improve shot patterns for turkey hunters. Now his focus is bolt-action hunting rifles, for which he furnishes his own synthetic stocks. They are hand-bedded to cradle the receiver without imposing stress points. Mark has formed High Tech Specialties to produce these lightweight stocks for sale to the trade.

At Bansner's shop, match-grade, hand-lapped Lilja barrels are fitted to actions trued to ensure concentric chambering. Mark and his craftsmen tune factory triggers or install aftermarket Jewell triggers for a crisp, consistent pull. Bansner rifles are guaranteed to deliver fine accuracy.

Trim but functional lines give Banser's rifles an elegant look. Myriad stock finish and color options include speckling and spider-webbing. Stock-to-steel fit is skin-tight except where the barrel is intentionally floated. The shop even makes muzzle brakes, which reduce recoil by up to 45 percent.

Mark ships about 200 custom-built rifles each year from his shop in Adamstown, Pennsylvania. Some are special-edition rifles that go to conservation organizations for fundraisers. The Bansner brochure shows standard rifle configurations and options, but the customer can make his rifle truly personal. Prices start at $4695.

The Biesens

Spokane, Washington

At 87, Alvin Biesen isn't turning out the number of rifles he once did But son Roger and grand-daughter Paula carry on the tradition. Al's basement shop always seemed too small and dark. Gun parts and tools lay askew below faded photos of Biesen rifles in the hands of hunters behind trophy game. But for decades it was a sanctuary for people who sought fine rifles

"Dad didn't force me into this," says Paula, who has become an accomplished engraver. "I got plenty of encouragement but no push. I began by etching into steel what I painted in school—mostly animals." Paula has proven herself against stiff competition.

David Malicki of Napa, California had less interest in Biesen rifles than in the pretty young blond engraving them and married her in 1992. David moved to Spokane, partly to let Paula continue work with Roger and Al. Her work has appeared on rifles commissioned for auction by the National Rifle Association, the Rocky Mountain Elk Foundation and Safari Club International. Paula has been accepted as a member of the Custom Gunmakers Guild

Strikingly evident in Paula's work is her clean detail, the mark of a careful and confident artist. The animals she

scribes appear lifelike. "You learn tricks," she shrugs. "Like never setting an animal face-on so you have to duplicate details right and left. Engraving game scenes is harder than painting with a brush because you can't just sweep over them and try again."

Kent Bowerly

Redmond, Oregon

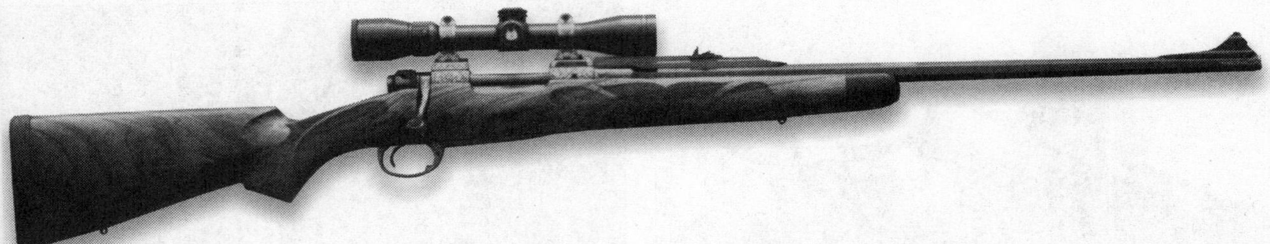

The year was 1958. Winchester announced its .338 Magnum and Roy Weatherby came up with the Mark V rifle. Young Kent Bowerly mated a Springfield 03-A3 to a Roberts semi-inletted stock. All three events were of lasting significance. Friends admired Kent's craftsmanship, and they offered to pay him for stockwork on their rifles. Eagerly, he obliged.

During the 1960s, Bowerly studied the work of Al Biesen and Earl Milliron, both masters of the trade and both living close by in the Pacific Northwest. He practiced their techniques on hunting rifle stocks he shaped, fitted and finished, mostly for Winchester Model 70s.

"In those days, you could still get the early 70s for a reasonable price, and a lot of hunters preferred them." He still likes those Winchester bolt guns, but he's also fitted walnut to Mausers and the occasional Dakota 76. He has fashioned stocks for Ruger Number Ones, a rifle that adds variety to his workbench in Redmond, Oregon. Kent says that his stocks are meant to be used, though they feature the lines and detailing that sophisticated gun enthusiasts admire. "If a rifle won't shoot well in your hands, if it's not responsive, if it lacks the fine balance to point itself and put your eye behind the sight automatically, it's not stocked properly." Wood and detail work, he insists, are of no value on a rifle that doesn't point naturally.

Since his early retirement from the boat-building industry in 1985, Bowerly has worked full-time as a stockmaker, applying his artistry on occasion to shotgun stocks.

David Christman

Delhi, Louisiana

Colville, Washington was David Christman's home for 20 years, until a downsizing at U.S. West freed him to return to his native Louisiana. There David has revved up his gun work, restocking Parker double shotguns and Stevens single-shot rifles, besides building the bolt-action rifles so popular with custom makers. David shows a rare versatility; he fashions both wood and metal work. Only the engraving gets outsourced. David offers a full suite of restocking and refinishing services, including rust bluing, in the same shop that turns out complete custom shotguns and rifles.

His favorite project? "Probably still a bolt rifle on a Mauser 98 or Winchester 70 action," he says. "A classic hunting rifle deserves a stock of fine English walnut, but Don Cantwell sells some very nice high-grade Claro." He'd not too fussy on action types. "Given the right parts and a little metal work, the Remington 700 can become a handsome custom rifle.

Melissa Dibbens
Harrisonville, Missouri

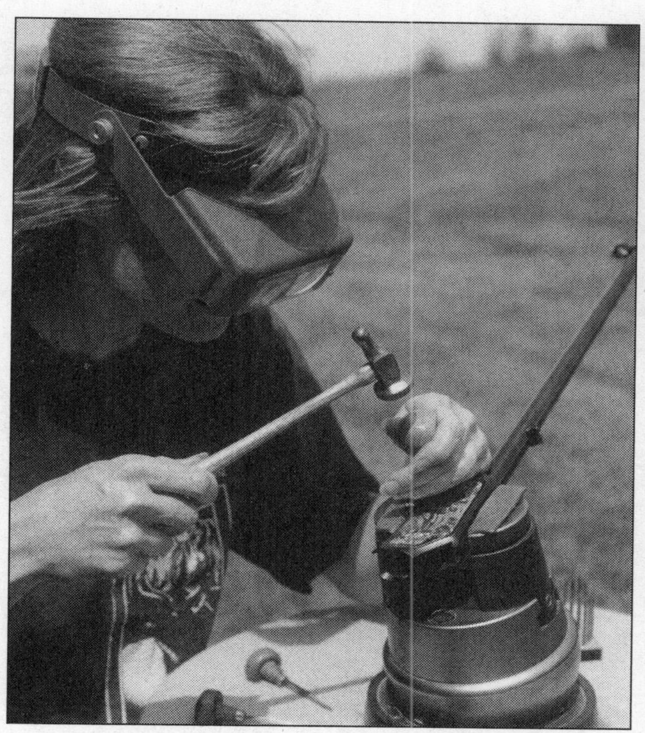

Melissa Dibben, an engraver from Harrisonville, Missouri, started sculpting gunmetal in 1982. "My grandfather built a local jewelry business during the 1940s, and my parents bought it in 1976. Engraving allowed me to live at home and put my imagination to work," she says. Melissa trained on the pneumatic Gravermeister tool in Little Rock, Arkansas, then put her bench in front of the jewelry store. A Remington Model 11-48 shotgun was her first project. Then she scrimshawed roses on revolver grips. "One of the store's customers saw me working and told me yellow roses had no place on a gun. That hurt a little, but not for long."

Since 1988, when her parents closed the jewelry store and moved to Corpus Christi, Melissa has worked mostly on guns. Active in Safari Club International, she has engraved three rifles for the Kansas City chapter.

Melissa, Dave and son Ben live on 20 acres with six dogs, two cats and two horses. The Dibbens also own 90 acres in northern Missouri, where they hunt deer and turkeys. Melissa also spends a good deal of time in Wyoming. Does she have a favorite canvas? "No. I don't want to do the same thing all the time. I'm easily bored. Variety and new challenge bring me back to the bench."

D'Arcy Echols
Providence, Utah

"I like to build rifles you'd hunt with," says gunmaker D'Arcy Echols. "The profile of a great rifle must serve a purpose, not just attract attention on a rack." Echols achieves superiority with straight lines and a mating of wood to metal that looks impossibly tight. His symetrical checkering adorns a grip and forend that all but grab your hands. Cast-off is standard, and D'Arcy's pantograph is adjustable to deliver cast-off (a slight angling of the butt away from the shooter's cheek).

To speed up production (in 1997Echols was turning out about four a year) he introduced the "Legend" rifle with a synthetic stock. Built on new Winchester 70 Classic actions, the Legend wears a McMillan stock that D'Arcy designed. He overhauls the action, modifying the magazine box to hold an extra round. Then he lengthens the loading port and bores out scope base holes to accept 8-40 screws. D'Arcy remachines and laps the lug seats and lugs, and squares up the receiver and bolt face. "I use Krieger cut-rifled barrels," he says. "And I make sure they're fitted on-axis with the receiver. He repins the trigger and bolt stop and grinds the sear surface for a consistent 3-pound pull.

After matte-bluing the metal and hand-bedding it in the stock, D'Arcy shoots each rifle at least 40 times to break in the barrel and make sure the rifle meets his accuracy standards. D'Arcy also builds a Dangerous Game Rifle with a barrel-mounted sling swivel and action work to accommodate round-nose bullets.

Kent "Buzz" Fletcher

Alamosa, Colorado

Buzz Fletcher had an early interest in guns, and longed to accompany his six brothers in the field. One of them pointed out that some hunters had money enough to buy custom rifles. "The notion that I could build fine rifles suddenly had never occurred to me."

He enrolled in gunsmithing school at Trinidad State Junior College and studied with Maurice Ottmar, Chuck Grace, Jim Turtin and others. He graduated in 1972, and worked in an Austrian gunshop for a year. Returning to Colorado, he set up shop in Alamosa to build bolt-action sporting rifles.

Kent is also an accomplished shotgun stocker. "British bird guns point like magic because the Brits know how to build stocks," he says. Kent's cast, pitch and drop, and the spartan lines of butt and forend, result from painstaking study of the British game gun. He strives to make a firearm handle like an extension of the shooter's body. As with his rifle stocks, shotgun wood in Buzz's shop is typically checkered 22 lines per inch, though he does cut some patterns at 24 lines-per-inch. He uses various fillers to get the stock surface he wants, but finishes only with Tung Oil.

Kent's most recent project is a rifle he calls the Still-Hunter. Very trim, the Still-Hunter that came to my door for testing was chambered in .256 Newton. The .256 matches the .257 Roberts Improved ballistically, though it uses .264 bullets, not .257s. Equipped with an aperture sight and a QD scope mount, and a stock of distinctive but conservative profile, the Still-Hunter emloys a Mauser action.

Rick Freudenberg

Everett, Washington

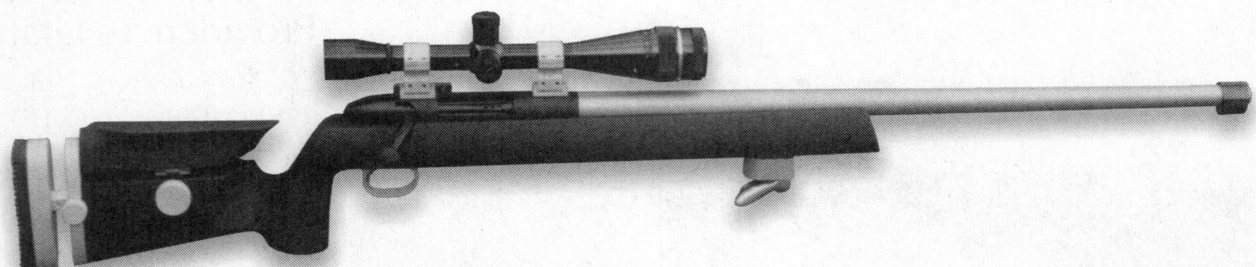

Hunting is still a passion for Rick Freudenberg. Big antlers adorn the walls of his well-equipped machine shop but once there you'll find that Rick is focused on building rifles. His match and hunting rifles are as accurate as he can make them, which means he prefers synthetic stocks. Rick also offers wood stocks but says that, properly fitted, a walnut-stocked rifle won't shoot as well as a synthetic.

Rick prefers Winchester 70 actions, pre-64s first and current Classics next. He's also built rifles on the Remington 700 action. He favors a three-groove Lilja barrel with a 1-11 twist for the .30-06, and commonly gets it to deliver sub-half-minute groups with Nosler Ballistic Tip bullets.

Rick's latest project is a lightweight hunting rifle with a #4 fluted barrel 23½ inches long. He trims a Remington 700 receiver and flutes the bolt, outfitting it with a Sako-type extractor. The S&K rings and bases add only another ounce, and with a 3-9x36 Swarovski scope, the rifle tips the scales at just 6½ pounds.

Jim Spradlin, in Colorado, finishes metal parts for Rick, using a Teflon-like material that comes in 11 colors and protect the metal as no bluing can.

Rick Freudenberg builds accurate hunting rifles because he assembles and uses super-accurate match rifles, shooting at ranges to 1000 yards. He'll chamber to just about any cartridge but prefers those "with legs" – like the 6.5/284 and the .300 Winchester. Many elk hunters have ordered a Freudenberg rifle in .330 Dakota. Rick's personal .300 Dakota will launch 180-grain Siroccos at 3360 fps from its 26-inch barrel. A rifle of this type, including a pre-64 M70 action, starts at about $3500.

Gary Goudy

Dayton, Washington

Semi-retired after 37 years fashioning elegant rifle stocks, Gary Goudy is still known in the trade as one of the most talented and productive of his fraternity.

A charter member of the American Custom Gunmakers Guild, Gary later became its Vice President. His work belies a perfectionist's obsession, and a genuine affinity for fine guns and the best walnut. "I work mainly with California English," he says. "Or Bastogne. I've not had good luck with European blanks." Unlike many of his colleagues, Gary buys most of his wood green, preferring to dry it himself. "Most blanks need a couple of years, but I like to give them four seasons before inletting." Gary is renowned for skin-tight wood-to-metal fit and impossibly detailed checkering that leaves ribbons the width of a pencil line and even as a lightbeam.

His favorite action? The Model 70 Winchester, "because it makes such a good hunting rifle." But he says that a 98 Mauser worked over by Hermann Waldron or Tom Burgess is every bit as desirable. He's stocked shotguns from time to time, almost all of them side-by-sides. The two most recent are Dakotas, a 12 and a 20. "They took a very long time to finish, the they're true exhibition-grade guns." Gary is also working on a Dakota take-down rifle for his own use.

Among relatively few rifle-makers who are also keen hunters, Gary spends much of the fall afield, some of it in the Blue Mountains within hiking distance of his Dayton, Washington shop. But he travels out-of-state too, and last year killed a bull elk that scored over 330 points. He isn't saying where. Gary often hunts with an ordinary Winchester Model 70 Featherweight. "It doesn't have one of my stocks," he laughs. "It shoots just fine in the factory wood, and I've been too busy to change it."

Chuck Grace

Trinidad, Colorado

In 1971 Chuck Grace left his Michigan home for gunsmithing school in Colorado. He stayed there to hone his skills and in 1980 became a full-time stockmaker. Three years later he joined the American Custom Gunmakers Guild as a charter member. His considerable talent was evident on the ACGG's 16th annual fundraising project: a Winchester Model 70 rifle in 7x57. His rifles, built on clean, classic lines, have open grips that make for fast handling.

Best known as a stockmaker, Chuck also takes on rifle restoration and custom metal work in his Trinidad shop. His perfect execution of "the simple things, like a straight line" have earned him widespread respect among gun enthusiasts. The rifles he stocks seem to point themselves, a mark of a master.

Darwin Hensley
Brightwood, Oregon

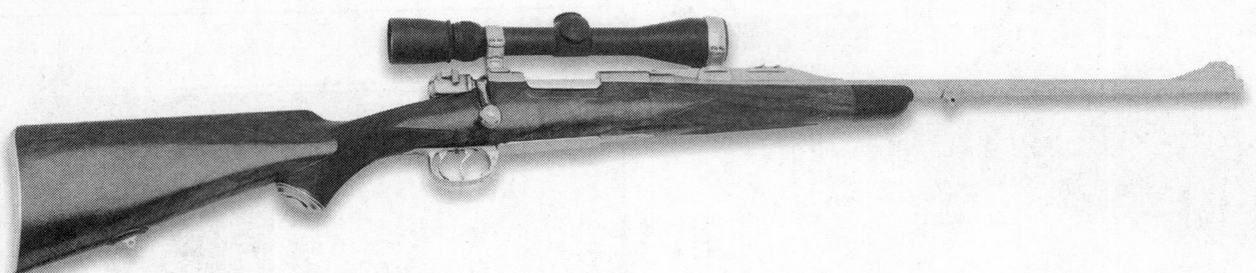

A childhood spent whittling might have given Darwin Hensley's parents a clue as to this talented stock-maker's future. Growing up on an Iowa farm in the 1940s allowed Darwin the time to do a lot of whittling. In 1952, when he was 10, the Hensleys moved into town, but Darwin still spent summers on the farm, where he entertained himself with an 1890 Winchester .22 pump.

Darwin taught art for two years after earning his B.A. and B.S. degrees. He left to earn more money in marketing. He stayed with that for 25 years, and raised a family. Always on the prowl for fine guns, he bought and sold many for profit. All the while he continued to whittle, but now on gunstocks. In 1985 he gave up "real work" and became a full-time stockmaker.

Darwin says "I've been blessed with wonderful clients. I wake up every day eager to go to work. It's not the life for everyone, but there's nothing I'd rather do." Darwin's commitment to superior craftsmanship is evident in his rifles, which show an artist's eye for line, and are notable for their trim profiling. "It's important that a rifle shoot and handle well; beyond that, its design should show a harmony of parts. Profile, components, engraving, checkering, fit and finish—all must work together to achieve the best effect. It's wrong for one part to draw attention from the whole."

Carefully fitting each rifle stock to its owner, Darwin ncludes detailing so subtle that it's often visible only upon close inspection. The single-shot rifles shown here—a miniature Gibbs Farquharson in .17 Hornet, a miniature Jeffery Farquharson in 2R Lovell and a miniature Alex Henry in .218 Bee—have the sleek, spare profiles that under Hensley's hand become elegant. Metalwork on the first two (and on the featured bolt rifles) is by Steve Heilmann.

Hill Country Rifle Company
New Braunfels, Texas

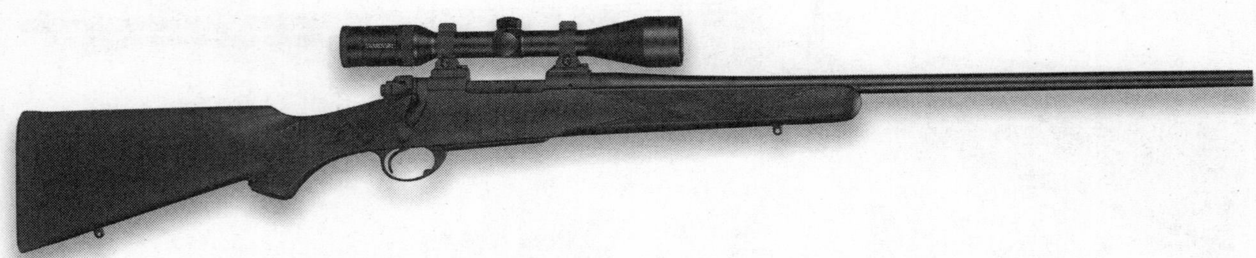

Hill Country Rifle Company is a semi-custom shop, specializing in high-end bolt-action rifles on commercial actions. Customers can order a McMillan synthetic stock—or French, English or Turkish walnut. Clarao and Bastogne walnut are also available. Lilja, Hart and Krieger barrels remain the top choices from this New Braunfels, Texas company, which routinely pillar-beds the actions and leaves barrels free-floating. Most rifles from the Hill Country shop are built on Winchester M70 actions. A test rifle I received on loan in 2003 wore a synthetic stock, pleasingly trim in the grip and straight enough to use comfortably with a scope. Exhibition-grade English walnut stocks are available too. Here are a few other components.

Bob Hisserich

Mesa, Arizona

"Accuracy comes from installing a good barrel on an action that's squared up," says Bob Hisserich. "Naturally, the bolt face must be true and the lugs made to bear evenly. And of course, the stock can't be allowed to interfere." It all sounds so simple. But pin him down, and Bob Hisserich admits that building an accurate rifle takes care as well as know-how.

Now 20 years into gunmaking career, Bob lives in Mesa, Arizona., where he is adapting to market demand by building big-bore rifles chambered to the likes of the .458 Lott, .500 Jeffery and .585 Nyati. His Sharpshooter Series for such rounds as the .300 Weatherby remains popular with deer and elk hunters. Bob employs a Honig/Rodman stock duplicator capable of .0001 precision. His rifle stocks—both laminated and traditional walnut—are all on classic patterns, though Bob will fashion a cross-over stock upon request. You'll find his stock work on shotguns as well as on rifles.

Patrick Holehan

Tucson, Arizona

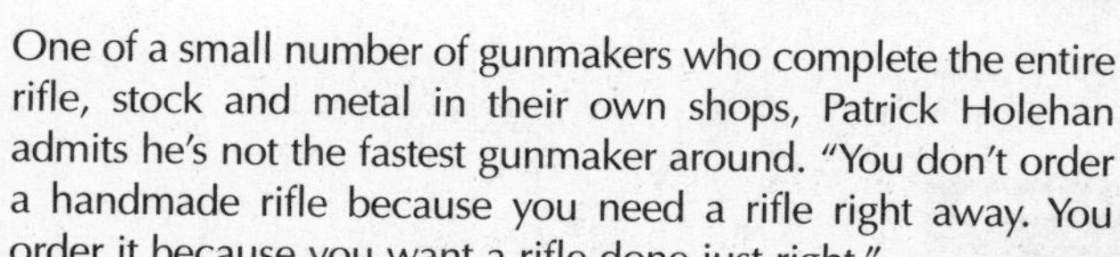

One of a small number of gunmakers who complete the entire rifle, stock and metal in their own shops, Patrick Holehan admits he's not the fastest gunmaker around. "You don't order a handmade rifle because you need a rifle right away. You order it because you want a rifle done just right."

Blending innovation with classic features, Patrick has earned quite a following. A lot of shooters have placed orders after seeing his Arizona Square Bridge actions. "I start with Model 70 Winchester metal, then add scope mount blocks, making them integral and contouring them into the receiver. They're machined on top to accept quick-detachable rings." This makes Holehan's rifles unique, as well as pleasing to the eye. "Of course," says Patrick, "every rifle must shoot well and function perfectly."

Homan's M70 bolt rifles include Long Range, Lightweight and Safari versions comprising the "Hunter" series, with walnut, laminated or high-quality synthetic stocks. He trues barrel seating surfaces, laps the locking lugs and hones and polishes the feed ramp and bolt face. His stocks fit skin-tight except where customers want barrels to float. A long list of options includes wildcat chamberings in cryogenically treated barrels.

Steven Dodd Hughes

Livingston, Montana

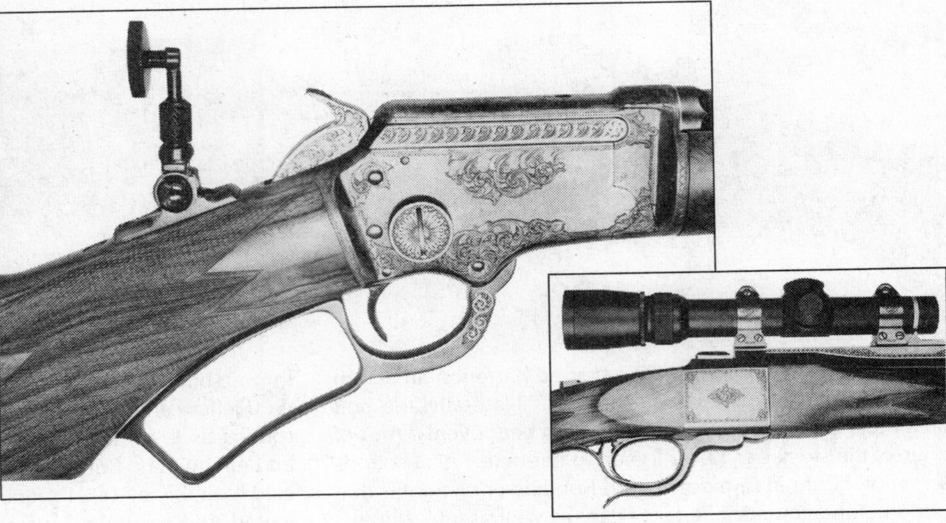

CUSTOM GUNMAKERS

For a decade after starting his career in 1978, Steven Hughes focused on muzzleloading firearms faithful to 18th and 19th century patterns. Now he works almost exclusively on cartridge guns, like the Marlin Model 39 lever rifle shown here with a 1920s-pattern Winchester High Wall.

"Bolt rifles don't interest me much anymore," says Steven. "I leave those to the masses." He adds that there are a dozen craftsmen building custom turnbolt guns for every one keen to tackle a single-shot. "I also like old lever-actions. One of my favorite projects was an original Winchester 1873. I stocked it like one of the original 1-of-1,000 rifles after refitting the action with new parts."

Hughes also builds first-class double shotguns, which he appreciates as much as the classic American hunting rifles that demand much of his time. Steven writes a column for *Shooting Sportsman* magazine and has authored a couple books as well, but this multi-talented resident of Livingston, Montana considers himself primarily a gunmaker.

David Miller

Tucson, Arizona

"It's not a cheap rifle," David Miller says without apology. "We don't build cheap rifles. We build very accurate rifles that look good, for people who want the best there is."

He's been doing that for decades now, from a Tucson shop that's also the workplace for Curt Crum, an equally talented gunmaker. Miller and Crum produce true custom rifles built to the highest standards. Miller Classic rifles have earned the spotlight at several SCI conventions.

Some years ago, David assembled a rifle for his own use, a .300 Weatherby on a Model 70 Winchester action, with a long, fluted barrel and a laminated stock. The rifle wore a Leupold 6.5-20x scope in David's own bomb-proof mount. This outfit had the same clean lines as David's Classic rifle, but not the hand-checkering and expensive wood. As soon as other hunters heard of the project, Miller's phone started ringing. Now David and Curt offer their Marksman rifle as an affordable alternative to the Classic. It's still not cheap, but it shoots extremely well. After killing a Coues deer with one, I fired a three-shot group that measured an inch and a half—at 400 yards!

Steve Nelson
Corvallis, Oregon

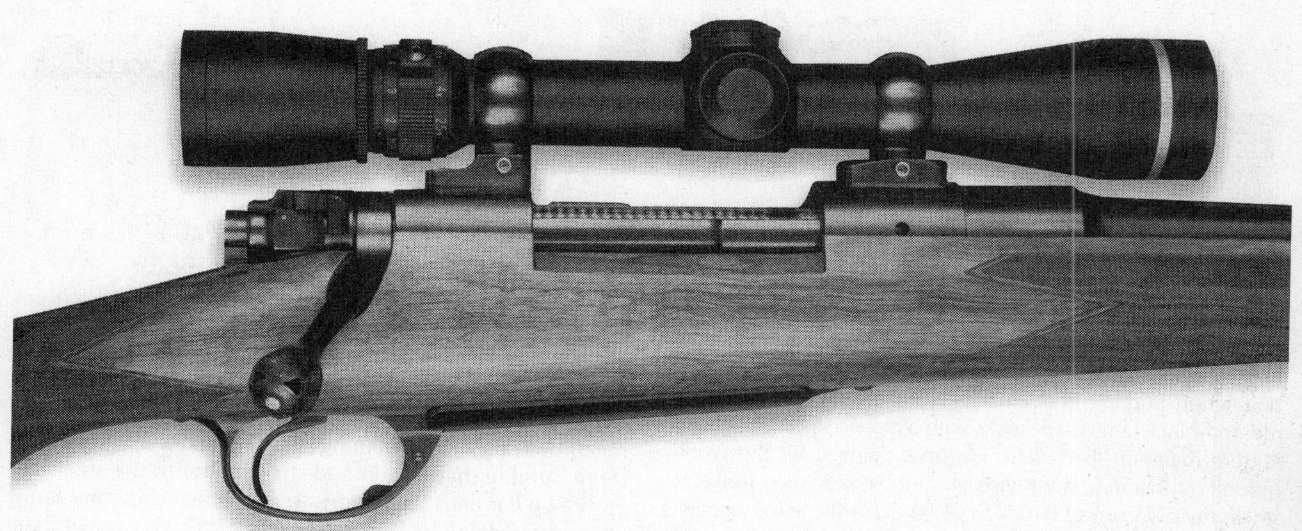

"Strictly defined, a custom firearm is one built for an individual," insists Steve Nelson. Steve should know about custom rifles. He built his first in 1974. "I like to think I'm a consultant as well as a gunbuilder," he says. "My aim is to deliver a rifle that meets the client's needs specifically. I do all the work—wood and metal—except the engraving. The firearm must satisfy me as regards craftmanship. If it fails that test, or if it won't shoot well, it doesn't go out the door."

CUSTOM GUNMAKERS

Dave Norin
Waukegan, Illinois

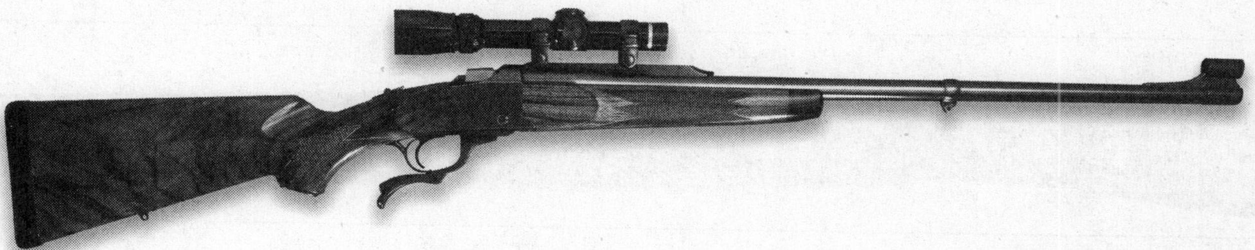

An early interest in firearms led Dave Norin to Trinidad State College in Colorado, there to study gunmaking. He graduated in 1972, joining a huge fraternity of custom gun-builders with that alma mater. But he has since distinguished himself from other craftsmen by steering toward unusual projects. "I have a broad range of interests," he says. "Obscure old guns fascinate me."

Dave's specialty these days is restoration of collector-quality firearms. Not long ago he was rebuilding a German 8x46R take-down target rifle and bringing an ultra-rare Farrow rifle back to life. He has restored Luger, Mauser and Mannlicher pistols and lever-action Winchester rifles. He admits to producing a few classic bolt rifles – "the kind everybody works on." But few other custom shops boast the suite of services available from Norin: rust bluing, Niter bluing, color case hardening, stocking from blanks and vintage wood finishes. Dave's work shows an artist's attention to detail, and a faithfulness to original color and form.

Dave Norin lives and works in Waukegan, Illinois. He and his wife have four children and a grandchild. "Even without the shop and my whitetail hunting, I'd be busy!" he says. In his spare time, Dave collects pre-1945 self-loading pistols, Winchesters and "any nice double I can afford...."

Ray Riganian
Glendale, California

In another life, Ray Riganian was a machinist in the aerospace industry, and he brings a machinist's eye for tight tolerances to his gun-building. Ray specializes in elegant and distinctive bolt-action hunting rifles, marrying such unlikely features as red-and-black laminated stocks with a classic stock profile and austere matte-finished steel. He does "almost all the work" himself. "I machine my own sight and scope bases from bar stock, my own swivel bands too," he explains. Some components come from other sources: Ted Blackburn bottom metal, for instance. He uses Talley scope rings. "Everything is carefully matched to the other components, and to the use the customer expects to make of his rifle."

Ray likes the Model 70 Winchester for hunting rifles, because of its beefy extractor—"also the 98 Mauser, but it requires a lot of work to finish." If the customer wants a Mauser, Ray recommends Searcy and Johannsen magnum actions. His varmint rifles are built on 700 Remingtons. Long-range target and bench rifles typically get Stolle or Nisika actions and Riganian uses Krieger barrels for big game rifles and Hart barrels on target guns. He sends the metal out for cold rust-bluing or a "special treatment that's more durable than Teflon and sticks better to the steel."

Ray pillar-beds the actions to stocks that show the same attention to detail he lavishes on metal. "I prefer to work on California English, but Circassian walnut makes a lovely stock. I buy dry blanks and will not shape any until it's down to 8 percent moisture. Though on high-quality wood I sometimes cut checkering as fine as 28 lines per inch, most of my checkering is 22 or 24 lpi, because hunters find it easier to grip. Rifles must be functional to be truly beautiful."

Tony Schuelke
Glencoe, Minnesota

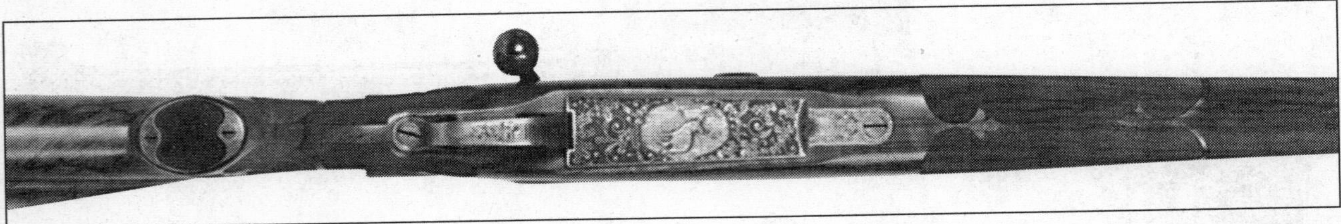

At 16 Tony Schuelke bought a shotgun and tried to refinish the wood. It was a start. But not until many years and countless amateur projects later did Tony start building guns. That was after stints in auto repair, life insurance, banking and real estate.

Tony says he's a machinist, but that label is inadequate.Tony has artistic talent, obvious when you look at what he's wrought with a file. Checkering not only stocks but bolt handles, and fabricating skeleton grip caps, he doesn't imitate anyone. He's constantly innovating. "If you're not a creative kind of a guy, there's not much interesting about building guns," he says, adding that the customer's ideas are very important. He'd rather respond to them than recommend his own design.

"Custom guns are more art than implements," he explains. "Customers have their own tastes, and they're paying the freight. So I listen." He adds that individuality can be important to gun people, and little details that have no bearing on performance often matter a great deal. He admits that untested ideas intrigue him. "But in this industry it's hard to find an idea that hasn't popped up sometime in wood or steel." Tony Schuelke's shop is in Glencoe, Minnesota, where he can hunt grouse with the double shotguns that get a lot of his attention, and where he says winters "are just right for working on guns."

Gene Simillion

Gunnison, Colorado

Gene Simillion's gun-building career started in Kalispell, Montana, where he worked under the tutelage of crack stockmaker Jerry Fisher. "Not far down the road was Tom Burgess," grins Gene. "He's forgotten more about metal-smithing than most gunmakers ever learn." Gene also credits D'Arcy Echols, Monte Mandarino and Don Klein for giving him " the best education a young fellow could hope for."

Gene has earned a reputation for building some of the classiest-looking rifles available. The classic bolt rifle is still his favorite and his aim is to produce a rifle with "fine accuracy, flawless function and elegant beauty."

Gene's best rifle he calls the "Premier." Each is built to customer's specifications, usually on a new Winchester Model 70 Classic action because that's what Gene prefers. But he's willing to substitute early Model 70s, Mauser 98s and Remington 700s. Stocks, sleek and spartan of line, are exquisitely checkered and fitted skin-tight to the metal. Magnums get a second recoil lug and a crossbolt in front of the magazine well. Quarter ribs and drop-box magazines are two of many options. Gene fashions his own scope mounts. His less costly Classic Hunter comes only on the new M70 action. It has fewer options and less detailing, but its cut-rifled barrel, hand-bedded to a checkered walnut stock, delivers the same level of performance.

Lately, Gene has begun marketing high-grade walnut blanks to other gunmakers. "There's a real shortage of fine wood, and I've managed to cultivate a reliable supply," he says.

Charlie Sisk

Dayton, Texas

Texas is home to several well-known gunmakers and shooters who appreciate accurate rifles. Charlie Sisk is right at home there, assembling synthetic-stocked bolt guns for hunters and tackling other projects he finds interesting. Charlie built his first gun in a high-school machine shop. "It was a .257 Roberts on a 98 Mauser action." And it's still in the rack. "My guns are more accurate now, but I'm still a two-minute shooter most of the time."

Charlie's rifles don't wear handsome wood or engraving. They're meant to be shot. In bolt rifles, Charlie prefers Model 700 Remingtons but says Winchester 70s come in a close second. He uses barrels from several top-brand suppliers, mainly from Krieger and Lilja, but air-gauges them to cull those that vary more than .0001. He inspects each barrel with a bore-scope. Chambering is done with match-grade live-pilot reamers to ensure concentricity.

Charlie's standard rifle jobs include "blueprinting" the action to square up the bolt with the bore. Charlie installs and adjusts aftermarket triggers, mainly Timneys but also Rifle Basix, Shilen and Jewell. And he takes care that his stocks fit each client perfectly. He obtains the stocks from the nation's top-rank makers but engineers and machines his own muzzle brakes and works up loads for customers who request that service.

Mark Stratton
Lynnwood, Washington

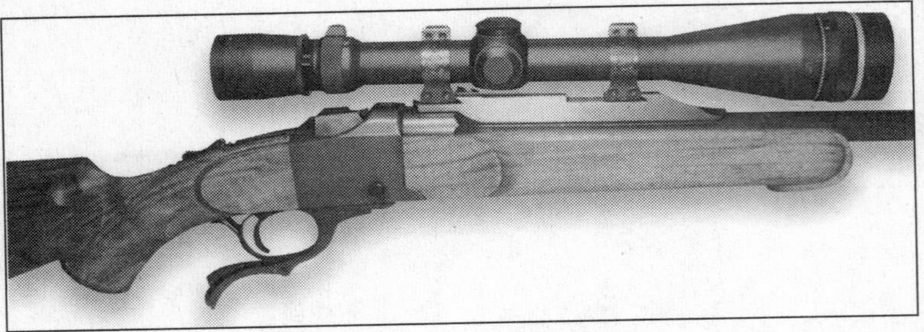

Early on, Mark Stratton found that his training as a gunsmith in Trinidad, Colorado, good as it was, did not guarantee financial security in his native southern California. So he worked as a machinist for an electronics firm, building rifles as a hobby during off-hours. He peddled his first rifle in 1974 to a friend for the cost of the parts; then he moved to Seattle and another job.

At the 1988 American Custom Gunmakers Guild show in Reno, Mark decided to turn his hobby into a career. "I saw the products of the country's finest craftsmen and wanted to become one. I was pretty good at metal work, but these fellows were way beyond me in the wood." Inspired, Mark set out to improve his stockmaking. By 1994, Mark was confident enough in his products to start advertising his work, which promptly brought kudos from customers. In 2001 Mark joined the ACGG and became one of its more accomplished members.

Z-Hat Custom
Casper, Wyoming

The shop in Casper, Wyoming is unpretentious. But Fred Zeglin's workmanship keeps hunters and handloaders coming back. Still young but well established as a custom diemaker and rifle-builder, Fred specializes in things that few others in the trade will tackle. His Z-Hat products include a Micrometer Inline Seating die similar to the Vickerman. It works with contemporary and obsolete rounds, also wildcats. The MIS die indexes on the datum line of the case shoulder and on the ogive of the bullet, so it can be used for most popular bullet diameters, .22 through .411.

Fred's rifle work ranges from ordinary bolt-action guns to take-down lever-action models like the 1895 Winchester. Based on a Thomas Bland design now a century old, the take-apart 95 features a heavy contact plate on the barrel assembly, so the barrel will always index to the same point. A simple lock screw holds the assembly in tight alignment with the receiver. "Switching barrels is no problem," says Fred. "You can do it easily in the field." He adds that Browning M95 replicas are as easy to convert as original 95s—and more affordable. He's now working on take-down designs for bolt rifles. "We have one ready to go for the Winchester M70."

Besides building guns, Fred works to protect them, with aluminum travel cases made for the take-down rifles. "Not only do they hold the rifles securely," explains Fred," they look more like luggage than gun cases, so they're less apt to be stolen."

One of the first gunsmiths to chamber the Hawk family of cartridges based on the .30-06 case, Fred offers loaded Hawk ammunition, brass and match-grade dies. Working on a wildcat with a bullet of unusual diameter? Fred markets a ring de that can size standard bullets to fit that bore.

SIGHTS & SCOPES

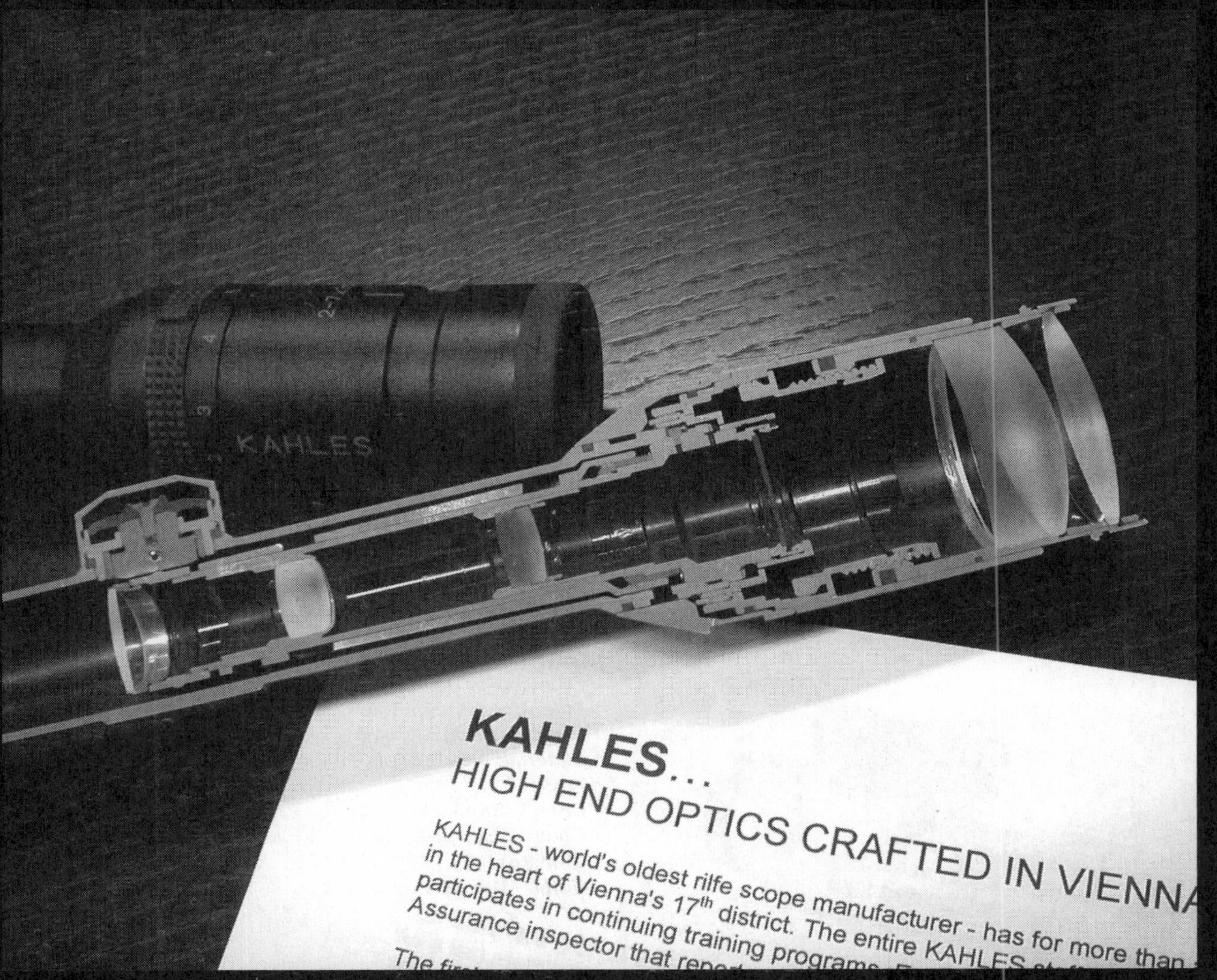
KAHLES
KAHLES...
HIGH END OPTICS CRAFTED IN VIENNA
KAHLES - world's oldest rilfe scope manufacturer - has for more than
in the heart of Vienna's 17th district. The entire KAHLES
participates in continuing training programs.
Assurance inspector that

Aimpoint Sights

7000S SIGHT

COMP M2 AND COMP ML2

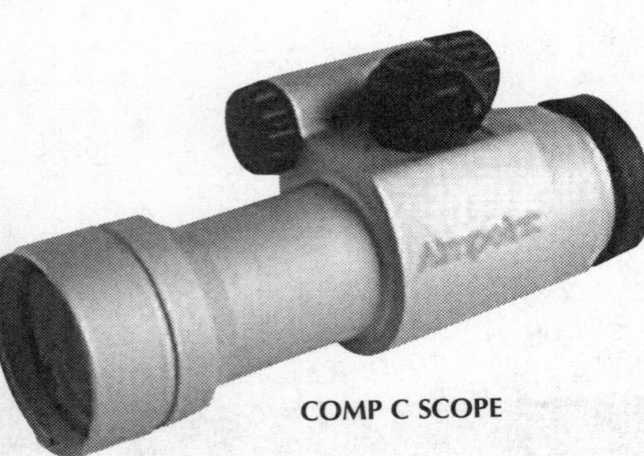

COMP C SCOPE

C SCOPE GUN

7000SC SIGHT

SPECIFICATIONS

System: Parallax free
Optical: Anti-reflex coated lenses
Adjustment: 1 click = ½ inch at 100 yards
Length: 6.3" ***Weight:*** 7.4 oz.
Objective diameter: 36mm
Mounting system: 30mm rings Magnification: 1X
Material: Anodized aluminum; black finish
Diameter of dot: Red dot, 4 MOA

7000SC (short) $319

Also Available:

7000L (length: 7.9") 319
7000SC 2X (fixed 2X) 416
7000L 2X (fixed2X) 416
7000SC SM (short silver metallic) 332

COMPC 2X

SPECIFICATIONS

System: Parallax free
Optical: Anti-reflex coated lens
Adjustment: 1 click = ½" at 100 yards
Length: 4.7"
Weight: 6.5 oz.
Objective diameter: 36 mm
Diameter of dot: 2 MOA
Mounting system: 30mm ring
Magnification: 2X fixed
Material: Anodized aluminum; black finish

Price:

CompC 2X black. $452
Comp ML2 410
Comp M2 457
Comp ML2 2X 535

COMPC

SPECIFICATIONS

System: 100% Parallax free
Optics: Anti-reflex coated lenses
Eye relief: Unlimited
Batteries: 3V Lithium
Adjustment: 1 click = ½-inch at 100 yards
Length: 4¾"
Weight: 6.5 oz.
Objective diameter: 36mm
Dot diameter: 4 MOA
Mounting system: 30mm ring Magnification: 1X
Material: Black or stainless finish

Price: $347
CompC SM (7 MOA silver metallic) 361
Also Available: heavy-duty, hard anodized, graphite gray, submersible to 80' 411

SIGHTS & SCOPES

Alpen Optics

APEX AND KODIAK SCOPES

Familiar to many outdoorsmen as a purveyor of binoculars and spotting scopes, Alpen Optics has announced two lines of riflescopes, comprising 11 models. Three Apex variables feature fully multi-coated lens systems, plus resettable finger-adjustable windage and elevation adjustments with ¼-minute clicks.

Three models are available: 3-9x42, 3.5-10x50 and 6-24x50. All have fast-focus eye-pieces and the Alpen AccuPlex reticle, plus a lifetime warranty.

The companion line to the Apex is called Kodiak. Its scopes are also fully waterproof, fog-proof and warranteed. They feature multi-coated lenses, but apparently not all lenses are treated. A 4x32 is the only fixed-power scope. The others range in magnification from the 1.5-4.5x32 to the 6-24x50. As with the Apex, eye relief is about 3 inches on all models save the 1.5-4x, which offers 4 inches of ER.

Apex scopes:. . . . . **$345 – 435**
Kodiak scopes: . . . . **75 – 238**

Browning Sport Optics

BROWNING SCOPES

These riflescopes have the Browning name but Bushnell lineage. Browning's line consists of 6 scopes—2-7x32, 3-9x40, 3-9x50, 4-12x40, 5-15x40 and 8-24x40. Claiming 94 percent light transmission people at Browning point out also the fast-focus eyepiece, finger-friendly, quarter-minute click adjustments and a one-piece tube guaranteed waterproof and fog-proof. Eye relief is a generous 3½ inches. The lenses are all multi-coated.

2-7x32 . . . . **$336**
3-9x40 . . . . **352**
3-9x50 . . . . **420**
4-12x40 . . . . **450**
5-15x40 . . . . **490**
8-24x40 . . . . **590**

BSA Scopes

HUNTSMAN 3-9X40

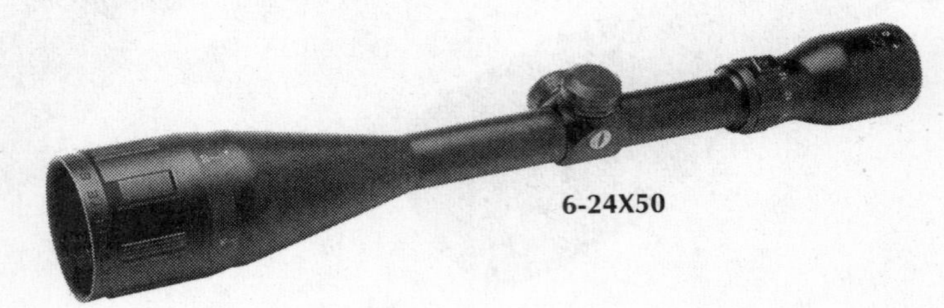

6-24X50

BSA CATSEYE

The Catseye line has multi-coated objective and ocular lenses and a European-style reticle for shooting in dim light. The PowerBright has the features of a BSA Catseye plus a PowerBright reticle that lights up bright red against dark backgrounds. The Big Cat has all the features wanted in a hunting scope: long eye relief, fully multicoated, very bright three piece objective lens.

Prices: Catseye
1.5-4.5x32 European reticle $120
with illuminated reticle 122
3-10x44 152
illum. reticle 172
3.5-10x50 172
illum. reticle 192
4-16x50 AO 192

BSA CATSEYE CE 6-24X50

SPECIFICATIONS
Magnification: 6x-24x
Objective Lens Diameter: 50mm
Exit Pupil Range: 8.3-2.0
Field of View at 100 yd: 16-3'
Optimum Eye Relief: 4.5"
Length/Weight: 16"/23 oz.
Price: $223

MIL-DOT SCOPES (NOT SHOWN)

4-16x40 . . . . $150
6-24x40 170
8-32x40 190
6-24x40 illum. 200
4-16x40 illum. 180

HUNTSMAN SERIES

The Huntsman series includes three 3-9x and a 6-18x AO, plus fixed-power and low-power variable models. A 3-12x and 4-16x have 50mm objectives. All tubes are 1-inch alloy, of one-piece construction. They feature finger-adjustable windage and elevation dials and generous eye relief. Multi-coated lenses are standard. Huntsman scopes are warranted waterproof, fog proof and shockproof.
Price: . . . . $90 to 150

BSA PLATINUM TARGET SCOPES

BSA Platinum target scopes are fitted with finger-adjustable windage and elevation dials that move point of impact in 1/8-minute clicks. BSA's Big Wheel is for long distance shooting when parallax adjustments are extremely critical. It has a convenient sidewheel for extra-sensitive focusing. Actually the side wheel is two wheels in one. The larger outer wheel is best for off-hand or prone shooting, and the smaller wheel for benchrest. You just snap off the outer wheel to use the smaller focusing wheel. These new scopes are more compact than older models and have three-piece objective lens systems for sharper resolution, better color and less distortion.

Prices: PT 6-24x44 AO $222
PT 8-32x44 AO. 242
PT 6-24x44 AO Mildot reticle. 200
PT 8-32x44 AO Mildot reticle. 230

SWEET 17 SCOPES (NOT SHOWN)

Designed for the .17 HMR
2-7x32 A/O $110
3-12x40 152
4-12x40 152
6-18x40 190

BSA Scopes

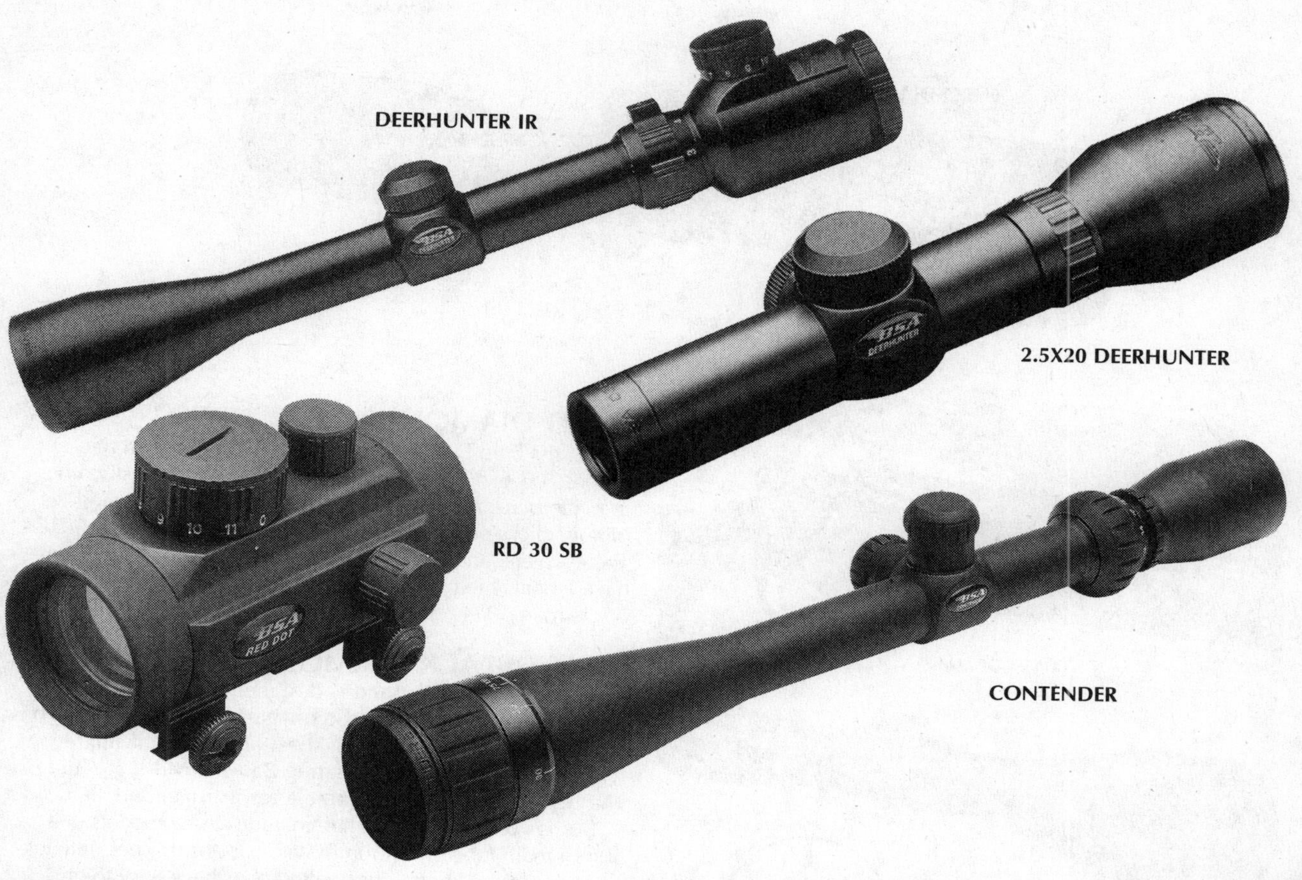

DEERHUNTER 3-9X40 ILLUMINATED RETICLE

SPECIFICATIONS
Magnification: 3x-9x
Objective Lens Diameter: 40mm
Exit Pupil Range: 13.3-4.4
Field of View at 100 yd: 26'
Eye Relief: 4.5"
Weight: 13 oz.
Price: $130
Also available:
Deerhunter models from 2.5x20 (shown) to 3-9x50.
Prices: .... $60 – 130

PANTHER SCOPE

The all-weather scope.
Preice: 3-10x40 .... $160
2.5-10x44 180
3.5-10x50 200
6.5-20x44 230

RED DOT SIGHTS

Prices: RD30 (30mm black matte or silver) $60
RD30SB (30mm shadow black) 70
RD42SB (42mm shadow black) 100
RD50SB (50mm shadow black) 130

DEERHUNTER DH 2.5X20 SHOTGUN

SPECIFICATIONS
Magnification: 2.5x
Objective Lens Diameter: 20mm
Exit Pupil Range: 8
Field of View at 100 yd: 72'
Optimum Eye Relief: 6"
Length/Weight: 7.5"/7.5 oz.
Price: $60

CONTENDER CT 6-24X40 TS

SPECIFICATIONS
Magnification: 6x-24x
Objective Lens Diameter: 40mm
Exit Pupil Range: 6.7-1.7
Field of View at 100 yd: 16'-4'
Optimum Eye Relief: 3"
Length/Weight: 15.5"/20 oz.
Price: $150
Also Available: 3-12x40 130
4-16x40 132
8-32x40 (silver: $160) 170
3-12x50 132
4-16x50 170
6-24x50 172
8-32x50 192

Burris Scopes

Black Diamond Riflescopes

EURO DIAMOND 3X-10X40

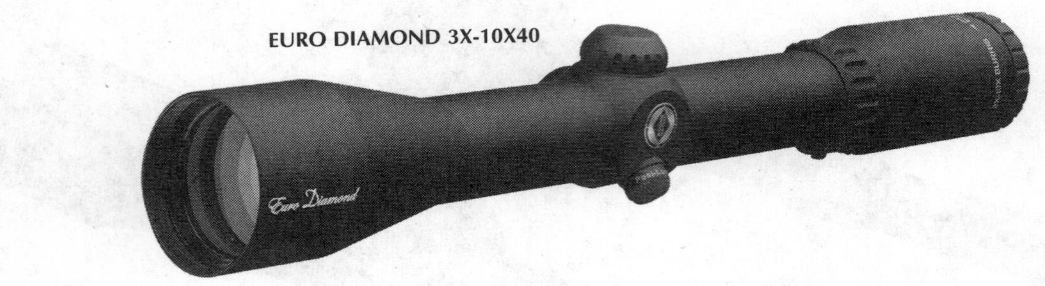

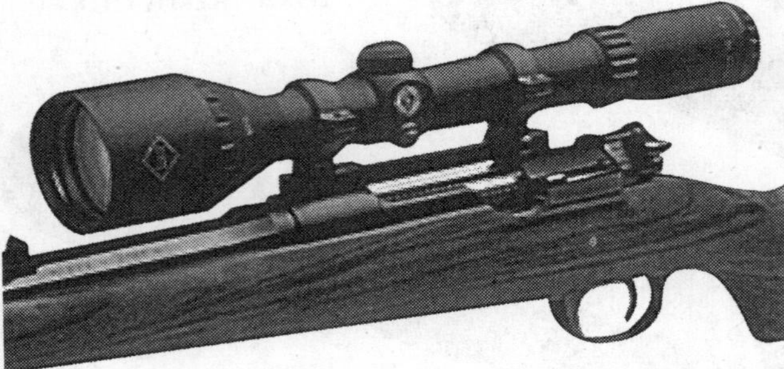

3X-12X-50MM

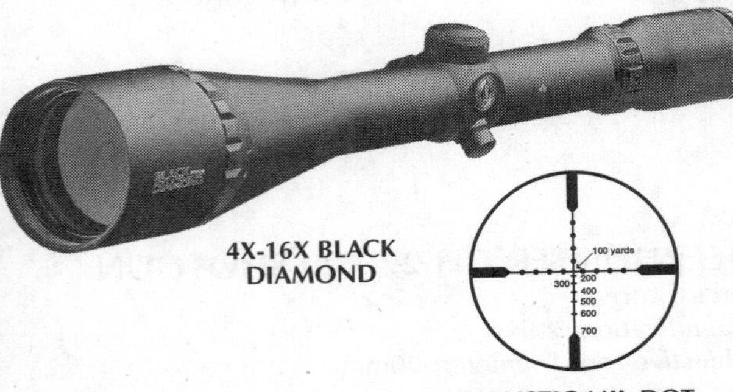

4X-16X BLACK DIAMOND

BALLISTIC MIL-DOT

2.75X SCOUT

SPEEDDOT 135

EURO DIAMOND

The Burris Euro Diamond line includes four 30mm riflescopes: 1.5-6x40, 3-10x40, 2.5-10x44, 3-12x50. All come in matte black finish, with fully multi-coated lenses and 1/4-minute clicks on re-settable dials. Eye relief is 3½ to 4 inches. The eyepiece and power ring are integrated and the scopes have a helical rear ocular ring. Options include: ballistic Plex or German 3P#4 reticle and Posi-Lock or illuminated.

4X-16X BLACK DIAMOND

The Burris Black Diamond is designed for long-range big game rifles and dual-purpose big game/varmint rifles, it has a 50mm objective and Burris' best optics. It is available with the trajectory-compensating Ballistic Mil-Dot reticle. The heavy 30mm tube is notable for its ruggedness.

Burris's Black Diamond line includes three models of a 30mm main tube 3-12X50mm with various finishes, reticles, and adjustment knobs. These riflescopes have easy-to-grip rubber-armored parallax-adjust rings, an adjustable and resettable adjustment dial, and an internal focusing eyepiece.

SPECIFICATIONS

Models: 3-12X50mm/4-16x50/6-24x50/8-32x50
Field of View (feet @ 100yds.): 34'-12'/18-6
Optimum eye relief: 3.5"-4.0"/3.5-4
Exit Pupil: 13.7mm-4.2mm/7.6-2.1
Click adjust value (@ 100 yds.): .25"/.125
Max. internal adj. (@ 100 yds.): 100"/52
Clear objective diameter: 50mm/50mm
Ocular end diameter: 42mm/42mm
Weight: 25 oz./25 oz.
Length: 13.8"/16.2"
Reticles available: Plex, Mil-Dot, Ballistic MDot, and Fine Plex

SCOUT SCOPES

For hunters who need a 7- to 14-inch eye relief for mounting in front of the ejection port; allows you to shoot with both eyes open. The 15-foot field of view and 2.75X magnification are ideal for brush guns and shotgunners. Rugged, reliable and fog proof.

SPEEDDOT 135

1x35mm pistol and shotgun sight. Electronic red dot reticle, 3 moa or 11 moa

Burris Riflescopes

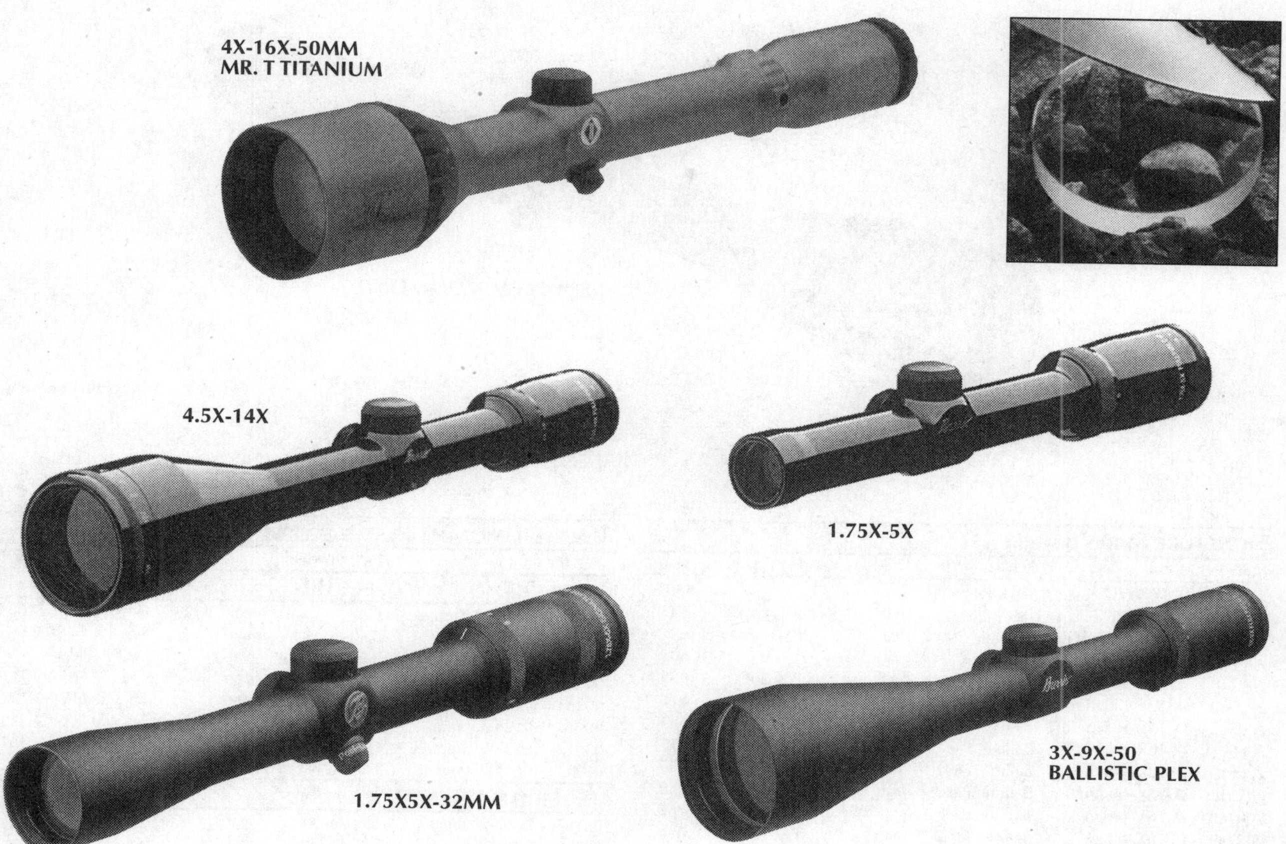

BURRIS "MR T" TITANIUM BLACK • DIAMOND SCOPES

This scope's tube is constructed of titanium, stronger than aluminum and much lighter than steel. Each scope is coated with a nitride harder than carbide or hard chrome. These nitrides are molecularly bonded to the titanium through high intensity physical vapor deposition for maximum adhesion that will not blister, flake, or chip. The result is an ultra-hard (up to 85 Rockwell C), abrasion resistant surface.

The lenses in this scope are as tough as the tube. A scratch-proof T-Plate coating applied to the objective and eyepiece lenses is remarkable. These lenses do not come with the warning of other "scratch-resistant" coatings about removing all dust before cleaning. T-plated lenses do not require a "soft clean lens cloth". Just knock the mud off the lens and wipe it clean with a dirty shirt tail. Ordinary dirt, dust, and grit won't touch it. This coating technology is prohibitively expensive for ordinary scopes. Mr. T is a premium-quality sight for discriminating hunters.

1.75X-5X-32MM SIGNATURE SAFARI TM

This optic system was designed to integrate a host of features into the ultimate riflescope for hunting in heavy brush, for heavy recoiling dangerous game rifles, and for magnum slug shotguns. The 1.75X-5X Signature SafariTM provides ¾" additional eye relief to save your brow while shooting from awkward positions. The 32mm objective allows for ultra-flexibility in eye position. The eyepiece and power ring are combined into a single sturdy unit that makes changing magnifications faster. The Post and Crosshair reticle is the fastest and most instinctive reticle pattern available. Because of its size, shape, ruggedness, and lighter weight, the 1.75X-5X also makes a great scope for all the new short magnum rifles.

BURRIS FULLFIELD II VARIABLE SCOPES

One of the most popular big game scopes around, the Fullfield II is more forgiving for eye positioning both fore and aft, and left and right, than its predecessor. Burris has shaved 4 ounces of weight off each model without affecting durability or optical performance. Overall, the Fullfield is about one inch shorter too—for a more compact look and feel. Like the Fullfield, and unlike other scopes, Fullfield II eyepieces are sealed with special quad seals rather than old-tech O-rings. And the eyepiece is now part of the power ring. To change magnification, simply turn the entire eyepiece. A European-style adjustable eyepiece is easy to use and requires no locking mechanism.

Burris Scopes

Signature Series

6X24X BLACK DIAMOND

Signature Series Scopes

Item	Model	Reticle	Finish	Features	List
200707	1.75X-5X-32 Safari	Taper Plex	mat		$607
200708	1.75X-5X-32 Safari	Taper Plex	mat	Posi-Lock	655
200713	1.75X-5X-32 Safari	German 3P#4	mat	Posi-Lock	691
200717	1.5X-6X-40mm	Taper Plex	mat		607
200718	1.5X-6x-40mm	Taper Plex	mat	Posi-Lock	655
200560	3X-10X-40mm	Ballistic Plex	mat		672
200562	3X-10X-40mm	Plex	mat		654
200561	3X-10X-40mm	Ballistic Plex	mat	Posi-Lock	715
200616	3X-12X-44mm	Ballistic Plex	mat		708
200617	3X-12X-44mm	Ballistic Plex	mat	Posi-Lock	756
200768	4X-16X-44mm	Ballistic Plex	mat	PA	767
200769	4X-16X-44mm	Ballistic Mdot	mat	PA	894
200770	4X-16X-44mm	Ballistic Plex	mat	Posi-Lock/PA	854
200822	6X-24X-44mm	Plex	mat	PA	794
200823	6X-24X-44mm	Fine Plex	mat	Target/PA	830
200824	6X-24X-44mm	Ballistic MDot	mat	Target/PA	957
200867	8X-32X	Fine Plex	mat	Target/PA	849
200868	8X-32X	Ballistic MDot	mat	Target/PA	975

Euro Diamond Scopes

Item	Model	Reticle	Finish	Features	List
200960	1.5X-6X-40mm	German 3P#4	mat	Posi-Lock	735
200961	1.5X-6X-40mm	German 3P#4	mat	Illuminated	879
200965	3X-10X-40mm	German 3P#4	mat	Posi-Lock	830
200967	3X-10X-40mm	German 3P#4	mat	Illuminated	975
200966	3X-10X-40mm	Ballistic Plex	mat		758
200919	2.5X-10X-44mm	German 3P#4	mat	Posi-Lock	863
200918	2.5X-10X-44mm	Ballistic Plex	mat		773
200914	3X-12X-50mm	German 3P#4	mat	Posi-Lock	935
200915	3X-12X-50mm	German 3P#4	mat	Illuminated	993
200916	3X-12X-50mm	Ballistic Plex	mat		849

Black Diamond T-Plates Scopes (30mm)

Item	Model	Reticle	Finish	Features	List
200929	4X-16X-50mm	Ballistic MDot	mat	PA	1,670

Black Diamond Scopes (30mm)

Item	Model	Reticle	Finish	Features	List
200954	4X-16X-50mm	Plex	mat	Side PA	988
200955	4X-16X-50mm	Ballistic MDot	mat	Side PA	1,130
200958	4X-16X-50mm	Ballistic MDot	mat	PLOCK/SideP	1,202
200926	4X-16X-50mm	Ballistic Plex	mat		1034
200933	6X-24X-50mm	Fine Plex	mat	Tar-Side /PA	1,109
200934	6X-24X-50mm	Ballistic MDot	mat	Tar-Side /PA	1,249
200942	8X-32X-50mm	Fine Plex	mat	Tar-Side /PA	1,161
200943	8X-32X-50mm	Ballistic MDot	mat	Tar-Side /PA	1,322

LRS Lighted Reticle Scopes

Item	Model	Reticle	Finish	Features	List
200167	3X-9X Fullfield II	Electro-Dot	mat		$523
200168	3X-9X FFII LRS	LRS Ball Plex	mat		563
200173	3.5X-10X-50 FFII LRS	LRS Ball Plex	mat		679
200710	1.75X-5X Sig LRS	LRS Fast Plex	mat		776
200179	3X-9X-40 Fullfield II	Plex	mat		563
200175	3X-10X-50 FFII	Plex	mat		679
200185	4.5X-14X-42 FFII	Ballistic Plex	mat		775
200186	4.5X-14X-42 FFII	Plex	mat		775
200719	1.5X-6X-40 Sig Select	Electro-Dot	mat		673
200565	3X-10X-40 Sig Select	Electro-Dot	mat		802
200566	3X-10X-40 Sig Select	Ballistic Plex	mat		846
200567	3X-10X-40 Sig Select	Ballistic Plex	mat	Posi-Lock	891
200771	4X-16X-44 Sig Select	Electro-Dot	mat	PA	932
200772	4X-16X-44 Sig Select	Ballistic Plex	mat	PA	976
200773	4X-16X-44 Sig Select	Ballistic Plex	mat	Posi-Lock/PA	1021

Eye relief is the distance from your eye to the scope's rear or ocular lens. Mount the scope well forward, to protect your brow and speed your aim as you shove your face forward on the comb.

Burris Scopes

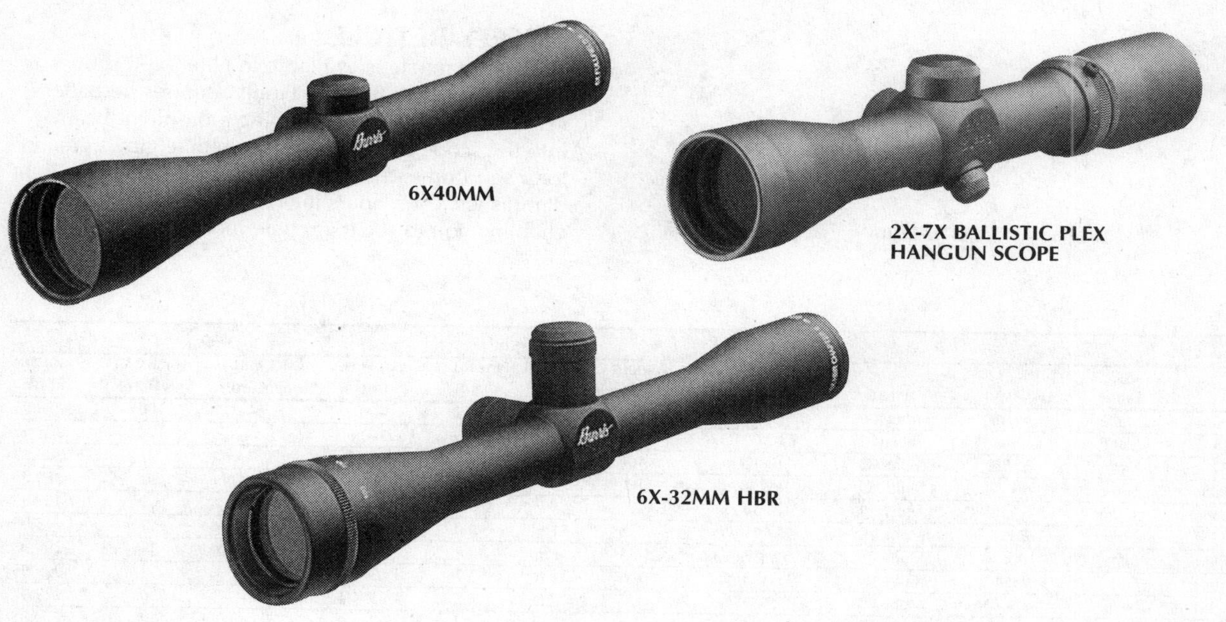

6X40MM

2X-7X BALLISTIC PLEX HANGUN SCOPE

6X-32MM HBR

FULLFIELD IITM SCOPES FIXED POWER WITH HI-LUME LENSES

Fullfield II Scopes

Item	Model	Reticle	Finish	Features	List
200052	6X-40mm	Plex	mat		$386
200057	6X-32mm HBRII	Superfine XHr	mat	Target /PA	515
200056	6X-32mm HBRII	.375 Dot	mat	Target /PA	538
200153	3X-9X-50mm	Plex	mat		481
200154	3X-9X-50mm	Ballistic Plex	mat		490
200089	1.75-5X-20mmPlex		camo		313
200087	1.75-5X-20mmPlex		mat		286
200160	3X-9X-40mm	Plex	blk		336
200161	3X-9X-40mm	Plex	mat		336
200162	3X-9X-40mm	Ballistic Plex	mat		354
200163	3X-9X-40mm	Plex	nic		372
200164	3X-9X-40mm	German 3P#4	mat		372
200166	3X-9X-40mm	Ballistic Plex	blk		354
200169	3X-9X-40mm	Ballistic Plex	nic		390
200174	3.5X-10X-50mm	3P#4	blk		579
200171	3.5X-10X-50mm	Plex	mat		561
200172	3.5X-10X-50mm	Ballistic Plex	mat		570
200180	4.5X-14X	Plex	blk	PA	585
200181	4.5X-14X	Plex	mat	PA	585
200183	4.5X-14X-42mm	Ballistic Plex	mat	PA	602
200184	4.5X-14X-42	German 3P#4	mat	PA	620
200191	6.5X-20X-50mm	Fine Plex	mat	PA	674
200192	6.5X-20X-50mm	Fine Plex	mat	Target /PA	715
200193	6.5X-20X-50mm	Ballistic MDot	mat	PA	808
200413	2.5X shotgun	Plex	mat		$307

Compact Scopes

Item	Model	Reticle	Finish	Features	List
200381	3X-9X	Sako Quad Ballistic Plex		mat	475
200384	3X-9X	Plex	mat	PA	460
200390	4X-12XPlex		blk	PA	540
200395	4X-12XPlex		mat	PA	547
200393	4X-12XFine Plex		blk	Target /PA	581
200394	4X-12XFine Plex		mat	Target /PA	601

Rimfire/Airgun Scopes

Item	Model	Reticle	Finish	Features	List
200384	3X-9X	Plex	mat	PA	$460
200390	4X-12X	Plex	blk	PA	540
200395	4X-12X	Plex	mat	PA	547
200396	4X-12X	Ballistic Plex	mat	PA	567
200393	4X-12X	Fine Plex	blk	Target /PA	581
200394	4X-12X	Fine Plex	mat	Target /PA	601
200858	8X-32X	Plex	blk	Target /PA	$835

Handgun Scopes

Item	Model	Reticle	Finish	Features	List
200299	2X-7X	Ballistic Plex	mat	Posi-Lock	$533
200309	3X-12X	Ballistic Plex	mat	PA	592
200424	1X XER	Plex	mat		324
200220	2X	Plex	blk		289
200218	2X	Plex	mat		282
200229	2X	Plex	nic		309
200228	2X	Plex	mat	Posi-Lock	338
200235	4X	Plex	blk		341
200242	4X	Plex	mat		341
200214	1.5X-4X	Plex	nic		415
200207	1.5X-4X	Plex	mat	Posi-Lock	453
200213	1.5X-4X	Plex	nic	Posi-Lock	455
200290	2X-7X	Plex	blk		462
200291	2X-7X	Plex	mat		473
200279	2X-7X	Ballistic Plex	mat		491
200298	2X-7X	Plex	nic		484
200299	2X-7X	Ballistic Plex	mat	Posi-Lock	533
200297	2X-7X	Plex	nic	Posi-Lock	525
200306	3X-12X	Plex	blk	PA	563
200307	3X-12X	Plex	mat	PA	574
200308	3X-12X	Plex	blk	PA	583
200305	3X-12X	Fine Plex	blk	Target /PA	576
200303	3X-12X	Plex	mat	Posi-Lock	614

Speeddot 135 Sights

Item	Model	Reticle	Finish	Features	List
300200	1X-35mm	3 MOA Dot	mat		$294
300201	1X-35mm	11 MOA Dot	mat		294
300203	1X-35mm	3MOA Dot	camo		338

Scout Scopes

Item	Model	Reticle	Finish	Features	List
200424	1X XER	Plex	mat		$324
200269	2.75X	Heavy Plex	mat		359

Bushnell Riflescopes

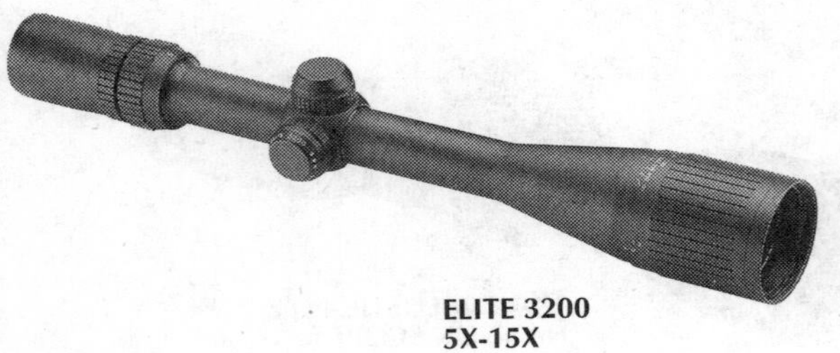

ELITE 3200
5X-15X

FIREFLY RETICLE

The Firefly reticle is available in Elite 3200 scopes, from 1.5-4x32 to 3-9x50. Firefly requires no batteries. You "energize" it by shining a flashlight beam into the scope for a minute. The reticle glows green for a short time, then fades to black. As shooting light diminishes, even hours later, the green glow returns, enabling you to see the reticle more clearly.

Elite 3200

Model	Finish	Power / Obj. Lens (mm)	Reticle	Field-of-View (ft@100yds)	Weight (oz)	Length (in)	Eye Relief (in)	Exit Pupil (mm)	Click Value (in@100yds)	Adj. Range (in@100yds)	Suggested Retail
32-1040M	Matte	10 x 40	Mil Dot	11	15.5	11.7	3.5	4.0	.25	100	$279.95
32-1546M	Matte	1.5–4.5 x 32	FireFly™	63/21@1.5x	13	12.5	3.6	21–7.6	.25	100	307.95
32-2632M	Matte	2–6 x 32	Multi-X®	10/3@2x	10	9	20	16–5.3	.25	50	389.95
32-2632S	Silver	2–6 x 32	Multi-X®	10/3@2x	10	9	20	16–5.3	.25	50	389.95
*32-2636M	Matte	2–6 x 32	FireFly™	10/3@2x	10	9	20	16–5.3	.25	50	431.95
32-2732M	Matte	2–7 x 32	Multi-X®	44.6/15@2x	12	11.6	3.0	12.2–4.6	.25	50	265.95
32-3104M	Matte	3-10 x 40	Multi-X®	35.5/11.803x	14.5	11	3.7	13.1-4	.25	85	297.95
32-3940G	Gloss	3–9 x 40	Multi-X®	33.8/11@3x	13	12.6	3.3	13.3–4.4	.25	50	279.95
32-3940S	Silver	3–9 x 40	Multi-X®	33.8/11@3x	13	12.6	3.3	13.3–4.4	.25	50	279.95
32-3944M	Matte	3–9 x 40	Multi-X®	33.8/11@3x	13	12.6	3.3	13.3–4.4	.25	50	279.95
32-3946M	Matte	3–9 x 40	FireFly™	33.8/11@3x	13	12.6	3.3	13.3–4.4	.25	50	321.95
32-3954M	Matte	3–9 x 50	Multi-X®	31.5/10@3x	19	15.7	3.3	16–5.6	.25	50	335.95
32-3955E	Matte	3–9 x 50	European	31.5/10@3x	22	15.6	3.3	16–5.6	.36	70	561.95
32-3956M	Matte	3–9 x 50	FireFly™	31.5/1.50@3x	19	15.7	3.3	16.7–5.6	.25	50	377.95
32-3957M	Matte	3–9 x 50	FireFly™	31.5/10.5@3x	22	15.6	3.3	16.7–5.6	.25	70	603.95
32-4124A	Matte	4–12 x 40	Multi-X®	26.9/9@4x	15	13.2	3.3	10–3.33	.25	50	411.95
32-4124B	Matte	4-12x40	Ballistic	26.9/9@4x	15	13.2	3.3	10-3.33	.25	50	531.95
32-5154M	Matte	5–15 x 40	Multi-X®	21/7@5x	19	14.5	4.3	9–2.7	.25	50	439.95
32-5155M	Matte	5–15 x 50	Multi-X®	21/7@5x	24	15.9	3.4	10–3.3	.25	40	463.95
*32-5156M	Matte	5–15 x 40	FireFly™	21/7@5x	19	14.5	4.3	9–2.7	.25	50	481.95
32-7214M	Matte	7-21 x 40	MilDot	13.5/4.5@7x	15	12.8	3.3	14.6-6	.25	40	549.95

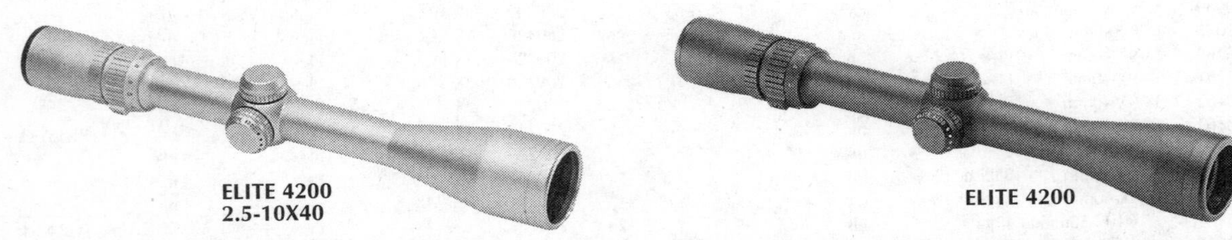

ELITE 4200
2.5-10X40

ELITE 4200

Elite 4200

Model	Finish	Power / Obj. Lens (mm)	Reticle	Field-of-View (ft@100yds)	Weight (oz)	Length (in)	Eye Relief (in)	Exit Pupil (mm)	Click Value (in@100yds)	Adj. Range (in@100yds)	Suggested Retail
42-1636M	Matte	1.5–6 x 36	Multi-X®	61.8/20.6@1.5x	15.4	12.8	3.3	14.6–6	.25	60	$533.95
42-1637m	Matte	1.5-6 x 36	FireFly™	61.8/20.6 @65x	15.4	12.8	3.3	14.6-6	.25	60	603.95
42-2104M	Matte	2.5–10 x 40	Multi-X®	41.5/13.8@2.5x	16	13.5	3.3	15.6–4	.25	50	563.95
42-2104G	Gloss	2.5–10 x 40	Multi-X®	41.5/13.8@2.5x	16	13.5	3.3	15.6–4	.25	50	563.95
42-2104S	Silver	2.5–10 x 40	Multi-X®	41.5/13.8@2.5x	16	13.5	3.3	15.6–4	.25	50	563.95
42-2105M	Matte	2.5–10 x 50	Multi-X®	40.3/13.4@2.5x	18	14.3	3.3	15–5	.25	50	669.95
42-2106M	Matte	2.5-10 x 50	FireFly™	40.3/13.4 @25x	18	14.3	3.3	15-5	.25	50	747.95
42-2146M	Matte	2.5–10 x 40	FireFly™	41.5/13.8@2.5x	16	13.5	3.3	15.6–4	.25	50	605.95
42-2151M	Matte	2.5–10 x 50	4A w/1 M.O.A Dot	40/13.3@2.5x	22	14.5	3.3	5–15	.25	60	699.95
42-4164M	Matte	4–16 x 40	Multi-X®	26/8.7@4x	18.6	14.4	3.3	10–25	.125	40	565.95
42-4165M	Matte	4–16 x 50	Multi-X®	26/9@4x	22	15.6	3.3	12.5–3.1	.125	50	731.95
42-6242M	Matte	6–24 x 40	Mil Dot	18/6@6x	20.2	16.9	3.3	6.7–1.7	.125	26	659.95
42-6243A	Matte	6–24 x 40	1/4 M.O.A. Dot	18/6@6x	20.2	16.9	3.3	6.7–1.7	.125	26	639.95
42-6244M	Matte	6–24 x 40	Multi-X®	18/4.5@6x	20.2	16.9	3.3	6.7–1.7	.125	26	639.95
42-8324M	Matte	8–32 x 40	Multi-X®	14/4.7@8x	22	18	3.3	5–1.25	.125	20	703.95

Bushnell Riflescopes

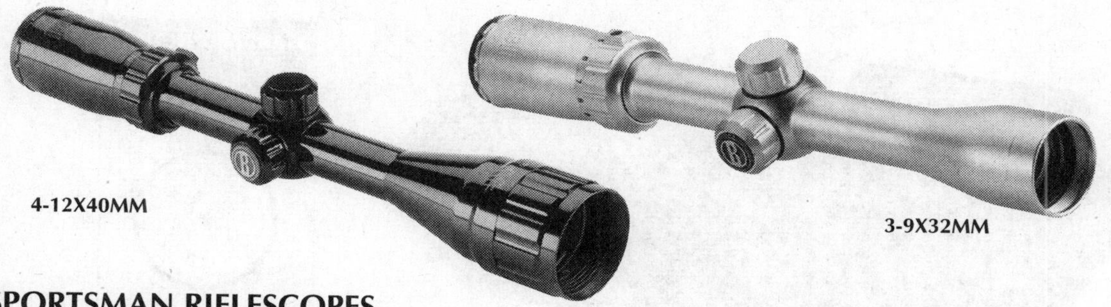

4-12X40MM

3-9X32MM

SPORTSMAN RIFLESCOPES

Sportsman Riflescopes have multi-coated optics, plus a long list of standard features, including a fast-focus eyepiece and ¼ M.O.A. fingertip windage and elevation adjustments. The easy-grip power change ring makes changing magnifications fast and easy. The rigid one-piece 1" tube is waterproof, fogproof and shockproof. 3-9x32mm: Gloss, 72-1393; Silver, 72-1393S; Matte, 72-13984-12x40mm: Gloss, 72-0412

BUSHNELL SPORTSMAN® RIFLESCOPES

Model	Finish	Power / Obj. Lens (mm)	Reticle	Field-of-View (ft@100yds)	Weight (oz)	Length (in)	Eye Relief (in)	Exit Pupil (mm)	Click Value (in@100yds)	Adj. Range (in@100yds)	Suggested Retail
*72-0038	Matte	3–9 x 32	Multi-X®	37–14	13.5	12	3.5	10.6–3.6	.25	100	$69.96
**72-0039	Gloss	3–9 x 32	Multi-X®	40 13.1	163	12.2	430	3.6–11	.25	100	101.95
72-0130	Matte	1 x 23	6 M.O.A. Red Dot	60	4.9	5.5	Unlimited	2.3	.5	50	73.95
72-1393	Gloss	3–9 x 32	Multi-X®	37–14	13.5	12	3.5	10–3.6	.25	100	59.95
72-1393S	Silver	3–9 x 32	Multi-X®	37–14	13.5	12	3.5	10–3.6	.25	100	59.95
72-1398	Matte	3–9 x 32	Multi-X®	37–14	13.5	12	3.5	10–3.6	.25	100	59.95
72-1403	Matte	4 x 32	Multi-X®	29	11	11.7	3.4	8	.25	110	49.95
72-1545	Matte	1.5–4.5 x 21	Multi-X®	24–69	11.7	10.1	3.3	10–3.6	.25	210	75.95
72-1548R	Camo	1.5–4.5 x 32	Circle-X®	46.2–19.3	13.5	11.7	4.3	21–7.1	.25	100	95.95
72-3940M	Matte	3–9 x 40	Multi-X®	37–12	15	13	3.5	13–4.4	.25	100	83.95
72-3943	Matte	3-9 x 40	Lowlight	37-12	15	13	3.5	13-4.4	.25	100	83.95

*Airgun scope **Target Airgun scope

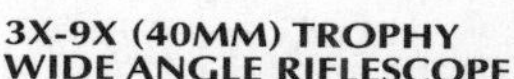

3X-9X (40MM) TROPHY WIDE ANGLE RIFLESCOPE

BUSHNELL TROPHY® RIFLESCOPES

Model	Finish	Power / Obj. Lens (mm)	Reticle	Field-of-View (ft@100yds)	Weight (oz)	Length (in)	Eye Relief (in)	Exit Pupil (mm)	Click Value (in@100yds)	Adj. Range (in@100yds)	Suggested Retail
73-0131	Matte	1 x 28	6 M.O.A. Red Dot	68–22.6	6	5.5	Unlimited	28	.5	50	$89.95
73-0134	Matte	1 x 28	4 Dial-In Electronic	68–22.6	6	5.5	Unlimited	28	.5	50	119.95
73-0135	Matte	1 x 30	4 Dial-Fn	68-22.6	6	5.5	Unlimited	28	.5	50	131.95
73-0232S	Silver	2 x 32	Multi-X®	20–7	7.7	8.7	18	16	.25	90	191.95
73-1421	Matte	1.75–4 x 32	Circle-X®	73–30	10.9	10.8	4.1	18@1.75x / 8@4x	.25	120	149.95
73-1422MO	Camo	1.75–4 x 32	Circle-X®	73–30	10.9	10.8	4.1	18@1.75x / 8@4x	.25	120	163.95
73-1500	Gloss	1.75–5 x 32	Multi-X®	68–23	12.3	10.8	4.1	18.3@1.75x / 6.4@5x	.25	120	155.95
73-2632	Matte	2–6 x 32	Multi-X®	11–4	10.9	9.1	9–26	16@2x / 5.3@6x	.25	50	251.95
73-2632S	Silver	2–6 x 32	Multi-X®	11–4	10.9	9.1	9–26	16@2x / 5.3@6x	.25	50	251.95
73-3940	Gloss	3–9 x 40	Multi-X®	42–14	13.2	11.7	3.4	13.3@3x / 4.4@9x	.25	60	139.95
73-3940S	Silver	3–9 x 40	Multi-X®	42–14	13.2	11.7	3.4	13.3@3x / 4.4@9x	.25	60	139.95
73-3946	Matte	3–9 x 40	Mil Dot	42–14	13.2	11.7	3.4	13.3@3x / 4.4@9x	.25	60	149.95
73-3948	Matte	3–9 x 40	Multi-X®	42–14	13.2	11.7	3.4	13.3@3x / 4.4@9x	.25	60	139.95
73-39481	Matte	3-9 x 40	TRX	42-14	13.2	11.7	3.4	13.3 @3x/4.4 @9x	.25	60	149.95
73-3949	Matte	3–9 x 40	Circle-X®	42–14	13.2	11.7	3.4	13.3@3x / 4.4@9x	.25	60	149.95
73-4124	Gloss	4–12 x 40	Multi-X®	32–11	16.1	12.6	3.4	10@4x / 3.3@12x	.25	60	263.95
73-4124M	Matte	4–12 x 40	Multi-X®	32–11	16.1	12.6	3.4	10@4x / 3.3@12x	.25	60	263.95
73-6184	Matte	6–18 x 40	Multi-X®	17.3–6	17.9	14.8	3.0	6.6@6x / 2.2@18x	.125	40	331.95

Bushnell Riflescopes

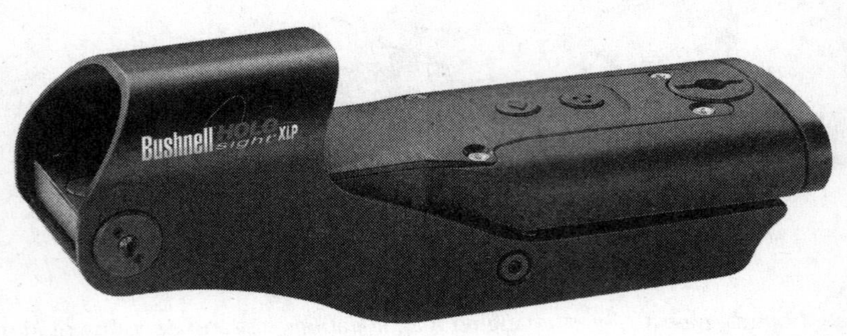

53-0027 HOLOSIGHT XLP

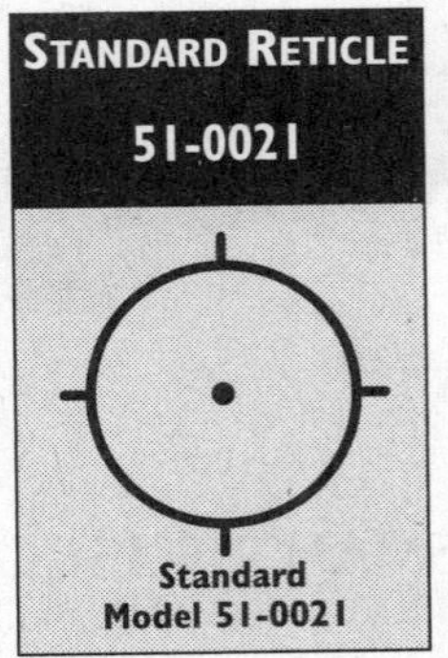

HOLOSIGHT

HOLOSIGHT

Unlike conventional sights, HOLOsight projects the appearance of an illuminated crosshair 50 yards in front of your gun, yet no forward light is projected. Sight from any distance behind the gun—with both eyes on the target. This fastest of all optical sights offers unlimited field of view and eye relief. Shockproof, waterproof and fogproof. Half the length and weight of conventional scopes. Fits easily on handguns, shotguns and rifles with a standard Weaver style mount. Available in two battery styles—N cell or AAA.

HOLOsight

Model	Reticle	Magnification @ 100 yds.	Field-of-View ft. @100yds.	Weight	Length	Eye relief	Batteries	Brightness adj.	Price
51-0021	Holographic	1x	Unlimited	6.4 oz.	4.12 in.	1/2-in.-10′	2 Type N	20 Levels	$389.95
53-0021	Holographic	1x	Unlimited	12 oz.	6 in.	Unlimited	AAA	20 Levels	299.95
53-0027	Holographic	1x	Unlimited	12 oz.	6 in.	Unlimited	AAA	20 Levels	299.95

5-15X40
LEGEND SCOPE

Legend

Model	Finish	Power / Obj. Lens (mm)	Reticle	Field-of-View (ft@100yds)	Weight (oz / g)	Length (in)	Eye Relief (in)	Exit Pupil (mm)	Click Value (in@100yds)	Adj. Range (in@100yds)	Suggested Retail
*75-2732M	Matte	2–7 x 32	Multi-X®	56–16	11.6	11.6	3.5	14.4–4.6	.25	60	$187.95
75-3940M	Matte	3–9 x 40	Multi-X®	36–13	14.6	13.1	3.5	13.3–4.4	.25	80	207.95
75-3950M	Matte	3–9 x 50	Multi-X®	36–13	16	13.1	3.5	16.7–5.6	.25	80	227.95
75-4124M	Matte	4-12 x 40	Multi-X®	30-10	17.3	14.4	3.9	10-3.4	.25	75	265.95
75-5154M	Matte	5–15 x 40	Mil Dot	23–8	17.7	14.6	3.5	8–2.7	.25	50	277.95

Bushnell Riflescopes

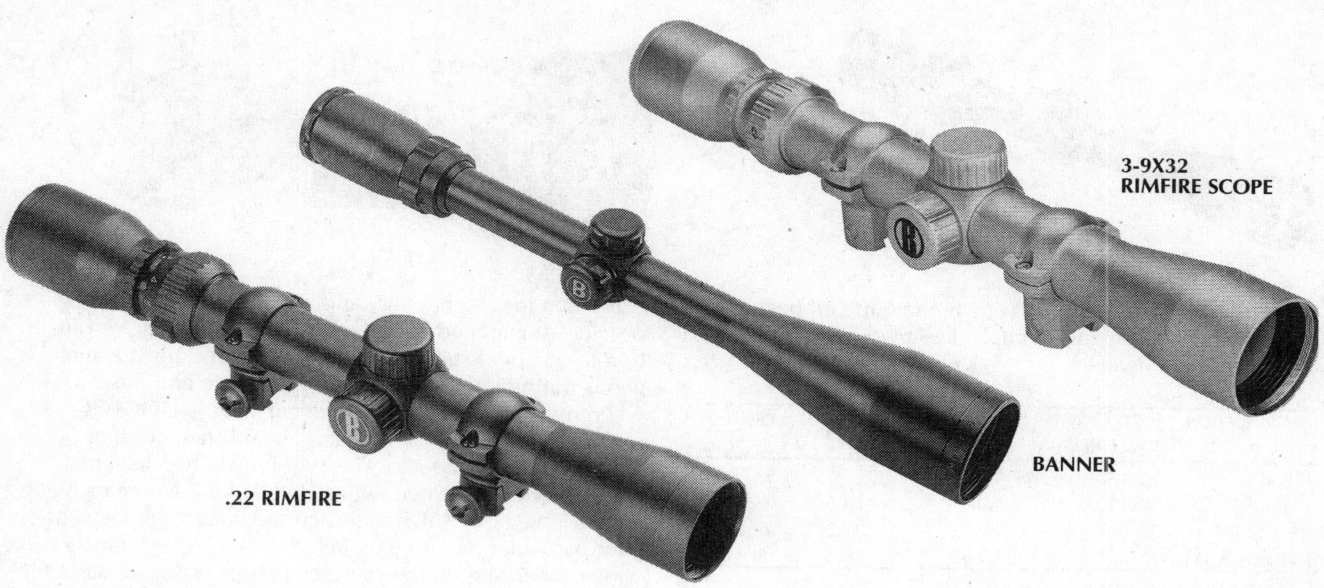

3-9X32 RIMFIRE SCOPE

BANNER

.22 RIMFIRE

.22 RIMFIRE

Bushnell .22 Rimfire scopes are designed with a 50-yard parallax setting and fully coated optics for low-light shooting The one-piece 1″ tube is waterproof and fogproof; ¼ M.O.A. windage and elevation adjustments are fingertip-easy to turn. These scopes come with rings for grooved receivers.

BANNER

Bushnell's Banner Dusk & Dawn riflescopes feature DDB multi-coated lenses to maximize dusk and dawn brightness for clarity in low and full light. A fast-focus eyepiece and wide-angle field of view complement a one-piece tube and ¼″ M.O.A. resettable windage and elevation adjustments. An easy-trip power change ring allows fast power changes. This scope is waterproof, fogproof and shockproof.

.22 Rimfire

Model	Finish	Power / Obj. Lens (mm)	Reticle	Field-of-View (ft@100yds)	Weight (oz)	Length (in)	Eye Relief (in)	Exit Pupil (mm)	Click Value (in@100yds)	Adj. Range (in@100yds)	Suggested Retail
76-2239	Matte	3–9 x 32	Multi-X®	40–13	11.2	11.75	3.0	10.6–3.6	.25	40	$53.95
76-2239S	Silver	3–9 x 32	Multi-X®	40–13	11.2	11.75	3.0	10.6–3.6	.25	40	53.95
76-2243	Matte	4 x 32	Multi-X®	30 / 10@4x	10	11.5	3.0	8	.25	40	45.95

Banner Dusk & Dawn

Model	Finish	Power / Obj. Lens (mm)	Reticle	Field-of-View (ft@100yds)	Weight (oz)	Length (in)	Eye Relief (in)	Exit Pupil (mm)	Click Value (in@100yds)	Adj. Range (in@100yds)	Suggested Retail
71-0432	Matte	4 x 32	Circle-X®	31.5–10.5@4x	11.1	11.3	3.3	8@4x	.25	50	$89.95
71-1432	Matte	1–4 x 32	Circle-X®	78.5–24.9	12.2	10.5	4.3	16.9@1x / 8@4x	.25	50	107.95
71-1436	Matte	1.75–4 x 32	Circle-X®	35–16	12.1	10.8	6	18.3@1.75x –6.4@4x	.25	100	101.95
71-1545	Matte	1.5–4.5 x 32	Multi-X®	67v23	10.5	10.5	4.0	17@1.5x / 7@4.5x	.25	60	101.95
71-3510	Matte	3.5-10 x 36	Multi-X®	30-10.415.0	12.5	3.4		10.3@ 3.5/3.6 @10	.25	85	133.95
71-3944	Matte	3–9 x 40	Circle-X®	36–13	12.5	11.5	4.0	13@3x / 4.4@9x	.25	60	109.95
71-3946	Matte	3–9 x 40	Multi-X®	40–14	13	12	4.0	13@3x / 4.4@9x	.25	60	101.95
*71-3947	Matte	3–9 x 40	Multi-X®	40–13.6	13	12	3.3	13@3x / 4.4@9x	.25	60	111.95
71-3948	Matte	3–9 x 40	Multi-X®	40–14	13	12	3.3	13.3@3x / 4.4@9x	.25	60	105.95
71-3950	Matte	3–9 x 50	Multi-X®	26–12	19	16	3.8	16@3x / 5.6@9x	.25	50	163.95
71-3951	Matte	3–9 x 50	3-2-1 Low Light™	26–12	19	16	3.8	16@3x / 5.6@9x	.25	50	163.95
71-4124	Matte	4–12 x 40	Multi-X®	29–11	15	12	3.3	10@4x / 3.3@12x	.25	60	138.95
71-6185	Matte	6–18 x 50	Multi-X®	17–6	18	16	3.5	8.3@6x / 2.8@18x	.25	40	183.95
*71-6244	Matte	6–24 x 40	Mil Dot	17–5	19.6	16.1	3.4	6.7@6x / 1.7@24x	.25	36	189.95

Docter Sports Optics

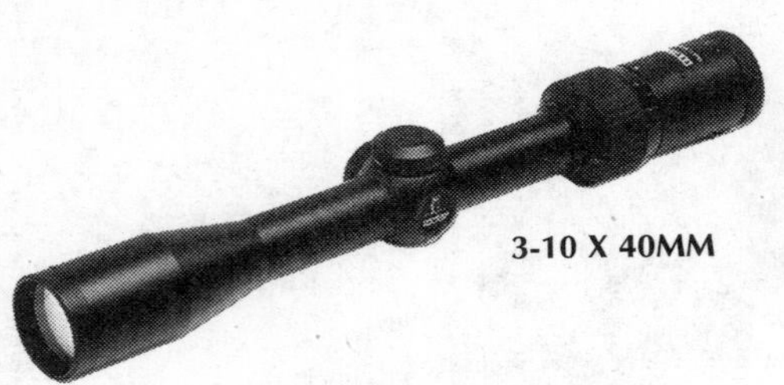

3-10 X 40MM

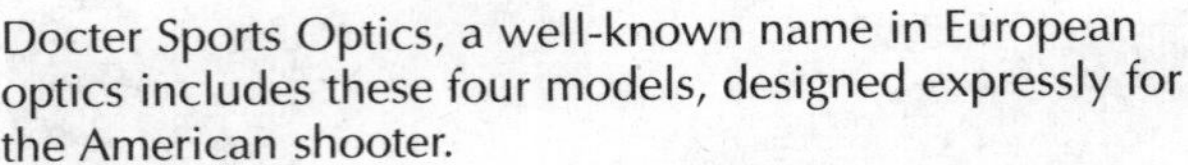

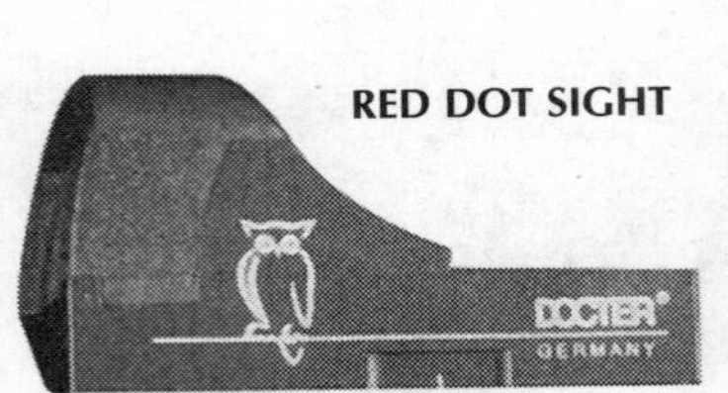

RED DOT SIGHT

Docter Sports Optics, a well-known name in European optics includes these four models, designed expressly for the American shooter.

Magnification x obj. dia.	Field Of View (ft., 100 yds)	Dia./Length (in.)	Weight (oz.)	Price
3-9x40	31-13	1/12.5	17	$378.00
3-10x40	34-12	1/13	18.5	626.00
4.5-14x40	23-8	1/13.5	21.5	652.00
8-25x50	13-4	1/16	26.5	901.00

Some of Docter Optic 30mm scopes feature aspherical lenses, as do the company's binoculars. All Docter scopes offer these advantages:

RIFLE SCOPE SPECIFICATIONS

- High strength, one-piece tube construction of aircraft-grade aluminum eliminates weak screw-together joints that can leak or break, won't rust or corrode in adverse weather.
- Precise click-stop adjustments of ¼" at 100 yards for windage and elevation. Wide range of adjustment (50") makes it easier to compensate for mounting errors.
- Advanced lens technology and high grade multi-coating provides unparalled light transmission and image resolution for crisp, clear sighting picture—especially advantageous during low light conditions at dawn and dusk when most animal movement occurs. Every DOCTER scope is subjected to stringent leak and shock testing before it leaves the factory.Every joint where a leak may possibly occur is sealed with statically and dynamically loaded ring gaskets. Diopter focusing adapts the focus to your particular needs.Eye relief of over 3 inches, plus a wide rubber ring on the eye-piece protects the shooter from half-moon cuts, even with heavy calibers.

DOCTER RED DOT SIGHT

A red dot sight is now available from Docter Sports Optics. Weighing just one ounce, it is not much bulkier than a standard rear aperture. A red dot appears to project itself on the target—there's nothing to line up. You can shoot more quickly than with any other type of sight. Coated, high-quality lenses ensure a clear sight picture. There is no battery switch; batteries last up to five years without rest. Available in 3.5 or 7 M.D.A.

Description	Magnification	Objective Lens Dia.	Color	Reticle
One-Inch Tube Scopes				
3-9 x 40 Variable	3x to 9x	40 mm	Matte Black	Plex
3-9 x 40 Variable	3x to 9x	40 mm	Matte Black	German #4
3-10 x 40 Variable	3x to 10x	40 mm	Matte Black	Plex
3-10 x 40 Variable	3x to 10x	40 mm	Matte Black	German #4
4.5-14 x 40 Variable	4.5x to 14x	40 mm	Matte Black	Plex
4.5-14 x 40 Variable	4.5x to 14x	40 mm	Matte Black	Dot
8-25 x 50 Variable	8x to 25x	50 mm	Matte Black	Dot
8-25 x 50 Variable	8x to 25x	50 mm	Matte Black	Plex
30 mm Tube Scopes				
1.5-6 x 42 Variable	1.5x to 6x	42 mm	Matte Black	Plex
1.5-6 x 42 Variable	1.5x to 6x	42 mm	Matte Black	German #4
1.5-6 x 42 Var., Aspherical Lens	1.5x to 6x	42 mm	Matte Black	Plex
1.5-6 x 42 Var., Aspherical Lens	1.5x to 6x	42 mm	Matte Black	German #4
2.5-10 x 48 Variable	2.5x to 10x	48 mm	Matte Black	Plex
2.5-10 x 48 Variable	2.5x to 10x	48 mm	Matte Black	German #4
2.5-10 x 48 Var., Aspherical Lens	2.5x to 10x	48 mm	Matte Black	Plex
2.5-10 x 48 Var., Aspherical Lens	2.5x to 10x	48 mm	Matte Black	German #4
3-12 x 56 Variable	3x to 12x	56 mm	Matte Black	Plex
3-12 x 56 Variable	3x to 12x	56 mm	Matte Black	German #4
3-12 x 56 Var., Aspherical Lens	3x to 12x	56 mm	Matte Black	Plex
3-12 x 56 Var., Aspherical Lens	3x to 12x	56 mm	Matte Black	German #4

Kahles Riflescopes

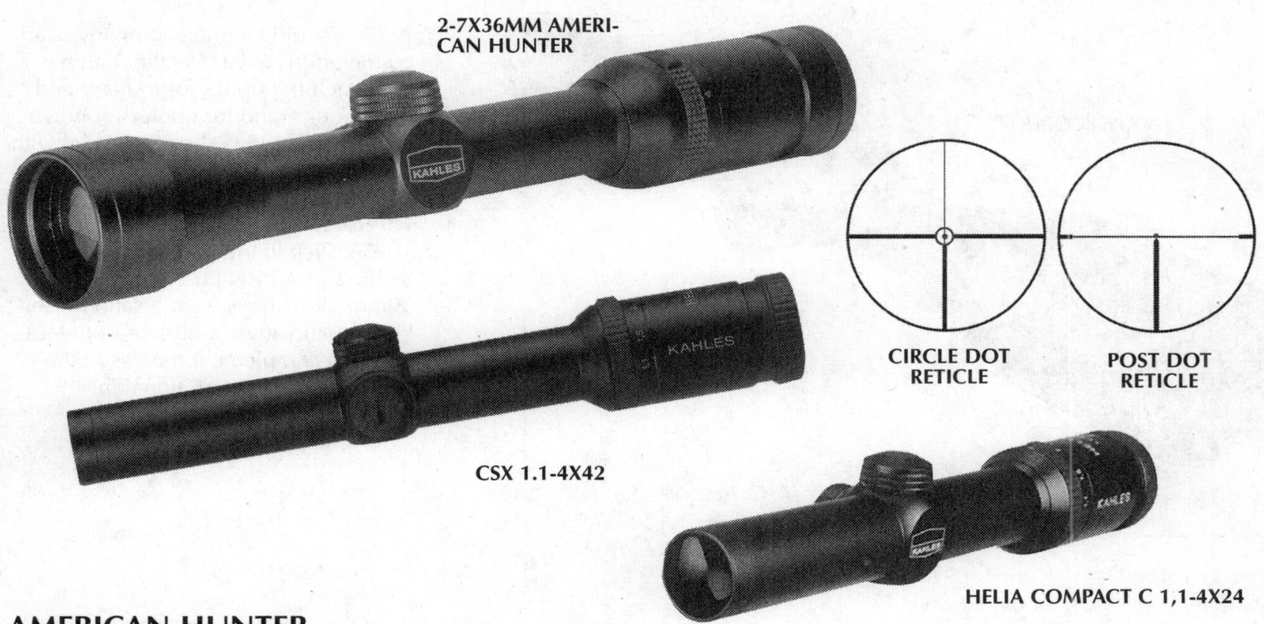

2-7X36MM AMERICAN HUNTER

CSX 1.1-4X42

CIRCLE DOT RETICLE

POST DOT RETICLE

HELIA COMPACT C 1,1-4X24

AMERICAN HUNTER

Kahles rifle scopes, manufactured in Austria, are compact and lightweight with excellent optical performance. The 1-inch tubes are of one piece construction, with hard anodized, scratch resistant finish. Shockproof and fogproof these scopes offer generous eye relief. The AH's reticle is mounted in the second image focal plane, so the reticle appears the same size at every power setting.

Prices: AH 2-7x36 (4A)........................ $621
AH 2-7x36 (Plex) 621
AH 2-7x36 (Circle Plex) 621
AH 2-7x36 (TDS) 688
AH 3-9x42 (4A) 732
AH 3-9x42 (Plex) 732
AH 3-9x42 (TDS) 799
AH 3.5-10x50 (4A)........................... 843
AH 3.5-10x50 (Plex).......................... 843
AH 3.5-10x50 (TDS).......................... 932

HELIA COMPACT

Kahles AMV-multi-coatings transmit up to 99.5% per air-to-glass surface. This ensures optimum use of incident light, especially in low light level conditions or at twilight.

These 30mm Kahles rifle scopes are shockproof, waterproof and fogproof, nitrogen purged several times to assure the elimination of any moisture.

Prices: C 1.1-4x24 (4A or 7A)................. $943
CSX 1.1-4x24 (circle, Post or D-Dot) 1477
C 1.5-6x42 (4A or 7A) 1043
CSX 1.5-6x42 (circle, Post or D-Dot) 1667
C 2.5-10x50 (7A or Plex) 1188
C 3-12x56 (7A, Plex or 4A) 1332
C 4x36 (1″ tube, 4A or 7A) 666
C 6x42 (1″ tube, 4A or 7A) 854
CSX 2.5-10x50 (circle, post or D-Dot) 1810
CSX 3-12x56 (circle, post or D-Dot)............ 1954

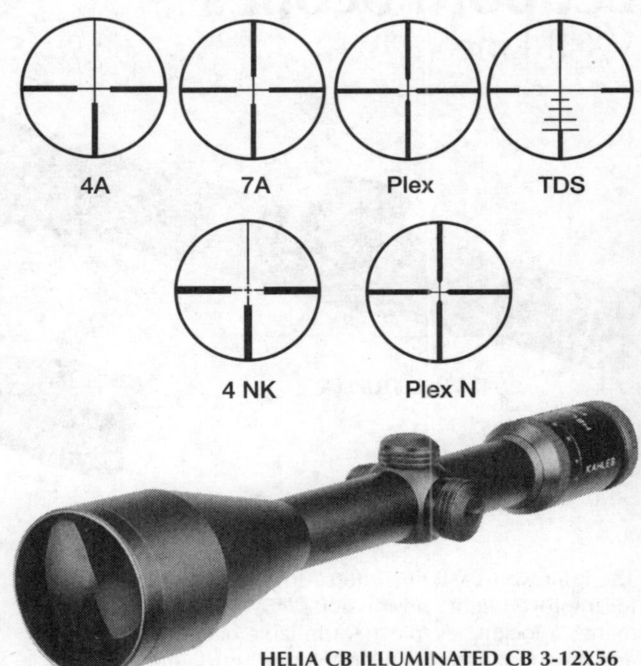

HELIA CB ILLUMINATED CB 3-12X56

HELIA CB ILLUMINATED

When you don't have the light to see a standard reticle, the illuminated crosswire of the Helia comes through. It's adjustable for illumination, and minimizes stray light. Battery life: 110 hours.

Prices: CB 1.5-6x42 (4NK or PlexN)............ $1499
CB 2.5-10x50 (4NK or PlexN) 1610
CB 3-12x56 (PlexN or 4NK).................. 1743

Kaps Optics

KAPS SCOPES

A 50-year-old German company headquartered in Asslar/Wetzlar, Kap has manufactured optics for military and police units, and for hunters. It now brings its riflescope line Stateside, with 4x36, 6x42 and 8x56 fixed-power models and five variables: 1-4x22, 1.5-6x42, 1-8x42, 2.5-10x50, 2.5-10x56. Pick illuminated reticles in 8x56, 2.5-10x50 and 2.5-10x56. The 30mm alloy tubes wear a satin finish. High-quality glass and state-of-the-art coatings complement reticles in the first focal plane—traditional in European scopes.

Leupold Scopes

VX-II Line

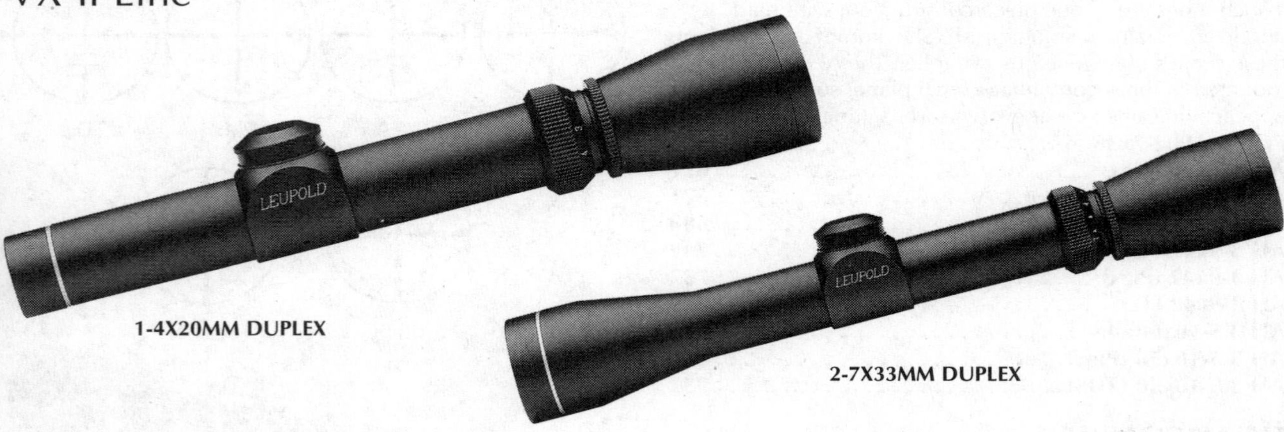

1-4X20MM DUPLEX

2-7X33MM DUPLEX

SIGHTS & SCOPES

The improved VX-II line offers Multi-Coated 4 lens coatings for improved light transmission, ¼ M.O.A. click adjustments, a locking eyepiece for reliable ocular adjustment, and a sealed, nitrogen-filled interior for fog-free sighting.

VX-II 1-4X20MM

This scope, the smallest of Leupold's VX-I line, is noted for its large field of view: 70 feet at 100 yards.

Matte finish only(Duplex) $375

VX-II 2-7X33MM

A compact scope, no larger than the Leupold FX-II 4X, the 2-7x33 is arguably the most useful big game scope.

VX II 2-7x 33 Shotgun (Duplex) matte $375
Leupold Dot 440

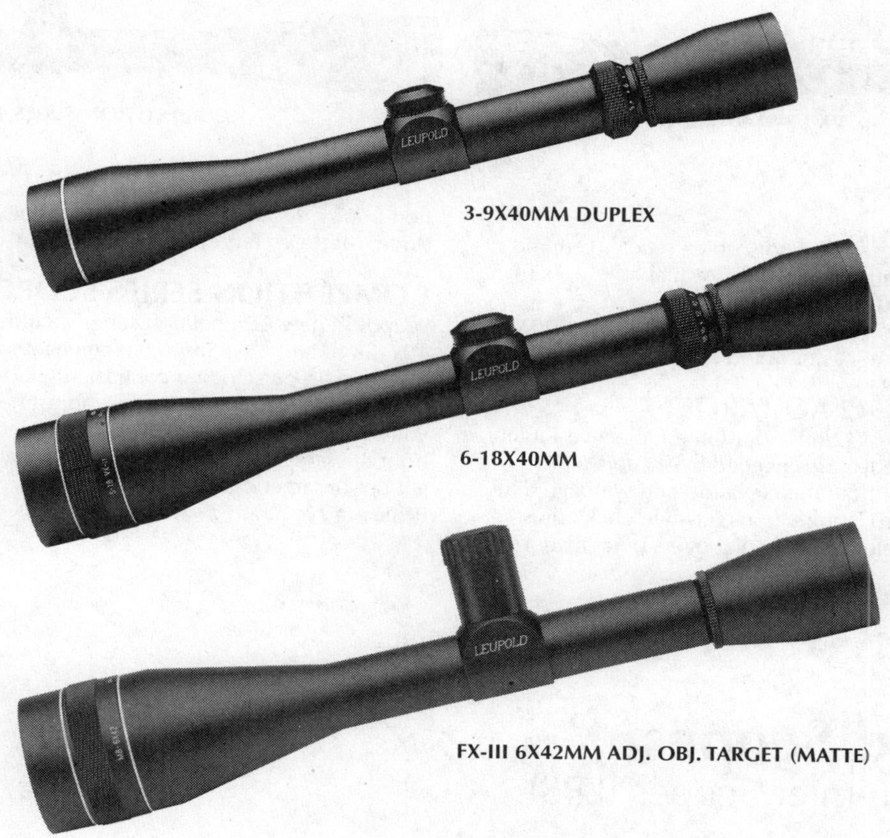

3-9X40MM DUPLEX

6-18X40MM

FX-III 6X42MM ADJ. OBJ. TARGET (MATTE)

VX-II 3-9X50MM

This LOV scope delivers a 5.5mm exit pupil for low-light visibility:

Gloss (Duplex) **$440**
Matte finish (Duplex) **440**
German #4 or Leupold dot (Matte) **490**

VX-II 3-9X40MM

A wide power range makes the 3-9 the most popular of hunting scopes. Many hunters use the 3X setting most of the time, cranking up to 9X for positive identification of game or for extremely long shots. The adjustable objective eliminates parallax and permits precise focusing on any object from less than 50 yards to infinity.

Gloss finish (Duplex) **$375**
In matte, silver (Duplex). **375**
Matte (Leupold Dot, German #1 or #4) **440**

VX-II 4-12X40MM

(Adj. Objective)

The ideal answer for big game and varmint hunters alike. At 12.25 inches, the 4X12 is virtually the same length as Vari-X II 3X9. New fixed objective has same long eye relief and is factory-set to be free of parallax at 150 yds.

Matte or silver finish (Duplex) **$500**
Leupold Dot **550**
VX-II 4-12x50mm . . . . **565 - 614**

VX-II 6-18X40MM ADJ. OBJ. TARGET

Features target-style click adjustments, fully coated lenses, adjustable objective for parallax-free shooting from 50 yards to infinity.

In matte, Fine or wide Duplex **$540**
Target Dot **590**
Dot w/Target knobs **615**
Duplex w/Target knobs. **565**

VX-III

The VX-III scopes, which replace the Vari-X III line, feature new lens coatings and the Index Matched Lens System (IMLS). The IMLS matches coatings to the different types of glass used in a scope's lens system. Other refinements include finger-adjustable dials with re-settable pointers to indicate zero, a fast-focus, lockable eyepiece and a 30mm main tube for scopes with side-mounted focus (parallax correction) dials. Thirteen models of VX-III scopes are available, from 1.5-5x20 to 8.5-25x50.

Price:. . . . . **$500 to $1160**

Leupold Scopes

VX-I Line

VX-I 3-9X40MM

COMPETITION SERIES 45X45MM

VX-I SERIES

A tough, gloss black finish and Duplex reticle. Leupold's high quality at an affordable price. Available in 2-7x33, 3-9x40, 3-9x50 and 4-12x40mm

Gloss **$225-350**
Matte **250-375**

LEUPOLD 6 X 42 AO TARGET

The Leupold FX-III 6x42mm Adjustable Objective Target Scope offers all the features needed by hunters and benchrest shooters. Both the elevation and windage dials of this scope feature ¼-minute, target-style click adjustments. An adjustable objective dial offers parallax correction from a distance of 50 yards to infinity.

Price: Matte w/Target Crosshair or Dot **$590**

COMPETITION SERIES SCOPES

Leupold's new Competition series includes the 35x45mm, 40x45mm and 45x45mm. Shooters get a bright, crisp sight picture with outstanding contrast, at extremely high magnification. The side-focus parallax adjustment knob allows you to adjust your scope to be parallax-free at distances from 40 yards to infinity. Available in matte finish with target dot or target crosshair reticle.

Price **$1250**

Leupold Scopes

Leupold Premier Scopes (LPS)

LPS 3.5-14X50MM SIDE FOCUS (SATIN FINISH)

VX-I 1-4X20MM SHOTGUN/MUZZLELOADER

Leupold's Premiere Scope (LPS) line features 30mm tubes, fast-focus eyepieces, armored power selector dials that can be read from the shooting position, 4-inch constant eye relief, Diamondcoat lenses for increased light transmission, scratch resistance, and finger adjustable, low-profile elevation and windage adjustments.

LPS 2.5-10X45

The magnification range of the new LPS 2.5-10x45mm is perfect for big game hunting. The unusually bright sight picture is due to 99.65% light transmission per lens surface. You get constant, non-critical eye relief, a scratch-resistant DiamondCoat anti-reflective lens coating on all interior and exterior lenses; fast-focus eyepiece; and all the other features of Leupold Premier Scopes.

Prices: 2.5-10x45 Duplex (satin) **$1125**
German #1 or #4 (satin) **1125**

LPS 3.5-14X50

The LPS 3.5-14x50mm has a turret-mounted side-focus parallax adjustment so you can change parallax settings easily, even from the shooting position. The 50mm objective lens produces a bright sight picture, in dim light. Finally, the long maintube allows generous ring mount space for rifles with long actions.

Prices: Duplex (satin) **$1250**
Target Dot, German #1 or #4 (satin) **1250**
Mil Dot (satin) **1250**

SHOTGUN & MUZZLELOADERS SCOPES

Leupold shotgun scopes are parallax-adjusted to deliver precise focusing at 75 yards. Each scope features a special Heavy Duplex reticle that is more effective against heavy, brushy backgrounds. All scopes have matte finish and Multicoat 4 lens coating.

Prices: VX-I 4X20mm Model Heavy Duplex **$225**
VX-I 2-7X33mm Heavy Duplex **250**

Leupold Scopes
Compact Scopes

FX-II 2.5X20MM COMPACT

VX-I 2-7X28 & RF SPECIAL

VX-II 3-9X33 ULTRALIGHT

COMPACT SCOPES
FX-II 2.5-20MM ULTRALIGHT

This small scope presents the shooter with an enormous field of view for fast target acquisition. It also features generous elevation and windage adjustment. Standard models are parallax adjusted to 100 yards. The Turkey Ranger model, with a special Post & Duplex reticle designed to subtend 9 inches from the post to crosswire at 40 yards, is parallax adjusted to 40 yards. Offered in a matte finish.

FX-II 2.5-20 Duplex or Heavy Duplex (matte) $340
FX-I 4x28mm Compact Rimfire Special
Fine Duplex (gloss) 250
Matte 275
VX-II 2-7x28mm Ultralight
Duplex (gloss) 400
VX-I 2-7x28mm Rimfire Special
Fine Duplex (gloss) 250
Matte 275
VX-II 3-9x33mm Ultralight Duplex
(matte, silver) 415

VX-II 3-9X33MM ULTRALIGHT AO

With an adjustable objective capable of correcting parallax as close as 10 meters, this scope is perfectly suited to .22 rimfire silhouette and air rifle shooting.

Duplex (gloss) $440
VX-II 3-9x33 AO Rimfire (matte, fine duplex) 440

Leupold Scopes
Tactical Scopes

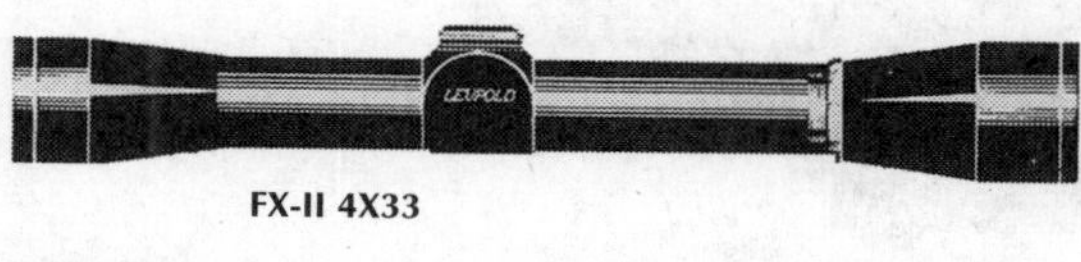
FX-II 4X33

FX-II 2.5X28MM IER SCOUT

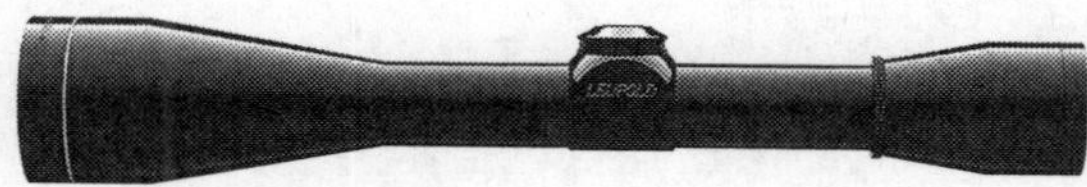
FX-II 6X42MM

FX-II 6X36

LEUPOLD TACTICAL SCOPES
FIXED AND VARIABLE POWER

Repeatable accuracy on all powers. ¼ MOA audible click windage and elevation adjustments (Except M-3s). Superior image quality and excellent light transmission. Duplex or Mil Dot reticle. Waterproof.

FX-II 2.5X28MM

Shooters worldwide are rediscovering the classic lever-action rifle, and for that, the M8-2.5x28mm IER Scout is the ideal sight. Designed specifically for lever- and scout-style rifles, it offers 9 to 17 inches of eye relief (IER stands for "Intermediate Eye Relief"). The Scout is mounted on the barrel, in front of the receiver.

Matte or silver (Duplex) 325

FX-II 4X33MM

The 4X delivers a magnification and a generous field of view.

Gloss, duplex $340
In black matte finish (wide duplex) 340

FX-II 6X36MM

The 6X extends the range for big-game hunting and doubles in some cases as a varmint scope.

Gloss or matte, duplex $350
matte, Post & Duplex or Leupold Dot 400

FX-II 6X42MM

Large 42mm objective lens features a 7mm exit pupil for increased light-gathering capability. Recommended for varmint shooting at night.

Duplex or Heavy Duplex $475
Wide Duplex or German #4 475-525

Leupold Scopes
Tactical Scopes

FX-II 12X40MM STANDARD

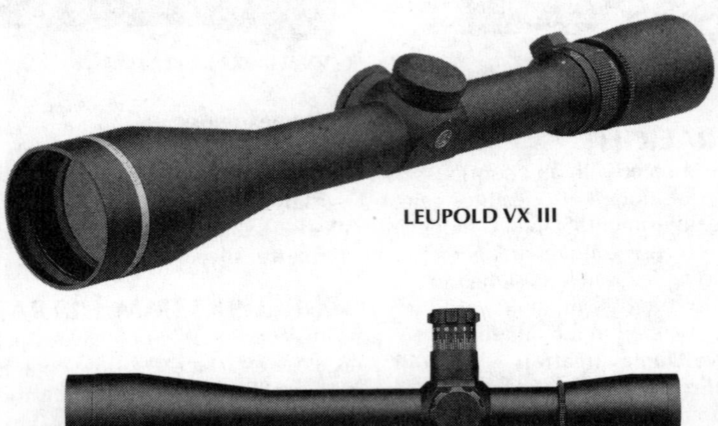

LEUPOLD VX III

MARK 4 M1-16X40MM

MARK 4 CQ/T 1-3X14MM

FX-III 12X40MM TARGET AO

Outstanding optical qualities, resolution and magnification make the 12X a natural for the varmint shooter. Adjustable objective is standard for parallax-free focusing.

Fine Duplex, matte **$665**
Leupold Dot, matte **715**

MARK 4 LR/T (LONG RANGE/TACTICAL) MARK 4 M1 10X40 (MATTE)/MARK 4 M1 16X40 (MATTE)

Duplex **$940**
Mil Dot **1100**
Mark 4 8.5-25x50, mil Dot **1400**
Mark 4 6.5-20x50, mil Dot **1225**
Mark 4 4.5-14x50, Duplex or mil Dot **1065-1165**
Mark 4 3.5-10x40, Duplex or mil Dot **1250-1275**
with illuminated reticle **1300**

MARK 4 CQ/T

The Leupold Mark 4 CQ/T 1-3x14mm is a revolutionary optical sight for tactical firearms. It combines the strengths of a red dot sight and variable-power riflescopes. Ten illumination settings match any light conditions; two low-intensity settings work with night-vision devices.

Price **$875**

Nikon Monarch Scopes

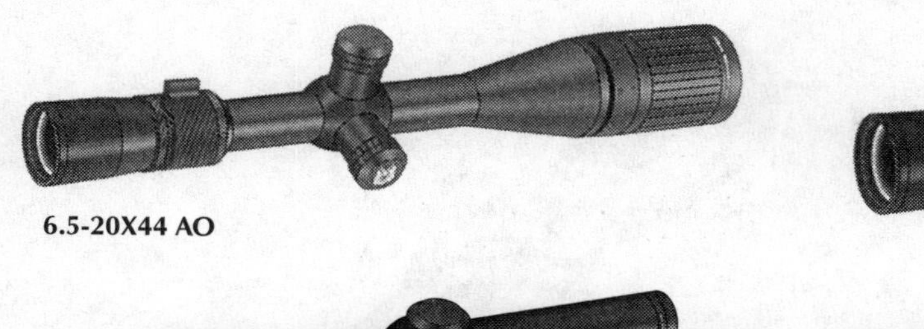
6.5-20X44 AO

2-7X32

1.5-4X20

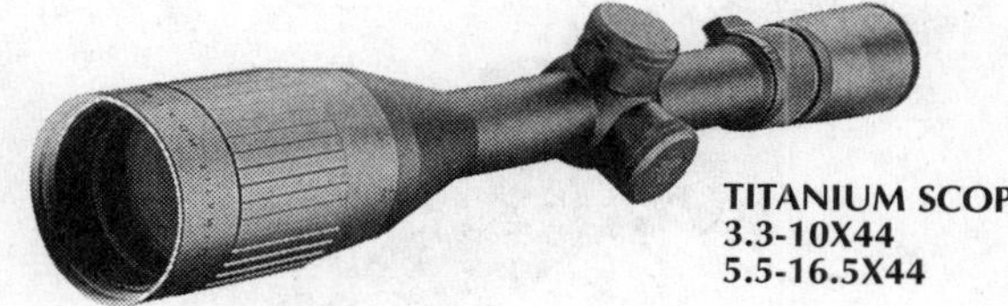
TITANIUM SCOPE
3.3-10X44
5.5-16.5X44

NIKON MONARCH RIFLE SCOPES

Model 6500 4x40 Lustre. $230
Model 6505 4x40 Matte. 240
Model 6506 6x42 Lustre. 240
Model 6508 6x42 Matte. 250
Model 6510 2-7x32 Lustre 270
Model 6515 2-7x32 Matte 280
Model 6520 3-9x40 Lustre 290
Model 6525 3-9x40 Matte 300
Model 6528 3-9x40 Silver Matte 310
Model 6530 3.5-10x50 Lustre 430
Model 6535 3.5-10x50 Matte. 440
Model 6537 3.3-10x44AO Lustre. 380
Model 6538 3.3-10X44AO Matte (Mildot) 390
Model 6539 3.3-10x44AO Matte 390
Model 6540 4-12x40 AO Lustre 370
Model 6545 4-12x40 AO Matte 380
Model 6580 5.5-16.5x44 AO Black Lustre 390
Model 6585 5.5-16.5x44 AO Black Matte 400
Model 6550 6.5-20x44 AO Lustre 460
Model 6555 6.5-20x44 AO Matte. 470
Model 6570 6.5-20x44 HV. 460
Model 6575 6.5-20x44 HV. 470
Model 6556 6.5-20x44 AO Lustre target Dot 460
Model 6558 6.5-20x44 AO Matte target Dot 470
Model 6630 3.3-10x44 AO (Titanium) 580
Model 6680 5.5-16.5x44 AO (Titanium). 600

Handgun and Shotgun Scopes

Model 6560 2x20 EER Black Lustre 170
Model 6562 2x20 EER Matte 180
Model 6565 2x20 EER Silver 180
Model 6590 1.5-4.5x20 Shotgun Black Matte 240
Model 6595 1.5-4.5x20 Sabot/Slug Black Matte. 240

Also Available:

Illuminated Scopes

3.5-10x50 (Nikoplex or Mildot) 600
6.5-20x44 (Nikoplex or Mildot) 680

Monarch Gold

1.5-6x42. 500
2.5-10x50. 600
2.5-10x56. 700

MONARCH™ UCC RIFLESCOPE SPECIFICATIONS

MODEL	4x40	1.5-4.5x20	2-7x32	3-9x40	3.5-10x50	4-12x40AO	5.5-16.5x44AO	6.5-20x44AO	2x20EER
Lustre	6500	N/A	6510	6520	6530	6540	6580	6550/6556	6560
Matte	6505	6595	6515	6525	6535	6545	6585	6555/6558	6562
Silver	N/A	N/A	N/A	6528	N/A	N/A	N/A	N/A	6565
Actual Magnification	4x	1.5x-4.5x	2x-7x	3x-9x	3.5x-10x	4x-12x	5.5x-16.5x	6.5x-19.46x	1.75x
Objective Diameter	40mm	20mm	32mm	40mm	50mm	40mm	44mm	44mm	20mm
Exit Pupil (mm)	10	13.3-4.4	16-4.6	13.3-4.4	14.3-5	10-3.3	8-2.7	6.7-2.2	11.4
Eye Relief (in)	3.5	3.7-3.5	3.9-3.6	3.6-3.5	3.9-3.8	3.6-3.4	3.2-3.0	3.5-3.1	26.4-10.5
FOV @ 100 yds (ft)	26.9	50.3-16.7*	44.5-12.7	33.8-11.3	25.5-8.9	25.6-8.5	19.1-6.4	16.1-5.4	22
Tube Diameter	1 in.	1 in.	1 in.	1 in.	1 in.	1 in.	1 in.	1 in.	1 in.
Objective Tube(mm/in)	47.3-1.86	25.4/1	39.3-1.5	47.3-1.86	57.3-2.2	53.1-2.09	54-2.13	54-2.13	25, 4/1
Eyepiece O.D. (mm)	38	38	38	38	38	38	38	38	38
Length (in)	11.7	10	11.1	12.3	13.7	13.7	13.4	14.6	8.1
Weight (oz)	11.2	9.3	11.2	12.6	15.5	16.9	18.4	20.1	6.6
Adjustment Gradation	1/4 MOA	1/4 MOA	1/4 MOA	1/4 MOA	1/4 MOA	1/4 MOA	1/4 MOA	1/8 MOA	1/4 MOA
Max Internal Adjustment	120 MOA	120 MOA	70 MOA	55 MOA	45 MOA	45 MOA	40 MOA	38 MOA	120 MOA
Parallax Setting (yds)	100	75	100	100	100	50 to ∞	50 to ∞	50 to ∞	100

*FOV @ 75 yds (ft) *FOV @ 50 yds (ft)

Nikon Buckmasters Scopes

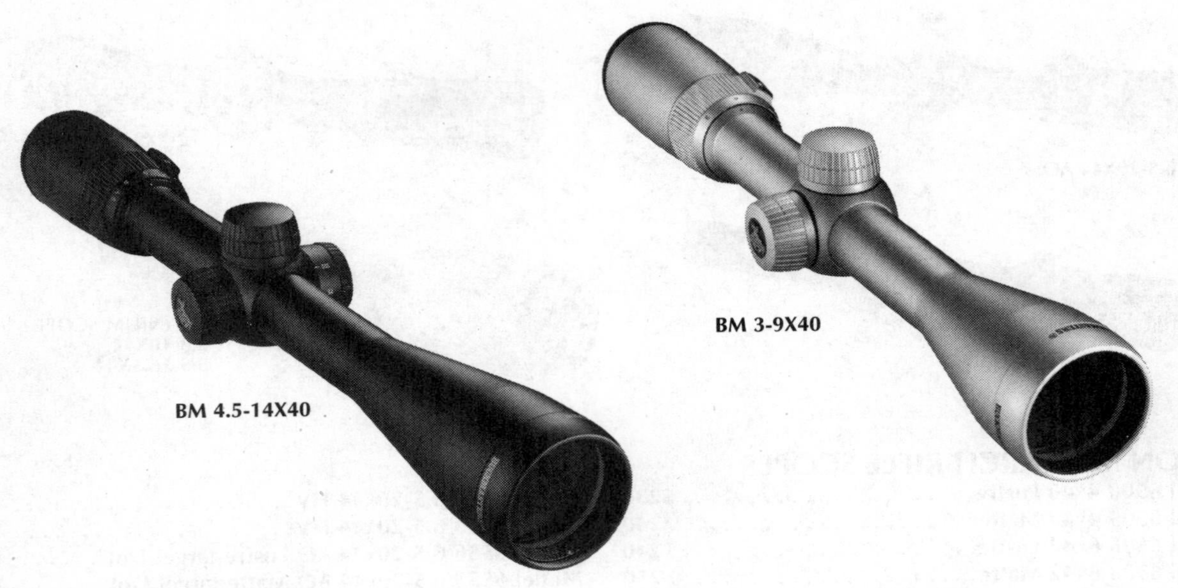

BM 4.5-14X40

BM 3-9X40

NIKON BUCKMASTERS SCOPES

Built to withstand the toughest hunting conditions, Nikon buckmaster scopes integrate shockproof, fogproof and waterproof construction, plus other features seldom found on riflescopes in this price range. Nikon's BrightvueTM anti-reflective system of high-quality, multicoated lenses provides over 93% anti-reflection capability for high levels of light transmission and dawn-to-dusk big game hunting. These riflescopes are parallax-adjusted at 100 yards and have durable matte finishes that reduce glare while afield. They also feature positive steel-to-brass, quarter-minute-click windage and elevation adjustments for instant, repeatable accuracy and a Nikoplex® reticle for quick target acquisition.

Prices:

Model 6465 1x20 .... $160
Model 6405 4x40 160
Model 6425 3-9x40 Black Matte 200
Model 6415 3-9x40 Silver 210
Model 6435 3-9x50 300
Model 6450 4.5-14x40 AO Blck Matte 280
Model 6455 4.5-14x40 AO Silver 290
Model 6466 4.5-14X40AO Matte Adj. Mildot 280
Model 6440 4-12x50 AO Matte 350
Model 6470 6-18x40 AO Matte 350
Model 6475 6-18x40 AO Matte 350

BUCKMASTERS SCOPES

MODEL	1x20	4x40	3-9x40	3-9x50	4.5-14x40AO
Model	1x20	4x40	3-9x40	3-9x50	4.5-14x40AO
Matte	6465	6405	6425	6435	6450
Silver	N/A	N/A	6415	N/A	6455
Actual Magnification	1x	4x	3.3-8.5x	3.3-8.5x	4.5-13.5x
Objective Diameter	20mm	40mm	40mm	50mm	40mm
Exit Pupil (mm)	20	10	12.1-4.7	15.1-5.9	8.9-2.9
Eye Relief (in)	4.3-13.0	3.5	3.5-3.4	3.5-3.4	3.6-3.4
FOV @ 100 yds (ft)	52.5	30.6	33.9-12.9	33.9-12.9	22.5-7.5
Tube Diameter	1 in.	1 in.	1 in.	1 in.	1 in.
Objective Tube (mm/in)	27/1.06	47.3/1.86	47.3/1.86	58.7/2.3	53/2.1
Eyepiece O.D. (mm)	37	42.5	42.5	42.5	38
Length (in)	8.8	12.7	12.7	12.9	14.8
Weight (oz)	9.2	11.8	13.4	18.2	18.7
Adjustment Gradation	1/4: 1 click	1/4: 1 click	1/4: 1 click	1/4: 1 click	
Max Internal Adjustment	50	80	80	70	40
Parallax Setting (yds)	75	100	100	100	50 to ∞

Nikon Scopes

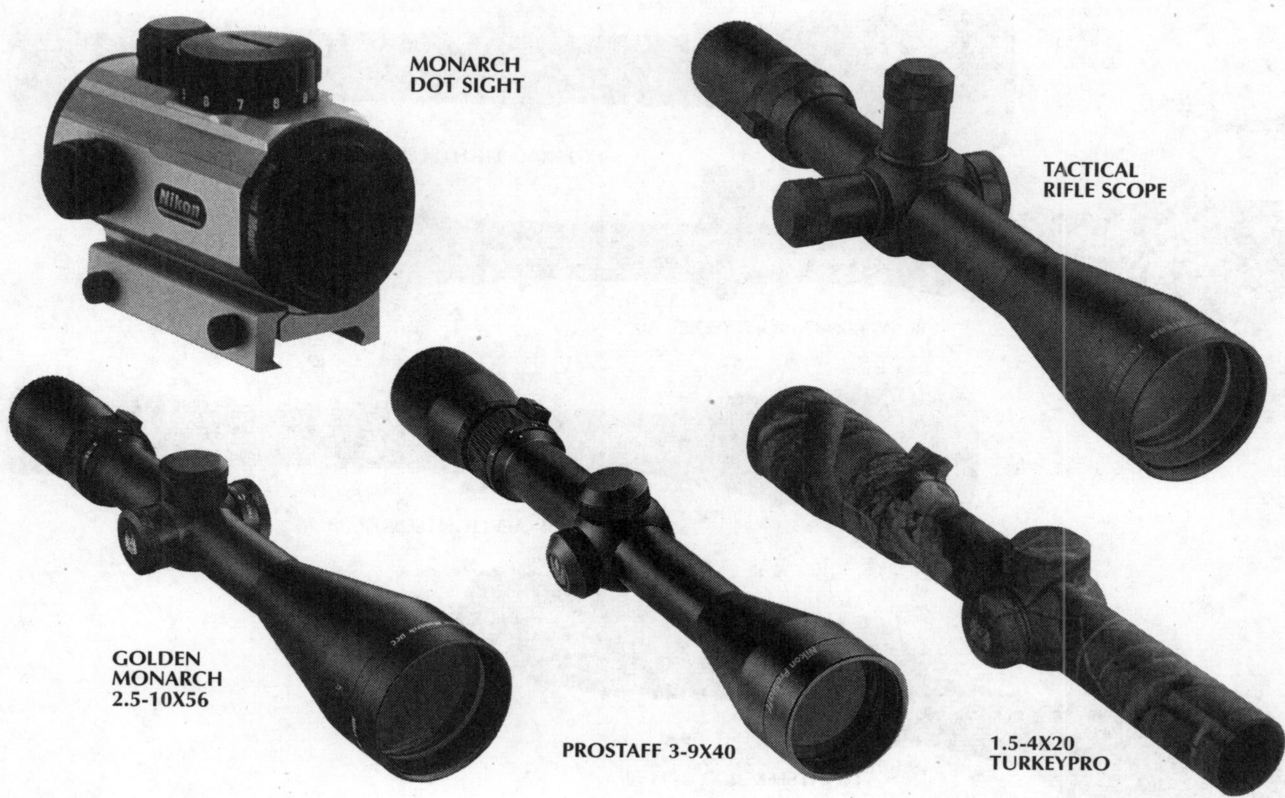

TACTICAL RIFLESCOPE

Nikon's Tactical Riflescopes are available in 2.5-10x44 and 4-16x50. The 2.5-10x44 features a choice of reticles: Nikoplex, Mildot, and Dual Illuminated Mildot. The 4-16 is offered with Nikoplex or Mildot. Both are equipped with turret mounted parallax adjustment knobs, have a tough, black-anodized matte finish and have easy-to-grip windage and elevation knobs for accurate field adjustments.

Prices:
Tactical 2.5-10x44 (Nikoplex or Mildot). $900
With Illuminated Mildot. 1050
Tactical 4-16x50 (Mildot or Nikoplex) 1000

PROSTAFF

Nikon's Prostaff line inclues the 4x32, 2-7x32 and 3-9x40 scopes. The 4x is parallax-corrected at 50 yards. It measures 11.2 inches long and weighs just 11.6 ounces, in silver, matte black or Realtree camo finish. The 2-7x, parallax-free at 75 yards, is a 12-ounce scope available in matte black or camo. You can get the 13-ounce 3-9x in all three finishes. The Prostaff scopes have multicoated lenses and quarter-minute adjustments. They're waterproof, fog proof and carry Nikon's Full Lifetime Warranty.

Prostaff 4x32 . . . . $100
2-7x32 130
309x40. 150

MONARCH DOT SIGHT

As fast a sight as you'll ever find, the Monarch Dot is fully waterproof, fogproof and shockproof. Objective and ocular lenses are 30mm diameter and are fully multicoated. Nikon Dot sights have zero magnification, providing unlimited eye relief and a 47.2' field of view at 100 yards, perfect for close up, fast shots. Brightness is controlled by a lithium battery. The standard Monarch Dot Sight is available in silver and black and has a 6 MOA dot. It is also available in Realtree camouflage.

Price: Standard. $250
VSD 280
VSD in camo 290

1.5-4.5X20 TURKEYPRO

Now available in Realtree Hardwoods camo, the 1.5-4x20 Monarch TurkeyPro is parallax-free at 50 yards. Kill more toms with precise pattern placement!

Price: $270

2.5-8X28 EER HANDGUN SCOPE

Nikon's 2.5-8x28 EER (Extended Eye Relief) should find favor with hunters, varminters and competitors. It has a wide field of view at low power, but a twist of the power ring instantly supplies 8x magnification for long shots.

Price: Matte $280
Silver 290

Pentax Scopes

4X-16XAO LIGHTSEEKER 30

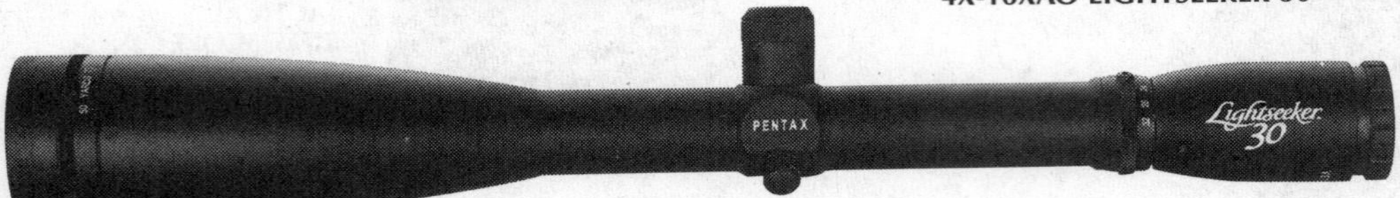

8.5X-32XAO LIGHTSEEKER 30

6X-24XAO LIGHTSEEKER 30

LIGHTSEEKER-XL 3-9X50

WHITETAILS UNLIMITED

LIGHTSEEKER

Among the brightest scopes available, Pentax sights are durable as well. The Lightseeker features:

- Scratch-resistant outer tube. Under ordinary wear and tear, the outer tube is almost impossible to scratch.
- High Quality cam zoom tube. No plastics are used. The tube is made of a bearing-type brass with precision machined cam slots. The zoom control screws are precision-ground to ½ of one thousandth tolerance.
- Leak Prevention. Power rings are sealed on a separate precision-machined seal tube. The scopes are then filled with nitrogen and double-sealed with heavy-duty "O" rings, making them leak-proof and fog-proof.
- Optics. Fully multi-coated, Lightseekers' optics are among the best in the industry, giving you a bright, sharp picture even in poor light.

The Lightseeker-30 has the same features as the Lightseeker II, but with a 30mm tube.

The purchase of every Pentax Whitetails Unlimited rifle or shotgun scope includes a free one-year membership in Whitetails Unlimited, and a portion of the purchase price goes to the organization to support its conservation efforts. Ballistic Plex reticles are available on the 3X-9X and 6.5X-20X Whitetails Unlimited Scopes.

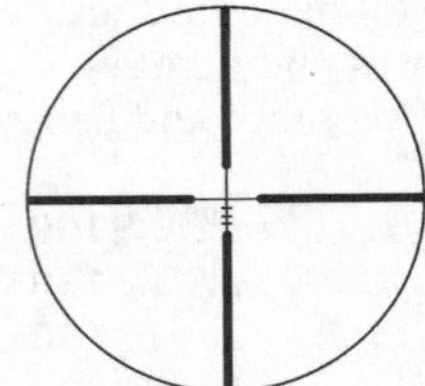

The Ballistic Plex Reticle is a copyrighted design on the lower vertical crosshair that compensates for bullet drop. The Ballistic Plex reticle is set to provide dead-on aiming from 100 yards to 500 yards for many of the most common hunting cartridges.

Pentax Rifle Scopes

LIGHTSEEKER 2.5xSG PLUS
MOSSY OAK BREAK-UP SCOPE

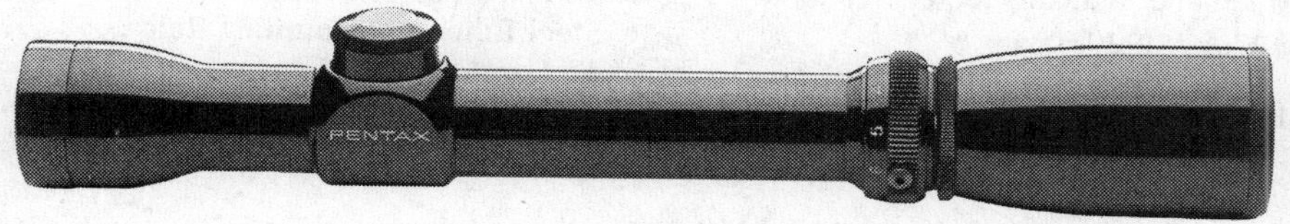

LIGHTSEEKER 1.75X-6X

LIGHTSEEKER RIFLESCOPE AND WHITETAILS UNLIMITED

	Tube Diameter (in)	Objective Diameter (mm)	Eyepiece Diameter (mm)	Exit Pupil (mm)	Eye Relief (in)	Field of View (ft@100 yd)	Adjustment Graduation (in@100 yd)	Maximum Adjustment (in@100 yd)	Length (in)	Weight (oz)	Reticle	Price
Rifle Scopes												
Lightseeker 3X - 9X	1	40	39	12.0-5.0	3.5-4.0	36-14	1/4	50	12.7	15	P, MD	495-523
Lightseeker 3X - 9X	1	50	39	16.1-5.6	3.5-4.0	35-12	1/4	50	13.0	19	TW, BP	582
Lightseeker 2.5X - 10X	1	50	39	16.3-4.6	4.2-4.7	35-10	1/4	100	14.1	23	TW	665
Lightseeker 4X - 16X	1	44	36	10.4-2.8	3.5-4.0	33-9	1/4	35	15.4	23.7	BP	682
Lightseeker 2.5X SG Plus	1	25	39	7.0	3.5-4.0	55	1/2	60	10.0	9	DW	292-303
Lightseeker-30												
3X-10X AO	30MM	40	35	13.3-4.4	3.5-4.0	34-14	1/4	90	13.1	20.0	BP	$599
4X-16X AO	30mm	50	42	12-3.1	3.3-3.8	27-7.5	1/4	74	15.2	23	TW, MD	715-798
6X-24X AO	30mm	50	42	7.6-2.1	3.2-3.7	18-5	1/8	52	16.9	27	MD, FP	746-832
8.5X-32X AO	30mm	50	42	6.2-1.7	3.0-3.5	14-4	1/8	39	18.0	27	MD, FP	782-865
Whitetails Unlimited												
2X-5X WTU	1	20	39	11.1-4.2	3.1-3.8	65-23	1/2	70	10.7	10	TW	332-348
3X-9X WTU	1	40	39	12.9-4.7	3.1-3.8	31-13	1/4	50	12.4	13	TW	348
3.5X-10X WTU	1	50	39	13-5.1	3.1-3.8	28-11	1/4	50	13.1	15	LBP	582
3.7X-11X WTU	1	42	39	13-5.1	3.1-3.8	28-11	1/4	50	13.1	15	TW	465
4.5X-14X WTU	1	42	39	9.3-3.0	3.7-4.2	23-8	1/4	52	12.9	17	BP	497
6.5X-20X WTU	1	50	39	7.6-2.6	3.1-3.6	17-6	1/4	30	14.6	19	BP	598
3X-9X WTU	1	50	39	16.0-5.3	3.1-3.8	32-13	1/4	50	13.2	17	BP	398

Scopes are available in high gloss black, matte black, or camouflage, depending on model.
P=Penta-Plex, FP=Fine-Plex, DW=Deepwoods Plex, MD=Mil-Dot, CP=Comp-Plex, TW=Twilight Plex, BP=Ballistic Plex, LBP=Laser Ballistic Plex

Schmidt & Bender Rifle Scopes

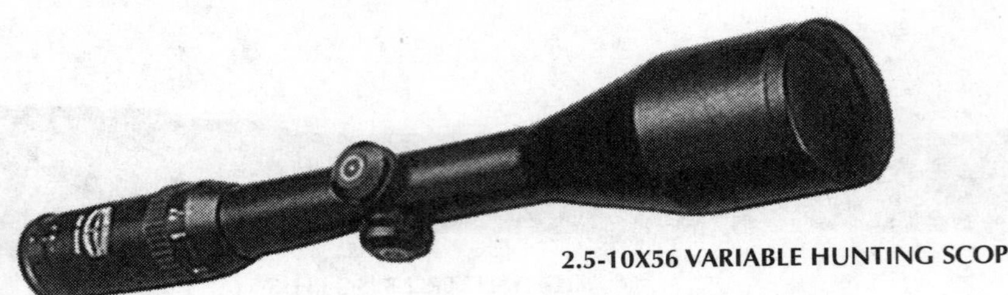

2.5-10X56 VARIABLE HUNTING SCOPE

This German firm manufactures carriage-class optics for discriminating sportsmen and tactical shooters. Variable scopes have 30mm and 34mm tubes.

2.5-10X56 Variable Hunting Scopes
Price: $1659
Also available:
1.5-6X42. 1449
3-12X42 1629
3-12X50 1629
4-16X50 1979
Note: All variable power scopes have glass reticles and aluminum tubes.

Also available:
4X36 Fixed Power Scope
1" Steel Tube w/o Mounting Rail $978
6X42 Fixed Power. 1069
8X56 Fixed Power. 1229
10X42 Fixed Power. 1129

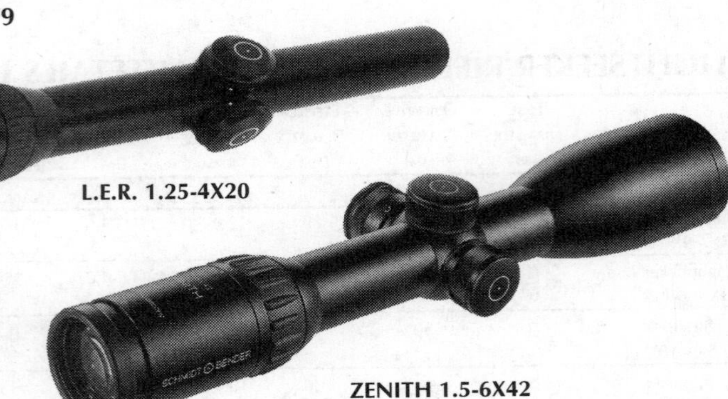

L.E.R. 1.25-4X20

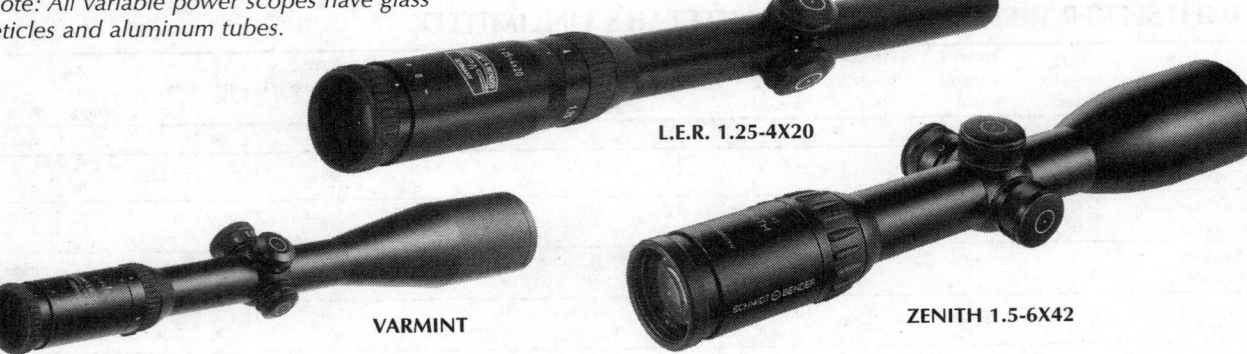

VARMINT

ZENITH 1.5-6X42

ILLUMINATED SCOPES

This 1.25-4x is designed for use on magnum rifles and for quick shots at dangerous game. Long eye relief, and a wide field of view (31.5 yards at 200 yards) speed your aim. The Flash Dot reticle shows up bright against the target at the center of the crosswire.
Magnification: 1.25-4X
Objective lens diameter: 12.7-20mm
Field of view at 100m: 32m-10m; at 100 yards: 96'-16'
Objective housing diameter: 30mm
Scope tube diameter: 30mm
Twilight factor: 3,7-8,9
Lenses: hard multi-coating
Click value 1 click @100 meters: 15mm; @100 yards: .540"
Price: $1819
Also available:
Illuminated reticles
1.5-6x42. 1869
3-12x50 or 3-12X42 2059
2.5-10x56 2089

ZENITH SERIES

1.1-4x24 . . . . $1389
1.5-6x42 1449
1.1-4x24 Ill. 1819
1.5-6x42 Ill. 1879
3.5-12x50 or 2.5-10X56 1759
2.5-10x56 Illuminated or 3-12X50 Ill. 2189

VARMINT SERIES

Designed for long-range target shooters and varmint hunters, Schmidt & Bender 4-16X50 "Varmint" riflescope features a precise parallax adjustment located in a third turret on the left side of the scope, making setting adjustments quick and convenient. The fine crosshairs of Reticle No. 6 and 8 cover only 1.5mm at 100 meters (.053" at 100 yards) throughout the entire magnification range.
Magnification: 4-16X
Objective lens diameter: 50mm
Field of view at 100m: 7.5-2.5m; at 100 yards: 22.5'-7.5'
Objective housing diameter: 57mm
Scope tube diameter: 30mm
Twilight factor: 14-28
Lenses: Hard multi-coating
Click value 1 click @100 meters: 10mm; @100 yards: .360"
Price: $1979

Schmidt & Bender Scopes

Police/Marksman II

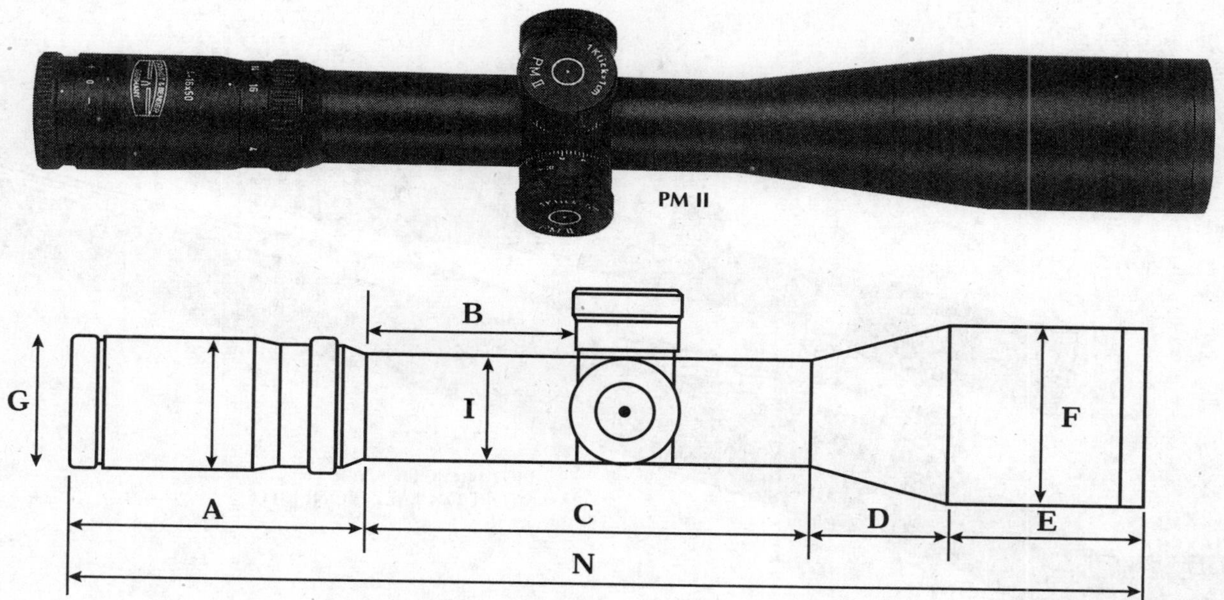

DIMENSIONS

Model	A	B	C	D	E	F	G	I	N
10x42	98mm 3.858″	56mm 2,204″	139mm 5.472″	55mm 2.165″	54mm 2.126″	50mm 1.969″	43mm 1.693″	30mm	346mm 13.622″
3-12x50	101.3mm 3.988″	68.3mm 2.689″	145.4mm 6.076″	43.5mm 1.713″	64.8mm 3.354″	57mm 2.244″	43mm 1.693″	34mm	355mm 13.976″
4-16x50	101.3mm 3.988″	68.3mm 2.689″	145.4mm 6.076″	85.2mm 1.713″	75.5mm 3.354″	57mm 2.244″	43mm 1.693″	34mm	405.7mm 15.972″

A big objective (front) lens will help you aim only if the scope is set at high magnification and the light is dim. Otherwise, it's a liability because it adds weight and bulk and raises line of sight.

Schmidt & Bender Scopes
Scopes For Long Range Shooting

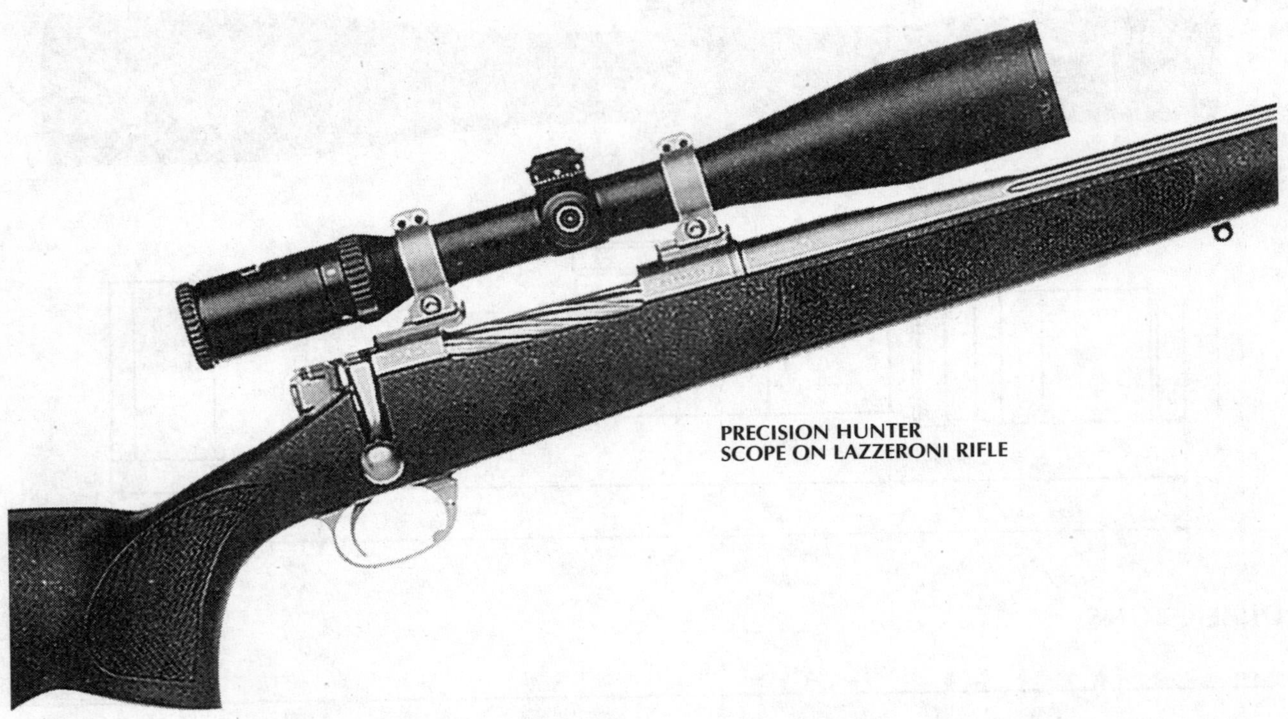

PRECISION HUNTER
SCOPE ON LAZZERONI RIFLE

SIGHTS & SCOPES

PRECISION HUNTER
Accurate rifles, high-speed cartridges and modern bullets make long-range hits possible. But the scope matters too. It must deliver a clear image but also help with range estimation and holdover.

Precision Hunter scopes combine the optical quality of S&B hunting scopes, with a sophisticated mil-dot reticle (developed by the U.S. Marine Corps) with a bullet drop compensator to give shooters the ability and confidence to place an accurate shot at up to 500 yards. Three models are available:

4-16 X 50 PRECISION HUNTER SCOPE WITH PARALLAX ADJUSTMENT
At 4 power, the mil-dot reticle with fine crosshairs and four posts allows quick target acquisition. This scope can be used in thickets or on the prairie. Turned up to 16 power, the mil-dots become visible and can be used for range, trajectory and windage calculations. The top-mounted bullet drop compensator has 5mm (1/5") clicks, permitting quick adjustments up to 500 yards. The windage adjustment also has 5mm (1/5") clicks, allowing for precise sighting in.

The standard elevation adjustment knob has graduations and numbers for creating a meaningful distance chart for preferred caliber. A blank elevation knob can be special-ordered with markings to be specified after sighting in rifle. A parallax adjustment is conveniently located in a third turret on the left side. This allows shooter to make necessary adjustments with the rifle shouldered, ready to shoot.

Price: **$2189**

3-12 X 50 PRECISION HUNTER & 3-12X42
Identical to the 4-16 x 50 with mil-dot reticle but 1cm (2/5") clicks and no parallax adjustment. It is factory-adjusted to be parallax free at 200 meters.

Price: **$1849**

2.5-10 X 56 PRECISION HUNTER
Identical to the 3-12 x 50, but with 1 cm (2/5") clicks for windage and elevation adjustment and with our Reticle No. 9, which makes it suitable for dangerous game.

Price: **$1879**

Sightron Scopes

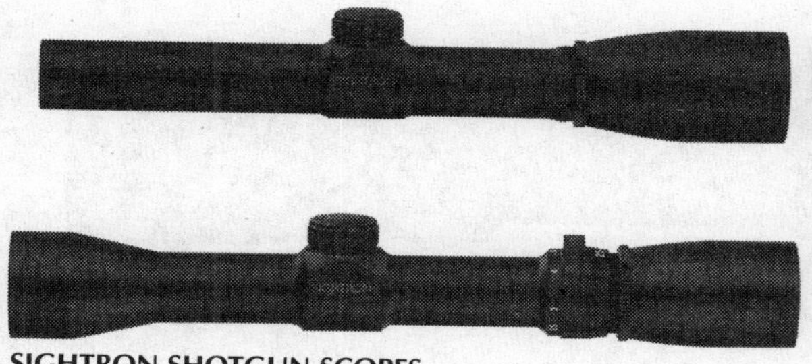

SIGHTRON SHOTGUN SCOPES

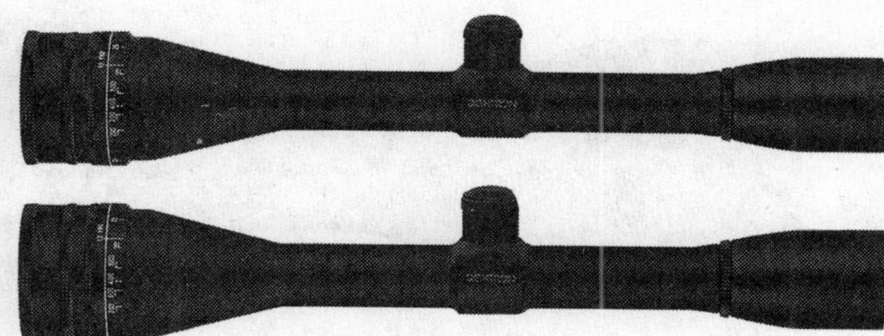

SIGHTRON BENCHREST SCOPES

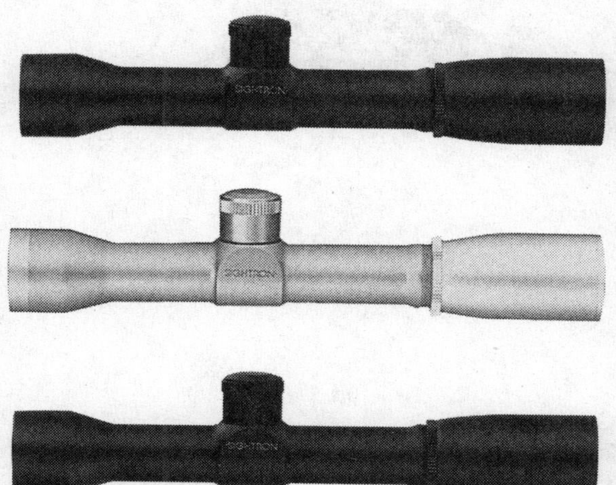

SIGHTRON PISTOL SCOPES

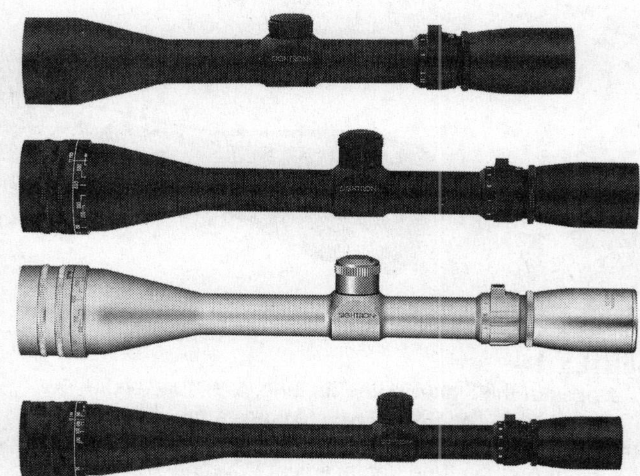

SIGHTRON HUNTING SCOPES

SIGHTRON SERIES III

With side-mounted ("saddle") parallax adjustment Sightron's expanded scope line offers nearly 40 models in fixed and variable power at modest prices. The SII series features 1-inch alloy tubes; the SIII series has 30 mm aluminum tubes, multicoated lenses, and "saddle" mounted parallax adjustments. Most target and competition scopes feature ⅛-minute clicks. Sightron offers stainless finish and a broad choice of reticles including the mil dot.

Prices:

SIII 3.5-10x44 mil dot $902
SIII 1.5-6x50 plex. 757
SIII 6-24x50 984
SIII 6-24x50 mil dot 1034
SII shotgun 2.5-7x32 315

SII hunting scopes:
3-9x36 . . . . $386
3-9x42 356
3-9x42 dot 419
3-9x50 440
1.5-6x42. 372
3-12x42 422
3-12x50 443
3.5-10x42. 421
3.5-10x50. 446
4.5-14x42. 481
4.5-14x50. 474

SII target scopes:
4-16x42 481
4-16x42 dot 534
6-24x42 510
6-24x42 dot 563

SII competition scopes:
3-12x42 mil dot 428
4-16x42 mil dot 568
4.5-14x42 mil dot. 730
6-24x42 mil dot 599
24x44 Dot 442
6x42 AO HBRD 442
6-24x42 510
36x42. 534

SII compact scopes:
4x32. 267
2.5-10x32. 338
2.5-7x32. 315
6x42. 291
12x42 Dot 390

Sightron Scopes

SI 3.510X50

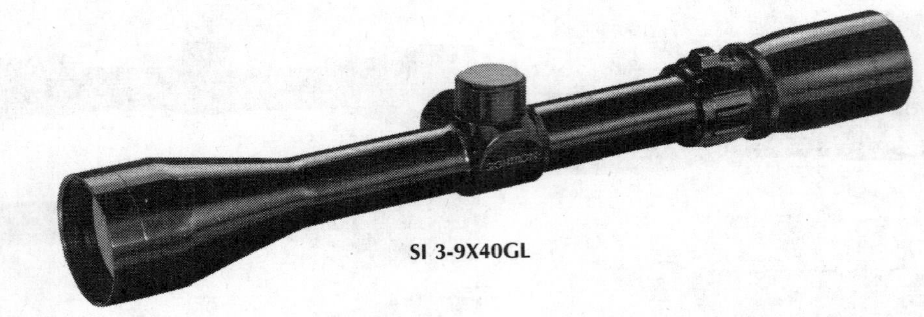

SI 3-9X40GL

SERIES 1

S1 scopes in the Sightron line include: 3-9x40, 3-9x50 and 3.5-10x50. The 3-9x40 MD features a mil dot rangefinding reticle. All have multi-coated optics and come with Sightron's Lifetime Replacement Warranty. The 4.5-14x42 IRMD has a three-position brightness switch. Battery life ranges from 100 to 400 hours, depending on intensity. The 3-9x features a plex reticle with a lighted center.

Series 1 1x20	**$162**
2.5-10x44	**249**
2.5x20	**115**
3-9x32RF	**156**
3-9x40	**205**
3-9x40GL	**205**
3-9x40MD	**248**
3.5-10x50	**276**

An adjustable objective (AO) enables you to eliminate parallax (image shift relative to the reticle) at a given range. It also allows you to bring the target sharply into focus.

SIGHTS & SCOPES

Sightron Scopes

In conventional scopes a curved erector tube surface contacts the flat surface of the adjustment peg. This contact is only complete at zero adjustment. As the adjustments press the erector tube in any direction, the contact becomes imperfect, causing the reticle to drift from the optical center. In many cases, since the point of contact is less than what is required to hold the erector tube in position, point of impact can shift. Sightron has developed a new erector tube with an integral ring. ExacTrack will keep constant and perfect point-of-impact, at or off zero. This constant pressure point will ensure the accuracy of all Sightron scopes under heavy recoil and severe use afield.

SIGHTRON COMPACT SCOPES

RETICLE DIMENSION REFERENCES

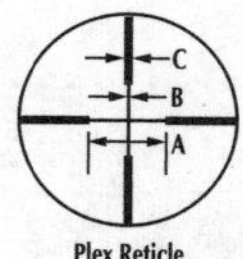

Plex Reticle

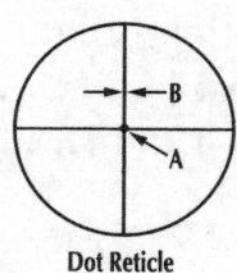

Dot Reticle

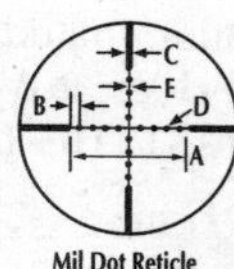

Mil Dot Reticle

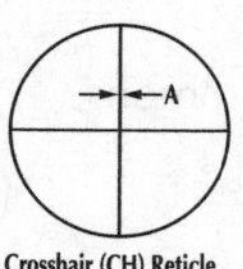

Crosshair (CH) Reticle

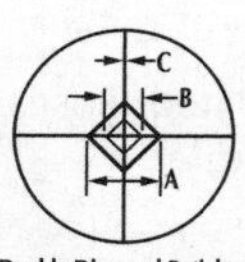

Double Diamond Reticle

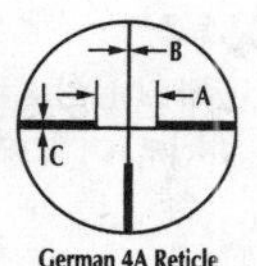

German 4A Reticle

Item Number	Magnification	Objective Dia. (mm)	Field of View (ft @ 100 yds)	Eye Relief (in.)	Reticle Type	Reticle Subtensions (in. @ 100 yds) Min. Power A/B/C/D/E	Max. Power A/B/C/D/E	Click Value	Windage/ Elevation Travel (in.)	Tube (Dia.)	Weight (oz.)	Finish
SIII Series Rifle Scopes												
30mm Side Saddle Rifle Scopes												
SIII3.510X44MD	3.5-10X	44	28-9.2	3.5	Mil-Dot	102.6/10.26/3.25/2.2/.6936/3.6/1.15/.8/.23		1/4 MOA	80	30mm	24.60	Satin Black
SIII1.56X50	1.5-6X	50	64-17	4.3-3.7	Plex	79.0/1.33/5.32	19.8/.33/1.32	1/4 MOA	70	30mm	21.00	Satin Black
SII Series Rifle Scopes												
Variable Power Rifle Scopes												
SII1.56X42	1.5-6X	42	50-15	4.0-3.8	Plex	79.0/1.33/5.32	19.8/.33/1.32	1/4 MOA	70	1.0 in.	14.00	Satin Black
SII2.58X42	2.5-8X	42	36-12	3.6-4.2	Plex	48.0/.80/3.20	15.0/.25/1.0	1/4 MOA	90	1.0 in.	12.82	Satin Black
SII39X42	3-9X	42	34-12	3.6-4.2	Plex	39.9/.66/2.66	13.2/.22/.88	1/4 MOA	95	1.0 in.	13.22	Satin Black
SII39X42ST	3-9X	42	34-12	3.6-4.2	Plex	39.9/.66/2.66	13.2/.22/.88	1/4 MOA	95	1.0 in.	13.22	Stainless
SII39X42D	3-9X	42	34-12	3.6-4.2	Dot	4/.66	1.3/.22	1/4 MOA	95	1.0 in.	13.22	Satin Black
SII312X42	3-12X	42	32-9	3.6-4.2	Plex	39.9/.66/2.66	9.9/.16/.66	1/4 MOA	80	1.0 in.	12.99	Satin Black
SII3.510X42	3.5-10X	42	32-11	3.6	Plex	34.2/.57/2.28	12.0/.20/.80	1/4 MOA	60	1.0 in.	13.80	Satin Black
SII4.514X42	4.5-14X	42	22-7.9	3.6	Plex	26.4/.44/1.76	8.5/.14/.56	1/4 MOA	50	1.0 in.	16.07	Satin Black
SII39X50	3-9X	50	34-12	4.2-3.6	Plex	39.9/.66/2.66	13.2/.22/.88	1/4 MOA	*	1.0 in.	15.40	Satin Black
SII312X50	3-12X	50	34-8.5	4.5-3.7	Plex	39.9/.66/2.66	9.9/.16/.66	1/4 MOA	*	1.0 in.	16.30	Satin Black
SII3.510X50	3.5-10X	50	30-10	4.0-3.4	Plex	34.2/.57/2.28	12.0/.20/.80	1/4 MOA	50	1.0 in.	15.10	Satin Black
SII4.514X50	4.5-14X	50	23-8	3.9-3.25	Plex	26.4/.44/1.76	8.4/.14/.56	1/4 MOA	60	1.0 in.	15.20	Satin Black
Variable Power Target Scopes												
SII416X42	4-16X	42	26-7	3.6	Plex	30/.50/2.0	7.5/.125/.50	1/8 MOA	56	1.0 in.	16.00	Satin Black
SII416X42ST	4-16X	42	26-7	3.6	Plex	30/.50/2.0	7.5/.125/.50	1/8 MOA	56	1.0 in.	16.00	Stainless
SII416X42D	4-16X	42	26-7	3.6	Dot	1.7/.10	.425/.025	1/8 MOA	56	1.0 in.	16.00	Satin Black
SII416X42DST	4-16X	42	26-7	3.6	Dot	1.7/.10	.425/.025	1/8 MOA	56	1.0 in.	16.00	Stainless
SII624X42	6-24X	42	15.7-4.4	3.6	Plex	19.8/.33/1.32	4.8/.08/.32	1/8 MOA	40	1.0 in.	18.70	Satin Black
SII624X42ST	6-24X	42	15.7-4.4	3.6	Plex	19.8/.33/1.32	4.8/.08/.32	1/8 MOA	40	1.0 in.	18.70	Stainless
SII624X42D	6-24X	42	15.7-4.4	3.6	Dot	1.12/.066	.27/.016	1/8 MOA	40	1.0 in.	18.70	Satin Black
SII624X42DST	6-24X	42	15.7-4.4	3.6	Dot	1.12/.066	.27/.016	1/8 MOA	40	1.0 in.	18.70	Stainless
Competition/Tactical Scopes												
SII312X42MD	3-12X	42	32-9	3.6-4.2	Mil-Dot	144/14/4.7/3.1/.7	36/3.6/1.2/.79/.1	1/4 MOA	80	1.0 in.	12.99	Satin Black
SII416X42MD	4-16X	42	26-7	3.6	Mil-Dot	144/14/4.7/3.1/.6	36/3.6/1.2/.79/.1	1/8 MOA	56	1.0 in.	16.00	Satin Black
SII416X42MDST	4-16X	42	26-7	3.6	Mil-Dot	144/14/4.7/3,1/.6	36/3.6/1.2/.79/.1	1/8 MOA	56	1.0 in.	16.00	Stainless
SII624X42MD	6-24X	42	15.7-4.4	3.6	Mil-Dot	144/14/4.7/3.1/.4	36/3.6/1.2/.79/.1	1/8 MOA	40	1.0 in.	18.70	Satin Black
SII624X42MDST	6-24X	42	15.7-4.4	3.6	Mil-Dot	144/14/4.7/3.1/.4	36/3.6/1.2/.79/.1	1/8 MOA	40	1.0 in.	18.70	Stainless
SII24X44D	24X	44	4.4	4.33	Dot	.27/.016		1/8 MOA	60	1.0 in.	15.87	Satin Black
SII6X42HBRD	6X	42	20	4.00	Dot	.375/.070		1/8 MOA	100	1.0 in.	16.00	Satin Black
Compact Rifle Scopes												
SII4X32	4X	32	25	4.52	Plex	30/.50/2.0		1/4 MOA	120	1.0 in.	9.80	Satin Black
SII2.57X32	2.5-7X	32	41-11.8	3.8-3.2	Plex	48/.80/3.20	17.2/.29/1.2	1/4 MOA	120	1.0 in.	11.60	Satin Black
SII2.510X32	2.5-10X	32	41-10.5	3.8-3.5	Plex	48/.80/3.20	12/.20/.80	1/4 MOA	120	1.0 in.	10.93	Satin Black
SII6X42	6X	42	20	3.60	Plex	19.8/.33/1.32		1/4 MOA	100	1.0 in.	12.69	Satin Black
Shotgun Scopes												
SII2.5X20SG	2.5X	20	41	4.33	Plex	48.0/.80/3.201/4 MOA		160	1.0 in.	9.00	Satin Black	
SII2.57X32SG	2.5-7X	32	41-11.8	3.8-3.2	DD	48/24/.60	17/8.5/.26	1/4 MOA	120	1.0 in.	11.60	Satin Black

*Specifications not available at press time

SIGHTS & SCOPES

Simmons Scopes
Aetec

AETEC 2.8-10X44

AETEC 2.8-10X44
Sleek and durable, with bright, coated lenses, Simmons scopes offers great value for the dollar.

MODEL 512100/512101/512102
2.8-10X44 WA Length: 11.9" Weight: 15.5 oz. Reticle: Truplex
Price: **$190**
Model 512104 3.8-12x44mm AO 215

MODEL 512103/512105
Illuminated Reticle, black matte
Prices: 2.8-10x44 . . . . **$220**
M512105 (3.8-12x44). **227**

Simmons Scopes
44 Mag Riflescopes

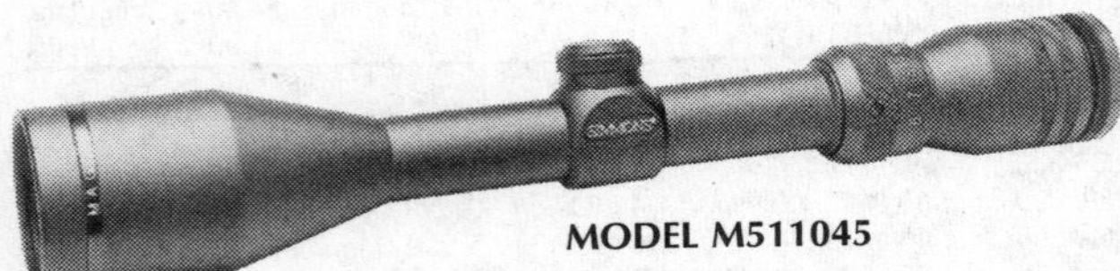

MODEL M511045

44 MAG RIFLESCOPES
MODEL M511044 (BLACK MATTE)
3-10X44mm Length: 12.75" Weight: 15.5 oz.
Price: **$220**

MODEL M511045 (BLACK MATTE)
4-12X44mm Length: 13.2" Weight: 18.25 oz.
Price: **$260**

MODEL M511047 (BLACK MATTE)
6.5-20X44mm Length: 12.8" Weight: 19.5 oz.
Price: **$270**

MODEL M511048
6.5-20X44 Target Turrets
Black Matte (1/8" MOA). **$280**

MODEL M511056
6.5-20X44 Mildot **$280**

Simmons Scopes
ProHunter Riflescopes

PROHUNTER SE MODEL 807729

PROHUNTER RIFLESCOPES
MODEL 517710
3-9X40mm Wide Angle Riflescope
Length: 12.6"
Weight: 13.5 oz.
Features: Truplex reticle; silver matte finish
Price: **$150**

Also available:
Model 517700 2-7X32 Black Matte **120**
Model 517716 4-12X40 Black Matte AO **220**
Model 511050 4-14x44 WA matte Diamond **270**
Model 517721 6-18X40 AO Black Matte **240**
Model 517722 6-18X40 AO Target Gray. **240**
Model 517740 6X40 Black Matte. **100**
Model 517711 3-9X40 WA Matte. **150**
Model 517702 3-9X40 Illum.. . . . . **200**
Model 17712 3-9X40 Gloss **150**
Model 517703 6-24X42 Mildot **290**

SIGHTS & SCOPES

Simmons Scopes

PRO50

Pro 50's have all the features of the Prohunter models, only with a 50mm lens.

Prices: 4-12x50mm, AO Black Matte $160
6-18x50mm, AO Black Matte 180
4-12x40 AO Gloss 140

PRO 50 MODEL

511072 RIMFIRE TARGET SCOPE

Magnification: 3-9X32mm WA/AO Finish: Black matte or silver Features: Adjustable for windage and elevation; adjustable objective lens, target knobs

Price: $90

Also available:
511022 4X32 black matte w/22 rings. 50
511033 4X32 silver matte (or gloss) w/22 rings 50
511037 3-9X32 silver matte w/22 rings 60
511039 3-9X32 black matte (or gloss) w/22 rings 60
511073 3-9x32 AO silver w/.22 rings. 90

511072 RIMFIRE TARGET SCOPE

Simmons Scopes

ProDiamond Shotgun Scopes

MODEL 517793

PRODIAMOND SHOTGUN SCOPES MODEL 517793

Magnification: 4X32 Finish: Black matte
Field of view: 17′ Eye relief: 5.5″ Reticle: ProDiamond
Length: 8.5″ Weight: 9.1 oz.
Price: $135

Also available:
Model 517789 2X32 Black matte (ProDiamond reticle) 130
Model 517791 1.5-5X20 WA Black matte (ProDiamond reticle) 150
Model 517792 1.5-5X32 Camo Pro Diamond 170
Model 517787 1.5-5x32 illum. Pro Diamond 200
Model 517788 1x32 Truplex 130

SIGHTS & SCOPES

Simmons Scopes

8-Point

SIMMONS 8 POINT
4X32 BLACK

SIMMONS 8-POINT SCOPES

The Simmons 8-Point series is aimed at the entry level or budget-minded shooter who needs a reliable scope at an affordable price. The 8-Point family includes seven scopes in popular configurations: 3-9x32mm, 3-9x40mm, 3-9x50mm, 4x32mm, 4-12x40mm AO, and 4x32 mm shotgun. All versions are offered in black matte finish, and the 3-9x40mm is also available in silver. Fully coated lenses enhance light transmission for low-light viewing and reduce reflections. Simmons' popular Truplex reticle is standard. Windage and elevation are adjusted in ¼-MOA increments. The 8-Point scopes are shockproof, waterproof, and fogproof.

8-POINT SCOPE 4-12X40MM AO

Magnification: 4-12X
Field of View: 29 - 10 ft. at 100 yards
Eye Relief: 3 inches at 4X and 2⅞ inches at 12X
Length: 13.5 inches
Weight: 15.75 oz.
Reticle: Duplex
Finish: Black Matte
Price: **$140**

8-POINT SCOPE 4X32MM

Magnification: 4X
Field of View: 28.75 ft. at 100 yards
Eye Relief: 3 inches
Length: 11.625 inches
Weight: 14.25 oz.
Reticle: Duplex
Finish: Black Matte
Price: **$90**

8-POINT SCOPE 3-9X32 MM

Magnification: 3-9X
Field of View: 37.5 - 13 ft. at 100 yards
Eye Relief: 3 inches at 3X and 2⅞ inches at 9X
Length: 11.875 inches
Weight: 11.5 oz.
Reticle: Duplex
Finish: Black Matte
Price: **$70**

8-POINT SCOPE 3-9X40MM

Magnification: 3-9X
Field of View: 37 - 13 ft. at 100 yards
Eye Relief: 3 inches at 3X and 2⅞ inches at 9X
Length: 12.25 inches
Weight: 12.25 oz.
Reticle: Duplex
Finish: Black Matte or Silver
Price: Black Matte or Silver **$100**
Camo **130**
Gloss **100**

8-POINT SCOPE 3-9X50MM

Magnification: 3-9X
Field of View: 32 - 11.75 ft. at 100 yards
Eye Relief: 3 inches at 3X and 2⅞ inches at 9X
Length: 13 inches
Weight: 15.25 oz.
Reticle: Duplex
Finish: Black Matte
Price: **$150**

Also available: 8-Point Shotgun Scopes
2.5x20, matte **$70**
4x32, matte **100**
1.5-5x32, matte **100**
1.5-5x32, camo **130**

SIGHTS & SCOPES

Simmons Scopes

Prohunter Handgun Scopes

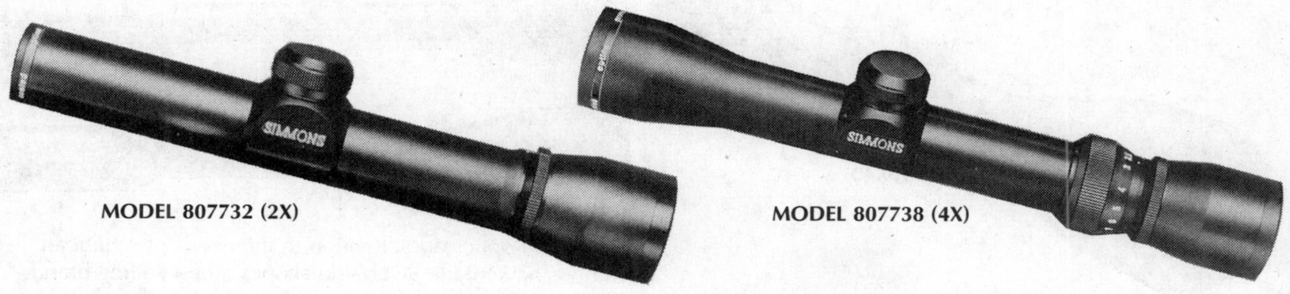

MODEL 807732 (2X)

MODEL 807738 (4X)

PROHUNTER HANDGUN SCOPES

Model #807732/807733 (Silver Matte)

SPECIFICATIONS

Magnification: 2X ***Field of View:*** 22' ***Eye Relief:*** 9-17"
Length: 8.75" ***Weight:*** 7 oz. ***Reticle:*** Truplex
Finish: Black matte
Price: **$140**

Model #807738/807739 (Silver Matte)

SPECIFICATIONS

Magnification: 4X ***Field of View:*** 15' ***Eye Relief:*** 11.8-17.6"
Length: 9" ***Weight:*** 8 oz. ***Reticle:*** Truplex
Finish: Black matte
Price: **$150**
Also: Prohunter 2-6X32, Matte or Silver........... **180**

Springfield Armory Optics

6-20X50

SPRINGFIELD ARMORY SCOPES

After significant redesign, Springfield Armory scopes feature range-finding reticles, ballistic drop compensators, illuminated crosswires and mil dots, only the 3-9x42 and the 3.5-10x50 are "hunting-style" sights, with plex reticles. Only four of the 15 scopes in Springfield's line have 1-inch tubes; the others are all 30mm. All have an internal bubble level at the bottom of the scope field to tell you if you're canting. Target knobs are standard on 4-16x50 models, BDC knobs on 6-20x50 scopes.

6x40 to 6-20x50:.................... **$419 to $899**

The ocular lens of a scope can be adjusted to sharpen the reticle image. Simply point the scope at the northern sky and turn the lens housing until the reticle appears crisp.

SIGHTS & SCOPES

Swarovski Scopes

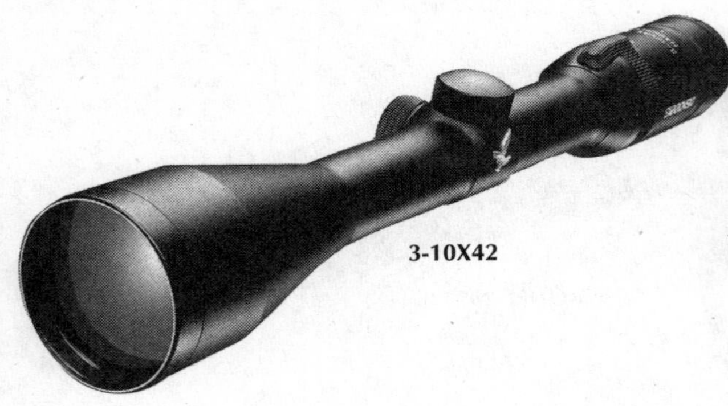
3-10X42

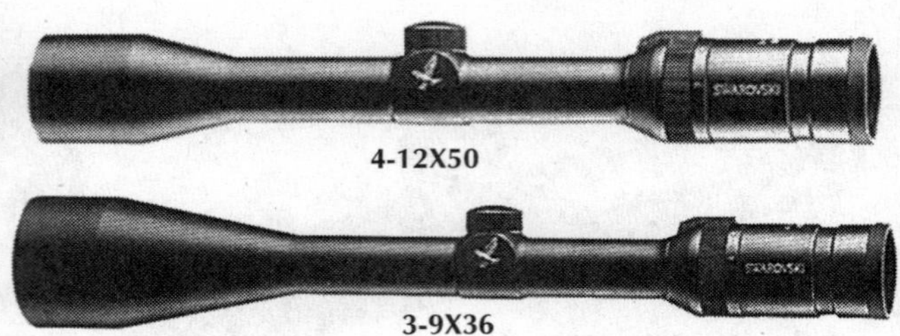
4-12X50

3-9X36

Top-grade optics and attention to the needs of American hunters have made Swarovski scopes a best-selling brand. When performance matters more than price, sportsmen are turning to Swarovski.

A-LINE RETICLES AVAILABLE:

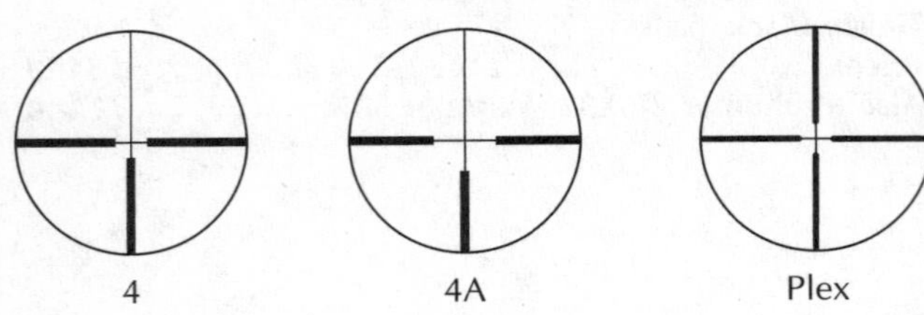

SWAROVSKI AV SERIES LIGHTWEIGHT 1-INCH SCOPES

Developed for American hunters, the AV scopes feature constant-size reticles, lightweight alloy tubes and satin finish. Totally waterproof even with caps removed, these scopes have fully multi-coated lenses and the quality that has made Swarovski famous.

Prices:
3-10x42 (TDS) $1021
3-10 x 42 (4A, Plex) 943
4-12 x 50 (4A, Plex) 988
3-9 x 36 (4A, Plex) 854
6-18x50 (4A, Plex) 1066
6-18x50 (TDS)1110
4-12X50 (TDS) 1057

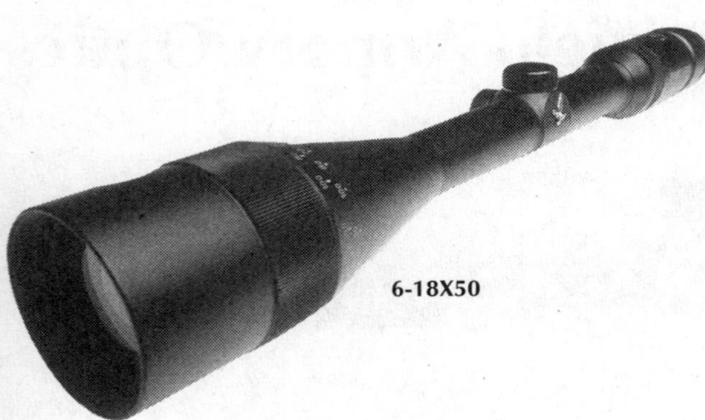
6-18X50

6-18X50

Swarovski's 6-18x50 incorporates a parallex adjustment ring that insures parallex free accuracy from 50 yds to beyond 500. The objective bell, 1" tube, turret housing and ocular bell are machined out of one solid piece of alloy bar stock for strength, weight and waterproof integrity.

Price: $1066
Also available:
AV series in SR Rail Mount
(3-10x42 and 4-12x50) . . . . $999 - 1099

	3-9x36	3-10x42	4-12x50	6-18x50
Magnification	3-9x	3.3-10x	4-12x	6-18x
Objective lens diameter: mm	36	42	50	50
in	1.42	1.55	1.97	1.97
Exit pupil, diameter: mm	12-4	12.6-4.2	12.5-4.2	8.3-2.8
Eye relief: in	3.5	3.5	3.5	3.5
Field of view, real: m/100m	13-4.5	11-3.9	9.7-3.3	17.4-6.5
ft/100yds	39-13.5	33-11.7	29.1-9.9	17.4-6.5
Diopter compensation (dpt)	± 2.6	± 2.5	± 2.5	± 2.5
Transission (%)	94	94	94	92
Twilight factor (DIN 58388)	9-18	9-21	11-25	17-30
Impact Point correction per click: in/100yds	0.25	0.25	0.25	0.25
Max. elevation/windage adjustment range: ft/100yds	4.8	4.2	3.6	3.9
Length, approx: in	11.8	12.44	13.5	14.85
Weight, approx (oz.): L	11.6	12.7	13.9	20.3
LS	–	13.6	15.2	–

L=light alloy • LS=light alloy with rail

Swarovski Scopes

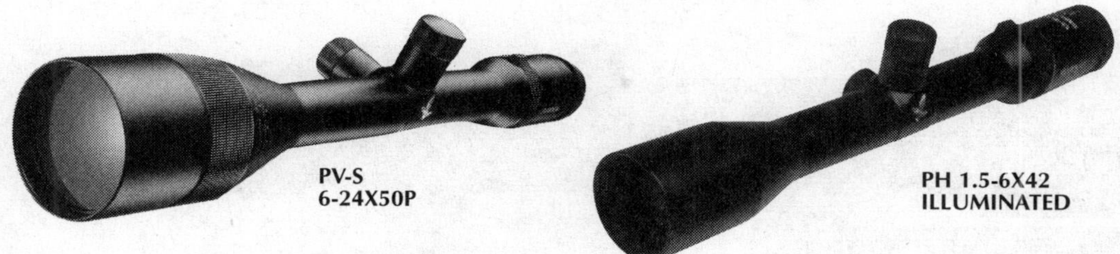
PV-S 6-24X50P

PH 1.5-6X42 ILLUMINATED

PH SERIES (PROFESSIONAL HUNTER)

The 6-24X50mm "PH" riflescope was developed by Swarovski for long-range target, big-game and varmint shooting. Its water-proof parallax adjustment system should be popular with whitetail "Bean Field Shooters" and long-range varmint hunters looking for a choice of higher powers in a premium rifle scope and still deliver accuracy. The scope will also appeal to many bench rest shooters who compete in certain classes where power and adjustment are limited. A non-magnifying, fine plex reticle and a fine crosshair reticle with 1/8" MOA dot are available in the 6-24x50mm scope. Reticle adjustment clicks are 1/4 1" (minute) by external, waterproof target knobs. The internal optical system features a patented coil spring suspension system for dependable accuracy and positive reticle adjustment. The objective bell, 30mm middle tube, turret housing and ocular bell are machined from one solid bar of aluminum.

Prices PH Series Riflescopes

PH 6x42 (4A) $1154
PH 8x50 (4A) 1199
PH 8x56 (4A) 1266
PH8x56 (Illum. ret. PLEXN) 1732
PH 1.25-4x24 (4A) 1277
PH 1.25-4x24 (Ill. ret. #24N, 3 post-dot) 1621
PH 1.5-6x42 (4A, 7A) 1432
PH 1.5-6x42 (Illum. ret. #24N, 3 post-dot, 4A-1K) . . 1732
PH 1.5-6x42 (#24) 1477
PH 2.5-10x42 (4A, 7A, PLEX) 1588
illum reticle (4NK) 1977
PH 2.5-10x56 (4A, 7A PLEX) 1654
w/illum reticle (4NK, PLEXN) 2143
PH 3-12x50 (4A, 7A, PLEX) 1677
TDS reticle 1754
w/illum reticle (4NK, PLEXN) 2143
PH 6-24x50 (Plex, dot, fine) 1977
PH 6-24x50 (4A, PLEX) with low turret 1866
PH 6-24x50 (low turrets, TDS) 1954
PH 4-16x50 (4A, PLEX) 1754
PH 4-16x50 (TDS) 1832

PF & PV

	PF	PF/PF-N	PF/PF-N	PV/PV-1	PV	PV/PV-N	PV/PV-N	PV/PV-N	PV	PV	PV-S
	6x42	8x50	8x56	1.25-4x24	1.5-6x42	2.5-10x42	2.5-10x56	3-12x50	4-16x50P	6-24x50P	6-24x50P
Magnification	6x	8x	8x	1.25-4x	1.5-6x	2.5-10x	2.5-10x	3-12x	4-16x	6-24x	6-24x
Objective lens											
diameter: mm	42	50	56	17-24	20-42	33-42	33-56	39-50	50	50	50
in	1.65	1.97	2.20	0.67-0.94	0.79-1.65	1.3-1.65	1.3-2.20	1.54-1.97	1.97	1.97	1.97
Exit pupil,											
diameter: mm	7	6.25	7	12.5-6	13.1-7	13.1-4.2	13.1-5.6	13.1-4.2	12.5-3.1	8.3-2.1	8.3-2.1
Eye relief: in	3.15	3.15	3.15	3.15	3.15	3.15	3.15	3.15	3.15	3.15	3.15
Field of view,											
real: m/100m	7	5.2	5	32.8-10.4	21.8-7	13.2-4.2	13.2-4.1	11-3.5	9.1-2.6	6.2-1.8	6.2-1.8
ft/100yds	21	15.6	15.6	98.4-31.2	65.4-21	39.6-12.6	39.6-12.3	33-10.5	27.3-7.8	18.6-5.4	18.6-5.4
Diopter com-											
pensation (dpt)	+2. -3	+2. -3	+2. -3	+2. -3	+2. -3	+2. -3	+2. -3	+2. -3	+2. -3	+2. -3	+2. -3
Transission (%)	94	94/92	93/91	93/91	93	94/92	93/91	94/92	90	90	90
Twilight factor											
(DIN 58388)	16	20	21	4-10	4-16	7-21	7-24	9-25	11-28	17-35	17-35
Impact Point correction											
per click: in/100yds	0.36	0.36	0.36	0.54	0.36	0.36	0.36	0.36	0.18	0.18	0.17
Max. elevation/windage											
adjustment range: ft/100yds	3.9	3.3	3.9	9.9	6.6	3.9	3.9	3.3	E:5.4/W:3	E:3.6/W:2.1	E:3.6/W:2.1
Length, approx: in	12.83	13.94	13.27	10.63	12.99	13.23	13.62	14.33	14.21	15.43	15.43
Weight, approx (oz.): L	12.0	14.8	15.9	12.7	16.2	15.2	18.0	16.9	22.2	23.6	24.5
LS	13.4	15.9	16.9	13.8	17.5	16.4	19.0	18.3	—	—	—

L=light alloy • LS=light alloy with rail

Swarovski Optics

SR RAIL MOUNT

SR RAIL PH SERIES

The Swarovski SR line uses an integral toothed rail on PH scopes that makes the tube stronger while eliminating the ring/tube juncture that can fail during heavy recoil.

PH 1.25-4x24SR $1333
PH 1.5-6x42SR 1483
PH 2.5-10x56SR 1706
PH 3-12x50SR 1728
PH 3-12x50SR 1810
also available with illum. reticle

SIGHTS & SCOPES

Lighted reticles can be easier to see in poor light; but remember that when an ordinary reticle is hard to see, so is the target. And you can't make targets brighter.

Swift Scopes

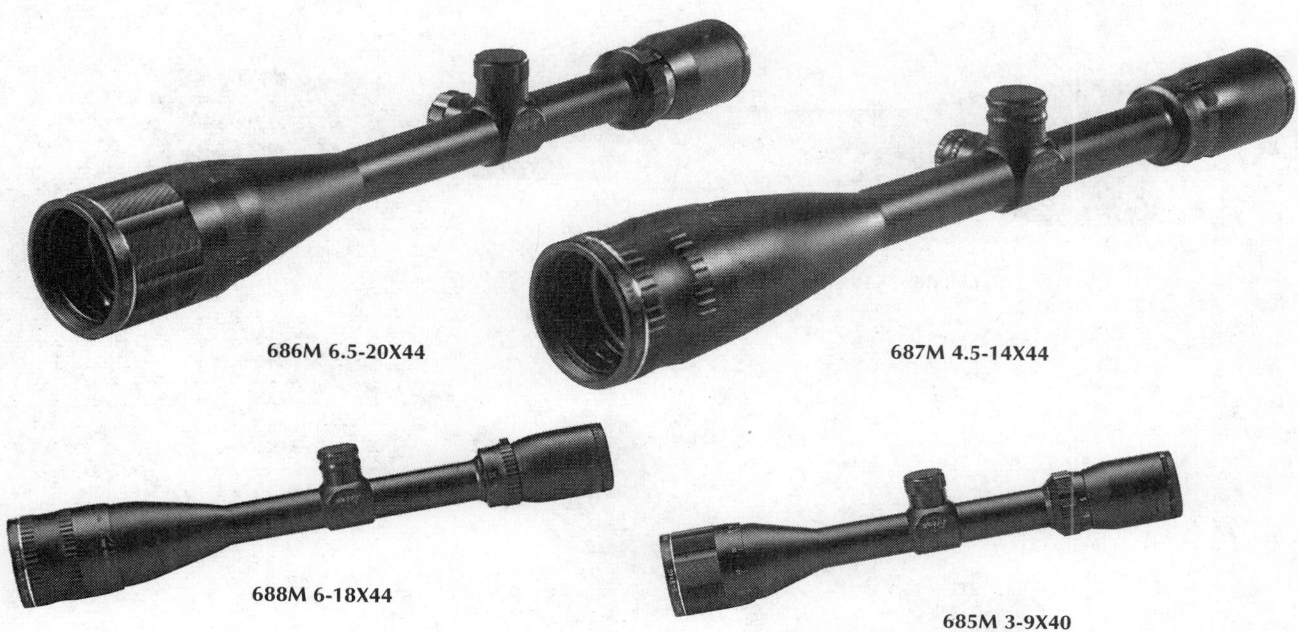

686M 6.5-20X44

687M 4.5-14X44

688M 6-18X44

685M 3-9X40

Swift Model's 685M and 686M were both designed for the rigors of airgun use. Strength and durability are the best terms used to describe these two scopes as they are constructed to withstand the severe reverse recoil of spring-loaded airguns. These versatile scopes have the Swift Quadraplex reticle, have been shock tested and are airgun rated.

MODEL 685M: SWIFT PREMIER 3-9X,40MM AIR GUN RATED RIFLESCOPE

Waterproof—Fully Multi-Coated—Speed Focus
Adjustable Objective
Comes Complete with Sunshade
Price: **$190**

MODEL 686M: SWIFT PREMIER 6.5-20X,44MM AIR GUN RATED RIFLESCOPE

Waterproof—Fully Multi-Coated—Speed Focus
Adjustable Objective
Comes Complete with Sunshade
Price: **$250**

Swift Model's 687M and 688M both feature a mil-dot reticle for pinpoint accuracy in long-range varmint or target shooting. The 44mm objective lens on these scopes allows for an exceptional light gathering capability.

MODEL 687M: SWIFT PREMIER 4.5-14X,44MM MIL-DOT RIFLESCOPE

Waterproof—Fully Multi-Coated—Speed Focus
Comes Complete with Sunshade
Price: **$220**

MODEL 688M: SWIFT PREMIER 6-18X,44MM MIL-DOT RIFLESCOPE

Waterproof—Fully Multi-Coated—Speed Focus
Comes Complete with Sunshade
Price: **$240**

Produced for the youth market, Swift's new Model 587 is a 4x, 32mm with a quadraplex reticle, this lightweight scope is designed for smaller caliber rimfires rifles.

MODEL 587: SWIFT 4X,32MM RIMFIRE RIFLESCOPE

Waterproof—Fully Coated
Comes Complete with Rings
Price: **$50**

The Swift Model 660M with a 2 - 6X zoom is a very versatile pistol scope that features full saddle construction and the Swift Speed Focus feature for optimum focusing ability at any power setting. Quadraplex reticle.

MODEL 660M: SWIFT PREMIER 2-6X,32MM PISTOL SCOPE

Waterproof—Fully Multi-Coated—Speed Focus
Price: **$250**

Swift Scopes

658M 2-7X40

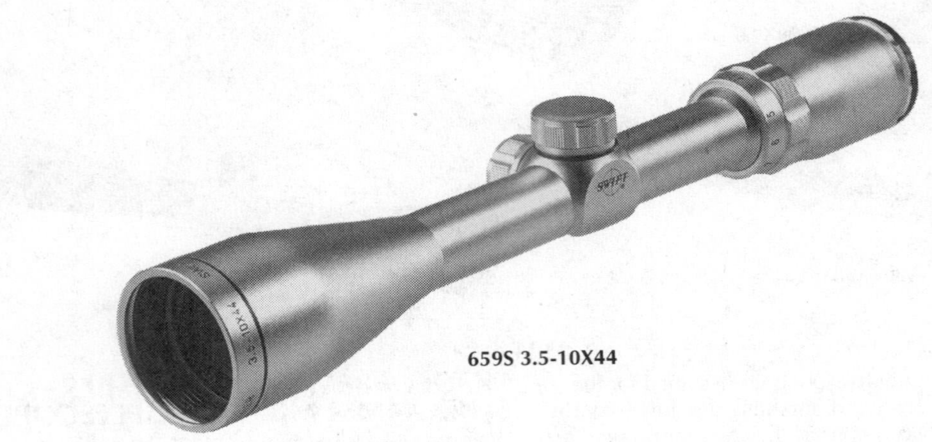

659S 3.5-10X44

669MA 6-18X44

Three of Swift's best selling standard line of riflescopes, models 658M, 659M, and 669MA will be upgraded to become part of the Swift Premier line. The upgrades to these scopes will include; full saddle construction, for added strength; 'Speed Focus', for a quick focus at any power setting; fully multi-coated optics for a brighter, glare free view at dawn and dusk, and; clear dust caps that will allow hunters to get off a quick shot if the need arises, without losing the time it takes to remove their dust caps.

MODEL 658M: SWIFT PREMIER 2-7X,40MM RIFLESCOPE

Waterproof—Fully Multi-Coated—Speed Focus
Finger Tip Adjustment System
Price: **$175**

MODEL 659M: SWIFT PREMIER 3.5-10X,44MM RIFLESCOPE

Waterproof—Fully Multi-Coated—Speed Focus
Also available in "blue" and "silver" finishes
Price: **$210**

MODEL 669MA: SWIFT PREMIER 6-18X,44MM RIFLESCOPE

Waterproof—Fully Multi-Coated—Speed Focus w/target turrets
Price: **$250**

Tasco Scopes

PROPOINT 1X25

RGD PRO POINT

PROPOINT RED DOT SIGHTING DEVICE

Propoint Red Dot Sights have been the choice for competitive shooters, turkey hunters and slug gun enthusiasts for years. Built to last, the Propoint features solid construction, flawless tracking and a rheostat-controlled illuminated red dot. Included accessories: rings to fit standard 5/8″ bases, extension tubes, polarizing filter and one lithium battery.

Model	Power	Objective Diameter	Finish	Reticle	Field of View @ 100 Yds.	Eye Relief	Tube Diam.	Scope Length	Scope Weight	Prices
Propoint Scopes										
PDP2	1X	25mm	Black Matte	5 M.O.A. Dot	40'	Unlimited	30mm	5"	5.5 oz.	$118
PDP2	1X	25mm	camo	5 M.O.A. Dot	40′	Unlimited	38mm	3.75″	6 oz.	138
PDP3	1X	25mm	Black Matte	5 M.O.A. Dot	52'	Unlimited	30mm	5"	5.5 oz.	138
PDP3ST	1X	25mm	Stainless	10 M.O.A. Dot	52'	Unlimited	30mm	5"	5.5 oz.	144
PDP3CMP	1X	30mm	Black Matte	10 M.O.A. Dot	68'	Unlimited	33mm	4.75"	5.4 oz.	158
PDPRG	1X	26mm	Black Matte	5 M.O.A. Dot	60'	Unlimited	38mm	5.4"	5.7 oz.	92
Red Dot Sights										
BKRD30	1X	30mm	Black Matte AWF	Illum. Red Dot	57"	Unlimited	38mm	3.75"	6 oz.	$46
BKRD30MD	1X	30mm	camo	Illum. Red Dot	57″	Unlimited	38mm	3.75″	6 oz.	60
BKRD30/22	1X	30mm	Black Matte AWF	Illum. Red Dot	57"	Unlimited	38mm	3.75"	6 oz.	46
BKRD42	1X	42mm	Black Matte AWF	Illum. Red Dot	62"	Unlimited	47mm	3.75"	6.7 oz.	58

Tasco Scopes

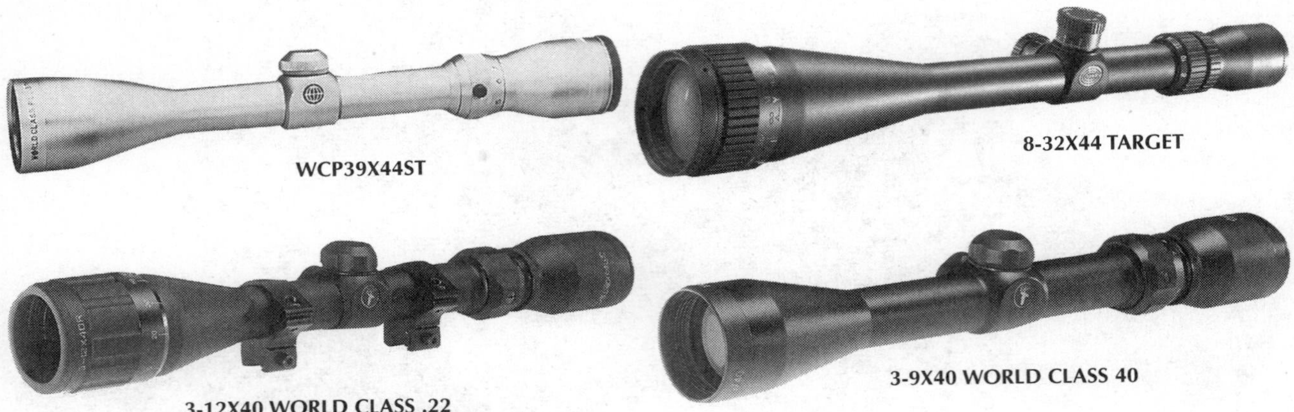
WCP39X44ST
8-32X44 TARGET
3-12X40 WORLD CLASS .22
3-9X40 WORLD CLASS 40

WORLD CLASS RIFLESCOPES

Wide-angle World Class Riflescopes have 1″ Advanced Monotube Construction to make them strong and shock resistant. SuperCon multi-layered coating on the objective and ocular lenses and fully-coated optics throughout increase light transmission. World Class Riflescopes are waterproof, fogproof and shock proof.

TITAN RIFLESCOPES

Titan 30mm riflescopes feature multi-coated lenses, finger adjustable windage and elevation controls and a fast-focus eyepiece. Available with a 30/30 or German-style 4A reticle, the Titan is waterproof, fogproof and shockproof.

TASCO RIFLESCOPES

Model	Power	Objective Diameter	F.O.V. @ 100 Yd.s	Eye Relief (inches)	Length	Weight	Prices
Titan							
DWCP351050	3.5-10	50	30-10.5	3.75	13	17.1	$191.95
DWCP39X44	3-9	44	39-14	3.5	12.75	16.5	173.95
T156X42N	1.5-6	42	59-20	3.5	12	16.4	293.95
T156X42N4A	1.5-6	42	59-20	3.5	12	16.4	293.95
T312X52N	3-12	52	27-10	4.5	14	20.7	335.95
T312X52N4A	3-12	52	27—10	4.5	14	20.7	335.95
T39X42N	3-9	42	37-13	3.5	12.5	16	281.95
Target & Varmint							
VAR251042M	2.5-10	42	35-9	3	14	19.1	$ 89.95
MAG624x40	6-24	40	17-4	3	16	19.1	113.95
VAR624X42M	6-24	42	13-3.7	7	16	19.6	113.95
TG624X44DS	6-24	44	15-4.5	3	16.5	19.6	199.95
TG104050DS	10-40	50	11-2.5	3.25	15.5	25.5	211.95
TG832X44DS	8-32	44	11-3.5	3.25	17	20	219.95
World Class							
BA1545X32	1.5-4.5	32	77-23	4	11.25	12	$59.95
DWC28X32	2-8	32	50-17	4	10.5	12.5	69.95
DWC39X40N	3-9	40	41-15	3.5	12.75	13	73.95
WA39X40N	3-9	40	41-15	3.5	12.75	13	73.95
WA39X40STN	3-9	40	41-15	3.5	12.75	13	73.95
DWC39X50N	3-9	40	41-13	3	12.5	15.8	87.95
DWC39X40M	3-9	40	41-15	3.5	12.75	13	73.95
MAG312X40	2-12	40	26.5-7.3	3	14	18	95.95
DWC416X40	4-16	40	22.5-5.9	3.7	14	16	103.95
DWC416X50	4-16	50	28-7	3	16	20.5	123.95
WC39X40IR	3-9	40	35-12	3.8	12.5	16.3	83.95
Pronghorn							
PH39X40D	3-9	40	39-13	3	13	12.1	$47.95
PH39X32D	3-9	32	39-13	3	12	11	41.95
PH4x32D	4	32	32	3	12	11	32.95
PH2533D	2.5	32	43	3.2	11.4	10.1	32.95
PH3950D	3-9	50	33	3.3	13	14.8	57.95

Tasco Riflescopes

VARMINT/TACTICAL SCOPES

Long range shooting is easier with Tasco's True Mil-Dot system. SuperCon multi-layered lens coatings and fully coated optics throughout provide clear resolution. With extra large 42mm objectives, this line of Varmint riflescopes transmit more light than standard 40mm scopes.

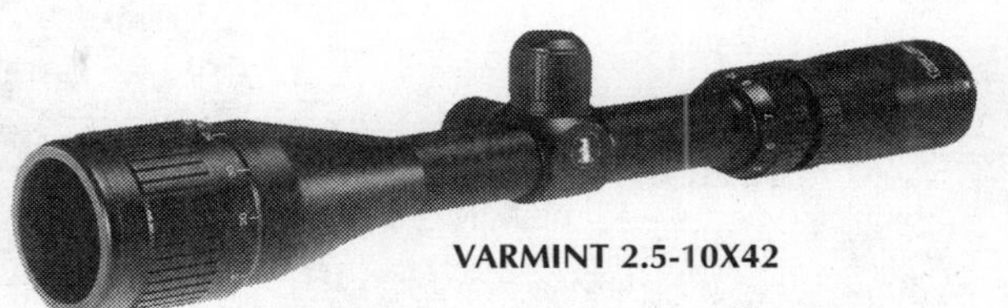

VARMINT 2.5-10X42

LER

Tasco's LER (Long Eye Relief) combines a lightweight, compact scope with illuminated technology (IT) to make these riflescopes perfect for rifles, shotgun, black powder, slug and brush. Available in fixed 4 power and variable 1.5 to 6 power.

LER4X32

MAG IV RIFLESCOPES

The large 40mm objective of MAG IV riflescopes delivers a full four times magnification with more zooming range than most variable scopes. In addition, a focusing objective provides valuable parallax correction. MAG IV scopes feature ¼-minute windage/elevation click stops and black matte finish. The result is a line of scopes that provide superior light transmission and clarity even at high magnifications. Waterproof, fogproof and shockproof.

3-12X40

GA 2.5X32 CB

SIGHTS & SCOPES

Tasco riflescopes

Model	Power	Objective Diameter	F.O.V. @ 100 Yd.s	Eye Relief (inches)	Length	Weight	Prices
.22 Riflescopes							
MAG39X32D	3-9	32	17.75-6	3	12.75	11.3	55.95
MAG4X32D	4	32	13.5	3	12.25	12.1	43.95
MAG4X32STD	4	32	13.5	3	12.25	12.1	43.95
Rimfire							
EZ01D	1	20	35	Unltd.	4.75	2.5	17.95
RF37X20D	3-7	20	24	2.5	11.5	5.7	23.95
RF4X15D	4	15	20.5	2.5	11	4	7.95
RF4X20WAD	4	20	23	2.5	10.5	3.8	9.95
Golden Antler							
DMGA39X32T	3-9	32	39-13	3	13.25	12.2	49.95
DMGA4X32T	4	32	32	3	12.75	11.	37.95
GA3940	3-9	40	41-15	3	12.75	13	57.95
GA2532	2.5	32	43	3.2	11.4	10.1	43.95
GA3932AGD	3-9	32	39	3	13.25	12	43.95

Trijicon Sights & Scopes

Fiber-Optic

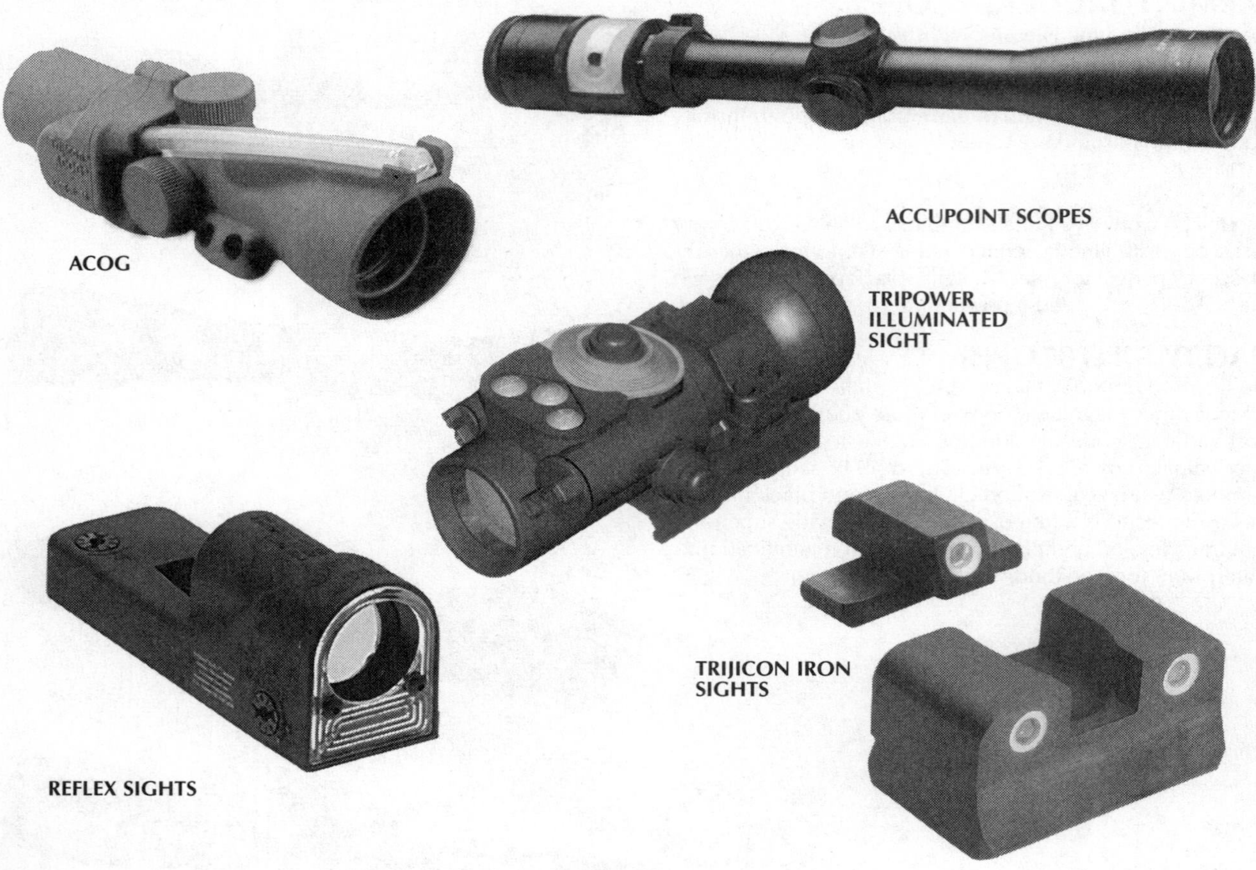

ACCUPOINT SCOPES

ACOG

TRIPOWER ILLUMINATED SIGHT

TRIJICON IRON SIGHTS

REFLEX SIGHTS

ACOG

The ACOGs are internally-adjustable, compact telescopic sights with tritium illuminated reticle patterns for use in low light or at night. Many models are dual-illuminated, featureing fiber optics which collect ambient light for maximum brightness in day-time shooting. The ACOGs combine traditional, precise distance marksmanship with close-in aiming speed.

Prices: . . . . **$950 to 1672**
Compact ACOG **950**

ACCUPOINT SCOPES

AccuPoint's dual-illuminated aiming point offers a major advancement over crosshairs that can disappear due to lack of contrast when aiming at a dark animal, or in low-light conditions. Reticle illumination is supplied by advanced fiber optics or, in low-light conditions, by a self-contained tritium lamp.

Prices: 3-9x40, red or amber triangle **$720**
1.2-4x24, red or amber triangle **700**
2.5-10x56 amber triangle (30mm tube) **950**

REFLEX SIGHTS

The dual-illuminated, Trijicon Reflex sight gives shooters next-generation technology for super-fast, any-light aiming-without batteries.

Developed for the military for use in both-eyes-open Close Quarters Battle (CQB) situations, the Reflex sight features an amber aiming dot or triangle that is illuminated both by light from the target area and from a tritium lamp.

Price: . . . . **$375 to 600**

TRIJICON NIGHT SIGHTS

Trijicon self-luminous iron sights give shooters greater night fire accuracy-with the same speed as instinctive shooting. Trijicon Bright & Tough night sights are the first choice of major handgun manufacturers and standard issue with hundreds of municipal and county departments, numerous state and police departments and several Federal agencies.

Price: . . . . **$100 to 150**

TRIPOWER ILLUMINATED SIGHT

The new TriPower features a red chevron-shaped reticle illuminated by three lighting sources: an integrated fiber optic system, a Tritium-Illuminated reticle and on-call battery backup. The TriPower has a 30mm tube, coated lenses, and is sealed for underwater use up to 100 feet. The TriPower is 5 inches long and weighs 6 oz.

Price: **$620**

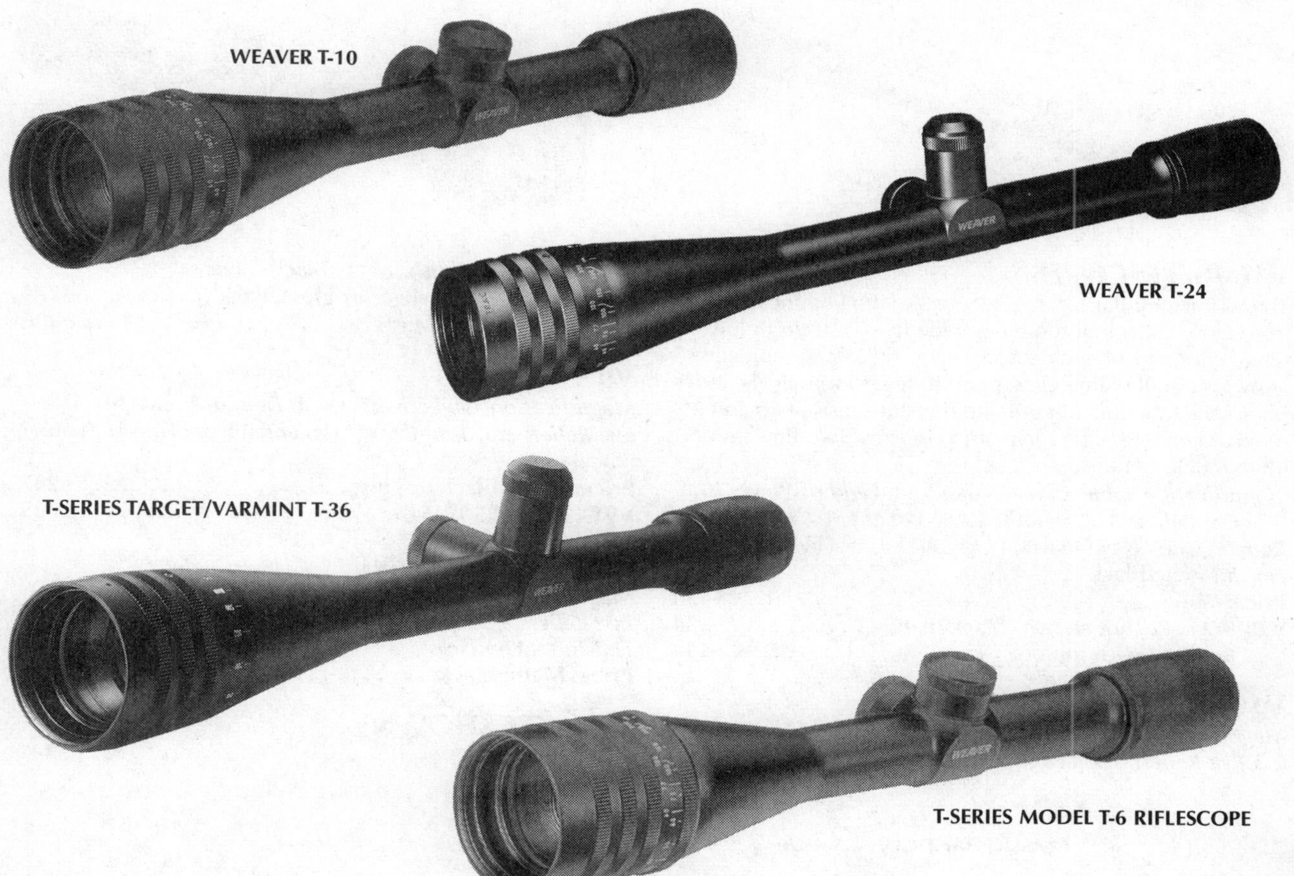

WEAVER T-10

WEAVER T-24

T-SERIES TARGET/VARMINT T-36

T-SERIES MODEL T-6 RIFLESCOPE

T-10 AND T-24TARGET

The T-10 target model (no AO) has quarter-minute click adjustments and a 1/8-minute dot reticle. It weighs just one pound, has a 40mm objective lens and comes in black satin finish—a fine choice for a light varmint rifle or a dual-purpose coyote/pronghorn rifle. The T-24 also has a 40mm front end. The parallax (AO) adjustment is the traditional forward ring. At 17 ounces, it is very light for its magnification. Choose a 1/8-minute dot or a 1/2-minute dot.

T-10 Target Scope: **$598**
T-24 Scope:. **$638**

T-SERIES TARGET/VARMINT T-36

You need high magnification for the greatest possible precision. Weaver's 36x gives it to you with patented Micro-Trac adjustments in a dual-spring, four-bearing housing that allows independent movement of windage and elevation. Optics are fully multi-coated, delivering premium image clarity in virtually all light conditions. An adjustable objective allows for parallax zero from 50′ to infinity. Choice of fine crosshair or dot reticles. Scopes come with sunshade, an extra pair of oversize benchrest adjustment knobs, and screw-in metal lens caps.
Model: T-36 ***Magnification/Objective:*** 36X40mm ***Field of View:*** 3.0' ***Eye Relief:*** 3.0" ***Length:*** 15.1" ***Weight:*** 16.7 oz. ***Reticle:*** 1/8 MOA Dot, Fine Crosshair ***Finish:*** Matte black or silver

Price: Matte **$670**
Silver **679**
Matte Dot. **678**
Silver Dot. **688**

T-SERIES MODEL T-6 RIFLESCOPE

Weaver's T-6 competition 6x scope is only 12.7 inches long and weighs less than 15 ounces. All optical surfaces are fully multi-coated for maximum clarity and light transmission. The T-6 features Weaver's Micro-Trac precision adjustments in 1/8-minute clicks to ensure parallel tracking. The protected target-style turrets are a low-profile configuration combining ease of adjustment with weight reduction. A 40mm adjustable objective permits parallax correction from 50 feet to infinity without shifting the point of impact. A special AO lock ring eliminates bell vibration or shift. The T-6 comes with screw-in metal lens caps and features a competition matte black finish. Reticles: dot, Fine Crosshair

Price: 6x40 Satin Black. **$474**

Weaver Scopes

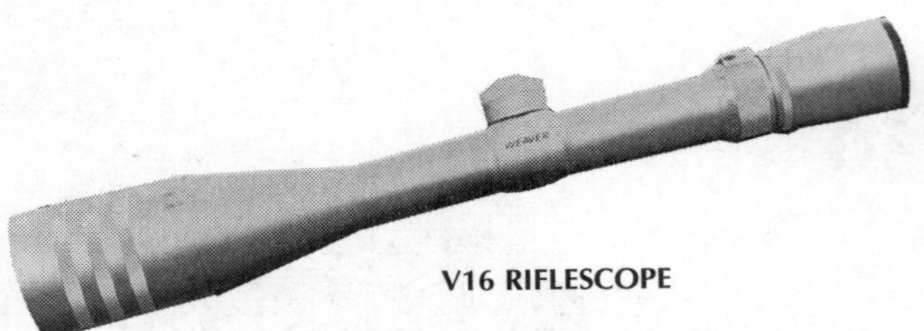

V16 RIFLESCOPE

CLASSIC V9

V16 RIFLESCOPES

The V16 is popular for a variety of shooting applications, from close shots that require a wide field of view to long-range varmint or benchrest shooting. Adjustable objective allows a parallax-free view from 30 feet to infinity. Features one-piece tube for strength and moisture resistance and multicoated lenses for clear, crisp images. Two finishes and three reticle options.

Magnification/Objective: 4-16X42mm ***Field of View:*** 26.8'-6.8' ***Eye Relief:*** 3.1" ***Length:*** 13.9" ***Weight:*** 16.5 oz.
Reticle: Choice of Dual-X, ¼ MOA Dot, or Fine Crosshair
Finish: Matte black

Price: $458
V24 6-24x42 (not shown) black matte 534
V24 6-24x42 with mil dot 554

V10 (NOT SHOWN)

Magnification/Objective: 2-10X38mm ***Field of View:*** 38.5-9.5 ***Eye Relief:*** 3.5" ***Length:*** 12.2" ***Weight:*** 11.2 oz.
Reticle: Dual-X ***Finish:*** Matte black, silver

Price: Matte black, silver or gloss black $274
V10x50 (2-10x50) Matte 386

V9

Magnification/Objective: 3-9x38 ***Field of View:*** 34-11' ***Eye Relief:*** 3.5" ***Length:*** 12" ***Weight:*** 11 oz. ***Finish:*** Matte black, gloss

Price: Matte black or gloss $247
V9XX50 (3-9x50) Matte 335

V3 (NOT SHOWN)

Magnification/Objective: 1-3x20 ***Field of View:*** 100x34 ***Eye Relief:*** 3.5" ***Length:*** 9" ***Weight:*** 9 oz.
Finish: Matte black

Price: Matte black $246

V7 (NOT SHOWN)

2-7x32 matte $247

CLASSIC HANDGUN 1.5-4X20

CLASSIC RIMFIRE RV7

WEAVER CLASSIC HANDGUN SCOPES

Fixed-power scopes include 2x28 and 4x28 scopes in gloss black or silver. Variables in 1.5-4x20 and 2.5-8x28 come with a gloss black finish. The 2.5-8x28 is also available in black matte. One-piece tubes, fully multi-coated lenses and generous eye relief (4-29") make these scopes top performers on hunting handguns.

Prices: 2x28 gloss black or silver $226
4x28 gloss black or silver 245
1.5-4x20 gloss black 300
2.5-8x28 gloss black or silver 320
2.5-8x28 matte 320
Also available:
Classic shotgun 4x32 246
1.5-5x32 260

CLASSIC RIMFIRE RV7

Lenses are multi-coated for bright, clear low-light performance and the one-piece tube design is shockproof and waterproof.

Prices: 2.5-7x28 Rimfire Matte black or silver..... $208

RIMFIRE SCOPE RV4 (NOT SHOWN)

This fixed 4x scope is ideal for a variety of shooting applications. It's durable, light-weight and waterproof.

Prices: Rimfire Matte Black 4x28 178
3-9x32 AO matte 338

SIGHTS & SCOPES

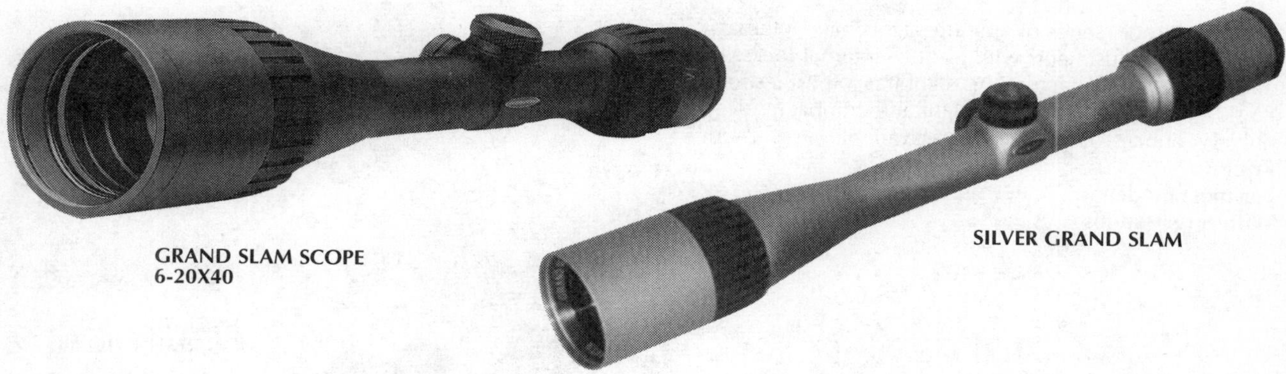

GRAND SLAM SCOPE
6-20X40

SILVER GRAND SLAM

WEAVER GRAND SLAM SCOPES

The Grand Slam series features Weaver's best optics, with an advanced one-piece tube design. A "sure-grip" power ring and AO adjustment let you easily adjust the variable scopes, even while wearing heavy gloves. An offset parallax indicator lets you remain in shooting position while adjusting the scope. The eyepiece has a fast-focus adjustment ring. Simply rotate the ring until the reticle becomes sharp.

Grand Slam configurations include: 4.75x40mm, a fixed-power scope with sufficient magnification for longer shots, yet a wide field of view for finding running game close in; 1.5-5x32mm, the ideal scope for short-range rifles and fast target acquisition in brushy country; 3.5-10x40mm, the traditional choice of big-game hunters for short- or long-range shooting; 3.5-10x50mm, which provides the brightest view in low-light situations; 4.5-14x40mm AO, possibly the most versatile Grand Slam scope, with a low range suitable for stand hunting and high enough magnification for target shooting or varmint hunting; and 6-20x40mm AO, two target/varminter models.Windage and elevation knobs have target-type finger adjustments so ¼-MOA adjustments can be made by gripping the rim of the knob between the thumb and index finger.

The Grand Slam scopes are also equipped with Micro-Trac, Weaver's patented four-point adjustment system. All Grand Slam scopes are offered with a plex reticle (except the 6-20x model, which is offered with a choice of Weaver's Varminter reticle or fine crosshairs with a dot). The scopes have a non-glare black matte or silver and black finish, featuring the green and gold oval Weaver logo medallion on the scope saddle and green ring inside the objective lens hood.

Prices: 6-20x40 AO black or silver $580
4.5-14x40 AO black or silver 570
3.5-10x50 black or silver 520
3-10x40 black or silver. 430
1.5-5x32 black 480
4.75x40 black. 400

CLASSIC 2.5 2.5X20MM

WEAVER CLASSIC K SERIES

Classic American scopes, the K2.5, K4 and K6 now have a sleeker look. They weigh less but deliver brighter images than ever before. New logos distinguish these versatile hunting scopes at a glance. Reasonably priced and great values, K scopes–including the target model, KT-15–have one-piece tubes.

Prices: KT-15 (15x42 gloss). $394
K6 (gloss) 208
K6 (matte) 208
K6 (matte, LER). 250
K4 (gloss) 195
K4 (matte) 195
K2.5 (2.5x20 gloss). 186

Williams Sights
FP Series

The "Foolproof" series of aperture sights have internal micrometer adjustments with positive internal locks. The alloy used to manufacture this sight has a tensile strength of 85,000 pounds. Yet, the FP is light and compact, weighing only 1½ ounces. Target knobs are available on all models.

Prices:

For most models $70

With target knobs 82

FP-GR-TK
ON REMINGTO 581

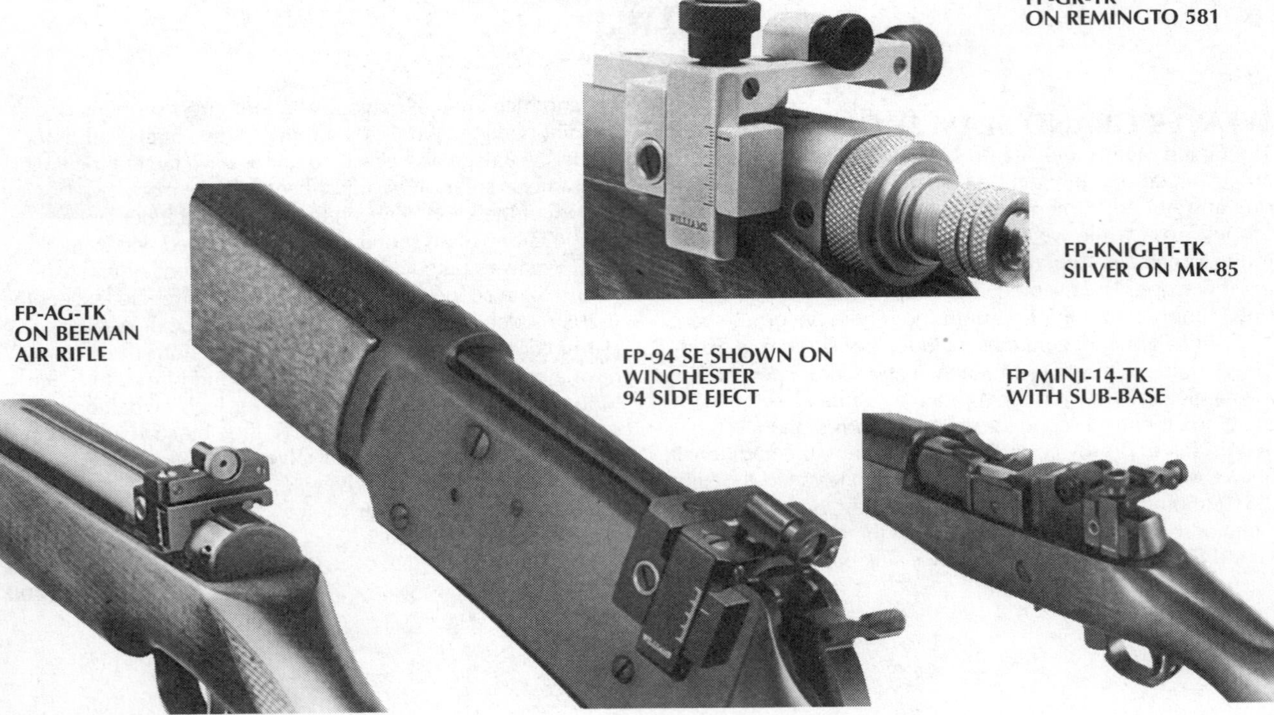

FP-KNIGHT-TK
SILVER ON MK-85

FP-AG-TK
ON BEEMAN
AIR RIFLE

FP-94 SE SHOWN ON
WINCHESTER
94 SIDE EJECT

FP MINI-14-TK
WITH SUB-BASE

FP RECEIVER SIGHT OPTIONS

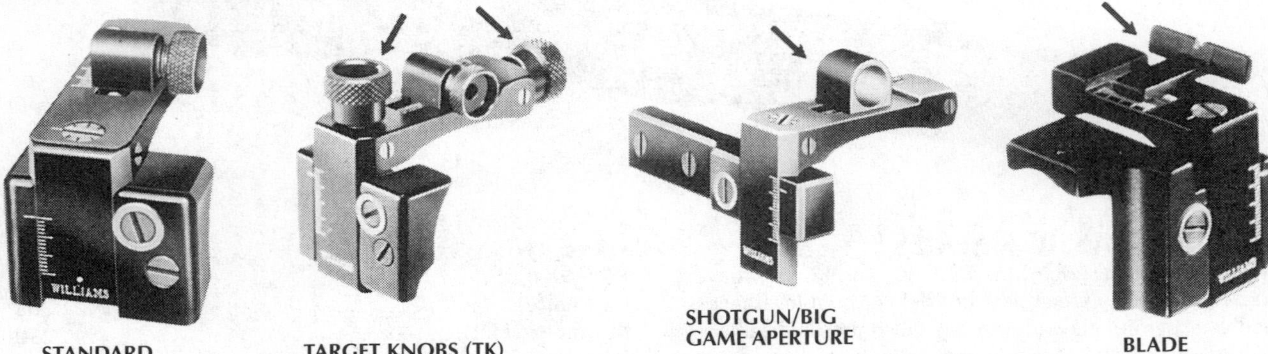

STANDARD

TARGET KNOBS (TK)

SHOTGUN/BIG
GAME APERTURE

BLADE

Williams Sights
Open Sights

WGOS SERIES
- Made from high tensile strength aluminum. Will not rust.
- All parts milled—no stampings.
- Streamlined and lightweight with tough anodized finish.
- Dovetailed windage and elevation - Easy to adjust, positive locks.
- Interchangeable blades available in four heights and four styles.

Price:. **$20-27**

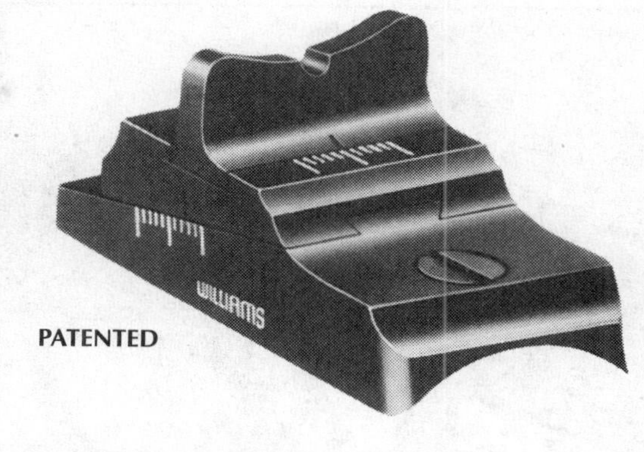

PATENTED

Blades are sold separately, except "U" blades are available installed on WGOS octagon T/C and CVA.
Price: **$7**

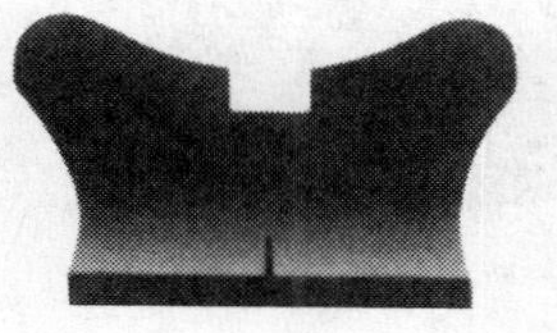
"SQ"

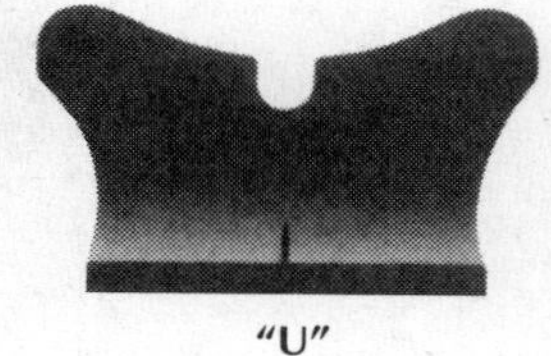
"U"

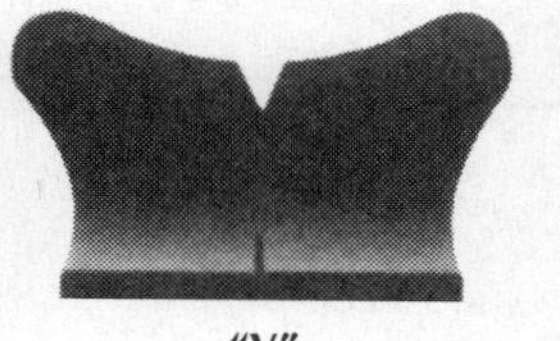
"V"

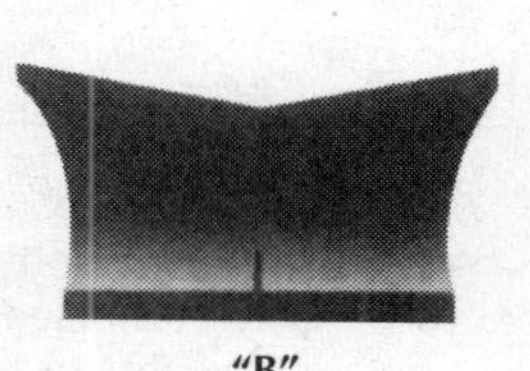
"B"

Williams Sights
Receiver Sights

RECEIVER SIGHTS
Military Sights
Open and aperture for:
- SKS (no drilling required)
- AK47 (no drilling required)
- **Mauser 96** **$20-26**

WGRS SERIES
- Compact Low Profile
- Lightweight, Strong, Rustproof
- Positive Windage and Elevation Locks

In most cases these sights utilize dovetail or existing screws on top of the receiver for installation. They are made from an aluminum alloy that is stronger than many steels. Light. Rustproof. Williams quality throughout.
Price: most models **$36**

WGRS-CVA ON CVA APOLLLO

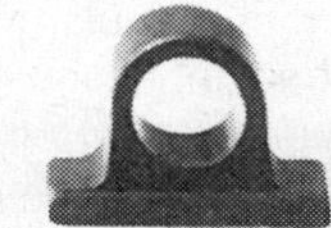
"GHOST RING" SHOTGUN APERTURE AVAILABLE FOR WGRS RECEIVER SIGHTS. SOLD SEPARATELY.

FIRE SIGHTS
Williams has introduced new "Fire Sights". These sights are machined from aircraft-strength aluminum and steel. This sight is lightweight, durable and brightens in low-light situations.
Prices:
Pistol Fire Sight Sets **$46**
Shotgun Fire Sight Sets . . . . **30 to 38**
Muzzleloader Fire Sight Sets . . . . **30 to 50**
Rifle Fire Sight Sets . . . . **30 to 42**
Peep Sets . . . . **48 to 81**
Rifle Beads **18**

FIRE SIGHTS

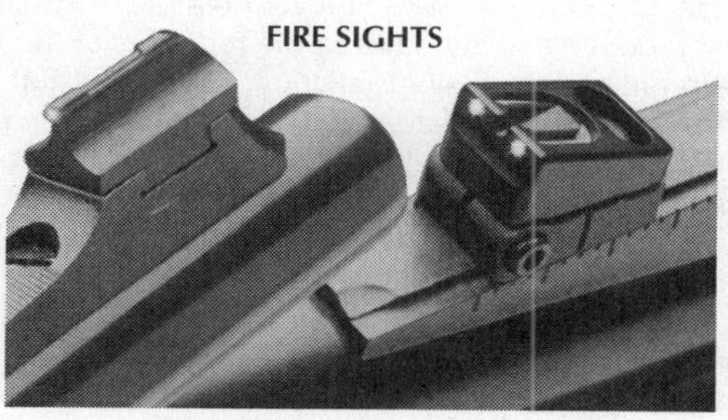

SIGHTS & SCOPES

Williams Sights
5D Series

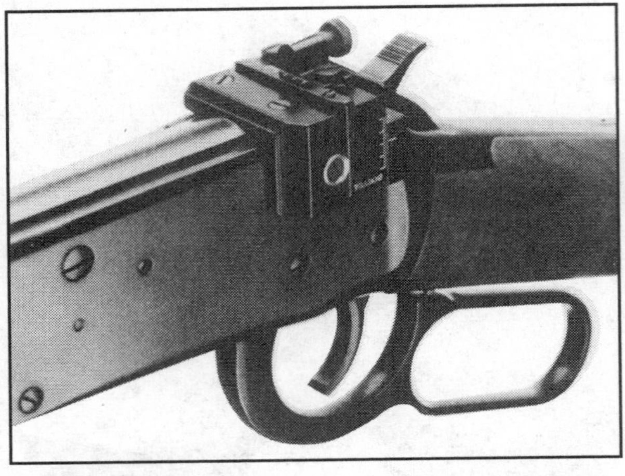

5D SERIES

5D SERIES

- For Big Game Rifles, 22's, Shotguns
- Positive Windage and Elevation Locks
- Lightweight, Strong, Accurate
- Williams Quality Throughout—Rustproof

TARGET - FP (HIGH)

TARGET - FP (LOW)

SIGHTS & SCOPES

Williams has offered the inexpensive, high-quality 5D sight for decades. Models are available for most popular rifles and shotguns. These sights have the strength, light weight, and neat appearance of the FP, without the micrometer adjustments. Designed for rugged hunting use, 5D sights offer unobstructed vision. No knobs or side plates to blot out shooter's field of vision. Wherever possible, the manufacturers' mounting screw holes in the receivers of the guns have been utilized for easy installation. The upper staff of the Williams 5D sight is readily detachable. Just loosen one screw. The angular bushing locks this upper staff. A set screw is provided as a stop screw so that the sight will return to absolute zero after reattaching. The Williams 5D sight is made of one of the highest grade alloys obtainable. Laboratory tests show that the material used has a tensile strength approximately 25% greater than mild steels.
Price: Most 5D models $38

TARGET—FP (HIGH)

Adjustable From 1.250" to 1.750"
Above Centerline of Bore.
Price: $78

TARGET FP-ANSCHUTZ

Designed to fit many of the Anschutz Lightweight .22 Cal. Target and Sporter Models. No Drilling and Tapping required.
Price: $83

TARGET—FP (LOW)

Adjustable From .750" to 1.250"
Above Centerline of Bore.
Price: $78

XS Sight Systems

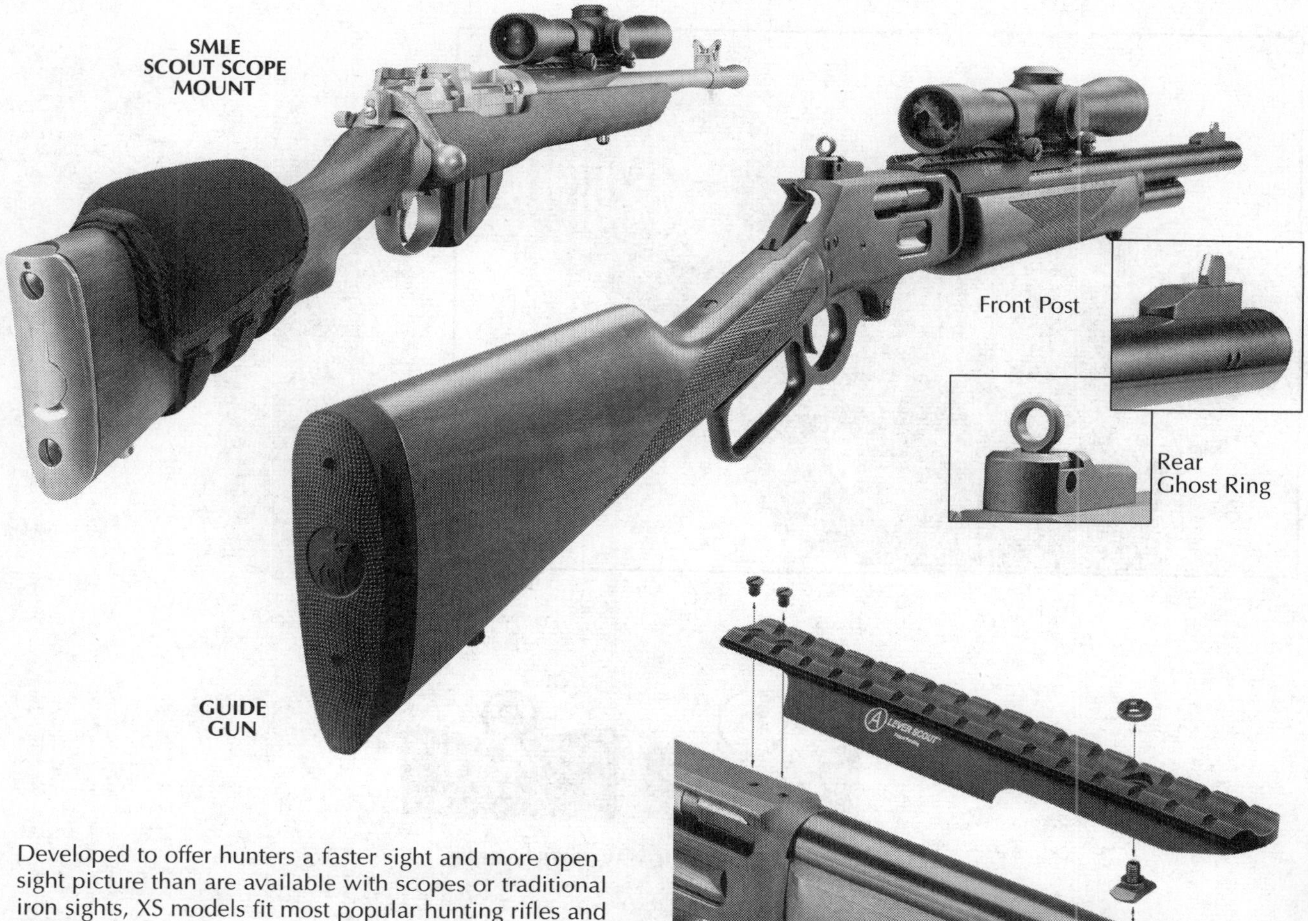

MOUNT INSTALLATION

.191 .230 .150 .218

Developed to offer hunters a faster sight and more open sight picture than are available with scopes or traditional iron sights, XS models fit most popular hunting rifles and shotguns.

XS SIGHT SYSTEMS GHOST-RING SIGHTS & LEVER SCOUT MOUNTS

• Scout Scope Mount with 8" long Weaver-style rail and cross slots on ½" Centers • Scope mounts ⅛" lower than previously possible on Marlin Lever Guns • Drop-in installation, no gunsmithing required • Installs using existing rear dovetail & front two screw holes on receiver • Allows fast target acquisition with both eyes open—better peripheral vision • Affords use of Ghost-Ring Sights with Scope dismounted • Recoil tested for even the stout 45/70 and .450 Loads • Available for Marlin Lever Models: 1895 Guide Series, new .450, .444P, the 336, and 1894.

Price: $50
XS Lever Scout Mount for Win 94 55

XS GHOST-RING HUNTING SIGHTS

• Fully adjustable for windage & elevation • Available for most rifles, including blackpowder • Minimum gunsmithing for most installations; matches most existing mounting holes • Compact design, CNC machined from steel and heat treated • Perfect for low light hunting conditions and brush/timer hunting, offers minimal target obstruction.

Price: AO Ghost-Ring Hunting Sight Set. . . . $90 for most

SMLE SCOUT SCOPE MOUNTS

• Offers Scout Scope Mount with 7" long Weaver style rail
• Requires no machining of barrel to fit—no drilling or tapping
• Tapered counter bore for snug fit of SMLE Barrels
• Circular Mount is final filled with Brownells Acraglass

Price: SMLE Scout Mount $60

XS Sight Systems

GLOCK 36
W/BIG DOT
TRITIUM

BIG DOT TRITIUM W/TRITIUM REAR

SIGHTS & SCOPES

XS 24/7 TRITIUM EXPRESS SIGHTS

The original fast aacquisition sight. Now enhanced with new 24/7 tritium sight.

24/7 Express sights are the finest sights made for fast sight acquisition under any light conditions. Light or dark just "dot the i" and put the dot on the target.

- Enhances low light sight acquisition
- Improves Low Light accuracy
- Low profile, snag free design
- Available for most pistols

Prices: XS 24/7 Big Dot or Standard
Express Sets. . . . . $90 - 120

XS ADJUSTABLE EXPRESS SIGHT SETS

Incorporates Adjustable Rear Express Sight with a white stripe rear, or Pro Express Rear with a Vertical Tritium Bar, fits Bomar style cut, LPA style cut, or a Kimber Target cut rear sight. Affords same Express Sight principles as fixed sight models.

Prices:
Adjustable Express w/White Stripe Rear and Big Dot Front or Standard Dot Front $120
Adjustable Express w/White Stripe Rear and Big Dot Tritium or Standard Dot Tritium Front. . . . 150
Adjustable Pro Express w/Tritium Rear and Big Dot Tritium or Standard Dot Tritium Front. 150

The 30mm scope tube is becoming more popular. But for most applications the smaller 1-inch tube suffices. It's lighter and just as strong. In some scopes, a big tube adds adjustment inches.

Zeiss Scopes

CONQUEST 3-9X50

CONQUEST 3.5-10X44
STAINLESS STEEL FINISH

CONQUEST 3-9X40

ZEISS CONQUEST SERIES RIFLESCOPES

The Conquest series has Zeiss' proprietary MC anti-reflective coating and is backed by a Lifetime Transferable Warranty. Couple this with Zeiss' world renowned low-light performance, new arsenic/lead-free glass technology, precision engineering, quick focus and constant eye relief design and you have one of the world's highest performance riflescope series.

CONQUEST 50MM

Zeiss' trio of Conquest scopes has 50mm objectives for enhanced light transmission at dawn and dusk. The 3-9x50, 3.5-10x50 and 4.5-14x50 weigh 17, 18 and 20 ounces and feature 1-inch alloy tubes and reticles in the second focal plane. All Conquest scopes have Zeiss MC multicoating. These scopes are waterproof and fog-proof and come with a plex reticle and quarter-minute click adjustments. Eye relief is 3.3 inches.

Zeiss also offers the 3-12x56 high-powered scope, with a huge objective on a 30mm alloy tube. It has 3.2 inches of eye relief and more than 30 inches of windage and elevation adjustment. Field of view: 9.9 to 27.6 feet at 100 yards. The scope weighs 25.8 ounces.

3-9x50: **$599**
3.5-10x50: **699**
4.5-14x50 AO: **799**
3-12x56 High-Powered Scope: **1069**
(stainless anodized): **1099**

CONQUEST 3-9X40

The 3-9x40 Conquest is the most versatile scope in the series, featuring a 4-inch eye-relief with unique European quick focus and advanced internal design, enabling the widest windage/elevation adjustment to 64 inches. All this combined with a solid one-piece alloy body manufactured to German standards makes the 3-9x40 Conquest a practical hunting sight.

Price: 3-9x40 MC **$519**
Stainless **549**

CONQUEST 3-9X40S

The 3-9x40S Conquest is designed to support sportsmen who demand a shotgun, airgun, or muzzleloader scope with heavy reticle. The 3-9x40S has the same glass and coating as the 3-9, with a safe 4-inch eye relief, etched glass reticle and one-piece alloy tube.

Price: 3-9x40S **$519**
w/turkey reticle **519**

CONQUEST 3.5-10X44

The 3.5-10x44 Conquest, designed to replace Zeiss' Diavari C 3-9x36, is superior in design and has all the standard Conquest features. Additionally, the 3.5-10x44 Conquest offers a 22-percent larger objective and a 66-inch windage/elevation adjustment. Combine these features with a weight of just 14 oz., the 3.5-10x44 Conquest makes it suitable for general big game hunting.

Price: 3.5-10x44 MC **$689**
Stainless **719**
Target **789**

CONQUEST 4.5-14X44

The 4.5-14x44 Conquest offers the first turret-mounted parallax adjustment from Zeiss. The 64-inch windage/elevation adjustment coupled with the 25-foot to 8.3-foot field of view made the 4.5-14x44 Conquest the selection of choice. The objective clarity and light transmission exceeds most models that have larger objectives and provides for perfect balance without adding weight or requiring raised mounts. Conquest riflescopes are water- and fog-proof, are free of lead and arsenic, and are backed by Zeiss' lifetime transferable warranty.

Price: 4.5-14x44 AO **$789**
Stainless **829**
Target **889**

CONQUEST 6.5-20X50 MC

The latest addition to the Conquest line of riflescopes is the 6.5-20X50. Developed for the American long-range shooter, this riflescope is ideal for big game hunting, varmint shooting or competition at great distances. Equipped with a turret-mounted parallax adjustment, the new 6.5-20X50 eliminates the need for the shooter to take his eye off the target. The external target turret knobs have no caps to lose and make it easier to view the windage and elevation. The riflescope does not require high mounts, allowing for a compact rifle profile and low line of sight.

Reticle: Z Plex or Fine Crosshair
Eye Relief: 3.5"
F.O.V.: 17.6'-5.8' at 100 yds.
Weight: 21.5 oz.
Price: Matte Black **$949**
Stainless **989**

Zeiss Scopes

Zeiss Premuim Sports Optics

1.1-4 X 24 T*

DIAVARI 1.1-4 X 24 T* VM/V

- Compact riflescope with 108 ft. field of view at 1.1 power
- Extremely lightweight—ideal for safari rifles
- With illuminated varipoint reticle for fast target acquisition clearly visible also in critical lighting conditions
- Especially designed for running shots and hunting in heavy brush
- Available with bullet drop compensator
- Eye relief: 3.74 in.

Price: $1800

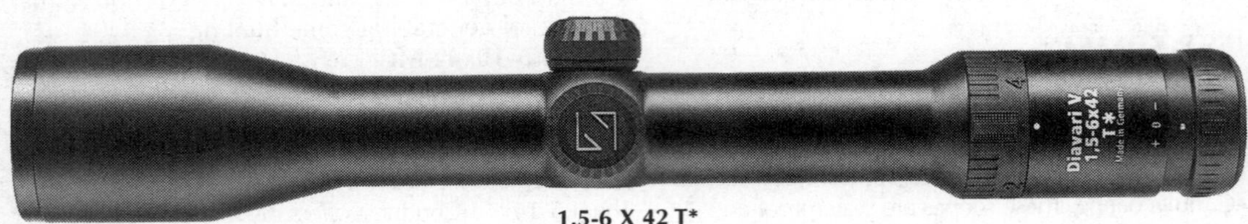

1.5-6 X 42 T*

DIAVARI 1.5-6 X 42 T* VM/V

- Excellent choice for white-tail or moose hunter
- Compact and easy to handle
- Lightest scope of its class
- 72 ft. field of view—largest field of view in premium class
- Easy-grip adjustment knob
- Available with bullet drop compensator
- Eye relief: 3.54 in.

Price: $1400
w/Varipoint, reticle. 1880
w/Varipoint 54 reticle. 1950

SIGHTS & SCOPES

Zeiss Scopes

Zeiss Premuim Sports Optics

DIAVARI VM/V 3-9X42 T*

Over the years, the 3-9x power range has proven its staying power. It is still the favorite power range of North American hunters. The 42 mm objective, coupled with the Zeiss T* coating, extends the hunting day. Whether the quarry is elk, Dall sheep or Boone and Crockett white-tail, the VM/V Diavari 3-9 x 42T* offers top quality and the right magnification.

Power **3-9x**
Effective Objective Diameter (mm) **30-42**
Exit Pupil Diameter (mm) **10-4.7**
Twilight Factor **8.5-18.4**
Field Of View At 100 Yards (feet) **36-12.9**
Minimum Square Adjustment Range . . . .
At 100 Yards (inch) **49.7**

Eye Relief (inch)3.74
Center Tube Diameter (inch) **1**
Objective Bell Diameter (inch) **1.89**
Length (inch) **13.3**
Weight (ounces) **15.2**
Parallax Free (yards) **109.4**
Price: **$1300**

2.5-10 X 50 T*

DIAVARI 2.5-10 X 50 T* VM/V

- High powered riflescope with superior twilight performance
- Light, compact with a wide field of view
- Available with an illuminated reticle
- Easy-grip adjustment knob
- Excellent choice for world-wide all-round hunting
- Available with bullet drop compensator
- Eye relief: 3.54 in.

Price: **$1570**
w/illuminated reticle **2000**

Zeiss Scopes

Zeiss Premuim Sports Optics

DIAVARI VM/V 5-15X42 T*

Precise windage and elevation adjustments make the Diavari VM/V 5 - 15 x 42 T* the perfect companion for a target or varmint rifle. The rugged adjustment system provides fast, accurate and repeatable adjustments. By aligning the optical and mechanical axes, Zeiss ensures full range of adjustment.

Power **5-15x**
Effective Objective Diameter (mm) **42-42**
Exit Pupil Diameter (mm) **8.4-2.8**
Twilight Factor **14.1-25.1**
Field Of View At 100 Yards (feet) **23.7-7.8**
Minimum Square Adjustment Range . . . .
At 100 Yards (inch) **30**
Eye Relief (inch) **3.74**
Center Tube Diameter (inch) **1**
Objective Bell Diameter (inch) **1.89**
Length (inch) **13.3**
Weight (ounces) **14**
Parallax Free (yards) **109.4**
Price: **$1500**

DIAVARI VM/V 6-24X56

The VM/V 6-24x56 has 57.6 inches of elevation with a 5.2-foot field at 24x and an 18.6-foot field at 6x. A quick-focus eyepiece and turret-mounted parallax adjustment (55 yards to infinity) deliver a perfect sight picture almost instantly.

The VM/V 6-24x56 features the "Advanced Optical System" lenses and Zeiss T* coatings. Eye relief is 3.1 inches.

6-24x56T **$1599**
6-24x56 with illuminated reticle: **$2000**

DIAVARI VM/V 3-12X56 T*

In the quiet haze of dawn or the fleeting light of sunset, a riflesope is put to the ultimate test. Under these conditions, the Diavari VM/V 3-12x56 T* excels. The patented Zeiss T* anti-reflection coating is designed to transmit the optimum percentage of light throughout the spectral range to take full advantage of your eye's sensitivity. Weighing in at 13.5 ounces, the VM/V 3-12x56 T* won't slow you down.

Power **3-12x**
Effective Objective Diameter (mm) **44.0-56**
Exit Pupil Diameter (mm) **14.7-4.7**
Twilight Factor **8.5-25.9**
Field Of View At 100 Yards (feet) **37.5-10.4**
Minimum Square . . . .
Adjustment Range . . . .
At 100 Yards (inch) **36.7**
Eye Relief (inch) **3.54**
Center Tube Diameter (inch) **1.18**
Objective Bell Diameter (inch) **2.44**
Length (inch) **13.54**
Weight (ounces) **17.8/16.8**
Parallax Free (yards) **109.4**
Price: **$1600**
w/illuminated reticle **$2000**

AMMUNITION

VARMINTS
CXP1
WINCHESTER
Ballistic Silvertip
223 WSSM
WINCHESTER SUPER SHORT MAGNUM
55 GR. BALLISTIC SILVERTIP
SBST223SS

Black Hills Ammunition

Noted for varmint and tactical ammo, Black Hills has expanded its big game hunting line to include softpoint offerings beginning with the .223 loaded with 60-grain Nosler Partition bullets. Velocity is 3150 fps from a 24-inch barrel. You'll also find a broad selection in the Black Hills Gold big game series. The .25-06 comes with 100-grain Nosler Ballistic Tips and 115-grain Barnes X-Bullets. Get 140-grain Ballistic Tips and X-Bullets in 7mm Remington Magnum cartridges. For 2005 Nosler's AccuBond joins the bullet line in several rounds, including .270 and .300 WSM, new Black Hills Gold cartridges are also available in .22-250, .243 Win, .25-06, 270, .308, .30-06, 7mm Rem. Mag. and .300 Win Mag.

The Cowboy line includes modern and traditional rounds from the .32 H&R to the .45-70. Black Hills, offers an expanding line of factory-new and remanufactured ammunition for handguns and rifles. The Cowboy Action Line includes loads for the .32 H+R, .357 Magnum, .38-40, .44-40, .45 Colt, .32-20, .44 Colt, .44 Spl., .45 Schofield, .38 Spl, .38 Long Colt, .44 Russian, .45-70. Modern handgun ammunition, from .40 S+W to .44 Magnum, features a variety of bullet types. Black Hills rifle cartridges include the popular .223, .308, 6.5-284, .300 Win. Mag, and the potent long-range tactical round, the .338 Lapua. There's also specialty ammo, with frangible or moly-coated bullets.

Brenneke USA Cartridges

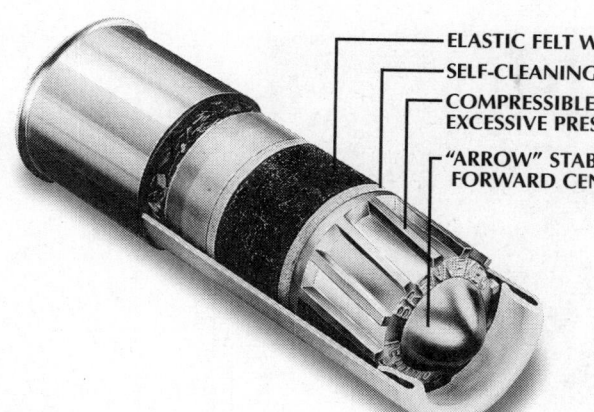

ELASTIC FELT WAD FOR OPTIMUM GAS PRESSURE RISE
SELF-CLEANING WAD PREVENTS LEAD BUILD-UP IN BORE
COMPRESSIBLE GUIDING RIBS PREVENT EXCESSIVE PRESSURE ON THE MUZZLE
"ARROW" STABILIZATION PROVIDED BY FORWARD CENTER OF GRAVITY

The Original Brenneke has been the standard against which other slugs have been measured for 100 years.

Specifications

Brenneke USA Load	Barrel	Distance (yds)	Velocity (ft./sec.)	Energy (ft./lbs.)	Trajectory (in)
SuperSabot 12 GA	Rifled only	Muzzle	1407	2157	-2.0
23/4"		25	1274	1770	+0.4
11/8 oz		50	1165	1478	+1.6
		75	1080	1272	+1.1
		100	1017	1127	-1.3
SuperSabot 12 GA	Rifled only	Muzzle	1526	2536	-2.0
3"		25	1376	2064	+0.2
11/8 oz		50	1248	1697	+1.2
		75	1144	1426	+0.9
		100	1065	1236	-1.1
K.O. Sabot 12 GA	Smooth or rifled	Muzzle	1509	2184	-2.0
23/4"		25	1344	1733	+0.3
1 oz		50	1206	1395	+1.3
		75	1101	1162	+0.9
		100	1024	1007	-1.3
K.O. Sabot 12 GA	Smooth or rifled	Muzzle	1673	2686	-2.0
3"		25	1487	2122	+0.0
1 oz		50	1325	1685	+1.0
		75	1191	1361	+0.7
		100	1090	1139	-1.1
Black Magic Short Mag 12 GA	Smooth or Rifled	Muzzle	1560	2375	-2.0
2 3/4"		25	1306	1664	+0.1
1 oz		50	1135	1258	+1.2
		75	1044	1063	+0.7
		100	929	842	-1.4
Black Magic	Smooth or rifled	Muzzle	1502	3014	-2.0
Magnum 12 GA		25	1295	2241	+0.4
3"		50	1136	1724	+1.6
13/8 oz		75	1030	1418	+1.0
		100	955	1219	-1.5
Magnum 20 GA	Smooth or rifled	Muzzle	1476	2120	-2.0
3"		25	1322	1701	+0.4
1 oz		50	1193	1385	+1.5
		75	1094	1165	+1.2
		100	1022	1016	-1.0
K.O. 12 GA	Smooth or rifled	Muzzle	1600	2491	-2.0
23/4"		25	1377	1845	+0.3
1 oz		50	1199	1399	+1.5
		75	1072	1118	+1.2
		100	987	948	-1.0
Heavy Field Short	Smooth or rifled	Muzzle	1476	2538	-2.0
Magnum 12 GA		25	1310	2000	+0.4
23/4"		50	1174	1606	+1.5
11/4 oz		75	1075	1346	+1.0
		100	1002	1170	-1.4
Tactical Home Defense	Smooth or rifled	Muzzle	1378	1854	-2.0
12 GA		25	1181	1362	+0.5
23/4"		50	1066	1110	0
1 oz		75	968	915	+0.4
		100	896	785	-2.9
Magnum .410	Smooth or rifled	Muzzle	1755	781	-2.0
3"		25	1427	517	+0.2
1/4 oz		50	1179	352	+1.4
		75	1025	266	+1.0
		100	930	219	-1.4
Heavy Field Short Mag 20 GA	Smooth or rifled	Muzzle	1392	1890	-2.0
23/4"		25	1209	1431	-0.4
1 oz.		50	1110	1201	+1.6
		75	950	884	-0.2
		100	881	761	-2.8

Federal Ammunition

The Premium label covers Federal's best big game loads, featuring bullets, including Nosler partition and AccuBond, Solid Base, Ballistic Tip, Trophy Bonded, and Sierra GameKing. The Barnes Triple-Shock X-Bullet are offered under the Vital Shok label. The Cape Shok list includes loads for the .375 H&H, .416 Rigby, .416 Remington Magnum, .458 Winchester and .470 Nitro Express. Choose a Partition, Bear Claw or Woodleigh Weldcore softpoint, or a Woodleigh or Trophy Bonded solid. V Shok ammunition features Ballistic Tip, Sierra Varminter and others.

The Power Shok line featuring hunting loads from the .222 to the .375 Holland and .45-70 Government, includes the .308 and .30-06 with low recoil loads. Also on the Power Shok list: the .270 and 7mm Winchester Short Magnums, with 130- and 150-grain loads at 3250 and 3200 fps.

Federal has added a .45 G.A.P. (Glock Automatic Pistol) 185-grain load to its American Eagle handgun offerings and a high-performance 3-inch 20-gauge listing that kicks a 5/8-ounce Barnes slug out the muzzle at 1900 fps.

Federal Ammunition

TROPHY BONDED BEAR CLAW

This legendary Jack Carter design is ideal for medium to large dangerous game and is loaded exclusivly by Federal. The jacket and core are 100% fusion-bonded for reliable bullet expansion from 25 yards to extreme ranges. The bullet retains 95% of its weight, assuring deep penetration. The bullet jacket features a hard solid copper base tapering to a soft, copper nose section for controlled expansion.

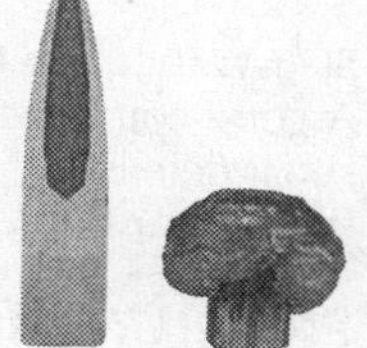

TROPHY BONDED SLEDGEHAMMER

Use it on the largest, most dangerous game in the world. This Jack Carter design maximizes stopping power and your confidence. It's a bonded bronze solid with a flat nose that minimizes deflection off bone and muscle for a deep, straight wound channel.

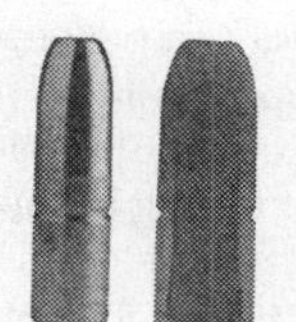

SIERRA GAMEKING BOAT-TAIL

Long ranges are its specialty. With varying calibers, it's an excellent choice for everything from varmints to big game animals. The GameKings's tapered, boat-tail design provides extremely flat trajectories. The design also gives it a higher downrange velocity, so there's more energy at the point of impact. Reduced wind drift makes it a good choice for long-range shots.

WOODLEIGH WELDCORE

Safari hunters have long respected this bonded Australian bullet for its superb accuracy and excellent stopping power. Its special heavy jacket provides 80-85% weight retention. These bullets are favored for large or dangerous game.

NOSLER PARTITION

This Nosler design is a proven choice for medium to large game animals. A partioned copper jacket allows the front half of the bullet to mushroom, while the rear core remains intact, driving forward for deep penetration and stopping power.

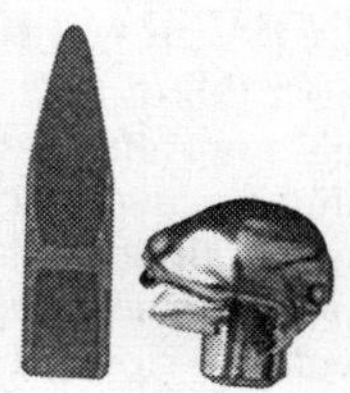

NOSLER BALLISTIC TIP

With proven fast, flat-shooting wind-defying performance, it's specially designed for long-range shots at varmints, predators and small to medium game. A color-coded polycarbonate tip provides easy identification, prevents deformation in the magazine and drives back on impact for expansion and immediate energy transfer.

NOSLER ACCUBOND

AccuBond combines the terminal performance of a bonded bullet with the accuracy and retained energy of a Ballistic Tip. Loads in .280 Rem., 7mm-08, 7mm Rem. Mag. and 7mm Win Short Mag.

BARNES TRIPLE SHOCK X-BULLET

The TSX-Bullet delivers superior expansion and deep penetration. The all-copper design provides high weight retention for knockdown power.

NOSLER SOLID BASE BOAT-TAIL

A Federal exclusive, Solid Base is accurate and consistent. Its tapered jacket and boat-tail design provides controlled expansion and reliable performance. Available in 21 configurations.

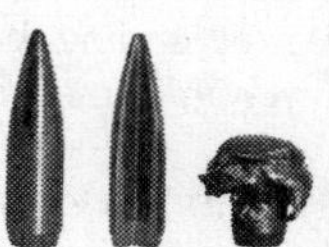

Federal Ammunition

POWER•SHOK CENTERFIRE RIFLE

Soft Point

It's a proven performer on small game and thin-skinned medium game. It has an aerodynamic tip for a flat trajectory. The exposed soft point expands rapidly for hard hits, even as velocity slows at longer ranges.

Soft Point Round Nose

For generations, hunters have made this bullet the choice for deer and bear in heavy cover. Its large exposed tip, good weight retention and specially tapered jacket provide controlled expansion for deep penetration.

Soft Point Flat Nose

This is the bullet hunters traditionally choose when headed into thick cover. It expands reliably and penetrates deep on light to medium game. The flat nose prevents accidental discharge in tubular magazines.

Full Metal Jacket Boat-Tail

These accurate, non-expanding bullets give you a flat shooting trajectory, leave a small exit hole in game, and puts clean holes in paper - great for sharpening your shooting eye. And they're famous for smooth, reliable feeding into semi-automatics too.

HANDGUN BULLET STYLES

Lead Round Nose

A great economical training round for practicing at the range. It dates back to the early part of this century. This bullet is 100% lead with no jacket. It provides excellent accuracy and is very economical.

Full Metal Jacket

A good choice for range practice and reducing lead fouling in the barrel. The jacket extends from the nose to the base, preventing bullet expansion and barrel leading. It is used primarily as military ammunition and for recreational shooting.

Hi-Shok Jacketed Soft Point

It's a proven performer on small to medium-sized game.

Lead Semi-Wadcutter

The most popular all-around choice for target and personal defense. a versatile design which cuts clean holes in targets and efficiently transfers energy.

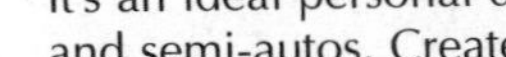

Jacketed Hollow Point

It's an ideal personal defense round in revolvers and semi-autos. Creates quick, positive expansion with proven accuracy. Specially designed jacket ensures smooth feeding into autoloading firearms.

Semi-Wadcutter Hollow Point

A good combination for both small game and personal defense. Hollow point design promotes uniform expansion.

PREMIUM HANDGUN BULLET STYLES

Hydra-Shok

The choice of law enforcement agencies nationwide. Federal's unique center-post design delivers controlled expansion, and the notched jacket provides efficient energy transfer to penetrate barriers while retaining stopping power. The deep penetration of this jacketed bullet satisfies even the FBI's stringent testing requirements.

Premium Personal Defense

We hope you never have to use our Premium Personal Defense ammunition in a critical situation. But, if you do, you'll appreciate the increased muzzle velocity and energy compared to standard loads, and the rapid bullet expansion that delivers instant stopping power. You'll also appreciate that recoil is significantly reduced. In addition, our unique clear packaging lets you see the ammo before you open the box.

An ideal choice for agencies that don't permit hollow point ammunition, this revolutionary barrier-penetrating design combines a scored metal nose over an internal rubber tip that collapses on impact. It never fills with barrier material and assures expansion on every shot. A lead core at the base maintains weight retension.

CastCore

Premium CastCore gives you a heavyweight, flat nosed, hard cast-lead bullet that smashes through bone, without breaking apart.

Trophy Bonded Bear Claw

The Trophy Bonded Bear Claw handgun bullet has a fusion-bonded jacket and core for up to 95% weight retention, better penetration and more knockdown power.

Fiocchi Ammunition

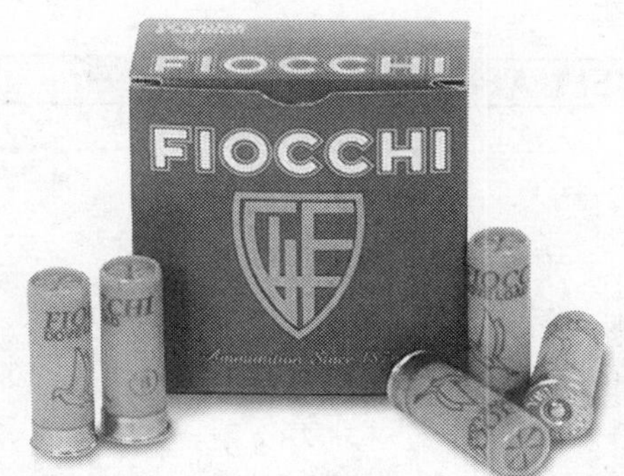

Known for its shotshells and .22 rimfire ammunition, Fiocchi also markets centerfire pistol and rifle cartridges. This Italian firm has been in business since 1876.

Fiocchi Target Loads offer you many choices to suit the shell to your game: Standard 1⅛-ounce loads for everything from registered trap and skeet to sporting clays. One-ounce loads that deliver superior performance with less recoil than a comparable 1⅛-ounce load. Also, a ⅞-ounce training load for new or recoil sensitive shooters. Fiocchi lilac-colored hulls are fully reloadable.

Stock #		Gauge	Shell Length	Dram. Equiv.	Muzzle Velocity	Shot Oz.	Shot Sizes	Rds./Box	Shot Type
Steel (Waterfowl Loads)									
1235ST	Speed Steel	12	3 1/2"	Max.	1520	1 3/8	T BBB BB 1 2	25	Treated Steel
1235SH	Heavy Steel	12	3 1/2"	Max.	1470	1 9/16	T BBB BB 1	25	Treated Steel
123ST	Speed Steel	12	3"	Max.	1475	1 1/8	BBB BB 1 2 3 4	25	Treated Steel
123S	Steel	12	3"	Max.	1320	1 1/4	T BBB BB 1 2 3 4	25	Treated Steel
12SLR7	Low Recoil Target	12	2 3/4"	Lite	1200	1	7	25	Treated Steel
12S78	Training Load	12	2 3/4"	Max.	1440	7/8	7	25	Treated Steel
12S1OZ	Upland Steel	12	2 3/4"	Max.	1400	1	4 6 7	25	Treated Steel
12S118	Steel	12	2 3/4"	Max.	1375	1 1/8	BB 1 2 3 4 6	25	Treated Steel
20SLR	Low Recoil Target	20	2 3/4"	Lite	1225	7/8	7	25	Treated Steel
20S	Upland Steel	20	2 3/4"	Max.	1470	3/4	3 4 6 7	25	Treated Steel
203ST	Speed Steel	20	3"	Max.	1500	7/8	2 3 4	25	Treated Steel
Field Loads (Upland Game Loads)									
12HF	Heavy Field	12	2 3/4"	3 1/4	1225	1 1/4	6 7-12/ 8 9	25	Lead
12FLD	Field Load	12	2 3/4"	3 1/4	1255	1 1/8	6 7-1/2 8 9	25	Lead
16FLD	Field Load	16	2 3/4"	2 3/4	1185	1 1/8	6 7-12 8	25	Lead
20FLD	Field Load	20	2 3/4"	2 1/2	1165	1	6 7-1/2 8 9	25	Lead
Dove Loads									
12MS3	Multi-Sport	12	2 3/4"	3	1250	1	7-1/2 8 9	25	Lead
12MS118	Multi-Sport	12	2 3/4"	2 3/4	1150	1 1/8	7 1/2 8	25	Lead
12GT	Game & Target	12	2 3/4"	3 1/4	1290	1	6 7-1/2 8 9	25	Lead
12GT118	Game & Target	12	2 3/4"	3	1200	1 1/8	7-1/2 8	25	Lead
16GT	Game & Target	16	2 3/4"	2 1/2	1165	1	7-1/2 8 9	25	Lead
20GT	Game & Target	20	2 3/4"	2 1/2	1210	7/8	7-1/2 8 9	25	Lead
28GT	Game & Target	28	2 3/4"	2	1200	3/4	8 9	25	Lead
410GT	Game & Target	410	2 1/2"	Max	1200	1/2	8 9	25	Lead
Target Loads									
12TL	Target Light	12	2 3/4"	2 3/4	1150	1	7-1/2 8 8-1/2 9	25	Hi-Antimony Lead
12TH	Target Heavy	12	2 3/4"	3	1200	1	7-1/2 8 8-1/2	25	Hi-Antimony Lead
12TX	Little Rhino	12	2 3/4"	HDCP	1250	1	7-1/2 8 8-1/2	25	Hi-Antimony Lead
12CRSR	Crusher	12	2 3/4"	Max	1300	1	7-1/2 8 8-1/2 9	25	Hi-Antimony Lead
12SCRS	Super Crusher	12	2 3/4"	Max.	1400	1	6 7 1/2	25	Hi-Antimony Lead
12LITE	Lite	12	2 3/4"	2 7/8	1165	1 1/8	7-1/2 8 9	25	Hi-Antimony Lead
12VIPL	VIP Light	12	2 3/4"	2 3/4	1150	1 1/8	7-1/2 8 9	25	Hi-Antimony Lead
12VIPH	VIP Heavy	12	2 3/4"	3	1200	1 1/8	7-1/2 8 9	25	Hi-Antimony Lead
12WRNO	White Rhino	12	2 3/4"	HDCP	1250	1 1/8	7-1/2 8 8-1/2 9	25	Hi-Antimony Lead
1278OZ	Training Load	12	2 3/4"	3	1200	7/8	7-1/2 8	25	Hi-Antimony Lead
12IN24	International	12	2 3/4"	Max	1350	24 grams	7-1/2 8 9	25	Hi-Antimony Lead
12TRAPL	Low Recoil Trap Light	12	2 3/4"	2 3/4	1140	1 1/8	7 1/2 8	25	Hi-Antimony Lead
12TRAPH	Low Recoil Trap Heavy	12	2 3/4"	3	1185	1 1/8	7 1/2 8	251	Hi-Antimony Lead
Golden Pheasant									
12GP	Field Load	12	2 3/4"	3 3/4	1250	1 3/8	4 5 6	25	Nickel Plated
12GPX	Field Load	12	2 3/4"	Max.	1485	1 3/8	4 5 6	25	Nickel Plated
123GP	Heavy Field	12	3"	Max.	1200	1 3/4	4 5 6	25	Nickel Plated
16GP	Field Load	16	2 3/4"	3 1/4	1310	1 1/8	5	25	Nickel Plated
20GP	Field Load	20	2 3/4"	2 7/8	1245	1	5 6 7 1/2	25	Nickel Plated
203GP	Heavy Field	20	3"	Max.	1200	1 1/4	4 5 6	25	Nickel Plated
28GP	Field Load	28	2 3/4"	Max.	1300	7/8	6 7 1/2	8 25	Nickel Plated
High Velocity									
12HV	High Velocity	12	2 3/4"	3 3/4	1330	1 1/4	4 5 6 7-1/2 8 9	25	Lead
123HV	High Velocity	12	3"	Max	1330	1 3/4	6	25	Lead
16HV	High Velocity	16	2 3/4"	3 1/8	1300	1 1/8	4 6 7-1/2 8	25	Lead
20HV	High Velocity	20	2 3/4"	2 3/4	1220	1	4 5 6 7-1/2 8 9	25	Lead
28HV	High Velocity	28	2 3/4"	2 1/4	1300	3/4	6 7-1/2 8 9	25	Lead
410HV	High Velocity	410	3"	Max	1140	11/16	6 7-1/2 8 9	25	Lead

Fiocchi Ammunition

SHOTSHELL APPLICATION GUIDE

Game	Lead Shot Size	Steel Shot Size	Recommended Loads
Geese	NA	T-BBB-BB-1	Heavy Steel, Speed Steel
Ducks	NA	BB-1-2-3-4-6	Heavy Steel, Speed Steel, Upland Steel
Pheasant	4-5-6	3-4-5-6	Golden Pheasant, HV, Speed Steel, Upland Steel, HVN
Turkey	4-5-6	4-5	Turkey Tunder, HV, HVN
Grouse/Partridge	5-6-7 1/2-8	4-6-7	Field Loads, Upland Steel, HV, HVN, HFN
Quail	7 1/2-8-9	7	Field Loads, HV, Upland Steel, HVN, HFN
Dove/Pigeon	6-7 1/2-8-9	6-7	Field Loads, GT, Dove, HV, HFN, HVN
Rabbit/Squirrel	4-5-6-7 1/2	6-7	Field Loads, HV, GT, Upland Steel, HFN, HVN
Deer/Boar	00-Slug	NA	12HV00BK, 12 Gauge Slug, 20 Gauge Slug
Trap	7 1/2-8-8 1/2	6-7	TL, TH, TX, VIP, LITE, WRNO, MS, TRAPH, TRAPL
Skeet	8-8 1/2-9	7	TL, TH, TX, VIP, LITE, WRNO, MS
Sporting Clays	7 1/2-8-8 1/2-9	7	TL, TH, TX, TIP, LITE, WRNO, MS
Steel Target			Upland Steel, Training Load

SHOT PELLET SIZES

Size #	9	8-1/2	8	7-1/2	6	5	4	3	2	1	BB	BBB	T	#4	00
Dia.In.	.08	.085	.09	.095	.11	.12	.13	.14	.15	.16	.18	.19	.20	.24	.33
Dia.MM	2.03	2.16	2.29	2.41	2.79	3.05	3.30	3.56	3.81	4.06	4.57	4.83	5.08	6.10	8.38

LEAD SHOT

Shot Size	1/2	1/16	3/4	7/8	1	1 1/8	1 1/4	1 3/8	1 3/4	2
9	290	398	434	507	579	685	724			
8 1/2				423	483					
8	204	280	305	356	407	458	509			
7 1/2		238	260	303	346	389	433			
6		153	167	194	222	250	278	305	389	444
5		118			171	192	214	235	299	342
4					135	152	169	186	236	270

STEEL SHOT

Shot Size	3/4	7/8	1	1 1/8	1 1/4	1 3/8	1 9/16
7	315	368	420				
6	237		316	356			
4	143	167	191	215	239	263	
3	115	134		172	191	210	
2		109		141	156	172	
1				116	129	142	161
BB				81	90	99	113
BBB				69	76	84	95
T					66	73	83

Note: When comparing steel shot to lead shot, increase shot size by two to get similar downrange results (i.e. Lead #4 to Steel #2). Check your shotgun and choke manufacturer for steel shot compatibility.

Fiocchi Ammunition

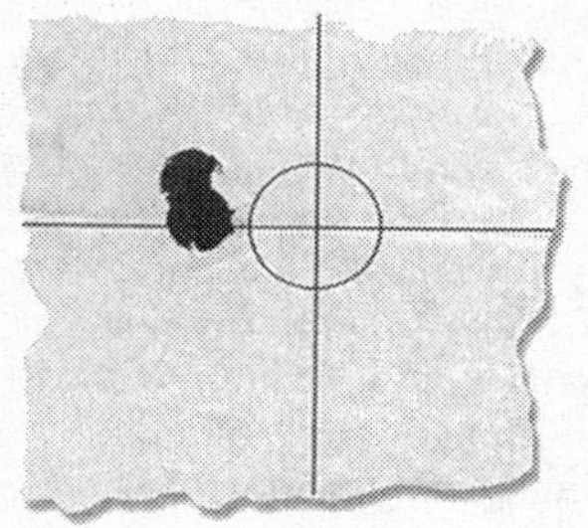

Stock #	Gauge	Shell Length	Dram. Equiv.	Muzzle Velocity	Pellet Ct.	Shot Sizes	Rds. Box	Shot Type
Buckshot								
12HV4BK Buckshot	12	2 3/4"	Max	1325	27 pell.	4 Buck	10	Hi-Antimony Nicke-Plated
12HV00BK Buckshot	12	2 3/4"	Max	1325	9 pell.	00 Buck	10	Hi-Antimony Nickel-Plated
12LE00BK Reduced Recoil*	12	2 3/4"	Lite	1150	9 pell.	00 Buck	10	Hi-Antimony Nickel-Plated

Stock #		Gauge	Shell Length	MM	Dram. Equiv.	Muzzle Velocity	Shot Oz.	Shot Sizes	Rds. Box	Shot Type
Slugs										
12SLUG	Trophy Slug	12	2 3/4"	70	Max	1560	1	Rifled Slug	5	Lead w/attached Wad
20TS78	Trophy Slug	20	2 3/4"	70	Max	1650	7/8	Rifled Slug	5	Lead w/attached Wad

Stock #	Gauge	Shell Length	Dram. Equiv.	Muzzle Velocity	Shot Oz.	Shot Sizes	Rds. Box	Shot Type
Nickel Plated Hunting Loads								
12HFN Heavy Field Nickel	12	2 3/4"	3 1/4	1225	1 1/4	7-1/2 8	25	Nickel-Plated Lead
12HVN High Velocity Nickel	12	2 3/4"	3 3/4	1330	1 1/4	4 5 6 7-1/2 8	25	Nickel-Plated Lead
12GP Golden Pheasant	12	2 3/4"	Max	1250	1 3/8	4 5 6	25	Nickel-Plated Lead
203GP Golden Pheasant 20	20	3"	Max	1200	1 1/4	4 5 6	25	Nickel-Plated Lead
Interceptor Spreader								
12CPTR Interceptor	12	2 3/4"	Max	1300	1	7-1/2 8 8-1/2 9	25	Lead
Sporting Clays Power Spreaders								
12SSCH Power Spreader	12	2 3/4"	3	1200	1 1/8	8 8-1/2	25	Lead
12SSCX Power Spreader	12	2 3/4"	Max	1250	1 1/8	8 8-1/2 9	25	Lead
Steel Target Load								
12S78 Steel Target Load	12	2 3/4"	Max	1440	7/8	7	25	Steel
12S1OZ Steel Target Load	12	2 3/4"	Max	1400	1	4 6 7	25	Steel
20S Steel Target Load	20	2 3/4"	Max	1470	3/4	3 4 6 7	25	
Ultra Low Recoil Loads								
1278OZ Trainer	12	2 3/4"	Lite	1200	7/8	7-1/2 8	25	Hi-Antimony Lead
20LITE Trainer	20	2 3/4″	Lite	1075	3/4	7 1/2	25	Hi-Antimony Lead
Multi-Sport Loads-Game & Target								
12MS3 Multi-Sport	12	2 3/4"	3	1250	1	7-1/2 8 9	25	Lead
12GT Game & Target	12	2 3/4"	3 1/4	1290	1	6 7-1/2 8 9	25	Lead
12GT118 Game & Target	12	2 3/4"	3	1200	1 1/8	7-1/2 8	25	Lead
Low Recoil Trap Loads								
12TRAPL Low-Recoil Trap Light	12	2 3/4"	2 3/4	1140	1 1/8	7-1/2 8	25	Hi-Antimony Lead
12TRAPH Low-Recoil Trap Heavy	12	2 3/4"	3	1185	1 1/8	7-1/2 8	25	Hi-Antimony
Steel Low Recoil Loads								
12SLR Low Recoil Steel	12	2 3/4″	Lite	1200	1	7	25	Treated Steel
20SLR Low Recoil Steel	20	2 3/4″	Lite	1225	7/8	7	25	Treated Steel

Note: When comparing steel shot to lead shot, increase shot size by two to get similar downrange results (i.e. Lead #4 to Steel #2). Check your shotgun and choke manufacturer for steel shot compatibility.

Hornady

Based on the high-performance .22 Stinger case, Hornady's .17 Mach 2 fits the mechanisms of ordinary .22s. It functions in self-loaders, and the tiny 17-grain V-Max bullet flies flatter than bullets from any .22 Long Rifle ammunition.

Hornady's .204 Ruger derives from the .222 Magnum. A 32-grain polymer-tipped, V-Max bullet, .204 in diameter, clocks 4200 fps. Hornady has cataloged a 40-grain load at 3900 fps. Ruger is chambering both its 77 bolt rifle and Number One dropping-block single-shot for the .204. An endearing quality of the .204 is its mild recoil.

Hornady offers a .500 Smith & Wesson handgun cartridge with a 350-grain XTP bullet that clocks 1900 fps at the muzzle of a 7½-inch barrel.

Hornady has brought the old war-horse favored by Teddy Roosevelt into the 21st century by designing a high-performance cartridge that delivers amazing power and accuracy from the .405 Winchester. The .405 Winchester cartridge is loaded with a 300-grain FP bullet at 2200 fps. Other big-bore ammo: the .444 Marlin Light Magnum with a 265-grain bullet at 2335 fps and, for dangerous African game, the.458 Lott with a 500-grain bullet at 2300 fps.

405 WINCHESTER

500 S&W

.204 RUGER

204 RUGER

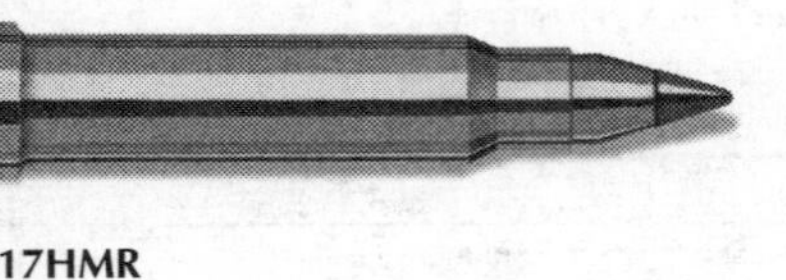

17HMR

17HMR 20 GR XTP

.17 MACH 2

Kynoch

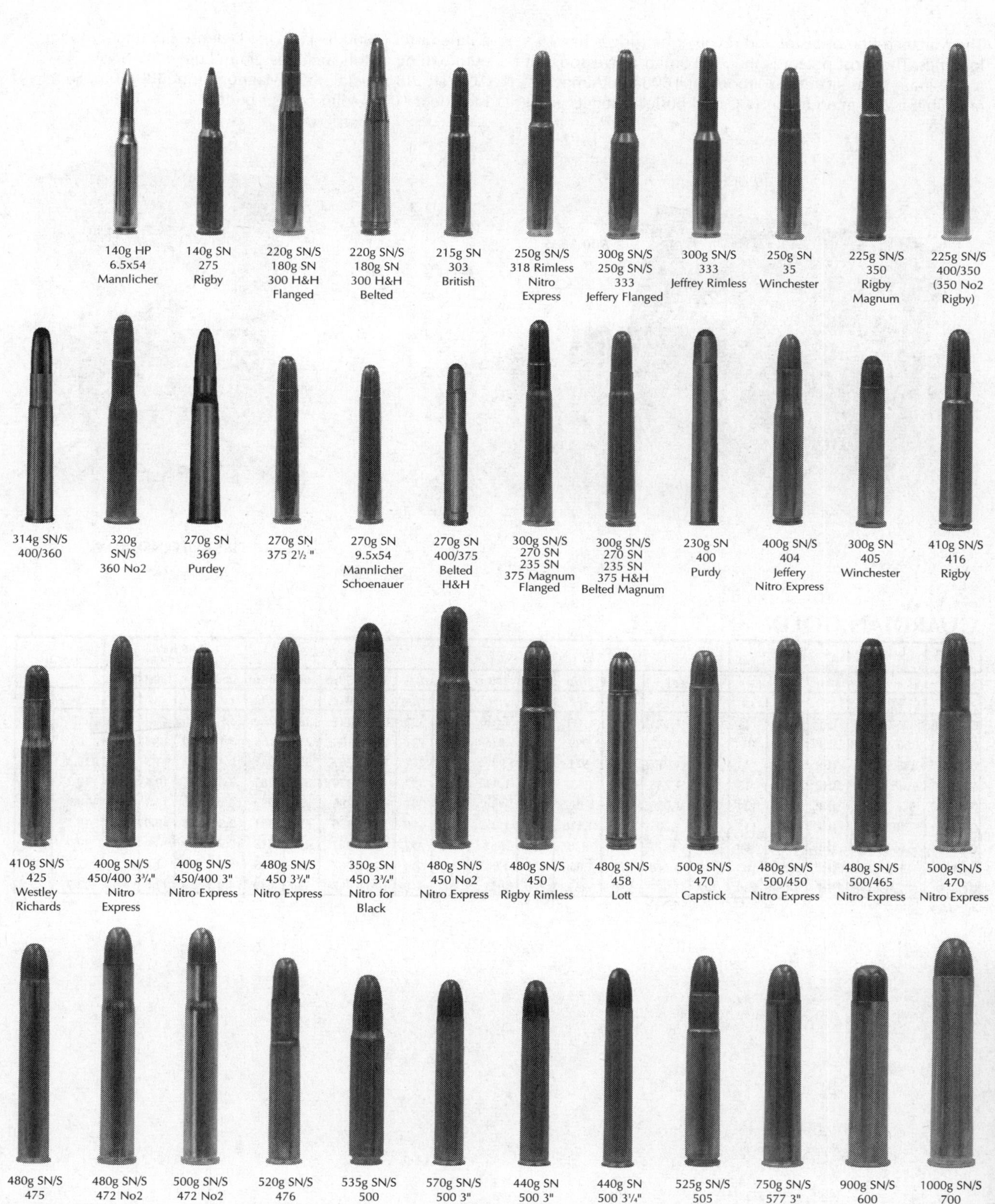
140g HP 6.5x54 Mannlicher
140g SN 275 Rigby
220g SN/S 180g SN 300 H&H Flanged
220g SN/S 180g SN 300 H&H Belted
215g SN 303 British
250g SN/S 318 Rimless Nitro Express
300g SN/S 250g SN/S 333 Jeffery Flanged
300g SN/S 333 Jeffrey Rimless
250g SN 35 Winchester
225g SN/S 350 Rigby Magnum
225g SN/S 400/350 (350 No2 Rigby)
314g SN/S 400/360
320g SN/S 360 No2
270g SN 369 Purdey
270g SN 375 2½ "
270g SN 9.5x54 Mannlicher Schoenauer
270g SN 400/375 Belted H&H
300g SN/S 270 SN 235 SN 375 Magnum Flanged
300g SN/S 270 SN 235 SN 375 H&H Belted Magnum
230g SN 400 Purdy
400g SN/S 404 Jeffery Nitro Express
300g SN 405 Winchester
410g SN/S 416 Rigby
410g SN/S 425 Westley Richards
400g SN/S 450/400 3¼" Nitro Express
400g SN/S 450/400 3" Nitro Express
480g SN/S 450 3¼" Nitro Express
350g SN 450 3¼" Nitro for Black
480g SN/S 450 No2 Nitro Express
480g SN/S 450 Rigby Rimless
480g SN/S 458 Lott
500g SN/S 470 Capstick
480g SN/S 500/450 Nitro Express
480g SN/S 500/465 Nitro Express
500g SN/S 470 Nitro Express
480g SN/S 475 Nitro Express
480g SN/S 472 No2 Eley
500g SN/S 472 No2 Jeffrey
520g SN/S 476 Nitro Express
535g SN/S 500 Jeffrey
570g SN/S 500 3" Nitro Express
440g SN 500 3" Nitro for Black
440g SN 500 3¼" Nitro for Black
525g SN/S 505 Gibbs
750g SN/S 577 3" Nitro Express
900g SN/S 600 Nitro Express
1000g SN/S 700 Nitro Express

Magtech Ammunition

The Magtech line of pistol and revolver cartridges has 15 loadings. The most potent is the .500 Smith & Wesson, with a 400-grain semi-jacketed softpoint at 1608 fps. Almost as crushing: a 260-grain FMJ.454 Casull bullet that gets going a little faster (1800 fps). A First Defense line of ammo for autoloading pistols includes: 9mm Luger, .40 S&W, .45 ACP +P, .38 Special, .357 Magnum and .380 Auto. Features include a 100% solid copper bullet.

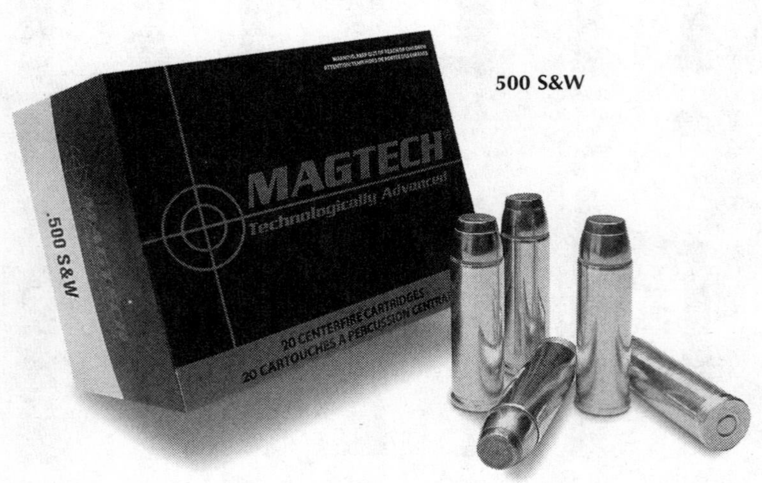

500 S&W

FIRST DEFENSE BOX

GUARDIAN GOLD

Symbol	Caliber	Bullet			Velocity						Energy						Mid-Range Trajectory				Test Barrel Length	
		Style	Weight		Muzzle		50m	50yd	100m	100yd	Muzzle		50m	50yd	100m	100yd	50m	50yd	100m	100yd		
			g	gr	m/s	fps	m/s	fps	m/s	fps	J	ft/lbs	J	ft/lbs	J	ft/lbs	cm	inch	cm	inch	cm	inch
GG357A	.357 Mag	JHP	8.10	125	420	1,378	353	1,170	307	1,020	714	527	505	381	382	289	1.5	0.5	7.5	2.5	10.2V	4-V
GG380A	.380 Auto+P	JHP	5.5	85	330	1,082	303	999	282	936	300	221	252	188	219	166	3.1	1.0	13.3	4.3	9.5	3¾
GG38A	.38 SPL+P	JHP	8.10	125	310	1,017	295	971	282	931	389	287	352	262	322	241	3.4	1.1	14.3	4.6	10.2	4
GG9A	9mm Luger+P	JHP	7.45	115	380	1,246	344	1,137	318	1,056	538	397	441	330	377	285	2.4	0.8	10.5	3.4	10.2	4
GG9B	9mm Luger	JHP	8.03	124	334	1,096	304	1,017	286	958	448	331	371	285	328	253	3.1	1.0	12.5	4.1	10.2	4
GG40A	.40 S&W	JHP	10.0	155	367	1,205	338	1,118	317	1,052	677	500	571	430	523	381	2.5	0.8	10.9	3.5	10.2	4
GG40B	.40 S&W	JHP	11.66	180	302	990	282	938	268	891	532	392	463	352	419	318	3.7	1.2	13.4	4.5	10.2	4
GG45A	.45 Auto+P	JHP	12.0	185	350	1,148	323	1,066	303	1,005	735	540	626	467	551	415	2.7	0.9	11.8	3.8	12.7	5
GG45B	.45 Auto+P	JHP	14.90	230	307	1,007	290	965	279	927	702	518	626	467	580	440	4.0	1.3	12.5	4.0	12.7	5

PMC Ammunition

SILVER RIFLE

PMC (PRECISION MADE CARTRIDGES) is the same firm as Eldorado Cartridge Company. It is a growing enterprise whose product line has expanded substantially this year, offering new sporting and tactical centerfire rounds from its rural Nevada digs. Handgun ammo, from .25 Auto to .44 Magnum, includes loads specifically for Cowboy Action shooting. The centerfire rifle stable has cowboy action loads in .30-30 and .45-70, plus a wide variety of hunting and match ammunition from .222 Remington to .375 H&H Magnum. The selection of .22 rimfire rounds features hunting, plinking and match loads.

A broad choice of pistol bullets is available from PMC. There's the quick-opening Starfire hollowpoint, a traditional jacketed hollowpoint, a jacketed softpoint and a full-metal-jacket (hardball) bullet—plus lead wadcutter, semi-wadcutter and round-nose options. Rifle bullets include the Barnes X-Bullet, .30-30 Starfire hollowpoint, Sierra boat-tail hollowpoint, Sierra boat-tail softpoint, pointed softpoint, softpoint, flat-nose softpoint and full metal jacket. PMC also manufactures shotshells, from light dove and quail and target loads to heavy steel-shot loads for geese.

PMC Ammunition

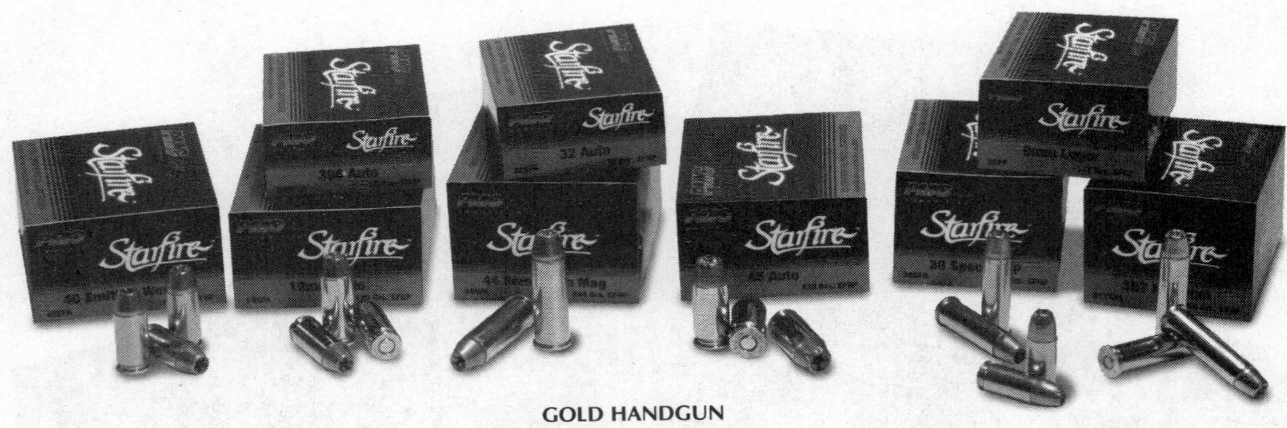

GOLD HANDGUN

GOLDLINE ULTIMATE HIGH VELOCITY

GREEN PISTOL

PMC FIELD & TARGET SHOTSHELLS

PMC's shotshell line includes the Gold Line Ultimate High Velocity shotshell. Available in $2\frac{3}{4}$-inch 12-, 20- and 28-gauge offerings and 3-inch .410, the new shells feature shot sizes ranging from 4 to 9. The 12-bore $1\frac{1}{4}$-ounce load chronographs 1400 fps. A 1-ounce 20-gauge charge leaves the muzzle at 1300, the $\frac{7}{8}$-ounce 28 at 1250 and the $\frac{11}{16}$-ounce .410 at 1135. Also: extra heavy Silver Line shotshells, 12-gauge only, with $1\frac{3}{8}$ ounces of shot at 1320 fps. Choose 4, 5, 6 or $7\frac{1}{2}$ shot size. PMC has included target loads for the .410 and 28 gauge both with a velocity of 1220 fps. To round out its shotgun ammo list, the firm has a 12-gauge deer load with a $\frac{7}{8}$-ounce slug in a sabot sleeve.

PMC "GREEN" LINE

In centerfire ammunition, there's a "PMC Green" line with non-toxic frangible loads for the .223, .308 and 7.62x39 (bullet weights 40, 120 and 100 grains). Seven pistol rounds, from .38 Special to .357 Sig and .45 ACP, are included.

PMC Gold, Silver and Bronze hunting loads range from .223 to .375 H&H, The Gold Line features Barnes XLC-HP bullets, the Silver Line Sierra BlitzKing and Match bullets, with softpoint boattails. The Bronze Line has softpoint and pointed softpoint bullets. New this year are .45-90 and .40-65 rifle cartridges for the Cowboy Action shooter, and Predator .22 WMR ammo with a 40-grain full-jacket bullet at 1910 fps.

PREMIER HEVI-SHOT MAGNUM TURKEY LOADS

If you're passionate about turkey hunting, Premier Hevi-Shot is the load for you. This load won all event classes at the 2001 National Wild Turkey Federation Annual Turkey Shoot. It routinely achieves patterns in excess of 90%. Shot material alloy of tungsten, nickel and iron features a 10% higher density than lead, which yields denser patterns and higher energy—a lead improvement. A superior product for serious turkey hunters.

PREMIER HEVI-SHOT NITRO MAGNUM WATERFOWL LOADS

Premier Hevi-Shot Nitro Magnums are manufactured of a non-toxic tungsten-nickel-iron alloy, Hevi-Shot is 10% denser than lead and an amazing 54% denser than steel. Shooting an equal payload and shot size, Hevi-Shot pellets have 25% more energy at 50 yards than steel pellets have at 30 yards. This allows you to drop down three shot sizes to maintain pattern energy and dramatically increase on-game pellet count. The resulting Hevi-Shot patterning, with full chokes, yields an average of 88% efficiency.

Density Comparison	
Density Of Steel	7.8
Density Of Lead	10.9
Density Of Hevi-Shot	12.0

Remington Ammunition

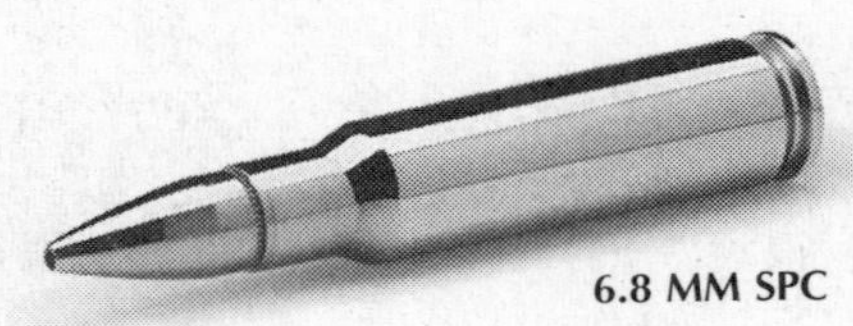

6.8 MM SPC

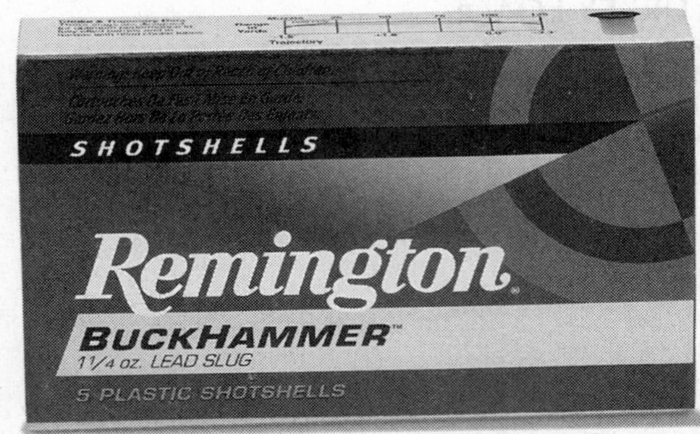

BUCKHAMMER

MANAGED RECOIL

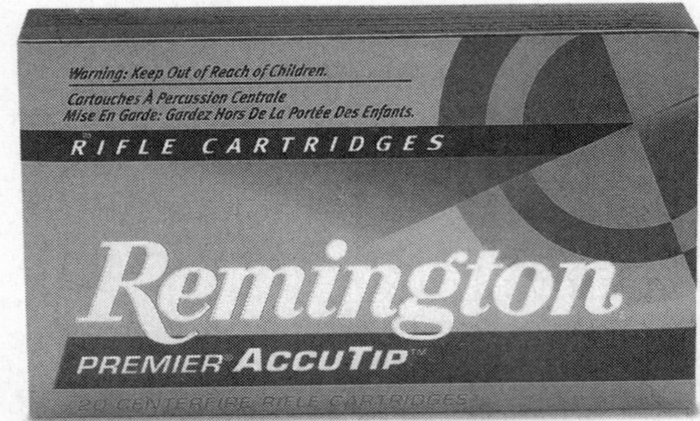

ACCUTIP BOX

NITRO STEEL HV

NITRO STEEL SHOTSHELL

The Nitro Steel high-velocity shotshell has a 1/8-ounce payload of 2s and 4s at 1390 fps. Also available in 3 1/2-inch options: a 1 3/8-ounce charge at 1450 fps. Available for 12-, 20-, 28-gauge and .410. Remington offers Sportsman steel shot in a 10-gauge 3 1/2-inch load (1 3/8 ounces of BBs or 2s at 1500 fps) and a 12-gauge 3-inch load (1 1/4, BB, 1, 2, 3, 4).

BUCKHAMMER SHOTGUN SLUG

The Buckhammer shotgun slug, is available 12-gauge 2 3/4-inch loads and 3-inch 12 and 2 3/4-inch 20-gage hulls. The new loads feature 1 3/8- and 1-ounce slugs respectively, at 1500 fps. Muzzle energy: 3232 and 2236 ft-lbs.

MANAGED RECOIL

The Managed Recoil loads generate half the kick of ordinary ammunition. The bullets are designed for 2x expansion and 75-percent weight retention between 50 and 200 yards. Managed Recoil loads are available in .270 (115-grain bullet), .30-06 (125-grain) and 7mm Rem. Mag. (140-grain). Muzzle velocities are 2710, 2660 and 2710 fps, respectively. All deliver more than 1100 ft-lbs of energy to 200 yards.

ACCUTIP

The Remington Premier AccuTip line includes the 6.8mm Remington SPC, .223, .308, .300 Winchester Magnum and .300 Remington Short Ultra Mag.

Remington Ammunition

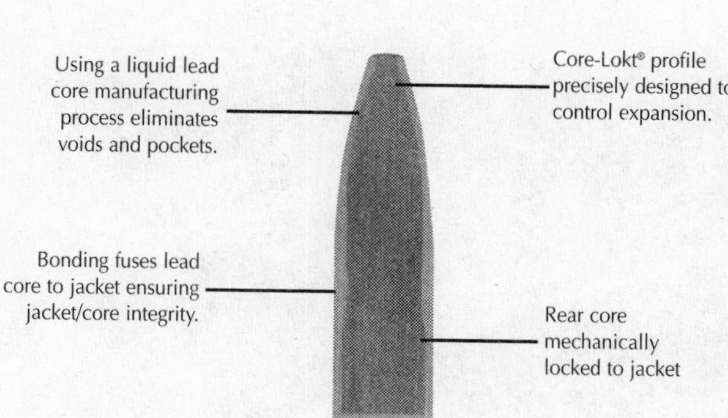
Using a liquid lead core manufacturing process eliminates voids and pockets.
Core-Lokt® profile precisely designed to control expansion.
Bonding fuses lead core to jacket ensuring jacket/core integrity.
Rear core mechanically locked to jacket

Remington.
RIFLE CARTRIDGES
PREMIER SHORT ACTION ULTRA MAG
300 REMINGTON SA ULTRA MAG

PREMIER SHORT-ACTION ULTRA MAG

Designed to offer belted magnum performance in a .308-length action, SA Ultra Mag cartridges headspace off the shoulder, rather than a belt, promoting more precise bore alignment and improved accuracy. Furthermore, the highly efficient case design duplicates or exceeds belted magnum ballistics with less powder, which in turn means less felt recoil. Finally, the entire package achieves greater down-range velocity and energy than traditional 300 Win Mag and 7mm Remington Mag calibers. SA Ultra Mag ammo will be available to match Remington's Model Seven Magnum rifles in two popular calibers: 300 Remington SA Ultra Mag and 7mm Remington SA Ultra Mag.

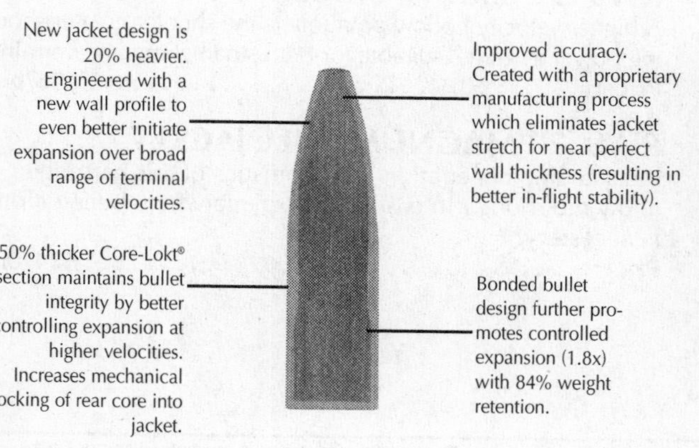
New jacket design is 20% heavier. Engineered with a new wall profile to even better initiate expansion over broad range of terminal velocities.
Improved accuracy. Created with a proprietary manufacturing process which eliminates jacket stretch for near perfect wall thickness (resulting in better in-flight stability).
50% thicker Core-Lokt® section maintains bullet integrity by better controlling expansion at higher velocities. Increases mechanical locking of rear core into jacket.
Bonded bullet design further promotes controlled expansion (1.8x) with 84% weight retention.

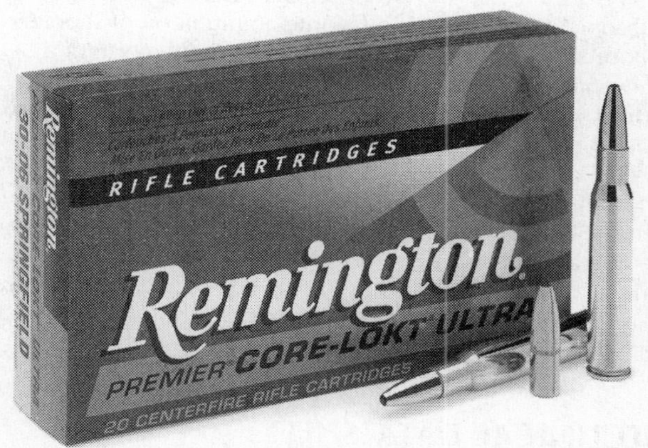
Remington.
RIFLE CARTRIDGES
30-06 SPRINGFIELD
PREMIER CORE-LOKT ULTRA
20 CENTERFIRE RIFLE CARTRIDGES

PREMIER CORE-LOKT ULTRA

Core-Lokt Ultra bonded bullets retain up to 90% of their original weight for maximum penetration and energy transfer. Featuring a progressively-tapered jacket, the Core-Lokt Ultra bullet initiates and controls expansion up to 1.8X. The unique design of the bullet, combined with the bonded lead core, provides the hunter with a Premier bullet that yields unmatched performance from 50 yards to 500 yards and all yardages in between.

RWS Rimfire Cartridges

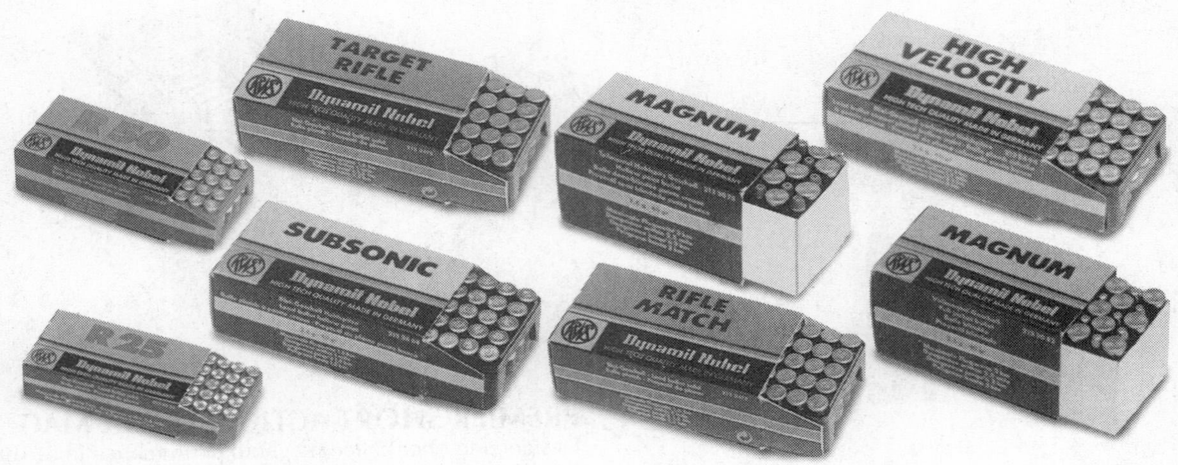

RWS .22 R50

For competitive shooters demanding the ultimate in precision. This cartridge has been used to establish several world records and is used by Olympic Gold Medalists. No finer cartridge can be bought at any price.

Price: $13/box

RWS .22 L.R. RIFLE MATCH

Perfect for the club level target competitor. Accurate and affordable.

Price:. $8/box

RWS .22 L.R. SUBSONIC HOLLOW POINT

Subsonic ammunition is a favorite ammunition of shooters whose shooting range is limited to where the noise of a conventional cartridge would be a problem.

Price:. $5/box

RWS .22 MAGNUM HOLLOW POINT

The soft point allows good expansion on impact, while preserving the penetration characteristics necessary for larger vermin and game.

Price:. $24/box

RWS .22 SHORT R25

Designed for world class Rapid Fire Pistol events, this cartridge provides the shooter with outstanding accuracy and minimal recoil. Manufactured to exacting standards, the shooter can be assured of consistent performance.

Price:. $9/box

RWS .22 L.R. TARGET RIFLE

An ideal training and field cartridge, the .22 Long Rifle Target also excels in informal competitions. The target .22 provides the casual shooter with accuracy at an economical price.

Price:. $4/box

RWS .22 L.R. HV HOLLOW POINT

A higher velocity hollow point offers the shooter greater shocking power in game, suitable for both small game and vermin.

Price:. $6/box

RWS .22 MAGNUM FULL JACKET

Outstanding penetration characteristics of this cartridge allow the shooter to easily tackle game where penetration is necessary.

Price:. $24/box

TECHNICAL DATA

			Max.	Velocity (ft./sec.)			Energy (ft./lbs.)			Trajectory inches above (+) or below (-) line of sight									
Cartridges	Bullet Style	Bullet Weight (grains)	Chamber Pressure (psi)	Muzzle	50Y	100Y	Muzzle	50Y	100Y	Open Sight At	25 yds	50 yds	75 yds	100yds	Scope sighted in at	25 yds	50 yds	75 yds	100 yds
.22 L.R. R 50	Lead	40	25.600	1.070	970	890	100	80	70	--	--	--	--	--	--	--	--	--	--
.22 Short R 25	Lead	28	18.500	560	490	---	20	15	--	--	--	--	--	--	--	--	--	--	--
.22 L.R. Rifle Match	Lead	40	25.600	1.035	945	860	95	80	65	50 yds.	+0.7		-3.2	-9.0	50 yds	+0.1		-2.6	-7.8
.22 L.R. Target Rifle	Lead	40	25.600	1.080	990	900	100	85	70	50 yds.	+0.6		-3.1	-8.7	50 yds	+0.1		-2.5	-7.5
.22 L.R. Subsonic	Hollow Point	40	25.600	1.000	915	835	90	75	60	50 yds.	+0.8		-3.4	-4.7	50 yds	+0.2		+2.8	-8.5
.22 L.R. HV	Lead	40	25.600	1.310	1.120	990	150	110	85		--	--	--	--	--	--	--	--	--
Hollow point	coppered																		
.22 Magnum	Soft Point	40	25.600	2.020	1.710	1.430	360	260	180	100 yds.	+0.6	+1.3	+1.1	0	100 yds	-0.3	+0.7	+0.8	0
.22 Magnum	Full Jacket	40	25.600	2.020	1.710	1.430	360	260	180	100 yds.	+0.6	+1.3	+1.1	0	100 yds	-0.3	+0.7	+0.8	0
.22 LR R100	Lead	40	25.600	1.175	1.065	970	100	80	70	100 yds.	+0.6	+13	+1.1	0	100 yds.	-0.3	+0.7	+0.8	0

WSSM: SPEED AND ACCURACY

Winchester's first Super Short Magnums—the .223 and .243—are so short that new rifle actions (Winchester M70 and Browning A-Bolt) were developed to accommodate them. The .223 is loaded with three bullets: the 55-grain Ballistic Silver-tip, the 55-grain Pointed Soft Point and 64-grain Power Point. They all shoot fast and barrels with over 1000 rounds still fired ½-minute groups. The newest WSSM is a 25-caliber round designed to duplicate or exceed the performance of the .25-06. Two other loads are available in the Supreme line: an 85-grain Ballistic Silvertip at 3470 fps, and a 115 Balllistic Silvertip at 3060.

Winchester Ammunition

SHORT MAGNUMS AND ACCUBONDS

Like the .270, 7mm and .300 WSM, the .325 WSM is loaded with several bullet types, including the Nosler AccuBond. Winchester offers CT (Combined Technology) AccuBond bullets in .270 Win. (140-gr.), .270 WSM, (140-gr.), 7mm Rem. Mag., (160-gr.), 7mm WSM, (160-gr.), .30-06, (180-gr.), .300 Win. Mag., (180-gr.), .300 WSM, (180-gr.), .325 WSM (200-gr.) and 338 Win. Mag., (225-gr.).

SHOTSHELL POTOURRI

Winchester's Super-Target shotshell line in 12 and 20 gauge, are inexpensive but effective on clays. Choose $7\frac{1}{2}$ or 8 shot. The 12-bore $1\frac{1}{8}$-ounce charge can be had with $2\frac{3}{4}$- or 3-dram equivalent thrust—1145 fps or 1200. The $2\frac{1}{2}$-dram 20-bore shells kick $\frac{7}{8}$-ounce shot columns downrange at 1200. Winchester is also fields a 3-inch 12-gauge slug load featuring the 385-grain Partition Gold slug in a sabot.

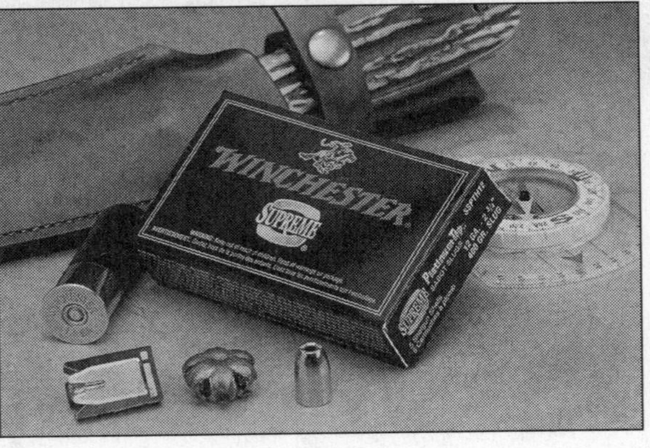

WINCHESTER SUPREME PLATINUM TIP

Winchester handgun ammunition includes the Platinum tip bullet with a notched, reverse-taper jacket with a two-step nose cavity. Supreme Platinum tip hunting ammo is available in .41 Magnum, .44 Magnum and .454 Casull. Platinum Tip Hollow Point Hunting Ammunition is also available in a 12 gauge sabot slug shotshell and as a 50-caliber Muzzleloading sabot bullet, the Platinum Tip Hollow Point bullet.

Centerfire Rifle Ballistics

Comprehensive Ballistics Tables for Currently Manufactured Sporting Rifle Cartridges

No more collecting catalogs and peering at microscopic print to find out what ammunition is offered for a cartridge, and how it performs relative to other factory loads! Shooter's Bible has assembled the data for you, in easy-to-read tables, by cartridge. Of course, this section will be updated every year to bring you the latest information.

Data is taken from manufacturers' charts; your chronograph readings may vary. Listings are current as of February the year Shooter's Bible appears (not the cover year). Listings are not intended as recommendations. For example, the data for the .44 Magnum at 400 yards shows its effective range is much shorter. The lack of data for a 285-grain .375 H&H bullet beyond 300 yards does not mean the bullet has no authority farther out. Besides ammunition, the rifle, sights, conditions and shooter ability all must be considered when contemplating a long shot. Accuracy and bullet energy both matter when big game is in the offing.

Barrel length affects velocity, and at various rates depending on the load. As a rule, figure 50 fps per inch of barrel, plus or minus, if your barrel is longer or shorter than 22 inches.

Bullets are given by make, weight (in grains) and type. Most type abbreviations are self-explanatory: BT=Boat-Tail, FMJ=Full Metal Jacket, HP=Hollow Point, SP=Soft Point—except in Hornady listings, where SP is the firm's Spire Point. TNT and TXP are trademarked designations of Speer and Norma. XLC identifies a coated Barnes X bullet. HE indicates a Federal High Energy load, similar to the Hornady LM (Light Magnum) and HM (Heavy Magnum) cartridges.

Arc (trajectory) is based on a zero range published by the manufacturer, from 100 to 300 yards. If a zero does not fall in a yardage column, it lies halfway between—at 150 yards, for example, if the bullet's strike is "+" at 100 yards and "-" at 200.

.17 REMINGTON TO .222 REMINGTON

.17 Remington

CARTRIDGE BULLET	RANGE, YARDS:	0	100	200	300	400
Rem. 20 AccuTip BT	velocity, fps:	4250	3594	3028	2529	2081
	energy, ft-lb:	802	574	407	284	192
	arc, inches:		+1.3	+1.3	-2.5	-11.8
Rem. 25 HP Power-Lokt	velocity, fps:	4040	3284	2644	2086	1606
	energy, ft-lb:	906	599	388	242	143
	arc, inches:		+1.8	0	-3.3	-16.6

.204 Ruger

CARTRIDGE BULLET	RANGE, YARDS:	0	100	200	300	400
Hornady 32 V-Max	velocity, fps:	4225	3632	3114	2652	2234
	energy, ft-lb:	1268	937	689	500	355
	arc, inches:		+0.6	0	-4.2	-13.4
Hornady 40 V-Max	velocity, fps:	3900	3451	3046	2677	2335
	energy, ft-lb:	1351	1058	824	636	485
	arc, inches:		+0.7	0	-4.5	-13.9
Rem. 32 AccuTip	velocity, fps:	4225	3632	3114	2652	2234
	Energy, ft-lb:	1268	937	689	500	355
	Arc, inches:		+0.6	0	-4.1	-13.1
Rem. 40 AccuTip	velocity, fps:	3900	3451	3046	2677	2336
	energy, ft-lb:	1351	1058	824	636	485
	arc, inches:		+0.7	0	-4.3	-13.2
Win. 34 HP	velocity, fps:	4025	3339	2751	2232	1775
	energy, ft-lb:	1223	842	571	376	238
	arc, inches:		+0.8	0	-5.5	-18.1

.218 Bee

CARTRIDGE BULLET	RANGE, YARDS:	0	100	200	300	400
Win. 46 Hollow Point	velocity, fps:	2760	2102	1550	1155	961
	energy, ft-lb:	778	451	245	136	94
	arc, inches:		0	-7.2	-29.4	

.22 Hornet

CARTRIDGE BULLET	RANGE, YARDS:	0	100	200	300	400
Hornady 35 V-Max	velocity, fps:	3100	2278	1601	1135	929
	energy, ft-lb:	747	403	199	100	67
	arc, inches:		+2.8	0	-16.9	-60.4
Rem. 35 AccuTip	velocity, fps:	3100	2271	1591	1127	924
	energy, ft-lb:	747	401	197	99	66
	arc, inches:		+1.5	-3.5	-22.3	-68.4
Rem. 45 Pointed Soft Point	velocity, fps:	2690	2042	1502	1128	948
	energy, ft-lb:	723	417	225	127	90
	arc, inches:		0	-7.1	-30.0	
Rem. 45 Hollow Point	velocity, fps:	2690	2042	1502	1128	948
	energy, ft-lb:	723	417	225	127	90
	arc, inches:		0	-7.1	-30.0	
Win. 34 Jacketed HP	velocity, fps:	3050	2132	1415	1017	852
	energy, ft-lb:	700	343	151	78	55
	arc, inches:		0	-6.6	-29.9	
Win. 45 Soft Point	velocity, fps:	2690	2042	1502	1128	948
	energy, ft-lb:	723	417	225	127	90
	arc, inches:		0	-7.7	-31.3	
Win. 46 Hollow Point	velocity, fps:	2690	2042	1502	1128	948
	energy, ft-lb:	739	426	230	130	92
	arc, inches:		0	-7.7	-31.3	

.221 Remington Fireball

CARTRIDGE BULLET	RANGE, YARDS:	0	100	200	300	400
Rem. 50 AccuTip BT	velocity, fps:	2995	2605	2247	1918	1622
	energy, ft-lb:	996	753	560	408	292
	arc, inches:		+1.8	0	-8.8	-27.1

.222 Remington

CARTRIDGE BULLET	RANGE, YARDS:	0	100	200	300	400
Federal 50 Hi-Shok	velocity, fps:	3140	2600	2120	1700	1350
	energy, ft-lb:	1095	750	500	320	200
	arc, inches:		+1.9	0	-9.7	-31.6

Centerfire Rifle Ballistics

.222 Remington to .223 Remington

CARTRIDGE BULLET	RANGE, YARDS:	0	100	200	300	400
Federal 55 FMJ boat-tail	velocity, fps:	3020	2740	2480	2230	1990
	energy, ft-lb:	1115	915	750	610	484
	arc, inches:		+1.6	0	-7.3	-21.5
Hornady 40 V-Max	velocity, fps:	3600	3117	2673	2269	1911
	energy, ft-lb:	1151	863	634	457	324
	arc, inches:		+1.1	0	-6.1	-18.9
Hornady 50 V-Max	velocity, fps:	3140	2729	2352	2008	1710
	energy, ft-lb:	1094	827	614	448	325
	arc, inches:		+1.7	0	-7.9	-24.4
Norma 50 Soft Point	velocity, fps:	3199	2667	2193	1771	
	energy, ft-lb:	1136	790	534	348	
	arc, inches:		+1.7	0	-9.1	
Norma 50 FMJ	velocity, fps:	2789	2326	1910	1547	
	energy, ft-lb:	864	601	405	266	
	arc, inches:		+2.5	0	-12.2	
Norma 62 Soft Point	velocity, fps:	2887	2457	2067	1716	
	energy, ft-lb:	1148	831	588	405	
	arc, inches:		+2.1	0	-10.4	
PMC 50 Pointed Soft Point	velocity, fps:	3044	2727	2354	2012	1651
	energy, ft-lb:	1131	908	677	494	333
	arc, inches:		+1.6	0	-7.9	-24.5
PMC 55 Pointed Soft Point	velocity, fps:	2950	2594	2266	1966	1693
	energy, ft-lb:	1063	822	627	472	350
	arc, inches:		+1.9	0	-8.7	-26.3
Rem. 50 Pointed Soft Point	velocity, fps:	3140	2602	2123	1700	1350
	energy, ft-lb:	1094	752	500	321	202
	arc, inches:		+1.9	0	-9.7	-31.7
Rem. 50 HP Power-Lokt	velocity, fps:	3140	2635	2182	1777	1432
	energy, ft-lb:	1094	771	529	351	228
	arc, inches:		+1.8	0	-9.2	-29.6
Rem. 50 AccuTip BT	velocity, fps:	3140	2744	2380	2045	1740
	energy, ft-lb:	1094	836	629	464	336
	arc, inches:		+1.6	0	-7.8	-23.9
Win. 40 Ballistic Silvertip	velocity, fps:	3370	2915	2503	2127	1786
	energy, ft-lb:	1009	755	556	402	283
	arc, inches:		+1.3	0	-6.9	-21.5
Win. 50 Pointed Soft Point	velocity, fps:	3140	2602	2123	1700	1350
	energy, ft-lb:	1094	752	500	321	202
	arc, inches:		+2.2	0	-10.0	-32.3

.223 Remington

CARTRIDGE BULLET	RANGE, YARDS:	0	100	200	300	400
Black Hills 40 Nosler B. Tip	velocity, fps:	3600				
	energy, ft-lb:	1150				
	arc, inches:					
Black Hills 50 V-Max	velocity, fps:	3300				
	energy, ft-lb:	1209				
	arc, inches:					
Black Hills 52 Match HP	velocity, fps:	3300				
	energy, ft-lb:	1237				
	arc, inches:					
Black Hills 55 Softpoint	velocity, fps:	3250				
	energy, ft-lb:	1270				
	arc, inches:					
Black Hills 60 SP or V-Max	velocity, fps:	3150				
	energy, ft-lb:	1322				
	arc, inches:					
Black Hills 60 Partition	velocity, fps:	3150				
	energy, ft-lb:	1322				
	arc, inches:					
Black Hills 68 Heavy Match	velocity, fps:	2850				
	energy, ft-lb:	1227				
	arc, inches:					
Black Hills 69 Sierra MK	velocity, fps:	2850				
	energy, ft-lb:	1245				
	arc, inches:					
Black Hills 73 Berger BTHP	velocity, fps:	2750				
	energy, ft-lb:	1226				
	arc, inches:					
Black Hills 75 Heavy Match	velocity, fps:	2750				
	energy, ft-lb:	1259				
	arc, inches:					
Black Hills 77 Sierra MKing	velocity, fps:	2750				
	energy, ft-lb:	1293				
	arc, inches:					
Federal 50 Jacketed HP	velocity, fps:	3400	2910	2460	2060	1700
	energy, ft-lb:	1285	940	675	470	320
	arc, inches:		+1.3	0	-7.1	-22.7
Federal 50 Speer TNT HP	velocity, fps:	3300	2860	2450	2080	1750
	energy, ft-lb:	1210	905	670	480	340
	arc, inches:		+1.4	0	-7.3	-22.6
Federal 52 Sierra MatchKing BTHP	velocity, fps:	3300	2860	2460	2090	1760
	energy, ft-lb:	1255	945	700	505	360
	arc, inches:		+1.4	0	-7.2	-22.4
Federal 55 Hi-Shok	velocity, fps:	3240	2750	2300	1910	1550
	energy, ft-lb:	1280	920	650	445	295
	arc, inches:		+1.6	0	-8.2	-26.1
Federal 55 FMJ boat-tail	velocity, fps:	3240	2950	2670	2410	2170
	energy, ft-lb:	1280	1060	875	710	575
	arc, inches:		+1.3	0	-6.1	-18.3
Federal 55 Sierra GameKing BTHP	velocity, fps:	3240	2770	2340	1950	1610
	energy, ft-lb:	1280	935	670	465	315
	arc, inches:		+1.5	0	-8.0	-25.3
Federal 55 Trophy Bonded	velocity, fps:	3100	2630	2210	1830	1500
	energy, ft-lb:	1175	845	595	410	275
	arc, inches:		+1.8	0	-8.9	-28.7
Federal 55 Nosler Bal. Tip	velocity, fps:	3240	2870	2530	2220	1920
	energy, ft-lb:	1280	1005	780	600	450
	arc, inches:		+1.4	0	-6.8	-20.8
Federal 55 Sierra BlitzKing	velocity, fps:	3240	2870	2520	2200	1910
	energy, ft-lb:	1280	1005	775	590	445
	arc, inches:		+-1.4	0	-6.9	-20.9
Federal 62 FMJ	velocity, fps:	3020	2650	2310	2000	1710
	energy, ft-lb:	1225	970	735	550	405
	arc, inches:		+1.7	0	-8.4	-25.5
Federal 64 Hi-Shok SP	velocity, fps:	3090	2690	2325	1990	1680
	energy, ft-lb:	1360	1030	770	560	400
	arc, inches:		+1.7	0	-8.2	-25.2
Federal 69 Sierra MatchKing BTHP	velocity, fps:	3000	2720	2460	2210	1980
	energy, ft-lb:	1380	1135	925	750	600
	arc, inches:		+1.6	0	-7.4	-21.9
Hornady 40 V-Max	velocity, fps:	3800	3305	2845	2424	2044
	energy, ft-lb:	1282	970	719	522	371
	arc, inches:		+0.8	0	-5.3	-16.6
Hornady 53 Hollow Point	velocity, fps:	3330	2882	2477	2106	1710
	energy, ft-lb:	1305	978	722	522	369
	arc, inches:		+1.7	0	-7.4	-22.7
Hornady 55 V-Max	velocity, fps:	3240	2859	2507	2181	1891
	energy, ft-lb:	1282	998	767	581	437
	arc, inches:		+1.4	0	-7.1	-21.4
Hornady 55 TAP-FPD	velocity, fps:	3240	2854	2500	2172	1871
	Energy, ft-lb:	1282	995	763	576	427
	Arc, inches:		+1.4	0	-7.0	-21.4
Hornady 55 Urban Tactical	velocity, fps:	2970	2626	2307	2011	1739
	energy, ft-lb:	1077	842	650	494	369
	arc, inches:		+1.5	0	-8.1	-24.9

Centerfire Rifle Ballistics

.223 REMINGTON TO .22-250 REMINGTON

BALLISTICS

CARTRIDGE BULLET	RANGE, YARDS:	0	100	200	300	400
Hornady 60 Soft Point	velocity, fps:	3150	2782	2442	2127	1837
	energy, ft-lb:	1322	1031	795	603	450
	arc, inches:		+1.6	0	-7.5	-22.5
Hornady 60 TAP-FPD	velocity, fps:	3115	2754	2420	2110	1824
	energy, ft-lb:	1293	1010	780	593	443
	arc, inches:		+1.6	0	-7.5	-22.9
Hornady 60 Urban Tactical	velocity, fps:	2950	2619	2312	2025	1762
	energy, ft-lb:	1160	914	712	546	413
	arc, inches:		+1.6	0	-8.1	-24.7
Hornady 75 BTHP Match	velocity, fps:	2790	2554	2330	2119	1926
	energy, ft-lb:	1296	1086	904	747	617
	arc, inches:		+2.4	0	-8.8	-25.1
Hornacy 75 TAP-FPD	velocity, fps:	2790	2582	2383	2193	2012
	energy, ft-lb:	1296	1110	946	801	674
	arc, inches:		+1.9	0	-8.0	-23.2
Hornady 75 BTHP Tactical	velocity, fps:	2630	2409	2199	2000	1814
	energy, ft-lb:	1152	966	805	666	548
	arc, inches:		+2.0	0	-9.2	-25.9
PMC 40 non-toxic	velocity, fps:	3500	2606	1871	1315	
	energy, ft-lb:	1088	603	311	154	
	arc, inches:		+2.6	0	-12.8	
PMC 50 Sierra BlitzKing	velocity, fps:	3300	2874	2484	2130	1809
	energy, ft-lb:	1209	917	685	504	363
	arc, inches:		+1.4	0	-7.1	-21.8
PMC 52 Sierra HPBT Match	velocity, fps:	3200	2808	2447	2117	1817
	energy, ft-lb:	1182	910	691	517	381
	arc, inches:		+1.5	0	-7.3	-22.5
PMC 53 Barnes XLC	velocity, fps:	3200	2815	2461	2136	1840
	energy, ft-lb:	1205	933	713	537	398
	arc, inches:		+1.5	0	-7.2	-22.2
PMC 55 HP boat-tail	velocity, fps:	3240	2717	2250	1832	1473
	energy, ft-lb:	1282	901	618	410	265
	arc, inches:		+1.6	0	-8.6	-27.7
PMC 55 FMJ boat-tail	velocity, fps:	3195	2882	2525	2169	1843
	energy, ft-lb:	1246	1014	779	574	415
	arc, inches:		+1.4	0	-6.8	-21.1
PMC 55 Pointed Soft Point	velocity, fps:	3112	2767	2421	2100	1806
	energy, ft-lb:	1182	935	715	539	398
	arc, inches:		+1.5	0	-7.5	-22.9
PMC 64 Pointed Soft Point	velocity, fps:	2775	2511	2261	2026	1806
	energy, ft-lb:	1094	896	726	583	464
	arc, inches:		+2.0	0	-8.8	-26.1
PMC 69 Sierra BTHP Match	velocity, fps:	2900	2591	2304	2038	1791
	energy, ft-lb:	1288	1029	813	636	492
	arc, inches:		+1.9	0	-8.4	-25.3
Rem. 50 AccuTip BT	velocity, fps:	3300	2889	2514	2168	1851
	energy, ft-lb:	1209	927	701	522	380
	arc, inches:		+1.4	0	-6.9	-21.2
Rem. 55 Pointed Soft Point	velocity, fps:	3240	2747	2304	1905	1554
	energy, ft-lb:	1282	921	648	443	295
	arc, inches:		+1.6	0	-8.2	-26.2
Rem. 55 HP Power-Lokt	velocity, fps:	3240	2773	2352	1969	1627
	energy, ft-lb:	1282	939	675	473	323
	arc, inches:		+1.5	0	-7.9	-24.8
Rem. 55 AccuTip BT	velocity, fps:	3240	2854	2500	2172	1871
	energy, ft-lb:	1282	995	763	576	427
	arc, inches:		+1.5	0	-7.1	-21.7
Rem. 55 Metal Case	velocity, fps:	3240	2759	2326	1933	1587
	energy, ft-lb:	1282	929	660	456	307
	arc, inches:		+1.6	0	-8.1	-25.5
Rem. 62 HP Match	velocity, fps:	3025	2572	2162	1792	1471
	energy, ft-lb:	1260	911	643	442	298
	arc, inches:		+1.9	0	-9.4	-29.9

CARTRIDGE BULLET	RANGE, YARDS:	0	100	200	300	400
Rem. 69 BTHP Match	velocity, fps:	3000	2720	2457	2209	1975
	energy, ft-lb:	1379	1133	925	747	598
	arc, inches:		+1.6	0	-7.4	-21.9
Win. 40 Ballistic Silvertip	velocity, fps:	3700	3166	2693	2265	1879
	energy, ft-lb:	1216	891	644	456	314
	arc, inches:		+1.0	0	-5.8	-18.4
Win. 45 JHP	velocity, fps:	3600				
	energy, ft-lb:	1295				
	arc, inches:					
Win. 50 Ballistic Silvertip	velocity, fps:	3410	2982	2593	2235	1907
	energy, ft-lb:	1291	987	746	555	404
	arc, inches:		+1.2	0	-6.4	-19.8
Win. 53 Hollow Point	velocity, fps:	3330	2882	2477	2106	1770
	energy, ft-lb:	1305	978	722	522	369
	arc, inches:		+1.7	0	-7.4	-22.7
Win. 55 Pointed Soft Point	velocity, fps:	3240	2747	2304	1905	1554
	energy, ft-lb:	1282	921	648	443	295
	arc, inches:		+1.9	0	-8.5	-26.7
Win. 55 Super Clean NT	velocity, fps:	3150	2520	1970	1505	1165
	energy, ft-lb:	1212	776	474	277	166
	arc, inches:		+2.8	0	-11.9	-38.9
Win. 55 FMJ	velocity, fps:	3240	2854			
	energy, ft-lb:	1282	995			
	arc, inches:					
Win. 55 Ballistic Silvertip	velocity, fps:	3240	2871	2531	2215	1923
	energy, ft-lb:	1282	1006	782	599	451
	arc, inches:		+1.4	0	-6.8	-20.8
Win. 64 Power-Point	velocity, fps:	3020	2656	2320	2009	1724
	energy, ft-lb:	1296	1003	765	574	423
	arc, inches:		+1.7	0	-8.2	-25.1
Win. 64 Power-Point Plus	velocity, fps:	3090	2684	2312	1971	1664
	energy, ft-lb:	1357	1024	760	552	393
	arc, inches:		+1.7	0	-8.2	-25.4

.5.6 x 52 R

CARTRIDGE BULLET	RANGE, YARDS:	0	100	200	300	400
Norma 71 Soft Point	velocity, fps:	2789	2446	2128	1835	
	energy, ft-lb:	1227	944	714	531	
	arc, inches:		+2.1	0	-9.9	

.22 PPC

CARTRIDGE BULLET	RANGE, YARDS:	0	100	200	300	400
A-Square 52 Berger	velocity, fps:	3300	2952	2629	2329	2049
	energy, ft-lb:	1257	1006	798	626	485
	arc, inches:		+1.3	0	-6.3	-19.1

.225 Winchester

CARTRIDGE BULLET	RANGE, YARDS:	0	100	200	300	400
Win. 55 Pointed Soft Point	velocity, fps:	3570	3066	2616	2208	1838
	energy, ft-lb:	1556	1148	836	595	412
	arc, inches:		+2.4	+2.0	-3.5	-16.3

.224 Weatherby Mag.

CARTRIDGE BULLET	RANGE, YARDS:	0	100	200	300	400
Wby. 55 Pointed Expanding	velocity, fps:	3650	3192	2780	2403	2056
	energy, ft-lb:	1627	1244	944	705	516
	arc, inches:		+2.8	+3.7	0	-9.8

.22-250 Remington

CARTRIDGE BULLET	RANGE, YARDS:	0	100	200	300	400
Black Hills 50 Nos. Bal. Tip	velocity, fps:	3700				
	energy, ft-lb:	1520				
	arc, inches:					
Black Hills 60 Nos. Partition	velocity, fps:	3550				
	energy, ft-lb:	1679				
	arc, inches:					
Federal 40 Nos. Bal. Tip	velocity, fps:	4150	3610	3130	2700	2300
	energy, ft-lb:	1530	1155	870	645	470
	arc, inches:		+0.6	0	-4.2	-13.2

CARTRIDGE BULLET	RANGE, YARDS:	0	100	200	300	400
Federal 40 Sierra Varminter	velocity, fps:	4000	3320	2720	2200	1740
	energy, ft-lb:	1420	980	660	430	265
	arc, inches:		+0.8	0	-5.6	-18.4
Federal 55 Hi-Shok	velocity, fps:	3680	3140	2660	2220	1830
	energy, ft-lb:	1655	1200	860	605	410
	arc, inches:		+1.0	0	-6.0	-19.1
Federal 55 Sierra BlitzKing	velocity, fps:	3680	3270	2890	2540	2220
	energy, ft-lb:	1655	1300	1020	790	605
	arc, inches:		+0.9	0	-5.1	-15.6
Federal 55 Sierra GameKing	velocity, fps:	3680	3280	2920	2590	2280
BTHP	energy, ft-lb:	1655	1315	1040	815	630
	arc, inches:		+0.9	0	-5.0	-15.1
Federal 55 Trophy Bonded	velocity, fps:	3600	3080	2610	2190	1810
	energy, ft-lb:	1585	1155	835	590	400
	arc, inches:		+1.1	0	-6.2	-19.8
Hornady 40 V-Max	velocity, fps:	4150	3631	3147	2699	2293
	energy, ft-lb:	1529	1171	879	647	467
	arc, inches:		+0.5	0	-4.2	-13.3
Hornady 50 V-Max	velocity, fps:	3800	3349	2925	2535	2178
	energy, ft-lb:	1603	1245	950	713	527
	arc, inches:		+0.8	0	-5.0	-15.6
Hornady 53 Hollow Point	velocity, fps:	3680	3185	2743	2341	1974
	energy, ft-lb:	1594	1194	886	645	459
	arc, inches:		+1.0	0	-5.7	-17.8
Hornady 55 V-Max	velocity, fps:	3680	3265	2876	2517	2183
	energy, ft-lb:	1654	1302	1010	772	582
	arc, inches:		+0.9	0	-5.3	-16.1
Hornady 60 Soft Point	velocity, fps:	3600	3195	2826	2485	2169
	energy, ft-lb:	1727	1360	1064	823	627
	arc, inches:		+1.0	0	-5.4	-16.3
Norma 53 Soft Point	velocity, fps:	3707	3234	2809	1716	
	energy, ft-lb:	1618	1231	928	690	
	arc, inches:		+0.9	0	-5.3	
PMC 50 Sierra BlitzKing	velocity, fps:	3725	3264	2641	2455	2103
	energy, ft-lb:	1540	1183	896	669	491
	arc, inches:		+0.9	0	-5.2	-16.2
PMC 50 Barnes XLC	velocity, fps:	3725	3280	2871	2495	2152
	energy, ft-lb:	1540	1195	915	691	514
	arc, inches:		+0.9	0	-5.1	-15.9
PMC 55 HP boat-tail	velocity, fps:	3680	3104	2596	2141	1737
	energy, ft-lb:	1654	1176	823	560	368
	arc, inches:		+1.1	0	-6.3	-20.2
PMC 55 Pointed Soft Point	velocity, fps:	3586	3203	2852	2505	2178
	energy, ft-lb:	1570	1253	993	766	579
	arc, inches:		+1.0	0	-5.2	-16.0
Rem. 50 AccuTip BT	velocity, fps:	3725	3272	2864	2491	2147
(also in EtronX)	energy, ft-lb:	1540	1188	910	689	512
	arc, inches:		+1.7	+1.6	-2.8	-12.8
Rem. 55 Pointed Soft Point	velocity, fps:	3680	3137	2656	2222	1832
	energy, ft-lb:	1654	1201	861	603	410
	arc, inches:		+1.9	+1.8	-3.3	-15.5
Rem. 55 HP Power-Lokt	velocity, fps:	3680	3209	2785	2400	2046
	energy, ft-lb:	1654	1257	947	703	511
	arc, inches:		+1.8	+1.7	-3.0	-13.7
Rem. 60 Nosler Partition	velocity, fps:	3500	3045	2634	2258	1914
(also in EtronX)	energy, ft-lb:	1632	1235	924	679	488
	arc, inches:		+2.1	+1.9	-3.4	-15.5
Win. 40 Ballistic Silvertip	velocity, fps:	4150	3591	3099	2658	2257
	energy, ft-lb:	1530	1146	853	628	453
	arc, inches:		+0.6	0	-4.2	-13.4
Win. 50 Ballistic Silvertip	velocity, fps:	3810	3341	2919	2536	2182
	energy, ft-lb:	1611	1239	946	714	529
	arc, inches:		+0.8	0	-4.9	-15.2

CARTRIDGE BULLET	RANGE, YARDS:	0	100	200	300	400
Win. 55 Pointed Soft Point	velocity, fps:	3680	3137	2656	2222	1832
	energy, ft-lb:	1654	1201	861	603	410
	arc, inches:		+2.3	+1.9	-3.4	-15.9
Win. 55 Ballistic Silvertip	velocity, fps:	3680	3272	2900	2558	2240
	energy, ft-lb:	1654	1307	1027	799	613
	arc, inches:		+0.9	0	-5.0	-15.4
Win. 64 Power-Point	velocity, fps:	3500	3086	2708	2360	2038
	Energy, ft-lb:	1741	1353	1042	791	590
	Arc, inches:		+1.1	0	-5.9	-18.0

.220 Swift

CARTRIDGE BULLET	RANGE, YARDS:	0	100	200	300	400
Federal 52 Sierra MatchKing	velocity, fps:	3830	3370	2960	2600	2230
BTHP	energy, ft-lb:	1690	1310	1010	770	575
	arc, inches:		+0.8	0	-4.8	-14.9
Federal 55 Sierra BlitzKing	velocity, fps:	3800	3370	2990	2630	2310
	energy, ft-lb:	1765	1390	1090	850	650
	arc, inches:		+0.8	0	-4.7	-14.4
Federal 55 Trophy Bonded	velocity, fps:	3700	3170	2690	2270	1880
	energy, ft-lb:	1670	1225	885	625	430
	arc, inches:		+1.0	0	-5.8	-18.5
Hornady 40 V-Max	velocity, fps:	4200	3678	3190	2739	2329
	energy, ft-lb:	1566	1201	904	666	482
	arc, inches:		+0.5	0	-4.0	-12.9
Hornady 50 V-Max	velocity, fps:	3850	3396	2970	2576	2215
	energy, ft-lb:	1645	1280	979	736	545
	arc, inches:		+0.7	0	-4.8	-15.1
Hornady 50 SP	velocity, fps:	3850	3327	2862	2442	2060
	energy, ft-lb:	1645	1228	909	662	471
	arc, inches:		+0.8	0	-5.1	-16.1
Hornady 55 V-Max	velocity, fps:	3680	3265	2876	2517	2183
	energy, ft-lb:	1654	1302	1010	772	582
	arc, inches:		+0.9	0	-5.3	-16.1
Hornady 60 Hollow Point	velocity, fps:	3600	3199	2824	2475	2156
	energy, ft-lb:	1727	1364	1063	816	619
	arc, inches:		+1.0	0	-5.4	-16.3
Norma 50 Soft Point	velocity, fps:	4019	3380	2826	2335	
	energy, ft-lb:	1794	1268	887	605	
	arc, inches:		+0.7	0	-5.1	
Rem. 50 Pointed Soft Point	velocity, fps:	3780	3158	2617	2135	1710
	energy, ft-lb:	1586	1107	760	506	325
	arc, inches:		+0.3	-1.4	-8.2	
Rem. 50 V-Max boat-tail	velocity, fps:	3780	3321	2908	2532	2185
(also in EtronX)	energy, ft-lb:	1586	1224	939	711	530
	arc, inches:		+0.8	0	-5.0	-15.4
Win. 40 Ballistic Silvertip	velocity, fps:	4050	3518	3048	2624	2238
	energy, ft-lb:	1457	1099	825	611	445
	arc, inches:		+0.7	0	-4.4	-13.9
Win. 50 Pointed Soft Point	velocity, fps:	3870	3310	2816	2373	1972
	energy, ft-lb:	1663	1226	881	625	432
	arc, inches:		+0.8	0	-5.2	-16.7

.223 WSSM

CARTRIDGE BULLET	RANGE, YARDS:	0	100	200	300	400
Win. 55 Ballistic Silvertip	velocity, fps:	3850	3438	3064	2721	2402
	energy, ft-lb:	1810	1444	1147	904	704
	arc, inches:		+0.7	0	-4.4	-13.6
Win. 55 Pointed Softpoint	velocity, fps:	3850	3367	2934	2541	2181
	energy, ft-lb:	1810	1384	1051	789	581
	arc, inches:		+0.8	0	-4.9	-15.1
Win. 64 Power-Point	velocity, fps:	3600	3144	2732	2356	2011
	energy, ft-lb:	1841	1404	1061	789	574
	arc, inches:		+1.0	0	-5.7	-17.7

Centerfire Rifle Ballistics

6MM PPC TO 6MM REMINGTON

6mm PPC

CARTRIDGE BULLET	RANGE, YARDS:	0	100	200	300	400
A-Square 68 Berger	velocity, fps:	3100	2751	2428	2128	1850
	energy, ft-lb:	1451	1143	890	684	516
	arc, inches:		+1.5	0	-7.5	-22.6

6x70 R

CARTRIDGE BULLET	RANGE, YARDS:	0	100	200	300	400
Norma 95 Nosler Bal. Tip	velocity, fps:	2461	2231	2013	1809	
	energy, ft-lb:	1211	995	810	654	
	arc, inches:		+2.7	0	-11.3	

.243 Winchester

CARTRIDGE BULLET	RANGE, YARDS:	0	100	200	300	400
Black Hills 55 Nosler B. Tip	velocity, fps:	3800				
	energy, ft-lb:	1763				
	arc, inches:					
Black Hills 95 Nosler B. Tip	velocity, fps:	2950				
	energy, ft-lb:	1836				
	arc, inches:					
Federal 70 Nosler Bal. Tip	velocity, fps:	3400	3070	2760	2470	2200
	energy, ft-lb:	1795	1465	1185	950	755
	arc, inches:		+1.1	0	-5.7	-17.1
Federal 70 Speer TNT HP	velocity, fps:	3400	3040	2700	2390	2100
	energy, ft-lb:	1795	1435	1135	890	685
	arc, inches:		+1.1	0	-5.9	-18.0
Federal 80 Sierra Pro-Hunter	velocity, fps:	3350	2960	2590	2260	1950
	energy, ft-lb:	1995	1550	1195	905	675
	arc, inches:		+1.3	0	-6.4	-19.7
Federal 85 Sierra GameKing	velocity, fps:	3320	3070	2830	2600	2380
BTHP	energy, ft-lb:	2080	1770	1510	1280	1070
	arc, inches:		+1.1	0	-5.5	-16.1
Federal 90 Trophy Bonded	velocity, fps:	3100	2850	2610	2380	2160
	energy, ft-lb:	1920	1620	1360	1130	935
	arc, inches:		+1.4	0	-6.1	-19.2
Federal 100 Hi-Shok	velocity, fps:	2960	2700	2450	2220	1990
	energy, ft-lb:	1945	1615	1330	1090	880
	arc, inches:		+1.6	0	-7.5	-22.0
Federal 100 Sierra GameKing	velocity, fps:	2960	2760	2570	2380	2210
BTSP	energy, ft-lb:	1950	1690	1460	1260	1080
	arc, inches:		+1.5	0	-6.8	-19.8
Federal 100 Nosler Partition	velocity, fps:	2960	2730	2510	2300	2100
	energy, ft-lb:	1945	1650	1395	1170	975
	arc, inches:		+1.6	0	-7.1	-20.9
Hornady 58 V-Max	velocity, fps:	3750	3319	2913	2539	2195
	energy, ft-lb:	1811	1418	1093	830	620
	arc, inches:		+1.2	0	-5.5	-16.4
Hornady 75 Hollow Point	velocity, fps:	3400	2970	2578	2219	1890
	energy, ft-lb:	1926	1469	1107	820	595
	arc, inches:		+1.2	0	-6.5	-20.3
Hornady 100 BTSP	velocity, fps:	2960	2728	2508	2299	2099
	energy, ft-lb:	1945	1653	1397	1174	979
	arc, inches:		+1.6	0	-7.2	-21.0
Hornady 100 BTSP LM	velocity, fps:	3100	2839	2592	2358	2138
	energy, ft-lb:	2133	1790	1491	1235	1014
	arc, inches:		+1.5	0	-6.8	-19.8
Norma 80 FMJ	velocity, fps:	3117	2750	2412	2098	
	energy, ft-lb:	1726	1344	1034	782	
	arc, inches:		+1.5	0	-7.5	
Norma 100 FMJ	velocity, fps:	3018	2747	2493	2252	
	energy, ft-lb:	2023	1677	1380	1126	
	arc, inches:		+1.5	0	-7.1	
Norma 100 Soft Point	velocity, fps:	3018	2748	2493	2252	
	energy, ft-lb:	2023	1677	1380	1126	
	arc, inches:		+1.5	0	-7.1	
Norma 100 Oryx	velocity, fps:	3018	2653	2316	2004	
	energy, ft-lb:	2023	1563	1191	892	
	arc, inches:		+1.7	0	-8.3	
PMC 80 Pointed Soft Point	velocity, fps:	2940	2684	2444	2215	1999
	energy, ft-lb:	1535	1280	1060	871	709
	arc, inches:		+1.7	0	-7.5	-22.1
PMC 85 Barnes XLC	velocity, fps:	3250	3022	2805	2598	2401
	energy, ft-lb:	1993	1724	1485	1274	1088
	arc, inches:		+1.6	0	-5.6	16.3
PMC 85 HP boat-tail	velocity, fps:	3275	2922	2596	2292	2009
	energy, ft-lb:	2024	1611	1272	991	761
	arc, inches:		+1.3	0	-6.5	-19.7
PMC 100 Pointed Soft Point	velocity, fps:	2743	2507	2283	2070	1869
	energy, ft-lb:	1670	1395	1157	951	776
	arc, inches:		+2.0	0	-8.7	-25.5
PMC 100 SP boat-tail	velocity, fps:	2960	2742	2534	2335	2144
	energy, ft-lb:	1945	1669	1425	1210	1021
	arc, inches:		+1.6	0	-7.0	-20.5
Rem. 75 AccuTip BT	velocity, fps:	3375	3065	2775	2504	2248
	energy, ft-lb:	1897	1564	1282	1044	842
	arc, inches:		+2.0	+1.8	-3.0	-13.3
Rem. 80 Pointed Soft Point	velocity, fps:	3350	2955	2593	2259	1951
	energy, ft-lb:	1993	1551	1194	906	676
	arc, inches:		+2.2	+2.0	-3.5	-15.8
Rem. 80 HP Power-Lokt	velocity, fps:	3350	2955	2593	2259	1951
	energy, ft-lb:	1993	1551	1194	906	676
	arc, inches:		+2.2	+2.0	-3.5	-15.8
Rem. 90 Nosler Bal. Tip	velocity, fps:	3120	2871	2635	2411	2199
(also in EtronX) or Scirocco	energy, ft-lb:	1946	1647	1388	1162	966
	arc, inches:		+1.4	0	-6.4	-18.8
Rem. 95 AccuTip	velocity, fps:	3120	2847	2590	2347	2118
	energy, ft-lb:	2053	1710	1415	1162	946
	arc, inches:		+1.5	0	-6.6	-19.5
Rem. 100 PSP Core-Lokt	velocity, fps:	2960	2697	2449	2215	1993
(also in EtronX)	energy, ft-lb:	1945	1615	1332	1089	882
	arc, inches:		+1.6	0	-7.5	-22.1
Rem. 100 PSP boat-tail	velocity, fps:	2960	2720	2492	2275	2069
	energy, ft-lb:	1945	1642	1378	1149	950
	arc, inches:		+2.8	+2.3	-3.8	-16.6
Speer 100 Grand Slam	velocity, fps:	2950	2684	2434	2197	
	energy, ft-lb:	1932	1600	1315	1072	
	arc, inches:		+1.7	0	-7.6	-22.4
Win. 55 Ballistic Silvertip	velocity, fps:	4025	3597	3209	2853	2525
	energy, ft-lb:	1978	1579	1257	994	779
	arc, inches:		+0.6	0	-4.0	-12.2
Win. 80 Pointed Soft Point	velocity, fps:	3350	2955	2593	2259	1951
	energy, ft-lb:	1993	1551	1194	906	676
	arc, inches:		+2.6	+2.1	-3.6	-16.2
Win. 95 Ballistic Silvertip	velocity, fps:	3100	2854	2626	2410	2203
	energy, ft-lb:	2021	1719	1455	1225	1024
	arc, inches:		+1.4	0	-6.4	-18.9
Win. 100 Power-Point	velocity, fps:	2960	2697	2449	2215	1993
	energy, ft-lb:	1945	1615	1332	1089	882
	arc, inches:		+1.9	0	-7.8	-22.6
Win. 100 Power-Point Plus	velocity, fps:	3090	2818	2562	2321	2092
	energy, ft-lb:	2121	1764	1458	1196	972
	arc, inches:		+1.4	0	-6.7	-20.0

6mm Remington

CARTRIDGE BULLET	RANGE, YARDS:	0	100	200	300	400
Federal 80 Sierra Pro-Hunter	velocity, fps:	3470	3060	2690	2350	2040
	energy, ft-lb:	2140	1665	1290	980	735
	arc, inches:		+1.1	0	-5.9	-18.2

CARTRIDGE BULLET	RANGE, YARDS:	0	100	200	300	400
Federal 100 Hi-Shok	velocity, fps:	3100	2830	2570	2330	2100
	energy, ft-lb:	2135	1775	1470	1205	985
	arc, inches:		+1.4	0	-6.7	-19.8
Federal 100 Nos. Partition	velocity, fps:	3100	2860	2640	2420	2220
	energy, ft-lb:	2135	1820	1545	1300	1090
	arc, inches:		+1.4	0	-6.3	-18.7
Hornady 100 SP boat-tail	velocity, fps:	3100	2861	2634	2419	2231
	energy, ft-lb:	2134	1818	1541	1300	1088
	arc, inches:		+1.3	0	-6.5	-18.9
Hornady 100 SPBT LM	velocity, fps:	3250	2997	2756	2528	2311
	energy, ft-lb:	2345	1995	1687	1418	1186
	arc, inches:		+1.6	0	-6.3	-18.2
Rem. 75 V-Max boat-tail	velocity, fps:	3400	3088	2797	2524	2267
	energy, ft-lb:	1925	1587	1303	1061	856
	arc, inches:		+1.9	+1.7	-3.0	-13.1
Rem. 100 PSP Core-Lokt	velocity, fps:	3100	2829	2573	2332	2104
	energy, ft-lb:	2133	1777	1470	1207	983
	arc, inches:		+1.4	0	-6.7	-19.8
Rem. 100 PSP boat-tail	velocity, fps:	3100	2852	2617	2394	2183
	energy, ft-lb:	2134	1806	1521	1273	1058
	arc, inches:		+1.4	0	-6.5	-19.1
Win. 100 Power-Point	velocity, fps:	3100	2829	2573	2332	2104
	energy, ft-lb:	2133	1777	1470	1207	983
	arc, inches:		+1.7	0	-7.0	-20.4

.243 WSSM

CARTRIDGE BULLET	RANGE, YARDS:	0	100	200	300	400
Win. 55 Ballistic Silvertip	velocity, fps:	4060	3628	3237	2880	2550
	energy, ft-lb:	2013	1607	1280	1013	794
	arc, inches:		+0.6	0	-3.9	-12.0
Win. 95 Ballistic Silvertip	velocity, fps:	3250	3000	2763	2538	2325
	energy, ft-lb:	2258	1898	1610	1359	1140
	arc, inches:		+1.2	0	5.7	16.9
Win. 100 Power Point	velocity, fps:	3110	2838	2583	2341	2112
	energy, ft-lb:	2147	1789	1481	1217	991
	arc, inches:		+1.4	0	-6.6	-19.7

.240 Weatherby Mag.

CARTRIDGE BULLET	RANGE, YARDS:	0	100	200	300	400
Wby. 87 Pointed Expanding	velocity, fps:	3523	3199	2898	2617	2352
	energy, ft-lb:	2397	1977	1622	1323	1069
	arc, inches:		+2.7	+3.4	0	-8.4
Wby. 90 Barnes-X	velocity, fps:	3500	3222	2962	2717	2484
	energy, ft-lb:	2448	2075	1753	1475	1233
	arc, inches:		+2.6	+3.3	0	-8.0
Wby. 95 Nosler Bal. Tip	velocity, fps:	3420	3146	2888	2645	2414
	energy, ft-lb:	2467	2087	1759	1475	1229
	arc, inches:		+2.7	+3.5	0	-8.4
Wby. 100 Pointed Expanding	velocity, fps:	3406	3134	2878	2637	2408
	energy, ft-lb:	2576	2180	1839	1544	1287
	arc, inches:		+2.8	+3.5	0	-8.4
Wby. 100 Partition	velocity, fps:	3406	3136	2882	2642	2415
	energy, ft-lb:	2576	2183	1844	1550	1294
	arc, inches:		+2.8	+3.5	0	-8.4

.25-20 Winchester

CARTRIDGE BULLET	RANGE, YARDS:	0	100	200	300	400
Rem. 86 Soft Point	velocity, fps:	1460	1194	1030	931	858
	energy, ft-lb:	407	272	203	165	141
	arc, inches:		0	-22.9	-78.9	-173.0
Win. 86 Soft Point	velocity, fps:	1460	1194	1030	931	858
	energy, ft-lb:	407	272	203	165	141
	arc, inches:		0	-23.5	-79.6	-175.9

.25-35 Winchester

CARTRIDGE BULLET	RANGE, YARDS:	0	100	200	300	400
Win. 117 Soft Point	velocity, fps:	2230	1866	1545	1282	1097
	energy, ft-lb:	1292	904	620	427	313
	arc, inches:		+2.1	-5.1	-27.0	-70.1

.250 Savage

CARTRIDGE BULLET	RANGE, YARDS:	0	100	200	300	400
Rem. 100 Pointed SP	velocity, fps:	2820	2504	2210	1936	1684
	energy, ft-lb:	1765	1392	1084	832	630
	arc, inches:		+2.0	0	-9.2	-27.7
Win. 100 Silvertip	velocity, fps:	2820	2467	2140	1839	1569
	energy, ft-lb:	1765	1351	1017	751	547
	arc, inches:		+2.4	0	-10.1	-30.5

.257 Roberts

CARTRIDGE BULLET	RANGE, YARDS:	0	100	200	300	400
Federal 120 Nosler Partition	velocity, fps:	2780	2560	2360	2160	1970
	energy, ft-lb:	2060	1750	1480	1240	1030
	arc, inches:		+1.9	0	-8.2	-24.0
Hornady 117 SP boat-tail	velocity, fps:	2780	2550	2331	2122	1925
	energy, ft-lb:	2007	1689	1411	1170	963
	arc, inches:		+1.9	0	-8.3	-24.4
Hornady 117 SP boat-tail LM	velocity, fps:	2940	2694	2460	2240	2031
	energy, ft-lb:	2245	1885	1572	1303	1071
	arc, inches:		+1.7	0	-7.6	-21.8
Rem. 117 SP Core-Lokt	velocity, fps:	2650	2291	1961	1663	1404
	energy, ft-lb:	1824	1363	999	718	512
	arc, inches:		+2.6	0	-11.7	-36.1
Win. 117 Power-Point	velocity, fps:	2780	2411	2071	1761	1488
	energy, ft-lb:	2009	1511	1115	806	576
	arc, inches:		+2.6	0	-10.8	-33.0

.25-06 Remington

CARTRIDGE BULLET	RANGE, YARDS:	0	100	200	300	400
Black Hills 100 Nos. Bal. Tip	velocity, fps:	3200				
	energy, ft-lb:	2273				
	arc, inches:					
Black Hills 100 Barnes XLC	velocity, fps:	3200				
	energy, ft-lb:	2273				
	arc, inches:					
Black Hills 115 Barnes X	velocity, fps:	2975				
	energy, ft-lb:	2259				
	arc, inches:					
Federal 90 Sierra Varminter	velocity, fps:	3440	3040	2680	2340	2030
	energy, ft-lb:	2365	1850	1435	1100	825
	arc, inches:		+1.1	0	-6.0	-18.3
Federal 100 Barnes XLC	velocity, fps:	3210	2970	2750	2540	2330
	energy, ft-lb:	2290	1965	1680	1430	1205
	arc, inches:		+1.2	0	-5.8	-17.0
Federal 100 Nosler Bal. Tip	velocity, fps:	3210	2960	2720	2490	2280
	energy, ft-lb:	2290	1940	1640	1380	1150
	arc, inches:		+1.2	0	-6.0	-17.5
Federal 115 Nosler Partition	velocity, fps:	2990	2750	2520	2300	2100
	energy, ft-lb:	2285	1930	1620	1350	1120
	arc, inches:		+1.6	0	-7.0	-20.8
Federal 115 Trophy Bonded	velocity, fps:	2990	2740	2500	2270	2050
	energy, ft-lb:	2285	1910	1590	1310	1075
	arc, inches:		+1.6	0	-7.2	-21.1
Federal 117 Sierra Pro Hunt.	velocity, fps:	2990	2730	2480	2250	2030
	energy, ft-lb:	2320	1985	1645	1350	1100
	arc, inches:		+1.6	0	-7.2	-21.4
Federal 117 Sierra GameKing	velocity, fps:	2990	2770	2570	2370	2190
BTSP	energy, ft-lb:	2320	2000	1715	1465	1240
	arc, inches:		+1.5	0	-6.8	-19.9
Hornady 117 SP boat-tail	velocity, fps:	2990	2749	2520	2302	2096
	energy, ft-lb:	2322	1962	1649	1377	1141
	arc, inches:		+1.6	0	-7.0	-20.7
Hornady 117 SP boat-tail LM	velocity, fps:	3110	2855	2613	2384	2168
	energy, ft-lb:	2512	2117	1774	1476	1220
	arc, inches:		+1.8	0	-7.1	-20.3

Centerfire Rifle Ballistics

.25-06 REMINGTON TO 6.5X55 SWEDISH

BALLISTICS

CARTRIDGE BULLET	RANGE, YARDS:	0	100	200	300	400
PMC 100 SPBT	velocity, fps:	3200	2925	2650	2395	2145
	energy, ft-lb:	2273	1895	1561	1268	1019
	arc, inches:		+1.3	0	-6.3	-18.6
PMC 117 PSP	velocity, fps:	2950	2706	2472	2253	2047
	energy, ft-lb:	2261	1900	1588	1319	1088
	arc, inches:		+1.6	0	-7.3	-21.5
Rem. 100 PSP Core-Lokt	velocity, fps:	3230	2893	2580	2287	2014
	energy, ft-lb:	2316	1858	1478	1161	901
	arc, inches:		+1.3	0	-6.6	-19.8
Rem. 115 Core-Lokt Ultra	velocity, fps:	3000	2751	2516	2293	2081
	energy, ft-lb:	2298	1933	1616	1342	1106
	arc, inches:		+1.6	0	-7.1	-20.7
Rem. 120 PSP Core-Lokt	velocity, fps:	2990	2730	2484	2252	2032
	energy, ft-lb:	2382	1985	1644	1351	1100
	arc, inches:		+1.6	0	-7.2	-21.4
Speer 120 Grand Slam	velocity, fps:	3130	2835	2558	2298	
	energy, ft-lb:	2610	2141	1743	1407	
	arc, inches:		+1.4	0	-6.8	-20.1
Win. 85 Ballistic Silvertip	velocity, fps	3470	3156	2863	2589	2331
	energy, ft-lb:	2273	1880	1548	1266	1026
	arc, inches:		+1.0	0	-5.2	-15.7
Win. 90 Pos. Exp. Point	velocity, fps:	3440	3043	2680	2344	2034
	energy, ft-lb:	2364	1850	1435	1098	827
	arc, inches:		+2.4	+2.0	-3.4	-15.0
Win. 110 AccuBond CT	velocity, fps:	3100	2870	2651	2442	2243
	energy, ft-lb:	2347	2011	1716	1456	1228
	arc, inches:		+1.4	0	-6.3	-18.5
Win. 115 Ballistic Silvertip	velocity, fps:	3060	2825	2603	2390	2188
	energy, ft-lb:	2391	2038	1729	1459	1223
	arc, inches:		+1.4	0	-6.6	-19.2
Win. 120 Pos. Pt. Exp.	velocity, fps:	2990	2717	2459	2216	1987
	energy, ft-lb:	2382	1967	1612	1309	1053
	arc, inches:		+1.6	0	-7.4	-21.8

.25 WINCHESTER SUPER SHORT MAG.

CARTRIDGE BULLET	RANGE, YARDS:	0	100	200	300	400
Win. 85 Ballistic Silvertip	velocity, fps:	3470	3156	2863	2589	2331
	energy, ft-lb:	2273	1880	1548	1266	1026
	arc, inches:		+1.0	0	-5.2	-15.7
Win. 110 AccuBond CT	velocity, fps:	3100	2870	2651	2442	2243
	energy, ft-lb:	2347	2011	1716	1456	1228
	arc, inches:		+1.4	0	-6.3	-18.5
Win. 115 Ballistic Silvertip	velocity, fps:	3060	2844	2639	2442	2254
	energy, ft-lb:	2392	2066	1778	1523	1298
	arc, inches:		+1.4	0	-6.4	-18.6
Win. 120 Pos. Pt. Exp.	velocity, fps:	2990	2717	2459	2216	1987
	energy, ft-lb:	2383	1967	1612	1309	1053
	arc, inches:		+1.6	0	-7.4	-21.8

.257 WEATHERBY MAG.

CARTRIDGE BULLET	RANGE, YARDS:	0	100	200	300	400
Federal 115 Nosler Partition	velocity, fps:	3150	2900	2660	2440	2220
	energy, ft-lb:	2535	2145	1810	1515	1260
	arc, inches:		+1.3	0	-6.2	-18.4
Federal 115 Trophy Bonded	velocity, fps:	3150	2890	2640	2400	2180
	energy, ft-lb:	2535	2125	1775	1470	1210
	arc, inches:		+1.4	0	-6.3	-18.8
Wby. 87 Pointed Expanding	velocity, fps:	3825	3472	3147	2845	2563
	energy, ft-lb:	2826	2328	1913	1563	1269
	arc, inches:		+2.1	+2.8	0	-7.1
Wby. 100 Pointed Expanding	velocity, fps:	3602	3298	3016	2750	2500
	energy, ft-lb:	2881	2416	2019	1680	1388
	arc, inches:		+2.4	+3.1	0	-7.7
Wby. 115 Nosler Bal. Tip	velocity, fps:	3400	3170	2952	2745	2547
	energy, ft-lb:	2952	2566	2226	1924	1656
	arc, inches:		+3.0	+3.5	0	-7.9
Wby. 115 Barnes X	velocity, fps:	3400	3158	2929	2711	2504
	energy, ft-lb:	2952	2546	2190	1877	1601
	arc, inches:		+2.7	+3.4	0	-8.1
Wby. 117 RN Expanding	velocity, fps:	3402	2984	2595	2240	1921
	energy, ft-lb:	3007	2320	1742	1302	956
	arc, inches:		+3.4	+4.31	0	-11.1
Wby. 120 Nosler Partition	velocity, fps:	3305	3046	2801	2570	2350
	energy, ft-lb:	2910	2472	2091	1760	1471
	arc, inches:		+3.0	+3.7	0	-8.9

6.53 (.257) SCRAMJET

CARTRIDGE BULLET	RANGE, YARDS:	0	100	200	300	400
Lazzeroni 85 Nosler Bal. Tip	velocity, fps:	3960	3652	3365	3096	2844
	energy, ft-lb:	2961	2517	2137	1810	1526
	arc, inches:		+1.7	+2.4	0	-6.0
Lazzeroni 100 Nosler Part.	velocity, fps:	3740	3465	3208	2965	2735
	energy, ft-lb:	3106	2667	2285	1953	1661
	arc, inches:		+2.1	+2.7	0	-6.7

6.5X50 JAPANESE

CARTRIDGE BULLET	RANGE, YARDS:	0	100	200	300	400
Norma 156 Alaska	velocity, fps:	2067	1832	1615	1423	
	energy, ft-lb:	1480	1162	904	701	
	arc, inches:		+4.4	0	-17.8	

6.5X52 CARCANO

CARTRIDGE BULLET	RANGE, YARDS:	0	100	200	300	400
Norma 156 Alaska	velocity, fps:	2428	2169	1926	1702	
	energy, ft-lb:	2043	1630	1286	1004	
	arc, inches:		+2.9	0	-12.3	

6.5X55 SWEDISH

CARTRIDGE BULLET	RANGE, YARDS:	0	100	200	300	400
Federal 140 Hi-Shok	velocity, fps:	2600	2400	2220	2040	1860
	energy, ft-lb:	2100	1795	1525	1285	1080
	arc, inches:		+2.3	0	-9.4	-27.2
Federal 140 Trophy Bonded	velocity, fps:	2550	2350	2160	1980	1810
	energy, ft-lb:	2020	1720	1450	1220	1015
	arc, inches:		+2.4	0	-9.8	-28.4
Federal 140 Sierra MatchKg.	velocity, fps:	2630	2460	2300	2140	2000
BTHP	energy, ft-lb:	2140	1880	1640	1430	1235
	arc, inches:		+16.4	+28.8	+33.9	+31.8
Hornady 129 SP LM	velocity, fps:	2770	2561	2361	2171	1994
	energy, ft-lb:	2197	1878	1597	1350	1138
	arc, inches:		+2.0	0	-8.2	-23.2
Hornady 140 SP Interlock	velocity, fps	2525	2341	2165	1996	1836
	energy, ft-lb:	1982	1704	1457	1239	1048
	arc, inches:		+2.4	0	-9.9	-28.5
Hornady140 SP LM	velocity, fps:	2740	2541	2351	2169	1999
	energy, ft-lb:	2333	2006	1717	1463	1242
	arc, inches:		+2.4	0	-8.7	-24.0
Norma 120 Nosler Bal. Tip	velocity, fps:	2822	2609	2407	2213	
	energy, ft-lb:	2123	1815	1544	1305	
	arc, inches:		+1.8	0	-7.8	
Norma 139 Vulkan	velocity, fps:	2854	2569	2302	2051	
	energy, ft-lb:	2515	2038	1636	1298	
	arc, inches:		+1.8	0	-8.4	
Norma 140 Nosler Partition	velocity, fps:	2789	2592	2403	2223	
	energy, ft-lb:	2419	2089	1796	1536	
	arc, inches:		+1.8	0	-7.8	
Norma 156 TXP Swift A-Fr.	velocity, fps:	2526	2276	2040	1818	
	energy, ft-lb:	2196	1782	1432	1138	
	arc, inches:		+2.6	0	-10.9	
Norma 156 Alaska	velocity, fps:	2559	2245	1953	1687	
	energy, ft-lb:	2269	1746	1322	986	
	arc, inches:		+2.7	0	-11.9	
Norma 156 Vulkan	velocity, fps:	2644	2395	2159	1937	
	energy, ft-lb:	2422	1987	1616	1301	
	arc, inches:		+2.2	0	-9.7	

CARTRIDGE BULLET	RANGE, YARDS:	0	100	200	300	400
Norma 156 Oryx	velocity, fps:	2559	2308	2070	1848	
	energy, ft-lb:	2269	1845	1485	1183	
	arc, inches:		+2.5	0	-10.6	
PMC 139 Pointed Soft Point	velocity, fps:	2850	2560	2290	2030	1790
	energy, ft-lb:	2515	2025	1615	1270	985
	arc, inches:		+2.2	0	-8.9	-26.3
PMC 140 HP boat-tail	velocity, fps:	2560	2398	2243	2093	1949
	energy, ft-lb:	2037	1788	1563	1361	1181
	arc, inches:		+2.3	0	-9.2	-26.4
PMC 140 SP boat-tail	velocity, fps:	2560	2386	2218	2057	1903
	energy, ft-lb:	2037	1769	1529	1315	1126
	arc, inches:		+2.3	0	-9.4	-27.1
PMC 144 FMJ	velocity, fps:	2650	2370	2110	1870	1650
	energy, ft-lb:	2425	1950	1550	1215	945
	arc, inches:		+2.7	0	-10.5	-30.9
Rem. 140 PSP Core-Lokt	velocity, fps:	2550	2353	2164	1984	1814
	energy, ft-lb:	2021	1720	1456	1224	1023
	arc, inches:		+2.4	0	-9.8	-27.0
Speer 140 Grand Slam	velocity, fps:	2550	2318	2099	1892	
	energy, ft-lb:	2021	1670	1369	1112	
	arc, inches:		+2.5	0	-10.4	-30.6
Win. 140 Soft Point	velocity, fps:	2550	2359	2176	2002	1836
	energy, ft-lb:	2022	1731	1473	1246	1048
	arc, inches:		+2.4	0	-9.7	-28.1

.260 Remington

CARTRIDGE BULLET	RANGE, YARDS:	0	100	200	300	400
Federal 140 Sierra GameKing	velocity, fps:	2750	2570	2390	2220	2060
BTSP	energy, ft-lb:	2350	2045	1775	1535	1315
	arc, inches:		+1.9	0	-8.0	-23.1
Federal 140 Trophy Bonded	velocity, fps:	2750	2540	2340	2150	1970
	energy, ft-lb:	2350	2010	1705	1440	1210
	arc, inches:		+1.9	0	-8.4	-24.1
Rem. 120 Nosler Bal. Tip	velocity, fps:	2890	2688	2494	2309	2131
	energy, ft-lb:	2226	1924	1657	1420	1210
	arc, inches:		+1.7	0	-7.3	-21.1
Rem. 120 AccuTip	velocity, fps:	2890	2697	2512	2334	2163
	energy, ft-lb:	2392	2083	1807	1560	1340
	arc, inches:		+1.6	0	-7.2	-20.7
Rem. 125 Nosler Partition	velocity, fps:	2875	2669	2473	2285	2105
	energy, ft-lb:	2294	1977	1697	1449	1230
	arc, inches:		+1.71	0	-7.4	-21.4
Rem. 140 PSP Core-Lokt	velocity, fps:	2750	2544	2347	2158	1979
(and C-L Ultra)	energy, ft-lb:	2351	2011	1712	1448	1217
	arc, inches:		+1.9	0	-8.3	-24.0
Speer 140 Grand Slam	velocity, fps:	2750	2518	2297	2087	
	energy, ft-lb:	2351	1970	1640	1354	
	arc, inches:		+2.3	0	-8.9	-25.8

6.5/284

CARTRIDGE BULLET	RANGE, YARDS:	0	100	200	300	400
Norma 120 Nosler Bal. Tip	velocity, fps:	3117	2890	2674	2469	
	energy, ft-lb:	2589	2226	1906	1624	
	arc, inches:		+1.3	0	-6.2	
Norma 140 Nosler Part.	velocity, fps:	2953	2750	2557	2371	
	energy, ft-lb:	2712	2352	2032	1748	
	arc, inches:		+1.5	0	-6.8	

6.5 Remington Mag.

CARTRIDGE BULLET	RANGE, YARDS:	0	100	200	300	400
Rem. 120 Core-Lokt PSP	velocity, fps:	3210	2905	2621	2353	2102
	energy, ft-lb:	2745	2248	1830	1475	1177
	arc, inches:		+2.7	+2.1	-3.5	-15.5

.264 Winchester Mag.

CARTRIDGE BULLET	RANGE, YARDS:	0	100	200	300	400
Rem. 140 PSP Core-Lokt	velocity, fps:	3030	2782	2548	2326	2114
	energy, ft-lb:	2854	2406	2018	1682	1389
	arc, inches:		+1.5	0	-6.9	-20.2

CARTRIDGE BULLET	RANGE, YARDS:	0	100	200	300	400
Win. 140 Power-Point	velocity, fps:	3030	2782	2548	2326	2114
	energy, ft-lb:	2854	2406	2018	1682	1389
	arc, inches:		+1.8	0	-7.2	-20.8

6.8mm Remington SPC

CARTRIDGE BULLET	RANGE, YARDS:	0	100	200	300	400
Rem. 115 Open Tip Match	velocity, fps:	2800	2535	2285	2049	1828
(and HPBT Match)	energy, ft-lb:	2002	1641	1333	1072	853
	arc, inches:		+2.0	0	-8.8	-26.2
Rem. 115 Metal Case	velocity, fps:	2800	2523	2262	2017	1789
	energy, ft-lb:	2002	1625	1307	1039	817
	arc, inches:		+2.0	0	-8.8	-26.2
Rem. 115 Sierra HPBT	velocity, fps:	2775	2511	2263	2028	1809
(2005; all vel. @ 2775)	energy, ft-lb:	1966	1610	1307	1050	835
	arc, inches:		+2.0	0	-8.8	-26.2
Rem. 115 CL Ultra	velocity, fps:	2775	2472	2190	1926	1683
	energy, ft-lb:	1966	1561	1224	947	723
	arc, inches:		+2.1	0	-9.4	-28.2

.270 Winchester

CARTRIDGE BULLET	RANGE, YARDS:	0	100	200	300	400
Black Hills 130 Nos. Bal. T.	velocity, fps:	2950				
	energy, ft-lb:	2512				
	arc, inches:					
Black Hills 130 Barnes XLC	velocity, ft-lb:	2950				
	energy, ft-lb:	2512				
	arc, inches:					
Federal 130 Hi-Shok	velocity, fps:	3060	2800	2560	2330	2110
	energy, ft-lb:	2700	2265	1890	1565	1285
	arc, inches:		+1.5	0	-6.8	-20.0
Federal 130 Sierra Pro-Hunt.	velocity, fps:	3060	2830	2600	2390	2190
	energy, ft-lb:	2705	2305	1960	1655	1390
	arc, inches:		+1.4	0	-6.4	-19.0
Federal 130 Sierra GameKing	velocity, fps:	3060	2830	2620	2410	2220
	energy, ft-lb:	2700	2320	1980	1680	1420
	arc, inches:		+1.4	0	-6.5	-19.0
Federal 130 Nosler Bal. Tip	velocity, fps:	3060	2840	2630	2430	2230
	energy, ft-lb:	2700	2325	1990	1700	1440
	arc, inches:		+1.4	0	-6.5	-18.8
Federal 130 Nos. Partition	velocity, fps:	3060	2830	2610	2400	2200
And Solid Base	energy, ft-lb:	2705	2310	1965	1665	1400
	arc, inches:		+1.4	0	-6.5	-19.1
Federal 130 Barnes XLC	velocity, fps:	3060	2840	2620	2420	2220
And Triple Shock	energy, ft-lb:	2705	2320	1985	1690	1425
	arc, inches:		+1.4	0	-6.4	-18.9
Federal 130 Trophy Bonded	velocity, fps:	3060	2810	2570	2340	2130
	energy, ft-lb:	2705	2275	1905	1585	1310
	arc, inches:		+1.5	0	-6.7	-19.8
Federal 140 Trophy Bonded	velocity, fps:	2940	2700	2480	2260	2060
	energy, ft-lb:	2685	2270	1905	1590	1315
	arc, inches:		+1.6	0	-7.3	-21.5
Federal 140 Tr. Bonded HE	velocity, fps:	3100	2860	2620	2400	2200
	energy, ft-lb:	2990	2535	2140	1795	1500
	arc, inches:		+1.4	0	-6.4	-18.9
Federal 140 Nos. AccuBond	velocity, fps:	2950	2760	2580	2400	2230
	energy, ft-lb:	2705	2365	2060	1790	1545
	arc, inches:		+1.5	0	-6.7	-19.6
Federal 150 Hi-Shok RN	velocity, fps:	2850	2500	2180	1890	1620
	energy, ft-lb:	2705	2085	1585	1185	870
	arc, inches:		+2.0	0	-9.4	-28.6
Federal 150 Sierra GameKing	velocity, fps:	2850	2660	2480	2300	2130
	energy, ft-lb:	2705	2355	2040	1760	1510
	arc, inches:		+1.7	0	-7.4	-21.4
Federal 150 Sierra GameKing	velocity, fps:	3000	2800	2620	2430	2260
HE	energy, ft-lb:	2995	2615	2275	1975	1700
	arc, inches:		+1.5	0	-6.5	-18.9

Centerfire Rifle Ballistics

.270 WINCHESTER TO .270 WINCHESTER SHORT MAG.

CARTRIDGE BULLET	RANGE, YARDS:	0	100	200	300	400
Federal 150 Nosler Partition	velocity, fps:	2850	2590	2340	2100	1880
	energy, ft-lb:	2705	2225	1815	1470	1175
	arc, inches:		+1.9	0	-8.3	-24.4
Hornady 130 SST (or Interbond)	velocity, fps:	3060	2845	2639	2442	2254
	energy, ft-lb:	2700	2335	2009	1721	1467
	arc, inches:		+1.4	0	-6.6	-19.1
Hornady 130 SST LM (or Interbond)	velocity, fps:	3215	2998	2790	2590	2400
	energy, ft-lb:	2983	2594	2246	1936	1662
	arc, inches:		+1.2	0	-5.8	-17.0
Hornady 140 SP boat-tail	velocity, fps:	2940	2747	2562	2385	2214
	energy, ft-lb:	2688	2346	2041	1769	1524
	arc, inches:		+1.6	0	-7.0	-20.2
Hornady 140 SP boat-tail LM	velocity, fps:	3100	2894	2697	2508	2327
	energy, ft-lb:	2987	2604	2261	1955	1684
	arc, inches:		+1.4	0	6.3	-18.3
Hornady 150 SP	velocity, fps:	2800	2684	2478	2284	2100
	energy, ft-lb:	2802	2400	2046	1737	1469
	arc, inches:		+1.7	0	-7.4	-21.6
Norma 130 SP	velocity, fps:	3140	2862	2601	2354	
	energy, ft-lb:	2847	2365	1953	1600	
	arc, inches:		+1.3	0	-6.5	
Norma 130 FMJ	velocity, fps:	2887	2634	2395	2169	
	energy, ft-lb:					
	arc, inches:		+1.8	0	-7.8	
Norma 150 SP	velocity, fps:	2799	2555	2323	2104	
	energy, ft-lb:	2610	2175	1798	1475	
	arc, inches:		+1.9	0	-8.3	
Norma 150 Oryx	velocity, fps:	2854	2608	2376	2155	
	Energy, ft-lb:	2714	2267	1880	1547	
	Arc, inches:		+1.8	0	-8.0	
PMC 130 Barnes X	velocity, fps:	2910	2717	2533	2356	2186
	energy, ft-lb:	2444	2131	1852	1602	1379
	arc, inches:		+1.6	0	-7.1	-20.4
PMC 130 SP boat-tail	velocity, fps:	3050	2830	2620	2421	2229
	energy, ft-lb:	2685	2312	1982	1691	1435
	arc, inches:		+1.5	0	-6.5	-19.0
PMC 130 Pointed Soft Point	velocity, fps:	2950	2691	2447	2217	2001
	energy, ft-lb:	2512	2090	1728	1419	1156
	arc, inches:		+1.6	0	-7.5	-22.1
PMC 150 Barnes X	velocity, fps:	2700	2541	2387	2238	2095
	energy, ft-lb:	2428	2150	1897	1668	1461
	arc, inches:		+2.0	0	-8.1	-23.1
PMC 150 SP boat-tail	velocity, fps:	2850	2660	2477	2302	2134
	energy, ft-lb:	2705	2355	2043	1765	1516
	arc, inches:		+1.7	0	-7.4	-21.4
PMC 150 Pointed Soft Point	velocity, fps:	2750	2530	2321	2123	1936
	energy, ft-lb:	2519	2131	1794	1501	1248
	arc, inches:		+2.0	0	-8.4	-24.6
Rem. 100 Pointed Soft Point	velocity, fps:	3320	2924	2561	2225	1916
	energy, ft-lb:	2448	1898	1456	1099	815
	arc, inches:		+2.3	+2.0	-3.6	-16.2
Rem. 115 PSP Core-Lokt mr	velocity, fps:	2710	2412	2133	1873	1636
	energy, ft-lb:	1875	1485	1161	896	683
	arc, inches:		+1.0	-2.7	-14.2	-35.6
Rem. 130 PSP Core-Lokt	velocity, fps:	3060	2776	2510	2259	2022
	energy, ft-lb:	2702	2225	1818	1472	1180
	arc, inches:		+1.5	0	-7.0	-20.9
Rem. 130 Bronze Point	velocity, fps:	3060	2802	2559	2329	2110
	energy, ft-lb:	2702	2267	1890	1565	1285
	arc, inches:		+1.5	0	-6.8	-20.0
Rem. 130 Swift Scirocco	velocity, fps:	3060	2838	2677	2425	2232
	energy, ft-lb:	2702	2325	1991	1697	1438
	arc, inches:		+1.4	0	-6.5	-18.8

CARTRIDGE BULLET	RANGE, YARDS:	0	100	200	300	400
Rem. 130 AccuTip BT	velocity, fps:	3060	2845	2639	2442	2254
	energy, ft-lb:	2702	2336	2009	1721	1467
	arc, inches:		+1.4	0	-6.4	-18.6
Rem. 140 Swift A-Frame	velocity, fps:	2925	2652	2394	2152	1923
	energy, ft-lb:	2659	2186	1782	1439	1150
	arc, inches:		+1.7	0	-7.8	-23.2
Rem. 140 PSP boat-tail	velocity, fps:	2960	2749	2548	2355	2171
	energy, ft-lb:	2723	2349	2018	1724	1465
	arc, inches:		+1.6	0	-6.9	-20.1
Rem. 140 Nosler Bal. Tip	velocity, fps:	2960	2754	2557	2366	2187
	energy, ft-lb:	2724	2358	2032	1743	1487
	arc, inches:		+1.6	0	-6.9	-20.0
Rem. 140 PSP C-L Ultra	velocity, fps:	2925	2667	2424	2193	1975
	energy, ft-lb:	2659	2211	1826	1495	1212
	arc, inches:		+1.7	0	-7.6	-22.5
Rem. 150 SP Core-Lokt	velocity, fps:	2850	2504	2183	1886	1618
	energy, ft-lb:	2705	2087	1587	1185	872
	arc, inches:		+2.0	0	-9.4	-28.6
Rem. 150 Nosler Partition	velocity, fps:	2850	2652	2463	2282	2108
	energy, ft-lb:	2705	2343	2021	1734	1480
	arc, inches:		+1.7	0	-7.5	-21.6
Speer 130 Grand Slam	velocity, fps:	3050	2774	2514	2269	
	energy, ft-lb:	2685	2221	1824	1485	
	arc, inches:		+1.5	0	-7.0	-20.9
Speer 150 Grand Slam	velocity, fps:	2830	2594	2369	2156	
	energy, ft-lb:	2667	2240	1869	1548	
	arc, inches:		+1.8	0	-8.1	-23.6
Win. 130 Power-Point	velocity, fps:	3060	2802	2559	2329	2110
	energy, ft-lb:	2702	2267	1890	1565	1285
	arc, inches:		+1.8	0	-7.1	-20.6
Win. 130 Power-Point Plus	velocity, fps:	3150	2881	2628	2388	2161
	energy, ft-lb:	2865	2396	1993	1646	1348
	arc, inches:		+1.3	0	-6.4	-18.9
Win. 130 Silvertip	velocity, fps:	3060	2776	2510	2259	2022
	energy, ft-lb:	2702	2225	1818	1472	1180
	arc, inches:		+1.8	0	-7.4	-21.6
Win. 130 Ballistic Silvertip	velocity, fps:	3050	2828	2618	2416	2224
	energy, ft-lb:	2685	2309	1978	1685	1428
	arc, inches:		+1.4	0	-6.5	-18.9
Win. 140 AccuBond	velocity, fps:	2950	2751	2560	2378	2203
	energy, ft-lb:	2705	2352	2038	1757	1508
	arc, inches:		+1.6	0	-6.9	-19.9
Win. 140 Fail Safe	velocity, fps:	2920	2671	2435	2211	1999
	energy, ft-lb:	2651	2218	1843	1519	1242
	arc, inches:		+1.7	0	-7.6	-22.3
Win. 150 Power-Point	velocity, fps:	2850	2585	2336	2100	1879
	energy, ft-lb:	2705	2226	1817	1468	1175
	arc, inches:		+2.2	0	-8.6	-25.0
Win. 150 Power-Point Plus	velocity, fps:	2950	2679	2425	2184	1957
	energy, ft-lb:	2900	2391	1959	1589	1276
	arc, inches:		+1.7	0	-7.6	-22.6
Win. 150 Partition Gold	velocity, fps:	2930	2693	2468	2254	2051
	energy, ft-lb:	2860	2416	2030	1693	1402
	arc, inches:		+1.7	0	-7.4	-21.6

.270 Winchester Short Mag.

CARTRIDGE BULLET	RANGE, YARDS:	0	100	200	300	400
Black Hills 140 AccuBond	velocity, fps:	3100				
	energy, ft-lb:	2987				
	arc, inches:					
Federal 130 Nos. Bal. Tip	velocity, fps:	3300	3070	2840	2630	2430
	energy, ft-lb:	3145	2710	2335	2000	1705
	arc, inches:		+1.1	0	-5.4	-15.8

CARTRIDGE BULLET	RANGE, YARDS:	0	100	200	300	400
Federal 130 Nos. Partition And Nos. Solid Base And Barnes TS	velocity, fps:	3280	3040	2810	2590	2380
	energy, ft-lb:	3105	2665	2275	1935	1635
	arc, inches:		+1.1	0	-5.6	-16.3
Federal 140 Nos. AccuBond	velocity, fps	3200	3000	2810	2630	2450
	energy, ft-lb:	3185	2795	2455	2145	1865
	arc, inches:		+1.2	0	-5.6	-16.2
Federal 140 Trophy Bonded	velocity, fps:	3130	2870	2640	2410	2200
	energy, ft-lb:	3035	2570	2160	1810	1500
	arc, inches:		+1.4	0	-6.3	18.7
Federal 150 Nos. Partition	velocity, fps:	3160	2950	2750	2550	2370
	energy, ft-lb:	3325	2895	2515	2175	1870
	arc, inches:		+1.3	0	-5.9	-17.0
Norma 130 FMJ	velocity, fps:	3150	2882	2630	2391	
	energy, ft-lb:					
	arc, inches:		+1.5	0	-6.4	
Norma 130 Ballistic ST	velocity, fps:	3281	3047	2825	2614	
	energy, ft-lb:	3108	2681	2305	1973	
	arc, inches:		+1.1	0	-5.5	
Norma 140 Barnes X TS	velocity, fps:	3150	2952	2762	2580	
	energy, ft-lb:	3085	2709	2372	2070	
	arc, inches:		+1.3	0	-5.8	
Norma 150 Nosler Bal. Tip	velocity, fps:	3280	3046	2824	2613	
	energy, ft-lb:	3106	2679	2303	1972	
	arc, inches:		+1.1	0	-5.4	
Norma 150 Oryx	velocity, fps:	3117	2856	2611	2378	
	energy, ft-lb:	3237	2718	2271	1884	
	arc, inches:		+1.4	0	-6.5	
Win. 130 Bal. Silvertip	velocity, fps:	3275	3041	2820	2609	2408
	energy, ft-lb:	3096	2669	2295	1964	1673
	arc, inches:		+1.1	0	-5.5	-16.1
Win. 140 AccuBond	velocity, fps:	3200	2989	2789	2597	2413
	energy, ft-lb:	3184	2779	2418	2097	1810
	arc, inches:		+1.2	0	-5.7	-16.5
Win. 140 Fail Safe	velocity, fps:	3125	2865	2619	2386	2165
	energy, ft-lb:	3035	2550	2132	1769	1457
	arc, inches:		+1.4	0	-6.5	-19.0
Win. 150 Ballistic Silvertip	velocity, fps:	3120	2923	2734	2554	2380
	energy, ft-lb:	3242	2845	2490	2172	1886
	arc, inches:		+1.3	0	-5.9	-17.2
Win. 150 Power Point	velocity, fps:	3150	2867	2601	2350	2113
	energy, ft-lb:	3304	2737	2252	1839	1487
	arc, inches:		+1.4	0	-6.5	-19.4

.270 Weatherby Mag.

CARTRIDGE BULLET	RANGE, YARDS:	0	100	200	300	400
Federal 130 Nosler Partition	velocity, fps:	3200	2960	2740	2520	2320
	energy, ft-lb:	2955	2530	2160	1835	1550
	arc, inches:		+1.2	0	-5.9	-17.3
Federal 130 Sierra GameKing BTSP	velocity, fps:	3200	2980	2780	2580	2400
	energy, ft-lb:	2955	2570	2230	1925	1655
	arc, inches:		+1.2	0	-5.7	-16.6
Federal 140 Trophy Bonded	velocity, fps:	3100	2840	2600	2370	2150
	energy, ft-lb:	2990	2510	2100	1745	1440
	arc, inches:		+1.4	0	-6.6	-19.3
Wby. 100 Pointed Expanding	velocity, fps:	3760	3396	3061	2751	2462
	energy, ft-lb:	3139	2560	2081	1681	1346
	arc, inches:		+2.3	+3.0	0	-7.6
Wby. 130 Pointed Expanding	velocity, fps:	3375	3123	2885	2659	2444
	energy, ft-lb:	3288	2815	2402	2041	1724
	arc, inches:		+2.8	+3.5	0	-8.4
Wby. 130 Nosler Partition	velocity, fps:	3375	3127	2892	2670	2458
	energy, ft-lb:	3288	2822	2415	2058	1744
	arc, inches:		+2.8	+3.5	0	-8.3
Wby. 140 Nosler Bal. Tip	velocity, fps:	3300	3077	2865	2663	2470
	energy, ft-lb:	3385	2943	2551	2204	1896
	arc, inches:		+2.9	+3.6	0	-8.4
Wby. 140 Barnes X	velocity, fps:	3250	3032	2825	2628	2438
	energy, ft-lb:	3283	2858	2481	2146	1848
	arc, inches:		+3.0	+3.7	0	-8.7
Wby. 150 Pointed Expanding	velocity, fps:	3245	3028	2821	2623	2434
	energy, ft-lb:	3507	3053	2650	2292	1973
	arc, inches:		+3.0	+3.7	0	-8.7
Wby. 150 Nosler Partition	velocity, fps:	3245	3029	2823	2627	2439
	energy, ft-lb:	3507	3055	2655	2298	1981
	arc, inches:		+3.0	+3.7	0	-8.

7-30 Waters

CARTRIDGE BULLET	RANGE, YARDS:	0	100	200	300	400
Federal 120 Sierra GameKing BTSP	velocity, fps:	2700	2300	1930	1600	1330
	energy, ft-lb:	1940	1405	990	685	470
	arc, inches:		+2.6	0	-12.0	-37.6

7mm Mauser (7x57)

CARTRIDGE BULLET	RANGE, YARDS:	0	100	200	300	400
Federal 140 Sierra Pro-Hunt.	velocity, fps:	2660	2450	2260	2070	1890
	energy, ft-lb:	2200	1865	1585	1330	1110
	arc, inches:		+2.1	0	-9.0	-26.1
Federal 140 Nosler Partition	velocity, fps:	2660	2450	2260	2070	1890
	energy, ft-lb:	2200	1865	1585	1330	1110
	arc, inches:		+2.1	0	-9.0	-26.1
Federal 175 Hi-Shok RN	velocity, fps:	2440	2140	1860	1600	1380
	energy, ft-lb:	2315	1775	1340	1000	740
	arc, inches:		+3.1	0	-13.3	-40.1
Hornady 139 SP boat-tail	velocity, fps:	2700	2504	2316	2137	1965
	energy, ft-lb:	2251	1936	1656	1410	1192
	arc, inches:		+2.0	0	-8.5	-24.9
Hornady 139 SP Interlock	velocity, fps:	2680	2455	2241	2038	1846
	energy, ft-lb:	2216	1860	1550	1282	1052
	arc, inches:		+2.1	0	-9.1	-26.6
Hornady 139 SP boat-tail LM	velocity, fps:	2830	2620	2450	2250	2070
	energy, ft-lb:	2475	2135	1835	1565	1330
	arc, inches:		+1.8	0	-7.6	-22.1
Hornady 139 SP LM	velocity, fps:	2950	2736	2532	2337	2152
	energy, ft-lb:	2686	2310	1978	1686	1429
	arc, inches:		+2.0	0	-7.6	-21.5
Norma 150 Soft Point	velocity, fps:	2690	2479	2278	2087	
	energy, ft-lb:	2411	2048	1729	1450	
	arc, inches:		+2.0	0	-8.8	
PMC 140 Pointed Soft Point	velocity, fps:	266[illegible]	2450	2260	2070	1890
	energy, ft-lb:	220[illegible]	1865	1585	1330	1110
	arc, inches:		+2.4	0	-9.6	-27.3
PMC 175 Soft Point	velocity, fps:	244[illegible]	2140	1860	1600	1380
	energy, ft-lb:	2315	1775	1340	1000	740
	arc, inches:		+1.5	-3.6	-18.6	-46.8
Rem. 140 PSP Core-Lokt	velocity, fps:	2660	2435	2221	2018	1827
	energy, ft-lb:	2199	1843	1533	1266	1037
	arc, inches:		+2.2	0	-9.2	-27.4
Win. 145 Power-Point	velocity, fps:	2660	2413	2180	1959	1754
	energy, ft-lb:	2279	1875	1530	1236	990
	arc, inches:		+1.1	-2.8	-14.1	-34.4

7x57 R

CARTRIDGE BULLET	RANGE, YARDS:	0	100	200	300	400
Norma 150 FMJ	velocity, fps:	2690	2489	2296	2112	
	energy, ft-lb:	2411	2063	1756	1486	
	arc, inches:		+2.0	0	-8.6	
Norma 154 Soft Point	velocity, fps:	2625	2417	2219	2030	
	energy, ft-lb:	2357	1999	1684	1410	
	arc, inches:		+2.2	0	-9.3	

Centerfire Rifle Ballistics

7X57 R TO .280 REMINGTON

CARTRIDGE BULLET	RANGE, YARDS:	0	100	200	300	400
Norma 156 Oryx	velocity, fps:	2608	2346	2099	1867	
	energy, ft-lb:	2357	1906	1526	1208	
	arc, inches:		+2.4	0	-10.3	

7MM-08 REMINGTON

CARTRIDGE BULLET	RANGE, YARDS:	0	100	200	300	400
Black Hills 140 AccuBond	velocity, fps:	2700				
	energy, ft-lb:					
	arc, inches:					
Federal 140 Nosler Partition	velocity, fps:	2800	2590	2390	2200	2020
	energy, ft-lb:	2435	2085	1775	1500	1265
	arc, inches:		+1.8	0	-8.0	-23.1
Federal 140 Nosler Bal. Tip And AccuBond	velocity, fps:	2800	2610	2430	2260	2100
	energy, ft-lb:	2440	2135	1840	1590	1360
	arc, inches:		+1.8	0	-7.7	-22.3
Federal 140 Tr. Bonded HE	velocity, fps:	2950	2660	2390	2140	1900
	energy, ft-lb:	2705	2205	1780	1420	1120
	arc, inches:		+1.7	0	-7.9	-23.2
Federal 150 Sierra Pro-Hunt.	velocity, fps:	2650	2440	2230	2040	1860
	energy, ft-lb:	2340	1980	1660	1390	1150
	arc, inches:		+2.2	0	-9.2	-26.7
Hornady 139 SP boat-tail LM	velocity, fps:	3000	2790	2590	2399	2216
	energy, ft-lb:	2777	2403	2071	1776	1515
	arc, inches:		+1.5	0	-6.7	-19.4
Norma 140 Ballistic ST	velocity, fps:	2822	2633	2452	2278	
	energy, ft-lb:	2476	2156	1870	1614	
	arc, inches:		+1.8	0	-7.6	
PMC 139 PSP	velocity, fps:	2850	2610	2384	2170	1969
	energy, ft-lb:	2507	2103	1754	1454	1197
	arc, inches:		+1.8	0	-7.9	-23.3
Rem. 120 Hollow Point	velocity, fps:	3000	2725	2467	2223	1992
	energy, ft-lb:	2398	1979	1621	1316	1058
	arc, inches:		+1.6	0	-7.3	-21.7
Rem. 140 PSP Core-Lokt	velocity, fps:	2860	2625	2402	2189	1988
	energy, ft-lb:	2542	2142	1793	1490	1228
	arc, inches:		+1.8	0	-7.8	-22.9
Rem. 140 PSP boat-tail	velocity, fps:	2860	2656	2460	2273	2094
	energy, ft-lb:	2542	2192	1881	1606	1363
	arc, inches:		+1.7	0	-7.5	-21.7
Rem. 140 AccuTip BT	velocity, fps:	2860	2670	2488	2313	2145
	energy, ft-lb:	2543	2217	1925	1663	1431
	arc, inches:		+1.7	0	-7.3	-21.2
Rem. 140 Nosler Partition	velocity, fps:	2860	2648	2446	2253	2068
	energy, ft-lb:	2542	2180	1860	1577	1330
	arc, inches:		+1.7	0	-7.6	-22.0
Speer 145 Grand Slam	velocity, fps:	2845	2567	2305	2059	
	energy, ft-lb:	2606	2121	1711	1365	
	arc, inches:		+1.9	0	-8.4	-25.5
Win. 140 Power-Point	velocity, fps:	2800	2523	2268	2027	1802
	energy, ft-lb:	2429	1980	1599	1277	1010
	arc, inches:		+2.0	0	-8.8	-26.0
Win. 140 Power-Point Plus	velocity, fps:	2875	2597	2336	2090	1859
	energy, ft-lb:	2570	1997	1697	1358	1075
	arc, inches:		+2.0	0	-8.8	26.0
Win. 140 Fail Safe	velocity, fps:	2760	2506	2271	2048	1839
	energy, ft-lb:	2360	1953	1603	1304	1051
	arc, inches:		+2.0	0	-8.8	-25.9
Win. 140 Ballistic Silvertip	velocity, fps:	2770	2572	2382	2200	2026
	energy, ft-lb:	2386	2056	1764	1504	1276
	arc, inches:		+1.9	0	-8.0	-23.8

7X64 BRENNEKE

CARTRIDGE BULLET	RANGE, YARDS:	0	100	200	300	400
Federal 160 Nosler Partition	velocity, fps:	2650	2480	2310	2150	2000
	energy, ft-lb:	2495	2180	1895	1640	1415
	arc, inches:		+2.1	0	-8.7	-24.9
Norma 140 AccuBond	velocity, fps:	2953	2759	2572	2394	
	energy, ft-lb:	2712	2366	2058	1782	
	arc, inches:		+1.5	0	-6.8	
Norma 154 Soft Point	velocity, fps:	2821	2605	2399	2203	
	energy, ft-lb:	2722	2321	1969	1660	
	arc, inches:		+1.8	0	-7.8	
Norma 156 Oryx	velocity, fps:	2789	2516	2259	2017	
	energy, ft-lb:	2695	2193	1768	1410	
	arc, inches:		+2.0	0	-8.8	
Norma 170 Vulkan	velocity, fps:	2756	2501	2259	2031	
	energy, ft-lb:	2868	2361	1927	1558	
	arc, inches:		+2.0	0	-8.8	
Norma 170 Oryx	velocity, fps:	2756	2481	2222	1979	
	energy, ft-lb:	2868	2324	1864	1478	
	arc, inches:		+2.1	0	-9.2	
Norma 170 Plastic Point	velocity, fps:	2756	2519	2294	2081	
	energy, ft-lb:	2868	2396	1987	1635	
	arc, inches:		+2.0	0	-8.6	
PMC 170 Pointed Soft Point	velocity, fps:	2625	2401	2189	1989	1801
	energy, ft lb:	2601	2175	1808	1493	1224
	arc, inches:		+2.3	0	-9.6	-27.9
Rem. 175 PSP Core-Lokt	velocity, fps:	2650	2445	2248	2061	1883
	energy, ft-lb:	2728	2322	1964	1650	1378
	arc, inches:		+2.2	0	-9.1	-26.4
Speer 160 Grand Slam	velocity, fps:	2600	2376	2164	1962	
	energy, ft-lb:	2401	2006	1663	1368	
	arc, inches:		+2.3	0	-9.8	-28.6
Speer 175 Grand Slam	velocity, fps:	2650	2461	2280	2106	
	energy, ft-lb:	2728	2353	2019	1723	
	arc, inches:		+2.4	0	-9.2	-26.2

7X65 R

CARTRIDGE BULLET	RANGE, YARDS:	0	100	200	300	400
Norma 150 FMJ	velocity, fps:	2756	2552	2357	2170	
	energy, ft-lb:	2530	2169	1850	1569	
	arc, inches:		+1.9	0	-8.2	
Norma 156 Oryx	velocity, fps:	2723	2454	2200	1962	
	energy, ft-lb:	2569	2086	1678	1334	
	arc, inches:		+2.1	0	-9.3	
Norma 170 Plastic Point	velocity, fps:	2625	2390	2167	1956	
	energy, ft-lb:	2602	2157	1773	1445	
	arc, inches:		+2.3	0	-9.7	
Norma 170 Vulkan	velocity, fps:	2657	2392	2143	1909	
	energy, ft-lb:	2666	2161	1734	1377	
	arc, inches:		+2.3	0	-9.9	
Norma 170 Oryx	velocity, fps:	2657	2378	2115	1871	
	energy, ft-lb:	2666	2135	1690	1321	
	arc, inches:		+2.3	0	-10.1	

.284 WINCHESTER

CARTRIDGE BULLET	RANGE, YARDS:	0	100	200	300	400
Win. 150 Power-Point	velocity, fps:	2860	2595	2344	2108	1886
	energy, ft-lb:	2724	2243	1830	1480	1185
	arc, inches:		+2.1	0	-8.5	-24.8

.280 REMINGTON

CARTRIDGE BULLET	RANGE, YARDS:	0	100	200	300	400
Federal 140 Sierra Pro-Hunt.	velocity, fps:	2990	2740	2500	2270	2060
	energy, ft-lb:	2770	2325	1940	1605	1320
	arc, inches:		+1.6	0	-7.0	-20.8
Federal 140 Trophy Bonded	velocity, fps:	2990	2630	2310	2040	1730
	energy, ft-lb:	2770	2155	1655	1250	925
	arc, inches:		+1.6	0	-8.4	-25.4
Federal 140 Tr. Bonded HE	velocity, fps:	3150	2850	2570	2300	2050
	energy, ft-lb:	3085	2520	2050	1650	1310
	arc, inches:		+1.4	0	-6.7	-20.0

Centerfire Rifle Ballistics

.280 REMINGTON TO 7MM REMINGTON MAG.

CARTRIDGE BULLET	RANGE, YARDS:	0	100	200	300	400
Federal 140 Nos. AccuBond And Bal. Tip And Solid Base	velocity, fps:	3000	2800	2620	2440	2260
	energy, ft-lb:	2800	2445	2130	1845	1590
	arc, inches:		+1.5	0	-6.5	-18.9
Federal 150 Hi-Shok	velocity, fps:	2890	2670	2460	2260	2060
	energy, ft-lb:	2780	2370	2015	1695	1420
	arc, inches:		+1.7	0	-7.5	-21.8
Federal 150 Nosler Partition	velocity, fps:	2890	2690	2490	2310	2130
	energy, ft-lb:	2780	2405	2070	1770	1510
	arc, inches:		+1.7	0	-7.2	-21.1
Federal 150 Nos. AccuBond	velocity, fps	2800	2630	2460	2300	2150
	energy, ft-lb:	2785	2455	2155	1885	1645
	arc, inches:		+1.8	0	-7.5	-21.5
Federal 160 Trophy Bonded	velocity, fps:	2800	2570	2350	2140	1940
	energy, ft-lb:	2785	2345	1960	1625	1340
	arc, inches:		+1.9	0	-8.3	-24.0
Hornady 139 SPBT LMmoly	velocity, fps:	3110	2888	2675	2473	2280
	energy, ft-lb:	2985	2573	2209	1887	1604
	arc, inches:		+1.4	0	-6.5	-18.6
Norma 156 Oryx	velocity, fps:	2789	2516	2259	2017	
	energy, ft-lb:	2695	2193	1768	1410	
	arc, inches:		+2.0	0	-8.8	
Norma 170 Plastic Point	velocity, fps:	2707	2468	2241	2026	
	energy, ft-lb:	2767	2299	1896	1550	
	arc, inches:		+2.1	0	-9.1	
Norma 170 Vulkan	velocity, fps:	2592	2346	2113	1894	
	energy, ft-lb:	2537	2078	1686	1354	
	arc, inches:		+2.4	0	-10.2	
Norma 170 Oryx	velocity, fps:	2690	2416	2159	1918	
	energy, ft-lb:	2732	2204	1760	1389	
	arc, inches:		+2.2	0	-9.7	
Rem. 140 PSP Core-Lokt	velocity, fps:	3000	2758	2528	2309	2102
	energy, ft-lb:	2797	2363	1986	1657	1373
	arc, inches:		+1.5	0	-7.0	-20.5
Rem. 140 PSP boat-tail	velocity, fps:	2860	2656	2460	2273	2094
	energy, ft-lb:	2542	2192	1881	1606	1363
	arc, inches:		+1.7	0	-7.5	-21.7
Rem. 140 Nosler Bal. Tip	velocity, fps:	3000	2804	2616	2436	2263
	energy, ft-lb:	2799	2445	2128	1848	1593
	arc, inches:		+1.5	0	-6.8	-19.0
Rem. 140 AccuTip	velocity, fps:	3000	2804	2617	2437	2265
	energy, ft-lb:	2797	2444	2129	1846	1594
	arc, inches:		+1.5	0	-6.8	-19.0
Rem. 150 PSP Core-Lokt	velocity, fps:	2890	2624	2373	2135	1912
	energy, ft-lb:	2781	2293	1875	1518	1217
	arc, inches:		+1.8	0	-8.0	-23.6
Rem. 165 SP Core-Lokt	velocity, fps:	2820	2510	2220	1950	1701
	energy, ft-lb:	2913	2308	1805	1393	1060
	arc, inches:		+2.0	0	-9.1	-27.4
Speer 145 Grand Slam	velocity, fps:	2900	2619	2354	2105	
	energy, ft-lb:	2707	2207	1784	1426	
	arc, inches:		+2.1	0	-8.4	-24.7
Speer 160 Grand Slam	velocity, fps:	2890	2652	2425	2210	
	energy, ft-lb:	2967	2497	2089	1735	
	arc, inches:		+1.7	0	-7.7	-22.4
Win. 140 Fail Safe	velocity, fps:	3050	2756	2480	2221	1977
	energy, ft-lb:	2893	2362	1913	1533	1216
	arc, inches:		+1.5	0	-7.2	-21.5
Win. 140 Ballistic Silvertip	velocity, fps:	3040	2842	2653	2471	2297
	energy, ft-lb:	2872	2511	2187	1898	1640
	arc, inches:		+1.4	0	-6.3	-18.4

7mm Remington Mag.

CARTRIDGE BULLET	RANGE, YARDS:	0	100	200	300	400
A-Square 175 Monolithic Solid	velocity, fps:	2860	2557	2273	2008	1771
	energy, ft-lb:	3178	2540	2008	1567	1219
	arc, inches:		+1.92	0	-8.7	-25.9
Black Hills 140 Nos. Bal. Tip	velocity, fps:	3150				
	energy, ft-lb:	3084				
	arc, inches:					
Black Hills 140 Barnes XLC	velocity, fps:	3150				
	energy, ft-lb:	3084				
	arc, inches:					
Black Hills 140 Nos. Partition	velocity, fps:	3150				
	energy, ft-lb:	3084				
	arc, inches:					
Federal 140 Nosler Bal. Tip And AccuBond	velocity, fps:	3110	2910	2720	2530	2360
	energy, ft-lb:	3005	2630	2295	1995	1725
	arc, inches:		+1.3	0	-6.0	-17.4
Federal 140 Nosler Partition	velocity, fps:	3150	2930	2710	2510	2320
	energy, ft-lb:	3085	2660	2290	1960	1670
	arc, inches:		+1.3	0	-6.0	-17.5
Federal 140 Trophy Bonded	velocity, fps:	3150	2910	2680	2460	2250
	energy, ft-lb:	3085	2630	2230	1880	1575
	arc, inches:		+1.3	0	-6.1	-18.1
Federal 150 Hi-Shok	velocity, fps:	3110	2830	2570	2320	2090
	energy, ft-lb:	3220	2670	2200	1790	1450
	arc, inches:		+1.4	0	-6.7	-19.9
Federal 150 Sierra GameKing BTSP	velocity, fps:	3110	2920	2750	2580	2410
	energy, ft-lb:	3220	2850	2510	2210	1930
	arc, inches:		+1.3	0	-5.9	-17.0
Federal 150 Nosler Bal. Tip	velocity, fps:	3110	2910	2720	2540	2370
	energy, ft-lb:	3220	2825	2470	2150	1865
	arc, inches:		+1.3	0	-6.0	-17.4
Federal 150 Nos. Solid Base	velocity, fps:	3100	2890	2690	2500	2310
	energy, ft-lb:	3200	2780	2405	2075	1775
	arc, inches:		+1.3	0	-6.2	-17.8
Federal 160 Barnes XLC	velocity, fps:	2940	2760	2580	2410	2240
	energy, ft-lb:	3070	2695	2360	2060	1785
	arc, inches:		+1.5	0	-6.8	-19.6
Federal 160 Sierra Pro-Hunt.	velocity, fps:	2940	2730	2520	2320	2140
	energy, ft-lb:	3070	2640	2260	1920	1620
	arc, inches:		+1.6	0	-7.1	-20.6
Federal 160 Nosler Partition	velocity, fps:	2950	2770	2590	2420	2250
	energy, ft-lb:	3090	2715	2375	2075	1800
	arc, inches:		+1.5	0	-6.7	-19.4
Federal 160 Nos. AccuBond	velocity, fps:	2950	2770	2600	2440	2280
	energy, ft-lb:	3090	2730	2405	2110	1845
	arc, inches:		+1.5	0	-6.6	-19.1
Federal 160 Trophy Bonded	velocity, fps:	2940	2660	2390	2140	1900
	energy, ft-lb:	3070	2505	2025	1620	1280
	arc, inches:		+1.7	0	-7.9	-23.3
Federal 165 Sierra GameKing BTSP	velocity, fps:	2950	2800	2650	2510	2370
	energy, ft-lb:	3190	2865	2570	2300	2050
	arc, inches:		+1.5	0	-6.4	-18.4
Federal 175 Hi-Shok	velocity, fps:	2860	2650	2440	2240	2060
	energy, ft-lb:	3180	2720	2310	1960	1640
	arc, inches:		+1.7	0	-7.6	-22.1
Federal 175 Trophy Bonded	velocity, fps:	2860	2600	2350	2120	1900
	energy, ft-lb:	3180	2625	2150	1745	1400
	arc, inches:		+1.8	0	-8.2	-24.0
Hornady 139 SPBT	velocity, fps:	3150	2933	2727	2530	2341
	energy, ft-lb:	3063	2656	2296	1976	1692
	arc, inches:		+1.2	0	-6.1	-17.7

Centerfire Rifle Ballistics

7MM REMINGTON MAG. TO 7MM REMINGTON MAG.

CARTRIDGE BULLET	RANGE, YARDS:	0	100	200	300	400
Hornady 139 SST	velocity, fps:	3150	2948	2754	2569	2391
(or Interbond)	energy, ft-lb:	3062	2681	2341	2037	1764
	arc, inches:		+1.1	0	-5.7	-16.7
Hornady 139 SST LM	velocity, fps:	3250	3044	2847	2657	2475
(or Interbond)	energy, ft-lb:	3259	2860	2501	2178	1890
	arc, inches:		+1.1	0	-5.5	-16.2
Hornady 139 SPBT HMmoly	velocity, fps:	3250	3041	2822	2613	2413
	energy, ft-lb:	3300	2854	2458	2106	1797
	arc, inches:		+1.1	0	-5.7	-16.6
Hornady 154 Soft Point	velocity, fps:	3035	2814	2604	2404	2212
	energy, ft-lb:	3151	2708	2319	1977	1674
	arc, inches:		+1.3	0	-6.7	-19.3
Hornady 154 SST	velocity, fps:	3035	2850	2672	2501	2337
(or Interbond)	energy, ft-lb:	3149	2777	2441	2139	1867
	arc, inches:		+1.4	0	-6.5	-18.7
Hornady 162 SP boat-tail	velocity, fps:	2940	2757	2582	2413	2251
	energy, ft-lb:	3110	2735	2399	2095	1823
	arc, inches:		+1.6	0	-6.7	-19.7
Hornady 175 SP	velocity, fps:	2860	2650	2440	2240	2060
	energy, ft-lb:	3180	2720	2310	1960	1640
	arc, inches:		+2.0	0	-7.9	-22.7
Norma 140 Nosler Bal. Tip	velocity, fps:	3150	2936	2732	2537	
	energy, ft-lb:	3085	2680	2320	2001	
	arc, inches:		+1.2	0	-5.9	
Norma 140 Barnes X TS	velocity, fps:	3117	2912	2716	2529	
	energy, ft-lb:	3021	2637	2294	1988	
	arch, inches:		+1.3	0	-6.0	
Norma 150 Scirocco	velocity, fps:	3117	2934	2758	2589	
	energy, ft-lb:	3237	2869	2535	2234	
	arc, inches:		+1.2	0	-5.8	
Norma 156 Oryx	velocity, fps:	2953	2670	2404	2153	
	energy, ft-lb:	3021	2470	2002	1607	
	arc, inches:		+1.7	0	-7.7	
Norma 170 Vulkan	velocity, fps:	3018	2747	2493	2252	
	energy, ft-lb:	3439	2850	2346	1914	
	arc, inches:		+1.5	0	-2.8	
Norma 170 Oryx	velocity, fps:	2887	2601	2333	2080	
	energy, ft-lb:	3147	2555	2055	1634	
	arc, inches:		+1.8	0	-8.2	
Norma 170 Plastic Point	velocity, fps:	3018	2762	2519	2290	
	energy, ft-lb:	3439	2880	2394	1980	
	arc, inches:		+1.5	0	-7.0	
PMC 140 Barnes X	velocity, fps:	3000	2808	2624	2448	2279
	energy, ft-lb:	2797	2451	2141	1863	1614
	arc, inches:		+1.5	0	-6.6	18.9
PMC 140 Pointed Soft Point	velocity, fps:	3099	2878	2668	2469	2279
	energy, ft-lb:	2984	2574	2212	1895	1614
	arc, inches:		+1.4	0	-6.2	-18.1
PMC 140 SP boat-tail	velocity, fps:	3125	2891	2669	2457	2255
	energy, ft-lb:	3035	2597	2213	1877	1580
	arc, inches:		+1.4	0	-6.3	-18.4
PMC 160 Barnes X	velocity, fps:	2800	2639	2484	2334	2189
	energy, ft-lb:	2785	2474	2192	1935	1703
	arc, inches:		+1.8	0	-7.4	-21.2
PMC 160 Pointed Soft Point	velocity, fps:	2914	2748	2586	2428	2276
	energy, ft-lb:	3016	2682	2375	2095	1840
	arc, inches:		+1.6	0	-6.7	-19.4
PMC 160 SP boat-tail	velocity, fps:	2900	2696	2501	2314	2135
	energy, ft-lb:	2987	2582	2222	1903	1620
	arc, inches:		+1.7	0	-7.2	-21.0
PMC 175 Pointed Soft Point	velocity, fps:	2860	2645	2442	2244	2957
	energy, ft-lb:	3178	2718	2313	1956	1644
	arc, inches:		+2.0	0	-7.9	-22.7

CARTRIDGE BULLET	RANGE, YARDS:	0	100	200	300	400
Rem. 140 PSP Core-Lokt mr	velocity, fps:	2710	2482	2265	2059	1865
	energy, ft-lb:	2283	1915	1595	1318	1081
	arc, inches:		+1.0	-2.5	-12.8	-31.3
Rem. 140 PSP Core-Lokt	velocity, fps:	3175	2923	2684	2458	2243
	energy, ft-lb:	3133	2655	2240	1878	1564
	arc, inches:		+2.2	+1.9	-3.2	-14.2
Rem. 140 PSP boat-tail	velocity, fps:	3175	2956	2747	2547	2356
	energy, ft-lb:	3133	2715	2345	2017	1726
	arc, inches:		+2.2	+1.6	-3.1	-13.4
Rem. 150 AccuTip	velocity, fps:	3110	2926	2749	2579	2415
	energy, ft-lb:	3221	2850	2516	2215	1943
	arc, inches:		+1.3	0	-5.9	-17.0
Rem. 150 PSP Core-Lokt	velocity, fps:	3110	2830	2568	2320	2085
	energy, ft-lb:	3221	2667	2196	1792	1448
	arc, inches:		+1.3	0	-6.6	-20.2
Rem. 150 Nosler Bal. Tip	velocity, fps:	3110	2912	2723	2542	2367
	energy, ft-lb:	3222	2825	2470	2152	1867
	arc, inches:		+1.2	0	-5.9	-17.3
Rem. 150 Swift Scirocco	velocity, fps:	3110	2927	2751	2582	2419
	energy, ft-lb:	3221	2852	2520	2220	1948
	arc, inches:		+1.3	0	-5.9	-17.0
Rem. 160 Swift A-Frame	velocity, fps:	2900	2659	2430	2212	2006
	energy, ft-lb:	2987	2511	2097	1739	1430
	arc, inches:		+1.7	0	-7.6	-22.4
Rem. 160 Nosler Partition	velocity, fps:	2950	2752	2563	2381	2207
	energy, ft-lb:	3091	2690	2333	2014	1730
	arc, inches:		+0.6	-1.9	-9.6	-23.6
Rem. 175 PSP Core-Lokt	velocity, fps:	2860	2645	2440	2244	2057
	energy, ft-lb:	3178	2718	2313	1956	1644
	arc, inches:		+1.7	0	-7.6	-22.1
Speer 145 Grand Slam	velocity, fps:	3140	2843	2565	2304	
	energy, ft-lb:	3174	2602	2118	1708	
	arc, inches:		+1.4	0	-6.7	
Speer 175 Grand Slam	velocity, fps:	2850	2653	2463	2282	
	energy, ft-lb:	3156	2734	2358	2023	
	arc, inches:		+1.7	0	-7.5	-21.7
Win. 140 Fail Safe	velocity, fps:	3150	2861	2589	2333	2092
	energy, ft-lb:	3085	2544	2085	1693	1361
	arc, inches:		+1.4	0	-6.6	-19.5
Win. 140 Ballistic Silvertip	velocity, fps:	3100	2889	2687	2494	2310
	energy, ft-lb:	2988	2595	2245	1934	1659
	arc, inches:		+1.3	0	-6.2	-17.9
Win. 140 AccuBond CT	velocity, fps:	3180	2965	2760	2565	2377
	energy, ft-lb:	3143	2733	2368	2044	1756
	arc, inches:		+1.2	0	-5.8	-16.9
Win. 150 Power-Point	velocity, fps:	3090	2812	2551	2304	2071
	energy, ft-lb:	3181	2634	2167	1768	1429
	arc, inches:		+1.5	0	-6.8	-20.2
Win. 150 Power-Point Plus	velocity, fps:	3130	2849	2586	2337	2102
	energy, ft-lb:	3264	2705	2227	1819	1472
	arc, inches:		+1.4	0	-6.6	-19.6
Win. 150 Ballistic Silvertip	velocity, fps:	3100	2903	2714	2533	2359
	energy, ft-lb:	3200	2806	2453	2136	1853
	arc, inches:		+1.3	0	-6.0	-17.5
Win. 160 AccuBond	velocity, fps:	2950	2766	2590	2420	2257
	energy, ft-lb:	3091	2718	2382	2080	1809
	arc, inches:		+1.5	0	-6.7	-19.4
Win. 160 Partition Gold	velocity, fps:	2950	2743	2546	2357	2176
	energy, ft-lb:	3093	2674	2303	1974	1682
	arc, inches:		+1.6	0	-6.9	-20.1
Win. 160 Fail Safe	velocity, fps:	2920	2678	2449	2331	2025
	energy, ft-lb:	3030	2549	2131	1769	1457
	arc, inches:		+1.7	0	-7.5	-22.0

CARTRIDGE BULLET	RANGE, YARDS:	0	100	200	300	400
Win. 175 Power-Point	velocity, fps:	2860	2645	2440	2244	2057
	energy, ft-lb:	3178	2718	2313	1956	1644
	arc, inches:		+2.0	0	-7.9	-22.7

7mm Remington Short Ultra Mag

CARTRIDGE BULLET	RANGE, YARDS:	0	100	200	300	400
Rem. 140 PSP C-L Ultra	velocity, fps:	3175	2934	2707	2490	2283
	energy, ft-lb:	3133	2676	2277	1927	1620
	arc, inches:		+1.3	0	-6.0	-17.7
Rem. 150 PSP Core-Lokt	velocity, fps:	3110	2828	2563	2313	2077
	energy, ft-lb:	3221	2663	2188	1782	1437
	arc, inches:		+2.5	+2.1	-3.6	-15.8
Rem. 160 Partition	velocity, fps:	2960	2762	2572	2390	2215
	energy, ft-lb:	3112	2709	2350	2029	1744
	arc, inches:		+2.6	+2.2	-3.6	-15.4
Rem. 160 PSP C-L Ultra	velocity, fps:	2960	2733	2518	2313	2117
	energy, ft-lb:	3112	2654	2252	1900	1592
	arc, inches:		+2.7	+2.2	-3.7	-16.2

7mm Winchester Short Mag.

CARTRIDGE BULLET	RANGE, YARDS:	0	100	200	300	400
Federal 140 Nos. AccuBond	velocity, fps:	3250	3040	2840	2660	2470
	energy, ft-lb:	3285	2875	2515	2190	1900
	arc, inches:		+1.1	0	-5.5	-15.8
Federal 140 Nos. Bal. Tip	velocity, fps:	3310	3100	2900	2700	2520
	energy, ft-lb:	3405	2985	2610	2270	1975
	arc, inches:		+1.1	0	-5.2	15.2
Federal 150 Nos. Solid Base	velocity, fps:	3230	3010	2800	2600	2410
	energy, ft-lb:	3475	3015	2615	2255	1935
	arc, inches:		+1.3	0	-5.6	-16.3
Federal 160 Nos. AccuBond	velocity, fps:	3120	2940	2760	2590	2430
	energy, ft-lb:	3460	3065	2710	2390	2095
	arc, inches:		+1.3	0	-5.9	-16.8
Federal 160 Nos. Partition	velocity, fps:	3160	2950	2750	2560	2380
	energy, ft-lb:	3545	3095	2690	2335	2015
	arc, inches:		+1.2	0	-5.9	-16.9
Federal 160 Barnes TS	velocity, fps:	2990	2780	2590	2400	2220
	energy, ft-lb:	3175	2755	2380	2045	1750
	arc, inches:		+1.5	0	-6.6	-19.4
Federal 160 Trophy Bonded	velocity, fps:	3120	2880	2650	2440	2230
	energy, ft-lb:	3460	2945	2500	2105	1765
	arc, inches:		+1.4	0	-6.3	-18.5
Win. 140 Bal. Silvertip	velocity, fps:	3225	3008	2801	2603	2414
	energy, ft-lb:	3233	2812	2438	2106	1812
	arc, inches:		+1.2	0	-5.6	-16.4
Win. 140 AccuBond CT	velocity, fps:	3225	3008	2801	2604	2415
	energy, ft-lb:	3233	2812	2439	2107	1812
	arc, inches:		+1.2	0	-5.6	-16.4
Win. 150 Power Point	velocity, fps:	3200	2915	2648	2396	2157
	energy, ft-lb:	3410	2830	2335	1911	1550
	arc, inches:		+1.3	0	-6.3	-18.6
Win. 160 AccuBond	velocity, fps:	3050	2862	2682	2509	2342
	energy, ft-lb:	3306	2911	2556	2237	1950
	arc, inches:		1.4	0	-6.2	-17.9
Win. 160 Fail Safe	velocity, fps:	2990	2744	2512	2291	2081
	energy, ft-lb:	3176	2675	2241	1864	1538
	arc, inches:		+1.6	0	-7.1	-20.8

7mm Weatherby Mag.

CARTRIDGE BULLET	RANGE, YARDS:	0	100	200	300	400
Federal 160 Nosler Partition	velocity, fps:	3050	2850	2650	2470	2290
	energy, ft-lb:	3305	2880	2505	2165	1865
	arc, inches:		+1.4	0	-6.3	-18.4
Federal 160 Sierra GameKing BTSP	velocity, fps:	3050	2880	2710	2560	2400
	energy, ft-lb:	3305	2945	2615	2320	2050
	arc, inches:		+1.4	0	-6.1	-17.4
Federal 160 Trophy Bonded	velocity, fps:	3050	2730	2420	2140	1880
	energy, ft-lb:	3305	2640	2085	1630	1255
	arc, inches:		+1.6	0	-7.6	-22.7
Hornady 154 Soft Point	velocity, fps:	3200	2971	2753	2546	2348
	energy, ft-lb:	3501	3017	2592	2216	1885
	arc, inches:		+1.2	0	-5.8	-17.0
Hornady 154 SST (or Interbond)	velocity, fps:	3200	3009	2825	2648	2478
	energy, ft-lb:	3501	3096	2729	2398	2100
	arc, inches:		+1.2	0	-5.7	-16.5
Hornady 175 Soft Point	velocity, fps:	2910	2709	2516	2331	2154
	energy, ft-lb:	3290	2850	2459	2111	1803
	arc, inches:		+1.6	0	-7.1	-20.6
Wby. 139 Pointed Expanding	velocity, fps:	3340	3079	2834	2601	2380
	energy, ft-lb:	3443	2926	2478	2088	1748
	arc, inches:		+2.9	+3.6	0	-8.7
Wby. 140 Nosler Partition	velocity, fps:	3303	3069	2847	2636	2434
	energy, ft-lb:	3391	2927	2519	2159	1841
	arc, inches:		+2.9	+3.6	0	-8.5
Wby. 150 Nosler Bal. Tip	velocity, fps:	3300	3093	2896	2708	2527
	energy, ft-lb:	3627	3187	2793	2442	2127
	arc, inches:		+2.8	+3.5	0	-8.2
Wby. 150 Barnes X	veloctiy, fps:	3100	2901	2710	2527	2352
	energy, ft-lb:	3200	2802	2446	2127	1842
	arc, inches:		+3.3	+4.0	0	-9.4
Wby. 154 Pointed Expanding	velocity, fps:	3260	3028	2807	2597	2397
	energy, ft-lb:	3634	3134	2694	2307	1964
	arc, inches:		+3.0	+3.7	0	-8.8
Wby. 160 Nosler Partition	velocity, fps:	3200	2991	2791	2600	2417
	energy, ft-lb:	3638	3177	2767	2401	2075
	arc, inches:		+3.1	+3.8	0	-8.9
Wby. 175 Pointed Expanding	velocity, fps:	3070	2861	2662	2471	2288
	energy, ft-lb:	3662	3181	2753	2373	2034
	arc, inches:		+3.5	+4.2	0	-9.9

7mm Dakota

CARTRIDGE BULLET	RANGE, YARDS:	0	100	200	300	400
Dakota 140 Barnes X	velocity, fps:	3500	3253	3019	2798	2587
	energy, ft-lb:	3807	3288	2833	2433	2081
	arc, inches:		+2.0	+2.1	-1.5	-9.6
Dakota 160 Barnes X	velocity, fps:	3200	3001	2811	2630	2455
	energy, ft-lb:	3637	3200	2808	2456	2140
	arc, inches:		+2.1	+1.9	-2.8	-12.5

7mm STW

CARTRIDGE BULLET	RANGE, YARDS:	0	100	200	300	400
A-Square 140 Nos. Bal. Tip	velocity, fps:	3450	3254	3067	2888	2715
	energy, ft-lb:	3700	3291	2924	2592	2292
	arc, inches:		+2.2	+3.0	0	-7.3
A-Square 160 Nosler Part.	velocity, fps:	3250	3071	2900	2735	2576
	energy, ft-lb:	3752	3351	2987	2657	2357
	arc, inches:		+2.8	+3.5	0	-8.2
A-Square 160 SP boat-tail	velocity, fps:	3250	3087	2930	2778	2631
	energy, ft-lb:	3752	3385	3049	2741	2460
	arc, inches:		+2.8	+3.4	0	-8.0
Federal 140 Trophy Bonded	velocity, fps:	3330	3080	2850	2630	2420
	energy, ft-lb:	3435	2950	2520	2145	1815
	arc, inches:		+1.1	0	-5.4	-15.8
Federal 150 Trophy Bonded	velocity, fps:	3250	3010	2770	2560	2350
	energy, ft-lb:	3520	3010	2565	2175	1830
	arc, inches:		+1.2	0	-5.7	-16.7
Federal 160 Sierra GameKing BTSP	velocity, fps:	3200	3020	2850	2670	2530
	energy, ft-lb:	3640	3245	2890	2570	2275
	arc, inches:		+1.1	0	-5.5	-15.7
Rem. 140 PSP Core-Lokt	velocity, fps:	3325	3064	2818	2585	2364
	energy, ft-lb:	3436	2918	2468	2077	1737
	arc, inches:		+2.0	+1.7	-2.9	-12.8

Centerfire Rifle Ballistics

7MM STW TO .30-30 WINCHESTER

CARTRIDGE BULLET	RANGE, YARDS:	0	100	200	300	400
Rem. 140 Swift A-Frame	velocity, fps:	3325	3020	2735	2467	2215
	energy, ft-lb:	3436	2834	2324	1892	1525
	arc, inches:		+2.1	+1.8	-3.1	-13.8
Speer 145 Grand Slam	velocity, fps:	3300	2992	2075	2435	
	energy, ft-lb:	3506	2882	2355	1909	
	arc, inches:		+1.2	0	-6.0	-17.8
Win. 140 Ballistic Silvertip	velocity, fps:	3320	3100	2890	2690	2499
	energy, ft-lb:	3427	2982	2597	2250	1941
	arc, inches:		+1.1	0	-5.2	-15.2
Win. 150 Power-Point	velocity, fps:	3250	2957	2683	2424	2181
	energy, ft-lb:	3519	2913	2398	1958	1584
	arc, inches:		+1.2	0	-6.1	-18.1
Win. 160 Fail Safe	velocity, fps:	3150	2894	2652	2422	2204
	energy, ft-lb:	3526	2976	2499	2085	1727
	arc, inches:		+1.3	0	-6.3	-18.5

7MM REMINGTON ULTRA MAG

CARTRIDGE BULLET	RANGE, YARDS:	0	100	200	300	400
Rem. 140 PSP Core-Lokt	velocity, fps:	3425	3158	2907	2669	2444
	energy, ft-lb:	3646	3099	2626	2214	1856
	arc, inches:		+1.8	+1.6	-2.7	-11.9
Rem. 140 Nosler Partition	velocity, fps:	3425	3184	2956	2740	2534
	energy, ft-lb:	3646	3151	2715	2333	1995
	arc, inches:		+1.7	+1.6	-2.6	-11.4
Rem. 160 Nosler Partition	velocity, fps:	3200	2991	2791	2600	2417
	energy, ft-lb:	3637	3177	2767	2401	2075
	arc, inches:		+2.1	+1.8	-3.0	-12.9

7.21 (.284) FIREHAWK

CARTRIDGE BULLET	RANGE, YARDS:	0	100	200	300	400
Lazzeroni 140 Nosler Part.	velocity, fps:	3580	3349	3130	2923	2724
	energy, ft-lb:	3985	3488	3048	2656	2308
	arc, inches:		+2.2	+2.9	0	-7.0
Lazzeroni 160 Swift A-Fr.	velocity, fps:	3385	3167	2961	2763	2574
	energy, ft-lb:	4072	3565	3115	2713	2354
	arc, inches:		+2.6	+3.3	0	-7.8

7.5X55 SWISS

CARTRIDGE BULLET	RANGE, YARDS:	0	100	200	300	400
Norma 180 Soft Point	velocity, fps:	2651	2432	2223	2025	
	energy, ft-lb:	2810	2364	1976	1639	
	arc, inches:		+2.2	0	-9.3	
Norma 180 Oryx	velocity, fps:	2493	2222	1968	1734	
	energy, ft-lb:	2485	1974	1549	1201	
	arc, inches:		+2.7	0	-11.8	

7.62X39 RUSSIAN

CARTRIDGE BULLET	RANGE, YARDS:	0	100	200	300	400
Federal 123 Hi-Shok	velocity, fps:	2300	2030	1780	1550	1350
	energy, ft-lb:	1445	1125	860	655	500
	arc, inches:		0	-7.0	-25.1	
Federal 124 FMJ	velocity, fps:	2300	2030	1780	1560	1360
	energy, ft-lb:	1455	1135	875	670	510
	arc, inches:		+3.5	0	-14.6	-43.5
PMC 123 FMJ	velocity, fps:	2350	2072	1817	1583	1368
	energy, ft-lb:	1495	1162	894	678	507
	arc, inches:		0	-5.0	-26.4	-67.8
PMC 125 Pointed Soft Point	velocity, fps:	2320	2046	1794	1563	1350
	energy, ft-lb:	1493	1161	893	678	505
	arc, inches:		0	-5.2	-27.5	-70.6
Rem. 125 Pointed Soft Point	velocity, fps:	2365	2062	1783	1533	1320
	energy, ft-lb:	1552	1180	882	652	483
	arc, inches:		0	-6.7	-24.5	
Win. 123 Soft Point	velocity, fps:	2365	2033	1731	1465	1248
	energy, ft-lb:	1527	1129	818	586	425
	arc, inches:		+3.8	0	-15.4	-46.3

.30 CARBINE

CARTRIDGE BULLET	RANGE, YARDS:	0	100	200	300	400
Federal 110 Hi-Shok RN	velocity, fps:	1990	1570	1240	1040	920
	energy, ft-lb:	965	600	375	260	210
	arc, inches:		0	-12.8	-46.9	
Federal 110 FMJ	velocity, fps:	1990	1570	1240	1040	920
	energy, ft-lb:	965	600	375	260	210
	arc, inches:		0	-12.8	-46.9	
Magtech 110 FMC	velocity, fps:	1990	1654			
	energy, ft-lb:	965	668			
	arc, inches:		0			
PMC 110 FMJ	(and RNSP)	velocity, fps:		1927	1548	1248
	energy, ft-lb:	906	585	380		
	arc, inches:		0	-14.2		
Rem. 110 Soft Point	velocity, fps:	1990	1567	1236	1035	923
	energy, ft-lb:	967	600	373	262	208
	arc, inches:		0	-12.9	-48.6	
Win. 110 Hollow Soft Point	velocity, fps:	1990	1567	1236	1035	923
	energy, ft-lb:	967	600	373	262	208
	arc, inches:		0	-13.5	-49.9	

.30-30 WINCHESTER

CARTRIDGE BULLET	RANGE, YARDS:	0	100	200	300	400
Federal 125 Hi-Shok HP	velocity, fps:	2570	2090	1660	1320	1080
	energy, ft-lb:	1830	1210	770	480	320
	arc, inches:		+3.3	0	-16.0	-50.9
Federal 150 Hi-Shok FN	velocity, fps:	2390	2020	1680	1400	1180
	energy, ft-lb:	1900	1355	945	650	460
	arc, inches:		+3.6	0	-15.9	-49.1
Federal 170 Hi-Shok RN	velocity, fps:	2200	1900	1620	1380	1190
	energy, ft-lb:	1830	1355	990	720	535
	arc, inches:		+4.1	0	-17.4	-52.4
Federal 170 Sierra Pro-Hunt.	velocity, fps:	2200	1820	1500	1240	1060
	energy, ft-lb:	1830	1255	845	575	425
	arc, inches:		+4.5	0	-20.0	-63.5
Federal 170 Nosler Partition	velocity, fps:	2200	1900	1620	1380	1190
	energy, ft-lb:	1830	1355	990	720	535
	arc, inches:		+4.1	0	-17.4	-52.4
Hornady 150 Round Nose	velocity, fps:	2390	1973	1605	1303	1095
	energy, ft-lb:	1902	1296	858	565	399
	arc, inches:		0	-8.2	-30.0	
Hornady 170 Flat Point	velocity, fps:	2200	1895	1619	1381	1191
	energy, ft-lb:	1827	1355	989	720	535
	arc, inches:		0	-8.9	-31.1	
Norma 150 Soft Point	velocity, fps:	2329	2008	1716	1459	
	energy, ft-lb:	1807	1344	981	709	
	arc, inches:		+3.6	0	-15.5	
PMC 150 Starfire HP	velocity, fps:	2100	1769	1478		
	energy, ft-lb:	1469	1042	728		
	arc, inches:		0	-10.8		
PMC 150 Flat Nose	velocity, fps:	2300	1943	1627		
	energy, ft-lb:	1762	1257	881		
	arc, inches:		0	-7.8		
PMC 170 Flat Nose	velocity, fps:	2150	1840	1566		
	energy, ft-lb:	1745	1277	926		
	arc, inches:		0	-8.9		
Rem. 55 PSP (sabot)	velocity, fps:	3400	2693	2085	1570	1187
"Accelerator"	energy, ft-lb:	1412	886	521	301	172
	arc, inches:		+1.7	0	-9.9	-34.3
Rem. 150 SP Core-Lokt	velocity, fps:	2390	1973	1605	1303	1095
	energy, ft-lb:	1902	1296	858	565	399
	arc, inches:		0	-7.6	-28.8	
Rem. 170 SP Core-Lokt	velocity, fps:	2200	1895	1619	1381	1191
	energy, ft-lb:	1827	1355	989	720	535
	arc, inches:		0	-8.3	-29.9	

Centerfire Rifle Ballistics

.30-30 WINCHESTER TO .308 WINCHESTER

CARTRIDGE BULLET	RANGE, YARDS:	0	100	200	300	400
Rem. 170 HP Core-Lokt	velocity, fps:	2200	1895	1619	1381	1191
	energy, ft-lb:	1827	1355	989	720	535
	arc, inches:		0	-8.3	-29.9	
Speer 150 Flat Nose	velocity, fps:	2370	2067	1788	1538	
	energy, ft-lb:	1870	1423	1065	788	
	arc, inches:		+3.3	0	-14.4	-43.7
Win. 150 Hollow Point	velocity, fps:	2390	2018	1684	1398	1177
	energy, ft-lb:	1902	1356	944	651	461
	arc, inches:		0	-7.7	-27.9	
Win. 150 Power-Point	velocity, fps:	2390	2018	1684	1398	1177
	energy, ft-lb:	1902	1356	944	651	461
	arc, inches:		0	-7.7	-27.9	
Win. 150 Silvertip	velocity,fps:	2390	2018	1684	1398	1177
	energy, ft-lb:	1902	1356	944	651	461
	arc, inches:		0	-7.7	-27.9	
Win. 150 Power-Point Plus	velocity, fps:	2480	2095	1747	1446	1209
	energy, ft-lb:	2049	1462	1017	697	487
	arc, inches:		0	-6.5	-24.5	
Win. 170 Power-Point	velocity, fps:	2200	1895	1619	1381	1191
	energy, ft-lb:	1827	1355	989	720	535
	arc, inches:		0	-8.9	-31.1	
Win. 170 Silvertip	velocity, fps:	2200	1895	1619	1381	1191
	energy, ft-lb:	1827	1355	989	720	535
	arc, inches:		0	-8.9	-31.1	

.300 Savage

CARTRIDGE BULLET	RANGE, YARDS:	0	100	200	300	400
Federal 150 Hi-Shok	velocity, fps:	2630	2350	2100	1850	1630
	energy, ft-lb:	2305	1845	1460	1145	885
	arc, inches:		+2.4	0	-10.4	-30.9
Federal 180 Hi-Shok	velocity, fps:	2350	2140	1940	1750	1570
	energy, ft-lb:	2205	1825	1495	1215	985
	arc, inches:		+3.1	0	-12.4	-36.1
Rem. 150 PSP Core-Lokt	velocity, fps:	2630	2354	2095	1853	1631
	energy, ft-lb:	2303	1845	1462	1143	806
	arc, inches:		+2.4	0	-10.4	-30.9
Rem. 180 SP Core-Lokt	velocity, fps:	2350	2025	1728	1467	1252
	energy, ft-lb:	2207	1639	1193	860	626
	arc, inches:		0	-7.1	-25.9	
Win. 150 Power-Point	velocity, fps:	2630	2311	2015	1743	1500
	energy, ft-lb:	2303	1779	1352	1012	749
	arc, inches:		+2.8	0	-11.5	-34.4

.307 Winchester

CARTRIDGE BULLET	RANGE, YARDS:	0	100	200	300	400
Win. 180 Power-Point	velocity, fps:	2510	2179	1874	1599	1362
	energy, ft-lb:	2519	1898	1404	1022	742
	arc, inches:		+1.5	-3.6	-18.6	-47.1

.30-40 Krag

CARTRIDGE BULLET	RANGE, YARDS:	0	100	200	300	400
Rem. 180 PSP Core-Lokt	velocity, fps:	2430	2213	2007	1813	1632
	energy, ft-lb:	2360	1957	1610	1314	1064
	arc, inches, s:		0	-5.6	-18.6	
Win. 180 Power-Point	velocity, fps:	2430	2099	1795	1525	1298
	energy, ft-lb:	2360	1761	1288	929	673
	arc, inches, s:		0	-7.1	-25.0	

7.62x54R Russian

CARTRIDGE BULLET	RANGE, YARDS:	0	100	200	300	400
Norma 150 Soft Point	velocity, fps:	2953	2622	2314	2028	
	energy, ft-lb:	2905	2291	1784	1370	
	arc, inches:		+1.8	0	-8.3	
Norma 180 Alaska	velocity, fps:	2575	2362	2159	1967	
	energy, ft-lb:	2651	2231	1864	1546	
	arc, inches:		+2.9	0	-12.9	

.308 Winchester

CARTRIDGE BULLET	RANGE, YARDS:	0	100	200	300	400
Black Hills 150 Nosler B. Tip	velocity, fps:	2800				
	energy, ft-lb:	2611				
	arc, inches:					
Black Hills 165 Nosler B. Tip (and SP)	velocity, fps:	2650				
	energy, ft-lb:	2573				
	arc, inches:					
Black Hills 168 Barnes X (and Match)	velocity, fps:	2650				
	energy, ft-lb:	2620				
	arc, inches:					
Black Hills 175 Match	velocity, fps:	2600				
	energy, ft-lb:	2657				
	arc, inches:					
Black Hills 180 AccuBond	velocity, fps:	2600				
	Energy, ft-lb:	2701				
	Arc, inches:					
Federal 150 Hi-Shok	velocity, fps:	2820	2530	2260	2010	1770
	energy, ft-lb:	2650	2140	1705	1345	1050
	arc, inches:		+2.0	0	-8.8	-26.3
Federal 150 Nosler Bal. Tip.	velocity, fps:	2820	2610	2410	2220	2040
	energy, ft-lb:	2650	2270	1935	1640	1380
	arc, inches:		+1.8	0	-7.8	-22.7
Federal 150 FMJ boat-tail	velocity, fps:	2820	2620	2430	2250	2070
	energy, ft-lb:	2650	2285	1965	1680	1430
	arc, inches:		+1.8	0	-7.7	-22.4
Federal 150 Barnes XLC	velocity, fps:	2820	2610	2400	2210	2030
	energy, ft-lb:	2650	2265	1925	1630	1370
	arc, inches:		+1.8	0	-7.8	-22.9
Federal 155 Sierra MatchKg. BTHP	velocity, fps:	2950	2740	2540	2350	2170
	energy, ft-lb:	2995	2585	2225	1905	1620
	arc, inches:		+13.2	+23.3	+28.1	+26.5
Federal 165 Sierra GameKing BTSP	velocity, fps:	2700	2520	2330	2160	1990
	energy, ft-lb:	2670	2310	1990	1700	1450
	arc, inches:		+2.0	0	-8.4	-24.3
Federal 165 Trophy Bonded	velocity, fps:	2700	2440	2200	1970	1760
	energy, ft-lb:	2670	2185	1775	1425	1135
	arc, inches:		+2.2	0	-9.4	-27.7
Federal 165 Tr. Bonded HE	velocity, fps:	2870	2600	2350	2120	1890
	energy, ft-lb:	3020	2485	2030	1640	1310
	arc, inches:		+1.8	0	-8.2	-24.0
Federal 168 Sierra MatchKg. BTHP	velocity, fps:	2600	2410	2230	2060	1890
	energy, ft-lb:	2520	2170	1855	1580	1340
	arc, inches:		+17.7	+31.0	+37.2	+35.4
Federal 180 Hi-Shok	velocity, fps:	2620	2390	2180	1970	1780
	energy, ft-lb:	2745	2290	1895	1555	1270
	arc, inches:		+2.3	0	-9.7	-28.3
Federal 180 Sierra Pro-Hunt.	velocity, fps:	2620	2410	2200	2010	1820
	energy, ft-lb:	2745	2315	1940	1610	1330
	arc, inches:		+2.3	0	-9.3	-27.1
Federal 180 Nosler Partition	velocity, fps:	2620	2430	2240	2060	1890
	energy, ft-lb:	2745	2355	2005	1700	1430
	arc, inches:		+2.2	0	-9.2	-26.5
Federal 180 Nosler Part. HE	velocity, fps:	2740	2550	2370	2200	2030
	energy, ft-lb:	3000	2600	2245	1925	1645
	arc, inches:		+1.9	0	-8.2	-23.5
Hornady 110 TAP-FPD	velocity, fps:	3165	2830	2519	2228	1957
	energy, ft-lb:	2446	1956	1649	1212	935
	arc, inches:		+1.4	0	-6.9	-20.9
Hornady 110 Urban Tactical	velocity, fps:	3170	2825	2504	2206	1937
	energy, ft-lb:	2454	1950	1532	1189	916
	arc, inches:		+1.5	0	-7.2	-21.2

Centerfire Rifle Ballistics

BALLISTICS

.308 WINCHESTER TO .308 WINCHESTER

CARTRIDGE BULLET	RANGE, YARDS:	0	100	200	300	400
Hornady 150 SP boat-tail	velocity, fps:	2820	2560	2315	2084	1866
	energy, ft-lb:	2648	2183	1785	1447	1160
	arc, inches:		+2.0	0	-8.5	-25.2
Hornady 150 SST (or Interbond)	velocity, fps:	2820	2593	2378	2174	1984
	energy, ft-lb:	2648	2240	1884	1574	1311
	arc, inches:		+1.9	0	-8.1	-22.9
Hornady 150 SST LM (or Interbond)	velocity, fps:	3000	2765	2541	2328	2127
	energy, ft-lb:	2997	2545	2150	1805	1506
	arc, inches:		+1.5	0	-7.1	-20.6
Hornady 150 SP LM	velocity, fps:	2980	2703	2442	2195	1964
	energy, ft-lb:	2959	2433	1986	1606	1285
	arc, inches:		+1.6	0	-7.5	-22.2
Hornady 155 A-Max	velocity, fps:	2815	2610	2415	2229	2051
	energy, ft-lb:	2727	2345	2007	1709	1448
	arc, inches:		+1.9	0	-7.9	-22.6
Hornady 155 TAP-FPD	velocity, fps:	2785	2577	2379	2189	2008
	energy, ft-lb:	2669	2285	1947	1649	1387
	arc, inches:		+1.9	0	-8.0	-23.3
Hornady 165 SP boat-tail	velocity, fps:	2700	2496	2301	2115	1937
	energy, ft-lb:	2670	2283	1940	1639	1375
	arc, inches:		+2.0	0	-8.7	-25.2
Hornady 165 SPBT LM	velocity, fps:	2870	2658	2456	2283	2078
	energy, ft-lb:	3019	2589	2211	1877	1583
	arc, inches:		+1.7	0	-7.5	-21.8
Hornady 165 SST LM (or Interbond)	velocity, fps:	2880	2672	2474	2284	2103
	energy, ft-lb:	3038	2616	2242	1911	1620
	arc, inches:		+1.6	0	-7.3	-21.2
Hornady 168 BTHP Match	velocity, fps:	2700	2524	2354	2191	2035
	energy, ft-lb:	2720	2377	2068	1791	1545
	arc, inches:		+2.0	0	-8.4	-23.9
Hornady 168 BTHP Match LM	velocity, fps:	2640	2630	2429	2238	2056
	energy, ft-lb:	3008	2579	2201	1868	1577
	arc, inches:		+1.8	0	-7.8	-22.4
Hornady 168 A-Max Match	velocity fps:	2620	2446	2280	2120	1972
	energy, ft-lb:	2560	2232	1939	1677	1450
	arc, inches:		+2.6	0	-9.2	-25.6
Hornady 168 A-Max	velocity, fps:	2700	2491	2292	2102	1921
	energy, ft-lb:	2719	2315	1959	1648	1377
	arc, inches:		+2.4	0	-9.0	-25.9
Hornady 168 TAP-FPD	velocity, fps:	2700	2513	2333	2161	1996
	energy, ft-lb:	2719	2355	2030	1742	1486
	arc, inches:		+2.0	0	-8.4	-24.3
Hornady 178 A-Max	velocity, fps:	2965	2778	2598	2425	2259
	energy, ft-lb:	3474	3049	2666	2323	2017
	arc, inches:		+1.6	0	-6.9	-19.8
Hornady 180 A-Max Match	velocity, fps:	2550	2397	2249	2106	1974
	energy, ft-lb:	2598	2295	2021	1773	1557
	arc, inches:		+2.7	0	-9.5	-26.2
Norma 150 Nosler Bal. Tip	velocity, fps:	2822	2588	2365	2154	
	energy, ft-lb:	2653	2231	1864	1545	
	arc, inches:		+1.6	0	-7.1	
Norma 150 Soft Point	velocity, fps:	2861	2537	2235	1954	
	energy, ft-lb:	2727	2144	1664	1272	
	arc, inches:		+2.0	0	-9.0	
Norma 165 TXP Swift A-Fr.	velocity, fps:	2700	2459	2231	2015	
	energy, ft-lb:	2672	2216	1824	1488	
	arc, inches:		+2.1	0	-9.1	
Norma 180 Plastic Point	velocity, fps:	2612	2365	2131	1911	
	energy, ft-lb:	2728	2235	1815	1460	
	arc, inches:		+2.4	0	-10.1	
Norma 180 Nosler Partition	velocity, fps:	2612	2414	2225	2044	
	energy, ft-lb:	2728	2330	1979	1670	
	arc, inches:		+2.2	0	-9.3	

CARTRIDGE BULLET	RANGE, YARDS:	0	100	200	300	400
Norma 180 Alaska	velocity, fps:	2612	2269	1953	1667	
	energy, ft-lb:	2728	2059	1526	1111	
	arc, inches:		+2.7	0	-11.9	
Norma 180 Vulkan	velocity, fps:	2612	2325	2056	1806	
	energy, ft-lb:	2728	2161	1690	1304	
	arc, inches:		+2.5	0	-10.8	
Norma 180 Oryx	velocity, fps:	2612	2305	2019	1755	
	energy, ft-lb:	2728	2124	1629	1232	
	arc, inches:		+2.5	0	-11.1	
Norma 200 Vulkan	velocity, fps:	2461	2215	1983	1767	
	energy, ft-lb:	2690	2179	1747	1387	
	arc, inches:		+2.8	0	-11.7	
PMC 147 FMJ boat-tail	velocity, fps:	2751	2473	2257	2052	1859
	energy, ft-lb:	2428	2037	1697	1403	1150
	arc, inches:		+2.3	0	-9.3	-27.3
PMC 150 Barnes X	velocity, fps:	2700	2504	2316	2135	1964
	energy, ft-lb:	2428	2087	1786	1518	1284
	arc, inches:		+2.0	0	-8.6	-24.7
PMC 150 Pointed Soft Point	velocity, fps:	2750	2478	2224	1987	1766
	energy, ft-lb:	2519	2045	1647	1315	1039
	arc, inches:		+2.1	0	-9.2	-27.1
PMC 150 SP boat-tail	velocity, fps:	2820	2581	2354	2139	1935
	energy, ft-lb:	2648	2218	1846	1523	1247
	arc, inches:		+1.9	0	-8.2	-24.0
PMC 168 Barnes X	velocity, fps:	2600	2425	2256	2095	1940
	energy, ft-lb:	2476	2154	1865	1608	1379
	arc, inches:		+2.2	0	-9.0	-26.0
PMC 168 HP boat-tail	velocity, fps:	2650	2460	2278	2103	1936
	energy, ft-lb:	2619	2257	1935	1649	1399
	arc, inches:		+2.1	0	-8.8	-25.6
PMC 168 Pointed Soft Point	velocity, fps:	2559	2354	2160	1976	1803
	energy, ft-lb:	2443	2067	1740	1457	1212
	arc, inches:		+2.4	0	-9.9	-28.7
PMC 168 Pointed Soft Point	velocity, fps:	2600	2404	2216	2037	1866
	Energy, ft-lb:	2476	2064	1709	1403	1142
	Arc, inches:		+2.3	0	-9.8	-28.7
PMC 180 Pointed Soft Point	velocity, fps:	2550	2335	2132	1940	1760
	energy, ft-lb:	2599	2179	1816	1504	1238
	arc, inches:		+2.5	0	-10.1	-29.5
PMC 180 SP boat-tail	velocity, fps:	2620	2446	2278	2117	1962
	energy, ft-lb:	2743	2391	2074	1790	1538
	arc, inches:		+2.2	0	-8.9	-25.4
Rem. 125 PSP C-L MR	velocity, fps:	2660	2348	2057	1788	1546
	energy, ft-lb:	1964	1529	1174	887	663
	arc, inches:		+1.1	-2.7	-14.3	-35.8
Rem. 150 PSP Core-Lokt	velocity, fps:	2820	2533	2263	2009	1774
	energy, ft-lb:	2648	2137	1705	1344	1048
	arc, inches:		+2.0	0	-8.8	-26.2
Rem. 150 PSP C-L Ultra	velocity, fps:	2620	2404	2198	2002	1818
	energy, ft-lb:	2743	2309	1930	1601	1320
	arc, inches:		+2.3	0	-9.5	-26.4
Rem. 150 Swift Scirocco	velocity, fps:	2820	2611	2410	2219	2037
	energy, ft-lb:	2648	2269	1935	1640	1381
	arc, inches:		+1.8	0	-7.8	-22.7
Rem. 165 AccuTip	velocity, fps:	2700	2501	2311	2129	1958
	energy, ft-lb:	2670	2292	1957	1861	1401
	arc, inches:		+2.0	0	-8.6	-24.8
Rem. 165 PSP boat-tail	velocity, fps:	2700	2497	2303	2117	1941
	energy, ft-lb:	2670	2284	1942	1642	1379
	arc, inches:		+2.0	0	-8.6	-25.0
Rem. 165 Nosler Bal. Tip	velocity, fps:	2700	2613	2333	2161	1996
	energy, ft-lb:	2672	2314	1995	1711	1460
	arc, inches:		+2.0	0	-8.4	-24.3

Centerfire Rifle Ballistics

.308 WINCHESTER TO .30-06 SPRINGFIELD

CARTRIDGE BULLET	RANGE, YARDS:	0	100	200	300	400
Rem. 165 Swift Scirocco	velocity, fps:	2700	2513	2233	2161	1996
	energy, fps:	2670	2313	1994	1711	1459
	arc, inches:		+2.0	0	-8.4	-24.3
Rem. 168 HPBT Match	velocity, fps:	2680	2493	2314	2143	1979
	energy, ft-lb:	2678	2318	1998	1713	1460
	arc, inches:		+2.1	0	-8.6	-24.7
Rem. 180 SP Core-Lokt	velocity, fps:	2620	2274	1955	1666	1414
	energy, ft-lb:	2743	2066	1527	1109	799
	arc, inches:		+2.6	0	-11.8	-36.3
Rem. 180 PSP Core-Lokt	velocity, fps:	2620	2393	2178	1974	1782
	energy, ft-lb:	2743	2288	1896	1557	1269
	arc, inches:		+2.3	0	-9.7	-28.3
Rem. 180 Nosler Partition	velocity, fps:	2620	2436	2259	2089	1927
	energy, ft-lb:	2743	2371	2039	1774	1485
	arc, inches:		+2.2	0	-9.0	-26.0
Speer 150 Grand Slam	velocity, fps:	2900	2599	2317	2053	
	energy, ft-lb:	2800	2249	1788	1404	
	arc, inches:		+2.1	0	-8.6	-24.8
Speer 165 Grand Slam	velocity, fps:	2700	2475	2261	2057	
	energy, ft-lb:	2670	2243	1872	1550	
	arc, inches:		+2.1	0	-8.9	-25.9
Speer 180 Grand Slam	velocity, fps:	2620	2420	2229	2046	
	energy, ft-lb:	2743	2340	1985	1674	
	arc, inches:		+2.2	0	-9.2	-26.6
Win. 150 Power-Point	velocity, fps:	2820	2488	2179	1893	1633
	energy, ft-lb:	2648	2061	1581	1193	888
	arc, inches:		+2.4	0	-9.8	-29.3
Win. 150 Power-Point Plus	velocity, fps:	2900	2558	2241	1946	1678
	energy, ft-lb:	2802	2180	1672	1262	938
	arc, inches:		+1.9	0	-8.9	-27.0
Win. 150 Partition Gold	velocity, fps:	2900	2645	2405	2177	1962
	energy, ft-lb:	2802	2332	1927	1579	1282
	arc, inches:		+1.7	0	-7.8	-22.9
Win. 150 Ballistic Silvertip	velocity, fps:	2810	2601	2401	2211	2028
	energy, ft-lb:	2629	2253	1920	1627	1370
	arc, inches:		+1.8	0	-7.8	-22.8
Win. 150 Fail Safe	velocity, fps:	2820	2533	2263	2010	1775
	energy, ft-lb:	2649	2137	1706	1346	1049
	arc, inches:		+2.0	0	-8.8	-26.2
Win. 168 Ballistic Silvertip	velocity, fps:	2670	2484	2306	2134	1971
	energy, ft-lb:	2659	2301	1983	1699	1449
	arc, inches:		+2.1	0	-8.6	-24.8
Win. 168 HP boat-tail Match	velocity, fps:	2680	2485	2297	2118	1948
	energy, ft-lb:	2680	2303	1970	1674	1415
	arc, inches:		+2.1	0	-8.7	-25.1
Win. 180 Power-Point	velocity, fps:	2620	2274	1955	1666	1414
	energy, ft-lb:	2743	2066	1527	1109	799
	arc, inches:		+2.9	0	-12.1	-36.9
Win. 180 Silvertip	velocity, fps:	2620	2393	2178	1974	1782
	energy, ft-lb:	2743	2288	1896	1557	1269
	arc, inches:		+2.6	0	-9.9	-28.9

.30-06 SPRINGFIELD

CARTRIDGE BULLET	RANGE, YARDS:	0	100	200	300	400
A-Square 180 M & D-T	velocity, fps:	2700	2365	2054	1769	1524
	energy, ft-lb:	2913	2235	1687	1251	928
	arc, inches:		+2.4	0	-10.6	-32.4
A-Square 220 Monolythic Solid	velocity, fps:	2380	2108	1854	1623	1424
	energy, ft-lb:	2767	2171	1679	1287	990
	arc, inches:		+3.1	0	-13.6	-39.9
Black Hills 150 Nosler B. Tip	velocity, fps:	2900				
	energy, ft-lb:	2770				
	arc, inches:					
Black Hills 165 Nosler B. Tip	velocity, fps:	2750				
	energy, ft-lb:	2770				
	arc, inches:					
Black Hills 168 Hor. Match	velocity, fps:	2700				
	energy, ft-lb:	2718				
	arc, inches:					
Black Hills 180 Barnes X	velocity, fps:	2650				
	energy, ft-lb:	2806				
	arc, inches:					
Black Hills 180 AccuBond	velocity, ft-lb:	2700				
	energy, ft-lb:					
	arc, inches:					
Federal 125 Sierra Pro-Hunt.	velocity, fps:	3140	2780	2450	2140	1850
	energy, ft-lb:	2735	2145	1660	1270	955
	arc, inches:		+1.5	0	-7.3	-22.3
Federal 150 Hi-Shok	velocity, fps:	2910	2620	2340	2080	1840
	energy, ft-lb:	2820	2280	1825	1445	1130
	arc, inches:		+1.8	0	-8.2	-24.4
Federal 150 Sierra Pro-Hunt.	velocity, fps:	2910	2640	2380	2130	1900
	energy, ft-lb:	2820	2315	1880	1515	1205
	arc, inches:		+1.7	0	-7.9	-23.3
Federal 150 Sierra GameKing BTSP	velocity, fps:	2910	2690	2480	2270	2070
	energy, ft-lb:	2820	2420	2040	1710	1430
	arc, inches:		+1.7	0	-7.4	-21.5
Federal 150 Nosler Bal. Tip	velocity, fps:	2910	2700	2490	2300	2110
	energy, ft-lb:	2820	2420	2070	1760	1485
	arc, inches:		+1.6	0	-7.3	-21.1
Federal 150 FMJ boat-tail	velocity, fps:	2910	2710	2510	2320	2150
	energy, ft-lb:	2820	2440	2100	1800	1535
	arc, inches:		+1.6	0	-7.1	-20.8
Federal 165 Sierra Pro-Hunt.	velocity, fps:	2800	2560	2340	2130	1920
	energy, ft-lb:	2875	2410	2005	1655	1360
	arc, inches:		+1.9	0	-8.3	-24.3
Federal 165 Sierra GameKing BTSP	velocity, fps:	2800	2610	2420	2240	2070
	energy, ft-lb:	2870	2490	2150	1840	1580
	arc, inches:		+1.8	0	-7.8	-22.4
Federal 165 Sierra GameKing HE	velocity, fps:	3140	2900	2670	2450	2240
	energy, ft-lb:	3610	3075	2610	2200	1845
	arc, inches:		+1.5	0	-6.9	-20.4
Federal 165 Nosler Bal. Tip	velocity, fps:	2800	2610	2430	2250	2080
	energy, ft-lb:	2870	2495	2155	1855	1585
	arc, inches:		+1.8	0	-7.7	-22.3
Federal 165 Trophy Bonded	velocity, fps:	2800	2540	2290	2050	1830
	energy, ft-lb:	2870	2360	1915	1545	1230
	arc, inches:		+2.0	0	-8.7	-25.4
Federal 165 Tr. Bonded HE	velocity, fps:	3140	2860	2590	2340	2100
	energy, ft-lb:	3610	2990	2460	2010	1625
	arc, inches:		+1.6	0	-7.4	-21.9
Federal 168 Sierra MatchKg. BTHP	velocity, fps:	2700	2510	2320	2150	1980
	energy, ft-lb:	2720	2350	2010	1720	1460
	arc, inches:		+16.2	+28.4	+34.1	+32.3
Federal 180 Hi-Shok	velocity, fps:	2700	2470	2250	2040	1850
	energy, ft-lb:	2915	2435	2025	1665	1360
	arc, inches:		+2.1	0	-9.0	-26.4
Federal 180 Sierra Pro-Hunt. RN	velocity, fps:	2700	2350	2020	1730	1470
	energy, ft-lb:	2915	2200	1630	1190	860
	arc, inches:		+2.4	0	-11.0	-33.6
Federal 180 Nosler Partition	velocity, fps:	2700	2500	2320	2140	1970
	energy, ft-lb:	2915	2510	2150	1830	1550
	arc, inches:		+2.0	0	-8.6	-24.6
Federal 180 Nosler Part. HE	velocity, fps:	2880	2690	2500	2320	2150
	energy, ft-lb:	3315	2880	2495	2150	1845
	arc, inches:		+1.7	0	-7.2	-21.0

Centerfire Rifle Ballistics

.30-06 SPRINGFIELD TO .30-06 SPRINGFIELD

CARTRIDGE BULLET	RANGE, YARDS:	0	100	200	300	400
Federal 180 Sierra GameKing	velocity, fps:	2700	2540	2380	2220	2080
BTSP	energy, ft-lb:	2915	2570	2260	1975	1720
	arc, inches:		+1.9	0	-8.1	-23.1
Federal 180 Barnes XLC	velocity, fps:	2700	2530	2360	2200	2040
	energy, ft-lb:	2915	2550	2220	1930	1670
	arc, inches:		+2.0	0	-8.3	-23.8
Federal 180 Trophy Bonded	velocity, fps:	2700	2460	2220	2000	1800
	energy, ft-lb:	2915	2410	1975	1605	1290
	arc, inches:		+2.2	0	-9.2	-27.0
Federal 180 Tr. Bonded HE	velocity, fps:	2880	2630	2380	2160	1940
	energy, ft-lb:	3315	2755	2270	1855	1505
	arc, inches:		+1.8	0	-8.0	-23.3
Federal 220 Sierra Pro-Hunt.	velocity, fps:	2410	2130	1870	1630	1420
RN	energy, ft-lb:	2835	2215	1705	1300	985
	arc, inches:		+3.1	0	-13.1	-39.3
Hornady 150 SP	velocity, fps:	2910	2617	2342	2083	1843
	energy, ft-lb:	2820	2281	1827	1445	1131
	arc, inches:		+2.1	0	-8.5	-25.0
Hornady 150 SP LM	velocity, fps:	3100	2815	2548	2295	2058
	energy, ft-lb:	3200	2639	2161	1755	1410
	arc, inches:		+1.4	0	-6.8	-20.3
Hornady 150 SP boat-tail	velocity, fps:	2910	2683	2467	2262	2066
	energy, ft-lb:	2820	2397	2027	1706	1421
	arc, inches:		+2.0	0	-7.7	-22.2
Hornady 150 SST	velocity, fps:	2910	2802	2599	2405	2219
(or Interbond)	energy, ft-lb:	3330	2876	2474	2118	1803
	arc, inches:		+1.5	0	-6.6	-19.3
Hornady 150 SST LM	velocity, fps:	3100	2860	2631	2414	2208
	energy, ft-lb:	3200	2724	2306	1941	1624
	arc, inches:		+1.4	0	-6.6	-19.2
Hornady 165 SP boat-tail	velocity, fps:	2800	2591	2392	2202	2020
	energy, ft-lb:	2873	2460	2097	1777	1495
	arc, inches:		+1.8	0	-8.0	-23.3
Hornady 165 SPBT LM	velocity, fps:	3015	2790	2575	2370	2176
	energy, ft-lb:	3330	2850	2428	2058	1734
	arc, inches:		+1.6	0	-7.0	-20.1
Hornady 165 SST	velocity, fps:	2800	2598	2405	2221	2046
(or Interbond)	energy, ft-lb:	2872	2473	2119	1808	1534
	arc, inches:		+1.9	0	-8.0	-22.8
Hornady 165 SST LM	velocity, fps:	3015	2802	2599	2405	2219
	energy, ft-lb:	3330	2878	2474	2118	1803
	arc, inches:		+1.5	0	-6.5	-19.3
Hornady 168 HPBT Match	velocity, fps:	2790	2620	2447	2280	2120
	energy, ft-lb:	2925	2561	2234	1940	1677
	arc, inches:		+1.7	0	-7.7	-22.2
Hornady 180 SP	velocity, fps:	2700	2469	2258	2042	1846
	energy, ft-lb:	2913	2436	2023	1666	1362
	arc, inches:		+2.4	0	-9.3	-27.0
Hornady 180 SPBT LM	velocity, fps:	2880	2676	2480	2293	2114
	energy, ft-lb:	3316	2862	2459	2102	1786
	arc, inches:		+1.7	0	-7.3	-21.3
Norma 150 Nosler Bal. Tip	velocity, fps:	2936	2713	2502	2300	
	energy, ft-lb:	2872	2453	2085	1762	
	arc, inches:		+1.6	0	-7.1	
Norma 150 Soft Point	velocity, fps:	2972	2640	2331	2043	
	energy, ft-lb:	2943	2321	1810	1390	
	arc, inches:		+1.8	0	-8.2	
Norma 180 Alaska	velocity, fps:	2700	2351	2028	1734	
	energy, ft-lb:	2914	2209	1645	1202	
	arc, inches:		+2.4	0	-11.0	
Norma 180 Nosler Partition	velocity, fps:	2700	2494	2297	2108	
	energy, ft-lb:	2914	2486	2108	1777	
	arc, inches:		+2.1	0	-8.7	

CARTRIDGE BULLET	RANGE, YARDS:	0	100	200	300	400
Norma 180 Plastic Point	velocity, fps:	2700	2455	2222	2003	
	energy, ft-lb:	2914	2409	1974	1603	
	arc, inches:		+2.1	0	-9.2	
Norma 180 Vulkan	velocity, fps:	2700	2416	2150	1901	
	energy, ft-lb:	2914	2334	1848	1445	
	arc, inches:		+2.2	0	-9.8	
Norma 180 Oryx	velocity, fps:	2700	2387	2095	1825	
	energy, ft-lb:	2914	2278	1755	1332	
	arc, inches:		+2.3	0	-10.2	
Norma 180 TXP Swift A-Fr.	velocity, fps:	2700	2479	2268	2067	
	energy, ft-lb:	2914	2456	2056	1708	
	arc, inches:		+2.0	0	-8.8	
Norma 180 AccuBond	velocity, fps:	2674	2499	2331	2169	
	energy, ft-lb:	2859	2497	2172	1881	
	arc, inches:		+2.0	0	-8.5	
\Norma 200 Vulkan	velocity, fps:	2641	2385	2143	1916	
	energy, ft-lb:	3098	2527	2040	1631	
	arc, inches:		+2.3	0	-9.9	
Norma 200 Oryx	velocity, fps:	2625	2362	2115	1883	
	energy, ft-lb:	3061	2479	1987	1575	
	arc, inches:		+2.3	0	-10.1	
PMC 150 X-Bullet	velocity, fps:	2750	2552	2361	2179	2005
	energy, ft-lb:	2518	2168	1857	1582	1339
	arc, inches:		+2.0	0	-8.2	-23.7
PMC 150 Pointed Soft Point	velocity, fps:	2773	2542	2322	2113	1916
	energy, ft-lb:	2560	2152	1796	1487	1222
	arc, inches:		+1.9	0	-8.4	-24.6
PMC 150 SP boat-tail	velocity, fps:	2900	2657	2427	2208	2000
	energy, ft-lb:	2801	2351	1961	1623	1332
	arc, inches:		+1.7	0	-7.7	-22.5
PMC 150 FMJ	velocity, fps:	2773	2542	2322	2113	1916
	energy, ft-lb:	2560	2152	1796	1487	1222
	arc, inches:		+1.9	0	-8.4	-24.6
PMC 168 Barnes X	velocity, fps:	2750	2569	2395	2228	2067
	energy, ft-lb:	2770	2418	2101	1818	1565
	arc, inches:		+1.9	0	-8.0	-23.0
PMC 180 Barnes X	velocity, fps:	2650	2487	2331	2179	2034
	energy, ft-lb:	2806	2472	2171	1898	1652
	arc, inches:		+2.1	0	-8.5	-24.3
PMC 180 Pointed Soft Point	velocity, fps:	2650	2430	2221	2024	1839
	energy, ft-lb:	2807	2359	1972	1638	1351
	arc, inches:		+2.2	0	-9.3	-27.0
PMC 180 SP boat-tail	velocity, fps:	2700	2523	2352	2188	2030
	energy, ft-lb:	2913	2543	2210	1913	1646
	arc, inches:		+2.0	0	-8.3	-23.9
PMC 180 HPBT Match	velocity, fps:	2800	2622	2456	2302	2158
	energy, ft-lb:	3133	2747	2411	2118	1861
	arc, inches:		+1.8	0	-7.6	-21.7
Rem. 55 PSP (sabot)	velocity, fps:	4080	3484	2964	2499	2080
"Accelerator"	energy, ft-lb:	2033	1482	1073	763	528
	arc, inches:		+1.4	+1.4	-2.6	-12.2
Rem. 125 PSP C-L MR	velocity, fps:	2660	2335	2034	1757	1509
	energy, ft-lb:	1964	1513	1148	856	632
	arc, inches:		+1.1	-3.0	-15.5	-37.4
Rem. 125 Pointed Soft Point	velocity, fps:	3140	2780	2447	2138	1853
	energy, ft-lb:	2736	2145	1662	1269	953
	arc, inches:		+1.5	0	-7.4	-22.4
Rem. 150 AccuTip	velocity, fps:	2910	2686	2473	2270	2077
	energy, ft-lb:	2820	2403	2037	1716	1436
	arc, inches:		+1.8	0	-7.4	-21.5
Rem. 150 PSP Core-Lokt	velocity, fps:	2910	2617	2342	2083	1843
	energy, ft-lb:	2820	2281	1827	1445	1131
	arc, inches:		+1.8	0	-8.2	-24.4

Centerfire Rifle Ballistics

.30-06 SPRINGFIELD TO .308 NORMA MAG.

CARTRIDGE BULLET	RANGE, YARDS:	0	100	200	300	400
Rem. 150 Bronze Point	velocity, fps:	2910	2656	2416	2189	1974
	energy, ft-lb:	2820	2349	1944	1596	1298
	arc, inches:		+1.7	0	-7.7	-22.7
Rem. 150 Nosler Bal. Tip	velocity, fps:	2910	2696	2492	2298	2112
	energy, ft-lb:	2821	2422	2070	1769	1485
	arc, inches:		+1.6	0	-7.3	-21.1
Rem. 150 Swift Scirocco	velocity, fps:	2910	2696	2492	2298	2111
	energy, ft-lb:	2820	2421	2069	1758	1485
	arc, inches:		+1.6	0	-7.3	-21.1
Rem. 165 AccuTip	velocity, fps:	2800	2597	2403	2217	2039
	energy, ft-lb:	2872	2470	2115	1800	1523
	arc, inches:		+1.8	0	-7.9	-22.8
Rem. 165 PSP Core-Lokt	velocity, fps:	2800	2534	2283	2047	1825
	energy, ft-lb:	2872	2352	1909	1534	1220
	arc, inches:		+2.0	0	-8.7	-25.9
Rem. 165 PSP boat-tail	velocity, fps:	2800	2592	2394	2204	2023
	energy, ft-lb:	2872	2462	2100	1780	1500
	arc, inches:		+1.8	0	-7.9	-23.0
Rem. 165 Nosler Bal. Tip	velocity, fps:	2800	2609	2426	2249	2080
	energy, ft-lb:	2873	2494	2155	1854	1588
	arc, inches:		+1.8	0	-7.7	-22.3
Rem. 168 PSP C-L Ultra	velocity, fps:	2800	2546	2306	2079	1866
	energy, ft-lb:	2924	2418	1984	1613	1299
	arc, inches:		+1.9	0	-8.5	-25.1
Rem. 180 SP Core-Lokt	velocity, fps:	2700	2348	2023	1727	1466
	energy, ft-lb:	2913	2203	1635	1192	859
	arc, inches:		+2.4	0	-11.0	-33.8
Rem. 180 PSP Core-Lokt	velocity, fps:	2700	2469	2250	2042	1846
	energy, ft-lb:	2913	2436	2023	1666	1362
	arc, inches:		+2.1	0	-9.0	-26.3
Rem. 180 PSP C-L Ultra	velocity, fps:	2700	2480	2270	2070	1882
	energy, ft-lb:	2913	2457	2059	1713	1415
	arc, inches:		+2.1	0	-8.9	-25.8
Rem. 180 Bronze Point	velocity, fps:	2700	2485	2280	2084	1899
	energy, ft-lb:	2913	2468	2077	1736	1441
	arc, inches:		+2.1	0	-8.8	-25.5
Rem. 180 Swift A-Frame	velocity, fps:	2700	2465	2243	2032	1833
	energy, ft-lb:	2913	2429	2010	1650	1343
	arc, inches:		+2.1	0	-9.1	-26.6
Rem. 180 Nosler Partition	velocity, fps:	2700	2512	2332	2160	1995
	energy, ft-lb:	2913	2522	2174	1864	1590
	arc, inches:		+2.0	0	-8.4	-24.3
Rem. 220 SP Core-Lokt	velocity, fps:	2410	2130	1870	1632	1422
	energy, ft-lb:	2837	2216	1708	1301	988
	arc, inches, s:		0	-6.2	-22.4	
Speer 150 Grand Slam	velocity, fps:	2975	2669	2383	2114	
	energy, ft-lb:	2947	2372	1891	1489	
	arc, inches:		+2.0	0	-8.1	-24.1
Speer 165 Grand Slam	velocity, fps:	2790	2560	2342	2134	
	energy, ft-lb:	2851	2401	2009	1669	
	arc, inches:		+1.9	0	-8.3	-24.1
Speer 180 Grand Slam	velocity, fps:	2690	2487	2293	2108	
	energy, ft-lb:	2892	2472	2101	1775	
	arc, inches:		+2.1	0	-8.8	-25.1
Win. 125 Pointed Soft Point	velocity, fps:	3140	2780	2447	2138	1853
	energy, ft-lb:	2736	2145	1662	1269	953
	arc, inches:		+1.8	0	-7.7	-23.0
Win. 150 Power-Point	velocity, fps:	2920	2580	2265	1972	1704
	energy, ft-lb:	2839	2217	1708	1295	967
	arc, inches:		+2.2	0	-9.0	-27.0
Win. 150 Power-Point Plus	velocity, fps:	3050	2685	2352	2043	1760
	energy, ft-lb:	3089	2402	1843	1391	1032
	arc, inches:		+1.7	0	-8.0	-24.3

CARTRIDGE BULLET	RANGE, YARDS:	0	100	200	300	400
Win. 150 Silvertip	velocity, fps:	2910	2617	2342	2083	1843
	energy, ft-lb:	2820	2281	1827	1445	1131
	arc, inches:		+2.1	0	-8.5	-25.0
Win. 150 Partition Gold	velocity, fps:	2960	2705	2464	2235	2019
	energy, ft-lb:	2919	2437	2022	1664	1358
	arc, inches:		+1.6	0	-7.4	-21.7
Win. 150 Ballistic Silvertip	velocity, fps:	2900	2687	2483	2289	2103
	energy, ft-lb:	2801	2404	2054	1745	1473
	arc, inches:		+1.7	0	-7.3	-21.2
Win. 150 Fail Safe	velocity, fps:	2920	2625	2349	2089	1848
	energy, ft-lb:	2841	2296	1838	1455	1137
	arc, inches:		+1.8	0	-8.1	-24.3
Win. 165 Pointed Soft Point	velocity, fps:	2800	2573	2357	2151	1956
	energy, ft-lb:	2873	2426	2036	1696	1402
	arc, inches:		+2.2	0	-8.4	-24.4
Win. 165 Fail Safe	velocity, fps:	2800	2540	2295	2063	1846
	energy, ft-lb:	2873	2365	1930	1560	1249
	arc, inches:		+2.0	0	-8.6	-25.3
Win. 168 Ballistic Silvertip	velocity, fps:	2790	2599	2416	2240	2072
	energy, ft-lb:	2903	2520	2177	1872	1601
	arc, inches:		+1.8	0	-7.8	-22.5
Win. 180 Ballistic Silvertip	velocity, fps:	2750	2572	2402	2237	2080
	energy, ft-lb:	3022	2644	2305	2001	1728
	arc, inches:		+1.9	0	-7.9	-22.8
Win. 180 Power-Point	velocity, fps:	2700	2348	2023	1727	1466
	energy, ft-lb:	2913	2203	1635	1192	859
	arc, inches:		+2.7	0	-11.3	-34.4
Win. 180 Power-Point Plus	velocity, fps:	2770	2563	2366	2177	1997
	energy, ft-lb:	3068	2627	2237	1894	1594
	arc, inches:		+1.9	0	-8.1	-23.6
Win. 180 Silvertip	velocity, fps:	2700	2469	2250	2042	1846
	energy, ft-lb:	2913	2436	2023	1666	1362
	arc, inches:		+2.4	0	-9.3	-27.0
Win. 180 AccuBond	velocity, fps:	2750	2573	2403	2239	2082
	energy, ft-lb:	3022	2646	2308	2004	1732
	arc, inches:		+1.9	0	-7.9	-22.8
Win. 180 Partition Gold	velocity, fps:	2790	2581	2382	2192	2010
	energy, ft-lb:	3112	2664	2269	1920	1615
	arc, inches:		+1.9	0	-8.0	-23.2
Win. 180 Fail Safe	velocity, fps:	2700	2486	2283	2089	1904
	energy, ft-lb:	2914	2472	2083	1744	1450
	arc, inches:		+2.1	0	-8.7	-25.5

.300 H&H Mag.

CARTRIDGE BULLET	RANGE, YARDS:	0	100	200	300	400
Federal 180 Nosler Partition	velocity, fps:	2880	2620	2380	2150	1930
	energy, ft-lb:	3315	2750	2260	1840	1480
	arc, inches:		+1.8	0	-8.0	-23.4
Win. 180 Fail Safe	velocity, fps:	2880	2628	2390	2165	1952
	energy, ft-lb:	3316	2762	2284	1873	1523
	arc, inches:		+1.8	0	-7.9	-23.2

.308 Norma Mag.

CARTRIDGE BULLET	RANGE, YARDS:	0	100	200	300	400
Norma 180 TXP Swift A-Fr.	velocity, fps:	2953	2704	2469	2245	
	energy, ft-lb:	3486	2924	2437	2016	
	arc, inches:		+1.6	0	-7.3	
Norma 180 Oryx	velocity, fps:	2953	2630	2330	2049	
	energy, ft-lb:	3486	2766	2170	1679	
	arc, inches:		+1.8	0	-8.2	
Norma 200 Vulkan	velocity, fps:	2903	2624	2361	2114	
	energy, ft-lb:	3744	3058	2476	1985	
	arc, inches:	0	+1.8	0	-8.0	

BALLISTICS

Centerfire Rifle Ballistics

.300 WINCHESTER MAGNUM TO .300 WINCHESTER MAGNUM

BALLISTICS

.300 Winchester Mag.

CARTRIDGE BULLET	RANGE, YARDS:	0	100	200	300	400
A-Square 180 Dead Tough	velocity, fps:	3120	2756	2420	2108	1820
	energy, ft-lb:	3890	3035	2340	1776	1324
	arc, inches:		+1.6	0	-7.6	-22.9
Black Hills 180 Nos. Bal. Tip	velocity, fps:	3100				
	energy, ft-lb:	3498				
	arc, inches:					
Black Hills 180 Barnes X	velocity, fps:	2950				
	energy, ft-lb:	3498				
	arc, inches:					
Black Hills 180 AccuBond	velocity, fps:	3000				
	energy, ft-lb:	3597				
	arc, inches:					
Black Hills 190 Match	velocity, fps:	2950				
	energy, ft-lb:	3672				
	arc, inches:					
Federal 150 Sierra Pro Hunt.	velocity, fps:	3280	3030	2800	2570	2360
	energy, ft-lb:	3570	3055	2600	2205	1860
	arc, inches:		+1.1	0	-5.6	-16.4
Federal 150 Trophy Bonded	velocity, fps:	3280	2980	2700	2430	2190
	energy, ft-lb:	3570	2450	2420	1970	1590
	arc, inches:		+1.2	0	-6.0	-17.9
Federal 180 Sierra Pro Hunt.	velocity, fps:	2960	2750	2540	2340	2160
	energy, ft-lb:	3500	3010	2580	2195	1860
	arc, inches:		+1.6	0	-7.0	-20.3
Federal 180 Barnes XLC	velocity, fps:	2960	2780	2600	2430	2260
	energy, ft-lb:	3500	3080	2700	2355	2050
	arc, inches:		+1.5	0	-6.6	-19.2
Federal 180 Trophy Bonded	velocity, fps:	2960	2700	2460	2220	2000
	energy, ft-lb:	3500	2915	2410	1975	1605
	arc, inches:		+1.6	0	-7.4	-21.9
Federal 180 Tr. Bonded HE	velocity, fps:	3100	2830	2580	2340	2110
	energy, ft-lb:	3840	3205	2660	2190	1790
	arc, inches:		+1.4	0	-6.6	-19.7
Federal 180 Nosler Partition	velocity, fps:	2960	2700	2450	2210	1990
	energy, ft-lb:	3500	2905	2395	1955	1585
	arc, inches:		+1.6	0	-7.5	-22.1
Federal 190 Sierra MatchKg.	velocity, fps:	2900	2730	2560	2400	2240
BTHP	energy, ft-lb:	3550	3135	2760	2420	2115
	arc, inches:		+12.9	+22.5	+26.9	+25.1
Federal 200 Sierra GameKing	velocity, fps:	2830	2680	2530	2380	2240
BTSP	energy, ft-lb:	3560	3180	2830	2520	2230
	arc, inches:		+1.7	0	-7.1	-20.4
Federal 200 Nosler Part. HE	velocity, fps:	2930	2740	2550	2370	2200
	energy, ft-lb:	3810	3325	2885	2495	2145
	arc, inches:		+1.6	0	-6.9	-20.1
Federal 200 Trophy Bonded	velocity, fps:	2800	2570	2350	2150	1950
	energy, ft-lb:	3480	2935	2460	2050	1690
	arc, inches:		+1.9	0	-8.2	-23.9
Hornady 150 SP boat-tail	velocity, fps:	3275	2988	2718	2464	2224
	energy, ft-lb:	3573	2974	2461	2023	1648
	arc, inches:		+1.2	0	-6.0	-17.8
Hornady 150 SST	velocity, fps:	3275	3027	2791	2565	2352
(and Interbond)	energy, ft-lb:	3572	3052	2593	2192	1842
	arc, inches:		+1.2	0	-5.8	-17.0
Hornady 165 SP boat-tail	velocity, fps:	3100	2877	2665	2462	2269
	energy, ft-lb:	3522	3033	2603	2221	1887
	arc, inches:		+1.3	0	-6.5	-18.5
Hornady 165 SST	velocity, fps:	3100	2885	2680	2483	2296
	energy, ft-lb:	3520	3049	2630	2259	1930
	arc, inches:		+1.4	0	-6.4	-18.6
Hornady 180 SP boat-tail	velocity, fps:	2960	2745	2540	2344	2157
	energy, ft-lb:	3501	3011	2578	2196	1859
	arc, inches:		+1.9	0	-7.3	-20.9
Hornady 180 SST	velocity, fps:	2960	2764	2575	2395	2222
	energy, ft-lb:	3501	3052	2650	2292	1974
	arc, inches:		+1.6	0	-7.0	-20.1
Hornady 180 SPBT HM	velocity, fps:	3100	2879	2668	2467	2275
	energy, ft-lb:	3840	3313	2845	2431	2068
	arc, inches:		+1.4	0	-6.4	-18.7
Hornady 190 SP boat-tail	velocity, fps:	2900	2711	2529	2355	2187
	energy, ft-lb:	3549	3101	2699	2340	2018
	arc, inches:		+1.6	0	-7.1	-20.4
Norma 150 Nosler Bal. Tip	velocity, fps:	3250	3014	2791	2578	
	energy, ft-lb:	3519	3027	2595	2215	
	arc, inches:		+1.1	0	-5.6	
Norma 150 Barnes TS	velocity, fps:	3215	2982	2761	2550	
	energy, ft-lb:	3444	2962	2539	2167	
	arc, inches:		+1.2	0	-5.8	
Norma 165 Scirocco	velocity, fps:	3117	2921	2734	2554	
	energy, ft-lb:	3561	3127	2738	2390	
	arc, inches:		+1.2	0	-5.9	
Norma 180 Soft Point	velocity, fps:	3018	2780	2555	2341	
	energy, ft-lb:	3641	3091	2610	2190	
	arc, inches:		+1.5	0	-7.0	
Norma 180 Plastic Point	velocity, fps:	3018	2755	2506	2271	
	energy, ft-lb:	3641	3034	2512	2062	
	arc, inches:		+1.6	0	-7.1	
Norma 180 TXP Swift A-Fr.	velocity, fps:	2920	2688	2467	2256	
	energy, ft-lb:	3409	2888	2432	2035	
	arc, inches:		+1.7	0	-7.4	
Norma 180 AccuBond	velocity, fps:	2953	2767	2588	2417	
	energy, ft-lb:	3486	3061	2678	2335	
	arc, inches:		+1.5	0	-6.7	
Norma 180 Oryx	velocity, fps:	2920	2600	2301	2023	
	energy, ft-lb:	3409	2702	2117	1636	
	arc, inches:		+1.8	0	-8.4	
Norma 200 Vulkan	velocity, fps:	2887	2609	2347	2100	
	energy, ft-lb:	3702	3023	2447	1960	
	arc, inches:		+1.8	0	-8.2	
Norma 200 Oryx	velocity, fps:	2789	2510	2248	2002	
	energy, ft-lb:	3455	2799	2245	1780	
	arc, inches:		+2.0	0	-8.9	
PMC 150 Barnes X	velocity, fps:	3135	2918	2712	2515	2327
	energy, ft-lb:	3273	2836	2449	2107	1803
	arc, inches:		+1.3	0	-6.1	-17.7
PMC 150 Pointed Soft Point	velocity, fps:	3150	2902	2665	2438	2222
	energy, ft-lb:	3304	2804	2364	1979	1644
	arc, inches:		+1.3	0	-6.2	-18.3
PMC 150 SP boat-tail	velocity, fps:	3250	2987	2739	2504	2281
	energy, ft-lb:	3517	2970	2498	2088	1733
	arc, inches:		+1.2	0	-6.0	-17.4
PMC 180 Barnes X	velocity, fps:	2910	2738	2572	2412	2258
	energy, ft-lb:	3384	2995	2644	2325	2037
	arc, inches:		+1.6	0	-6.9	-19.8
PMC 180 Pointed Soft Point	velocity, fps:	2853	2643	2446	2258	2077
	energy, ft-lb:	3252	2792	2391	2037	1724
	arc, inches:		+1.7	0	-7.5	-21.9
PMC 180 SP boat-tail	velocity, fps:	2900	2714	2536	2365	2200
	energy, ft-lb:	3361	2944	2571	2235	1935
	arc, inches:		+1.6	0	-7.1	-20.3
PMC 180 HPBT Match	velocity, fps:	2950	2755	2568	2390	2219
	energy, ft-lb:	3478	3033	2636	2283	1968
	arc, inches:		+1.5	0	-6.8	-19.7

.300 WINCHESTER MAGNUM TO .300 WINCHESTER SHORT MAG.

CARTRIDGE BULLET	RANGE, YARDS:	0	100	200	300	400
Rem. 150 PSP Core-Lokt	velocity, fps:	3290	2951	2636	2342	2068
	energy, ft-lb:	3605	2900	2314	1827	1859
	arc, inches:		+1.6	0	-7.0	-20.2
Rem. 150 PSP C-L MR	velocity, fps:	2650	2373	2113	1870	1646
	energy, ft-lb:	2339	1875	1486	1164	902
	arc, inches:		+1.0	-2.7	-14.3	-35.8
Rem. 150 PSP C-L Ultra	velocity, fps:	3290	2967	2666	2384	2120
	energy, ft-lb:	3065	2931	2366	1893	1496
	arc, inches:		+1.2	0	-6.1	-18.4
Rem. 180 AccuTip	velocity, fps:	2960	2764	2577	2397	2224
	energy, ft-lb:	3501	3053	2653	2295	1976
	arc, inches:		+1.5	0	-6.8	-19.6
Rem. 180 PSP Core-Lokt	velocity, fps:	2960	2745	2540	2344	2157
	energy, ft-lb:	3501	3011	2578	2196	1424
	arc, inches:		+2.2	+1.9	-3.4	-15.0
Rem. 180 PSP C-L Ultra	velocity, fps:	2960	2727	2505	2294	2093
	energy, ft-lb:	3501	2971	2508	2103	1751
	arc, inches:		+2.7	+2.2	-3.8	-16.4
Rem. 180 Nosler Partition	velocity, fps:	2960	2725	2503	2291	2089
	energy, ft-lb:	3501	2968	2503	2087	1744
	arc, inches:		+1.6	0	-7.2	-20.9
Rem. 180 Nosler Bal. Tip	velocity, fps:	2960	2774	2595	2424	2259
	energy, ft-lb:	3501	3075	2692	2348	2039
	arc, inches:		+1.5	0	-6.7	-19.3
Rem. 180 Swift Scirocco	velocity, fps:	2960	2774	2595	2424	2259
	energy, ft-lb:	3501	3075	2692	2348	2039
	arc, inches:		+1.5	0	-6.7	-19.3
Rem. 190 PSP boat-tail	velocity, fps:	2885	2691	2506	2327	2156
	energy, ft-lb:	3511	3055	2648	2285	1961
	arc, inches:		+1.6	0	-7.2	-20.8
Rem. 190 HPBT Match	velocity, fps:	2900	2725	2557	2395	2239
	energy, ft-lb:	3547	3133	2758	2420	2115
	arc, inches:		+1.6	0	-6.9	-19.9
Rem. 200 Swift A-Frame	velocity, fps:	2825	2595	2376	2167	1970
	energy, ft-lb:	3544	2989	2506	2086	1722
	arc, inches:		+1.8	0	-8.0	-23.5
Speer 180 Grand Slam	velocity, fps:	2950	2735	2530	2334	
	energy, ft-lb:	3478	2989	2558	2176	
	arc, inches:		+1.6	0	-7.0	-20.5
Speer 200 Grand Slam	velocity, fps:	2800	2597	2404	2218	
	energy, ft-lb:	3481	2996	2565	2185	
	arc, inches:		+1.8	0	-7.9	-22.9
Win. 150 Power-Point	velocity, fps:	3290	2951	2636	2342	2068
	energy, ft-lb:	3605	2900	2314	1827	1424
	arc, inches:		+2.6	+2.1	-3.5	-15.4
Win. 150 Fail Safe	velocity, fps:	3260	2943	2647	2370	2110
	energy, ft-lb:	3539	2884	2334	1871	1483
	arc, inches:		+1.3	0	-6.2	-18.7
Win. 165 Fail Safe	velocity, fps:	3120	2807	2515	2242	1985
	energy, ft-lb:	3567	2888	2319	1842	1445
	arc, inches:		+1.5	0	-7.0	-20.0
Win. 180 Power-Point	velocity, fps:	2960	2745	2540	2344	2157
	energy, ft-lb:	3501	3011	2578	2196	1859
	arc, inches:		+1.9	0	-7.3	-20.9
Win. 180 Power-Point Plus	velocity, fps:	3070	2846	2633	2430	2236
	energy, ft-lb:	3768	3239	2772	2361	1999
	arc, inches:		+1.4	0	-6.4	-18.7
Win. 180 Ballistic Silvertip	velocity, fps:	2950	2764	2586	2415	2250
	energy, ft-lb:	3478	3054	2673	2331	2023
	arc, inches:		+1.5	0	-6.7	-19.4
Win. 180 AccuBond	velocity, fps:	2950	2765	2588	2417	2253
	energy, ft-lb:	3478	3055	2676	2334	2028
	arc, inches:		+1.5	0	-6.7	-19.4

CARTRIDGE BULLET	RANGE, YARDS:	0	100	200	300	400
Win. 180 Fail Safe	velocity, fps:	2960	2732	2514	2307	2110
	energy, ft-lb:	3503	2983	2528	2129	1780
	arc, inches:		+1.6	0	-7.1	-20.7
Win. 180 Partition Gold	velocity, fps:	3070	2859	2657	2464	2280
	energy, ft-lb:	3768	3267	2823	2428	2078
	arc, inches:		+1.4	0	-6.3	-18.3

.300 Remington Short Ultra Mag

CARTRIDGE BULLET	RANGE, YARDS:	0	100	200	300	400
Rem. 150 PSP C-L Ultra	velocity, fps:	3200	2901	2672	2359	2112
	energy, ft-lb:	3410	2803	2290	1854	1485
	arc, inches:		+1.3	0	-6.4	-19.1
Rem. 165 PSP Core-Lokt	velocity, fps:	3075	2792	2527	2276	2040
	energy, ft-lb:	3464	2856	2339	1828	1525
	arc, inches:		+1.5	0	-7.0	-20.7
Rem. 180 Partition	velocity, fps:	2960	2761	2571	2389	2214
	energy, ft-lb:	3501	3047	2642	2280	1959
	arc, inches:		+1.5	0	-6.8	-19.7
Rem. 180 PSP C-L Ultra	velocity, fps:	2960	2727	2506	2295	2094
	energy, ft-lb:	3501	2972	2509	2105	1753
	arc, inches:		+1.6	0	-7.1	-20.9
Rem. 190 HPBT Match	velocity, fps:	2900	2725	2557	2395	2239
	energy, ft-lb:	3547	3133	2758	2420	2115
	arc, inches:		+1.6	0	-6.9	-19.9

.300 Winchester Short Mag.

CARTRIDGE BULLET	RANGE, YARDS:	0	100	200	300	400
Black Hills 175 Sierra MKing	velocity, fps:	2950				
	energy, ft-lb:	3381				
	arc, inches:					
Black Hills 180 AccuBond	velocity, fps:	2950				
	energy, ft-lb:	3478				
	arc, inches:					
Federal 150 Nosler Bal. Tip	velocity, fps:	3200	2970	2755	2545	2345
	energy, ft-lb:	3410	2940	2520	2155	1830
	arc, inches:		+1.2	0	-5.8	-17.0
Federal 165 Nos. Partition	velocity, fps:	3130	2890	2670	2450	2250
	energy, ft-lb:	3590	3065	2605	2205	1855
	arc, inches:		+1.3	0	-6.2	-18.2
Federal 165 Nos. Solid Base	velocity, fps:	3130	2900	2690	2490	2290
	energy, ft-lb:	3590	3090	2650	2265	1920
	arc, inches:		+1.3	0	-6.1	-17.8
Federal 180 Barnes TS And Nos. Solid Base	velocity, fps:	2980	2780	2580	2400	2220
	energy, ft-lbs:	3550	3085	2670	2300	1970
	arc, inches:		+1.5	0	-6.7	-19.5
Federal 180 Grand Slam	velocity, fps:	2970	2740	2530	2320	2130
	energy, ft-lb:	3525	3010	2555	2155	1810
	arc, inches:		+1.5	0	-7.0	-20.5
Federal 180 Trophy Bonded	velocity, fps:	2970	2730	2500	2280	2080
	energy, ft-lb:	3525	2975	2500	2085	1725
	arc, inches:		+1.5	0	-7.2	-21.0
Federal 180 Nosler Partition	velocity, fps:	2975	2750	2535	2290	2126
	energy, ft-lb:	3540	3025	2570	2175	1825
	arc, inches:		+1.5	0	-7.0	-20.3
Federal 180 Nos. AccuBond	velocity, fps:	2960	2780	2610	2440	2280
	energy, ft-lb:	3500	3090	2715	2380	2075
	arc, inches:		+1.5	0	-6.6	-19.0
Federal 180 Hi-Shok SP	velocity, fps:	2970	2520	2115	1750	1430
	energy, ft-lb:	3525	2540	1785	1220	820
	arc, inches:		+2.2	0	-9.9	-31.4
Norma 150 FMJ	velocity, fps:	2953	2731	2519	2318	
	energy, ft-lb:					
	arc, inches:		+1.6	0	-7.1	
Norma 150 Barnes X TS	velocity, fps:	3215	2982	2761	2550	
	energy, ft-lb:	3444	2962	2539	2167	
	arc, inches:		+1.2	0	-5.7	

Centerfire Rifle Ballistics

.300 WINCHESTER SHORT MAG. TO .300 PEGASUS

CARTRIDGE BULLET	RANGE, YARDS:	0	100	200	300	400
Norma 180 Nosler Bal. Tip	velocity, fps:	3215	2985	2767	2560	
	energy, ft-lb:	3437	2963	2547	2179	
	arc, inches:		+1.2	0	-5.7	
Norma 180 Oryx	velocity, fps:	2936	2542	2180	1849	
	energy, ft-lb:	3446	2583	1900	1368	
	arc, inches:		+1.9	0	-8.9	
Win. 150 Power-Point	velocity, fps:	3270	2903	2565	2250	1958
	energy, ft-lb:	3561	2807	2190	1686	1277
	arc, inches:		+1.3	0	-6.6	-20.2
Win. 150 Ballistic Silvertip	velocity, fps:	3300	3061	2834	2619	2414
	energy, ft-lb:	3628	3121	2676	2285	1941
	arc, inches:		+1.1	0	-5.4	-15.9
Win. 165 Fail Safe	velocity, fps:	3125	2846	2584	2336	2102
	energy, ft-lb:	3577	2967	2446	1999	1619
	arc, inches:		+1.4	0	-6.6	-19.6
Win. 180 Ballistic Silvertip	velocity, fps:	3010	2822	2641	2468	2301
	energy, ft-lb:	3621	3182	2788	2434	2116
	arc, inches:		+1.4	0	-6.4	-18.6
Win. 180 AccuBond	velocity, fps:	3010	2822	2643	2470	2304
	energy, ft-lb:	3622	3185	2792	2439	2121
	arc, inches:		+1.4	0	-6.4	-18.5
Win. 180 Fail Safe	velocity, fps:	2970	2741	2524	2317	2120
	energy, ft-lb:	3526	3005	2547	2147	1797
	arc, inches:		+1.6	0	-7.0	-20.5
Win. 180 Power Point	velocity, fps:	2970	2755	2549	2353	2166
	energy, ft-lb:	3526	3034	2598	2214	1875
	arc, inches:		+1.5	0	-6.9	-20.1

.300 Weatherby Mag.

CARTRIDGE BULLET	RANGE, YARDS:	0	100	200	300	400
A-Square 180 Dead Tough	velocity, fps:	3180	2811	2471	2155	1863
	energy, ft-lb:	4041	3158	2440	1856	1387
	arc, inches:		+1.5	0	-7.2	-21.8
A-Square 220 Monolythic Solid	velocity, fps:	2700	2407	2133	1877	1653
	energy, ft-lb:	3561	2830	2223	1721	1334
	arc, inches:		+2.3	0	-9.8	-29.7
Federal 180 Sierra GameKing BTSP	velocity, fps:	3190	3010	2830	2660	2490
	energy, ft-lb:	4065	3610	3195	2820	2480
	arc, inches:		+1.2	0	-5.6	-16.0
Federal 180 Trophy Bonded	velocity, fps:	3190	2950	2720	2500	2290
	energy, ft-lb:	4065	3475	2955	2500	2105
	arc, inches:		+1.3	0	-5.9	-17.5
Federal 180 Tr. Bonded HE	velocity, fps:	3330	3080	2850	2750	2410
	energy, ft-lb:	4430	3795	3235	2750	2320
	arc, inches:		+1.1	0	-5.4	-15.8
Federal 180 Nosler Partition	velocity, fps:	3190	2980	2780	2590	2400
	energy, ft-lb:	4055	3540	3080	2670	2305
	arc, inches:		+1.2	0	-5.7	-16.7
Federal 180 Nosler Part. HE	velocity, fps:	3330	3110	2810	2710	2520
	energy, ft-lb:	4430	3875	3375	2935	2540
	arc, inches:		+1.0	0	-5.2	-15.1
Federal 200 Trophy Bonded	velocity, fps:	2900	2670	2440	2230	2030
	energy, ft-lb:	3735	3150	2645	2200	1820
	arc, inches:		+1.7	0	-7.6	-22.2
Hornady 150 SST (or Interbond)	velocity, fps:	3375	3123	2882	2652	2434
	energy, ft-lb:	3793	3248	2766	2343	1973
	arc, inches:		+1.0	0	-5.4	-15.8
Hornady 180 SP	velocity, fps:	3120	2891	2673	2466	2268
	energy, ft-lb:	3890	3340	2856	2430	2055
	arc, inches:		+1.3	0	-6.2	-18.1
Hornady 180 SST	velocity, fps:	3120	2911	2711	2519	2335
	energy, ft-lb:	3890	3386	2936	2535	2180
	arc, inches:		+1.3	0	-6.2	-18.1
Rem. 180 PSP Core-Lokt	velocity, fps:	3120	2866	2627	2400	2184
	energy, ft-lb:	3890	3284	2758	2301	1905
	arc, inches:		+2.4	+2.0	-3.4	-14.9
Rem. 190 PSP boat-tail	velocity, fps:	3030	2830	2638	2455	2279
	energy, ft-lb:	3873	3378	2936	2542	2190
	arc, inches:		+1.4	0	-6.4	-18.6
Rem. 200 Swift A-Frame	velocity, fps:	2925	2690	2467	2254	2052
	energy, ft-lb:	3799	3213	2701	2256	1870
	arc, inches:		+2.8	+2.3	-3.9	-17.0
Speer 180 Grand Slam	velocity, fps:	3185	2948	2722	2508	
	energy, ft-lb:	4054	3472	2962	2514	
	arc, inches:		+1.3	0	-5.9	-17.4
Wby. 150 Pointed Expanding	velocity, fps:	3540	3225	2932	2657	2399
	energy, ft-lb:	4173	3462	2862	2351	1916
	arc, inches:		+2.6	+3.3	0	-8.2
Wby. 150 Nosler Partition	velocity, fps:	3540	3263	3004	2759	2528
	energy, ft-lb:	4173	3547	3005	2536	2128
	arc, inches:		+2.5	+3.2	0	-7.7
Wby. 165 Pointed Expanding	velocity, fps:	3390	3123	2872	2634	2409
	energy, ft-lb:	4210	3573	3021	2542	2126
	arc, inches:		+2.8	+3.5	0	-8.5
Wby. 165 Nosler Bal. Tip	velocity, fps:	3350	3133	2927	2730	2542
	energy, ft-lb:	4111	3596	3138	2730	2367
	arc, inches:		+2.7	+3.4	0	-8.1
Wby. 180 Pointed Expanding	velocity, fps:	3240	3004	2781	2569	2366
	energy, ft-lb:	4195	3607	3091	2637	2237
	arc, inches:		+3.1	+3.8	0	-9.0
Wby. 180 Barnes X	velocity, fps:	3190	2995	2809	2631	2459
	energy, ft-lb:	4067	3586	3154	2766	2417
	arc, inches:		+3.1	+3.8	0	-8.7
Wby. 180 Bal. Tip	velocity, fps:	3250	3051	2806	2676	2503
	energy, ft-lb:	4223	3721	3271	2867	2504
	arc, inches:		+2.8	+3.6	0	-8.4
Wby. 180 Nosler Partition	velocity, fps:	3240	3028	2826	2634	2449
	energy, ft-lb:	4195	3665	3193	2772	2396
	arc, inches:		+3.0	+3.7	0	-8.6
Wby. 200 Nosler Partition	velocity, fps:	3060	2860	2668	2485	2308
	energy, ft-lb:	4158	3631	3161	2741	2366
	arc, inches:		+3.5	+4.2	0	-9.8
Wby. 220 RN Expanding	velocity, fps:	2845	2543	2260	1996	1751
	energy, ft-lb:	3954	3158	2495	1946	1497
	arc, inches:		+4.9	+5.9	0	-14.6

.300 Dakota

CARTRIDGE BULLET	RANGE, YARDS:	0	100	200	300	400
Dakota 165 Barnes X	velocity, fps:	3200	2979	2769	2569	2377
	energy, ft-lb:	3751	3251	2809	2417	2070
	arc, inches:		+2.1	+1.8	-3.0	-13.2
Dakota 200 Barnes X	velocity, fps:	3000	2824	2656	2493	2336
	energy, ft-lb:	3996	3542	3131	2760	2423
	arc, inches:		+2.2	+1.5	-4.0	-15.2

.300 Pegasus

CARTRIDGE BULLET	RANGE, YARDS:	0	100	200	300	400
A-Square 180 SP boat-tail	velocity, fps:	3500	3319	3145	2978	2817
	energy, ft-lb:	4896	4401	3953	3544	3172
	arc, inches:		+2.3	+2.9	0	-6.8
A-Square 180 Nosler Part.	velocity, fps:	3500	3295	3100	2913	2734
	energy, ft-lb:	4896	4339	3840	3392	2988
	arc, inches:		+2.3	+3.0	0	-7.1
A-Square 180 Dead Tough	velocity, fps:	3500	3103	2740	2405	2095
	energy, ft-lb:	4896	3848	3001	2312	1753
	arc, inches:		+1.1	0	-5.7	-17.5

Centerfire Rifle Ballistics

.300 REMINGTON ULTRA MAG TO 8MM MAUSER (8X57)

.300 Remington Ultra Mag

CARTRIDGE BULLET	RANGE, YARDS:	0	100	200	300	400
Federal 180 Trophy Bonded	velocity, fps:	3250	3000	2770	2550	2340
	energy, ft-lb:	4220	3605	3065	2590	2180
	arc, inches:		+1.2	0	-5.7	-16.8
Rem. 150 Swift Scirocco	velocity, fps:	3450	3208	2980	2762	2556
	energy, ft-lb:	3964	3427	2956	2541	2175
	arc, inches:		+1.7	+1.5	-2.6	-11.2
Rem. 180 Nosler Partition	velocity, fps:	3250	3037	2834	2640	2454
	energy, ft-lb:	4221	3686	3201	2786	2407
	arc, inches:		+2.4	+1.8	-3.0	-12.7
Rem. 180 Swift Scirocco	velocity, fps:	3250	3048	2856	2672	2495
	energy, ft-lb:	4221	3714	3260	2853	2487
	arc, inches:		+2.0	+1.7	-2.8	-12.3
Rem. 180 PSP Core-Lokt	velocity, fps:	3250	2988	2742	2508	2287
	energy, ft-lb:	3517	2974	2503	2095	1741
	arc, inches:		+2.1	+1.8	-3.1	-13.6
Rem. 200 Nosler Partition	velocity, fps:	3025	2826	2636	2454	2279
	energy, ft-lb:	4063	3547	3086	2673	2308
	arc, inches:		+2.4	+2.0	-3.4	-14.6

.30-378 Weatherby Mag.

CARTRIDGE BULLET	RANGE, YARDS:	0	100	200	300	400
Wby. 165 Nosler Bal. Tip	velocity, fps:	3500	3275	3062	2859	2665
	energy, ft-lb:	4488	3930	3435	2995	2603
	arc, inches:		+2.4	+3.0	0	-7.4
Wby. 180 Nosler Bal. Tip	velocity, fps:	3420	3213	3015	2826	2645
	energy, ft-lb:	4676	4126	3634	3193	2797
	arc, inches:		+2.5	+3.1	0	-7.5
Wby. 180 Barnes X	velocity, fps:	3450	3243	3046	2858	2678
	energy, ft-lb:	4757	4204	3709	3264	2865
	arc, inches:		+2.4	+3.1	0	-7.4
Wby. 200 Nosler Partition	velocity, fps:	3160	2955	2759	2572	2392
	energy, ft-lb:	4434	3877	3381	2938	2541
	arc, inches:		+3.2	+3.9	0	-9.1

7.82 (.308) Warbird

CARTRIDGE BULLET	RANGE, YARDS:	0	100	200	300	400
Lazzeroni 150 Nosler Part.	velocity, fps:	3680	3432	3197	2975	2764
	energy, ft-lb:	4512	3923	3406	2949	2546
	arc, inches:		+2.1	+2.7	0	-6.6
Lazzeroni 180 Nosler Part.	velocity, fps:	3425	3220	3026	2839	2661
	energy, ft-lb:	4689	4147	3661	3224	2831
	arc, inches:		+2.5	+3.2	0	-7.5
Lazzeroni 200 Swift A-Fr.	velocity, fps:	3290	3105	2928	2758	2594
	energy, ft-lb:	4808	4283	3808	3378	2988
	arc, inches:		+2.7	+3.4	0	-7.9

7.65x53 Argentine

CARTRIDGE BULLET	RANGE, YARDS:	0	100	200	300	400
Norma 174 Soft Point	velocity, fps:	2493	2173	1878	1611	
	energy, ft-lb:	2402	1825	1363	1003	
	arc, inches:		+2.0	0	-9.5	
Norma 180 Soft Point	velocity, fps:	2592	2386	2189	2002	
	energy, ft-lb:	2686	2276	1916	1602	
	arc, inches:		+2.3	0	-9.6	

.303 British

CARTRIDGE BULLET	RANGE, YARDS:	0	100	200	300	400
Federal 150 Hi-Shok	velocity, fps:	2690	2440	2210	1980	1780
	energy, ft-lb:	2400	1980	1620	1310	1055
	arc, inches:		+2.2	0	-9.4	-27.6
Federal 180 Sierra Pro-Hunt.	velocity, fps:	2460	2230	2020	1820	1630
	energy, ft-lb:	2420	1995	1625	1315	1060
	arc, inches:		+2.8	0	-11.3	-33.2
Federal 180 Tr. Bonded HE	velocity, fps:	2590	2350	2120	1900	1700
	energy, ft-lb:	2680	2205	1795	1445	1160
	arc, inches:		+2.4	0	-10.0	-30.0
Hornady 150 Soft Point	velocity, fps:	2685	2441	2210	1992	1787
	energy, ft-lb:	2401	1984	1627	1321	1064
	arc, inches:		+2.2	0	-9.3	-27.4
Hornady 150 SP LM	velocity, fps:	2830	2570	2325	2094	1884
	energy, ft-lb:	2667	2199	1800	1461	1185
	arc, inches:		+2.0	0	-8.4	-24.6
Norma 150 Soft Point	velocity, fps:	2723	2438	2170	1920	
	energy, ft-lb:	2470	1980	1569	1228	
	arc, inches:		+2.2	0	-9.6	
PMC 174 FMJ (and HPBT)	velocity, fps:	2400	2216	2042	1876	1720
	energy, ft-lb:	2225	1898	1611	1360	1143
	arc, inches:		+2.8	0	-11.2	-32.2
PMC 180 SP boat-tail	velocity, fps:	2450	2276	2110	1951	1799
	energy, ft-lb:	2399	2071	1779	1521	1294
	arc, inches:		+2.6	0	-10.4	-30.1
Rem. 180 SP Core-Lokt	velocity, fps:	2460	2124	1817	1542	1311
	energy, ft-lb:	2418	1803	1319	950	687
	arc, inches, s:		0	-5.8	-23.3	
Win. 180 Power-Point	velocity, fps:	2460	2233	2018	1816	1629
	energy, ft-lb:	2418	1993	1627	1318	1060
	arc, inches, s:		0	-6.1	-20.8	

7.7x58 Japanese Arisaka

CARTRIDGE BULLET	RANGE, YARDS:	0	100	200	300	400
Norma 174 Soft Point	velocity, fps:	2493	2173	1878	1611	
	energy, ft-lb:	2402	1825	1363	1003	
	arc, inches:		+2.0	0	-9.5	
Norma 180 Soft Point	velocity, fps:	2493	2291	2099	1916	
	energy, ft-lb:	2485	2099	1761	1468	
	arc, inches:		+2.6	0	-10.5	

.32-20 Winchester

CARTRIDGE BULLET	RANGE, YARDS:	0	100	200	300	400
Rem. 100 Lead	velocity, fps:	1210	1021	913	834	769
	energy, ft-lb:	325	231	185	154	131
	arc, inches:		0	-31.6	-104.7	
Win. 100 Lead	velocity, fps:	1210	1021	913	834	769
	energy, ft-lb:	325	231	185	154	131
	arc, inches:		0	-32.3	-106.3	

.32 Winchester Special

CARTRIDGE BULLET	RANGE, YARDS:	0	100	200	300	400
Federal 170 Hi-Shok	velocity, fps:	2250	1920	1630	1370	1180
	energy, ft-lb:	1910	1395	1000	710	520
	arc, inches:		0	-8.0	-29.2	
Rem. 170 SP Core-Lokt	velocity, fps:	2250	1921	1626	1372	1175
	energy, ft-lb:	1911	1393	998	710	521
	arc, inches:		0	-8.0	-29.3	
Win. 170 Power-Point	velocity, fps:	2250	1870	1537	1267	1082
	energy, ft-lb:	1911	1320	892	606	442
	arc, inches:		0	-9.2	-33.2	

8mm Mauser (8x57)

CARTRIDGE BULLET	RANGE, YARDS:	0	100	200	300	400
Federal 170 Hi-Shok	velocity, fps:	2360	1970	1620	1330	1120
	energy, ft-lb:	2100	1465	995	670	475
	arc, inches:		0	-7.6	-28.5	
Hornady 195 SP	velocity, fps:	2550	2343	2146	1959	1782
	energy, ft-lb:	2815	2377	1994	1861	1375
	arc, inches:		+2.3	0	-9.9	-28.8
Hornady 195 SP (2005)	velocity, fps:	2475	2269	2074	1888	1714
	energy, ft-lb:	2652	2230	1861	1543	1271
	arc, inches:		+2.6	0	-10.7	-31.3
Norma 123 FMJ	velocity, fps:	2559	2121	1729	1398	
	energy, ft-lb:	1789	1228	817	534	
	arc, inches:		+3.2	0	-15.0	
Norma 196 Oryx	velocity, fps:	2395	2146	1912	1695	
	energy, ft-lb:	2497	2004	1591	1251	
	arc, inches:		+3	0	-12.6	

Centerfire Rifle Ballistics

8MM MAUSER (8X57) TO .338 WINCHESTER MAG.

BALLISTICS

CARTRIDGE BULLET	RANGE, YARDS:	0	100	200	300	400
Norma 196 Vulkan	velocity, fps:	2395	2156	1930	1720	
	energy, ft-lb:	2497	2023	1622	1289	
	arc, inches:		3.0	0	-12.3	
Norma 196 Alaska	velocity, fps:	2395	2112	1850	1611	
	energy, ft-lb:	2714	2190	1754	1399	
	arc, inches:		0	-6.3	-22.9	
Norma 196 Soft Point (JS)	velocity, fps:	2526	2244	1981	1737	
	energy, ft-lb:	2778	2192	1708	1314	
	arc, inches:		+2.7	0	-11.6	
Norma 196 Alaska (JS)	velocity, fps:	2526	2248	1988	1747	
	energy, ft-lb:	2778	2200	1720	1328	
	arc, inches:		+2.7	0	-11.5	
Norma 196 Vulkan (JS)	velocity, fps:	2526	2276	2041	1821	
	energy, ft-lb:	2778	2256	1813	1443	
	arc, inches:		+2.6	0	-11.0	
Norma 196 Oryx (JS)	velocity, fps:	2526	2269	2027	1802	
	energy, ft-lb:	2778	2241	1789	1413	
	arc, inches:		+2.6	0	-11.1	
PMC 170 Pointed Soft Point	velocity, fps:	2360	1969	1622	1333	1123
	energy, ft-lb:	2102	1463	993	671	476
	arc, inches:		+1.8	-4.5	-24.3	-63.8
Rem. 170 SP Core-Lokt	velocity, fps:	2360	1969	1622	1333	1123
	energy, ft-lb:	2102	1463	993	671	476
	arc, inches:		+1.8	-4.5	-24.3	-63.8
Win. 170 Power-Point	velocity, fps:	2360	1969	1622	1333	1123
	energy, ft-lb:	2102	1463	993	671	476
	arc, inches:		+1.8	-4.5	-24.3	-63.8

.325 WSM

CARTRIDGE BULLET	RANGE, YARDS:	0	100	200	300	400
Win. 180 Ballistic ST	velocity, fps:	3060	2841	2632	2432	2242
	energy, ft-lb:	3743	3226	2769	2365	2009
	arc, inches:		+1.4	0	-6.4	-18.7
Win. 200 AccuBond CT	velocity, fps:	2950	2753	2565	2384	2210
	energy, ft-lb:	3866	3367	2922	2524	2170
	arc, inches:		+1.5	0	-6.8	-19.8
Win. 220 Power-Point	velocity, fps:	2840	2605	2382	2169	1968
	energy, ft-lb:	3941	3316	2772	2300	1893
	arc, inches:		+1.8	0	-8.0	-23.3

8MM REMINGTON MAG.

CARTRIDGE BULLET	RANGE, YARDS:	0	100	200	300	400
A-Square 220 Monolythic Solid	velocity, fps:	2800	2501	2221	1959	1718
	energy, ft-lb:	3829	3055	2409	1875	1442
	arc, inches:		+2.1	0	-9.1	-27.6
Rem. 200 Swift A-Frame	velocity, fps:	2900	2623	2361	2115	1885
	energy, ft-lb:	3734	3054	2476	1987	1577
	arc, inches:		+1.8	0	-8.0	-23.9

.338-06

CARTRIDGE BULLET	RANGE, YARDS:	0	100	200	300	400
A-Square 200 Nos. Bal. Tip	velocity, fps:	2750	2553	2364	2184	2011
	energy, ft-lb:	3358	2894	2482	2118	1796
	arc, inches:		+1.9	0	-8.2	-23.6
A-Square 250 SP boat-tail	velocity, fps:	2500	2374	2252	2134	2019
	energy, ft-lb:	3496	3129	2816	2528	2263
	arc, inches:		+2.4	0	-9.3	-26.0
A-Square 250 Dead Tough	velocity, fps:	2500	2222	1963	1724	1507
	energy, ft-lb:	3496	2742	2139	1649	1261
	arc, inches:		+2.8	0	-11.9	-35.5
Wby. 210 Nosler Part.	velocity, fps:	2750	2526	2312	2109	1916
	energy, ft-lb:	3527	2975	2403	2074	1712
	arc, inches:		+4.8	+5.7	0	-13.5

.338 WINCHESTER MAG.

CARTRIDGE BULLET	RANGE, YARDS:	0	100	200	300	400
A-Square 250 SP boat-tail	velocity, fps:	2700	2568	2439	2314	2193
	energy, ft-lb:	4046	3659	3302	2972	2669
	arc, inches:		+4.4	+5.2	0	-11.7
A-Square 250 Triad	velocity, fps:	2700	2407	2133	1877	1653
	energy, ft-lb:	4046	3216	2526	1956	1516
	arc, inches:		+2.3	0	-9.8	-29.8
Federal 210 Nosler Partition	velocity, fps:	2830	2600	2390	2180	1980
	energy, ft-lb:	3735	3160	2655	2215	1835
	arc, inches:		+1.8	0	-8.0	-23.3
Federal 225 Sierra Pro-Hunt.	velocity, fps:	2780	2570	2360	2170	1980
	energy, ft-lb:	3860	3290	2780	2340	1960
	arc, inches:		+1.9	0	-8.2	-23.7
Federal 225 Trophy Bonded	velocity, fps:	2800	2560	2330	2110	1900
	energy, ft-lb:	3915	3265	2700	2220	1800
	arc, inches:		+1.9	0	-8.4	-24.5
Federal 225 Tr. Bonded HE	velocity, fps:	2940	2690	2450	2230	2010
	energy, ft-lb:	4320	3610	3000	2475	2025
	arc, inches:		+1.7	0	-7.5	-22.0
Federal 225 Barnes XLC	velocity, fps:	2800	2610	2430	2260	2090
	energy, ft-lb:	3915	3405	2950	2545	2190
	arc, inches:		+1.8	0	-7.7	-22.2
Federal 250 Nosler Partition	velocity, fps:	2660	2470	2300	2120	1960
	energy, ft-lb:	3925	3395	2925	2505	2130
	arc, inches:		+2.1	0	-8.8	-25.1
Federal 250 Nosler Part HE	velocity, fps:	2800	2610	2420	2250	2080
	energy, ft-lb:	4350	3775	3260	2805	2395
	arc, inches:		+1.8	0	-7.8	-22.5
Hornady 225 Soft Point HM	velocity, fps:	2920	2678	2449	2232	2027
	energy, ft-lb:	4259	3583	2996	2489	2053
	arc, inches:		+1.8	0	-7.6	-22.0
Norma 225 TXP Swift A-Fr.	velocity, fps:	2740	2507	2286	2075	
	energy, ft-lb:	3752	3141	2611	2153	
	arc, inches:		+2.0	0	-8.7	
Norma 230 Oryx	velocity, fps:	2756	2514	2284	2066	
	energy, ft-lb:	3880	3228	2665	2181	
	arc, inches:		+2.0	0	-8.7	
Norma 250 Nosler Partition	velocity, fps:	2657	2470	2290	2118	
	energy, ft-lb:	3920	3387	2912	2490	
	arc, inches:		+2.1	0	-8.7	
PMC 225 Barnes X	velocity, fps:	2780	2619	2464	2313	2168
	energy, ft-lb:	3860	3426	3032	2673	2348
	arc, inches:		+1.8	0	-7.6	-21.6
Rem. 200 Nosler Bal. Tip	velocity, fps:	2950	2724	2509	2303	2108
	energy, ft-lb:	3866	3295	2795	2357	1973
	arc, inches:		+1.6	0	-7.1	-20.8
Rem. 210 Nosler Partition	velocity, fps:	2830	2602	2385	2179	1983
	energy, ft-lb:	3734	3157	2653	2214	1834
	arc, inches:		+1.8	0	-7.9	-23.2
Rem. 225 PSP Core-Lokt	velocity, fps:	2780	2572	2374	2184	2003
	energy, ft-lb:	3860	3305	2815	2383	2004
	arc, inches:		+1.9	0	-8.1	-23.4
Rem. 225 PSP C-L Ultra	velocity, fps:	2780	2582	2392	2210	2036
	energy, ft-lb:	3860	3329	2858	2440	2071
	arc, inches:		+1.9	0	-7.9	-23.0
Rem. 225 Swift A-Frame	velocity, fps:	2785	2517	2266	2029	1808
	energy, ft-lb:	3871	3165	2565	2057	1633
	arc, inches:		+2.0	0	-8.8	-25.2
Rem. 250 PSP Core-Lokt	velocity, fps:	2660	2456	2261	2075	1898
	energy, ft-lb:	3927	3348	2837	2389	1999
	arc, inches:		+2.1	0	-8.9	-26.0
Speer 250 Grand Slam	velocity, fps:	2645	2442	2247	2062	
	energy, ft-lb:	3883	3309	2803	2360	
	arc, inches:		+2.2	0	-9.1	-26.2
Win. 200 Power-Point	velocity, fps:	2960	2658	2375	2110	1862
	energy, ft-lb:	3890	3137	2505	1977	1539
	arc, inches:		+2.0	0	-8.2	-24.3

Centerfire Rifle Ballistics

.338 WINCHESTER MAG. TO .357 MAGNUM

BALLISTICS

CARTRIDGE BULLET	RANGE, YARDS:	0	100	200	300	400
Win. 200 Ballistic Silvertip	velocity, fps:	2950	2724	2509	2303	2108
	energy, ft-lb:	3864	3294	2794	2355	1972
	arc, inches:		+1.6	0	-7.1	-20.8
Win. 225 AccuBond	velocity, fps:	2800	2634	2474	2319	2170
	energy, ft-lb:	3918	3467	3058	2688	2353
	arc, inches:		+1.8	0	-7.4	-21.3
Win. 230 Fail Safe	velocity, fps:	2780	2573	2375	2186	2005
	energy, ft-lb:	3948	3382	2881	2441	2054
	arc, inches:		+1.9	0	-8.1	-23.4
Win. 250 Partition Gold	velocity, fps:	2650	2467	2291	2122	1960
	energy, ft-lb:	3899	3378	2914	2520	2134
	arc, inches:		+2.1	0	-8.7	-25.2

.340 Weatherby Mag.

CARTRIDGE BULLET	RANGE, YARDS:	0	100	200	300	400
A-Square 250 SP boat-tail	velocity, fps:	2820	2684	2552	2424	2299
	energy, ft-lb:	4414	3999	3615	3261	2935
	arc, inches:		+4.0	+4.6	0	-10.6
A-Square 250 Triad	velocity, fps:	2820	2520	2238	1976	1741
	energy, ft-lb:	4414	3524	2781	2166	1683
	arc, inches:		+2.0	0	-9.0	-26.8
Federal 225 Trophy Bonded	velocity, fps:	3100	2840	2600	2370	2150
	energy, ft-lb:	4800	4035	3375	2800	2310
	arc, inches:		+1.4	0	-6.5	-19.4
Wby. 200 Pointed Expanding	velocity, fps:	3221	2946	2688	2444	2213
	energy, ft-lb:	4607	3854	3208	2652	2174
	arc, inches:		+3.3	+4.0	0	-9.9
Wby. 200 Nosler Bal. Tip	velocity, fps:	3221	2980	2753	2536	2329
	energy, ft-lb:	4607	3944	3364	2856	2409
	arc, inches:		+3.1	+3.9	0	-9.2
Wby. 210 Nosler Partition	velocity, fps:	3211	2963	2728	2505	2293
	energy, ft-lb:	4807	4093	3470	2927	2452
	arc, inches:		+3.2	+3.9	0	-9.5
Wby. 225 Pointed Expanding	velocity, fps:	3066	2824	2595	2377	2170
	energy, ft-lb:	4696	3984	3364	2822	2352
	arc, inches:		+3.6	+4.4	0	-10.7
Wby. 225 Barnes X	velocity, fps:	3001	2804	2615	2434	2260
	energy, ft-lb:	4499	3927	3416	2959	2551
	arc, inches:		+3.6	+4.3	0	-10.3
Wby. 250 Pointed Expanding	velocity, fps:	2963	2745	2537	2338	2149
	energy, ft-lb:	4873	4182	3572	3035	2563
	arc, inches:		+3.9	+4.6	0	-11.1
Wby. 250 Nosler Partition	velocity, fps:	2941	2743	2553	2371	2197
	energy, ft-lb:	4801	4176	3618	3120	2678
	arc, inches:		+3.9	+4.6	0	-10.9

.330 Dakota

CARTRIDGE BULLET	RANGE, YARDS:	0	100	200	300	400
Dakota 200 Barnes X	velocity, fps:	3200	2971	2754	2548	2350
	energy, ft-lb:	4547	3920	3369	2882	2452
	arc, inches:		+2.1	+1.8	-3.1	-13.4
Dakota 250 Barnes X	velocity, fps:	2900	2719	2545	2378	2217
	energy, ft-lb:	4668	4103	3595	3138	2727
	arc, inches:		+2.3	+1.3	-5.0	-17.5

.338 Remington Ultra Mag

CARTRIDGE BULLET	RANGE, YARDS:	0	100	200	300	400
Federal 210 Nosler Partition	velocity, fps:	3025	2800	2585	2385	2190
	energy, ft-lb:	4270	3655	3120	2645	2230
	arc, inches:		+1.5	0	-6.7	-19.5
Federal 250 Trophy Bonded	velocity, fps:	2860	2630	2420	2210	2020
	energy, ft-lb:	4540	3850	3245	2715	2260
	arc, inches:		+0.8	0	-7.7	-22.6
Rem. 250 Swift A-Frame	velocity, fps:	2860	2645	2440	2244	2057
	energy, ft-lb:	4540	3882	3303	2794	2347
	arc, inches:		+1.7	0	-7.6	-22.1
Rem. 250 PSP Core-Lokt	velocity, fps:	2860	2647	2443	2249	2064
	energy, ft-lb:	4540	3888	3314	2807	2363
	arc, inches:		+1.7	0	-7.6	-22.0

.338 Lapua

CARTRIDGE BULLET	RANGE, YARDS:	0	100	200	300	400
Black Hills 250 Sierra MKing	velocity, fps:	2950				
	energy, ft-lb:	4831				
	arc, inches:					
Black Hills 300 Sierra MKing	velocity, fps:	2800				
	energy, ft-lb:	5223				
	arc, inches:					

.338-378 Weatherby Mag.

CARTRIDGE BULLET	RANGE, YARDS:	0	100	200	300	400
Wby. 200 Nosler Bal. Tip	velocity, fps:	3350	3102	2868	2646	2434
	energy, ft-lb:	4983	4273	3652	3109	2631
	arc, inches:	0	+2.8	+3.5	0	-8.4
Wby. 225 Barnes X	velocity, fps:	3180	2974	2778	2591	2410
	energy, ft-lb:	5052	4420	3856	3353	2902
	arc, inches:	0	+3.1	+3.8	0	-8.9
Wby. 250 Nosler Partition	velocity, fps:	3060	2856	2662	2475	2297
	energy, ft-lb:	5197	4528	3933	3401	2927
	arc, inches:	0	+3.5	+4.2	0	-9.8

8.59 (.338) Titan

CARTRIDGE BULLET	RANGE, YARDS:	0	100	200	300	400
Lazzeroni 200 Nos. Bal. Tip	velocity, fps:	3430	3211	3002	2803	2613
	energy, ft-lb:	5226	4579	4004	3491	3033
	arc, inches:		+2.5	+3.2	0	-7.6
Lazzeroni 225 Nos. Partition	velocity, fps:	3235	3031	2836	2650	2471
	energy, ft-lb:	5229	4591	4021	3510	3052
	arc, inches:		+3.0	+3.6	0	-8.6
Lazzeroni 250 Swift A-Fr.	velocity, fps:	3100	2908	2725	2549	2379
	energy, ft-lb:	5336	4697	4123	3607	3143
	arc, inches:		+3.3	+4.0	0	-9.3

.338 A-Square

CARTRIDGE BULLET	RANGE, YARDS:	0	100	200	300	400
A-Square 200 Nos. Bal. Tip	velocity, fps:	3500	3266	3045	2835	2634
	energy, ft-lb:	5440	4737	4117	3568	3081
	arc, inches:		+2.4	+3.1	0	-7.5
A-Square 250 SP boat-tail	velocity, fps:	3120	2974	2834	2697	2565
	energy, ft-lb:	5403	4911	4457	4038	3652
	arc, inches:		+3.1	+3.7	0	-8.5
A-Square 250 Triad	velocity, fps:	3120	2799	2500	2220	1958
	energy, ft-lb:	5403	4348	3469	2736	2128
	arc, inches:		+1.5	0	-7.1	-20.4

.338 Excaliber

CARTRIDGE BULLET	RANGE, YARDS:	0	100	200	300	400
A-Square 200 Nos. Bal. Tip	velocity, fps:	3600	3361	3134	2920	2715
	energy, ft-lb:	5755	5015	4363	3785	3274
	arc, inches:		+2.2	+2.9	0	-6.7
A-Square 250 SP boat-tail	velocity, fps:	3250	3101	2958	2684	2553
	energy, ft-lb:	5863	5339	4855	4410	3998
	arc, inches:		+2.7	+3.4	0	-7.8
A-Square 250 Triad	velocity, fps:	3250	2922	2618	2333	2066
	energy, ft-lb:	5863	4740	3804	3021	2370
	arc, inches:		+1.3	0	-6.4	-19.2

.348 Winchester

CARTRIDGE BULLET	RANGE, YARDS:	0	100	200	300	400
Win. 200 Silvertip	velocity, fps:	2520	2215	1931	1672	1443
	energy, ft-lb:	2820	2178	1656	1241	925
	arc, inches:		0	-6.2	-21.9	

.357 Mag.

CARTRIDGE BULLET	RANGE, YARDS:	0	100	200	300	400
Federal 180 Hi-Shok HP	velocity, fps:	1550	1160	980	860	770
Hollow Point	energy, ft-lb:	960	535	385	295	235
	arc, inches:		0	-22.8	-77.9	-173.8

Centerfire Rifle Ballistics

.357 MAGNUM TO .375 H&H MAGNUM

CARTRIDGE BULLET	RANGE, YARDS:	0	100	200	300	400
Win. 158 Jacketed SP	velocity, fps:	1830	1427	1138	980	883
	energy, ft-lb:	1175	715	454	337	274
	arc, inches:		0	-16.2	-57.0	-128.3

.35 Remington

CARTRIDGE BULLET	RANGE, YARDS:	0	100	200	300	400
Federal 200 Hi-Shok	velocity, fps:	2080	1700	1380	1140	1000
	energy, ft-lb:	1920	1280	840	575	445
	arc, inches:		0	-10.7	-39.3	
Rem. 150 PSP Core-Lokt	velocity, fps:	2300	1874	1506	1218	1039
	energy, ft-lb:	1762	1169	755	494	359
	arc, inches:		0	-8.6	-32.6	
Rem. 200 SP Core-Lokt	velocity, fps:	2080	1698	1376	1140	1001
	energy, ft-lb:	1921	1280	841	577	445
	arc, inches:		0	-10.7	-40.1	
Win. 200 Power-Point	velocity, fps:	2020	1646	1335	1114	985
	energy, ft-lb:	1812	1203	791	551	431
	arc, inches:		0	-12.1	-43.9	

.356 Winchester

CARTRIDGE BULLET	RANGE, YARDS:	0	100	200	300	400
Win. 200 Power-Point	velocity, fps:	2460	2114	1797	1517	1284
	energy, ft-lb:	2688	1985	1434	1022	732
	arc, inches:		+1.6	-3.8	-20.1	-51.2

.358 Winchester

CARTRIDGE BULLET	RANGE, YARDS:	0	100	200	300	400
Win. 200 Silvertip	velocity, fps:	2490	2171	1876	1610	1379
	energy, ft-lb:	2753	2093	1563	1151	844
	arc, inches:		+1.5	-3.6	-18.6	-47.2

.35 Whelen

CARTRIDGE BULLET	RANGE, YARDS:	0	100	200	300	400
Federal 225 Trophy Bonded	velocity, fps:	2600	2400	2200	2020	1840
	energy, ft-lb:	3375	2865	2520	2030	1690
	arc, inches:		+2.3	0	-9.4	-27.3
Rem. 200 Pointed Soft Point	velocity, fps:	2675	2378	2100	1842	1606
	energy, ft-lb:	3177	2510	1958	1506	1145
	arc, inches:		+2.3	0	-10.3	-30.8
Rem. 250 Pointed Soft Point	velocity, fps:	2400	2197	2005	1823	1652
	energy, ft-lb:	3197	2680	2230	1844	1515
	arc, inches:		+1.3	-3.2	-16.6	-40.0

.358 Norma Mag.

CARTRIDGE BULLET	RANGE, YARDS:	0	100	200	300	400
A-Square 275 Triad	velocity, fps:	2700	2394	2108	1842	1653
	energy, ft-lb:	4451	3498	2713	2072	1668
	arc, inches:		+2.3	0	-10.1	-29.8
Norma 250 TXP Swift A-Fr.	velocity, fps:	2723	2467	2225	1996	
	energy, ft-lb:	4117	3379	2748	2213	
	arc, inches:		+2.1	0	-9.1	
Norma 250 Woodleigh	velocity, fps:	2799	2442	2112	1810	
	energy, ft-lb:	4350	3312	2478	1819	
	arc, inches:		+2.2	0	-10.0	
Norma 250 Oryx	velocity, fps:	2756	2493	2245	2011	
	energy, ft-lb:	4217	3451	2798	2245	
	arc, inches:		+2.1	0	-9.0	

.358 STA

CARTRIDGE BULLET	RANGE, YARDS:	0	100	200	300	400
A-Square 275 Triad	velocity, fps:	2850	2562	2292	2039	1764
	energy, ft-lb:	4959	4009	3208	2539	1899
	arc, inches:		+1.9	0	-8.6	-26.1

9.3x57

CARTRIDGE BULLET	RANGE, YARDS:	0	100	200	300	400
Norma 232 Vulkan	velocity, fps:	2329	2031	1757	1512	
	energy, ft-lb:	2795	2126	1591	1178	
	arc, inches:		+3.5	0	-14.9	
Norma 232 Oryx	velocity, fps:	2362	2058	1778	1528	
	energy, ft-lb:	2875	2182	1630	1203	
	arc, inches:		+3.4	0	-14.5	
Norma 285 Oryx	velocity, fps:	2067	1859	1666	1490	
	energy, ft-lb:	2704	2188	1756	1404	
	arc, inches:		+4.3	0	-16.8	
Norma 286 Alaska	velocity, fps:	2067	1857	1662	1484	
	energy, ft-lb:	2714	2190	1754	1399	
	arc, inches:		+4.3	0	-17.0	

9.3x62

CARTRIDGE BULLET	RANGE, YARDS:	0	100	200	300	400
A-Square 286 Triad	velocity, fps:	2360	2089	1844	1623	1369
	energy, ft-lb:	3538	2771	2157	1670	1189
	arc, inches:		+3.0	0	-13.1	-42.2
Norma 232 Vulkan	velocity, fps:	2625	2327	2049	1792	
	energy, ft-lb:	3551	2791	2164	1655	
	arc, inches:		+2.5	0	-10.8	
Norma 232 Oryx	velocity, fps:	2625	2294	1988	1708	
	energy, ft-lb:	3535	2700	2028	1497	
	arc, inches:		+2.5	0	-11.4	
Norma 250 A-Frame	velocity, fps:	2625	2322	2039	1778	
	energy, ft-lb:	3826	2993	2309	1755	
	arc, inches:		+2.5	0	-10.9	
Norma 286 Plastic Point	velocity, fps:	2362	2141	1931	1736	
	energy, ft-lb:	3544	2911	2370	1914	
	arc, inches:		+3.1	0	-12.4	
Norma 286 Alaska	velocity, fps:	2362	2135	1920	1720	
	energy, ft-lb:	3544	2894	2342	1879	
	arc, inches:		+3.1	0	-12.5	

9.3x64

CARTRIDGE BULLET	RANGE, YARDS:	0	100	200	300	400
A-Square 286 Triad	velocity, fps:	2700	2391	2103	1835	1602
	energy, ft-lb:	4629	3630	2808	2139	1631
	arc, inches:		+2.3	0	-10.1	-30.8

9.3x74 R

CARTRIDGE BULLET	RANGE, YARDS:	0	100	200	300	400
A-Square 286 Triad	velocity, fps:	2360	2089	1844	1623	
	energy, ft-lb:	3538	2771	2157	1670	
	arc, inches:		+3.6	0	-14.0	
Norma 232 Vulkan	velocity, fps:	2625	2327	2049	1792	
	energy, ft-lb:	3551	2791	2164	1655	
	arc, inches:		+2.5	0	-10.8	
Norma 232 Oryx	velocity, fps:	2526	2191	1883	1605	
	energy, ft-lb:	3274	2463	1819	1322	
	arc, inches:		+2.9	0	-12.8	
Norma 285 Oryx	velocity, fps:	2362	2114	1881	1667	
	energy, ft-lb:	3532	2829	2241	1758	
	arc, inches:		+3.1	0	-13.0	
Norma 286 Alaska	velocity, fps:	2362	2135	1920	1720	
	energy, ft-lb:	3544	2894	2342	1879	
	arc, inches:		+3.1	0	-12.5	
Norma 286 Plastic Point	velocity, fps:	2362	2135	1920	1720	
	energy, ft-lb:	3544	2894	2342	1879	
	arc, inches:		+3.1	0	-12.5	

.375 Winchester

CARTRIDGE BULLET	RANGE, YARDS:	0	100	200	300	400
Win. 200 Power-Point	velocity, fps:	2200	1841	1526	1268	1089
	energy, ft-lb:	2150	1506	1034	714	
	arc, inches:		0	-9.5	-33.8	

.375 H&H Mag.

CARTRIDGE BULLET	RANGE, YARDS:	0	100	200	300	400
A-Square 300 SP boat-tail	velocity, fps:	2550	2415	2284	2157	2034
	energy, ft-lb:	4331	3884	3474	3098	2755
	arc, inches:		+5.2	+6.0	0	-13.3
A-Square 300 Triad	velocity, fps:	2550	2251	1973	1717	1496
	energy, ft-lb:	4331	3375	2592	1964	1491
	arc, inches:		+2.7	0	-11.7	-35.1

.375 H&H MAGNUM TO .378 WEATHERBY MAGNUM

CARTRIDGE BULLET	RANGE, YARDS:	0	100	200	300	400
Federal 250 Trophy Bonded	velocity, fps:	2670	2360	2080	1820	1580
	energy, ft-lb:	3955	3100	2400	1830	1380
	arc, inches:		+2.4	0	-10.4	-31.7
Federal 270 Hi-Shok	velocity, fps:	2690	2420	2170	1920	1700
	energy, ft-lb:	4340	3510	2810	2220	1740
	arc, inches:		+2.4	0	-10.9	-33.3
Federal 300 Hi-Shok	velocity, fps:	2530	2270	2020	1790	1580
	energy, ft-lb:	4265	3425	2720	2135	1665
	arc, inches:		+2.6	0	-11.2	-33.3
Federal 300 Nosler Partition	velocity, fps:	2530	2320	2120	1930	1750
	energy, ft-lb:	4265	3585	2995	2475	2040
	arc, inches:		+2.5	0	-10.3	-29.9
Federal 300 Trophy Bonded	velocity, fps:	2530	2280	2040	1810	1610
	energy, ft-lb:	4265	3450	2765	2190	1725
	arc, inches:		+2.6	0	-10.9	-32.8
Federal 300 Tr. Bonded HE	velocity, fps:	2700	2440	2190	1960	1740
	energy, ft-lb:	4855	3960	3195	2550	2020
	arc, inches:		+2.2	0	-9.4	-28.0
Federal 300 Trophy Bonded	velocity, fps:	2530	2160	1820	1520	1280
Sledgehammer Solid	energy, ft-lb:	4265	3105	2210	1550	1090
	arc, inches, s:		0	-6.0	-22.7	-54.6
Hornady 270 SP HM	velocity, fps:	2870	2620	2385	2162	1957
	energy, ft-lb:	4937	4116	3408	2802	2296
	arc, inches:		+2.2	0	-8.4	-23.9
Hornady 300 FMJ RN HM	velocity, fps:	2705	2376	2072	1804	1560
	energy, ft-lb:	4873	3760	2861	2167	1621
	arc, inches:		+2.7	0	-10.8	-32.1
Norma 300 Soft Point	velocity, fps:	2549	2211	1900	1619	
	energy, ft-lb:	4329	3258	2406	1747	
	arc, inches:		+2.8	0	-12.6	
Norma 300 TXP Swift A-Fr.	velocity, fps:	2559	2296	2049	1818	
	energy, ft-lb:	4363	3513	2798	2203	
	arc, inches:		+2.6	0	-10.9	
Norma 300 Oryx	velocity, fps:	2559	2292	2041	1807	
	energy, ft-lb:	4363	3500	2775	2176	
	arc, inches:		+2.6	0	-11.0	
Norma 300 Barnes Solid	velocity, fps:	2493	2061	1677	1356	
	energy, ft-lb:	4141	2829	1873	1234	
	arc, inches:		+3.4	0	-16.0	
PMC 270 PSP	velocity, fps:					
	energy, ft-lb:					
	arc, inches:					
PMC 270 Barnes X	velocity, fps:	2690	2528	2372	2221	2076
	energy, ft-lb:	4337	3831	3371	2957	2582
	arc, inches:		+2.0	0	-8.2	-23.4
PMC 300 Barnes X	velocity, fps:	2530	2389	2252	2120	1993
	energy, ft-lb:	4263	3801	3378	2994	2644
	arc, inches:		+2.3	0	-9.2	-26.1
Rem. 270 Soft Point	velocity, fps:	2690	2420	2166	1928	1707
	energy, ft-lb:	4337	3510	2812	2228	1747
	arc, inches:		+2.2	0	-9.7	-28.7
Rem. 300 Swift A-Frame	velocity, fps:	2530	2245	1979	1733	1512
	energy, ft-lb:	4262	3357	2608	2001	1523
	arc, inches:		+2.7	0	-11.7	-35.0
Speer 285 Grand Slam	velocity, fps:	2610	2365	2134	1916	
	energy, ft-lb:	4310	3540	2883	2323	
	arc, inches:		+2.4	0	-9.9	
Speer 300 African GS	velocity, fps:	2609	2277	1970	1690	
Tungsten Solid	energy, ft-lb:	4534	3453	2585	1903	
	arc, inches:		+2.6	0	-11.7	-35.6
Win. 270 Fail Safe	velocity, fps:	2670	2447	2234	2033	1842
	energy, ft-lb:	4275	3590	2994	2478	2035
	arc, inches:		+2.2	0	-9.1	-28.7

CARTRIDGE BULLET	RANGE, YARDS:	0	100	200	300	400
Win. 300 Fail Safe	velocity, fps:	2530	2336	2151	1974	1806
	energy, ft-lb:	4265	3636	3082	2596	2173
	arc, inches:		+2.4	0	-10.0	-26.9

.375 Dakota

CARTRIDGE BULLET	RANGE, YARDS:	0	100	200	300	400
Dakota 270 Barnes X	velocity, fps:	2800	2617	2441	2272	2109
	energy, ft-lb:	4699	4104	3571	3093	2666
	arc, inches:		+2.3	+1.0	-6.1	-19.9
Dakota 300 Barnes X	velocity, fps:	2600	2316	2051	1804	1579
	energy, ft-lb:	4502	3573	2800	2167	1661
	arc, inches:		+2.4	-0.1	-11.0	-32.7

.375 Weatherby Mag.

CARTRIDGE BULLET	RANGE, YARDS:	0	100	200	300	400
A-Square 300 SP boat-tail	velocity, fps:	2700	2560	2425	2293	2166
	energy, ft-lb:	4856	4366	3916	3503	3125
	arc, inches:		+4.5	+5.2	0	-11.9
A-Square 300 Triad	velocity, fps:	2700	2391	2103	1835	1602
	energy, ft-lb:	4856	3808	2946	2243	1710
	arc, inches:		+2.3	0	-10.1	-30.8
Wby. 300 Nosler Part.	velocity, fps:	2800	2572	2366	2140	1963
	energy, ft-lb:	5224	4408	3696	3076	2541
	arc, inches:		+1.9	0	-8.2	-23.9

.375 JRS

CARTRIDGE BULLET	RANGE, YARDS:	0	100	200	300	400
A-Square 300 SP boat-tail	velocity, fps:	2700	2560	2425	2293	2166
	energy, ft-lb:	4856	4366	3916	3503	3125
	arc, inches:		+4.5	+5.2	0	-11.9
A-Square 300 Triad	velocity, fps:	2700	2391	2103	1835	1602
	energy, ft-lb:	4856	3808	2946	2243	1710
	arc, inches:		+2.3	0	-10.1	-30.8

.375 Remington Ultra Mag

CARTRIDGE BULLET	RANGE, YARDS:	0	100	200	300	400
Rem. 270 Soft Point	velocity, fps:	2900	2558	2241	1947	1678
	energy, fps:	5041	3922	3010	2272	1689
	arc, inches:		+1.9	0	-9.2	-27.8
Rem. 300 Swift A-Frame	velocity, fps:	2760	2505	2263	2035	1822
	energy, fps:	5073	4178	3412	2759	2210
	arc, inches:		+2.0	0	-8.8	-26.1

.375 A-Square

CARTRIDGE BULLET	RANGE, YARDS:	0	100	200	300	400
A-Square 300 SP boat-tail	velocity, fps:	2920	2773	2631	2494	2360
	energy, ft-lb:	5679	5123	4611	4142	3710
	arc, inches:		+3.7	+4.4	0	-9.8
A-Square 300 Triad	velocity, fps:	2920	2596	2294	2012	1762
	energy, ft-lb:	5679	4488	3505	2698	2068
	arc, inches:		+1.8	0	-8.5	-25.5

.376 Steyr

CARTRIDGE BULLET	RANGE, YARDS:	0	100	200	300	400
Hornady 225 SP	velocity, fps:	2600	2331	2078	1842	1625
	energy, ft-lb:	3377	2714	2157	1694	1319
	arc, inches:		+2.5	0	-10.6	-31.4
Hornady 270 SP	velocity, fps:	2600	2372	2156	1951	1759
	energy, ft-lb:	4052	3373	2787	2283	1855
	arc, inches:		+2.3	0	-9.9	-28.9

.378 Weatherby Mag.

CARTRIDGE BULLET	RANGE, YARDS:	0	100	200	300	400
A-Square 300 SP boat-tail	velocity, fps:	2900	2754	2612	2475	2342
	energy, ft-lb:	5602	5051	4546	4081	3655
	arc, inches:		+3.8	+4.4	0	-10.0
A-Square 300 Triad	velocity, fps:	2900	2577	2276	1997	1747
	energy, ft-lb:	5602	4424	3452	2656	2034
	arc, inches:		+1.9	0	-8.7	-25.9
Wby. 270 Pointed Expanding	velocity, fps:	3180	2921	2677	2445	2225
	energy, ft-lb:	6062	5115	4295	3583	2968
	arc, inches:		+1.3	0	-6.1	-18.1

Centerfire Rifle Ballistics

.378 WEATHERBY MAGNUM TO 10.57 (.416) METEOR

BALLISTICS

CARTRIDGE BULLET	RANGE, YARDS:	0	100	200	300	400
Wby. 270 Barnes X	velocity, fps:	3150	2954	2767	2587	2415
	energy, ft-lb:	5948	5232	4589	4013	3495
	arc, inches:		+1.2	0	-5.8	-16.7
Wby. 300 RN Expanding	velocity, fps:	2925	2558	2220	1908	1627
	energy, ft-lb:	5699	4360	3283	2424	1764
	arc, inches:		+1.9	0	-9.0	-27.8
Wby. 300 FMJ	velocity, fps:	2925	2591	2280	1991	1725
	energy, ft-lb:	5699	4470	3461	2640	1983
	arc, inches:		+1.8	0	-8.6	-26.1

.38-40 Winchester

CARTRIDGE BULLET	RANGE, YARDS:	0	100	200	300	400
Win. 180 Soft Point	velocity, fps:	1160	999	901	827	
	energy, ft-lb:	538	399	324	273	
	arc, inches:		0	-23.4	-75.2	

.38-55 Winchester

CARTRIDGE BULLET	RANGE, YARDS:	0	100	200	300	400
Black Hills 255 FN Lead	velocity, fps:	1250				
	energy, ft-lb:	925				
	arc, inches:					
Win. 255 Soft Point	velocity, fps:	1320	1190	1091	1018	
	energy, ft-lb:	987	802	674	587	
	arc, inches:		0	-33.9	-110.6	

.41 Mag.

CARTRIDGE BULLET	RANGE, YARDS:	0	100	200	300	400
Win. 240 Platinum Tip	velocity, fps:	1830	1488	1220	1048	
	energy, ft-lb:	1784	1180	792	585	
	arc inches:		0	-15.0	-53.4	

.450/.400 (3")

CARTRIDGE BULLET	RANGE, YARDS:	0	100	200	300	400
A-Square 400 Triad	velocity, fps:	2150	1910	1690	1490	
	energy, ft-lb:	4105	3241	2537	1972	
	arc, inches:		+4.4	0	-16.5	

.450/.400 (3 1/4")

CARTRIDGE BULLET	RANGE, YARDS:	0	100	200	300	400
A-Square 400 Triad	velocity, fps:	2150	1910	1690	1490	
	energy, ft-lb:	4105	3241	2537	1972	
	arc, inches:		+4.4	0	-16.5	

.404 Jeffery

CARTRIDGE BULLET	RANGE, YARDS:	0	100	200	300	400
A-Square 400 Triad	velocity, fps:	2150	1901	1674	1468	1299
	energy, ft-lb:	4105	3211	2489	1915	1499
	arc, inches:		+4.1	0	-16.4	-49.1

.405 Winchester

CARTRIDGE BULLET	RANGE, YARDS:	0	100	200	300	400
Hornady 300 Flatpoint	velocity, fps:	2200	1851	1545	1296	
	energy, ft-lb:	3224	2282	1589	1119	
	arc, inches:		0	-8.7	-31.9	
Hornady 300 SP Interlock	velocity, fps:	2200	1890	1610	1370	
	energy, ft-lb:	3224	2379	1727	1250	
	arc, inches:		0	-8.3	-30.2	

.416 Taylor

CARTRIDGE BULLET	RANGE, YARDS:	0	100	200	300	400
A-Square 400 Triad	velocity, fps:	2350	2093	1853	1634	1443
	energy, ft-lb:	4905	3892	3049	2371	1849
	arc, inches:		+3.2	0	-13.6	-39.8

.416 Hoffman

CARTRIDGE BULLET	RANGE, YARDS:	0	100	200	300	400
A-Square 400 Triad	velocity, fps:	2380	2122	1879	1658	1464
	energy, ft-lb:	5031	3998	3136	2440	1903
	arc, inches:		+3.1	0	-13.1	-38.7

.416 Remington Mag.

CARTRIDGE BULLET	RANGE, YARDS:	0	100	200	300	400
A-Square 400 Triad	velocity, fps:	2380	2122	1879	1658	1464
	energy, ft-lb:	5031	3998	3136	2440	1903
	arc, inches:		+3.1	0	-13.2	-38.7

CARTRIDGE BULLET	RANGE, YARDS:	0	100	200	300	400
Federal 400 Trophy Bonded Sledgehammer Solid	velocity, fps:	2400	2150	1920	1700	1500
	energy, ft-lb:	5115	4110	3260	2565	2005
	arc, inches:		0	-6.0	-21.6	-49.2
Federal 400 Trophy Bonded	velocity, fps:	2400	2180	1970	1770	1590
	energy, ft-lb:	5115	4215	3440	2785	2245
	arc, inches:		0	-5.8	-20.6	-46.9
Rem. 400 Swift A-Frame	velocity, fps:	2400	2175	1962	1763	1579
	energy, ft-lb:	5115	4201	3419	2760	2214
	arc, inches:		0	-5.9	-20.8	

.416 Rigby

CARTRIDGE BULLET	RANGE, YARDS:	0	100	200	300	400
A-Square 400 Triad	velocity, fps:	2400	2140	1897	1673	1478
	energy, ft-lb:	5115	4069	3194	2487	1940
	arc, inches:		+3.0	0	-12.9	-38.0
Federal 400 Trophy Bonded	velocity, fps:	2370	2150	1940	1750	1570
	energy, ft-lb:	4990	4110	3350	2715	2190
	arc, inches:		0	-6.0	-21.3	-48.1
Federal 400 Trophy Bonded Sledgehammer Solid	velocity, fps:	2370	2120	1890	1660	1460
	energy, ft-lb:	4990	3975	3130	2440	1895
	arc, inches:		0	-6.3	-22.5	-51.5
Federal 410 Woodleigh Weldcore	velocity, fps:	2370	2110	1870	1640	1440
	energy, ft-lb:	5115	4050	3165	2455	1895
	arc, inches:		0	-7.4	-24.8	-55.0
Federal 410 Solid	velocity, fps:	2370	2110	2870	1640	1440
	energy, ft-lb:	5115	4050	3165	2455	1895
	arc, inches:		0	-7.4	-24.8	-55.0
Norma 400 TXP Swift A-Fr.	velocity, fps:	2350	2127	1917	1721	
	energy, ft-lb:	4906	4021	3266	2632	
	arc, inches:		+3.1	0	-12.5	
Norma 400 Barnes Solid	velocity, fps:	2297	1930	1604	1330	
	energy, ft-lb:	4687	3310	2284	1571	
	arc, inches:		+3.9	0	-17.7	

.416 Rimmed

CARTRIDGE BULLET	RANGE, YARDS:	0	100	200	300	400
A-Square 400 Triad	velocity, fps:	2400	2140	1897	1673	
	energy, ft-lb:	5115	4069	3194	2487	
	arc, inches:		+3.3	0	-13.2	

.416 Dakota

CARTRIDGE BULLET	RANGE, YARDS:	0	100	200	300	400
Dakota 400 Barnes X	velocity, fps:	2450	2294	2143	1998	1859
	energy, ft-lb:	5330	4671	4077	3544	3068
	arc, inches:		+2.5	-0.2	-10.5	-29.4

.416 Weatherby

CARTRIDGE BULLET	RANGE, YARDS:	0	100	200	300	400
A-Square 400 Triad	velocity, fps:	2600	2328	2073	1834	1624
	energy, ft-lb:	6004	4813	3816	2986	2343
	arc, inches:		+2.5	0	-10.5	-31.6
Wby. 350 Barnes X	velocity, fps:	2850	2673	2503	2340	2182
	energy, ft-lb:	6312	5553	4870	4253	3700
	arc, inches:		+1.7	0	-7.2	-20.9
Wby. 400 Swift A-Fr.	velocity, fps:	2650	2426	2213	2011	1820
	energy, ft-lb:	6237	5227	4350	3592	2941
	arc, inches:		+2.2	0	-9.3	-27.1
Wby. 400 RN Expanding	velocity, fps:	2700	2417	2152	1903	1676
	energy, ft-lb:	6474	5189	4113	3216	2493
	arc, inches:		+2.3	0	-9.7	-29.3
Wby. 400 Monolithic Solid	velocity, fps:	2700	2411	2140	1887	1656
	energy, ft-lb:	6474	5162	4068	3161	2435
	arc, inches:		+2.3	0	-9.8	-29.7

10.57 (.416) Meteor

CARTRIDGE BULLET	RANGE, YARDS:	0	100	200	300	400
Lazzeroni 400 Swift A-Fr.	velocity, fps:	2730	2532	2342	2161	1987
	energy, ft-lb:	6621	5695	4874	4147	3508
	arc, inches:		+1.9	0	-8.3	-24.0

.425 Express

CARTRIDGE BULLET	RANGE, YARDS:	0	100	200	300	400
A-Square 400 Triad	velocity, fps:	2400	2136	1888	1662	1465
	energy, ft-lb:	5115	4052	3167	2454	1906
	arc, inches:		+3.0	0	-13.1	-38.3

.44-40 Winchester

CARTRIDGE BULLET	RANGE, YARDS:	0	100	200	300	400
Rem. 200 Soft Point	velocity, fps:	1190	1006	900	822	756
	energy, ft-lb:	629	449	360	300	254
	arc, inches:		0	-33.1	-108.7	-235.2
Win. 200 Soft Point	velocity, fps:	1190	1006	900	822	756
	energy, ft-lb:	629	449	360	300	254
	arc, inches:		0	-33.3	-109.5	-237.4

.44 Remington Mag.

CARTRIDGE BULLET	RANGE, YARDS:	0	100	200	300	400
Federal 240 Hi-Shok HP	velocity, fps:	1760	1380	1090	950	860
	energy, ft-lb:	1650	1015	640	485	395
	arc, inches:		0	-17.4	-60.7	-136.0
Rem. 210 Semi-Jacketed HP	velocity, fps:	1920	1477	1155	982	880
	energy, ft-lb:	1719	1017	622	450	361
	arc, inches:		0	-14.7	-55.5	-131.3
Rem. 240 Soft Point	velocity, fps:	1760	1380	1114	970	878
	energy, ft-lb:	1650	1015	661	501	411
	arc, inches:		0	-17.0	-61.4	-143.0
Rem. 240 Semi-Jacketed Hollow Point	velocity, fps:	1760	1380	1114	970	878
	energy, ft-lb:	1650	1015	661	501	411
	arc, inches:		0	-17.0	-61.4	-143.0
Rem. 275 JHP Core-Lokt	velocity, fps:	1580	1293	1093	976	896
	energy, ft-lb:	1524	1020	730	582	490
	arc, inches:		0	-19.4	-67.5	-210.8
Win. 210 Silvertip HP	velocity, fps:	1580	1198	993	879	795
	energy, ft-lb:	1164	670	460	361	295
	arc, inches:		0	-22.4	-76.1	-168.0
Win. 240 Hollow Soft Point	velocity, fps:	1760	1362	1094	953	861
	energy, ft-lb:	1650	988	638	484	395
	arc, inches:		0	-18.1	-65.1	-150.3
Win. 250 Platinum Tip	velocity, fps:	1830	1475	1201	1032	931
	energy, ft-lb:	1859	1208	801	591	481
	arc, inches:		0	-15.3	-54.7	-126.6

.444 Marlin

CARTRIDGE BULLET	RANGE, YARDS:	0	100	200	300	400
Rem. 240 Soft Point	velocity, fps:	2350	1815	1377	1087	941
	energy, ft-lb:	2942	1755	1010	630	472
	arc, inches:		+2.2	-5.4	-31.4	-86.7
Hornady 265 FP LM	velocity, fps:	2335	1913	1551	1266	
	energy, ft-lb:	3208	2153	1415	943	
	arc, inches:		+ 2.0	-4.9	-26.5	

.45-70 Government

CARTRIDGE BULLET	RANGE, YARDS:	0	100	200	300	400
Black Hills 405 FPL	velocity, fps:	1250				
	energy, ft-lb:					
	arc, inches:					
Federal 300 Sierra Pro-Hunt. HP FN	velocity, fps:	1880	1650	1430	1240	1110
	energy, ft-lb:	2355	1815	1355	1015	810
	arc, inches:		0	-11.5	-39.7	-89.1
PMC 350 FNSP	velocity, fps:					
	energy, ft-lb:					
	arc, inches:					
Rem. 300 Jacketed HP	velocity, fps:	1810	1497	1244	1073	969
	energy, ft-lb:	2182	1492	1031	767	625
	arc, inches:		0	-13.8	-50.1	-115.7
Rem. 405 Soft Point	velocity, fps:	1330	1168	1055	977	918
	energy, ft-lb:	1590	1227	1001	858	758
	arc, inches:		0	-24.0	-78.6	-169.4
Win. 300 Jacketed HP	velocity, fps:	1880	1650	1425	1235	1105
	energy, ft-lb:	2355	1815	1355	1015	810
	arc, inches:		0	-12.8	-44.3	-95.5
Win. 300 Partition Gold	velocity, fps:	1880	1558	1292	1103	988
	energy, ft-lb:	2355	1616	1112	811	651
	arc, inches:		0	-12.9	-46.0	-104.9

.450 Marlin

CARTRIDGE BULLET	RANGE, YARDS:	0	100	200	300	400
Hornady 350 FP	velocity, fps:	2100	1720	1397	1156	
	energy, ft-lb:	3427	2298	1516	1039	
	arc, inches:		0	-10.4	-38.9	

.450 Nitro Express (3 1/4")

CARTRIDGE BULLET	RANGE, YARDS:	0	100	200	300	400
A-Square 465 Triad	velocity, fps:	2190	1970	1765	1577	
	energy, ft-lb:	4952	4009	3216	2567	
	arc, inches:		+4.3	0	-15.4	

.450 #2

CARTRIDGE BULLET	RANGE, YARDS:	0	100	200	300	400
A-Square 465 Triad	velocity, fps:	2190	1970	1765	1577	
	energy, ft-lb:	4952	4009	3216	2567	
	arc, inches:		+4.3	0	-15.4	

.458 Winchester Mag.

CARTRIDGE BULLET	RANGE, YARDS:	0	100	200	300	400
A-Square 465 Triad	velocity, fps:	2220	1999	1791	1601	1433
	energy, ft-lb:	5088	4127	3312	2646	2121
	arc, inches:		+3.6	0	-14.7	-42.5
Federal 350 Soft Point	velocity, fps:	2470	1990	1570	1250	1060
	energy, ft-lb:	4740	3065	1915	1205	870
	arc, inches:		0	-7.5	-29.1	-71.1
Federal 400 Trophy Bonded	velocity, fps:	2380	2170	1960	1770	1590
	energy, ft-lb:	5030	4165	3415	2785	2255
	arc, inches:		0	-5.9	-20.9	-47.1
Federal 500 Solid	velocity, fps:	2090	1870	1670	1480	1320
	energy, ft-lb:	4850	3880	3085	2440	1945
	arc, inches:		0	-8.5	-29.5	-66.2
Federal 500 Trophy Bonded	velocity, fps:	2090	1870	1660	1480	1310
	energy, ft-lb:	4850	3870	3065	2420	1915
	arc, inches:		0	-8.5	-29.7	-66.8
Federal 500 Trophy Bonded Sledgehammer Solid	velocity, fps:	2090	1860	1650	1460	1300
	energy, ft-lb:	4850	3845	3025	2365	1865
	arc, inches:		0	-8.6	-30.0	-67.8
Federal 510 Soft Point	velocity, fps:	2090	1820	1570	1360	1190
	energy, ft-lb:	4945	3730	2790	2080	1605
	arc, inches:		0	-9.1	-32.3	-73.9
Hornady 500 FMJ-RN HM	velocity, fps:	2260	1984	1735	1512	
	energy, ft-lb:	5670	4368	3341	2538	
	arc, inches:		0	-7.4	-26.4	
Norma 500 TXP Swift A-Fr.	velocity, fps:	2116	1903	1705	1524	
	energy, ft-lb:	4972	4023	3228	2578	
	arc, inches:		+4.1	0	-16.1	
Norma 500 Barnes Solid	velocity, fps:	2067	1750	1472	1245	
	energy, ft-lb:	4745	3401	2405	1721	
	arc, inches:		+4.9	0	-21.2	
Rem. 450 Swift A-Frame PSP	velocity, fps:	2150	1901	1671	1465	1289
	energy, ft-lb:	4618	3609	2789	2144	1659
	arc, inches:		0	-8.2	-28.9	
Speer 500 African GS Tungsten Solid	velocity, fps:	2120	1845	1596	1379	
	energy, ft-lb:	4989	3780	2828	2111	
	arc, inches:		0	-8.8	-31.3	
Speer African Grand Slam	velocity, fps:	2120	1853	1609	1396	
	energy, ft-lb:	4989	3810	2875	2163	
	arc, inches:		0	-8.7	-30.8	
Win. 510 Soft Point	velocity, fps:	2040	1770	1527	1319	1157
	energy, ft-lb:	4712	3547	2640	1970	1516
	arc, inches:		0	-10.3	-35.6	

Centerfire Rifle Ballistics

.458 LOTT TO .700 NITRO EXPRESS

CARTRIDGE BULLET	RANGE, YARDS:	0	100	200	300	400
.458 Lott						
A-Square 465 Triad	velocity, fps:	2380	2150	1932	1730	1551
	energy, ft-lb:	5848	4773	3855	3091	2485
	arc, inches:		+3.0	0	-12.5	-36.4
Hornady 500 RNSP or solid	velocity, fps:	2300	2022	1776	1551	
	energy, ft-lb:	5872	4537	3502	2671	
	arc, inches:		+3.4	0	-14.3	
Hornady 500 InterBond	velocity, fps:	2300	2028	1777	1549	
	energy, ft-lb:	5872	4535	3453	2604	
	arc, inches:		0	-7.0	-25.1	
.450 Ackley						
A-Square 465 Triad	velocity, fps:	2400	2169	1950	1747	1567
	energy, ft-lb:	5947	4857	3927	3150	2534
	arc, inches:		+2.9	0	-12.2	-35.8
.460 Short A-Square						
A-Square 500 Triad	velocity, fps:	2420	2198	1987	1789	1613
	energy, ft-lb:	6501	5362	4385	3553	2890
	arc, inches:		+2.9	0	-11.6	-34.2
.450 Dakota						
Dakota 500 Barnes Solid	velocity, fps:	2450	2235	2030	1838	1658
	energy, ft-lb:	6663	5544	4576	3748	3051
	arc, inches:		+2.5	-0.6	-12.0	-33.8
.460 Weatherby Mag.						
A-Square 500 Triad	velocity, fps:	2580	2349	2131	1923	1737
	energy, ft-lb:	7389	6126	5040	4107	3351
	arc, inches:		+2.4	0	-10.0	-29.4
Wby. 450 Barnes X	velocity, fps:	2700	2518	2343	2175	2013
	energy, ft-lb:	7284	6333	5482	4725	4050
	arc, inches:		+2.0	0	-8.4	-24.1
Wby. 500 RN Expanding	velocity, fps:	2600	2301	2022	1764	1533
	energy, ft-lb:	7504	5877	4539	3456	2608
	arc, inches:		+2.6	0	-11.1	-33.5
Wby. 500 FMJ	velocity, fps:	2600	2309	2037	1784	1557
	energy, ft-lb:	7504	5917	4605	3534	2690
	arc, inches:		+2.5	0	-10.9	-33.0
.500/.465						
A-Square 480 Triad	velocity, fps:	2150	1928	1722	1533	
	energy, ft-lb:	4926	3960	3160	2505	
	arc, inches:		+4.3	0	-16.0	
.470 Nitro Express						
A-Square 500 Triad	velocity, fps:	2150	1912	1693	1494	
	energy, ft-lb:	5132	4058	3182	2478	
	arc, inches:		+4.4	0	-16.5	
Federal 500 Woodleigh Weldcore	velocity, fps:	2150	1890	1650	1440	1270
	energy, ft-lb:	5130	3965	3040	2310	1790
	arc, inches:		0	-9.3	-31.3	-69.7
Federal 500 Woodleigh Weldcore Solid	velocity, fps:	2150	1890	1650	1440	1270
	energy, ft-lb:	5130	3965	3040	2310	1790
	arc, inches:		0	-9.3	-31.3	-69.7
Federal 500 Trophy Bonded	velocity, fps:	2150	1940	1740	1560	1400
	energy, ft-lb:	5130	4170	3360	2695	2160
	arc, inches:		0	-7.8	-27.1	-60.8
Federal 500 Trophy Bonded Sledgehammer Solid	velocity, fps:	2150	1940	1740	1560	1400
	energy, ft-lb:	5130	4170	3360	2695	2160
	arc, inches:		0	-7.8	-27.1	-60.8
Norma 500 Woodleigh SP	velocity, fps:	2165	1975	1795	1627	
	energy, ft-lb:	5205	4330	3577	2940	
	arc, inches:		0	-7.4	-25.7	

CARTRIDGE BULLET	RANGE, YARDS:	0	100	200	300	400
Norma 500 Woodleigh FJ	velocity, fps:	2165	1974	1794	1626	
	energy, ft-lb:	5205	4328	3574	2936	
	arc, inches:		0	-7.5	-25.7	
.470 Capstick						
A-Square 500 Triad	velocity, fps:	2400	2172	1958	1761	1553
	energy, ft-lb:	6394	5236	4255	3445	2678
	arc, inches:		+2.9	0	-11.9	-36.1
.475 #2						
A-Square 480 Triad	velocity, fps:	2200	1964	1744	1544	
	energy, ft-lb:	5158	4109	3240	2539	
	arc, inches:		+4.1	0	-15.6	
.475 #2 Jeffery						
A-Square 500 Triad	velocity, fps:	2200	1966	1748	1550	
	energy, ft-lb:	5373	4291	3392	2666	
	arc, inches:		+4.1	0	-15.6	
.495 A-Square						
A-Square 570 Triad	velocity, fps:	2350	2117	1896	1693	1513
	energy, ft-lb:	6989	5671	4552	3629	2899
	arc, inches:		+3.1	0	-13.0	-37.8
.500 Nitro Express (3")						
A-Square 570 Triad	velocity, fps:	2150	1928	1722	1533	
	energy, ft-lb:	5850	4703	3752	2975	
	arc, inches:		+4.3	0	-16.1	
.500 A-Square						
A-Square 600 Triad	velocity, fps:	2470	2235	2013	1804	1620
	energy, ft-lb:	8127	6654	5397	4336	3495
	arc, inches:		+2.7	0	-11.3	-33.5
.505 Gibbs						
A-Square 525 Triad	velocity, fps:	2300	2063	1840	1637	
	energy, ft-lb:	6166	4962	3948	3122	
	arc, inches:		+3.6	0	-14.2	
.577 Nitro Express						
A-Square 750 Triad	velocity, fps:	2050	1811	1595	1401	
	energy, ft-lb:	6998	5463	4234	3267	
	arc, inches:		+4.9	0	-18.5	
.577 Tyrannosaur						
A-Square 750 Triad	velocity, fps:	2460	2197	1950	1723	1516
	energy, ft-lb:	10077	8039	6335	4941	3825
	arc, inches:		+2.8	0	-12.1	-36.0
.600 Nitro Express						
A-Square 900 Triad	velocity, fps:	1950	1680	1452	1336	
	energy, ft-lb:	7596	5634	4212	3564	
	arc, inches:		+5.6	0	-20.7	
.700 Nitro Express						
A-Square 1000 Monolithic Solid	velocity, fps:	1900	1669	1461	1288	
	energy, ft-lb:	8015	6188	4740	3685	
	arc, inches:		+5.8	0	-22.2	

Centerfire Handgun Ballistics

Centerfire Handgun Ballistics

Data shown here is taken from manufacturers' charts; your chronograph readings may vary. Barrel lengths for pistol data vary, and depend in part on which pistols are typically chambered in a given cartridge. Velocity variations due to barrel length depend on the baseline bullet speed and the load. Velocity for the .30 Carbine, normally a rifle cartridge, was determined in a pistol barrel.

Listings are current as of February the year Shooter's Bible appears (not the cover year). Listings are not intended as recommendations. For example, the data for the .25 Auto gives velocity and energy readings to 100 yards. Few handgunners would call the little .25 a 100-yard cartridge.

Abbreviations: Bullets are designated by loading company, weight (in grains) and type, with these abbreviations for shape and construction: BJHP=brass-jacketed hollowpoint; FN=Flat Nose; FMC=Full Metal Case; FMJ=Full Metal Jacket; HP=Hollowpoint; L=Lead; LF=Lead-Free; +P=a more powerful load than traditionally manufactured for that round; RN=Round Nose; SFHP=Starfire (PMC) Hollowpoint; SP=Softpoint; SWC=Semi Wadcutter; TMJ=Total Metal Jacket; WC=Wadcutter; CEPP, SXT and XTP are trademarked designations of Lapua, Winchester and Hornady, respectively.

.25 AUTO TO .32 S&W LONG

.25 Auto

CARTRIDGE BULLET	RANGE, YARDS:	0	25	50	75	100
Federal 50 FMJ	velocity, fps:	760	750	730	720	700
	energy, ft-lb:	65	60	60	55	55
Hornady 35 JHP/XTP	velocity, fps:	900		813		742
	energy, ft-lb:	63		51		43
Magtech 50 FMC	velocity, fps:	760		707		659
	energy, ft-lb:	64		56		48
PMC 50 FMJ	velocity, fps:	754	730	707	685	663
	energy, ft-lb:	62				
Rem. 50 Metal Case	velocity, fps:	760		707		659
	energy, ft-lb:	64		56		48
Speer 35 Gold Dot	velocity, fps:	900		816		747
	energy, ft-lb:	63		52		43
Speer 50 TMJ (and Blazer)	velocity, fps:	760		717		677
	energy, ft-lb:	64		57		51
Win. 45 Expanding Point	velocity, fps:	815		729		655
	energy, ft-lb	66		53		42
Win. 50 FMJ	velocity, fps:	760		707		
	energy, ft-lb	64		56		

.30 Luger

CARTRIDGE BULLET	RANGE, YARDS:	0	25	50	75	100
Win. 93 FMJ	velocity, fps:	1220		1110		1040
	energy, ft-lb	305		255		225

7.62x25 Tokarev

CARTRIDGE BULLET	RANGE, YARDS:	0	25	50	75	100
PMC 93 FMJ	velocity and energy figures not available					

.30 Carbine

CARTRIDGE BULLET	RANGE, YARDS:	0	25	50	75	100
Win. 110 Hollow SP	velocity, fps:	1790		1601		1430
	energy, ft-lb	783		626		500

.32 Auto

CARTRIDGE BULLET	RANGE, YARDS:	0	25	50	75	100
Federal 65 Hydra-Shok JHP	velocity, fps:	950	920	890	860	830
	energy, ft-lb:	130	120	115	105	100
Federal 71 FMJ	velocity, fps:	910	880	860	830	810
	energy, ft-lb:	130	120	115	110	105
Hornady 60 JHP/XTP	velocity, fps:	1000		917		849
	energy, ft-lb:	133		112		96
Hornady 71 FMJ-RN	velocity, fps:	900		845		797
	energy, ft-lb:	128		112		100
Magtech 71 FMC	velocity, fps:	905		855		810
	energy, ft-lb:	129		115		103
Magtech 71 JHP	velocity, fps:	905		855		810
	energy, ft-lb:	129		115		103
PMC 60 JHP	velocity, fps:	980	849	820	791	763
	energy, ft-lb:	117				
PMC 70 SFHP	velocity, fps:	velocity and energy figures not available				
PMC 71 FMJ	velocity, fps:	870	841	814	791	763
	energy, ft-lb:	119				
Rem. 71 Metal Case	velocity, fps:	905		855		810
	energy, ft-lb:	129		115		97
Speer 60 Gold Dot	velocity, fps:	960		868		796
	energy, ft-lb:	123		100		84
Speer 71 TMJ (and Blazer)	velocity, fps:	900		855		810
	energy, ft-lb:	129		115		97
Win. 60 Silvertip HP	velocity, fps:	970		895		835
	energy, ft-lb	125		107		93
Win. 71 FMJ	velocity, fps:	905		855		
	energy, ft-lb	129		115		

.32 S&W

CARTRIDGE BULLET	RANGE, YARDS:	0	25	50	75	100
Rem. 88 LRN	velocity, fps:	680		645		610
	energy, ft-lb:	90		81		73
Win. 85 LRN	velocity, fps:	680		645		610
	energy, ft-lb	90		81		73

.32 S&W Long

CARTRIDGE BULLET	RANGE, YARDS:	0	25	50	75	100
Federal 98 LWC	velocity, fps:	780	700	630	560	500
	energy, ft-lb:	130	105	85	70	55
Federal 98 LRN	velocity, fps:	710	690	670	650	640
	energy, ft-lb:	115	105	100	95	90
Lapua 83 LWC	velocity, fps:	240		189*		149*
	energy, ft-lb:	154		95*		59*
Lapua 98 LWC	velocity, fps:	240		202*		171*
	energy, ft-lb:	183		130*		93*
Magtech 98 LRN	velocity, fps:	705		670		635
	energy, ft-lb:	108		98		88
Magtech 98 LWC	velocity, fps:	682		579		491
	energy, ft-lb:	102		73		52
Norma 98 LWC	velocity, fps:	787	759	732		683
	energy, ft-lb:	136	126	118		102

Centerfire Handgun Ballistics

.32 S&W LONG TO 9MM LUGER

CARTRIDGE BULLET	RANGE, YARDS:	0	25	50	75	100
PMC 98 LRN	velocity, fps:	789	770	751	733	716
	energy, ft-lb:	135				
PMC 100 LWC	velocity, fps:	683	652	623	595	569
	energy, ft-lb:	102				
Rem. 98 LRN	velocity, fps:	705		670		635
	energy, ft-lb:	115		98		88
Win. 98 LRN	velocity, fps:	705		670		635
	energy, ft-lb:	115		98		88

.32 Short Colt

CARTRIDGE BULLET	RANGE, YARDS:	0	25	50	75	100
Win. 80 LRN	velocity, fps:	745		665		590
	energy, ft-lb	100		79		62

.32-20

CARTRIDGE BULLET	RANGE, YARDS:	0	25	50	75	100
Black Hills 115 FPL	velocity, fps:	800				
	energy, ft-lb:					

.32 H&R Mag

CARTRIDGE BULLET	RANGE, YARDS:	0	25	50	75	100
Black Hills 85 JHP	velocity, fps	1100				
	energy, ft-lb	228				
Black Hills 90 FPL	velocity, fps	750				
	energy, ft-lb					
Black Hills 115 FPL	velocity, fps	800				
	energy, ft-lb					
Federal 85 Hi-Shok JHP	velocity, fps:	1100	1050	1020	970	930
	energy, ft-lb:	230	210	195	175	165
Federal 95 LSWC	velocity, fps:	1030	1000	940	930	900
	energy, ft-lb:	225	210	195	185	170

9mm Makarov

CARTRIDGE BULLET	RANGE, YARDS:	0	25	50	75	100
Federal 90 Hi-Shok JHP	velocity, fps:	990	950	910	880	850
	energy, ft-lb:	195	180	165	155	145
Federal 90 FMJ	velocity, fps:	990	960	920	900	870
	energy, ft-lb:	205	190	180	170	160
Hornady 95 JHP/XTP	velocity, fps:	1000		930		874
	energy, ft-lb:	211		182		161
PMC 100 FMJ-TC	velocity, fps:	velocity and energy figures not available				
Speer 95 TMJ Blazer	velocity, fps:	1000		928		872
	energy, ft-lb:	211		182		161

9x21 IMI

CARTRIDGE BULLET	RANGE, YARDS:	0	25	50	75	100
PMC 123 FMJ	velocity, fps:	1150	1093	1046	1007	973
	energy, ft-lb:	364				

9mm Luger

CARTRIDGE BULLET	RANGE, YARDS:	0	25	50	75	100
Black Hills 115 JHP	velocity, fps:	1150				
	energy, ft-lb:	336				
Black Hills 115 FMJ	velocity, fps:	1150				
	energy, ft-lb:	336				
Black Hills 115 JHP +P	velocity, fps:	1300				
	energy, ft-lb:	431				
Black Hills 115 EXP JHP	velocity, fps:	1250				
	energy, ft-lb:	400				
Black Hills 124 JHP +P	velocity, fps:	1250				
	energy, ft-lb:	430				
Black Hills 124 JHP	velocity, fps:	1150				
	energy, ft-lb:	363				
Black Hills 124 FMJ	velocity, fps:	1150				
	energy, ft-lb:	363				
Black Hills 147 JHP subsonic	velocity, fps:	975				
	energy, ft-lb:	309				
Black Hills 147 FMJ subsonic	velocity, fps:	975				
	energy, ft-lb:	309				
Federal 105 EFMJ	velocity, fps:	1225	1160	1105	1060	1025
	energy, ft-lb:	350	315	285	265	245

CARTRIDGE BULLET	RANGE, YARDS:	0	25	50	75	100
Federal 115 Hi-Shok JHP	velocity, fps:	1160	1100	1060	1020	990
	energy, ft-lb:	345	310	285	270	250
Federal 115 FMJ	velocity, fps:	1160	1100	1060	1020	990
	energy, ft-lb:	345	310	285	270	250
Federal 124 FMJ	velocity, fps:	1120	1070	1030	990	960
	energy, ft-lb:	345	315	290	270	255
Federal 124 Hydra-Shok JHP	velocity, fps:	1120	1070	1030	990	960
	energy, ft-lb:	345	315	290	270	255
Federal 124 TMJ TMF Primer	velocity, fps:	1120	1070	1030	990	960
	energy, ft-lb:	345	315	290	270	255
Federal 124 Truncated FMJ Match	velocity, fps:	1120	1070	1030	990	960
	energy, ft-lb:	345	315	290	270	255
Federal 124 Nyclad HP	velocity, fps:	1120	1070	1030	990	960
	energy, ft-lb:	345	315	290	270	255
Federal 124 FMJ +P	velocity, fps:	1120	1070	1030	990	960
	energy, ft-lb:	345	315	290	270	255
Federal 135 Hydra-Shok JHP	velocity, fps:	1050	1030	1010	980	970
	energy, ft-lb:	330	315	300	290	280
Federal 147 Hydra-Shok JHP	velocity, fps:	1000	960	920	890	860
	energy, ft-lb:	325	300	275	260	240
Federal 147 Hi-Shok JHP	velocity, fps:	980	950	930	900	880
	energy, ft-lb:	310	295	285	265	255
Federal 147 FMJ FN	velocity, fps:	960	930	910	890	870
	energy, ft-lb:	295	280	270	260	250
Federal 147 TMJ TMF Primer	velocity, fps:	960	940	910	890	870
	energy, ft-lb:	300	285	270	260	245
Hornady 115 JHP/XTP	velocity, fps:	1155		1047		971
	energy, ft-lb:	341		280		241
Hornady 124 JHP/XTP	velocity, fps:	1110		1030		971
	energy, ft-lb:	339		292		259
Hornady 124 TAP-FPD	velocity, fps:	1100		1028		967
	energy, ft-lb:	339		291		257
Hornady 147 JHP/XTP	velocity, fps:	975		935		899
	energy, ft-lb:	310		285		264
Hornady 147 TAP-FPD	velocity, fps:	975		935		899
	energy, ft-lb:	310		285		264
Lapua 116 FMJ	velocity, fps:	365		319*		290*
	energy, ft-lb:	500		381*		315*
Lapua 120 FMJ CEPP Super	velocity, fps:	360		316*		288*
	energy, ft-lb:	505		390*		324*
Lapua 120 FMJ CEPP Extra	velocity, fps:	360		316*		288*
	energy, ft-lb:	505		390*		324*
Lapua 123 HP Megashock	velocity, fps:	355		311*		284*
	energy, ft-lb:	504		388*		322*
Lapua 123 FMJ	velocity, fps:	320		292*		272*
	energy, ft-lb:	410		342*		295*
Lapua 123 FMJ Combat	velocity, fps:	355		315*		289*
	energy, ft-lb:	504		397*		333*
Magtech 115 JHP +P	velocity, fps:	1246		1137		1056
	energy, ft-lb:	397		330		285
Magtech 115 FMC	velocity, fps:	1135		1027		961
	energy, ft-lb:	330		270		235
Magtech 115 JHP	velocity, fps:	1155		1047		971
	energy, ft-lb:	340		280		240
Magtech 124 FMC	velocity, fps:	1109		1030		971
	energy, ft-lb:	339		292		259
Norma 84 Lead Free Frangible (Geco brand)	velocity, fps:	1411				
	energy, ft-lb:	371				
Norma 124 FMJ (Geco brand)	velocity, fps:	1120				
	energy, fps:	341				
Norma 123 FMJ	velocity, fps:	1099	1032	980		899
	energy, ft-lb:	331	292	263		221

Centerfire Handgun Ballistics

9MM LUGER TO .380 AUTO

CARTRIDGE BULLET	RANGE, YARDS:	0	25	50	75	100
Norma 123 FMJ	velocity, fps:	1280	1170	1086		972
	energy, ft-lb:	449	375	323		259
PMC 75 Non-Toxic Frangible	velocity, fps:	1350	1240	1154	1088	1035
	energy, ft-lb:	303				
PMC 95 SFHP	velocity, fps:	1250	1239	1228	1217	1207
	energy, ft-lb:	330				
PMC 115 FMJ	velocity, fps:	1157	1100	1053	1013	979
	energy, ft-lb:	344				
PMC 115 JHP	velocity, fps:	1167	1098	1044	999	961
	energy, ft-lb:	350				
PMC 124 SFHP	velocity, fps:	1090	1043	1003	969	939
	energy, ft-lb:	327				
PMC 124 FMJ	velocity, fps:	1110	1059	1017	980	949
	energy, ft-lb:	339				
PMC 124 LRN	velocity, fps:	1050	1006	969	937	908
	energy, ft-lb:	304				
PMC 147 FMJ	velocity, fps:	980	965	941	919	900
	enerby, ft-lb:	310				
PMC 147 SFHP	velocity, fps:	velocity and energy figures not available				
Rem. 101 Lead Free Frangible	velocity, fps:	1220		1092		1004
	energy, ft-lb:	334		267		226
Rem. 115 FN Enclosed Base	velocity, fps:	1135		1041		973
	energy, ft-lb:	329		277		242
Rem. 115 Metal Case	velocity, fps:	1135		1041		973
	energy, ft-lb:	329		277		242
Rem. 115 JHP	velocity, fps:	1155		1047		971
	energy, ft-lb:	341		280		241
Rem. 115 JHP +P	velocity, fps:	1250		1113		1019
	energy, ft-lb:	399		316		265
Rem. 124 JHP	velocity, fps:	1120		1028		960
	energy, ft-lb:	346		291		254
Rem. 124 FNEB	velocity, fps:	1100		1030		971
	energy, ft-lb:	339		292		252
Rem. 124 BJHP	velocity, fps:	1125		1031		963
	energy, ft-lb:	349		293		255
Rem. 124 BJHP +P	velocity, fps:	1180		1089		1021
	energy, ft-lb:	384		327		287
Rem. 124 Metal Case	velocity, fps:	1110		1030		971
	energy, ft-lb:	339		292		259
Rem. 147 JHP subsonic	velocity, fps:	990		941		900
	energy, ft-lb:	320		289		264
Rem. 147 BJHP	velocity, fps:	990		941		900
	energy, ft-lb:	320		289		264
Speer 90 Frangible	velocity, fps:	1350		1132		1001
	energy, ft-lb:	364		256		200
Speer 115 JHP Blazer	velocity, fps:	1145		1024		943
	energy, ft-lb:	335		268		227
Speer 115 FMJ Blazer	velocity, fps:	1145		1047		971
	energy, ft-lb:	341		280		241
Speer 115 FMJ	velocity, fps:	1200		1060		970
	energy, ft-lb:	368		287		240
Speer 115 Gold Dot HP	velocity, fps:	1200		1047		971
	energy, ft-lb:	341		280		241
Speer 124 FMJ Blazer	velocity, fps:	1090		989		917
	energy, ft-lb:	327		269		231
Speer 124 FMJ	velocity, fps:	1090		987		913
	energy, ft-lb:	327		268		230
Speer 124 TMJ-CF (and Blazer)	velocity, fps:	1090		989		917
	energy, ft-lb:	327		269		231
Speer 124 Gold Dot HP	velocity, fps:	1150		1030		948
	energy, ft-lb:	367		292		247
Speer 124 Gold Dot HP+P	velocity, fps:	1220		1085		996
	energy, ft-lb:	410		324		273

CARTRIDGE BULLET	RANGE, YARDS:	0	25	50	75	100
Speer 147 TMJ Blazer	velocity, fps:	950		912		879
	energy, ft-lb:	295		272		252
Speer 147 TMJ	velocity, fps:	985		943		906
	energy, ft-lb:	317		290		268
Speer 147 TMJ-CF (and Blazer)	velocity, fps:	985		960		924
	energy, ft-lb:	326		300		279
Speer 147 Gold Dot	velocity, fps:	985		960		924
	energy, ft-lb:	326		300		279
Win. 105 Jacketed FP	velocity, fps:	1200		1074		989
	energy, ft-lb:	336		269		228
Win. 115 Silvertip HP	velocity, fps:	1225		1095		1007
	energy, ft-lb:	383		306		259
Win. 115 Jacketed HP	velocity, fps:	1225		1095		
	energy, ft-lb:	383		306		
Win. 115 FMJ	velocity, fps:	1190		1071		
	energy, ft-lb:	362		293		
Win. 115 EB WinClean	velocity, fps:	1190		1088		
	energy, ft-lb:	362		302		
Win. 124 FMJ	velocity, fps:	1140		1050		
	energy, ft-lb:	358		303		
Win. 124 EB WinClean	velocity, fps:	1130		1049		
	energy, ft-lb:	352		303		
Win. 147 FMJ FN	velocity, fps:	990		945		
	energy, ft-lb:	320		292		
Win. 147 SXT	velocity, fps:	990		947		909
	energy, ft-lb:	320		293		270
Win. 147 Silvertip HP	velocity, fps:	1010		962		921
	energy, ft-lb:	333		302		277
Win. 147 JHP	velocity, fps:	990		945		
	energy, ft-lb:	320		291		
Win. 147 EB WinClean	velocity, fps:	990		945		
	energy, ft-lb:	320		291		

9 x 23 Winchester

CARTRIDGE BULLET	RANGE, YARDS:	0	25	50	75	100
Win. 124 Jacketed FP	velocity, fps:	1460		1308		
	energy, ft-lb:	587		471		
Win. 125 Silvertip HP	velocity, fps:	1450		1249		1103
	energy, ft-lb:	583		433		338

.38 S&W

CARTRIDGE BULLET	RANGE, YARDS:	0	25	50	75	100
Rem. 146 LRN	velocity, fps:	685		650		620
	energy, ft-lb:	150		135		125
Win. 145 LRN	velocity, fps:	685		650		620
	energy, ft-lb:	150		135		125

.38 Short Colt

CARTRIDGE BULLET	RANGE, YARDS:	0	25	50	75	100
Rem. 125 LRN	velocity, fps:	730		685		645
	energy, ft-lb:	150		130		115

.38 Long Colt

CARTRIDGE BULLET	RANGE, YARDS:	0	25	50	75	100
Black Hills 158 RNL	velocity, fps:	650				
	energy, ft-lb:					

.380 Auto

CARTRIDGE BULLET	RANGE, YARDS:	0	25	50	75	100
Black Hills 90 JHP	velocity, fps:	1000				
	energy, ft-lb:	200				
Black Hills 95 FMJ	velocity, fps:	950				
	energy, ft-lb:	190				
Federal 90 Hi-Shok JHP	velocity, fps:	1000	940	890	840	800
	energy, ft-lb:	200	175	160	140	130
Federal 90 Hydra-Shok JHP	velocity, fps:	1000	940	890	840	800
	energy, ft-lb:	200	175	160	140	130
Federal 95 FMJ	velocity, fps:	960	910	870	830	790
	energy, ft-lb:	190	175	160	145	130

Centerfire Handgun Ballistics

BALLISTICS

.380 AUTO TO .38 SPECIAL

CARTRIDGE BULLET	RANGE, YARDS:	0	25	50	75	100
Hornady 90 JHP/XTP	velocity, fps:	1000		902		823
	energy, ft-lb:	200		163		135
Magtech 85 JHP + P	velocity, fps:	1082		999		936
	energy, ft-lb:	221		188		166
Magtech 95 FMC	velocity, fps:	951		861		781
	energy, ft-lb:	190		156		128
Magtech 95 JHP	velocity, fps:	951		861		781
	energy, ft-lb:	190		156		128
PMC 77 NT/FR	velocity, fps:	1200	1095	1012	932	874
	energy, ft-lb:	223				
PMC 90 FMJ	velocity, fps:	910	872	838	807	778
	energy, ft-lb:	165				
PMC 90 JHP	velocity, fps:	917	878	844	812	782
	energy, ft-lb:	168				
PMC 95 SFHP	velocity, fps:	925	884	847	813	783
	energy, ft-lb:	180				
Rem. 88 JHP	velocity, fps:	990		920		868
	energy, ft-lb:	191		165		146
Rem. 95 FNEB	velocity, fps:	955		865		785
	energy, ft-lb:	190		160		130
Rem. 95 Metal Case	velocity, fps:	955		865		785
	energy, ft-lb:	190		160		130
Rem. 102 BJHP	velocity, fps:	940		901		866
	energy, ft-lb:	200		184		170
Speer 88 JHP Blazer	velocity, fps:	950		920		870
	energy, ft-lb:	195		164		148
Speer 90 Gold Dot	velocity, fps:	990		907		842
	energy, ft-lb:	196		164		142
Speer 95 TMJ Blazer	velocity, fps:	945		865		785
	energy, ft-lb:	190		160		130
Speer 95 TMJ	velocity, fps:	950		877		817
	energy, ft-lb:	180		154		133
Win. 85 Silvertip HP	velocity, fps:	1000		921		860
	energy, ft-lb:	189		160		140
Win. 95 SXT	velocity, fps:	955		889		835
	energy, ft-lb:	192		167		147
Win. 95 FMJ	velocity, fps:	955		865		
	energy, ft-lb:	190		160		
Win. 95 EB WinClean	velocity, fps:	955		881		
	energy, ft-lb:	192		164		

.38 Special

CARTRIDGE BULLET	RANGE, YARDS:	0	25	50	75	100
Black Hills 125 JHP +P	velocity, fps:	1050				
	energy, ft-lb:	306				
Black Hills 148 HBWC	velocity, fps:	700				
	energy, ft-lb:					
Black Hills 158 SWC	velocity, fps:	850				
	energy, ft-lb:					
Black Hills 158 CNL	velocity, fps:	800				
	energy, ft-lb:					
Federal 110 Hydra-Shok JHP	velocity, fps:	1000	970	930	910	880
	energy, ft-lb:	245	225	215	200	190
Federal 110 Hi-Shok JHP +P	velocity, fps:	1000	960	930	900	870
	energy, ft-lb:	240	225	210	195	185
Federal 125 Nyclad HP	velocity, fps:	830	780	730	690	650
	energy, ft-lb:	190	170	150	130	115
Federal 125 Hi-Shok JSP +P	velocity, fps:	950	920	900	880	860
	energy, ft-lb:	250	235	225	215	205
Federal 125 Hi-Shok JHP +P	velocity, fps:	950	920	900	880	860
	energy, ft-lb:	250	235	225	215	205
Federal 125 Nyclad HP +P	velocity, fps:	950	920	900	880	860
	energy, ft-lb:	250	235	225	215	205
Federal 129 Hydra-Shok JHP+P	velocity, fps:	950	930	910	890	870
	energy, ft-lb:	255	245	235	225	215
Federal 130 FMJ	velocity, fps:	950	920	890	870	840
	energy, ft-lb:	260	245	230	215	205
Federal 148 LWC Match	velocity, fps:	710	670	630	600	560
	energy, ft-lb:	165	150	130	115	105
Federal 158 LRN	velocity, fps:	760	740	720	710	690
	energy, ft-lb:	200	190	185	175	170
Federal 158 LSWC	velocity, fps:	760	740	720	710	690
	energy, ft-lb:	200	190	185	175	170
Federal 158 Nyclad RN	velocity, fps:	760	740	720	710	690
	energy, ft-lb:	200	190	185	175	170
Federal 158 SWC HP +P	velocity, fps:	890	870	860	840	820
	energy, ft-lb:	280	265	260	245	235
Federal 158 LSWC +P	velocity, fps:	890	870	860	840	820
	energy, ft-lb:	270	265	260	245	235
Federal 158 Nyclad SWC-HP+P	velocity, fps:	890	870	860	840	820
	energy, ft-lb:	270	265	260	245	235
Hornady 125 JHP/XTP	velocity, fps:	900		856		817
	energy, ft-lb:	225		203		185
Hornady 140 JHP/XTP	velocity, fps:	825		790		757
	energy, ft-lb:	212		194		178
Hornady 140 Cowboy	velocity, fps:	800		767		735
	energy, ft-lb:	199		183		168
Hornady 148 HBWC	velocity, fps:	800		697		610
	energy, ft-lb:	210		160		122
Hornady 158 JHP/XPT	velocity, fps:	800		765		731
	energy, ft-lb:	225		205		188
Lapua 123 HP Megashock	velocity, fps:	355		311*		284*
	energy, ft-lb:	504		388*		322*
Lapua 148 LWC	velocity, fps:	230		203*		181*
	energy, ft-lb:	254		199*		157*
Lapua 150 SJFN	velocity, fps:	325		301*		283*
	energy, ft-lb:	512		439*		388*
Lapua 158 FMJLF	velocity, fps:	255		243*		232*
	energy, ft-lb:	332		301*		275*
Lapua 158 LRN	velocity, fps:	255		243*		232*
	energy, ft-lb:	332		301*		275*
Magtech 125 JHP +P	velocity, fps:	1017		971		931
	energy, ft-lb:	287		262		241
Magtech 148 LWC	velocity, fps:	710		634		566
	energy, ft-lb:	166		132		105
Magtech 158 LRN	velocity, fps:	755		728		693
	energy, ft-lb:	200		183		168
Magtech 158 LFN	velocity, fps:	800		776		753
	energy, ft-lb:	225		211		199
Magtech 158 SJHP	velocity, fps:	807		779		753
	energy, ft-lb:	230		213		199
Magtech 158 LSWC	velocity, fps:	755		721		689
	energy, ft-lb:	200		182		167
Magtech 158 FMC-Flat	velocity, fps:	807		779		753
	energy, ft-lb:	230		213		199
PMC 85 Non-Toxic Frangible	velocity, fps:	1275	1181	1109	1052	1006
	energy, ft-lb:	307				
PMC 110 SFHP +P	velocity, fps:	velocity and energy figures not available				
PMC 125 SFHP +P	velocity, fps:	950	918	889	863	838
	energy, ft-lb:	251				
PMC 125 JHP +P	velocity, fps:	974	938	906	878	851
	energy, ft-lb:	266				
PMC 132 FMJ	velocity, fps:	841	820	799	780	761
	energy, ft-lb:	206				
PMC 148 LWC	velocity, fps:	728	694	662	631	602
	energy, ft-lb:	175				

CARTRIDGE BULLET	RANGE, YARDS:	0	25	50	75	100
PMC 158 LRN	velocity, fps:	820	801	783	765	749
	energy, ft-lb:	235				
PMC 158 JSP	velocity, fps:	835	816	797	779	762
	energy, ft-lb:	245				
PMC 158 LFP	velocity, fps:	800		761		725
	energy, ft-lb:	225		203		185
Rem. 101 Lead Free Frangible	velocity, fps:	950		896		850
	energy, ft-lb:	202		180		162
Rem. 110 SJHP	velocity, fps:	950		890		840
	energy, ft-lb:	220		194		172
Rem. 110 SJHP +P	velocity, fps:	995		926		871
	energy, ft-lb:	242		210		185
Rem. 125 SJHP +P	velocity, ft-lb:	945		898		858
	energy, ft-lb:	248		224		204
Rem. 125 BJHP	velocity, fps:	975		929		885
	energy, ft-lb:	264		238		218
Rem. 125 FNEB	velocity, fps:	850		822		796
	energy, ft-lb:	201		188		176
Rem. 125 FNEB +P	velocity, fps:	975		935		899
	energy, ft-lb:	264		242		224
Rem. 130 Metal Case	velocity, fps:	950		913		879
	energy, ft-lb:	261		240		223
Rem. 148 LWC Match	velocity, fps:	710		634		566
	energy, ft-lb:	166		132		105
Rem. 158 LRN	velocity, fps:	755		723		692
	energy, ft-lb:	200		183		168
Rem. 158 SWC +P	velocity, fps:	890		855		823
	energy, ft-lb:	278		257		238
Rem. 158 SWC	velocity, fps:	755		723		692
	energy, ft-lb:	200		183		168
Rem. 158 LHP +P	velocity, fps:	890		855		823
	energy, ft-lb:	278		257		238
Speer 125 JHP +P Blazer	velocity, fps:	945		898		858
	energy, ft-lb:	248		224		204
Speer 125 Gold Dot +P	velocity, fps:	945		898		858
	energy, ft-lb:	248		224		204
Speer 158 TMJ +P (and Blazer)	velocity, fps:	900		852		818
	energy, ft-lb:	278		255		235
Speer 158 LRN Blazer	velocity, fps:	755		723		692
	energy, ft-lb:	200		183		168
Speer 158 Trail Blazer LFN	velocity, fps:	800		761		725
	energy, ft-lb:	225		203		184
Speer 158 TMJ-CF +P	velocity, fps:	900		852		818
(and Blazer)	energy, ft-lb:	278		255		235
Win. 110 Silvertip HP	velocity, fps:	945		894		850
	energy, ft-lb:	218		195		176
Win. 110 Jacketed FP	velocity, fps:	975		906		849
	energy, ft-lb:	232		201		176
Win. 125 Jacketed HP	velocity, fps:	945		898		
	energy, ft-lb:	248		224		
Win. 125 Jacketed HP +P	velocity, fps:	945		898		858
	energy, ft-lb:	248		224		204
Win. 125 Jacketed FP	velocity, fps:	850		804		
	energy, ft-lb:	201		179		
Win. 125 Silvertip HP + P	velocity, fps:	945		898		858
	energy, ft-lb:	248		224		204
Win. 125 JFP WinClean	velocity, fps:	775		742		
	energy, ft-lb:	167		153		
Win. 130 FMJ	velocity, fps:	800		765		
	energy, ft-lb:	185		169		
Win. 130 SXT +P	velocity, fps:	925		887		852
	energy, ft-lb:	247		227		210
Win. 148 LWC Super Match	velocity, fps:	710		634		566

CARTRIDGE BULLET	RANGE, YARDS:	0	25	50	75	100
	energy, ft-lb:	166		132		105
Win. 150 Lead	velocity, fps:	845		812		
	energy, ft-lb:	238		219		
Win. 158 Lead	velocity, fps:	800		761		725
	energy, ft-lb:	225		203		185
Win. 158 LRN	velocity, fps:	755		723		693
	energy, ft-lb:	200		183		168
Win. 158 LSWC	velocity, fps:	755		721		689
	energy, ft-lb:	200		182		167
Win. 158 LSWC HP +P	velocity, fps:	890		855		823
	energy, ft-lb:	278		257		238

.38-40

CARTRIDGE BULLET	RANGE, YARDS:	0	25	50	75	100
Black Hills 180 FPL	velocity, fps:	800				
	energy, ft-lb:					

.38 Super

CARTRIDGE BULLET	RANGE, YARDS:	0	25	50	75	100
Federal 130 FMJ +P	velocity, fps:	1200	1140	1100	1050	1020
	energy, ft-lb:	415	380	350	320	300
PMC 115 JHP	velocity, fps:	1116	1052	1001	959	923
	energy, ft-lb:	318				
PMC 130 FMJ	velocity, fps:	1092	1038	994	957	924
	energy, ft-lb:	348				
Rem. 130 Metal Case	velocity, fps:	1215		1099		1017
	energy, ft-lb:	426		348		298
Win. 125 Silvertip HP +P	velocity, fps:	1240		1130		1050
	energy, ft-lb:	427		354		306
Win. 130 FMJ +P	velocity, fps:	1215		1099		
	energy, ft-lb:	426		348		

.357 Sig

CARTRIDGE BULLET	RANGE, YARDS:	0	25	50	75	100
Federal 125 FMJ	velocity, fps:	1350	1270	1190	1130	1080
	energy, ft-lb:	510	445	395	355	325
Federal 125 JHP	velocity, fps:	1350	1270	1190	1130	1080
	energy, ft-lb:	510	445	395	355	325
Federal 150 JHP	velocity, fps:	1130	1080	1030	1000	970
	energy, ft-lb:	420	385	355	330	310
Hornady 124 JHP/XTP	velocity, fps:	1350		1208		1108
	energy, ft-lb:	502		405		338
Hornady 147 JHP/XTP	velocity, fps:	1225		1138		1072
	energy, ft-lb:	490		422		375
PMC 85 Non-Toxic Frangible	velocity, fps:	1480	1356	1245	1158	1092
	energy, ft-lb:	413				
PMC 124 SFHP	velocity, fps:	1350	1263	1190	1132	1083
	energy, ft-lb:	502				
PMC 124 FMJ/FP	velocity, fps:	1350	1242	1158	1093	1040
	energy, ft-lb:	512				
Rem. 104 Lead Free Frangible	velocity, fps:	1400		1223		1094
	energy, ft-lb:	453		345		276
Rem. 125 Metal Case	velocity, fps:	1350		1146		1018
	energy, ft-lb:	506		422		359
Rem. 125 JHP	velocity, fps:	1350		1157		1032
	energy, ft-lb:	506		372		296
Speer 125 TMJ (and Blazer)	velocity, fps:	1350		1177		1057
	energy, ft-lb:	502		381		307
Speer 125 TMJ-CF	velocity, fps:	1350		1177		1057
	energy, ft-lb:	502		381		307
Speer 125 Gold Dot	velocity, fps:	1375		1203		1079
	energy, ft-lb:	525		402		323
Win. 105 JFP	velocity, fps:	1370		1179		1050
	energy, ft-lb	438		324		257
Win. 125 FMJ FN	velocity, fps:	1350		1185		
	energy, ft-lb	506		390		

Centerfire Handgun Ballistics

.357 SIG TO .40 S&W

CARTRIDGE BULLET	RANGE, YARDS:	0	25	50	75	100
.357 MAGNUM						
Black Hills 125 JHP	velocity, fps:	1500				
	energy, ft-lb:	625				
Black Hills 158 CNL	velocity, fps:	800				
	energy, ft-lb:					
Black Hills 158 SWC	velocity, fps:	1050				
	energy, ft-lb:					
Black Hills 158 JHP	velocity, fps:	1250				
	energy, ft-lb:					
Federal 110 Hi-Shok JHP	velocity, fps:	1300	1180	1090	1040	990
	energy, ft-lb:	410	340	290	260	235
Federal 125 Hi-Shok JHP	velocity, fps:	1450	1350	1240	1160	1100
	energy, ft-lb:	580	495	430	370	335
Federal 130 Hydra-Shok JHP	velocity, fps:	1300	1210	1130	1070	1020
	energy, ft-lb:	490	420	370	330	300
Federal 158 Hi-Shok JSP	velocity, fps:	1240	1160	1100	1060	1020
	energy, ft-lb:	535	475	430	395	365
Federal 158 JSP	velocity, fps:	1240	1160	1100	1060	1020
	energy, ft-lb:	535	475	430	395	365
Federal 158 LSWC	velocity, fps:	1240	1160	1100	1060	1020
	energy, ft-lb:	535	475	430	395	365
Federal 158 Hi-Shok JHP	velocity, fps:	1240	1160	1100	1060	1020
	energy, ft-lb:	535	475	430	395	365
Federal 158 Hydra-Shok JHP	velocity, fps:	1240	1160	1100	1060	1020
	energy, ft-lb:	535	475	430	395	365
Federal 180 Hi-Shok JHP	velocity, fps:	1090	1030	980	930	890
	energy, ft-lb:	475	425	385	350	320
Federal 180 Castcore	velocity, fps:	1250	1200	1160	1120	1080
	energy, ft-lb:	625	575	535	495	465
Hornady 125 JHP/XTP	velocity, fps:	1500		1314		1166
	energy, ft-lb:	624		479		377
Hornady 125 JFP/XTP	velocity, fps:	1500		1311		1161
	energy, ft-lb:	624		477		374
Hornady 140 Cowboy	velocity, fps:	800		767		735
	energy, ft-lb:	199		183		168
Hornady 140 JHP/XTP	velocity, fps:	1400		1249		1130
	energy, ft-lb:	609		485		397
Hornady 158 JHP/XTP	velocity, fps:	1250		1150		1073
	energy, ft-lb:	548		464		404
Hornady 158 JFP/XTP	velocity, fps:	1250		1147		1068
	energy, ft-lb:	548		461		400
Lapua 150 FMJ CEPP Super	velocity, fps:	370		527*		303*
	energy, ft-lb:	664		527*		445*
Lapua 150 SJFN	velocity, fps:	385		342*		313*
	energy, ft-lb:	719		569*		476*
Lapua 158 SJHP	velocity, fps:	470		408*		359*
	energy, ft-lb:	1127		850*		657*
Magtech 158 SJSP	velocity, fps:	1235		1104		1015
	energy, ft-lb:	535		428		361
Magtech 158 SJHP	velocity, fps:	1235		1104		1015
	energy, ft-lb:	535		428		361
PMC 85 Non-Toxic Frangible	velocity, fps:	1325	1219	1139	1076	1025
	energy, ft-lb:	331				
PMC 125 JHP	velocity, fps:	1194	1117	1057	1008	967
	energy, ft-lb:	399				
PMC 150 JHP	velocity, fps:	1234	1156	1093	1042	1000
	energy, ft-lb:	512				
PMC 150 SFHP	velocity, fps:	1205	1129	1069	1020	980
	energy, ft-lb:	484				
PMC 158 JSP	velocity, fps:	1194	1122	1063	1016	977
	energy, ft-lb:	504				

CARTRIDGE BULLET	RANGE, YARDS:	0	25	50	75	100
PMC 158 LFP	velocity, fps:	800		761		725
	energy, ft-lb:	225		203		185
Rem. 110 SJHP	velocity, fps:	1295		1094		975
	energy, ft-lb:	410		292		232
Rem. 125 SJHP	velocity, fps:	1450		1240		1090
	energy, ft-lb:	583		427		330
Rem. 125 BJHP	velocity, fps:	1220		1095		1009
	energy, ft-lb:	413		333		283
Rem. 125 FNEB	velocity, fps:	1450		1240		1090
	energy, ft-lb:	583		427		330
Rem. 158 SJHP	velocity, fps:	1235		1104		1015
	energy, ft-lb:	535		428		361
Rem. 158 SP	velocity, fps:	1235		1104		1015
	energy, ft-lb:	535		428		361
Rem. 158 SWC	velocity, fps:	1235		1104		1015
	energy, ft-lb:	535		428		361
Rem. 165 JHP Core-Lokt	velocity, fps:	1290		1189		1108
	energy, ft-lb:	610		518		450
Rem. 180 SJHP	velocity, fps:	1145		1053		985
	energy, ft-lb:	542		443		388
Speer 125 Gold Dot	velocity, fps:	1450		1240		1090
	energy, ft-lb:	583		427		330
Speer 158 JHP Blazer	velocity, fps:	1150		1104		1015
	energy, ft-lb:	535		428		361
Speer 158 Gold Dot	velocity, fps:	1235		1104		1015
	energy, ft-lb:	535		428		361
Speer 170 Gold Dot SP	velocity, fps:	1180		1089		1019
	energy, ft-lb:	525		447		392
Win. 110 JFP	velocity, fps:	1275		1105		998
	energy, ft-lb:	397		298		243
Win. 110 JHP	velocity, fps:	1295		1095		
	energy, ft-lb:	410		292		
Win. 125 JFP WinClean	velocity, fps:	1370		1183		
	energy, ft-lb:	521		389		
Win. 145 Silvertip HP	velocity, fps:	1290		1155		1060
	energy, ft-lb:	535		428		361
Win. 158 JHP	velocity, fps:	1235		1104		1015
	energy, ft-lb:	535		428		361
Win. 158 JSP	velocity, fps:	1235		1104		1015
	energy, ft-lb:	535		428		361
Win. 180 Partition Gold	velocity, fps:	1180		1088		1020
	energy, ft-lb:	557		473		416
.40 S&W						
Black Hills 155 JHP	velocity, fps:	1150				
	energy, ft-lb:	450				
Black Hills 165 EXP JHP	velocity, fps:	1150 (2005: 1100)				
	energy, ft-lb:	483				
Black Hills 180 JHP	velocity, fps:	1000				
	energy, ft-lb:	400				
Black Hills 180 JHP	velocity, fps:	1000				
	energy, ft-lb:	400				
Federal 135 Hydra-Shok JHP	velocity, fps:	1190	1050	970	900	850
	energy, ft-lb:	420	330	280	245	215
Federal 155 FMJ Ball	velocity, fps:	1140	1080	1030	990	960
	energy, ft-lb:	445	400	365	335	315
Federal 155 Hi-Shok JHP	velocity, fps:	1140	1080	1030	990	950
	energy, ft-lb:	445	400	365	335	315
Federal 155 Hydra-Shok JHP	velocity, fps:	1140	1080	1030	990	950
	energy, ft-lb:	445	400	365	335	315
Federal 165 EFMJ	velocity, fps:	1190	1060	970	905	850
	energy, ft-lb:	520	410	345	300	265

Centerfire Handgun Ballistics

.40 S&W TO 10 MM AUTO

BALLISTICS

CARTRIDGE BULLET	RANGE, YARDS:	0	25	50	75	100
Federal 165 FMJ	velocity, fps:	1050	1020	990	960	935
	energy, ft-lb:	405	380	355	335	320
Federal 165 FMJ Ball	velocity, fps:	980	950	920	900	880
	energy, ft-lb:	350	330	310	295	280
Federal 165 Hydra-Shok JHP	velocity, fps:	980	950	930	910	890
	energy, ft-lb:	350	330	315	300	290
Federal 180 High Antim. Lead	velocity, fps:	990	960	930	910	890
	energy, ft-lb:	390	365	345	330	315
Federal 180 TMJ TMF Primer	velocity, fps:	990	960	940	910	890
	energy, ft-lb:	390	370	350	330	315
Federal 180 FMJ Ball	velocity, fps:	990	960	940	910	890
	energy, ft-lb:	390	370	350	330	315
Federal 180 Hi-Shok JHP	velocity, fps:	990	960	930	910	890
	energy, ft-lb:	390	365	345	330	315
Federal 180 Hydra-Shok JHP	velocity, fps:	990	960	930	910	890
	energy, ft-lb:	390	365	345	330	315
Hornady 155 JHP/XTP	velocity, fps:	1180		1061		980
	energy, ft-lb:	479		387		331
Hornady 155 TAP-FPD	velocity, fps:	1180		1061		980
	energy, ft-lb:	470		387		331
Hornady 180 JHP/XTP	velocity, fps:	950		903		862
	energy, ft-lb:	361		326		297
Hornady 180 TAP-FPD	velocity, fps:	950		903		862
	energy, ft-lb:	361		326		297
Magtech 155 JHP	velocity, fps:	1025		1118		1052
	energy, ft-lb:	500		430		381
Magtech 180 JHP	velocity, fps:	990		933		886
	energy, ft-lb:	390		348		314
Magtech 180 FMC	velocity, fps:	990		933		886
	energy, ft-lb:	390		348		314
PMC 115 Non-Toxic Frangible	velocity, fps:	1350	1240	1154	1088	1035
	energy, ft-lb:	465				
PMC 155 SFHP	velocity, fps:	1160	1092	1039	994	957
	energy, ft-lb:	463				
PMC 165 JHP	velocity, fps:	1040	1002	970	941	915
	energy, ft-lb:	396				
PMC 165 FMJ	velocity, fps:	1010	977	948	922	899
	energy, ft-lb:	374				
PMC 180 FMJ/FP	velocity, fps:	985	957	931	908	885
	energy, ft-lb:	388				
PMC 180 SFHP	velocity, fps:	985	958	933	910	889
	energy, ft-lb:	388				
Rem. 141 Lead Free Frangible	velocity, fps:	1135		1056		996
	energy, ft-lb:	403		349		311
Rem. 155 JHP	velocity, fps:	1205		1095		1017
	energy, ft-lb:	499		413		356
Rem. 165 BJHP	velocity, fps:	1150		1040		964
	energy, ft-lb:	485		396		340
Rem. 180 JHP	velocity, fps:	1015		960		914
	energy, ft-lb:	412		368		334
Rem. 180 FN Enclosed Base	velocity, fps:	985		936		893
	energy, ft-lb:	388		350		319
Rem. 180 Metal Case	velocity, fps:	985		936		893
	energy, ft-lb:	388		350		319
Rem. 180 BJHP	velocity, fps:	1015		960		914
	energy, ft-lb:	412		368		334
Speer 105 Frangible	velocity, fps:	1380		1128		985
	energy, ft-lb:	444		297		226
Speer 155 TMJ Blazer	velocity, fps:	1175		1047		963
	energy, ft-lb:	475		377		319
Speer 155 TMJ	velocity, fps:	1200		1065		976
	energy, ft-lb:	496		390		328

CARTRIDGE BULLET	RANGE, YARDS:	0	25	50	75	100
Speer 155 Gold Dot	velocity, fps:	1200		1063		974
	energy, ft-lb:	496		389		326
Speer 165 TMJ Blazer	velocity, fps:	1100		1006		938
	energy, ft-lb:	443		371		321
Speer 165 TMJ	velocity, fps:	1150		1040		964
	energy, ft-lb:	484		396		340
Speer 165 Gold Dot	velocity, fps:	1150		1043		966
	energy, ft-lb:	485		399		342
Speer 180 HP Blazer	velocity, fps:	985		951		909
	energy, ft-lb:	400		361		330
Speer 180 FMJ Blazer	velocity, fps:	1000		937		886
	energy, ft-lb:	400		351		313
Speer 180 FMJ	velocity, fps:	1000		951		909
	energy, ft-lb:	400		361		330
Speer 180 TMJ-CF (and Blazer)	velocity, fps:	1000		951		909
	energy, ft-lb:	400		361		330
Speer 180 Gold Dot	velocity, fps:	1025		957		902
	energy, ft-lb:	420		366		325
Win. 140 JFP	velocity, fps:	1155		1039		960
	energy, ft-lb:	415		336		286
Win. 155 Silvertip HP	velocity, fps:	1205		1096		1018
	energy, ft-lb	500		414		357
Win. 165 SXT	velocity, fps:	1130		1041		977
	energy, ft-lb:	468		397		349
Win. 165 FMJ FN	velocity, fps:	1060		1001		
	energy, ft-lb:	412		367		
Win. 165 EB WinClean	velocity, fps:	1130		1054		
	energy, ft-lb:	468		407		
Win. 180 JHP	velocity, fps:	1010		954		
	energy, ft-lb:	408		364		
Win. 180 FMJ	velocity, fps:	990		936		
	energy, ft-lb:	390		350		
Win. 180 SXT	velocity, fps:	1010		954		909
	energy, ft-lb:	408		364		330
Win. 180 EB WinClean	velocity, fps:	990		943		
	energy, ft-lb:	392		356		

10 MM AUTO

CARTRIDGE BULLET	RANGE, YARDS:	0	25	50	75	100
Federal 155 Hi-Shok JHP	velocity, fps:	1330	1230	1140	1080	1030
	energy, ft-lb:	605	515	450	400	360
Federal 180 Hi-Shok JHP	velocity, fps:	1030	1000	970	950	920
	energy, ft-lb:	425	400	375	355	340
Federal 180 Hydra-Shok JHP	velocity, fps:	1030	1000	970	950	920
	energy, ft-lb:	425	400	375	355	340
Federal 180 High Antim. Lead	velocity, fps:	1030	1000	970	950	920
	energy, ft-lb:	425	400	375	355	340
Federal 180 FMJ	velocity, fps:	1060	1025	990	965	940
	energy, ft-lb:	400	370	350	330	310
Hornady 155 JHP/XTP	velocity, fps:	1265		1119		1020
	energy, ft-lb:	551		431		358
Hornady 180 JHP/XTP	velocity, fps:	1180		1077		1004
	energy, ft-lb:	556		464		403
Hornady 200 JHP/XTP	velocity, fps:	1050		994		948
	energy, ft-lb:	490		439		399
PMC 115 Non-Toxic Frangible	velocity, fps:	1350	1240	1154	1088	1035
	energy, ft-lb:	465				
PMC 170 JHP	velocity, fps:	1200	1117	1052	1000	958
	energy, ft-lb:	543				
PMC 180 SFHP	velocity, fps:	950	926	903	882	862
	energy, ft-lb:	361				
PMC 200 TC-FMJ	velocity, fps:	1050	1008	972	941	912
	energy, ft-lb:	490				

Centerfire Handgun Ballistics

10 MM AUTO TO .44-40

CARTRIDGE BULLET	RANGE, YARDS:	0	25	50	75	100
Rem. 180 Metal Case	velocity, fps:	1150		1063		998
	energy, ft-lb:	529		452		398
Speer 200 TMJ Blazer	velocity, fps:	1050		966		952
	energy, ft-lb:	490		440		402
Win. 175 Silvertip HP	velocity, fps:	1290		1141		1037
	energy, ft-lb:	649		506		418

.41 Remington. Magnum

CARTRIDGE BULLET	RANGE, YARDS:	0	25	50	75	100
Federal 210 Hi-Shok JHP	velocity, fps:	1300	1210	1130	1070	1030
	energy, ft-lb:	790	680	595	540	495
PMC 210 TCSP	velocity, fps:	1290	1201	1128	1069	1021
	energy, ft-lb:	774				
PMC 210 JHP	velocity, fps:	1289	1200	1127	1068	1020
	energy, ft-lb:	774				
Rem. 210 SP	velocity, fps:	1300		1162		1062
	energy, ft-lb:	788		630		526
Win. 175 Silvertip HP	velocity, fps:	1250		1120		1029
	energy, ft-lb:	607		488		412
Win. 240 Platinum Tip	velocity, ft-lb:	1250		1151		1075
	energy, ft-lb:	833		706		616

.44 Colt

CARTRIDGE BULLET	RANGE, YARDS:	0	25	50	75	100
Black Hills 230 FPL	velocity, fps:	730				
	energy, ft-lb:					

.44 Russian

CARTRIDGE BULLET	RANGE, YARDS:	0	25	50	75	100
Black Hills 210 FPL	velocity, fps:	650				
	energy, ft-lb:					

.44 Special

CARTRIDGE BULLET	RANGE, YARDS:	0	25	50	75	100
Black Hills 210 FPL	velocity, fps:	700				
	energy, ft-lb:					
Federal 200 SWC HP	velocity, fps:	900	860	830	800	770
	energy, ft-lb:	360	330	305	285	260
Federal 250 CastCore	velocity, fps:	1250	1200	1150	1110	1080
	energy, ft-lb:	865	795	735	685	645
Hornady 180 JHP/XTP	velocity, fps:	1000		935		882
	energy, ft-lb:	400		350		311
Magtech 240 LFN	velocity, fps:	750		722		696
	energy, ft-lb:	300		278		258
PMC 180 JHP	velocity, fps:	980	938	902	869	839
	energy, ft-lb:	383				
PMC 240 SWC-CP	velocity, fps:	764	744	724	706	687
	energy, ft-lb:	311				
PMC 240 LFP	velocity, fps:	750		719		690
	energy, ft-lb:	300		275		253
Rem. 246 LRN	velocity, fps:	755		725		695
	energy, ft-lb:	310		285		265
Speer 200 HP Blazer	velocity, fps:	875		825		780
	energy, ft-lb:	340		302		270
Speer 200 Trail Blazer LFN	velocity, fps:	750		714		680
	energy, ft-lb:	250		226		205
Speer 200 Gold Dot	velocity, fps:	875		825		780
	energy, ft-lb:	340		302		270
Win. 200 Silvertip HP	velocity, fps:	900		860		822
	energy, ft-lb:	360		328		300
Win. 240 Lead	velocity, fps:	750		719		690
	energy, ft-lb	300		275		253
Win. 246 LRN	velocity, fps:	755		725		695
	energy, ft-lb:	310		285		265

.44 Remington Magnum

CARTRIDGE BULLET	RANGE, YARDS:	0	25	50	75	100
Black Hills 240 JHP	velocity, fps:	1260				
	energy, ft-lb:	848				
Black Hills 300 JHP	velocity, fps:	1150				
	energy, ft-lb:	879				
Federal 180 Hi-Shok JHP	velocity, fps:	1610	1480	1370	1270	1180
	energy, ft-lb:	1035	875	750	640	555
Federal 240 Hi-Shok JHP	velocity, fps:	1180	1130	1080	1050	1010
	energy, ft-lb:	740	675	625	580	550
Federal 240 Hydra-Shok JHP	velocity, fps:	1180	1130	1080	1050	1010
	energy, ft-lb:	740	675	625	580	550
Federal 240 JHP	velocity, fps:	1180	1130	1080	1050	1010
	energy, ft-lb:	740	675	625	580	550
Federal 300 CastCore	velocity, fps:	1250	1200	1160	1120	1080
	energy, ft-lb:	1040	960	885	825	775
Hornady 180 JHP/XTP	velocity, fps:	1550		1340		1173
	energy, ft-lb:	960		717		550
Hornady 200 JHP/XTP	velocity, fps:	1500		1284		1128
	energy, ft-lb:	999		732		565
Hornady 240 JHP/XTP	velocity, fps:	1350		1188		1078
	energy, ft-lb:	971		753		619
Hornady 300 JHP/XTP	velocity, fps:	1150		1084		1031
	energy, ft-lb:	881		782		708
Magtech 240 SJSP	velocity, fps:	1180		1081		1010
	energy, ft-lb:	741		632		623
PMC 180 JHP	velocity, fps:	1392	1263	1157	1076	1015
	energy, ft-lb:	772				
PMC 240 JHP	velocity, fps:	1301	1218	1147	1088	1041
	energy, ft-lb:	900				
PMC 240 TC-SP	velocity, fps:	1300	1216	1144	1086	1038
	energy, ft-lb:	900				
PMC 240 SFHP	velocity, fps:	1300	1212	1138	1079	1030
	energy, ft-lb:	900				
PMC 240 LSWC-GCK	velocity, fps:	1225	1143	1077	1025	982
	energy, ft-lb:	806				
Rem. 180 JSP	velocity, fps:	1610		1365		1175
	energy, ft-lb:	1036		745		551
Rem. 210 Gold Dot HP	velocity, fps:	1450		1276		1140
	energy, ft-lb:	980		759		606
Rem. 240 SP	velocity, fps:	1180		1081		1010
	energy, ft-lb:	721		623		543
Rem. 240 SJHP	velocity, fps:	1180		1081		1010
	energy, ft-lb:	721		623		543
Rem. 275 JHP Core-Lokt	velocity, fps:	1235		1142		1070
	energy, ft-lb:	931		797		699
Speer 240 JHP Blazer	velocity, fps:	1200		1092		1015
	energy, ft-lb:	767		636		549
Speer 240 Gold Dot HP	velocity, fps:	1400		1255		1139
	energy, ft-lb:	1044		839		691
Speer 270 Gold Dot SP	velocity, fps:	1250		1142		1060
	energy, ft-lb:	937		781		674
Win. 210 Silvertip HP	velocity, fps:	1250		1106		1010
	energy, ft-lb:	729		570		475
Win. 240 Hollow SP	velocity, fps:	1180		1081		1010
	energy, ft-lb:	741		623		543
Win. 240 JSP	velocity, fps:	1180		1081		
	energy, ft-lb:	741		623		
Win. 250 Partition Gold	velocity, fps:	1230		1132		1057
	energy, ft-lb:	840		711		620
Win. 250 Platinum Tip	velocity, fps:	1250		1148		1070
	energy, ft-lb:	867		732		635

.44-40

CARTRIDGE BULLET	RANGE, YARDS:	0	25	50	75	100
Black Hills 200 RNFP	velocity, fps:	800				
	energy, ft-lb:					

Centerfire Handgun Ballistics

.44-40 TO .45 AUTOMATIC (ACP)

CARTRIDGE BULLET	RANGE, YARDS:	0	25	50	75	100
Hornady 205 Cowboy	velocity, fps:	725		697		670
	energy, ft-lb:	239		221		204
Magtech 225 LFN	velocity, fps:	725		703		681
	energy, ft-lb:	281		247		232
PMC 225 LFP	velocity, fps:	725		723		695
	energy, ft-lb:	281		261		242
Win. 225 Lead	velocity, fps:	750		723		695
	energy, ft-lb:	281		261		242

.45 Automatic (ACP)

CARTRIDGE BULLET	RANGE, YARDS:	0	25	50	75	100
Black Hills 185 JHP	velocity, fps:	1000				
	energy, ft-lb:	411				
Black Hills 200 Match SWC	velocity, fps:	875				
	energy, ft-lb:	340				
Black Hills 230 FMJ	velocity, fps:	850				
	energy, ft-lb:	368				
Black Hills 230 JHP	velocity, fps:	850				
	energy, ft-lb:	368				
Black Hills 230 JHP +P	velocity, fps:	950				
	energy, ft-lb:	460				
Federal 165 Hydra-Shok JHP	velocity, fps:	1060	1020	980	950	920
	energy, ft-lb:	410	375	350	330	310
Federal 165 EFMJ	velocity, fps:	1090	1045	1005	975	942
	energy, ft-lb:	435	400	370	345	325
Federal 185 Hi-Shok JHP	velocity, fps:	950	920	900	880	860
	energy, ft-lb:	370	350	335	315	300
Federal 185 FMJ-SWC Match	velocity, fps:	780	730	700	660	620
	energy, ft-lb:	245	220	200	175	160
Federal 200 Exp. FMJ	velocity, fps:	1030	1000	970	940	920
	energy, ft-lb:	470	440	415	395	375
Federal 230 FMJ	velocity, fps:	850	830	810	790	770
	energy, ft-lb:	370	350	335	320	305
Federal 230 FMJ Match	velocity, fps:	855	835	815	795	775
	energy, ft-lb:	375	355	340	325	305
Federal 230 Hi-Shok JHP	velocity, fps:	850	830	810	790	770
	energy, ft-lb:	370	350	335	320	300
Federal 230 Hydra-Shok JHP	velocity, fps:	850	830	810	790	770
	energy, ft-lb:	370	350	335	320	305
Federal 230 FMJ	velocity, fps:	850	830	810	790	770
	energy, ft-lb:	370	350	335	320	305
Federal 230 TMJ TMF Primer	velocity, fps:	850	830	810	790	770
	energy, ft-lb:	370	350	335	315	305
Hornady 185 JHP/XTP	velocity, fps:	950		880		819
	energy, ft-lb:	371		318		276
Hornady 200 JHP/XTP	velocity, fps:	900		855		815
	energy, ft-lb:	358		325		295
Hornady 200 HP/XTP +P	velocity, fps:	1055		982		925
	energy, ft-lb:	494		428		380
Hornady 200 TAP-FPD	velocity, fps:	1055		982		926
	energy, ft-lbs:	494		428		380
Hornady 230 FMJ/RN	velocity, fps:	850		809		771
	energy, ft-lb:	369		334		304
Hornady 230 FMJ/FP	velocity, fps:	850		809		771
	energy, ft-lb:	369		334		304
Hornady 230 HP/XTP +P	velocity, fps:	950		904		865
	energy, ft-lb:	462		418		382
Hornady 230 TAP-FPD	velocity, fps:	950		908		872
	energy, ft-lb:	461		421		388
Magtech 185 JHP +P	velocity, fps:	1148		1066		1055
	energy, ft-lb:	540		467		415
Magtech 200 LSWC	velocity, fps:	950		910		874
	energy, ft-lb:	401		368		339

CARTRIDGE BULLET	RANGE, YARDS:	0	25	50	75	100
Magtech 230 FMC	velociy, fps:	837		800		767
	energy, ft-lb:	356		326		300
Magtech 230 FMC-SWC	velocity, fps:	780		720		660
	energy, ft-lb:	310		265		222
PMC 145 Non-Toxic Frangible	velocity, fps:	1100	1045	999	961	928
	energy, ft-lb:	390				
PMC 185 JHP	velocity, fps:	903	870	839	811	785
	energy, ft-lb:	339				
PMC 200 FMJ-SWC	velocity, fps:	850	818	788	761	734
	energy, ft-lb:	321				
PMC 230 SFHP	velocity, fps:	850	830	811	792	775
	energy, ft-lb:	369				
PMC 230 FMJ	velocity, fps:	830	809	789	769	749
	energy, ft-lb:	352				
Rem. 175 Lead Free Frangible	velocity, fps:	1020		923		851
	energy, ft-lb:	404		331		281
Rem. 185 JHP	velocity, fps:	1000		939		889
	energy, ft-lb:	411		362		324
Rem. 185 BJHP	velocity, fps:	1015		951		899
	energy, ft-lb:	423		372		332
Rem. 185 BJHP +P	velocity, fps:	1140		1042		971
	energy, ft-lb:	534		446		388
Rem. 185 MC	velocity, fps:	1015		955		907
	energy, ft-lb:	423		375		338
Rem. 230 FN Enclosed Base	velocity, fps:	835		800		767
	energy, ft-lb:	356		326		300
Rem. 230 Metal Case	velocity, fps:	835		800		767
	energy, ft-lb:	356		326		300
Rem. 230 JHP	velocity, fps:	835		800		767
	energy, ft-lb:	356		326		300
Rem. 230 BJHP	velocity, fps:	875		833		795
	energy, ft-lb:	391		355		323
Speer 140 Frangible	velocity, fps:	1200		1029		928
	energy, ft-lb:	448		329		268
Speer 185 Gold Dot	velocity, fps:	1050		956		886
	energy, ft-lb:	453		375		322
Speer 185 TMJ/FN	velocity, fps:	1000		909		839
	energy, ft-lb:	411		339		289
Speer 200 JHP Blazer	velocity, fps:	975		917		860
	energy, ft-lb:	421		372		328
Speer 200 Gold Dot +P	velocity, fps:	1080		994		930
	energy, ft-lb:	518		439		384
Speer 200 TMJ/FN	velocity, fps:	975		897		834
	energy, ft-lb:	422		357		309
Speer 230 FMJ (and Blazer)	velocity, fps:	845		804		775
	energy, ft-lb:	363		329		304
Speer 230 TMJ-CF (and Blazer)	velocity, fps:	845		804		775
	energy, ft-lb:	363		329		304
Speer 230 Gold Dot	velocity, fps:	890		845		805
	energy, ft-lb:	405		365		331
Win. 170 JFP	velocity, fps:	1050		982		928
	energy, ft-lb:	416		364		325
Win. 185 Silvertip HP	velocity, fps:	1000		938		888
	energy, ft-lb:	411		362		324
Win. 185 FMJ FN	velocity, fps:	910		861		
	energy, ft-lb:	340		304		
Win. 185 EB WinClean	velocity, fps:	910		835		
	energy, ft-lb:	340		286		
Win. 230 JHP	velocity, fps:	880		842		
	energy, ft-lb:	396		363		
Win. 230 FMJ	velocity, fps:	835		800		
	energy, ft-lb:	356		326		

Centerfire Handgun Ballistics

.45 AUTOMATIC (ACP) TO .500 SMITH & WESSON

CARTRIDGE BULLET	RANGE, YARDS:	0	25	50	75	100
Win. 230 SXT	velocity, fps:	880		846		816
	energy, ft-lb:	396		366		340
Win. 230 JHP subsonic	velocity, fps:	880		842		808
	energy, ft-lb:	396		363		334
Win. 230 EB WinClean	velocity, fps:	835		802		
	energy, ft-lb:	356		329		

.45 GAP

CARTRIDGE BULLET	RANGE, YARDS:	0	25	50	75	100
Federal 185 Hydra-Shok JHP	velocity, fps:	1090	1020	970	920	890
And Federal TMJ	energy, ft-lb:	490	430	385	350	320
Federal 230 Hydra-Shok	velocity, fps:	880	870	850	840	820
And Federal FMJ	energy, ft-lb:	395	380	3760	355	345
Win. 185 STHP	velocity, fps:	1000		938		887
	energy, ft-lb:	411		361		323
Win. 230 JHP	velocity, fps:	880		842		
	energy, ft-lb:	396		363		
Win. 230 EB WinClean	velocity, fps:	875		840		
	energy, ft-lb:	391		360		
Win. 230 FMJ	velocity, fps:	850		814		
	energy, ft-lb:	369		338		

.45 Winchester Magnum

CARTRIDGE BULLET	RANGE, YARDS:	0	25	50	75	100
Win. 260 Partition Gold	velocity, fps:	1200		1105		1033
	energy, ft-lb:	832		705		616
Win. 260 JHP	velocity, fps:	1200		1099		1026
	energy, ft-lb:	831		698		607

.45 Schofield

CARTRIDGE BULLET	RANGE, YARDS:	0	25	50	75	100
Black Hills 180 FNL	velocity, fps:	730				
	energy, ft-lb:					
Black Hills 230 RNFP	velocity, fps:	730				
	energy, ft-lb:					

.45 Colt

CARTRIDGE BULLET	RANGE, YARDS:	0	25	50	75	100
Black Hills 250 RNFP	velocity, fps:	725				
	energy, ft-lb:					
Federal 225 SWC HP	velocity, fps:	900	880	860	840	820
	energy, ft-lb:	405	385	370	355	340
Hornady 255 Cowboy	velocity, fps:	725		692		660
	energy, ft-lb:	298		271		247
Magtech 250 LFN	velocity, fps:	750		726		702
	energy, ft-lb:	312		293		274
PMC 250 LFP	velocity, fps:	800		767		736
	energy, ft-lb:	355		331		309
PMC 300 +P+	velocity, fps:	1250	1192	1144	1102	1066
	energy, ft-lb:	1041				
Rem. 225 SWC	velocity, fps:	960		890		832
	energy, ft-lb:	460		395		346
Rem. 250 RLN	velocity, fps:	860		820		780
	energy, ft-lb:	410		375		340
Speer 200 FMJ Blazer	velocity, fps:	1000		938		889
	energy, ft-lb:	444		391		351
Speer 230 Trail Blazer LFN	velocity, fps:	750		716		684
	energy, ft-lb:	287		262		239
Speer 250 Gold Dot	velocity, fps:	900		860		823
	energy, ft-lb:	450		410		376
Win. 225 Silvertip HP	velocity, fps:	920		877		839
	energy, ft-lb:	423		384		352
Win. 255 LRN	velocity, fps:	860		820		780
	energy, ft-lb:	420		380		345
Win. 250 Lead	velocity, fps:	750		720		692
	energy, ft-lb:	312		288		266

.454 Casull

CARTRIDGE BULLET	RANGE, YARDS:	0	25	50	75	100
Federal 300 Trophy Bonded	velocity, fps:	1630	1540	1450	1380	1300
	energy, ft-lb:	1760	1570	1405	1260	1130
Federal 360 CastCore	velocity, fps:	1500	1435	1370	1310	1255
	energy, ft-lb:	1800	1640	1500	1310	1260
Hornady 240 XTP-MAG	velocity, fps:	1900		1679		1483
	energy, ft-lb:	1923		1502		1172
Hornady 300 XTP-MAG	velocity, fps:	1650		1478		1328
	energy, ft-lb:	1813		1455		1175
Magtech 260 SJSP	velocity, fps:	1800		1577		1383
	energy, ft-lb:	1871		1437		1104
Rem. 300 Core-Lokt Ultra	velocity, fps:	1625		1472		1335
	energy, ft-lb:	1759		1442		1187
Speer 300 Gold Dot HP	velocity, fps:	1625		1477		1343
	energy, ft-lb:	1758		1452		1201
Win. 250 JHP	velocity, fps:	1300		1151		1047
	energy, ft-lb:	938		735		608
Win. 260 Partition Gold	velocity, fps:	1800		1605		1427
	energy, ft-lb:	1871		1485		1176
Win. 260 Platinum Tip	velocity, fps:	1800		1596		1414
	eneryg, ft-lb:	1870		1470		1154
Win. 300 JFP	velocity, fps:	1625		1451		1308
	energy, ft-lb:	1759		1413		1141

.460 Smith & Wesson

CARTRIDGE BULLET	RANGE, YARDS:	0	25	50	75	100
Hornady 200 SST	velocity, fps:	2250		2003		1772
	energy, ft-lb:	2248		1395		1081

.475 Linebaugh

CARTRIDGE BULLET	RANGE, YARDS:	0	25	50	75	100
Hornady 400 XTP-MAG	velocity, fps:	1300		1179		1093
	energy, ft-lb:	1501		1235		1060

.480 Ruger

CARTRIDGE BULLET	RANGE, YARDS:	0	25	50	75	100
Hornady 325 XTP-MAG	velocity, fps:	1350		1191		1076
	energy, ft-lb:	1315		1023		835
Hornady 400 XTP-MAG	velocity, fps:	1100		1027		971
	energy, ft-lb:	1075		937		838
Speer 275 Gold Dot HP	velocity, fps:	1450		1284		1152
	energy, ft-lb:	1284		1007		810
Speer 325 SP	velocity, fps:	1350		1224		1124
	energy, ft-lb:	1315		1082		912

.50 Action Express

CARTRIDGE BULLET	RANGE, YARDS:	0	25	50	75	100
Speer 300 Gold Dot HP	velocity, fps:	1550		1361		1207
	energy, ft-lb:	1600		1234		970
Speer 325 UCHP	velocity, fps:	1400		1232		1106
	energy, ft-lb:	1414		1095		883

.500 Smith & Wesson

CARTRIDGE BULLET	RANGE, YARDS:	0	25	50	75	100
Hornady 350 XTP Mag	velocity, fps:	1900		1656		1439
	energy, ft-lb:	2805		2131		1610
Hornady 500 FP-XTP	velocity, fps:	1425		1281		1164
	energy, ft-lb:	2254		1823		1505
Win. 400 Platinum Tip	velocity, fps:	1800		1647		1505
	energy, ft-lb:	2877		2409		2012

HANDLOADING

Barnes Bullets

The All Copper Barnes X-Bullet

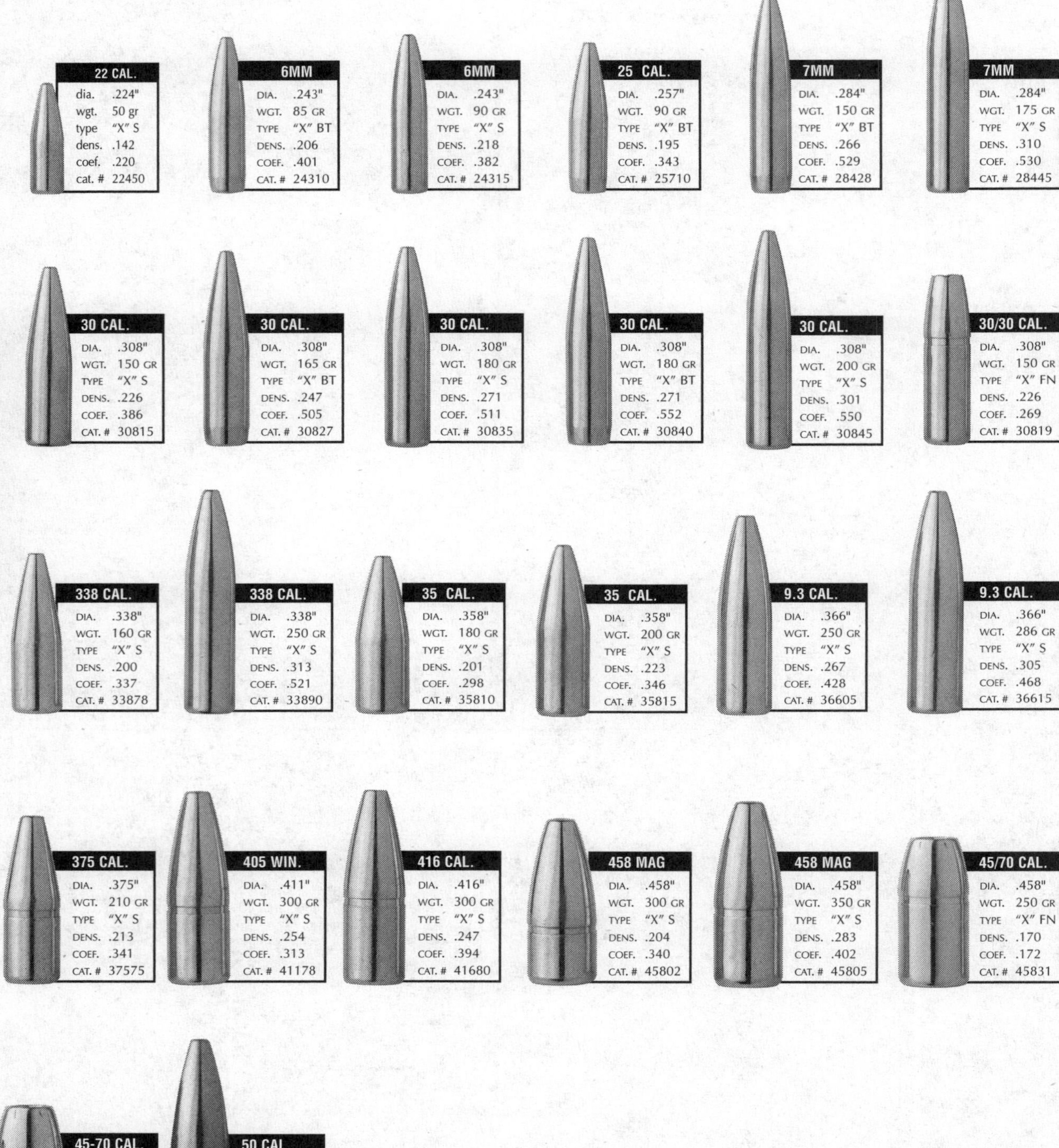

22 CAL. dia. .224" wgt. 50 gr type "X" S dens. .142 coef. .220 cat. # 22450
6MM DIA. .243" WGT. 85 GR TYPE "X" BT DENS. .206 COEF. .401 CAT. # 24310
6MM DIA. .243" WGT. 90 GR TYPE "X" S DENS. .218 COEF. .382 CAT. # 24315
25 CAL. DIA. .257" WGT. 90 GR TYPE "X" BT DENS. .195 COEF. .343 CAT. # 25710
7MM DIA. .284" WGT. 150 GR TYPE "X" BT DENS. .266 COEF. .529 CAT. # 28428
7MM DIA. .284" WGT. 175 GR TYPE "X" S DENS. .310 COEF. .530 CAT. # 28445
30 CAL. DIA. .308" WGT. 150 GR TYPE "X" S DENS. .226 COEF. .386 CAT. # 30815
30 CAL. DIA. .308" WGT. 165 GR TYPE "X" BT DENS. .247 COEF. .505 CAT. # 30827
30 CAL. DIA. .308" WGT. 180 GR TYPE "X" S DENS. .271 COEF. .511 CAT. # 30835
30 CAL. DIA. .308" WGT. 180 GR TYPE "X" BT DENS. .271 COEF. .552 CAT. # 30840
30 CAL. DIA. .308" WGT. 200 GR TYPE "X" S DENS. .301 COEF. .550 CAT. # 30845
30/30 CAL. DIA. .308" WGT. 150 GR TYPE "X" FN DENS. .226 COEF. .269 CAT. # 30819
338 CAL. DIA. .338" WGT. 160 GR TYPE "X" S DENS. .200 COEF. .337 CAT. # 33878
338 CAL. DIA. .338" WGT. 250 GR TYPE "X" S DENS. .313 COEF. .521 CAT. # 33890
35 CAL. DIA. .358" WGT. 180 GR TYPE "X" S DENS. .201 COEF. .298 CAT. # 35810
35 CAL. DIA. .358" WGT. 200 GR TYPE "X" S DENS. .223 COEF. .346 CAT. # 35815
9.3 CAL. DIA. .366" WGT. 250 GR TYPE "X" S DENS. .267 COEF. .428 CAT. # 36605
9.3 CAL. DIA. .366" WGT. 286 GR TYPE "X" S DENS. .305 COEF. .468 CAT. # 36615
375 CAL. DIA. .375" WGT. 210 GR TYPE "X" S DENS. .213 COEF. .341 CAT. # 37575
405 WIN. DIA. .411" WGT. 300 GR TYPE "X" S DENS. .254 COEF. .313 CAT. # 41178
416 CAL. DIA. .416" WGT. 300 GR TYPE "X" S DENS. .247 COEF. .394 CAT. # 41680
458 MAG DIA. .458" WGT. 300 GR TYPE "X" S DENS. .204 COEF. .340 CAT. # 45802
458 MAG DIA. .458" WGT. 350 GR TYPE "X" S DENS. .283 COEF. .402 CAT. # 45805
45/70 CAL. DIA. .458" WGT. 250 GR TYPE "X" FN DENS. .170 COEF. .172 CAT. # 45831
45-70 CAL. DIA. .458" WGT. 300 GR TYPE "X" FN DENS. .206 COEF. .204 CAT. # 45832
50 CAL. DIA. .510" WGT. 647 GR TYPE "X" BT D.S. .355 B.C. .592 CAT. # 51064

Barnes Bullets

Triple-Shock and Expander MZ Muzzleloader Bullets

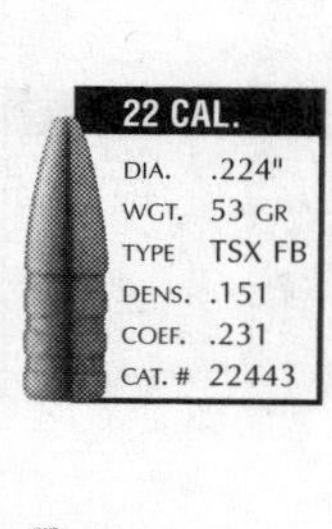

22 CAL.
DIA. .224"
WGT. 53 GR
TYPE TSX FB
DENS. .151
COEF. .231
CAT. # 22443

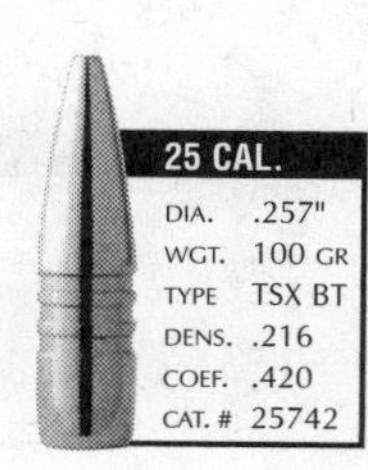

25 CAL.
DIA. .257"
WGT. 100 GR
TYPE TSX BT
DENS. .216
COEF. .420
CAT. # 25742

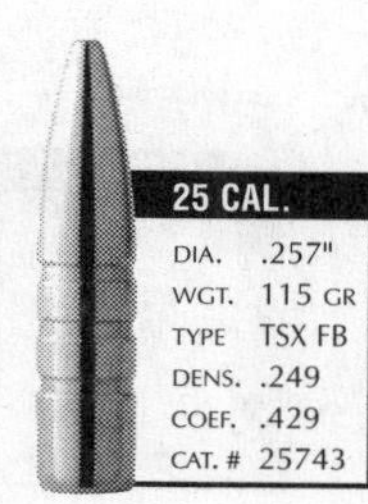

25 CAL.
DIA. .257"
WGT. 115 GR
TYPE TSX FB
DENS. .249
COEF. .429
CAT. # 25743

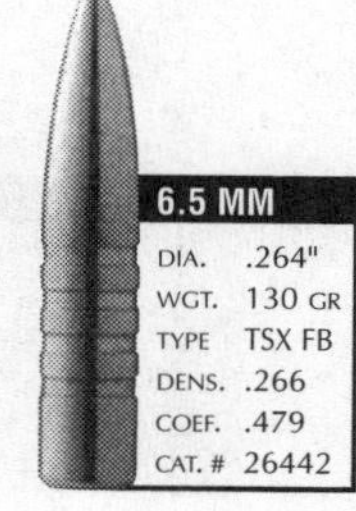

6.5 MM
DIA. .264"
WGT. 130 GR
TYPE TSX FB
DENS. .266
COEF. .479
CAT. # 26442

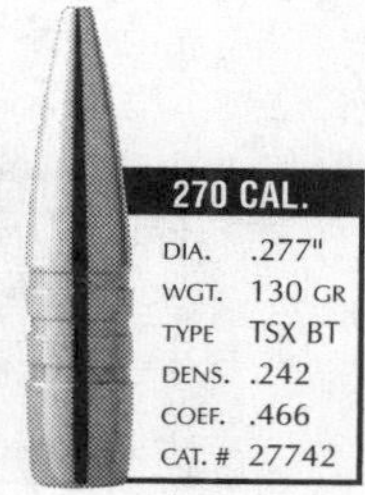

270 CAL.
DIA. .277"
WGT. 130 GR
TYPE TSX BT
DENS. .242
COEF. .466
CAT. # 27742

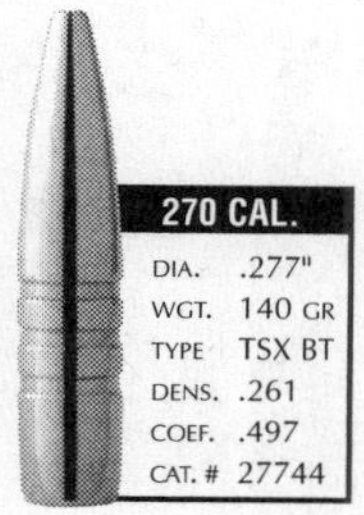

270 CAL.
DIA. .277"
WGT. 140 GR
TYPE TSX BT
DENS. .261
COEF. .497
CAT. # 27744

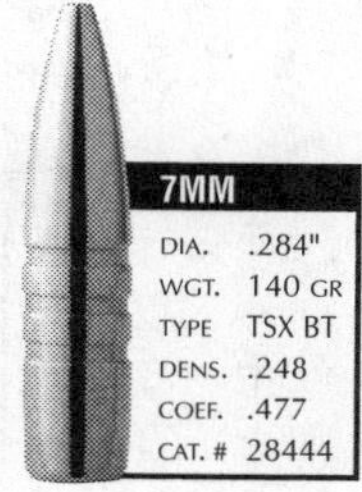

7MM
DIA. .284"
WGT. 140 GR
TYPE TSX BT
DENS. .248
COEF. .477
CAT. # 28444

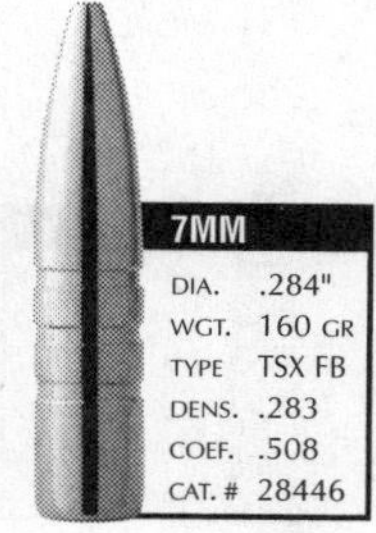

7MM
DIA. .284"
WGT. 160 GR
TYPE TSX FB
DENS. .283
COEF. .508
CAT. # 28446

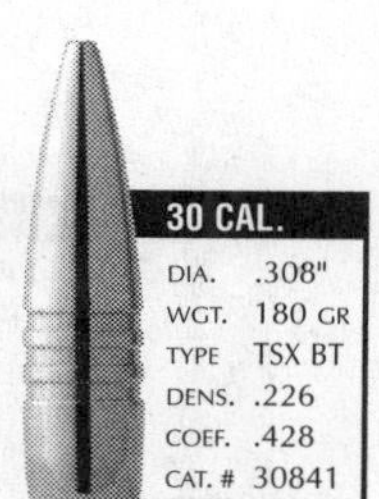

30 CAL.
DIA. .308"
WGT. 180 GR
TYPE TSX BT
DENS. .226
COEF. .428
CAT. # 30841

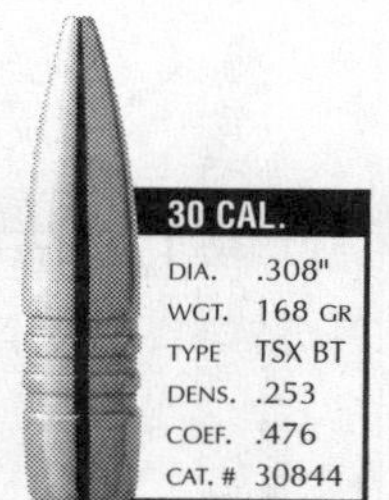

30 CAL.
DIA. .308"
WGT. 168 GR
TYPE TSX BT
DENS. .253
COEF. .476
CAT. # 30844

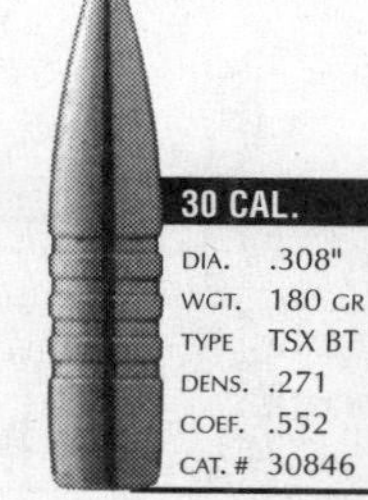

30 CAL.
DIA. .308"
WGT. 180 GR
TYPE TSX BT
DENS. .271
COEF. .552
CAT. # 30846

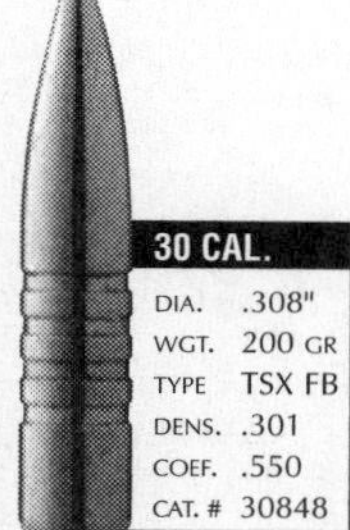

30 CAL.
DIA. .308"
WGT. 200 GR
TYPE TSX FB
DENS. .301
COEF. .550
CAT. # 30848

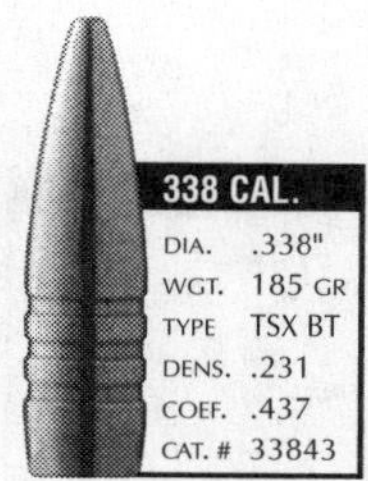

338 CAL.
DIA. .338"
WGT. 185 GR
TYPE TSX BT
DENS. .231
COEF. .437
CAT. # 33843

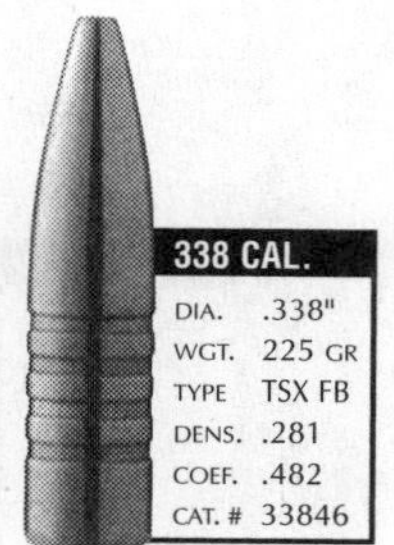

338 CAL.
DIA. .338"
WGT. 225 GR
TYPE TSX FB
DENS. .281
COEF. .482
CAT. # 33846

Triple-Shock Barnes X-Bullet

Greater velocity, lower pressure, and less fouling.

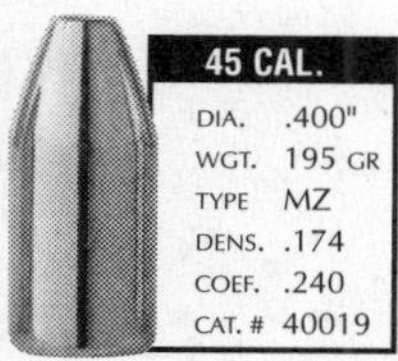

45 CAL.
DIA. .400"
WGT. 195 GR
TYPE MZ
DENS. .174
COEF. .240
CAT. # 40019

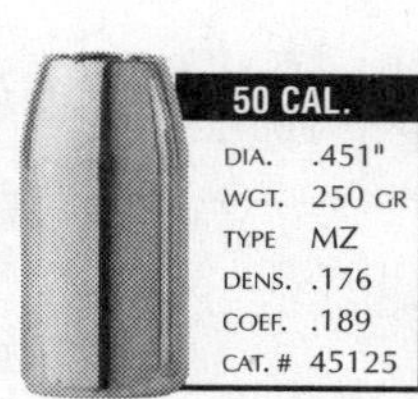

50 CAL.
DIA. .451"
WGT. 250 GR
TYPE MZ
DENS. .176
COEF. .189
CAT. # 45125

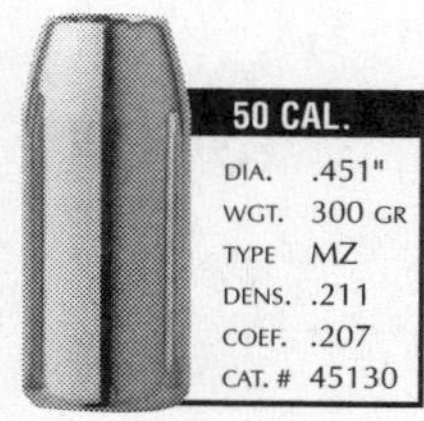

50 CAL.
DIA. .451"
WGT. 300 GR
TYPE MZ
DENS. .211
COEF. .207
CAT. # 45130

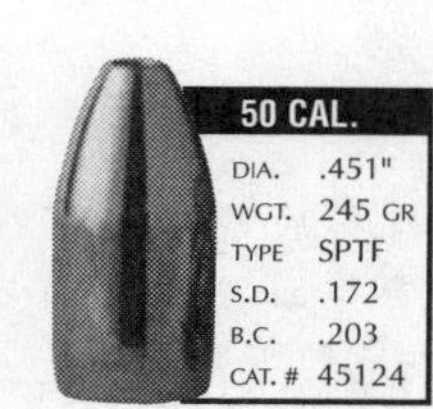

50 CAL.
DIA. .451"
WGT. 245 GR
TYPE SPTF
S.D. .172
B.C. .203
CAT. # 45124

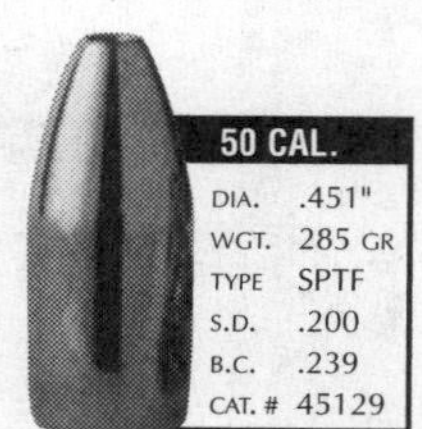

50 CAL.
DIA. .451"
WGT. 285 GR
TYPE SPTF
S.D. .200
B.C. .239
CAT. # 45129

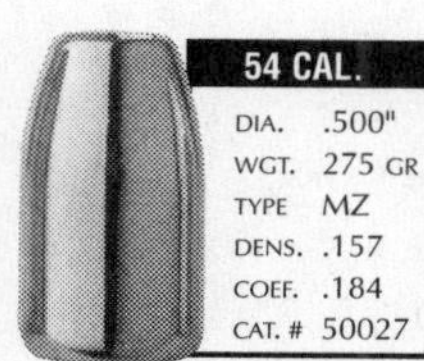

54 CAL.
DIA. .500"
WGT. 275 GR
TYPE MZ
DENS. .157
COEF. .184
CAT. # 50027

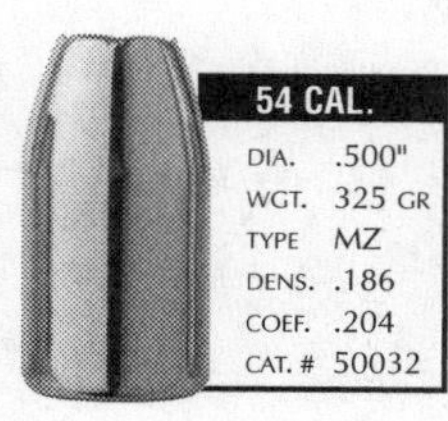

54 CAL.
DIA. .500"
WGT. 325 GR
TYPE MZ
DENS. .186
COEF. .204
CAT. # 50032

Expander MZ Muzzleloader Bullets

With only one shot available, it better be with the best.

Barnes Bullets

XLC Coated X-Bullets

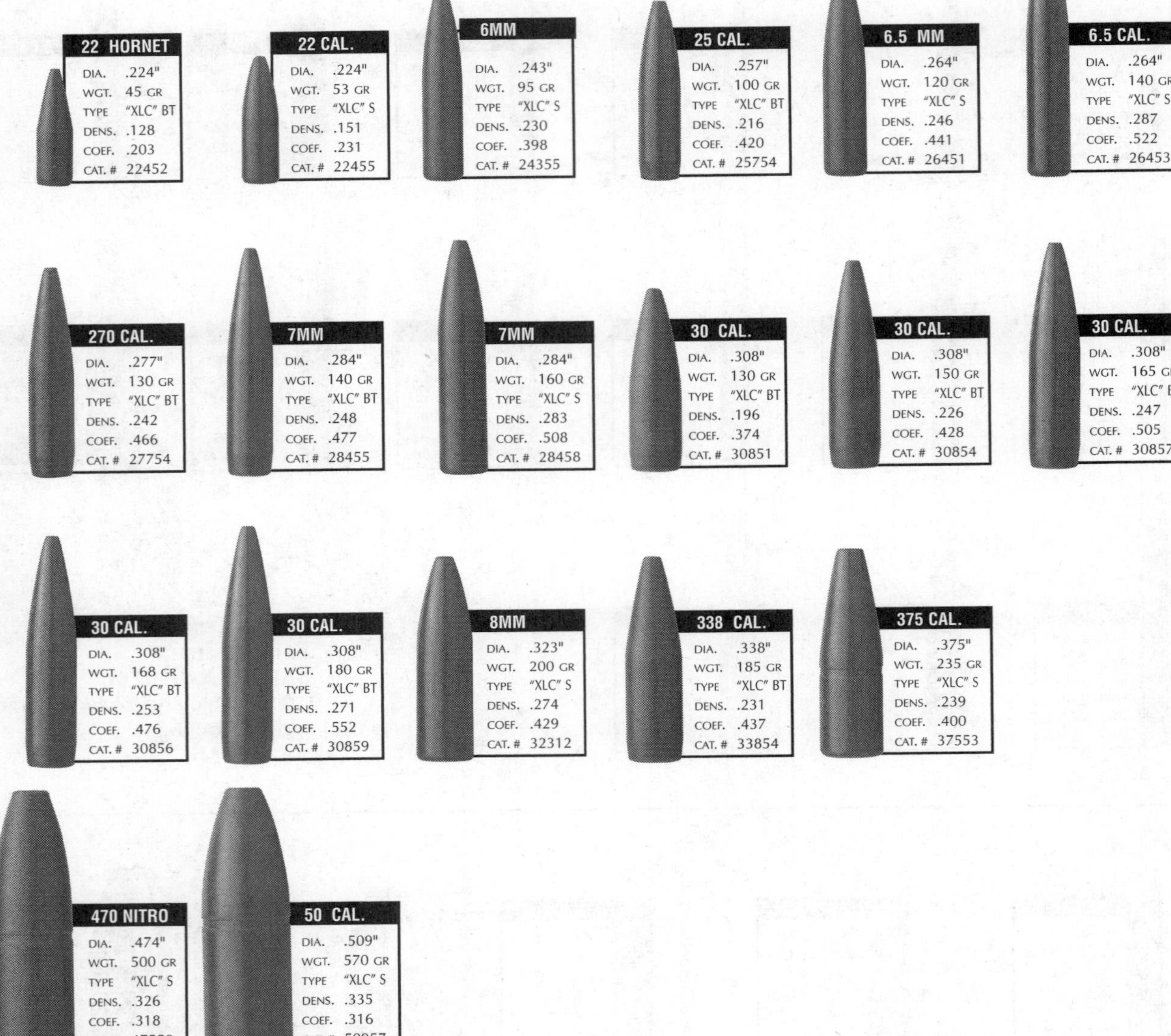

22 HORNET
DIA. .224" WGT. 45 GR TYPE "XLC" BT DENS. .128 COEF. .203 CAT. # 22452
22 CAL.
DIA. .224" WGT. 53 GR TYPE "XLC" S DENS. .151 COEF. .231 CAT. # 22455
6MM
DIA. .243" WGT. 95 GR TYPE "XLC" S DENS. .230 COEF. .398 CAT. # 24355
25 CAL.
DIA. .257" WGT. 100 GR TYPE "XLC" BT DENS. .216 COEF. .420 CAT. # 25754
6.5 MM
DIA. .264" WGT. 120 GR TYPE "XLC" S DENS. .246 COEF. .441 CAT. # 26451
6.5 CAL.
DIA. .264" WGT. 140 GR TYPE "XLC" S DENS. .287 COEF. .522 CAT. # 26453
270 CAL.
DIA. .277" WGT. 130 GR TYPE "XLC" BT DENS. .242 COEF. .466 CAT. # 27754
7MM
DIA. .284" WGT. 140 GR TYPE "XLC" BT DENS. .248 COEF. .477 CAT. # 28455
7MM
DIA. .284" WGT. 160 GR TYPE "XLC" S DENS. .283 COEF. .508 CAT. # 28458
30 CAL.
DIA. .308" WGT. 130 GR TYPE "XLC" BT DENS. .196 COEF. .374 CAT. # 30851
30 CAL.
DIA. .308" WGT. 150 GR TYPE "XLC" BT DENS. .226 COEF. .428 CAT. # 30854
30 CAL.
DIA. .308" WGT. 165 GR TYPE "XLC" BT DENS. .247 COEF. .505 CAT. # 30857
30 CAL.
DIA. .308" WGT. 168 GR TYPE "XLC" BT DENS. .253 COEF. .476 CAT. # 30856
30 CAL.
DIA. .308" WGT. 180 GR TYPE "XLC" BT DENS. .271 COEF. .552 CAT. # 30859
8MM
DIA. .323" WGT. 200 GR TYPE "XLC" S DENS. .274 COEF. .429 CAT. # 32312
338 CAL.
DIA. .338" WGT. 185 GR TYPE "XLC" BT DENS. .231 COEF. .437 CAT. # 33854
375 CAL.
DIA. .375" WGT. 235 GR TYPE "XLC" S DENS. .239 COEF. .400 CAT. # 37553
470 NITRO
DIA. .474" WGT. 500 GR TYPE "XLC" S DENS. .326 COEF. .318 CAT. # 47550
50 CAL.
DIA. .509" WGT. 570 GR TYPE "XLC" S DENS. .335 COEF. .316 CAT. # 50957

Barnes Bullets

Barnes Burner Varmin-A-Tor Bullet

Taking varmint hunting to new extremes in explosive accuracy.

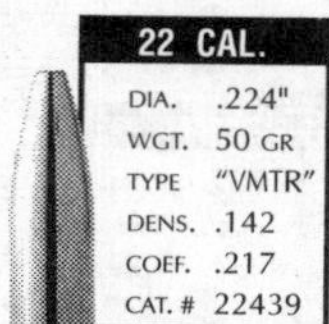
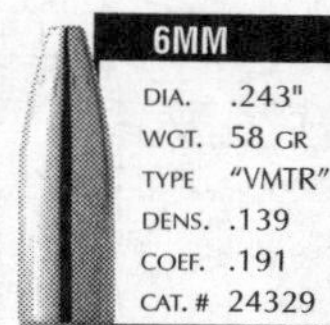
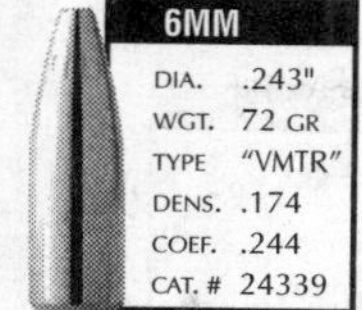

	DIA.	WGT.	TYPE	DENS.	COEF.	CAT. #
22 CAL.	.224"	40 GR	"VMTR"	.114	.175	22429
22 CAL.	.224"	50 GR	"VMTR"	.142	.217	22439
6MM	.243"	58 GR	"VMTR"	.139	.191	24329
6MM	.243"	72 GR	"VMTR"	.174	.244	24339

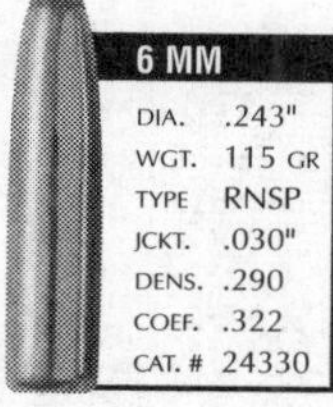

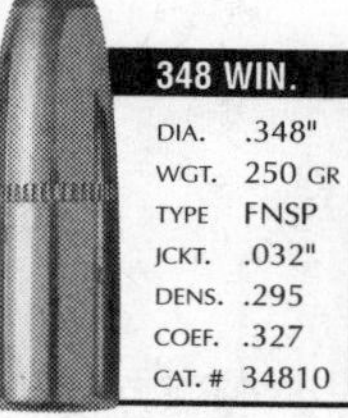

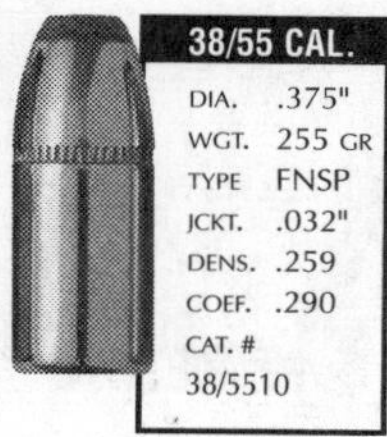
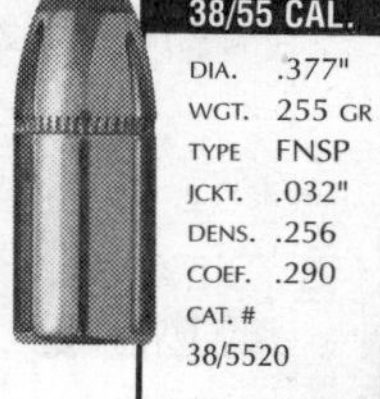

	DIA.	WGT.	TYPE	JCKT.	DENS.	COEF.	CAT. #
6 MM	.243"	115 GR	RNSP	.030"	.290	.322	24330
348 WIN.	.348"	220 GR	FNSP	.032"	.260	.301	34805
348 WIN.	.348"	250 GR	FNSP	.032"	.295	.327	34810
375 WIN.	.375"	255 GR	FNSP	.032"	.259	.290	375W20
38/55 CAL.	.375"	255 GR	FNSP	.032"	.259	.290	38/5510
38/55 CAL.	.377"	255 GR	FNSP	.032"	.256	.290	38/5520

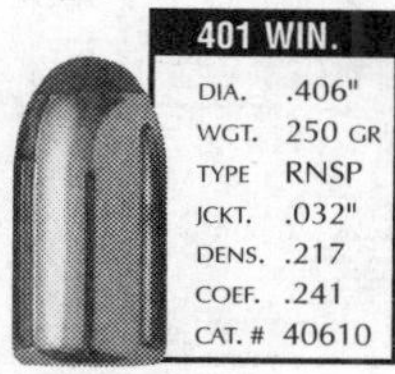

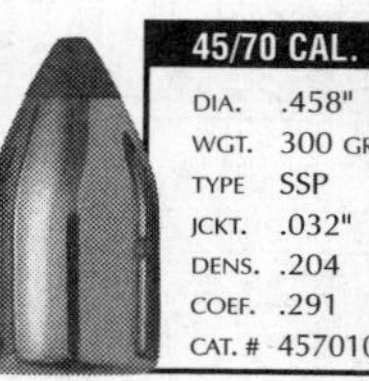
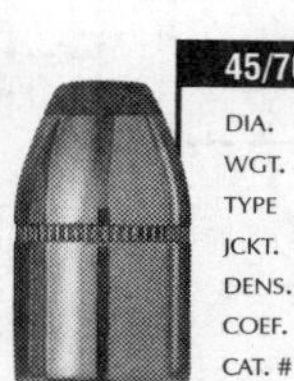
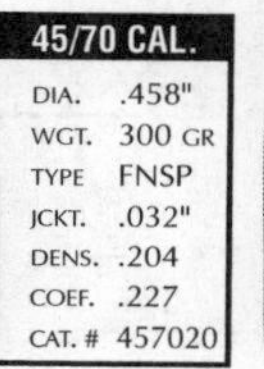
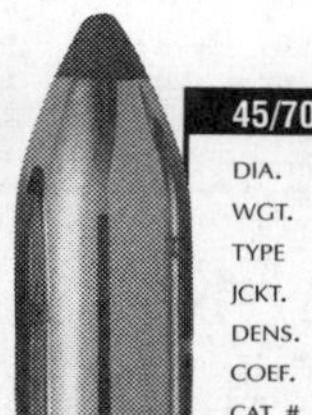

	DIA.	WGT.	TYPE	JCKT.	DENS.	COEF.	CAT. #
401 WIN.	.406"	250 GR	RNSP	.032"	.217	.241	40610
40/65 WIN.	.406"	250 GR	FNSP	.032"	.217	.231	40611
45/70 CAL.	.458"	300 GR	SSP	.032"	.204	.291	457010
45/70 CAL.	.458"	300 GR	FNSP	.032"	.204	.227	457020
45/70 CAL.	.458"	400 GR	SSP	.032"	.272	.389	457030
45/70 CAL.	.458"	400 GR	FNSP	.032"	.272	.302	457040

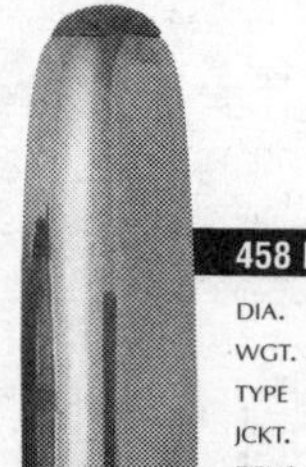
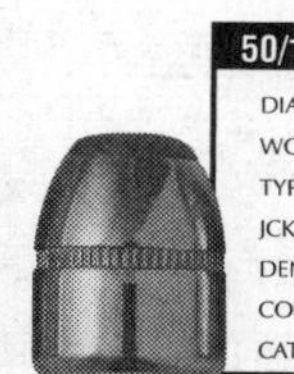
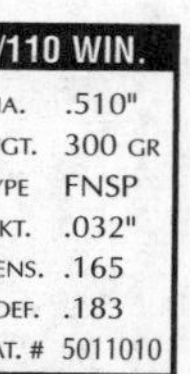
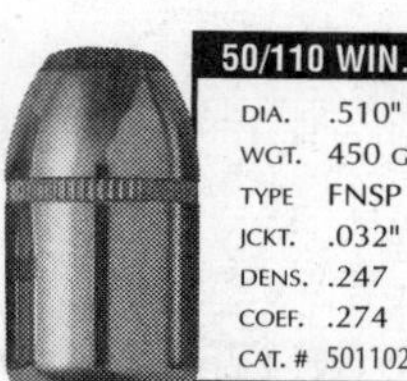

	DIA.	WGT.	TYPE	JCKT.	DENS.	COEF.	CAT. #
458 MAG.	.458"	600 GR	RNSP	.049"	.409	.454	45860
50/110 WIN.	.510"	300 GR	FNSP	.032"	.165	.183	5011010
50/110 WIN.	.510"	450 GR	FNSP	.032"	.247	.274	5011020

Copper-Jacket/Lead Core Barnes Original

XPB Pistol Bullet Features

- X-Bullet technology
- Increased penetration over jacketed lead-core bullets
- Expands like no other
- Superior weight retention
- Available in factory ammunition

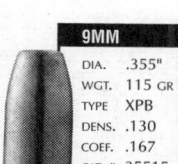

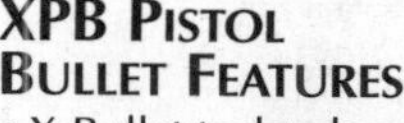

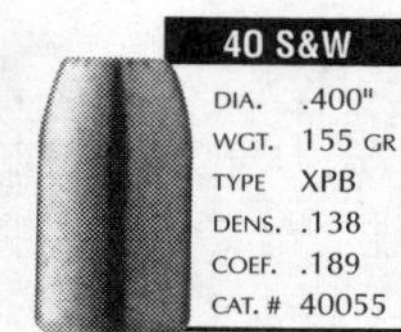
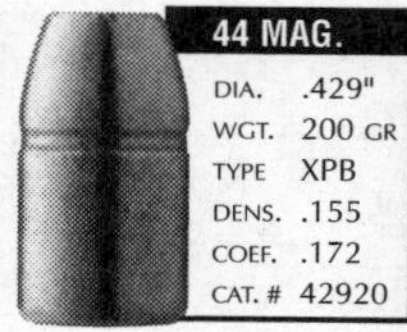
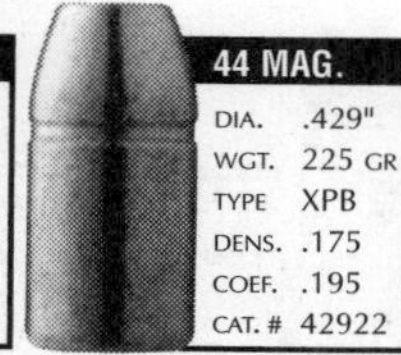
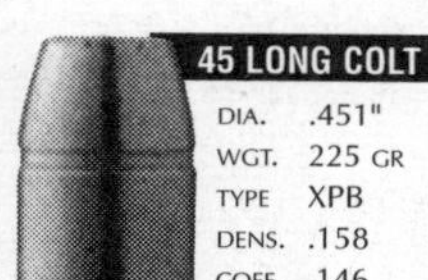

	DIA.	WGT.	TYPE	DENS.	COEF.	CAT. #
9MM	.355"	115 GR	XPB	.130	.167	35515
40 S&W	.400"	155 GR	XPB	.138	.189	40055
44 MAG.	.429"	200 GR	XPB	.155	.172	42920
44 MAG.	.429"	225 GR	XPB	.175	.195	42922
45 LONG COLT	.451"	225 GR	XPB	.158	.146	45120

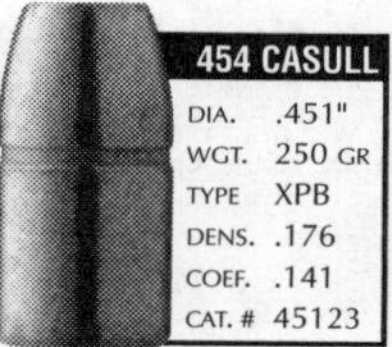
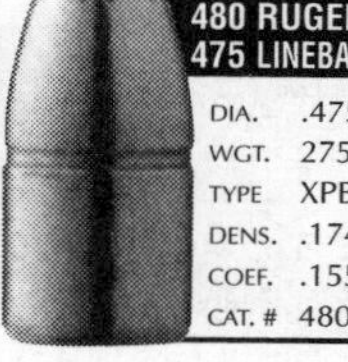
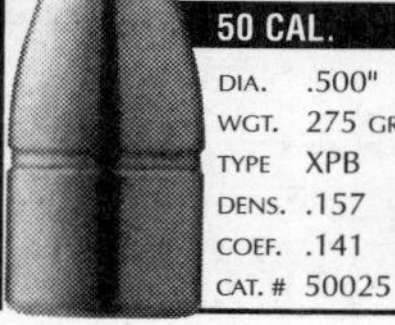
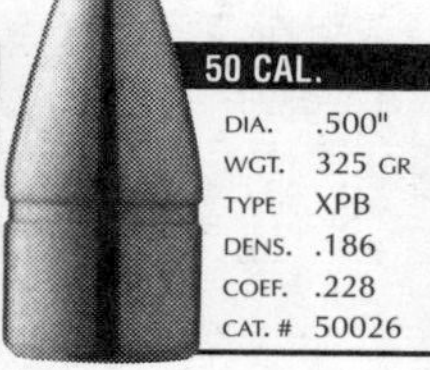
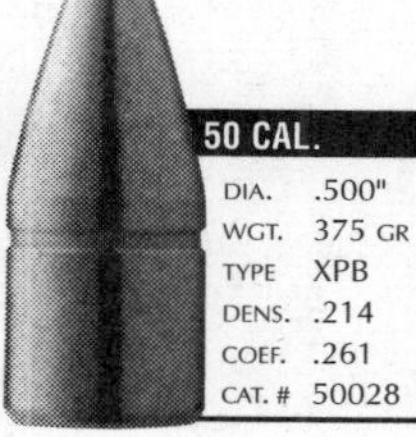

	DIA.	WGT.	TYPE	DENS.	COEF.	CAT. #
44 ACP	.451"	185 GR	XPB	.130	.167	45185
454 CASULL	.451"	250 GR	XPB	.176	.141	45123
480 RUGER 475 LINEBAUGH	.475"	275 GR	XPB	.174	.155	48010
50 CAL.	.500"	275 GR	XPB	.157	.141	50025
50 CAL.	.500"	325 GR	XPB	.186	.228	50026
50 CAL.	.500"	375 GR	XPB	.214	.261	50028

Barnes Bullets

Barnes Solids

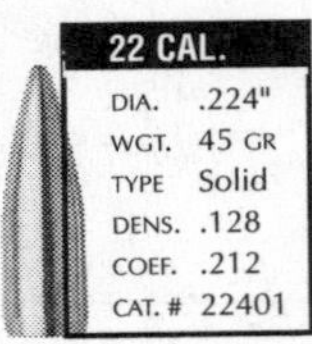

22 CAL.
DIA. .224"
WGT. 45 GR
TYPE Solid
DENS. .128
COEF. .212
CAT. # 22401

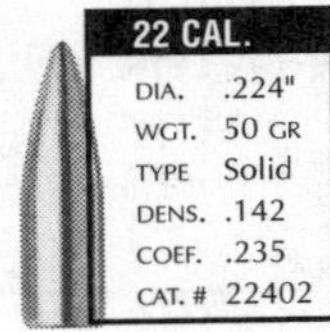

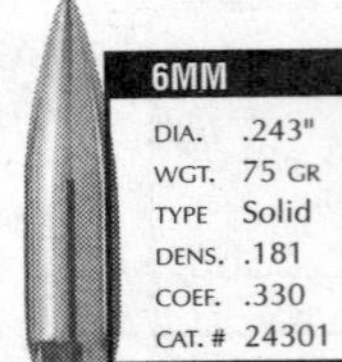

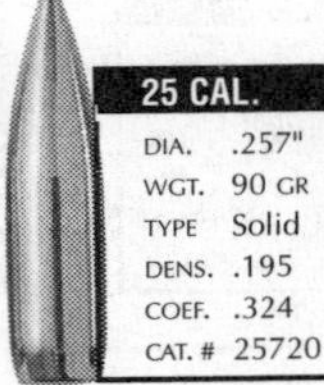

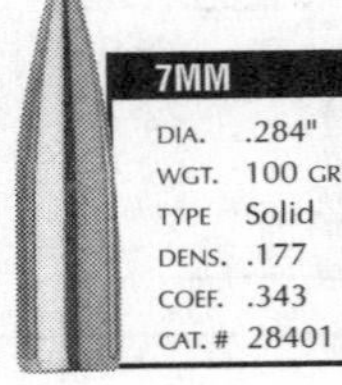

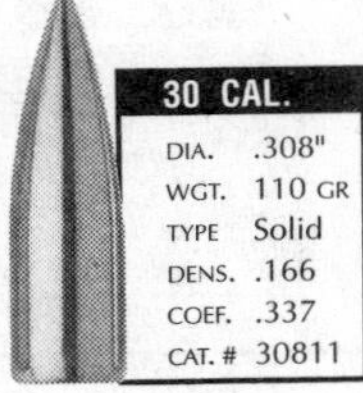

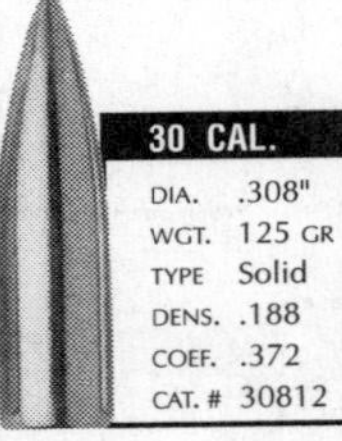

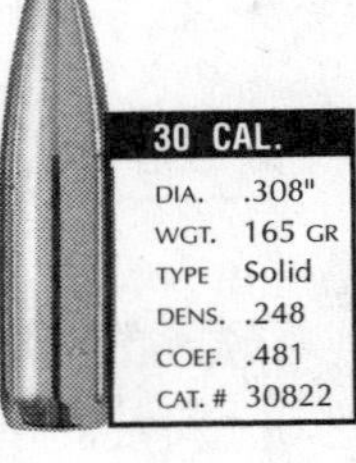

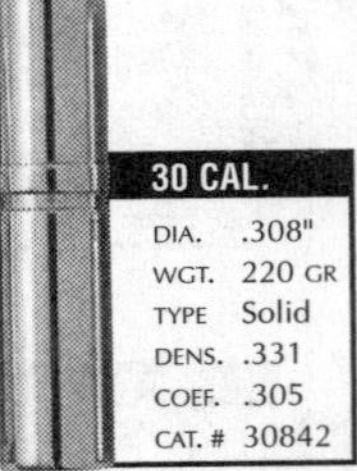

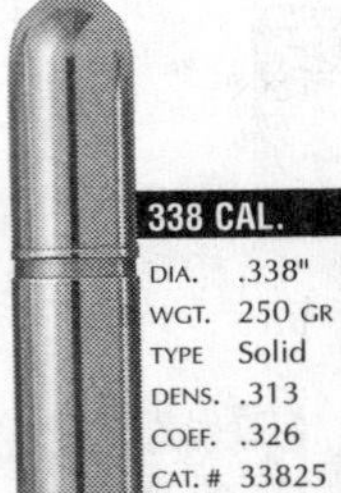

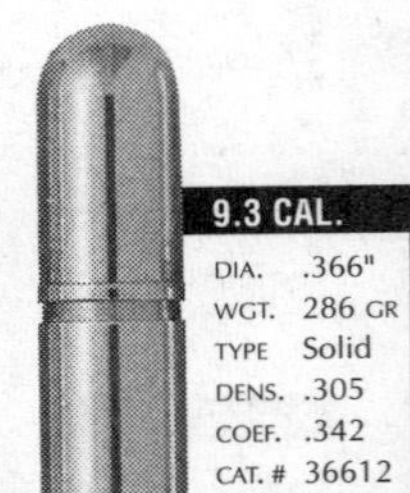

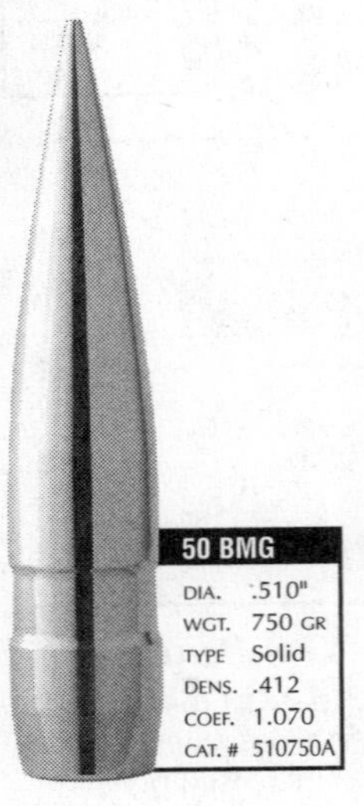

50 BMG
DIA. .510"
WGT. 750 GR
TYPE Solid
DENS. .412
COEF.
CAT. # 510750

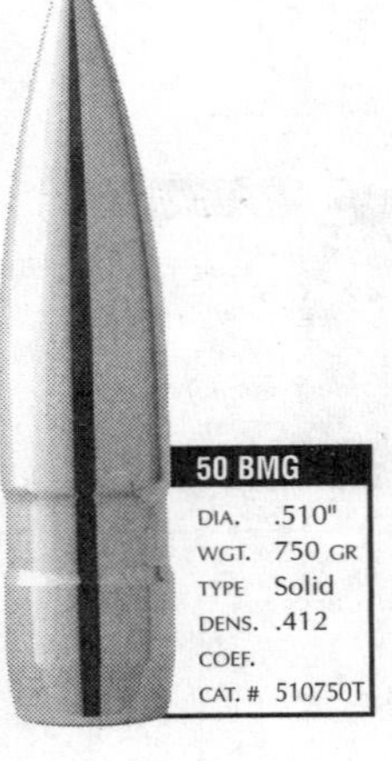

50 BMG
DIA. .510"
WGT. 750 GR
TYPE Solid
DENS. .412
COEF.
CAT. # 510750T

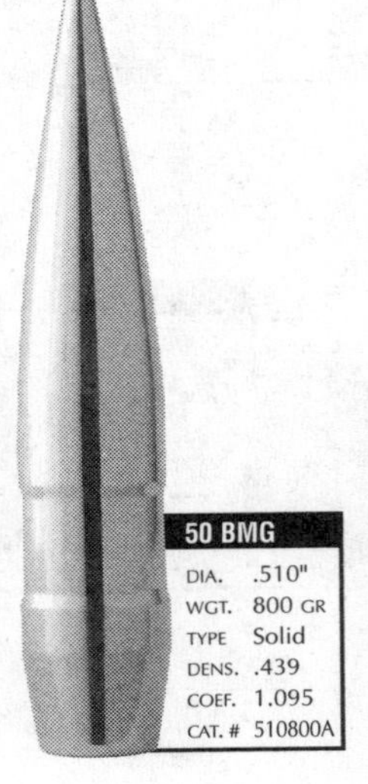

50 BMG
DIA. .510"
WGT. 800 GR
TYPE Solid
DENS. .439
COEF. 1.095
CAT. # 510800A

Berger Bullets

Famous for their superior performance in benchrest matches, Berger bullets now include hunting designs. From .17 to .30, all Bergers feature 14 jackets with wall concentricity tolerance of .0003. Lead cores are 99.9% pure and swaged in dies to within .0001 of round. Berger's line includes several profiles: Low Drag, Very Low Drag, Length Tolerant, Maximum-Expansion, besides standard flat-base and standard boat-tail.

ITEM	WEIGHT	TWIST
17 Cal.	15 Gr. Varmint	12
17 Cal.	18 Gr. Varmint	12
17 Cal.	20 Gr.*	12
17 Cal.	22 Gr.*	11
17 Cal.	25 Gr.*	10
17 Cal.	37 Gr. VLD	6
20 Cal.	30 Gr. Varmint	14
20 Cal.	35 Gr. Varmint	14
20 Cal.	40 Gr. BT Varmint	12
20 Cal.	50 Gr. BT Varmint	9
22 Cal.	30 Varmint	15
22 Cal.	35 Varmint	15
22 Cal.	40 Varmint	15
22 Cal.	45 Gr.*	15
22 Cal.	50 Gr.*	14
22 Cal.	52 Gr.*	14
22 Cal.	55 Gr.*	14
22 Cal.	60 Gr.*	12
22 Cal.	62 Gr.*	12
22 Cal.	64 Gr.*	12
22 Cal.	70 Gr. VLD	9
22 Cal.	70 Gr.BT	10
22 Cal.	73 Gr. BT	9
22 Cal.	75 Gr. VLD	9
22 Cal.	80 Gr. VLD	8
(6mm) Cal.	60 Gr.*	14
(6mm) Cal.	62 Gr.*	14
(6mm) Cal.	65 Gr.*	13
(6mm) Cal.	65 Gr. Short	14
(6mm) Cal.	65 Gr. BT	13
(6mm) Cal.	66 Gr. High BC FB	13
(6mm) Cal.	68 Gr.*	13
(6mm) Cal.	69 Gr. High BC FB	12
(6mm) Cal.	70 Gr.*	13
(6mm) Cal.	71 Gr. BT*	12
(6mm) Cal.	74 Gr.*	13
(6mm) Cal.	80 Gr.*	12
(6mm) Cal.	88 Gr. High BC FB	10
(6mm) Cal.	90 Gr. BT*	10
(6mm) Cal.	95 Gr. VLD	9
(6mm) Cal.	105 Gr. LTB	9
(6mm) Cal.	105 Gr. VLD	8
(6mm) Cal.	115 Gr. VLD	7
25 Cal.	72 Gr.*	15
25 Cal.	78 Gr.*	13
25 Cal.	82 Gr.*	14
25 Cal.	87 Gr.*	13
25 Cal.	95 Gr.*	12
25 Cal.	110 Gr.*	12
25 Cal.	115 Gr. VLD	10
(6.5mm) Cal.	140 Gr. VLD	9
(7mm) Cal.	168 Gr. VLD	10
(7mm) Cal.	180 Gr. VLD	9
30 Cal.	110 Gr.*	19
30 Cal.	125 Gr.*	19
30 Cal.	135 Gr.*	16
30 Cal.	150 Gr.*	15
30 Cal.	155 Gr. LTB	14
30 Cal.	155 Gr. VLD	14
30 Cal.	168 Gr. LTB	13
30 Cal.	168 Gr. VLD	13
30 Cal.	175 Gr. VLD	13
30 Cal.	185 Gr. VLD	12
30 Cal.	190 Gr. VLD	12
30 Cal.	210 Gr. VLD	11

15 Gr. Varmint · 18 Gr. Varmint · 20 Gr. · 22 Gr. · 25 Gr. · 30 Gr. · 37 Gr. VLD

30 Gr. Varmint · 35 Gr. Varmint · 40 Gr. BT Varmint · 50 Gr. BT Varmint

30 Gr. Varmint · 35 Gr. Varmint · 40 Gr. Varmint · 45 Gr. · 50 Gr. · 52 Gr. · 55 Gr. · 60 Gr. · 62 Gr. · 64 Gr. · 70 Gr. VLD · 70 Gr. BT · 73 Gr. BT · 75 Gr. VLD · 80 Gr. VLD

60 Gr. · 62 Gr. · 65 Gr. · 65 Gr. Short · 65 Gr. BT · 65 Gr. High BC FB · 68 Gr. · 69 Gr. High BC FB

70 Gr. · 71 Gr. BT · 74 Gr. · 80 Gr. · 88 Gr. High BC FB · 90 Gr. BT · 95 Gr. VLD · 105 Gr. LTB · 105 Gr. VLD · 115 Gr. VLD

140 Gr. VLD · 168 Gr. VLD · 180 Gr. VLD

72 Gr. · 78 Gr. · 87 Gr. · 95 Gr. · 110 Gr. · 115 Gr. VLD

110 Gr. · 125 Gr. · 135 Gr. · 150 Gr. · 155 Gr. VLD · 155 Gr. BT · 168 Gr. BT · 168 Gr. VLD · 175 Gr. VLD · 185 Gr. VLD · 190 Gr. VLD · 210Gr. VLD

Cor-Bon Handloading

Specializing in high-performance handgun ammo, Cor-Bon collaborated with Smith & Wesson to develop the .500 S&W cartridge. From the S&W X-Frame revolver, it easily outperforms the .454 Casull. A 275-grain Barnes X-Bullet clocks 1665 fps – about the same speed as a 400-grain Hawk Softpoint, which turns up 2500 foot-pounds of energy. The 440 lead bullet from Cast Performance leaves at 1625 fps, to generate 2580 foot-pounds. The newest in Cor-Bon's line is ammunition loaded with Pow'Rball, a controlled expansion bullet with a polymer ball in the nose. It's designed to penetrate glass and light sheet metal but expand readily in flesh.

Lapua Handloading

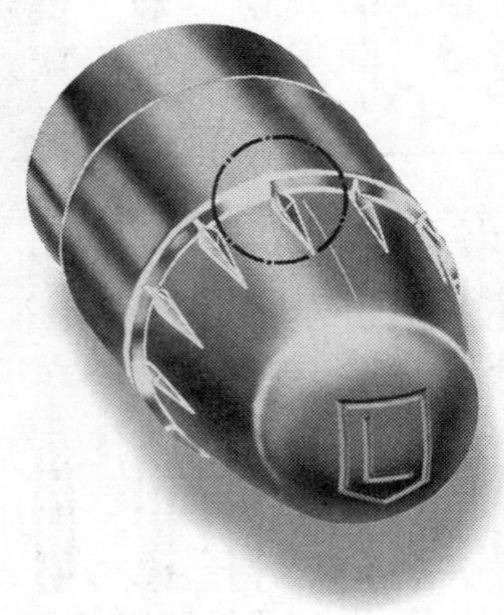

Naturalis is Lapua's copper expanding bullet with a hollow, polymer-capped nose. Factory loads include 130-grain 6.5x55, 180-grain .308 Winchester, 180-grain .30-06 and 270-grain 9.3x62. Lapua Aficionado centerfire target loads are available in .223 and .308 with 69-grain and 167-grain match bullets. A line of .22 rim fire rounds carries the Lapua Signum bullet, whose tiny lube grooves on the front of a diving band minimize gumming in bore and chamber. The bullet's design reduces pressure by 15 percent, say the people who've tested them. Lapua offers 13 kinds of .22 ammo, including specialty rounds for pistol and biathlon competition.

Hornady Rifle Bullets

The Hornady SST bullet is now available for black powder shooters. The 200-grain .40 and 250- and 300-grain .45 bullets are meant for use in sabot sleeves. They feature a jacketed lead core with the signature red polymer tip. The SST has lead also to Hornady's newest big game bullet, the Interbond. Essentially, it's an SST with a thicker jacket that has an inner "expansion control ring" near the front of the shank. Jacket and core are also bonded to ensure deep penetration and high weight retention. Though it typically opens to double its initial diameter, the Interbond bullet can be expected to hold 90 percent of its weight in the animal.

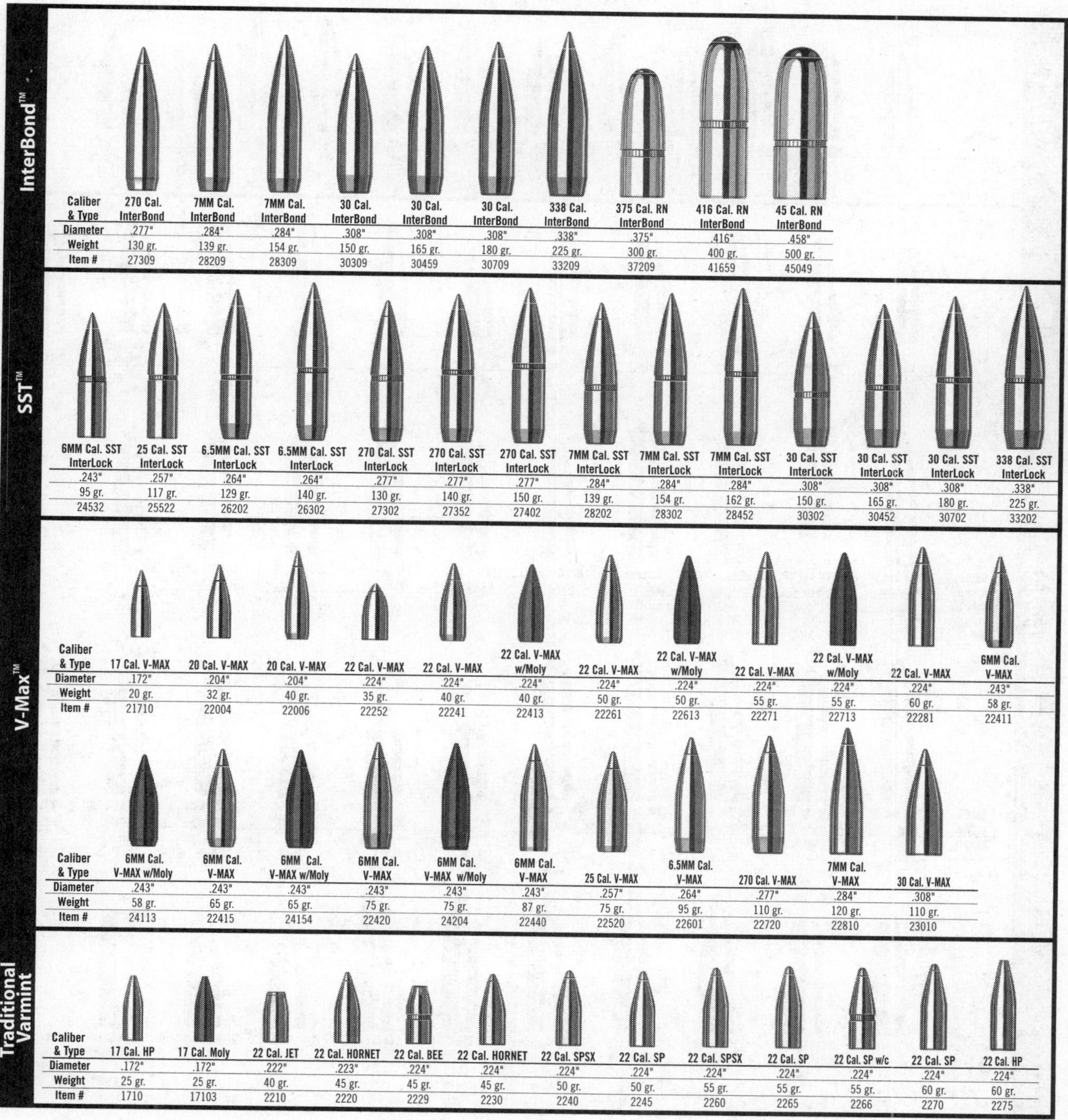

InterBond™

Caliber & Type	270 Cal. InterBond	7MM Cal. InterBond	7MM Cal. InterBond	30 Cal. InterBond	30 Cal. InterBond	30 Cal. InterBond	338 Cal. InterBond	375 Cal. RN InterBond	416 Cal. RN InterBond	45 Cal. RN InterBond
Diameter	.277"	.284"	.284"	.308"	.308"	.308"	.338"	.375"	.416"	.458"
Weight	130 gr.	139 gr.	154 gr.	150 gr.	165 gr.	180 gr.	225 gr.	300 gr.	400 gr.	500 gr.
Item #	27309	28209	28309	30309	30459	30709	33209	37209	41659	45049

SST™

6MM Cal. SST InterLock	25 Cal. SST InterLock	6.5MM Cal. SST InterLock	6.5MM Cal. SST InterLock	270 Cal. SST InterLock	270 Cal. SST InterLock	270 Cal. SST InterLock	7MM Cal. SST InterLock	7MM Cal. SST InterLock	7MM Cal. SST InterLock	30 Cal. SST InterLock	30 Cal. SST InterLock	30 Cal. SST InterLock	338 Cal. SST InterLock
.243"	.257"	.264"	.264"	.277"	.277"	.277"	.284"	.284"	.284"	.308"	.308"	.308"	.338"
95 gr.	117 gr.	129 gr.	140 gr.	130 gr.	140 gr.	150 gr.	139 gr.	154 gr.	162 gr.	150 gr.	165 gr.	180 gr.	225 gr.
24532	25522	26202	26302	27302	27352	27402	28202	28302	28452	30302	30452	30702	33202

V-Max™

Caliber & Type	17 Cal. V-MAX	20 Cal. V-MAX	20 Cal. V-MAX	22 Cal. V-MAX	22 Cal. V-MAX	22 Cal. V-MAX w/Moly	22 Cal. V-MAX	22 Cal. V-MAX w/Moly	22 Cal. V-MAX	22 Cal. V-MAX w/Moly	22 Cal. V-MAX	6MM Cal. V-MAX
Diameter	.172"	.204"	.204"	.224"	.224"	.224"	.224"	.224"	.224"	.224"	.224"	.243"
Weight	20 gr.	32 gr.	40 gr.	35 gr.	40 gr.	40 gr.	50 gr.	50 gr.	55 gr.	55 gr.	60 gr.	58 gr.
Item #	21710	22004	22006	22252	22241	22413	22261	22613	22271	22713	22281	22411

Caliber & Type	6MM Cal. V-MAX w/Moly	6MM Cal. V-MAX	6MM Cal. V-MAX w/Moly	6MM Cal. V-MAX	6MM Cal. V-MAX w/Moly	6MM Cal. V-MAX	25 Cal. V-MAX	6.5MM Cal. V-MAX	270 Cal. V-MAX	7MM Cal. V-MAX	30 Cal. V-MAX
Diameter	.243"	.243"	.243"	.243"	.243"	.243"	.257"	.264"	.277"	.284"	.308"
Weight	58 gr.	65 gr.	65 gr.	75 gr.	75 gr.	87 gr.	75 gr.	95 gr.	110 gr.	120 gr.	110 gr.
Item #	24113	22415	24154	22420	24204	22440	22520	22601	22720	22810	23010

Traditional Varmint

Caliber & Type	17 Cal. HP	17 Cal. Moly	22 Cal. JET	22 Cal. HORNET	22 Cal. BEE	22 Cal. HORNET	22 Cal. SPSX	22 Cal. SP	22 Cal. SPSX	22 Cal. SP	22 Cal. SP w/c	22 Cal. SP	22 Cal. HP
Diameter	.172"	.172"	.222"	.223"	.224"	.224"	.224"	.224"	.224"	.224"	.224"	.224"	.224"
Weight	25 gr.	25 gr.	40 gr.	45 gr.	45 gr.	45 gr.	50 gr.	50 gr.	55 gr.	55 gr.	55 gr.	60 gr.	60 gr.
Item #	1710	17103	2210	2220	2229	2230	2240	2245	2260	2265	2266	2270	2275

HANDLOADING

Hornady Rifle Bullets

Traditional Varmint

Caliber & Type	6MM SP	6MM HP	6MM BTHP	25 Cal. HP	25 Cal. SP	270 Cal. SP	270 Cal. HP	7MM HP	7MM SP	7MM HP	30 Cal. SJ	30 Cal. SP
Diameter	.243"	.243"	.243"	.257"	.257"	.277"	.277"	.284"	.284"	.284"	.308"	.308"
Weight	70 gr.	75 gr.	87 gr.	75 gr.	87 gr.	100 gr.	110 gr.	100 gr.	120 gr.	120 gr.	100 gr.	110 gr.
Item #	2410	2420	2442	2520	2530	2710	2720	2800	2810	2815	3005	3010

Traditional Hunting

Caliber & Type	22 Cal. SP	6MM SP	6MM SP InterLock	6MM BTSP InterLock	6MM RN InterLock	25 Cal. FP	25 Cal. SP InterLock	25 Cal. BTSP InterLock	25 Cal. RN InterLock	25 Cal. HP InterLock	6.5MM Cal. SP
Diameter	.227"	.243"	.243"	.243"	.243"	.257"	.257"	.257"	.257"	.257"	.264"
Weight	70 gr.	87 gr.	100 gr.	100 gr.	100 gr.	60 gr.	100 gr.	117 gr.	117 gr.	120 gr.	100 gr.
Item #	2280	2440	2450	2453`	2455	2510	2540	2552	2550	2560	2610

Caliber & Type	6.5MM Cal. SP InterLock	6.5MM Cal. SP InterLock	6.5MM Cal. RN InterLock	Carcano 6.5MM Cal. RN	270 Cal. SP InterLock	270 Cal. BTSP InterLock	270 Cal. SP InterLock	270 Cal. RN InterLock	7MM Cal. SP InterLock	7MM Cal. BTSP InterLock
Diameter	.264"	.264"	.264"	.267"	.277"	.277"	.277"	.277"	.284"	.284"
Weight	129 gr.	140 gr.	160 gr.	160 gr.	130 gr.	140 gr.	150 gr.	150 gr.	139 gr.	139 gr.
Item #	2620	2630	2640	2645	2730	2735	2740	2745	2820	2825

Caliber & Type	7MM Cal. SP InterLock	7MM Cal. RN InterLock	7MM Cal. BTSP InterLock	7MM Cal. SP InterLock	7MM Cal. RN InterLock	30 Cal. RN	30 Cal. SP	30 Cal. SP InterLock	30 Cal. BTSP InterLock	30 Cal. RN (30-30) InterLock	30 Cal. SP InterLock
Diameter	.284"	.284"	.284"	.284"	.284"	.308"	.308"	.308"	.308"	.308"	.308"
Weight	154 gr.	154 gr.	162 gr.	175 gr.	175 gr.	110 gr.	130 gr.	150 gr.	150 gr.	150 gr.	165 gr.
Item #	2830	2835	2845	2850	2855	3015	3020	3031	3033	3035	3040

Caliber & Type	30 Cal. BTSP InterLock	30 Cal. FP (30-30) InterLock	30 Cal. SP InterLock	30 Cal. BTSP InterLock	30 Cal. RN InterLock	30 Cal. BTSP InterLock	30 Cal. RN InterLock	7.62 X 39MM Cal. SP	303 Cal. SP InterLock	303 Cal. RN InterLock
Diameter	.308"	.308"	.308"	.308"	.308"	.308"	.308"	.310"	.312"	.312"
Weight	165 gr.	170 gr.	180 gr.	180 gr.	180 gr.	190 gr.	220 gr.	123 gr.	150 gr.	174 gr.
Item #	3045	3060	3070	3072	3075	3085	3090	3140	3120	3130

Hornady Rifle Bullets

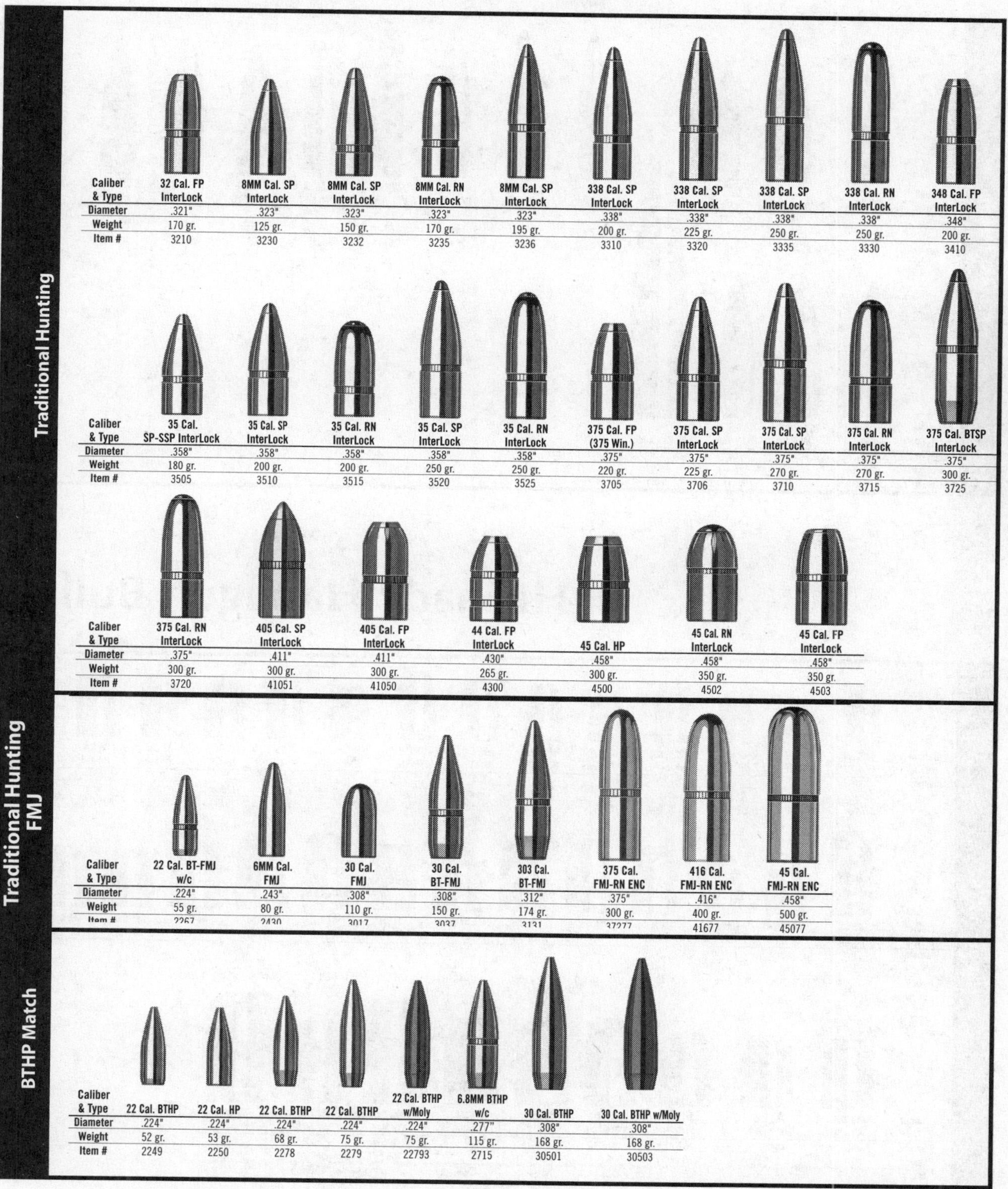

Traditional Hunting

Caliber & Type	32 Cal. FP InterLock	8MM Cal. SP InterLock	8MM Cal. SP InterLock	8MM Cal. RN InterLock	8MM Cal. SP InterLock	338 Cal. SP InterLock	338 Cal. SP InterLock	338 Cal. SP InterLock	338 Cal. RN InterLock	348 Cal. FP InterLock
Diameter	.321"	.323"	.323"	.323"	.323"	.338"	.338"	.338"	.338"	.348"
Weight	170 gr.	125 gr.	150 gr.	170 gr.	195 gr.	200 gr.	225 gr.	250 gr.	250 gr.	200 gr.
Item #	3210	3230	3232	3235	3236	3310	3320	3335	3330	3410

Caliber & Type	35 Cal. SP-SSP InterLock	35 Cal. SP InterLock	35 Cal. RN InterLock	35 Cal. SP InterLock	35 Cal. RN InterLock	375 Cal. FP (375 Win.)	375 Cal. SP InterLock	375 Cal. SP InterLock	375 Cal. RN InterLock	375 Cal. BTSP InterLock
Diameter	.358"	.358"	.358"	.358"	.358"	.375"	.375"	.375"	.375"	.375"
Weight	180 gr.	200 gr.	200 gr.	250 gr.	250 gr.	220 gr.	225 gr.	270 gr.	270 gr.	300 gr.
Item #	3505	3510	3515	3520	3525	3705	3706	3710	3715	3725

Caliber & Type	375 Cal. RN InterLock	405 Cal. SP InterLock	405 Cal. FP InterLock	44 Cal. FP InterLock	45 Cal. HP	45 Cal. RN InterLock	45 Cal. FP InterLock
Diameter	.375"	.411"	.411"	.430"	.458"	.458"	.458"
Weight	300 gr.	300 gr.	300 gr.	265 gr.	300 gr.	350 gr.	350 gr.
Item #	3720	41051	41050	4300	4500	4502	4503

Traditional Hunting FMJ

Caliber & Type	22 Cal. BT-FMJ w/c	6MM Cal. FMJ	30 Cal. FMJ	30 Cal. BT-FMJ	303 Cal. BT-FMJ	375 Cal. FMJ-RN ENC	416 Cal. FMJ-RN ENC	45 Cal. FMJ-RN ENC
Diameter	.224"	.243"	.308"	.308"	.312"	.375"	.416"	.458"
Weight	55 gr.	80 gr.	110 gr.	150 gr.	174 gr.	300 gr.	400 gr.	500 gr.
Item #	2267	2430	3017	3037	3131	37277	41677	45077

BTHP Match

Caliber & Type	22 Cal. BTHP	22 Cal. HP	22 Cal. BTHP	22 Cal. BTHP	22 Cal. BTHP w/Moly	6.8MM BTHP w/c	30 Cal. BTHP	30 Cal. BTHP w/Moly
Diameter	.224"	.224"	.224"	.224"	.224"	.277"	.308"	.308"
Weight	52 gr.	53 gr.	68 gr.	75 gr.	75 gr.	115 gr.	168 gr.	168 gr.
Item #	2249	2250	2278	2279	22793	2715	30501	30503

HANDLOADING

Hornady Rifle Bullets

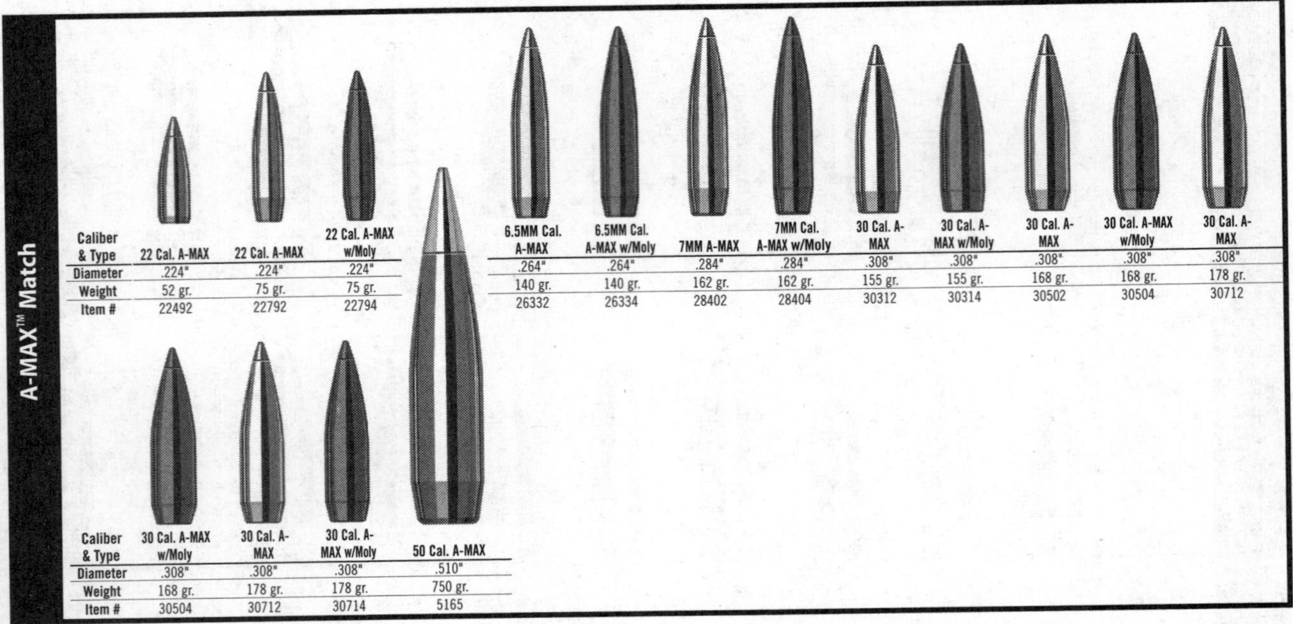

A-MAX™ Match

Caliber & Type	22 Cal. A-MAX	22 Cal. A-MAX	22 Cal. A-MAX w/Moly	6.5MM Cal. A-MAX	6.5MM Cal. A-MAX w/Moly	7MM A-MAX	7MM Cal. A-MAX w/Moly	30 Cal. A-MAX	30 Cal. A-MAX w/Moly	30 Cal. A-MAX	30 Cal. A-MAX w/Moly	30 Cal. A-MAX
Diameter	.224"	.224"	.224"	.264"	.264"	.284"	.284"	.308"	.308"	.308"	.308"	.308"
Weight	52 gr.	75 gr.	75 gr.	140 gr.	140 gr.	162 gr.	162 gr.	155 gr.	155 gr.	168 gr.	168 gr.	178 gr.
Item #	22492	22792	22794	26332	26334	28402	28404	30312	30314	30502	30504	30712

Caliber & Type	30 Cal. A-MAX w/Moly	30 Cal. A-MAX	30 Cal. A-MAX w/Moly	50 Cal. A-MAX
Diameter	.308"	.308"	.308"	.510"
Weight	168 gr.	178 gr.	178 gr.	750 gr.
Item #	30504	30712	30714	5165

Hornady Handgun Bullets

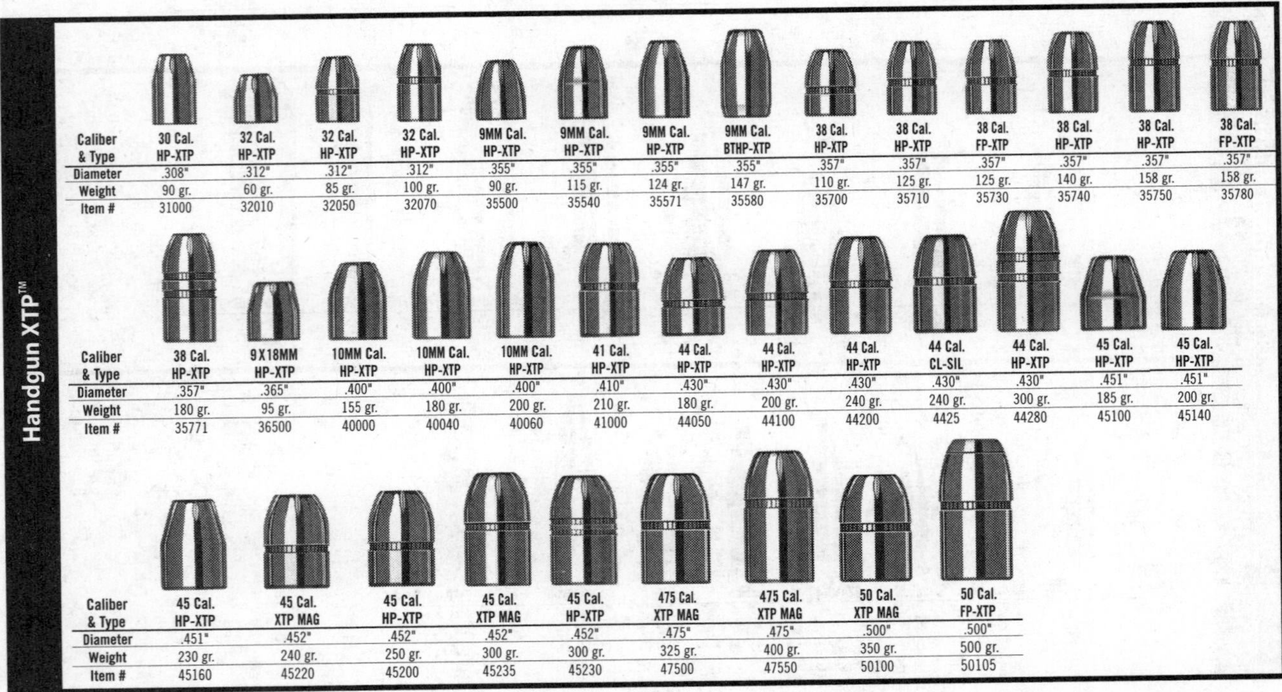

Handgun XTP™

Caliber & Type	30 Cal. HP-XTP	32 Cal. HP-XTP	32 Cal. HP-XTP	32 Cal. HP-XTP	9MM Cal. HP-XTP	9MM Cal. HP-XTP	9MM Cal. HP-XTP	9MM Cal. BTHP-XTP	38 Cal. HP-XTP	38 Cal. HP-XTP	38 Cal. FP-XTP	38 Cal. HP-XTP	38 Cal. HP-XTP	38 Cal. FP-XTP
Diameter	.308"	.312"	.312"	.312"	.355"	.355"	.355"	.355"	.357"	.357"	.357"	.357"	.357"	.357"
Weight	90 gr.	60 gr.	85 gr.	100 gr.	90 gr.	115 gr.	124 gr.	147 gr.	110 gr.	125 gr.	125 gr.	140 gr.	158 gr.	158 gr.
Item #	31000	32010	32050	32070	35500	35540	35571	35580	35700	35710	35730	35740	35750	35780

Caliber & Type	38 Cal. HP-XTP	9X18MM HP-XTP	10MM Cal. HP-XTP	10MM Cal. HP-XTP	10MM Cal. HP-XTP	41 Cal. HP-XTP	44 Cal. HP-XTP	44 Cal. HP-XTP	44 Cal. HP-XTP	44 Cal. CL-SIL	44 Cal. HP-XTP	45 Cal. HP-XTP	45 Cal. HP-XTP
Diameter	.357"	.365"	.400"	.400"	.400"	.410"	.430"	.430"	.430"	.430"	.430"	.451"	.451"
Weight	180 gr.	95 gr.	155 gr.	180 gr.	200 gr.	210 gr.	180 gr.	200 gr.	240 gr.	240 gr.	300 gr.	185 gr.	200 gr.
Item #	35771	36500	40000	40040	40060	41000	44050	44100	44200	4425	44280	45100	45140

Caliber & Type	45 Cal. HP-XTP	45 Cal. XTP MAG	45 Cal. HP-XTP	45 Cal. XTP MAG	45 Cal. HP-XTP	475 Cal. XTP MAG	475 Cal. XTP MAG	50 Cal. XTP MAG	50 Cal. FP-XTP
Diameter	.451"	.452"	.452"	.452"	.452"	.475"	.475"	.500"	.500"
Weight	230 gr.	240 gr.	250 gr.	300 gr.	300 gr.	325 gr.	400 gr.	350 gr.	500 gr.
Item #	45160	45220	45200	45235	45230	47500	47550	50100	50105

Hornady Handgun Bullets

Handgun FMJ

Caliber & Type	9MM Cal. FMJ RN-ENC	9MM Cal. FMJ FP-ENC	9MM Cal. FMJ RN-ENC	45 Cal. FMJ SWC-ENC	45 Cal. FMJ CT-ENC	45 Cal. FMJ RN-ENC	45 Cal. FMJ FP-ENC
Diameter	.355"	.355"	.355"	.451"	.451"	.451"	.451"
Weight	115 gr.	124 gr.	124 gr.	185 gr.	200 gr.	230 gr.	230 gr.
Item #	35557	35567	35577	45137	45157	45177	45187

Handgun HAP™

Caliber & Type	9MM Cal. HAP	9MM Cal. HAP	10MM Cal. HAP	10MM Cal. HAP	45 Cal. HAP
Diameter	.356"	.356"	.400"	.400"	.451"
Weight	121 gr.	125 gr.	180 gr.	200 gr.	230 gr.
Item #	35530B	35572B	40042B	40061B	45161B

Frontier™/Lead

Caliber & Type	32 Cal. SWC	32 Cal. HBWC	38 Cal. FP Cowboy	38 Cal. HBWC	38 Cal. SWC	38 Cal. HP-SWC	38 Cal. LRN	44 Cal. FP Cowboy	44 Cal. FP Cowboy	44 Cal. SWC	44 Cal. HP-SWC	45 Cal. SWC	45 Cal. L-C/T	45 Cal. LRN	45 Cal. FP Cowboy
Diameter	.314"	.314"	.358"	.358"	.358"	.358"	.358"	.427"	.430"	.430"	.430"	.452"	.452"	.452"	.454"
Weight	90 gr.	90 gr.	140 gr.	148 gr.	158 gr.	158 gr.	158 gr.	205 gr.	180 gr.	240 gr.	240 gr.	200 gr.	200 gr.	230 gr.	255 gr.
Item #	10008	10028	10078	10208	10408	10428	10508	11208	11058	11108	11118	12108	12208	12308	12458

Nosler Bullets

HANDLOADING

Custom Competition™

Caliber/ Diameter	Bullet Weight & Style	Sectional Density	Ballistic Coefficient	Part #
22/ .224"	69 Gr. HPBT 250 Ct. Bulk Pack	0.196	0.305	17101 53065
	77 Gr. HPBT 250 Ct. Bulk Pack	0.219	0.340	22421 53064
	80 Gr. HPBT 250 Ct. Bulk Pack	0.228	0.415	25116 53080
30/ .308"	155 Gr. HPBT 250 Ct. Bulk Pack	0.233	0.450	53155 53169
	168 Gr. HPBT 250 Ct. Bulk Pack	0.253	0.462	53164 53168
45/ .451"	185 Gr. JHP 250 Ct. Bulk Pack	0.130	0.142	44847

Partition®

Caliber/ Diameter	Bullet Weight & Style	Sectional Density	Ballistic Coefficient	Part #
22/ .224"	60 Gr. Spitzer	0.171	0.228	16316
6mm/ .243"	85 Gr. Spitzer	0.206	0.315	16314
	95 Gr. Spitzer	0.230	0.365	16315
	100 Gr. Spitzer	0.242	0.384	35642
25/ .257"	100 Gr. Spitzer	0.216	0.377	16317
	115 Gr. Spitzer	0.249	0.389	16318
	120 Gr. Spitzer	0.260	0.391	35643
6.5mm/ .264"	100 Gr. Spitzer	0.205	0.326	16319
	125 Gr. Spitzer	0.256	0.449	16320
	140 Gr. Spitzer	0.287	0.490	16321
270/ .277"	130 Gr. Spitzer	0.242	0.416	16322
	140 Gr. Spitzer	0.261	0.432	35200
	150 Gr. Spitzer	0.279	0.465	16323
	160 Gr. Semi Spitzer	0.298	0.434	16324

Partition®

Caliber/ Diameter	Bullet Weight & Style	Sectional Density	Ballistic Coefficient	Part #
7mm/ .284"	150 Gr. Spitzer	0.266	0.456	16326
	160 Gr. Spitzer	0.283	0.475	16327
	175 Gr. Spitzer	0.310	0.519	35645
30/ .308"	150 Gr. Spitzer	0.226	0.387	16329
	165 Gr. Spitzer	0.248	0.410	16330
	170 Gr. Round Nose	0.256	0.252	16333
	180 Gr. Protected Point	0.271	0.361	25396
	180 Gr. Spitzer	0.271	0.474	16331
	200 Gr. Spitzer	0.301	0.481	35626
	220 Gr. Semi Spitzer	0.331	0.351	16332
8mm/ .323"	200 Gr. Spitzer	0.274	0.350	35277
338/ .338"	210 Gr. Spitzer	0.263	0.400	16337
	225 Gr. Spitzer	0.281	0.454	16336
	250 Gr. Spitzer	0.313	0.473	35644
35/ .358"	225 Gr. Spitzer	0.251	0.430	44800
	250 Gr. Spitzer	0.279	0.446	44801
9.3mm/ .366"	286 Gr. Spitzer (18.5 gram)	0.307	0.482	44750
375/ .375"	260 Gr. Spitzer	0.264	0.314	44850
	300 Gr. Spitzer	0.305	0.398	44845
416/ .416"	400 Gr. Spitzer	0.330	0.390	45200
45-70/ .458"	300 Gr. Protected Point	0.204	0.199	45325

Nosler Bullets

Ballistic Tip® Hunting

Caliber/ Diameter	Bullet Weight & Style	Sectional Density	Ballistic Coefficient	Part #
6mm/ .243"	90 Gr. Spitzer (Purple Tip)	0.218	0.365	24090
	95 Gr. Spitzer (Purple Tip)	0.230	0.379	24095
25/ .257"	100 Gr. Spitzer (Blue Tip)	0.216	0.393	25100
	115 Gr. Spitzer (Blue Tip)	0.249	0.453	25115
6.5mm/ .264"	100 Gr. Spitzer (Brown Tip)	0.205	0.350	26100
	120 Gr. Spitzer (Brown Tip)	0.246	0.458	26120
270/ .277"	130 Gr. Spitzer (Yellow Tip)	0.242	0.433	27130
	140 Gr. Spitzer (Yellow Tip)	0.261	0.456	27140
	150 Gr. Spitzer (Yellow Tip)	0.279	0.496	27150
7mm/ .284"	120 Gr. Spitzer (Red Tip)	0.213	0.417	28120
	140 Gr. Spitzer (Red Tip)	0.248	0.485	28140
	150 Gr. Spitzer (Red Tip)	0.266	0.493	28150
30/ .308"	125 Gr. Spitzer (Green Tip)	0.188	0.366	30125
	150 Gr. Spitzer (Green Tip)	0.226	0.435	30150
	165 Gr. Spitzer (Green Tip)	0.248	0.475	30165
	180 Gr. Spitzer (Green Tip)	0.271	0.507	30180
8mm/ .323"	180 Gr. Spitzer (Gunmetal Tip)	0.247	0.357	32180
338/ .338"	180 Gr. Spitzer (Maroon Tip)	0.225	0.372	33180
	200 Gr. Spitzer (Maroon Tip)	0.250	0.414	33200
35/ .358"	225 Gr. Whelen (Buckskin Tip)	0.251	0.421	35225
9.3mm/ .366"	250 Gr. Spitzer (Olive Tip)	0.267	0.494	36250

Ballistic Tip® Varmint

Caliber/ Diameter	Bullet Weight & Style	Sectional Density	Ballistic Coefficient	Part #
22/ .224"	40 Gr. Spitzer (Orange Tip) 250 Ct. Varmint Pak™	0.114	0.221	39510 39555
	45 Gr. Hornet (Soft Lead Tip)	0.128	0.144	35487
	50 Gr. Spitzer (Orange Tip) 250 Ct. Varmint Pak™	0.142	0.238	39522 39557
	55 Gr. Spitzer (Orange Tip) 250 Ct. Varmint Pak™	0.157	0.267	39526 39560
6mm/ .243"	55 Gr. Spitzer (Purple Tip) 250 Ct. Varmint Pak™	0.133	0.276	24055 39565
	70 Gr. Spitzer (Purple Tip) 250 Ct. Varmint Pak™	0.169	0.310	39532 39570
	80 Gr. Spitzer (Purple Tip)	0.194	0.329	24080
25/ .257"	85 Gr. Spitzer (Blue Tip)	0.183	0.329	43004

CT® Ballistic Silvertip® Hunting

Caliber/ Diameter	Bullet Weight & Style	Sectional Density	Ballistic Coefficient	Part #
6mm/ .243"	95 Gr. Spitzer	0.230	0.379	51040
25/ .257"	85 Gr. Spitzer	0.183	0.329	51045
	115 Gr. Spitzer	0.249	0.453	51050
270/ .277"	130 Gr.Spitzer	0.242	0.433	51075
	150 Gr. Spitzer	0.279	0.496	51100
7mm/ .284"	140 Gr. Spitzer	0.248	0.485	51105
	150 Gr. Spitzer	0.266	0.493	51110
30/ .308"	150 Gr. Spitzer	0.226	0.435	51150
	168 Gr. Spitzer	0.253	0.490	51160
	180 Gr. Spitzer	0.271	0.507	51170
338/ .338"	200 Gr. Spitzer	0.250	0.414	51200

Nosler Bullets

HANDLOADING

CT® Fail Safe®

Caliber/ Diameter	Bullet Weight & Style	Sectional Density	Ballistic Coefficient	Part #
270/ .277"	140 Gr. HP Spitzer	0.261	0.322	53140
7mm/ .284"	140 Gr. HP Spitzer	0.248	0.323	53150
	160 Gr. HP Spitzer	0.283	0.382	53160
30/ .308"	150 Gr. HP Spitzer	0.226	0.310	53170
	165 Gr. HP Spitzer	0.248	0.314	53175
	180 Gr. HP Spitzer	0.271	0.391	53180
338/ .338"	230 Gr. HP Spitzer	0.288	0.436	53230
375/ .375"	270 Gr. HP Spitzer	0.274	0.393	53350
	300 Gr. HP Spitzer	0.305	0.441	53360

AccuBond®

Caliber/ Diameter	Bullet Weight & Style	Sectional Density	Ballistic Coefficient	Part #
25/ .257"	110 Gr. Spitzer	0.238	0.418	53742
270/ .277"	140 Gr. Spitzer	0.261	0.496	54765
7mm/ .284"	140 Gr. Spitzer	0.248	0.485	59992
	160 Gr. Spitzer	0.283	0.531	54932
30/ .308"	150 Gr. Spitzer	0.226	0.435	56719
	180 Gr. Spitzer	0.271	0.507	54825
	200 Gr. Spitzer	0.301	0.588	54618
8mm/ .323"	200 Gr. Spitzer	0.274	0.379	54374
338/ .338"	180 Gr. Spitzer	0.225	0.372	57625
	225 Gr. Spitzer	0.281	0.550	54357
375/ .375"	260 Gr. Spitzer	0.264	0.473	54413

CT® Ballistic Silvertip® Varmint

Caliber/ Diameter	Bullet Weight & Style	Sectional Density	Ballistic Coefficient	Part #
22/ .224"	40 Gr. Spitzer	0.114	0.221	51005
	50 Gr. Spitzer	0.142	0.238	51010
	55 Gr. Spitzer	0.157	0.267	51031
6mm/ .243"	55 Gr. Spitzer	0.133	0.276	51030

Partition-HG™

Caliber/ Diameter	Bullet Weight & Style	Sectional Density	Ballistic Coefficient	Part #
38/ .357"	180 Gr. HP	0.202	0.201	35180
44/ .429"	250 Gr. HP	0.194	0.200	44250
45/ .451"	260 Gr. HP	0.182	0.174	45260
	300 Gr. Protected Point	0.211	0.199	45350

Sporting Handgun™

Caliber/ Diameter	Bullet Weight & Style	Sectional Density	Ballistic Coefficient	Part #
9mm/ .355"	115 Gr. JHP 250 Ct. Bulk Pack	0.130	0.109	44848
38/ .357"	158 Gr. JHP 250 Ct. Bulk Pack	0.177	0.182	44841
10mm/ .400"	135 Gr. JHP 250 Ct. Bulk Pack	0.121	0.093	44852
	150 Gr. JHP 250 Ct. Bulk Pack	0.134	0.106	44860
41/ .410"	210 Gr. JHP	0.178	0.170	43012
44/ .429"	200 Gr. JHP 250 Ct. Bulk Pack	0.155	0.151	44846
	240 Gr. JHP 250 Ct. Bulk Pack	0.186	0.173	44842
	240 Gr. JSP 250 Ct. Bulk Pack	0.186	0.177	44868
	300 Gr. JHP	0.233	0.206	42069
45 Colt/ .451"	250 Gr. JHP	0.176	0.177	43013

Sierra Bullets

Rifle Bullets

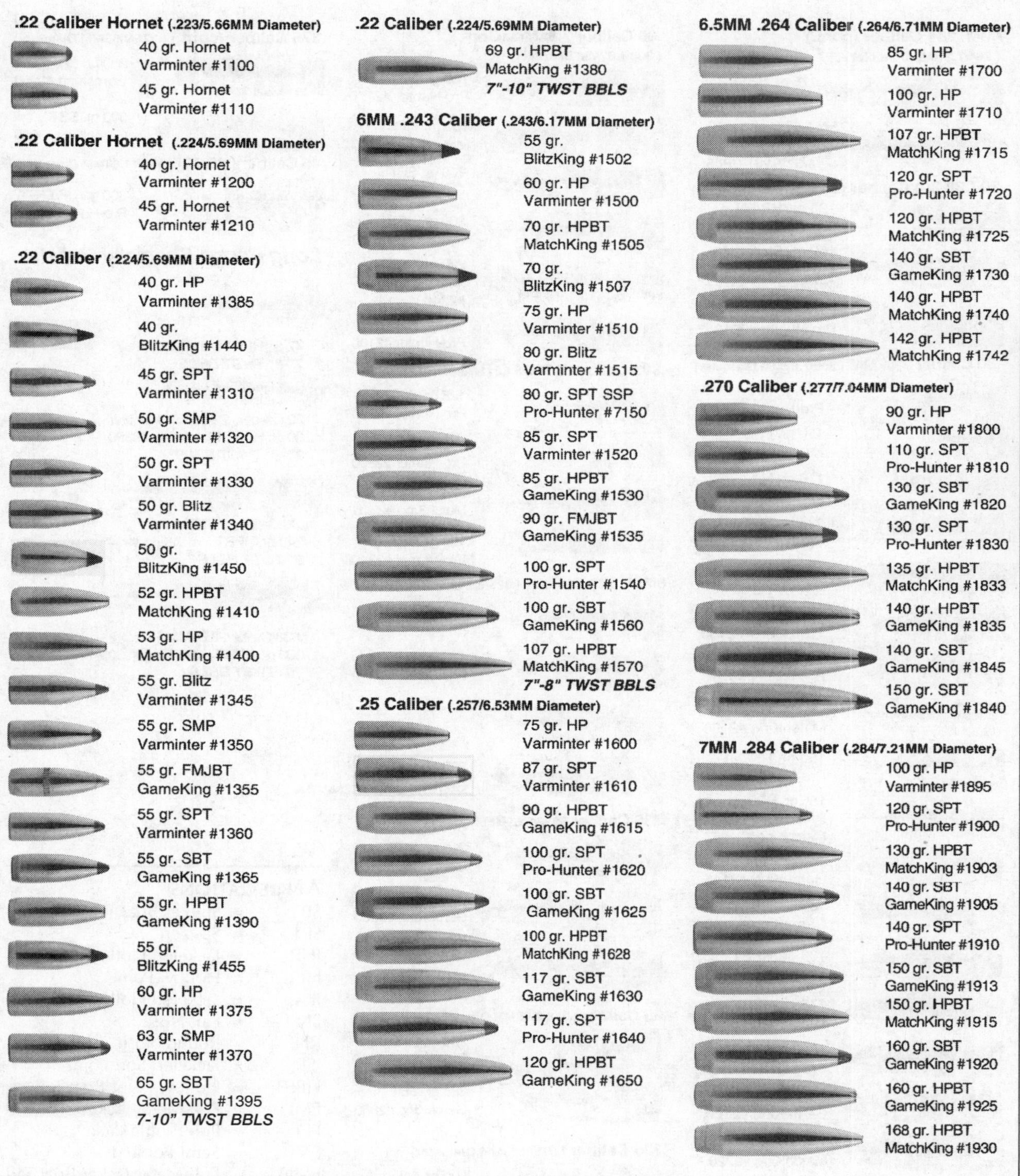
.22 Caliber Hornet (.223/5.66MM Diameter)
40 gr. Hornet Varminter #1100
45 gr. Hornet Varminter #1110
.22 Caliber Hornet (.224/5.69MM Diameter)
40 gr. Hornet Varminter #1200
45 gr. Hornet Varminter #1210
.22 Caliber (.224/5.69MM Diameter)
40 gr. HP Varminter #1385
40 gr. BlitzKing #1440
45 gr. SPT Varminter #1310
50 gr. SMP Varminter #1320
50 gr. SPT Varminter #1330
50 gr. Blitz Varminter #1340
50 gr. BlitzKing #1450
52 gr. HPBT MatchKing #1410
53 gr. HP MatchKing #1400
55 gr. Blitz Varminter #1345
55 gr. SMP Varminter #1350
55 gr. FMJBT GameKing #1355
55 gr. SPT Varminter #1360
55 gr. SBT GameKing #1365
55 gr. HPBT GameKing #1390
55 gr. BlitzKing #1455
60 gr. HP Varminter #1375
63 gr. SMP Varminter #1370
65 gr. SBT GameKing #1395
7-10" TWST BBLS
.22 Caliber (.224/5.69MM Diameter)
69 gr. HPBT MatchKing #1380
7"-10" TWST BBLS
6MM .243 Caliber (.243/6.17MM Diameter)
55 gr. BlitzKing #1502
60 gr. HP Varminter #1500
70 gr. HPBT MatchKing #1505
70 gr. BlitzKing #1507
75 gr. HP Varminter #1510
80 gr. Blitz Varminter #1515
80 gr. SPT SSP Pro-Hunter #7150
85 gr. SPT Varminter #1520
85 gr. HPBT GameKing #1530
90 gr. FMJBT GameKing #1535
100 gr. SPT Pro-Hunter #1540
100 gr. SBT GameKing #1560
107 gr. HPBT MatchKing #1570
7"-8" TWST BBLS
.25 Caliber (.257/6.53MM Diameter)
75 gr. HP Varminter #1600
87 gr. SPT Varminter #1610
90 gr. HPBT GameKing #1615
100 gr. SPT Pro-Hunter #1620
100 gr. SBT GameKing #1625
100 gr. HPBT MatchKing #1628
117 gr. SBT GameKing #1630
117 gr. SPT Pro-Hunter #1640
120 gr. HPBT GameKing #1650
6.5MM .264 Caliber (.264/6.71MM Diameter)
85 gr. HP Varminter #1700
100 gr. HP Varminter #1710
107 gr. HPBT MatchKing #1715
120 gr. SPT Pro-Hunter #1720
120 gr. HPBT MatchKing #1725
140 gr. SBT GameKing #1730
140 gr. HPBT MatchKing #1740
142 gr. HPBT MatchKing #1742
.270 Caliber (.277/7.04MM Diameter)
90 gr. HP Varminter #1800
110 gr. SPT Pro-Hunter #1810
130 gr. SBT GameKing #1820
130 gr. SPT Pro-Hunter #1830
135 gr. HPBT MatchKing #1833
140 gr. HPBT GameKing #1835
140 gr. SBT GameKing #1845
150 gr. SBT GameKing #1840
7MM .284 Caliber (.284/7.21MM Diameter)
100 gr. HP Varminter #1895
120 gr. SPT Pro-Hunter #1900
130 gr. HPBT MatchKing #1903
140 gr. SBT GameKing #1905
140 gr. SPT Pro-Hunter #1910
150 gr. SBT GameKing #1913
150 gr. HPBT MatchKing #1915
160 gr. SBT GameKing #1920
160 gr. HPBT GameKing #1925
168 gr. HPBT MatchKing #1930

Sierra Bullets

7MM .284 Caliber (cont.) (.284/7.21MM Diameter)

175 gr. SBT GameKing #1940

175 gr. HPBT MatchKing #1975 *8.5" TWST BBLS*

.30 (.30-30) Caliber (.308/7.82MM Diameter)

125 gr. HP/FN Pro-Hunter #2020

150 gr. FN Pro-Hunter #2000 POWER JACKET

170 gr. FN Pro-Hunter #2010 POWER JACKET

.30 Caliber 7.62MM (.308/7.82MM Diameter)

110 gr. RN Pro-Hunter #2100

110 gr. FMJ Pro-Hunter #2105

110 gr. HP Varminter #2110

125 gr. SPT Pro-Hunter #2120

150 gr. FMJBT GameKing #2115

150 gr. SPT Pro-Hunter #2130

150 gr. SBT GameKing #2125

150 gr. HPBT MatchKing #2190

150 gr. RN Pro-Hunter #2135

155 gr. HPBT PALMA MatchKing #2155

165 gr. SBT GameKing #2145

165 gr. HPBT GameKing #2140

168 gr. HPBT MatchKing #2200

175 gr. HPBT MatchKing #2275

180 gr. SPT Pro-Hunter #2150

180 gr. SBT GameKing #2160

180 gr. HPBT MatchKing #2220

.30 Caliber 7.62MM (Cont.) (.308/7.82MM Diameter)

180 gr. RN Pro-Hunter #2170

190 gr. HPBT MatchKing #2210

200 gr. SBT GameKing #2165

200 gr. HPBT MatchKing #2230

220 gr. HPBT MatchKing #2240

220 gr. RN Pro-Hunter #2180

.303 Caliber 7.7MM (.311/7.90MM Diameter)

125 gr. SPT Pro-Hunter #2305

150 gr. SPT Pro-Hunter #2300

174 gr. HPBT MatchKing #2315

180 gr. SPT Pro-Hunter #2310

8MM .323 Caliber (.323/8.20MM Diameter)

150 gr. SPT Pro-Hunter #2400

175 gr. SPT Pro-Hunter #2410

220 gr. SBT GameKing #2420

.338 Caliber (.338/8.59MM Diameter)

215 gr. SBT GameKing #2610

250 gr. SBT GameKing #2600

.35 Caliber (.358/9.09MM Diameter)

200 gr. RN Pro-Hunter #2800

225 gr. SBT GameKing #2850

.375 Caliber (.375/9.53MM Diameter)

200 gr. FN Pro-Hunter #2900 POWER JACKET

.375 Caliber (cont.) (.375/9.53MM Diameter)

250 gr. SBT GameKing #2950

300 gr. SBT GameKing #3000

.45 Caliber (.45-70) (.458/11.63MM Diameter)

300 gr. HP/FN Pro-Hunter #8900

Long Range Specialty Bullets

77 gr. HPBT MatchKing #9377
7"-8" TWST BBLS

22 Caliber, .224/5.69 Diameter
80 gr. HPBT MatchKing #9390
7"- 8" TWST BBLS

.30 Caliber, 7.62MM
240 gr. HPBT MatchKing #9245
9" TWST BBLS

.338 Caliber, 8.59MM
300 gr. HPBT MatchKing #9300
10" TWST BBLS

Abbreviations

SBT = Spitzer Boat Tail
SPT = Spitzer
JHP = Jacketed Hollow Point
HP = Hollow Point
JHC = Jacketed Hollow Cavity
FN = Flat Nose
RN = Round Nose
JSP = Jacketed Soft Point
HPBT = Hollow Point Boat Tail
FMJ = Full Metal Jacket
FPJ = Full Profile Jacket
SMP = Semi-Pointed
FMJBT = Full Metal Jacket Boat Tail
SSP = Single Shot Pistol

Sierra Bullets
Handgun Bullets

.25 Caliber (.251/6.38MM Diameter)

50 gr. FMJ
Tournament Master #8000

.30 Caliber (.308/7.82MM Diameter)

85 gr. RN
Sports Master #8005

.32 Caliber 7.65MM (.312/7.92MM Diameter)

71 gr. FMJ
Tournament Master #8010

.32 Mag. (.312/7.92MM Diameter)

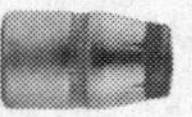
90 gr. JHC
Sports Master #8030
POWER JACKET

9MM .355 Caliber (.355/9.02MM Diameter)

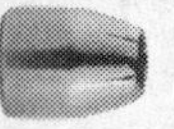
90 gr. JHP
Sports Master #8100
POWER JACKET

95 gr. FMJ
Tournament Master #8105

115 gr. JHP
Sports Master #8110
POWER JACKET

115 gr. FMJ
Tournament Master #8115

125 gr. JHP Sports Master
#8125 POWER JACKET

125 gr. FMJ
Tournament Master #8120

.38 Caliber (.357/9.07MM Diameter)

110 gr. JHC Blitz
Sports Master #8300
POWER JACKET

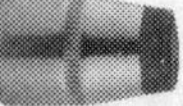
125 gr. JSP
Sports Master #8310

125 gr. JHC
Sports Master #8320
POWER JACKET

140 gr. JHC
Sports Master #8325
POWER JACKET

158 gr. JSP
Sports Master #8340

158 gr. JHC
Sports Master #8360
POWER JACKET

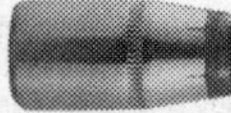
170 gr. JHC
Sports Master #8365
POWER JACKET

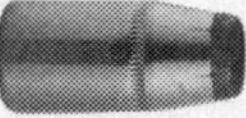
180 gr. FPJ Match
Tournament Master #8370

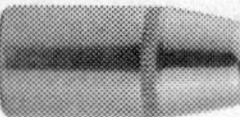

9MM Makarov (.363/9.22MM Diameter)

100 gr. FPJ
Tournament Master #8210

10MM .400 Caliber (.400/10.16MM Diameter)

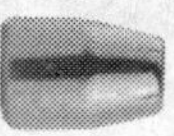
135 gr. JHP
Sports Master #8425
POWER JACKET

150 gr. JHP
Sports Master #8430
POWER JACKET

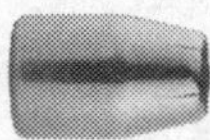
165 gr. JHP
Sports Master #8445
POWER JACKET

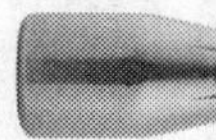
180 gr. JHP
Sports Master #8460
POWER JACKET

190 gr. FPJ
Tournament Master #8480

.41 Caliber (.410/10.41MM Diameter)

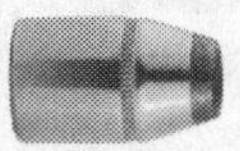
170 gr. JHC
Sports Master #8500
POWER JACKET

210 gr. JHC
Sports Master #8520
POWER JACKET

.44 Caliber (.4295/10.91MM Diameter)

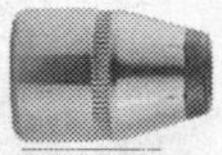
180 gr. JHC
Sports Master #8600
POWER JACKET

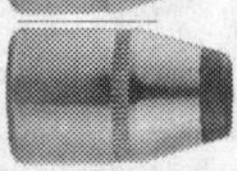
210 gr. JHC
Sports Master #8620
POWER JACKET

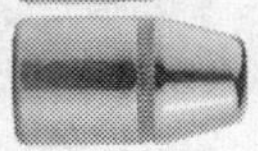
220 gr. FPJ Match
Tournament Master #8605

240 gr. JHC
Sports Master #8610
POWER JACKET

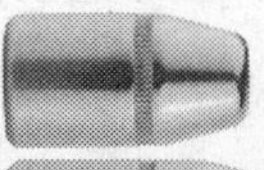
250 gr. FPJ Match
Tournament Master #8615

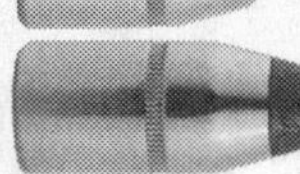
300 gr. JSP
Sports Master #8630

.45 Caliber (.4515/11.47MM Diameter)

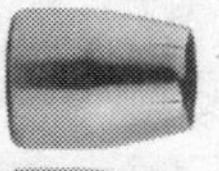
185 gr. JHP
Sports Master #8800
POWER JACKET

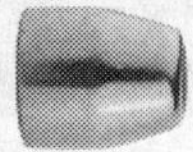
185 gr. FPJ Match
Tournament Master #8810

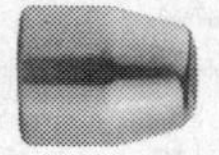
200 gr. FPJ Match
Tournament Master #8825

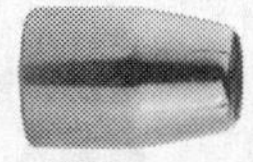
230 gr. JHP
Sports Master #8805
POWER JACKET

230 gr. FMJ Match
Tournament Master #8815

240 gr. JHC
Sports Master #8820
POWER JACKET

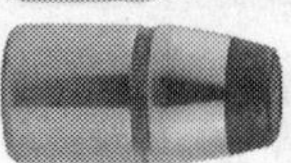
300 gr. JSP
Sports Master #8830

.50 Caliber (.5000/12.7mm Diameter)

350 gr. JHP
Sports Master #5350
POWER JACKET

400 gr. JHP
Sports Master #5400
POWER JACKET

Abbreviations

SBT = Spitzer Boat Tail
SPT = Spitzer
JHP = Jacketed Hollow Point
HP = Hollow Point
JHC = Jacketed Hollow Cavity
FN = Flat Nose
RN = Round Nose
JSP = Jacketed Soft Point
HPBT = Hollow Point Boat Tail
FMJ = Full Metal Jacket
FPJ = Full Profile Jacket
SMP = Semi-Pointed
FMJBT = Full Metal Jacket Boat Tail
SSP = Single Shot Pistol

Speer Bullets

Gold Dot Handgun Bullets

Caliber & Description	25 Auto Gold Dot HP	32 Auto Gold Dot HP	380 Auto Gold Dot HP	9mm Luger Gold Dot HP	9mm Luger Gold Dot HP	9mm Luger Gold Dot HP SB	9mm Luger Gold Dot HP	357 SIG/38 Super Gold Dot HP	38 Special Gold Dot HP SB	38 Spl 357 Mag Gold Dot HP SB	38 Spl 357 Mag Gold Dot HP SB	357 Magnum Gold Dot HP	357 Magnum Gold Dot HP	357 Magnum Gold Dot SP	9x18mm Makarov Gold Dot HP	40/10mm Gold Dot HP	40/10mm Gold Dot HP
Diameter, Inches	.251	.312	.355	.355	.355	.355	.355	.355	.357	.357	.357	.357	.357	.357	.364	.400	.400
Weight, grains	35	60	90	115	124	124	147	125	110	135	147	125	158	170	90	155	165
BC	.091	.118	.101	.125	.134		.164	.141	.117	.141	.153	.140	.168	.185	.107	.123	.138
Part Number	3985	3986	3992	3994	3998	4000	4002	4360	4009	4014	4016	4012	4215	4230	3999	4400	4397
Bullets/box	100	100	100	100	100	100	100	100	100	100	100	100	100	100	100	100	100
Bullet Construction	UC	UC	UC	UC	UC	UC	UC	UC	UC	UC	UC	UC	UC	UC	UC	UC	UC

44 Special Gold Dot HP	44 Magnum Gold Dot HP	44 Magnum Gold Dot HP	44 Magnum Gold Dot SP	44 Magnum Gold Dot SP	45 Auto Gold Dot HP	45 Auto Gold Dot HP	45 Auto Gold Dot HP	45 Auto Gold Dot HP SB	45 Colt Gold Dot HP	454 Casull Gold Dot HP	480 Ruger Gold Dot HP	480 Ruger Gold Dot SP	475 Linebaugh® Gold Dot SP†	50 Action Express Gold Dot HP
.429	.429	.429	.429	.429	.451	.451	.451	.451	.452	.452	.475	.475	.475	.500
200	210	240	240	270	185	200	230	230	250	300	275	325	400	300
.145	.154	.175	.175	.193	.109	.138	.143		.165	.233	.162	.191	.242	.155
4427	4428	4455	4456	4461	4470	4478	4483		4484	3974	3973	3978	3976	4493
100	100	100	100	50	100	100	100	100	50	50	50	50	50	50
UC	UC	UC	UC	UC	UC	UC	UC	UC	UC	UC	UC	UC	UC	UC

†=475 linebaugh is a registered trademark of Timothy B. Sundles

Uni-Cor Handgun Bullets

Caliber & Description	25 Auto TMJ	380 Auto TMJ	9mm Luger TMJ	9mm Luger UCSP	9mm Luger TMJ Match	9mm Luger TMJ	357 SIG 38 Super TMJ	38 Spl 357 Magnum UCHP	38 Spl 357 Magnum UCSP	38 Spl 357 Magnum UCHP	38 Spl 357 Magnum TMJ	38 Spl 357 Magnum UCHP	357 Magnum UCHP	357 Magnum UCSP	357 Magnum TMJ	357 Magnum Sil. Match TMJ	357 Magnum Sil. Match TMJ
Diameter, Inches	.251	.355	.355	.355	.355	.355	.355	.357	.357	.357	.357	.357	.357	.357	.357	.357	.357
Weight, grains	50	95	115	124	130	147	125	110	125	125	125	140	158	158	158	180	200
BC	.110	.131	.151	.115	.165	.188	.147	.113	.129	.129	.146	.145	.163	.164	.173	.230	.236
Part Number	3982	4001	3995	3997	4010	4006	4362	4007	4011	4013	4015	4203	4211	4217	4207	4229	4231
Bullets/box	100	100	100	100	100	100	100	100	100	100	100	100	100	100	100	100	100
Bullet Construction	UC	UC	UC	UC	UC	UC	UC	UC	UC	UC	UC	UC	UC	UC	UC	UC	UC

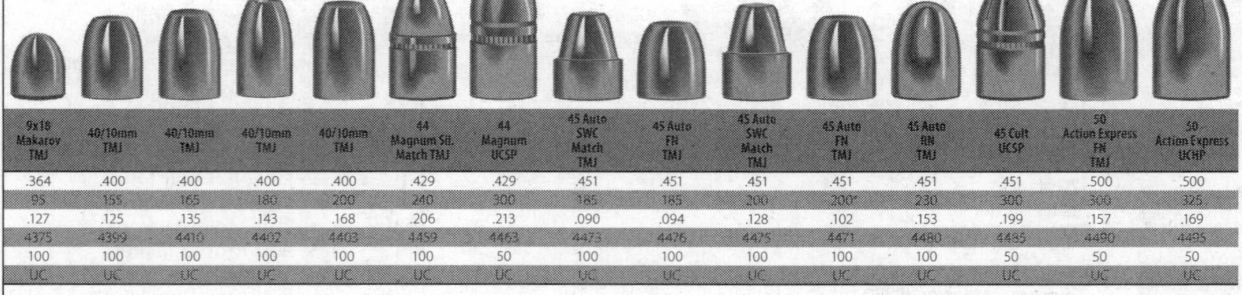

9x18 Makarov TMJ	40/10mm TMJ	40/10mm TMJ	40/10mm TMJ	40/10mm TMJ	44 Magnum Sil. Match TMJ	44 Magnum UCSP	45 Auto SWC Match TMJ	45 Auto FN TMJ	45 Auto SWC Match TMJ	45 Auto FN TMJ	45 Auto RN TMJ	45 Colt UCSP	50 Action Express FN TMJ	50 Action Express UCHP
.364	.400	.400	.400	.400	.429	.429	.451	.451	.451	.451	.451	.451	.500	.500
95	155	165	180	200	240	300	185	185	200	200*	230	300	300	325
.127	.125	.135	.143	.168	.206	.213	.090	.094	.128	.102	.153	.199	.157	.169
4375	4399	4410	4402	4403	4459	4463	4473	4476	4475	4471	4480	4485	4490	4495
100	100	100	100	100	100	50	100	100	100	100	100	50	50	50
UC	UC	UC	UC	UC	UC	UC	UC	UC	UC	UC	UC	UC	UC	UC

HANDLOADING

Speer Bullets

Jacketed Handgun Bullets

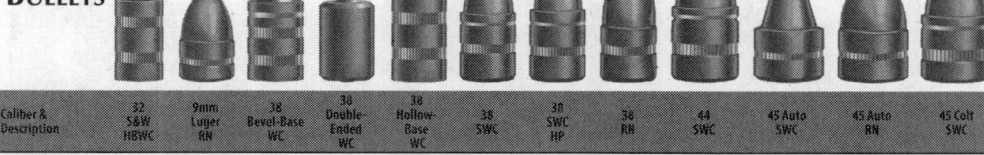

Caliber & Description	32 Revolver JHP	32 Revolver JHP	38 Spl 357 Magnum SWC-JHP	41 Magnum SWC-JHP	41 Magnum SWC-JSP	44 Magnum JHP	44 Magnum SWC-JHP	44 Magnum SWC-JSP	44 Magnum JHP	44 Magnum JSP	45 Colt JHP	45 Colt JHP
Diameter, Inches	.312	.312	.357	.410	.410	.429	.429	.429	.429	.429	.451	.451
Weight, grains	85	100	146	200	220	200	225	240	240	240	225	260
BC	.121	.167	.159	.113	.137	.122	.146	.157	.165	.164	.169	.183
Part Number	3987	3981	4205	4405	4417	4425	4435	4447	4453	4457	4479	4481
Bullets/box	100	100	100	100	100	100	100	100	100	100	100	100
Bullet Construction	C	C	C	C	C	C	C	C	C	C	C	C

Lead Handgun Bullets

Caliber & Description	32 S&W HBWC	9mm Luger RN	38 Bevel-Base WC	38 Double-Ended WC	38 Hollow-Base WC	38 SWC	38 SWC HP	38 RN	44 SWC	45 Auto SWC	45 Auto RN	45 Colt SWC
Diameter, Inches	.314	.356	.358	.358	.358	.358	.358	.358	.430	.452	.452	.452
Weight, grains	98	125	148	148	148	158	158	158	240	200	230	250
Part No	–	4601	4605	–	4617	4623	4627	4647	4660	4677	4690	4683
Box Count	–	100	100	–	100	100	100	100	100	100	100	100
Bulk Part No.	4600	4602	4606	4611	4618	4624	4628	4648	4661	4678	4691	4684
Bulk Count	1000	500	500	500	500	500	500	500	500	500	500	500

Idaho Territory Bullets

Caliber & Description	38 FN Lead	44 FN Lead	45 FN Lead	45-70 FN Lead
Diameter, Inches	.358	.430	.454	.459
Weight, grains	158	200	230	405
BC	.136	.130	.139	.224
Part No	4629	4662	4680	2480
Box Count	100	100	100	25
Bulk Part No.	4630	4663	4681	2481
Bulk Count	500	500	500	350

Abbreviation Key

BT—boat tail
C—conventional construction
FB—fusion bonded
FMJ—full metal jacket
FN—flat nose
GD—Gold Dot®
HC—Hot-Cor®
HP—hollow point
L—lead
MHP™—molybdenum disulfide impregnated
SB™—for short-barrel firearms
SP—soft point
TMJ®—encased-core full jacket
RN—round nose
SWC—semi-wadcutter
UC—Uni-Cor®
WC—wadcutter

TNT Rifle Bullets

Caliber & Description	22 Hornet TNT	22 TNT HP	22 TNT HP Hi-Vel.	6mm TNT HP	25 TNT HP	6.5mm TNT HP	270 TNT HP	7mm TNT HP	30 TNT HP
Diameter, Inches	.224	.224	.224	.243	.257	.264	.277	.284	.308
Weight, grains	33	50	55	70	87	90	90	110	125
BC	.080	.228	.233	.279	.337	.281	.303	.384	.341
Part Number	1014	1030	1032	1206	1246	1445	1446	1616	1986
Bullets/box	100	100	100	100	100	100	100	100	100
Bullet Construction	UC	C	C	C	C	C	C	C	C

MHP Rifle Bullets

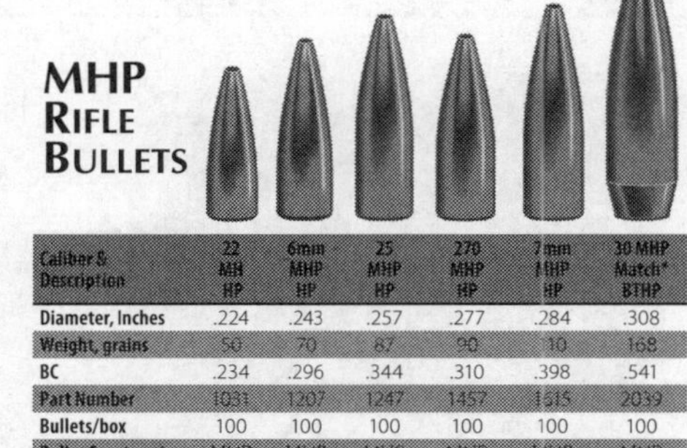

Caliber & Description	22 MH HP	6mm MHP HP	25 MHP HP	270 MHP HP	7mm MHP HP	30 MHP Match* BTHP
Diameter, Inches	.224	.243	.257	.277	.284	.308
Weight, grains	50	70	87	90	10	168
BC	.234	.296	.344	.310	.398	.541
Part Number	1031	1207	1247	1457	1615	2039
Bullets/box	100	100	100	100	100	100
Bullet Construction	MHP	MHP	MHP	MHP	MHP	MHP

Speer Bullets

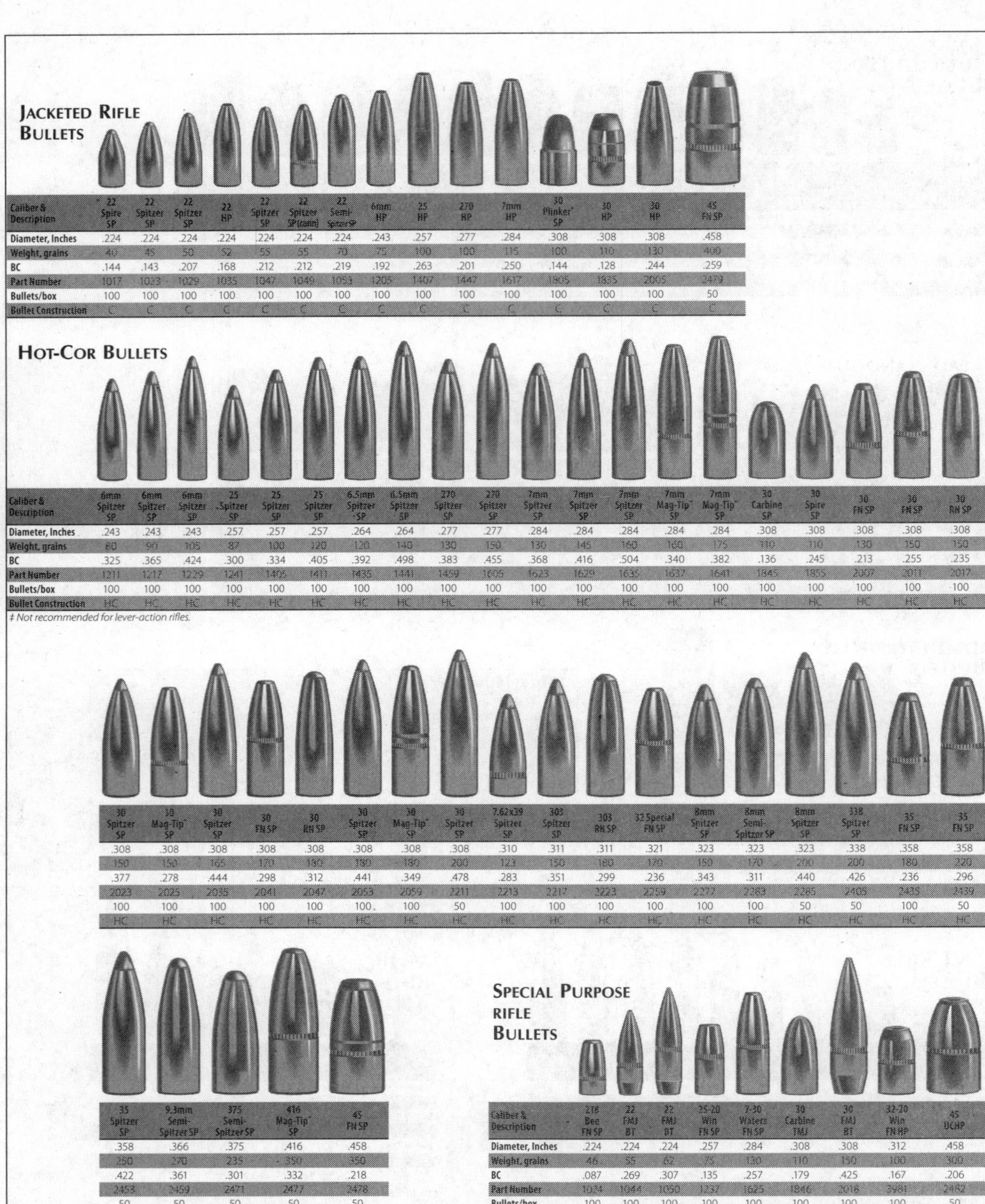

Jacketed Rifle Bullets

Caliber & Description	22 Spire SP	22 Spitzer SP	22 Spitzer SP	22 HP	22 Spitzer SP	22 Spitzer SP(cann)	22 Semi-Spitzer SP	6mm HP	25 HP	270 HP	7mm HP	30 Plinker‡ SP	30 HP	30 HP	45 FN SP
Diameter, Inches	.224	.224	.224	.224	.224	.224	.224	.243	.257	.277	.284	.308	.308	.308	.458
Weight, grains	40	45	50	52	55	55	70	75	100	100	115	100	110	130	400
BC	.144	.143	.207	.168	.212	.212	.219	.192	.263	.201	.250	.144	.128	.244	.259
Part Number	1017	1023	1029	1035	1047	1049	1053	1205	1407	1447	1617	1805	1835	2005	2479
Bullets/box	100	100	100	100	100	100	100	100	100	100	100	100	100	100	50
Bullet Construction	C	C	C	C	C	C	C	C	C	C	C	C	C	C	C

Hot-Cor Bullets

Caliber & Description	6mm Spitzer SP	6mm Spitzer SP	6mm Spitzer SP	25 Spitzer SP	25 Spitzer SP	25 Spitzer SP	6.5mm Spitzer SP	6.5mm Spitzer SP	270 Spitzer SP	270 Spitzer SP	7mm Spitzer SP	7mm Spitzer SP	7mm Spitzer SP	7mm Mag-Tip‡ SP	7mm Mag-Tip‡ SP	30 Carbine SP	30 Spire SP	30 FN SP	30 FN SP	30 RN SP
Diameter, Inches	.243	.243	.243	.257	.257	.257	.264	.264	.277	.277	.284	.284	.284	.284	.284	.308	.308	.308	.308	.308
Weight, grains	80	90	105	87	100	120	120	140	130	150	130	145	160	160	175	110	110	130	150	150
BC	.325	.365	.424	.300	.334	.405	.392	.498	.383	.455	.368	.416	.504	.340	.382	.136	.245	.213	.255	.235
Part Number	1211	1217	1229	1241	1405	1411	1435	1441	1459	1605	1623	1629	1635	1637	1641	1845	1855	2007	2011	2017
Bullets/box	100	100	100	100	100	100	100	100	100	100	100	100	100	100	100	100	100	100	100	100
Bullet Construction	HC	HC	HC	HC	HC	HC	HC	HC	HC	HC	HC	HC	HC	HC	HC	HC	HC	HC	HC	HC

‡ *Not recommended for lever-action rifles.*

30 Spitzer SP	30 Mag-Tip‡ SP	30 Spitzer SP	30 FN SP	30 RN SP	30 Spitzer SP	30 Mag-Tip‡ SP	30 Spitzer SP	7.62x39 Spitzer SP	303 Spitzer SP	303 RN SP	32 Special FN SP	8mm Spitzer SP	8mm Semi-Spitzer SP	8mm Spitzer SP	338 Spitzer SP	35 FN SP	35 FN SP
.308	.308	.308	.308	.308	.308	.308	.308	.310	.311	.311	.321	.323	.323	.323	.338	.358	.358
150	150	165	170	180	180	180	200	123	150	180	170	150	170	200	200	180	220
.377	.278	.444	.298	.312	.441	.349	.478	.283	.351	.299	.236	.343	.311	.440	.426	.236	.296
2023	2025	2035	2041	2047	2053	2059	2211	2213	2217	2223	2259	2277	2283	2285	2405	2435	2439
100	100	100	100	100	100.	100	50	100	100	100	100	100	100	50	50	100	50
HC	HC	HC	HC	HC	HC	HC	HC	HC	HC	HC	HC	HC	HC	HC	HC	HC	HC

35 Spitzer SP	9.3mm Semi-Spitzer SP	375 Semi-Spitzer SP	416 Mag-Tip‡ SP	45 FN SP
.358	.366	.375	.416	.458
250	270	235	350	350
.422	.361	.301	.332	.218
2453	2459	2471	2477	2478
50	50	50	50	50
HC	HC	HC	HC	HC

Special Purpose Rifle Bullets

Caliber & Description	218 Bee FN SP	22 FMJ BT	22 FMJ BT	25-20 Win FN SP	7-30 Waters FN SP	30 Carbine TMJ	30 FMJ BT	32-20 Win FN HP	45 UCHP
Diameter, Inches	.224	.224	.224	.257	.284	.308	.308	.312	.458
Weight, grains	46	55	62	75	130	110	150	100	300
BC	.087	.269	.307	.135	.257	.179	.425	.167	.206
Part Number	1024	1044	1050	1237	1625	1846	2018	3981	2482
Bullets/box	100	100	100	100	100	100	100	100	50
Bullet Construction	C	C	C	HC	HC	UC	C	C	UC

‡ *Recommended for twist rates of 1 in 10" or faster.*

Speer Bullets

HANDLOADING

Boat Tail Rifle Bullets

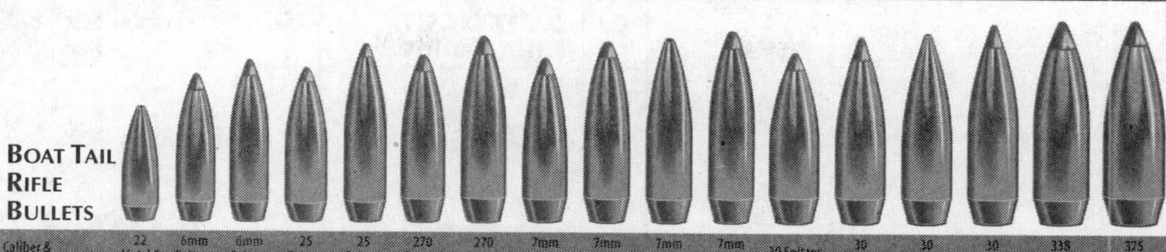

Caliber & Description	22 Match* BTHP	6mm Spitzer BTSP	6mm Spitzer BTSP	25 Spitzer BTHP	25 Spitzer BTSP	270 Spitzer BTSP	270 Spitzer BTSP	7mm Spitzer BTSP	7mm Spitzer BTSP	7mm Match* BTHP	7mm Spitzer BTSP	30 Spitzer BTSP	30 Spitzer BTSP	30 Match* BTHP	30 Spitzer BTSP	338 Spitzer BTSP	375 Spitzer BTSP
Diameter, Inches	.224	.243	.243	.257	.257	.277	.277	.284	.284	.284	.284	.308	.308	.308	.308	.338	.375
Weight, grains	52	85	100	100	120	130	150	130	145	145	160	150	165	168	180	225	270
BC	.230	.380	.446	.393	.480	.412	.489	.424	.472	.468	.519	.417	.520	.534	.545	.497	.478
Part Number	1036	1213	1220	1408	1410	1458	1604	1624	1628	1631	1634	2022	2034	2040	2052	2406	2472
Bullets/box	100	100	100	100	100	100	100	100	100	100	100	100	100	100	100	50	50
Bullet Construction	C	C	C	C	C	C	C	C	C	C	C	C	C	C	C	C	C

*Match bullets are not recommended for use on game animals.

Grand Slam

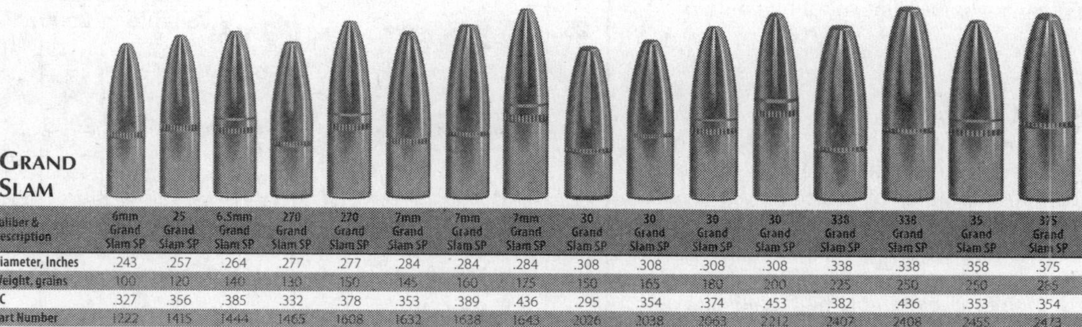

Caliber & Description	6mm Grand Slam SP	25 Grand Slam SP	6.5mm Grand Slam SP	270 Grand Slam SP	270 Grand Slam SP	7mm Grand Slam SP	7mm Grand Slam SP	7mm Grand Slam SP	30 Grand Slam SP	30 Grand Slam SP	30 Grand Slam SP	30 Grand Slam SP	338 Grand Slam SP	338 Grand Slam SP	35 Grand Slam SP	375 Grand Slam SP
Diameter, Inches	.243	.257	.264	.277	.277	.284	.284	.284	.308	.308	.308	.308	.338	.338	.358	.375
Weight, grains	100	120	140	130	150	145	160	175	150	165	180	200	225	250	250	265
BC	.327	.356	.385	.332	.378	.353	.389	.436	.295	.354	.374	.453	.382	.436	.353	.354
Part Number	1222	1415	1444	1465	1608	1632	1638	1643	2026	2038	2063	2212	2407	2408	2455	2473
Bullets/box	50	50	50	50	50	50	50	50	50	50	50	50	50	50	50	50
Bullet Construction	HC	HC	HC	HC	HC	HC	HC	HC	HC	HC	HC	HC	HC	HC	HC	HC

Tropty Bonded Bear Claw

Caliber & Description	22 TBBC	25 TBBC	6.5mm TBBC	270 TBBC	7mm TBBC	7mm TBBC	7mm TBBC	30 TBBC	30 TBBC	30 TBBC	30 TBBC	338 TBBC	35 Whelen TBBC	375 TBBC	375 TBBC	416 TBBC	458 TBBC	470 Nitro Express TBBC
Diameter, Inches	.224	.257	.264	.277	.284	.284	.284	.308	.308	.308	.308	.338	.358	.375	.375	.416	.458	.474
Weight, grains	55	115	140	140	140	160	175	150	165	180	200	225	225	250	300	400	500	500
BC	.201	.372	.405	.392	.360	.380	.400	0.335	.342	.357	.392	.376	350	.286	.336	.374	.340	.330
Part Number	1725	1730	1735	1740	1745	1750	1755	1759	1760	1765	1770	1775	1777	1778	1780	1785	1790	1795
Bullets/box	50	25	25	25	25	25	25	25	25	25	25	25	25	25	25	25	25	25
Bullet Construction	FB	FB	FB	FB	FB	FB	FB	FB	FB	FB	FB	FB	FB	FB	FB	FB	FB	FB

Abbreviation Key

- BT—boat tail
- C—conventional construction
- FB—fusion bonded
- FMJ—full metal jacket
- FN—flat nose
- GD—Gold Dot®
- HC—Hot-Cor®
- HP—hollow point
- L—lead
- MHP™—molybdenum disulfide impregnated
- SB™—for short-barrel firearms
- SP—soft point
- TMJ®—encased-core full jacket
- RN—round nose
- SWC—semi-wadcutter
- UC—Uni-Cor®
- WC—wadcutter

Swift

A-Frame and Scirocco Bullets

SWIFT SCIROCCO BONDED 30 CAL. (.308″) 180-GR. POLYMER TIP/BOAT TAIL SPITZER
Tapered jacket and proprietary bonding process produce controlled mushrooming with high weight retention. Ideally suited to fast, flat-shooting calibers.

Cal.	Scirocco Rifle Bullet	Dia.	Wt. (gr.)	Profile	Sect. Den.	Ball. Coef.
224		Available in 2005				
224	1.085"	.224"	75	BTS	.214	.419
6mm	1.132"	.243"	90	BTS	.218	.419
25		Available in 2005				
6.5mm		Available in 2005				
270	1.315"	.277"	130	BTS	.242	.450
7mm	1.385"	.284"	150	BTS	.266	.515
30	1.270"	.308"	150	BTS	.226	.430
30	1.350"	.308"	165	BTS	.248	.470
30	1.435"	.308"	180	BTS	.271	.520
338	1.393"	.338"	210	BTS	.263	.507

THE SWIFT BULLET COMPANY

The Scirocco rifle bullet starts with a tough, pointed polymer tip that reduces air resistance, prevents tip deformation, and blends into the radius of its secant ogive nose section. A moderate 15-degree boat-tail base reduces drag and eases seating. The thick base prevents bullet deformation during launch. Scirocco's shape creates two other significant advantages. One is an extremely high ballistic coefficient. The other, derived from the secant ogive nose, is a comparatively long bearing surface for a sharply pointed bullet, a feature that improves rotational stability.

Inside, the Scirocco has a bonded-core construction with a pure lead core encased in a tapered, progressively thickening jacket of pure copper. Pure copper was selected because it is more malleable and less brittle than less expensive gilding metal. Both jacket and core are bonded by Swift's proprietary process so that the bullet expands without break-up as if the two parts were the same metal. In tests, the new bullet mushroomed effectively at velocities as low as 1440 fps, yet stayed together at velocities in excess of 3,000 fps, with over 70 percent weight retention.

Swift A-Frame bullet, with its mid-section wall of copper, is still earning praise for its deep-driving dependability in tough game. Less aerodynamic than the Scirocco, it produces a broad mushroom while carrying almost all its weight through muscle and bone. Available in a wide range of weights and diameters, it is also a bonded-core bullet.

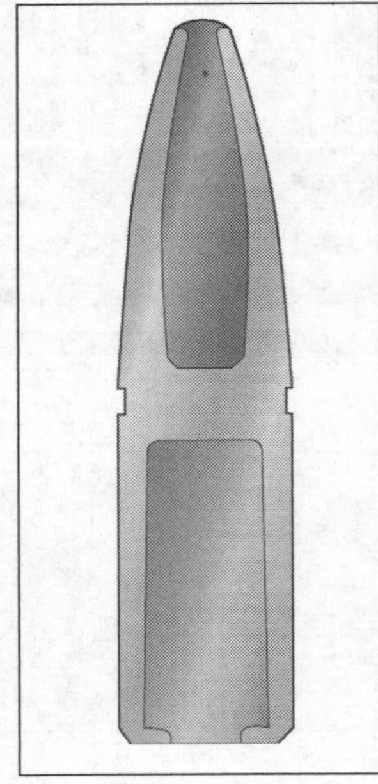

A-Frame Bullet

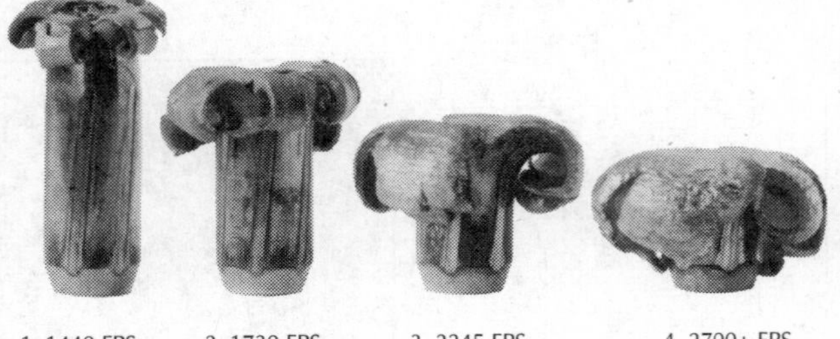

1. 1440 FPS 2. 1730 FPS 3. 2245 FPS 4. 2700+ FPS

Swift SciroccoTM Expands dependably over a wide range of velocities, and maintains high jacket/core integrity.

Swift

A-Frame Rifle Bullet Specifications

Cal.	A-Frame Rifle Bullet	Dia.	Wt. (gr.)	Profile	Sect. Den.	Ball. Coef.
25	1.015"	.257"	100	AF/SS	.216	.318
25	1.150"	.257"	120	AF/SS	.260	.382
6.5	1.115"	.264"	120	AF/SS	.246	.344
6.5	1.245"	.264"	140	AF/SS	.287	.401
270	1.090"	.277"	130	AF/SS	.242	.323
270	1.190"	.277"	140	AF/SS	.261	.414
270	1.230"	.277"	150	AF/SS	.279	.444
7mm	1.115"	.284"	140	AF/SS	.248	.335
7mm	1.270"	.284"	160	AF/SS	.283	.450
7mm	1.365"	.284"	175	AF/SS	.310	.493
30	1.140"	.308"	165	AF/SS	.248	.367
30	1.215"	.308"	180	AF/SS	.271	.400
30	1.315"	.308"	200	AF/SS	.301	.444

Cal.	A-Frame Rifle Bullet	Dia.	Wt. (gr.)	Profile	Sect. Den.	Ball. Coef.
8mm	1.235"	.323"	200	AF/SS	.274	.357
8mm	1.325"	.323"	220	AF/SS	.301	.393
338	1.245"	.338"	225	AF/SS	.281	.384
338	1.335"	.338"	250	AF/SS	.313	.427
338	1.435"	.338"	275	AF/SS	.344	.469
35	1.140"	.358"	225	AF/SS	.251	.312
35	1.237"	.358"	250	AF/SS	.279	.347
35	1.345"	.358"	280	AF/SS	.312	.388
9.3mm	1.120"	.366"	250	AF/SS	.267	.285
9.3mm	1.310"	.366"	300	AF/SS	.320	.342
375	1.085"	.375"	250	AF/SS	.254	.271
375	1.200"	.375"	270	AF/SS	.274	.349
375	1.270"	.375"	300	AF/SS	.305	.325

BTS = ***Boat Tail Spitzer*** **AF/SS =** ***A-Frame Semi-Spitzer*** **AF/FN =** ***A-Frame Flat Nose*** **AF/RN =** ***A-Frame Round Nose*** **AF/HP =** ***A-Frame Hollow Point***

HANDLOADING

Swift

A-Frame Rifle, Revolver and muzzle Loader Bullets

HANDLOADING

Cal.	A-Frame Rifle Bullet	Dia.	Wt. (gr.)	Profile	Sect. Den.	Ball. Coef.
416	1.260"	.416"	350	AF/SS	.289	.321
416	1.405"	.416"	400	AF/SS	.330	.367
404	1.380"	.423"	400	AF/SS	.319	.375
458	.960"	.458"	350	AF/FN	.238	.170
458	1.130"	.458"	400	AF/FN	.272	.258
458	1.310"	.458"	450	AF/SS	.307	.325
458	1.430"	.458"	500	AF/SS	.341	.361
470	1.280"	.475"	500	AF/RN	.329	.364

Cal.	A-Frame Revolver Bullet	Dia.	Wt. (gr.)	Profile	Sect. Den.	Ball. Coef.
357		Available in 2005				
41		Available in 2005				
44	.755"	.430"	240	AF/HP	.185	.119
44	.845"	.430"	280	AF/HP	.216	.139

Cal.	A-Frame Revolver Bullet	Dia.	Wt. (gr.)	Profile	Sect. Den.	Ball. Coef.
44	.910"	.430"	300	AF/HP	.232	.147
45	.750"	.452"	265	AF/HP	.185	.129
45	.840"	.452"	300	AF/HP	.210	.153
45	.895"	.452"	325	AF/HP	.227	.171
50		Available in 2005				

Cal.	A-Frame Muzzle Loader	Dia.	Wt. (gr.)	Profile	Sect. Den.	Ball. Coef.
50		.430"	240	AF/HP	.185	.119
50		.430"	300	AF/HP	.232	.147
54		.452"	265	AF/HP	.185	.129
54		.452"	325	AF/HP	.227	.153

The Swift A-Frame, noted for deep penetration in tough game, is loaded in Remington Premier ammunition.

Woodleigh Premium Bullets

WELDCORE SOFT NOSE

A product of Australia, Woodleigh weldcore Soft Nose bullets are made from 90/100 gilding metal (90% copper; 10% zinc) 1.6 mm thick. Maximum retained weight is obtained by fusing the pure lead to the gilding metal jacket, hence the name "Weldcore."

FULL METAL JACKET

Fashioned from gilding metal-clad steel 2mm thick, jackets on FMJ bullets are heavy at the nose for extra impact resistance. The jacket then tapers towards the base to assist rifling engraving.

Calibre Diameter	Type	Weight Grain	SD	BC
700 Nitro	SN	1000	.292	.340
.700″	FMJ	1000	.292	.340
600 Nitro	SN	900	.334	.371
.620″	FMJ	900	.334	.334
577 Nitro	SN	750	.313	.346
.585″	FMJ	750	.313	.351
	SN	650	.271	.292
	FMJ	650	.271	.292
577 B.P.	SN	650	.271	.320
.585″				
500 Nitro	SN	570	.313	.474
.510″	FMJ	570	.313	.434
500 B.P.	SN	440	.242	.336
.510″				
500	PP	535	.304	.460
Jeffery	SN	535	.304	.460
.510″	FMJ	535	.304	.422
	PP	600	.330	.423
	FMJ	600	.330	.330
505	PP	600	.336	.450
Gibbs	SN	525	.294	.445
.505″	FMJ	525	.294	.408
	FMJ	600	.366	.450
475 No2	SN	500	.300	.420
Jeffery .488″	FMJ	500	.300	.416
475 No2	SN	480	.303	.400
.483″	FMJ	480	.303	.410
476 W.R.	SN	520	.328	.420
.476″	FMJ	520	.328	.455
475 Nitro	SN	480	.227	.307
.476″	FMJ	480	.227	.257
470 Nitro	SN	500	.318	.411
.474″	FMJ	500	.318	.410
465 Nitro	SN	480	.318	.410
.468″	FMJ	480	.318	.407
450 Nitro	SN	480	.327	.419
.458″	FMJ	480	.327	.410
458 Mag.	SN	500	.341	.430
.458″	SN	550	.375	.480
	FMJ	500	.341	.405
	FMJ	550	.375	.426
	PP	400	.272	.420
	RN	350	.238	.305
45/70	FN	405	.276	.250
.458″				
11.3x62				
Schuler	SN	401	.296	.411
.440″				
425 W.R.	SN	410	.310	.344
.435″	FMJ	410	.310	.336
404	SN	400	.319	.354
Jeffery	FMJ	400	.319	.358
.423″	SN	350	.279	.357
10.75x68mm	SN	347	.277	.355
.423″	FMJ	347	.277	.307
416	SN	410	.338	.375
Rigby	FMJ	410	.338	.341
.416″	PP	340	.281	.425
	SN	450	.372	.402
450/400	SN	400	.338	.384
Nitro .411″	FMJ	400	.338	.433
or .408″				

Calibre Diameter	Type	Weight Grain	SD	BC
.408	SN	400	.338	.384
.408	FMJ	400	.338	.433
375 Mag.	PP	235	.239	.331
.375″	RN	270	.275	.305
	SP	270	.275	.380
	PP	270	.275	.352
	RN	300	.305	.340
	SP	300	.305	.425
	PP	300	.305	.420
	FMJ	300	.305	.307
	RN	350	.354	.354
	PP	350	.354	.440
	FMJ	350	.354	.372
405 Win., .411″	SN	300	.254	.194
9.3mm	SN	286	.305	.331
.366″	PP	286	.305	.381
	FMJ	286	.305	.324
	SN	250	.267	.296
360 No2	SN	320	.341	.378
.366″	FMJ	320	.341	.362
	PP	320	.343	.428
358 Cal	SN	225	.250	.277
.358″	FMJ	225	.250	.298
	SN	250	.285	.365
	SN	310	.346	.400
	FMJ	310	.346	.378
338 Mag	PP	225	.281	.425
.338″	SN	250	.313	.332
	PP	250	.313	.470
	FMJ	250	.313	.326
	SN	300	.375	.416
	FMJ	300	.375	.398
333	SN	250	.328	.400
Jeffery	SN	300	.386	.428
.333″	FMJ	300	.386	.419
318 W.R.	SN	250	.328	.420
.330″	FMJ	250	.328	.364
8mm	SN	196	.268	.370
.323″	SN	220	.302	.363
	SN	250	.343	.389
8X57	SN	200	.282	.370
303	SN	174	.257	.342
British .312	PP	215	.316	.359
308 Cal	FMJ	220	.331	.359
.308″	RN	220	.331	.367
	PP	180	.273	.376
	PP	165	.250	.320
	PP	150	.226	.301
Win Mag.	PP	180	.273	.435
	PP	200	.301	.450
275 H&H	PP	160	.275	.474
.287″	PP	175	.301	.518
7mm	PP	140	.247	.436
.284″	PP	160	.282	.486
	PP	175	.312	.530
270 Win	PP	130	.241	.409
.277″	PP	150	.278	.463

SP = Semi-point • PP = Protected Point • FN = Flat Nose • RN = Round Nose • FMJ = Full Metal Jacket
All PP, FN, RN, SP, SN bullets are Weldcore Softnose

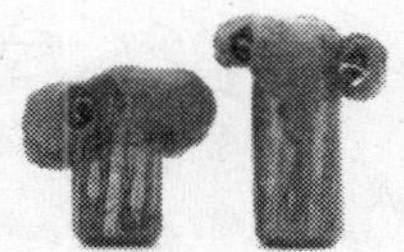

98% & 95% RETAINED WEIGHT 300 WIN MAG 180GR PP

458 X 500GN SN RECOVERED FROM BUFFALO

270 WIN 150GN PP 86% RETAINED WEIGHT

94% RETAINED WEIGHT 300 WIN MAG 180GR PP

500/465 RECOVERED FROM BUFFALO

Accurate Powder

Accurate Powder Specifications

	NG*	Avg. Length/Thickness		Avg. Diameter		Bulk Density	VMD	Comparative Powders***	
		inches	mm	Inches	mm	Gram/cc	cc/grain	Ball	Extruded
Ball Propellants									
Handguns/Shotshell									
No.2 Imp.	14.0			0.018	0.457	0.650	0.100	WIN 231	Bullseye
No. 5	18.0			0.027	0.686	0.950	0.068	WIN 540	
No. 7	12.0			0.012	0.305	0.985	0.066	WIN 630	
No. 9	10.0			1.015	0.381	0.935	0.069	WIN 296	
1680	10.0			0.014	0.356	0.950	0.068	WIN 680	
Solo 4100	10.0			0.011	0.279	0.960	0.068	WIN 296	
Rifle									
2230	10.0			0.022	0.559	0.980	0.066	BL C2, WIN 748	
2460	10.0			0.022	0.559	0.990	0.065	BL C2, WIN 748	
2520	10.0			0.022	0.559	0.970	0.067		
2700	10.0			0.022	0.559	0.960	0.068	WIN 760	
MAGPRO	9.0			0.030	0.762	0.970	0.067		
8700	10.0			0.030	0.762	0.960	0.068	H870	
Extruded Propellants									
Shotshell/Handguns									
Nirto 100	21.0	0.010	0.254	0.058	1.473	0.505	0.128		700X, Red Dot
Solo 1000		0.010	0.254	0.052	1.321	0.510	0.127		Green Dot
Solo 1250		0.013	0.033	0.051	1.295	0.550	0.118		PB
Rifle/handgun									
5744	20.00	0.048	1.219	0.033	0.838	0.880	0.074		
Rifle									
2015		0.039	0.991	0.031	0.787	0.880	0.074		H322,N201 IMR 4198
2495		0.068	1.727	0.029	0.737	0.880	0.074		IMR 4895
4064		0.050	1.270	0.035	0.889	0.890	0.072		IMR 4064
4350		0.083	0.038	0.038	0.965	0.890	0.072		IMR 4350
3100		0.083	0.038	0.038	0.965	0.920	0.070		IMR 4831

*NG-NItroglycerin ***For comparison only, not a loading recommendation

Alliant Smokeless Powders

BULLSEYE

America's best known pistol powder. Unsurpassed for .45 ACP target loads. ***Available in 8-lb., 4-lb., and 1-lb. canisters.***

POWER PISTOL

Designed for high performance in semi-automatic pistols and is the powder of choice for 9mm, .40 S&W and .357 SIG. ***Available in 4-lb. and 1-lb. canisters.***

2400

Legendary for its performance in .44 magnum and other magnum pistol loads. Originally developed for the .22 Hornet, it's also the shooter's choice for .410 bore. ***Available in 8-lb., 4-lb., and 1-lb. canisters.***

UNIQUE

The most versatile shotgun/handgun powder made. Great for 12, 16, 20 and 28 gauge. loads. Use with most hulls, primers and wads. ***Available in 8- lb., 4-lb., and 1- lb. canisters.***

RELODER 7

Designed for small caliber varmint loads, it meters consistently, and meets the needs of the most demanding bench rest shooter. Great in .45-70 and .450 Marlin. ***Available in 5-lb. and 1-lb. canisters.***

RELODER 10X

Best choice for light bullet applications in .222 Rem, .223 Rem, .22-250 Rem and key bench rest calibers. Also great in light bullet .308 Win loads. ***Available in 5 lb. and 1 lb. containers.***

RELODER 15

The best all-around medium speed rifle powder. It provides excellent .223 and .308 cal. performance. Selected as the powder for U.S. Military's M118 Special Ball Long Range Sniper Round. ***Available in 5-lb. and 1-lb. canisters.***

RELODER 19

Provides superb accuracy in most medium and heavy rifle loads and is the powder of choice for 30-06 and .338 calibers. ***Available in 5-lb. and 1-lb. canisters.***

RELODER 22

This top performing powder for big game loads provides excellent metering, and is the powder of choice for .270, 7mm magnum and .300 Win. magnum. ***Available in 5-lb. and 1-lb. canisters.***

RELODER 25

This new, advanced powder for big game hunting features improved slower burning, and delivers the high ener-gy that heavy magnum loads need. ***Available in 5-lb. and 1-lb. canisters.***

Alliant Shotshell Powders

RED DOT
America's #1 choice for clay target loads, now 50% cleaner. Since 1932, more 100 straights than any other powder. ***Available in 8-lb., 4-lb., and 1-lb. canisters.***

E^3
The first of a new generation of high performance powders.

GREEN DOT
It delivers precise burn rates for uniformly tight patterns, and you'll appreciate the lower felt recoil. Versatile for target and field. ***Available in 8-lb., 4-lb., and 1-lb. canisters.***

AMERICAN SELECT
Our "ultra clean" burning premium powder makes a versatile target load and superior 1-oz. load for improved clay target scores. Great for Cowboy Action handgun loading too! ***Available in 8-lb., 4-lb., and 1-lb. canisters.***

410
Cleanest .410 bore powder on the market.

STEEL
Designed for waterfowl shotshell. Gives steel shot high velocity within safe pressure limits for 10 and 12 gauge loads. ***Available in 4-lb. and 1-lb. canisters.***

BLUE DOT
The powder of choice for magnum lead shotshell loads. 10, 12, 16, and 20 gauge. Consistent and accurate. Doubles as magnum handgun powder. ***Available in 5-lb., and 1-lb. canisters.***

HERCO
Since 1920, a proven powder for heavy shotshell loads, including 10, 12, 16, 20 and 28 gauge target loads. The ultimate in 12 gauge, 1¼ oz. upland game loads. ***Available in 8-lb., 4-lb., and 1-lb. canisters.***

Hodgdon Smokeless Powder

Hodgdon Powder Company offers its popular sulfur-free Triple Seven powder in 50-grain pellets. Formulated for use with 209 shotshell primers, Triple Seven leaves no rotten egg smell, and the residue is easy to clean from the bore with water only. The pellets are sized for 50-caliber muzzleloaders and can be used singly (for target shooting or small game) as well as two at a time (for a 100-grain big game charge). Also available in .45 caliber/50 grain and .50 caliber/30 grain sizes.

PYRODEX PELLETS
Both rifle and pistol pellets eliminate powder measures, speeds shooting for black powder enthusiasts.

EXTREME H4198
H4198 was developed especially for small and medium capacity cartridges.

EXTREME H322
This powder fills the gap between H4198 and BL-C9(2). Performs best in small to medium capacity cases.

EXTREME BENCHMARK
A fine choice for small rifle cases like the .223 Rem and PPC competition rounds. Appropriate also for the 300-30 and 7x57.

SPHERICAL BL-C2
Best performance is in the 222, .308 other cases smaller than 30/06.

SPHERICAL H335
Similar to BL-C(2), H335 is popular for its performance in medium capacity cases, especially in 222 and 308 Winchester.

EXTREME VARGET
Features small extruded grain powder for uniform metering, plus higher velocities/normal pressures in such calibers as .223, 22-250, 306, 30-06, 375 H&H

EXTREME H4895
4895 gives desirable performance in almost all cases from 222 Rem. to 458 Win. Reduced loads, to as low as 3/5 maximum, still give target accuracy.

SPHERICAL H380
This number fills a gap between 4320 and 4350. It is excellent in 22/250, 220 Swift, the 6mm's, 257 and 30/06.

SPHERICAL H414
In many popular medium to medium-large calibers, pressure velocity relationship is better.

EXTREME H4350
This powder gives superb accuracy at optimum velocity for many large capacity metallic rifle cartridges.

EXTREME H4831
Outstanding performance with medium and heavy bullets in the 6mm's, 25/06, 270 and Magnum calibers. Also available with shortened grains (H4831SC) for easy metering.

EXTREME H1000 EXTRUDED POWDER
Fills the gap between H4831 and H870. Works especially well in overbore capacity cartridges (1,000-yard shooters take note).

EXTREME H50 BMG
Designed for the 50 Browning Machine Gun cartridge.

RETUMBO

A true magnum rifle powder, designed for such cartridges as the 300 Rem. Ultra Mag., 30-378 Weatherby, the 7mm STW and other cases with large capacities and small bores. Shooters can expect up to 40-100 feet per second more velocity than other magnum powders.

TRIPLE SEVEN

A muzzleloading propellant that does not use sulfur, keeping shooter's hand clean. No offensive odor and cleaning is as easy as running a water soaked patch down the barrel followed by 3 or 4 dry patches!

Highly insensitive to extreme temperature changes.

CLAYS
Tailored for use in 12 ga., 7/8, 1-oz. and 1 1/8-oz. loads. Also performs well in many handgun applications, including .38 Special, .40 S&W and 45 ACP. Perfect for 1 1/8 and 1 oz. loads.

UNIVERSAL CLAYS
Loads nearly all of the straight-wall pistol cartridges as well as 12 ga. 1.25 oz. thru 28 ga. 3/4 oz. target loads.

INTERNATIONAL CLAYS
Ideal for 12 and 20 ga. autoloaders who want reduced recoil.

TITEWAD
This 12 ga. flattened spherical shotgun powder is ideal for 7/8, 1 and 1 1/8 oz. loads, with minimum recoil and mild muzzle report. The fastest fuel in Hodgdon's line.

HS-6 AND HS-7
HS-6 and HS-7 for Magnum field loads are unsurpassed, since they do not pack in the measure. They deliver uniform charges and are dense to allow sufficient wad column for best patterns.

LONGSHOT
A spherical powder for heavy shotgun loads.

HP38
A fast pistol powder for most pistol loading. Especially recommended for mid-range 38 specials.

TITEGROUP
Excellent for most straight-walled pistol cartridges, incl. 38 Spec., 44 Spec., 45 ACP. Low charge weights, clean burning; position insensitive and flawless ignition.

H110
A spherical powder made especially for the 30 M1 carbine. H110 also does very well in 357, 44 spec., 44 Mag. or 410 ga. shotshell. Magnum primers are recommended for consistent ignition.

H4227
An extruded powder similar to H110, it is recommended for the 22 Hornet and some specialized loading in the 45-70 caliber. Also excellent in magnum pistol and .410 shotgun.

LIL' GUN
This powder was developed specifically for the .410 shotgun but works very well in rifle cartridges like the .22 Hornet and in the .44 magnum.

IMR Powders

E.I. DuPont de Nemours began its corporate life in 1802, on Delaware's Brandywine River. The varied product line that evolved over the next couple of centuries could hardly have been imagined by its founder, French immigrant Eleuthere Irenee DuPont.

"I can make better black powder than what your country has in its magazines," DuPont told Alexander Hamilton. The enterprising engineer got the help he needed to build a plant in Wilmington. The new propellant satisfied U.S. ordnance officers, and DuPont put down roots. Gunpowder was the firm's primary product for most of the 19th century. In the 1880s, DuPont built a plant at Carney's Point to boost capacity. During World War I, 25,000 people went to work at this facility on the Brandywine, providing more than 80 percent of the military powders used by the Allies (the British, French, Danes, and Russians as well as U.S. troops.

Soon after the transition from black to smokeless powders at the close of the 19th century, "MR" began appearing on canisters of DuPont powders. It meant "military rifle." The IMR line of "improved military rifle" powders came along in the 1920s, when four-digit numbers replaced two-digit numbers in DuPont designations. MR 10 and the like died out. IMR fuels, beginning with 4198, supplanted them. The first had relatively fast burn rates, because in those days, rifle cartridges were small. In 1934, DuPont introduced IMR 4227. In the early 1940s, IMR 4895 came along, specifically for the .30-06 in the M1 Garand service rifle. About that time the first slow IMR propellant made its debut. Developed for 20mm cannons, IMR 4831 would become one of the most popular powders for high-capacity rifle cartridges developed by wildcatters like Roy Weatherby and P.O. Ackley. Incidentally, label numbers have nothing to do with burning rate. According to long-time DuPont engineer Larry Werner, powder is labeled chronologically. The highest numbers indicate the most recent propellants.

You'll find differences in charts ranking the burn rates of IMR and other smokeless powders. The reason: powders can behave differently as you change case shape and bore diameter, fuel charge and bullet weight. IMR gives all its powders a Relative Quickness value, assigning IMR 4350 an arbitrary value of 100. According to Larry Werner, quick-burning IMR 4227 has an RQ of 180; IMR 4198 comes in at 165 and IMR 3031 at 135. IMR 4064, 4320 and 4895 are listed at 120, 115 and 110 respectively, though some loading manuals suggest a different order. IMR 4831 and 7828 burn more slowly. "Closed bomb" tests are used to gauge burn rate. A unit charge of powder ignited in a chamber of known volume produces a pressure curve that's then compared to the curves from other propellants.

DuPont's MR line included single-base (nitrocellulose) and double-base (nitrocellulose with nitroglycerine) powders. "The nitro gives you more energy per grain," explains Larry, "and it reduces the tendency for the grains to pick up moisture. Its drawback is more residue. Double-base powders generally don't burn as clean. To get the full effect of nitroglycerine, you really need 8 to 12 percent in the mix, but some powders claimed to be double-base contain less." All commercial ball powders are double-base, he says. The current IMR line includes only single-base propellants.

IMR powders are no longer made by DuPont. The IMR trademark belongs to EXPRO, another chemical firm. The transfer has its roots in the Depression, which DuPont weathered. But scathing political attacks from certain U.S. senators accused the company of war-mongering. As Hitler tuned his war machine and the U.S. prepared to re-arm, DuPont boosted its production capacity. "But the company was fed up with the treatment it had received from Congress," Larry remembers. Rather than build new plants, it contracted to operate government facilities for one dollar a year. That way, it could not be said to have had a stake in the hostilities. Of course, the government had no powder works that could match DuPont's, so the firm supervised construction of seven factories modeled on the Carney's Point plant. Another was built in Canada. At the height of the Second World War, these facilities shipped a million pounds of powder a day.

In the summer of 1978, DuPont contracted with Valleyfield Chemical Products in Quebec to produce its commercial smokeless propellants. (The Valleyfield plant was the Canadian factory built during World War II. It had been operated by CIL, or Canadian Industries, Ltd., a branch of the government.) In 1982, Valleyfield Chemical sold to Welland Chemical, which became EXPRO.

In December, 1986, DuPont sold its smokeless powder business to EXPRO. The IMR Powder Company became a testing and marketing firm for EXPRO propellants. IMR's laboratory and offices in Plattsburg, New York, developed ballistics data for IMR powders and packaged and distributed them to dealers. EXPRO, with an annual manufacturing capacity of more than 10 million pounds, also made other powders, including Alliant. Though DuPont owned 70 percent of Remington for decades, it has from time to time provided powder for competing ammunition firms.

In October 2003, Hodgdon Powder Company purchased IMR and retains it as a division. IMR powders are still available under their familiar product names. The phone number for IMR is now 913-362-9455. Learn more at www.imrpowder.com

Ramshot Powders

Ramshot (Western Powders, Inc.) powders are all double-base propellants, meaning they contain nitrocellulose and nitroglycerine. While some spherical or ball powders are known for leaving plenty of residue in barrels, Ramshots people say these new fuels burn very clean. They meter easily, as do all ball powders. Plastic canisters are designed for spill-proof use and include basic loading data on the labels.

RAMSHOT COMPETITION is for the clay target shooter. A fast-burning powder comparable to 700-X or Red Dot it performs well in a variety of 12-gauge target loads, offering low recoil, consistent pressures and clean combustion.

RAMSHOT TRUE BLUE was designed for small to medium-size handgun cartridges. Similar to Winchester 231 and Hodgdon HP-38, it has enough bulk to nearly fill most cases, thereby better positioning the powder for ignition.

RAMSHOT ZIP, a fast-burning target powder for cartridges like the .38 Special and .45 ACP, gives competitors uniform velocities.

RAMSHOT SILHOUETTE is ideal for the 9mm handgun cartridge, from light to heavy loads. It also works well in the .40 Smith & Wesson and combat loads for the .45 Auto.

RAMSHOT ENFORCER is a match for high-performance handgun hulls like the .40 Smith & Wesson. It is designed for full-power loading and high velocities. Ramshot X-Terminator, a fast-burning rifle powder, excels in small-caliber, medium-capacity cartridges. It has the versatility to serve in both target and high-performance varmint loads.

RAMSHOT TAC was formulated for tactical rifle cartridges, specifically the .223 and .308. It has produced exceptional accuracy with a variety of bullets and charge weights.

RAMSHOT BIG GAME is a versatile propellant for cartridges as diverse as the .30-06 and the .338 Winchester, and for light-bullet loads in small-bore magnums.

RAMSHOT MAGNUM is the slowest powder of the Western line, and does its best work in cartridges with lots of case volume and small to medium bullet diameter. It is the powder of choice in 7mm and .30 Magnums.

RAMSHOT X-TERMINATOR is a clean burning powder designed for the .222 Rem., 223 Rem., and .22 Benchrest calibers.

Vihtavuori

Kaltron-Pettibone imports Vihtavuori propellants (and Lapua ammunition in the U.S.) The powders, only recently available Stateside, have become popular with American shooters, who applaud their consistency. Their burning rates complement those of powders from IMR, Accurate, Hodgdon and Alliant (the ReLoder series). Here's a synopsis. Note that "similar" in these descriptions does NOT connote interchangeability!

N11O: very fast, for rifle cartridges like the .22 Hornet and .25-20, and for powerful handgun rounds like the .357 and .44 Magnums; similar powders include H110, Winchester 296, Alliant 2400.

N120: a fast powder that requires high pressure for complete and efficient burn; similar to IMR 4227 and best used in small-capacity .22 centerfires.

N130: . . a bit slower than 4227 but still quick; a standard propellant in the .22 and 6mm PPC.

N133: slow enough for use in medium-capacity .22 cartridges like the .223; also useful in the .45-70 and similar cartridges with little or no neck restriction; similar to IMR 4198.

N135: a versatile powder of medium burn rate, ideal in the .308 and close derivatives, as well as the .30-06; applications from the various 17-calibers to the .458 Winchester; similar to RL-12.

N140: . . slightly slower than N135, but useful in the same cartridges and any that would be served with RL-15 or IMR 4320; a fine choice for the .30-06 and .375 H&H.

N150: a medium-slow powder for light-bullet loads in the .270 and the 30-caliber magnums; an excellent alternative to Winchester 760, Hodgdon H414, IMR 4350.

N160: a workhorse powder for magnum cases and high-velocity rounds on the .308 and .30-06 hulls; similar to RL-19, IMR 4831, Accurate 3100; useful in the .243, .270, 7mm Remington and .300 and .338 Winchester Magnums.

N165: a slow powder for "overbore" magnum cases and for heavy-bullet loads in the medium-bore magnums; ideal for high-performance .300s with all bullet weights; similar to H4831 and RL-22.

N170: the slowest-burning of Vihtavuori's propellants, for small-bore magnums like the .257 Weatherby and .264 Winchester; similar to H1000 and RL-25.

Unlike the single-base (nitrocellulose) N100 series, the N500 series of Vihtavuori powders has a nitroglycerol component (up to 25 percent, by impregnation). There's also a special stabilizer, a flame reducing agent, a wear-reducing agent and coating agents that ensure progressive burning in the case to provide uniform and efficient pressure curves. These high-energy double-base powders are available in three burning rates, equivalent to the 100-series powders with the same last digits. N540 is applicable in the same cartridges as N140. N550 is a match for N150. N560 is the slowest, an ideal propellant for the .270 Winchester and 6.5x55 Swedish Mauser.

Vihtavuori also makes single-base powders for the .50 BMG. The 24N41 is slightly faster than the 20N29. Eight Vihtavuori pistol powders complete the 2003 line:

N310: as fast as Bullseye, for small-capacity cartridges like the .25 ACP up to the 9mm Luger.

N320: slightly faster than Winchester 231, a versatile powder for the most popular of pistol rounds, including the .38 Special, .357 Magnum, .45 ACP, .44 Magnum and .45 Long Colt.

N330: useful in medium- to large-capacity cases from the .38 Special to the various .44s and .45s; similar to Green Dot.

N340: slow enough for high-performance loads in the .357 and .44 Magnums, also useful in the .38 Super and .30 Luger; similar to Winchester 540.

N350: a slow powder for magnum and heavy-bullet handgun loads; burning rate like that of Blue Dot or Hi-Skor 800-X.

3N37: between N340 and N350 in burn rate; recommended for competitive shooters.

3N38: a competition powder specifically for high-speed loads in the .38 Super and 9mm Luger.

N105 Super Magnum: a very slow pistol powder for heavy-bullet loads in magnum cases; almost as slow as N110.

Dillon Precision Reloaders

DILLON PRECISION RELOADERS

Besides manufacturing high-speed metallic cartridge reloading machines, Dillon Precision is a leader in the shotshell reloading market with its SL 900 progressive press. Based on Dillon's proven XL 650 O-frame design, it incorporates the same powerful compound linkage. The automatic case insert system, fed by an electric case collator, ranks high among the new features of this reloader. Adjustable shot and powder bars come as standard equipment. Both the powder and shot bars are case-activated, so no powder or shot can spill when no shell is at that station. Should the operator forget to insert a wad during the reloading process, the SL 900 will not dispense shot into the powder-charged hull. Both powder and shot systems are based on Dillon's adjustable powder bar design, which is accurate to within a few tenths of a grain. These systems also eliminate the need for fixed-volume bushings. Simply adjust the measures to dispense the exact charges required.

The Dillon SL 900 is the first progressive shotshell loader on which it is practical to change gauges. An interchangeable toolhead makes it quick and easy to change from one gauge to another. The SL 900 also has an extra large, remote shot hopper that holds an entire 25-pound bag of shot, making it easy to fill with a funnel. The unique shot reservoir/dispenser helps ensure that a consistent volume of shot is delivered to each shell.

For shotgunners who shoot and load for multiple gauges or different kinds of shooting, the SL 900's interchangeable toolhead feature makes quick work of changing from one gauge to another. It uses a collet-type sizing die that re-forms the base of the shotshell to factory specifications—a feature that ensures reliable feeding in all shotguns. The heat-treated steel crimp-die forms and folds the hull before the final taper crimp die radiuses and blends the end of the hull and locks the crimp into place.

HANDLOADING

MODEL RL550B PROGRESSIVE LOADER

- Accommodates over 120 calibers
- Interchangeable toolhead assembly
- Auto/Powder priming systems
- Uses standard 7/8" by 14 dies
- Loading rate: 500-600 rounds per hour

Prices on request

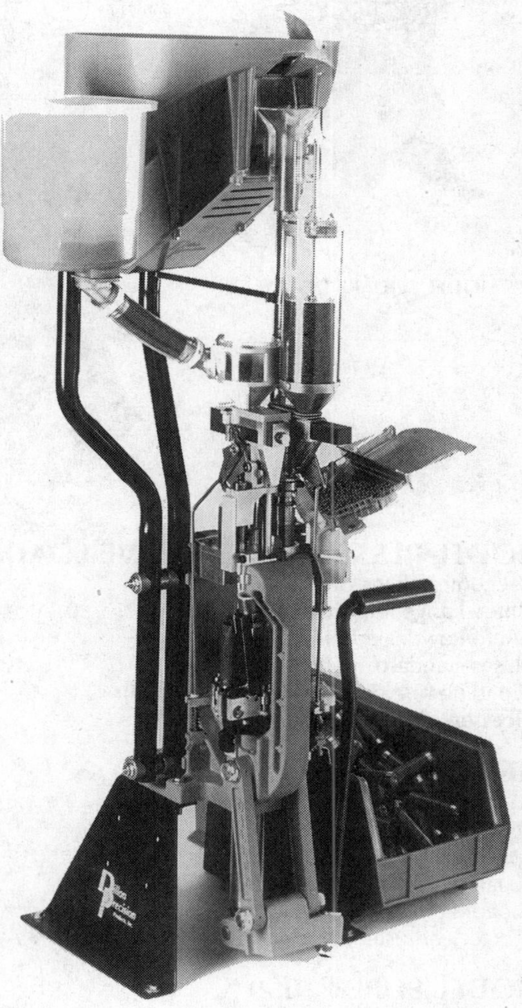

MODEL SL900

Price on request

Dillon Precision Reloaders

MODEL SQUARE DEAL B

MODEL XL 650

MODEL AT-500

MODEL SUPER 1050 AND RL 1050

MODEL RL550B PROGRESSIVE LOADER

- Accommodates over 120 calibers
- Interchangeable toolhead assembly
- Auto/Powder priming systems
- Uses standard ⅞″ by 14 dies
- Loading rate: 500-600 rounds per hour

Prices on request

MODEL SQUARE DEAL B

- Automatic indexing
- Auto Powder/Priming Systems
- Available in 14 handgun calibers
- Loading rate: 400-500 rounds per hour
- Loading dies standard
- Factory adjusted, ready-to-use

MODEL SUPER 1050

- Automatic indexing
- Auto powder/priming systems
- Automatic casefeeder
- Commercial grade machine
- Swages military primer pockets
- Loading rate: 1000-1200 rounds per hour
- Weighs 54 lbs.
- Eight stations

MODEL XL 650

- Rotary indexing plate for primers
- Automatic indexing
- Uses standard ⅞″ x 14 dies
- Loading rate: 800-1000 rounds per hour
- Five-station interchangeable toolhead

MODEL AT-500

- Loads over 40 calibers
- Uses standard ⅞″ by 14 dies
- Upgradeable to Model RL 550B
- Interchangeable toolhead
- Switch from one caliber to another in 30 seconds
- Universal shellplate

Forster Reloading

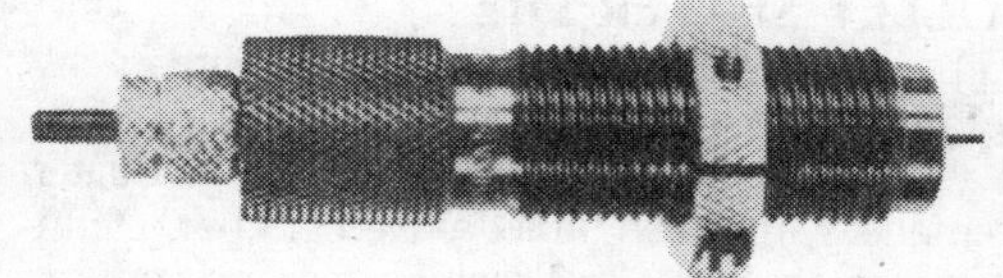

CO-AX BENCH REST RIFLE DIES

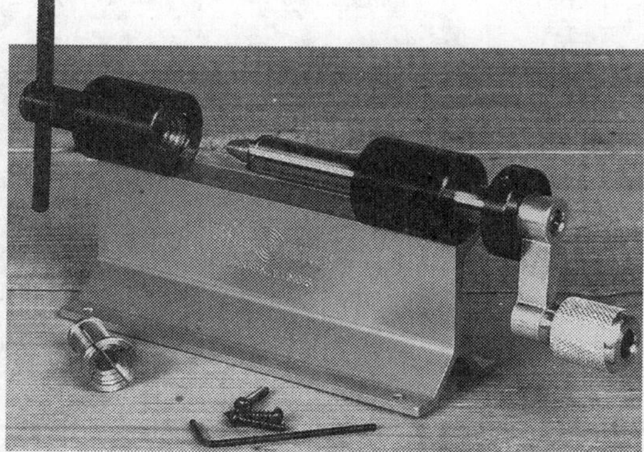

HAND CASE TRIMMER

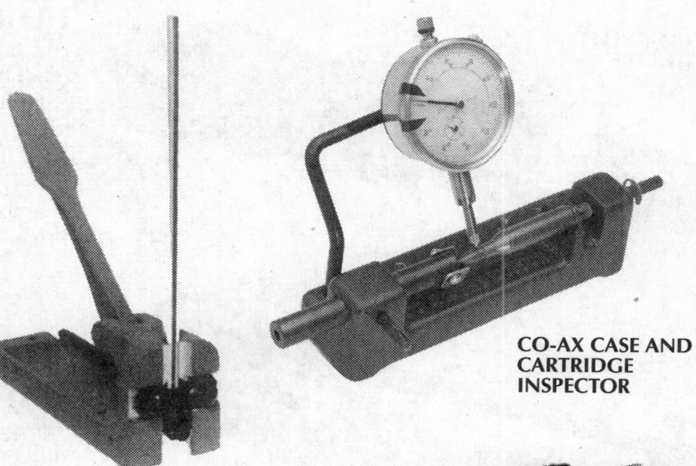

PRIMER SEATER

CO-AX CASE AND CARTRIDGE INSPECTOR

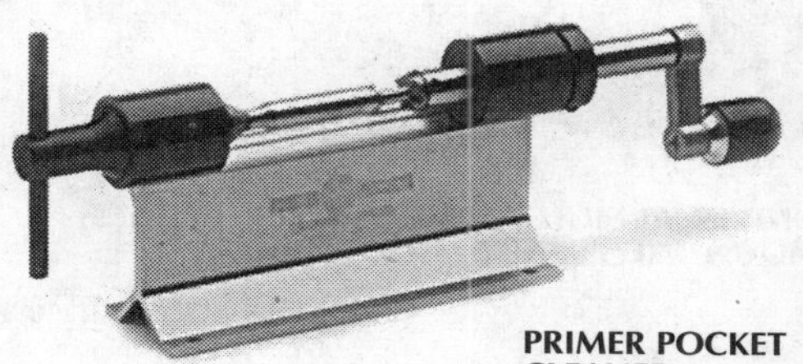

PRIMER POCKET CLEANER

CO-AX BENCH REST RIFLE DIES

Bench Rest Rifle Dies are glass-hard and polished mirror-smooth with special attention given to headspace, tapers and diameters. Sizing die has an elevated expander button to ensure better alignment of case and neck.

Bench Rest® Die Set **$82**
Ultra Bench Rest Die Set **112**
Full Length Sizer **39**
Bench Rest Seating Die......................... **47**

HAND CASE TRIMMER

Shell holder is a Brown & Sharpe-type collet. Case and cartridge conditioning accessories include inside neck reamer, outside neck turner, deburring tool, hollow pointer and primer pocket cleaners. The case trimmer trims all cases, ranging from 17 to 458 Winchester caliber.

Price: **$69**

PRIMER SEATER WITH "E-Z-JUST" SHELLHOLDER

The Bonanza Primer Seater is designed so that primers are seated co-axially (primer in line with primer pocket). Mechanical leverage allows primers to be seated fully without crushing. With the addition of one extra set of disc shell holders and one extra Primer Unit, all modern cases, rim or rimless, from 222 up to 458 Magnum, can be primed. Shell holders are easily adjusted to any case by rotating to contact rim or cannelure of the case.

Primer Seater **$80**

"CLASSIC 50" CASE TRIMMER (NOT SHOWN)

Handles more than 100 different big bore calibers–500 Nitro Express, 416 Rigby, 50 Sharps, 475 H&H, etc. Also available: .50 BMG Case Trimmer, designed specifically for reloading needs of .50 Cal. BMG shooters.

Price: "Classic 50" Case Trimmer **$99**
.50 BMG Case Trimmer........................... **$103**

CO-AX CASE AND CARTRIDGE INSPECTOR

One tool to perform three vital measurements. Accurate performance from ammunition is dependent on uniformity of both the bullet and the case. Forster's exclusive Co-Ax® Case & Cartridge Inspector provides the ability to ensure uniformity by measuring three critical dimensions: • Neck wall thickness • Case neck concentricity • Bullet run-out.

Measurements are in increments of one-thousandth of an inch. The Inspector is unique because it checks both the bullet and case alignment in relation to the centerline (axis) of the entire cartridge or case.

Price: **$93**

PRIMER POCKET CLEANER

The Primer Pocket Cleaner helps ensure consistent ignition and reduce the incidence of misfires by removing powder and primer residue from the primer pockets of your cases. This simple took is easy to use: Just hold the case mouth over the Primer Pocket Center with one hand while you quickly and easily clean the primer pockets by turning the Case Trimmer Handle.

Price: **$8**

Forster Reloading

ULTRA BULLET SEATER DIE

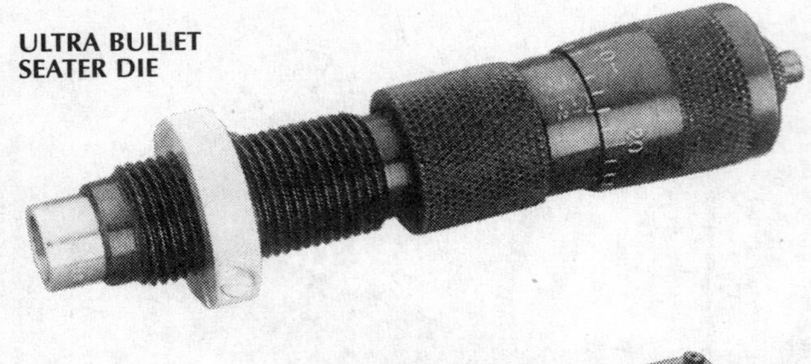

ULTRA BULLET SEATER DIE

Forster's Ultra Die is available in 61 calibers, more than any other brand of micrometer-style seater. Adjustment is identical to that of a precision micrometer—the head is graduated to .001" increments with .025" bullet movement per revolution. The cartridge case, bullet and seating stem are completely supported and perfectly aligned in a close-fitting chamber before and during the bullet seating operation.

Price: **$75**

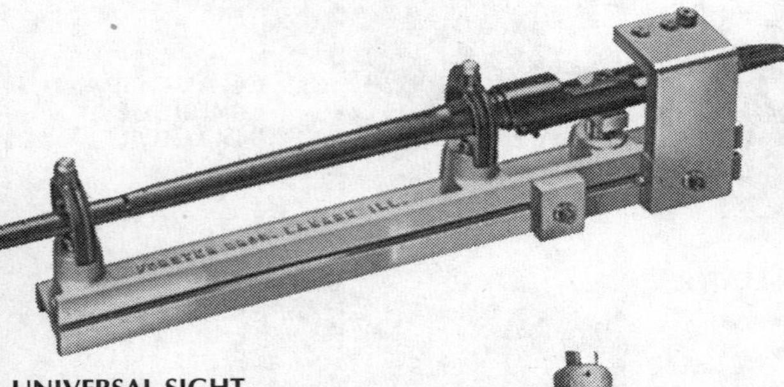

UNIVERSAL SIGHT MOUNTING FIXTURE

UNIVERSAL SIGHT MOUNTING FIXTURE

This product fills the exacting requirements needed for drilling and tapping holes for the mounting of scopes, receiver sights, shotgun beads, etc. The fixture handles any single-barrel gun—bolt-action, lever-action or pump-action—as long as the barrel can be laid into the "V" blocks of the fixture. Rifles with tube magazines are drilled in the same manner by removing the magazine tube. The fixture's main body is made of aluminum casting. The two "V" blocks are adjustable for height and are made of hardened steel ground accurately on the "V" as well as the shaft.

Price: **$403**

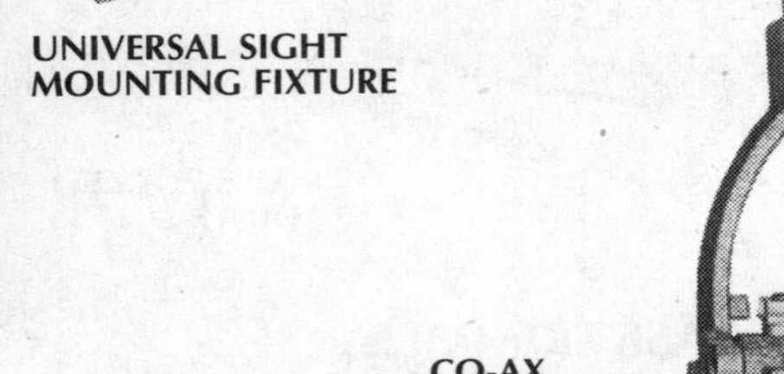

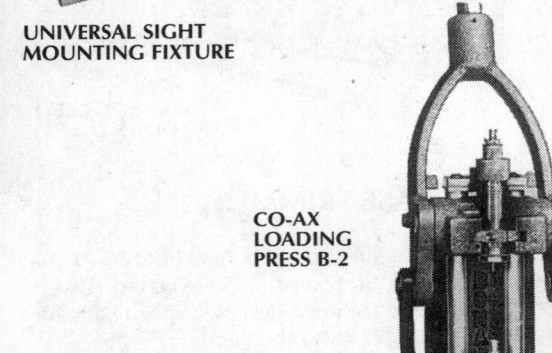

CO-AX LOADING PRESS B-2

CO-AX LOADING PRESS MODEL B-2

Designed to make reloading easier and more accurate, this press offers the following features: Snap-in and snap-out die change • Positive spent primer catcher • Automatic self-acting shell holder • Floating guide rods • Working room for right- or left-hand operators • Top priming device seats primers to factory specifications • Uses any standard ⅞" x 14 dies • No torque on the head • Perfect alignment of die and case • Three times the mechanical advantage of a "C" press

Price: **$336**

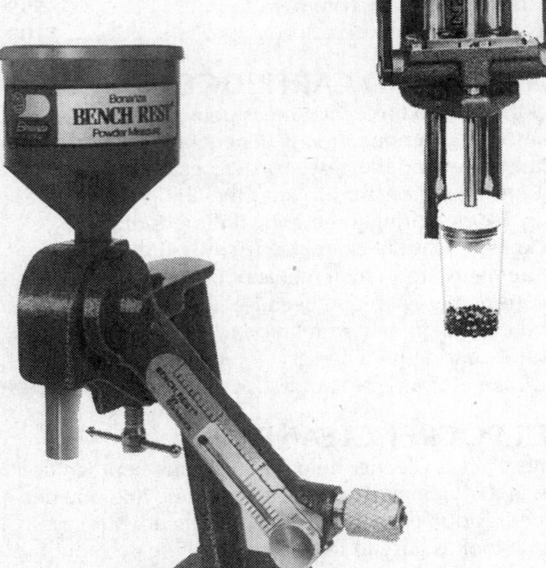

BENCH REST POWDER MEASURE

BENCH REST POWDER MEASURE

When operated uniformly, this measure will throw uniform charges from 2½ grains Bullseye to 95 grains #4320. No extra drums are needed. Powder is metered from the charge arm, allowing a flow of powder without extremes in variation while minimizing powder shearing. Powder flows through its own built-in baffle, entering the charge arm uniformly.

Price: **$123**

Hornady

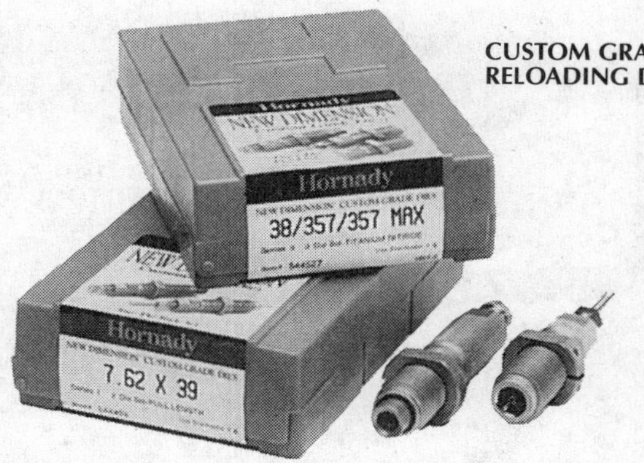

CUSTOM GRADE RELOADING DIES

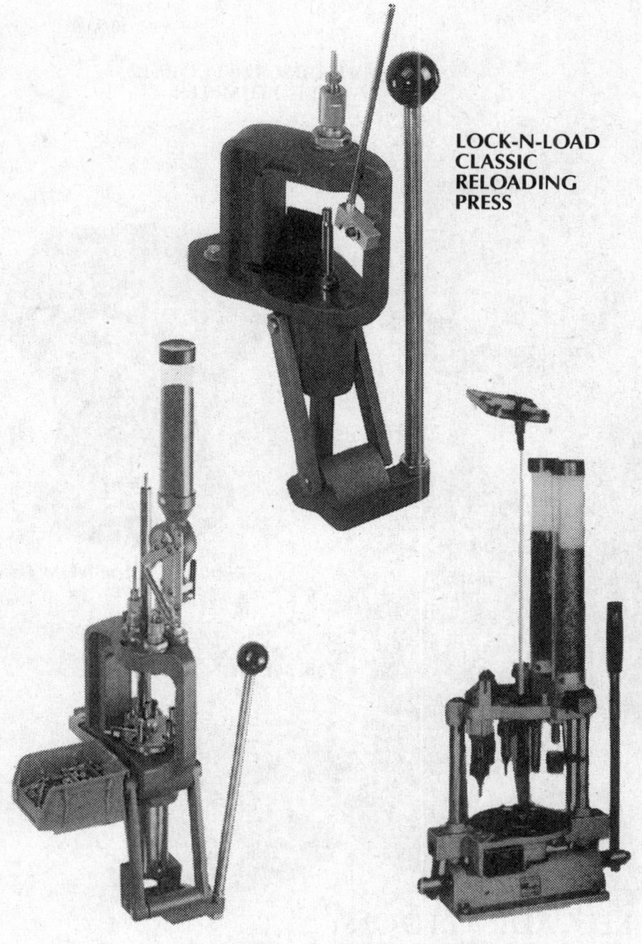

LOCK-N-LOAD CLASSIC RELOADING PRESS

LOCK-N-LOAD

MODEL 366

CUSTOM GRADE RELOADING DIES

An Elliptical Expander in Hornady dies minimizes friction and reduces case neck stretch. (No need for a tapered expander for "necking up" to the next larger caliber.) Other design changes include a hardened steel decap pin that will not break, bend or crack even when depriming stubborn military cases. A bullet seater alignment sleeve guides the bullet and case neck into the die for in-line benchrest alignment. All New Dimension Reloading Dies include: collar and collar lock to center expander precisely; one-piece expander spindle with tapered bottom for easy cartridge insertion; wrench flats on die body, Sure-Loc™ lock rings and collar lock for easy tightening; and built-in crimper.

Prices:

New Dimension Custom Grade Reloading Dies:

Series I **$33**

Series II Three-die Rifle Set **36**

Series III **40**

Match Grade **39**

LOCK-N-LOAD CLASSIC PRESS

Lock-N-Load is available on Hornady's single stage and progressive reloader models. This bushing system locks the die into the press like a rifle bolt. Instead of threading dies in and out of the press, you simply lock and unlock them with a slight twist. Dies are held firmly in a die bushing that stays with the die and retains the die setting. The Lock-N-Load Classic Press features an easy-grip handle, an O-style frame made of high-strength alloy, and a positive priming system that feeds, aligns and seats the primer smoothly and automatically.

Prices: Lock-N-Load Press **$123**

Lock-N-Load Classic Press Kit **292**

Also Available: Lock-N-Load

50 BMG Press **353**

50 BMG Press Kit **575**

LOCK-N-LOAD AUTO PROGRESSIVE PRESS

The Lock-N-Load Automatic Progressive reloading press featuring the Lock-N-Load bushing system offers the flexibility to add a roll or taper crimp die. Dies and powder measure are inserted into Lock-N-Load die bushings, which lock securely into the press. The bushings remain with the die and powder measure and can be removed in seconds. They also fit on other presses. Other features include: deluxe powder measure, automatic indexing, off-set handle, power-pac linkage, case ejector.

Price:

Lock-N-Load Auto Progressive Press (includes five die bushings, shellplate, primer catcher, Positive Priming System, powder drop, Deluxe Powder Measure, automatic primer feed) **$397**

MODEL 366 AUTO SHOTSHELL RELOADER

The 366 Auto features full-length resizing with each stroke, automatic primer feed, swing-out wad guide, three-state crimping featuring Taper-Loc for factory tapered crimp, automatic advance to the next station and automatic ejection. The turntable holds 8 shells for 8 operations with each stroke. Automatic charge bar loads shot and powder, dies and crimp starters for 6 point, 8 point and paper crimps.

Price:

Model 366 Auto Shotshell Reloader:

12, 20, 28 gauge or .410 bore **$557**

Lyman Reloading Tools

MODEL 1200 CLASSIC TURBO TUMBLER

"INSIDE/OUTSIDE" DEBURRING TOOL

MASTER CASTING KIT

2500 PRO MAGNUM TUMBLER

TURBO TWIN TUMBLER

HANDLOADING

RELOADING TOOLS

Model 1200 Classic Turbo Tumbler

This sturdy case tumbler features a redesigned base and drive system, plus a stronger suspension system and built-in exciters for better tumbling action and faster cleaning.

Model 1200 Classic $100
Model 1200 Auto-Flo 100
Also available:
Model 600 70
Model 2200 Auto-Flo 136
Model 3200 Auto-Flo 185

2500 PRO MAGNUM TUMBLER

Prep your cases with a new Lyman 2500 Pro Magnum tumbler. The bin handles up to 900 .38 Special cartridges at once.

2500 Pro Magnum Tumbler $95
with Auto Flow feature. 130

"INSIDE/OUTSIDE" DEBURRING TOOL

This tool features an adjustable cutting blade that adapts easily to the mouth of any rifle or pistol case from 22 caliber to 45 caliber with a simple hex wrench adjustment. Inside deburring is completed by a conical internal section with slotted cutting edges, thus providing uniform inside and outside deburring in one simple operation. The deburring tool is mounted on an anodized aluminum handle that is machine-knurled for a sure grip.

Deburring Tool $14

TURBO TWIN TUMBLER

The Twin features Lyman 1200 Pro Tumbler with an extra, 600 bowl system. Reloaders may use each bowl interchangeably for small or large capacity loads. 1200 Pro Bowl System has a built-in sifter lid for easy sifting of cases and media at the end of the polishing cycle. The Twin Tumbler features the Lyman Hi-Profile base design with built-in exciters and anti-rotation pads for faster, more consistent tumbling action.

Turbo Twin Tumbler 110V. $80

MASTER CASTING KIT

Designed especially to meet the needs of blackpowder shooters, this kit features Lyman's combination round ball and maxi ball mould blocks. It also contains a combination double cavity mould, mould handle, mini-mag furnace, lead dipper, bullet lube, a user's manual and a cast bullet guide. Kits are available in 45, 50 and 54 caliber.

Master Casting Kit $185

Lyman Reloading Tools

POWER CASE TRIMMER

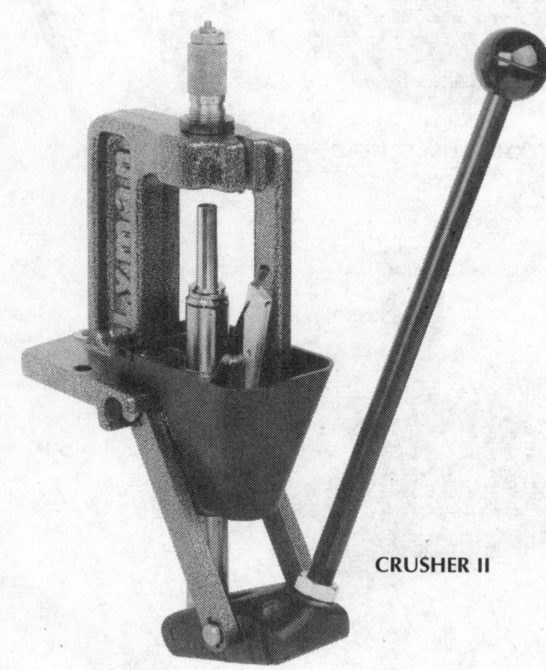
CRUSHER II

ACCULINE OUTSIDE NECK TURNER (NOT SHOWN)

To obtain perfectly concentric case necks, Lyman's Outside Neck Turner assures reloaders of uniform neck wall thickness and outside neck diameter. The unit fits Lyman's Universal Trimmer and AccuTrimmer. In use, each case is run over a mandrel, which centers the case for the turning operation. The cutter is carefully adjusted to remove a minimum amount of brass. Rate of feed is adjustable and a mechanical stop controls length of cut. Mandrels are available for calibers from .17 to .375; cutter blade can be adjusted for any diameter from .195″ to .405″.

Outside Neck Turner w/extra blade, 6 mandrels $31
Individual Mandrels 4

POWER CASE TRIMMER

The Lyman Power Trimmer is powered by a fan-cooled electric motor designed to withstand the severe demands of case trimming. The unit, which features the Universal™ Chuckhead, allows cases to be positioned for trimming or removed with fingertip ease. The Power Trimmer package includes Nine-Pilot Multi-Pack. Two cutter heads and a pair of wire end brushes for cleaning primer pockets are included. Other features include safety guards, on-off rocker switch, heavy cast base with receptacles for nine pilots, and bolt holes for mounting on a work bench. Available for 110-volt or 220-volt systems.

Prices: 110 V Model $230
220 V Model 237

CRUSHER II PRO KIT

Includes press, loading block, case lube kit, primer tray, Model 500 Pro scale, powder funnel and Lyman Reloading Handbook.

Starter Kit $185

LYMAN CRUSHER II RELOADING PRESS

The only press for rifle or pistol cartridges that offers the advantage of powerful compound leverage combined with a true Magnum press opening. A unique handle design transfers power easily to the center of the ram. A 4½-inch press opening accommodates even the largest cartridges.

With Priming Arm and Catcher $130

Lyman Reloading Tools

T-MAG II TURRET RELOADING PRESS

With the T-Mag II, up to six different reloading dies can be mounted on one turret. This means all dies can be set up, precisely mounted, locked in and ready to reload at all times. The T-Mag works with all 7/8 x 14 dies. The T-Mag II turret with its quick-disconnect release system is held in rock-solid alignment by a 3/4-inch steel stud.

Also featured is Lyman's Crusher II compound leverage system. It has a longer handle with a ball-type knob that mounts easily for right- or left-handed operation.

T-Mag II Press w/Priming Arm & Catcher $180
Extra Turret Head 42
Also available:
Expert Kit that includes T-MAG II Press, Universal Case Trimmer and pilot Multi-Pak, Model 500 powder scale and Model 50 powder measure, plus accessories and Reloading Manual. Available in calibers 30-06,270 and 308
Price: $390

T-MAG II PRESS W/PRIMING ARM & CATCHER

EXTRA TURRET HEAD

MODEL 1200 DPS II

ELECTRONIC DIGITAL MICROMETER $95

BLACK POWDER MEASURE

MODEL 1200 DPS II (DIGITAL POWDER SYSTEM)

The 1200 DPS dispenses powder quickly, with .1-grain precision. The 4500 Lube sizer, with a one-piece base casting and a built-in heating element (choose 110- or 220-volt). The long ball-knob handle offers the leverage for sizing and lubricating big bullets. It comes with a gas check seater.

1200 DPS $350
4500 Lube sizer 170

55 CLASSIC BLACK POWDER MEASURE

Lyman's 55 Classic Powder Measure is ideal for the Cowboy Action Competition or black powder cartridge shooters. The one-pound-capacity aluminum reservoir and brass powder meter eliminate static. The internal powder baffel assures highly accurate and consistent charges. The 24" powder compacting drop tube allows the maximum charge in each cartridge. Drop tube works on calibers 38 through 50 and mounts easily to the bottom of the measure. Clamp on back allows easy mounting of the measure at a convenient height, when using long drop tubes.

55 Classic Powder Measure (std model-no tubes) . . . $120
55 Classic Powder Measure (with drop tubes) 138
Powder Drop Tubes Only 38

Lyman Reloading Tools

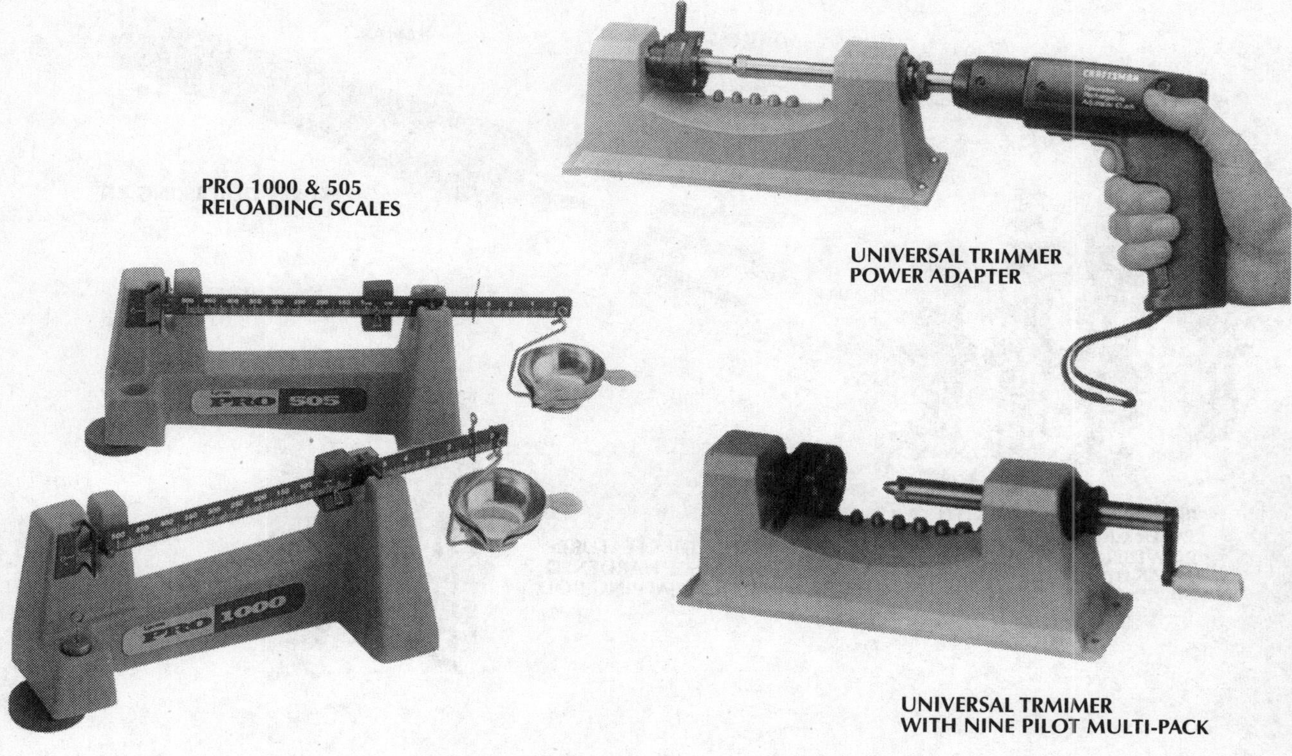

PRO 1000 & 505
RELOADING SCALES

UNIVERSAL TRIMMER
POWER ADAPTER

UNIVERSAL TRMIMER
WITH NINE PILOT MULTI-PACK

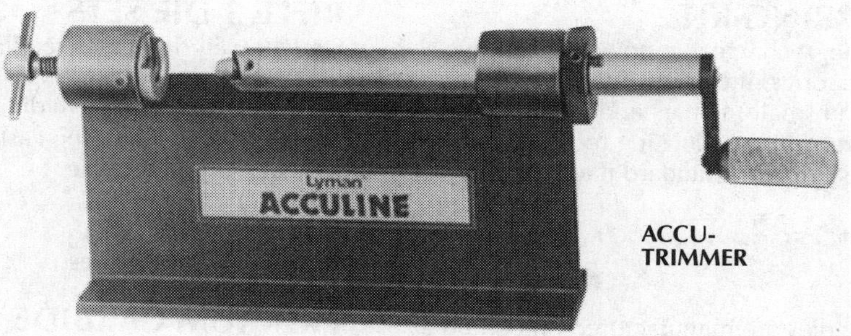

ACCU-
TRIMMER

ACCU-TRIMMER

Lyman's Accu Trimmer can be used for all rifle and pistol cases from 22 to 458 Winchester Magnum. Standard shell-holders are used to position the case, and the trimmer incorporates standard Lyman cutter heads and pilots. Mounting options include bolting to a bench, C-clamp or vise.

Accu Trimmer w/9-pilot multi-pak **$48**

UNIVERSAL TRMIMER

This trimmer with patented chuckhead accepts all metallic rifle or pistol cases, regardless of rim thickness. To change calibers, simply change the case head pilot. Other features include coarse and fine cutter adjustments, an oil-impregnated bronze bearing, and a rugged cast base to assure precision alignment. Optional carbide cutter available. Trimmer Stop Ring includes 20 indicators as reference marks.

Trimmer Multi-Pack (incl. 9 pilots: 22, 24, 27, 28/7mm, 30, 9mm, 35, 44 and 4A) **$73**

Nine Pilot Multi-Pack **13**

Universal Trimmer Power Adapter **20**

Power Trimmer, 110 V. **230**

PRO 1000 & 505 RELOADING SCALES

Features include improved platform system; hi-tech base design of high-impact styrene; extra-large, smooth leveling wheel; dual agate bearings; larger damper for fast zeroing; built-in counter weight compartment; easy-to-read beam.

Pro 1000 Scale **$70**

Pro 500 Scale **50**

Metric scale **54**

Lyman Reloading Tools

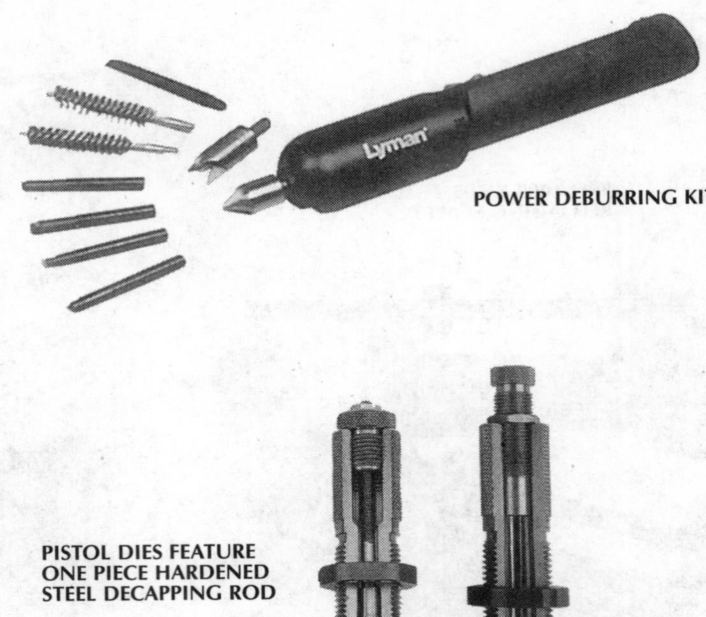

POWER DEBURRING KIT

PREMIUM 4-DIE SET WITH TAPER CRIMP AND POWDER CHARGE EXPANDING DIE

PISTOL DIES FEATURE ONE PIECE HARDENED STEEL DECAPPING ROD

POWER DEBURRING KIT

Features a high torque, rechargeable power driver plus a complete set of accessories, including inside and outside deburr tools, large and small reamers and cleaners and case neck brushes. No threading or chucking required. Set also includes battery recharger and standard flat and phillips driver bits.

Power Deburring Kit. $55

RIFLE DIE SETS

Lyman precision rifle dies are manufactured on computer controlled equipment ensuring th extra smoothness. Fine adjustment threads on the bullet seating stem allow for precision adjustments of bullet seating depth. Lyman dies fit all popular presses using industry standard ⅞ x 14 threads, including RCBS, Lee, Hornady, Dillon, Redding and others.at each die is chambered perfectly and has a smooth finish. Each sizing die for bottle-necked rifle cartridges is then carefully vented. This vent hole is precisely placed to prevent air traps that can damage cartridge cases. Each sizing die is polished, then heat treated for toughness.

RIFLE 2-DIE SETS

Set consists of a full length resizing die with decapping stem and neck expanding button and a bullet seating die for loading jacketed bullets in bottlenecked rifle cases. For those who load cast bullets, use a neck expanding die, available separately.

Price: $32

RIFLE 3-DIE SETS

Straight wall rifle cases require these three die sets consisting of a full length resizing die with decapping stem, a two step neck expanding (M) die and a bullet seating die. These sets are ideal for loading cast bullets due to the inclusion of the neck expanding die.

Price: $42
Classic Calibers. 51
Classic Neck Size Dies 35

PREMIUM CARBIDE 4-DIE SETS FOR PISTOLS

Lyman 4-Die Sets feature a separate taper crimp die and powder charge/expanding die. The powder charge/expand die has a special hollow 2-step neck expanding plug which allows powder to flow through the die from a powder measure directly into the case. The powder charge/expanding die has a standard ⅞ x 14 thread and will accept Lyman's 55 Powder Measure, or most other powder measures.

Price:. $58

3-DIE CARBIDE PISTOL DIE SETS

Lyman originated the Tungsten Carbide (T-C) sizing die and the addition of extra seating screws for pistol die sets and the two step neck expanding die. Multi-Deluxe Die sets offer these features; a one-piece hardened steel decapping rod and extra seating screws for all popular bullet nose shapes; all-steel construction.

Price: $45

MEC Shotshell Reloaders

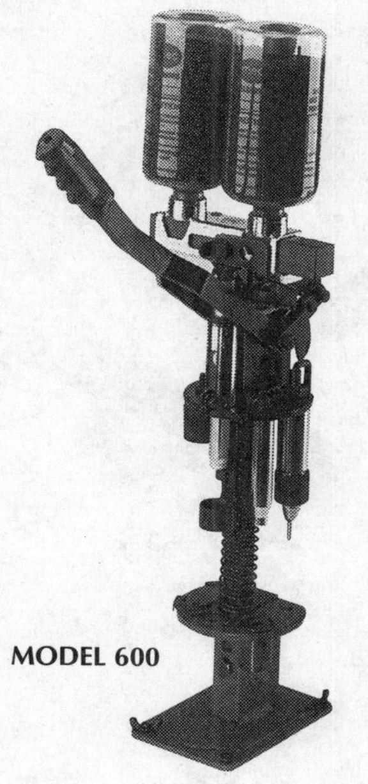

MODEL 600

MODEL 600 JR. MARK V

This single-stage reloader features a cam-action crimp die to ensure that each shell returns to its original condition. MEC's 600 Jr. Mark 5 can load 6 to 8 boxes per hour and can be updated with the 285 CA primer feed. Press is adjustable for 3" shells.

Price: **$118**

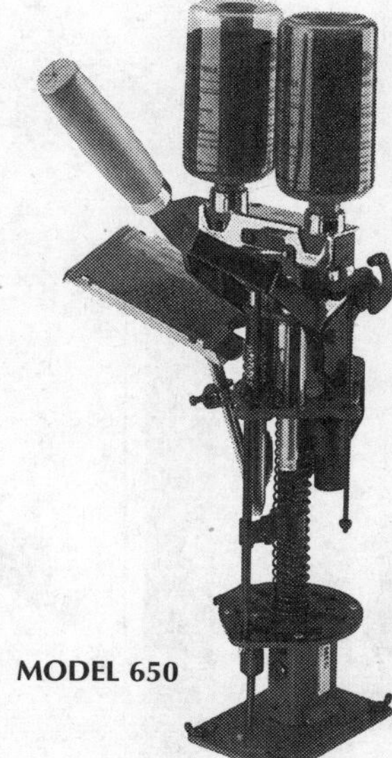

MODEL 650

MODEL 650

This reloader works on 6 shells at once. A reloaded shell is completed with every stroke. The MEC 650 does not resize except as a separate operation. Automatic Primer feed is standard. Simply fill it with a full box of primers and it will do the rest. Reloader has 3 crimping stations: the first one starts the crimp, the second closes the crimp, and the third places a taper on the shell. Available in 12, 16, 20 and 28 gauge and .410 bore. No die sets available.

Price: **$240**

MODEL 8567

MODEL 8567 GRABBER

This reloader features 12 different operations at all 6 stations, producing finished shells with each stroke of the handle. It includes a fully automatic primer feed and Auto-Cycle charging, plus MEC's exclusive 3-stage crimp. The "Power Ring" resizer ensures consistent, accurately sized shells without interrupting the reloading sequence. Simply put in the wads and shell casings, then remove the loaded shells with each pull of the handle. Optional kits to load 3" shells and steel shot make this reloader tops in its field. Resizes high and low base shells. Available in 12, 16, 20, 28 gauge and .410 bore. No die available.

Price: **$338**

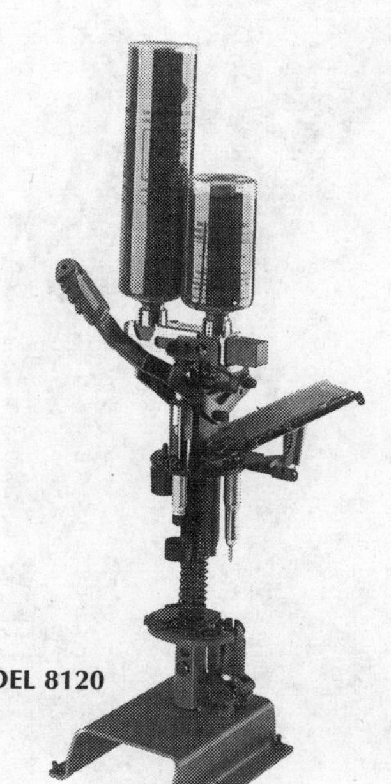

MODEL 8120

MODEL 8120 SIZEMASTER

Sizemaster's "Power Ring" collet resizer returns each base to factory specifications. This resizing station handles brass or steel heads, both high and low base. An 8-fingered collet squeezes the base back to original dimensions, then opens up to release the shell easily. The E-Z Prime auto primer feed is standard equipment (not offered in .410 bore). Press is adjustable for 3" shells and is available in 10, 12, 16, 20, 28 gauge and .410 bore. Die sets are available at: $88.67 ($104.06 in 10 ga.)

Price: **$179**

MEC Reloading

STEELMASTER SINGLE STATE

The only shotshell reloader equipped to load steel shotgshells as well as lead ones. Every base is resized to factory specs by a precision "power ring" collet. Handles brass or steel heads in high or low base. The E-Z prime auto primer feed dispenses primers automatically and is standard equipment. Separate presses are available for 12 gauge 2¾", 3", 3½" and 10 gauge.

8639 Steelmaster 10 & 12 ga.. . . . . $193
8755 Steelmaster 12 ga. 3½" only 220

9000 SERIES SHOTSHELL RELOADER

Mdec's 9000 Series features automatic indexing and finished shell ejection for quicker and easier reloading. The factory set speed provides uniform movement through every reloading stage. Dropping the primer into the reprime station no longer requires operator "feel." The reloader requires only a minimal adjustment from low to high brass domestic shells, any one of which can be removed for inspection from any station. Can be set up for automatic or manual indexing. Available in 12, 16, 20 and 28 gauge and .410 bore. No die sets are available.

MEC 9000HN $958
MEC 9001HN without pump 525
MEC 9000GN Series. 407
Also available: Mec Super Sizer
Resize shotgun shells back to factory specs.
Price: $67

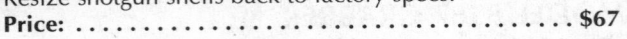

STEEL MASTER

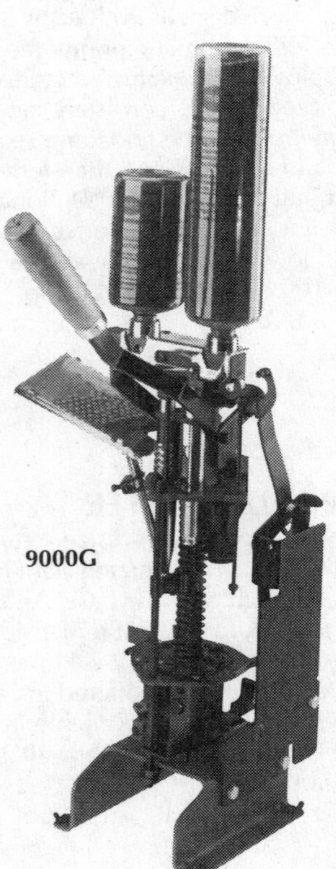

9000G

9000H

MTM Reloading

GUNSMITH'S MAINTENANCE CENTER

CASE-GARD IN WILD CAMO

PISTOL REST MODEL PR-30

HANDLOADING

GUNSMITH'S MAINTENANCE CENTER

MTM's Gunsmiths Maintenance Center (RMC-5) is designed for mounting scopes and swivels, bedding actions or for cleaning rifles and shotguns. Multi-positional forks allow for eight holding combinations, making it possible to service firearm level, upright or upside down. The large middle section keeps tools and cleaning supplies in one area. Individual solvent compartments help to eliminate accidental spills. Cleaning rods stay where they are needed with the two built-in holders provided. Both forks (covered with a soft molded-on rubber pad) grip and protect the firearm. The RMC-5 is made of engineering- grade plastic.

Dimensions: 29.5″ X 9.5″

Model RMC-5-30 . . . . $34

PISTOL REST MODEL PR-30

MTM's PR-30 Pistol Rest will accommodate any size handgun, from a Derringer to a 14″ Contender. A locking front support leg adjusts up or down, allowing 20 different positions. Rubber padding molded to the tough polypropylene fork protects firearms from scratches. Fork clips into the base when not in use for compact storage.

Dimensions: 6″ x 11″ x 2.5

Pistol Rest Model PR-30 . . . . $19

CASE-GARD IN WILD CAMO

The CASE-GARD SF-100 holds 100 shotshells in two removable trays. Designed primarily for hunters, this dust and moisture resistant carrier features a heavy-duty latch, fold-down handle, integral hinge and textured finish.

Price: SF-100 12 or 20 ga.
Wild Camo Shotshell Box 18

RCBS Reloading Tools

ROCK CHUCKER SUPREME PRESS

With its easy operation, outstanding strength and versatility, a Rock Chucker Supreme press serves beginner and pro alike. It can also be upgraded to a progressive press with an optional Piggyback conversion unit.

- Heavy-duty cast iron for easy case-resizing
- Larger window opening to accommodate longer cartridges
- 1″ ram held in place by 12.5 sq. in. of rambearing surface
- Ambidextrous handle
- Compound leverage system
- ⅞″-14 thread for all standard reloading dies and accessories

Price: **$156**

ROCK CHUCKER SUPREME MASTER RELOADING KIT

The Rock Chucker Master Reloading Kit includes all the tools and accessories needed to start handloading: • Rock Chucker Press • RCBS 505 Reloading Scale • Speer Manual #13 • Uniflow Powder Measure • deburring tool • case loading block • Primer Tray-2 • Hand priming tool • powder funnel • case lube pad • case neck brushes • fold-up hex key set • Trim Pro Manual Case Trimmer Kit

Price: **$359**

.50 BMG PACK

The Pack includes the press, dies, and accessory items needed, all in one box. The press is the Ammo Master® Single Stage rigged for 1.5-inch dies. It has a 1.5-inch solid steel ram and plenty of height for the big .50. The kit also has a set of RCBS .50 BMG, 1.5-inch reloading dies, including both full-length sizer and seater. Other items are a shell holder, ram priming unit, and a trim die.

Price: **$617**

AMMOMASTER-2 RELOADING SYSTEM

The AmmoMaster offers handloaders the freedom to configure a press to his particular needs and preferences. It covers the complete spectrum of reloading, from single stage through fully automatic progressive reloading, from .25 Auto to .50 caliber. The AmmoMaster Auto has all the features of a five-station press.

Single Stage **$259**

RELOADER SPECIAL-5

The Reloader Special press features a comfortable ball handle and a primer arm so that cases can be primed and resized at the same time.

- Compound leverage system
- Solid aluminum black "O" frame offset for unobstructed access
- Corrosion-resistant baked-powder finish
- Can be upgraded to progressive reloading with an optional Piggyback II conversion unit
- ⅞″ - 14 thread for all standard reloading dies and accessories

Price: **$127**
Reloading Starter Kit........................... **290**

ROCK CHUCKER SUPREME

RELOADER SPECIAL-5

AMMOMASTER-2 SINGLE STAGE

PIGGYBACK III CONVERSION KIT (NOT SHOWN)

- The Piggyback III conversion unit moves from single-stage reloading to 5-station, manual-indexing, progressive reloading in one step
- Increases output from 50 rounds an hour to well over 400

The Piggyback III will work with the RCBS Rock Chucker, Reloader Special-3, and Reloader Special-5.

Price: **$344**

HANDLOADING

RCBS Reloading Tools

APS PRIMER STRIP LOADER

APS HAND PRIMING TOOL

RELOADING SCALE MODEL 5-0-5

TRIM PRO™ CASE TRIMMER

HANDLOADING

HAND PRIMING TOOL

A patented safety mechanism separates the seating operation from the primer supply, virtually eliminating the possibility of tray detonation. Fits in your hand for portable primer seating. Primer tray installation requires no contact with the primers. Uses the same RCBS shell holders as RCBS presses. Made of cast metal. Includes large and small primer plugs.

APS PRIMER STRIP LOADER

For those who keep a supply of CCI primers in conventional packaging, the APS primer strip loader allows quick filling of empty strips. Each push of the handle seats 25 primers.

Price: **$30**

POW'R PULL BULLET PULLER

The RCBS Pow'r Pull bullet puller features a three-jaw chuck that grips the case rim—just rap it on any solid surface like a hammer, and powder and bullet drop into the main chamber for re-use. A soft cushion protects bullets from damage. Works with most centerfire cartridges from .22 to .45 (not for use with rimfire cartridges).

Price: **$16**

RELOADING SCALE MODEL 5-0-5

This 511-grain capacity scale has a three-poise system with widely spaced, deep beam notches to keep them in place. Two smaller poises on right side adjust from 0.1 to 10 grains, larger one on left side adjusts in full 10-grain steps. The first scale to use magnetic dampening to eliminate beam oscillation, the 5-0-5 also has a sturdy die-cast base with large leveling legs for stability. Self-aligning agate bearings support the hardened steel beam pivots for a guaranteed sensitivity to 0.1 grains.

Price: **$92**

TRIM PROTM CASE TRIMMER

Cartridge cases are trimmed quickly and easily with a few turns of the RCBS Trim Pro case trimmer. The lever-type handle is more accurate to use than draw collet systems. A flat plate shell holder keeps cases locked in place and aligned. A micrometer fine adjustment bushing offers trimming accuracy to within .001″. Made of die-cast metal with hardened cutting blades. The power model is like having a personal lathe, delivering plenty of torque. Positive locking handle and in-line power switch make it simple and safe.

Price: Power 120 Vac Kit **$276**
Manual Kit **101**
Also available:
Trim Pro Case Trimmer Stand **21**

RCBS Reloading Tools

RANGEMASTER 750

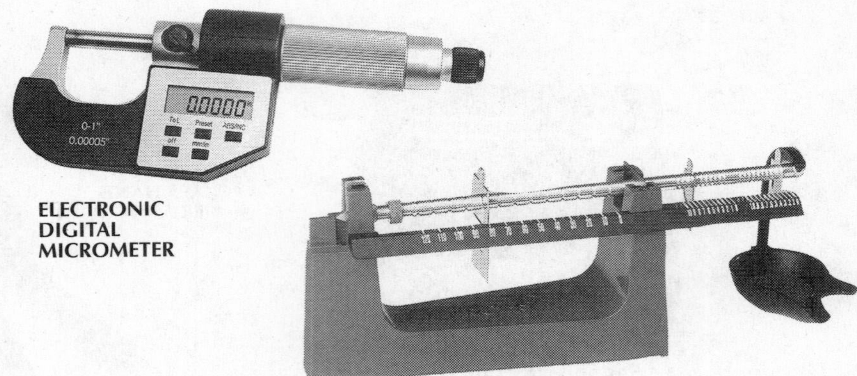

ELECTRONIC DIGITAL MICROMETER

RC-130 MECHANICAL SCALE

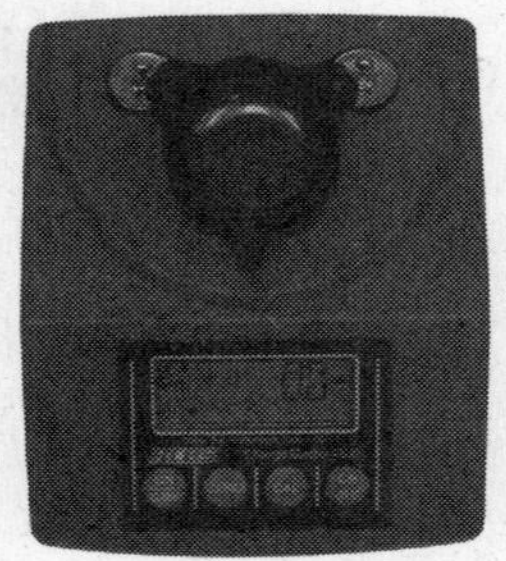

CHARGEMASTER 1500

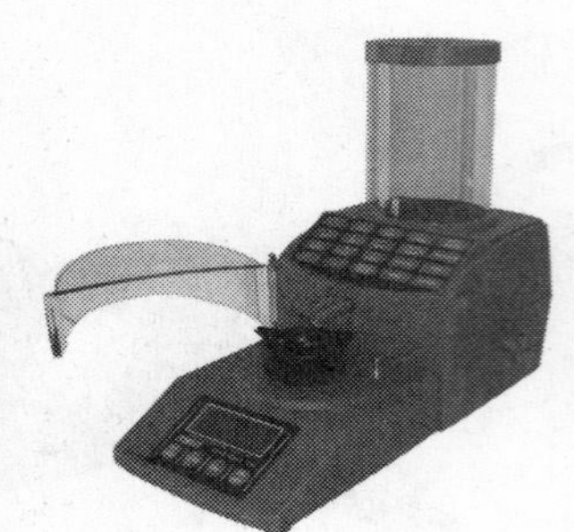

CHARGEMASTER COMBO

RELOADING SCALE MODEL 10-10
UP TO 1010 GRAIN CAPACITY

RELOADING SCALE MODEL 1010 UP TO 1010 GRAIN CAPACITY

Normal capacity is 510 grains, which can be increased without loss of sensitivity by attaching the included extra weight. Features include micrometer poise for quick, precise weighing, special approach-to-weight indicator, easy-to-read graduation, magnetic dampener, agate bearings, anti-tip pan, and dustproof lid snaps on to cover scale for storage. Sensitivity is guaranteed to 0.1 grains.

Price: **$154**

RC-130 MECHANICAL SCALE

The RC130 features a 130 grain capacity and maintenance-free movement, plus a magnetic dampening system for fast readings. A 3-poise design incorporates easy adjustments with a beam that is graduated in increments of 10 grains and one grain. A micrometer poise measures in 0.1 grain increments with acuracy to ±0.1 grain.

Price: **$46**

ELECTRONIC DIGITAL MICROMETER

•Instant reading • Large, easy to read numbers for error reduction with instant inch/millimeter conversion • Zero adjust at any position • thimble lock for measuring like objects • replaceable silver oxide cell—1.55 Volt • auto off after 5 minutes for longer battery life • adjustment wrench included • fitted wooden storage cases

Price: **$114**

RANGEMASTER 750 SCALE

• Compact, lightweight and portable • 750-grain capacity • reads in grams or grains • accurate to + or – 1/10 of a grain • fast calibration; weights included • AC or 9-volt battery powdered • AC adaptor included • 110 volt or 220 volt available

Price: **$129**

CHARGEMASTER 1500 SCALE

• High performance reloading scale • 1500 grain capacity • weighs in grains or grams • calibration weights included • AC adaptor included • 110 volt or 220 volt available • upgrade to an automatic dispensing system with the RCBS ChargeMaster

Price: **$203**

CHARGEMASTER COMBO

• Performs as a scale or as a complete powder dispensing system • scale can be removed and used separately • accurate with all types of powder • dispenses from 2.0 to 300 grains • reads and dispenses in grains or grams mode • quick powder drain feature reduces spills • no powder calibration required • stores up to 30 charges in memory for quick recall of favorite loads • 110 volt or 220 volt adaptor included

Price: **$387**

TURRET PRESS

Handloaders who want to speed up the loading process without giving up the level of control offered by a single-stage press can boost their output fourfold with the RCBS Turret Press. With pre-set dies in the six-station turret head, the Turret Press can increase production from 50 to 200 rounds per hour with a simple manual operation.

The frame, links, and toggle block of the press are constructed of strong, reliable, cast iron. The handle offers compound leverage for full-length sizing of any caliber from .25 ACP to .460 Wea-therby Magnum. Priming is accomplished with a reliable tube feed priming system.

Six stations allow the handloader to customize his set-up with the options of using a lube die in station one and seating and crimping bullets in separate operations. The quick-change turret head makes caliber changes fast and easy. Dies can be left in the turret head to eliminate set-up and tear-down time. This press accepts all standard 7/8 - 14 dies and shell holders. Lifetime warranty.

Price: **$225**
Turret Deluxe Reloading Kit **435**

PRO 2000 PROGRESSIVE PRESS

Constructed of cast iron, the Pro 2000 features five reloading stations. It can be set up with a lube die in station one, sizing dies in station two and three, a Powder Checker or Lock Out Die in station four and seating die in station five. Bullet seating and crimping can also be done in separate operations in station four and five.

The case-actuated powder measure assures repeatability of dispensing powder and eliminates spillage. A Micrometer Adjustment Screw allows precise return to previously recorded powder charges. All dies are standard 7/8-14, including the Expander Die.

The press incorporates RCBS's exclusive APS Priming System. Using preloaded plastic priming strips, it eliminates handling of primers and loading tube priming. Compound leverage in the press allows effortless full-length sizing in any caliber, from .32 Auto to the .460 Weatherby Magnum. Lifetime Warranty.

Prices: Pro 2000 Progressive Press **$560**
Pro 2000 Deluxe Reloading Kit **959**

GRAND SHOTSHELL PRESS

Features: The combination of the Powder system and shot system and Case Holders allows the user to reload shells without fear of spillage. The powder system is case-actuated: no hull, no powder. Cases are easily removed with universal 12 and 20 gauge case holders allowing cases to be sized down to the rim. Priming system: Only one primer feeds at a time. Steel size ring: Provides complete resizing of high and low base hulls. Holds 25 lbs of shot and 1½ lbs. of powder. Lifetime warranty.

Price. **$775**
Grand Conversion kit **370**

MINI-GRAND SHOTSHELL PRESS

The Mini-Grand shotgun press, a seven-station single-stage press, loads 12- and 20-gauge hulls, from 2¾ to 3½ inches in length. It utilizes RCBS, Hornady and Ponsness Warren powder and shot bushings, with a half-pound capacity powder hopper and 12½-pound capacity shot hopper. The machine will load both lead and steel shot, though steel requires optional accessories.

TURRET PRESS
PRO 2000 PROGRESSIVE PRESS
GRAND SHOTSHELL PRESS
MINI-GRAND SHOTGUN PRESS

Redding Reloading Tools

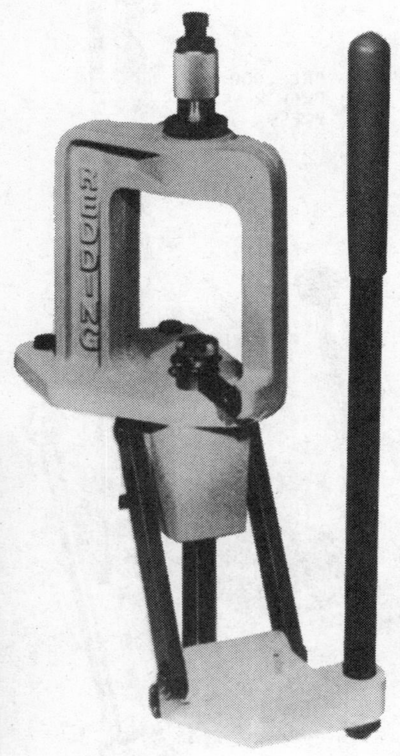

MODEL 721

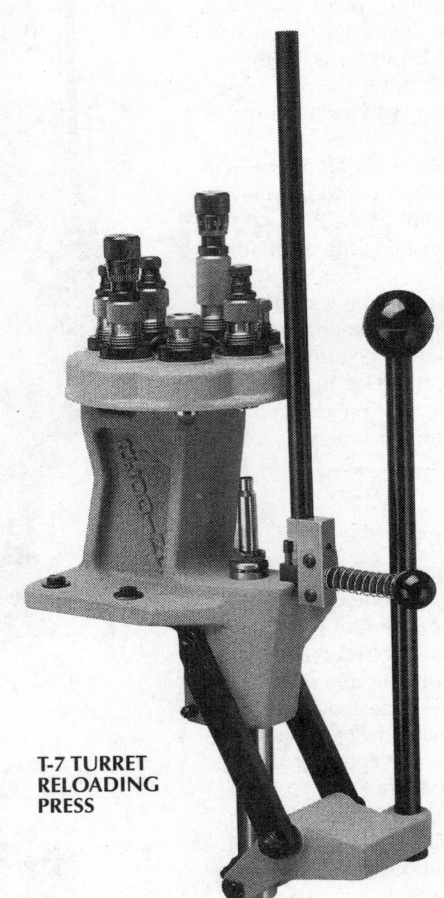

T-7 TURRET RELOADING PRESS

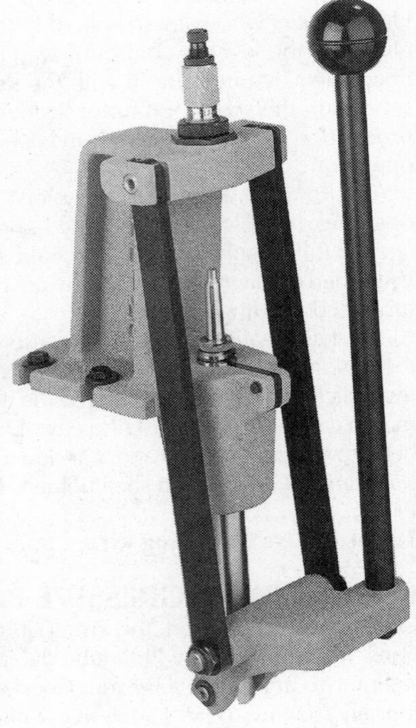

MODEL 7000

HANDLOADING

MODEL 721 "THE BOSS" PRESS

This "O" type reloading press features a rigid cast iron frame whose 36° offset provides the best visibility and access of comparable presses. Its "Smart" primer arm moves in and out of position automatically with ram travel. The priming arm is positioned at the bottom of ram travel for lowest leverage and best feel. Model 721 accepts all standard 7/8-14 threaded dies and universal shell holders.

Model 721 "The Boss" $156
With Shellholder and 10A Dies. 207
Also available:
Boss Pro-Pak Reloading Kit.
Includes Boss Reloading Press, #2 Powder and Bullet Scale, Powder Trickler, Reloading 10A Dies $419
w/o dies and shellholder. 360
Boss Deluxe Reloading Kit
Includes all items in the Pro-Pak plus:
Match-Grade Model 3BR Powder Measure and Model 1400 case trimmer $648
Big Boss Reloading Press
All the features of the Boss with a heavier frame. . . . $195
Big Boss Kit. 245

ULTRAMAG MODEL 7000

Unlike other reloading presses that connect the linkage to the lower half of the press, the Ultramag's compound leverage system is connected at the top of the press frame. This allows the reloader to develop tons of pressure without the usual concern about press frame deflection. Huge frame opening will handle 50 x 3¼-inch Sharps with ease.

Press $351
Kit, includes shell holder and one set of 10A dies . . . 396

T-7 TURRET RELOADING PRESS

Features: 7 station turret head, heavy duty cast iron frame, 1" diameter ram, optional "Slide Bar Automatic Primer Feeder System". This feeder eliminates handling of primers during sizing and speeds up reloading operations.

T-7 Turret Press $336
Kit, including press, shellholder and 10A dies. 383
Slide Bar Automatic Primer Feeder System. 50

Redding Reloading Dies

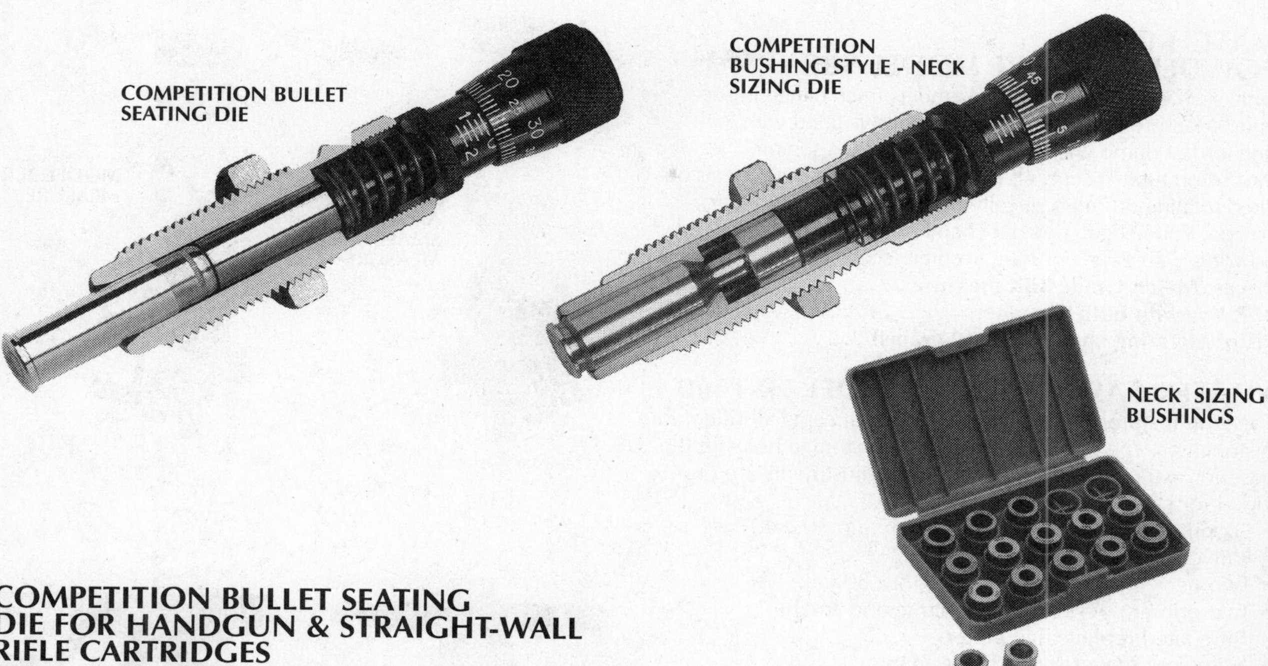

COMPETITION BULLET SEATING DIE FOR HANDGUN & STRAIGHT-WALL RIFLE CARTRIDGES

Positive alignment between the bullet and cartridge case prior to bullet seating is essential to fine accuracy. Here is how this die works:

The precision fitting seating stem is allowed to move well down into the chamber of the die to accomplish early bullet contact. The spring loading of the seating stem provides the positive alignment bias between its tapered nose and the bullet ogive. Thus spring loading and bullet alignment are maintained as the bullet and cartridge case move upward until the actual seating of the bullet begins.

Micrometer Adjustment

The micrometer adjustment simplifies setting and recording bullet seating depth. By recording the micrometer setting of reloads one can return to that same overall length by simply "dialing it in." The micrometer is calibrated in .001" increments, is infinitely adjustable and has a "zero" set feature that allows setting desired load to zero if desired.

Separate Crimp

Competition shooters generally prefer bullet crimping as a separate operation from bullet seating. A superior crimp will be acomplished by using a Redding "Profile Crimp" or "Taper Crimp" die.

Progressive Press Compatible

The Competition Seating Die for straight-wall cartridges has been made compatible with all popular progressive reloading presses. The industry standard 7/8 x 14 threaded die bodies have been slightly extended to allow full thread engagement of the lock ring. An oversize bell-mouth chamfer with smooth radius has been added to the bottom of the die to ease case and bullet entry in progressive presses.

Price: **$90**

COMPETITION BUSHING STYLE - NECK SIZING DIE

This die allows you to fit the neck of your case perfectly in the chamber. As in the Competition Seating Die, the cartridge case is completely supported and aligned with the sizing bushing and remains supported in the sliding sleeve as it moves upward while the resizing bushing self-centers on the case neck.

The micrometer adjustment of the bushing position delivers precise control to the desired neck length. All dies are supplied without bushings.

Category I **$122**
Category II **147**
Category III **179**

REDDING NECK SIZING BUSHINGS

Redding Neck Sizing Bushings are available in two styles. Both share the same external dimensions (1/2" O.D. x 3/8" long) and freely interchange in all Redding Bushing style Neck Sizing Dies.

They are available in .001" size increments throughout the range of .185" thru .365", covering all calibers from .17 to .338.

By selecting the correct bushing, the right amount of neck tension is provided to properly hold the bullet.

Part No. 73185 thru 73365 .... **$15**
Heat treated steel. The sizing diameters are hand-polished with a surface hardness of Rc 60-62 to reduce sizing effort.

Part No. 76185 thru 76365 .... **27**
Heat treated steel as above but with the addition of a Titanium Nitride surface treatment to further increase the effective surface hardness and reduce sizing friction.

Redding Reloading Tools

MATCH-GRADE POWDER MEASURE MODEL 3BR

Universal- or pistol-metering chambers interchange in seconds. Measures charges 100 grains. Unit is fitted with lock ring for fast dump with large "clear" plastic reservoir. "See-thru" drop tube accepts all calibers from 22 to 600. Precision-fitted rotating drum is critically honed to prevent powder escape. Knife-edged powder chamber shears coarse-grained powders with ease, ensuring accurate charges.

Prices: Match Grade 3BR measure $189
3BR Kit, with both Chambers 234
Pistol Metering chamber (0-10 grains) 57

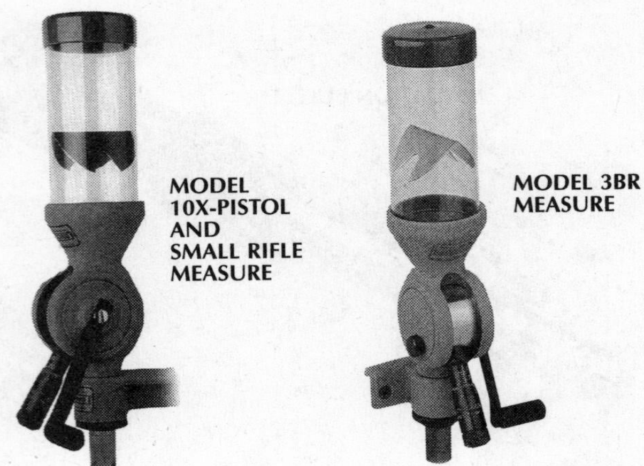

MODEL 10X-PISTOL AND SMALL RIFLE MEASURE

MODEL 3BR MEASURE

MASTER CASE TRIMMER MODEL TR-1400

This unit features a universal collet that accepts all rifle and pistol cases. The frame is cast iron with storage holes in the base for extra pilots. Coarse and fine adjustments are provided for case length.

- Six pilots (22, 6mm, 25, 270, 7mm and 30 cal.)
- Universal collet
- Two neck cleaning brushes (22 thru 30 cal.)
- Two primer pocket cleaners (large and small)
- Tin coated replaceable cutter
- Accessory power screwdriver adaptor

Prices: Master Case Trimmer. $108
Pilots. 5

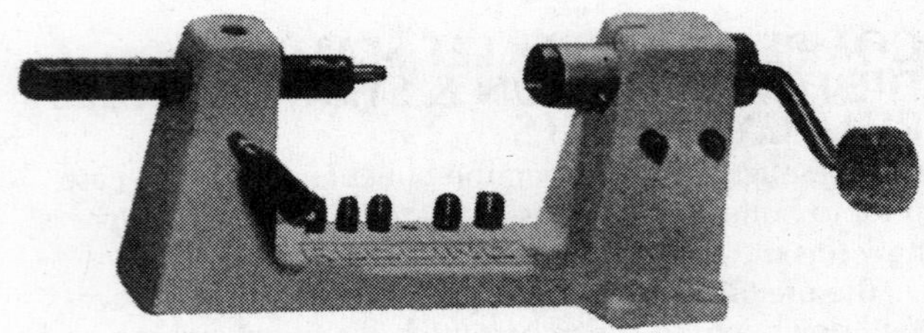

MODEL TR-1400 TRIMMER

COMPETITION MODEL BR-30 POWDER MEASURE (NOT SHOWN)

This powder measure features a drum and micrometer that limit the overall charging range from a low of 10 grains to a maximum of 50 grains. The diameter of Model 3BR's metering cavity has been reduced, and the metering plunger has a unique hemispherical shape, creating a powder cavity that resembles the bottom of a test tube. The result: irregular powder settling is alleviated and charge-to-charge uniformity is enhanced.

Price: $228

Model No. 2 Master Powder and Bullet Scale

- 505-grain capacity
- dampened beam
- 1/10-grain accuracy
- hardened knife edges and milled stainless bearing seats for smooth, consistent operation and a high level of durability

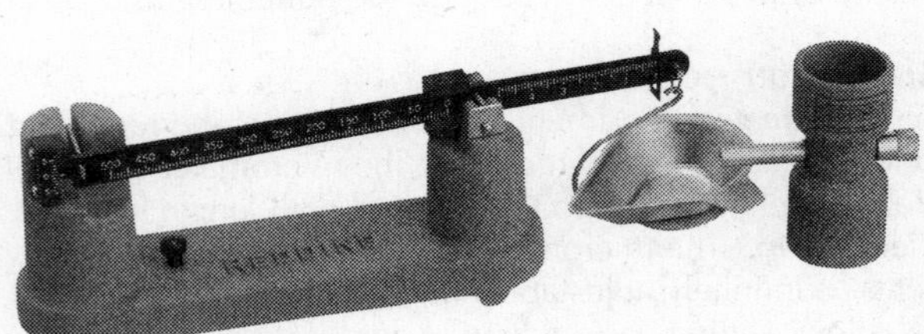

MODEL NO. 2SCALE

COMPETITION MODEL 10X-PISTOL AND SMALL RIFLE POWDER MEASURE

This powder measure uses all of the features of Competition Model BR-30, combined with new drum and metering unit designed to provide uniform metering of small charge weights. To achieve the best metering possible at the targeted charge weight of approximately 10 grains, the diameter of the metering cavity is reduced and the metering plunger is given a unique hemispherical shape. Charge range: 1 to 25 grains.

To provide increased versatility, the 10X-Pistol Powder Measure has a drum assembly that can be easily changed from right to left-handed operation.

Price: Powder Measure $228

HANDLOADING

Redding Reloading Accessories

"INSTANT INDICATOR" HEADSPACE AND BULLET COMPARATOR

The Instant Indicator checks the headspace from the case shoulder to the base. Bullet seating depths can be compared and bullets can be sorted by checking the base of bullet to give dimension. Case length can be measured. Available for 33 cartridges from .222 Rem to .338 Win. Mag., including new WSSM cartridges.

Price: w/Dial Indicator **$135**
w/o Dial Indicator **104**

"EZ FEED" SHELLHOLDERS

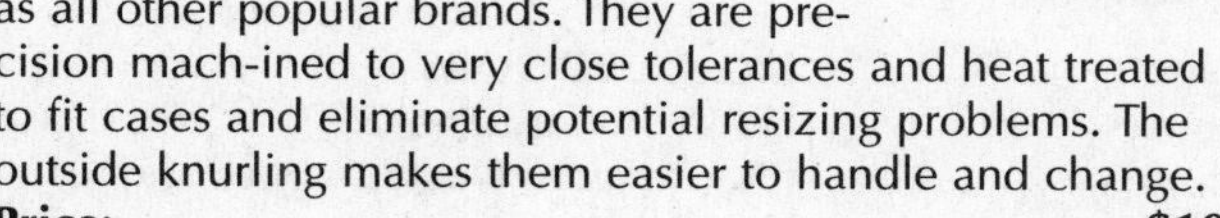

Redding shellholders are of a Universal "snap-in" design recommended for use with all Redding dies and presses, as well as all other popular brands. They are precision mach-ined to very close tolerances and heat treated to fit cases and eliminate potential resizing problems. The outside knurling makes them easier to handle and change.
Price: **$10**

FORM & TRIM DIES

Redding trim dies file trim cases without unnecessary resizing because they are-made to chamber dimensions. For case forming and necking brass down from another caliber, Redding trim dies can be the perfect intermediate step before full length resizing.

Prices:
Series A **$32**
Series B **44**
Series C **54**
Series D **60**

NECK SIZING DIES

These dies size only the necks of bottleneck cases to prolong brass life and improve accuracy. These dies size only the neck and not the shoulder or body, fired cases should not be interchanged between rifles of the same caliber. Available individually or in Deluxe Die Sets.
Prices:
Series A **$36**
Series B **48**
Series C **62**
Series D **69**

PISTOL TRIM DIES

Redding trim dies for pistol calibers allow trimming cases without excessive resizing. Pistol trim dies require extended shellholders.
Series A **$32**
Series B **44**
Series C **54**
Series D **60**

PROFILE CRIMP DIES

For handgun cartridges which do not headspace on the case mouth. These dies were designed for those who want the best possible crimp. Profile crimp dies provide a tighter, more uniform roll type crimp, and require the bullet to be seated to the correct depth in a previous operation.

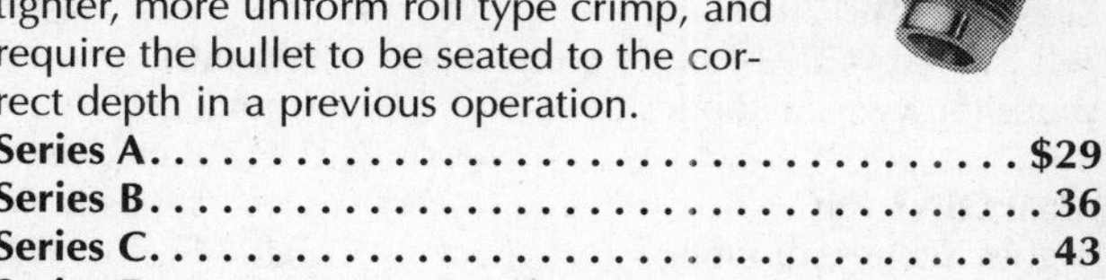

Series A **$29**
Series B **36**
Series C **43**
Series D **48**

CARBIDE SIZE BUTTON KITS

Make inside neck sizing smoother and easier without lubrication. Now die sets can be upgraded with a carbide size button kit. Available for bottleneck cartridges 22 thru 338 cal. The carbide size button is free-floating on the decap rod, allowing it to self-center in the case neck. Kits contain: carbide size button, retainer and spare decapping pin. These kits also fit all Type-S dies
Price: **$28**

EXTENDED SHELL HOLDERS

Extended shellholders are required when trimming short cases under 1½" O.A.L. They are machined to the same tolerances as standard shellholders except they're longer.
Price: **$16**

TAPER AND CRIMP DIES

Designed for handgun cartridges which headspace on the case mouth where conventional roll crimping is undesirable. Also available for some revolver cartridges, for those who prefer the uniformity of a taper crimp. Now available in the following rifle calibers: 223 Rem., 7.62MM x 39, 30-30, 308 Win, 30-06, 300, Win Mag
Prices:
Series A **$29**
Series B **36**
Series C **43**
Series D **48**

Directory of Manufacturers & Suppliers

The following manufacturers, suppliers and distributors of firearms, reloading equipment, sights, scopes, ammo and accessories all appear with their products in the "Specifications" and/or "Manufacturers' Showcase" sections of this edition of Shooter's Bible.

ACCURATE ARMS CO., INC.
(gunpowder, reloading)
5891 Hwy. 230 W
McEwen TN 37101
Tel: 931-729-4207; 800-416-3006
Fax: 931-729-4211
Website: www.accuratepowder.com

ADIRONDACK OPTICS
(scopes and sights)
1512 Front St. P.O. Box 303
Keesville NY 12944
Tel: 518-834-7093 Fax: 518-834-7061
Website: www.adkoptics.com

AIMPOINT INC.
(sights, scopes, mounts)
3989 HWY 62 West
Berryville AR 72616
Tel: 870-423-3398 Fax: 870-423-2960
Website: www.aimpoint.com
E-mail: info@aimpoint.com

ATK AMMUNITION
(Federal, Speer, RCBS, Alliant)
900 Ehlen Drive
Anoka MN 55303
Tel: 763-2300 Fax: 763-323-2506
Website: www.atk.com

ALLIANT POWDER
(gunpowder)
Route 114, P.O. Box 6 Bldg. 229
Radford VA 24143-0096
Tel: 540-639-7805; 800-276-9337
Fax: 540-639-8496
Website: www.alliantpowder.com

ALPEN OUTDOOR CORP.
(optics)
10329 Dorset St.
Rancho Cucamonga CA 91730
Tel: 909-987-8370
Fax: 909-987-8661
Website: www.alpenoutdoor.com

AMERICAN DERRINGER CORP.
(handguns)
127 North Lacy Drive
Waco TX 76705
Tel: 817-799-9111 Fax: 817-799-7935
Website: www.amderringer.com

AMERICAN HUNTING RIFLES, INC.
(AHR rifles)
P.O. Box 300
Hamilton MT 59840
Tel: 406-961-1410
Website: www.hunting-rifles.com

A.G. ANSCHUTZ GMBH
(rifles, pistols)
Website: www.anschutz-sporters.com
Available through Tristar Sporting Arms

ARMSCO
(shotguns)
1247 Rand Road
Des Plaines IL 60016
Tel: 847-768-1000
Fax: 847-768-1001
Website: www.armsco.net

AUSTIN & HALLECK
2150 South 950 East
Provo UT 84606-6285
Tel: 801-371-0412
Fax: 801-374-9998
Website: www.austinhalleck.com

AUTO-ORDNANCE CORP.
Available through Kahr Arms

AYA (shotguns)
Available through New England
Custom Gun Service

LES BAER CUSTOM, INC.
29601 34th St.
Hillsdale IL 61257
Tel: 309-658-2716 Fax: 309-658-2610

BANSNER'S ULTIMATE RIFLES L.L.C.
Mark Bansner (custom guns)
P.O. Box 839
261 East Main St.
Adamstown PA 19501
Tel: 717-484-2370 Fax: 717-484-0523
Website: www.bansnersrifle.com

BARNES BULLETS
P.O. Box 215
American Fork UT 84003
Tel: 385-756-4222; 800-574-9200
Fax: 385-756-2465
E-mail: email@barnesbullets.com
Website: www.barnesbullets.com

BARRETT FIREARMS MFG.
P.O. Box 1077
Murfreesboro TN 37133-1077
Tel: 615-896-2938 Fax: 615-896-7313
Website: www.barrettrifles.com

BATTENFELD TECHNOLOGIES, INC.
(reloading equipment)
5885 West Van Horn Tavern Rd.
P.O. Box 1035
Columbia MO 65203
Tel: 573-445-9200 Fax: 573-447-4158
Website: www.battenfeldtechnologies.com

B.C. OUTDOORS
Eldorado Cartridge Co.
(PMC ammo, Docter scopes and Verona shotguns)
PO Box 61497
Boulder City NV 89006
Tel: 702-294-3056 Fax: 702-294-0413
Website: www.pmcammo.com

BENELLI U.S.A. CORP.
(shotguns)
17603 Indian Head Hwy, Suite 200
Accokeek MD 20607-2501
Tel: 301-283-6981 Fax: 301-283-6988
Website: www.benelliusa.com
E-mail benusa1@aol.com

BERETTA U.S.A. CORP.
(handguns, rifles, shotguns; Sako,Tikka)
17601 Beretta Drive
Accokeek MD 20607
Tel: 301-283-2191 Fax: 301-283-0189
Website: www.berettausa.com

BERGER BULLETS, INC.
4275 N. Palm St.
Fullerton CA 92835
Tel: 714-447-5456 Fax: 714-447-5407
www.bergerbullets.com
Website: www.bergerbullets.com

BERNARDELLI
(handguns, shotguns)
Available through Armsport

BERSA
(handguns)
Available through Eagle Imports Inc.

Directory of Manufacturers & Suppliers

ROGER BIESEN
(custom guns)
10323 N. Woodridge Dr.
Spokane WA 99208-8644
Tel: 509-328-9340

BLACK HILLS AMMUNITION
P.O. Box 3090
3050 Eglin
Rapid City SD 57709-3090
Tel: 605-348-5150 Fax: 605-348-9827
Website www.black-hills.com
E-mail: black-hills.com

BLACKPOWDER PRODUCTS, INC.
(CVA & Winchester Blackpowder)
5988 Peachtree Corners East
Norcross GA 30071
Tel: 770-449-4687 Fax: 770-242-8546
Website: www.bpiguns.com

BLASER USA, INC.
(rifles)
Available through Sig Arms

BONANZA
(reloading tools)
See Forster Products

BOND ARMS INC.
(handguns)
204 Alpha Lane
P.O. Box 1296
Granbury TX 76048
Tel: 817-573-4445 Fax: 817-573-5636

KENT BOWERLY
(custom guns)
710 Golden Pheasant Drive
Redmond OR 97756
Tel: 541-923-3501

BRENNEKE OF AMERICA LTD.
(ammunition)
P.O. Box 1481
Clinton IA 52733-1481
Tel.: 800-753-9733 Fax: 563-244 7421
Website: www.brennekeusa.com

ED BROWN PRODUCTS, INC.
(rifles, handguns)
P.O. Box 492
Perry MO 63462
Tel: 573-565-3261 Fax: 573-565-2791
Website: www.edbrown.com

BROWNING
(handguns, rifles, shotguns, blackpowder guns)
One Browning Place
Morgan UT 84050
Tel: 801-876-2711 Fax: 801-876-3331
Website: www.browning.com

BROWNING SPORT OPTICS
Available through Bushnell

BROWN PRECISION, INC.
(custom rifles)
7786 Molinos Avenue
P.O. Box 270 W.
Los Molinos CA 96055
Tel: 530-384-2506 Fax: 530-384-1638

BRUNTON
(spotting scopes)
620 East Monroe Ave.
Riverton WY 82501
Tel: 307-856-6559 Fax: 307-856-1840
Website: www.brunton.com

BSA OPTICS, INC.
3911 SW 47th Ave., Ste 914
Ft. Lauderdale FL 33314
Tel: 954-581-2144
Fax: 954-581-3165
Website: www.bsa.optic.com
E-mail: bsaoptic@bellsouth.net

BURRIS COMPANY, INC.
(scopes)
331 East Eighth Street
P.O. Box 1899
Greeley CO 806321-1899
Tel: 970-356-1670; 888-228-7747
Fax: 970-356-8702
Website: www.burrisoptics.com

BUSHMASTER FIREARMS INC.
P.O. Box 1479
Windham, ME 04062
1-800-998-7928

BUSHNELL
(scopes, Tasco scopes, Browning Sport Optics)
Performance Optics
9200 Cody
Overland Park KS 66214
Tel: 913-752-3400 Fax: 913-752-3550
Website: www.bushnell.com

CABELA'S INC.
(blackpowder rifles)
One Cabela Drive
Sidney NE 69160
Tel: 308-254-5505 Fax: 308-254-6669

CCI/SPEER-BLOUNT, INC.
(ammunition, bullets)
2299 Snake River Ave., P.O. Box 856
Lewiston ID 83501
Tel: 208-746-2351 Fax: 208-746-3904
Website: www.cci-ammunition.com
www.speer-bullets.com

CHEVY TAC ASSOCIATES LTD.
185 Arco Ave.
Arco, ID 83213
888-807-8611

CHRISTENSEN ARMS
(rifles)
192 E. 100 N.
Fayette UT 84630
Tel: 801-528-7199
Website: www.christensenarms.com

CIMARRON FIREARMS CO.
(revolvers, rifles)
P.O. Box 906
Fredericksburg TX 78624
Website: www.cimarron-firearms.com
E-mail:cimarron@fbg.net

COLT BLACKPOWDER ARMS CO.
(handguns)
110 8th street
Brooklyn NY 11215
Tel: 718-499-4678 Fax: 718-768-8056

COLT DEFENSE, LLC
(handguns, rifles)
P.O. Box 118
Hartford CT 06141
Tel: 800-962-COLT
Fax: 860-244-1467
Website: www.colt.com

COMANCHE
Available through Eagle Imports

CONNECTICUT SHOTGUN MFG. CO.
(A.H. Fox shotguns)
35 Woodland Street, P.O. Box 1692
New Britain CT 06051-1692
Tel: 860-225-6581 Fax: 860-832-8707

Directory of Manufacturers & Suppliers

COOPER FIREARMS OF MONTANA, INC.
P.O. Box 114
Stevensville MT 59870
Tel: 406-777-5534
Website: www.cooperfirearms.com

COR-BON/GLASER
(reloading)
1311 Industry Rd.
P.O. Box 369
Sturgis SD 57785
Tel: 605-347-4544 Fax: 605-347-5055
Website: www.corbon.com

CVA
(blackpowder arms)
5988 Peachtree Corners East
Norcross GA 30071
Tel: 800-320-8767 Fax: 770-242-8546
Website: www.cva.com
E-mail: sales@cva.com

CZ-USA (pistols, rifles)
P.O. Box 171073
Kansas City KS 66117-0073
Tel: 913-321-1811; 800-955-4486
Fax: 913-321-2251
Website: www.cz-usa.com
E-mail: cz-usa@qvl.net

DAKOTA ARMS
(rifles, shotguns)
1310 Industry Road
Sturgis SD 57785
Tel:605-347-4686
Fax: 605-347-4459; 508-302-4784
Website: www.dakotarms.com
E-mail: dakarms@sturgis.com

CHARLES DALY (pistols, shotguns)
Available through K.B.I., Inc.

DAYTONA (shotguns)
Available through Renato Gamba U.S.A.

DESERT EAGLE (handguns)
Available through Magnum Research Inc.

DILLON PRECISION PRODUCTS, INC. (reloading equipment)
8009 East Dillon's Way
Scottsdale AZ 85260-9865
Tel: 800-223-4570; 602-948-8009
Fax: 602-998-2786
Website: www.dillonprecision.com

DIXIE GUN WORKS
(blackpowder guns)
P.O. Box 130
Union City TN 38281
Tel: 800-238-6785
Fax: 901-885-0440
info: 901-885-0700
Website: www.dixiegun.com

DKG TRADING INC.
(Eley ammuniton, Famous Maker scopes)
8791 Stringtown Rd.
Evansville IL 62242
Tel: 877-354-2666 Fax: 618-785-2120
Website: www.dkgtrading.com

DOCTER SCOPES
Available through B.C. Outdoors

DOWNSIZER CORPORATION
(handguns)
P.O. Box 710316
Santee CA 92072-0316
Tel: 619-448-5510 Fax: 619-448-5780
Website: www.downsizer.com

DYNAMIT NOBEL/RWS
(Rottweil shotguns and ammunition, Steyr Mannlicher)
81 Ruckman Road
Closter NJ 07624
Tel: 201-767-1995
Fax: 201-767-1589

EAGLE IMPORTS, INC.
(Bersa, Comanche, Llama and Firestorm handguns)
1750 Brielle Avenue, Unit B1
Wanamassa NJ 07712
Tel: 732-493-0302 Fax: 732-493-0301

E.D.M. ARMS
(rifles, handguns)
421 Business Center Ct.
Redlands, CA 92373
909-798-2770

E.M.F. COMPANY, INC.
(Dakota handguns; Uberti handguns, blackpower arms, rifles)
1900 East Warner Avenue,
Suite 1-D
Santa Ana CA 92705
Tel: 714-261-6611 Fax: 714-756-0133
Website: www.emf-company.com

ELEY LIMITED
(ammunition; see Zander's Sporting Goods)
Selco Way, 1st Ave.
Minworth Industrial Estate
Sutton Coldfield
West Midlands, England B76 1BA
Tel: 011 (44) 121 313 4567
Website: www.eley.co.uk

ENTRÉPRISE ARMS
(handguns)
15861 Busines Center Drive
Irwindale CA 91706-2062
Tel: 626-962-8712 Fax: 626-962-4692
Website: www.entreprise.com

ESCORT
(shotguns)
Available through Legacy Sports Intl.

EUROARMS OF AMERICA INC.
(blackpowder arms)
P.O. Box 3277
Winchester VA 22604
Tel: 540-662-1863

EUROPEAN AMERICAN ARMORY CORP.
(E.A.A. handguns, rifles)
P.O. Box 1299
Sharpes FL 32959
Tel: 800-536-4442 Tel: 321-639-4842
Fax: 321-639-7006
Website: www.eaacorp.com

FABARMS
(shotguns)
Available through Heckler & Koch

FAMOUS MAKER SCOPES
Available through DKG Trading Inc.

FEDERAL CARTRIDGE CO.
(ammunition, ballistics)
900 Ehlen Drive
Anoka MN 55303-7503
Tel: 800-322-2342; 763-323-2300
Fax: 763-323-2506
Website: www.federalcartridge.com

KENT "BUZZ" FLETCHER
(custom gunmaker)
121 Sunset Dr.
Espanola NM 87532
Tel: 505-753-5434

Directory of Manufacturers & Suppliers

FLODMAN GUNS SWEDEN
640 60 Akers styckebruk
Jarsta, Sweden
Tel: 46 159308 61 Fax: 46 159300 61
Website: www.flodman.com

FIRESTORM PISTOLS
Available through Eagle Imports

FIOCCHI OF AMERICA
(ammunition)
6930 Fremont Rd.
Ozark MO 65721
Tel: 800-721-AMMO; 417-725-4118
Fax: 417-725-1039
Website: www.fiocchiusa.com

FLINTLOCKS, ETC.
(Pedersoli replica rifles)
160 Rossiter Road, P.O. Box 181
Richmond MA 01254
Tel: 413-698-3822
Fax: 1-888-GUNCLIP
Website: www.GUNMAGS.com

FNH USA, INC.
(tactical rifles, shotguns, handguns)
P.O. Box 697
McLean VA 22101
Tel: 703-288-1292 Fax: 703-288-1730
Website: www.fnhusa.com

FORSTER PRODUCTS
(reloading)
310 East Lanark Avenue
Lanark IL 61046
Tel: 815-493-6360 Fax: 815-493-2371
Website: forsterproducts.com
E-mail: infor@forsterproducts.com

A.H. FOX (shotguns)
Available through Connecticut
Shotgun Mfg. Co.

FRANCHI
(shotguns)
Available through Beretta

FREEDOM ARMS
(handguns)
314 Hyw. 239, P.O. Box 150
Freedom WY 83120-0150
Tel: 307-883-2468 Fax: 307-883-2005
Website: www.freedomarms.com
E-mail: freedom@freedomarms.com

GLOCK, INC. (pistols)
6000 Highland Parkway
Smyrna GA 30082
Tel: 770-432-1202 Fax: 770-433-8719

GONIC ARMS
134 Flagg Rd.
Gonic NH 03839

GARY GOUDY
(custom gunmaker)
1512 S. 5th St.
Dayton WA 99328
Tel: 509-382-2726

CHARLES GRACE
(custom gunmaker)
718 E. 2nd
Trinidad CO 81082
Tel: 719-846-9435

GSI (GUN SOUTH INC.)
(Mauser rifles; Merkel shotguns)
7661 Commerce Lane, P.O. Box 129
Trussville AL 35173
Tel: 800-821-3021; 205-655-8299
Fax: 205-655-7078
Website: www.gsifirearms.com
E-mail: infor@gsifirearms.com

H&R 1871 INC.
(Harrington & Richardson shotguns, NEF shotguns)
Available through New England Firearms
Website: www.hr1871.com

H-S PRECISION
(rifles, pistols)
1301 Turbine Drive
Rapid City SD 57703
Tel: 605-341-3006 Fax: 605-342-8964
Website: www.hsprecision.com

HAMMERLI U.S.A.
(handguns)
19296 Oak Grove Circle
Groveland CA 95321
Tel: 209-962-5311 Fax: 209-962-5931

HECKLER & KOCH
(handguns, rifles; and Fabarm shotguns)
21480 Pacific Blvd.
Sterling VA 20166
Tel: 703-450-1900
Fax: 703-450-8160
Website: www.hecklerkoch-usa.com

HENRY REPEATING ARMS CO.
(rifles)
110 8th Street
Brooklyn NY 11215
Tel: 718-499-5600 Fax: 718-768-8056
Website: www.henryrepeating.com

HERITAGE MANUFACTURING
(handguns)
4600 NW 135 St.
Opa Locka FL 33054
Tel: 305-685-5966
Fax: 305-687-6721
Website: www.heritagemfg.com

HEYM RIFLE
Available through PSI
Email: 0422@frontiernet.net

HI-POINT FIREARMS
(handguns)
MKS Supply, Inc.
8611-A North Dixie Drive
Dayton OH 45414
Tel/Fax: 877-425-48671
Website: www.hi-pointfirearms.com

HIGH STANDARD MFG. CO., INC.
5200 Mitchelldale Suite E-17
Houston TX 77092
Tel: 800-272-7816; 713-462-4200
Fax: 713-681-5665

HILL COUNTRY RIFLE CO.
5726 Morningside Dr.
New Braunfels TX 78132
Tel: 830-609-3139
Website: www.hillcountryrifle.com

BOB HISSERICH
(custom gunmaker)
StockWorks Rifles
1843 S. Los Alamos
Mesa AZ 85204
Tel: 480-545-2994
Fax: 480-507-7560
Website: www.stockworks.net

HODGDON POWDER CO., INC.
(gunpowder, IMR)
6231 Robinson, P.O. Box 2932
Shawnee Mission KS 66201
Tel: 913-362-9455
Fax: 913-362-1307
Website: www.hodgdon.com
E-mail: info@hodgdon.com

Directory of Manufacturers & Suppliers

PATRICK HOLEHAN
(custom rifles)
5758 E. 34th St.
Tucson AZ 85711
Tel: 520-745-0622
E-mail: plholehan@juno.com

HORNADY MFG. CO.
(ammunition, reloading)
P.O. Box 1848; 3625 Old Potash Hwy.
Grand Island NE 68803
Tel: 308-382-1390 Fax: 308-382-5761
Website: www.hornady.com

HOWA (rifles)
Available through Legacy Sports Intl.

HUNTER COMPANY, INC.
(Hunter Wicked Optics)
3300 West 71st Ave.
Westminster CO 80030
Tel: 303-427-4626 Fax: 303-428-3980
Website: www.huntercompany.com

IMR POWDER CO. INC.
See Hodgdon Powder
Website: www.imrpowder.com

ITHACA GUN CO. (shotguns)
901 Route 34-B
Kings Ferry NY 13081
Tel: 315-364-7171 Fax: 315-364-5134
Website: www.ithacagun.com

JARRETT RIFLES INC.
(custom rifles, ammuniton)
383 Brown Road
Jackson SC 29831
Tel: 803-471-3616 Fax: 803-471-9246
Website: www.jarrettrifles.com

JOHANNSEN EXPRESS RIFLE
(available through New England
Custom Guns)

KAHLES (scopes)
2 Slater Rd.
Cranston RI 02920
Tel: 800-426-3089 Fax: 401-734-5888
Website: www.kahlesoptik.com

KAHR ARMS
(handguns, Auto-Ordnance)
630 Route 303, POB 220
Blauvelt NY 10913
Tel: 508-795-3919 Fax: 508-795-7046
Website: www.kahr.com

KAPS OPTICS
Karl Kaps Gmbh
Europastrasse
35614 Asslar/Wetzlar
Germany
Tel: 49-6441-80704
Fax: 49-6441-85985

K.B.I., INC.
(rifles, handguns, shotguns; Charles
Daly rifles, shotguns; FEG handguns)
P.O. box 6625
Harrisburg PA 17112-0625
Tel: 717-540-8518 Fax: 717-540-8567
Website: www.kbi-inc.com or
www.charlesdaly.com
E-mail: sales @kbi-inc.com

KEL-TEC CNC IND INC.
(handguns)
P.O. Box 236009
Cocoa FL 32926
Tel: 321-631-0068 Fax: 231-631-1169
Website: www.kel-tec.com
E-mail: aimkeltec@aol.com

KIMBER MANUFACTURING, INC.
(handguns, rifles)
1 Lawton Street
Yonkers NY 10705
Tel: 914-964-0771; 888-243-4522
E-mail: info@kimberamerica.com

KNIGHT RIFLES
(blackpowder rifles)
P.O. Box 130, 21852 Hwy. J46
Centerville IA 52544-0130
Tel: 515-856-2626 Fax: 515-856-2628
Website: www.knightrifles.com
E-mail: knightrifles@lisco.net

KRIEGHOFF INTERNATIONAL INC.
(rifles, shotguns)
337A Route 611, P.O. Box 549
Ottsville PA 18942
Tel: 610-847-5173 Fax: 610-847-8691

KYNOCH AMMUNITION
Kynamco Limited -
The Old Railway Station
Mildenhall, IP28 7DT England
Tel: +44 (0) 1638 711999
Fax: +44 (0) 1638 515251

LAPUA (ammunition)
Available through Vihtavuori
Website: www.lapua.com

L.A.R. MANUFACTURING, INC.
(Grizzly rifles)
4133 West Farm Rd.
West Jordan UT 84088-4997
Tel: 801-280-3505
Fax: 801-280-1972
Website: www.largrizzly.com
E-mail: guns@largrizzly.com

LAZZERONI ARMS CO.
1415 South Cherry Ave.
Tucson AZ 85713
Tel: 888-4-WAR-BIRD
Fax: 520-624-4250
Website: www.lazzeroni.com

LEGACY SPORTS INTL.
(Howa & Mauser rifles,
Escort shotguns)
206 S. Union St.
Alexandria VA 22314
Tel: 703-548-4837 Fax: 703-549-7826
Website: www.legacysports.com

LENARTZ MUZZLOADING
(blackpowder guns)
8001 Whitneyville Rd.
Alto MI 49302

LEUPOLD & STEVENS, INC.
(scopes, mounts)
14400 N.W. Greenbriar Parkway,
P.O. Box 688
Beaverton OR 97075
Tel: 503-646-9171 Fax: 503-526-1475
Website: www.leupold.com

LLAMA
(handguns)
Available through Eagle Imports

LONE STAR RIFLE CO., INC.
11231 Rose Road
Conroe TX 77303
Tel: 409-856-3363
Website: www.lonstarrifle.com

LYMAN PRODUCTS CORP.
(blackpowder guns, reloading tools)
475 Smith Street
Middletown CT 06457
Tel: 800-225-9626; 860-632-2020
Fax: 860-632-1699
Website: ww.lymanproducts.com
E-mail: lymansales@cshore.com

Directory of Manufacturers & Suppliers

MAGNUM RESEARCH INC.
(handguns, rifles, Desert Eagle)
7110 University Avenue N.E.
Minneapolis MN 55432
Tel: 612-574-1868 Fax: 612-574-0109
Website: www.magnumresearch.com

MAGTECH AMMUNITION CO.INC
6845 20th Ave. South
Suite 120
Centerville MN 55038
Tel: 800-466-7191 Fax: 651-429-9485

MARKESBERY MUZZLELOADERS, INC. (blackpowder guns)
7785 Foundation Drive, Suite 6
Florence KY 41042
Tel: 606-342-5553 Fax: 606-342-2380
Website: www.markesbery.com

MARLIN FIREARMS COMPANY
(rifles, shotguns, blackpowder)
100 Kenna Drive, P.O. Box 248
North Haven CT 06473
Tel: 203-239-5621 Fax: 203-234-7991
Website: www.marlinfirearms.com

MAROCCHI
(Conquista shotguns)
Available through Precision Sales Int'l.

MEADE INSTRUMENTS
(Scopes: Simmons, Redfield, Weaver)
6001 Oak Canyon
Irvine CA 92618
Website: www.meade.com

MEC INC.
(reloading tools)
c/o Mayville Engineering Co.
715 South Street
Mayville WI 53050
Tel: 800-797-4MEC; 920-387-4500
Fax: 920-387-5802
Website: www.mecreloaders.com
E-mail: reloaders@mayvl.com

MERKEL (shotguns, rifles)
Available through GSI
(Gun South Inc.)
Website: www.gsifirearms.com

M.O.A. CORP.
(handguns)
2451 Old Camden Pike
Eaton OH 45302
Tel: 937-456-3669 Fax: 937-456-9331
Website: moaguns.com

O.F. MOSSBERG & SONS, INC.
(shotguns, rifles)
7 Grasso Avenue, P.O. Box 497
North Haven CT 06473
Tel: 203-230-5300 Fax: 203-230-5420
Website: www.mossberg.com

MTM MOLDED PRODUCTS
(cases, reloading accessories)
P.O. Box 13117
Dayton OH 45413
Tel: 937-890-7461 Fax: 937-890-1747
Website: www.mtmcase-gard.com

NAVY ARMS COMPANY, INC.
(handguns, rifles, blackpowder guns)
219 Lawn St.
Martinsburg WV 25401
Tel: 800-669-6289 Fax: 304-262-1658
Website: www.navyarms.com

NELSON'S CUSTOM GUNS, INC.
Stephen Nelson
7430 NW Valley View Dr.
Corvallis OR 97330
Tel: 541-745-5232

NEW ENGLAND ARMS CORP./FAIR TECHNI MEC
6 Lawrence Lane,
P.O. Box 278
Kittery Point ME 03905
Tel: 207-439-0593 Fax: 207-439-6726

NEW ENGLAND CUSTOM GUN LTD.
(AYA shotguns and Schmidt-Bender Scopes)
438 Willow Brook Rd.
Plainfield NH 03781
Tel: 603-469-3450 Fax 603-469-3471

NEW ENGLAND FIREARMS CO. INC.
(handguns, rifles, shotguns, H&R 1871)
60 Industrial Rowe
Gardner MA 01440
Tel: 978-632-9393
Fax: 978-632-2300

NEW ULTRA LIGHT ARMS, LLC
(rifles, black powder)
1024 Grafton Road
Morgantown WV 26508
Tel: 304-292-0600 Fax: 304-292-9662
E-mail: newultralightarm@cs.com

NIKON INC.
(scopes)
1300 Walt Whitman Road
Melville NY 11747-3064
Tel: 631-547-4200
Fax: 631-547-4040
Website: www.nikonusa.com

DAVE NORIN
(custom gunmaker)
2010 Washington St.
Waukegan IL 60085
Tel: 847-662-4034

NORTH AMERICAN ARMS
(handguns)
2150 South 950 East
Provo UT 84606-6285
Tel: 800-821-5783; 801-374-9990
Fax: 801-374-9998
Website: www.naaminis.com

NOSLER BULLETS, INC.
(bullets)
P.O. Box 671, 107 SW Columbia
Bend OR 97709
Tel: 541-382-3921 Fax: 541-388-4667
Website: www.nosler.com

OLIN/WINCHESTER
(ammunition, primers, cases)
427 No. Shamrock St.
East Alton IL 62024-1174
Tel: 618-258-3692 Fax: 618-258-3609
Website: www.winchester.com

PARA-ORDNANCE MFG, INC.
(handguns)
980 Tapscott Road
Toronto ON M1X 1C3
Tel: 416-297-7855 Fax: 416-297-7855
Website: www.paraord.com
E-mail: info@paraord.com

PEDERSOLI, DAVIDE
(replica arms)
Available through Flintlocks Etc.
Website: www.davide-pedersoli.com

PENTAX USA
(scopes)
600 12th St. Suite 300
Golden CO 80401
Tel: 800-729-1419
Website: www.pentax.com

Directory of Manufacturers & Suppliers

PERAZZI U.S.A.
1010 W. 10th St.
Azusa CA 91702
Tel: 626-334-1234 Fax: 626-334-0344
PerazziUSA@aol.com

PMC CARTRIDGES
Available through B.C. Outdoors
Website: www.pmcammo.com

PGW DEFENSE TECHNOLOGIES
(Prairie Gun Works rifles)
1-761 Marion St.
Winnipeg, Manitoba,
Canada R2J0K6
Tel: 204-231-2976 Fax: 204-231-8566
Website: www.prairiegunworks.com

RAMSHOT PROPELLANT
(gunpowder)
Available through Western Powders

RCBS (reloading equipment)
605 Oro Dam Blvd.
Oroville CA 95965
Tel: 916-533-5191 Fax: 916-533-1647
Website: www.rcbs.com

REDDING RELOADING EQUIPMENT
(reloading tools)
1089 Starr Road
Cortland NY 13045
Tel: 607-753-3331 Fax: 607-756-8445
Website: www.redding-reloading.com
E-mail: techline@redding-reloading.com

REDFIELD
Available through Simmons
(scopes)
P.O. Box 38
Onalaska WI 54650
Tel: 608-781-5800 Fax: 608-781-0368
Website: www.redfieldoptics.com

REMINGTON ARMS COMPANY, INC.
(rifles, shotguns, blackpowder arms, ammunition)
870 Remington Drive, P.O. Box 700
Madison NC 27025-0700
Tel: 800-243-9700 Fax: 336-548-7741
Website: www.remington.com

RENATO GAMBA U.S.A. INC.
(Daytona shotguns)
25063 Gardone Val Trompia
Brescia, Itlay
Tel: +39 308911640

RIFLES, INC.
3580 Leal Rd.
Pleasanton TX 78064
Tel: 830-569-2055 Fax: 830-569-2297

RIZZINI
(shotguns)
Available through Traditions Firearms
Website: www.rizzini.it

ROGUE RIFLE CO.
1140 36th St. North, Suite B
Lewiston ID 83501
Tel: 208-743-4355 Fax: 208-743-4163
Website: www.roguerifle.com

ROSSI FIREARMS
(handguns, rifles, shotguns)
BrazTech Intl.
16175 NW 49th Ave.
Miami FL 33014
Tel: 305-624-1115 Fax: 305-623-7506
Website: www.rossiusa.com

ROTTWEIL BRENNEKE
(see Brenneke)

RUGER
(handguns, rifles, shotguns, blackpowder guns)
See Sturm, Ruger & Co., Inc.

RWS
Available through
Dynamit Nobel

OLYMPIC ARMS, INC.
(handguns)
624 Old Pacific Hwy SE
Olympia WA 98513
Tel: 360-459-7940, 800-228-3471
Fax: 360-491-3447
Website: www.olyarms.com

SAKO
(rifles, actions, scope mounts, ammo)
Available through
Beretta U.S.A. Corp.

SAUER
(rifles)
c/o Paul Company, Inc.
27385 Pressonville Road
Wellsville KS 66092
Tel: 913-883-4444 Fax: 913-883-1515

SAVAGE ARMS, INC.
(handguns, rifles, shotguns)
100 Springdale Road
Westfield MA 01085
Tel: 413-568-7001
Fax: 413-562-7764
Website: www.savagearms.com

SCHMIDT AND BENDER INC.
(scopes)
Schmidt & Bender U.S.A.
P.O. Box 134
Meriden NH 03770
Tel: 800-468-3450 Fax: 603-469-3471
Website: www.schmidt-bender.de

SHILOH RIFLE MANUFACTURING
(blackpowder guns)
PO Box 279
Big Timber MT 59011
Tel: 406-932-4454 Fax: 406-932-5627
Website: www.Shilohrifle.com

SIERRA BULLETS
(bullets)
P.O. Box 818
1400 West Henry Steet
Sedalia MO 65301
Tel: 888-223-3006; 660-827-6300
Fax: 660-827-4999
Website: www.sierrabullets.com
E-mail: sierra@sierrabullets.com

SIGARMS INC.
(Sig-Sauer shotguns, handguns, Blaser rifles)
18 Industrial Dr.
Exeter NH 03833
Tel: 603-772-2302 Fax: 603-772-1481
Website: www.sigarms.com

SIGHTRON, INC.
(scopes)
100 Jeffrey Way, Suite A
Youngville NC 27596
Tel: 919-562-3000 Fax: 919-556-0157
Website: www.sightron.com

GENE SIMILLION
(custom guns)
220 S. Wisconsin
Gunnison CO 81230
Tel: 970-641-1126

Directory of Manufacturers & Suppliers

SIMMONS Outdoor corp.
(scopes, Weaver, Redfield)
201 Plantation Oak Drive
Thomasville GA 31792
Tel: 229-227-9053 Fax: 229-227-6454
Website: www.simmonsoptics.com

SISK RIFLES (cusom rifles)
Charlie Sisk
400 County Road
Dayton TX 77535-3294
Tel: 936-258-4984

SKB SHOTGUNS
(shotguns)
4325 S. 120th Street
Omaha NE 68137-1253
Tel: 800-752-2767 Fax: 402-330-8040
Website: www.skbshotguns.com
E-mail: SKB@radiks.net

SMITH & WESSON
(handguns)
2100 Roosevelt Avenue, P.O. Box 2208
Springfield MA 01102-2208
Tel: 413-781-8300; 800-331-0852
Fax: 413-747-3317
Website: www.smith-wesson.com

SPEER (bullets)
Available through CCI/Speer-Blount, Inc.

SPRINGFIELD ARMORY
(handguns, rifles, Aimpoint scopes, & sights)
420 West Main Street
Geneseo IL 61254
Tel: 800-680-6866; 309-944-5631
Fax: 309-944-3676
Website: www.springfield-armory.com

STEVENS
(a Savage Arms Co.)
118 Mountain Rd.
Suffield CT 06078

STEYR-MANNLICHER
(rifles)
Available through Dynamit/Nobel
Website: www.dnrws.com

STOEGER INDUSTRIES
(shotguns)
17603 Indian Head Hwy., Suite 200
Accokeek MD 20607
Tel: 301-283-6300 Fax: 301-283-6586

STURM, RUGER AND COMPANY, INC.
(Ruger handguns, rifles, shotguns, blackpower, revolvers)
200 Ruger Road
Prescott AZ 86301
Tel: 203-259-7843 Fax: 203-256-3367
Website: www.ruger-firearms.com

SWAROVSKI OPTIK NORTH AMERICA
(scopes)
2 Slater Road
Cranston RI 02920
Tel: 800-426-3089; 401-734-1800
Fax: 401-734-5888; 877-287-8517
Website: www.swarovskioptik.com

SWIFT BULLET CO.
(bullets)
201 Main Street
P.O. Box 27
Quinter KS 67752
Tel: 785-754-3959 Fax: 785-754-2359

SWIFT INSTRUMENTS, INC.
(scopes, mounts)
952 Dorchester Avenue
Boston MA 02125
Tel: 800-446-1116 Fax: 617-436-3232
Website: www.swift-optics.com

SWISS ARMS AG
Industrieplatz
8212 Neuhausen am Rheinfall
Switzerland
Tel: +41 52 674 6565
Email: info@swissarms.ch

SZECSEI & FUCHS
(custom rifles)
450 Charles Street
Windsor, Ontario N8X 371 Canada
Tel: 001 519 966 1234

TACTICAL FIREARMS
19250 Hwy. 301
Dade City FL 33523

TASCO WORLDWIDE, INC.
See Bushnell
(scopes, mounts)
Website: www.tasco.com

TAURUS INT'L, INC.
(handguns)
16175 N.W. 49th Avenue
Miami FL 33014-6314
Tel: 800-327-3776; 305-624-1115
Fax: 305-623-7506
Website: www.taurususa.com

TAYLOR'S & CO. INC.
(rifles, carbines)
304 Lenoir Drive
Winchester VA 22603
Tel: 540-722-2017 Fax: 540-722-2018
Website: ww.taylorsfirearms.com
E-mail: info@taylorsfirearms.com

THOMPSON & CAMPBELL
(custom rifles)
Cromarty – The Black Isle
Ross-Shire IV11 8YB Scotland
Tel: +44 (0) 1381 600 536
Fax: +44 (0) 1381 600 767

THOMPSON/CENTER ARMS
(handguns, rifles, reloading, blackpowder arms)
Farmington Road, P.O. Box 5002
Rochester NH 03867
Tel: 603-332-2394 Fax: 603-332-5133
Website: www.tcarms.com

TIKKA (rifles, shotguns))
Available through Beretta U.S.A.

TRADITIONS PERFORMANCE FIREARMS
(blackpowder arms, Rizzini Shotguns)
1375 Boston Post Road
P.O. Box 776
Old Saybrook CT 06475-0776
Tel: 860-388-4656 Fax: 860-388-4657
Website: www.traditionfirearms.com
E-mail: info@traditionsfirearms.com

TRIJICON
(rifle scopes)
49385 Shafer Ave. P.O. Box 930059
Wixom MI 48393
Tel: 248-960-7700; 800-338-0563
Fax: 248-960-7725
Website: www.trijikon-inc.com

TRISTAR SPORTING ARMS, LTD.
1814-16 Linn St.
North Kansas City MO 64116
Tel: 816-421-1400
Fax: 816-421-4182
Website: www.tristarsportingarms.com

Directory of Manufacturers & Suppliers

UBERTI USA, INC.
(handguns, rifles, blackpowder guns)
Stoeger Industries
17603 Indian Head Hwy, Suite 200
Accokeek MD 20607
Tel: 301-283-6300

U.S. REPEATING ARMS CO.
(Winchester rifles, shotguns)
275 Winchester Ave.
Morgan UT 84050-9326
Tel: 801-876-3440 Fax: 801-876-3737
Website: www.winchesterguns.com

VERONA SHOTGUNS
Available through B.C. Outdoors

VIHTAVUORI
(powder and Lapua ammunition)
1241 Ellis St.
Bensenville IL 60106
Tel: 630-350-1116 Fax: 630-350-1606

WALTHER U.S.A.
(handguns)
2100 Roosevelt Ave.
Springfield MA 01104
Tel: 800-372-6454 Fax: 413-747-3592
Website: www.walther-usa.com

WEATHERBY, INC.
(rifles, shotguns, ammunition)
3100 El Camino Real
Atascadero CA 93422
Tel: 800-227-2016; 805-466-1767
Fax: 805-466-2527
Website: www.weatherby.com

WEAVER
(scopes)
Available through
Simmons
Website: www.weaveroptics.com

WESTERN POWDER
(Ramshot powder)
P.O. Box 158
Miles City MT 59301
Tel: 406-232-0422 Fax: 406-232-0430
Website: www.westernpowders.com

WHITE RIFLES
(blackpowder)
P.O. Box 1044
Orem UT 84059-1044
Tel: 877-684-4867
Fax: 801-932-7959
Website: www.whiterifles.com

WILDEY F.A. INC.
(handguns)
45 Angevine Road
Warren CT 06754
Tel: 860-355-9000 Fax: 860-354-7759
Website: www.wildeyguns.com

WILD WEST GUNS, INC.
(Summit rifles)
7521 Old Seward Hwy., Unit A
Anchorage AK 99518
Tel: 800-992-4570 Fax: 907-344-4005
Website: www.wildwestguns.com
E-mail: wwguns@ak.net

WILLIAMS GUN SIGHT CO.
7389 Lapeer Road
P.O. Box 329
Davison MI 48423
Tel: 800-530-9028; 810-653-2131
Fax: 810-658-2140
Website: www.williamsgunsight.com

WINCHESTER
(ammunition, primers,
cases, ballistics)
Available through Olin/Winchester
Website: www.winchester.com

WINCHESTER FIREARMS
(rifles, shotguns)
Available through U.S. Repeating
Arms Co.
Website: www.winchester-guns.com

WINCHESTER MUZZLELOADING
Available through Blackpowder
Products

WOODLEIGH BULLETS
Huntingtons
POB 991
601 Oro Dam Blvd.
Oroville CA 95965
Fax: 530-534-1212

XS SIGHT SYSTEMS
2401 Ludelle St.
Forth Worth TX 76105
Tel: 817-536-0136; 888-744-4880
Fax: 817-536-3517
Website: www.xssights.com

CARL ZEISS OPTICAL, INC.
13017 N. Kingston Ave.
Chester VA 23836
Tel: 804-530-8300
Fax: 804-530-8325

Z-HAT CUSTOM DIES
(reloading)
4010A S. Poplar, Suite 72
Casper WY 82601
Tel: 307-577-7443
Website: www.z-hat.com
E-mail: RifleBuilder@z-hat.com

ZANDER'S SPORTING GOODS
(Eley ammunition)
Available through DKG Trading Inc.

Manufacturer's Showcase

Specifications:
- Motor: 1½ HP, 110V/220V single-phase
- Precision ground cast iron table: 10" x 33¾"
- Table travel (longitudinal): 17¾"
- Table travel (cross): 12"
- Spindle taper: R-8
- Spindle travel: 3½"
- Max. spindle to column: 16½"
- Max. spindle to table: 20 7/16"
- 9 Speeds: 420-5000 RPM
- Approx. shipping wt: 1610 lbs.

Includes:
- Way chip protectors
- Drawbar

The **G9977** is **$2,595.00** and is shipped in the lower 48 states for $210.00.

Please check current pricing before ordering!

3 LOCATIONS
Bellingham, WA / Muncy, PA / Springfield, MO

514003658

grizzly.com **Visit our Web site!**
TEL: 1-800-523-4777 · FAX: 1-800-438-5901
MEDIA CODE SBIBLE06

Specifications:
- Motor: 2 HP, 220V, single-phase
- Swing over bed: 12"
- Swing over gap: 18⅞"
- Distance between centers: 37"
- Spindle nose taper: MT#5
- Spindle bore: 1 7/16"
- Speeds: 12, 50-1200 RPM
- Tailstock barrel taper: MT#3
- Tailstock barrel travel: 3"
- Approx. shipping weight: 1136 lbs.

Includes:
- 6" 3-jaw chuck • 8" 4-jaw chuck
- 10" face plate • Steady rest
- Follow rest • Chip tray
- Heavy-duty stand • 4 way tool post
- Dual inch/metric dials

The **G9249** is **$2,095.00** and is shipped in the lower 48 states for $210.00.

Please check current pricing before ordering!

3 LOCATIONS
Bellingham, WA / Muncy, PA / Springfield, MO

514003658

grizzly.com **Visit our Web site!**
TEL: 1-800-523-4777 · FAX: 1-800-438-5901
MEDIA CODE SBIBLE06

MODEL G4016
13½" x 40"
GEAR-HEAD LATHE
WITH STAND

Specifications:
- Motor: 2 HP, 220V, single-phase
- Swing over bed: 13½"
- Swing over gap: 19"
- Distance between centers: 40"
- Spindle: D1-4 Camlock
- Spindle bore: 1 7/16"
- 8 Speeds: 78-2100 RPM
- Tailstock barrel taper: MT#3
- Tailstock barrel travel: 3½"
- Approx. shipping weight: 1330 lbs.

Includes:
- 6" 3-jaw chuck • 8" 4-jaw chuck
- 12" face plate
- 4-way turret tool post
- Two MT#3 dead centers
- Live center
- Steady rest • Follow rest
- Jog button & emergency stop
- Tool box
- Stand, chip pan & splash guard

The **G4016** is **$2,895.00** and is shipped in the lower 48 states for $210.00.

Please check current pricing before ordering!

3 LOCATIONS
Bellingham, WA / Muncy, PA / Springfield, MO

514003658

grizzly.com **Visit our Web site!**
TEL: 1-800-523-4777 · FAX: 1-800-438-5901
MEDIA CODE SBIBLE06

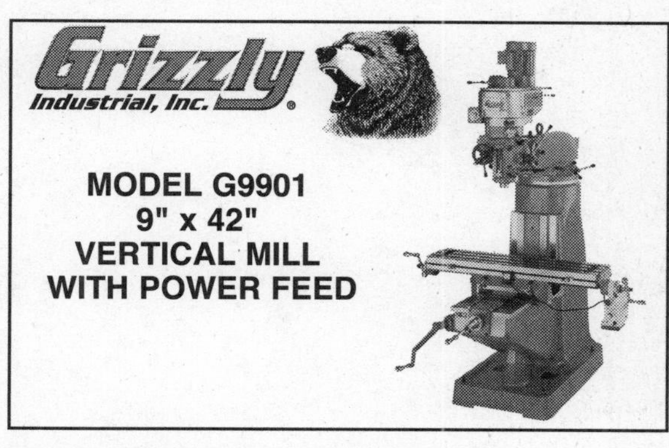

Specifications:
- Motor: 2 HP, 110V/220V single-phase
- Precision ground cast iron table: 9" x 42"
- Table travel (longitudinal): 25⅞"
- Table travel (cross): 12½"
- Max. dist. spindle to table: 18"
- Max. dist. spindle to column: 17½"
- 8 Speeds: 78-2000 R.P.M.
- Approx. shipping weight: 2379 lbs.

Features:
- One-shot pump lubrication
- Power down feed • R-8 spindle
- Quill feeds/Spindle rev.: .0019", .0035", .0058"
- Auto stop w/ micro adjustable stop
- Longitudinal power feed
- Adjustable micrometer quill depth stop
- Hardened & ground table surface
- Chrome plated, precision ground quill

The **G9901** is **$3,495.00** and is shipped in the lower 48 states for $375.00.

Please check current pricing before ordering!

3 LOCATIONS
Bellingham, WA / Muncy, PA / Springfield, MO

514003658

grizzly.com **Visit our Web site!**
TEL: 1-800-523-4777 · FAX: 1-800-438-5901
MEDIA CODE SBIBLE06

MANUFACTURERS

Manufacturer's Showcase

MANUFACTURERS

Gunfinder Index

To help you find the model of your choice, the following index includes every firearm found in this edition of Shooter's Bible, listed by type of gun.

GUNFINDER INDEX

Gunfinder Index

GUNFINDER INDEX

Gunfinder Index

Gunfinder Index

Gunfinder Index

Gunfinder Index

GUNFINDER INDEX

Gunfinder Index

Gunfinder Index

Revolvers

Revolvers – Single Action

Gunfinder Index

Gunfinder Index

GUNFINDER INDEX